policyAMERICA

Online advocacy . . .

The development of public policy is increasingly being influenced by **online advocacy.** Online advocacy can be as simple as sending an email to a legislator or as complex as launching a major Internet-based campaign. Like any grassroots advocacy tool, the Internet does have its limits. An e-mail is not a replacement for a personal visit with one's representative. And nothing is more effective in persuading a member of Congress to pay attention to your cause than the sound of his staffers' telephones ringing off the hook with constituent calls. However, there can be no question that the Internet revolution holds tremendous promise for the future of politics and political activism.

One organization that is taking online advocacy to the arena of social welfare is policyAmerica, a nonprofit organization whose purpose is to develop the next agenda in American social policy. The purpose of policyAmerica is to create and foster an electronic network of current and retired policy administrators, scholars, and advocates who propose, discuss, and craft innovations in social policy. The organization focuses on child protection, poverty, employment, health insurance, long-term care, and other social welfare issues.

The goal of policyAmerica is to exploit information technology and the capacity of the Internet to bridge the chasm between grassroots advocates and national policy makers. Its website allows participants to post position papers, monographs, and opinions on issues of compelling public interest. Equally important, policyAmerica provides the tools to encourage interaction with national policy makers and the media.

To find out how to get involved . . .

www.policyamerica.org

American Social Welfare Policy

FIFTH EDITION

American Social Welfare Policy

A PLURALIST APPROACH

Howard Jacob Karger

University of Houston

David Stoesz

Virginia Commonwealth University

Boston • New York • San Francisco
Mexico City • Montreal • Toronto • London • Madrid • Munich • Paris
Hong Kong • Singapore • Tokyo • Cape Town • Sydney

Series Editor: *Patricia Quinlin*
Editorial Assistant: *Sara Holliday*
Marketing Manager: *Laura Lee Manley*
Editorial-Production Administrator: *Anna Socrates*
Editorial-Production Service: *Omegatype Typography, Inc.*
Developmental Editor: *Janice M. Wiggins*
Manufacturing Buyer: *JoAnne Sweeney*
Composition and Prepress Buyer: *Linda Cox*
Cover Administrator: *Linda Knowles*
Electronic Composition: *Omegatype Typography, Inc.*
Photo Research: *Helane M. Prottas, Posh Pictures*
Interior Designer: *Roy Neuhaus*

For related titles and support materials, visit our online catalog at www.ablongman.com.

Between the time website information is gathered and then published, it is not unusual for some sites to have closed. Also, the transcription of URLs can result in unintended typographical errors. The publisher would appreciate notification where these occur so that they may be corrected in subsequent editions.

Library of Congress Cataloging-in-Publication Data

Karger, Howard Jacob
American social welfare policy : a pluralist approach / Howard Jacob Karger, David Stoesz.—5th ed.
p. cm.
Includes bibliographical references and index.
ISBN 0-205-40182-1
1. Public welfare—United States. 2. United States—Social policy. 3. Welfare state—United States. I. Stoesz, David. II. Title.

HV95.K354 2006
361.973—dc22

2005042914

Printed in the United States of America

10 9 8 7 6 5 4 3 VHP 10 09 08 07

Photo Credits: Photo credits appear on page 520, which constitutes an extension of the copyright page.

For Anna and my children, Aaron, Saul, and Rafi

H. J. K.

For Marc, Darcy, and Tim

D. S.

Brief Contents

Contents

CHAPTER 3

Howard Jacob Karger and Peter A. Kindle

CHAPTER 4

CHAPTER 5

PART TWO

THE VOLUNTARY AND FOR-PROFIT SOCIAL SECTORS

CHAPTER 6

The Voluntary Sector Today 145

CHAPTER 7

Privatization and Human Service Corporations 168

PART THREE
THE GOVERNMENT SECTOR

CHAPTER 8
The Making of Governmental Policy 205

CHAPTER 9
Tax Policy and Income Distribution 232

CHAPTER 10

Social Insurance Programs 251

CHAPTER 11

Public Assistance Programs 269

CHAPTER 12

The American Health Care System 301

CHAPTER 13

Mental Health and Substance Abuse Policy 337

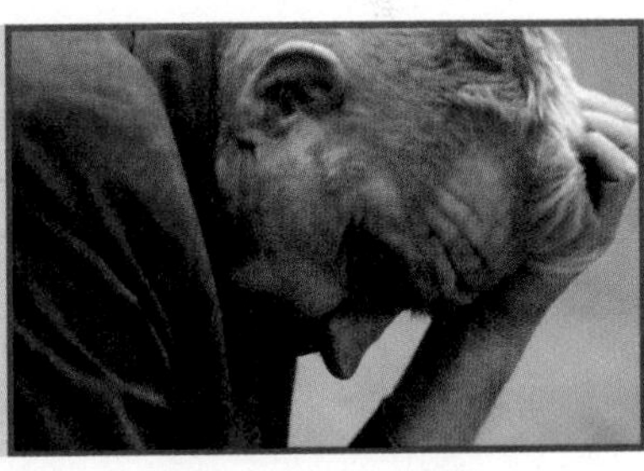

CHAPTER 14
Criminal Justice 368

CHAPTER 15
Child Welfare Policy 389

CHAPTER 16
Housing Policies 416

CHAPTER 17

The Politics of Food Policy and Rural Life 442

PART FOUR

THE AMERICAN WELFARE STATE IN PERSPECTIVE

CHAPTER 18

The American Welfare State in International Perspective 471

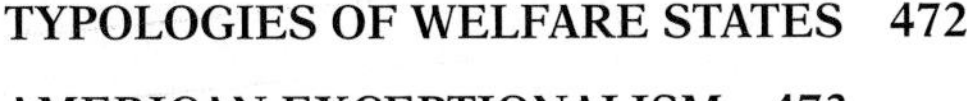

Preface

The four years since the publication of the fourth edition have been characterized by dramatic changes on numerous fronts. On September 11, 2001, almost 3,000 people were killed and as many as 8,000 injured in the most devastating terrorist attack in the nation's history. The attacks were the first highly lethal attack by a foreign force on the mainland United States since 1814 and many pundits claim that America will never be the same after that event. Shortly afterward, the United States declared that the militant Islamic group al-Qaeda and its leader, Osama bin Laden, were the prime suspects. This led to what the Bush administration called the War on Terrorism, which included the U.S. removal of the Afghanistan's Taliban government in October 2001. In the aftermath of the World Trade Center attacks, the U.S. government increased military operations, economic measures, and political pressure on groups it accused of being terrorists, as well as on governments and countries accused of harboring them. The September 11 attacks on the World Trade Center and the Pentagon led to a renewed focus on domestic security and the creation of a new cabinet-level federal agency, the Department of Homeland Security. These attacks also precipitated important changes in our concept of civil liberties and in a wide range of immigration policies.

The invasion of Afghanistan was eclipsed by the Bush administration's contention that strong links existed between Osama bin Laden and Saddam Hussein, that Iraq had weapons of mass destruction and the means to deliver and develop them, and that Iraq was a major supporter of international terrorism. This argument was used to justify the invasion of Iraq on March 19, 2003. In 2004, the National Commission on Terrorist Attacks upon the United States, also known as the 9/11 Commission, concluded that there was no credible evidence that Saddam Hussein had assisted al-Qaeda in preparing for or carrying out the 9/11 attacks. Nor were any weapons of mass destruction ever found. Nevertheless, by April 2005 more than 1,500 U.S. troops had been killed and more than 11,000 wounded (estimates run even higher if other factors are added). As many as 100,000 Iraqis may have also been killed.[1]

The domestic front was equally problematic. The flush economy of the Clinton years was eclipsed by a recession that left the federal and state governments with unprecedented deficits. The low unemployment, rising wages, and a drop in poverty during the middle 1990s gave way to rising unemployment, stagnant wages, and increases in poverty by 2004. The slight budget surplus of the Clinton administration was quickly eclipsed by a record $450 billion federal budget deficit in 2004. Indeed, the gains made during the Clinton era proved to be fragile, as the massive tax cuts enacted under George W. Bush exacerbated the impoverishment of the public sector. Not surprisingly, Bush's "compassionate conservatism" proved to be 90 percent hard-edged conservatism laced with 10 percent compassion. The dismantling of the American welfare state that began 30 years ago was hastened by the promise of more stringent work requirements for welfare recipients, a drug benefit for Medicare that benefits drug companies over elderly beneficiaries, and an educational system that is leaving more children behind. At the end of the first Bush term, the nation found itself ensconced in a seemingly intractable war complemented by a social service system that is breaking under the weight of increased clients and fewer resources. On November 2, 2004, George W. Bush won a second term in what was one of the closest presidential races in recent memory. Much of the country was stunned by the results.

Since the "revolution" that installed Ronald Reagan in the White House, the ideological right has defined the discussion of social policy. The Clinton interregnum, afforded by the leveraging of the

[1]See "Too Many Killed: A New, Preliminary Study Puts Iraq's Civilian Deaths at 100,000," *Houston Chronicle* (November 2, 2004), p. 6; and Michael Ewen, "Casualties in Iraq: The Human Cost of Occupation," The Randolph Bourne Institute, retrieved October 20, 2004, from http://antiwar.com/casualties.

Democratic party to the center by means of the Democratic Leadership Council (DLC), was an accommodation to regnant conservatism. Aside from his peccadilloes, Clinton will be remembered as a centrist president, one who behaved more like a moderate Republican than like a liberal Democrat. The DLC interlude, however, witnessed two classically liberal initiatives—both of which failed spectacularly. The first was the effort to pass a Health Security Act, an attempt to universalize health care in the United States, the only industrial country without such a policy. Despite being drafted in a manner that appeased the health industry, the measure failed. The second was the Gore presidential campaign. Despite unprecedented economic prosperity that should have made for certain victory, an incumbent vice president running a campaign heavily laden with liberal themes was trumped by a second-term governor of Texas.

While liberal human service professionals have continued to lick their ideological wounds, conservatives have made serious inroads into the U.S. welfare state. To date, the hallmark has been the 1996 Personal Responsibility and Work Opportunity Reconciliation Act, which terminated the 60-year entitlement to family assistance, converting the welfare system to a block grant program devolved to the states. Federal welfare reform may serve as a prelude for more draconian ventures under the presidency of George W. Bush, who has advocated privatizing Social Security. The message is clear: Not only have liberals lost the public support undergirding welfare programs, but they have watched the foundation of social insurance erode as well.

The irony is that the current policy environment could offer social welfare advocates multiple opportunities, if they were willing to shed their insistence on federal entitlements as a basis for social policy. Consider several of the conservative themes that are driving public philosophy: "Privatization" has long been part of human services in the United States, as is amply evident in nonprofit organizations as well as private practitioners. "Devolution" is familiar to providers of child welfare, mental health, and corrections—traditionally state-controlled programs—to say nothing of professionals who have served as elected officials in state and local governments. "Faith-based social service" has been a cornerstone of the nonprofit sector, evident in such agencies as Catholic Charities, the Salvation Army, and Jewish community services, among others. As these examples suggest, advocates of social justice already have substantial expertise in domains that conservatives have appropriated; this expertise could be mobilized to enhance the public interest, and social work would benefit as a result.

Several changes will be required, however, if human service professionals are to reclaim a prominent role in social policy. Foremost, "compassionate conservatism" must be taken seriously along with traditional liberal prescriptions in social affairs. Markets have been a primary means of distributing goods and services to the nonpoor, and the application of market dynamics to low-income families should be evaluated on merit, not discarded out of ideological preference. State and local politics have been important as arenas for introducing innovations in social welfare as well as for providing social workers a first step on the ladder of public service; such opportunities should be celebrated, not dismissed.

If social work is to reassert its role in public policy, acceptance of privatization and devolution by itself will be insufficient if the profession is to be an influential player. The currency of the realm in public policy is power, and power occurs in three basic forms: money, votes, and networks. These resources have been the staple of politics, but the information age has introduced a higher level of sophistication. Money means access to capital and various means for increasing its value; votes are massaged by constant polling; networks are identified and modified depending on the objective at hand. In a postindustrial policy environment, influence is a function of a player's facility in manipulating these three resources. To be competitive, one must have command of information systems, large data sets, and complex decision menus.

If social work can educate students about these methods and begin to insert them into the policy environment, the profession will become an influential force in social policy. On the other hand, if the profession rests on the laurels of the New Deal and the War on Poverty, all the while denigrating the rapacity of "special interests," it will remain a bit player. Such an eventuality would essentially waste the substantial assets that social work brings to social affairs: a distinguished legacy, the altruism of the young, and a unique moral imperative. Just as the foundation of the conservative juggernaut can be attributed to the anguish of young Republicans in the aftermath of the 1964 presidential election, so the rebirth of Progressivism may be found in the dismay of the 2000 and 2004 presidential elections. Social workers can be among the catalysts in this rebirth.

This fifth edition of *American Social Welfare Policy* attempts to provide the information necessary for the reemergence of social work in social policy, nationally and internationally. In addition to discussing the basic concepts, policies, and programs that have typified the U.S. welfare state, the text includes separate chapters on the voluntary nonprofit sector (Chapter 6) and the for-profit corporate sector (Chapter 7). Chapter 9 directs attention to a new strategy in social policy: tax expenditures. Chapter 3 discusses the often neglected role of religion in the formation of social welfare policy. The final chapter, Chapter 18, examines the influence of global capitalism, a development that not only weds the developed nations with the undeveloped nations but also, in the process, shifts capital and jobs in unprecedented volumes.

New to this edition are Spotlight boxes; at least one of these boxes is included in each chapter. At the end of each chapter are discussion questions. Many of these discussion questions can be enhanced by using the policyAmerica website for students at www.policyamerica.org/policyamerica/legproc.html.

We owe many debts in writing the fifth edition. The reviewers of this and previous editions have provided an invaluable service in identifying deficiencies. We would like to thank the reviewers of the fifth edition for their insightful comments and suggestions: Lowell J. Bishop, University of Maryland Eastern Shore; Patricia Brownell, Fordham University; Edward J. Gumz, Loyola University Chicago; Mark Hanna, California State University Fresno; and Thomas McLaughlin, University of New England.

In addition, we would also like to thank our student assistants, including Kari Miller, who provided research for select chapters. We owe a huge debt to Nancy Jane Otto, Brett Needham, Kristen Russo, and David Aurisano. Peter Kindle deserves a major "thank you" for helping to write a remarkable chapter on religion and social policy. Finally, thanks to our families for suffering our many absences with patience. In anticipation of a sixth edition, comments by students and faculty are welcome.

H. J. K.
D. S.

About the Authors

Howard Karger is a professor in the Graduate School of Social Work at University of Houston; David Stoesz is a professor at Virginia Commonwealth University. Howard and David have been friends and colleagues for more than twenty years. In 2001 they collaborated on the creation of policyAmerica, a nonprofit organization dedicated to disseminating innovations in social policy. In addition to five editions of *American Social Welfare Policy,* they have coauthored two other books: *The Politics of Child Abuse in America* (with Lela Costin) (Oxford University Press, 1996) and *Reconstructing the American Welfare State* (Rowman and Littlefield, 1992). Howard's newest book, *Shortchanged: Life and Debt in the Fringe Economy* (Berret-Koehler, 2005), examines the financial practices and products that exploit millions of American families. David's latest book, *Quixote's Ghost: The Right, the Liberati, and the Future of Social Policy* (Oxford University Press, 2005), explains how conservatives have assumed control of domestic policy and proposes a new framework for social policy. Howard and Anna live in Houston, Texas, and Cloudcroft, New Mexico; David lives in Alexandria, Virginia, with his son, Julio.

American Social Welfare Policy

CHAPTER 1

Social Policy and the American Welfare State

This chapter provides an overview of the American welfare state. In particular, it examines various definitions of social welfare policy, the relationship between social policy and social problems, and the values and ideologies that drive social welfare in the United States. In addition, the chapter examines the effects of ideology on the U.S. welfare state, including the important roles played by conservatism and liberalism (and their variations) in shaping welfare policy. The chapter also explores the political economy of welfare in this country, including the roles played by the Keynesians, free market economics, socialism, and communitarianism, among others.

American social welfare is in transition. Starting with the Social Security Act of 1935, liberals argued that federal social programs were the best way to help the disadvantaged. Now, after 70 years of experimenting with the **welfare state,** a discernible shift has occurred. The conservatism of U.S. culture—so evident in the Reagan, Bush, and even Clinton presidencies—has left private institutions to shoulder more of the welfare burden. For proponents of social justice, the suggestion that the private sector should assume more responsibility for welfare represents a retreat from the hard-won governmental social legislation that provided essential benefits to millions of Americans. Justifiably, these groups fear the loss of basic goods and services during the transition in social welfare.

A pluralistic mix of private and public services is an overriding feature of U.S. social welfare. As in other realms, such as education, in social welfare private institutions coexist alongside those of the public sector. American social welfare has a noble tradition of voluntary citizen groups taking the initiative to solve local problems. Today, private voluntary groups provide important services to AIDS patients, the homeless, immigrants, victims of domestic violence, and refugees.

Social welfare is also big business. During the last 30 years the number of human service corporations—for-profit firms providing social welfare through the marketplace—has increased dramatically. Human service corporations are prominent in long-term nursing care, health maintenance, child day care, psychiatric and substance abuse services, and even corrections. For many welfare professionals the privatizing of social services is troubling, occurring as it does at a time when government has reduced its commitment to social programs. Yet human service corporations will likely continue to be prominent players in shaping the nation's social welfare policies. As long as U.S. culture is democratic and capitalistic, entrepreneurs will be free to establish social welfare services in the private sector, both as nonprofit agencies and as for-profit corporations.

The **mixed welfare economy** of the United States, in which the voluntary, governmental, and corporate sectors coexist, poses important questions for social welfare policy. To what extent can voluntary groups be held responsible for public welfare, given their limited fiscal resources? For which groups of people, if any, should government divest itself of responsibility? Can human service corporations care for poor and multiproblem clients while continuing to generate profits? Equally important, how can welfare professionals shape coherent social welfare policies, given the fragmentation inherent in such pluralism? Clearly, the answers to these questions have much to say about how social welfare programs are perceived by human service professionals, their clients, and the taxpayers who continue to subsidize social programs.

The multitude of questions posed by the transition of social welfare in this country is daunting. Temporarily satisfied by the draconian 1996 welfare reform bill (and the dramatic cuts in the nation's public assistance rolls), conservatives have shifted their attention to "reforming" social insurance programs such as Social Security and Medicare through privatization. Yet past advocates of social justice such as Jane Addams, Whitney Young Jr., and Wilbur Cohen, to name a few, interpreted the inadequacy of social welfare provision and the confusion of their times as an opportunity to further social justice. It remains for another generation of welfare professionals to demonstrate the same imagination, perseverance, and courage to advance social welfare in the years ahead. Those accepting this challenge will need to be familiar with the various meanings of social welfare policy, differing political and economic explanations of social welfare, and the multiple interest groups that have emerged within the American social welfare system.

Definitions of Social Welfare Policy

The English social scientist Richard Titmuss has defined **social services** as "a series of collective interventions that contribute to the general welfare by assigning claims from one set of people who are said to produce or earn the national income to another set of people who may merit compassion and charity."[1] Welfare policy, whether it is the product of governmental, voluntary, or corporate institutions, is concerned with allocating goods, services, and opportunities to enhance social functioning.

William Epstein defines social policy as "social action sanctioned by society."[2] Social policy can also be defined as the formal and consistent ordering of human affairs. **Social welfare policy,** a subset of social policy, regulates the provision of benefits to people to meet basic life needs, such as employment, income, food, housing, health care, and relationships.[3]

Social welfare policy is influenced by the context in which benefits are provided. For example, social welfare is often associated with legislatively mandated programs of the **governmental sector,** such as **Temporary Assistance for Needy Families (TANF).** In the TANF program, social welfare policy consists of the rules by which the federal and state governments apportion cash benefits to an economically disadvantaged population. TANF benefits are derived from general revenue taxes (often paid by citizens who are better off). But this is a simplification of benefits provided to those deemed needy. Benefits provided through governmental social welfare policy include cash, but also noncash or in-kind benefits, including personal social services.[4] Cash benefits can be further divided into social insurance and public assistance grants.

In-kind benefits (provided as proxies for cash) include benefits such as food stamps, Medicaid, housing vouchers, Women, Infants, and Children (WIC) coupons, and low-income energy assistance. Personal social services are services designed to enhance relationships between people as well as institutions, such as individual, family, and mental health treatment; child welfare services; rehabilitation counseling; and so forth. While complicated, this classification reflects a common theme—namely, the redistribution of resources from those who are better off to those who are disadvantaged. This redistributional aspect of social welfare policy is generally accepted by those who view social welfare as a legitimate function of the state. Governmental social welfare policy is often referred to as "public" policy, because it is the result of decisions reached through a legislative process that is intended to represent the entire population.

But social welfare is also provided by nongovernmental entities, in which case social welfare policy is a manifestation of "private" policy. For example, a nonprofit agency with a high demand for its services and limited resources may establish a waiting list as agency policy. As other agencies in similar circumstances adopt the same strategy for rationing services, clients begin to pile up on waiting lists. Eventually, some clients are denied services because of the waiting lists. Hence, the policies of independent private agencies have a significant impact on the welfare of clients. Or consider the practice of "dumping," a policy that has been used by some private health care providers that abruptly transfer uninsured patients to public hospitals while they are suffering from traumatic injuries. Some patients have died as a result of private social welfare policy.

Because U.S. social welfare has been shaped by policies of governmental and nonprofit agencies, confusion exists about the role of for-profit social service firms. The distinction between the public and private sectors was traditionally marked by the boundary between governmental and nonprofit agencies. Profit-making firms are also "private," being nongovernmental entities, but they differ from the traditional private voluntary agencies in that they operate on a for-profit basis. Consequently, within private social welfare it is important to distinguish between policies of for-profit and policies of nonprofit organizations. A logical way to redraw the social welfare map is to adopt the following definitions: *Governmental social welfare policy* refers to decisions made by the state; *voluntary social welfare policy* refers to decisions reached by nonprofit agencies; and *corporate social welfare policy* refers to decisions made by for-profit firms.

Social Problems and Social Welfare Policy

Social welfare policy often develops in response to social problems. The relationship between social problems and social welfare policy is not linear, however; not all social problems result in social welfare policies. In many instances, social welfare policies exist but are funded at ineffectual levels. For example, the Child Abuse Prevention and Treatment Act of 1974 was designed to ameliorate the problem of child abuse, yet underbudgeting left Child Protective

Service (CPS) workers in a catch-22 situation. The act required CPS workers to promptly investigate child abuse reports, but agencies had inadequate staff resources to deal with the skyrocketing number of complaints. Caught in a resources crunch, many CPS workers were unable to properly investigate allegations of abuse. As a result, many children died or were seriously injured.

Social welfare is not merely an expression of social altruism; it contributes to the maintenance and survival of society. In this respect, social welfare policy helps hold together a society that may fracture along social, political, and economic stress lines. Social welfare policy is also useful in enforcing social control, especially as a proxy for other coercive measures such as law enforcement and the courts.[5] When their basic minimum needs are met, the disadvantaged are less inclined to revolt against the unequal distribution of resources. Social welfare policies also subsidize employers, because welfare benefits supplement low and nonlivable wages. If wages are insufficient to meet basic human needs for food, clothing, and shelter, there is little incentive for workplace participation. Without social welfare benefits tied to employment, such as the earned income tax credit (EITC), employers would have to raise wages and thereby prices would rise for all consumers. Social welfare also supports important industries, such as agriculture (food stamps), housing (Section 8 and various other housing programs), and health care (Medicaid and Medicare). Indeed, if social welfare benefits were suddenly eliminated, a segment of U.S. business would collapse and/or prices for commodities and services would rise dramatically. Hence, social welfare benefits help maintain stable price structures and economic growth.

Social welfare policies also relieve the social and economic dislocations caused by the uneven nature of economic development. For example, one of the main features of capitalism and economic globalism is a constantly changing economy where jobs are created in one sector and lost (or exported) in another. The result is large islands of unemployment as workers transition from one employment sector to the other, or are lost in the shuffle. Myriad social welfare programs, such as unemployment insurance, food stamps, and so forth, help soften the transition. Without such social benefits, fundamental questions would also arise about the moral, spiritual, and ethical nature of U.S. society. Finally, social welfare policies are a means for rectifying past and current injustices. For example, affirmative action was designed to remedy the historical discrimination that has denied large numbers of Americans access to economic opportunities and positions of power. School breakfast and lunch programs, teacher incentive pay, and other policies are designed to help ameliorate the unequal distribution of resources between underfunded inner-city and better-funded suburban school systems.

Social Work and Social Policy

Social work practice is driven by social policies, which dictate how the work is done, with whom, for how much, and toward what ends. For example, a social worker employed in a public mental health center may have a caseload of well over 200 clients. Given that caseload size, it is unlikely that a worker can engage in any kind of sustained psychotherapeutic intervention with clients; caseload constraints permit little more than superficial case tracking. Or consider the JOBS (Jobs Opportunities and Basic Skills) worker required to find employment for mothers on public assistance who are about to lose benefits because of the imposition of time limits but who are unlikely to find adequate work because of high unemployment in their area. In these instances, social, ideological, and economic factors contribute to policies that determine the ability of the social worker and the agency to accomplish their mission.

Since 1980, an ideological preference among policymakers for private sector social services has resulted in less funding for public agencies. A conservative emphasis on cutting taxes—evident in the dramatic tax cuts of the Bush administration—has led to reductions in public revenues, which, in turn, has translated into reductions for social programs. As a result of diminishing revenues, public agencies are taking predictable measures to adjust, including reductions in the number of qualified staff (existing staff is expected to do more with less), the utilization of less-qualified and less-expensive staff, the promotion of short-term or group interventions designed to process more clients less expensively, and stagnant or reduced salaries and benefits for professional staff. All of these strategies help shape an agency geared to processing more clients rather than to helping clients in any real sense. What a trained social worker is able to accomplish depends, in part, on the available resources within the agency.

Although this may not be obvious at first glance, the same is true for many social workers in private practice who depend on managed care plans for reimbursement. Specifically, managed care plans dictate how much a social worker will be paid and how often they will see a client; accordingly, care management dictates the kinds of interventions that will be practical in the allotted time. The rationing of client services by managed care companies has become a volatile issue. Thus, social policy and its components—ideology and values—greatly influence social work practice. In fact, policies have as much impact on clients and social workers as the microlevel theories that guide much of social work education. Moreover, these multilevel policies shape much of what is being taught in direct social work practice.

Values, Ideology, and Social Welfare Policy

Social welfare policies are shaped by a set of social and personal values that reflect the preferences of those in decision-making capacities. According to David Gil, "Choices in social welfare policy are heavily influenced by the dominant beliefs, values, ideologies, customs, and traditions of the cultural and political elites recruited mainly from among the more powerful and privileged strata."[6] Charles Prigmore and Charles Atherton list no fewer than 15 values that influence social welfare policy: achievement and success, activity and work, public morality, humanitarian concerns, efficiency and practicality, material comfort, equality, freedom, external conformity, science and secular rationality, nationalism and patriotism, democracy and self-determination, individualism, racism and group superiority, and belief in progress.[7] How these values are played out in the realm of social welfare is the domain of the policy analyst.

Despite the best of intentions, social welfare policy is often not based on a rational set of assumptions and reliable research. One view of a worthwhile social policy is that it should leave no one worse off and at least one person better off, at least as that person judges his or her needs. In the real world of policy that is rarely the case. More often, the policy game is played as a zero-sum game, in which some people are advantaged at the expense of others. In fact, it can be argued that major social policies are based on values, not on the careful consideration of alternative policies.

Of course, there are serious consequences when social welfare policy is determined to a high degree by values. Since the late 1970s, social welfare policy has been largely shaped by values that emphasize individualism, self-sufficiency, work, and the omniscience of the marketplace. Because policymakers expected disadvantaged people to be more independent, supports from government social programs were cut significantly. Although these reductions saved money in the short run, most of the beneficiaries whose supports fell to the budget ax were children. Eventually, cuts in social programs may well lead to greater expenditures, as the generation of children who have gone without essential services begin to require programs to remedy problems associated with poor maternal and infant health care, poverty, illiteracy, and family disorganization. As Silvia Ann Hewlett poignantly observed, "Although the United States ranks No. 2 worldwide in per capita income, this country does not even make it into the top ten on any significant indicator of child welfare."[8]

Social values are organized through the lens of ideology. Simply put, an **ideology** is the framework of commonly held beliefs through which we view the world. It is a set of assumptions about how the world works: what has value, what is worth living and dying for, what is good and true, and what is right. For the most part, these beliefs are rarely examined and are simply assumed to be true. Hence, the ideological tenets around which society is organized exist as a collective social consciousness that defines the world for the society's members. All societies reproduce themselves, in part, through reproducing ideology; in this way, each generation accepts the basic ideological suppositions of the preceding generation. When widely held ideological beliefs are questioned, society often reacts with strong sanctions. Ideological trends influence social welfare directly when adherents of one orientation hold a majority in decision-making bodies, such as a state or national legislature.

Ideology strongly influences social welfare policy during periods of social and economic instability, such as the current "War on Terror." In this instance, issues around social welfare policy retreat to the background as the perceived need for personal and national security takes center stage. The continuity of American social history has been intermittently shattered when certain oppressed groups have asserted their rights in the face of mainstream norms. Such periods of social unrest strain the capacity of conventional ideologies to explain social problems and offer solutions. Sometimes social unrest is met with force, as during the period of the great labor strikes of 1877. In other instances, such as the Great Depression, social unrest is met with the expansion of social welfare programs.

The Political Economy of American Social Welfare

The term **political economy** refers to the interaction of political and economic institutions in a society. The political economy of the United States has been labeled **democratic capitalism;** that is, in this country an open, representative form of government coexists with a market economy. The interaction of political and economic institutions is frequently irregular, however, and social welfare functions make society more stable. The main function of social welfare is to modify the play of market forces and to moderate the social and economic inequities that the market generates.[9] To that end, two sets of activities are necessary: state provision of social services (benefits of cash, in-kind benefits, and personal social services) and state regulation of private activities to alter (though not necessarily improve) the lives of citizens. In short, social welfare bolsters ideology by helping to remedy the problems associated with economic dislocation, thereby allowing society to remain in a state of more or less controlled balance.

Although Americans are assured of their political rights by a constitution that mandates a representative democracy, there is no corresponding document guaranteeing economic rights. Such a document would be undesirable in a free market economy, because it would allow government to interfere in the operations of the marketplace. In the absence of any guaranteed economic rights, large numbers of Americans find the economy unresponsive to their needs, and the political system is the only vehicle through which to seek redress. But because access to the political system often presupposes wealth and status, it is a less than optimal method for achieving social justice for many citizens. To some extent, social welfare programs compensate for deficiencies in the U.S. political economy by appeasing dissident groups.

It is important to understand the political economy in order to comprehend the intense disagreement around the optimal way to enhance the general welfare. Yet there is little common understanding of how this nation's political economy works or how it should work. Instead, several competing schools of thought purport to explain how the political economy functions and how best to deploy it to solve new problems. The stakes are high: Major institutions—government, corporations, organized labor, and the social welfare industry—stand to lose or gain considerable power based on how the political economy should be defined. Invariably, any given explanation of the political economy will benefit some institutions more than others. Because social welfare is advantaged or disadvantaged based on which school of political economy holds sway at any given moment, policy analysts pay close attention to important schools of thought.

As noted earlier, the U.S. welfare state is driven by political economy. While ideally the political economy of the welfare state should be viewed as an integrated fabric of politics and economics, in reality some schools of thought or movements contain more political than economic content, and vice versa. For example, most economic schools of thought contain sufficient political implications to qualify them as both economic and political dogmas. Conversely, most political schools of thought contain significant economic content. It is therefore often difficult to separate political from economic schools of thought. For the purposes of this chapter, though, we will organize the political economy of American welfare into two separate categories: (1) predominantly economic schools of thought, and (2) predominantly political schools of thought. The careful reader will find a significant overlap among and between these categories.

The U.S. Economic Continuum

In large measure, economics forms the backbone of the political system. For example, we would not have the modern welfare state without the contributions of economist John Maynard Keynes. Conversely, we would not have the conservative movement without the contributions of classical or free market economists such as Adam Smith or Milton Friedman. Virtually every political movement is in some way or another grounded in economic thought. The three major schools of economics that have traditionally dominated American economic thought are Keynesian economics; classical or free market economics (and its variants); and, to a lesser degree, democratic socialism.

Keynesian Economics

Keynesian economics drives liberalism and most welfare state ideology. Albeit indirectly, John Maynard Keynes was the economic architect of the modern welfare state, and virtually all welfare societies are built along his principles. Sometimes called demand or consumer-side economics, this model emerged from Keynes's book *The General Theory of Employment, Interest and Money,* published in 1936.

John Maynard Keynes is best known as the economic architect of the modern welfare state.

An Englishman, Keynes took the classical model of economic analysis (self-regulating markets, perfect competition, the laws of supply and demand, etc.) and added the insight that macroeconomic stabilization by government is necessary to keep the economic clock ticking smoothly.[10] He rejected the laissez-faire idea that a perfectly competitive economy tended automatically toward full employment and that the government should not interfere in the process. Keynes argued that instead of being self-correcting and readily able to pull themselves out of recessions, modern economies were recession prone and had problems providing full employment.

According to Keynes, periodic and volatile economic situations that cause high unemployment are primarily caused by an instability in investment expenditures. The government can stabilize and correct recessionary or inflationary trends by increasing or decreasing total spending on output. A government can accomplish this by increasing or decreasing taxes, thereby increasing or decreasing consumption, and by the transfer of public goods or services. For Keynes, the "good" government is an activist government in economic matters, especially when the economy gets out of a full employment mode. Keynesians hypothesize that social welfare expenditures are investments in human capital that eventually increase the national wealth (e.g., by increasing productivity) and thereby boost everyone's net income.

Keynes's doctrine emerged from his attempt to understand the nature of recessions and depressions. Specifically, he saw recessions and depressions as emerging from businesses' loss of confidence in investments (e.g., focusing on risk rather than gain), which in turn causes the hoarding of cash. The loss of confidence eventually leads to a shortage of money as everyone tries to hoard cash simultaneously. Keynes's answer to this problem is that government should make it possible for people to satisfy their economic needs without cutting their spending, which will prevent the spiral of shrinking incomes and shrinking spending. Simply put, the government should print more money and get it into circulation.[11]

Keynes also understood that this policy alone would not suffice if a recession were allowed to get out of control, as in the Depression of the 1930s. In a depression businesses and households will not increase spending regardless of how much cash they have. To help an economy exit this "liquidity trap," government must do what the private sector will not—namely, spend. This spending can take the form of public works projects (financed by borrowing programs) or by direct governmental subsidization of demand (welfare entitlements). To be fair, Keynes saw public spending only as a last resort to be employed if monetary expansion failed. Moreover, he sought an economic balance: Print money and spend in a recession, but stop printing and stop spending once it is over. Keynes understood that too much money in circulation, especially when production is active and there is full employment, leads to inflation. Although relatively simple, Keynes's theories represent one of the great insights of twentieth-century economic thought.[12] Keynes's ideas also form the economic basis for the modern welfare state.

Conservative or Free Market Economics

Whereas liberalism is guided by Keynesian economics, the conservative view of social welfare is guided by free market economics. The ascendence of the conservative economic (and social) argument accelerated after 1973, when the rise in living standards began to slow for most Americans. Conservatives blamed this economic slowdown on governmental policies—specifically, deficit spending, progressive taxes, excessive regulations, and monetary policies.[13]

Milton Friedman, considered by some to be the father of modern conservative economics, was one of Keynes's more ardent critics. In opposition to Keynes, Friedman argues that using fiscal and monetary policy to smooth out the business cycle is harmful to the economy and worsens economic instability.[14] Friedman contends that the Depression did not occur because people were hoarding money; rather, there was a fall in the quantity of money in circulation. He argues that Keynesian economic policies should be replaced by simple monetary rules (hence the term *monetarism*). In effect, Friedman believes that the role of government should be to keep the money supply growing slowly and steadily at a rate that is consistent with stable prices and long-term economic growth.[15]

Friedman counsels against active efforts to stabilize the economy. Instead of pumping money into the economy, government should simply make sure that enough cash is in circulation. He calls for government to be relatively inactive in economic affairs and not try to manage or intervene in the business cycle. For Friedman, welfare spending would exist only for altruistic rather than economic reasons.[16] To the right of Milton Friedman is Robert Lucas, 1994 Nobel Prize winner and developer of the "theory of rational expectations." Lucas argues that Friedman's monetary policy is still too interventionist and will invariably do more harm than good.[17]

Developing outside of conventional economics, **supply-side economics** enjoyed considerable popularity during the early 1980s. Led by Robert Barth, editorial page head of the *Wall Street Journal,* supply-siders were journalists, policymakers, and maverick economists who argued that demand-side policies and monetary policies were ineffective.[18] They maintained that the incentive effects of reduced taxation would be so large that tax cuts would dramatically increase economic activity—to the point where tax revenues would rise, not fall. (Former president George H. W. Bush referred to this as *voodoo economics* in 1980.[19]) Specifically, supply-siders argued that tax cuts would lead to a large increase in labor supply and investment and therefore to a large expansion in economic output. The budget deficit would not be problematic, because taxes, increased savings, and higher economic output would offset the deficit. In the early 1980s supply-siders seized power not only from the Keynesians, but also from more mainstream conservative economists, many of whom believed in the same things but wanted to move more slowly.[20]

Although some supporters preferred to think of supply-side economics as pure economics, the theory contained enough political implications to qualify as a political as well as an economic approach. Popularized by supporters such as Jack Kemp, Arthur Laffer, and Ronald Reagan, supply-side economics provided the major rationale for cuts in social programs executed under the Reagan administration.

Despite their popularity in the early years of the Reagan administration, supply-side ideas fell out of favor when it became evident that massive tax cuts for the wealthy and corporations did not result in increased capital formation and economic activity. Instead, the wealthy spent their tax savings on luxury items, and corporations used their tax savings to purchase other companies in a merger mania that took Wall Street by surprise. In addition, many corporations took advantage of temporary tax savings to transfer their operations abroad, further reducing the supply of high-paying industrial jobs in the United States. For these and other reasons, the budget deficit grew from about $50 billion a year in the Carter term to $352 billion a year in 1992.[21] Although the term "supply side economics" fell out of favor by the late 1980s, many of its basic tenets, such as massive tax cuts and cuts in social welfare spending, were adopted by the G. W. Bush administration. The result mirrored the earlier effects of supply side policies: huge federal and state budget shortfalls, corporate hoarding, greater economic inequality, and stagnant wages.[22] In fact, by 2004 the federal budget deficit had reached a record $450 billion.[23]

Conservative economists argue that large social welfare programs—including unemployment benefits and public service jobs—are detrimental to the society in two ways. First, government social programs erode the work ethic by supporting those not in the labor force. Second, because they are funded by taxes, public sector social welfare programs divert money that could otherwise be invested in the private sector. These conservative economists believe that economic growth helps everyone since overall prosperity creates more jobs, income, and goods, and these will eventually filter down to the poor. For conservative economists, investment is the key to prosperity and the engine that drives the economic machine. Accordingly, many conservative economists favor tax breaks for the wealthy based on the premise that such breaks will result in more disposable after-tax income freed up for investment. High taxes are an impediment to economic progress because they channel money into "public" investments and away from "private" investments.

In the neoconservative paradigm, opportunity is based on one's relationship to the marketplace. Thus, legitimate rewards can occur only through marketplace participation. In contrast to liberals who emphasize mutual self-interest, interdependence, and social equity, conservative economists argue that the highest form of social good is realized by the maximization of self-interest. In the conservative view (as epitomized by author Ayn Rand[24]) the best society is one in which everyone actively pursues their own good. Through a leap of faith, the maximization of self-interest can be transformed into a mutual good. In that sense, conservatives occupy the opposite end of the philosophical spectrum from liberals.

Conservative economists maintain not only that high taxation and government regulation of business serve as disincentives to investment, but that individual claims on social insurance and public welfare grants discourage work. Together these factors lead to a decline in economic growth and an increase in the expectations of beneficiaries of welfare programs. For conservatives the only way to correct the irrationality of governmental social programs is to eliminate them. Charles Murray has suggested that the entire federal assistance and income support structure for working-aged persons (Medicaid, the former AFDC, food stamps, etc.) should be scrapped. This would leave working-aged persons no recourse except to actively engage the job market or turn to family, friends, or privately funded services.[25]

Many conservative economists argue that economic insecurity is an important part of the entrepreneurial spirit. Unless people are *compelled* to work, they will choose leisure over work. Conversely, providing economic security for large numbers of people through welfare programs leads to diminished ambition and fosters an unhealthy dependence on the state. Conservatives further argue that self-realization can occur only through marketplace participation. Hence, social programs harm rather than help the most vulnerable members of society. This belief in the need for economic insecurity forms the basis for the 1996 welfare reform bill that includes a maximum time limit on welfare benefits.

Some conservative economists are influenced by "public choice" theory. The **public choice school** gained adherents among conservative analysts as faith ebbed in the supply-side school. Not widely known beyond academic circles until its major proponent, James Buchanan, was awarded the Nobel Prize for economics in 1986, the public choice model states that public sector bureaucrats are self-interested utility-maximizers, and that strong incentives exist for interest groups to make demands on government. The resulting concessions from this arrangement flow directly to the interest group while their costs are spread among all taxpayers. Initial concessions lead to demands for further concessions, which are likely to be forthcoming so long as interest groups are vociferous in their demands. Under such an incentive system, different interests are also encouraged to band together to make demands, because there is no reason for one interest group to oppose the demands of others. But while demands for goods and services increase, revenues tend to decrease. This happens because interest groups resist paying taxes directed specifically toward them and because no interest group has much incentive to support general taxes. The result of this scenario is predictable: Strong demands for government benefits accompanied by declining revenues lead to government borrowing, which in turn results in large budget deficits.[26] Adherents of public choice theory view social welfare as a series of endless concessions to disadvantaged groups that will eventually bankrupt the government. On the other hand, it would be logical also to apply public choice theory to defense industry interest groups, which make similar demands on government while not paying a fair share of taxes. Despite such contradictions, the public choice school is likely to remain influential and continue to shape social welfare policy by calling for further reductions in public expenditures for social programs.

Democratic Socialism

Democratic socialism (as opposed to old Soviet-style socialism) is based on the belief that radical economic change can occur within a democratic context. While eschewing capitalism, democratic socialists, such as the late Michael Harrington, have a fundamental belief in the democratic process.

Democratic socialism differs from both Keynesianism and conservative economics in an important way. Specifically, Keynesians have a basic faith in the market economy but want to make it more responsive to human needs. They want to retain capitalism, albeit with economic reforms that would smooth out the rough edges. Most conservatives believe that the economy should be left alone except for a few minor tweaks, such as regulating the money flow. Other conservative economists believe that the market should be left totally alone. On balance, both Keynesians and economic conservatives have a basic faith that capitalism can advance the public good and is not antithetical to human needs. In that sense, Keynesianism and economic conservatism have more in common with each other than with a radical leftist perspective.

In contrast, proponents of **socialism** argue that the fundamental nature of capitalism is anathema to advancing the public good. They contend that a system predicated on the pursuit of profit and individual self-interest can lead only to greater inequality. The creation of a just society requires a fundamental transformation of the economic system, and democratic socialists argue that the pursuit of profit and self-interest should be replaced by the collective pursuit of the common good. Not surprisingly, democratic socialists rebuff Keynesianism because of its inherent belief that economic problems can be fixed by simple technicalities as opposed to major institutional change. They dislike conservatism for more obvious reasons, such as the primary importance it places on markets, its belief in subordinating individual interests to market forces, and its overall social conservatism.

Left-wing theorists maintain that the failure of capitalism has led to political movements that have pressured institutions to respond with increased social welfare services. They believe that real social welfare must be structural and can be accomplished only by redistributing resources. In a just society where goods, resources, and opportunities are made available to everyone, all but the most specific forms of welfare (health care, rehabilitation, counseling, etc.) would be unnecessary. In this radical worldview, poverty is inextricably linked to structural inequality. People need welfare because they are exploited and denied access to resources. In an unjust society, welfare functions as a substitute, albeit a puny one, for social justice.[27]

For some socialists, social welfare is an ingenious arrangement on the part of business to have the public assume the costs caused by the social and economic dislocations inherent in capitalism. According to these theorists, social welfare expenditures "socialize" the costs of capitalist production by making public the costs of private enterprise. Thus, social welfare serves both the needs of people and the needs of capitalism. For other socialists, social welfare programs support an unjust economic system, which in turn, continues to generate problems requiring social programs.

Radicals maintain that social welfare programs function like junk food for the impoverished: They provide just enough sustenance to discourage revolution but not enough to make a real difference in the lives of the poor. Within this radical framework, social welfare is seen as a form of social control. Frances Fox Piven and Richard Cloward summarize the socialist argument:

> Relief arrangements are ancillary to economic arrangements. Their chief function is to regulate labor, and they do that in two general ways. First, when mass unemployment leads to outbreaks of turmoil, relief programs are ordinarily initiated or expanded to absorb or control enough of the unemployed to restore order; then, as turbulence subsides, the relief system contracts, expelling those who are needed to populate the labor markets.[28]

In place of liberal welfare reforms, the radical vision proposes that the entire social, political, and especially economic system undergo a major overhaul. In short, the radical position is that real welfare reform (i.e., a complete redistribution of goods, income, and services) can occur only in the context of a socialist economic system.

The U.S. Political Continuum

Various understandings of the political economy produce differing conceptions of the ultimate public good. Competition among ideas about the public good and the welfare state has long been a knotty issue in the political economy of the United States. Because any shift in government policy is driven largely by an ideologically determined view of the public good, any analysis must be based on whose definition is being examined. In a democratic capitalist society, beliefs about the public good often vary depending on the proponent's position in the social order.

The major American ideologies, (neo)liberalism and (neo)conservatism, hold vastly different views of social welfare and the public good. Conservatives believe that the public good is best served when individuals and families meet their needs through marketplace participation. Accordingly, conservatives prefer private sector approaches over governmental welfare and advocate for smaller government social welfare programs. Conservatives are not antiwelfare per se; they simply believe that government should have a minimal role (i.e., serve as a "safety net") in ensuring the social welfare of citizens. Traditional liberals, on the other hand, view government as the only institution capable of bringing about a measure of **social justice** to millions of Americans who cannot fully participate in the U.S. mainstream because of obstacles such as racism, poverty, and sexism, among others. Traditional liberals therefore view governmental social welfare programs as a key component in promoting the public good. One of the major differences between conservatives and liberals lies in their differing perceptions on how the public good is enhanced or hurt by the welfare state.

The definition of "the public good" is lodged in the political and ideological continuum that makes up American political economy. An appreciation of this continuum requires an understanding of the interaction of schools of political thought and how they evolved. These ideological tenets also shape the platforms of the major political parties and can be divided into two categories: (1) liberalism and left-of-center movements, and (2) traditional conservatives and the far right.

Liberalism and Left-of-Center Movements

Liberalism Since Franklin Delano Roosevelt's **New Deal,** advocates of liberalism have argued for advancing the public good by promoting an expanding economy coupled with the growth of universal, non-means–tested social welfare and health programs. Traditional liberals used Keynesian concepts as the economic justification for building the welfare state. As such, the general direction of policy from the 1930s to the early 1970s was for the federal government to assume greater amounts of responsibility for the public good.

American liberals established the welfare state with the passage of the Social Security Act of 1935. Harry Hopkins—a social worker, the head of the Federal Emergency Relief Administration, a confidant of President Roosevelt, a coarchitect of the New Deal, and a consummate political operative—developed the calculus for American liberalism: "tax, tax; spend, spend; elect, elect."[29] This liberal approach was elegant in its simplicity: The government taxes the wealthy, thereby securing the necessary revenues to fund social programs for workers and the poor. This approach dominated social policy for almost 50 years. In fact, it was so successful that by 1980 social welfare accounted for 57 percent of all federal expenditures.[30]

By the middle 1960s the welfare state was an important fixture in America's social landscape, and politicians sought to expand its benefits to more constituents. Focusing on the expansion of middle-class programs such as FHA home mortgages, federally insured student loans, Medicare, and veterans' pensions, liberal policymakers secured the political loyalty of the middle class. Even conservative politicians respected voter support for the middle-class welfare state, and not surprisingly, the largest expansion of social welfare spending occurred under Richard Nixon, a Republican president.

Yet the promise of the U.S. welfare state to provide social protection similar to that in industrialized European nations never materialized. By the middle 1970s the hope of traditional liberals to build a welfare state mirroring those of northern Europe had been replaced by an incremental approach that narrowly focused on consolidating and fine-tuning the programs of the Social Security Act. One reason for this failure was the ambivalence of many Americans toward centralized government. "The emphasis consistently has been on the local, the pluralistic, the voluntary, and the business-like over the national, the universal, the legally entitled, and the governmental," observed policy analyst Marc Bendick.[31] Having lost the public policy debate to conservatives, liberals were in a poor position to press for additional programs to serve vulnerable populations neglected by the "reluctant" U.S. welfare state.[32]

Liberalism lost ground for another reason. The Social Security Act of 1935—the hallmark of American liberalism—was primarily a self-financing social insurance program that rewarded working people. Public assistance programs that contained less political capital and were therefore a better measure of public compassion, were rigorously means tested, sparse in their benefits, and operated by the less than generous states. For example, while Social Security benefits were indexed to the cost of living in the mid-1970s, AFDC benefits deteriorated so badly that it lost about half its value from 1975 to 1992. At the same time that Social Security reforms reduced the elderly poverty rate by 50 percent, the plight of poor families worsened.

Neoliberalism By the late 1970s, the liberal belief that the welfare state was the best mechanism to advance the public good was in retreat. What remained of traditional liberalism was replaced by a **neoliberalism** that was more cautious of government, less antagonistic toward big business, and more skeptical about the value of universal entitlements.

The defeat of Jimmy Carter and the election of a Republican Senate in 1980 forced many liberal Democrats to reevaluate their party's traditional position on domestic policy. This reexamination, which Charles Peters christened "neoliberalism" to differentiate it from old-style liberalism, attracted only a small following in the early 1980s.[33] However, by the middle 1990s most leading Democrats could be classified as neoliberal. Randall Rothenberg charted signs of the influence of neoliberalism on the Democratic domestic policy platform as early as 1982, when he observed that the party's midterm convention did not endorse a large-scale federal jobs program, did not endorse a plan for national health insurance, and did not submit a plan for a guaranteed annual income.[34]

In the late 1980s a cadre of prominent mainstream Democrats, among them Paul Tsongas, Richard Gephardt, Sam Nunn, and Bill Bradley, established the Democratic Leadership Council (DLC). In part, their goal was to wrest control of the Democratic Party from traditional liberals (who were presumably easily exploited by the Republican Party) and to create a new Democratic Party that was more attuned to the beliefs of the traditional core voters. In 1989 the DLC released *The New Orleans Declaration: A Democratic Agenda for the 1990s,* which promised that Democratic Party politics would shift toward a middle ground combining a corporatist economic analysis with Democratic compassion. Two of the founders of the DLC were Al Gore and Bill Clinton, who chaired the DLC just before announcing his presidential candidacy.[35]

Compared to traditional liberals, neoliberals were more forgiving of the behavior of large corporations and were opposed to economic protectionism. Adherents of *realpolitik,* neoliberals viewed the New Deal approach (with the exception of Social Security) as too expensive and antiquated to address the current mood of voters and the new global realities. As such, neoliberals distanced themselves from the large-scale governmental welfare programs associated with Democrats since the New Deal. Like their neoconservative counterparts, they called for reliance on personal responsibility, work, and thrift as an alternative to governmental programs. Accordingly, their welfare proposals emphasized labor market participation (workfare), personal responsibility (time-limited welfare benefits), family obligations (child support enforcement), and frugality in governmental spending ("reinventing government"). As a substitute for comprehensive welfare reform, neoliberals argued for reduced governmental spending while encouraging businesses to assume more responsibility for the welfare of the population.

Former Secretary of Labor Robert Reich, a former Harvard professor and DLC advisor, advocated a postliberal formulation that replaced social welfare entitlements with investments in **human capital.** Public spending was divided into "good" and "bad" categories: "Bad" was consumption, such as unproductive expenditures on welfare and price supports; "good" was investments in human capital, such as expenditures on education, research, and job training.[36] In 1983, Reich anticipated that a significant part of the present welfare system would be replaced by government grants to businesses that agreed to hire the chronically unemployed; he also made these predictions:

> Other social services—health care, social security, day care, disability benefits, unemployment benefits, relocation assistance—will become part of the process of structural adjustment. Public funds now spent directly on these services will instead be made available to businesses, according to the number of people they agree to hire. Government bureaucracies that now administer these programs to individuals will be supplanted, to a large extent, by companies that administer them to their employees. Companies, rather than state and local governments, will be the agents and intermediaries through which such assistance is provided.[37]

Neoliberalism altered the traditional liberal concept of the public good. Instead of viewing the best interests of large corporations as antithetical to the best interests of society, neoliberals argued for free trade, less regulation of corporate activity, and a more laissez-faire approach to social problems. Neoliberals also viewed longtime Democratic Party supporters such as labor unions with caution. For example, when labor unions fought to stop NAFTA (the North American Free Trade Agreement), President Clinton continued to endorse it, despite labor's threats to oppose his reelection bid in 1996. The same was true for the GATT (General Agreement on Tariffs and Trade) agreement. In both instances Clinton was firmly aligned with conservative Democrats and Republicans. Traditional liberal Democrats found themselves alone, bereft of support from the first Democratic White House in 14 years. In effect, the new shapers of the public good had systematically excluded key actors of the old liberal coalition.

The neoliberal view of the public good reflects a kind of postmodern perspective. For neoliberals, the public good is elusive, and its form is fluid. Definitions of the public good change as a social order evolves and new power relationships emerge. Thus, neoliberals do not define the public good as tethered to industrial era allegiances but look to a postindustrial society composed of new opportunities and new institutional forms.

Neoliberalism, then, is more a political strategy and pragmatic mode of operation than a political philosophy embodying a firm view of the public good. This is both its strength and its weakness. Specifically, the strength of neoliberalism lies in its ability to compromise and therefore to accomplish things. Its weakness is that when faced with an ideological critique (such as the Republicans' Contract with America), neoliberals are incapable of formulating a cogent ideological response. When G. W. Bush argued for staying the course in 2004, voters knew exactly what he meant even if they disagreed with him. When Clinton argued for staying the course in 1994, the public was unsure as to what the course was.

In the American and British contexts, neoliberalism represents a "third way." Anthony Giddens offers a philosophical rationale for neoliberalism: "We should speak of a *positive welfare,* to which individuals and other agencies besides government contribute—and which is functional for wealth creation. The guideline for investment is *human capital* wherever possible, rather than the direct provision of economic maintenance. In place of the welfare state we should put the *social investment state,* operating in the context of a positive welfare society."[38]

The Greens/Green Party A loosely knit national organization that is part of a worldwide movement that began in Germany, **Greens** promote ecological awareness, social justice, grassroots democracy, and nonviolence. In the United States, the movement is organized into state Green parties and Green locals. By 1996 the Green Party had run Senate or House candidates in Alaska, New Mexico, Maine, California, Massachusetts, New York, and Rhode Island. Running as the Green Party's 2000 presidential candidate, Ralph Nader made it onto the ballot in several key states.[39]

The U.S. Green Party promotes ten core values: ecological wisdom, grassroots democracy, nonviolence, social justice, decentralization, community-based economics, feminism, respect for diversity, personal and global responsibility, and future focus. In addition, Greens argue for policies that promote economic and environmental sustainability, and encourage their members to live green lifestyles and to organize local groups in urban and rural areas; work on community issues such as toxic dumping, homelessness, equal rights and recycling; field ballot initiatives, referendums, and challenge restrictive election laws; work for or against legislation; and take nonviolent direct action.[40]

Communitarianism Sometimes known as civic republicans,[41] communitarians represent a loose-knit group of intellectuals who propose a middle ground between radical individualism and excessive statism. In part, **communitarianism** arose in the late 1980s as a response to the lacuna that emerged when the political center began to erode in the late 1970s and the United States moved markedly to the right. Groups that were once considered fringe, such as the Christian fundamentalist right, now found themselves in mainstream positions of power. At the same time, there was an uneasy sense among certain intellectuals and political leaders that the moral and social fabric of the nation was unwinding along with its political center.

According to Peter Steinfels, "Communitarians essentially staked out political territory somewhere between the liberal advocates of the welfare state and civil liberties entrenched in one corner, and conservative devotees of laissez-faire and traditional values on the other."[42] Communitarians generally agree with liberals on issues of individual rights, equality, and democratic change. They argue, however, that none of these values can be preserved unless basic communities and institutions (e.g., families, schools, neighborhoods, unions, local governments, religious institutions, and ethnic groups) succeed in rebuilding individual character and promoting the virtues of citizenship.[43]

Communitarians are concerned with rebuilding communities. For them, radical individualism is responsible for the breakdown of society. In addition, they advocate for strong two-parent families (although they do acknowledge that some single-parent families succeed), which they view as the main conduit for socialization and good citizenship. In communitarian philosophy, the family is where each new generation acquires its moral anchor.[44]

Communitarians attempt to balance conservatism with liberalism. On the one hand, communitarians—like traditional conservatives—fault liberals for consistently citing economic and political forces as the causes of poverty, drug abuse, crime, and urban problems while neglecting the importance of personal responsibility. On the other hand, they blame conservatives for overemphasizing the value of the free market and for promoting the pursuit of self-interest as the answer to social problems. Conservatives, as communitarians see it, ignore the corrosive effects of the market and the subsequent economic pressure it places on family life and community spirit. Communitarians take no positions on abortion or gay rights.[45]

On the surface, communitarians appear more conservative than traditional liberals. They argue for adolescent curfews, work requirements for welfare, family values, "drug-free" zones, more emphasis on public safety, less access to legal redress for criminals, and the need for government to create more obstacles to divorce. Communitarians also reject the view that Americans are so divided over basic values that teaching moral education is impossible. They argue that moral education and character building should be part of curricula from kindergarten to college. Although communitarians advocate the protection of basic rights, they also call for "sensible limits on freedom," including driver sobriety checkpoints and mandatory drug testing for those in public jobs. Echoing anti-federal–government sentiment, communitarians call for shifting power out of Washington and into the private sector and local government. But, lest communitarians sound too conservative, they also advocate European-style child allowance benefits, extended paid and unpaid parental leaves, and flexible working hours. Communitarians also call for national service and an end to private gun ownership.

Communitarians maintain that the terms *liberal* and *conservative* are antiquated. Amitai Etzioni argues that "When it comes to freedom of speech, enforcement of law, public safety, the family and schools, we find it better to talk about authoritarians who want to impose their moral solution on everybody, libertarians who oppose any voice other than that of the individual, and communitarians who want new moral standards reached through consensus."[46] Evidence of the bridging effects of communitarianism was reflected in an agenda developed in the early 1990s that was endorsed by leaders from across the political spectrum, among them Democrats Daniel P. Moynihan and Al Gore and Republicans David Durenberger and Jack Kemp.

The Self-Reliance School A perspective gaining influence in economically distressed areas of the United States and in developing countries is the **self-reliance school** of political economy.[47] This school maintains that industrial economic models are irrelevant to the economic needs of poor communities and are often damaging to the spiritual life of people.[48] Adherents of self-reliance repudiate the emphasis of Western economic philosophies on economic growth and the belief that the quality of life can be measured by material acquisitions. These political economists stress a balanced economy based on the real needs of people, production designed for internal consumption rather than export, productive technologies that are congruent with the culture and background of the population, the use of appropriate and manageable technologies, and a small-scale and decentralized form of economic organization.[49] Simply put, proponents of self-reliance postulate that more is less and less is more. The objective of self-reliance is the creation of a no-poverty society in which economic life is organized around issues of subsistence rather than trade and economic expansion. Accepting a world of finite resources and inherent limitations to economic growth, proponents argue that the true question of social and economic development is not what people think they want or need but what they require for survival. The self-reliance school accepts the need for social welfare programs that ameliorate the dislocations caused by industrialization, but it prefers low-technology and local solutions to social problems. This contrasts with the conventional wisdom of the welfare state, which is predicated on a prescribed set of programs on a national scale, administered by large bureaucracies using sophisticated management systems.

Classical Conservatives and the Far Right

Classic Conservatism Former conservative political leaders such as Nelson Rockefeller, Richard Nixon, and Barry Goldwater represented traditional conservatism. Virtually no traditional conservatives now occupy important leadership positions in the Republican party since most have been replaced by cultural conservatives.

On one level, all U.S. conservatives agree on important values relating to social policy. They are anti-union, oppose aggressive governmental regulations, demand lower taxes and less governmental spending, want local control of public education, oppose extending civil rights legislation, and believe strongly in states' rights. Beneath this agreement, however, important differences exist among various conservative factions.

Older, traditional conservatives diverge with the newer cultural conservatives on a range of social issues. First, as strict constitutionalists, traditional or classical conservatives believe strongly in the separation of church and state. They see prayer and religion as personal choices in which government has no legitimate right to intervene. Second, although both classical conservatives and cultural conservatives advocate a less powerful federal government, cultural conservatives also demand that the federal government use its power to implement their domestic agenda in areas they consider immoral, including abortion and homosexuality.

Third, classical conservatives are more socially liberal than cultural conservatives. For example, the late Barry Goldwater, a conservative former U.S. senator and 1964 presidential candidate, stated that "I have been, and am still, a traditional conservative, focusing on three general freedoms—economic, social, and political. . . . The conservative movement is founded on the simple tenet that people have the right to live life as they please, as long as they don't hurt anyone else in the process."[50] Goldwater's outspoken support of homosexuals in the military was in direct opposition to the principles of neoconservatives. Regarding reproductive freedom, classical conservatives might challenge cultural conservatives on various measures that limit or ban abortions.

From the late 1970s until the present, factions within the conservative movement became more pronounced. Old-style conservatives such as Nelson Rockefeller, Barry Goldwater, and William Cohen, who were more concerned with foreign policy than with domestic issues, were replaced by a new breed of radical cultural conservatives, such as Dick Armey, Newt Gingrich, Phil Gramm, and others. These cultural conservatives were adamant about reversing a half century of liberal influence in social policy. How the cultural conservatives came to shape social policy warrants elaboration, although it is first important to examine the forerunners of cultural conservatism, the neoconservatives.

Neoconservatism Before the 1970s, conservatives seemed content merely to snipe at welfare programs, reserving their attention for areas more in line with their traditional concerns such as the economy, defense spending, and foreign affairs. However, by the mid-1970s, younger conservative intellectuals recognized that this classically conservative stance toward social welfare was no longer tenable: Welfare had become too important to be dismissed so lightly. Consequently, **neoconservatism** emerged as a movement seeking to arrest the growth in governmental welfare programs while simultaneously transferring as much welfare responsibility as possible from government to the private sector.[51] Neoconservatives faulted government programs for a breakdown in the mutual obligation between groups; the lack of attention to efficiencies in the way programs were operated and benefits awarded; the dependency of recipients on programs; and the growth of the welfare industry and its special interest groups,

President George W. Bush has labeled himself a compassionate conservative.

particularly professional associations.[52] To counter the liberal goals of full employment, national health care, and a guaranteed annual income, neoconservatives maintained that high unemployment was good for the economy, that health care should remain in the private marketplace, and that competitive income structures were critical to productivity. Neoconservative economists argued that income inequality was socially desirable, contending that social policies that promote equality encourage coercion, limit individual freedom, and damage the economy.[53]

The neoconservative attack on the welfare state was particularly pointed since many neoconservatives, among them Irving Kristol and Norman Podhoretz, were former liberals who had developed such misgivings about the welfare state that they joined the conservative movement. These neoconservatives were effective in critiquing the welfare state, in large measure because they were so familiar with its philosophical origins. Despite their opposition to the welfare state, former liberals found their new conservative home anything but tidy. Born out of an urban environment, neoconservatives fashioned themselves as cosmopolitan intellectuals and free thinkers. Social issues such as abortion, school prayer, and the like were not a hot button for this movement. As a whole, neoconservatives were more urban and sophisticated then their cultural conservatives counterparts.

By the late 1970s, however, the position that the neoconservatives occupied in the conservative movement began to be usurped by the emerging cultural conservatives. Although the neoconservatives had provided the intellectual wedge that fractured the liberal consensus around the welfare state, it was cultural conservatives such as Trent Lott and Tom DeLay who attained the leadership positions necessary to take down what was left of the institutional structure of liberal public philosophy. Properly understood, neoconservatism is at odds with the culturally conservative social agenda promoted by the Republicans for the past 30-plus years.

Cultural Conservatism The neoconservative assault on liberal social policy was soon taken over by cultural conservatives, who raged against governmental intrusion in the marketplace while simultaneously attempting to use the authority of government to advance their social objectives in the areas of antiwelfare planks, sexual abstinence, school prayer, abortion, and anti-gay rights proposals. Cultural conservatives cleverly promoted a dual attitude toward the role of government. Mimicking their classical conservative predecessors in demanding a laissez-faire approach to economics, they steadfastly refused to translate that orientation to social affairs. Instead, cultural conservatives argued for social conformity and a level of governmental intrusion into private affairs that made most classical conservatives gag. In contrast to the classical conservative skepticism about blending religion and politics, cultural conservatives opportunistically embraced the rising tide of fundamentalist religion. As a measure of their success, this cobbled-together coalition of economic conservatives, right-wing Christians, and opportunistic politicians had by the late 1980s virtually decimated what remained of Republican liberalism, whose adherents had become an endangered species like liberal Democrats.

For liberals, the state represents the best vehicle for achieving the public good and is an ally in promoting social change. In contrast, cultural conservatives view the state as the cause of rather than the solution to social problems. With the exception of protecting people (police and defense) and property, cultural conservatives argue that the very existence of the state is antithetical to the public good since government interferes with the maximization of individual self-interest. Hence, their posture toward government is adversarial, except when the state is used to further their social agenda. While cultural conservatives argue for a minimalist state, they have been willing to compromise these libertarian leanings by adopting the agenda of traditionalists in myriad social issues such as school prayer, abortion, sexual orientation, and drug testing.

The conservative agenda of the 1980s was fourfold: (1) end the liberal hegemony in social policy, (2) reroute public policy through the private sector, (3) curtail costly social programs that lessen profits and restrict the global competitiveness of corporations, and (4) preclude the possibility of a resurgence in social programs. In tandem with this agenda, conservative presidents such as Reagan and the two Bushes prohibited the future growth of the welfare state by employing multiple strategies such as tax policy and federal budget deficits.

Despite important victories, cultural conservatives were unable to construct a programmatic alternative to the welfare state. After hammering away at social programs, conservatives had accomplished relatively little by the late 1980s in terms of replacing liberal social policies. As an example, costs for social insurance and entitlement programs such as Social Security, Medicare, and Medicaid continued to soar. In the end, cultural conservatives had underestimated three important factors: (1) the resiliency of the welfare state, (2) the continued support (however ambivalent) it enjoyed among the middle

Spotlight 1.1

Two groups that exemplify the differences between liberal and conservative political movements are the Green Party and the Moral Majority.

The Green Party

Ten key values serve as guiding principles for the Green Party—grassroots democracy, social justice and equal opportunity, ecological wisdom, nonviolence, decentralization, community-based economics and economic justice, feminism and gender equity, respect for diversity, personal and global responsibility, and future focus and sustainability. To learn more about these key values, go to the Green Party's website at **www.gp.org/tenkey.html.**

The Moral Majority

Traditionalists are characterized by conservative evangelical groups such as the Moral Majority. The Moral Majority and other traditional groups believe that God's laws must be translated into politics, and "higher laws" must become the laws of the state. Traditionalists are highly critical of governmental social programs, which they associate with a liberal social philosophy that is eroding traditional social institutions, particularly the family and the church. To learn more about the Moral Majority platform, visit the group's website at **www.faithandvalues.us.**

class, and (3) the difficulty of translating rhetoric into viable reform proposals.

Nevertheless, in 1994 frustrated voters seemed ready to offer the right a second chance by giving them control of the Senate and the House. Cultural conservatives had learned from past mistakes. Instead of toying with incremental policies, they proposed bold new social initiatives that were incorporated into the Contract with America (designed to alter most of the safety net programs within a two-year period), a document signed by more than 300 House Republicans in 1994.[54] In the end, the crowning victory of the conservative movement occurred with the passage of the Personal Responsibility and Work Opportunity Reconciliation Act (PRWORA) in 1996.

Traditionalism Proponents of **traditionalism** have a Christian religious orientation to social policy and emphasize a moral relationship between politics and religion. Although similar to cultural conservatives, they are even more extreme in their beliefs. Traditionalists are characterized by evangelical groups such as the Moral Majority. According to traditionalists, God's laws must be translated into politics, and "higher laws" must become the laws of the state. Because traditionalists presume the United States to be a Christian nation, they see the separation between church and state as unnatural. Traditionalists emphasize the Christian value of hard work and see little value for welfare, except for the most needy.

Traditionalists are highly critical of governmental social programs, which they associate with a liberal social philosophy (secular humanism) that is eroding traditional social institutions, particularly the family and the church. Lightning-rod issues for traditionalists are abortion, prohibition of prayer in school, affirmative action, and school integration—all of which traditionalists associate with the increasing liberalism of society.

Libertarianism **Libertarians** reflect another perspective. Specifically, this school of thought believes in virtually no government regulation.

> We, the members of the Libertarian Party, challenge the cult of the omnipotent state and defend the rights of the individual. We hold that all individuals . . . have the right to live in whatever manner they choose, so long as they do not forcibly interfere with the equal right of others to live in whatever manner they choose. We . . . hold that governments . . . must not violate the rights of any individual: namely, (1) the right to life—accordingly we support the prohibition of the initiation of physical force against others; (2) the right to liberty of speech and action—accordingly we oppose all attempts . . . [at] . . . government censorship in any form; and (3) . . . we oppose all government interference with private property. . . .[55]

Libertarians argue that governmental growth occurs at the expense of individual freedom. They also believe that the proper role for government is to provide a police force and a military that possesses only defensive weapons. Libertarians are highly critical of taxation since it fuels governmental growth. Apart from advocating minimal taxation earmarked for defense and police activities, libertarians oppose the income tax. Because libertarians emphasize individual freedom and personal responsibility, they advocate the decriminalization of narcotics. They also believe that government should only intercede in social affairs when the behavior of an individual threatens the safety of another. The Libertarian Party critique of social welfare is based on the belief that the state should not be involved in social and economic activities, except in very limited circumstances.

The Welfare Philosophers and the Neoconservative Think Tanks

Many welfare professionals envisioned a U.S. welfare state based on a European model.[56] This vision was shared by virtually every social welfare scholar writing in the late 1960s and early 1970s.[57] In turn, most social workers adhered to a liberal welfare philosophy grounded in a system of national social programs that would be deployed as more citizens demanded greater services and benefits. This framework was informed by European welfare states, especially the Scandinavian variant that spread health care, housing, income benefits, and employment opportunities equitably across the population.[58] It also led Richard Titmuss to hope that the welfare state, as an instrument of government, would eventually lead to a "welfare world."[59]

For U.S. welfare philosophers, government programs that ameliorated the caprices of capitalism were both desirable and inevitable. In their classic *Industrial Society and Social Welfare,* Harold Wilensky and Charles Lebeaux suggested that "under continuing industrialization all institutions will be oriented toward and evaluated in terms of social welfare aims. The 'welfare state' will become the 'welfare society,' and both will be more reality than epithet."[60]

This vision of the role of social welfare in U.S. society was accepted for decades by welfare professionals who took jobs with governmental agencies or in voluntary sector organizations that were heavily dependent on governmental contracts. In fact, the combination of government bureaucracy and agency casework was so prevalent that Wilensky and Lebeaux concluded that "virtually all welfare service is dispensed through social agencies . . . and virtually all social workers operate through such agencies."[61] For most social welfare professionals, the welfare state was not a philosophical abstraction but the basis of their livelihood.

Despite the widespread acceptance of this liberal vision, an alternative one arose that questioned the fundamental nature of welfare and social services. Throughout the 1970s and 1980s, conservatives (especially right-wing **think tanks,** or conservative policy institutes) busily made proposals for welfare reform. In fact, no policy institute on the right could prove its mettle until it produced a plan to clean up "the welfare mess." The Hoover Institution at Stanford University helped shape the early conservative position on welfare. "There is no inherent reason that Americans should look to government for those goods and services that can be individually acquired," argued Hoover's Alvin Rabushka, who listed four strategies for reforming welfare: (1) let users pay, (2) contract for services, (3) fund mandated services through the states, and (4) emphasize private substitution.[62] Martin Anderson, a Hoover senior fellow and later a domestic policy adviser to the Reagan administration, elaborated the conservative position on welfare in terms of the need to (1) reaffirm the need-only philosophical approach to welfare and state it as explicit national policy; (2) increase efforts to eliminate fraud; (3) establish and enforce a fair, clear work requirement; (4) remove inappropriate beneficiaries from the welfare rolls; (5) enforce support of dependents by those who have the responsibility and are shirking it; (6) improve the efficiency and effectiveness of welfare administration; and (7) shift more responsibility from the federal government to state and local governments and private institutions.[63] It was precisely these recommendations that formed the backbone of the 1996 PRWORA.

Another conservative think tank, the American Enterprise Institute (AEI), commissioned sociologist Peter Berger and theologian Richard John Neuhaus to prepare a theoretical analysis of U.S. society. Berger and Neuhaus's *To Empower People: The Role of Mediating Structures in Public Policy* identified the fundamental problem confronting the culture such as the growth of megastructures (big government, big business, big labor, and professional bureaucracies) and the corresponding diminution in the value of the individual. The route to empowerment was to revitalize "mediating structures," among them the neighborhood, family, church, and voluntary associations.[64] In a subsequent analysis an AEI scholar recategorized the corporation from a megastructure to a mediating structure, thus leaving the basic institutions of liberal social reform—government, the professions, and labor—as the sources of mass alienation.[65]

Not to be outdone, the Heritage Foundation featured *Out of the Poverty Trap: A Conservative Strategy for Welfare Reform* by Stuart Butler and Anna Kondratas.[66] Following along the same lines, the Free Congress Research and Education Foundation proposed reforming welfare through "cultural conservatism"; that is, by reinforcing "traditional values such as delayed gratification, work and saving, commitment to family and to the next generation, education and training, self-improvement, and rejection of crime, drugs, and casual sex."[67]

A handful of other works also served as beachheads for the conservative assault on the liberal welfare state. George Gilder's *Wealth and Poverty* argued that beneficent welfare programs represented a "moral hazard," insulating people against risks essential to capitalism and thus contributing to dependency.[68] Martin Anderson contended that income calculations should include the cash equivalent of in-kind benefits such as food stamps, Medicaid, and housing vouchers, thus effectively lowering the poverty rate by 40 percent.[69] Taken together, these ideas and recommendations provided a potent critique of liberal governmental welfare programs. Unlike classical conservatives of an earlier generation, neoconservatives not only did their homework on social welfare policy but they also prepared serious proposals for welfare reform.

Conclusion

John Judis and Michael Lind argue that "Ultimately American economic policy must meet a single test: Does it, in the long run, tend to raise or depress the incomes of most Americans? A policy that tends to impoverish the ordinary American is a failure, no matter what its alleged benefits are for U.S. corporations or for humanity as a whole."[70] To this we would add: "What are the effects of an economic policy on the social health of the nation?" Researchers at Fordham University's Institute for Innovation in Social Policy contend that the nation's quality of life has become unhinged from its economic growth. "We really have to begin to reassess this notion that the gross domestic product—the overall growth of the society—necessarily is going to produce improvements in the quality of life."[71] Constructing an Index for Social Health that encompassed governmental data from 1970 to 1993, researchers found that in six categories—children in poverty, child abuse, health insurance coverage, average weekly earnings adjusted for inflation, out-of-pocket health costs for senior citizens, and the gap between rich and poor—"social health" hit its lowest point in 1993. These indicators have worsened in the years since 1993 and we can therefore presume that the downward trend continues.

As this chapter has demonstrated, social welfare in the United States is characterized by a high degree of diversity and is not a monolithic, highly centralized, well-coordinated system of programs. Rather, a great variety of organizations provide a wide range of benefits and services to different client populations. The vast array of social welfare organizations contributes to what is commonly called "the welfare mess." Consequently, different programs serving different groups through different procedures have engendered an impenetrable tangle of institutional red tape that is problematic for administrators, human service professionals, and clients.

The complexity of U.S. social welfare policy can be attributed to several cultural influences, some of which are peculiar to the American experience. For instance, the U.S. Constitution outlines a federal system whereby states vest certain functions in the national government. Although the states have assumed primary responsibility for social welfare through much of U.S. history, this changed with the New Deal of Franklin Delano Roosevelt, which ushered in a raft of federal programs. Over subsequent decades, federal social welfare initiatives played a dominant role in the nation's welfare effort. Still, states continued to manage important social welfare programs, such as mental health, corrections, and social services. Over time, the relationship between the federal government and the states has changed. From the New Deal of the 1930s through the Great Society of the 1960s, federal welfare programs expanded, forming the American version of the "welfare state." Beginning in the 1980s, the Reagan administration sought to return more of the responsibility for welfare to the states, a process called devolution.[72] This devolution was furthered by the Clinton administration with the signing of the PRWORA.

A second confounding element can be attributed to the relatively open character of U.S. society. Often referred to as a melting pot, the national culture is a protean brew of immigrant groups that competed with one another to become an established part of national life.[73] A staggering influx of Europeans in the late nineteenth century gave way to waves of Hispanics and Asians entering the United States a century later.[74] Historically, social welfare programs have played an important role in the acculturation of these groups. At the same time, many ethnic groups brought with them their own fraternal and community associations, which not only provide welfare benefits to members of the community but also serves to maintain its norms. Other groups that have exerted important influences on U.S. social welfare are African Americans, the aged, women, and Native Americans. The very pluralism of U.S. society—a diverse collection of peoples, each with somewhat different needs—contributes to the complexity of social welfare.

The economic system also exacerbates the complexity of social welfare. With important exceptions, the U.S. economy is predominantly capitalist, with most goods and services being owned, produced, and distributed through the marketplace. In a capitalist economy people are expected to meet their basic needs in the marketplace through labor force participation. When people are unable to participate fully in the labor market, like the aged or the handicapped, "social" programs are deployed to support these groups. These programs take various forms. Many are governmental programs mandated by legislation. Private sector programs often complement those of the public sector. Within the private sector, two organizational forms are common—nonprofit organizations and for-profit corporations. Often these private sector organizations coexist, proximate to one another.[75] For instance, in many communities, family planning services are provided by the public health department; by Planned Parenthood, a private nonprofit agency; and by a private for-profit health maintenance organization.

Finally, various religious or faith-based organizations strongly influence social welfare in the United States. This is seen most clearly in the range of faith-based agencies that offer social services, such as Jewish Family Services, Lutheran Social Services, Catholic Charities, and the Salvation Army, among others. In many cases, religious-based agencies provide services to groups that would not otherwise receive them. When the federal government experimented with contracting out some services to the private sector in the 1970s, faith-based agencies frequently competed for these contracts. Today many faith-based agencies receive federal funds for various services they provide to the public. It is likely that this trend will grow.

The pluralism of this nation's culture is of increasing interest to social welfare policy analysts as the influence of the federal government in social policy diminishes. In light of reductions in many federal social programs and calls for the private sector to assume more responsibility for welfare, the prospect of molding the diverse entities involved in American social welfare into one unified whole under the auspices of a central federal authority seems remote. This vision of a unified whole is implicit in the proposals of advocates for nationalized programs that ensure basic goods and services such as food, housing, education, health, and income as a right of citizenship. While programs of this nature have been integral to the welfare states of northern Europe for decades, there is a serious question as to their plausibility for the United States, which has so much complexity built into its social welfare system.[76]

Questions about the proper role of the federal government in social welfare had reached a fever pitch by the late 1980s. Proponents of a strong federal role conceded that the U.S. welfare state was, by European standards, incomplete. For these analysts the "reluctant welfare state"[77] or the "semi-welfare state"[78] required further elaboration through social programs in primary areas such as income supports, health, and employment. The principle that social welfare should be a "national effort on behalf of those in need," noted Robert Reich, has been central to American social welfare for a half-century. According to Reich, "The theme permeated Roosevelt's New Deal, Truman's Fair Deal, Johnson's Great Society: America is a single, national community, bound by a common ideal of equal opportunity and generosity toward the less fortunate. *E Pluribus Unum.*"[79] For proponents of more state intervention in social welfare, the growth of nongovernmental initiatives represented the abandonment of the most effective method for assuring the protection of vulnerable populations. "Conservatives," some observed, "continually assert that many social services in the public sector can be transferred to the voluntary sector."[80]

Advocates of more nongovernmental activity in social welfare trace their argument to the American colonial era. Daniel Boorstin, former librarian of Congress, has written passionately about the unique role played by voluntary organizations in the United States. Boorstin maintains that voluntary organizations "have many unique characteristics and a spirit all their own. . . . [Voluntary organizations are no less than] monuments to what in the Old World was familiar neither as private charity nor as governmental munificence. They are monuments to community. They originate in the community, depend on the community, are developed by the community, serve the community, and rise or fall with the community."[81]

Can the problems of the postindustrial nation be addressed adequately without massive federal social programs? The late Daniel Patrick Moynihan, former U.S. senator and an authority on welfare, claimed that we have no choice but to think about new ways to solve social problems. According to Moynihan, "The issues of social policy the United States faces today have no European counterpart nor any European model of a viable solution. They are American problems, and we Americans are going to have to think them through by ourselves."[82] To the extent that Moynihan is correct, future welfare initiatives are increasingly likely to reflect the diversity of American social welfare.

The complexity of social welfare in the United States helps account for changes in welfare policies and programs. For example, since 1980 a convergence of social, political, and economic forces has led to a reappraisal of welfare. Both liberal and conservative scholars have questioned the dominance of government programs in welfare provision. At the same time, a firestorm of fundamentalism has swept across the nation, attracting the allegiance of groups associated with evangelicalism. The traditionalist movement flexed its muscles through the elections of Ronald Reagan, the two Bush administrations, the installation of a Republican Senate in the early 1980s and a conservative House of Representatives in 1994, and an effective grassroots mobilization that challenged government policies on issues ranging from the family to affirmative action. By the early 1990s, social conservatism had begun to influence Democratic party leaders, traditional supporters of government welfare programs. To reestablish credibility in an increasingly conservative political milieu, liberals distanced themselves from the large-scale government welfare programs they had been associated with since the New Deal. In place of these programs, many liberals called for a reliance on personal responsibility, work, and thrift.

Conservative public sentiment currently serves as a backdrop for the debate on the future of welfare policy.[83] An ascendant conservatism has not only checked further expansion of federal social programs, but the unprecedented tax cuts engineered by the George W. Bush administration threaten to dry up the revenues upon which social programs are dependent. The magnitude of this cannot be overstated: The tax cuts of the George W. Bush presidency eliminated the federal surplus; after September 11, 2001, Social Security and Medicare funds that had been set aside for retiring baby boomers were diverted to national security. As a result, the current, unfunded obligations of Social Security and Medicare total 10.1 *trillion*.[84] The impact of this on social programs is profound, and the future solvency of social insurances for retirees would require a 91 percent increase in the withholding tax or an 81 percent increase in the income tax paid by individuals. If future workers reject such tax increases, pressure will build to convert Social Security and Medicare to means-tested, welfare programs. "This is the death trap of the welfare state," concluded Paul Samuelson, "here and in Europe and Asia."[85] Given these developments, welfare professionals face a formidable challenge: How can basic goods and services be brought to vulnerable populations within a context of such complexity and uncertainty?

Discussion Questions

1. According to the authors, American social welfare is undergoing a transition. Which ideologies, schools of political economy, and interest groups within social welfare stand to gain most from this transition?
2. Ideology tends to parallel schools of political economy. How would classical conservatives and liberals address current social welfare issues such as health care, long-term care for the aged, and substance abuse? How would neoconservatives and neoliberals diverge from traditional conservatives and liberals on these issues?
3. Which schools of political, social, and economic thought discussed in this chapter would come closest to being classified as moderate? Why?
4. The chapter argues that in large measure social policy dictates social work practice. Do you agree with that premise? Explain your position. Can you think of any instances (historic or otherwise) in which social work practice has led to changes in social welfare policy?
5. In your opinion, which schools of economic and political thought are the most compatible with social work practice? Why? What are the incompatibilities in the various schools of thought with macro- and micro-level social work practice?

Notes

1. Richard Titmuss, *Essays on the Welfare State* (Boston: Beacon Press, 1963), p. 16.
2. Contained in personal correspondence between David Stoesz and William Epstein, April 2000.
3. Education would logically be included here, except that in the American experience it has been treated separately.
4. See Alfred Kahn, *Social Policy and Social Services* (New York: Random House, 1979).
5. Frances Fox Piven and Richard Cloward, *Regulating the Poor* (New York: Vintage, 1971).
6. David Gil, *Unraveling Social Policy* (Boston: Shenkman, 1981), p. 32.
7. Charles Prigmore and Charles Atherton, *Social Welfare Policy* (Lexington, MA: D.C. Heath, 1979), pp. 25–31.
8. Silvia Ann Hewlett, *When the Bough Breaks* (New York: Basic Books, 1991), p. 12.

9. Claus Offe, *Contradictions of the Welfare State* (Cambridge, MA: MIT Press, 1984).
10. John Maynard Keynes, *The General Theory of Employment, Interest and Money* (London: Macmillan, 1936).
11. Paul R. Krugman, *Peddling Prosperity: Economic Sense and Nonsense in the Age of Diminished Expectations* (New York: W. W. Norton, 1994).
12. Ibid.
13. Ibid.
14. Milton Friedman, *Money Mischief: Episodes in Monetary History* (New York: Harcourt Brace, 1992).
15. Milton Friedman, *Capitalism and Freedom* (Chicago: University of Chicago Press, 1962).
16. Ibid.
17. Robert E. Lucas, *Studies in Business Cycle Theory* (Cambridge, MA: MIT Press, 1981).
18. Krugman, *Peddling Prosperity.*
19. Ibid.
20. Ibid.
21. Congressional Budget Office, *The Economic and Budget Outlook: Fiscal Years 1993–1997* (Washington, DC: Congressional Budget Office, 1992), p. 28.
22. See Beth Shulman, *The Betrayal of Work: How Low Wage Jobs Fail 35 Million Americans* (New York: The New Press, 2003); Lawrence Mishel, Jared Bernstein, and John Schmitt, *The State of Working America 2000/2001* (Ithaca, NY: Cornell University Press, 2001); and Jared Bernstein, "Economic Growth Not Reaching Middle- and Lower Wage Earners," January 28, 2004, retrieved 2004 from www.epinet.org/content.cfm/webfeatures_snapshots
23. Reuters, "White House Forecasts Record Budget Deficit," July 30, 2004. Retrieved 2004 from www.reuters.com/financeNewsArticle.jhtml?type=bondsNews&storyID=5831525
24. See Ayn Rand, *The Fountainhead* (New York: New American Library, 50th Anniversary Edition, 1996); *Atlas Shrugged* (New York: Signet Book; 35th Anniversary Edition, 1996).
25. Charles Murray, *Losing Ground* (New York: Basic Books, 1984), pp. 227–228.
26. *Privatization: Toward More Effective Government* (Washington, DC: U.S. Government Printing Office, 1988), pp. 233–234.
27. Jeffry Galper, "Introduction of Radical Theory and Practice in Social Work Education: Social Policy." Mimeographed paper, Michigan State University School of Social Work, ca. 1978.
28. Piven and Cloward, *Regulating the Poor,* pp. 3–4.
29. Harry Hopkins, *Spending to Save: The Complete Story of Relief* (Seattle: University of Washington Press, 1936).
30. Neil Gilbert, Harry Specht, and Paul Terrell, *Dimensions of Social Welfare Policy* (Englewood Cliffs, NJ: Prentice-Hall, 1993).
31. Marc Bendick, *Privatizing the Delivery of Social Welfare Service* (Washington, DC: National Conference on Social Welfare, 1985), p. 1.
32. Bruce Jansson, *The Reluctant Welfare State* (Belmont, CA: Wadsworth, 1988).
33. Charles Peters, "A New Politics," *Public Welfare* 41, no. 2 (Spring 1983), pp. 34, 36.
34. Randall Rothenberg, *The Neoliberals* (New York: Simon & Schuster, 1984), pp. 244–245.
35. David Stoesz, *Small Change* (New York: Longman, 1995).
36. Robert Reich, *The Next American Frontier* (New York: Times Books, 1983).
37. Ibid., p. 248.
38. Anthony Giddens, *The Third Way* (Cambridge: Polity Press, 1999), p. 117.
39. Politics Now. Retrieved 2000 from www.politicsnow.com/campaign/wh_house/green/index.htm
40. Nationwide Green Organizations in the USA. Retrieved 2000 from www.greens.org/usa
41. Michael J. Sandel, *Democracy's Discontent* (Cambridge, MA: Belknap Press/Harvard University Press, 1996).
42. Peter Steinfels, "A Political Movement Blends Its Ideas from Left and Right," *New York Times* (May 24, 1992), p. B16.
43. Peter Steinfels, "A Political Movement Blends Its Ideas from Left and Right," *New York Times* (May 24, 1992), p. B16.
44. Amitai Etzioni (ed.), *New Communitarian Thinking: Persons, Virtues, Institutions, Communities* (Charlottesville and London: University Press of Virginia, 1995).
45. Katha Pollitt, "Subject to Debate," *The Nation* (July 25/August 1, 1994), p. 118.
46. Richard Benedetto, "A New Approach to Nation's Problems. Interview with Amitai Etzioni," *USA Today* (April 23, 1992), p. 13A.
47. Bruce Stokes, *Helping Ourselves: Local Solutions to Global Problems* (New York: W. W. Norton, 1981).
48. Sugata Dasgupta, "Towards a No-Poverty Society," *Social Development Issues* 12 (Winter 1983), pp. 85–93.
49. Some of these economic principles were addressed by E. F. Schumacher in *Small Is Beautiful* (New York: Harper & Row, 1973).
50. Barry M. Goldwater, *The Conscience of a Conservative* (New York: Putnam, 1960), pp. 109–110.
51. See Peter Steinfels, *The Neoconservatives* (New York: Simon & Schuster, 1979).
52. Interview with Stuart Butler, Director of Domestic Policy at the Heritage Foundation, October 4, 1984.
53. Alan Walker, "The Strategy of Inequality: Poverty and Income Distribution in Britain 1979–89," in I. Taylor (ed.), *The Social Effects of Free Market Policies* (Sussex, England: Harvester-Wheatsheaf, 1990), pp. 43–66.
54. Kristen Geiss-Curran, Sha'ari Garfinkle, Fred Knocke, Terri Lively, and Sue McCullough, "The Contract with

America and the Budget Battle," unpublished manuscript, University of Houston, Spring 1996.

55. The Libertarian Party, "Statement of Principles," The Libertarian Party, 2600 Virginia Ave, NW, Washington, DC, 1996.
56. Daniel Patrick Moynihan, *Came the Revolution* (New York: Harcourt Brace Jovanovich, 1988), p. 291.
57. See Harold Wilensky and Charles Lebeaux, *Industrial Society and Social Welfare* (New York: Free Press, 1965); and Mimi Abramovitz, "The Privatization of the Welfare State," *Social Work* 31 (July–August 1986), pp. 257–264.
58. R. Erikson, E. Hansen, S. Ringen, and H. Uusitalo, *The Scandinavian Model* (Armonk, NY: M. E. Sharpe, 1987).
59. Richard Titmuss, *Commitment to Welfare* (New York: Pantheon, 1968), p. 127.
60. Wilensky and Lebeaux, *Industrial Society and Social Welfare*, p. 147.
61. Wilensky and Lebeaux, *Industrial Society and Social Welfare*, p. 231.
62. Alvin Rabushka, "Tax and Spending Limits," in Peter Duignan and Alvin Rabushka (eds.), *The United States in the 1980s* (Stanford, CA: Hoover Institution, 1980), pp. 104–106.
63. Martin Anderson, "Welfare Reform," in Peter Duignan and Alvin Rabushka (eds.), *The United States in the 1980s*, pp. 171–176.
64. Peter Berger and John Neuhaus, *To Empower People: The Role of Mediating Structures in Public Policy* (Washington, DC: American Enterprise Institute, 1977).
65. Michael Novak, *Toward a Theology of the Corporation* (Washington, DC: American Enterprise Institute, 1981), p. 5.
66. Stuart Butler and Anna Kondratas, *Out of the Poverty Trap: A Conservative Strategy for Welfare Reform* (New York: Free Press, 1987).
67. William Lind and William Marshner, *Cultural Conservatism: Toward a New National Agenda* (Washington, DC: Free Congress Research and Education Foundation, 1987), p. 83.
68. George Gilder, *Wealth and Poverty* (New York: Basic Books, 1981), p. 118.
69. Anderson, "Welfare Reform," p. 145.
70. John Judis and Michael Lind, "For a New Nationalism," *The New Republic* (March 27, 1995), p. 26.
71. Mitchell Landsberg, "Nation's Social Health Declined in '93," *Houston Chronicle* (October 16, 1995), p. 1C.
72. Domestic Policy Council, Up from Dependency (Washington, DC: White House Domestic Policy Council, December 1986).
73. For a classic description of the assimilation phenomenon, see Nathan Glazer and Daniel Patrick Moynihan, *Beyond the Melting Pot* (Cambridge, MA: MIT Press, 1970).
74. Thomas Muller et al., *The Fourth Wave* (Washington, DC: Urban Institute, 1985).
75. The three auspices of social welfare in the United States have been termed the mixed economy of welfare. See Sheila Kamerman, "The New Mixed Economy of Welfare," *Social Work* 28 (January–February 1983), pp. 43–50.
76. Marc Bendick, Privatizing the Delivery of Social Welfare Service (Washington, DC: National Conference on Social Welfare, 1985).
77. Jansson, *The Reluctant Welfare State.*
78. Michael Katz, *In the Shadow of the Poorhouse* (New York: Basic Books, 1986).
79. Robert Reich, *Tales of a New America* (New York: Vintage, 1987), p. 11.
80. Robert Schilling, Steven Schinke, and Richard Weatherly, "Service Trends in a Conservative Era: Social Workers Rediscover the Past," *Social Work* 33 (January–February 1988), p. 7.
81. Daniel Boorstin, *Hidden History* (New York: Harper and Row, 1987), p. 194.
82. Daniel Patrick Moynihan, *Came the Revolution* (New York: Harcourt Brace Jovanovich, 1988), p. 291.
83. For further details, see David Stoesz, "The Functional Conception of Social Welfare," *Social Work* 34 (March 1989), pp. 86–91.
84. Howell E. Jackson, "It's Even Worse than You Think," *The New York Times* (October 9, 2003), p. A35.
85. Paul Samuelson, "The Deficit Chicken Hawks," *Washington Post* (October 10, 2003), p. A27.

CHAPTER 2

Social Welfare Policy Research: A Framework for Policy Analysis

Policy analysts engage in the systematic investigation of a social policy or a set of policies. They are employed in a variety of settings, including federal, state, and local governments; think tanks; universities; social justice or public interest groups, or community organizations; and larger social agencies. The goals of policy analysis can range from pure research to providing information to legislators (i.e., congressional researchers) and to advocacy research. This chapter examines one of the major tools used by the policy researcher, a systematic and structured framework for policy analysis. In addition, the authors propose a model for policy analysis.

Chapter 1 examined the impact of ideology, economic theories, and political ideas on the social welfare state. The ways in which concepts such as social justice and equity play a central role in the formation of social welfare policy are also examined. A **policy framework**—a systematic model for examining a specific social welfare policy or a series of policies—is one means analysts use to evaluate the congruence of a policy with the mission and goals of the social welfare state. Analysts can also employ policy frameworks to assess whether key social welfare values—such as social justice, redistribution, or equity—are incorporated within a given policy. Moreover, policy frameworks help us determine if a policy is consistent with established social welfare values or the historical precedents that have guided social welfare initiatives. For example, let us consider the proposal that foster care should be abolished and that all children suspected of being abused or neglected should be placed in orphanages. The use of a policy framework would illustrate that this proposal reflects a clear break with the general drift of child welfare policy at the beginning of the twenty-first century and, moreover, that it repudiates established values such as family reunification. In addition, a systematic analysis would reveal that this policy is not economically, politically, or socially feasible.

Apart from examining a given policy, an analytic framework is also useful for comparing existing policies. For example, comparing the mental health policies of Missouri with those of Massachusetts and Minnesota would yield valuable information for all three states. A comparative analysis of the health systems of the United States, Canada, and Sweden would also provide useful information for decision makers. Lastly, analytic frameworks can be used to evaluate competing policies and help the analyst make a recommendation as to which policy will most effectively address a problem or remedy a need.

Policy analysis frameworks can be useful for social work practitioners on several levels, and can address agency policies as well as those at the statewide or national level. Agency policies dictate what a social worker will do, with whom, and for how long. They also define who is (or is not) a client and what services will be provided for them. Social work practitioners can also examine agency policies around issues such as flextime, merit pay, agency-based day care services, job shifting, and so forth. Child welfare workers can use policy analysis to evaluate impending state or federal legislation and the concomitant fiscal allocations. Social workers in health care can analyze managed care policies in terms of equity, effectiveness, and a wide range of other issues. Social work practice is clearly influenced—if not driven—by social policy.

Policy analysis is also useful in the environmental scanning activities of non- and for-profit agencies. As the delivery of social services becomes more grounded in the competitive marketplace, social agencies are forced to replicate successful private sector corporate behavior. This includes being aware of changing demographic trends (doing market analyses) and monitoring new legislation. In some social welfare sectors, events change so rapidly that agencies must quickly modify their operations if they are to remain viable. Data-based environmental scanning allows agencies to make long- and short-term plans based on changing demographics, new competing organizations, or the effects of impending legislation. Environmental scanning also allows agencies to discover new markets and to protect their existing ones.[1]

Social welfare policies and programs are complex phenomena. For example, it is easy to propose a social policy such as mandatory drug testing for all governmental employees. On the surface, the policy may appear simple: Drug users are discovered through testing and then forced to seek treatment. On closer scrutiny, however, the hidden issues become problematic. Is it constitutional to require drug treatment if a positive result is found? Is occasional use of marijuana sufficient grounds for requiring drug treatment? Because alcohol is a legal substance, drug tests do not detect it. Is alcohol less debilitating than marijuana? Can mandatory drug testing be misused by supervisors to harass employees? Will drug testing produce the desired results? Without a systematic means to analyze the effects

The policy analyst is expected to evaluate policies and make recommendations. To succeed, the analyst must accept his or her own values while basing the analysis on objective criteria.

of a policy, decisions become arbitrary and may produce consequences that are worse than the original problem.

All well-designed policy frameworks are characterized by eight key elements:

- Policy frameworks attempt to systematically analyze a social policy or program.
- Policy frameworks reflect the understanding that social policy is context sensitive, and that policy options usually contain a set of competing priorities.
- Policy frameworks employ rational methods of inquiry and analysis. The data used in policy analysis must be derived from objective scientific inquiry, and it must come from legitimate sources. Data should be interpreted and analyzed as objectively as possible.
- While open to interpretation, the analytic method is explicit, and all succeeding policy analyses should be able to approximate the same conclusion.
- Policy analysis is based on the commitment to derive the largest possible social benefit at the least possible social cost. A good social policy is one that benefits at least one person (as they perceive their own self-interest) while at the same time hurting no one. Although that goal is rarely achieved in the real world of finite resources—and of proliferating claims on them—policy analysts should nevertheless strive to realize that aim.
- Policy frameworks should attempt to take into account the unintended consequences of a particular policy or program.
- Policy frameworks should examine a particular policy within the context of alternatives. Specifically, analysts should consider alternative social policies and/or alternative uses of present or future resources allocated to a given policy.
- Policy frameworks should examine the potential impact of a policy (or a series of policies) on other social policies, social problems, and the overall public good.

A policy framework can provide decision makers and the general public with information, an understanding of the ramifications of a policy on the target problem as well as on other problems and policies, and alternative policies that might more effectively address the problem. Untoward costs and injuries are more likely when the decision-making process is not based on a systematic framework for policy analysis.

History is replete with examples of well-intentioned policies that proved catastrophic. For example, in 1919 the U.S. Congress enacted a law prohibiting the manufacture, sale, or transport of alcohol in an effort to cut down on crime, familial instability, unemployment, and other social problems. Advocates of Prohibition, including many social workers, touted the end of alcohol as a major step forward in the social evolution of the United States. However, when Prohibition was repealed in 1932, most of the original supporters were relatively quiet. Despite their hopes, Prohibition did not decrease crime or lead to more family stability and greater social order; instead, it encouraged the growth of an organized crime industry that fed the ongoing taste of Americans for alcohol. Instead of curbing alcohol-related nightlife, Prohibition led to the creation of illegal and well-attended speakeasies. Even many supporters conceded that alcohol was almost as abundant as before Prohibition. A systematic analysis of prohibition done before the passage of the bill might have demonstrated the futility of this policy initiative.

A similar argument can be made for the current policy of drug interdiction and enforcement. After almost a half-century of vigorous drug enforcement, marijuana, heroin, cocaine, and other drugs continue to be readily available. Vigilant drug enforcement has not necessarily resulted in less drug use but in a doubling of the prison population from 1980 to 2004 (more than 2 million Americans are now incarcerated). The "war on drugs" has also resulted in the added public expense of new prison construction (about 1,000 new prisons were built from 1990 to 2004[2]), the creation of international drug cartels whose wealth and power rival that of many national governments and multinational corporations, a dramatic increase in the drug-related homicide rate, and the deterioration of inner-city neighborhoods racked by a gang warfare nourished by the lucrative drug trade. While drug enforcement policies have not resulted in the end of illegal drugs, they have fostered the creation of a vibrant industry that includes government officials, contractors, private correctional corporations, police departments, and large segments of the legal and judicial system. These groups have a vested interest in maintaining a status quo drug policy, regardless of its efficacy. In short, a social problem led to a social policy; but the policy, in turn, has led to a powerful industry that depends for its very existence on the continuation of that ineffective policy. As this example suggests, social policy is often driven by politics and rarely, if ever, systematically analyzed. Policy analysis often occurs only after a bill or policy is enacted. As a result, analysts are often asked to perform an autopsy to determine why a specific bill or policy failed.

The purpose of a policy framework is to provide the analyst with a model or a set of questions for systematically analyzing a policy. Consequently, the choice of a policy framework must fit the requirements of the project as well as the resources available to the analyst. Every policy framework can be either fine-tuned or modified. In fact, the best policy framework may result from a synthesis of existing models.[3]

A Proposed Model for Policy Analysis

Policy analysts are expected to evaluate a policy and make recommendations. To succeed, the analyst must acknowledge his or her own values, while at the same time, basing the analysis on objective criteria. The policy framework proposed in this text is divided into four sections: (1) the historical background of the policy, (2) a description of the problem(s) that necessitated the policy, (3) a description of the policy, and (4) the policy analysis (see Figure 2.1).

Historical Background of the Policy

The policy analyst should examine similar policies that were adopted in the past and assess how they fared. Understanding the historical antecedents of a policy is important for two reasons. First, continuity requires that the analyst identify the historical problems that led to the original policy. Questions might include: What historical problems led to the creation of the policy? How important were they? How were these problems previously handled?

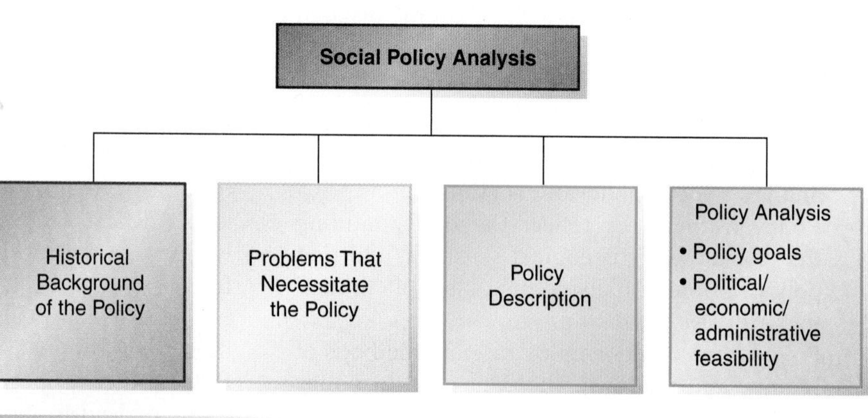

Figure 2.1

Proposed Framework for Policy Analysis

When did the policy originate and how has it changed over time? What is the legislative history of the policy?

Second, a historical analysis helps to curb the tendency of decision makers to reinvent the wheel. Policies that were previously unsuccessful may continue to be so; or the analyst may find that circumstances have changed, thus creating a climate in which a previously failed policy might now be viable. A historical analysis also helps the analyst to understand the forces that were mobilized to support or oppose a given policy. In short, this part of the analysis locates a particular policy within a historical framework, thus helping to explain the evolutionary nature of a social policy or series of policies.

Spotlight 2.1

A Model for Policy Analysis

The model for policy analysis can be divided into four sections—the historical background of the policy, a description of the problem that necessitated the policy, a description of the policy, and the policy analysis. Each of these sections requires the policy analyst to ask specific questions.

Historical Background of the Policy

- What historical problems led to the creation of the policy?
- How important have these problems been historically?
- How was the problem previously handled?
- What is the historical background of the policy?
- When did the policy originate?
- How has the original policy changed over time?
- What is the legislative history of the policy?

Description of the Problem That Necessitated the Policy

- What is the nature of the problem?
- How widespread is it?
- How many people are affected by it?
- Who is affected and how?
- What are the causes of the problem?

Policy Description

- How is the policy expected to work?
- What resources or opportunities is the policy expected to provide?
- Who will be covered by the policy and how?
- How will the policy be implemented?
- What are the short- and long-term goals and outcomes of the policy?
- What are the administrative auspices under which the policy will be lodged?
- What is the funding mechanism for the policy?
- Who will be the agencies or organizations charged with overseeing, evaluating, and coordinating the policy?
- What is the formal or informal criteria that will be used to determine the effectiveness of the policy?
- For what length of time is the policy expected to be in existence?
- What is the knowledge base or scientific grounding on which the policy rests?

Policy Analysis

- Are the goals of the policy legal?
- Are the goals of the policy just and democratic?
- Do the goals of the policy contribute to greater social equality?
- Do the goals of the policy positively affect the redistribution of income, resources, rights, entitlements, rewards, opportunities, and status?
- Do the goals of the policy contribute to a better quality of life for the target population?
- Will the goals adversely affect the quality of life of the target population?
- Does the policy contribute to positive social relations between the target population and the overall society?
- Are the goals of the policy consistent with the values of professional social work?

Problems That Necessitate the Policy

The second step in policy analysis is an examination of the problems that led to the creation of the policy. To fully assess whether a proposed policy will successfully remedy a social problem, the analyst must understand the parameters of the problem. Furthermore, the analyst must be familiar with the nature, scope, and magnitude of the problem and with the affected populations. In this way, the analyst can discern early whether the policy is appropriate. Specific questions might include: What is the nature and causes of the problem? How widespread is it? Who and how many people are affected by it?

Policy Description

The next step is the description of the policy. This section requires a detailed explanation of the policy, including a description of (1) how the policy is expected to work; (2) the resources or opportunities the policy is expected to provide (power, cash, economic opportunity, in-kind benefits, status redistribution, goods and services, and so forth); (3) who will be covered by the policy and how (e.g., universal versus selective entitlement, means testing, and so forth); (4) how the policy will be implemented; (5) the expected short- and long-term goals and outcomes of the policy; (6) the administrative auspices under which the policy will be lodged; (7) the funding mechanism, including short- and long-term funding commitments; (8) the agencies or organizations that have overall responsibility for overseeing, evaluating, and coordinating the policy; (9) the criteria used to determine the effectiveness of the policy; (10) the length of time the policy is expected to be in existence (i.e., is it a "sunset law" designed to end at a certain date?); and (11) the knowledge base or scientific undergirding for the policy.

Policy Analysis

This section is the heart of any policy analysis. In this section, the analyst engages in a *systematic* analysis of the policy.

Policy Goals The policy goals are the criteria by which all else is measured. Often the analyst must conjecture on the overall goals of the policy since they may not be explicitly stated. The following questions can help to explicate the goals of a particular policy.

- Are the goals legal, just, and democratic?
- Do they contribute to greater social equality?
- Do the goals positively affect the redistribution of income, resources, rights, entitlements, rewards, opportunities, and status?
- Do the goals contribute to a better quality of life for the target population? Will they adversely affect the quality of life of the target group?
- Does the policy contribute to positive social relations between the target population and the overall society?
- Are the policy goals consistent with the values of professional social work (i.e., self-determination, client rights, self-realization, and so forth)?

Analysts must understand the value premises of the policy as well as the ideological assumptions underlying it. To this end, several questions should be asked: What are the hidden ideological assumptions in the policy? How is the target population viewed in the context of the policy? What social vision, if any, does the policy contain? Does the policy encourage the status quo or does it represent a radical departure from it? Who are the major beneficiaries of the policy? Is the policy designed to foster real social change or to placate a potentially insurgent group? Uncovering the hidden ideological dimensions of a policy is frequently the most difficult task for the policy analyst.

Despite good intentions, a prospective policy must be viable if it is to be successful. American history is littered with worthy policies that were simply not viable at the time they were proposed. For example, at the height of the Great Depression, a California physician named Francis Townsend proposed that all citizens over the age of 65 be given a flat governmental pension of $200 a month. Although in more prosperous times this proposal might have been granted at least a cursory hearing, in the midst of one of the greatest depressions in U.S. history, policymakers dismissed the proposal as not viable. The overall viability of a policy is based on three factors: political feasibility, economic feasibility, and administrative feasibility.

Political Feasibility The political feasibility of a policy is a subjective assessment. In order to evaluate a policy, the analyst must assess which groups will oppose or support a particular policy, and they must estimate the constituency and power base of each group. However, in U.S. politics the size of the constituency base and its relative power are sometimes unrelated. For example, despite its relatively small numbers, the American Medical Association (AMA) is a powerful lobby. Conversely, although more than 30 million Americans are poor, they have negligible political clout.

The political viability of a policy is subject to the public's perception of its feasibility. In other words, for a policy to be feasible, it must be perceived as being feasible. For example, although a sizable portion of the public would welcome some form of national health care, none exists. While the United States lacks a national health care partly because of the power of the health care industry, in part it has not been enacted because the public believes it cannot happen. Thus is born a public myth around what is and what is not possible.

In assessing the political feasibility of a policy, the analyst must examine the public's sentiment toward it. Is a large segment of the public concerned about the policy? Do people feel they will be directly affected by the policy? Does the policy threaten fundamental social values? Is the policy compatible with the present social and political climate? Can either side marshal substantial public support for or against the policy? The answers to these questions will help the policy analyst determine the political feasibility of the policy.

The political feasibility of a policy also encompasses a smaller, but no less important, dimension. In their assessment, the analyst must understand the relationship between the policy and external factors in agencies and institutions. For example, which social welfare agencies, institutions, or organizations support or oppose the policy? What is the relative strength of each group? How strong is their support or opposition to the policy? Which federal, state, or local agencies would be affected by the policy? The world of social policy is highly political and some governmental and private social welfare agencies have political power on par with elected officials and other decision makers. Groups of institutions often coalesce around issues or policies that directly affect them, and, through lobbying efforts, they can defeat legislation. In cases where they cannot defeat a policy outright, these administrative units can implement a policy in ways that ensure its failure. The analyst must therefore take into account whether key administrative units support or oppose a new or existing policy.

Economic Feasibility Most social policies require some form of direct or indirect funding. In assessing the economic feasibility of a policy, the analyst must ask several questions: What is the minimum level of funding necessary for successfully implementing the policy? Does adequate funding for the policy currently exist? If not, what is the public sentiment toward increased funding for the policy? What are the future funding needs of the policy likely to be?

Given the current political and economic climate, it appears unlikely that new social policy initiatives requiring large revenues will be successful. Perhaps new revenue-based policy legislation will be based on the reallocation of existing resources (budget-neutral policies) rather than on new revenue sources. This approach—taking money from one program to fund another—is called **pay-go** financing. The danger in this approach is that thinning out fiscal resources among many programs may mean that none will be adequately funded. The analyst must therefore decide whether a new policy initiative should be recommended regardless of the funding prospects. The parameters of this decision are complex. If a new policy is recommended despite insufficient resources, the chances of its failure are greater. If a policy is not recommended, however, the possibility that fiscal resources may be allocated in the future is precluded. As a result, many policy analysts lean toward incremental approaches, tending to recommend policies in the hope that future funding will become available.

Administrative Feasibility The analyst must also be concerned with the administrative viability of a policy. Regardless of the potential value of a policy, responsible administrative and supervisory agencies must possess the personnel, resources, skills, and expertise needed to effectively implement the policy. In addition, directors and supervisors must be sympathetic to the goals of the policy, have the expertise and skill necessary to implement or oversee the policy, and possess an understanding of the fundamental objectives of the policy. Policy analysts focus on two key aspects of administrative feasibility: effectiveness and efficiency.

Effectiveness is based on the likelihood that the policy will accomplish what its designers intended. This encompasses several questions: Is the policy broad enough to accomplish its stated goals? Will the benefits of the policy reach the target group? Is the implementation of the policy likely to cause new or other social problems? What are the ramifications of the policy on the nontarget sector (i.e., higher taxes, reduced opportunities, diminished freedom, etc.)?

Another challenge facing policy analysts is the nature and extent of the unintended consequences of a policy. Virtually all policies have unforeseen consequences. One example of this is methadone, a drug legally administered to addicts as a substitute for heroin. When introduced in the 1960s, methadone was thought to be a safe way to wean addicts away from heroin. However, by the mid-1970s health experts realized that methadone was almost as addictive as heroin and that some addicts were selling their methadone as a street drug. Despite this unintended outcome, some addicts were able to withdraw from heroin, and on balance, the methadone program was a positive development. Because policy analysts cannot see into the future, recommendations are made on the basis of available data. Nevertheless, analysts must try to investigate the possibility of adverse future consequences.

Policy analysts look closely at *efficiency,* or the cost-effectiveness of the proposed policy compared to alternative policies, no policy, or the present policy. Social policy always involves trade-offs. Even in the best of economic times, fiscal resources are always inadequate to meet the breadth of human need. For example, virtually everyone could benefit from some form of social welfare, whether it be counseling, food stamps, or free health care. But because resources are finite, society must choose the primary beneficiaries for its social allocations. Publicly financed services are often provided on the basis of two criteria: (1) the severity of the problem (services go to those who most need them) and (2) means (services go to those who can least afford them). As a result, adequately funding one policy often means denying or curbing the allocations to another. This is the essential trade-off in social welfare policy. When analysts evaluate a policy, they are cognizant that promoting one policy often means that needs in other areas may go unmet. Hence, important questions remain: Is the policy important enough to justify the allocation of scarce resources? Are there other areas where scarce resources could be better used?

The policy analyst often compares the cost-effectiveness of a proposed policy with an alternative policy. Will the proposed policy have better results than the present policy or no policy at all? Is it advantageous to enlarge or modify the present policy rather than create a new one? Can an alternative policy provide better results at a lower cost? Can an alternative policy achieve the same results? These questions are often addressed in a thorough policy analysis.

Researching and Analyzing Social Policies

There are two major hurdles in policy analysis. The first is finding and focusing on a manageable social policy, and the second is finding or generating information relevant to it.

One of the most difficult tasks the analyst faces is choosing the actual policy. To do a careful policy analysis, the analyst must select a policy that is specific and discrete. For example, it would be virtually impossible to do an exhaustive analysis of child welfare policy in the United States. For one thing, the United States lacks an integrated child welfare policy; instead, child welfare is characterized by a patchwork quilt of myriad programs. Second, differing child welfare policies on the national, state, and community levels make such a policy analysis even more daunting.

A second task involves locating policy-relevant information. There are seven major avenues for finding information. First, policy analysts may choose to generate their own data through primary research, including surveys, opinion polls, experimental research, longitudinal studies, and so forth. Although this method can yield a rich body of information, time and cost constraints may prove an impossible obstacle. Moreover, the same research may already exist in other places, in which case the replication of the effort would be unwarranted.

Second, governmental or agency records are often useful sources for relevant data. These can include archival material; memos; minutes of boards of directors, governmental officials, and staff meetings; policy manuals; and departmental records. A surprising amount of information can be found online in government or agency websites.

A third avenue for policy research is the records and published minutes of legislative bodies and committees. On the federal level these sources include the *Congressional Record* and the minutes of the various House and Senate committees and subcommittees. All state legislatures have similar record-keeping procedures, and most of these records can be found in regional or university libraries or online.

A fourth source of information is governmental publications. For example, the U.S. Government Printing Office maintains catalogues of all government documents published. Other documents include the Census Bureau's population studies (often updated annually); publications of the Departments of Labor, Commerce,

Housing, and Health and Human Services; and the *Green Book* of the House Committee on Ways and Means, a yearly publication containing comprehensive information on social programs and participants.

A fifth source of policy-relevant information are think tanks, advocacy organizations, and professional associations. All think tanks (many of which are also advocacy organizations) employ research staff who evaluate and analyze social policies. Examples of these include the Brookings Institute, the American Enterprise Institute, the Heritage Foundation, the Hoover Institute, the Urban Institute, the Center on Budget and Policy Priorities, the Reason Foundation, the Hudson Institute, the Progressive Policy Institute, the Economic Policy Institute, and the Independent Sector. Again, much of this information can be accessed through the Internet. Since most think tanks are affiliated with particular political or economic ideologies or political parties, their data and policy recommendations should be viewed critically.

Many national advocacy organizations retain research staff and publish reports that are helpful to the policy analyst. Some of these organizations include the Urban League, the NAACP, the Children's Defense Fund, the National Farm Organization, and the National Organization for Women. Many professional associations, such as the American Medical Association, the American Public Welfare Association, the National Association of Social Workers, and the American Psychological Association, also publish policy-relevant information.

A sixth data source is professional journals, books, and monographs. Articles or books on specific policy topics can be found in various places, including the Social Science Index and the subject headings in library catalogues. Commercial electronic databases such as Lexis/Nexis and Westlaw are also useful. Lastly, policy-relevant information can be derived from interviews with principals in the policy process, advocates, recipients of services, and government officials. Personal interviews may also help gauge public opinion and assess the opposition or support for a particular policy. Taken together, these sources can be a gold mine for the policy analyst.

Social Policy Research and the Internet

The Internet, e-mail, Listservs, and FTP (File Transfer Protocol) sites have made the job of the policy analyst immeasurably easier, more efficient, and even more fun. Policy analysts no longer have to wait months before their library receives the report or data they are seeking; no longer must they contend with lost, misplaced, or checked-out documents; or wade through library stacks filled with endless feet of government reports. Instead, analysts can now download the newest government data, legislative reports, and governmental bills from the comfort of home. Policy analysts engage in different types of research activities. Although the Internet can provide access to vast stores of information, the degree to which it will facilitate your research will vary. It is helpful at the outset to know your research needs and how the Internet can help.

Journals and Online Research

Although titles, tables of contents, and article abstracts of many professional journals can be found online, the full text is often not available electronically. Full library searches remain the most fruitful way to conduct research when the full texts of print journals are required. While many professional journals are beginning to convert to an electronic format, this remains a costly and time-consuming process. Since journals provide income for their publishers, there is little incentive to provide free what journal subscribers must pay for. Still, when research requirements involve locating the most current information available, the Internet is a good starting place. This is especially true since virtually all major newspapers and news services are now online.

Although the full texts of many journal articles are often not available online, there are web-based databases that provide those services. These vary in cost. Some are free, but the majority charge an initial sign-up fee; an annual maintenance fee; fees for time spent searching the database; and a fee for each full article or abstract that is viewed or downloaded.

Online Data Collection

Recruiting subjects and collecting data online for research that requires more formalized qualitative and quantitative data collection has several advantages:

- Posting messages on e-mail lists or newsgroups to recruit and interview subjects is more efficient and less costly than traditional forms of data collection such as mailing questionnaires or using field researchers.

- Data obtained online does not require transcription, which lowers research costs.
- Subjects living anywhere in the world can respond to questionnaires at their convenience.
- Principal investigators living in various parts of the country can quickly and conveniently communicate with each other to clarify aspects of the research, provide feedback, and share reactions to the findings.[4]

There are also disadvantages to relying on the Internet for data collection. First, the danger exists that convenience and cost will dictate sampling methods, resulting in a biased sample. Second, the pool of people available to the researcher is limited to those who possess

- sufficient education to enable them to express themselves in written form
- the ability to operate a computer and Internet software
- adequate financial resources to maintain an Internet account, or have access through their place of employment
- the inclination to use the Internet and to participate in research[5]

Ethical Concerns Related to Online Research Involving Human Subjects

Just as copyright and fair use laws dictate the use of online information, ethical principles also apply to research activities. Two major areas that demand vigilance are informed consent and confidentiality.

The rights of research subjects have been codified into laws and codes of professional ethics. Violating these codes puts the researcher not only at risk of incurring professional sanctions but also legal ones. At the heart of this protection is informed consent. The fundamental ethical principle underlying informed consent is respect for subjects' autonomy—their right to make an informed decision about whether to participate in a research activity based on their understanding of the process, risks, and benefits.

Confidentiality involving the subjects and their responses is another hallmark of ethical research. Challenges to confidentiality arise in online research when identifying information on subjects and/or their responses are published on an online forum, especially since there are no guarantees that all forum users will honor professional ethics. E-mail presents similar concerns since there is no way to ensure that the person accessing the e-mail is the research subject. Opportunities for Internet-related research are abundant since many individuals openly discuss personal information in public forums, such as chat rooms or newsgroups. Unfortunately, there are reports of some researchers who have opportunistically exploited this situation, conducting naturalistic studies by observing a support Listserv or newsgroup.[6] This kind of research is in clear violation of the informed consent rule that guides professionals engaging in responsible human subjects research.

Finding and Accessing Online Information

Searching for information on the Internet may initially appear daunting, especially since Internet traffic is growing rapidly with more than 100 million Americans now online.[7] Fortunately, tools for searching the Internet allow users to quickly locate and access the data they need. These include (1) search engines, (2) subject directory guides, and (3) meta-search engines.

Search engines collect and index online data. They are easy to use, and the information is returned ranked by relevancy to the search topic. Some well-known search engines include Google (www.google.com); Yahoo (www.yahoo.com); Excite (www.excite.com), HotBot (www.hotbot.com), and Lycos (www.Lycos.com). One drawback of search engines is that all online data are included, thereby forcing the user to sort through many irrelevant hits. To be efficient, search engines require specificity in the choice of words or phrases.[8]

Subject directory guides are helpful when the user knows the broad topic but has not yet decided on a narrower subtopic. The information obtained will be an index of the World Wide Web's contents by subject category, with the results provided in a subject directory. Information in this type of search reflects efforts by editors who have searched for information and reviewed its contents. As with most search engines, retrieved information will be ranked by relevancy. Because of the editorial review of material in these databases, users generally obtain more relevant responses than using search engines. Examples of subject guides include the Library of Congress web page (http://lcweb.loc.gov), the Argus Clearinghouse (www.clearinghouse.net), Mental

Health Net (www.cmhc.com), and Medical Matrix (www.medmatrix.org).

Meta-search engines search across all the other online search engines. Although this search yields a vast amount of information, it collates the results, removes duplications and links that are no longer valid, and then rank orders the results. Examples of meta-search engines include Meta-Crawler (www.metacrawler.com/), SavvySearch (www.cs.colostate.edu/~dreiling/smartform.html), and Inference Find (http://m5.inference.com/ifind).

Citing and Documenting Information Obtained Online

Correctly citing online sources is as important as citing print references. Moreover, intellectual property rights apply to online material in much the same way as printed material. While electronic information technologies have transformed the flow of information, they have not changed our concept of intellectual property ownership. Copyright laws cover online public messages, collections of messages (i.e., message threads), e-mail, computer program files, text files, image files, sound and MIDI files, and electronic databases and trademarks. Shareware, freeware, and public domain software are the only types of software that can move through online networks without potentially violating copyrights.[9] In short, it is important to carefully cite online sources in research papers to avoid plagiarism.

Evaluating Reliable and Legitimate Internet Sources

We all are familiar with the saying "Don't believe everything you read." This warning also applies to information obtained online.

- The Internet is home to many bogus "professional" and hate-based websites containing questionable "facts." Obviously, information obtained from these sources should be avoided.
- Certain types of legal or technical information obtained online may be inappropriate because the website providing the information may be in a different country and subject to different jurisdictions.[10]
- The quality of online information varies from up-to-date research from leading policy institutes to out-of-date or inaccurate research. Information from websites that do not contain a date or a "modified on" notation should be avoided.

The Internet poses a challenge to policy analysts because of the mismatch between the speed with which new data can be disseminated and the length of time required for careful peer review.[11] One strategy for mitigating this problem is to develop innovative peer-reviewed approaches to Internet publishing.

Electronic Journals: An Increasingly Popular Venue

Electronic journals often take two forms: print journals with a website that contains an online copy of articles, and electronic journals with no print counterpart.[12] Online journals are increasingly seen as a way to address the problems libraries have with print journal collections, such as storage, preservation, accessibility, and cost. One project that has facilitated the availability of online information is Journal Storage (JSTOR), a not-for-profit organization of approximately 200 libraries, including Columbia, Harvard, Princeton, and Yale. JSTOR (www.jstor.org/about) has digitalized all or some of more than 52 core journal titles in 12 disciplines, including economics, political science, sociology, and anthropology.

Online Publishing

Electronically distributed information should be subject to the same standards of validity and reliability as printed materials. This is important to keep in mind when considering whether to publish online. For example, publishing an article on an Internet mailing list typically does not carry formal academic recognition. Peer-reviewed journals that appear in print are still considered the normative venue by which to achieve academic distinction. Moreover, if an article is published electronically many print journals will reject it since prior publication has already occurred. Online publishing may therefore be a problem for policy analysts who must formally document their publications.

Fortunately, there are a growing number of legitimate online publications. One way to discern whether an online journal is legitimate is to determine whether it is peer-reviewed. Specifically, the journal should have a masthead listing an editor, an editorial board, and guidelines for submission and review. In addition, legitimate online journals are sometimes issued an International Standard Serial Number (ISSN) through the Library of Congress or another official agency.[13] The Internet facilitates a wide range of research activities that range from conducting literature searches to publishing in online journals. Just as we adopt a critical stance when evaluating the credibility and quality of print sources, it is important to maintain a critical perspective when evaluating information obtained online.

Conclusion

The choice of a policy analysis framework depends on several factors, including (1) the kind of problem or policy that is being analyzed; (2) the resources available to the analyst, such as time, money, staff, facilities, and the availability of data; (3) the needs of the decision maker requesting the analysis; and (4) the time frame within which the analysis must be completed.

Because it is impossible to evaluate all of the data (data are essentially infinite) and to ask all of the possible questions, no policy analysis is ever complete. Policy analysis is always an approximation of the ideal, and therefore decisions are inevitably made on the basis of incomplete information. How incomplete the information is and how close an approximation to a rational decision is offered to decision makers will depend on the skills of the analyst, the available resources, and the time allotted for the project.

Despite its reliance on an analytic framework, social policy analysis is largely subjective. Because a policy is analyzed by human beings, it is always done through the lens of the analyst's value system, ideological beliefs, and their particular understanding of the goals and purposes of social welfare. Subjectivity may be evident in the omission of facts or questions or in the relative weight given to one variable over another. Other forms of subjectivity include asking the wrong questions about the policy, evaluating it on the basis of expectations that it cannot meet, or expecting it to tackle a problem the policy was not designed to remedy. Finally, political pressure can be put on the policy analyst to come up with recommendations that are acceptable to a certain interest group. Regardless of the causes of subjectivity, policy analysis always approximates the ideal and always involves an informed hunch as to the effects of a policy or a set of policies.

Discussion Questions

1. What are the main advantages of using an analytic framework for social policy analysis? Describe the benefits of using such a framework. What, if any, are the potential drawbacks?
2. Although the *unintended* consequences of a social policy are obviously unpredictable, what can a policy analyst do to minimize the risk? Describe a social policy that has produced unintended consequences that were either positive or harmful.
3. Can a policy researcher neutralize his or her personal values when conducting a policy analysis? If so, describe ways in which this can be done.
4. What components should be added to the proposed policy framework presented in this chapter? Which of the components provided in this framework are the most important, and why?
5. Are most social policies analyzed rationally? If not, why not? Describe the factors that stand in the way of a systematic and rational analysis of social policy in the U.S. context. How much value do decision makers place on social policy research? Why?
6. Since any analysis of social policy is by nature incomplete, should decision makers minimize policy studies? What alternatives, if any, can be used in lieu of a thorough and systematic policy analysis?
7. Because of its long reach and low costs, the Internet is the perfect breeding ground for the growth of hate groups. Should legislative controls be placed on the Internet to limit its use by hate groups?
8. What are some of the strengths and weaknesses of Internet research?

Notes

1. Thanks to Brene Brown for her ideas on environmental scanning. Dr. Brown has repeatedly pointed out that environmental scanning is a concept that successful agencies must adopt.
2. Lionheart Foundation, "Corrections in the U.S.—The Picture Today . . ." Retrieved 2004 from www.lionheart.org/prison_proj/corrections.html
3. Many social policy writers have developed excellent policy frameworks, among them Elizabeth Huttman, *Introduction to Social Policy* (New York: McGraw-Hill, 1981); Neil Gilbert and Harry Specht, *Dimensions of Social Welfare Policy,* 2nd ed. (Englewood Cliffs, NJ: Prentice-Hall, 1986); Gail Marker, "Guidelines for Analysis of a Social Welfare Program," in John E. Tropman et al. (eds.), *Strategic Perspectives on Social Policy* (New York: Pergamon Press, 1976); David Gil, *Unraveling Social Policy* (Boston: Shenkman, 1981); and Charles Prigmore and Charles Atherton, *Social Welfare Policy* (New York: D. C. Heath, 1979).
4. Richard Lakeman, "Using the Internet for Data Collection in Nursing Research," *Computers in Nursing* 15, no. 5 (1997), pp. 269–275.
5. Ibid.
6. John Grohol, "Best Practices in E-Therapy: Confidentiality & Privacy." Retrieved 1999 from www.ismho.org/issues/99901.htm
7. Elizabeth Weise, "Net Use Doubling Every 100 Days," *USA Today* (April 16, 1998), p. 6.
8. Joanne Yaffe, *Quick Guide to the Internet for Social Work* (Boston: Allyn & Bacon, 1998).
9. Lance Rose, *Netlaw: Your Rights in the Online World* (Berkeley: McGraw-Hill, 1995).
10. Alan Parkin and David Stretch, "Facilities on the Internet May Be Abused," *British Medical Journal* 313, no. 4 (November 11, 1997), pp. 67–69.
11. Enrico Coiera, "The Internet's Challenge to Health Care Provision," *British Medical Journal* 312, no. 3–4 (January 6, 1996), pp. 8–16.
12. John Grohol, *The Insider's Guide to Mental Health Resources Online* (New York: Guilford Press, 1997).
13. Ibid.

CHAPTER 3

Religion and Social Welfare Policy

Howard Jacob Karger and Peter A. Kindle

Every week more than 300,000 congregations, mosques, temples, and ashrams meet to conduct religious services across the United States.[1] Over 80 percent of the American population report a religious affiliation, over 90 percent report a personal belief in the existence of a supreme being, and more than $179.4 billion was donated to churches and charities in 2003.[2] Not only are the American people the most religious western democracy in the world, the variety of religious expression in this country is unequaled.

There are more Jews practicing their faith in the United States than there are in Israel. There are more Muslim adherents in the United States than there are in Kuwait, Oman, Qatar, Lebanon, or the United Arab Emirates.[3] There were almost 1,200 congregations practicing the Bahai faith in 2000, over 1,600 Buddhist worship centers, and over 600 Hindu temples.[4] To one accustomed to the variety of religious expressions and practices that are part of contemporary America, it may be difficult to recognize that this diversity has not always been the case.

While we understand and appreciate the important contributions made by the world's religions to American social policy, the vast majority of this chapter will focus on Christianity. This is not because we are Christocentric. On the contrary. However, American social welfare history has been more strongly influenced by Christianity than by any other world religion. In order to understand how religion has influenced the development of social welfare policy, it is necessary to understand the major historical trends that have shaped religion in America. As such, this chapter examines the religious roots for the development of the welfare state, and how changes in religious thought and expression have been reflected in social welfare policies.

Religious Antecedents of Welfare Statism

The roots of social welfare go deep into the soil of Judeo-Christian tradition. It was the disfavored son Cain who repudiated his responsibility to his brother with the defensive, "Am I my brother's keeper?"[5] Societal structures in ancient Judaism encoded protections for the most powerless (e.g., the poor, the orphan, and the widow). The poor were allowed to glean the remains and corners of the fields at harvest time, and brothers-in-law were commanded to marry their brother's widow and to raise her children as his own.[6]

Christian traditions build on Jewish foundations. Jesus himself is said to value the "cup of cold water" given in faith, and early gatherings of Christians were reputedly communitarian in that they appear to have shared material provision for daily living in an egalitarian fashion.[7] "No one claimed that any of his possessions was his own, but they shared everything they had."[8] In fact, there are interpreters of religious history that attribute the survival of Jewish and Christian sects during the first and second centuries to this communitarian impulse.

While there are other traditions of compassion that could be related to the development of welfare statism, the dominance of Judeo-Christian compassion and community is without peer as the source in Western societies. The eventual dominance of the Christian tradition in Europe, and the near-identification of church with state government during the medieval period, led to the gradual assumption of government responsibility for social welfare.

The English Poor Laws

Early social welfare relief in England was considered a private and church matter. For example, individual benefactors took responsibility for building almshouses, hospitals, and even bridges and roads. Despite private philanthropy, the main burden for the poor rested on the shoulders of the church; however, it would be a mistake to interpret this to mean that the English government assumed little or no responsibility for the care of the poor. The Church of England has been an integral part of the English government since the sixteenth century, and there has been a sense in which government responsibility for social welfare has continually been, at least partially, discharged through this established church.

In 1601, the English government established the Elizabethan Poor Laws which were largely administered through church parishes. In essence, these laws, which remained active for almost 250 years, established the responsibility of the English government to provide relief to the needy. Furthermore, the laws decreed that the needy had a legal right to receive governmental assistance. In order to define the boundaries of government help, the law distinguished among three classes of dependents and proposed remedial measures: Needy children were given apprenticeships, the able-bodied were given work, and the worthy poor were provided either indoor (institutional) or outdoor (home) relief. Finally, the law ordered local governments to assume responsibility for the needy.[9] The English Poor Laws formed the basis for statutes that were enacted in both colonial and postcolonial America.[10]

Church, State, and Social Welfare in Colonial America

Most settlers in colonial America were poor; however, unlike their European ancestors, they were not destitute.[11] The undeveloped resources of the frontier provided opportunities for colonists that were not available in the social milieu of Europe, and, therefore, pauperism was not widespread. According to Robert Morris, fewer than 1 percent of American colonists received help from outside sources.[12] The new frontier provided ample opportunity for work, and the ready availability of work allowed for the reinterpretation of European religious perspectives.

European Protestants valued work. Martin Luther viewed work as a responsibility to God. Furthermore, work conferred dignity and was a "calling" by God. In Luther's view, a person served God by doing the work of his vocation. Therefore, those who are able-bodied and yet unemployed are sinners. John Calvin took Luther's argument one step further by claiming that work carried out the will of God and, as such, would ultimately help to create God's kingdom on earth. According to both Luther and Calvin, God-fearing people must work regardless of their wage or type of employment.[13]

God commanded work, America provided opportunity, and economic success became a sign of divine favor. This Protestant ethic (Roman Catholics were less than 2 percent of the population in 1776) fueled the creation of a work-oriented society and provided a religious foundation for the condemnation of the poor.[14] If prosperity was a sign of God's favor, then poverty was a sign of God's judgment. When assistance was required, it was provided on a case-by-case basis in town meetings. When the number of cases increased as a result of indentured servants and abandoned children, the English system of overseers was introduced. It was not uncommon for the town council to auction off the poor to neighboring farmers, apprentice out children, place the poor in private homes at public expense, or send them to privately operated almshouses. Settlers believed that children should be part of a family unit, and thus the practice of indenture became widespread; however, by the end of the colonial period, the locus of responsibility for the poor began to shift from the town to the province.[15] It was inconceivable until the mid-1800s that there could be any federal responsibility for social welfare.

The Second Great Awakening

The nineteenth century opened (1800–1830) with a period of unusually intense religious fervor termed the *Second Great Awakening.* At least in part a reaction to the disestablishment of religion codified in the Bill of Rights (eight of the original 13 colonies had an established church on the European pattern) and in part millennial enthusiasm, the religion sparked by the Second Great Awakening contributed to the a general spirit of reform.[16] The Puritans' vision of America as "a city set on a hill" was renewed across the nation. America's destiny was to be a pure and holy nation.

Church attendance doubled in comparison to the revolutionary era,[17] but the organizational structure of most denominations was still quite rudimentary. Those denominations with the most adherents in 1776 were in serious decline, and the more evangelistic denominations were on the rise. In 1776 Congregationalists, Episcopalians, and Presbyterians made up 55.1 percent of religious adherents; by 1850 these denominations represented only 19.1 percent. The Baptists and Methodists, who made up 19 percent of adherents in 1776, had grown to 55 percent by 1850. Catholics, who encompassed less than 2 percent of the population in 1776, in spite of western expansion into Texas and French Catholic lands to the Mississippi River, remained a modest minority of 14 percent in 1850.[18]

Voluntary associations were formed to promote causes the existing denominational structures could not support. For example, the American Board for Foreign Missions (1810), the American Tract Society (1814), the American Bible Society (1816), and the American Sunday School Union (1824) were organized.[19] However, this optimistic religious fervor was not contained solely within the churches and religious endeavors, but was also channeled into moral and social reform.

From his pulpit at Hanover Street Congregational Church in Boston, Lyman Beecher (1775–1863) railed against moral license. Largely due to his efforts, the Connecticut Society for the Reformation of Morals (1823) and later the American Temperance Union (1836) were formed.[20] The casual and heavy drinking of alcohol that had been the American custom since the first colonists came under attack. Abstinence from all strong drink became the new moral standard, if not the actual practice, of the average American citizen. It would be more than a century before the temperance movement would culminate in the 18th Amendment prohibiting the manufacturing, transportation, or sale of alcoholic beverages.[21]

The tone was set for future clashes between church and state by the New England Sabbatarian campaign (1828–1832). Although ultimately unsuccessful, the clergy-led campaign to end mail delivery on Sunday did "recruit moral reformers and give them their political baptism."[22] "They raised funds, held rallies, published tracts, signed petitions, and failed. . . ."[23] This experience was to prove invaluable for abolitionists that followed, and according to James A. Morone, established a new institutional symbiosis between private organizations and the public bureaucracy that was instrumental in melding local and national interests in this geographically dispersed nation.[24]

Perhaps no reform movement shows more clearly the intricate interweaving of religion and politics more than the abolition movement. While the former editor of a small Baptist temperance journal, William Lloyd Garrison (1805–1879), thundered against the evils of slavery in his *Public Liberator and Journal of the Times* (in press from 1831–1843), Charles G. Finney (1792–1875) led religious revivals throughout the northern states that led converts to support the abolition movement. Many, if not the majority, of these converts were women who stepped forward with Garrison's support to take an active role in the leadership of the movement.[25]

While there was little sympathy for the abolitionists in the southern states, the religious fervor of the Second Great Awakening had its influence. The Cane Ridge camp meeting in Kentucky (1801) is often cited as the beginning of the awakening, and its influence was felt in both Tennessee and Ohio.[26] The Baptists and Methodists were quick to adopt the revival patterns that fueled their rapid growth. For the first time conversion efforts were directed toward the slave population of the south with considerable success. Sydney Ahlstrom notes that "the evangelization of the slaves was prosecuted with increased vigor" as though it was a direct response to northern abolitionists.[27]

Three products of the Second Great Awakening had a lasting influence on what was to become social welfare policy. First, the religious impulse for reform was channeled into private organizations attempting to affect public change. Second, a cadre of female leaders were mobilized and trained. Third, an African American clergy began to form to lead the African American converts. While the egalitarianism associated with the religious revival had produced tumult, social welfare reform proceeded at a slower pace.

The Civil War Era

Those denominations with national constituencies split over the slavery issue prior to the beginning of the Civil War. In 1845 the Methodists and Baptists divided into autonomous northern and southern denominations. The Presbyterians followed in 1857. Those denominations without national membership (e.g., Congregationalists, Unitarians, and Universalists), those whose congregational polity had yet to produce denominational structures (e.g., Jews and Disciples of Christ), and those that were withdrawn or isolated from public life (e.g., Latter Day Saints and Mennonites) did not separate into distinct denominations. Lutherans, Episcopalians, and Catholics did not take a denominational stand on slavery prior to the outbreak of war in 1860. They did not split into distinct national churches until there were two separate nations—the United States and the Confederate States of America.[28]

During the course of the Civil War (1860–1864), the evangelistic fervor of the Second Great Awakening was rekindled. Soldiers on both sides of the conflict required assistance, and the existing churches and private organizations were generous in meeting these needs. In the North the Christian Commission raised more than $3 million in cash, millions more in supplies and services, and recruited over 5,000 volunteers to assist Northern soldiers. While the work of the Southern churches is less well documented, the religious support was no less fervent. Linus P. Brockett wrote in his 1864 book, *The Philanthropic Results of the War in America,* "neither in ancient nor modern times has there been so vast an outpouring of a nation's wealth for the care, the comfort, and the physical and moral welfare of those who have fought the nation's battles or been the sufferers from its condition of war."[29] This philanthropic impulse was to continue to influence America's early social welfare for some time.

For example, Dorothea Dix, a Sunday School teacher, led a campaign to reform the care of the mentally ill. She was successful in lobbying for state actions, but became convinced that federal assistance was needed due to the large expenditures required. In 1854 both houses of Congress passed a bill to assist the mentally ill. It was vetoed by President Franklin Pierce with these words, "If Congress has the power to make provisions for the indigent insane . . . it has the same power for the indigent who are not insane. . . . I cannot find any authority in the Constitution for making the Federal Government the great almoner of public charity throughout the United States."[30] Federal responsibility for social welfare was to develop slowly and gradually.

However, the Civil War did usher in a new period for relief activities. Families who had lost a breadwinner or who had a breadwinner return from the war permanently disabled could not be blamed for their misfortunes. As a response to this hardship, localities passed laws that raised funds for the sick and needy and, in some instances, for the founding of homes for disabled soldiers. Another concern was the increasing numbers of freed slaves, and freedman relief societies with religious ties were organized in most northern cities during the first year of the war.[31]

Other welfare issues during the Civil War included the disease and filth rampant in army camps and hospitals and the shortage of trained medical personnel. In an effort to remedy this situation, Unitarian minister Henry W. Bellows and a group of citizens (mainly women) organized the U.S. Sanitary Commission in 1861, the first important national public health group. Functioning as a quasi-governmental body, the commission was financed and directed by the private voluntary sector. Working initially in the area of preventive health education, the commission eventually became involved in serving the needs of soldiers.[32]

Another social welfare institution that emerged from the Civil War was the Freedmen's Bureau. By the close of the war, political leaders realized that the emancipation of millions of slaves would create serious social problems. Former slaves having no occupational training, land, or jobs would require assistance. In 1865, following the earlier example of local freedman's relief societies, Congress established the Bureau of Refugees, Freedmen, and Abandoned Lands. The Freedmen's Bureau, as it was commonly called, was responsible for directing a program of temporary relief for the duration of the war and one year afterward. After a bitter struggle, Congress extended the Freedmen's Bureau for an additional six years.

Under General Oliver Howard the bureau performed a variety of services designed to help African Americans make the transition from slavery to freedom. For example, the bureau served as an emergency relief center that distributed 22 million rations to needy Southerners. The bureau also functioned as an African American employment agency, a settlement agency, a health center that employed doctors and operated hospitals, an educational agency that encouraged the funding of African American colleges and provided financial aid, and, finally, as a legal agency that maintained courts in which civil and criminal cases involving African Americans were heard. The Freedmen's Bureau set an important precedent for federal involvement in a variety of human services. In 1872 the bureau was dissolved by Congress.[33] Northern denominations continued the work, sponsoring thousands of educational missionaries to teach in African American schools, and founding Lincoln University in Pennsylvania, Morehouse College and Atlanta University in Georgia, Talladega College in Alabama, Tougaloo University in Mississippi, Hampton Institute in Virginia, and Fisk University in Tennessee.[34]

Following the war and the end of Reconstruction in 1877, only the Catholic and Episcopal churches immediately reunited. Methodists reunited in 1939, Presbyterians in 1983, and the division between northern and southern Baptists continues to this day.[35] Further divisions occurred as each denomination tended to segregate African Americans. The Colored Primitive Baptists (1866), the Colored Cumberland Presbyterian Church (1869), and the National Baptist Convention (1895) joined the older African Methodist Episcopal Church, Bethel (1816) and African Methodist Episcopal Church, Zion (1821) as institutional organizations for African Americans. By 1900 2.7 million out of 8.3 million African Americans would identify with one of these denominations.[36]

The Late Nineteenth and Early Twentieth Centuries

Although Catholic immigration increased the size of this denomination until it was the largest in America by 1890, the Protestant hegemony over America was unchallenged. Protestant discrimination led to Catholic sectarianism. Parochial schools, Catholic versions of professional organizations and semi-professional guilds, even a Catholic alternative to fraternal lodges "created a parallel society within which [Catholics] were protected from Protestant insults as well as from Protestant influences."[37] As late as 1866, white, American Protestant denominations were capable of forming into a single ecumenical association called the Evangelical Alliance to assert "the claim that Protestantism was the only true religion of the republic."[38] This alliance was short-lived, but provided the development of a Protestant confidence in large-scale organizations and affirmed an "optimism about realizing God's kingdom in this world."[39] Other circumstances—social, philosophical, and theological—in the late nineteenth century would cause this optimism to crumble.

Immigration and industrialization made significant impacts on Protestant optimism. Prior to industrialization, most people lived in small, rural communities with an array of institutions that afforded a high degree of self-sufficiency. Chief among these institutions were the local churches. Survival necessitated a degree of solidarity, or interdependence, and the local churches were an apt institution to fill this need. From 1890 to 1920, 22 million immigrants came to the United States. At the same time, the American people became more urban. Seventy-five percent of foreign immigrants lived in the cities and, during the decade following 1920, 6 million people moved from farms to cities.[40] Community solidarity was no longer the norm, and an urban/rural dichotomy became more apparent in the Protestant denominations.

Philosophically, many people looked to the developing social sciences for guidance in redefining social policy. There, prominent scholars drew lessons from the natural sciences that could be used for purposes of social engineering. Borrowing from biology, some American proponents of the new science of sociology applied the idea of natural selection to social affairs.

Social Darwinism was a bastard outgrowth of Charles Darwin's theory of evolution as described in his 1859 classic, *The Origin of Species*.[41] Social theorists such as Herbert Spencer and America's William Graham Sumner reasoned that if Darwin's laws of evolution determined the origin and development of species, then they might also be applied to understanding the laws of society.[42]

Applying Darwin's rules to society and then adapting laissez-faire principles of economics to sociology led to a problematic set of assumptions. First, if the "survival of the fittest" (a term coined by Spencer) was a law governing the lower species, then it must also govern the higher species. Because subsidizing the poor allowed them to survive, this circumvented the law of nature, and because the poor reproduced more rapidly than the middle classes, society was thus subsidizing its own demise. Social Darwinists believed essentially that the poor would eventually overrun society and bring down the general level of civilization.

Social Darwinists believed that, although unfortunate, the poor must pay the price demanded by nature and be allowed to die out. According to the Social Darwinists, social welfare thwarts nature's plan of evolutionary progress toward higher forms of social life. Speaking for many intellectuals, the British theorist Herbert Spencer drew this conclusion:

> It seems hard that widows and orphans should be left to struggle for life or death. Nevertheless, when regarded not separately but in connexion with the interests of universal humanity, these harsh fatalities are seen to be full of beneficence the same beneficence which brings to early graves the children of diseased parents, and singles out the intemperate and the debilitated as the victims of an epidemic.[43]

Social Darwinism in the north, and white indifference to the freedman's condition in the south, set a secular tone for the nation that denied the most basic assumption of Protestant optimism—that America was to be a holy nation, a "city set upon a hill." The Protestant establishment was not unanimous in its response to these threats and began to separate into what would become mainline and evangelical traditions.

This cleavage among Protestants was to be accelerated by theological conflicts. German higher criticism challenged the infallibility of scripture. Evolution provided a natural alternative to supernatural explanations as did Freudian psychology and Marxian socialism. The success of the scientific method elevated confidence in human reason. Protestants responded in two ways. First, conservative, evangelical theologians reverted to traditional interpretations. Biblical infallibility, miracles, and the existence of the supernatural were reasserted. Conversion and personal piety were emphasized as essential elements of Christian faith. Within this religious framework, poverty was related to improvidence: People were poor because they engaged in drinking, slothfulness, licentious behavior, and gambling.

This evangelical Protestant response to theological challenges was not without opposition. A movement known as the Social Gospel emerged. Composed of theologians concerned with the abuses created by industrialization and the excesses of capitalism, Social Gospelists such as Josiah Strong, Graham Taylor, and others believed that the church should recapture the militant spirit of Christ by taking on the issues of social justice and poverty. The critique posed by the Social Gospelists called for fair play and simple justice for the worker.[44]

Proponents of the Social Gospel movement maintained that churches wrongfully stressed spirituality rather than morality.[45] The condemnation of classical economics, business ethics, and the lawlessness of the plutocracy was centered on a moral rather than a spiritual plane. For the Social Gospelists, social reformation could not occur without a regeneration of character.[46] Although the movement contained degrees of radicalism, all Social Gospelists were moved by a sense of social crisis, and all believed in the necessity of a Christian solution.[47]

At the turn of the twentieth century, an outside observer may have had great difficulty in identifying the distinction between these two Protestant factions. Both were heavily committed to the tradition of religious social relief. Postmillennialism, the belief that Christian preaching will result in a gradually and steadily improving society so that, when Christ returns a second time, God's kingdom will be established without additional radical change, was the dominant eschatological view.[48]

The cleavage began to be apparent in 1908 when the more conservative and evangelical denominations declined to join the Federal Council of Churches.[49] Walter Rauschenbusch's 1907 book, *Christianity and the Social Crisis,* provided a ready statement of the Social Gospel that was later countered by publication of twelve volumes called *The Fundamentals* (1910–1915) that were distributed without charge to Protestant ministers.[50] Postmillennial optimism did not survive the first world war among evangelical Protestants who began to embrace dispensational premillennialism. This new eschatological view, originating with the Englishman John Nelson Darby (1800–1882) and popularized by the Scofield Reference Bible, expected human society to become steadily more ungodly and evil until, in a secret rapture of the true Christians, a seven-year period of tribulation would signal the second return of Christ.[51] By 1920 evangelical Protestants had discontinued most social relief work, at least in part, as a means of distinguishing themselves from the more public and liberal theology of the mainline Protestants.[52]

The Rise of Social Work as a Profession

Religion and social welfare in nineteenth-century America were inextricably linked. Almost all forms of relief emanated from church groups, and all major denominations had some mechanism for providing social welfare, at least until the early twentieth century.[53] For example, as early as 1880 there were 500 private, church-related social welfare organizations in New York City alone, with the largest network for social services provided by Protestant churches. Christian charity suffused the Charity Organization Societies (COSs) and Settlement Houses that assumed a major share of the responsibility for urban social welfare during the late nineteenth century.

It was thought that in order to reclaim providence the poor must be taught to live a moral and self-disciplined life. While early religious social workers clung tenaciously to their desire to teach the moral life, they also understood the need to provide material assistance.[54] The major emphasis of the early social worker, however, was more often on spiritual guidance than on material aid.

The relief assistance provided by these religious social workers was often linked to harsh criteria. For example, it was not uncommon for social workers to appraise the worth of the family's possessions and then instruct them to sell off everything in order to qualify for relief. Nor was it uncommon for social workers to deny relief because they felt that the poor family was intemperate and not sufficiently contrite. Although social workers dispensed relief, they were basically opposed to the concept of it. In effect, they believed that distributing relief was imprudent because a reliance on charity would weaken the moral fabric of the poor and provide a disincentive for work.

Urban Needs during Industrialization

Life in late nineteenth-century America was hard. The dream of milk and honey that motivated many immigrants to leave their homelands became, for many, a nightmare. The streets of American cities were not paved with gold; instead, they were overcrowded, rampant with disease and crime, and economically destitute. Many tenement houses in the larger cities contained neither windows nor indoor plumbing. Tuberculosis was widespread, and among some groups, infant mortality ran as high as 50 percent. Scant medical care existed for the poor; there was no public education; and insanity and prostitution rates among immigrants were high.[55] Industrial and economic prospects were equally bleak. Factory conditions were deplorable: Workers were expected to labor six or seven days a week (often on Sunday), and 18-hour days were not unusual, especially in summer.[56] Factories were poorly lit and unsanitary, easily turned into fire traps, and offered almost no job security. Moreover, homework (taking piecework home, usually for assembly by whole families in one- or two-room tenements) was common. Women were forced to work night shifts and then take care of their homes and children by day.[57] No special protective legislation for women existed until the early 1900s, and child labor was legal.

Charity Organization Societies

First evident in the 1870s, Charity Organization Societies (COSs) had offices in most American cities by 1900.[58] With the exception of meager state-sponsored indoor and outdoor relief, the COS movement was a major provider of care to the destitute. COSs varied in their structures and methods. In general, they coordinated relief giving by operating community-wide registration bureaus, providing direct relief, and "educating" both the upper and lower classes as to their mutual obligations.

The work of the COS was carried out by a committee of volunteers and agency representatives who examined "cases" of needy applicants and decided on a course of action. The agent of the COS was the "friendly visitor," whose task was to conduct an investigation of the circumstances surrounding the cases and to instruct the poor in ways of better managing their lives. Friendly visitors, drawn from the upper classes, often held a morally superior attitude toward their clientele, and their intervention in the lives of the poor was interpreted by some observers as a form of social control as well as a means of providing assistance.[59] In any case, the charity provided by these organizations was often less than generous. Leaders of the movement drew an important lesson from Social Darwinism and the Protestant work ethic in believing that beneficent charity was counterproductive because it contributed to sloth and dependency. Josephine Shaw Lowell, president of the New York Charity Organization Society, believed that charity should be dispensed "only when starvation was imminent."[60] To be sure, it was difficult for friendly visitors to maintain a sense of Christian duty in the midst of immoral behavior. In such instances, when some wretched soul seemed beyond instruction and charity, more radical measures were in order.

Settlement Houses

Begun in the 1880s, the settlement house movement had emerged in most of the big cities over the next two decades. Settlement houses were primarily set

One of the best-known settlement houses, Hull House was established by Jane Addams in 1889.

up in immigrant neighborhoods by wealthy people, college students, unattached women, teachers, doctors, and lawyers, who themselves moved into the slums as residents. Rather than simply engaging in friendly visiting, the upper- and middle-class settlement leaders tried to bridge class differences and to develop a less patronizing form of charity. Rather than coordinating the existing charities like the COS movement, they sought to help the people in the neighborhoods to organize themselves. Because they actually lived in the same neighborhoods as the impoverished immigrants, settlement workers could provide fresh and reliable knowledge about the social and economic conditions of American cities.

Jane Addams established Hull House in 1889. She approached the project and the Chicago ethnic community in which it was based with a sense of Christian Socialism that was derived from a "rather strenuous moral purgation"[61] rather than a sense of *noblesse oblige.* By 1915, this altruism was shared by enough settlement workers so that more than 300 settlements had been established, and most large American cities boasted at least one or more settlement houses.[62]

While providing individual services to the poor, the larger settlements were essentially reform-oriented. These reforms were achieved not only by organizing the poor to press for change but also by using interest groups formed by elite citizens, as well as by the formation of national alliances. Settlement-pioneered reforms included tuberculosis prevention, the establishment of well-baby clinics, the implementation of housing codes, the construction of outdoor playgrounds, the enactment of child labor and industrial safety legislation, and the promotion of some of the first studies of the urban black in America, such as W. E. B. Du Bois's *The Philadelphia Negro.*

The Social Casework Agency

Charity Organization Societies and settlement houses served as models for the delivery of social welfare services in the voluntary sector organizations that emerged during the Progressive Era. Similar in many respects, these organizations evolved to form the social casework agency. Both were of modest size in terms of staff, both were located in the communities of the clientele they served, both served a predominantly poor population, and both relied on contributions from a variety of sources for private donations, the Community Chest, and foundations.[63] Typically, workers in these agencies were female volunteers. COS techniques for investigation were refined, their aim being the identification of a "social diagnosis" as the basis for case intervention.[64] Subsequently, these activities, along with the community-oriented work of the settlement reformers gave birth to the profession of social work.

As predominant service delivery forms, COSs and settlement houses were shaped by two influences: the need for scientifically based techniques, and the socialization of charity. Together, these contributed to the emergence of the social casework agency. COSs and settlement houses had provided meaningful activity for upper- and middle-class women who found it necessary to ground their work in techniques that were derived from science. This necessity had been driven home in 1915 during the National Conference of Charities and Correction, when Abraham Flexner, a renowned authority on professional graduate education, was asked to address the question of whether social work was a profession. Much to the disappointment of the audience, Flexner judged that social work lacked all the requirements of a profession, particularly a scientifically derived knowledge base that was transmittable.[65]

Spotlight 3.1

Jane Addams and Hull House

In 1889, Jane Addams established Hull House to serve residents of the Chicago community in which she lived. To learn more about Jane Addams and Hull House, go to **www.uic.edu/jaddams/hull/urbanexp.** Using historical photos and narrative, this website presents a comprehensive overview of Hull House and its surrounding neighborhoods.

The Progressive Movement

A reaction to the heartlessness that characterized a large segment of American society came in the form of the Progressive movement, a social movement that was popular from the early 1900s to World War I. Progressive Era philosophy intended to inject a measure of public credibility and Christian morality into social, political, and economic affairs. As a result, it reflected a unique blend of social reform encompassing anti–big business attitudes, a belief that government should regulate the public good, a strong emphasis on ethics in business and personal life, a commitment to social justice, a concern for the "common man," and a strong sense of paternalism. Progressives believed that the state had a responsibility for protecting the interests of the public, especially those who were vulnerable. Supported by the nation's most respected social workers, including Jane Addams, Lillian Wald, and Paul U. Kellogg, the Progressive Party presented a presidential ticket in 1912. The advent of World War I diminished the liberal fervor that had characterized the Progressive Era of the late 1800s and early 1900s. In the wake of the disillusionment that followed the war, the mood of the country became conservative. Progressive ideas were treated skeptically by the 1920s and activists were often accused of being Bolsheviks.

Religion and the Welfare State

On January 16, 1920, the 18th Amendment went into effect and Prohibition became the law throughout the country. This single event, the culmination of religious and moral reforms that had begun more than a century before, signaled the high point of Protestant dominance in the United States, but this was to be short-lived.

The Fundamentalist Controversy and Its Aftermath

The Protestantism of the 1920s held little resemblance to its nineteenth-century predecessor. Those mainline denominations that associated with the Federal Council of Churches were characterized by large denominational bureaucracies, significant interdenominational cooperation, and a new form of religious intellectualism.[66] Theologically, the mainline tended to embrace the findings of the natural sciences and the new social sciences in preference to biblical and historical traditions. Post-war patriotism was bolstered by economic prosperity, leading to the uncritical conclusion that capitalism and the Protestant work ethic had divine favor. Paradoxically, one-third of Americans continued to live in poverty.[67] Although the Social Gospel had waned, it maintained a presence in the larger urban congregations that were most proximate to those living in urban poverty and in the voices of social conscience best personified by Reinhold Niebuhr of Union Theological Seminary in New York.[68]

The cleavage in American Protestantism became the focus of national attention during the so-called Scopes monkey trial. "In the course of a few days in July 1923 two million words of newspaper reportage were telegraphed from Dayton, Tennessee."[69] John Scopes, a recent college graduate and novice high school teacher, was on trial for teaching the theory of evolution in violation of Tennessee law. Conservative and evangelical Protestants were subjected to national scorn and ridicule as Fundamentalists, exacerbating sectarian tendencies. For the most part, conservative and evangelical Protestant organizations withdrew from public life. The prosperous twenties abruptly ended in late 1929 as stock market values crashed. Within four years over a quarter of Americans were unemployed, Prohibition had been repealed, and Franklin D. Roosevelt was president.

The Great Depression and New Deal

It is difficult to appreciate the significance of the Great Depression from the position of the relatively prosperous twenty-first century; however, it can be safely concluded that religion had a more significant impact on the private lives of Americans than it did on public policy. The economic crisis called for emergency measures and Roosevelt's New Deal programs were the response. Social and policy changes took place with blinding speed as the federal government became "the great almoner of public charity."[70] Billions of dollars were spent on relief efforts to provide food, clothing, and shelter. Public works projects were to employ as many as 3.2 million a month by 1938. A minimum wage, a maximum work week, collective bargaining, and the abolishment of child labor were established in 1937. The apogee of the New Deal was the Social Security Act of 1935 which included a national old-age retirement system; federal grants to states for maternal, child, and disabled welfare services; and a federal-state unemployment system.[71]

Churchmen could not keep pace, and even the liberal mainline tended to withdraw into a quiescent spirituality. At best the mainline waged an ineffective post hoc critique of the New Deal while the conservative and evangelical groups tended to become more isolated and sectarian. Social workers and others with tenancy experience in a settlement house stepped to the forefront to provide the moral leadership previously provided by religion. Edith Abbott, president of the National Conference of Social Welfare and Dean of the University of Chicago School of Social Service Administration, participated in the drafting of the Social Security Act. Frances Perkins became the first Secretary of Labor. Harry Hopkins is credited as the primary architect of the New Deal. Both the National Association for the Advancement of Colored People (NAACP) and the National Urban League included key social workers in their early formation.[72]

Patterns of Religious Change

The abdication of public moral leadership did not mean that religious change did not occur. In a pattern that has held true since the Congregationalists yielded numerical dominance to the Methodists between 1776 and 1850, mainline denominations tended to decline in membership and sectarian groups tended to grow.[73] Dean M. Kelley, an executive with the National Council of Churches (which replaced the Federal Council in 1950), was the first to publicize this historical trend in his book *Why Conservative Churches Are Growing*. While many aspects of Kelley's analysis were flawed, for example his claim that the decline in mainline membership was a sudden change due to cultural shifts in the 1960s, his explanation for the trend has survived all challenges: Strong congregations are strict.[74] Finke and Stark explain:

> High cost [of association with sectarian groups] serve to screen out potential members whose commitment and participation would otherwise be low. The costs act as nonrefundable registration fees which, as in secular markets, measure seriousness of interest in the product. As a result the demanding sects speak of "conversions," "being born again," and "submitting their lives to the Lord." The less demanding churches refer to affiliations that are seldom life-altering events. Sectarian members are either in or out; they must follow the demands of the group or withdraw.[75]

Of course, it is not impossible for a sect to require too much of potential members, but in general, "the higher the costs of membership, the greater the material and social, as well as religious, benefits of membership."[76] Many, if not all, of the conservative and evangelical denominations benefited by their withdrawal from public life.

A comparison of the Methodist and Baptist traditions is one of the clearest examples of the declining trend associated with the mainline, and the corresponding growth associated with a more sectarian identity. Both groups grew during the first half of the nineteenth century, but the stricter Methodists clearly outshined the Baptists. Between 1776 and 1850, Baptist adherents grew by a respectable 21 percent; Methodists by more than 1,268 percent.[77] As the largest religious Protestant denomination in the late nineteenth century, Methodism began to change. Circuit riding lay preachers gave way to seminary trained ministers, the emotion-packed worship style of the camp meeting yielded to a more sedate middle-class conformity, and strict behavioral codes were relaxed.[78] By 1926, Baptists outnumbered Methodists.[79]

This trend continued unabated in virtually every religious group in America throughout the twentieth century. For example the market share for major mainline denominations (United Methodists, Presbyterian, USA, Episcopal, Christian [Disciples], and United Church of Christ) declined by more than 50 percent from 1940 to 1985. During the same time period, the more sectarian conservative and evangelical groups (Southern Baptists, Assemblies of God, Church of the Nazarene, and Church of God [Cleveland, Tennessee]) grew by more than 47 percent. Catholics, despite massive Latin American immigration, grew by only 12 percent.[80]

In the decades prior to World War II (1941–1945), there were specific individuals who made significant contributions that helped change the face of American religious life after the war. On the left, Reinhold Niebuhr, a theologian at Union Seminary in New York, articulated a neoorthodox theology aimed at reforming liberal thought. His work produced a renewed mainline appreciation for the reality of human evil and the need for social change.[81] Both Martin Luther King Jr. and president Jimmy Carter were to list Neibuhr as a major influence on their faith and political activism.[82]

On the right, J. Gresham Machen authored *Christianity and Liberalism* (1923), which remains one of the crown jewels of the conservative evangelical defense of biblical inerrancy.[83] A controversial figure within his own Presbyterian tradition, he was defrocked in 1936, yet his impassioned defense of traditional Christian orthodoxy influenced many conservative and evangelical leaders.[84] Carl F. H. Henry honored Machen in 1956 by naming his new evangelical magazine, *Christianity Today,* after a failed publication founded by Machen.[85]

Other theologians of public note included the Protestant Paul Tillich, the Catholic Jacques Maritain, and the Jewish Will Herberg. One historian concluded that "the 1950's were the last decade in which theologians played a major role in American public life."[86] The careful words and fine distinctions characteristic of theological reflection could not prevail in the new religious arena dominated by radio and television.

Religion and the New Media

Regular radio broadcasting began in 1920, and from the start the Federal Communications Commission required specific time to be set aside for public service broadcasting. As the sole interdenominational organization available, the mainline churches of the Federal Council of Churches soon developed a near monopoly on this free, religion-based programming. By 1931, only one radio network was willing to sell commercial time to conservative and evangelical Protestants.[87] Despite such restrictions, Charles Fuller's *Old Time Gospel Hour* aired in 1937 and had captured a weekly audience of over 20 million by 1943.[88] When the mainline churches were successful in lobbying all broadcast companies to stop selling commercial time to conservative evangelicals in 1944, the conservative evangelicals went directly to local stations to buy airtime, thereby creating radio syndication.[89]

Ironically, the mainline monopoly on radio broadcasting served to strengthen conservative and evangelical commitment to the use of new media. Without the largesse of free public service airtime, the conservative evangelicals developed successful self-funded programs. When the Federal Communications Commission rules changed in 1960, it was the conservative evangelicals who were best able to compete for available time slots on both television and radio.[90] Conservative evangelicals claimed their own television network that same year as Pat Robertson founded the Christian Broadcasting Network (CBN) with the purchase of a small UHF television station.[91] Today CBN broadcasts internationally in 77 different languages. Another network, Trinity Broadcasting (founded in 1973), currently boasts 5,000 local affiliates, 33 satellites links, and thousands of cable systems carrying their message worldwide.[92] By 1990, conservative and evangelical ministers controlled 90 percent of all religious broadcasting in the country.[93]

Conservative evangelicals were not the only ones to take advantage of new media. As early as 1926 Father Charles Coughlin of Michigan, a Catholic priest, gained national attention for airing his "America First" isolationist, anti-communist, and ultimately anti-Semitic and anti-Roosevelt message.[94] The almost rabid anti-communist stance of the Roman Catholics may have been the primary means by which this once highly sectarian group merged more fully into the American mainstream.[95] In the 1950s, Bishop Fulton Sheen's popular television series, *Life is Worth Living,* provided additional impetus.[96] By 1960, not only could a Catholic run for high office, but John F. Kennedy in fact became the first American Catholic president.

Television and radio were to make a significant impact on American religious life. For example, in 1955 only one out of 25 Americans had left their childhood faith for a new religious home. By 1985 one in three had done so.[97] Denominational growth was no longer merely a consequence of family size or immigration as Americans changed denominational affiliation as religious consumers. Religious use of the new media accelerated the commercialization of religious life and subordinated the relationship of pastor–pew to that of media–audience.

Secularization

The 1st Amendment to the U.S. Constitution states that "Congress shall make no law respecting an establishment of religion, or prohibiting the free exercise thereof."[98] Despite this sentence, often referred to as the establishment clause, Protestants had enjoyed considerable influence in virtually every public arena, and restrictions were few. Beginning in 1940 with the extension of the establishment clause to state governments in *Cantwell v. Connecticut,* but rapidly accelerating after the end of World War II in 1945, the Supreme Court began to dismantle Protestant privilege. Conservative and evangelical churchmen tended to view this loss of privilege as an attack on traditional Christian values. For example, public schools and public school teachers were prohibited from promoting religion in 1948; prayer in public schools was declared unconstitutional in 1962 and Bible reading was prohibited in 1963.[99] State laws preventing the teaching of evolution were overturned in 1968 and tax support of parochial schools was prohibited in 1971.[100] These cases specifically impacted long-standing, local privileges, but the social changes mandated by an activist court received even greater opposition. The 1954 *Brown v. Board of Education* decision undermining the legal foundation for segregation and the 1973 decision in *Roe v. Wade* banning state limits on abortion were particularly onerous to the conservative groups.[101] The first threatened white, Protestant dominance; the second threatened the Christian ideal of the sanctity of human life.

The mainline response to this secularizing trend may be best exemplified by Harvey Cox's *The Secular City* (1965). As Patrick Allitt describes Cox's views:

> . . . Christianity had itself been a powerful force for secularization. Ancient religions had had a great pantheon of gods. . . . Judaism and Christianity, however, had swept away the whole lot and left just one remote, omnipotent God presiding over the world. People were then free to manipulate and organize the world without fear that they were stepping on the gods' toes. And having learned that the world was not crammed with divinities, they had learned to take the logical next step of pushing back further and further their need for any god at all. Secularization and urbanization are the not the enemies of Christianity . . . but its logical end product.[102]

This radical theology culminated in the ultimate liberal claim: "God is dead." To conservative and evangelical ears there could be no greater challenge.

The Reawakening of a Religious Social Conscience and the Great Society

The liberal, moral leadership provided during the New Deal yielded the framework for the modern social welfare state. Income disparities were mitigated and federal responsibility for social welfare was well established. Despite this progress, irreligious liberal thinkers recognized the disadvantages reason held in comparison with the conservatives appeal to traditional faith. None attempted to face this disadvantage with more honesty than John Dewey in *A Common Faith* (1934) and *Liberalism and Social Action* (1935). His attempt to dislodge the "impulses of generosity and self-sacrifice, of humility and communal solidarity" from religious roots proved unsuccessful.[103] Liberal social action grinded to a halt following World War II until it was re-energized by a prophetic religious voice.

On December 1, 1955, Rosa Parks refused to give up her seat to a white man on a Montgomery, Alabama, city bus. Female co-workers at the local NAACP office and some local students distributed bus boycott leaflets to Montgomery's African American clergy that very day. Martin Luther King Jr. was elected president of the hastily organized Montgomery Improvement Association.[104] A prophet had been found.

Rejecting liberal, white leadership and, in most cases, counsel, King led a nonviolent activist movement confronting discrimination and segregation that was opposed by white southerners and his own African American denomination. Northern, white liberal churchmen offered weak support.[105] Recent scholarship has challenged the typical classification of this movement as mere civil protest:

> Participants often recalled the movement years as a heady, life-transforming era touched with divine significance. . . . Such testimony suggests that it may be misleading to view the civil rights movement as a social and political event that had religious overtones. . . . To take the testimony of intense religious transformation seriously is to consider the civil rights movement as part of the historical tradition of religious revivals. . . .[106]

Lyndon B. Johnson, president following John F. Kennedy's assassination in 1963, tapped into the religious and moral ideals sparked by King and the sacrifices made in the name of desegregation. He declared a "War on Poverty" in his State of the Union address on January 8, 1964.[107] Over 1,000 pieces of legislation were passed as part of Johnson's Great Society including the Civil Rights Act in 1964 and the Voting Rights Act in 1965.[108] White churchmen continued to lag behind the waves of social change, and social workers were among those who stepped forward to lead. For example the Secretary of Health, Education, and Welfare, Wilbur Cohen, played a major role in the passage of the Medicare and Medicaid Acts of 1965, only two of his 65 innovations in social welfare policy.[109] Even though the Vietnam War was to prove a fatal distraction, Johnson's War on Poverty and Great Society had some success. By 1969 the number of Americans living below the poverty line had fallen by more than half.[110]

The Continuing Decline of Mainline Influence

White religious leadership, in comparison to the courage and conviction of the African American churches, proved to be distracted by internal issues or radical irrelevancy. Roman Catholics were preoccupied with Vatican II (1962–1965). This reform movement, led by Pope John XXIII, ended the last vestiges of isolation and parochialism for American Catholics. Liturgical reforms included enhanced lay participation, the elimination of Latin during mass, and the loosening of behavioral codes. Faithful Catholics were no longer required to avoid meat on Fridays, except during Lent. As American Catholicism lost its sectarian identity, church attendance and seminary enrollments dropped.[111]

Twenty-nine Protestant and Orthodox denominations had reorganized the mainline into the National Council of Churches in 1950, largely because the *cause celebre* of the Federal Council, the religious delivery of social services, had become the purview of government after the New Deal. The new focus was on ecumenism. The Consultation on Church Union (COCU) was initiated in 1960. Although COCU was largely ineffective at producing broad denominational merger, some progress was made within major historical traditions. Unitarians and Universalists merged in 1961. The Methodist Church and Evangelical United Brethren became the United Methodists in 1968. The Civil War breach between Presbyterian groups ended with the Presbyterian Church in the United States of America in 1984, and several Lutheran bodies created the Evangelical Lutheran Church in America in 1988.[112]

Despite claims to the contrary, the National Council of Churches never represented a majority of religious adherents in the country, and the embrace of liberation theologies did little to maintain public influence or lay support. Developed in the class struggles and economic disparities of Latin America, "liberation theology employs a Marxist-style class analysis, which divides the culture between oppressors and oppressed. . . . But unlike Marxism, liberation theology turns to the Christian faith for bringing about liberation."[113] The goal is the radical transformation of society. James Cone applied the insights of liberation theology to the African American struggle for civil rights in his *Black Theology of Liberation* (1970), and Mary Daly did the same for women in her *Beyond God the Father* (1973).

The influence of liberation theology on mainline thought was evident as early as 1964 when the National Council of Churches criticized Great Society reforms as inadequate.[114] President Richard M. Nixon took office in 1968, and became an unlikely champion of the mainline goal—a guaranteed annual income as a fundamental right of citizenship. National Council of Churches' support quickly turned to opposition when Nixon refused to triple the proposed benefit level.[115] Nixon's Family Assistance Plan was ultimately to fail in the Senate. President Jimmy Carter (1976–1980) was to court mainline support for his own watered-down version which also failed.[116] Mainline influence has yet to recover. Martin Marty, a leading church historian, has written that "everybody knows that when the mainline churches take a position, it is only six people in a room on Riverside Drive."[117] Riverside Drive is the local address of the National Council offices in New York, and hyperbole aside, political events since the presidential election in 1980 indicate that there is some truth in Marty's observation.

The New Christian Right

In 1965 Jerry Falwell, senior minister at Thomas Road Baptist Church in Lynchburg, Virginia, preached that "believing the Bible as I do, I would find it impossible to stop preaching the pure saving gospel of Jesus Christ and begin doing anything else—including fighting Communism, or participating in Civil Rights reforms."[118] By 1979 he had changed his mind and founded the Moral Majority, a political action group committed to overturning the secular trends Falwell interpreted as moral deterioration. The Moral Majority was for prayer and the teaching of creationism in public schools, but was opposed to abortion, feminist issues such as the Equal Rights Amendment, homosexual rights, and even peace talks with the Soviet Union.[119]

Falwell had picked an opportune time to organize the Moral Majority. The two largest conservative evangelical denominations, Southern Baptists and Missouri-Synod Lutherans, had largely remained aloof from the fundamentalist controversy in the 1920s, but each had recently began internal struggles over the challenges of theological liberalism. Each rejected liberalism in favor of a traditional conservative theology. The Missouri-Synod Lutherans purged its leading seminary of liberal influence in 1976[120] while Paige Patterson and Paul Pressler

Jerry Falwell founded the Moral Majority, a political action group that supports prayer and the teaching of creationism in public schools and opposes abortion, the Equal Rights Amendment, and gay and lesbian rights.

led a well-coordinated and successful plan to gain control of the Southern Baptist Convention and its seminaries and agencies that began in 1979.[121] Lay support for theological conservatism was easily converted into sympathy for Falwell's political agenda.

The conservative dominance of religious media also furthered Falwell's agenda, as did the growth of megachurches across the country. With care he nurtured relationships with the leading religious personalities of the day. Pat Robertson of *The 700 Club,* Jim and Tammy Bakker of *The PTL Club,* and Jimmy Swaggert became colleagues in Falwell's campaign for moral and political reform, and even Catholics and Jews were included in Falwell's embrace.[122] While there have always been a few very large churches, the increase in megachurches is a peculiarly late twentieth-century phenomenon. Utilizing the best business management practices, the allure of charismatic preachers, a smorgasbord of family-oriented recreational services, contemporary professional music, and a traditional but undemanding theology, these large churches which number their members in the thousands have sprung up across the nation since the 1970s. In a country where the average non-Catholic church attendance is 84 persons a week (Catholics average 375 in mass), approximately 50 percent of all church attendance is in the top 10 percent of congregations in size.[123] In part, the lower levels of denominational loyalty noted earlier have been fueled by the existence of these megachurches. Those who prefer this style of worship are less concerned with denominational *brand* and more concerned with the megachurch *style.* The leaders of these new congregations also proved ready allies in Falwell's cause.

Was Falwell's Moral Majority a success? If success is measured by the number of column inches and the minutes of television and radio time devoted to the discussion of the Christian Right, the Moral Majority was an unqualified success. As previously stated, the conservative and evangelical perspective dominated religious broadcasting, and in like fashion, the colorful characters leading this movement were quick to provide useful sound bites and controversial opinions. Falwell, who remains active as the senior minister at Thomas Road Baptist Church, has been one of the primary foci of at least 16 books since 1979.[124]

Has the public relations victory of the Christian Right been equally overwhelming at the polls? Beginning with Ronald Reagan's election in 1980 and 1984, and through the election of George H. W. Bush in 1988, and again in George W. Bush's election in 2000 and 2004, the Christian Right has been quick to claim credit for each victory. In fact, advocates of this viewpoint have interpreted Bill Clinton's election in 1992 as the consequence of the financial scandals and sexual improprieties of Jim and Tammy Bakker, Jimmy Swaggert, and Oral Roberts in 1987.[125] In part a reaction to these scandals and in part evangelical disillusionment that Pat Robertson did not claim the Republican nomination in 1987, Falwell disbanded the Moral Majority in 1989, and consequently, Clinton's 1992 victory was due to the absence of organized opposition by the Christian Right. Unsurprisingly, others offer alternative interpretations.

While a consensus has yet to develop among religious scholars, preliminary studies seem to indicate that the influence of the Christian Right on social policy and politics is not so simply determined. Analyses of the National Election Studies indicate, that with the exception of conservative and evangelical support in 1976 for the Southern Baptist candidate, Jimmy Carter, there has been no significant change in the voting patterns of white, conservative Protestants. This group comprised 20 percent of the Democratic voters in 1972 and 18 percent in 1996, and it comprised 27 percent and 30 percent of Republican voters in 1972 and 1996, respectively. In comparison, the largest change was noted among white, mainline Protestants who were 45 percent of the Republican voters in 1972 but fell significantly to only 33 percent of the Republicans in 1996.[126] Other studies also seem to support a more limited political orientation, especially during congregational activities, for white, conservative Protestants.[127] If the Christian Right has influenced national elections since 1980, it has not been by changing the pattern of voting among white conservative evangelicals.

Conclusion

Progressives initially rejoiced at Clinton's election the first time in 16 years that a Democrat had captured the presidency. By the end of Clinton's first term, many of those same liberals were left more cautious or, in some cases, despondent because even the important policy successes of the Clinton administration were tinged with conservatism. For example, he signed into law the Personal Responsibility and Work Opportunity Reconciliation Act of 1996 (PRWORA), a bill that capped public assistance benefits, ended AFDC, and eliminated recipients' entitlement to public assistance. Equally important, Section 104 of the PRWORA contained what has been called the Charitable Choice provision:

> The purpose of this section is to allow States to contract with religious organizations, or to allow religious organizations to accept certificates, vouchers, or other forms of disbursement . . . on the same basis as any other non-governmental provider without impairing the religious character of such organizations, and with diminishing the religious freedom of beneficiaries of assistance funded under such program. [Section 104(b)].

George W. Bush has been a strong advocate of Charitable Choice. As governor of Texas he aggressive pursued welfare reform through a faith-based initiative as early as 1996. In his second week in office as president, he established the White House Office of Faith-Based and Community Initiatives with units in the Departments of Labor, Justice, Housing and Urban Development, Education, and Health and Human Services.[128] Executive orders expanded faith-based involvement to the Department of Agriculture and the U.S. Agency for International Development in 2002.[129]

Federal funding is available for faith-based organizations (FBOs) through state channels, but the states have been almost unanimous in their tepid response. "For the most part, it appears that state officials have not felt that there is a need to make substantive changes—FBOs are already active players in delivering services . . . and their involvement is not a subject of controversy. . . ."[130] Despite a lack of significant change in state policies and procedures, nearly two-thirds of states have pursued outreach efforts to FBOs and more than half have a faith representative on welfare advisory committees. On the other hand, less than one-third of the states provide technical assistance to FBOs, fewer than one-quarter have modified proposal notification processes, and only two states have provided capacity building or start-up grants.[131]

Federal guidelines make funding potentially available through Temporary Assistance for Needy Families, Welfare-to-Work, the Emergency Food and Shelter Program, the Emergency Shelter Grant program, and the Community Development Block Grant program. Educational funding is more problematic due to a long history of Supreme Court limitations on tax support for private schools.[132]

Michigan, Ohio, and Texas have been most aggressive in facilitating funding for FBOs, but the research to date seems to indicate that most of this funding is directed to older, established nonprofit agencies with religious roots (e.g., Catholic Charities, Catholic Social Services, Jewish Family Services, Lutheran Social Services, Salvation Army, and Young Women's Christian Association).[133] Congregations of all denominational varieties have been reluctant to pursue Charitable Choice funding. Even though more than half of all congregations provide some type of social service, primarily emergency food and shelter, only 3 percent receive public funds.[134] In the mainline it seems reasonable to assume that the sense of congregational participation in social services has been delegated to these volunteer associations for decades; among conservative evangelicals the reluctance may be due to concerns about government intervention.[135]

Marvin Olasky was among the first to advocate for faith-based provision of social services.[136] His rationale was clear: "holistic service delivery that focuses on personal transformation and provides long-term, lasting solutions to poor people's problems" are best provided in a faith context.[137] Besides, churches were awash in well-intentioned volunteers. The problem is that neither of these assumptions are actually correct. The National Congregations Study indicates that congregation-based social services are advanced by the smallest handful of volunteers, and that these services are overwhelming dispensed at arm's length. "If congregations' social services are imagined to be more effective than secular social services because they are more holistic, neither quantitative nor qualitative evidence supports the idea."[138]

Is the availability of funding likely to change the attitudes of religious organizations to social services? Frankly, it is too soon to tell. The decentralized channels through which the federal monies flow has hindered the collection of reliable information on the recipients; outcome studies have been rare, methodologically flawed, and frequently ambiguous; and there has been a tendency for Charitable Choice to simply expand the degree of competition for access to an ever-decreasing amount of social service funding.[139] One conclusion does seem obvious. Provision of social services through FBOs will always be limited to some extent; if not by the fluctuating availability of resources, then by the vision of church leaders and the limitations of theological perspectives. Some have already reported a reluctance by those with needs to obtain help through FBOs, and others have reported apparent abuses and financial irregularities by FBOs.[140] Charitable Choice may remain a permanent part of the federal provision of social services, but it is unlikely that FBOs have the capacity and commitment to sustain comprehensive and long-term services on a level comparable to federal and state bureaucracies.

Discussion Questions

1. Since the establishment of the English Poor Laws, there has been a tendency for social welfare programs to distinguish between the "worthy needy" and those less worthy of assistance. What, if any, are the religious foundations for such a distinction? Is this distinction still evident in American social welfare policies?
2. How has the Protestant work ethic affected American social welfare policy? Is there any recent evidence that suggests that this theological perspective has a continuing influence today? Is it compatible with macro- and micro-level social work practice? Give specific examples to support your answer.
3. What are the causes of the division of American Protestantism into mainline and evangelical camps? Describe the form of social welfare each camp is most likely to promote.
4. The authors present religion as having an important role in the development of professional social work. Does religion continue to have a significant influence on social work policies, values, and/or practice? If you agree, give specific examples. If you disagree, explain how social work now differs from its religious roots with specific policy and practice examples.
5. How would social welfare policy change if the theological movements of the Protestant mainline (the Social Gospel and liberation theology) were the dominant influences?
6. Interpret the Personal Responsibility and Work Opportunity Reconciliation Act from a religious perspective. What theological orientations seem to be most evident? Which religious groups are most likely to be pleased with its provisions?
7. The authors are pessimistic that Charitable Choice and faith-based initiatives are likely to solve America's social welfare problems. Why would they reach this conclusion?

Notes

1. American Religion Data Archive. Retrieved November 2004 from www.thearda.com
2. See Ontario Consultants on Religious Tolerance, 2003, retrieved October 2004 from www.religioustolerance.org/welcome.htm#new; and "The Bottom Line," *The Week* 4, no. 176 (October 1, 2004), p. 36.
3. Authors' conclusion based on comparison of Allied Media Corp. demographic information (at www.

allied-media.com) with population statistics reported in the *CIA World Factbook* (at www.cia.gov/cia/publications/factbook/geos/ba.html).

4. American Religion Data Archive. Retrieved November 2004 from www.thearda.com
5. Genesis 4:7 (New International Version).
6. Gary V. Smith, "Poor, Orphan, Widow," in *Holman Bible Dictionary* (Nashville, TN: Holman Bible Publishers, 1991), pp. 1124–1125.
7. Matthew 10:41 (New International Version).
8. Acts of the Apostles 4:32 (New International Version).
9. Howard Karger and David Stoesz, *American Social Welfare Policy: A Structural Approach*, 3rd ed. (NY: Longman, 1998), p. 34.
10. Ibid., p. 35.
11. David Rothman and Sheila Rothman (eds.), *On Their Own: The Poor in Modern America* (Reading, MA: Addison-Wesley, 1972).
12. Robert Morris, *Rethinking Social Welfare* (New York: Ketev Press, 1972), p. 143.
13. David Macarov, *The Design of Social Welfare* (New York: Holt, Rinehart and Winston, 1978).
14. Roger Finke and Rodney Stark, *The Churching of America. 1776–1990: Winners and Losers in our Religious Economy* (New Brunswick, NJ: Rutgers University Press, 1992).
15. Nathan Edward Cohen, *Social Work in the American Tradition* (New York: Holt, Rinehart and Winston, 1958), pp. 23–24.
16. Peter W. Williams, *American's Religions: From Their Origins to the Twenty-First Century* (Urbana, IL: University of Illinois Press, 2002), pp. 181–190.
17. Finke and Stark, *The Churching of America,* p. 16.
18. Ibid., p. 55.
19. Sydney E. Ahlstrom, *A Religious History of the American People* (New Haven, CT: Yale University Press, 1972), pp. 423–425.
20. p. 426.
21. James Morone, *Hellfire Nation* (NY: Knopf, 2001), pp. 311–317.
22. Ibid., p. 189.
23. Ibid., p. 25.
24. Ibid., pp. 186–189.
25. Ibid., pp. 159–168.
26. Ahlstrom, *A Religious History,* pp. 432–435.
27. Ibid., p. 659.
28. Ibid., pp. 659–668.
29. Quoted in Ahlstrom, *A Religious History,* p. 681.
30. Quoted in Walter Trattner, *From Poor Law to Welfare State* (New York: Free Press, 1974), p. 62.
31. Ahlstrom, *A Religious History,* p. 680.
32. Trattner, *From Poor Law to Welfare State,* p. 63.
33. Ibid., p. 87.
34. Ahlstrom, *A Religious History,* pp. 694–695.
35. Peter J. Thuesen, "The Logic of Mainline Churches: Historical Background since the Reformation," in Robert Wuthnow and John H. Evans (eds.), *The Quiet Hand of God: Faith-Based Activism and the Public Role of Mainline Protestantism* (Berkeley: University of California Press), p. 37.
36. Ahlstrom, *A Religious History,* pp. 707–709.
37. Finke and Stark, *The Churching of America,* p. 139.
38. Thuesen, *The Logic of Mainline Churches,* p. 35.
39. Ibid., p. 35.
40. June Axinn and Herman Levin, *Social Welfare* (New York: Dodd, Mead, 1975), p. 129.
41. Charles Darwin, *On the Origin of Species by Means of Natural Selection* (London: John Murray, 1859).
42. See Herbert Spencer, *An Autobiography,* 2 vols. (New York: D. Appleton, 1904); William Graham Sumner, *Social Darwinism* (Englewood Cliffs, NJ: Prentice-Hall, 1963); and Richard Hofstadter, *Social Darwinism in American Thought* (Boston: Beacon Press, 1959).
43. Spencer, *An Autobiography,* p. 186.
44. Charles Howard Hopkins, *The Rise of the Social Gospel in American Protestantism, 1865–1915* (New Haven, CT: Yale University Press, 1940).
45. Ibid.
46. Henry F. May, *Protestant Churches in Industrial America* (New York: Octagon Books, 1963).
47. Howard Jacob Karger, *The Sentinels of Order: A Study of Social Control and the Minneapolis Settlement House Movement, 1915–1950* (Lanham, MD: University Press of America, 1987).
48. R. G. Clouse, "Views of the Millennium," *Evangelical Dictionary of Theology* (Grand Rapids, MI: Baker Book House, 1984), p. 714.
49. Ahlstrom, *A Religious History,* pp. 802–804.
50. C. T. McIntire, "The Fundamentals," *Evangelical Dictionary of Theology* (Grand Rapids, MI: Baker Book House, 1984), p. 436.
51. Clouse, "Views of the Millennium," *Evangelical Dictionary of Theology* (Grand Rapids, MI: Baker Book House, 1984), p. 717.
52. George M. Marsden, *Fundamentalism and American Culture: The Shaping of Twentieth Century Evangelicalism, 1870–1925* (New York: Oxford University Press, 1980).
53. Macarov, *The Design of Social Welfare.*
54. Roy Lubove, *The Professional Altruist: The Emergence of Social Work as a Career, 1880–1930* (New York: Atheneum Books, 1975).
55. Robert Bremner, *From the Depths: The Discovery of Poverty in the United States* (New York: New York University Press, 1956).
56. David Montgomery, *Workers' Control in America* (Cambridge, England: Cambridge University Press, 1979).
57. Ibid.
58. Lubove, *The Professional Altruist,* pp. 1–21.
59. Ibid., p. 14.
60. Axinn and Levin, *Social Welfare,* p. 100.

61. Hofstadter, *The Age of Reform,* p. 211.
62. Ibid., p. 92.
63. H. L. Weissman, "Settlements and Community Centers," *Encyclopedia of Social Work,* 18th ed. (Silver Spring, MD: NASW Press, 1987), p. 21.
64. Mary Richmond, *Social Diagnosis* (New York: Russell Sage Foundation, 1917).
65. Maryann Syers, "Abraham Flexner," *Encyclopedia of Social Work,* 18th ed. (Silver Spring, MD: NASW Press, 1987), p. 923.
66. Ahlstrom, *A Religious History,* pp. 895–917.
67. Clark Chambers, *Seedtime of Reform* (Ann Arbor, MI: University of Michigan Press, 1967), p. 211.
68. Ahlstrom, *A Religious History,* pp. 939–943.
69. Ibid., p. 909.
70. President Franklin Pierce quoted in Trattner, *From Poor Law to Welfare State,* p. 62.
71. Cohen, *Social Work in the American Tradition,* p. 169.
72. Biographical information from *Encyclopedia of Social Work,* 18th ed.
73. Finke and Stark, *The Churching of America,* pp. 66–71.
74. Dean M. Kelley, *Why Conservative Churches are Growing* (New York: Harper and Row, 1972), pp. 95–96.
75. Finke and Stark, *The Churching of America,* p. 254.
76. Ibid., p. 255.
77. Ibid., p. 55.
78. Ibid., p. 161.
79. Ibid., p. 146.
80. Ibid., p. 248.
81. Ahlstrom, *A Religious History,* p. 942.
82. Patrick Allitt, *Religion in America Since 1945: A History* (New York: Columbia University Press, 2003), pp. 48, 149.
83. Ahlstrom, *A Religious History,* p. 912.
84. D. R. Kelly, "John Gresham Machen," *Evangelical Dictionary of Theology* (Grand Rapids, MI: Baker Book House, 1984), pp. 673–674.
85. Ahlstrom, *A Religious History,* p. 958.
86. Allitt, *Religion in America Since 1945,* p. 26.
87. Finke and Starke, *The Churching of America,* pp. 218–219.
88. Allitt, *Religion in America Since 1945,* p. 13.
89. Ibid., p. 223.
90. Ibid.
91. Christian Broadcasting Network. Retrieved October 2004 from www.cbn.com
92. Trinity Broadcasting Network. Retrieved October 2004 from www.tbn.org/index.php/3/18.html
93. Ahlstrom, *A Religious History,* pp. 928–930.
94. Ibid., p. 151.
95. Allitt, *Religion in America Since 1945,* p. 23.
96. Williams, *America's Religions,* p. 416.
97. Robert Wuthnow, *The Restructuring of American Religion: Society and Faith Since World War II* (Princeton, NJ: Princeton University Press, 1988), p. 88.
98. Williams, *America's Religions,* p. 181.
99. The New York Public Library, *American History Desk Reference* (New York: MacMillan, 1997), p. 415.
100. See Allitt, *Religion in America Since 1945,* p. 181; and New York Public Library, *American History Desk Reference,* p. 410.
101. Allitt, *Religion in America,* pp. 321–322, 356.
102. Allitt, *Religion in America Since 1945,* p. 75.
103. David L. Chappell, *A Stone of Hope: Prophetic Religion and the Death of Jim Crow* (Chapel Hill: University of North Carolina Press, 2004), pp. 12–18.
104. Allett, *Religion in America Since 1945,* pp. 47–48.
105. Chappell, *A Stone of Hope,* pp. 26–43.
106. Ibid., p. 87.
107. Michael B. Katz, *The Undeserving Poor: From the War on Poverty to the War on Welfare* (New York: Pantheon Books, 1989), p. 80.
108. New York Public Library, *American History Desk Reference,* pp. 112–113.
109. Charles Schottland, "Wilbur Joseph Cohen: Some Recollections," *Social Work* 32, no. 5 (September/October 1987), pp. 371–372.
110. Katz, *The Undeserving Poor,* pp. 113–114.
111. Finke and Stark, *The Churching of America, 1776–1990,* pp. 255–261.
112. Williams, *America's Religions,* pp. 352–356.
113. See Gustavo Gutierrez, *A Theology of Liberation* (Maryknoll, NY: Orbis, 1973). Quoted in D. D. Webster, "Liberation Theology," *Evangelical Dictionary of Theology* (Grand Rapids, MI: Baker Book House, 1984), p. 636.
114. Brian Steensland, "The Hydra and the Swords," in Robert Wuthnow and John H. Evans (eds.), *The Quiet Hand of God: Faith-Based Activism and the Public Role of Mainline Protestantism* (Berkeley: University of California Press), p. 214.
115. Ibid., pp. 215–217.
116. Ibid., pp. 217–218.
117. Quoted in Finke and Stark, *The Churching of America,* p. 224.
118. Quoted in Allitt, *Religion in America Since 1945,* p. 151.
119. "Moral Majority," *The Columbia Encyclopedia.* Retrieved November 2004 from www.bartleby.com/65/e-/E-MoralMajo.html
120. Williams, *America's Religions,* pp. 359–360.
121. Finke and Stark, *The Churching of America, 1776–1990,* pp. 187–198.
122. Allitt, *Religion in America Since 1945,* p. 153.
123. U.S. Congregational Life Survey, 2001. Retrieved November 2004 from www.uscongregations.org/myths.htm
124. Authors count of title available in subject search on Amazon.com on December 7, 2004.
125. Allitt, *Religion in America Since 1945,* pp. 194–195.
126. Jeff Manza and Clem Brooks, "The Changing Political Fortunes of Mainline Protestants," in Robert

Wuthnow and John H. Evans (eds.), *The Quiet Hand of God: Faith-Based Activism and the Public Role of Mainline Protestantism* (Berkeley: University of California Press), pp. 163–167.

127. Mark Chaves, *Congregations in America* (Cambridge, MA: Harvard University Press, 2004), pp. 94–126.
128. Ram A. Cnaan and Stephanie C. Boddie, "Charitable Choice and Faith-Based Welfare: A Call for Social Work," *Social Work* 47, no. 3 (July 2002), p. 225.
129. Lisa M. Montiel, "The Use of Public Funds for Delivery of Faith-Based Human Services." The Roundtable on Religion and Social Welfare Policy, 2003, p. 18. Retrieved December 2004 from www.religionandsocialpolicy.org
130. Mark Ragan, Lisa M. Montiel, and David J. Wright, "Scanning the Policy Environment for Faith-Based Social Services in the United States." The Roundtable on Religion and Social Welfare Policy, 2003, p. 18. Retrieved December 2004 from www.religionandsocialpolicy.org
131. Ibid., p. 11.
132. Montiel, *The Use of Public Funds*, pp. 4–11.
133. Ibid., p. 13.
134. Chavez, *Congregations in America*, p. 66.
135. Dave Donaldson and Stanley Carlson-Thies, *A Revolution of Compassion: Faith-Based Groups as Full Partners in Fighting America's Social Problems* (Grand Rapids, MI: Baker Books, 2003).
136. Marvin Olasky, *The Tragedy of American Compassion* (Washington, DC: Regnery Gateway, 1992).
137. Chavez, *Congregations in America*, p. 58.
138. Ibid., p. 65.
139. See Montiel, *The Use of Public Funds*, p. 22; Jason D. Scott, "The Scope and Scale of Faith-Based Social Services," The Roundtable on Religion and Social Welfare Policy, 2003, retrieved December 2004 from www.religionandsocialpolicy.org; and Byron R. Johnson, "Objective Hope: Assessing the Effectiveness of Faith-Based Organizations: A Review of the Literature," Center for Research on Religion and Urban Civil Society, 2002, retrieved December 2004 from www.manhattan-institute.org/crrucs_objective_hope.pdf
140. See Robert Wuthnow, Conrad Hackett, and Becky Yang Hsu, "The Effectiveness and Trustworthiness of Faith-Based and Other Service Organizations: A Study of Recipients' Perceptions," *Journal for the Scientific Study of Religion* 43, no. 1, 1–17; and Texas Freedom Network, "The Texas Faith-Based Initiative at Five Years: Warning Signs as President Bush Expands Texas-Style Program to National Level," 2002, retrieved December 2004 from www.tfn.org/issues/charitablechoice/report02.html

CHAPTER 4

Discrimination in American Society

Discrimination and poverty are inextricably linked to the fabric of American social welfare. Economic, social, and political discrimination often leads to poverty, which in turn, results in the need for income maintenance and other social programs. Realizing that discrimination leads to poverty, some policymakers have tried to address this cycle by attacking discrimination. These policymakers hope that if discriminatory practices and attitudes are curtailed, the result will be equal opportunities for achievement and success. This chapter probes discrimination based on race, gender, sexual orientation, disability, and age.

Discrimination

The causes of discrimination in U.S. society are complex. A range of literature explores the motives for discrimination. Broken down, the main theories fall into three broad categories: psychological, normative-cultural, and economic.

Psychological interpretations attempt to explain discrimination in terms of intrapsychic variables.[1] A theory called the frustration-aggression hypothesis, formulated by J. Dollard, maintains that discrimination is a form of aggression that is activated when individual needs become frustrated.[2] Dollard argues that when people cannot direct their aggression at the real sources of their rage, they seek a substitute target. Thus, relatively weak minority groups become an easy and safe target for the aggression and frustration of slightly stronger discontented groups. For example, poor Southern whites have been viewed as an outwardly racist group. Exploited by the rigid economic and social class system of the old South, they often focused their rage on African Americans, a group even weaker than themselves. African Americans therefore served a twin purpose for poor whites: On the one hand, they formed a lower socioeconomic group, making poor whites feel better about their own standing; on the other, they functioned as a scapegoat for the frustrations of poor whites. Women, racial minorities, homosexuals, and other disenfranchised groups often serve the same function for those on a slightly higher social rung.

Another psychological approach, the "authoritarian personality" theory developed by Theodore Adorno and other psychoanalysts, posited that discriminatory behavior is determined by personality traits that involve a reaction to authority.[3] Persons who exhibit the traits of irrationality, rigidity, conformity, xenophobia, and so forth are more likely to discriminate against minorities than are people lacking those traits. Other authors, such as Wilhelm Reich, argued that discriminatory attitudes arise from a sense of insecurity, self-hatred, deep-seated fears, and unresolved childhood needs and frustrations.[4]

The normative–cultural explanation suggests that individuals hold prejudicial attitudes because of their socialization. That is, through both overt and covert messages, a society teaches discrimination and rewards those who conform to prevailing attitudes and behaviors. Because of strong societal pressures to conform to established norms, resistance to discriminatory practices becomes difficult.[5] For example, special opprobrium in the old South was reserved for liberal whites who broke the norms governing interactions with African Americans. Often, societies are more tolerant of outsiders who break the norms than they are of insiders who "betray" the group. This theory suggests that as social and institutional norms supporting discriminatory practices change, individual attitudes will follow suit.

One economic theory contends that dominant groups discriminate to maintain their economic and political advantages. This theory is based on the belief that relative group advantages are gained from discrimination. For example, male workers may discriminate against female workers because they perceive them as encroaching on their employment prospects. These males may fear that they will be replaced by a female worker who will accept lower wages. And employers themselves may uphold discriminatory attitudes because as long as women workers are stigmatized, they will command a lower salary and thereby serve as a cheap labor pool. In that sense, the increasing racial tensions in U.S. society can be understood partly as reflecting the job advancements made by minority groups.

A Marxian analysis sees sexism, racism, homophobia, and other forms of discrimination as economically useful to the capitalist class. According to Marxists, capitalism requires a marginal and unskilled labor pool willing to take the jobs rejected by economically franchised groups. Specifically, industrialization requires a labor force willing to relocate to meet shifting employment needs. In this framework, discrimination forces disenfranchised groups to relocate in order to flee persecution based on ethnic, religious, or racial differences. There are various levels of stigma, and not all out-groups experience it with the same intensity. In the extreme, however, stigma can reduce the economic currency of whole populations and thereby create an underclass forced to take whatever jobs are available at whatever wages are offered.

By manipulating stigmatized groups against each other, employers can curtail wage demands. Specifically, they can force wage concessions by threatening to replace relatively well-paid employees with lower-paid workers from a stigmatized group. Paradoxically, the lower economic status of disenfranchised groups increases their value to the economic order. Simply put, discrimination determines who will flip the burgers and supersize the drinks.

To maintain an air of legitimacy, discrimination must have moral, social, and theological underpinnings. To that end, some have used the Bible to explain the inferiority of women, the "sin" of homosexuality, and the necessity of separating the races. To augment or replace biblical interpretations, spurious scientific explanations have been developed, such as Social Darwinism and pseudoanthropological treatises regarding the attributes of stigmatized groups. For example, some people maintain that menstrual cycles cause severe mood swings that make women incapable of holding positions of power. Others believe that African Americans are descended from Ham and have therefore committed biblical sins that justify discrimination. Some members of the Ku Klux Klan claim that African Americans are racially inferior, based on theories grounded in shaky anthropological research supported by dubious intelligence testing. Some white supremacist groups believe that Jews are descendants of Satan and that the "true Israelites" (i.e., the lost tribes of Israel) are Aryans. These stereotypes have little to do with reality. Moreover, it is difficult to imagine that skinheads or those living in white supremacist enclaves represent the hope of the white race or are the "true Israelites." Without the legitimation offered by moral, religious, social, and "scientific" sources, discrimination is devoid of social validity and becomes naked exploitation.

Social stigma and discrimination can lead to the transformation of disenfranchised groups into a lower socioeconomic class. Alternatively, as in the case of gays, lesbians, and the aged, social stigma and discrimination can result in social marginalization without triggering statistically observable economic discrimination. For example, although the individual incomes of gays and lesbians (and the assets of the elderly) are higher than the national averages, people in these groups often experience economic discrimination in the form of restricted career choices, including forced occupational clustering, limited access to upper managerial positions, discrimination in hiring practices, forced retirement, and so forth. In addition, discrimination can also turn violent. For example, from 1990 to 1996 there were more than 243 attacks against religious institutions—black churches and white churches, synagogues and mosques. About 78 percent of all suspicious black church fires during that period occurred in the Southeast. In response, Congress passed the Church Arson Prevention Act of 1996, which broadened the ability of the federal government to seek criminal penalties in cases involving vandalism or destruction of religious buildings.

The following sections will examine some core components of discrimination and social stigma, including racism, sexism, homophobia, ageism, and discrimination against people with disabilities.

Racism

Federal and state governments often accumulate data based on dividing U.S. society along the lines of whites and people of color. Today, however, clumping white Americans into a single category is as misleading as not understanding the important cultural differences among people of color. For example, in 1850 it was relatively easy to describe white Americans; in all probability they were Protestant and of Anglo-Saxon or Teutonic backgrounds. But after the Civil War vast numbers of immigrants began to arrive from southern and central Europe. They were not Protestant, they were not Anglo-Saxon, and they had different languages and cultures from those who preceded them. About 200 million Americans can trace at least some of their ancestry back to the following groups (in descending size order): English, German, Irish, French, Italian, Scottish, Polish, Dutch, Swedish, Norwegian, Russian, Czech, Slovakian, Hungarian, Welsh, Danish, and Portuguese.[6] In addition, while some white Americans have an Hispanic surname, they have no Hispanic cultural memory. This is complicated by a large migration of people from Arabic-speaking countries, who while they may experience discrimination, are classified as white. Although most white groups have generally assimilated into American culture, many still maintain some of the characteristics that have contributed to the particular attributes of white American society. It is therefore not surprising that the field of white studies is becoming popular at schools such as the University of California at Berkeley, Northwestern University, Harvard University, and the University of Massachusetts.[7]

Throughout America's history, whites have been a clear majority. But according to Census Bureau projections, this is rapidly changing. By the year 2050, minority groups are expected to account for almost 50 percent of the population. The Census Bureau projects that between 2004 and 2050, Asians and Hispanics will see the most dramatic increases, as the U.S. population grows by almost 50 percent to reach 420 million.[8]

While whites represented about 69 percent of the population in 2002, their growth is slowing because of low birth rates and high rates of immigration. The total white population is expected to increase 7 percent to 210 million in 2050, or to 50 percent of the population. In fact, the Census Bureau expects the non-Hispanic white population will decline slightly between 2040 and 2050, because of the expected deaths of baby boomers, many of whom will be 76 by 2040.[9] A good deal of social history in the next several decades will reflect how the United States addresses this changing demography and whether these changes result in greater equality. Regardless, major social institutions will undoubtedly be transformed as a result of this demographic shift.

The term **racism** refers to discrimination against and prejudicial treatment of a racially different minority group. This prejudicial treatment may take the form of differential hiring and firing practices and promotions, differential resource allocations in health care and education, a two-tier structure in transportation systems, segregation in housing policies, discriminatory behavior of judicial and law enforcement agencies, and/or stereotypical and prejudicial media images. A pattern of racial discrimination that is strongly entrenched in a society is called *institutional racism.*

The Minority Middle Class

Although the idea of "middle class" is central to American life, there is no official definition of the middle class, no agreed-on classification of those who are middle class, and no reliable income figure that connotes a middle-class lifestyle.[10] Moreover, the Census Bureau has no official definition of the middle class. As such, the middle class has come to represent a large portion of the U.S. population with incomes between 200 percent of the federal poverty

Spotlight 4.1

The Minority Middle Class

Minority groups have made concrete gains in entering the middle class. African Americans, for example, have not only improved their socioeconomic position in recent years, but have done so at a relatively faster rate than whites. One of the most noticeable gains has been in the area of professional employment. There is a variety of media outlets that offer business and financial information to the African American community. One of these outlets is *Black Enterprise* magazine, which has been in existence since 1970. The magazine provides information on financial management, entrepreneurship, and careers to professionals, corporative executives, entrepreneurs, and decision makers. To learn more about *Black Enterprise,* visit its website at **http://www.blackenterprise.com.**

The Hispanic population has also experienced important economic successes. Hispanics have achieved impressive gains in household income, educational attainment, and homeownership. *Hispanic Business* magazine, a publication of Hispanic Business Incorporated, provides current business-related news, covers the growth of the U.S. Hispanic market, economic trends within the Americas, best business practices, and career development opportunities. To learn more about *Hispanic Business,* visit its website at **www.hispanicbusiness.com.**

African Americans have made significant gains in professional employment.

threshold and those in the nation's top 5 percent of income earners. Some analysts classify households with total annual incomes between $40,000 and $140,000 as middle class.[12] Other analysts categorize middle-class families as having annual incomes between $25,000 and $75,000. Still others use annual incomes of $50,000 as a marker. In addition, middle-class incomes are not adjusted geographically or by an urban/rural designation. In short, the designation of "middle class" has been rendered virtually meaningless by the enormous income spread and the failure to adjust income levels to high- and low-cost regions.

Despite these definitional problems, the minority middle class is nearly invisible to the general public partly because of the intense (and generally negative) attention paid to poor urban populations. Debates about public assistance, child welfare, crime, school dropout rates, teenage pregnancy, and drug use are almost always directed toward the poor. Since almost 25 percent of Hispanics and African Americans live below the poverty line, this attention is not a wholly unreasonable bias. However, rarely do social researchers focus on the other three-fourths who may be the teachers, university professors, police officers, computer technicians, secretaries, managers, or corporate CEOs. This research bias is based on the belief that upwardly mobile minority groups are gaining a strong foothold in formerly all-white occupations, businesses, neighborhoods, and social clubs. As a result, social researchers have relatively little information on who makes up the minority middle class and what their lives are really like.

Minority groups have made concrete gains in entering the middle class. For instance, many African Americans have not only improved their socioeconomic position in recent years, but have done so at a relatively faster rate than whites. The most noticeable gains have occurred in the areas of professional employment, incomes (including two-earner family incomes), higher education, and home ownership. For example, the typical black family earned $3,000 more in 1995 than in 1992.[13] In 1995, African Americans were the only group whose inflation-adjusted median income exceeded that of 1989. In 1995 black married couples earned 87 percent as much as white married couples, up from 79 percent in 1989.[14] For two-earner black couples between 24 and 35, average annual income was less than $3,000 compared to white couples, a significant improvement over earlier decades. The black median family income in 2002 was $29,177, an all-time high first reached in 1997. Nearly one-third of all African American families reported total income in 2001 or $50,000 or more; for African American married couples it was nearly 52 percent. On the other hand, per capita income for African Americans decreased 1 percent between 2002 and 2003 to $15,775.[15]

The number of black businesses increased by 46 percent (from 424,165 to 620,912) between 1987 and 1992. (The nation's total number of firms increased only 26 percent in that same period.) Receipts for black firms increased by 63 percent, from $20 to $32 billion.[16] The number of African Americans in technical, professional, and managerial positions increased by 57 percent from 1973 to 1982. By 2002, 18 percent of African American men and 26 percent of women worked in managerial and professional occupations. Partly resulting from increased incomes, blacks recorded a 47 percent increase in home ownership during the 1970s compared to 30 percent for whites.[17] By 2003, 48 percent of black households owned their own homes, an increase of 2 percent since 1999.[18]

Education is an important indicator of middle-class status, and African American youngsters recorded a substantial gain in SAT scores from 1976 to 1989, scoring 19 percent higher in verbal and 32 percent higher in math scores. By comparison, white SAT scores dropped by 5 and 2 percent, respectively.[19] In 2002, 79 percent of blacks aged 25 to 29 were high school graduates, and 17 percent had baccalaureate degrees. There is now no statistical difference in high school graduation rates between whites and blacks. More than 800,000 African Americans have an advanced degree. A slightly higher percentage of black women than men aged 25 and over have at least a bachelor's degree (18 versus 16 percent). The number of African Americans under 35 enrolled in college in 1998 (1.7 million) was 50 percent higher than the number enrolled in 1988.[20] In addition, between 1985 and 1995, the homicide rate for African Americans dropped by 17 percent.[21]

The Hispanic population has also experienced important economic successes. Between 1979 and 1999, the Hispanic middle class grew by 71 percent to 9.5 million. At the same time, Hispanics achieved impressive gains in household income, educational attainment, and homeownership. From 1998 to 2000, aggregate Hispanic net worth jumped 31 percent to $512 billion. Hispanic families earning between $40,000 and $140,000 a year reached 2.5 million in 1999, or about one-third of all Hispanic households. (From 1995 to 2001, Hispanic household median income grew by 27 percent.) In 2000, 64 percent of middle-class Hispanic households (48 percent of *all* Hispanic households) either owned or were buying a home, and 20 percent were headed by someone with a bachelor's or an advanced degree. By 1999 total Hispanic purchasing power was estimated at $272.7 billion. Much of this economic growth was fueled by Hispanic business formation, which increased 39 percent from 1992 to 1997. In 1990, Hispanic businesses reported cumulative revenues of $8.3 billion; by 1999 that figure had more than doubled to $17.4 billion.[22]

Much of the recent growth of the minority middle class has resulted from the prosperity of the middle 1990s. However, this may be changing. According to a 2004 Census Bureau report, real median income did not change between 2001 and 2003 for non-Hispanic white (about $48,000), black (about $30,000) or Asian households (about $55,500). Hispanic households experienced a 2.6 percent decline in median income between 2002 and 2003. Real median earnings of men age 15 and older who worked full-time, year-round in 2003 ($40,668) remained unchanged from 2002. Women with similar work experience saw their real earnings decline—0.6 percent to $30,724—the first drop since 1995. As a result, the ratio of female-to-male earnings for full-time, year-round workers was 76 cents for every dollar in 2003, down from 77 cents in 2002.[23] Since 2001, the middle-income group (defined here as $50,000 a year or more) has declined by 1.2 percent. At the same time, households with annual incomes of less than $25,000 grew by 1.5 percent and now make up 29 percent of all households. In effect, a growing number of households are slipping from the middle class into the lower-income group.[24]

The sparse research that exists on middle class minorities indicates the continuing economic, residential, occupational, wealth, and social disparities between minority groups and whites, even within the middle class. As such, a more appropriate label for many members of the minority middle class is "lower middle class." The one doctor who lives in an exclusive white suburb and the few lawyers who work at a large firm are not representative of the overall black middle class. While most whites are also not doctors or lawyers, the lopsided occupational distribution favors whites for professional and managerial jobs, whereas the black middle class is clustered in sales, clerical fields, and governmental or civil sector jobs. The huge wealth disparity between whites and African Americans (the median net worth of all non-Hispanic white U.S. families was $121,000 in 2001 compared with $19,000 for African Americans) regardless of income, education, or occupation is a powerful indicator of social injustice and mitigates against putting too much emphasis on the term "middle class."[25]

African Americans

The Demography of African Americans

The nation's African American population was estimated in 2002 at 36.7 million, or almost 13 percent of the total population (this excludes 2 million people who chose the multi-racial options offered in the 2000 census and identified themselves as black and at least one other race). From 2000 to 2002, the African American population increased by 1.2 million people or 3.3%; meanwhile, the total U.S. population grew by 2.5 percent.[26] According to projections, the African American population may increase from 35 million in 1999 to 61 million by 2050, a 74 percent rise. The black population is young, with almost 33 percent under age 18 in 2002. This compares with 23 percent of the white population. In 2002, the median African American age was thirty, five years younger than the U.S. population as a whole. Conversely, 8 percent of African Americans were 65 years old and over versus 14 percent of whites.[27]

African Americans are concentrated in the South (55 percent resided there in 2002). They are also more likely to live in metro areas (87.5% versus 78% for whites). More than 52 percent of African Americans live in central cities within metro areas. The 10 states with the largest African American populations in 2002 were New York (3.5 million), Florida (2.7 million), California and Texas (2.6 million each), Georgia (2.5 million), Illinois (2 million), North Carolina (1.8 million) and Maryland (1.6 million), Michigan (1.5 million), and Louisiana (1.4 million).[28]

African Americans in Poverty

After having dropped in the mid-1990s, the number of poor African Americans rose from 8.1 million in 2001 to 8.9 million in 2002, while their poverty rate increased from 22.7 to 23.9 percent. For African American families, the number and percent in poverty fell from 2.2 million to 2.0 million and from 26.1 to 23.6 percent, respectively, from 1996 to 1997. African Americans accounted for 60 percent of the decline in the number of poor persons in the United States between 1996 and 1997. Similarly, about 400,000 fewer families were poor in 1997 than in 1996 and more than half of them were African American. African American families with a female householder (no husband present), experienced a drop in both the number and percentage of families who were poor: 1.4 million and 35% in 2001, down from 1.5 million and 39.3% in 2000. Although the 2001 poverty rate for African Americans is 22.7% (or 8.1 million people), it remained statistically unchanged from 2000 and represented the lowest rate since the Census Bureau began collecting poverty data in 1959.[29]

The "Diswelfare" of African Americans

Millions of African Americans have not seen positive changes in their living conditions; instead, they experienced a significant erosion in living standards. The effects of discrimination are illustrated by key socioeconomic indicators in the areas of poverty, family structure, African American businesses, labor force participation and income, crime, housing, health, education, and welfare dependency.

Poverty Despite a drop in the mid-1990s (and a rise in the early 2000s), black poverty rates continue to be much higher than for non-Hispanic whites. Some 8 percent of whites were poor in 2002, a rate less than one-third that for blacks. Similarly, median household income in 2003 was more than 38 percent higher for non-Hispanic whites than for blacks. The 2003 poverty rate was also higher than the poverty rates for every year of the 1970s, even though the unemployment rate was lower.[30]

Family Structure In 2002, 48% of African American families were married couples, 43% of families were single female-headed households, and 9% were maintained by men only. African American families are larger than non-Hispanic white families: 20%

had five or more members in contrast to 12% of white families. (Larger family sizes result in lower per capita income.) Four million African American children (36 percent) resided with both parents in 1998. In 2002, 30% (1.1 million) of all children living in a grandparent's home were African American.[31]

African American Businesses As mentioned earlier, black-owned businesses grew 46 percent between 1987 and 1992, and business receipts grew at the same rate as for white firms. However, receipts in black-owned businesses constituted only about 1 percent of total U.S. business receipts in 1992. Receipts for black-owned firms averaged $52,000 per firm, compared with $193,000 for all U.S. firms. Fifty-six percent of black-owned firms had receipts of under $10,000, and less than 1 percent had receipts of $1 million or more.[32] Overall, the annual combined revenue of the 25 largest U.S. black-owned businesses in 2002 was only $7.8 billion.[33]

Labor Force Participation and Income Discrimination continues in the areas of employment and wages. Although laws and regulations addressing racial discrimination in employment have had some success, they have not adequately prevented widespread discrimination against African Americans. The Urban Institute compared the experiences of comparable African American and white male job seekers. Using hiring audits, the study found that black applicants were subject to unfavorable treatment during the application process 20 percent of the time, compared with 7 percent for white applicants. Unfavorable treatment included (1) not advancing to the next level of the hiring process, (2) encountering more questions or resistance before receiving an application form, (3) being steered toward less desirable positions than white counterparts, (4) being forced to wait longer for interviews, (5) receiving only cursory interviews, (6) hearing discouraging or derogatory remarks, and (7) being turned down for a position when it was offered to a white applicant.[34]

Despite the narrowing of some important economic indicators, the unemployment rate for blacks is still almost twice that of whites. While the national employment rate stood at about 5.4 percent in mid-2004, the black adult unemployment rate was 10.4 percent, and among black teenagers it was 37 percent.[35]

Discrimination carries into income. Not surprisingly, the lowest income gap is found between blacks and whites without a high school diploma. The more education people attain, the greater the income gap. In 2003, white males with a master's degree earned $75,187 a year; African American males, $60,824. This $14,363 translates into a salary differential of almost 20 percent. In varying degrees, the same salary gap is evident between minority and white women. (See Table 4.1.)

Table 4.1

2003 Salary and Educational Attainment for Workers over Age 25

	Asian		White		Black		Hispanic	
	Men	Women	Men	Women	Men	Women	Men	Women
No H.S. Diploma	18,102	15,538	23,250	13,163	20,539	13,656	21,610	13,694
H.S. Grad	29,493	20,242	34,909	21,762	25,510	20,137	27,992	18,810
Some College	30,945	19,417	38,886	22,672	31,615	22,373	31,545	20,707
Assoc. Arts Degree	36,280	26,065	44,099	27,564	36,554	26,966	37,365	25,888
BA Degree	54,683	38,447	66,638	38,049	46,942	38,447	46,115	35,357
Master's Degree	73,788	47,999	75,187	46,729	60,824	47,999	59,901	57,447
Ph.D.	82,148	NA	103,311	63,883	NA	NA	NA	NA
Prof. Degree	117,707	NA	143,863	61,115	NA	NA	90,767	NA

*NA = The sample size was too small for accurate calculation.

Source: Adapted from American Council on Education (ACE), Center for Policy Analysis, *ACE Fact Sheet on Higher Education* (Washington, DC: American Council on Education, May 2004).

Jared Bernstein offers several explanations for the African American wage gap. These include discrimination in employment (aided by the lax enforcement of antidiscrimination laws); more frequent employment in vulnerable sectors of the labor economy; a combination of regional, industrial, and occupational choices; lower rates of unionization in the labor market; and the general erosion of worker rights.[36] Another explanation suggests that as middle-class African Americans advance, greater unemployment occurs among those with less education and skills. But this explanation does not address the large African American/white unemployment differential among college-educated men, a disparity that is greater in central cities of the East and North. According to Franklin Wilson, the cause of this discrepancy can be found in two factors: (1) the decline during the 1980s in the number of jobs traditionally filled by college-educated African American men (e.g., public sector jobs dealing with affirmative action, social welfare, and criminal justice); and (2) the inability of educated African Americans to penetrate the professional/technical occupations that entail managerial or supervisory responsibilities. Not surprisingly, these positions usually involve higher salaries and more job security.[37] Also, personnel cutbacks in federal and state governments are likely to exacerbate the income differential of African Americans, because one of the major opportunities for their employment has been in the governmental sector. Regardless of the causes, African Americans continue to earn less than whites, irrespective of household composition, education, region, or religion.

Crime In 1999, 603,000 black men were enrolled in higher education in the United States. The total number of black men incarcerated in federal, state, or local prisons was 757,000.[38] More than 5.6 million Americans are in prison or have served time. Given current trends, a black male in the United States has a one in three chance of going to prison during his lifetime. For a Hispanic male, it is one in six; for a white male, one in seventeen.[39] Among women, 3.6 percent of blacks and 0.5 percent of whites will enter prison at least once. Based on current rates of incarceration, an estimated 7.9 percent of black males (compared to 0.7 percent of white males) will enter state or federal prison before they reach age 20, and 21.4 percent of black males (versus 1.4 percent of white males) will be incarcerated before age 30. Some important factors influence these numbers. About 62 percent of first-time offenders admitted to federal prison and 31 percent of those admitted to state prison are sentenced because of drug offenses. About 12 percent of drug users are black, but blacks make up nearly 50 percent of all drug possession arrests in the United States.[40] Moreover, the racial composition of the 3,517 people on death row in 2003 was 46 percent white, 42 percent African American, and 10 percent Latino. Given that African Americans make up only 13 percent of the U.S. population, they were overrepresented on death row by more than three times their number in the population.[41]

Blacks were six times more likely than whites to be murdered in 2002.[42] Although the homicide rate for black males in the United States has fallen in recent years, the rate remains unacceptably high. Black males 18–24 years old have the highest homicide rates. Compared to the next highest rates, their rates are more than three times the rates of black males 14–17 years old and 4 times the rates of black males age 25 and older. For African American males, the probability of being murdered before age 45 in 1995 was 2.21 percent, compared with 0.29 percent for white males. In Washington, D.C., 1 in 12 black 15-year-old males (about 8 percent) will be murdered before age 45. By comparison, the death rate for U.S. soldiers serving in the military during World War II was 2.5 percent; during World War I, it was 2.4 percent; and during the Vietnam War, 1.2 percent.[43]

Housing Housing patterns reflect the economic gulf between African Americans and whites. Minority (African American, Hispanic, and Native American) households are both poorer and more likely to be renters than white households. This encourages a home ownership rate of only 48 percent for African Americans compared to about 70 percent for non-Hispanic whites.[44] In 1995, 78 percent of poor black renters paid more than 30 percent of their income for housing; 54 percent paid more than 50 percent. Only 49 percent of poor black households received housing assistance. Nineteen percent of poor black families live in physically deficient housing (e.g., in substandard structures, or in overcrowded or doubled-up housing), and 21 percent of poor black households have affordability problems and live in physically deficient housing.[45]

Health The effects of racism can also be seen in health issues. The black infant mortality rate in the United States in 2000 was 13.6 per 1,000 live births, more than twice that of whites (5.7 deaths). Taken by itself, the U.S. black infant mortality rate ranks high internationally (see Table 4.2). The rate of sudden infant death syndrome (SIDS) among African Americans was 113.5 deaths per 100,000 live infant births in 2001 compared to 45.6 for whites. Although blacks comprise about 12 percent of the population, they account for more than half of all new HIV diagnoses each year. The 2001 rate of reported AIDS cases among blacks is 59.6 per 100,000 population, approximately three times higher than the rate for Hispanics and nine times the rate for whites.[46] The pediatric AIDS rate for African American children under age 14 in 1998 was 3.2 per 100,000, compared to 0.2 for white children.[47] Not surprisingly, life expectancy is lower for African Americans. In 2001, black males had a life expectancy of 68.6 years compared to 75 years for Whites. For African American women, the life expectancy was 75.5 years compared to 80.2 years for white women.[48]

A major factor affecting infant mortality is low birth weight. Although the cause is unknown, low birth weight (less than 5.5 pounds) increases the chances of infant death during the first month by 40 percent. In 2002, 7.8 percent of babies were born at low birth weight; for African American babies it was 13.4 percent.[49]

Education As a high school diploma becomes less valuable in the marketplace, only educational upgrading can protect workers' incomes. In fact, on the average, college graduates in 2004 earned almost

Table 4.2

Infant Mortality Rates and Ranks: Selected Countries, 2002 (deaths per 1,000 live births)

Rank	Country	Rate	Rank	Country	Rate
1	Japan	3.3	20	U.S. (Overall)	6.8
2	Sweden	3.4	21	South Korea	7.3
3	Finland	3.7	22	Israel	7.4
4	Norway	3.9	23	Cyprus	7.5
5	Germany	4.2	*	U.S. (Amer. Indian)	8.3
6	Austria	4.3	24	Slovakia	8.6
7	Switzerland	4.4	25	Hungary	8.6
8	France	4.4	26	Chile	8.9
9	Spain	4.5	27	Poland	8.9
10	Australia	4.8	28	Costa Rica	10.6
11	Canada	4.9	*	U.S. (Black rate)	13.6
12	Denmark	4.9	29	Sri Lanka	15.2
13	United Kingdom	5.3	30	Russia	19.5
14	Ireland	5.3	31	Panama	21.4
15	Czech Republic	4.4	32	Mexico	23.7
16	Portugal	5.7	33	Venezuela	23.8
*	U.S. (White only)	5.7	34	China	25.3
17	Greece	6.1	35	Brazil	31.7
18	New Zealand	6.1	36	Syria	31.7
19	Italy	6.2	37	Ecuador	32.0

Sources: Adapted from U.S. Census Bureau, International Database, "Life Expectancy and Infant Mortality in Selected Countries, 2003," retrieved August 2004 from www.infoplease.com/ipa/A004393.html; and Centers for Disease Control, "Infant Mortality Statistics from the 2000 Period Linked Birth/Infant Death Data Set" *National Vital Statistics Reports* 50, no. 12 (August 28, 2002), retrieved August 2004 from www.cdc.gov/nchs/data/nvsr/nvsr50/nvsr50_12.pdf.

$43,000 a year compared to $21,000 for high school graduates.[50] As an example, between 1979 and 1987 the annual wage of a high school graduate fell 8.6 percent while the income of a college graduate rose by 9.2 percent.[51]

By 2004, continuing an upward trend in black educational attainment that began in 1940, there was no statistical difference in high school completion rates between African American and white students (around 86 percent). Although the high school dropout rate is now relatively low, it is still significant because the failure to complete high school is strongly correlated with poverty. According to the American Public Human Services Association, in 1989 nearly half of all female heads of families and 60 percent of parents receiving welfare in 36 of the previous 60 months did not finish high school.[52] Furthermore, an estimated 85 percent of juveniles appearing in court are functionally illiterate.[53]

Although the same proportions of black and white students graduate from high school, college completion rates differ. By 2000, of the over-25 age group, about 34 percent of whites were college graduates compared to only 18 percent of African Americans.[54] The strong correlation between higher education and higher salaries suggests that the disparity between African American and white college completion rates will have a long-term impact on the economic well-being of these groups. In addition, fewer minority college graduates go on to obtain advanced degrees.[55] For example, only 1,604 African Americans earned a doctoral degree in 2001.[56]

Welfare Dependency Welfare dependency is another indicator of racism. Although welfare dependency is decreasing for African Americans, 7.7 percent received more than 50 percent of their total annual family income from means-tested public assistance programs compared to 1.9 percent of the non-Hispanic white population.[57]

Hispanic Americans

Although the history of race relations in the United States is older than the nation itself, the issue is rising in importance with the coming of a "minority majority"—the name given by some to the changing demographics expected in U.S. society over the next 50 years. There are "two Americas." One is the aging, white society that is still found in smaller metropolitan areas, smaller towns and rural areas; the second is a younger, more multicultural society that is growing rapidly in the most visible cultural centers of the country.

The Demography of Hispanic Americans

In 2002, Hispanics became the nation's largest minority community. It is projected that from 2002 to 2050, Hispanics will increase their ranks by 188 percent to 102.6 million, or roughly one-quarter of the U.S. population. The Hispanic population in the United States is young, with more than one-third under age 18. Between 2000 and 2002, the nation's Hispanic population grew much faster than the population as a whole, increasing from 35.3 million to 38.8 million. According to Census Bureau estimates, Hispanics accounted for 3.5 million, or fully one-half, of the population increase of 6.9 million from 2000 to 2002.[58]

The use of the term *Hispanic* masks a rich diversity within this group. U.S. Hispanics have roots in 22 different countries; their family histories are from Mexico, Puerto Rico, Cuba and other Caribbean islands, and Central and South America as well as the United States. Some 60 percent of Hispanics in the United States are more comfortable speaking Spanish, 20 percent speak mostly English, and nearly 20 percent speak both.[59]

The diversity of the various Hispanic groups is reflected in the percentages of those 25 and older who had graduated from high school by 2002. These high school graduates ranged from 74 percent of "other Hispanic origin" to 71 percent for Cubans and 51 percent for Mexican Americans. Although Latinos pump $300 billion into the U.S. economy, 21 percent of Hispanics lived below the poverty line in 2001. Hispanic children represented 18 percent of all children in the United States but comprised 28 percent of all children in poverty.[60] Of those living below the poverty line in 2001, nearly 21 percent were Mexican American, 26 percent were Puerto Ricans living in the U.S. mainland, 16.5 percent were Cuban Americans, and 15 percent were from Central and South America.[61] This compares to just 8 percent of whites and 24.4 percent of African Americans who lived below the poverty line.[62]

Because of the large number of undocumented workers coming from Central America and Mexico, the Hispanic population of the United States is difficult to measure accurately. Although some estimates of the number of undocumented workers in the United States (most of them from Spanish-speaking countries) are in the 12 million range, other researchers have estimated this population to be 3 to 6 million.[63] Nevertheless, it is known that the total Hispanic population is growing rapidly.[64] The Hispanic population is also geographically concentrated, with 65 percent living in just three states: California, Texas, and New York. Eighty-eight percent of all Latinos live in nine states, and 88 percent live in urban areas (a figure 13 percent higher than the national average).[65]

Hispanic Poverty and Income

The poverty status of Hispanics worsened from the 1980s onward in relation to other groups, including African Americans. For example, the overall poverty rate for African Americans declined from 1992 (33 percent) to 2004 (24 percent); during those same years the poverty rate for Hispanics rose, surpassing the black poverty rate for the first time.[66] However, by 2003 the poverty rate for Hispanics was 22 percent. The median household net worth for Latino households between 1995 and 1998 fell 24 percent, from $12,170 in 1995 to $9,200 in 1998. Part of this drop may have resulted from the continuing immigration of poor and unskilled workers.

In 2001 Hispanic children represented almost 18 percent of all U.S. children but made up 30 percent of all children living in poverty. By comparison, only 9.5 percent of white children were living in poverty. All told, 28 percent of Hispanic children lived below the poverty line in 2002.[67] In 2003 Hispanics earned $33,102, slightly more than African Americans who earned $29,177. These 2003 earnings represented a fall of 2.9 percent compared to 2002.[68]

Diversity in the Hispanic Population

Although for statistical purposes the Hispanic population is often considered as a single group, the various Latino subgroups have distinct social and historical backgrounds. For example, Cubans living in Florida may have little in common historically or politically with Mexican Americans living in California, and Puerto Ricans living in New York may have little understanding of the culture of either Cuban Americans or Mexican Americans. These differences are also reflected in income. Among Latino full-time, year-round workers in 2002, Mexicans had the lowest proportion earning $35,000 or more.[69]

Mexican Americans constitute about 67 percent (17.1 million) of all Hispanics in the United States and are the fastest growing Spanish-speaking subgroup. According to the Census Bureau there were about 20.6 million Mexican Americans in the United States in 2000, a substantial increase over the 13 million in 1989.[70] In part, the poverty of Mexican Americans is correlated to deficits in educational attainment. More than two in five Hispanics aged 25 and older have not graduated from high school. The Hispanic population aged 25 and older was less likely to have graduated from high school than non-Hispanic whites (57 percent and 89 percent, respectively). In addition, more than one-quarter of Hispanics had less than a ninth-grade education (27 percent), compared with only 4 percent of non-Hispanic whites. The proportion with a bachelor's degree or more was much lower for Hispanics (11 percent) than for non-Hispanic whites (29 percent). Educational attainment varies among Hispanics. Among Latinos 25 years and older, other Hispanics, Cubans, Puerto Ricans, and Central and South Americans were more likely to have at least graduated from high school (74 percent, 67 percent, 71 percent, and 65 percent, respectively) than were Mexicans (51 percent). Similarly, the proportion that had attained at least a bachelor's degree ranged from 19 percent for Cubans, 17 percent for Central and South Americans, and 20 percent for other Hispanics to 7.6 percent for Mexicans.[71]

Puerto Ricans constituted 8.6 percent of the Hispanic population and less than 1 percent of the total U.S. population in 2002. They also had the highest unemployment rate (9.6 percent) among Hispanic groups and their poverty rate was 26 percent, again the highest of any Hispanic group.[72]

The economic data on Hispanics suggest two subgroups with different characteristics. For example, while average household worth fell, the Latino community's total wealth rose. Not surprisingly, the number of Hispanic businesses increased 76 percent (from 490,000 to 862,600) between 1987 and 1992 and their receipts rose by 134 percent.[73] This phenomenon is explained by the increasing numbers of poor households on the rich–poor continuum and by the increasing wealth on the rich end. Overall, however, the economic data clearly suggest a worsening picture for most of America's Hispanic communities.

American Indians

Oppression and exploitation are by no means limited to African Americans and Hispanics. American Indians, in some ways the poorest group in the United

States, experience similar oppression as other disenfranchised populations.

From 1970 to 2000, the reported American Indian population grew from 574,000 to more than 2 million. This population rise was due to a lower infant mortality rate, a high birthrate, and the fact that more individuals of mixed American Indian descent were reporting their race as American Indian. This last factor may be partly correlated with the resurgence of American Indian pride that began in the 1970s. In 2000, American Indian and Alaska Natives numbered about 2.5 million or 0.9 percent of the U.S. population. In combination with other races they total 4.2 million or 1.5 percent. According to BIA estimates, about 1.5 million American Indians live on or near reservations and about another 356,000 live in urban areas.[74]

Although there are 562 federally recognized tribes (including 223 Alaskan Native groups) and 275 American Indian reservations, there is no single definition of an American Indian.[75] The Bureau of Indian Affairs (BIA) considers someone to be an American Indian if the person is a member of a recognized American Indian tribe and has one-fourth or more American Indian blood. The Bureau of the Census uses self-identification.

The history of American Indians is marked by hardship, deprivation, and gross injustice. Before the arrival of Christopher Columbus, American Indians in the territorial United States numbered somewhere between 900,000 and 12 million.[76] This indigenous population was dramatically reduced as a result of disease and the westward expansion of whites and the wars and genocidal policies that followed. By 1880 the census reported only 250,000 American Indians.[77] Moreover, American Indians were not granted citizenship until 1924, and New Mexico did not allow them to vote until 1940.

The social and economic problems faced by American Indians is similar to those of other at-risk minority populations (see Table 4.3). After generations as the nation's poorest and most overlooked minority, American Indians continue to suffer from what a 2003 U.S. Commission on Civil Rights report called a "quiet crisis" of discrimination, poverty, and unmet promises. Unemployment, substance abuse, and school dropout rates are among the highest in the nation, and American Indians face staggering health problems.[78] In 2004, American Indians were 770 percent more likely to die from alcoholism, 650 percent more likely to die from tuberculosis, 420 percent more likely to die from diabetes, 280 percent more likely to die from accidents, and 52 percent more likely to die from pneumonia or influenza than the rest of the United States, including other minority populations. As a result of these increased mortality rates, the life expectancy for American Indians is 71 years of age, nearly five years less than the rest of the U.S. population.[79]

American Indian tribes are sovereign nations under federal law, and states may not enforce their

Table 4.3

Selected Indicators of American Indian Social and Economic Well-Being, 1999

	American Indian Only White, Non-Hispanic	Combination of American Indian and Other Race	White Non-Hispanic
% of female-headed households with children	45.7	42.9	26.0
H.S. dropout rate	16.1	14.5	6.9
% of those age 16–19 not in school or working	16.0	13.9	6.3
% of children in poverty	31.6	27.1	9.3
% of married couples with children in poverty	15.5	12.9	3.9
Median income	$33,144	$36,120	$54,698

Source: Adapted from Annie E. Casey Foundation, "American-Indian Children: State-Level Measures of Child Well-Being from the 2000 Census," *Kids Count* (Baltimore, MD: Annie E. Casey Foundation 2003).

civil codes on reservations within a state's borders. After the federal government gave tribes more control over their economic development, some began operating gaming places that conflicted with state and local laws. A number of states challenged these operations, but a series of Supreme Court cases were decided in the tribes' favor. To clarify the law, the Indian Gaming Regulatory Act was passed in 1988. Tribes could operate full-scale casino gambling on reservations in any state that allowed such gambling anywhere within its borders, provided the details of the operation were set forth under a tribal–state compact.

By the late 1990s there were over 310 gaming operations run by more than 200 of the nations' 562 federally recognized tribes. Of these operations, about 220 were "Las Vegas" style casinos with slot machines and/or table games. Examining the effects of casinos after at least four years of operation, economists William Evans and Julie Topoleski found that positive changes included young adults moving back to reservations (fueling a 12 percent population increase); adult employment increased by 26 percent; the number of working poor declined by 14 percent; and mortality rates fell by 2 percent. Evans and Topoleski concluded that tribal gaming operations had both positive and negative spillovers in the surrounding communities. Given the size of tribes relative to their counties, most of the growth in employment was due to growth in non–American Indian employment (most of those employed by casinos are not American Indians). Four years after a casino opens, negative changes include a 10 percent increase in auto thefts, larceny, violent crime, and an increase in bankruptcies within 50 miles of a new casino. Moreover, because casino profits are not taxable, their presence in many states may divert funds from a taxable activity.[80]

Caught in the paternalistic and authoritarian web of the Bureau of Indian Affairs, American Indians continue to struggle for their identity. Having been robbed of their land, murdered indiscriminately by encroaching white settlers (as well as by the U.S. Cavalry), and treated alternately as children and pests by the federal government, for many years American Indians were further oppressed by having their children taken away by welfare officials. This widespread abuse by welfare workers, who evaluated American Indian child-rearing practices as neglectful in the context of white middle-class family values, was partially remedied by the **Indian Child Welfare Act of 1978,** which restored child-placement decisions to the individual tribes. As a result of this act, priority in placement choices for American Indian children was given to tribal members rather than white families.[81] In an attempt to remedy historical injustices, the Indian Self-Determination Act of 1975 emphasized tribal self-government; self-sufficiency; and the establishment of independent health, education, and welfare services.[82] Despite these limited gains, the plight of American Indians serves as a reminder of the mistakes made by the United States in both its past and its present policies toward disenfranchised minority groups.

Asian Americans

The 2000 census reported more than 25 Asian-Pacific subgroups in the United States, including Chinese, Filipino, Japanese, Asian-Indian, Korean, Vietnamese, Laotian, Thai, Cambodian, Polynesian (Hawaiian, Samoan, and Tongan), Micronesian (Guamain), and Melanesian (Fijian). The six largest Asian population groups in the United States are: Chinese (2.7 million), Filipino (2.4 million), Japanese (1.1 million), Asian-Indian (1.9 million), Korean (1.2 million), and Vietnamese (1.2 million).[83] In 1970 there were 1.5 million Asians living in the United States; by 1980 there were 3.7 million; and by 1990, 7.3 million. This growth represented an astounding 475 percent increase over 20 years and made Asians the fastest growing minority group in the U.S. population. It is projected that because of above-average birthrates and accelerating legal and illegal immigration, the Asian population will more than triple to 33 million by 2050, and by 2080 it will make up about 12 percent of the population compared with 4 percent in 2002.[84]

While the social and economic data on Asians is mixed, perhaps the most striking feature is their median family income in 2003 (see Figure 4.1). Economic and social data point to a population that has made great strides, especially in the educational area. For example, in 2003, 88 percent of Asians were high school graduates, compared with 89 percent of whites, 80 percent of blacks, and 57 percent of Hispanics.[85] In 1989, college-bound Asian seniors had a high school grade point average of 3.25 out of 4.0 versus 3.08 for all other students.[86] In 1992 the nation's most elite universities reported 14 percent Asian American enrollment, almost five times their representation in the general population.[87] While Asians made up only 3 percent of the population in 1990, they represented 12 percent of the students at Harvard University; 20 percent at Stanford; and in 2003, 45 percent at the University of California.[88] In 1986, all five top scholarships of the

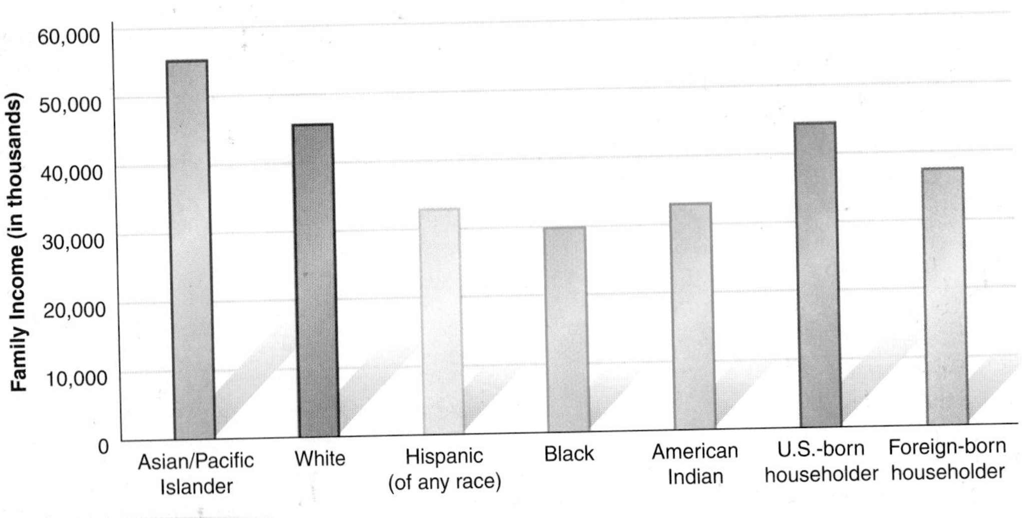

Figure 4.1

Median Family Income, 2003 (in thousands)

Source: U.S. Census Bureau, "Income Stable, Poverty Up, Numbers of Americans with and without Health Insurance Rise, Census Bureau Reports," August 26, 2004. Retrieved October 2004 from www.census.gov/Press-Release/www/releases/archives/income_wealth/002484.html.

Westinghouse Science Talent Search scholarships went to Asians.[89] In 2003, 29 percent of all males had completed college. Of that number, 28 percent were white, 17 percent black, 11 percent Hispanic, and 50 percent Asian.[90] In 2002, Asian Americans had approximately the same unemployment rate (6 percent) as whites (5 percent), yet their poverty rate in 2003 was 11.8 percent, up from 10.1 percent in 2002.[91]

In 1997, over 50 percent of all minority-owned businesses whose sales exceeded one million dollars were Asian American owned. In 1997 there were 913,000 Asian businesses in the U.S. with $307 billion in sales. Each firm averaged $336,000 in annual receipts and they employed 2.2 million people. Additionally, from 1992 to 1997, Asian-owned firms grew 30 percent with revenue growth of 46 percent. In comparison, the number of Hispanic-owned businesses stood at 1.1 million and black-owned businesses at 823,500.[92]

Impressive as these economic statistics are, they conceal several things. First, most Asians live in expensive urban areas where salaries are higher than the U.S. average. Second, economic statistics for Asian Americans obscure the problems of many low-wage recent immigrants who work in sweatshops in urban Chinatowns. For example, in 1980 the average suburban Chinese household earned $16,790 compared to $9,059 for the average Chinatown household.[93] A 2002 study by the Asian American Federation of New York found that garment workers in New York's Chinatown earned $112 a week. Restaurant workers, many of which were illegal, earned only $124 a week.[94] Third, although many Chinese and Japanese Americans have achieved economic success, Southeast Asians are at higher risk of poverty than whites. Fourth, Asians are underrepresented in the higher-salaried public and private career positions and their salaries tend to be lower than whites.[95] Fifth, although a large number of Asian immigrants have become successful entrepreneurs and own and operate their own small retail businesses, for some this role was forced on them as a result of discrimination.

Asian Americans have been stigmatized in U.S. society in several ways. Most dramatic was the internment of Japanese Americans in detention camps during World War II. However, Asians in this country have also experienced more subtle forms of discrimination. For example, because of their economic and educational achievements, Asians are often thought of as a "model minority." Because of this status many Asians experience pressure from the white majority as well as from other minority groups. An example of this tension is evident in the hostility between Korean shopkeepers and inner-city African American residents. Asians have also been the victims of hate crimes, some motivated by mudslinging that goes on periodically between Japan,

China, and the United States over recurrent trade problems and the resulting lay-offs of U.S. blue-collar workers. In addition, some Asian Americans complain that they are discriminated against in colleges and universities because of their superior academic performance.[96] Facing this backlash, some Asians have redoubled their efforts to become mainstream U.S. citizens—to be in the center of the society rather than on the margins as "hyphenated Americans."

Many Asians point to contributions to U.S. society that results from the input of Oriental cultural values. For example, Asian culture often includes an emphasis on frugality that leads to environmental conservation, greater consideration for the feelings of others, and a balance between group and individual welfare. According to sociologist Tu Weiming, the less individualistic culture of Asians, their lower sense of self-interest, their less adversarial nature, and their less legalistic approach have important applications for the United States.[97]

Immigrants and Immigration

In less than 50 years, the U.S. Census Bureau projects that immigration will cause the population of the United States to increase from 290 million to more than 400 million. Between January 2000 and March 2002, 3.3 million illegal immigrants arrived in the United States. Mexicans made up over half of undocumented immigrants (57 percent), with another 23 percent coming from other Latin American countries, 10 percent are from Asia, 5 percent from Europe and Canada, and 5 percent from the rest of the world. Almost two-thirds (65 percent) of the undocumented population lives in just six states: California (27 percent), Texas (13 percent), New York (8 percent), Florida (7 percent), Illinois (6 percent), and New Jersey (4 percent). However, the most rapid growth in the undocumented population since the mid-1990s has been outside these states.[98] In 2002, the foreign-born population of the United States was 33.1 million, equal to 11.5 percent of the U.S. population. The U.S. Office of Immigration Statistics (OIS) estimates that in 2002 the legal permanent resident (LPR) population and those eligible to naturalize were 11.4 million and 7.8 million, respectively.[99]

Although poverty rates are higher for immigrants, naturalized citizens have lower poverty rates (10 percent) than native-born Americans (11.8 percent).[100] Moreover, a significant portion of Hispanic poverty is attributable to the large numbers of illegal immigrants entering the United States and to the low-paying menial jobs they occupy. Asian Americans have also felt the backlash from mainstream Americans who are worried about the consequences of admitting non-Europeans into U.S. society.

The pace of economic growth in the 1990s would have been impossible without immigration. Since 1990, immigrants have contributed to job growth in three ways: (1) by filling an increasing share of jobs, (2) by taking jobs in labor-scarce regions, and (3) by filling the types of jobs shunned by native workers. Although the foreign-born make up only 11.3 percent of the U.S. population and 14 percent of the labor force, the flow of foreign-born is so large that immigrants currently account for a larger share of labor force growth than natives. For example, in the 1990s, the labor force grew by 16.7 million workers, with 6.4 million of them being foreign-born. The majority of foreign-born workers (4.2 million) came during the boom of 1996–2000, when their share of job growth rose to 44 percent. In fact, immigrants filled four of every 10 job openings at a time when the unemployment rate hit record lows in the mid-1990s.[101]

The number of jobs immigrants fill is important, but where these jobs are filled is also important. In the 1990s, there was large-scale geographic dispersion among recent immigrants. Whereas in earlier years most new immigrants from Latin America and Asia clustered in a few large cities—such as Los Angeles, New York, and Chicago—the 1990s witnessed a spread to the western Midwest, New England, and the Mid- and South Atlantic regions. In some parts of the country, almost all labor force growth between 1996 and 2000 was due to immigration.[102]

New immigrants commonly fill low-skill, blue-collar jobs because a large number have less than a high school education. About 33 percent of immigrants have not finished high school, compared with 13 percent of natives. Immigrants are not only low-skilled compared with native workers, but many of their skills do not translate into the U.S. workplace. Although immigrants overwhelmingly fill blue-collar jobs, they also account for as much as half the growth in categories such as administrative support and services.[103]

Legal immigration to the United States has undergone several important changes since the mid-1980s. From 1985 to 1988 the total number of immigrants into the United States remained relatively constant; it then rose sharply from 1988 to 1991. The sharp rise after 1988 was due to the impact of the Immigration Reform and Control Act of 1986 (IRCA), which granted legal status to undocumented immigrants who had been in the United States continuously since 1982 or had worked in agriculture. In 1995 the total number of immigrants admitted to the United States was 720,461, less than half of the 1,827,167 admitted in 1991.[104]

Major changes have occurred in the structure of U.S. immigration from the 1950s onward. According to the Immigration and Naturalization Service (INS), the most notable change was the shift of immigration from Europe and Canada (almost 52 percent of all immigrants to the United States in 1964) to Asia (27 percent of all immigrants in 2002). By 2002 Asian immigration was highest, at 27 percent, followed by Mexico at 18 percent and European immigration at 15 percent. (See Figure 4.2.) Most immigrants (65.3 percent) to the U.S. choose to settle in just six states: 26.6 percent in California, 10.7 percent in New York, 9.8 percent in Florida, 8.1 percent in Texas, 5.6 percent in New Jersey, and 4.5 percent in Illinois.[105]

In 1996, Congress passed the **Personal Responsibility and Work Opportunity Reconciliation Act (PRWORA).** The most comprehensive welfare reform legislation passed since the New Deal of 1935, the 900-page bill contained profound implications for both legal and illegal immigrants (PRWORA will be discussed more fully in Chapter 11).[106] Specifically, the PRWORA disentitled most legal immigrants (including many who had been living in the United States for years but had not elected to become citizens) from food stamps, Aid to Families with Dependent Children (AFDC), and Supplemental Security Income (SSI). (Illegal immigrants were never entitled to these benefits.) Based on the PRWORA, the only immigrants still entitled to benefits were (1) those who had become citizens or who had worked in the United States and paid Social Security taxes for at least 10 years; and (2) veterans of the U.S. Army who were noncitizens. In addition, the bill gave states the option to deny Medicaid benefits to immigrants.[107] Although some of the provisions were later rescinded, the sentiment that fueled the bill remains.

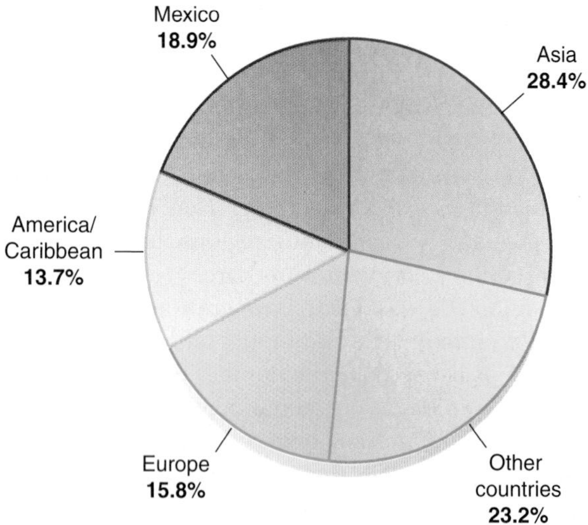

Figure 4.2

Immigrants by Place of Origin, 2002

Source: U.S. Office of Immigration Statistics, 2003. Retrieved October 2004 from www.uscis.gov/graphics/shared/aboutus/statistics/IMM02yrbk/IMMExcel/table2.xls.

In September 1996, Congress revisited immigration, this time voting to double the size of the Border Patrol, stiffen penalties for document fraud and immigrant smuggling, bar illegal immigrants from qualifying for Social Security benefits or public housing, give states the right to deny illegal immigrants drivers' licenses, and slightly increase the earnings requirements for U.S. residents wishing to sponsor foreign family members.[108]

Immigration policy has changed dramatically since the World Trade Center attacks of September 11, 2001. After 9/11 three important acts were passed: (1) the USA Patriot Act, (2) the Enhanced Border Security Act, and (3) the Homeland Security Act of 2002. While these acts do not address immigration per se, they affect it by more carefully screening and monitoring foreigners who temporarily visit (and sometimes wish to resettle in) the United States. The most important changes have been stricter background checks for visa applicants and requirements for tamper-proof, machine-readable travel documents. In addition, American consulates have raised fees, and wait times for visa approvals have gone from less than a month to several months. Those applying for visas are now paying more and are more likely to be denied entry. This stricter process has led to drastic declines in visas issued to tourists and businesspeople, with B1/B2 visas dropping 37 percent from 2001 to 2003.[109]

Two other groups have also been impacted by stricter procedures: foreign students and refugees.

Foreign students have been especially affected by stricter immigration procedures.

Background checks on foreign students and stricter requirements on the universities and schools that admit them have reduced the number of student visas issued. For instance, students must have a confirmation of acceptance from a United States school before they enter the country and are no longer allowed to apply to a school from the United States (i.e., they must first return to their home country). As a result of these policies, 299,000 student visas were issued in 2001 compared to 210,000 in 2003, a 26 percent drop. These policies have also affected U.S. universities who rely on foreign students to fill graduate programs and for the tuition they generate.[110]

Refugee resettlement has also slowed. Although 90,000 refugee applications were filed in 2002, only 19,000 were approved, a 72 percent drop from 2001. This decline is partly explained by stricter security procedures for natives of countries linked to terrorism, such as Sudan and Somalia.[111] Although the number of foreigners temporarily entering the United States has declined, there was no slowdown in the number of people granted permanent legal status. About 1.1 million green cards were issued in 2001 and 2002. However, since a portion of legal immigration often originates from foreign students, refugee resettlement, and sometimes through tourist and business visits, this decline may eventually lead to fewer permanent immigrants.[112]

A report released by the Migration Policy Institute analyzing post–September 11th policy changes, found an emerging pattern of violations of due process and harsh law enforcement measures directed against males from Arab and Muslim countries. The report also investigated the impact of current policy on U.S. Arab and Muslim communities and found that governmental actions have frightened and alienated this community. Programs such as special registration became a vehicle to arrest those with even minor immigration violations, and the threat of deportation was always looming in the background.[113] According to report co-author Muzaffar Chishti, "The experience of Muslim and Arab communities post–Sept. 11 is, in many ways, an impressive story of a community that first felt intimidated but has since started to assert its place in the American body politic."[114]

Women and Society

Sexism is a term that denotes the discriminatory and prejudicial treatment of women based on their gender, and sexism is a problem that U.S.

society has wrestled with since the beginning of the nation.

Sexism can manifest itself in a variety of ways. It can be social, as when women are kept out of military academies, private clubs, and certain sports. It can take the form of occupational boundaries that keep women from operating heavy construction machinery, being involved in skilled trades such as bricklaying, or flying commercial or military jets. It can take political forms, like appointing or electing token women to offices or cabinet positions or creating "special appointments" to placate feminist groups.

Violence and Sexism

Sexism can also manifest itself in crime and family violence. Violence against women is primarily partner violence.[115] According to a study by Patricia Tjaden and Nancy Thoennes:

- Nearly 25 percent of surveyed women said they were raped and/or physically assaulted by a current or former spouse, cohabiting partner, or date at some time in their lifetime.
- Approximately five percent (1.5 million) of women are raped and/or physically assaulted by an intimate partner annually in the United States. Almost 5 million (victims are often victimized more than once) intimate partner rapes and physical assaults are perpetrated against U.S. women annually.
- Almost 5 percent of women reported being stalked by a current or former spouse, cohabiting partner, or date at some time in their lifetime: 503,485 women are stalked by an intimate partner annually in the United States.
- The researchers found that women who were physically assaulted by an intimate partner averaged almost 7 physical assaults by the same partner. The survey also found that 41.5 percent of the women who were physically assaulted by an intimate partner were injured during their most recent assault.
- The U.S. medical community treats millions of intimate partner rapes and physical assaults annually. Of the estimated 4.9 million intimate partner rapes and physical assaults perpetrated against women annually, about 2 million will result in an injury to the victim, and 570,457 will result in some type of medical treatment.
- Most intimate partner victimizations are not reported to the police. Only one-fifth of all rapes, one-quarter of all physical assaults, and one-half of all stalkings perpetrated against women by intimates are reported to the police.[116]

Congress passed the Violence against Women Act (VAWA), which was signed into law by President Bill Clinton in 1994. VAWA represents a comprehensive approach to domestic violence and sexual assault, combining a broad array of legal and other reforms. Specifically, it was designed to improve the response of police, prosecutors, and judges to these crimes; force sex offenders to pay restitution to their victims; and increase funding for battered women's shelters. VAWA mandates a nationwide enforcement of protection orders entered in any court and provides penalties for crossing state lines to abuse a spouse or violate a protection order. It also prohibits anyone facing a restraining order for domestic abuse from possessing a firearm.[117] The act provides grants for training police, prosecutors, and judges in domestic abuse; provides grants for battered women's shelters; assists victims of sexual assault, including providing educational seminars, hotlines, and more programs to increase awareness (as well as targeted efforts to underserved racial and ethnic minority communities); provides grants for safety-related improvements to public transportation, national park systems, and public parks; funds efforts to prevent youth violence; assists funding for rape crisis centers; and allocates funds for the treatment and counseling of youth subjected to or at risk of sexual abuse (e.g., runaways, homeless youth, and street people).[118] In 2004, overall funding for VAWA was $567 million.[119]

The Feminization of Poverty

Sexism also has an economic face. Women's wages are lower than those of men, and women more often have to resort to public welfare programs. The term **feminization of poverty** was coined by Diana Peirce in a 1978 article in *Urban and Social Change Review* in which she argued that poverty was rapidly becoming a female phenomenon and that women accounted for an increasingly larger proportion of the economically disadvantaged.[120] Advocates maintain that the feminization of poverty is best illustrated by the demographics of poverty. In 2003 real median earnings of women 15 and older fell 0.6 percent to $30,724, the first annual decline since 1995. During that same period, the number of women and girls without health insurance rose to 21.2 million, an increase of 927,000 over 2002. In 2003, the poverty rate for women and girls increased for the third year in a row, to 13.7 percent (40 percent higher than for men). In turn, the poverty rate for single-mother families increased to 35.5 percent in 2003, up from 33.7 percent in 2002. In comparison, the poverty rate for married-couple families with children increased to 7 percent in 2003.[121]

The effects of female poverty are staggering. For example, in the United States in 2000 two out of three poor adults were women, and in 2003 nearly 4 out of 10 families headed by women lived in poverty in 2003.[122] There were almost 13 million female-headed families (about 7.5 million with children) in 2003—a figure more than double that of 1970.[123] Not surprisingly, this leads to a strong dependence of poor women on the welfare system, which is illustrated by the huge increase in the welfare rolls from 1960 (3 million) to 1992 (13.5 million).[124]

The causes of the feminization of poverty are complex. When women are deserted or divorced, many must find jobs immediately or go on public assistance. According to Ann Withorn, women generally enter the welfare system only after exhausting other possibilities for income support.[125] Those who choose welfare are held in poverty by the low benefits; those who opt to work are kept in poverty by the low wages that characterize service jobs. Low-paying service employment, such as jobs in fast-food outlets and retail stores, make welfare benefits seem attractive because at least staying at home involves no child care costs.

Women and Low-Income Work

Women frequently enter the workforce through the service and retail trades, doing clerical jobs, cleaning, food preparation or service, personal service work, or auxiliary health service work. These occupations are characterized by low pay, a low level of unionization, little status, meager work benefits, and limited prospects for job advancement. Thus, much of the increase of women in the workforce is in the "secondary labor market" (see Chapter 5), a marginal area of employment. When economists cite the creation of millions of jobs in the 1980s and 1990s, much of what they refer to was in the secondary labor market. For example, of the 18.8 million jobs created between 1979 and 1989, 14.4 million were in retail trade and in services (i.e., business, personal, and health services), the two lowest-paid economic sectors.[126]

The economics of low-wage service work are gloomy. For example, if a single mother[127] with one child in day care chooses to avoid the stigma of welfare and finds work at near the minimum wage, her prospects for economic survival are bleak. The mock budget in Table 4.4 illustrates the dilemma of a single mother who finds full-time employment at

Table 4.4

Monthly Budget for a Working Mother with One Child in School and One Infant in Day Care (Gross Monthly Income for a Full-Time Worker @ $6.00 an hour: $960)

Expenses	Monthly Total
Day care for 1 child	$ 540.83[a]
Rent	$ 337.53[b]
Health care	$ 93.75[c]
Utilities	$ 60.00[c]
Food	$ 259.00[d]
Clothing	$ 62.00[a]
Transportation	$ 200.00[c]
Entertainment	$ 50.00[c]
Sundry items (e.g., soap, cleaners, repairs, sheets, blankets, etc.)	$ 100.00[c]
Total approximate cost	$1,703.11[c]
Monthly deficit between income and budget	-$ 743.11[c]

a. Child care costs are calculated based on the average of the most and least expensive cities for child care according to the Runzheimer International survey of childcare costs. Retrieved September 2004 from www.runzheimer.com/corpc/news/scripts/012004.asp.

b. Rent was calculated on the basis of the average of HUD-determined fair market rents in the lowest-cost metropolitan areas in a state. The average rent of all these states totaled $450.00. See Department of Housing and Urban Development (2003), "Fair Market Rents for the Housing Choice Voucher Program and Moderate Rehabilitation Single Room Occupancy Program Fiscal Year 2004," *Federal Register, 68*(190). Retrieved August 2004 from www.huduser.org/datasets/fmr.html.

c. This amount was based on figures provided in John E. Schwartz and Thomas J. Volgy, "A Cruel Hoax Upon the Poor," *The San Diego Union Tribune,* November 9, 1992, p. 5.

d. The amount for food is based on the maximum Food Stamp allocation that this mother would receive in 2004 if she had no countable income.

$6.00 an hour (85 cents an hour above the minimum wage).

Work at or slightly above the minimum wage is problematic, limiting the economic choices for the unskilled female household head. Moreover, the National Commission on Children estimates that the typical family spends about $6,000 annually on expenses associated with raising a child. This would mean that, excluding a mother's personal expenses, having two children requires a minimum income of $12,000 per year. According to the National Commission on Children, "If a single mother with two children moved from welfare to a full-time, minimum wage job in 1991, her net income would have increased by only about $50 per week."[129] The stagnancy of the minimum wage combined with the effects of inflation to make a single mother's plight even more dire in 2004. In short, neither welfare nor low-income work provides single female-headed households with viable economic choices.

Indeed, single-mother families in the United States fare worse than their counterparts in many European industrial nations. In a study of the relative economic well-being of single-mother families in eight nations, Yin-Ling Wong, Irwin Garfinkel, and Sara McLanahan found that compared with two-parent families, single mothers in the United States are considerably worse off financially than single mothers in the eight countries surveyed. The United States ranked last, surpassed by Canada, Australia, France, Germany, Norway, Sweden, and the United Kingdom.[130]

Inequities in **public transfer programs** also exacerbate the economic problems of low-income women. For example, Social Security and public assistance are often the only viable options for women, and about 8 out of 10 poor, female-headed families rely on public cash transfers through public welfare programs.[131] Although median transfers to women are lower than to men, they constitute a higher share of the recipients' total income: about one-third for female-headed households as compared with one-tenth for male-headed households. Moreover, Social Security is often the only source of income for elderly women. Like other public transfer programs, Social Security is riddled with pitfalls. In large part, many problems with Social Security are based on the assumptions that all families are nuclear and that families with young children need more per capita income than aged couples or single individuals. Some of the inequities in Social Security include:

- Because women's wages are lower than men's, their retirement benefits are also lower.
- Married female workers fare better on Social Security than single women. Married individuals who never worked can benefit from Social Security payments made by a spouse.
- Couples in which one worker earned most of the wages may fare better than couples in which the husband and wife earned equal wages.
- Homemakers are not covered on their own unless they held a job in the past. Widows do not qualify for benefits unless they are 60 years old or have a minor in the house.
- Regardless of the length of the marriage, divorced women are entitled to only one-half of their ex-husband's benefits. If this partial payment is the divorced woman's only income, it is usually inadequate. Furthermore, divorced women must have been married to the beneficiary of Social Security for at least 10 years to qualify for his benefits.
- Because of child care responsibilities, women typically spend less time in the workforce than men and their benefits are usually lower.[132]

As a result of the Social Security amendments of 1983, several sex-based qualifications were eliminated: Divorced persons can qualify for benefits at age 62 (even if the ex-spouse has not yet claimed benefits), and divorced husbands can claim benefits based on the earnings records of their ex-wives.[133] Although these changes are important, they have led to only minor improvements in the system. Other reforms under discussion include an earnings-sharing option that would equally divide a couple's income between husband and wife (thereby eliminating the category of a primary wage earner and a dependent spouse) and a double-decker option in which everyone would be eligible for basic benefits regardless of whether they contributed to the system (individuals who contributed to the paid labor force would receive a higher benefit).

Women and Work

Myths abound in attempting to explain why women consistently earn less than men:[134]

Myth 1. A working mother's wages are not necessary to her family's survival; her job is a secondary activity that usually ceases with marriage or childbirth.

Fact. Most families require two paychecks to maintain the same standard of living as their parents. Twenty percent of working mothers are heads of households; two out of three working mothers report that they cannot decrease their working hours because of economic need. According to a 2004 AFL-CIO study, three in ten working women reported making all or almost all of their families' incomes. Three in five earned half or more of their families income.[135] The only families that realized an increase in their real incomes and living standards in the last two decades were ones with two college-educated working parents. And three-fourths of these gains came not from higher wages, but from the longer hours women added to the labor force.[136]

Myth 2. A working mother is unreliable, because her family is her primary concern.

Fact. Although some working mothers choose the "mommy track" (work affording flexible and/or shorter hours), others are forced into it by a lack of affordable quality day care. (Parenthetically, many men would choose the family as their first priority if they were forced to make the decision. However, they are usually not asked to make that choice.) Seventy-five percent of mothers return to work within a year after childbirth. Even without family assistance programs, most working mothers continue to maintain employment.

Myth 3. Large numbers of working women leave the workforce to return home to raise their children.

Fact. Statistics show an opposite trend. In 1978 mothers of infants had a labor force participation rate of 35.7 percent; by 2003 it had risen to 53.7 percent.[137] The choice of mothers to become full-time homemakers is the exception, not the rule (see Figure 4.3).

Myth 4. The cost to business of providing benefits to working mothers is prohibitive. Small businesses cannot afford to provide benefits and services such as child care, maternity leave, and flextime. For large businesses, such costs decrease their international competitiveness.

Fact. Family assistance programs raise productivity, increase worker loyalty, decrease turnover, and curb absenteeism costs. The majority of employers report no change in costs owing to family leave legislation.[138] In an AFL-CIO study, 64 percent of working women reported having no control over their work hours; 79 percent lacked child care benefits.[139]

Myth 5. Women are doing better economically. In fact, they are rapidly closing the wage gap and are forging ahead of men.

Fact. In 1979 women earned 64 percent of a male wage; by 1993 it was 71 percent; and by 1999, 77 percent. By 2004 the trend was slightly reversed and the wage differential had risen to

There were 112 million women age 16 and over in the United States in 2002. Of that 112 million, a record 67 million were in the civilian labor force. In 2002, the Bureau of Labor Statistics noted that 63 million women were working, 75 percent full time and 25 percent part time. Nearly sixty percent of women age 16 and over were in the labor force. Women between the ages of 20 and 54 had labor force participation rates of at least 72 percent. Over half of teenage women ages 16–19 were labor force participants. In 1990, nearly 40 percent of the 56.6 million workers in the United States were mothers, an increase of 4.4 million since 1980. Women's labor force participation grew from almost 38 percent in 1960 to 48 percent in 1995, a rise that accounted for 60 percent of the total growth in the workforce. Almost 72 percent of mothers with children under 18 worked in 2002, compared with 56.6 percent in 1980. When broken down, almost 60 percent of women with children under age three were in the labor force in 2002. Of the total female labor force, nearly 62.5 percent were married. African American women are more than three times as likely to be single heads of families than White women, those with children under 18 have the same labor force participation as their White counterparts.

In 1999, Black women had a participation rate of 64.8 percent, while white women participated 66.8 percent and Hispanics at 69.1 percent. There were 3.4 million women who were multiple job holders compared to 4.2 million men.

Figure 4.3

Who Is in the Work Force?

Source: U.S. Department of Labor, Bureau of Labor Statistics, *Women in the Labor Force: A Databook*, 2004. Retrieved October 2004 from www.bls.gov/cps/wlf-databook.pdf.

76 percent. Not only are their wages lower, but one-quarter to one-third of working women also lack basic benefits. Four in 10 working women work evenings, nights or weekends on a regular basis, and one-third work shifts different than their spouses or partners. Thirty-one percent of working women have no sick leave and 34 percent do not have access to these benefits through their employers.[140]

Income and Job Disparities between Men and Women

Some of the income disparity between men and women can be traced to **occupational segregation.** Occupations such as cashier, receptionist, and home health aides are traditional female jobs in which 75 percent or more of the workers are women. But they are also typically among the lowest paying jobs. And although women have gained ground in acquiring more managerial and professional positions, the clerical and teaching fields are still among the most likely female occupations.

There are about 100 employment categories in which women's participation is slight. For example, fewer than 25 percent of truck drivers, geologists, aircraft engine mechanics, airplane pilots and navigators, firefighters, and automobile mechanics are women. In 2002, the largest category of women workers were teachers (5.6 million, excluding those in colleges and universities), and women secretaries numbered 3 million.[141]

About half of all working women are in occupations in which 80 percent of coworkers are women.[142] In fact, 98.6 percent of secretaries are women, 92.7 percent of bookkeepers, 93 percent of nurses, and 78.5 percent of administrative/clerical staff. Between 1988 and 2002, the number of women in nontraditional jobs remained relatively unchanged at around 3 percent of the total number of employed workers. In 2003 women still made up only 3.4 percent of firefighters; 18.3 percent of state and local police officers; 2.4 percent of construction workers; 11.8 percent of college presidents; and 3 to 5 percent of senior-level management positions in corporations.[143]

The women with the highest earnings in 1999 were those employed as pharmacists, lawyers, electrical engineers, computer system analysts, teachers in colleges and universities, and physical thera-

Table 4.5

Salary Survey, 1996

	Women	Men	Average
Accounting auditor	$ 28,340	$ 37,648	$ 32,032
Advertising CEO	100,800	126,800	123,160
Art director	45,600	50,700	48,609
Computer systems analyst	39,572	45,760	43,992
Computer operator	19,084	26,000	21,268
College dean of arts and sci.	106,428	104,030	106,088
College prof., pub. inst.	56,050	63,000	62,000
Teacher, secondary school	34,528	37,856	35,880
Engineering, 10–14 yrs exp.	64,108	63,520	64,000
Engineering, 3–4 yrs exp	44,000	45,577	45,000
Financial serv. salesperson	26,936	48,932	37,366
Food serv. supervisor	15,288	19,344	16,848
Medicine health manager	30,212	44,200	32,396
Insurance sales person	30,160	36,660	31,772
General counsel	291,096	304,658	297,877
Attorney	84,200	89,500	88,862
Lawyer (overall)	47,684	64,324	58,032
Orthopedic surgeon	222,478	298,444	292,000
Internist	119,258	138,240	133,581
Psychiatrist	115,297	143,739	132,929
Family practitioner	109,000	125,333	122,000
Registered nurse	35,360	36,868	35,464
Pharmacist, chain	56,577	56,844	56,776
Real estate salesperson	24,908	37,960	30,836
Retail/personal sales	12,584	19,032	14,712
Executive travel services	30,800	38,600	32,500
Front-line travel agent	22,000	27,200	22,700
Mixed animal vet	35,500	40,900	39,700

Source: Based on data from Bureau of Labor Statistics and *Working Woman,* "Working Woman's 1996 Salary Survey."

pists. In the 20 leading occupations of employed women in 1998, the ratio of women's to men's earnings was highest in the category of registered nurses (94.8 percent) and lowest in Managers and Administrators (66.9 percent). When women work in the same occupations as men, they usually earn less. And women's wages lag behind men's even in female-dominated professions (see Tables 4.5, 4.6, and 4.7). In 2002 male computer system analysts earned $1,172 weekly compared to $962 for women. Even women therapists, who outnumber men three to one, have average weekly earnings of $832 compared to $879 for men.[144] Moreover, female attorneys earn at only 63 percent of the level of their male counterparts (and comprised only 12 percent of law firm partners in 1993); female sales representatives earn between 62 and 72 cents of every dollar earned by a male in the same position; and female social workers earn only 73 cents for each dollar earned by a male social worker.[145] Employment and earnings rise with educational attainment for both males and females. As Table 4.5 illustrates, earnings are considerably lower for females with the same education as males in most professions.[146]

Upward mobility is a key factor in male–female wage discrepancies. In 1995 a 21-member bipartisan Glass Ceiling Commission was created under the Civil Rights Act of 1991. The task of the commission was to study ways to eliminate barriers to advancement by minorities and women. Its recommendations included the enforcement of existing antidiscrimination laws and suggestions that businesses should more actively use affirmative action policies, that they should initiate work/life and family-friendly policies, and that CEOs should demonstrate greater commitment to the process of equal opportunity.[147]

The commission reported that 97 percent of senior managers of Fortune 1000 and Fortune 500 companies were white and that 95 to 97 percent were male. They also found that if women or minorities did achieve top jobs, they did not receive the same paycheck.[148] *Catalyst* looked at proxy statements from each Fortune 500 company. What they found was that the highest-paid female corporate executives earned 68 cents of every dollar earned by the highest-paid men.

Catalyst later found that in 1999 women represented 12 percent of corporate officers in the 500 largest U.S. companies, a 37 percent increase since 1995. Despite this, men still hold 93 percent of the high-profile jobs with profit-and-loss responsibility. Many women in executive or management level positions are in "staff" positions such as human resources or public relations.[149] And women still hold only 1 in 10 board seats. As such, women must break through two separate glass ceilings: getting into top executive positions and receiving salaries in those

Table 4.6

Median Weekly Earnings, Selected Traditionally Female Occupations, 2003

Occupation	Earnings: Women	Earnings: Men
Registered nurses	$870	$957
Elementary school teachers	750	836
Cashiers	307	324
General office clerks	474	521
Health aides, except nursing	367	380

Source: U.S. Department of Labor, Bureau of Labor Statistics, *Highlights of Women's Earnings: 2002, 2003.* Retrieved September 2004 from www.bls.gov/cps/cpswom2002.pdf.

Table 4.7

Median Income of Persons, by Educational Attainment and Sex, Year-Round, Full-Time Workers, 2003

Level of Education	Women	Men
9th to 12th grade (no diploma)	$ 9,299	$16,029
High school graduate	15,440	28,037
Some college, no degree	17,011	29,035
Associate degree	22,524	36,546
Bachelor's degree or more	31,170	49,074

Source: U.S. Census Bureau, *Educational Attainment in the United States, 2003.* Retrieved August 2004 from www.census.gov/prod/2004pubs/p20–550.pdf.

positions that are commensurate with their male counterparts.[150]

Many women face extraordinary challenges in finding and securing adequate employment for fair wages. Some of the obstacles faced by working women include the difficulty of finding high-quality and affordable day care, the existence of limited family leave policies, inflexible working conditions, inadequate health insurance, and problems of sexual harassment.

Day Care: A Barrier to Female Employment

A major barrier to female employment involves day care and subsidized child care leaves. Child care is a necessity for most working families. A 1982 Census Bureau survey found that 45 percent of single mothers would seek employment if affordable quality child care were made available. But infant and toddler care is more expensive than care for preschoolers, and care provided in a center is more expensive than family day care.

Only 12 percent of women with children under age six were in the workforce in 1947; by 2004 that number rose to 63 percent.[151] A Census Bureau survey found that 35 percent of children under age five of full-time employed mothers and 23 percent of children under age five of part-time employed mothers were cared for in organized day care settings.[152] A study by the Institute of Applied Research found that because of the lack of accessible and affordable child care, only 25 percent of low-income working mothers left their children in an organized child care setting.[153] On the other hand, a study by the U.S. Department of Health and Human Services found that more than two-thirds of low-income parents reported that they had no problems in finding child care centers.[154]

The availability of day care has increased rapidly, both in the number of vacancies and in the number of available day care centers. In the early 1990s there were three times as many child care centers as in the mid-1970s, and four times as many children were enrolled in such programs.[155] In 1996 the Children's Foundation reported that there were more than 93,000 regulated day care centers in the United States offering 5.3 million slots. Of that number, approximately 4.2 million were for preschool-aged children and 1.1 million were for school-aged children. The study also found that on average, 88 percent of the available spaces in day care centers were filled.[156]

In a given city, child care can cost between $3,600 and $12,500 a year. According to the Runzheimer International research group, the monthly cost of full-time child care ranges from under $400 a month to more than $1,000 per month, depending on the city. This expenditure can put a severe financial strain on both single- and two-parent families. As shown in Table 4.8, a single mother in New York earning $6.00 an hour would have to spend her entire salary just to pay for day care for one child.

First instituted in the 1970s, the Title XX Social Services Block Grant program is the largest federal program for child care services. In 1990 the U.S. Congress passed additional legislation that in-

Table 4.8

Cities with the Most and Least Expensive Monthly Child Care Costs, 2003

Most Expensive Cities	
New York, NY	$1,058
Boston, MA	977
Manchester, NH	799
Washington, DC	773
New London, CT	748
Portland, OR	737
Milwaukee, WI	674
San Francisco, CA	665
Chicago, IL	657
Least Expensive Cities	
Baton Rouge, LA	339.44
Mobile, AL	346.67
Winter Haven, FL	347.00
Jackson, MS	362.92
Macon, GA	364.00
Billings, MT	373.33
New Orleans, LA	374.11
Jacksonville, FL	375.56
Casper, WY	376.00
Little Rock, AR	379.00

Source: Based on data from Runzheimer International. Retrieved October 2004 from www.runzheimer.com/corpc/news/scripts/012004.asp.

creased the supply of child care and expanded early childhood education. Through child care and development block grants and amendments to Title IV-A of the Social Security Act, Congress provided new funds to help families with child care costs and to help states improve the quality and supply of child care services.[157]

The lack of subsidized child care leaves poses a major problem for America's working women. Sheila Kammerman reported on a study of working mothers in five industrialized countries—Sweden, East and West Germany, Hungary, and France.[158] In all those countries except West Germany, a higher proportion of women were employed than in the United States. All nations, except the United States, provided a tax-free family allowance that ranged from $300 to $600 yearly. Guaranteed maternity leave (in Sweden the leave also pertains to fathers) ranged from 14 weeks in West Germany to eight months in Sweden. In most places, guaranteed maternity leave also included full pay. Although the 1993 Family and Medical Leave Act (FMLA) allows for maternity leave, it is unpaid maternity leave. The child care system in the United States has two-tiers: Those with adequate incomes can afford first-rate child care or, if they desire, can stay at home; those with low wages are at the mercy of the ebb and flow of funding for publicly supported day care.[159]

Other Obstacles Faced by Working Women

Apart from low wages and difficulties in securing child care, many working mothers also require flexible family leave arrangements. Although 30 states had some form of parental or medical leave law in the past, no such law existed on the national level until 1993. In 1992 former President George Bush vetoed the Family and Medical Leave Act after it had passed the House and Senate for a second time. With the election of President Bill Clinton, the FMLA was rushed through Congress and was signed into law on February 5, 1993.

The FMLA requires public employers, and private employers with 50 or more workers, to offer job-protected family or medical leave for up to 12 weeks to qualifying employees (those who worked for the employer at least 1,250 hours in the previous year) who need to be absent from work for reasons that meet the terms of the law. Reasons include an employee's illness (including maternity-related disability), or the need to care for a newborn or an ill family member. The law does not require employers to provide paid leave, but it does mandate that those who provide health coverage continue to do so during the leave period. If a worker uses the FMLA, they are guaranteed the same or a comparable job upon returning to work. Those who work in firms with fewer than 50 employees are not protected by the FMLA. Because the FMLA only provides unpaid leave, many workers cannot afford to take advantage of it.

Another issue affecting working women is health insurance. Women working in traditionally female occupations (the largest share of working women) have the highest uninsured rate. More than 15 million women of childbearing age in the United States have no public or private medical coverage for maternity care, even though the average cost of having a baby is more than $4,300. Half of all women earning $6.00 an hour or less are without health care, and divorced and separated women are twice as likely to be uninsured as married women. Of the 4 million births each year in the United States, 500,000 are not covered by any health insurance plan. About 5 million women of reproductive age have private insurance policies that do not cover maternity care. Moreover, health insurance frequently does not cover important women's health services, such as family planning, long-term care, reproductive care, elective abortions, and maternity care and childbirth.[160] If women are to participate more fully in the labor force, health care insurance must be available to everyone.

Still another issue affecting working women is sexual harassment, an issue brought to the forefront by Anita Hill in the 1990 Senate confirmation hearing of Supreme Court Justice Clarence Thomas. Sexual harassment is defined as unwelcome sexual behaviors, including jokes, teasing, remarks, questions, and deliberate touching; letters, telephone calls, or materials of a sexual nature; pressure for sexual favors; and sexual assault. Although sexual harassment is against the law (Title VII of the 1964 Civil Rights Act has been interpreted as prohibiting sexual harassment), it remains all too common in the workplace.[161]

Finally, a major obstacle faced by many working women is the inflexibility of work. Because women frequently take on the major responsibility for child care, elder care, and home management, they often forgo educational or training opportunities. To help working women balance family and work responsibilities, options such as flexible hours, job sharing, and part-time work with benefits need to be expanded.

Fighting Back: The Equal Rights Amendment and Comparable Worth

The Nineteenth Amendment to the U.S. Constitution gave women the right to vote in 1920. That, however, did not seem to lessen their economic and social plight, and shortly after winning the vote the Women's Party proposed the first **Equal Rights Amendment (ERA)** to the Constitution. In 1972, Congress passed a newly drafted ERA and set a 1979 date for state ratification. When the ERA had not been ratified by 1978, Congress extended the deadline to June 30, 1982. Despite the endorsement of 450 organizations representing 50 million members, opponents of the ERA were able to defeat the amendment in 1982, just 3 states short of the 38 required for ratification.

The ERA read as follows: "Equality of rights under the law shall not be denied or abridged by the United States or any other State on account of sex. . . . The Congress shall have the power to enforce, by appropriate legislation, the provisions of this article. . . . This amendment shall take effect two years after the date of ratification."[162] Contrary to popular misconceptions, the ERA would not have nullified all laws on the basis of gender; instead, it would have required men and women to be treated equally. Most alimony, child support, and custody laws would not have been invalidated, although laws giving preference to one gender would have been struck down. On the other hand, special restrictions on the property rights of married women would have been invalidated, and wives would have been free to manage their own separate finances and property. Again, contrary to popular myth, the ERA would have affected only public employment; private employment practices would not have been changed.[163]

The battle for women's rights has also been fought around **comparable worth**—the idea that workers should be paid equally for different types of work, if those jobs require the same levels of skill, education, knowledge, training, responsibility, and effort. The desire to equalize incomes through comparable worth is based on the belief that the **dual labor market** has created a situation in which "women's work" (e.g., secretarial work, teaching, social work, nursing, child care) is less highly valued than traditional male occupations.

An illustration of the debate around comparable worth is provided in Table 4.9, which lists average wages for jobs typically occupied by women and men. Although the policy is controversial, 20 states have passed laws making comparable worth a requirement or goal of state employment. Although comparable worth is a good idea in theory, it brings up a difficult question: What criteria should be used to determine the comparability of different jobs? Moreover, some critics have rejected the idea of full-scale enforcement of comparable worth on the grounds that the economic costs would be catastrophic.

In 1963 Congress passed the Equal Pay Act, which required employers to compensate male and female workers equally for performing the same job under the same conditions (not all jobs were covered by the bill). Another protective measure was Title VII of the Civil Rights Act of 1964,

Table 4.9

Comparable Worth and Average Annual Income, 2003

	2003 Average Annual Income
Child care workers	$17,400
Teacher assistants	20,220
Nursing aides	21,050
Hairdressers and cosmetologists	21,810
Preschool teachers	22,190
Home health aides	22,750
Social and human services assistants	25,450
Fitness trainers	30,590
Auto mechanics	33,320
Truck drivers	34,330
Maintenance and repair workers	31,300
Machinists	33,900
Auto body mechanics	35,760

Source: U.S. Department of Labor, Bureau of Labor Statistics, *National Occupational Employment and Wage Estimates, All Occupations,* May 2003. Retrieved October 2004 from http://stats.bls.gov/oes/2003/may/oes_00Al.htm.

which prohibited sex discrimination in employment practices and provided the right of redress in the courts. In 1972, Presidential Executive Order 11375 mandated that employers practicing sex discrimination be prohibited from receiving federal contracts. Title IX of the Educational Amendments of 1972 prohibited discrimination in educational institutions receiving federal funds. Finally, the Equal Credit Act of 1975 prohibited discrimination by lending institutions on the basis of sex or marital status.

Abortion and Women's Rights

Feminists often point to the abortion debate as another area in which women's rights are threatened. Specifically, pro-choice advocates argue that where abortion is concerned, some male legislators and judges have promulgated laws and regulations to control the behavior of women by denying them full reproductive freedom. They argue that the choice of an abortion is a personal matter involving only a woman and her conscience. Antiabortion forces claim that life begins at conception and that, therefore, abortion is murder. Moreover, they point to the 32.5 million legal abortions performed in the United States in 1998, while at the same time pointing to the scarcity of adoptable infants.[164]

In 1973, Sarah Weddington, a young attorney from Austin, Texas, argued *Roe v. Wade* before the U.S. Supreme Court. Though her client had long since relinquished her child for adoption, Weddington argued that a state could not unduly burden a woman's right to choose an abortion by making regulations that prohibited her from carrying out that decision. The Court ruled in favor of Weddington, and abortion was legalized in the United States, thereby nullifying all state laws that made abortion illegal during the first trimester of pregnancy. (Before 1970, four states—New York, Alaska, Hawaii, and Washington—had already made abortion legal contingent upon the agreement of a physician.) Within a decade after *Roe v. Wade,* almost 500 bills were introduced in Congress, most of which sought to restrict abortions through a constitutional amendment outlawing abortion, by transferring the power to regulate abortion decisions to the states, or by limiting federal funding of abortions.[165]

Abortion has been marked by several key issues: (1) clinic access, (2) fetus viability testing, (3) parental consent for minors, (4) waiting periods, (5) insurance regulations, (6) public funding, and (7) partial birth abortions (abortions beyond the first trimester). The abortion debate has also been marked by Byzantine maneuvers and complex twists. In 1977 the Hyde Amendment prohibited the federal government from funding abortions except to save the life of a mother. Also in 1977 the federal government lifted its ban on funding abortions for promptly reported cases of rape and incest and in cases where severe and long-lasting harm would be caused to a woman by childbirth. The 1980 Supreme Court decision in *Harris v. McRae* upheld the constitutionality of the Hyde Amendment. In 1981 the government again reversed its position, this time cutting federal funding of abortions except to save the life of the mother. By 1990 federal funds paid for only 165 abortions, a dramatic drop from the almost 300,000 federally funded abortions in 1977.[166] In 1994, the Freedom of Access to Clinic Entrances Act was signed into law. This bill expanded the civil liberty of persons to have unobstructed access to any abortion or reproductive health services clinic. Any person or group that interferes with the right of such persons is subject to legal penalties, which range from a high fine to imprisonment. While 80 percent of non-hospital facilities that provide abortions reported picketing in 2000, the percentage that received bomb threats dropped to 15 percent compared to 48 percent in 1985.[167]

The strategy of the antiabortion movement has been to whittle away at *Roe v. Wade* by attempting to restrict abortions on the state level. For example, in Akron, Ohio, rules were promulgated that required a minor to receive parental consent for an abortion and that imposed a one-day moratorium between a woman's signing the consent form and the actual performance of the abortion. In a 1989 landmark decision, the Supreme Court upheld a Missouri law that prohibited public hospitals and public employees from performing an abortion (except to save the life of the mother), required physicians to determine whether a woman who is at least 20 weeks pregnant is carrying a fetus able to survive outside the womb, and declared that life starts at conception. In 1991 the Court ruled in *Rust v. Sullivan* that the United States can prohibit federally financed family planning programs from giving out abortion information (i.e., the gag rule). On former President Clinton's second day in office, he signed a bill overturning this "gag rule"; on the same day, in another blow to antiabortion advocates, he overturned the federal ban on using fetal tissue matter gained from abortions in scientific experiments.

Partial birth abortion is a common term for the Intact Dilation and Extraction (D&X) procedure. After former President Clinton vetoed a bill banning partial abortion twice, George W. Bush signed the ban into law in November 2003. Proponents of this ban believe that the procedure is gruesome, and is not medically necessary to save the life of the mother. Opponents of the ban believe that it is about abortion politics, not a true effort to limit late-term abortions. They argue that this legislation compromises women's health and limits a physician's ability to determine the appropriate abortion method for a patient. What many people did not realize was that the ban prohibited women from having an abortion after the first trimester. Unfortunately, many birth defects cannot be detected until well into the second trimester, and oftentimes if a birth defect is found, women choose to have an abortion after their 18–20-week ultrasound.[168] Pro-choice groups are currently attempting to overturn the law by having it declared unconstitutional.

The abortion rate in the United States decreased by 11 percent from 1994 to 2000. A substantial proportion of this decline was due to the use of emergency contraception. This decline, however, was not shared equally among all groups, and abortion rates increased among economically disadvantaged women. In 2000, 21 out of every 1,000 women of reproductive age had an abortion. Women aged 18–29, unmarried, black or Hispanic, or economically disadvantaged had higher abortion rates. The overall decline in abortions was greatest for 15- to 17-year-olds, women in the highest income category, those with college degrees, and those with no religious affiliation. Abortion rates for women with incomes below 200 percent of poverty and for women with Medicaid coverage increased between 1994 and 2000.[169]

Since 1973, abortion has proved to be one of the most divisive issues in American public life. The public itself is ambivalent. According to a 2000 Gallup poll, 51 percent of American adults believe that abortions should be legal under some circumstances; 28 percent believe that they should be legal under all circumstances; and 19 percent believe they should be illegal, even to save the life of the mother. The same poll revealed that 50 percent of adults identified themselves as pro-choice and 40 percent as pro-life. Other polls directly contradict the 2000 Gallup poll.[170]

Gays and Lesbians: Two Populations at Risk

In today's culture wars one of the most intense controversies surrounds the issue of whether homosexuality is an acceptable lifestyle and, if so, whether those who are openly gay and lesbian should enjoy protected minority status under civil rights laws. Only 40 years ago, few in public or religious sectors even dared to raise the possibility that it might be acceptable to be openly gay in the United States. For example, in 1960, all 50 states maintained laws criminalizing sodomy by consenting adults. In 1970, 84 percent of respondents to a national Gallup poll agreed that homosexuality was "social corruption that can cause the downfall of a civilization." Two-thirds of those polled thought homosexuals should not be allowed to work as schoolteachers, church pastors, or even government employees.

In recent decades there has been a slow but dramatic shifts in public attitudes toward homosexuality. After years of concerted pressure by gay activists, in 1993 the American Psychiatric Association removed homosexuality from its *DSM-III* list of "objective disorders" and declared it "a normal, if divergent lifestyle." Throughout the 1970s and 1980s, laws forbidding sodomy were repealed in state after state. Although the United States has no federal law protecting against discrimination in employment by private sector employers based on sexual orientation, 14 states, the District of Columbia, and over 140 cities and counties have enacted such bans. As of July 2003, the states banning sexual orientation discrimination in private sector employment are California, Connecticut, Hawaii, Maryland, Massachusetts, Minnesota, Nevada, New Hampshire, New Jersey, New Mexico, New York, Rhode Island, Vermont, and Wisconsin. Many of these laws also ban discrimination in other contexts, such as housing or public accommodation.[171] By 2004, 35 states had rescinded laws that criminalized consensual sodomy. In a crucial decision the U.S. Supreme Court invalidated the Texas sodomy law in 2003, holding private consensual sexual conduct to be constitutionally protected. Some 75 percent of Americans polled nationwide in the early 1990s felt that homosexuals should not be discriminated against in employment, housing, or public accommodations.[172] These policies and polls reflect a significant shift in public opinion about homosexuality.

Despite these limited successes, many homosexuals continue to be forced to live in the closet, concealing their sexual orientation in order to survive in a hostile world. Often the objects of ridicule, homosexuals have been denied housing and employment, harassed on the job, assaulted, and even killed because of their sexual orientation. In many states, homosexuality is still considered a criminal or felony offense, and in some of these states the police systematically raid homosexual bars and randomly arrest the patrons. For instance:

- Students describing themselves as lesbian, gay, bisexual, or transgendered are five times more likely to miss school because of feeling unsafe—28 percent are forced to drop out.
- The vast majority of victims of anti-lesbian/gay violence—possibly more than 80 percent—never report the incident because they fear being "outed."
- Eighty-five percent of teachers oppose integrating lesbian, gay, and bisexual themes in their curricula.
- Due to discrimination, lesbians earn up to 14 percent less than their heterosexual female peers with similar jobs, education, age, and residence.
- Forty-two percent of homeless youth identify as lesbian, gay, or bisexual.
- More than 84 percent of Americans oppose employment discrimination on the basis of sexual orientation.
- Seventy-five percent of people committing hate crimes are under age 30—one in three are under 18—and some of the most pervasive anti-gay violence occurs in schools.
- Lesbian and gay youth are at a four times higher risk for suicide than their straight peers.
- A survey of employers found that 18 percent would fire, 27 percent would not hire and 26 percent would refuse to promote a person perceived to be lesbian, gay, or bisexual.[173]

Represented in all occupations and socioeconomic strata, gays and lesbians make up anywhere from 1 to 10 percent of the population.[174] (Recent research suggests the percentage may be closer to 4.9 percent of men and 4.1 percent of women.[175]) Similar to Asian Americans, discrimination against gays and lesbians is not always reflected in income. For example, male homosexuals have per capita incomes ranging from $38,000 to $42,000, versus about $12,300 for heterosexuals.[176] According to one market analyst, "America's gay and lesbian community is emerging as one of the nation's most educated and affluent, and Madison Avenue is beginning to explore the potential for a market that may be worth hundreds of billions of dollars. . . . It's a market that screams opportunity."[177]

Violence against Gays and Lesbians

In his 1999 State of the Union address, former President Clinton referred to the murder of Matthew Shepard: "We saw a young man murdered in Wyoming just because he was gay."[178] The total number of anti-LGBT (lesbian, gay, bisexual, and transgendered) incidents was 2,051 in 2003 and 27 percent of victims suffered some level of injury. Sixty-one percent of victims were male and 34 percent female.[179]

Gay Rights

When gays and lesbians have demanded equal rights under the law, the result has been mixed—and generally negative. During the 1970s, Miami gays tried to pass a civil rights amendment that would have prevented discrimination based on sexual orientation. This referendum failed, and similar efforts were defeated in St. Paul and other cities. In 1986, Houston voters defeated two gay rights proposals, one calling for an end to discrimination in city employment practices based on sexual orientation, the other calling for an end to the maintenance of sexual orientation data in city employment records. In Tampa, Florida, and in Portland, Maine, voters overturned city ordinances protecting gays and lesbians.[180] By the late 1990s there were 13 states with anti-discrimination laws. While all of these laws protect at least lesbian and gay employees, some go further. In addition, municipalities across the country have also adopted civil rights ordinances to cover lesbians and gay men in areas such as employment, public accommodations, housing, and credit.[181]

For almost 20 years the Supreme Court refused to hear cases concerning gay rights, but in 1985 it heard *Oklahoma City Board of Education v. The National Gay Task Force*. In this case the Supreme Court ruled that public schoolteachers cannot be forbidden to advocate homosexuality (e.g., by way of public demonstrations), but they can be prohibited from engaging in homosexual acts in public. In 1988 the Supreme Court ruled that the Central Intelligence Agency could not dismiss a homosexual without a reason for justifying the dismissal. In 1992 Colorado voters passed a referendum (Amendment 2), which would have prevented any law banning discrimination against gays. This amendment would have nullified gay rights laws that already existed in Aspen, Denver, and Boulder. On May 20, 1996, the U.S. Supreme Court ruled that Colorado's Amendment 2 was unconstitutional. On the other hand, the Supreme Court has refused to rule on whether homosexuals have equal protection under the Fourteenth Amendment of the U.S. Constitution, including the right to serve in the military.

Gays and Lesbians in the Military

The United States armed forces have generally not tolerated homosexuality in their ranks. Draft board physicians in 1940 were ordered to screen out homosexuals on the basis of such characteristics as a man's lisp or a woman's deep voice. These instructions were often overlooked, because World War II created a desperate need for soldiers. After the war, however, gay and lesbian military personnel were discharged, and exclusionary policies were again enforced. A similar situation occurred during the Vietnam War; once the conflict ended, gays and lesbians were again persecuted and their careers terminated.[182] The policy of the U.S. armed forces that excludes gays and lesbians from military service reads as follows: "Homosexuality is incompatible with military service. The presence in the military environment of persons who engage in homosexual conduct or who, by their statements, demonstrate a propensity to engage in homosexual conduct, seriously impairs the accomplishment of the military mission."[183] Those who admit to homosexuality at the time of enlistment are rejected; if homosexuality comes to light later on, the individual is separated. Although more liberal policies were put into effect during the 1970s and 1980s, they were directed at the type of separation, not at the morality of the separation itself.[184]

One of the principal justifications for excluding gays and lesbians from military service has been their supposed vulnerability to blackmail by enemy agents threatening to expose their secret. The Defense Department conducted at least three separate studies to justify this belief, but no findings supported the exclusionary policy.[185] In fact, the Personnel Security Research and Education Center of the Defense Department conducted an examination of the homosexual exclusion policy and found no evidence that gays and lesbians disrupt any branch of the military; instead, its report praised their dedication and superior performance.[186] Support for homosexuals in the military came from other sources, including conservative former senator Barry Goldwater, who argued that "you don't need to be straight to fight and die for your country, you just need to shoot straight."[187] By the 1990s the argument against gays and lesbians serving in the armed forces changed. The "unit cohesion" argument was developed, which predicts a breakdown of the social bonds necessary for accomplishing a military mission if combat groups include a homosexual. The underlying belief is that heterosexuals will place the good of their unit first, except when it comes to working with gay people. In that case, they cannot or are unwilling to set aside their personal prejudices.[188]

The U.S. military's policy of excluding homosexuals has far-reaching consequences. First, it adversely affects the career prospects of uniformed gays and lesbians. Second, people discharged from military service without an honorable discharge may have difficulty finding employment and may be ineligible to obtain benefits associated with military service. Even an honorable discharge given on the grounds of homosexual conduct carries grave consequences for the future of ex-servicepeople.

One campaign promise of former president Bill Clinton was to end discrimination against homosexuals in the military. As one of his first official acts, Clinton signed an order that prohibited military recruiters from inquiring about the sexual orientation of potential recruits. Shortly afterward, he proposed wide-ranging reforms aimed at ensuring equal rights for gays and lesbians serving in the military. Proponents of the plans argued that discrimination against homosexuals in the military was no different from the discrimination practiced against African American soldiers in World Wars I and II. For these activists, discrimination in the military was a civil rights issue. Critics, on the other hand, argued that homosexuality was a lifestyle choice rather than a factor of birth such as skin color. Facing criticism from the Joint Chiefs of Staff and many influential members of Congress, Clinton retreated from his earlier position and instead supported a "don't ask, don't tell, don't pursue, and don't harass" policy that prohibited the military from asking questions as long as a homosexuals behaved discreetly. However, under this rule servicepeople can be discharged if they state they are gay, lesbian, or bisexual or make a statement that indicates a propensity to engage in a homosexual act.

By the end of 2003, 9682 service members were discharged from the military under the "don't ask, don't tell" policy. A 1999 report by the Servicemembers Legal Defense Network (SLDN), a gay rights group, noted that in the first five years of the "don't ask, don't tell" policy, there was a 92 percent increase in gay-related discharges. According to the military, these were the result of service persons' voluntarily "outing" themselves. The SLDN notes, however, that these "voluntary statements" include statements made in confidential settings such as counseling sessions, court testimony, and personal diaries. The SLDN report claims that many discharges are the result of coercion that circumvents the "don't ask, don't tell" policy.[189] An additional concern is violence directed toward gays in the military. In 1999 Pfc. Barry Winchell was murdered by soldiers on a Kentucky army base. The accused soldiers admitted that their motivation involved Winchell's sexual orientation. That murder spurred on the military to more proactively protect lesbian and gay service members. The two most significant outcomes of the Winchell murder was the addition of the "don't harass" prong, and the second was the Pentagon's adoption of an anti-harassment action plan.[190]

The ban on gays and lesbians serving in the military puts the United States among interesting company. Countries which allow gays and lesbians to serve in the military include Australia, Austria, Bahamas, Belgium, Britain, Canada, the Czech Republic, Denmark, Estonia, Finland, France, Ireland, Israel, Italy, Lithuania, Luxembourg, the Netherlands, New Zealand, Norway, Slovenia, South Africa, Spain, Sweden, and Switzerland. In addition to the United States, countries which ban gay military service include Argentina, Belarus, Brazil, Croatia, Greece, Poland, Peru, Portugal, Russia, Turkey, and Venezuela. The list does not include countries in which homosexuality is banned outright, such as several Middle East nations.[191]

Gay and Lesbian Family Life

African Americans were not permitted to marry in many parts of the United States until after the civil war, and mixed race couples could not marry in many states until a 1967 Supreme Court decision made it legal. A long-standing issue for gays and lesbians has been the recognition of gay unions. In 2001, the Netherlands became the first country to recognize same-sex marriages (SSM). Belgium followed suit, and by late 2004 six Canadian provinces and Massachusetts allowed SSMs. Denmark, Norway, Sweden, Finland, Greenland, Iceland, Germany, France, and Vermont allow same-sex couples to enter into legal partnerships, and although they have many of the benefits and protections of civil marriage, they are not legally married. While same-sex couples were able to obtain marriage licenses in San Francisco, and in various towns in New Mexico and New York for short intervals during 2004, none were able to register their marriages. Conversely, 38 states had enacted legislation banning SSMs by late 2004.

- Three states (Alaska, Nebraska, and Nevada) have amended their state constitutions to ban SSM.
- Four states (Maryland, Oregon, Wisconsin, and Wyoming) have marriage laws that specifically prohibit SSM.
- Five states (Connecticut, New Jersey, New Mexico, New York, and Rhode Island) and Washington, D.C., do not explicitly prohibit SSM.
- Only Massachusetts allows SSM, but only to residents of the state.[192]

By 1996 the question of gay marriages had become an issue, because it appeared that Hawaii might soon recognize such marriages. Other states were concerned that a same-sex couple could relocate to a state allowing such unions, fulfill whatever residency standards are required for marriage, and then move to another state that did not recognize the union. States were quick to react, and by late 1996 one-third of all states had passed legislation prohibiting the recognition of SSMs from another state. The federal government entered the fray by passing the Defense of Marriage Act (DOMA), which effectively established that the only legitimate marriage was with a member of the opposite sex. Ironically, in the same month that Congress passed DOMA, both IBM and the city of Denver extended domestic partnership benefits (e.g., health insurance) to their gay and lesbian employees.

A 1999 decision by the Vermont Supreme Court found no compelling reason to not recognize a civil union for same-sex couples and ruled that they should be granted the same rights and responsibilities as married Vermonters. In 2000, the Vermont

A long-standing issue for gays and lesbians has been the recognition of gay unions.

governor signed into law a "civil union" bill granting Vermont gay and lesbian couples most of the rights and benefits available to married couples under the law.[193] These protections included insurance benefits, inheritance, medical decision-making rights, and state tax benefits and obligations. The one exception was the right to have a same-sex union legally called a marriage. The concept of civil union has been criticized because it creates a separate and thereby unequal set of rights.[194]

In February 2004, San Francisco Mayor Gavin Newsom authorized granting marriage licenses to same-sex couples. In August 2004, the California Supreme Court unanimously struck down San Francisco's attempt to legalize SSMs, saying that Newsom had illegally defied the state law that defines marriage as a union between a man and a woman. The court also ruled that none of the almost 4,000 same-sex couples married in San Francisco were legally married or entitled to the rights of spouses. The court then ordered the city to refund each couple's $82 license fee and $62 fee for the wedding ceremony.[195]

In April 2001, seven Massachusetts gay and lesbian couples filed a lawsuit (*Goodridge et al. v. Department of Public Health*) attempting to obtain the right to marry. In November 2003 the Massachusetts Supreme Judicial Court ruled that the state constitution allowed SSMs and that the state had to issue marriage licenses starting in May 2004. Instead of accepting the ruling, the Massachusetts legislature passed a constitutional amendment overturning the court's decision, prohibiting SSMs but allowing civil unions for gay and lesbian couples. Before becoming effective the amendment must first be passed again by the legislature in 2005 and then voted on in the 2006 general election. The possibility for non-Massachusetts gay and lesbian couples to marry is unclear, since an ancient miscegenation law prevents out-of-state inter-racial couples from coming to Massachusetts to marry.[196]

Prompted by the Massachusetts same-sex marriage victory, the Senate proposed an amendment in 2004 stating that "Marriage in the United States shall consist only of the union of a man and a woman. Neither this Constitution, nor the constitution of any State, shall be construed to require that marriage or the legal incidents thereof be conferred upon any union other than the union of a man and a woman."[197] Although unlikely to pass, this amendment was strongly supported by the Bush administration.

In the 2004 elections, 11 states approved state constitutional amendments banning same-sex marriage. The antigay measures passed in Arkansas, Georgia, Kentucky, Michigan, Mississippi, Montana, North Dakota, Ohio, Oregon, Oklahoma, and Utah. Even though most of the states that passed the anti–gay marriage constitutional amendments already had laws on the books prohibiting same-sex marriage, antigay groups felt that amending the state constitutions would prevent court rulings like the one in Massachusetts.

Voters approved the measures despite vigorous campaigns against them by advocacy groups. The Human Rights Campaign (HRC) alone spent more than $6.5 million nationwide to defeat antigay ballot measures.

The constitutional amendments varied in severity from state to state. The measures in Oregon, Mississippi, and Montana only ban same-sex marriage. The rest also prohibit recognizing civil unions.

Ohio's measure is considered the most repressive. It bans same-sex marriage and civil unions, and denies any legal status to all unmarried couples. It also prohibits two unmarried people from jointly adopting a child. The Ohio measure could also deter private companies and universities from offering domestic partner benefits.[198]

The question of parental rights is linked to the recognition of same-sex unions. Specifically, sexual orientation is often a factor in issues of family law, including custody, visitation, and foster/adoptive parent eligibility. Because homosexuality does not enjoy a constitutionally protected status, it can be considered in legal actions surrounding the rights of parents and would-be parents. In some jurisdictions it effectively blocks adoption and foster care placement. Although most states have no statute explicitly prohibiting gay and lesbian adoption or foster care placement, several states do not permit it.[199]

AIDS and the Gay Community

The AIDS crisis has been used to justify omnipresent homophobic attitudes. In the early days of the epidemic (i.e., the 1980s), there were recommendations for quarantining AIDS victims, renewed attempts at punishing homosexual behavior, increased job discrimination, and a generally hostile climate for both gays and lesbians. At the federal level, former senator Jesse Helms successfully introduced a bill that prevented the Centers for Disease Control from using AIDS education funds in ways that could foster homosexuality. Although in the United States AIDS still predominantly affects gay and bisexual men, intravenous drug users, and African American women, the movement of AIDS into the heterosexual community has fueled a certain sympathy toward the gay population. But positive change has come only after the documentation of more than a million AIDS cases in the United States, resulting in about 500,000 deaths through mid-2002.[200] Robert Walker writes of the early days of the AIDS epidemic:

> This was the time, the early 1980s, when the AIDS epidemic and its costs might have been contained, but effectively raising the alarm entailed serious political risks in all the affected communities—the political, the religious, and the homosexual. Political leaders took their cue from President Reagan's deafening silence, and most national, state, and local public and private institutions dithered through the critical years.[201]

The AIDS crisis has had a devastating effect on the lives of gay men. There are few gays in larger cities who have not lost either a lover or many close friends to the disease. This suffering, combined with AIDS education, has led to the galvanizing of the gay community. Comprehensive medical and support services have been developed in several larger cities, and many members of the gay community are exercising increased caution in the choice of sexual partners and in the sexual act itself. As a result of these measures, there has been a perceptible decrease in the numbers of AIDS cases in some cities. Despite these advances, AIDS remains one of the most significant health problems facing both gay and heterosexual communities.

Homophobia—the irrational fear of homosexuality—is a social phenomenon that has led to numerous attempts to limit the civil rights and legal protections of gays and lesbians. Justifications for this attitude have been found in traditional religious dogma that treats homosexuality as a sin against God, and in psychological explanations that view homosexuality as a disease or symptom of arrested development or a fear of intimacy. Nevertheless, the self-perception of gays and lesbians has undergone a dramatic shift since the 1960s. Gays and lesbians have begun to identify themselves as members of an oppressed minority, similar to other oppressed minority groups. As gays and lesbians have become more visible, they have organized support groups; religious groups such as Dignity (Roman Catholics), Integrity (Episcopalians), Mishpachat Am (Jews), and Lutherans Concerned; social service organizations; subchapters of professional associations; and political action groups. The political power of gays and lesbians had grown to the point that by 1984 activists were successful in inserting a gay civil rights plank in the Democratic Party platform. These changing attitudes have encouraged some political leaders to openly court the gay vote by supporting gay issues. The Clinton administration was the first to endorse gay rights openly (albeit erratically). For example, Clinton's administration backed the Employment Non-Discrimination Act (a gay civil rights bill); appointed more than 100 openly gay and lesbian persons to administrative jobs; nominated the first-ever open lesbian to the U.S. District Court; helped defeat antigay initiatives in Oregon, Maine, and Idaho; mandated that all federal agencies add sexual orientation to their affirmative action policies; stopped the practice of denying security clearance based on sexual orientation; granted political asylum to people at risk of persecution in their home countries based on their sexual orientation; and increased public health spending on AIDS.[202]

Gays and lesbians face discrimination in social and economic areas that is manifested in the absence of gay and lesbian rights in employment and employment benefits, housing, immigration and naturalization, insurance, and custody and adoption.[203] Moreover, some social service agencies refuse to allow foster care in gay or lesbian homes; insurance companies deny workers the right to cover same-sex partners under their health insurance; and gays and lesbians are often refused the right to name their partner as next of kin in medical emergencies.

Ageism

Ageism is a problem in a consumer-oriented society that idolizes youth. Like other minority groups, the aged face significant social and economic barriers. For example, workers over 50 often find it difficult to find equivalent employment if they lose their jobs. The aged in the United States are seldom respected for their wisdom and experience; nor do they occupy elevated social positions protected by tradition. Instead, once they have lost their earning potential, the aged are often perceived as a financial albatross around the neck of an economically productive society. Socially isolated in retirement communities, low-income housing, or other old-age ghettos, the aged often become invisible.

America is getting older—nearly 21 percent of the U.S. population will be 65 or older by 2050, compared with 12 percent in 2004. Largely due to healthier lifestyles and better medical treatment, 5 percent of the country will be 85 or older in 2050, compared with 1.5 percent in 2003. For the first 99 percent of human history, the average life expectancy was approximately 18 years. Over the past 100 years, life expectancy rose from 47 in the year 1900 to 77.2 in 2002.[204] Over the same century, the percentage of the U.S. population over age 65 more than tripled—from 4.1 percent in 1900 to 12.7 percent in 1998. The over-65 population in the United States totaled 35.6 million in 2002.[205]

In addition to the increase in the elderly population, there is an increase in the number of very elderly people, those over age 85. In 2002, more than 4 million of the 35 million elderly were over age 85. It is estimated that by the year 2030, 71.5 million people in the United States will be over age 65, and 9.5 million will be over age 85.[206] This trend will have important consequences for health care costs, because disabilities increase with age. Whereas only about 20 percent of people aged 65 to 74 need help with daily activities such as eating, bathing, and dressing, 52.5 percent of those over age 85 need assistance with daily activities.[207] Similarly, although only a small percentage (4.2 percent) of all elderly people live in nursing homes, these numbers vary dramatically with age. For example, in 1996 only 1.1 percent of people aged 65 to 74 lived in nursing homes, compared with 19.8 percent of those over age 85.[208]

In 2002 more than 57 percent of people over age 65 were women, and among people over 85 there were 2.2 women for every man.[209] The longer life expectancy of women, combined with the tendency of wives to be younger than husbands, means that on average women outlive their husbands by 10 years, a pattern that results in four times as many widows as widowers.[210]

Elderly Poverty and Social Programs

The percentage of seniors living below the poverty line dropped from 35.2 percent in 1960 to less than 12 percent in 2002. Seniors in 2002 received about $22,000 in Social Security benefits and approximately $12,000 in Medicare benefits.[211] Despite the drop in poverty, elderly women had a higher poverty rate (12.4 percent) than men (7.7 percent) in 2002, with half of all single women over age 65 having a yearly income of less than $12,000.[212] In that same year, the median income for men age 65 and over was $19,346 compared to $111,046 for women.[213]

Women tend to work fewer years than men and earn less in their jobs. Hence, on the average, women receive less Social Security benefits than men. In fact, in 1999 the average Social Security benefit for a woman was about $600 per month compared to $800 for a man.[214] Lower economic status and greater longevity means that women are more likely to require public assistance programs as they grow older.

The great majority (84.7 percent) of elderly seniors are white, a disproportionately high ratio due in part to the failure of non-Hispanic populations to obtain adequate medical care. However, this pattern is changing. It is estimated that by the year 2030 African American elders will increase by 265 percent and the population of Hispanic elders will increase by 530 percent. These numbers compare to a relatively low anticipated (97 percent) increase in the number of white elders. Given their lower average incomes, fewer assets, and less access to health insurance programs, it is likely that many minority elderly will require governmental assistance.[215] Clearly, policymakers must calculate the impact of increasing numbers of minority elderly in determining the future funding needs of health and income-based social programs.

Many elderly do not fit the stereotypes of poverty, neglect, and despair so often associated with old age. As such, many are doing well financially and have accumulated considerable wealth and assets. According to one study, "average income and assets for persons over 65 have risen dramatically, from a median per capita income of $3,408 in 1975 to $10,808 in 1993."[216] Controlled for inflation, this rise represented an 18 percent increase in purchasing power.

In 2000, the net worth of elderly households was $108,885 compared to $55,000 for the total population. The largest asset type is home ownership (78 percent of the elderly own their own home), which accounts for 78.5 percent of this net worth. There are major differences in the median net worth of different household types. Elderly married couple households have a median net worth of $173,950 ($57,586 when home equity is excluded).[217]

While representing about 13 percent of the U.S. population, the elderly receive 60 percent of federal social spending. This is four times the amount spent on children and represents higher per capita spending than in Japan or any western European country.[218] Other than the very poor, seniors are the only group with universal health coverage and the only group to receive non-means–tested government assistance. In contrast, younger workers today are less likely to have health insurance or pension benefits than retired seniors.[219]

Health Care and the Elderly

As a group, a substantial number (3.6 million or 10.4 percent) of the elderly lived below the poverty line in 2002. Another 2.2 million or 6.4 percent were classified as "near-poor" (income less than 125 percent of the poverty line). Those living in poverty include a disproportionate number of women and minorities. As Judy Ochoa and Barbara Navarro argue, "In reality, both the stereotype from a few years ago of forgotten elders subsisting on dog food and the present day stereotype of `country club' seniors have some basis in fact, but are only parts of a varied group with varying needs."[220] As the numbers of the very old and the minority elderly increase, we can expect a dramatic increase of seniors who are in financial need.

These trends have important implications for social welfare policy. For one, as the numbers of elderly increase, their demands on society for housing, health, and recreational services will become greater. The stresses put on the health care system by an increasingly aging population are already evident in the near insolvency of Medicare. For example, in 1989 the elderly accounted for 33 percent of all hospital stays and 45 percent of all days of hospital care. The average stay for older people was 8.9 days compared with 5.3 days for persons under 65. The average length of stay for older people has increased 5.3 days since 1968 and 1.8 days since 1980. Although the elderly account for about 13 percent of the population, they account for 36 percent of personal health care expenditures.[221] As more of the population ages in the coming decades, and as the group aged 85 and over grows rapidly, the burden of health care expenses will become even more problematic.

Elderly women live longer than men—in 2002 there were 141 elderly women for every 100 elderly men—yet they have only 58 percent of their income. As such, more of elderly women's health care costs will have to be paid by the government or by their families, putting increasing burdens on both. In addition, as people live longer and require more care—especially in-home care—more pressure will be put on family members to provide or pay for that care. Because families are already stressed by increasing workloads, other family pressures, and the often large geographic distances between children and parents, the state may be pressed to provide even more care for greater numbers of the elderly.

The elderly vote in large numbers, and over the years their voices have been heard more clearly by politicians than those of African Americans and other minorities. In the 1960s policymakers responded to the needs of the elderly by passing the Older Americans Act (OAA) of 1965. The objectives of the OAA included (1) an adequate retirement income that corresponds to the general standard of living; (2) the promotion of good physical and mental health, regardless of economic status; (3) the provision of centrally located, adequate, and affordable housing; (4) the availability of meaningful employment, with the elimination of age-specific and discriminatory employment practices; (5) the provision of civic, cultural, and recreational opportunities; and (6) adequate community services, including low-cost transportation and supported living arrangements.[222]

Despite federal policies and vigorous advocacy by the American Association of Retired Persons (AARP) and other groups, ageism still persists. Negative stereotypes of elderly persons continue to be perpetuated by the media and the film industry. Moreover, the elderly continue to be victimized by crime, abuse by family members, and job discrimination. Perhaps the clearest expression of continuing ageism is seen in employment policies. The 1967 Age Discrimination in Employment Act (ADEA) protected most workers age 40 to 69 from discrimination in hiring, job retention, and promotion. However, for most workers the protection of the ADEA stops when they reach age 70. Legislation to remove the "70 cap" has consistently failed in Congress, as employer lobbies have argued that they require a free hand in personnel policies. Like race, gender, and sexual orientation, age is a social stigma that impacts social and economic justice.

People with Disabilities

People with disabilities are another group that experience the effects of discrimination. About 20 percent of the U.S. population have disabilities that limit their ability to work.[223] (See Tables 4.10 and 4.11.)

Table 4.10

Disabled Persons, Age 21–64

Disability	Percent Employed*
Difficulty hearing	64.4
Difficulty seeing	43.7
Mental disability	41.3
Difficulty walking	33.5

*Persons may have more than one type of disability.

Source: U.S. Census Bureau, *Disabilities Affect One-Fifth of All Americans Proportion Could Increase in Coming Decades* (Washington, DC: U.S. Department of Commerce, Economics, and Statistics Administration, December 1997).

Disability is a difficult term to define. One medical definition is based on the assumption that a disability is a chronic disease requiring various forms of treatment. Another definition derived from the medical model—a definition used as a basis for determining eligibility in the Social Security Disability Insurance program—characterizes people with disabilities as those unable to work (or unable to work as frequently) in the same range of jobs as nondisabled people.[224] People with disabilities are viewed as inherently less productive than other members of society. A third model defines disability based on what those with disabilities cannot do, seeing the disabled in terms of their inability to perform certain functions expected of the able-bodied population. As William Roth maintains, "The functional limitation, economic, and medical models all define disability by what a person is not—the medical model as not healthy, the economic model as not productive, the functional limitation model as not capable."[225]

A newer definition—the psychosocial model—views disability as a socially defined category. In other words, people with disabilities constitute a minority group, and if a person with disabilities is poor, it is because of discrimination rather than personal inadequacy. This definition locates the problem in the interaction between disabled people and the social environment. Therefore, the adjustment to disability is not a personal problem but a social challenge requiring the adjustment of society. This definition requires that society reevaluate its attitudes and remove the physical and transportation barriers placed in the way of people with disabilities. It also requires the elimination of stereotypes. In part, this newer definition of disability was expressed in Section 504 of the Rehabilitation Act of 1973 (PL 93-112).

Although the range of disabilities is large, people with disabilities share a central experience rooted in stigmatization, discrimination, and oppression. Like other stigmatized groups, those with disabilities experience poverty in numbers disproportionately larger than the general population. Perhaps not surprisingly, rates of disability are greatest among the aged, African Americans, the poor, and blue-collar workers.[226] Compared to the able-bodied, people with disabilities tend to be more frequently unemployed and underemployed and, as a consequence, often fall below the poverty line. Because disability is often correlated with poor education, age, and poverty, it is not surprising that African Americans are twice as likely as whites to have some level of disability (their representation is even greater in the fully disabled population), and that more women are disabled than men. The problems of low wages and unemployment are exacerbated because people with disabilities often need more medical and hospital care than others, are less likely to have health insurance, and spend three times more of their own money on medical care than do the able-bodied.[227]

Although discrimination continues to exist, major strides have been made to integrate people with disabilities into the social mainstream. These advances have often resulted from organized political activity on the part of the disabled and their families. For example, an outgrowth of this political activity is Title V of the Rehabilitation Act of 1973, which mandates the following rules for all programs and facilities that receive federal funds:

- Federal agencies must have affirmative action programs designed to hire and promote people with disabilities.
- The Architectural and Transportation Barriers Compliance Board must enforce a 1968 rule mandating that all buildings constructed with federal funds, including buildings owned or leased by federal agencies, be accessible to people with disabilities.
- All businesses, universities, and other institutions having contracts with the federal government must implement affirmative action programs targeted for people with disabilities.
- Discrimination against people with disabilities is prohibited in all public and private institutions receiving federal assistance.

Table 4.11

Characteristics of the Civilian Noninstitutionalized Population by Age, Disability Status, and Type of Disability, 2000

	Number	Percent
Total Population 5 years and over	257,167,527	100.00
With any disability	49,746,248	19.3
Total Population 5 to 15 years	45,133,667	100.00
With any disability	2,614,919	5.8
sensory	442,894	1.0
physical	455,461	1.0
mental	2,078,502	4.6
self-care	419,018	0.9
Total Population 16 to 64 years	178,687,234	100.00
With any disability	33,153,211	18.6
sensory	4,123,902	2.3
physical	11,150,365	6.2
mental	6,764,439	3.8
self-care	3,149,875	1.8
going outside the home	11,414,508	6.4
employment disability	21,287,570	11.9
Population 65 years and over	33,346,626	100.00
With any disability	13,978,118	41.9
sensory	4,738,479	14.2
physical	9,545,680	28.6
mental	3,592,912	10.8
self-care	3,183,840	9.5
going outside the home	6,795,517	20.4

Source: U.S. Census Bureau, *Census 2000, Summary File 3,* July 8, 2004. Retrieved October 2004 from www.census.gov/hhes/www/disable/disabstat2k/table1.html.

The greatest stride was made on July 26, 1990, when former president George Bush signed the Americans with Disabilities Act (ADA) (PL 101-336) into law (see Figure 4.4). This act is the most comprehensive legislation for people with disabilities ever passed in the United States. The ADA lays a foundation of equality for people with disabilities, and it extends to disabled people civil rights similar to those made available on the basis of race, sex, color, national origin, and religion through the Civil Rights Act of 1964. For example, the ADA prohibits discrimination on the basis of disability in private sector employment; in state and local government

I. Employment

A. Employers may not discriminate against an individual with a disability in hiring or promotion if the person is otherwise qualified for the job.

B. Employers can ask about one's ability to perform a job but cannot inquire if someone has a disability; nor can employers subject a person to tests that tend to screen out people with disabilities.

C. Employers must provide "reasonable accommodation" to employees with disabilities. This includes job restructuring and modification of equipment. Employers are not required to provide accommodations that impose an "undue hardship" on business operations.

D. All employers with 15 or more employees must comply with the ADA.

II. Transportation

A. New public transit buses and rail cars must be accessible to individuals with disabilities.

B. Transit authorities must provide comparable para-transit or other special transportation services to individuals with disabilities who cannot use fixed bus services, unless an undue burden would result.

C. Existing rail systems must have one accessible car per train.

D. New bus and train stations must be accessible. Key stations in rapid, light, and commuter rail systems must be made accessible. All existing Amtrak stations must be accessible by July 26, 2010.

III. Public Accommodations

A. Private entities such as restaurants, hotels, and retail stores may not discriminate against individuals with disabilities.

B. Auxiliary aids and services must be provided to individuals with vision or hearing impairments, unless an undue burden would result.

C. If removal is readily achievable, physical barriers in existing facilities must be removed. All new construction and alterations of facilities must be accessible.

IV. State and Local Government

A. State and local governments may not discriminate against individuals with disabilities.

B. All government facilities, services, and communications must be accessible, consistent with the requirements of Section 504 of the Rehabilitation Act of 1973.

V. Telecommunications

A. Companies offering telephone service to the general public must offer telephone relay services to individuals who use telecommunications services for the deaf (TDDs) or similar devices.

Figure 4.4

A Summary of the Americans with Disabilities Act

activities; and in public accommodations and services, including transportation provided by both public and private entities. Some policies of the ADA went into effect immediately, whereas others were to be phased in over several years.[228]

In spite of loopholes, the ADA is an important step forward for disabled people. Nevertheless, some argue that while the ADA is a good law in principle, abuses are stirring up widespread resistance. Specifically, disability is often defined so broadly that virtually anyone with a problem, regardless of its extent, can claim protection under the ADA. Moreover, some people seek to use this protection to excuse incompetence or inappropriateness on the job or in school. On the other hand, any social policy that addresses the widespread needs of a large constituent is inherently vulnerable to abuse.

Despite the ADA and other federal laws, discrimination is still widespread against people with disabilities. For instance, most buildings still do not meet the needs of the physically handicapped in terms of access, exits, restrooms, parking lots, warning systems, and so forth. Many apartment complexes and stores continue to be built without allowing for the needs of people with disabilities. The struggle for full integration remains an ongoing battle.

Legal Attempts to Remedy Discrimination

Attempts to eliminate discrimination are a relatively recent phenomenon. Although the Fourteenth Amendment of the Constitution guaranteed all citizens equal protection under the law, it was also used to perpetuate discrimination on the basis of "separate but equal" treatment. In fact, overt segregation existed in the South until the middle of the twentieth century, and separate but (supposedly) equal public facilities characterized much of the social and economic activity of the United States. The extensive system of Southern segregation included public transportation, schools, private economic activities, and even public drinking fountains. It was only in the mid-1950s that the U.S. Supreme Court overturned the ***Plessy v. Ferguson*** (1896) decision that had formed the basis for the separate but equal doctrine.

Desegregation and the Civil Rights Movement

In a landmark decision on ***Brown v. Board of Education of Topeka, Kansas,*** the U.S. Supreme Court ruled in 1954 that separate but equal facilities in education were inherently unequal. The Court ruled that separating the races was a way of denoting the inferiority of African Americans. In addition, the court ruled that segregation hindered the educational and mental development of black children. Although the Supreme Court ruled against officially sanctioned segregation in public schools, **de facto segregation** was not addressed until the ***Swann v. Charlotte-Mecklenburg Board of Education*** ruling of 1971. This ruling approved court-ordered busing to achieve racial integration of school districts with a history of discrimination.

The gains made by African Americans were won through bitter struggle. Up to the middle 1960s, Southern blacks enjoyed few rights, with total segregation enforced in almost all spheres of social, economic, political, and public life. Segregation in the North occurred through de facto, or unofficial, rather than de jure, or legal means, although the net effect was almost the same.

In 1955 Rosa Parks, too tired to stand in the "colored" section in the back of a bus in Montgomery, Alabama, sparked a nonviolent bus boycott led by Martin Luther King Jr. Still another protest was begun when African American students in North Carolina were refused service at an all-white lunch counter. The Civil Rights movement grew rapidly and resulted in widespread demonstrations (in Selma, Alabama, one march drew more than 100,000 people), picket lines, sit-ins, and other forms of political protest. Gaining international publicity, the protests of the late 1950s and early 1960s attracted Northern religious leaders, students, and white liberals—some of whom would lose their lives. By the time the Reverend Martin Luther King Jr. was assassinated in 1968, many demands of the Civil Rights movement had been incorporated in the Civil Rights Act of 1964. Ironically, Congress exempted itself from complying with the act until 1988. The 1964 Civil Rights Act did not live up to its implicit promise. The balance of racial power had not shifted and African American and other minority groups continued to be disenfranchised economically, politically, and socially. It soon became apparent that other remedies were required. One of those was affirmative action, a set of policies designed to provide equal opportunities for minorities and women.

Affirmative Action

Two basic strategies have been employed to address racial, economic, and other injustices. The first is nondiscrimination, in which no preferential treatment is given to selected groups. The second is **affirmative action,** whose overall goal is to ensure that women and minorities are admitted, hired, and promoted in direct proportion to their numbers in the population. Affirmative action policies and legislation represent an aggressive step beyond the largely reactive stance taken by simple nondiscrimination policies. As such, affirmative action policies give preferential treatment to minority and female applicants. The ostensible goal of affirmative action is to right past wrongs done to groups of people throughout the country's history.

As a response to the Civil Rights movement, Presidents Kennedy, Johnson, and Nixon initiated affirmative plans to move the country toward nondiscrimination. Designed initially to address discrimination against African Americans, affirmative action policies were expanded to address discrimination based on gender, age, and disability.

There are three types of affirmative action programs: (1) employers and schools can adopt voluntary programs to increase the hiring of minorities and women; (2) the courts can order an employer or school to create an affirmative action plan; and (3) federal, state, and local governments can require contractors to adopt affirmative action plans to remain eligible for government contracts.[229]

As Table 4.12 illustrates, affirmative action and civil rights legislation affect a much wider group of Americans than minorities. Moreover, as the table demonstrates, rulings on affirmative action and civil rights cases have been inconsistent, characterized by two steps forward and one or two steps backward. This has occurred partly because civil rights and affirmative action policies have emerged from often conflicting legislation and court decisions.

Opponents of affirmative action argue that it leads to racial quota systems, preferential treatment and reverse discrimination. They argue that it violates the equal protection under the laws guaranteed in the Fourteenth Amendment. Still others argue that affirmative action benefits minority group members who do not need the help while placing whites who are innocent of any wrongdoing at a disadvantage. These critics maintain that rights inhere in individuals, not in groups. Other conservatives, such as Supreme Court Justice Antonin Scalia, argue that there never was a justification for affirmative action because the Constitution is "colorblind."[230] Moderates such as former president Bill Clinton note that "Affirmative action has been good for America. Affirmative action has not always been perfect, and affirmative action should not go on forever. . . . We should reaffirm the principle of affirmative action and fix the practices. We should have a simple slogan: Mend it, but don't end it."[231] Yet attacks on affirmative action have also come from liberal quarters. Columnist Roger Hernandez argues:

> Admittedly, affirmative action offers protection from discrimination. But the price it exacts is too high. Affirmative action reinforces the degrading notion that certain cultures are so inferior they render all individuals brought up in it [sic]—regardless of their socioeconomic status—into incompetent fools who cannot get along without special attention. . . . The sense of ethnic inferiority such a philosophy encourages does more harm than the outright discrimination affirmative action is supposed to prevent. . . . Ending affirmative action attacks the idea that every member of certain ethnic groups is a muddle of social pathologies.[232]

William Julius Wilson, an African American sociologist, criticizes the ability of affirmative action strategies to help the most disadvantaged members of society:

> Programs based solely on [race-specific solutions] are inadequate . . . to deal with the complex problems of race in America. . . . This is because the most disadvantaged members of racial minority groups, who suffer the cumulative effects of both race and class subjugation . . . are disproportionately represented amongst the segment of the general population that has been denied the resources to compete effectively in a free and open market. . . . On the other hand, the competitive resources developed by the advantaged minority members . . . result in their benefitting disproportionately from policies that promote the rights of minority individuals by removing artificial barriers to valued positions. . . . [If] policies of preferential . . . treatment are developed in terms of racial group membership rather than real disadvantages suffered by individuals, then these policies will further improve the opportunities of the advantaged without necessarily addressing the problems of the truly disadvantaged such as the ghetto underclass.[233]

Affirmative action is one of the most controversial issues in U.S. social policy. Moreover, it is open to a wide array of moral conundrums. For example, how much discrimination does a group have to encounter to justify preferential treatment? Although Asian Americans have encountered (and continue to encounter) significant discrimination, their income levels and educational attainment arguably mitigate against the need for preferential treatment. Moreover, if historical social discrimination were a basis for affirmative action, then Jews, Catholics, Irish, Eastern Europeans, and other groups who have historically been squeezed out of the U.S. social mainstream should also be eligible. Moreover, poor whites are discriminated against in U.S. society because of their class background. Should they be covered under affirmative action? Women who grow up in upper-class families and attend Ivy League universities are covered under affirmative action by virtue of their gender. Do they experience more discrimination than a poor white Appalachian male who is marked by language, culture, and class background? These are some issues that plague the development of clear and fair affirmative action guidelines.

Table 4.12

Milestones in Civil Rights and Affirmative Action Rulings

Legislation or Court Ruling	Summary
Plessy v. Ferguson (1896)	The U.S. Supreme Court established the "separate but equal" doctrine.
Fair Employment Practices Committee (1935)	Employers are directed to not discriminate in hiring based on race.
Brown v. Board of Education of Topeka, Kansas (1954)	The Supreme Court ruled that "separate but equal" facilities in education were inherently unequal.
Equal Pay Act of 1963	Men and women have a right to equal pay for doing the same work
Civil Rights Act of 1964, including amendments added in 1972, 1978, and 1991	1. Voter registration is a legal right that cannot be tampered with. 2. It is unlawful to discriminate or segregate based on race, color, religion, or national origin in any public accommodation, including hotels, motels, theaters, and other public places. 3. The attorney general will undertake civil action on the part of any person who is denied access to a public accommodation. If the owner continues to discriminate, a court fine and imprisonment will result. 4. The attorney general must represent anyone who undertakes the desegregation of a public school. 5. Each federal department must take action to end discrimination in all programs or activities receiving federal assistance. 6. Public or private employers, employment agencies, or labor unions with more than 15 employees cannot discriminate against an individual because of their race, color, religion, national origin, or sex. An Equal Opportunity Commission will be established to enforce this provision. A 1968 amendment to this act prohibited discrimination in housing.
Age Discrimination Act of 1967	Persons over 40 may not be discriminated against in any terms or conditions of their employment.
Griggs v. Duke Power Co. (1971)	The Court prohibited discriminatory employment practices. It put the burden of proof on the employer to show that hiring criteria have a direct relationship to the job. Griggs was overturned by *Wards Cove Packing Co. Inc. v. Atonio* (1989), in which the Court imposed tougher standards for proving discrimination and shifted the burden of proof onto the employee.
Swann v. Charlotte-Mecklenburg Board of Education (1971)	The Court ruled in favor of court-ordered busing to achieve racial integration of school districts with a history of discrimination.
Title IX of Education Amendments of 1972	Institutions receiving federal financial assistance may not discriminate based on sex.
Rehabilitation Act of 1973	Discrimination on the basis of mental or physical disability is prohibited.
Vietnam Era Veterans Readjustment Act of 1974	Employers with federal contracts must take steps to employ and advance qualified disabled veterans.
Milliken v. Brady (1974)	The Court ruled that mandatory school busing across city-suburban boundaries to achieve racial integration was not required unless segregation had resulted from an official action.
Marco DeFunis v. University of Washington Law School (1974)	DeFunis claimed that he was denied admission to law school even though his grades and test scores were higher than those of minorities who were admitted. The Supreme Court ruled in his favor.

(continued)

Table 4.12 (continued)

Legislation or Court Ruling	Summary
Age Discrimination Act of 1975	Employers who receive federal financial assistance cannot discriminate based on age.
Regents of the University of California v. Bakke (1978)	The Supreme Court ruled that Alan Bakke was unfairly denied admission to the University of California-Davis Medical School. Like DeFunis, Bakke argued that his qualifications were stronger than those of many of the minority candidates who were admitted.
United Steelworkers v. Weber (1979)	The Court upheld an affirmative action plan to erase entrenched racial biases in employment.
Fullilove v. Klutznick (1980)	The court ruled that federal public works contracts may require 10 percent of the work to go to minority firms.
Firefighters Local Union No. 1784 v. Stotts (1984)	The Court ruled that an employer may use seniority rules in laying off employees, even when those rules adversely affect minority employees. This ruling was a blow to affirmative action, because it perpetuated the dilemma that minorities are the last to be hired and the first to be fired. The Department of Justice used this decision to force Indianapolis and 49 other jurisdictions to abandon their use of hiring quotas.
Wyatt v. Jackson Board of Education (1986)	An affirmative action plan must have a strong basis in evidence for remedial action.
United States v. Paradise (1987)	The Court found that a judge may order racial quotas in promoting and hiring to address "egregious" past discrimination.
Johnson v. Transportation Agency (1987)	The Court permitted the use of gender as a factor in hiring and promotion.
City of Richmond v. J. A. Croson (1989)	The Court imposed standards of "strict scrutiny." Racial or ethnic classifications must serve a compelling interest and be narrowly tailored.
Martin v. Wilks (1989)	The Court imposed tougher standards for Asian Americans to be included in affirmative action plans and made it easier to challenge settlements of those plans.
Metro Broadcasting Inc. v. FCC (1990)	The Court allowed minority preferences to promote diverse viewpoints across the airwaves.
Adarand Constructors Inc. v. Pena (1995)	The Court ruled that federal affirmative measures using racial and ethnic criteria in decision making must meet the same standards of strict scrutiny imposed in *Croson*.
Hopwood v. State of Texas (1996 5th Cir.)	The appeals court ruled that the University of Texas's goal of achieving a diverse student body did not justify its affirmative action program, suggesting that achieving diversity does not represent a compelling state interest.
California Proposition 209 (California Civil Rights Initiative) (1996). Now Article I, Section 31 of the California Constitution	Racial or gender preferences in public education, employment, and state contracting are prohibited. In 1997 a three-judge panel of the Ninth Circuit Court of Appeals upheld the referendum passed by California voters. The U.S. Supreme Court refused to consider the appeal.[a] The passage of the CCRI effectively put an end to affirmative action in California.
Washington State I-200 (1998)	"Preferences" in state and municipal hiring and recruitment to the state university system are prohibited. This 1998 ballot measure effectively repealed affirmative action in Washington state.

Table 4.12 (continued)

Legislation or Court Ruling	Summary
One Florida Plan (1999)	Racial preferences in university admissions and state contracting are prohibited. In November 1999 Florida Gov. Jeb Bush ordered an end to racial preference programs in agencies under his control. The One Florida plan replaces race and ethnicity with criteria such as a student's socioeconomic background, geographical diversity, status as a first generation college student, or preparation in a low-performing D or F school.
Grutter v. Bollinger and *Gratz v. Bollinger* (2003)	The U.S. Supreme Court ruled that race can be a factor in university admission decisions but limited the extent of it. In two separate but related decisions, the Court ruled that the University of Michigan's law school affirmative action policy (*Grutter v. Bollinger*) that favors minorities is legal. In the second decision (*Gratz v. Bollinger*) it ruled that the University of Michigan's undergraduate admissions, which awards 20 points on a 100 point scale to blacks, Hispanics, and Native Americans, violated equal protection provisions of the Constitution.

[a] D.D. Gehring (ed.), *Responding to the New Affirmative Actions Climate: New Directions for Student Services* (San Francisco: Jossey-Bass, 1998).

Sources: Adapted from ACLU, "Affirmative Action," ACLU Briefing Paper No. 17 (New York: ACLU, n.d.); American Council on Education, "Major Civil Rights and Equal Opportunity Legislation Since 1963," retrieved from www.berkshire-aap.com/ace; Winnie Chen, Vilma Hernandez, Erin Townsend, and Carol Wyatt, "Affirmative Action," unpublished class paper, Graduate School of Social Work, University of Houston, 1996; Marjorie Blythe and Anna Conaty, "Affirmative Action and the State of America's Minorities," unpublished paper, Graduate School of Social Work, University of Houston, 2000; and National Public Radio, "Split Ruling on Affirmative Action High Court Rules on Race as Factor in University Admissions," June 23, 2003, retrieved October 2004 from www.npr.org/news/specials/michigan.

Conclusion

Discrimination takes many forms in the United States. It can be targeted against African Americans, Hispanics, Native Americans, Asians, women, gays and lesbians, people with disabilities, and poor whites. Because discrimination often leads to poverty, it can result in the creation of income maintenance and poverty programs designed to meliorate its effects. Those who become beneficiaries of these programs soon find themselves with a second handicap—the stigma of being on public assistance.

Some policymakers have tried to reduce the need for long-term and expensive social welfare programs by attempting to arrest the cycle of discrimination and stigma. They often undertake this effort by advocating for policies and legislation designed to attack discrimination at its roots. Antidiscrimination programs, policies, and legislation often includes affirmative action policies, women's rights legislation, city and state gay and lesbian ordinances, and legislation protecting the rights of the physically and mentally challenged. Policymakers hope that by curtailing discrimination, U.S. society can offer at-risk populations equal opportunities for achievement and success. At best, the scorecard on these well-intentioned policies has been mixed. Despite a strong start, affirmative action programs have not led to widespread economic success for women and minorities. Gays and lesbians continue to be discriminated against, even in places that have passed civil rights ordinances. Although women have made significant gains over the past few decades, they still earn less than males in comparable jobs. Poverty rates for minority groups are three times higher than for whites and their median family incomes are lower.

When added together the vast majority of the U.S. population experiences discrimination: 51 percent of the population are women; almost 13 percent are over age 65; almost 20 percent are disabled; and roughly one in three Americans are either Hispanic,

African American, or Asian. Hence, discrimination in U.S. society is not about numbers per se, but reflects the relative lack of political, social, and economic power of marginalized groups.

Discussion Questions

1. The effects of racism can take many forms, including overt discrimination, poverty, housing problems, high rates of underemployment and unemployment, wage differentials, family disruption, inferior educational opportunities, high crime rates, and welfare dependency. The relationship between racism and poverty is clear. Less clear, however, are the causes of racism. Describe what you believe to be the primary causes of both individual and institutional racism. How are these factors nourished or condemned by society?
2. In recent years there has been a marked increase in the number of racially-based incidents, especially against African Americans, Asian Americans, gays and lesbians, Jews and Muslims, and those of Arabic descent. What factors explain the rise of such incidents?
3. Over the past four decades, numerous legal and judicial decisions have attempted to eradicate racism, including the 1964 Civil Rights Act and various Supreme Court rulings. Were these attempts successful? If not, why not? What, if anything, can be done to eliminate racism?
4. It is generally acknowledged that sexism is a powerful and pervasive force permeating much of U.S. society. How is sexism manifested? What strategies, if any, can be employed to lessen the impact of sexism in society?
5. Most women in U.S. society work to either provide a necessary second income or as the family's primary wage earner. Describe some of the major obstacles faced by working women. What can be done to eliminate some of these obstacles?
6. Gays and lesbians face severe economic and social problems apart from AIDS. What are some of the most important social, political, and economic hurdles standing in the way of full equality for gays and lesbians? What can be done to ameliorate these obstacles?
7. Being elderly in U.S. society is in many ways a social handicap. Describe some key social, economic, and political indicators that illustrate this belief.
8. It is generally agreed that people with disabilities face significant discrimination. What is the evidence, if any, to support this belief?
9. The Americans with Disabilities Act (ADA) is often considered the most important piece of legislation affecting people with disabilities. Why do policy analysts consider the ADA such an important act? What are its loopholes, if any?
10. After reviewing the various causes of discrimination discussed in this chapter, describe what you believe to be the major cause of discrimination today. Why is this more important than others? Using this cause as a framework, what can be done to counteract the effects of discrimination?

Notes

1. Billy J. Tidwell, "Racial Discrimination and Inequality," *Encyclopedia of Social Work,* 18th ed. (Silver Spring, MD: NASW, 1987), p. 450.
2. J. Dollard et al., *Frustration and Aggression* (New Haven, CT: Yale University Press, 1939).
3. Theodore W. Adorno et al., *The Authoritarian Personality* (New York: Harper & Row, 1950).
4. Wilhelm Reich, *Listen Little Man* (Boston: Beacon Press, 1971).
5. Tidwell, "*Racial Discrimination and Inequality.*"
6. Stephanie Bernardo, *The Ethnic Almanac* (Garden City, NY: Doubleday, 1981).
7. V. Dion Haynes, "Movement Aims to Explain and Deflate White Power," *Daily Titan,* 1999. Retrieved 2000 from http://dailytitan.fullerton.edu/issues/spring_98/dti_03_04/movementaims.html
8. Lee Hubbard, "Running the Numbers on Black Population Patterns," *Africana,* September 13, 2001. Retrieved 2001 from www.africana.com/articles/daily/index_20010913.asp
9. Department of Commerce, U.S. Census Bureau, "Young, Diverse, Urban: Hispanic Population Reaches All-Time High of 38.8 Million, New Census Bureau

Estimates Show." Public Information Office, Washington, D.C., June 18, 2003.

10. Mary Pattillo-McCoy, *Black Picket Fences: Privilege and Peril Among the Black Middle Class* (Chicago, IL: University of Chicago Press, 1999).
11. Frank D. Bean, Stephen J. Trejo, Randy Crapps, and Michael Tyler, "The Latino Middle Class: Myth, Reality and Potential." The Tomás Rivera Policy Institute, University of Southern California, April 2001.
12. See Andrew Cassel, "Black Middle Class Continues to Grow, but Gaps Remain," *Philadelphia Inquirer* (July 12, 2004), p. B6.
13. Ibid.
14. Steven A. Holmes, "Quality of Life Is Up for Many Blacks, Data Say," *New York Times* (November 18, 1996), pp. A1, A13.
15. See U.S. Census Bureau, "Census Bureau Facts for Features, African American History Month," Washington, D.C.; February 14, 2000; and U.S. Census Bureau, "Census Bureau Facts for Features, African American History Month 2004," January 7, 2004, retrieved July 2004 from the www.census.gov/Press-Release/www/releases/archives/facts_for_features/001645.html
16. U.S. Census Bureau, "Black-Owned Business Firms Up 46 Percent over Five Years, Census Bureau Survey Shows," December 12, 1995. Retrieved 2000 from www.census.gov/ftp/pub/agfs/smobe/view/b_press.txt
17. William Julius Wilson, *The Truly Disadvantaged: The Inner City, the Underclass, and Public Policy* (Chicago: University of Chicago Press, 1987), p. 109.
18. U.S. Census Bureau, "Census Bureau Facts for Features, African American History Month 2004."
19. Lawrence Mishel and David M. Frankel, *The State of Working America* (Armonk, NY: M. E. Sharpe, 1991), p. 251.
20. U.S. Census Bureau, "Census Bureau Facts for Features, African American History Month 2004."
21. Holmes, "Quality of Life Is Up for Many Blacks."
22. See Joel Russell, "The Hispanic Middle Class Emerges," *Hispanic Business* (May 2004), retrieved September 2004 from www.hispanicbusiness.com/news/newsbyid.asp?id=15962&page=2; and Robert R. Brischetto, "The Hispanic Middle Class Comes of Age," *Hispanic Business* (December 2001), retrieved September 2004 from www.hispanicbusiness.com/news/newsbyid.asp?id=5808&page=2
23. U.S. Census Bureau, "Income Stable, Poverty Up, Numbers of Americans With and Without Health Insurance Rise, Census Bureau Reports." Press Release, August 26, 2004. Retrieved September 27, 2004, from www.census.gov/Press-Release/www/releases/archives/income_wealth/002484.html
24. Annenberg Political Fact-Check, "Update on Kerry's "Shrinking Middle Class"—Still Shrinking in 2003." Annenberg Public Policy Center of the University of Pennsylvania, September 1, 2004. Retrieved September 2004 from www.factcheck.org/article.aspx?docID=249
25. Pattillo-McCoy, *Black Picket Fences.*
26. U.S. Census Bureau, "Facts for Features, African American History Month 2004."
27. U.S. Census Bureau, "Projected Population of the United States, by Race and Hispanic Origin: 2000 to 2050," March 18, 2004. Retrieved July 2004 from www.census.gov/ipc/www/usintermproj/natprojtab01a.pdf
28. U.S. Census Bureau, "State Population Estimates by Race Alone or in Combination and Hispanic or Latino Origin: July 1, 2002." Retrieved October 2004 from www.census.gov/popest/data/states/ST-EST2002-ASRO-04.php
29. See "Family Income Finally Rises," *The New York Times* (September 27, 1996), p. 18; and U.S. Census Bureau, "The Black Population in the United States, March 2002," retrieved July 2004 from www.census.gov/prod/2003pubs/p20–541.pdf
30. U.S. Census Bureau, "Income, Poverty and Health Insurance Coverage in the United States: 2003," 2004. Retrieved August 2004 from www.census.gov/prod/2004pubs/p60–226.pdf
31. U.S. Census Bureau, "Census Bureau Facts for Features, African American History Month, 2004."
32. United States Department of Commerce, Bureau of the Census, "Black-Owned Businesses: Strongest in Services," August 1996. Retrieved 2000 from www.census.gov/Press-Release/cb98–127.html
33. *The Journal of Blacks in Higher Education,* "Vital Statistics," 40 (Summer 2003), p. 9.
34. Jared Bernstein, *Where's the Payoff?* (Washington, DC: Economic Policy Institute, 1995).
35. Bureau of Labor Statistics, Employment Situation Summary, 2003. Retrieved September 2004 from www.bls.gov/news.release/empsit.nr0.htm.
36. Bernstein, *Where's the Payoff?*
37. Franklin D. Wilson, Marta Tienda, and Lawrence Wu, "Racial Equality in the Labor Market: Still an Elusive Goal?" Institute for Research on Poverty, Madison, WI, 1992, Discussion Paper no. 968–992.
38. *The Journal of Blacks in Higher Education,* "Vital Statistics."
39. Gail Russell Chaddock, "U.S. Notches World's Highest Incarceration Rate, a Report Highlights Extent to Which Many Citizens Have Served Time in Prison," *The Christian Science Monitor* (August 18, 2003), p. 9.
40. Thomas P. Bonczar and Allen J. Beck, "Special Report: Lifetime Likelihood of Going to State or Federal Prison," Publication NCJ-160092, U.S. Department of Justice, Office of Justice Programs, Bureau of Justice Statistics (Washington, DC: BJS Clearinghouse, March 1997).
41. See American Bar Association, "A Statistical Look at Criminal Justice and Injustice" *Human Rights Magazine* (Winter 2004), p. 19; and Matthew Klein, "Death

Row in Black and White," *American Demographics* (May 1998), retrieved 2000 from www.demographics.com/publications/ad/98_ad/9805_ad/ad980522.htm

42. U.S. Department of Justice, Bureau of Justice Statistics, "Homicide Trends in the U.S. Trends by Race, 2004." Retrieved September 2004 from www.ojp.usdoj.gov/bjs/homicide/race.htm
43. Gareth G. Davis and David B. Mulhausen, "Young African-American Males: Continuing Victims of High Homicide Rates in Urban Communities," Heritage Organization. Retrieved 2000 from www.heritage.org/library/cda/cda00-05.html
44. Cushing N. Dolbeare, *The Widening Gap* (Washington, DC: Low Income Housing Information Service, 1992), p. 11.
45. Jennifer Daskal, *In Search of Shelter* (Washington, DC: Center on Budget and Policy Priorities, June 15, 1998).
46. Centers for Disease Control, *Morbidity and Mortality Weekly Report,* "National Black HIV/AIDS Awareness Day—February 7, 2003," February 7, 2003, 52(05), p. 81.
47. The Department of Health and Human Services, Race and Health Home Page. Retrieved 2000 from http://raceandhealth.hhs.gov/sidebars/sbinitOver.htm
48. The Centers for Disease Control, "Deaths: Preliminary Data for 2001," *National Vital Statistics* 51, no. 5. Retrieved August 2004 from www.cdc.gov/nchs/data/nvsr/nvsr51/nvsr51_05.pdf
49. Centers for Disease Control, "Births: Final Data for 2002," *National Vital Statistics Reports* 52, no. 10 (2003). Retrieved September 2004 from www.cdc.gov/nchs/data/nvsr/nvsr52/nvsr52_10.pdf
50. U.S. Census Bureau, "Earnings By Occupation and Education, 2004." Retrieved October 2004 from www.census.gov/hhes/income/earnings/call1usboth.html
51. Mishel and Frankel, *The State of Working America,* p. 219.
52. Children's Defense Fund, *The State of America's Children,* p. 25.
53. Ibid., p. 92
54. See Kathryn Hoffman and Charmaine Llagas, "Status and Trends in the Education of Blacks," *Educational Statistics Quarterly* 5, no. 4 (2003), p.1; and Jennifer Day, "Young African Americans Boost High-School Completion Rate," United States Census Bureau, June 29, 1998, retrieved 2000 from www.census.gov/Press-Release/cb98-106.html
55. Mishel and Frankel, *The State of Working America,* p. 253.
56. *The Journal of Blacks in Higher Education,* "Vital Statistics."
57. See U.S. Department of Health and Human Services, Indicators of Welfare Dependence: Annual Report to Congress, 2003, HHS, Washington, D.C.
58. Department of Commerce, "Young, Diverse, Urban: Hispanic Population Reaches All-Time High of 38.8 Million."
59. U.S. Bureau of the Census, "Poverty," 1998. Retrieved 2000 from www.census.gov/hhes/www/poverty.html
60. Department of Commerce, "Young, Diverse, Urban: Hispanic Population Reaches All-Time High of 38.8 Million."
61. U.S. Census Bureau, "The Hispanic Population in the United States: March 2002," June 2003. Retrieved August 2004 from www.census.gov/prod/2003pubs/p20-545.pdf
62. U.S. Census Bureau, "Income, Poverty and Health Insurance Coverage in the United States: 2003," August 2004. Retrieved September 2004 from www.census.gov/prod/2004pubs/p60-226.pdf
63. L. Lowell, F. Bean, and R. De La Garza, "The Dilemmas of Undocumented Immigration: An Analysis of the 1984 Simpson-Mazzoli Vote," *Social Service Quarterly* 67 (1986), pp. 118–126.
64. Hispanic News Link, "Hispanics Who Defy Averages," *The Numbers News* (September 1995), p. 1.
65. U.S. Bureau of the Census, *The Hispanic Population in the United States* (Washington, DC: U.S. Government Printing Office, March 1989).
66. See U.S. House of Representatives, Committee on Ways and Means, *Overview of Entitlement Programs: 1992 Green Book* (Washington, DC: U.S. Government Printing Office, 1992), p. 1275; and Barbara Vobjeda and Steven Pearlstein, "Household Income Climbs," *Washington Post* (September 27, 1996), p. A1.
67. Roberto R. Ramirez and G. Patricia de la Cruz, "The Hispanic Population in the United States: March 2002," *Current Population Reports,* U.S. Census Bureau, Washington, D.C., June 2003.
68. See Ibid., pp. 590–591; and U.S. Census Bureau, "Poverty, Income See Slight Changes: Child Poverty Rate Unchanged," Press Release, September 26, 2003, retrieved October 2004 from www.census.gov/Press-Release/www/2003/cb03-153.html
69. U.S. Census Bureau, "Poverty, Income See Slight Changes; Child Poverty Rate Unchanged."
70. See Ramirez and de la Cruz, "The Hispanic Population in the United States: March 2002"; and Guadalupe Gibson, "Mexican Americans," *Encyclopedia of Social Work,* 18th ed. (Silver Spring, MD: NASW, 1987), p. 139.
71. Ramirez and de la Cruz, "The Hispanic Population in the United States: March 2002."
72. Ibid.
73. U.S. Census Bureau, "Number of Hispanic Businesses Up 76 Percent in Five Years, Census Bureau Reports," July 10, 1996. Retrieved 2000 from www.census.gov/Press-Release/cb96–110.html
74. See Evelyn Lance Blanchard, "American Indians and Alaska Natives," *Encyclopedia of Social Work,* 18th ed. (Silver Spring, MD: NASW, 1987), p. 61; U.S. Bureau of the Census, *Census of Population and Housing Summary* (Washington, DC: U.S. Government Printing Office, 1990), p. 93; and U.S. Department of

the Interior, Bureau of Indian Affairs, "Statistical-Abstract-on-the-Web."

75. Compiled from Bureau of Indian Affairs, Answers to Frequently Asked Questions, 2001. Retrieved August 2004 from http://usinfo.state.gov/russki/infousa/society/bia.pdf. See also U.S. Department of the Interior, Orientation to the U.S. Department of the Interior: Bureau of Indian Affairs. Retrieved August 2004 from www.doiu.nbc.gov/orientation/bia2.cfm.
76. H. F. Dobyns, *Native American Historical Demography: A Critical Bibliography* (Bloomington, IN: Indiana University Press, 1976), p. 32.
77. H. E. Fey and D. McNickle, *Indians and Other Americans: Two Ways of Life Meet* (New York: Harper & Row, 1970), pp. 9–12.
78. Thomas Hayden, "A Modern Life: After Decades of Discrimination, Poverty, and Despair, American Indians Can Finally Look Toward a Better Future," *U.S. News and World Report* (October 4, 2004), p. 20.
79. U.S. Commission on Civil Rights, Office of the General Counsel, *Broken Promises: Evaluating the Native American Health Care System,* Draft Report for Commissioners' Review, Washington, D.C., July 2, 2004.
80. William N. Evans and Julie H. Topoleski, "The Social and Economic Impact of Native American Casinos," *NBER Working Paper No. w9198,* National Bureau of Economic Research, September 2002. Retrieved October 2004 from www.bsos.umd.edu/econ/evans/wpapers/evans_topoleski_casinos.pdf
81. B. J. Jones, "The Indian Child Welfare Act: The Need for a Separate Law," American Bar Association, 1995. Retrieved October 2004 from www.abanet.org/genpractice/compleat/f95child.html
82. U.S. Department of Justice, Coverage Issues under the Indian Self-determination Act, Memorandum for the Assistant Attorney General Civil Division, April 22, 1998. Retrieved October 2004 from www.usdoj.gov/olc/isdafin.htm
83. U.S. Census Bureau, "The Asian Population, 2000," February 2002. Retrieved September 2004 from www.census.gov/prod/2002pubs/c2kbr01–16.pdf
84. Felicity Barringer, "U.S. Asian Population Up 70% in 80's," *New York Times* (March 2, 1990), p. 1.
85. U.S. Census Bureau, "Educational Attainment in the United States: 2003," June 2004. Retrieved August 2004 from www.census.gov/prod/2002pubs/c2kbr01-16.pdf
86. Daniel Goleman, "Probing School Success of Asian-Americans," *New York Times* (September 11, 1990), p. B5.
87. Arthur Hu, "Hu's on First: Asian Males Lose Again," *Asian Week* (February 12, 1993), p. 15.
88. See Goleman, "Probing School Success of Asian-Americans"; and Kelly St. John, "U.C.'s Top Ranks Found Lacking in Diversity," *San Francisco Chronicle* (February 6, 2003), p. A18.
89. Ibid.
90. U.S. Bureau of the Census, Educational Attainment in the United States: 2003.
91. See Rich Connell and Sonia Nazario, "Affirmative Action: Fairness or Favoritism?" *Los Angeles Times* (September 10, 1995), pp. A1, A26–A28; U.S. Commission on Civil Rights, "Civil Rights Issues Facing Asian-Americans in the 1990s" (Washington, DC: U.S. Commission on Civil Rights, February 1992), p. 17; U.S. Census Bureau, "The Asian and Pacific Islander Population in the United States: March 2002," May 2003, retrieved September 2004 from www.census.gov/prod/2003pubs/p20–540.pdf; and U.S. Census Bureau, "Income Stable, Poverty Up, Numbers of Americans with and without Health Insurance Rise, Census Bureau Reports."
92. U.S. Pan Asian American Chamber of Commerce, "AA Facts and Statistics," U.S. Pan Asian American Chamber of Commerce, Washington, D.C., 2004.
93. Rockefeller Foundation, Research Briefs on Poverty, "Poverty and Asian Americans." Retrieved 2000 from www.cdinet.com/Rockefeller/Briefs/brief27.html
94. U.S. Department of State, Bureau of International Information Programs, "September 11 Hurt New York's Chinatown, But Human Smuggling Continues to Flourish," June 17, 2004. Washington, D.C.
95. Bruce Brown, "Evidence of a Glass-Ceiling for Asian-Americans," Cal State Polytechnic University, WEAI Conference, Denver CO, July 12, 2003. Retrieved October 2004 from www.csupomona.edu/~bbrown
96. Sussumu Awanchara, "Hit by a Backlash," *Far Eastern Economic Review* 155, no. 2 (March 26, 1992), p. 30.
97. Ibid.
98. Jeffrey S. Passel, Randy Capps, and Michael Fix, *Undocumented Immigrants: Facts and Figures,* Urban Institute Immigration Studies Program, Washington, D.C., January 12, 2004.
99. Nancy F. Rytina, Estimates of the Legal Permanent Resident Population and Population Eligible to Naturalize in 2002, U.S. Department of Homeland Security, Office of Immigration Statistics, Washington, D.C., May 2004.
100. U.S. Census Bureau, "Income, Poverty and Health Insurance Coverage in the United States, 2003," August 2004. Retrieved September 2004 from www.census.gov/prod/2004pubs/p60-226.pdf
101. Pia M. Orrenius, Federal Reserve Bank of Dallas, "U.S. Immigration and Economic Growth: Putting Policy on Hold,"*Southwest Economy* (6), (November/December 2003), p. 3.
102. Ibid.
103. Ibid.
104. U.S. Department of Justice, Immigration and Naturalization Service, "Immigration to the United States in Fiscal Year 1995" (Washington, DC: USDOJ, August 5, 1996).

105. Office of Immigration Statistics, "2003 Yearbook of Immigrations Statistics," September 2004. Retrieved August 2004 from http://uscis.gov/graphics/shared/aboutus/statistics/2003Yearbook.pdf
106. HR 3734: Personal Responsibility and Work Opportunity Reconciliation Act (Immigration Provisions)—Conference Committee Version: Title IV, Restricting Welfare and Public Benefits for Aliens (Washington, DC: U.S. House of Representatives, Conference Committee, August 5, 1996), p. 16.
107. Patty Reinert, "Federal Welfare Plan Hits Legal Immigrants," *Houston Chronicle* (August 2, 1996), pp. 1A and 16A.
108. Greg McDonald, "House Passes $600 Billion Spending Bill," *Houston Chronicle* (September 29, 1996), pp. 1A and 32A.
109. Orrenius, U.S. Immigration and Economic Growth.
110. Ibid.
111. Ibid.
112. Ibid.
113. Muzaffar A. Chishti, Doris Meissner, Demetrios G. Papademetriou, Jay Peterzell, Michael J. Wishnie, and Stephen W. Yale-Loehr, *America's Challenge: Domestic Security, Civil Liberties, and National Unity After September 11.* (Washington, D.C.: Migration Policy Institute, Washington, 2003).
114. Ibid, p. 18.
115. U.S. Department of Justice, "National Crime Victimization Survey," August 1995. Quoted in U.S. Department of Justice, "The Violence against Women Act," September 23, 1996. Retrieved 2000 from www.usdoj.gov/vawo/vawafct.htm
116. Patricia Tjaden and Nancy Thoennes, "Extent, Nature, and Consequences of Intimate Partner Violence: Findings from the National Violence against Women Survey," National Institute of Justice, NCJ 181867, July 2000. Retrieved October 2004 from http://ncjrs.org/txtfiles1/nij/181867.txt
117. U.S. Department of Justice, National Crime Victimization Survey.
118. Update on VAWA, *National NOW Times* (January 1995). Retrieved 1999 from www.now.org
119. Jan Erickson, "Legislative Update: End of Year Funding Bills Leave Lives in the Balance," *National NOW Times* (Winter 2003/2004), p. 24.
120. Diana Pierce, quoted in S. Bianchi, "Feminization and Juvenilization of Poverty: Trends, Relative Risks, Causes and Consequences," *Annual Review of Sociology* 25 (1999), pp. 307–333.
121. Marianne Sullivan, "Women's Poverty Deepens Amid Slow 2003 Recovery," *Women's eNews,* August 30, 2004. Retrieved October 7, 2004, from www.womensenews.org/article.cfm/dyn/aid/1968/context/archive
122. Ruth Sidel, *Women and Children Last* (New York: Harper, 1984).
123. See Women's Bureau, "Women Who Maintain Families," U.S. Department of Labor, Washington, D.C., June 1993; Appalachian Regional Commission, Households and Families in Appalachia, 2003. Retrieved October 2004 from www.arc.gov/index.do?nodeId=2166; and National Women's Law Center, "Many Women Still Not Benefitting from Overall Declines in U.S. Poverty," Washington, D.C., September 30, 1999.
124. National Commission on Children, Poverty, *Welfare and America's Families: A Hard Look* (Washington, DC: National Commission on Children, 1992), p. 3.
125. Ann Withorn, quoted in M. A. Jimenez, "A Feminist Analysis of Welfare Reform: The Personal Responsibility Act of 1996," *Affilia* 14 (Fall 1999), pp. 278–293.
126. Mishel and Frankel, *The State of Working America,* p. 105.
127. Although we have stressed single female-headed families here, it is important to acknowledge that single male-headed families are growing even more rapidly. From 1959 to 1989 single male-headed families grew from 350,000 to 1.4 million, compared with 7.4 million mother-only and 25.5 million two-parent households. From 1960 to 1990, the percentage of father-only households increased 300 percent. See Daniel R. Mayer and Steven Garasky, Custodial Fathers: Myths, Realities, and Child Support Policy, Institute for Research on Poverty, Madison, WI, August 1992, Discussion Paper no. 982-992, pp. 8–9.
128. National Commission on Children, *Poverty, Welfare and America's Families,* p. 3.
129. National Commission on Children, *Beyond Rhetoric: A New Economic Agenda for Children and Families* (Washington, D.C.: National Commission on Children, 1991), p. 90.
130. Yin-Ling Irene Wong, Irwin Garfinkel, and Sara McLanahan, "Single-Mother Families in Eight Countries: Economic Status and Social Policy," Institute for Research on Social Policy, Madison, WI, 1992, Discussion Paper no. 970-992.
131. Winifred Bell, *Contemporary Social Welfare* (New York: Macmillan, 1983), p. 129.
132. Martha N. Ozawa, "Gender and Ethnicity in Social Security," *Conference Proceedings,* Nelson A. Rockefeller Institute of Government, State University of New York at Albany, November 1985, pp. 2–6.
133. Ibid.
134. Much of the following section is based on information found in *Wider Opportunities for Women, Making Both Ends Meet* (Washington, DC: Wider Opportunities for Women, 1991), pp. 4–9.
135. AFL-CIO, "Ask a Working Woman Survey Report," Washington, D.C., 2004.
136. Thomas A. Kochan, "Bringing Family Values to the Workplace," *The Boston Globe,* (August 29, 2004), p. 18.
137. U.S. Bureau of Labor Statistics, "Labor Force Participation of Mothers with Infants in 2003," April

22, 2004. Retrieved October 2004 from www.bls.gov/opub/ted/2004/apr/wk3/art04.htm

138. Family assistance was one of the major thrusts of the former Clinton administration. It is also an issue that crosses racial and social class lines.
139. AFL-CIO, "Ask a Working Woman Survey Report."
140. Ibid.
141. Department of Labor, Bureau of Labor Statistics, *Women in the Labor Force—A Databook*, 2004. Retrieved October 2004 from www.bls.gov/cps/wlf-databook.pdf
142. Bell, *Contemporary Social Welfare*, p. 126.
143. See Feminist Majority Foundation, "Women in Business," 1995, retrieved 1999 from www.feminist.org/research/ewb_myths.html; and the Department of Labor, Bureau of Labor Statistics, *Women in the Labor Force—A Databook*, 2004.
144. See U.S. Department of Labor, Women's Bureau, *Equal Pay: A Thirty-Five Year Perspective*, 1998, retrieved 2000 from www.dol.gov/dol/wb; Bureau of Labor Statistics, *Equal Pay: A Thirty-Five Year Perspective*, 1998; and *Highlights of Women's Earnings: 2002*, 2003, retrieved August 2004 from www.bls.gov/cps/cpswom2002.pdf
145. See National Commission on Working Women of Wider Opportunities for Women, *Women and Nontraditional Work* (Washington, DC: Wider Opportunities for Women, n.d.).
146. See Nijole V. Benokraitis and Joe R. Feagin, *Modern Sexism: Blatant, Subtle, and Covert Discrimination* (Englewood Cliffs, NJ: Prentice-Hall, 1986); and U.S. Department of Labor, Women's Bureau, "20 Facts about Women Workers," 2000, retrieved 2000 from www.dol.gov/dol/wb
147. U.S. Department of Labor, Office of Public Affairs, *The Glass Ceiling Commission Unanimously Agrees on 12 Ways to Shatter Barriers*, 1995. Retrieved 2000 from www.dol.gov/dol
148. U.S. Department of Labor, Women's Bureau, *Median Annual Earnings for Year-Round Full-Time Workers by Sex in Current and Real Dollars, 1951–98, 1999*. Retrieved 2000 from www.dol.gov/dol
149. Associated Press, "Glass Ceiling Shows Some Cracks." *New York Times* (April 23, 2000). Retrieved 2000 from www.nyt.com
150. Feminist Majority Foundation, "Women in Business."
151. See P. Anderson and B. Levine, *Working Paper Series: Child Care and Mothers' Employment Decisions* (Massachusetts: National Bureau of Economic Research, 1999); and The White House, *America's Workforce: Ready for the 21st Century*, August 5, 2004, retrieved October 2004 from www.whitehouse.gov/news/releases/2004/08/20040805-6.html
152. U.S. House of Representatives, "Child Care," *Green Book, 1998* (Washington, DC: U.S. Government Printing Office, 1998).
153. Ibid.
154. K. Miller and G. Schultz, "Survey Finds Former Welfare Recipients' Wages Highest in Nation," 1999. Retrieved 2000 from www.aphsa.org
155. S. Hofferth, "Childcare, Maternal Employment and Public Policy," *Annals of the American Academy of Political and Social Sciences* 563 (May 1999), pp. 20–38.
156. U.S. House of Representatives, *Green Book, 1998*, p. 1123.
157. Children's Defense Fund, *The State of America's Children*, p. 37.
158. Sheila B. Kammerman, "Child Care and Family Benefits: Policies of Six Industrialized Countries," *Monthly Labor Review* 103 (November 1980), pp. 23–28.
159. Sidel, *Women and Children Last*, p. 123.
160. National Commission on Working Women of Wider Opportunities for Women, "Women, Work and Health Insurance" (Washington, DC: Wider Opportunities for Women, n.d.).
161. National Commission on Working Women, "Women and Nontraditional Work."
162. Jim Harris, *The Complete Text of the Equal Rights Amendment* (New York: Ganis & Harris, 1980), p. 7.
163. "Fighting Discrimination," *The Legal Advisor* (Spring 1982), pp. 457–458.
164. Alan Guttmacher Institute, *Facts of Abortion* (Washington, DC: Alan Guttmacher Institute, September 1995).
165. Nanneska Magee, "Should the Federal Government Fund Abortions? No," in Howard Jacob Karger and James Midgley (eds.), *Controversial Issues in Social Policy* (Boston: Allyn & Bacon, 1993).
166. R. B. Gold and D. Daley, "Public Funding of Contraceptive, Sterilization and Abortion Services, Fiscal Year 1990," *Family Planning Perspectives* 23 (September/October 1991), pp. 204–211.
167. Tanya Albert, "Abortion, Legal since 1973, Still Shapes, Divides Doctors," *AMNews*, January 27, 2003, p. 30.
168. ACOG, "Statement on So-Called 'Partial Birth Abortion' Laws," The American College of Obstetricians and Gynecologists, February 13, 2002. Retrieved October 2004 from www.acog.org/from_home/publications/press_releases/nr02-13-02.cfm
169. Rachel K. Jones, Jacqueline E. Darroch and Stanley K. Henshaw, "Patterns in the Socioeconomic Characteristics of Women Obtaining Abortions in 2000–2001," *Perspectives on Sexual and Reproductive Health* 34, no. 5 (September/October 2002), pp. 18–31.
170. Religious Tolerance, Abortion: Public Opinion Polls: Year 2000, 2004. Retrieved October 2004 from www.religioustolerance.org/abo_poll2.htm
171. Campusprogram.com, "Gay Rights, 2004." Retrieved October 2004 from www.campusprogram.com/reference/en/wikipedia/g/ga/gay_rights.html
172. Robert Williams, *Just As I Am* (New York: Crown, 1992).

173. Cited in National Organization of Women, "Come out Against Homophobia! Did You Know? Retrieved October 2004 from www.now.org/issues/lgbi/stats.html
174. A. P. Bell and M. S. Weinberg, *Homosexualities: A Study of Diversity among Men and Women* (New York: Simon & Schuster, 1978), p. 101.
175. Edward O. Laumann, John H. Gagnon, Robert T. Michael, and Stuart Michaels, *The Social Organization of Sexuality in the United States* (Chicago: University of Chicago Press, 1994).
176. See "Overcoming a Deep Rooted Reluctance, More Firms Advertise to Gay Community," *Wall Street Journal* (July 18, 1991), p. 48; and "Gay Market a Potential Gold Mine," *San Francisco Chronicle* (August 27, 1991), p. C30.
177. "Gay Market a Potential Gold Mine"; also "For Gays, Ship Charters Are a Boon, Say Two Travel Companies," *Travel Weekly* (August 5, 1991), p. 2; and "Where the Money Is: Travel Industry Eyeing Gay/Lesbian Tourism," *Bay Area Reporter* (September 19, 1991), p. 53.
178. "State of the Union Address 2000," *Washington Post.* Retrieved November 2001 from www.washingtonpost.com/wp-srv/politics/special/states/docs/sou00.htm
179. National Coalition of Anti-Violence Programs, *Anti-Lesbian, Gay, Bisexual and Transgender Violence in 2003* (New York: National Coalition of Anti-Violence Programs, 2004).
180. Kent Kilpatrick, "Oregon Voters Reject Stigmatizing Homosexuals," *The Advocate* (November 5, 1992), p. 2C.
181. Lambda Legal, "Anti-Discrimination, 2004." Retrieved October 2004 from www.lambdalegal.org/cgi-bin/iowa/issues/record?record=18
182. Much of the section on gays and lesbians in the military was derived from Rivette Vullo, "Homosexuals in the Military," unpublished paper, Louisiana State University School of Social Work, Baton Rouge, LA, December 4, 1991. See also K. Dyer (ed.), *Gays in Uniform: The Pentagon's Secret Reports* (Boston: Alyson, 1990).
183. Dyer, *Gays in Uniform,* p. xiv.
184. Joseph Harry, "Homosexual Men and Women Who Served Their Country," *Journal of Homosexuality* 10 (1984), pp. 117–125.
185. Dyer, *Gays in Uniform,* p. xv.
186. Conrad K. Harper and Jane E. Booth, "End Military Intolerance," *National Law Journal* 13 (1991), pp. 17–18.
187. Barry M. Goldwater, "Ban on Gays Is Senseless Attempt to Stall the Inevitable," *Los Angeles Times* (September 23, 1993), C7.
188. Gregory M. Herek, "A Shift From 'Don't Ask' to Heterosexual Exception," *San Francisco Chronicle* (March 6, 2000), p. A8.
189. Servicemembers Legal Defense Network, "Gay Discharge Figures at Highest Level Since 1987," 1999. Retrieved 2000 from www.sldn.org/scripts/sldn.ixe?page=alert_01_23_99
190. Travis D. Bone, "Serving in Silence: Don't Ask, Don't Tell Deconstructed," *San Diego Gay & Lesbian Times* (September 16, 2004), p. 2.
191. Center for the Study of Sexual Minorities in the Military, "Russia Joins U.S. & Turkey in Barring Gays from Military Service, New Data Analysis Finds American Policy Out of Step with Other Democratic Nations," University of California, Santa Barbara, 2003.
192. B. A. Robinson, "Same-Sex Marriages (SSM) & Civil Unions," Ontario Consultants on Religious Tolerance, August 30, 2004. Retrieved September 2004 from www.religioustolerance.org/hom_marr.htm
193. R. Sneyd, "Same-Sex Bill Not about Marriage, Legislators Say," *Patriot Ledger* (March 18, 2000), p. 18.
194. Ibid.
195. Bob Egelko, "Top State Court Voids S.F.'s Gay Marriages, a Mayor Overruled: Newsom Found to Violate California Law by Issuing Same-Sex Licenses," *San Francisco Chronicle* (August 13, 2004), p. 1.
196. See B. A. Robinson, "Same-Sex Marriages (SSM) & Civil Unions"; and Rose Arce, "Same-Sex Couples Ready to Make History in Massachusetts, First State in U.S. to Allow Such Unions," *CNN,* May 17, 2004, retrieved September 28, 2004, from www.cnn.com/2004/LAW/05/17/mass.gay.marriage
197. Tom Curry, "Gay Marriage Vote Appears Doomed, Senate Leaders Unable to Agree on Procedure," *MSNBC,* July 14, 2004. Retrieved September 28, 2004 from www.msnbc.msn.com/id/5416297
198. "Marriage Rights for Same-Sex Couples," Gay.com, 2004. Retrieved from www.gay.com
199. See J. J. Sampson et al., *Texas Family Code Annotated* (Eagan, MN: West Group, August 1999); and N. D. Hunter et al., *The Rights of Lesbians and Gay Men: The Basic ACLU Guide to a Gay Person's Rights,* 3rd ed. (Carbondale & Edwardsville, IL: Southern Illinois University Press, 1992).
200. National Institute of Allergy and Infectious Diseases, "HIV/AIDS Statistics," National Institutes of Health, July 2004. Retrieved October 2004 from www.niaid.nih.gov/factsheets/aidsstat.htm.
201. Robert Searles Walker, *AIDS: Today, Tomorrow* (Atlantic Highlands, NJ: Humanities Press International, 1992), p. 119.
202. Joann Szabo, Phyllis Tonkin, Veronique Vaillancourt, Philip Winston, and Deidre Wright, "The Clinton Scorecard," unpublished paper, University of Houston Graduate School of Social Work, Houston, TX, April 25, 1996.
203. Norman Wyers, "Is Gay Rights Necessary for the Well-Being of Gays and Lesbians?" in Howard Jacob

Karger and James Midgley (eds.), *Controversial Issues in Social Welfare* Policy (Boston: Allyn & Bacon, 1994).

204. See K. Dychtwald, *Age Power* (New York: Putnam 1999); and National Center for Health Statistics, "U.S. Life Expectancy at All-Time High, But Infant Mortality Increases," Centers for Disease Control, February 11, 2004, retrieved October 2004 from www.cdc.gov/nchs/pressroom/04news/infantmort.htm
205. U.S. Department of Health and Human Services, Administration on Aging, *A Profile of Older Americans:2003.* Retrieved October 2004 from www.aoa.gov/prof/statistics/profile/2003/2003profile.pdf
206. See Ibid.; and C. Adamec, *The Unofficial Guide to Eldercare* (New York: McMillan Press, 1999).
207. C. Cozic (ed.), *An Aging Population: Opposing Viewpoints* (San Diego, CA: Greenhaven Press, 1996).
208. U.S. Department of Health and Human Services, Administration on Aging, *A Profile of Older Americans: 2003.*
209. U.S. Census Bureau, "The Older Population in the United States: March 2002," April 2003. Retrieved October 2004 from www.census.gov/prod/2003pubs/p20-546.pdf
210. Dychtwald, *Age Power.*
211. Ibid.
212. Cozic, *An Aging Population.*
213. U.S. Department of Health and Human Services, Administration on Aging, *A Profile of Older Americans: 2003.*
214. D. Olsen, "Testimony in Hearings before the Task Force on Social Security of the Committee on the Budget, House of Representatives, 106th Congress, First Session," May–June 1999. Retrieved from http://frwebgate.access.gpo.gov/cg . . . diskb/wais/data/106_house_hearings
215. Adamec, *The Unofficial Guide to Eldercare.*
216. M. Moon and J. Mulvey, *Entitlements and the Elderly: Protecting Promises, Recognizing Reality* (Washington DC: Urban Institute, 1996), p. 9.
217. U.S. Department of Health and Human Services, Administration on Aging, *A Profile of Older Americans: 2003.*
218. Cozic, *An Aging Population.*
219. Ibid.
220. Ibid., p. 7.
221. U.S. Census Bureau, "Sixty-Five Plus in the United States," May 1995. Retrieved from www.census.gov/socdemo/agebrief.html
222. L. D. Haber, "Trends and Demographic Studies on Programs for Disabled Persons," in L. G. Perlman and G. Austin (eds.), *A Report of the Ninth Annual Mary E. Switzer Memorial Seminar* (Alexandria, VA, 1985), pp. 27–29.
223. Bureau of the Census, "Disabilities Affect One-Fifth of All Americans Proportion Could Increase in Coming Decades," U.S. Department of Commerce, Economics and Statistics Administration, Washington, D.C., December 1997.
224. William Roth, "Disabilities: Physical," *Encyclopedia of Social Work,* 18th ed. (Silver Spring, MD: NASW, 1987), p. 86.
225. Ibid.
226. Haber, "Trends and Demographic Studies," p. 32.
227. Bell, *Contemporary Social Welfare,* p. 174.
228. Administration on Developmental Disabilities, *Fact Sheet* (Washington, DC: Administration on Developmental Disabilities, n.d.).
229. Kathy Brown, "Mend It, Don't End It," *Outlook* 90, no. 3 (Fall 1996), p. 9.
230. Brown, "Mend It, Don't End It," p. 11.
231. Bill Clinton, "Mend, Don't End, Affirmative Action," *Congressional Quarterly Weekly Report* 53 (July 22, 1995), pp. 2208–2209.
232. Roger Hernandez, "End Affirmative Action, but for the Right Reason," syndicated column, King Features, 1995.
233. Wilson, *The Truly Disadvantaged,* pp. 146–147.

CHAPTER 5

Poverty in America

This chapter examines the characteristics of poverty in the United States, focusing particular attention on the wide range of theories that attempt to explain why some people become poor and why many remain poor. Also examined are demographic aspects and ways of measuring poverty; family constitution and poverty; child poverty and elderly poverty; the urban and rural poor; and the connections between poverty and work-related issues such as the minimum wage, structural unemployment, dual labor markets, job training programs, and the alternative financial sector or the fringe economy. Lastly, this chapter surveys key strategies developed to combat poverty.

Some Theoretical Formulations about Poverty

Poverty is at once a simple and a complex phenomenon. People living in poverty can be seen as falling into three general categories: (1) those making only minimum wage (the working poor); (2) the unemployed; and (3) those who have human capital deficits, such as poor health, poor education, or a lack of training and skills.

The word *poverty* can be defined as deprivation—either absolute or relative deprivation. **Absolute poverty** refers to an unequivocal standard necessary for survival (e.g., the calories necessary for physical survival, adequate shelter for protection against the elements, and proper clothing). Those who fall below that absolute standard of poverty are considered poor. **Relative poverty** refers to deprivation that is relative to the standard of living enjoyed by other members of society. Although basic needs are met, a segment of the population may be considered poor if they possess fewer resources, opportunities, or goods than other citizens. Relative poverty (or deprivation) can be understood as inequality in the distribution of income, goods, or opportunities. Little attention is currently being focused on relative deprivation.

The Culture of Poverty

Culture of poverty (COP) theorists maintain that poverty and, more specifically, poverty traits are transmitted intergenerationally in a self-perpetuating cycle. According to this theory the COP transcends regional, rural/urban, and national differences and everywhere shows striking similarities in family structure, interpersonal relations, time orientation, value systems, and patterns of spending.[1]

Oscar Lewis maintained that the COP flourishes in certain types of societies where there is a cash economy based on wage labor and production for profit; there is a high rate of under- and

Spotlight 5.1

Poverty

People living in poverty fall into three general categories:

1. Those making only minimum wage (the working poor)
2. The unemployed
3. Those who have poor health or an occupational disability (e.g., a deficit in human capital such as poor education or a low quality and quantity of training and skills)

RESULTS is a nonprofit grassroots advocacy organization committed to creating the political will to end hunger and the worst aspects of poverty. RESULTS members lobby elected officials for effective solutions and key policies that affect hunger and poverty. To learn more about RESULTS, go to the organization's website at www.results.org.

unemployment for unskilled workers; low wages are common; there is a failure to provide low-income groups with social, political, and economic organization, either on a voluntary basis or by governmental imposition; and a set of values held by the dominant class that stresses the accumulation of wealth and property, the possibility of upward mobility, thrift, and the idea that low economic status results from personal inadequacy.

According to Lewis, the culture of poverty is characterized by hopelessness, indifference, alienation, apathy, and a lack of effective participation in or integration into the social and economic fabric of society. Key COP elements are a present-tense time orientation; cynicism toward and mistrust of those in authority; strong feelings of marginality, helplessness, dependence, and inferiority; a high incidence of maternal deprivation and a weak ego structure; lack of impulse control and the inability to defer gratification; a sense of resignation and fatalism; a widespread belief in male superiority; a high tolerance for psychological pathology of all kinds; the absence of childhood as a specially protected and prolonged state; early initiation into sexual unions or nonlegal marriages; a high incidence of abandonment of wives and children; a matriarchal family structure with an emphasis on family solidarity; a proclivity toward authoritarianism; and a minimal level of community organization combined with a strong sense of territoriality.

Adherents believe that simply being poor does not initiate one into the COP. Banfield and Lewis argue that most people who are poor because of the loss of a breadwinner, involuntary unemployment, or illness are able to overcome their impoverishment. Lewis suggests that only 20 percent of those living in poverty are actually ensconced in the culture of poverty. That is, they remain poor regardless of how the economy functions.

Some opponents argue that COP theories divert attention away from the real factors that cause poverty. Other critics argue that supposed characteristics of the COP are also evident in the middle and upper classes. For example, the inability to defer gratification underlies many credit card purchases. Sexual unions and informal marriages are a common occurrence among the middle classes. The lack of community is an earmark of the modern suburb; the inability to achieve family solidarity is widespread in U.S. culture; and feelings of indifference, helplessness, alienation, and dependence also afflict much of the middle classes.

Eugenics and Poverty

Theories based on eugenics and genetic inferiority have periodically surfaced as explanations for poverty, crime, and disease. In 1877, Richard Dugdale reported on a study of the New York penal system that found crime, pauperism, and disease were transmitted intergenerationally.[2] Henry Goddard's *The Kallikak Family* was an account of a Revolutionary War soldier who had an affair with a feebleminded servant girl before marrying a "respectable" woman.[3] Goddard meticulously listed the disreputable descendants of the servant girl and compared them with the respectable achievers of the wife's descendants. Generations of students were taught the dogma of eugenics.

The eugenics movement went into remission in response to the racial and genetic theories that Hitler's used to justify his genocidal policies. However, the movement reemerged with the publication of Arthur Jensen's 1969 article "How Much Can We Boost IQ and Scholastic Achievement?"[4] Jensen concluded that compensatory education was doomed to failure since 80 percent of intelligence (measured by IQ tests) was inherited. Jensen thereby concluded that money spent on compensatory education was wasted.[5]

William Shockley was a Nobel laureate in physics who became interested in genetics. Shockley advocated paying the "unfit poor" (those who paid no income taxes) $1,000 for each point they fell below an IQ of 100, if they agreed to be sterilized.[6] Richard Herrnstein, a Harvard psychologist and a colleague of Shockley and Jensen, claimed that income and wealth are distributed among Americans based on their abilities, which in turn, is related to their IQ score. Herrnstein argued that the United States should become a "hereditary meritocracy," where the most capable citizens receive the greatest rewards as an incentive for assuming leadership.[7]

The eugenics argument was rekindled by Richard Herrnstein and Charles Murray's *The Bell Curve,* which argued that socioeconomic inequality in the United States is not due to capitalism or racism but to the lack of genetic intelligence.[8] Armed with statistics, tables, and charts, Herrnstein and Murray tried to demonstrate that those in the lower socioeconomic classes have lower IQ scores, which explains why white males (who test higher) control so many of society's institutions.[9] They argue that affirmative action programs overlook intellectual meritocracy, and spending money to educate the poor is wasteful given their innate deficiencies.

The scholarship in *The Bell Curve* has been attacked by a wide range of critics in the scientific and educational communities.[10] These critics argue that Herrnstein and Murray exaggerate IQ as a predictor of job performance, attribute inaccurate validities to IQ scores, and substitute hypotheticals for reality.[11] Assertions about genetic inferiority fail to hold up under scrutiny, and the theories of Shockley, Jensen, Herrnstein, and Murray have been repudiated by scores of educators, psychologists, sociologists, and anthropologists.[12]

The Radical School and Poverty

Radicals define poverty as the result of exploitation by the ruling or dominant class under **capitalism.** According to socialists (see Chapter 1), poverty provides capitalists with an army of surplus laborers who can be used to depress the wages of workers. For example, employers can use an oversupply of workers to drive down wages in the knowledge that there will be an abundance of job takers. Using an oversupply of labor, employers can more easily threaten recalcitrant workers with dismissal since there is an intense competition for their jobs. Surplus labor is linked to poverty by using the *threat* of poverty (through unemployment) to discipline the labor force and demand concessions from it.

According to David Gil, poverty can be understood in terms of status, resource allocation, and the division of labor.[13] Most developed societies manipulate these factors. For instance, societies must develop resources—symbolic, material, life-sustaining, and life-enhancing goods and services. They must also develop a division of labor and must assign individuals or groups to specific tasks related to developing, producing, or distributing the resources of the society. This division of labor is used as the basis for assigning statuses to individuals and groups; that is, the more highly a society prizes the function an individual or group performs, the higher the status and the reward accrued. By manipulating the division of labor, a society is able to assign individuals to specific statuses within the total array of statuses and functions available.

The assignment of status roles is complemented by the distribution of rights. Higher-status roles implicitly demand greater compensation than lower-status ones, and such rewards come by way of the distribution of rights. Higher-status groups are rewarded by a substantial and liberal distribution of general entitlements and rights to material and symbolic resources, goods, and services. Conversely, lower-status groups are denied these resources through formal and informal constraints. Societies rationalize this form of status and goods allocation by an expressed belief in the omniscience of the marketplace. This ideology is well-masked and rarely questioned. Socialists argue that poverty will be omnipresent so long as society reproduces itself on the basis of the private ownership of the means of production. They believe that poverty cannot be altered without fundamentally rearranging the economic fabric of U.S. society.

Who Makes Up the Poor?

For most Americans, poverty is a fluid rather than static process. The University of Michigan's Panel Study of Income Dynamics (PSID) followed 5,000 U.S. families for almost 10 years (1969–1978) and found that only 2 percent of families were persistently poor throughout the entire period.[14] In fact, about one-third of the individuals who were poor in any given year escaped from poverty the following year, and only about one-third of the poor families in any given year had been poor for at least eight of the preceding years. The data showed that as people gained (or lost) jobs, as marriages were created (or dissolved), or as offspring were born (or left home), people either were pushed into poverty or escaped from it.[15] Changes in family composition, especially divorce or separation, were the leading causes of poverty. Conversely, **spells of poverty** were most often ended by family reconstitution (e.g., remarriage).

"Mobility in the United States is substantial, according to the evidence," concluded researchers from the Urban Institute, "Large portions of the population move into a new income quintile with estimates ranging from about 25 to 40 percent in a single year. The mobility rate is even higher over longer periods—about 45 percent over a 5-year period and about 60 percent over both 9-year and 17-year periods."[16] Bradley Schiller found that upward mobility is also experienced by the poor. According to Schiller, one-third of minimum wage workers had received a raise within a year, and that 60 percent were beyond the minimum wage within two years. "The longitudinal experiences of minimum-wage youth . . . refute the notion of a 'minimum-wage trap,'" he concluded. "Youth who started at the minimum wage in 1980 recorded impressive wage gains over the subsequent seven years both in absolute and relative terms."[17] W. Michael Cox and Richard Alm confirmed significant upward movement of the poor:

> Only 5 percent of those in the bottom fifth in 1975 were still there in 1991. Where did they end up? A majority made it to the top three fifths of the income distribution—middle class or better. Most amazing of all, almost 3 out of 10 of the low-income earners from 1975 had risen to the uppermost 20 percent by 1991. More than three-quarters found their way into the two highest tiers of income earners for at least one year by 1991.[18]

Delving deeper into the labor market, David Howell and Elizabeth Howell constructed a matrix of "job contours" consisting essentially of self-employed, white collar, blue collar, and low-wage jobs, then analyzed the mobility of workers according to race, gender, and immigrant status. During a period of enormous compression in job opportunities due to an influx of immigrants, the researchers found that among workers who had worked at least 20 weeks in the previous year, "male and female African American and female new immigrant workers show[ed] substantial improvements in their employment distribution, shifting from the two 'worst' (secondary) job contours toward the two 'best' (independent primary) contours."[19] There is much more to mobility than just income distribution, including education, occupation, and place of residence; yet, income data show that poverty is not a permanent status for many, if not the majority, of the poor.

The following statistics from 2003 suggest some important trends in poverty in the United States.

- The poverty rate in 2003 was 12.5 percent (35.9 million people), up from 12.1 percent (34.5 million) in 1998.
- The poverty rate for children under 18 was 17.6 percent, up from 16.7 percent in 1998. The poverty rate for people over 65 was 12.2 percent, the same rate as in 2002.
- Beginning in 2001 poverty rates also grew for every racial and ethnic group. The poverty rate for blacks was 24.4 percent in 2003, up from 24.1 percent in 2002 and more than twice the poverty rate for whites (10.6 percent). The non-Hispanic white poverty rate rose to 10.6 percent. For Hispanics the poverty rate rose to 22.5 percent, up from 21.8 percent in 2002. The poverty rate for Asians and Pacific Islanders rose to 11.8 percent in 2003, up from 10.0 percent in 2002. The 1997–1999 poverty rate for American Indians and Alaska Natives was 25.9 percent, not statistically different from those of blacks and Hispanics. This represents a dramatic turn since poverty rates had been edging downward throughout the 1990s. However, by 2001 the cycle was reversing and poverty rates began climbing upward.
- Poverty rates were 11.3 percent in the Northeast, 10.7 percent in the Midwest, 14.1 percent in the South, and 12.6 percent in the West. The rates remained the same as in 2002.
- Since 1993, poverty rose by 1.3 million to 28.4 million in metropolitan central cities.[20]

Table 5.1 describes the characteristics and numbers of poor over a 40-year period.

Measuring Poverty

There are two versions of the federal poverty measure: (1) the poverty threshold and (2) the poverty guideline. The poverty threshold, also called the **poverty line,** is the official federal poverty measure and is used primarily for statistical purposes, such as estimating the number of Americans in poverty each year. All official population figures are calculated using the poverty threshold. The poverty guideline uses a slightly lower poverty level than the poverty threshold; for example, for a family of four in 2003 the poverty guideline was $18,400 versus $18,810. The poverty guideline is used for determining eligibility requirements for federal programs such as Head Start, food stamps, the National School Lunch Program, and Low-Income Home Energy Assistance Program. Other federal programs, including TANF and Supplemental Security Income, use the poverty threshold. In 2003 the federal poverty index for a family of four was $18,810,[21] up from $8,414 in 1980.[22] (See Table 5.2 on page 116.) These increases do not reflect more liberal standards but are due solely to the effects of inflation.

Set by the Social Security Administration (SSA), absolute poverty is defined by a poverty line drawn at a given income. The poverty threshold used by the federal government was developed by taking the cost of the least expensive food plan (the Thrifty Food Plan developed by the Department of Agriculture) and multiplying that number by 3. This formula was based on 1955 survey data showing that the average family spent about one-third of its budget on food. Formally adopted by the SSA in 1969, the official pov-

Table 5.1

Persons below the Poverty Line, Selected Years and Characteristics, 1959–2002 (number and percentage below poverty, in thousands)

Year	Overall	Aged	Children[a]	Individuals in Female-Headed Families[b]	Blacks	Hispanic Origin[c]	White
+2002	34,570	3,578	12,133	11,667	8,884	8,556	24,074
	12.1%	10.4	16.7	26.5	24.1	21.8	10.3
1999	32,258	3,167	12,109	12,687	9,091	7,439	21,922
	11.8%	9.7	18.9	27.8	22.7	22.8	9.8
1995	36,425	3,318	13,999	12,315	9,872	8,574	24,423
	13.8%	10.5	20.2	32.4	29.3	30.3	11.2
1990	33,585	3,658	14,431	12,578	9,837	6,006	22,326
	13.5%	12.2	20.6	37.2	31.9	28.1	10.7
1986	32,370	3,477	12,876	11,944	8,983	5,117	22,183
	13.6%	12.4	20.5	38.3	31.3	27.3	11.0
1980	29,272	3,871	11,543	10,120	8,579	3,491	19,699
	13.0%	15.7	18.3	36.7	32.5	25.7	10.2
1978	24,497	3,233	9,931	9,269	7,626	2,607	16,259
	11.4%	14.0	15.9	35.6	30.6	21.6	8.7
1969	21,147	4,787	9,961	6,879	7,095	NA	16,659
	12.1%	25.3	14.0	38.2	32.2	NA	9.5
1959	39,490	5,481	17,552	7,014	9,927	NA	28,484
	22.4%	35.2	27.3	49.4	55.1	NA	18.1

\+ These numbers may appear inconsistent because the U.S. Census Bureau changed the classification of races in the 2000 census to include the designation of more than one race. In addition, the statistics were calculated slightly differently in different years.
a All children, including unrelated children.
b Does not include females living alone.
c People of Hispanic origin may be of any race; it is an overlapping category.

Sources: Compiled from Committee on Ways and Means, U.S. House of Representatives, *Overview of Entitlement Programs: 1992 Green Book* (Washington, DC: U.S. Government Printing Office, 1992), Tables 2 and 3, pp. 1274–1275; and U.S. Census Bureau, "Poverty 1995," September 26, 1996, retrieved from www.census.gov/hhes/poverty/pov95/thresh95.html; Joseph Dalaker and Bernadette D. Proctor, U.S. Census Bureau, "Poverty in the United States: 1999," *Current Population Reports,* Ser. P60-210 (Washington, DC: U.S. Government Printing Office, 2000); and Bernadette D. Proctor and Joseph Dalaker, U.S. Census Bureau, "Poverty in the United States: 2002, Demographic Programs," *Current Population Reports: Consumer Income, U.S. Department of Commerce, Economics and Statistics Administration* (Washington, DC: U.S. Government Printing Office, September 2003).

erty measure provides a set of income cutoffs adjusted for household size, the number of children under age 18, and the age of the household head. To ensure constant purchasing power, the SSA adjusts the poverty line yearly, using the consumer price index (CPI).

The poverty index is plagued by a variety of structural problems. A 1995 National Academy of Sciences (NAS) report noted the following problems in calculating the current poverty threshold:[24]

- It excludes in-kind benefits when counting family income.
- It ignores the cost of earning income when calculating the net income of working families. For example, $5,000 in wage income is treated as the equivalent of $5,000 in welfare benefits, despite inherent work-related costs such as clothing, transportation, and so on.
- It disregards regional variation in the cost of living, especially the cost of housing.
- It ignores the impact of tax payments, such as income, sales, payroll, and property taxes.
- It ignores the effects of earned income tax credits.

Table 5.2

Changes in the Poverty Line Based on Income and Family Size, 1975–2003

	Income, Selected Years					
Family Size	1975	1980	1985	1990	1995	2003
1	$2,724	$4,190	$5,250	$6,652	$7,763	$9,393
2	3,506	5,363	7,050	8,509	9,933	12,015
3	4,293	6,565	8,850	10,419	12,158	14,680
4	5,500	8,414	10,650	13,359	15,569	18,810
5	6,499	9,966	12,450	15,572	18,408	22,245
6	7,316	11,269	14,250	17,839	20,804	25,122
7	9,022	13,955	16,050	20,241	23,552	28,544

Source: Compiled from U.S. Census Bureau, *Technical Paper 56*, ser. P-60, nos. 134 and 149 (Washington, DC: U.S. Government Printing Office, 1992); U.S. Census Bureau, "Poverty 1995," retrieved September 1996 from www.census.gov/hhes/poverty/pov95/thresh95.html; and Carmen DeNavas-Walt, Bernadette D. Proctor, and Robert J. Mills, U.S. Census Bureau, "Income, Poverty and Health Insurance Coverage in the United States: 2003," *Current Population Reports*, ser. p. 60–226, retrieved October 2004 from www.census.gov/prod/2004pubs/p60-226.pdf.

- It ignores the value of health coverage in determining family income, and ignores medical care costs in determining family consumption needs.
- It has never been updated to account for changing consumption patterns and expenses. For example, although food accounted for one-third of all family expenditures in the 1950s, it now accounts for about one-seventh.[25]

The NAS panel made three important recommendations:

1. Change the measure of income by adding noncash benefits and by subtracting taxes and work-related expenses, child support payments, and out-of-pocket medical expenses.
2. Create a new poverty threshold that is based on clothing, food, shelter, and "a little bit more." The panel also suggested new ways of estimating the poverty threshold for families of different sizes and composition, allowing for geographic variation. They further suggested that annual updates of the threshold be based not simply on inflation but on the growth of median expenditures on basic goods (food, clothing, and shelter).
3. Replace the current use of the *March Current Population Survey* with data from the *Survey of Income and Program Participation*, a measure that would change the percentage and distribution of the poor.

Legitimizing the NAS panel recommendations, former Democratic senator Daniel Patrick Moynihan introduced the *Poverty Data Correction Act of 1999*, which would have required that any data relating to poverty be adjusted for geographic differences in the cost of living. Moynihan argued that because the current poverty calculations do not allow for geographical differences, they distort the true incidence of poverty.[26] Indeed, one would be hard-pressed to argue that the cost of living in Houma, Louisiana, is equivalent to Los Angeles or New York.

Families and Poverty

Family composition is strongly correlated to poverty, and the families at greatest risk of poverty in the United States are those headed by single females. In 2003 the poverty rate for male-present families was 5.4 percent; for female-headed households it was 28.0 percent. These figures become even starker when disaggregated: Families headed by non-Hispanic white women had a poverty rate of 25.8 percent; families headed by African American and Hispanic women had poverty rates of 39.3 and 38.8 percent, respectively.[27]

More than 1 million American children see their parents divorce or separate each year, and more than half will spend some time in a single-parent family.

Using six nationally representative data sets tracking more than 25,000 children, Sara McLanahan and Gary Sandefur found that children raised with only one biological parent are disadvantaged in myriad ways. Compared to children who grow up in two-parent families, they are (1) twice as likely to drop out of school; (2) 2.5 times as likely to become teen mothers; (3) 1.4 times as likely to be idle—out of work and out of school; (4) likely to have lower grade point averages, lower college aspirations, poorer academic attendance records, and higher rates of divorce in adulthood. These patterns persist even after adjustments for differences in race, the education of parents, the number of siblings, and the child's geographic location.[28]

The families at greatest risk of poverty in the United States are those headed by single females. This poverty is compounded when child support payments are withheld.

Child Support Enforcement

A 1995 Census Bureau study reported that slightly more than half of families with an absent parent have child support orders in place. Of those with orders, half received full payment and half received partial or no payment.[29] In 1975 Congress enacted Title IV-D, which was later amended by the Child Support Enforcement Amendments of 1984, the Family Support Act of 1988, and the Personal Responsibility and Work Opportunity Reconciliation Act of 1996. Title IV-D of the federal Social Security Act funds state programs designed to recover child support payments. A case is considered IV-D if the family has received public assistance benefits, or if an application for services was filed with a public welfare agency. The attention focused on "deadbeat dads" has important political overtones. Some argue that focusing on deadbeat dads has allowed policymakers to blame a variety of social ills, from poverty to high welfare costs to social pathology, squarely on fathers.[30]

Nevertheless, child support is important for families with only one custodial parent. According to the Census Bureau, almost 75 percent (6.9 million of 7.9 million) custodial parents received some child support in 2002. The proportion of custodial parents receiving every payment they were due increased from 37 percent to 46 percent between 1993 and 1997, with the 2001 proportion remaining unchanged at 45 percent. Custodial parents reported receiving about 63 percent of child support due in 2001.[31] When the 5.9 million custodial parents without any agreements or with informal agreements were asked why a legal agreement was not established, the reason most often cited was that they did not feel the need to go to court or get legal agreements (32.7 percent). Among the other reasons given were that the other parent provided what they could for support (26.3 percent), and the other parent could not afford to pay (23.3 percent).[32] Arguably, child support is even more important for low-income families.

- In 2001 child support constituted 16 percent of family income ($4,300) for households that received it.
- Child support constitutes 26 to 29 percent of the income of divorced families and reduces their poverty rate by 7 to 11 percent.
- Child support is an important income source for poverty-level families. In 2001 about 66 percent of custodial parents with incomes below the poverty line that were due child support received at least some payment. The average amount was $3000 and constituted 40 percent of their total family income.

- Child support lifts about 500,000 children out of poverty and reduces the poverty rate by 8 percent.
- Child support is an important income source for families leaving welfare. About 42 percent of families leaving welfare receive child support, which makes up 30 percent ($2562) of their income.
- Child support is important for families affected by welfare time limits. The percentage of these families receiving child support and the amounts they receive increase after public assistance is terminated.
- Child support is important for families leaving the TANF program for work. Between 25 and 33 percent of those leaving welfare for work receive between $250 and $400 a month in child support.
- One study of families leaving welfare with regular child support payments found that they had a slower rate of welfare reentry, a faster rate of finding work, and a slower rate of job loss compared to families without steady child support income.[33]

In 1996, President Clinton signed into law the Personal Responsibility and Work Opportunity Reconciliation Act (PRWORA). The PRWORA was intended to broadly reform the public assistance system, but it also addressed child support enforcement. Specifically, failure to meet child support obligations could result in revocation of driver's and professional licenses; expanded wage garnishment; liens; and/or denial, revocation, or limitation of passports. Delinquent support obligations could also be collected through unemployment and disability insurance benefits.

Children in Poverty

There were 12.9 million poor children in the United States in 2003. The poverty rate for children is higher than for any other age group: 17.6 percent in 2003 compared to an overall poverty rate of 12.5 percent. For children under age six, the poverty rate was even higher, at 19.8 percent (4.7 million children). While high, this rate is eclipsed by the almost 53 percent poverty rate for children under six living in female-headed households.[34] More than 10 percent of U.S. children live in extreme poverty (family incomes below 50 percent of the poverty line) and 40 percent of children live in or near poverty (family incomes below 200 percent of the poverty line). Compared to poverty in later childhood, research indicates that extreme poverty during a child's first five years has especially deleterious effects on their future life chances.[35]

White children account for the highest number of children in poverty, almost 15 million (poverty rates for white children rose more than 25 percent in the 1980s).[36] In 2003, 33.1 percent of African American children were poor. For Hispanic children the poverty rate was 29.4 percent, up from 28 percent in 1995.[37] The probability of children growing up poor is strongly correlated with family composition. In 1987, for example, the Census Bureau estimated that 61 percent of the children born in that year would spend some part of their childhood in single-parent families, which are five times more likely to be poor than two-parent families.[38]

Poverty and the Elderly

On the surface, the poverty picture for the elderly (once the poorest group in the country) seems to be growing less bleak. In 1959 the poverty rate for those over 65 was 35.2 percent; by 2003 it had dropped to 10.2 percent. Despite the downward trend, more than 3.5 million elderly citizens live in poverty, and almost 33 percent live near the poverty line.[39]

Senior poverty is disproportionately experienced by minority groups. Almost 24 percent of African Americans over age 65 were poor in 2003, and more than 49 percent were "near poor" (with incomes less than 175 percent of the poverty line). For African American women those numbers were 27.1 percent and 55.1 percent, respectively. More than 20 percent of elderly Hispanics were poor, and more than 47 percent were near poor. Among women the numbers rose to 21.7 percent and 48.6 percent, respectively.[40]

The federal government's estimate of the elderly poor is questionable. Specifically, the poverty line is calculated using two classifications: (1) families headed by persons under age 65, and (2) families headed by persons 65 or older, for whom the poverty line is set lower. For example, the poverty line in 1998 for unrelated individuals 65 or older was $7,818 compared to $8,480 for their younger counterparts—a difference of 8 percent or $662. This differential is based on the belief that the elderly spend less on food than their younger counterparts because physiologically they require less food to absorb the same amount of nutrients. Had the 1990 poverty line for the elderly been equivalent to the rest of the population, their poverty rate would have exceeded the rate for the population as a whole, raising by 25 percent the number of elderly people designated as poor.[42]

The Urban and Rural Poor

About 7.5 million Americans live in rural poverty. This segment of the population is generally overlooked because of the national attention directed toward urban poverty.[43] Although rural poverty does not receive significant media attention, many rural areas have poverty rates equal to those of central cities. In 2002, 14.2 percent of nonmetro residents had income levels below the poverty line compared to 11.6 percent of the metro population.[44]

More than half of the rural poor live in the South, 21 percent in the Midwest, 16 percent in the West, and 9 percent in the Northeast. Since the farming population accounts for only 10 percent of the rural population, the rural poor are mostly nonfarmers.[45] The number of poor rural communities has dropped since 1960, when 2083 counties had a poverty rate of 20 percent or more. By 2004 the number of persistently poor counties designated by the USDA as having poverty rates of 20 percent or more had dropped to 386. Traditionally poor rural areas include the Colonias of the Southwest, the Mississippi Delta, Appalachia, and Indian reservations.[46]

Rural minority members experience considerable. The figures are striking:

- More than 25 percent of nonmetro Hispanics, blacks, and American Indians are poor.
- The nonmetro poverty rates in 2002 for blacks (33 percent) and American Indians (35 percent) were more than three times the nonmetro poverty rate for whites (11 percent). The rate for Hispanics (27 percent) was more than twice as high.
- Sixty-eight percent of poor nonmetro Hispanics have less than a high school education, compared with 40 percent of nonmetro poor whites. Fifty-two percent of poor nonmetro American Indians have incomes less than half of the poverty line.
- Poverty rates for African Americans and American Indians are more than 10 percentage points higher in nonmetro areas than in metro areas, the largest gap among minority population groups.[47]

The rural poor are more likely than the urban poor to be in chronic long-term poverty. Though unemployment is generally higher in rural areas, the rural poor rely less on public assistance than the urban poor. Lack of information and access to services, fear of stigma, and reliance on informal employment sources may help explain some of this difference.[48] Family structure has a significant bearing on poverty.

- Over 75 percent of all nonmetro families are headed by a married couple. About 15 percent are headed by a single female.
- Nonmetro people living in families headed by a married couple have the lowest rate of poverty, at 7.2 percent.
- In nonmetro areas, 16.6 percent of the people in male-headed, single-adult families are poor, while the poverty rate is 37.1 percent for members of female-headed families.
- The poverty rate for nonmetro female-headed families is 10 percentage points greater than in metro areas.
- Approximately 2.6 million children living in nonmetro areas are poor, constituting 35 percent of the nonmetro poverty population. In 2002, one out of every five children living in nonmetro areas was poor.[49]

Several factors contribute to chronic rural poverty, including high levels of illiteracy, low levels of education, a dearth of highly trained workers, high numbers of low-skill and low-paying jobs, high levels of underemployment and unemployment, and an deficient physical infrastructure. Rural county and city managers also find it difficult to attract major industries. Not surprisingly, the absence of economic opportunity has resulted in the outmigration of many rural families, especially when the primary earner possesses higher-level skills and education.[50]

Work and Poverty

Almost one in four U.S. workers live in or around the edges of poverty. Thirty-five million Americans work full time but fail to make an adequate living. They are the nursing home aides, poultry processors, pharmacy assistants, child care workers, data entry keyers, janitors, and other employees of the secondary and tertiary labor markets. Except for short periods, the relative wages of these workers have declined since the 1980s, and the number of poor working people aged 22 to 64 rose more than 50 percent between 1979 and 1991.[51]

A Profile of the Working Poor

As a group, the **working poor** represent a growing sector of the poverty population. People who worked at any time during 1999 had a lower overall poverty rate (6.1 percent) than nonworkers (19.9 percent). More than 24 percent of female-headed households with one worker were poor, compared to 68 percent of households with no workers.[52] The following represents some of the demographics of the working poor in 2001.

- The working poor are defined as individuals who spend at least 27 weeks in the labor force (working or looking for work) but whose family or personal incomes fall below the poverty line. About 6.8 million persons were classified as the working poor in 2001, nearly 319,000 more than in 2000.
- Working wives are less likely than working husbands to be poor, because they are more likely to be in families with a second earner. In 2001 about 1.7 percent of married women in the labor force for 27 weeks or more were poor, compared to 3.1 percent of married men. In contrast, 17 percent of families headed by a single female in the labor force for at least six months were in poverty.
- About 5.3 percent of non-Hispanic whites were classified as working poor, compared to 9.6 percent of African Americans and 10.1 percent of Hispanics.
- Almost 13.1 percent of high school dropouts were classified as working poor, more than double that of high school graduates (5.8 percent). The poverty rates were even lower for workers with an associate degree (2.4 percent) and for college graduates (1.5 percent). Poverty rates at all levels of educational attainment were higher for women and African Americans than for white men.
- Nearly 11 percent of people who were in the labor force for at least 27 weeks but whose longest job was a service occupation lived below the poverty line. The 2 million working poor in these occupations accounted for nearly 32 percent of all workers in poverty.
- A sizable group of full-time workers live below the poverty threshold and are affected by three primary labor market problems: unemployment, low earnings, and involuntary part-time employment. In 2001 about 83 percent of the full-time working poor experienced at least one of these major labor market problems.[53]

Why Are There Working Poor?

Part of the problems of the working poor are related to the recent business cycle and its four phases: a downward spiral from 1989 to 1993 (family income fell $1,572 from 1989–1992), a slow recovery up to 1995, rapid growth from 1995 to 2001 (family income grew $4,555 from 1995–1999), and a drop in income from 2001 onward. One indicator to measure the economic well-being of workers is the hourly wage of the median male and female worker. Throughout the 1980s and early 1990s, the median male wage fell dramatically, dropping 9.1 percent. Although the male median wage rose 5.5 percent from 1995 to 1999, this was insufficient to offset earlier declines. In contrast, the median female wage grew slowly over the 1980s, rising 5.7 percent from 1979 to 1989 and then dipping slightly in the early 1990s. However, women's wages grew 5.8 percent from 1995 to 1999. Although there was a marked increase in wages during the mid-1990s, much of this increase was offset by the wage declines in the 1980s and early 1990s and by the higher prices of necessities such as housing, health care, education, and pharmaceuticals.[54] While corporate profits rose in 2003, median- and below-median wage earners were losing ground and the gains made in the mid-1990s had virtually evaporated.[55]

The large numbers of working poor are related to other factors, including the replacement of high-paying industrial jobs with low-paying service jobs. Millions of Americans who were working full time, year-round earned less than the official poverty level for a family of four. In 2002, that number was 16.1 million or 16.1 percent of full-time workers. Roughly one in five women and one in eight men who had full-time jobs the year round earned less than the poverty level for a family of four.[56]

This employment trend reflects a clear movement away from higher-paying manufacturing jobs to low-wage service employment. By the 1980s corporations had eliminated 300,000 manufacturing jobs. Continuing this trend, a million more manufacturing jobs were eliminated during the 1990s. In the 1950s, 33 percent of all workers were employed in primary manufacturing industries (e.g., cars, radios, refrigerators, clothing). By 1992 only 17 percent were employed in those industries. While manufacturing jobs have declined, service jobs have increased. According to the Bureau of Labor Statistics, service-providing industries are expected to account for approximately 20.8 million of the 21.6 million new wage and salary jobs generated from 2002 to 2012.[57]

Underemployment and Unemployment

The failure of the labor market to meet the economic needs of the population has been the source of important distinctions in employment policy. For example, those over 16 who are looking for work are counted by the Department of Labor as unemployed. But the **unemployment** rate does not assess the adequacy of employment. For example, part-time workers who wish to work full time are counted as employed; and workers holding jobs below their skill levels are not identified, even though such workers are **underemployed.** Finally, **discouraged workers** who simply give up and stop looking for work, relying on other methods to support themselves, do not appear in the unemployment statistics because they are not actively seeking work.

A second set of distinctions relates to economic performance. In a robust economy businesses start up and close down in significant numbers, leaving workers temporarily out of work until they find other jobs. Such **frictional unemployment** is considered to be unavoidable, the cost of a constantly changing economy. **Structural unemployment,** in contrast, refers to "deeper and longer-lasting maladjustments in the labor market," such as changes in the technical skills required for new forms of production.[58] Because of swings in economic performance, some unemployment may be cyclical, as when recessions pitch the rate upward; but because certain groups of workers in certain regions have persistent difficulty finding work owing to an absence of jobs, some unemployment may be chronic. Michael Sherraden has examined how these components vary in the composition of the unemployment rate and concludes that structural and frictional factors account for about one-third, **cyclical unemployment** for about one-fourth, and **chronic unemployment** for about one-half.[59]

These distinctions are important because social welfare is connected directly to the employment experience of Americans. When people are out of work, they frequently rely on welfare benefits to tide them over. Thus, welfare programs are often designed to complement the labor market. This has led some observers to refer to welfare as a **social wage;** in other words, the amount the government pays to workers through welfare programs when they are not able to participate in the labor market. Logically, much of welfare could be eliminated if well-paying jobs were plentiful, but such has not been the case in the United States. Policymakers have tacitly accepted an unemployment rate of 5 percent or more, which means that at any given time 5 to 8 million workers are unemployed.[60] Yet in 1978 Congress enacted the Humphrey–Hawkins Full Employment Act, which set an unemployment rate of 3 percent—equivalent to frictional unemployment—as a national goal. Since then, many government programs to aid unemployed, underemployed, and discouraged workers have been reduced or eliminated, leaving many Americans dependent on welfare programs for support.

The outsourcing of U.S. jobs to low-wage countries, such as India and China, may also be exacerbating unemployment. A report by the U.S. Department of Labor on mass layoffs found that in the first quarter of 2004, 4,633 workers were laid off because their jobs were moved overseas. However, other economists argue that the report undercounted the total number of jobs lost offshore, with the real number being between 250,000 to 350,000 jobs a year. (This is still a relatively small number in a labor force of more than 130 million people.) The report also did not account for jobs created by American companies overseas that did not involve a direct layoff in the United States. Nonetheless, the trend of outsourcing work overseas raises concerns about the potential loss of the high-wage white-collar jobs (especially in information technology) that were once considered safe from global competition. It also raises the specter that competition from less expensive overseas workers will slow the wage growth of American workers.[61]

The absence of employment opportunities contributes to other social problems. Research by M. Harvey Brenner shows that a seemingly small increase in the unemployment rate is associated with an increase in several social problems. During the 1973–1974 recession, for example, the unemployment rate increased by 14.3 percent, a change

Table 5.3

Consequences of Increases in Unemployment

Pathological Indicator	Percentage Increase due to Rise in Unemployment Increase	Rise in Incidence of Pathology
Total mortality	2.3	45,936
Cardiovascular mortality	2.8	28,510
Cirrhosis mortality	1.4	430
Suicide	1.0	270
Population in mental hospitals	6.0	8,416
Total arrests	6.0	577,477
Arrests for fraud and embezzlement	4.0	11,552
Assaults reported to police	1.1	7,035
Homicide	1.7	403

Source: Reprinted from M. Harvey Brenner, *Estimating the Effects of Economic Change on National Health and Social Well-Being* (Washington, DC: U.S. Government Printing Office, 1984), p. 2.

associated with the pathologies shown in Table 5.3. Brenner calculated that the combination of the 1973–1974 increase in the unemployment rate, the decrease in real per capita income, and an increase in the business failure rate was related to "an overall increase of more than 165,000 deaths [from cardiovascular disease] over a ten-year period (the greatest proportion of which occurs within three years)."[62] Overall, the total economic, social, and health care costs of this seemingly slight increase in unemployment cost $24 billion.[63]

As noted earlier, underemployment and unemployment constitute a major factor in determining poverty. Between 1981 and 1986, 10.8 million workers lost their jobs because of plant shutdowns, layoffs, or other forms of job termination. Five million of these workers had been at their jobs for at least three years.[64] From 1979 to 1984 the Department of Labor conducted a study of 5.1 million workers whose jobs were lost between January 1979 and January 1984. This study reported that in 1984, 40 percent of these workers were still unemployed or out of the workforce. Of the remainder, close to half were employed at either part-time jobs or jobs with lower weekly earnings than they had previously received. The majority experienced significant economic losses for a lengthy time after their jobs were lost.[65]

Job Training Programs

The failure of the labor market to provide adequate employment opportunities to large numbers of workers has also led to a series of governmental efforts to better prepare the unemployed and underemployed. The first of these was the Manpower Development and Training Act (MDTA) of 1962. Designed to assist workers displaced by technological and economic change, the MDTA was also expected to serve the disadvantaged when the **Office of Economic Opportunity (OEO)** was established in 1964. As one of the primary weapons in the Johnson administration's newly declared War on Poverty or Great Society plan, the MDTA grew rapidly, from $93 million in 1964 to $358 million in 1973. Still, the MDTA was only one among several **Great Society** job programs to aid the disadvantaged, including the Neighborhood Youth Corps, the Job Corps, and the Work Incentive Program (for AFDC recipients).[66]

By the mid-1970s the proliferation and cost of job training programs prompted the Nixon administration and Congress to consolidate MDTA and other job training programs under the Comprehensive Employment and Training Act (CETA) of 1973. In addition to consolidating federal job training programs, CETA also decentralized program responsibilities to local governments. By 1978 CETA was budgeted at $11.2 billion and enrolled 3.9 million persons.[67] Yet the nation's most ambitious program for contending with joblessness soon became the center of controversy. The recession of the 1970s placed financial burdens on local governments, at the same time as budget-limiting acts capped their fiscal capacity. Consequently, strong incentives were created for local governments to use the CETA program to fill civil service positions left vacant because of budget retrenchments. Because many of these jobs required work experience, CETA became a means by which a local government could subsidize its personnel budget—often by hiring relatively skilled persons and neglecting the chronically unemployed. Superseding CETA, the Job Training and Partnership Act (JTPA) of 1982 attempted to focus training on the hard-core unemployed to make them economically self-sufficient through private sector employment. Approximately 600 Private Industry Councils were created locally to synchronize training and job opportunities.[68]

Dual Labor Markets

According to Piore, the labor market can be divided into two segments, or "dual labor markets"—a **primary labor market** and a **secondary labor market:**

> The primary market offers jobs which possess several of the following traits: high wages, good working conditions, employment stability and job security, equity and due process in the administration of work rules, and chances for advancement. The other, secondary sector, has jobs which, relative to those in the primary sector, are decidedly less attractive. They tend to involve low wages, poor working conditions, considerable variability in employment, harsh and often arbitrary discipline, and little opportunity to advance. The poor are confined to the secondary labor market.[69]

Researchers calculated that in 1970 36.2 percent of workers fell into the secondary labor market, a modest increase over 1950's 35 percent.[70] By the 2000s, however, two factors increased the proportion of workers in the secondary labor market. First, membership in labor unions—the best security for nonprofessional workers—fell from 30.8 percent of nonagricultural workers in 1970 to 12.9 percent in 2003, leaving millions of workers vulnerable to the employment insecurity typical of the secondary labor market.[71] Second, a higher proportion of the new jobs created were in the service sector, which consists largely of secondary labor market jobs.[72]

Wages and Poverty

The Minimum Wage The low minimum wage is another factor that explains the growth of the working poor. In contrast to the current $5.15-an-hour minimum wage, the Economic Policy Institute estimates that households with one adult and two children require $14 an hour to live barely above the poverty line. Sixty percent of American workers earn less than $14 an hour and unskilled entry-level workers in many service occupations earn $7 an hour or less.[73] In 2003 about 2.1 million hourly workers (2.9 percent of the workforce) earned the minimum wage.[74] The following employment sectors have the highest percentage of minimum wage jobs:

Private household services (36.8 percent)
Retail trade—eating and drinking places (24.5 percent)

The minimum wage has been criticized by both conservatives and liberals.

Food service workers (23.8 percent)
All service occupations (14.1 percent)
Retail trade (11.5 percent)
Personal service workers (10.7 percent)
Farming, forestry and fishing (8.4 percent)
Agriculture (7.8 percent)
Cleaning and building service workers (6.9 percent)[75]

Unlike other programs, the minimum wage is not adjusted annually to the cost of living. Congress must pass a bill and the president must sign it into law for the minimum wage to rise. Minimum wage increases have been signed into law by Presidents Truman, Eisenhower, Kennedy, Johnson, Nixon, Carter, George H. W. Bush, and Clinton. The minimum wage has risen only slightly during the past 15 years, increasing to $4.25 an hour by 1991, then remaining at that level for more than five years. By 1996 approximately 10 million American workers were earning between $4.25 and $5.14 per hour. In 1997 the federal minimum wage was again raised, this time to $5.15 an hour. The minimum wage has not risen since 1997.

In 1950 the minimum wage brought a worker to 56 percent of the median wage. Throughout the 1950s and 1960s (see Table 5.4), the minimum wage hovered between 44 and 56 percent of the average wage. By 1980, however, the minimum wage had fallen to 46.5 percent of the average wage, and in 1988 it dropped even farther to 35.7 percent. Overall, from 1979 to 1996 the minimum wage dropped 29 percent. Even the increase to $5.15 an hour in 1997 raised the minimum wage to only 42 percent of the average wage, bringing a family of three to 83 percent of the poverty line[76] (considerably lower than the 120 percent of the poverty level reached by the minimum wage in 1968[77]). Moreover, the minimum wage increase in 1997 needed to be $6.07 (almost $1.00 higher) to have the same purchasing power as in the 1970s.[78]

The minimum wage has been criticized by both liberals and conservatives. Examining the persistently high unemployment rate among younger workers—including roughly 35 percent of African American teenagers—some conservatives have

Table 5.4

Value of the Minimum Wage, Selected Years

Year	Percent of Poverty Line for a Family of Three	Percent of Average Wage	Value of the Minimum Wage, 1995 Dollars	Minimum Wage, Nominal Dollars
1955	73	44	$3.94	$0.75
1960	88	48	4.75	1.00
1965	103	51	5.59	1.25
1968	120	56	6.49	1.60
1970	107	50	5.92	1.60
1975	101	46	5.71	2.10
1980	98	47	5.76	3.10
1985	81	39	4.76	3.35
1988	73	36	4.33	3.35
1989	71	35	4.13	3.35
1990	79	38	4.44	3.80
1993	75	39	4.50	4.25
1995	72	37	4.25	4.25
1997	83	42	NA	5.15

Sources: Based on data from Isaac Shapiro, *The Minimum Wage and Job Loss* (Washington, DC: Center on Budget and Policy Priorities, 1988), p. 3; U.S. Census Bureau, "Income 1995" (Washington, DC: U.S. Government Printing Office, September 26, 1996); and Center on Budget and Policy Priorities, "Assessing the $5.15 an Hour Minimum Wage," March 1996, retrieved from http://epn.org/cpbb/cbwage.html.

argued that the minimum wage deters employers from hiring unproven workers.[79] Lowering (or eliminating) the minimum wage, conservatives suggest, would encourage employers to make more jobs available to the disadvantaged. Liberals, on the other hand, argue that the minimum wage is inadequate. At its present level, a worker employed 40 hours a week would earn approximately $10,712 a year, $4,792 below the 2003 poverty line of $14,680 for a family of three.

Companies in metropolitan areas experiencing labor shortages use a "real" minimum wage that is often $1 to $2 above the federal level. Jared Bernstein maintains that a rise in the minimum wage would affect workers making just above the minimum wage through a "spillover effect." Workers in this group are more likely to be older (87 percent are adults) and to work more hours (69 percent work full time) than minimum wage workers.

The Living Wage Movement An alliance between labor and religious leaders in Baltimore in 1994 led to a campaign for a local law requiring city service contractors to pay a living wage. These kinds of campaigns seek to pass local ordinances requiring private businesses that benefit from public money to pay their workers a living wage. Commonly, these ordinances cover employers who hold large city or county service contracts or receive substantial financial assistance from the city in the form of grants, loans, bond financing, tax abatements, or other economic development subsidies. Since the Baltimore campaign 1994, community, labor, and religious coalitions have fought for and won similar ordinances in St. Louis, Boston, Los Angeles, Tucson, San Jose, Portland, Milwaukee, Detroit, Minneapolis, and Oakland. By 2000, there were more than 75 living wage campaigns under way in cities, counties, and states.

The justification for these campaigns is that when subsidized employers pay workers less than a living wage, taxpayers pay a double bill: the initial subsidy plus increased taxes to pay for food stamps and other social services low-wage workers require to support themselves and their families. Many citywide campaigns have defined the living wage as equivalent to the poverty line for a family of four, although ordinances that have passed stipulate wages ranging from $6.25 to $11.42 an hour, with some campaigns pushing for even higher wages. Increasingly, living wage coalitions are proposing other community standards in addition to a wage requirement, such as health benefits, vacation days, community hiring goals, public disclosure, community advisory boards, environmental standards, and language that supports union organizing.[80]

In addition to the federal minimum wage, states can institute their own higher minimum wage. (See Table 5.5.) By 2003, 12 states and the District of Columbia had a higher minimum wage, with Washington and Oregon linking it automatically to the cost of living.[81]

Table 5.5

States with Minimum Wages above the Federal Rate, 2003

State	Minimum Wage
Alaska	$7.15
California	6.75
Connecticut	6.90
Delaware	6.15
Washington, D.C.	6.15
Hawaii	6.25
Illinois	6.00
Maine	6.25
Massachusetts	6.75
Oregon	6.90
Rhode Island	6.15
Vermont	6.25
Washington	7.01

Source: Based on data from Jeff Chapman, "States Move on Minimum Wage, Federal Inaction Forces States to Raise Wage Floor to Protect Low-Wage Workers," *EPI Issue Brief #195* (June 11, 2003).

Strategies Developed to Combat Poverty

Former Senator Bob Kerrey stated that "In a global economy, your economic health and security is measured by what you own in addition to what you earn."[82] Michael Sherraden concurs: "Despite the prominence of asset ownership in American values and American history, social policy in the modern welfare state—and especially means-tested policy for the poor—has been focused almost exclusively on the distribution of income for consumption. Indeed, means-tested policy usually prohibits savings and the accumulation of assets. . . . After more than 50 years of income maintenance policy, we have confirmed that it is correctly named—it provides only maintenance, not development."[83] Sherraden goes on to suggest that "We should consider a different approach. Social policy, including welfare policy, should promote asset accumulation. In addition to the income and consumption policy of the current welfare state, asset-based policy would focus on savings and investment."[84] For the vast majority of households, the road to ending poverty involves savings, accumulation and assets. These are important prerequisites for purchasing a home, sending a child to college, starting a small business, and for reaching other economic goals. Moreover, when people begin to accumulate assets, their thinking and behavior changes, leading to important psychological and social effects that are not achieved when simply receiving and spending regular income.[85]

Until recently, the importance of asset accumulation for the poor has been virtually ignored in welfare state policies. Nevertheless, the tax system does support asset accumulation for the non-poor in two primary areas: tax benefits for home equity and for retirement pension accounts. In these two areas alone, the federal government spends well over $100 billion each year and the total is rising rapidly.[86] Unfortunately, poor people fail to benefit from asset accumulation tax policies because they have marginal tax rates that are either zero or too low to receive significant tax benefits. Even worse, means-tested welfare programs count assets and savings as income in calculating eligibility. As such, the poor who have accumulated assets or savings must spend these down in order to qualify for assistance.

IDAs

The concept of individual development accounts (IDAs) was introduced in 1991 by Michael Sherraden in *Assets and the Poor.*[87] IDAs are part of an asset-building policy strategy designed to reduce wealth inequality by enabling asset-poor individuals to accumulate assets. Low-income individuals establish savings accounts matched by public and private resources, which are then used for home purchases, business capitalization, and post-secondary education.[88]

In Sherraden's framework, IDA accounts would be established for all low-income individuals, and would be tax benefitted to foster asset accumulation. Depending on the financial circumstances of the depositor, individual savings would be matched by federal, state, or private contributions at varying rates. For instance, a very low–income family might have a match as high as 90 percent while a working family with a relatively good income would receive no match at all but might receive tax benefits. The matching system would be flexible and permit the government to supplement savings as the economic circumstances of individuals change. IDA accounts would be managed by individuals so that they become familiar with investment options. Despite the flexibility, IDA withdrawals would be restricted to approved purposes such as home purchases, education, retirement, or the creation of a business. IDA assets could be transferred to children at death or prior to death.[89]

The Assets for Independence Act (AFIA) became law in 1998. AFIA was essentially a five year, $125 million federal demonstration project. Although funding was anemic at best, it represented one of the first anti-poverty programs to emerge from Congress in many years. By 2002, approximately 250 IDA initiatives were in operation and 35 states had some sort of IDA policy. Moreover, Congress was deliberating on the Savings for Working Families Act (SWFA)—a multibillion-dollar tax bill promoting IDAs.[90]

Three Approaches to Combat Poverty

Policy analysts have identified three basic strategies for combating poverty. The first strategy, used by Lyndon Johnson in the War on Poverty and Great Society programs, was to apply a curative strategy to the problems of the poor. The **curative approach to poverty** aims to end chronic and persistent poverty by helping the poor to become self-supporting through changes in their personal lives and in their environment. By breaking the self-perpetuating cycle of poverty, the curative approach strives to initiate the poor into the employment and, later, the middle class. The goal of the curative approach is rehabilitation, and its target is the causes of poverty.

The second strategy is the **alleviative approach to poverty,** which is exemplified by public assistance programs that attempt to ease the suffering of the poor rather than ameliorate the causes of poverty. The third strategy is the **preventive approach to poverty,** exemplified by social insurance programs such as Social Security. In this approach, people are required to utilize social insurance to insure against the costs of accidents, sickness, death, old age, unemployment, and disability. The preventive strategy sees the state as a large insurance company whose umbrella shelters its members against the vicissitudes of life.

John Kenneth Galbraith's *The Affluent Society* identified two kinds of poverty: **case poverty** and **area poverty.** According to Galbraith, case poverty was the outgrowth of personal deficiencies (i.e., deficits in human capital). Area poverty was related to economic problems endemic to a region. "Pockets of poverty" or "depressed areas" resulted from a lack of industrialization in a region or the inability of an area to adjust to technological change. This kind of poverty was a function of the changing nature of the marketplace.[91]

One example of a case poverty approach is the federal government's attempt to promote education as a means to increase human capital. Poverty is highly correlated with educational deficits, and adolescent parenthood is strongly associated with low levels of basic skills and high dropout rates.[92] To help address these educational deficits, the federal government initiated the Head Start program, which was targeted at poor children age three to five and their families.[93]

Area poverty is illustrated by reviewing poverty rates on a state-by-state basis (see Table 5.6). While the overall national poverty rate in 2003 was 12.5 percent, some states that were poverty pockets had much higher poverty rates, including New Mexico (18.1 percent), Mississippi (16.0 percent), Alabama (15.0 percent), Louisiana (17.0 percent), West Virginia (17.4 percent), and Texas (17 percent). By contrast, other states like New Hampshire (5.8 percent), Alaska (9.6 percent), New Jersey (8.6 percent), and Delaware (7.3 percent) had poverty rates below the national average.[94]

The various approaches to poverty are not merely hypothetical formulations; they formed the basis for social welfare policy throughout much of the 1960s and beyond. Between 1965 and 1980, social welfare policies were grounded in the view that public expenditures should be used to stimulate opportunities for the poor. As a result, major social welfare legislation was enacted and billions of dollars were earmarked for the remediation of poverty. However, beginning with the Reagan administration in 1980, there was a move away from reliance on

Table 5.6

Strategies Developed to Combat Poverty Percent of Persons in Poverty by State, 2003

State	Average Percentage in Poverty 2003	State	Average Percentage in Poverty 2003
United States	12.5	Missouri	10.7
Alabama	15.0	Montana	15.1
Alaska	9.6	Nebraska	9.8
Arizona	13.5	Nevada	10.9
Arkansas	17.8	New Hampshire	5.8
California	13.1	New Jersey	8.6
Colorado	9.7	New Mexico	18.1
Connecticut	8.1	New York	14.3
Delaware	7.3	North Carolina	15.7
Dist. of Columbia	16.8	North Dakota	9.7
Florida	12.7	Ohio	10.9
Georgia	11.9	Oklahoma	12.8
Hawaii	9.3	Oregon	12.5
Idaho	10.2	Pennsylvania	10.5
Illinois	12.6	Rhode Island	11.5
Indiana	9.9	South Carolina	12.7
Iowa	8.9	South Dakota	12.7
Kansas	10.8	Tennessee	14.0
Kentucky	14.4	Texas	17.0
Louisiana	17.0	Utah	9.1
Maine	11.6	Vermont	8.5
Maryland	8.6	Virginia	10.0
Massachusetts	10.3	Washington	12.6
Michigan	11.4	West Virginia	17.4
Minnesota	7.4	Wisconsin	9.8
Mississippi	16.0	Wyoming	9.8

Source: Carmen DeNavas-Walt, Bernadette D. Proctor, and Robert J. Mills, U.S. Census Bureau, "Income, Poverty and Health Insurance Coverage in the United States: 2003," *Current Population Reports,* ser. P60-226. Retrieved September 2004 from www.census.gov/prod/2004pubs/p60-226.pdf.

social welfare expenditures and toward an emphasis on ending poverty through economic growth.

Consequently, public expenditures for poverty programs decreased and tax cuts—intended to give people incentives to work and save money—increased. The Reagan approach belied the belief that the poor should wait for gains through increased economic activity rather than rely on welfare programs. This perspective assumed that the trickle-down effect of economic growth would benefit the poor more than direct economic subsidies. According to analyst Kevin Phillips, "Low-income families, especially the working poor, lost appreciably more by cuts in government services than they gained in tax reductions."[95] Despite the nation's long-standing belief in eradicating poverty through market incomes, the major factors influencing the general decrease in poverty from the 1960s to the late 1970s were governmental cash and in-kind transfers.[96]

Employment opportunities are increasingly being based on the acquisition of technological skills, something which is directly impacted by the relationship between poverty and the digital divide.

The Digital Divide

The Internet and related information technologies represent a major technological breakthrough. However, there are also important policy concerns arising from the use of new technologies, including the balance between social well-being and the free flow of information in a democracy. For those with access, the Internet is fast becoming a marketplace of ideas as well as a marketplace for a wide range of goods and services. But this technology is also leaving some people behind, especially the poor.

The term *digital divide* refers to the information "haves" and "have-nots"—the differential access to technology that exists along income, class, and racial lines. The digital divide in the United States is an important social equity issue. For example, those with telecommunications services, such as a home telephone and a computer with Internet access, can effectively engage the global economy, participate in political debates, and interact within the "global village." People without this access risk being left behind, disconnected from the global community, the political system, and the information-driven market economy.

People use the Internet and related technologies for many different purposes. Among those accessing the Internet at home, 84 percent use it for e-mail; 67 percent for information searches; and 54 percent of unemployed persons use it for job searches. Pursuing online courses and school research is also popular inside and outside the home. Despite its popularity, certain groups still cannot access the Internet and are unable to benefit from its growing list of uses.[97] Although greater numbers of people are using the World Wide Web, the disparity in access is wide along racial, ethnic, and class lines. In fact, the digital divide between certain groups of Americans has actually increased since 1994. For example, while all racial groups now own more computers than in 1994, African Americans and Hispanics now lag farther behind non-Hispanic whites in their levels of PC ownership and online access.[98]

Central city rates of PC ownership (51 percent) and online access (46 percent) lag behind the national averages, as do rural areas (56 percent and 49 percent). Moreover, households earning below $35,000 a year have fewer PCs (50 percent) and less online access (42.2 percent) than the national averages. Rural households earning between $5,000 and $10,000 account for the lowest penetration rate for computers (16 percent) and for online access (11 percent). The digital divide cuts across all income levels. For example, whites earning $75,000 a year are more likely to have PCs (90 percent) than African Americans (83 percent). Similarly, the rate for online access is nearly twice as high for whites (55 percent) as for African Americans (31 percent) or Hispanics (32 percent).[99] America's digital divide is fast becoming a racial divide. As access to computer technology becomes increasingly important to economic and social success, many people in central cities and isolated rural areas are failing to acquire the necessary skills.

The digital divide has occupied policy discussions in national legislative bodies, state capitals, industry boardrooms, and grassroots community organizations since 1998. These discussions, and the media attention surrounding them, are causing society to become increasingly aware of the detrimental effects of the lack of Internet access for e-commerce, civic engagement, political organization, and the like. Several organizations such as Jesse Jackson's Rainbow/PUSH, the Benton Foundation, and notably the National Telecommunications and Information Administration (NTIA) of the U.S. Department of Commerce have identified the digital divide as a major social problem.

To narrow the digital gap, the Clinton administration initiated the E-Rate program, which was designed to provide schools and libraries with lower-cost Internet access and other telecommunication services. By 1999 E-Rate had funded more than 45,000 schools with more than $2.5 billion in telecommunications subsidies. Despite these efforts, the digital divide between low-poverty schools and high-poverty schools still exists. In 1998 51 percent of all classrooms nationally were wired to the Internet, but only 39 percent of schools with high levels of poverty were online.[100]

Welfare retrenchment, deep federal and state budget cuts, the growth of the working poor, under- and unemployment, dual labor markets and a frozen minimum wage have coalesced into creating an alternative financial services sector, or a fringe economy. The following section will examine this growing economic sector.

America's Fringe Economy[101]

While much of the economic life of the middle class is rooted in credit,[102] many poor people encounter obstacles to basic credit and are vulnerable to exploitation by fringe businesses. The often shoddy storefronts of fringe economy hide the true scope of this economic sector. Check cashers, payday lenders, pawnshops, rent-to-own stores, and the like engaged in at least 280 million transactions in 2001, generating about $78 billion in gross revenues.[103] By 2003, more than 15,000 payday lenders extended about $25 billion in short-term loans to millions of households.[104] The 11,000 storefronts of the check cashing industry alone process at least 180 million checks a year with a face value of $55 billion.[105] Started in 1968, ACE Cash Express (one of the nation's largest check-cashers) had more than 1,000 stores with 36 million yearly customers and 100,000 new customers a month by 2003.[106] There were 4,500 U.S. pawnshops in 1985; by 2000 that number rose to 14,000 including five publicly traded chains. Just three of those chains—Cash America, EZ Pawn, and First Cash—had combined annual revenues of nearly $1 billion in 2003.[107] The $6-billion-a-year furniture and appliance rent-to-own industry alone serves 3 million customers.[108] Low-income consumers paid almost $1.75 billion in fees for tax refund loans in 2002.[109]

The fringe economy is also robust in the housing sector. Subprime (loans to marginal borrowers that carry a higher interest rate) mortgages rose from 80,000 in 1993 to 790,000 by 1998, an 880 percent increase.[110] In short, America's fringe economy is not a mom-and-pop operation composed of small storefronts that generate moderate family incomes; instead, it is a multi-billion parallel economy that provides low-income consumers with a full spectrum of cash, commodities, and credit lines. While pawnshops, check cashers, and payday lenders are a major part of the fringe economy, they are only the tip of the iceberg. This subeconomy also includes mainstream banks issuing high-interest credit cards and expensive check overdraft protection, high interest subprime home financing and refinancing loans, and deferred interest retail payments. Fringe economic services exist in every sector where people borrow or spend money. The prices of commodities and financial services in the fringe economy are virtually removed from the real value of these goods and services in the mainstream marketplace. As such, prices in the fringe economy are based on the supposedly higher risk of serving a poor or credit-challenged population. In this economic bubble, used cars can cost twice their book value, housing prices are determined by the financial desperation of home buyers rather than the home's value, a 14-day $200 payday loan can cost $40 in interest/fees, and credit cards come with yearly and monthly service fees plus annual percentage rates (APR) of 30 percent or more. In the fringe economy, economic distress, and low credit scores translates into high corporate profits.

The Unbanked and the Functionally Poor

An important client base for the fringe economy is the unbanked (e.g., individuals and families without accounts at deposit institutions). About 12 million U.S. households (one-fourth of all low-income families) have no relationship with a mainstream financial service provider, such as a bank, savings institution, or credit union.[111] The unbanked report they do not have checking accounts because (1) they do not write enough checks to warrant one; (2) they have almost no month-to-month financial savings to deposit; (3) they cannot afford high bank fees; (4) they cannot meet minimum bank balance requirements; (5) they want to keep their financial records private; and (6) they experience discomfort dealing with banks. Almost 85 percent of the unbanked have yearly incomes below $25,000.[113]

One industry-funded study found that the average payday-loan customer was female with children living at home, was between 24 and 44, earned less than $40,000 a year, was a high school graduate, was a renter, was transient (most had lived in the same home for less than five years), and had little job tenure.[114] This group represents the lower- and moderate-income working class rather than the poorest of the poor.

The misconception that only the poor use the fringe economy overlooks the convergence of the traditional poor with growing segments of the middle class. For instance, the functionally poor can include homeowners who use their houses like ATM machines, regularly drawing out equity to finance credit card debts or other purchases. It also includes the middle class with tarnished credit who carry high-interest-rate credit cards or finance their purchases through tricky time-deferred payments. In that sense, a burgeoning sector of the middle class is economically closer to the traditional poor than the traditional middle class.

Total U.S. household debt (including vehicles and mortgages) was $8.4 trillion in 2003 (the equivalent of $29,000 per person), a 483 percent increase since 1957. Personal savings rates and home equity were the lowest in recent history. In the 1980s, consumers saved roughly 10 percent of their disposable income; by 2003 it was only 2.5 percent. In 2002, homeowners initiated $97 billion in home equity loans, nearly five times the amount in 1993.[115] Consumers spent almost all of it and about 500,000 homeowners are in the foreclosure process.[116] Credit card debt is another factor in the new poverty. Consumers who did not pay off monthly balances in 2002 owed an average of $8,940 in credit card debt compared to $3,275 in 1992. Overall, credit card holders carried more than $1.7 trillion in debt in 2002, up from $1.1 trillion in 1995.[117]

Credit and the Poor

Credit is a bridge between real household earnings and consumption decisions, offering relief during periods of economic distress and uncertainty.[118] Payment options are flexible for those with good credit and collateral is not required. Hence, the middle class can purchase goods, services or borrow cash without parting with their possessions. On the other hand, neither trust nor the presumption of goodwill exists in the fringe economy. A borrower with compromised credit typically must provide collateral such as a secured bank account, a post-dated check, household goods, or a car title. Those who find unsecured credit are often charged high interest rates combined with onerous loan terms.

Credit card use is a way of life in the United States. Renting a car or reserving a hotel room or flight is almost impossible without a credit card.[119] The average American credit card holder has ten cards—four retail cards, three bank cards, one phone card, almost one gasoline card, and one travel and entertainment card. Not surprisingly, bank write-offs for uncollectible credit card debt reached an 11-year high of 6.6 percent in early 2002.[120]

There are two basic types of credit cards: unsecured and secured cards. The cornerstones of unsecured credit are the cardholder's creditworthiness, past use of credit, and ability to repay debt. Conversely, secured credit cards require cardholders to guarantee their credit line by providing cash collateral which makes it difficult for them to default.

Unsecured Credit Cards Widespread credit card use by consumers with poor credit is a relatively recent phenomenon. Until the 1990s, banks limited their exposure on credit cards by refusing poor credit risks. However, as the credit card market became saturated and more competitive, banks were forced to examine ways to make money from riskier customers. Since bankruptcy laws prevent refiling for six years, banks began to promote "special offers" to newly bankrupted consumers with an income source.[121] Although the default rate for these individuals is high, the cards carry such low credit lines—coupled with high interest rates and fees—that banks can still make money. Terms are strict and only one late payment can result in a cardholder being moved into the default rate category, which carries a 23 percent or higher APR.

Some credit cards require no security deposit but credit limits are low (in the $100 to $500 range) and cardholders must earn at least $12,000 a year. Fees on these unsecured cards can cost hundreds and interest rates are close to 30 percent. For example, Centennial MasterCard/Visa advertises a low 9.9% APR. However, two late payments in six months results in the rate jumping to almost 24 percent. Fees for this credit card are $178, including a

$48 annual fee and a $6 monthly participation fee. The maximum credit limit is only $250. The Plains Commerce Bank Visa charges $281 for a credit card with a limit of $300, leaving only $19 when the card arrives.[122] This is predatory lending, especially when compared to mainstream credit cards that charge no setup or monthly fees, charge nothing to increase credit limits, and have free electronic access for account management.

Secured Credit Cards Responding to consumers with problematic credit, the industry created a class of credit cards securitized by a cardholder's collateral. Like their unsecured cousins, secured cards are emblazoned with Visa and MasterCard logos. Although these cards require a credit check, they are really quasi credit cards since no line of credit is actually extended. The major advantage of secured cards for credit card issuers (CCIs) is that they can easily liquidate a cardholder's collateral and apply it to the outstanding balance.

To receive a secured credit card, the customer must open an interest-bearing savings account for the amount of the credit line, usually a minimum of $200 to $5000. (Some banks only allow customers a credit line equal to 50 percent of their collateral.) Funds in the savings account are jointly owned by the bank and cannot be accessed by the cardholder. In turn, cardholders are given a Visa or MasterCard with a credit line equal to the collateral. Credit card balances are not subtracted from the savings account; instead, cardholders pay those charges as they would any other credit card. Despite the collateral, fees and interest rates are high: Cross Country Bank charges a $50 origination fee, a 24 percent APR, and a hefty late fee. There is also a 50 cent minimum finance charge and a $10 monthly fee. Because this credit card has no grace period, interest begins with each purchase. Wells Fargo's secured credit card has an $18 annual fee, a $300 security deposit, a late and over-the-limit fee of $30, and a 17 percent APR for purchases and 21.8 percent for cash advances.[123]

Preloaded or Stored Value Debit Cards A variation of the secured credit card is the preloaded debit card, sometimes called a stored value card. Using a Visa or MasterCard logo, stored value cards are similar to prepaid phone cards in that they are preloaded with funds. When the funds are exhausted, the card must be reloaded or it becomes inactive. Unlike secured credit cards, prepaid cards are not dependent on credit or banking history since they are not linked to a bank account. (Customers can use the entire amount loaded onto the card.) There is also no debt to repay. Like any fringe economy transaction there is a downside. For example, WiredPlastic charges an initial $50 fee, a one-time activation fee of $30, a monthly maintenance fee of $7 and $2 for each cash withdrawal (plus any other fees charged by ATM owner/operators). Money can be loaded directly through payroll transfers and government checks, such as Social Security.[124]

Secured and preloaded debit cards reflect the inherent inequities in the fringe economy. For instance, if banks demanded that the middle class securitize their $10,000 Visa or MasterCard credit lines, most would return to cash or checks. Secured credit card are exploitive in other ways. For one, customers are compelled to deposit money in a low-interest bearing savings account. Simultaneously, they are charged a 24 percent APR for purchases, plus other fees to essentially borrow against their own money. Since the credit line is guaranteed by collateral, banks cannot argue that high costs reflect an exceptional risk. The most viable explanation for the high costs is simple avarice. Lastly, secured credit cards are often marketed as a way to build or rebuild credit histories. However, if the CCI does not report the transaction to a credit bureau—which many do not—a cardholder cannot build or rebuild their credit history. In effect, stored value debit cards are essentially expensive gift cards.

Telecommunications and the Alternative Services Market The effects of poor credit are evident in the telecommunication services industry. Consumer telecommunications are divided into two groups: post- and pre-paid services. For post-paid (i.e., paying *after* a charge is accrued) telephone services, customers are required to undergo credit checks and those without an acceptable credit score are denied local and long-distance service. Denied mainstream telecommunications services, consumers are forced into the more expensive prepaid sector.

Consumers can opt for alternative prepaid local phone service from Competitive Local Exchange Carriers (CLECs), which are small companies that compete with regional carriers such as the Bell companies and GTE. DPI, a CLEC, charges $39 a month for basic local phone service with no option for long distance or directory assistance. Others, such as Direct Telephone, charge $50 a month for local service bundled with some options.[125] In comparison,

Southwest Bell charges about $19 a month for full-service local phone service.

Postpaid cell phone service is also dependent on good credit scores and clients with problematic credit are a lucrative part of the wireless industry. For example, wireless consumers with good credit can get Sprint's $35 postpaid cell phone service, which includes 300 daytime minutes and unlimited night and evening minutes. AT&T's $30 plan includes 200 daytime and unlimited nighttime minutes.[126] On the other hand, Verizon charges prepaid customers 10 cents a minute and 25 cents for each call (35 cents for the first minute). Cingular charges prepaid customers 35 cents a minute and 10 cents a minute on weekends or 10 cents a minute and $1 a day. AT&T bases its prepaid pricing on the amount of refills a customer buys. For example, customers who can only afford a $10 refill pay from 50 to 85 cents a minute while the costs for those who can afford a $100 refill range from 12 to 22 cents a minute.[127]

Since prepaying customers cannot default, the high costs of these services are based on the customer's economic vulnerability. Prepayment schemes are also unfair since they allow corporations to use a consumer's money without paying interest. While a single $100 prepayment to AT&T will not generate much interest, multiplied by tens of thousands of prepaid cell phone customers the float (i.e., the lag time between when money is received or requested and when the financial institution actually releases it) is sizeable. Prepaid consumers are therefore penalized twice—once by paying higher prices and then again when the company uses their money without paying interest. Consumers trying to build or rebuild their credit history derive little benefit from prepaying since no credit is extended and therefore there is nothing to report to a credit agency. Lacking cash and mainstream credit, many low-income and credit-impaired consumers also turn to the furniture and appliance rental industry.

The Furniture and Appliance Rental Industry

The rent-to-own (RTO) sector targets low- and moderate-income consumers. RTOs advertise no credit checks, weekly or monthly payments, and offer a choice of appliances, furniture, and jewelry that would otherwise be unaffordable if low-income consumers bought them outright.[128]

The $6 billion a year RTO industry serves almost 3 million customers and is a major player in the fringe economy. Rent-A-Center (the largest RTO) began with eight stores in 1986; by 2003 it had more than 2,500 stores in 50 states with $2 billion in revenues. Aaron Rents started in 1955 by renting folding chairs to auction houses for 10 cents a day. By 2003, it had 644 stores with annual revenues of more than $735 million.[129]

The RTO industry employs two approaches to transactions: (1) customers rent goods and pay weekly or monthly fees; or (2) they rent-to-own with payments extending from 12 to 24 months. In either case, customers can usually cancel the agreement without further cost or obligation. Customers take ownership of the property if the contract is renewed a prescribed number of times (usually 12 to 24 months) or if they complete the lease agreement. No credit bureau reports are obtained or filed since RTO customers make advanced payments.[130]

Renting or leasing is an expensive option. Rainbow Rentals, the nation's fourth largest RTO, leases/rents a Frigidaire washer and dryer for $19 a week or $69 a month for 21 months. The total cost is between $1,450 and $1,600 for a washer and dryer that could be purchased for $700–$800 at a local discount store. A Compaq Presario notebook rents for $38 a week or $144 a month for 24 months, raising the total cost to about $3,500. The same computer can be bought for one-third of the price—about $1,200 to $1,300—at major discount retailers. A 32-inch Toshiba flat screen television costs $1,800 to rent for 24 months while Best Buy sells the same set for $650. The list goes on and on. RTO customers generally pay at least two to three times more than the retail price for furniture or appliances.[131] The RTO industry argues that high prices reflect two variables: The cost of free repairs and the risk of doing business with customers who have poor credit histories and unstable incomes.

RTOs make money in other ways. For one, RTOs retailers offer merchandise at a "cash price and carry" price. According to a 1997 PIRG study, the typical RTO cash price on an item was $389 compared with the average department store price of $217.[132] For example, one Aaron Rents store in Houston was selling a used GE refrigerator for $1,134—about the same price as a new one in a discount appliance store. RTOs also make money by repossessions and re-rents. For instance, a 32-inch Toshiba television may cost the RTO store $500. If the set is rented for $69 a month, they will make up the $500 in only seven months and realize a gross profit of $1,173 at the end of the two-year lease term. If the set is repossessed after seven months, the retailer can re-rent it for another two years at a slightly lower rental price.

In this way, merchandise can be recycled often. One Rent-A-Center store had a $119 VCR that brought in more than $5,000 over a five-year period.[133] Typical RTO stores have revenues of almost $500,000 a year.[134]

The RTO industry is hounded by a controversy over whether transactions are credit sales or purchase option leases. As a credit sale, RTO transactions would carry a 100–200% APR and would therefore clash with many state anti-usury laws. In addition, federal truth-in-lending laws would apply in a credit sale, triggering interest rate disclosures and other consumer information. Forty-six states currently have laws regulating RTO transactions as leases, mandating a variety of disclosures and other requirements. Consumer groups argue that RTO transactions should be treated as credit sales.[135]

Many fringe businesses long ago realized the importance of treating low-income customers well. Good customer service is important to low-income consumers, especially those who have been subjected to humiliation by mainstream merchants after bad credit checks. Some consumers are so sensitive to poor treatment that they will pay more, sometimes much more, to feel they are being respected. As one former Rent-A-Center manager stated, "if you treat the customer like royalty, you can bleed them through the nose."[136]

Cash Loans Cash loans serve the same purpose for the poor as credit card cash advances for the middle class: They provide quick cash for a medical or familial emergency, or when income is insufficient to make ends meet on a short-term basis. Cash loans can be divided into two categories: collateral-based loans and non-secured or promissory loans. In the former, the borrower provides collateral (either property or guaranteed anticipated income) to the lender that is worth as much or more than the loan. While much of the middle class receive unsecured loans, they are often denied to the poor or those with bad credit. As such, loans available to the poor are generally collateral-based loans such as pawnshop transactions.

Pawnshops Pawnshops are a high growth industries and at least five chains are publicly traded (i.e., EZ Pawn, Cash America Pawn, Express Cash, Famous Pawn and First Cash Pawn). In 2001, there were about 12,000 to 14,000 pawnshops nationwide (more than twice the number in 1985), outnumbering both credit unions and banks.[137]

A pawnshop loan is a relatively simple transaction. A pawnbroker makes a fixed-term loan, which is guaranteed by collateral. The customer is given a pawn ticket that includes their name, address, a description of the pledged good, the amount lent, the maturity date, and the amount that must be repaid to reclaim the property. The property is returned when the customer presents the ticket and pays the loan and the fees within the agreed-on time. If the loan is not repaid, the collateral becomes the property of the pawnbroker and the customer's debt is extinguished. Customers can repay a loan at any time during the loan term and redeem the collateral. Pawnshops are typically regulated by state and sometimes local governments, and interest rates can range from 1.5 percent to 25 percent a month, depending on the regulations of the state. The average pawn shop loan is about $75 but can go as low as $15.[139]

In Houston, Texas, pawnshop transactions work in the following way. A customer brings in an item, which is then appraised by the broker. This appraisal is typically very low, with jewelry appraised at wholesale prices, guns appraised at less than 60 percent of their Blue Book value, and appliances at a fraction of their original cost. Many pawnshops have a maximum loan limit on items (usually $500 to $1,000) regardless of the value of the property. Hence, even if an item is worth $2,000, the pawnshop may only lend up to a maximum of $500 or $1,000 (although on higher priced items some pawnshops exercise flexibility).

Pawnshops allow customers to borrow all or part of the appraised value of an item for 30-days, which is then renewable for up to 90 days. However, many pawnshops have an open-ended policy whereby the customer can extend the pawn indefinitely by paying only the interest on the loan. In most Houston pawnshops, the interest on a $500 loan is $75 for the first month and $75 a month for the fixed term of the three-month loan. At the end of the first 30 days it would cost $575 to redeem the item; after 60 days the price would rise to $650; and at the end of 90 days it would cost $725, or 45 percent of the value of the collateral. One pawnshop manager stated that some people renew their loans for a year or more, which translates into $1,800 in interest charges on a $1,000 loan. Although some state laws cap interest rates, loopholes often allow "lease back" agreements to add fees, sometimes effectively doubling interest rates.[140]

Car Title Pawns Cart title pawns (vehicle title lenders) operate similarly to pawnshops. A customer needs a short-term loan, but instead of using their television or stereo as collateral, they use their vehicle title. In most cases, this will substantially increase the amount that can be borrowed since vehicles generally have more value than televisions, stereos or microwaves. Unlike pawnshop transactions, the borrower does not forego the use of their property during the course of the loan, even though the vehicle is technically owned by the lender until the loan is repaid.

Car title pawns operate in the following way. A borrower provides the lender with a free and paid-up vehicle title and an extra set of keys. In return for the loan, the borrower either allows the title lender to keep the title or to put a lien on the vehicle.

The vehicle is appraised based on the lowest possible value, which is the wholesale price in poor condition. For example, a 1993 Oldsmobile Cutlass Ciera would have a retail value of $2,217 if bought from a dealer in June 2002. The resale value of the car to a private party would be $1,530, and the dealer trade-in would be $1,118.[141] Since car title pawn companies generally lend up to 50 percent of the value of a vehicle, the maximum loan would be $559. A loan default would therefore provide the lender with a car worth $2,217 for $559 plus the interest payments already made by the borrower. Moreover, if a vehicle is repossessed the borrower does not receive any proceeds from the sale, even if the resale amount exceeds the loan amount.

Vehicle title loans are usually for one month and often involve an APR of 300 percent or more. Although loan terms vary slightly between companies, one large title loan company operates in the following way. A vehicle is appraised at $2,000 (the wholesale price in poor condition) and a 30-day loan is given for 50 percent of the car's value or $1,000. After 30 days the loan payoff is $1,246.57 (almost 25 percent in interest and fees). If the loan is not repaid, the car is repossessed on the 31st day. The borrower may ask for a 30-day extension after paying the interest and fees. After only 60 days the interest and fees will total almost 50 percent of the original $1,000 loan. The borrower may then ask for a third extension after paying the interest charges of $493 for the first two loan periods. This extension is for a maximum of one year. At that point, the monthly payment rises to $346.57 since the borrower is now expected to pay down $100 a month toward the loan principal as well as pay the interest. By the fourth month, the principal will be only $900 and so on until the loan is paid off or the car is repossessed.[142] If the borrower keeps the loan for 12 months, they will have paid almost $3,000 in interest charges/fees for a $1,000 loan. Borrowers will have also paid more than the value of the vehicle.

Payday Loans Although pawnshops are profitable, the payday loan market (sometimes called deferred deposit services) is even more robust. For example, while the average pawnshop loan is $75 the average payday loan ranges from $100 to $500 or more.[143] Nationwide, the number of payday lenders grew from a few hundred in 1990 to more than 25,000 in 2002.[144] About 65 million payday loans totaling $45 billion were originated in 2002 and low-income consumers paid $2.4 billion in fees for two-week loans.[145]

To qualify for a payday loan, the customer must have a valid checking account from which a check is issued (or electronically debited) to cover the interest and principal for the loan. On a $300 payday loan the lender may ask for a $300 check and then deduct the interest from the amount received by the borrower. Borrowers must also provide recent pay stubs and valid identification. Many payday lenders consider benefits as income and will give loans to those on public assistance, recipients of child support or alimony, and Social Security beneficiaries.[146]

Payday loans are typically issued for a maximum of $300 ($500–$1,000 for established customers) and are usually given for 14 or 18 days. The average fees are almost $20 per $100 borrowed (fees can be as high as $37 per hundred), or 20 percent for the two week loan period. Since the borrower repays $360 on a $300 loan this translates into a 500% APR. (Nationally, the average APR for payday loans is 474 percent.[147]) Because the lender may extend the loan (called a rollover) for additional 14- or 18-day periods (after the interest is paid), a $300 payday loan extended to 42 days or three loan periods will accrue $180 in interest charges alone, elevating the full loan repayment to $480 in less than two months. Unlike pawnshop transactions where a customer loses their collateral if they default, payday loans can inflict potentially greater damage on borrowers. For instance, defaulting on a payday loan will mar the credit worthiness of the borrower, if not destroy it. It may also result in criminal prosecution for writing a hot check.[148]

Collection tactics for payday loans can be aggressive. If a borrower cannot repay the loan, it may be turned over to a collection agency and result in the loss of a house, car or the garnishing of wages. In some cases, the collection agency can add additional interest to the original debt.[149] The payday lender may prosecute the customer for writing a "hot check," even though they knew the customer did not have sufficient funds in their checking account when they wrote it. Some payday loan companies require borrowers to agree beforehand to pay all fees related to the collection of their account, including attorney fees, collection fees, and court costs.[150] A default on a payday loan involves a worthless check, and some state credit laws allow for triple damages when a bad check is used in a retail transaction. Lenders may also require that customers sign statements authorizing them to go directly to the borrower's employer and ask for the amount owed to be deducted from their paychecks.

Tax Refund Anticipation Loans Refund anticipation loans (RALs) are short-term loans secured by an expected tax refund. RALs are expensive and similar to other forms of fringe credit with an APR ranging from 67 to 774 percent.[151] About 11 million taxpayers received RALs in 2000, almost half through H&R Block, the nation's largest tax preparer.[152]

RALs are common in low-income neighborhoods where there are a large number of tax refunds associated with the federal earned income tax credit (EITC) program (see Chapter 9). Under EITC, the working poor receive refunds that exceed what they paid in taxes. In addition to EITC, low- and moderate-income families with children are also eligible for the federal child tax credit (CTC), worth up to $1,000 a child. The EITC and CTC tax refunds created a powerful incentive for mainstream tax preparers to enter the poverty services market.

Sixty-eight percent of EITC- and CTC-eligible families use tax preparers and electronic return originators (EROs), which are authorized by the IRS to electronically transmit federal income tax returns. Low-income tax filers use EROs for several reasons: (1) the EITC and the CTC filing process is complicated;[153] (2) low-income working families can receive large tax refunds and many are eager to claim them quickly, sometimes on the day they file; (3) tax preparers are ubiquitous in lower-income neighborhoods (there are 50 percent more EROs in zip codes with high numbers of EITC recipients than zip codes with fewer recipients);[154] (4) free tax assistance is scarce; and (5) the poor cannot afford to pay upfront the $100 plus in tax-preparation fees.

Commercial tax preparers earn high profits by providing financial services to some of the poorest of the poor. According to one study, RAL customers tend to have annual incomes between $10,000 and $15,000, are unemployed or employed in service occupations, and possess less than a high school education.[155] About 40 percent of taxpayers who use RALs are EITC recipients.[156] Moreover, many of the poor are unaware that RALs are actually loans since they are often advertised as "Quick Cash," "Super Fast Refunds," or "Instant Money." In April 2001, H&R Block received 2,230 citations from the New York City Department of Consumer Affairs for misrepresenting RALs and luring customers into accepting loans they did not fully understand. The company settled for $4 million and paid $2.4 million in restitution to 61,700 customers. Block also settled a RAL-related class-action suit in Texas for $41.7 million.[157]

RALs are expensive. For example, a tax filer eligible for a $1,900 EITC refund who takes out a RAL will pay $248 (see Table 5.7), thereby reducing the original $1,900 to $1,652.[158] Most of these costs are incurred simply to get an EITC refund a few days

Table 5.7

Draining EITC: 2002 Tax Preparation, RAL Fees, and Check Cashing

Type of Fee	Cost to Tax Filer	Drain on EITC Program (in millions)
RAL loan fee	$ 75	$363
Electronic filing fee	$ 40	194
Document preparation/ application/handling fee	$ 33	160
Tax preparation fee	$100	484
Check cashing fee	$ 57	110*
Total	$305	1,311

*This was based on 40 percent of low-income tax filers using a check cashing service.

Source: Based on Chi Chi Wu and Jean Ann Fox, *The High Cost of Quick Tax Money: Tax Preparation, "Instant Refund" Loans, and Check Cashing Fees Target the Working Poor.* (Washington, DC: National Consumer Law Center, Consumer Federation of America, January 2003). Reprinted with permission of the National Consumer Law Center, www.consumerlaw.org, 617-542-9595.

earlier compared to filing electronically and having the IRS directly deposit the refund into a checking account. RALs are also risky for low-income tax filers. Since a RAL is a loan from a bank in partnership with a tax preparer, it must be repaid even if the IRS denies or delays the refund, or if the refund is smaller than expected. Moreover, when tax filers apply for RALs, they give the lender the right to use the tax refund to pay for old tax-preparation debts that may be owed.

If low-income consumers are fleeced when they enter a tax-preparation office, they are ripped off again on their way out. About 45 percent of RAL customers use commercial check cashing outlets (CCOs) to cash their refund checks, paying fees that range from 3 to 10 percent of the face value of the check. Responding to this captive market, ACE installed check-cashing machines in some H&R Block lobbies and charge roughly 3 percent to cash a secure check, thereby further lowering the $1,900 refund to $1,602.[159] All told, EITC-eligible families using EROs and check cashers can lose more than 16 percent of the value of their tax refund.

Tax-preparation fees can take other forms. For example, a consumer is charged a tax-preparation fee of $100–$118, which they are expected to pay out-of-pocket.[160] Since some families cannot pay the fee or do not have a checking account, tax preparers offer a "refund transfer." While not a loan per se, the filer pays about $28 to establish a dummy bank account into which the IRS directly deposits a tax refund check. After the deposit, the tax preparer subtracts their fees, issues a paper check, and closes the account. The $28 fee is high for a 10-day bank account designed for a single lump sum, especially since for a few dollars more the consumer can maintain a checking account for a full year. The advantage to low-income consumers is that tax-preparation fees can be deducted directly from the dummy account, thereby relieving them from paying those fees upfront. In effect, dummy accounts are actually disguised loans since they defer tax-preparation fees. Another variation is an assisted refund transfer or, as Jackson Hewitt calls it, "IRS Direct." With this product, a consumer pays the tax preparer to be an intermediary in processing a tax refund into the tax filer's *own* bank account.[161]

High tax-preparation and RAL fees hurt poor working families and substantially diminish the economic impact of the EITC and CTC. In 2001, tax filers paid almost $1.8 billion in RAL and other fees,[162] which took a substantial chunk out of the $31 billion EITC program that Congress had targeted for the poor.[163] Table 5.7 illustrates the impact of tax-preparation fees and RALs on tax filers and the EITC program.

Check Cashing In large urban areas, from 20 to 40 percent of the unbanked pay fees to cash their paychecks through CCOs.[164] Many larger CCOs are one-stop financial service centers in that they offer a wide range of services in one location: (1) check cashing; (2) utility and other bill pay services; (3) money transfers; (4) payday loans; (5) money orders; (6) telecommunications products (e.g., prepaid long distance calling cards, prepaid local phone service, cell phones and beepers); and (7) other services such as fax transmissions, copy services, stamps and envelopes, notary services, mailboxes and lottery tickets.[165]

CCOs with names like ACE Cash Express, Check 'N Go, Mr. Payroll, Dollar, and Money Mart are common sights in inner-city neighborhoods. Behind these 11,000 plus storefronts lies an industry that cashes upwards of 180 million checks a year with a face value of more than $55 billion. The CCO industry generates nearly $1.5 billion a year in revenues.[166]

CCOs are an expensive way to cash checks. Most check-cashing fees range from 1 to 10 percent (plus a service fee in some states) of the face value of a check.[167] Check cashing charges are often based on a sliding scale, and Dollar—the second largest CCO—charges 3.5 percent, or $35 to cash a $1,000 payroll check.[168] Fees for cashing personal checks can run as high as 10–12 percent of the value of the check. If a customer cashes twenty $800 paychecks a year through Dollar, they will pay $560—far more than the costs of even a deluxe checking account. The price list at one ACE Cash Express in Houston, Texas, is typical of the industry:

Cashier's check	5.0%
Government check	2.7%
Handwritten payroll check	2.7%
Insurance drafts/checks	5.0%
Money orders	5.0%
Tax refund checks	3.9%
No I.D. checks	5.0%
Special risk	5.0%
Bank processing fee	.49
Minimum charge per item	$1.99
Returned check charge	$25.00

High check-cashing fees do not correspond to high risk since about 70 to 90 percent of all checks cashed at CCOs are relatively secure payroll checks with an average value of $500 to $600.[169] Losses are also extremely low. For example, ACE uses a system for verifying and assessing the risk of each check-cashing transaction and reports losses of less than one quarter of 1 percent.[170] The profitability of the check cashing is stunning. In 2002, 797 ACE company-owned stores posted average revenues of $237,000, or a store profit of almost 43 percent.[171] This profitability is leading even non-finance-related industries into the fray. For example, the Eastern Division of the Safeway supermarket chain is now the largest CCO in Maryland. Supermarket chains such as H.E.B. and Kroger's have also established check-cashing operations, although often charging slightly less than commercial CCOs.

Transportation in the Fringe Economy

For the poor who can afford a used vehicle, the path to car ownership is mined with high downpayments, dead-end financing, extortionate interest rates, and overpriced insurance. Understanding the used-car industry is necessary to appreciate the obstacles faced by the poor. About 40 million used vehicles are sold annually in the United States—11 million by franchised new-car dealers and the remaining 29 million by independent used-car lots.[172] Used-car lots fall into two categories: independent lots and franchised dealerships. Independent or non-franchised dealers frequently sell older and less expensive vehicles. Franchised used-car lots are part of new-car dealerships and their cars tend to be newer, cleaner, and more expensive. Because of this market segmentation, most poor buyers end up in independent car lots, many of which are "here today and gone tomorrow."

A major obstacle faced by the poor is based on how mainstream financial institutions make loans in the $370 billion used-car industry. Most mainstream lenders like Bank of America, Wells Fargo Bank, and Chase refuse to lend money on vehicles four to six years or older, and those with more than 100,000 miles. Some lenders only finance vehicles purchased through dealerships, and some further restrict that to dealerships that also sell new cars. These restrictions limit the choices for the poor, since used cars sold by a dealer are more expensive than private party sales. According to the Kelly Blue Book, a 1996 Chevrolet Lumina with 76,000 miles bought from an auto dealer in New York City costs 30 percent more than one purchased privately.

Three tiers of financing exist for used-car buyers. The first is prime lending, which is offered to borrowers with a higher income and a good credit history. Interest rates are low because they are tied to the prime rate. The second tier is subprime lending, which is geared toward buyers with credit problems but who still have sufficient creditworthiness to secure a loan. Subprime loans carry higher interest rates, involve a substantial down payment, and often require that a vehicle be purchased from a franchised dealership. The third tier is nonprime lending or dealer financing, whereby vehicles are financed in-house. This type of financing often carries the highest interest rates and often require weekly payments.

Buy-Here, Pay-Here used-car lots provide in-house financing, and they do not require buyers to undergo a credit check because the payment history is not reported to a credit bureau. Dealer-financed cars require a hefty downpayment (typically $1,000 on a $5,000 vehicle) and late payments can result in immediate repossession.

Buy-Here, Pay-Here used-car lots are more profitable than franchised car dealerships. In 2002, the average retail price of used cars sold by franchised car lots was $11,793 with a gross profit of $1,741. In that same year, the average retail price of a used car in a Buy-Here, Pay-Here lot was $7,810, with a gross profit of $3,772—more than double that of franchised dealers. Lest one believe these dealerships are just small mom-and-pop operations, the National Association of Buy-Here, Pay-Here dealers held an annual convention in 2001 with over 800 attendees and 60 sponsors, including Bank of America, Bank One, SeaWest, and Wells Fargo. The Buy-Here, Pay-Here sector will likely grow as more subprime lenders—some of whom have lost money in recent years—further tighten their credit standards.

Auto insurance is another area where the poor are hard hit. For example, many people with older cars insure them only for state-mandated liability rather than for collision (damage to their vehicle) coverage. It makes little sense to pay $600 a year for collision coverage on a car worth $1,000, especially after a $500 deductible. Unfortunately, consumers who finance through Buy-Here, Pay-Here dealerships or subprime lenders must insure their vehicles for liability *and* collision, regardless of whether it is cost effective.

The poor are hard hit by high auto-insurance rates. According to one study, 92 percent of large insurance companies run credit checks on potential customers, which translate into insurance scores.[176] These insurance scores determine whether the carrier will insure an applicant and for how much. Those with poor or no credit will be denied coverage, while those with limited credit will pay high premiums. Although there is no evidence that residents in low-income or high minority zip codes are involved in more accidents, they pay more for basic auto insurance, even if they have been accident- and ticket-free for years.[177] Mounting consumer complaints have aroused the suspicion of some state insurance regulators that this may be a new form of redlining—a practice outlawed by the Fair Housing Act of 1968—since it discriminates against low-income, single-parent, young, and minority consumers whose credit histories may be less than perfect.[178]

While mainstream auto insurers calculate premiums based on six-month or one-year period, fringe auto insurers usually provide only monthly quotations. Many also require a sizeable downpayment and a service fee. The premiums charged by fringe insurers are exorbitant compared with mainstream auto insurers. For example, GEICO charges $700 a year for full coverage on 1991 Chrysler minivan for a Houston driver with an excellent driving record. In comparison, minimally regulated, high-rate local insurance agencies like Houston's Alamo Insurance charge $2,100 a year for the same vehicle, or three times the $700 quoted by GEICO.

Fringe auto insurers get away with charging high premiums for several reasons. For one, they have captive consumers who are rejected by large insurance carriers. Secondly, the insurance demands of Buy-Here, Pay-Here dealers and subprime lenders create a steady stream of car buyers desperate for insurance. Third, many fringe auto insurers are minimally regulated and state insurance agencies are lax in rooting out predatory insurers, especially those serving the poor. Not coincidentally, fringe auto insurers take the pressure off mainstream carriers to provide coverage for the poor. Lastly, many state vehicle inspections require a proof-of-insurance card before a vehicle can pass inspection. Some car owners will pay the high monthly premium only to get the card and pass inspection, after which they drop the coverage. This may explain why fringe auto insurance rates are quoted monthly rather than bi-annually.

The low-income population pays more than the middle class for financial services in both absolute dollars and relative to their income.[179] These costs are exacerbated by the bifurcation of financial services that results in one system for the poor and another for the middle and upper class. This bifurcation leads to even greater inequality: Banks for the middle class and check cashers for the poor; access to savings tools for the middle class and barriers to savings for the poor; low-cost financial services for the middle class and high fee–based services for the poor. The fringe economy represents the financial exploitation of the poor by a predatory market designed to deplete rather than enhance the resources of poor families and communities. To better understand the poor, policy analysts must be aware of the myriad ways in which they are economically exploited. The regulation of the fringe economy is an economic justice issue that should be a central focus of any progressive social welfare agenda.

Conclusion

Poverty is one of the most intractable problems in U.S. society. Because poverty is both a political and a social issue, the policies surrounding it are often less than objective. For example, one can halve the poverty rate simply by redefining the poverty index. One can also cut poverty rates by placing a high dollar value on in-kind benefits such as food stamps and Medicaid. Conversely, one can swell the ranks of the poor by moving the poverty line upward; that is, by increasing the income level at which people are defined as poor. Like all social policies, poverty-related policies exist in a context marked by political exigencies, public opinion, the economic health of a society, and the complex mask of ideology.

Although various kinds of poverty-related data are available, policymakers remain uncertain as to the precise causes of poverty. What is known is that they are complex and involve, among other things, the effects of discrimination; the composition of family life, including the rise in single, female-headed families and teenage pregnancies; geographical location; and age. In large measure, the determination of whether a child is poor depends on chance; that is, on the family the child is born into. Policymakers also know that the skewed distribution of income in society and governmental tax and investment policies have major impacts on the numbers of people in poverty and on the extent of their poverty.

Most policymakers agree that employment is the best antipoverty program. Thus, work-related factors such as the value of the minimum wage (especially its relationship to mean incomes), the level of under- and unemployment, the rise or decrease in family incomes, and the general state of the economy all have a major impact on the level and extent of poverty. The availability of job training programs and the regulation of the dual labor market helps determine the salaries workers will make. Taken together, these factors have caused poverty rates to remain higher in the United States than in many other industrialized nations. They have also helped make poverty seem like an intractable problem with few viable solutions.

Questions of poverty have long plagued social scientists. Specifically, these questions revolve around why some groups are able to rise out of poverty but others appear only to fall deeper into the poverty trap. Although several theorists have offered explanations for poverty, none hold up to empirical testing. This is because there is no simple or single answer to poverty. The causes of poverty involve a wide range of social, economic, political, and cultural factors. Poverty is one of the most elusive—if not the most elusive—problems facing U.S. social policy. Theories and strategies that address single explanations or single causes of poverty are doomed to failure, only aggravating a public that is already suspect of most antipoverty measures.

Discussion Questions

1. The measurement of poverty is both complex and controversial. Nevertheless, the way that poverty is measured has important consequences for the development of social policy in the United States. Describe some of the potential pitfalls in measuring poverty rates and discuss how the calculation of poverty rates affects the creation of social policy.
2. Working families make up an important and growing segment of the poor. What is causing the increase in the numbers of working poor? What specific policies should be implemented to reduce the number of working poor families?
3. Several theories have been advanced to explain why some individuals and groups of people are persistently poor while others are not. Theorists who have tried to tackle this problem include Daniel Patrick Moynihan, Oscar Lewis, and Edward Banfield, among others. Although all theories of poverty have intrinsic flaws, which theory or combination of theories described in this book (or elsewhere) do you think best explains the dynamics of poverty?
4. Many strategies have been developed to fight poverty, including the curative approach, the alleviative approach, and the preventive approach. Of these strategies, which is the most effective in fighting poverty and why? What alternative strategies, if any, could be developed that would be more effective in combating poverty?
5. Policy analysts have traditionally argued that jobs are preferable to welfare and that the lack of employment opportunities results in increasing needs for social welfare. Is this relationship apparent in your community? What is the evidence?
6. A commonly held belief is that government make-work jobs are inferior to private sector employment. Yet many New Deal jobs programs have made important contributions to the infrastructure of the nation's cities. What New Deal projects are evident in your community? If a new governmental jobs program were initiated, what community needs might it address?
7. The Job Training and Partnership Act has attempted to enhance opportunities for workers in the secondary labor market. What has been the track record of this and other programs in your community? Has one been more successful than another? How would you change these programs to more adequately address the needs of the poor in your community?
8. The fringe economy is a high-growth sector that is adversely affecting the economic lives of the poor. What policies or programs would you propose that could regulate, constrain or abolish the fringe economic sector? What legislative or policy reforms are needed?

Notes

1. See Edward C. Banfield, *The Unheavenly City* (Boston: Little, Brown, 1966) and Oscar Lewis, *La Vida* (New York: Harper & Row, 1965).
2. Richard Dugdale, *The Jukes* (New York: G. P. Putnam's Sons, 1910).
3. Henry Goddard, *The Kallikak Family* (New York: Arno Publishers, 1911).
4. Arthur R. Jensen, "How Much Can We Boost IQ and Scholastic Achievement?" *Harvard Educational Review* 39 (Winter 1969), pp. 1–23.
5. Winifred Bell, *Contemporary Social Welfare* (New York: Macmillan, 1983), p. 261.
6. William Shockley, "Sterilization: A Thinking Exercise," in Carl Bahema (ed.), *Eugenics: Then and Now* (Stroudsburg, PA: Doidon, Hutchinson & Ross, 1976); see also Bell, *Contemporary Social Welfare,* p. 263.
7. Richard Herrnstein, *IQ and the Meritocracy* (Boston: Little, Brown, 1973).
8. Richard Herrnstein and Charles Murray, *The Bell Curve* (New York: Free Press, 1994).
9. Winnie Chen, Vilma Hernandez, Erin Townsend, and Carol Wyatt, "Affirmative Action," unpublished paper, University of Houston Graduate School of Social Work, Houston, TX, May 1, 1996.
10. T. Beardsley, "For Whom the Bell Curve Really Tolls," *Scientific American* 272, no. 1 (1995), pp. 14–17; Stephen Gould, "Ghosts of Bell Curves Past," *Natural History* 104, no. 2 (1995), pp. 12–19; and C. Lane, "The Tainted Sources of the Bell Curve," *The New York Review of Books* 41, no. 20 (1994), pp. 14–19.
11. Gould, "Ghosts of Bell Curves Past," p. 14.
12. Bell, Contemporary Social Welfare, p. 264.
13. David Gil, *Unraveling Social Policy* (Boston: Shenkman, 1981).
14. Blanche Bernstein, "Welfare Dependency," in Lee D. Bawden (ed.), *The Social Contract Revisited* (Washington, DC: Urban Institute Press, 1984), p. 129.
15. Greg J. Duncan et al., *Years of Poverty, Years of Plenty* (Ann Arbor, MI: Institute for Social Research, 1984).
16. Daniel McMurer and Isabel Sawhill, *Getting Ahead* (Washington, DC: Urban Institute, 1998), p. 33.
17. Bradley Schiller, "Relative Earnings Redux." *Review of Income and Wealth* 40, no. 4 (1994), p. 629.
18. W. Michael Cox and Richard Alm, *Myths of Rich & Poor* (New York: Basic Books, 1999), p. 73.
19. David Howell and Elizabeth Howell, *The Effects of Immigrants on African American Earnings* (New York: New School for Social Research, 1997), p. 23.
20. U.S. Census Bureau, "Income, Poverty and Health Insurance Coverage in the United States: 2003." Retrieved September 2004 from www.census.gov/prod/2004pubs/p60-226.pdf
21. U.S. Census Bureau, "Poverty 1995," September 26, 1996, retrieved 1996 from www.census.gov/hhes/poverty/pov95/thresh95.html; U.S. Census Bureau, "Income, Poverty and Health Insurance Coverage: 2003," Washington, D.C., 2004.
22. Committee on Ways and Means, U.S. House of Representatives, *Overview of Entitlement Programs: 1992 Green Book* (Washington, DC: U.S. Government Printing Office, 1992), p. 1272.
23. William O'Hare, Taynia Mann, Kathryn Porter, and Robert Greenstein, *Real Life Poverty in America: Where the Public Would Set the Poverty Line* (Washington, DC: Center on Budget and Policy Priorities, and Families USA Foundation Report, July 1990), p. viii.
24. Institute for Research on Poverty, "Improving the Measurement of American Poverty," *Focus* 19, no. 2 (Spring 1998), p. 2.
25. Ibid.
26. U.S. Senate, "Introduction of the Poverty Data Correction Act of 1999." Retrieved 2000 from www.senate.gov/~moynihan/0119povd.htm, p. 1.
27. U.S. Census Bureau, "Income, Poverty and Health Insurance Coverage: 2003." Retrieved September 2004 from www.census.gov/prod/2004pubs/p60-226.pdf
28. Sara McLanahan and Gary Sandefur, *Growing Up with a Single Parent* (Cambridge, MA: Harvard University Press, 1997).
29. ACF Press Release, December, 1995. Retrieved 1998 from www.acf.dhhs.gov/ACFNews
30. Ron Dean, "Myths, Legends and the American Way: Deadbeat Dads," August 15, 1995. Retrieved 1997 from soc.men newsgroup.
31. Timothy S. Grall, "Custodial Mothers and Fathers and Their Child Support: 2001," U.S. Census Bureau, U.S. Department of Commerce, Economics and Statistics Administration, Washington, D.C., October 2003.
32. Ibid.
33. Center for Law and Social Policy, "Child Support Substantially Increases Economic Well-Being of Low- and Moderate-Income Families," Washington, D.C., 2004.
34. U.S. Census Bureau, "Income, Poverty and Health Insurance Coverage in the United States: 2003." Retrieved September 2004 from www.census.gov/prod/2004pubs/p60-226.pdf
35. Bennett, Li, Song, and Yang, "Young Children in Poverty."
36. Children's Defense Fund, *The State of America's Children* (Washington, DC: Children's Defense Fund, 1991), pp. 23–24.

37. U.S. Census Bureau, "Income, Poverty and Health Insurance Coverage in the United States: 2003." Retrieved September 2004 from www.census.gov/prod/2004pubs/p60-226.pdf
38. See Congressional Record, Senate, vol. 133, no. 120 (Washington, DC: U.S. Government Printing Office, July 21, 1987), pp. S10400–S10404; and Sheldon Danziger and Marcia Carlson, "Cohabitation and the Measurement of Child Poverty," Poverty Measurement Working Papers, U.S. Bureau of the Census, February 1998, retrieved 2000 from www.census.gov/hhes/poverty/povmeas/papers/cohabit.html.
39. U.S. Census Bureau, "Income, Poverty and Health Insurance Coverage in the United States: 2003." Retrieved September 2004 from www.census.gov/prod/2004pubs/p60-226.pdf
40. Ibid.
41. Kelly A. Olson, "Application of Experimental Poverty Models to the Aged," *Social Security Bulletin* 62, no. 3 (1999), p. 4.
42. O'Hare et al., *Real Life Poverty in America,* p. 9.
43. Cynthia M. Duncan (ed.), *Rural Poverty in America* (Westport, CT: Auburn House, 1992).
44. U.S. Census Bureau, "Income, Poverty and Health Insurance Coverage in the United States: 2003. Retrieved September 2004 from www.census.gov/prod/2004pubs/p60-226.pdf
45. Ibid.
46. See Ibid. Economic Research Center, "Measuring Rurality: 2004 County Typology Codes," U.S. Department of Agriculture, 2004; Kathryn Porter, *Poverty in Rural America* (Washington, DC: Center on Budget and Policy Priorities, 1989), pp. 7–11; and Scott Barancik, *The Rural Disadvantage: Growing Income Disparities between Rural and Urban Areas* (Washington, DC: Center on Budget and Policy Priorities, April 1990), pp. ix–x.
47. Economic Research Center, "Rural Poverty at a Glance." U.S. Department of Agriculture, 2003. Retrieved October 2004 from www.ers.usda.gov/publications/rdrr100/rdrr100.pdf
48. Porter, *Poverty.*
49. Economic Research Center, Rural Poverty at a Glance.
50. See Economic Research Service, "Rural America at a Glance," USDA, Rural Development Briefing Room, retrieved 1999 from www.ers.usda.gov/briefing/rural/Ruralecn/index.htm#pov; and Ohio State University Extension, "Poverty Fact Sheet Series—Rural Poverty," Family and Consumer Sciences, retrieved 2000 from http://ohioline.ag.ohio-state.edu/hyg-fact/5000/5709.html
51. See Beth Shulman, *The Betrayal of Work: How Low Wage Jobs Fail 35 Million Americans* (New York: The New Press, 2003); and the Center on Budget and Policy Priorities, "Number in Poverty Hits 20-Year High, As Recession Adds 2 Million Poor, Analysis Finds" (Washington, DC: Center on Budget and Policy Priorities, September 3, 1992), p. 4.
52. Dalaker and Proctor, *Poverty in the United States: 1999.*
53. Abraham T. Mosisa,"The Working Poor in 2001," *Monthly Labor Review* 126 (Nov/Dec 2003), pp. 11–12.
54. Lawrence Mishel, Jared Bernstein, and John Schmitt, *The State of Working America 2000 /2001* (Ithaca, NY: Cornell University Press, 2001).
55. Jared Bernstein, "Economic Growth Not Reaching Middle- and Lower Wage Earners," January 28, 2004. Retrieved 2004 from www.epinet.org/content.cfm/webfeatures_snapshots
56. Bureau of the Census, October 2003. Retrieved December 2003 from http://ferret.bls.census.gov/macro/032003/perinc/new05_001.htm
57. Bureau of Labor Statistics, "Tomorrow's Jobs," U.S. Department of Labor, June 2, 2004. Retrieved October 2004 from http://stats.bls.gov/oco/oco2003.htm
58. Michael Sherraden, "Chronic Unemployment: A Social Work Perspective," *Social Work* (September–October 1985), p. 403.
59. Ibid., pp. 404–406.
60. As Sherraden notes, the common understanding that an unemployment rate of 5 is "normal" is not supported by economists, who calculate that structural and frictional unemployment can be reduced to 3 percent through astute social policies.
61. *New York Times,* "Not Many Jobs Are Sent Abroad, U.S. Report Says" (June 11, 2004).
62. M. Harvey Brenner, *Estimating the Effects of Economic Change on National Health and Social Well-Being* (Washington, DC: U.S. Government Printing Office, 1984), pp. 2–4.
63. Ibid.
64. Harrington, *Who Are the Poor?* p. 10.
65. Center on Budget and Policy Priorities, "Smaller Pieces of the Pie" (Washington, DC: Center on Budget and Policy Priorities, 1987).
66. Sar A. Levitan and Joyce Zickler, *The Quest for a Federal Manpower Partnership* (Cambridge, MA: Harvard University Press, 1974), pp. 1–6.
67. Lawrence Mead, *Beyond Entitlement* (New York: Free Press, 1986), p. 27.
68. David Rosenbaum, "Federal Job Program Aids the More Able, According to Critics," *New York Times* (July 22, 1984), p. 9.
69. Michael Piore, "The Dual Labor Market," in David Gordon (ed.), *Problems in Political Economy* (Lexington, MA: D. C. Heath, 1977), p. 94.
70. David Gordon, Richard Edwards, and Michael Reich, *Segmented Work, Divided Workers* (New York: Cambridge University Press, 1982), p. 211.
71. U.S. Bureau of the Census, *Statistical Abstract of the United States 1982–83,* p. 409.
72. Harrington, *Who Are the Poor?* p. 10.

73. Barbara Ehrenreich, *Nickel and Dimed* (New York: Owl Books, 2001).
74. U.S. Bureau of Labor Statistics, "Characteristics of Minimum Wage Workers: 2003." U.S. Department of Labor. Retrieved October 2004 from www.bls.gov/cps/minwage2003.htm
75. The Bureau of Labor Statistics, Household Data and Averages, "Wage and Salary Workers Paid Hourly Rates with Earnings at or below Prevailing Minimum Wage by Occupation and Industry," Table 45. Retrieved 2000 from http://stats.bls.gov/pdf/cpsaat45.pdf
76. Center on Budget and Policy Priorities, "Assessing the $5.15 an Hour Minimum Wage," March 1996. Retrieved 1997 from http://epn.org/cpbb/cbwage.html
77. Isaac Shapiro, *The Minimum Wage and Job Loss* (Washington, DC: Center on Budget and Policy Priorities, 1988).
78. Center on Budget and Policy Priorities, "Assessing the $5.15 an Hour Minimum Wage."
79. Michael Novak (ed.), *The New Consensus on Family and Welfare* (Washington, DC: American Enterprise Institute, 1987), p. 32.
80. Acorn, National Living Wage Resource Center, "Introduction to ACORN's Living Wage Web Site." Retrieved 2000 from www.livingwagecampaign.org
81. Jeff Chapman, "States Move on Minimum Wage, Federal Inaction Forces States to Raise Wage Floor to Protect Low-Wage Workers," *EPI Issue Brief #195*, Economic Policy Institute, Washington, D.C., June 11, 2003.
82. Cited in Michal Grinstein-Weiss and Jami Curley, "Individual Development Accounts in Rural Communities: Implications for Research." Working Paper No. 03-21, Washington University, Center for Social Development, George Warren Brown School of Social Work Washington University, St. Louis, MO, 2003.
83. Michael Sherraden, "Can Asset-Based Welfare Policy Really Help the Poor?" In Howard Jacob Karger, James Midgley and Brene Brown, *Controversial Issues in Social Policy*, 2nd ed. (Boston: Allyn & Bacon, 2003), p. 50.
84. Ibid., 51.
85. Ibid.
86. Ibid.
87. Michael Sherraden, *Assets and the Poor: A New American Welfare Policy* (Armonk, NY: M. E. Sharpe, 1991).
88. Ibid.
89. Ibid.
90. CFED, "History and Highlights," 2004. Retrieved September 20, 2004 from www.cfed.org/about.m?id=27
91. John Kenneth Galbraith, *The Affluent Society* (Boston: Houghton Mifflin, 1958).
92. Harrington, *Who Are the Poor?* p. 17.
93. Ibid., p. 22.
94. Christine M. Ross, "Poverty Rates by State, 1979 and 1985: A Research Note," *Focus* 10, no. 3 (Fall 1987), pp. 1–5.
95. Kevin Phillips, *The Politics of Rich and* Poor (New York: Random House, 1990), p. 87.
96. Sheldon Danziger, "Poverty," *Encyclopedia of Social Work*, 18th ed. (Silver Spring, MD: NASW Press, 1987), pp. 301–302.
97. National Telecommunications and Information Agency, *A Nation Online: How Americans Are Expanding Their Use of the Internet*, U.S. Department of Commerce, February 2002. Retrieved August 2004 from www.ntia.doc.gov/ntiahome/dn/index.html
98. Ibid.
99. Ibid.
100. Ekaterina Walsh, Shelley Morrisette, and Nicky Maraganore, "The Digital Melting Pot," *The Forrester Review*. Retrieved 1999 from www.forrester.com/ER/Research/Brief/Excerpt/0,1317,5703,FF.html
101. For a fuller examination of the fringe economy see Howard Jacob Karger, *Not Only for the Poor: America's Fringe Economy* (San Francisco: Berrett-Koehler, 2005).
102. Robert D. Manning, *Credit Card Nation* (New York: Basic Books, 2000).
103. Fannie Mae Foundation, "Low-Income and Minority Families Rely Increasingly on High-Cost Financial Services," August 2, 2001. Retrieved 2002 from www.fanniemaefoundation.org/news/pr/2001sum/010802.shtml
104. Community Financial Services Association of America. "The Payday Advance Service, 2003." Retrieved 2004 from www.cfsa.net/genfo/ageninf.html
105. See Financial Service Centers of America (FiSCA). "Quick Facts about Fisca, 2003." Retrieved 2004 from www.fisca.org/q&a.htm; and Sougata Mukherjee, "Consumer Group Pushes for Regulation of Check Cashing Industry," *Houston Business Journal* (August 29, 1997), p. 18.
106. ACE Cash Express, Inc., *2003 Annual Report*. Retrieved 2004 from www.acecashexpress.com/investor/ACE03.pdf
107. Nasdaq Stock Report, "Cash America, EZ Pawn, and First Cash, November 28, 2003." Retrieved 2003 from www.nasdaq.com
108. APRO, "RTO Industry Stats, 2003." Retrieved 2004 from www.aprovision.org/industrystats.html
109. Consumer Federation of America, "Predatory Lending, 2002." Retrieved 2002 from www.consumerfed.org/backpage/predatory.html
110. Edward Gramlich, Remarks by Governor Edward M. Gramlich at the Federal Reserve Bank of Philadelphia. Community and Consumer Affairs Department Conference on Predatory Lending, December 6, 2000. Washington, D.C.: Federal Reserve Bank.
111. Fannie Mae Foundation, 2001.

112. Federal Reserve Board, "The Unbanked—Who Are They?" *Capital Connections* 3, no. 2, retrieved 2002 from www.federalreserve.gov/dcca/newsletter/2001/spring01/unbank.htm; Booz-Allen & Hamilton Shugoll Research, *Mandatory EFT Demographic Study: A Report Prepared for the U.S. Department of Treasury, September 15, 1997,* Washington, D.C.: U.S. Department of the Treasury; and John Caskey, *Lower Income American, Higher Cost Financial Services* (Madison, WI: Filene Research Institute, 1997).
113. Federal Reserve Board, 2002; Io Data Corporation, *Payday Advance Customer Research: Cumulative State Research Report, September 2002.* IO Data Corporation, Salt Lake City, UT.
114. Io Data Corporation, 2002.
115. Joint Center for Housing Studies of Harvard University *The State of the Nation's Housing* (Cambridge, MA: Harvard University, 2003); Theresa Murray, "Experts Warn Against Milking Home Equity to Extend Debt," *Minneapolis St. Paul Star Tribune* (November 4, 2000), p. B-5.
116. See Noel Paul, "Culture of Consumption," *Christian Science Monitor* (June 12, 2003), 18; and Joint Center for Housing Studies of Harvard University, 2003.
117. Paul, "Culture of Consumption," 2003.
118. Manning, *Credit Card Nation,* 2000.
119. Lloyd Klein, *It's in the Cards: Consumer Credit and the American Experience* (Westport, CT: Praeger Publishers, 1999).
120. CNN, "Late Payments at 5-Year High, Past-Due Credit Card Debt Highest Since '97," April 29, 2002. Retrieved 2002 from www.cnn.com
121. Joanna Stavins, "Credit Card Borrowing, Delinquency and Personal Bankruptcy," *Questia* (2000). Retrieved 2003 from http://www.questia.com
122. Ibid.
123. Cardweb.com. Retrieved 2003 from www/cardweb.com
124. Wired Plastic. Retrieved 2003 from www.wiredplastic.com
125. Direct Telephone Company, Inc., Houston, TX.
126. See Sprint PCS, retrieved 2004 from www.sprintpcs.com; and AT&T Wireless, retrieved 2004 from www.attwireless.com
127. Ibid.
128. See APRO 2003; and James M. Lacko, Signe-Mary McKernan, and Manoj Hastak, *Survey of Rent-to-Own Customers, Federal Trade Commission* (Bureau of Economics, Washington, D.C., 1999).
129. Rent-A-Center, retrieved January 2, 2004, from www.rentacenter.com; ColorTyme, retrieved January 2, 2004, from www.colortyme.com; Aaron Rents, retrieved 2004 from www.aaronrents.com; RentWay, retrieved 2004 from www.rentway.com; Rent Rite, retrieved 2003 from www.rentrite.com
130. Ibid.
131. Public Interest Research Group (PIRG), "Don't Rent to Own: The 1997 PIRG Rent-to-Own Survey," U.S. Public Interest Research Group, Washington, D.C., June 11, 1997.
132. Ibid.
133. Alix M. Freedman, "Peddling Dreams: A Market Giant Uses Its Sales Prowess to Profit on Poverty," *Wall Street Journal* (September 22, 1993), p. D15.
134. APRO, 2003.
135. John Seward, "Tales of the Tape: Rent-to-Owns Seek Definition in Law," *Wall Street Journal* (October 22, 2003), p. D15.
136. Quoted in Freedman, 1993, p. D16.
137. Fannie Mae Foundation, 2001; and Michael Hudson, (Ed.), *Merchants of Misery* (Monroe, ME: Common Courage Press, 1996).
138. John Caskey, *Fringe Banking* (New York: Russell Sage Foundation, 1994).
139. American Financial Services Association, "Pawnshops Struggle, 2002." Retrieved 2002 from www.spotlightonfinance.org/issues/August/Stories/story13.htm
140. Caskey, 1994.
141. *Edmund's Used Cars & Trucks Prices: 1992–2001, American & Import,* Spring/Summer, 2002 (Chicago, IL: Edmunds, 2002).
142. Personal Communication with Car Title Loans of America, Inc., Missouri office, Columbia, MO, June 5, 2002.
143. American Financial Services Association, 2002.
144. See Ibid; and Charles Gerena, "Need Quick Cash?" *IssueArchives,* Federal Reserve Bank of Richmond (Summer 2002), retrieved 2003 from www.rich.frb.org/pubs/regionfocus/summer02/payday.html.
145. Jean Ann Fox and Edmund Mierzwinski, "Rent-A-Bank Payday Lending: How Banks Help Payday Lenders Evade State Consumer Protections." Consumer Federation of America and U.S. Public Interest Group. Consumer Federation, Washington, D.C., November 2001.
146. Ibid.
147. Consumer Federation of America, 2002.
148. AARP, "Payday Loans Don't Pay, 2000." Retrieved 2002 from www.aarp.org/confacts/money/payday-loans.html
149. Editors, Nolo Press, "The 'Lectric' Law Library, 1995." Retrieved 2002 from www.lectlaw.com/files/ban05.htm
150. Quik Payday, "APR Disclosure, 2002." Retrieved 2002 from www.quikpayday.com/apr-disclosure.html
151. Consumer Federation of America, 2002.
152. Ibid.
153. Ibid.
154. Ibid.
155. Alan Berube, Anne Kim, Benjamin Forman, and Megan Burns, *The Price of Paying Taxes: How Tax*

Preparation and Refund Loan Fees Erode the Benefits of the EITC. Center on Urban & Metropolitan Policy, The Brookings Institution and The Progressive Policy Institute, Washington, D.C.: The Brookings Institution, May 2002.

156. Consumer Federation of America, 2002.
157. See New York City Department of Consumer Affairs, "Department of Consumer Affairs Announces More than $4 Million in Restitution, Fines and EITC Outreach Funds from H&R Block in Largest Settlement in Agency's History," December 12, 2002, retrieved 2003 from www.nyc.gov/html/dca/pdf/hr_block.pdf; *The Business Journal,* "Block Faces Another Shareholder Class Action," December 16, 2002, retrieved 2003 from http://kansascity.bizjournals.com/kansascity/stories/2002/12/16/daily1.html
158. Chi Chi Wu and Jean Ann Fox, "The High Cost of Quick Tax Money: Tax Preparation, 'Instant Refund' Loans, and Check Cashing Fees Target the Working Poor," National Consumer Law Center, Consumer Federation of America, January 2003. Washington, D.C.
159. Ibid.
160. This is based on national averages.
161. Wu and Fox, 2003.
162. Ibid.
163. Ibid.
164. John Caskey, "Bringing Unbanked Households into the Banking System," *Capitol Xchange,* The Brookings Institution, January 2002. Retrieved 2002 from www.brook.edu/dybdocroot/es/urban/capitalxchange/article10.htm.
165. ACE Cash Express, "ACE Store Services, 2002." Retrieved 2002 from www.acecashexpress.com/general/services.html.
166. See Anne Kim, "The Unbanked and the Alternative Financial Sector. Discussion Comments to the Changing Financial Markets and Community Development Conference." Federal Reserve Bank of Chicago, transcript, April 5, 2001. Retrieved 2002 from www.ppionline.org/ppi_ci.cfm?cp=3&knlgAreaID=114&subsecid=236&contentid=3843; and Financial Service Centers of America, 2003.
167. Mukherjee, 1997, p. 25.
168. Kim 2001, op cit.
169. Financial Service Centers of America (FiSCA), 2003.
170. See ACE Cash Express Inc., *Annual Report on Form 10-K for the Fiscal Year Ended June 30, 2000.* Filed with the Securities and Exchange Commission; and Dollar Financial Group, Inc., *Annual Report on Form 10-K for the Fiscal Year Ended June 30, 2000,* filed with the Securities and Exchange Commission.
171. ACE Cash Express, "ACE Cash Express Extends Money Order Relationship with Travelers Express, ACE to Receive $3.4 Million in Signing and Annual Bonuses," October 20, 2003. Retrieved 2003 from www.acecashexpress.com/investor/press/2004/Money%20Order%20Deal.html
172. *Consumer Reports,* "The Certified Option, 2000." Retrieved 2002 from www.consumerreports.org/main/detailv2.jsp?CONTENT%3C%3Ecnt_id=160483&FOLDER%3C%3Efolder_id=21135
173. National Association of Automobile Dealers, "NADA Data: Dealership Financial Trends." Retrieved 2002 from www.nada.org/Content/NavigationMenu/MediaCenter/NADAData/20021/NADAData_dft.pdf
174. *Automotive Digest,* "Average Retail vs. Buy-Here-Pay-Here Dealer Sales Data—2002." Retrieved 2002 from www.automotivedigest.com/research/research_results.asp?sigstats_id=201
175. *Dealer's Edge,* "Buy-Here, Pay-Here Business Continues to Grow," June 26, 2000. Retrieved 2002 from www.dealersedge.com/nlcontent/ded/2000/06262000.pdf
176. "Conning & Co. Study Says Auto Insurers are Paying Closer Attention to Credit Scores," *Insurance Journal* (August 2, 2001).
177. Consumers Union, "Reducing the Number of Uninsured Motorists," *Consumers Union SWRO Issue Pages for the 77th Texas Legislature* (January 2001).
178. A.M. Best Company, Inc., "Insurers Expect Battle on Use of Credit Scores in About Half the United States," *BestWire* (January 30, 2002).
179. Caskey, 1997.

CHAPTER 6

The Voluntary Sector Today

This chapter locates the voluntary sector with respect to the other institutions involved in social welfare in the United States. The heart of the **voluntary sector** is made up of the private, nonprofit organizations that are ubiquitous at the local level. Supporting the voluntary sector are philanthropic contributions that have been an important source of revenues for social service initiatives. The chapter describes the work of prominent human service agencies and examines the role of voluntary agencies in advocating social justice. The fiscal crisis of the voluntary sector is discussed, as are the recession of the early 1980s and the scandal that shook the United Way during the early 1990s, thus further compounding the funding problems of nonprofit service agencies. Finally, the chapter examines the response to September 11, 2001, as well as emerging trends in the voluntary sector.

As the twenty-first century begins, welfare professionals are reassessing the capacity of the voluntary sector to meet the nation's social welfare needs. The primary reason for renewed interest in the voluntary sector has been the reluctance of taxpayers and politicians to authorize major new governmental welfare initiatives. As governmental expenditures for social welfare fail to increase in the face of rising demand for human services, the voluntary sector has been called on to shoulder more of the welfare burden. This shift in responsibilities was stated explicitly by President Reagan, who appealed to the charitable impulses of Americans as a way for the nation to address human needs while reducing federal appropriations to social programs; the idea was restated by George H. W. Bush in his reference to "a thousand points of light" during his 1988 presidential campaign. Although President Clinton made no comparable gesture to the nonprofit sector, his statement that "the era of big government is over" had enormous implications for nonprofit agencies. Finally, the emergence of "compassionate conservatism" and its corollary, "faith-based social services," by George W. Bush restates the conservative case for a reinvigorated voluntary sector.

Although many liberals of the 1980s were skeptical about the sincerity of conservatives in championing the virtues of the voluntary sector, suspecting that it was a ruse to gut governmental social programs, other events conspired to focus attention on this sector. A wave of conservatism since the 1980s and 1990s may have stalled the introduction of liberally inspired social legislation, but the conservative imprint on social welfare could be traced as far back as the late 1970s. During the Carter presidency conservatives began to challenge welfare programs on the grounds that they divided the family, eroded the work ethic, and subverted communal norms. A widely distributed monograph by analysts from the American Enterprise Institute criticized social "megastructures" for contributing to alienation among Americans, and called for stronger "mediating structures"—voluntary entities—to empower people.[1] During the 1990s, Democrats responded to these conservative trends by jettisoning from their party platform traditional welfare planks that called for major new federal social programs in favor of more pluralist strategies that included the voluntary sector.

Accompanying these ideological developments, leaders of the voluntary sector sparked the imagination of other human service professionals by mounting important initiatives. The Catholic Campaign for Human Development allocated $11.5 million for anti-poverty programs in 2002, among them the Colonias Development Council serving Latinos on the Texas-Mexico border.[2] In 2003 the Rotary Club of Washington, DC marked the fifteenth anniversary of its international campaign to eradicate polio in India and other developing nations.[3] In July 2004, thousands of residents of southwestern Virginia stood in lines up to eight hours for free dental care arranged by the Remote Area Medical Volunteer Corps and the Virginia Dental Association.[4] As these projects attest, the voluntary sector remains a vital part of social welfare, not only in the United States, but internationally as well.

Structural Interests within Social Welfare

Organized responses to the needs of Americans have undergone fundamental change since European settlement. In a sense, the voluntary sector is the first modern welfare institution, with a long legacy in American social welfare. Over the centuries the voluntary sector has witnessed the emergence of competing institutions: the state and federal governmental programs of the public sector, the private practices of professional entrepreneurs, and a corporate sector accountable to chief executive officers and stockholders. Reflecting this transformation, David Stoesz has posited that four groups can be identified within U.S. social welfare: traditional providers, welfare bureaucrats, clinical entrepreneurs, and human service executives.[5] Because these groups have become integrated into the nation's political economy, they are termed *structural interests.*

Traditional Providers

The heart of the voluntary sector consists of professionals and laypersons who seek to maintain and enhance traditional relations, values, and structures in their communities through private, nonprofit agencies. **Traditional providers** hold an organic conception of social welfare, seeing it as tightly interwoven with other community institutions. According to traditional providers, voluntary nonprofit agencies offer the advantages of neighborliness, a reaffirmation of community values, a concern for community as opposed to personal gain, and freedom to alter programming so as to conform to changes in local priorities.

Much of the heritage of social welfare can be traced to early proponents of this structural interest-people such as Mary Richmond of the **Charity Organization Society** (COS) movement and Jane Addams of the settlement house movement. Charity Organization Societies and **settlement houses** were transformed by two influences: the need for scientifically based treatment techniques and the socialization of charity. Together, these factors functioned as an anchor for the social casework agencies in U.S. industrial society. The agency provided the grist for scientific casework that was instrumental in the emergence of the social work profession. The new schools of social work, in turn, relied on casework agencies for internship training, a substantial portion of a professional's education. Once graduated, many professionals elected to work in the voluntary sector, ensuring agencies of a steady supply of personnel.

Voluntary agencies routinized philanthropic contributions by socializing charity. Beginning with Denver's Associated Charities in 1887, the concept of a community appeal spread so rapidly that by the 1920s more than 200 cities had "community chests." The needs of social workers for effective treatment techniques and the economic imperatives for organizational survival functioned together to standardize the social agency. Perhaps the best description of the casework agency is found in the 1923 Milford Conference Report, *Social Casework: Generic and Specific,* which comprehensively outlined the organization through which professional caseworkers delivered services.[6] By the 1940s the social casework agency had become a predominant form of service delivery. Today, much social service provision exists in the form of United Way–subsidized sectarian and nonsectarian agencies, whose member groups collected $3.91 billion in 2000–2001.[7]

Welfare Bureaucrats

Welfare bureaucrats are public functionaries who maintain the welfare state in much the same form in which it was conceived during the New Deal. "Their ideology," according to Robert Alford, "stresses a rational, efficient, cost-conscious, coordinated . . . delivery system."[8] These functionaries view federal government intervention vis-à-vis social problems as legitimate and necessary, considering the apparent lack of concern by the private sector and local governments. Moreover, they contend that federal intervention is more effective than other forms, because authority is centralized, guidelines are standardized, and benefits are allocated according to principles of equity and equality.

The influence of welfare bureaucrats grew as a result of the Social Security Act of 1935. To a limited extent, the larger community chests "exerted a pressure toward rationalization of the professional welfare machinery,"[9] but this did not diminish the effect of the federal welfare bureaucracy, which soon eclipsed the authority of traditional providers. Actually, a unilinear evolution between these interests could have occurred had Harry Hopkins, head of the Federal Emergency Relief Administration in the 1930s, not prohibited states from turning federal welfare funds over to private agencies.[10] Denied the resources to address significantly the massive social problems caused by the Great Depression, private agencies lapsed into a secondary role while federal and state agencies ascended in importance. An array of welfare legislation followed the Social Security Act, including the Housing Act of 1937, the G. I. Bill of 1944, the Community Mental Health Centers Act of 1963, the Civil Rights Act of 1964, the Food Stamp Act of 1964, the Economic Opportunity Act of 1964, the Elementary and Secondary Education Act of 1965, the Medicare and Medicaid Acts of 1965, Supplemental Security Income in 1974, Title XX of the Social Security Act of 1975, the Full Employment Act of 1978, and the Americans with Disabilities Act of 1980.

The flourishing of bureaucratic rationality concomitant with this legislative activity represented the institutionalization of liberal thought, which sought to control the caprice of the market, ensure a measure of equality among widely divergent economic classes, and establish an administrative apparatus to ensure the continuity of these principles. Confronted with a rapidly industrializing society lacking basic programs for ameliorating social and economic catastrophes, progressives perceived the state as a vehicle for social reform. Their solutions focused on "coordinating fragmented services, instituting planning, and extending public funding."[11] Implicit in the methods advocated by welfare bureaucrats is an expectation, if not an assumption, that the social welfare administration should be centralized, that eligibility for benefits should be universalized, and that social welfare should be firmly anchored in the institutional fabric of society.

The influence of welfare bureaucrats had been curtailed somewhat since the mid-1980s. The Reagan administration all but capped the growth of public social welfare, expenditures of which as a percent of GDP hovered at 18.5 percent through the 1980s until increasing under the Clinton presidency to 21.8 percent in 1994.[12] The presidency of George W. Bush transmitted a mixed message to welfare bureaucrats: while a series of tax cuts reduced federal revenues for social programs, the addition of a prescription benefit to Medicare strengthened their relations to the pharmaceutical industry. Smarting from election losses in the 1980s and 2000, liberal Democrats had begun to reconsider their objections to private sector solutions to social problems. Still, the volume of resources and the number of people dependent on public welfare, especially those reliant on Social Security and Medicare, assure welfare bureaucrats of a dominant and continuing role in the foreseeable future.

Clinical Entrepreneurs

Clinical entrepreneurs are professional service providers, chiefly social workers, psychologists, and physicians, who work for themselves instead of being salaried employees. Important to clinical entrepreneurs in each specialty is the establishment of a **professional monopoly,** the evolution of which represents a concern on the part of practitioners that their occupational activity not be subject to political interference from the state or the ignorance of the lay public. In the United States the professions found that a market economy was conducive to occupational success. In the most fundamental sense, private practice reconciles the professionals' desire for autonomy with the imperatives of a market economy. The transition from entrepreneur to professional monopolist is a matter of obtaining legislation restricting practice to those duly licensed by the state. "Professionalism provides a way of preserving monopolistic control over services without the risks of competition."[13] As an extension of the entrepreneurial model of service delivery, professional monopoly offers privacy in practice, freedom to establish one's worth by setting fees, and the security ensured by membership in the professional monopoly.

The social worker as clinical entrepreneur is a relatively recent phenomenon, and the **National Association of Social Workers (NASW)** did not officially sanction this form of service delivery until 1964. Before that, privately practicing social workers identified themselves as psychotherapists and lay analysts. Typically, they relied on referrals from physicians and psychiatrists, and after World War II they began to establish "flourishing and lucrative"[14] practices. By the 1970s, **private practice** in social work was developing as an important form of service delivery, although analysts disagreed about the number of social workers engaged in independent practice. In 1975 NASW estimated that 10,000 to 20,000 social workers were engaged in private practice. By 1983 Robert Barker, author of *Social Work in Private Practice* and a columnist on private practice in *NASW News,* speculated that about 30,000 social workers, or 32 percent of all social workers, engaged in private practice on a full- or part-time basis.[15] By 1985 a large portion of psychotherapy was being done by social workers, and the *New York Times* noted that "growing numbers of social workers are treating more affluent private clients, thus moving into the traditional preserve of the elite psychiatrists and clinical psychologists."[16] Yet in the early 1990s, NASW reported that only about 15,000 of its members—11.1 percent—were in solo or partnership practice as private practitioners, compared to about one-third of NASW members employed in for-profit firms.[17]

Clinical entrepreneurs are an emerging interest in social welfare. Continued growth of this group is likely for several reasons. Through local and state chapters, NASW has been effective in expanding the scope of its professional monopoly. In 1983, 31 states had passed legislation regulating the practice of social work; by 1992 all 50 states regulated social work practice. At the same time, professional groups have lobbied for vendorship privileges that allow them more regular income through insurance held by clients. Finally, large numbers of students entering graduate schools of social work do so with the expressed intent of setting up in private practice.[18] Clinical entrepreneurs would be well positioned to become a more influential interest in social welfare in the United States were it not for the incursion of managed care: the attempt of human service corporations to diminish the influence of clinical entrepreneurs.

Human Service Executives

Human service executives share an important characteristic with clinical entrepreneurs: Both groups represent ways of organizing service delivery in the context of the market. However, in some important ways they differ. Unlike clinical entrepreneurs, **human service executives** are salaried employees of proprietary firms and, as such, have less autonomy. As administrators or chief executive officers of large corporations, human service executives advance market strategies for promoting social welfare. Whereas welfare bureaucrats emphasize the planning and regulatory functions of the state, human service executives favor the rationality of the marketplace in allocating resources and evaluating programs. In the present circumstances, human service executives are advocating market reform of the welfare state—the domain of welfare bureaucrats—and thus are in a position to challenge the bureaucratic interest.

For-profit firms became prominent in social welfare in the United States during the 1960s, when Medicaid and Medicare funds were paid to proprietary nursing homes and hospitals.[19] Since then, human service executives have been rapidly creating independent, for-profit human service corporations that provide an extensive range of nationwide services. Human service corporations have established prominent, if not dominant, positions in several human service markets, including nursing home care, hospital management, health maintenance, child care, home care, and even corrections and welfare. Most recently, human service corporations have aggressively exploited the managed care market. In 1981 there were 34 human service corporations, reporting annual revenues above $10 million; by 1985 the number of firms had increased to 66; and by 2000 the number had soared to 268. Of these, 16 corporations reported revenues higher than the total annual contributions to all of the United Ways of America; by 2004 the number had exceeded 20.

As the proprietary sector expands to dominate different human service markets, oligopolies emerge and a fundamental change occurs. No longer passively dependent on government appropriations, proprietary firms are in a strong position to shape the very markets they serve, influencing not only consumer demand but governmental policy as well. It is this capacity to determine or control a market that qualitatively distinguishes corporate welfare from the earlier form of business involvement in social welfare—that is, from philanthropic contributions to nonprofit agencies of the voluntary sector. For these reasons, human service executives are now well positioned to challenge the power of welfare bureaucrats.

The structural interests just described can be located in relation to two variables: span of influence and type of economy. As Figure 6.1 indicates, power shifts as a result of significant social influences: privatization and bureaucratization. The consequences of these forces will be evident throughout this book.

Marginal Interests

Social welfare in the United States is also populated by numerous groups that have not become as symbiotically attached to the social structure as have the structural interests just described. These marginal interest groups usually represent special populations

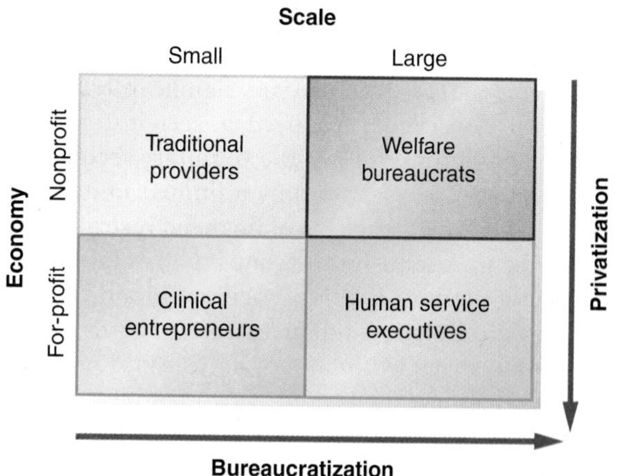

Figure 6.1

Dynamics of Structural Interests

Source: David Stoesz, "A Theory of Social Welfare," *Social Work* 34, no. 2 (March 1989), p. 106.

that have been ignored, excluded, or oppressed by mainstream society. Their number reflects the capacity of U.S. culture to maintain its equilibrium while excluding many groups from full social participation. A partial list of marginal interest groups includes African Americans, poor women, Native Americans, homosexuals, residents of isolated rural areas, and Hispanic Americans. These groups are of concern to welfare professionals because typically they have not had the same opportunities as mainstream populations; in other words, they have been denied social justice. Within the context of democratic capitalism, elevating marginal interests remains extraordinarily difficult.

The marginal status of many groups relates to the nature of the social welfare industry. In U.S. culture, groups excluded from the mainstream are expected to gather their resources and identify leaders who will mount programs to serve their particular group. Although this expectation is congruent with traditional values such as self-sufficiency and community solidarity, that solidarity approach does not necessarily ensure success. Significant variations are evident within regions of the United States with respect to generosity. For example, the Generosity Index reveals that residents of some states are more willing to contribute a portion of their income to social causes than others. For 2004 the most generous states were Mississippi, Arkansas, Oklahoma, Louisiana, and Alabama while the stingiest were New Hampshire, Massachusetts, Rhode Island, New Jersey, and Wisconsin. The Generosity Index suggests that a state's charity is inversely related to its wealth.[20]

Metropolitan areas also vary significantly in their generosity toward those in need, as seen in Table 6.1. In light of such variations, the voluntary sector may be able to accommodate only a limited number of marginal interests because of financial restraints, or it may be unresponsive to groups that violate traditional community norms. Programs to aid victims of domestic violence and the homeless, for example, have often struggled to mount and sustain minimal services, because the United Way often has funding priorities consonant with the needs of clientele more highly regarded in the community.

In a democratic polity, marginal groups can also make claims on the social order by seeking benefits through governmental programs; but to do so presents other problems. Government programs are likely to be managed by welfare bureaucrats, who have their own understanding of what is best for the marginal interest. For a marginal group to get benefits through government programs, its claim must be mandated through legislation, which requires the approval of a majority of legislators. Once enacted, benefits for marginal groups must be programmed, and monitored by agents of the welfare state, who often have a welfare ideology that differs from that of oppressed groups. The result is likely to be a program that is more consonant with the ideology of the welfare bureaucrats than with that of the marginal group. During the 1980s, the effort to combat AIDS was plagued by volatile disagreements between gay advocacy organizations and the public health bureaucrats who run the Centers for Disease Control and Prevention.

Despite such obstacles, members of marginal groups have powerful incentives to work within existing structures if their needs are to be met at all. Usually, their success in this regard is mixed. As a result of affirmative action, African Americans have

Table 6.1

Donations by Metropolitan Area

Area	% of Discretionary Income Given to Charity
Salt Lake City/Ogden	14.9
Grand Rapids, Michigan	10.0
Minneapolis/St. Paul	8.5
Greensboro/Winston-Salem	8.5
Memphis	8.4
Dallas/Fort Worth	8.4
Nashville	8.3
San Antonio	8.1
Houston/Galveston	8.1
Oklahoma City	8.0
Norfolk/Virginia Beach/ Newport News	8.0
Charlotte/Rock Hill	7.9
Seattle/Tacoma	7.7
Washington/Baltimore	7.6

Source: Adapted from Jacqueline Salmon and Hamil Harris, "Pr. George's a Leader in Giving," *Washington Post* (April 29, 2003), p. A7.

been able to secure positions within the welfare bureaucracy in relatively significant numbers and are now well established among welfare bureaucrats. White women have found independent practice a desirable framework within which to provide services and are well represented among clinical entrepreneurs. In contrast, many marginal groups continue to struggle against a welfare industry that is controlled by structural interests indifferent to minority concerns. The structural interest of human service executives, for example, remains a bastion of white patriarchy. Activists from the African American community struggle to contain gang violence, reduce the number of teen pregnancies, and halt the scourge of illegal drugs, often with inadequate resources. Indeed, one of the most glaring contradictions of American social welfare are state-of-the-art medical centers controlled by human-service executives located right next to inner city ghettoes inhabited by the poorest and most neglected Americans. How has the American welfare state come to assure wealth for health and human service executives while generating, at the same time, an underclass?

The Forgotten Sector

As a result of the dynamic expansion of other structural interests over the course of the twentieth century, the voluntary sector lapsed in importance.[21] Following the triumph of the New Deal, leading welfare theoreticians expected government to dominate in the creation and administration of the welfare state. In fact, so complete was the expectation that the government-driven welfare state would dominate social welfare in the United States that references to private voluntary agencies became scant in the professional literature. There was little room within welfare state ideology for a dynamic voluntary sector, and references to private, nonprofit agencies virtually disappeared from discussions of social welfare. When discussed at all, voluntary agencies were viewed as vestiges from an earlier time. Rediscovered during the 1980s, the voluntary sector quickly attracted converts. Perhaps the most notable of the new adherents to the promise of nonprofits was business guru Peter Drucker. Citing the capacity of the "social sector" to address local problems, Drucker recited the virtues of the nonprofit sector in books such as *The New Realities;*[22] in 1990 he even went so far as to establish the Peter F. Drucker Foundation for Nonprofit Management.[23] The Republican Party embraced the voluntary sector as a means to address social problems while containing federal social programs; subsequently, serving as the institutional basis for "compassionate conservatism."

To the extent that the voluntary sector has been related to the governmental welfare state, it has been as a subcontractor of social services. This role was made possible through an amendment to the Social Security Act, Title XX, which allowed for the "purchase of service" from private providers. Under purchase-of-service contracts, government could avoid the costs and responsibilities of administering programs directly. Because of an open-ended funding formula, however, federal costs for Title XX services escalated sharply. Congress later capped Title XX expenditures, initially at $2.5 billion, in order to contain program costs, and still later the Reagan administration was successful in having the program placed under a Social Services Block Grant, with further funding restrictions.[24] Consequently, in response to Title XX, many voluntary social service agencies secured purchase-of-service contracts, the funding for which allowed nonprofit agencies to expand programs in the late 1960s and early 1970s. Then, when funding was reduced, voluntary sector agencies were heavily penalized. Federal expenditures for Title XX fell from $2.8 billion in 1980 to $2.7 billion in 1992, a significant reduction in that it occurred at a time when demand for service was rising sharply.[25] By 2000, Title XX had eroded still further; only $1.775 billion of a possible $2.380 was allocated for social services.[26]

When policymakers turned to the voluntary sector in the 1980s to compensate for reductions in the governmental welfare effort, little was known about nonprofit social service agencies. Lester Salamon and Alan Abramson, authorities on the voluntary sector, observed that "despite their importance, these organizations have tended to be ignored in both public policy debates and scholarly research."[27] As government assumed a dominant role in U.S. social welfare, the voluntary sector receded in importance. If the Reagan-Bush presidencies rekindled interest in the voluntary sector, the 1994 Republican takeover of Congress created a small firestorm. As part of their Contract with America, congressional Republicans promised to reform welfare as part of an extensive overhaul of the whole welfare state. Government, they argued, had induced the dependency of millions of families on public assistance; welfare programs largely benefited the welfare professionals who worked in them; and all of this diluted the influence of community institutions. Congressional conservatives had a strategy in mind when they critiqued federal social programs: Replace governmental welfare programs with private, voluntary sector initiatives. "The crisis of the modern welfare state is not just a crisis of government," contended conservative scholar Marvin Olasky. "The more effective provision of social services will ultimately depend on their return to private and especially religious institutions."[28] Suddenly, after half a century of neglect, the "forgotten sector" was being called on to assume unprecedented responsibilities in caring for the needy.

Beginning in the 1970s, researchers had begun to investigate the scope of the voluntary sector. Their task has not been an easy one. The voluntary sector is composed of tens of thousands of organizations, many of which are not associated with any national umbrella association. The picture that is emerging from preliminary investigations reveals a sector that, if small by economic standards, is extraordinarily rich socially. Perhaps the most convenient measure of the scale of the voluntary sector is to count the voluntary and philanthropic associations that have received tax-exempt status as social service agencies from the Internal Revenue Service—177,604 in 1996, of which 66,514 are engaged in human services.[29] From 1977 to 1998, the number of nonprofit organizations increased by 500,000, from 1.12 million to 1.62 million.[30] A sizable number of these organizations are religious in nature. In 2002 the IRS reported 909,574 organizations with 501(c)(3) status.[31] Despite their proliferation, the voluntary sector accounts for only half of national economic activity attributed to government and one-tenth that of business.[32]

Generally, the expansion of the voluntary sector has paralleled economic growth; for example, between 1960 and 1995 per capita charitable giving increased from $280 to $522 in constant dollars.[33] Charitable giving for 1999 totaled $190 billion, having increased by $15 billion over each of the previous two years; by 2002 it had increased to $240.92 billion.[34] Total donations accounted for 2002 represented 2.3 percent of gross domestic product (GDP). Three-fourths of contributions emanate from individuals, with foundations accounting for about 10 percent and corporations about 5 percent.[35] Religious institutions receive more than 40 percent of philanthropic contributions, followed by education and health. While human service organizations received 7.7 percent of donations in 2002, their receipts represented an 11.4 percent decrease from the year before.[36]

In 2000 the American Association of Fund Raising Councils noted that the expansion of giving to human services "is part of a recent pattern of strong performance,"[37] yet events unforeseen would overshadow this projection. The economic reverberations of September 11, 2001, dampened philanthropic activity; between 2001 and 2002, charitable contributions fell by 1.2 percent.[38] Despite the infusion of $2.6 billion of charitable contributions to victims of the September 11 attacks,[39] subsequent mismanagement of nonprofit organizations reduced public philanthropy. A poll conducted by the Brookings Institution, the Chronicle of Philanthropy, and Independent Sector revealed that 42 percent of respondents had less confidence in charities after September 11, 2001.[40]

The voluntary sector rebounded modestly in 2003, though not enough to make up for the previous year's losses. Notably, foundation funding plummeted.

Despite financial fluctuations, the voluntary sector persevered, embedded in the social fabric of the nation. In 1998 the nonprofit sector employed 10.9 million staff and supervised 9.3 million full-time equivalent volunteers, the volunteer effort representing $225.9 billion in economic activity.[41] This voluntary activity shows a steady increase over the last quarter of the twentieth century: In 1977, 26 percent of Americans reported that they were involved in charitable work with the needy; by 1998 that figure had increased to 55 percent.[42] As noted Table 6.2, contrary to popular assumption, the voluntary sector is not bankrolled by wealthy philanthropists and their foundations. Foundations and corporations account for only 15 percent of voluntary sector contributions; "about half of all charitable dollars comes from families with incomes under $25,000."[43]

Nonprofit human service organizations have their share of organizational difficulties, of course. Notably during the Reagan presidency, charitable revenues dropped because of a severe recession, reductions in government assistance, and adverse changes in tax law. The 1980s were hard times for nonprofit organizations, particularly social service agencies. Federal spending in areas served by nonprofit social service programs was negative for more than a decade, and direct federal support of nonprofit social service agencies was not positive until the early 1990s. Although private giving increased

Table 6.2

Charitable Donations

	$ (billions)	% Change from 2002
2003 contributions	240.7	+0.5
Sources of donations		
living individuals	179.4	+0.2
bequests	21.6	+10.3
foundations	26.3	–4.7
corporations	13.5	+1.9
Beneficiary organizations		
religious	86.4	+2.0
educational	31.6	–3.0
foundations	21.4	–26.5
health	20.9	+8.2
human services	18.9	–1.0
arts, culture	13.1	+4.9
public society	12.1	+2.3
environment, animals	7.0	+3.1
international affairs	5.3	+12.1

Source: Adapted from Stephanie Strom, "Charitable Giving Holds Steady, Report Finds," *New York Times* (June 22, 2004), p. A11.

fairly steadily during the late 1980s and early 1990s, it has not compensated for overall federal rescissions. The end of the second millennium provided an answer to an important question: Can charitable giving replace federal social welfare? This question has been central to the thinking of conservatives who have criticized the welfare state and advanced the nonprofit sector as an alternative. During the Reagan-Bush presidencies federal social welfare expenditures plummeted, as did federal assistance to nonprofits; and, although private contributions did increase during this period, they were insufficient to compensate for federal cuts. It was not until the Clinton administration that the rise in private giving eclipsed federal cuts in social welfare and the trend in federal aid to nonprofits became positive. Although conservatives were correct in suggesting that there was untapped capacity in the philanthropic sector for social welfare, between 1982 and 1995 this voluntary capacity never made up for federal cuts in benefits to the poor. Consequently, most scholars of the voluntary sector concluded that rather than trying to replace governmental social welfare activities, nonprofit agencies should adopt practices "in support of an expansion of the welfare state."[44]

While the last decades of the twentieth century raised profound questions about the plausibility that the voluntary sector could replace government social programs, there was little doubt that philanthropy would expand significantly during the twenty-first century. Aside from normal economic growth, the massive tax cuts engineered by the administration of George W. Bush which favored the wealthy, presage a new era of philanthropy. The value of the four tax cuts enacted by the Bush administration is projected to total $1.9 trillion over ten years, much of it benefiting corporations and the wealthy.[45] Paul Schervish has outlined the philanthropic consequences of this massive expansion of wealth in America:

> We estimate that an unprecedented $45 to $150 trillion in wealth transfer is in the offing over the next five decades, that this will produce at least $21 trillion to $55 trillion of charitable giving, and that between 52 percent and 65 percent of this amount will be contributed by households with $1 million in net worth.[46]

The extent to which such unprecedented wealth will be used to amplify *moral citizenship*—fulfilling the inclinations and obligations of caring—will be one of the challenges of the twenty-first century.[47]

Advancing Social Justice

In addition to providing social services, the voluntary sector has been important in U.S. social welfare because it has been the source of efforts to advance the rights of disenfranchised populations. In this respect the voluntary sector is essential to the nation's culture, in that it is a correcting influence to the indifference often shown to marginal populations by governmental and corporate bureaucracies. This case has been argued vigorously by John W. Gardner, former secretary of Health, Education, and Welfare and former chairman of the board of Independent Sector. According to Gardner, the voluntary sector fosters much of the pluralism in the life of this country, taking on those concerns that do not attract the broad spectrum of public support necessary for the legislation that mandates governmental programs, and concerns that do not represent the commercial prospects necessary to attract the interests of the business community. In other words, the voluntary sector serves as the best—and, in some cases, the only—vehicle for addressing certain social needs. Indeed, much of what Americans would identify as central to their culture can be attributed to organizations of the voluntary sector: hospitals, schools, religious institutions, welfare agencies, fraternal associations, symphonies, and museums, to name of few. According to Gardner,

> Institutions of the nonprofit sector are in a position to serve as the guardians of intellectual and artistic freedom. Both the commercial and political marketplaces are subject to leveling forces that may threaten standards of excellence. In the non-profit sector, the fiercest champions of excellence may have their say. So may the champions of liberty and justice.[48]

Gardner's last reference here is not merely rhetorical but has its basis in history. As Alexis de Tocqueville observed in the 1830s, Americans have long depended on voluntary organizations to solve communal problems. And in addressing these problems, the voluntary sector has compiled an impressive list of positive additions to American life. Those seeking solutions to current problems often find inspiration in voluntary sector initiatives of the past. Gardner noted that "At a time in our history when we are ever in need of new solutions to new problems, the private sector is remarkably free to innovate, create, and engage in controversial experiments." He went on to observe, "In fact, virtually every far-reaching social change in our history has come up in the private sector: the abolition of slavery, the reforms of populism, child labor laws, the vote for women, civil rights, and so on."[49]

Important social welfare initiatives have also originated in the voluntary sector. The inspiration for the Great Society initiative, during which new social programs such as Medicaid, food stamps, and the Job Corps were launched, can be traced to Mobilization for Youth, a voluntary sector poverty program in New York City funded by the Ford Foundation. Two champions of community organization, the late Saul Alinsky and the late César Chávez of the United Farm Workers Union, were also influenced by the privately run Industrial Areas Foundation of Chicago. More recently, services to battered women, patients with AIDS, and the homeless have been pioneered by voluntary sector organizations. Given public apathy toward these groups, for many years the voluntary sector was the only source of service for these groups.

That social change begins in the voluntary sector has a particular lesson for human service professionals: The openness of democratic American culture means that anyone is free to organize for purposes of rectifying past injustices. Well within the reach of social welfare professionals are the building blocks of every voluntary sector initiative: recruiting participants, forming a board of directors, filing for tax-exempt status under Internal Revenue Service Code section 501(c)(3) or (4), soliciting contributions, and applying for grants and contracts. Wendy Kopp's Teach for America (TFA) is a good illustration. In 1988, armed with a vision of a Peace Corps–like program for inner cities and rural areas, the then 23-year-old Kopp began to hustle corporate contributions to match idealistic professionals to disadvantaged communities. In 1996 TFA boasted a $5.5 million budget and was graduating 500 volunteers annually;[50] by 2004 3,500 volunteers were teaching 297,500 students through a TFA budget of $34 million.[51] What Wendy Kopp accomplished illustrates the promise of the voluntary sector in every U.S. community.

Contemporary Nonprofit Human Service Organizations

The voluntary human service sector consists of a large constellation of organizations that are instantly recognizable by most Americans (see Table 6.3 on pages 155–157).

The United Way

Perhaps the best recognized of voluntary sector organizations is the United Way. Local United Ways, as well as the United Way of America, are nonprofit organizations themselves. The purpose of local United Ways is to raise funds that are then disbursed to nonprofit agencies in the community, most of which are United Way members. Local United Ways also contribute a small percentage of funds to the national headquarters, the United Way of America,

Table 6.3

Nonprofit Human Service Organizations, 2004

Name	Budget	Affiliates	Services	Issues
Alliance for Children and Families	$5 million (over $2 billion for all member organizations)	320 member organizations	Residential care, adoption, foster care, child care, job counseling, family and individual and family counseling, substance abuse counseling, and elder care—serving more than 8 million people	Drug and alcohol abuse, family violence, teenage pregnancy, juvenile delinquency, family preservation, and homelessness. Current key issues included obtaining funding, public policy, and at the headquarters, providing training and services to the member organizations
American Foundation for the Blind	$19.8 million	NYC central office and 5 field offices	Information and referral, education, research, and policy research	Encourage independent living; promote technological innovation for the vision impaired. Employment and Braille literacy are two key issues
American Red Cross	$3.2 billion	Nearly 900 chapters, 35 Blood Services regions, 9 National Testing Laboratories	Provide relief to victims of disasters and help people prevent, prepare for, and respond to emergencies	Maintain quality of blood supply; tsunami relief efforts
Arthritis Foundation	$118 million	48 chapters	Information, education, research, and support	Research, public policy, education
Association of Retarded Citizens	$3.2 million (national office)*	40 state chapters, and 1000 local chapters	Research, education, and prevention of mental retardation	Promoting and improving supports and services for people with mental retardation and their families
Boy Scouts	$499 million*	More than 300 local councils	Character building programs emphasizing leadership, citizenship, personal development, and physical fitness	Expand values based experiences
Camp Fire Boys and Girls	$4.2 million (national office)	120 local councils	Youth leadership, self-reliance, after school groups, camping, environmental education, and child care for more than 750,000 youth	Reduce sex-role, racial and cultural stereotypes
Catholic Charities	$2.3 million (national office)*	1,417 affiliates	Social services to people in need	Disaster response; policy division is focused on building and preserving affordable housing and reducing homelessness

(continued)

Table 6.3

(continued)

Name	Budget	Affiliates	Services	Issues
Child Welfare League of America	$21 million (national office)	6 regional groups; 1,100 member agencies	Program and policy advocacy on a full range of child-related problems	Serving troubled families, substance abuse, child welfare policy, dependency courts
Girl Scouts	$67.9 million	315 local councils	Values-based activities to enhance development of girls	Prepare girls for leadership roles
Goodwill Industries	$13.6 million (national office)	207 member organizations	Rehabilitation, training, placement and employment services for those with disabilities and other barriers to employment	Reduce barriers to employment for people with disabilities and other disadvantages (e.g., welfare dependency)
National Council on Alcoholism and Drug Dependence	$1.3 million (national office)*	100 councils	Information, education, research, and policy related to substance abuse issues	Eliminate the stigma associated with alcoholism and other drug additions
National Easter Seal Society	$472 million*	More than 450 service sites	Medical rehabilitation, job training and employment, child care, camping, and adult day services	Reducing employment barriers and facilitating greater independence for people with disabilities
National Mental Health Association	$10.9 million	More than 340 affiliates	Advocacy, education, research, and service to improve mental health	Reducing stigma and prejudice associated with mental illness; improving mental health care treatment; ensuring adequate funding for mental health services
National Urban League	$43.7 million	Over 100 affiliates	Programs in education, job training and placement, housing, business development, crime prevention	Enable African Americans to secure economic self-reliance, parity, power, and civil rights
Planned Parenthood Federation of America	$775 million	123 affiliates, 5 national offices	Sexual and reproductive health care, education, and information	Ensure access to reproductive and sexual health care; preserve reproductive freedom
Salvation Army	$1.8 billion*	More than 9000 service units in 109 countries	Full range of Christian programming to those in need	Restore Christian values as a basis for social services
United Jewish Communities	$40 million (national office)*	155 Jewish Federations and 400 independent Jewish communities	Full range of services to the Jewish Community	Improve the quality of Jewish life worldwide

Table 6.3

(continued)

Name	Budget	Affiliates	Services	Issues
United Service Organizations (USO)	$114 million	124 centers around the world (71 in the continental U.S.)	Information and support services to military personnel and their families	Morale, welfare, and recreation services to military personnel
Young Men's Christian Association (YMCA)	$61 million (national office)*	More than 2,500	Health, fitness, and recreation programs; child care and community development programs	Develop values and behavior consistent with Christian principles
Young Women's Christian Association (YWCA)	$81 million (national office)*	300 local associations in the U.S.	Health, youth development and women's leadership (nationwide initiatives). Sports and fitness programs for women and girls; shelter, support, and child care services for women and their families; advocacy for women and families	Racial justice and women's economic advancement

* Figures are for 2000.

which is located in suburban Washington, D.C. Because the United Way is a confederation of organizations, power resides within the local United Ways. The United Way of America provides support services nationwide but has no direct authority over local United Ways.

In 2000/2001 the United Ways in the United States raised $3.91 billion, an amount that, once adjusted for inflation, was comparable to contributions in 1990.[52] United Way contributions have oscillated over time, often failing to keep pace with inflation. Two recent events account for marked drops in contributions. First, the recession of the early 1980s, the worst since the Great Depression, accounted for a significant loss in contributions. Second, revelations of managerial improprieties on the part of United Way CEO William Aramony in the early 1990s precipitated another reduction in donations (adjusted for inflation) to United Ways. Muckraking journalists reported that Aramony had supplemented his $390,000 annual salary by authorizing excessive perks, including a New York penthouse, limousine service, and European trips on the Concorde. Using United Way funds for seed money, Aramony had also authorized the creation of three independent corporations, which later employed his son.[53] The final chapter in the Aramony scandal was not written until 1995, when a jury found Aramony and two associates guilty of multiple counts of conspiracy, fraud, and filing false tax returns. Aramony was found to have misappropriated $1.2 million in United Way funds, was sentenced to seven years in federal prison, and was fined $522,000.[54]

In late 1995, leaders of major foundations met in New York to survey the damage. Noting that the philanthropic community "seems to have lost a large part of its claim on the sympathies of the American public," Lester Salamon, director of the Johns Hopkins Institute for Policy Studies, suggested the establishment of a special commission that would "rethink the role, function and operation of the nonprofit sector for the next century." Citing "a growing mismatch between the actual operation of the voluntary sector and popular conceptions of what this

One of the most well-known nonprofit human service organizations is the United Way.

sector is supposed to be like," Salamon argued that the major philanthropies were vulnerable to "cheap shots and exposés" when a management scam hit the headlines.[55]

Thus, while overall charitable contributions actually increased during the early 1990s, donations to the United Way fell. This blow was felt especially acutely by some of the larger metropolitan United Ways. Between 1991 and 1997, United Way gifts in Los Angeles fell 41.3 percent, San Diego 35.6 percent, Cleveland 29.4 percent, Boston 25.3 percent, Chicago 24.3 percent, Detroit 23.1 percent, and New York 17.5 percent. Meanwhile, contributions to suburban United Ways increased.[56] The consequence was a reduction in funding for services to the poor. In 1970 Giving USA had reported that 13.9 percent of charitable donations went to the poor; by 1998, 9.2 percent were so dedicated.[57]

At the same time, traditional United Way agencies were faced with diminishing revenues as a result of competition from nontraditional organizations that were also seeking charitable contributions. For example, until recently the United Way claimed about 90 percent of all contributions to the Combined Federal Campaign (a campaign directed at federal employees) that were not specifically designated for other purposes. As a result of challenges brought by agencies as diverse as environmental groups and the National Rifle Association, however, nondesignated contributions are now apportioned among a larger number of organizations. Consequently, the United Way receives less than it did in the past from the Combined Federal Campaign.[58]

In response to increased competition for charitable dollars, many United Ways have evolved donor-friendly policies. For example, 76.9 percent of United Ways now offer individuals the option of designating the recipient agency, and 37.7 percent of United Ways allow the designation of a recipient agency even if it is not a United Way member.[59] But an unintended consequence of "donor choice" has been the diversion of United Way contributions from urban agencies serving the chronically ill to suburban agencies providing service to a less-disadvantaged clientele, as noted above. In 1996, for example, more than 70 percent

Spotlight 6.1

Nonprofit Human Service Organizations

Well-known nonprofit human service organizations include United Way, the American Red Cross, the Child Welfare League of America, Goodwill Industries, United Jewish Communities, and Catholic Charities. To learn more about each of these organizations, visit their websites using the links below:

The United Way: **http://national.unitedway.org**

The American Red Cross: **www.redcross.org**

The Child Welfare League of America: **www.cwla.org**

Goodwill Industries: **www.goodwill.org**

United Jewish Communities: **www.ujc.org**

Catholic Charities: **www.catholiccharitiesusa.org**

of Washington, D.C., United Way contributions were designated to suburban agencies. This, of course, left urban United Way member agencies with fewer resources. Subsequently the Salvation Army withdrew from the United Way on the basis that its services were not adequately valued by contributors.[60]

Revenues of the United Way are derived from multiple sources. As is generally true of charitable contributions, about half of the funds contributed to the United Way are from employees and small businesses. Corporations account for somewhat less than a fourth of United Way revenues. Financial support that the United Way provides to local agencies is also varied. Health, family services, and youth services account for the largest categories of expenditures. Smaller percentages go to agencies providing food, clothing, and housing; day care; public safety; community development; income and jobs support; education; and other kinds of assistance. Of course, the amounts actually allocated in communities vary considerably according to the different priorities of each local United Way.

Elite Philanthropy

The United Ways that dot the nation's landscape, which pursue relatively modest goals, can be classified as "bourgeois" philanthropy. "Elite" philanthropy, on the other hand, has much grander expectations. During the late 1990s, Ted Turner announced an unprecedented $1 billion contribution to the United Nations; this gift was matched by Bill Gates, whose foundation pledged $1 billion for various disease prevention initiatives in the Third World, notably work on HIV/AIDS in sub-Saharan Africa.[61] By 2004 the Gates Foundation was investing $600 million annually on diseases that ravaged developing nations, significantly outspending other charities.[62] These contributions were all the more poignant given the United States government's failure to pay the dues it owed to the United Nations.

As government funding for social services has stagnated, private foundations have supported local initiatives. Between 1975 and 1995, foundation grants increased from $1.94 billion to $12.26 billion.[63] Yet, foundations have not demonstrated consistent generosity; while foundation grants increased 7.7 percent in 2000–2001, they fell to minus 2.7 percent the following year—a drop for which corporations compensated by an 8.8 percent increase in giving.[64]

The major philanthropic foundations are identified by the names of the titans of American capitalism. (See Table 6.4.) Despite the substantial philanthropic activity of foundations—gifts of $27 billion in 2002—critics questioned their generosity. Accusations of impropriety, fraudulent activity, and inefficiency plagued the foundation world. Subsequently, the Charitable Giving Act of 2003 was introduced which would require foundations to spend 5 percent of their endowments annually on charity. Under current law foundations are allowed to include administrative expenses, such as rent, travel, and salaries, in that 5 percent requirement, so disallowing administrative expenses were projected to increase gifts to nonprofits by $4.3 billion.[65] In response, 18 major foundations secured the services of former congressman Bill Paxon who worked for a major lobbying firm.[66] The strategy succeeded; subsequently, the bill died in the House Ways and Means Committee.

In addition to criticisms of fund misuse, many people question the motives of large philanthropies and the individuals who support these organizations. "Elite American philanthropy serves the interests of the rich to a greater extent than it does the interests of the poor, disadvantaged, or disabled," argues Teresa Odendahl; it is "a system of 'generosity' by which the wealthy exercise social control and help

Table 6.4

Largest U.S. Foundations

Foundation	Assets (billions)
Bill & Melinda Gates Foundation	$32.8
Lilly Endowment	12.8
Ford Foundation	10.8
Robert Wood Johnson Foundation	9.0
J. Paul Getty Trust	8.8
David and Lucille Packard Foundation	6.2
William and Flora Hewlett Foundation	6.1
W.K. Kellogg Foundation	5.5
Starr Foundation	4.8
Pew Charitable Trusts	4.4

Source: Adapted from Stephanie Strom, "Gates Aims Billions to Attack Illnesses of World's Neediest," *New York Times* (July 13, 2002), p. 1.

themselves more than they do others."[67] In 1987, for example, Odendahl calculates that contributions totaling $47 billion, about one-half of all gifts itemized on income tax returns, were made by the wealthy.[68] For what purposes do the rich demonstrate such beneficence? They give to institutions that "sustain their culture, their education, their policy formulation, their status-in short, their interests."[69] In other words, wealthy Americans usually use the tax code to maintain institutions of elite culture, such as private schools, museums, symphony orchestras, and opera companies. These institutions often announce generosity of sufficient magnitude to the public by naming an important structure or endowment after the benefactor, a tradition that is maintained by cultural elites in major U.S. cities. The use of funds that have been withdrawn from public use by the tax code in order to reproduce the social institutions of the rich is unacceptable to Odendahl, who proposes reforms that would require philanthropy to be put to public benefit in different ways.

Impropriety within Nonprofits

The United Way scandal and other questionable practices refocused attention on the informal norms of propriety existing within the philanthropic community. In the aftermath of the Aramony scandal, *The Chronicle of Philanthropy* surveyed 117 of the nation's largest nonprofits and reported that one-fourth paid chief executives annual salaries of more than $200,000. As examples, Ben Love, chief executive of the Boy Scouts, was being paid $223,375; Robert Ross of the Muscular Dystrophy Association, $284,808; and Dudley Hafner, executive vice president of the American Heart Association, $246,000.[70] Yet even these salaries often paled in comparison to the salaries commanded by the executives of major foundations, as suggested by the examples in Table 6.5. Why are nonprofit executives paid so well? Presumably because, in order to secure charitable contributions, they are expected to associate with the cultural elites who populate the corporate world of the United States. To do so requires a substantial enough salary to cover the entertainment, club memberships, and other incidental costs associated with such socialization. The upscale lifestyle of executives of prominent nonprofits seems to validate this supposition. While there are no limits on salaries paid to voluntary sector executives, compensation must be comparable to private organizations of comparable scale; moreover, there are laws regulating fraudulent financial practices. When some foundations were found to have paid more for executive compensation than charitable giving, excessive salaries and exotic compensation packages attracted the scrutiny of the Internal Revenue Service in 2004 which announced a formal investigation of the 2,000 largest nonprofits.[71]

One incident that prompted the IRS inquiry was another scandal within the United Way. Oral Suer, head of the United Way of the National Capital Area (Washington, D.C.), was found to have misappropriated $1.5 million through various financial arrangements. In the process Suer had made himself a "paragon of personal virtue" by pledging $9,000 annually to the United Way, then paid off his pledge through unauthorized payments from the United Way.[72] Suer was subsequently sentenced to a 27 months in prison; but the credibility of the United Way serving the nation's capital had been severely damaged. In 2001, the United Way of the National Capital Area had raised $90 million; after the Suer scandal, contributions fell to $19 million, causing the organization to lay off half of its staff, close several satellite offices, and forfeit its lucrative fundraising contract with federal employees.[73] In a sector where credibility is a virtue, such damage requires years to repair.

Table 6.5

Compensation for Executives of Selected Foundations

Foundation	Executive	1997 Salary
Lilly Endowment	Thomas Lofton	$450,000
Ford Foundation	Susan Berresford	440,500
Packard Foundation	Colburn Wilbur	272,549
Kellogg Foundation	William Richardson	400,000
RW Johnson Foundation	Steven Schroeder	367,000
Pew Charitable Trusts	Rebecca Rimel	339,734
Rob't Woodruff Foundation	Charles McTier	270,000

Source: Adapted from Judith Havemann, "Top Foundations Gave Chiefs a Bountiful Raise," *Washington Post* (July 5, 1998), p. A1.

The Future of the Voluntary Sector

Despite the excesses of elite philanthropy, most Americans voiced preference for voluntary efforts to address social problems. Of respondents to a 2001 poll of the public's perception of problem solving, 56 percent ranked sectarian agencies as important for "solving social problems in their communities," compared to 53 percent for local nonprofits, 39 percent for the United Way, 33 percent for state government, and 28 percent for the federal government.[74] Several forces have transformed the nonprofit sector, including the intrusion of commercial firms, the rise of faith-based social services, and the emergence of social entrepreneurship. While each of these remains important issues within the nonprofit sector, they were eclipsed by the outpouring of charity after the terrorist attacks of September 11, 2001.

Commercialization

The **commercialization** issue is particularly important for financially strapped nonprofit agencies. Faced with static, if not declining, revenues, some voluntary sector agencies have experimented with commercial activities in order to supplement income derived from traditional sources (contributions, grants, and fees). That nonprofit organizations should be allowed to engage in commercial endeavors without restriction is "unfair competition," according to business operators, who note that nonprofits do not ordinarily pay taxes on their income. Exempt from taxation, nonprofits could lower their prices, increasing pressure on tax-paying businesses operating in the same market.

Limits on the freedom of nonprofit organizations to engage in commercial activities were highlighted in a celebrated case involving New York University Law School and the Mueller Macaroni Company. Seeking a way to enhance revenues to the law school and thereby lighten the burden of contributing to their alma mater, enterprising alumni acquired Mueller and reorganized it as a nonprofit organization registered in Delaware. Income from the macaroni company was thus redefined as nontaxable income and diverted to the law school as a charitable contribution. This clever arrangement, however, did not go unnoticed by Mueller's competitors, who saw the possibility that Mueller might be able to use its newly acquired tax-exempt status to cut prices and drive other macaroni companies from the market. Further, they argued, what was to prevent any well-endowed nonprofit institution from acquiring profitable businesses as a way of supplementing its income while dodging any tax obligation? The situation soon proved so embarrassing to the law school that it sent no representatives to the congressional hearings convened to deliberate on the ethics of the arrangement. Eventually the tax code was altered, making income from commercial activities that are not related to the service function of a nonprofit organization taxable.[75] Since 1950, revenue obtained by nonprofit organizations from commercial activity has been taxable under the unrelated business income tax (UBIT).

Conflicts between nonprofit and for-profit organizations were aired during hearings held by the House Ways and Means Committee in 1987.[76] At the hearings representatives of the business community complained that nonprofits were engaging in "unfair competition" with for-profit businesses in two ways. First, they argued, the UBIT is inconsistent in distinguishing between related and unrelated business activities. For example, a nonprofit hospital's pharmacy is considered related to the hospital's mission and is therefore exempt from paying taxes on profit, but a for-profit hospital's pharmacy is part of the business and its profit is therefore taxable. Second, nonprofit organizations benefit from the "halo effect"—that is, the public's perception that their services are superior because they do not operate from the profit motive. Thus, health spas complain that YMCAs benefit from a philanthropic "halo," and the revenues of the Ys are tax exempt. Yet Ys use many commercial business practices, such as marketing and advertising, to promote their services.

Although complaints of unfair competition on the part of nonprofit organizations appear to be academic, the accusations open the possibility of further restrictions on the revenue base of voluntary sector agencies. For example, some Ys have stopped advertising their programs for fear that local authorities may interpret those programs as commercial and thereby attempt to tax income derived from them. Thus, the unfair competition issue presents some very disturbing questions for administrators of nonprofit organizations. Facing intense competition from for-profit hospitals, some nonprofit health care institutions have not only charged indigent patients for care, but hounded them into bankruptcy as well, raising fundamental questions about the virtue of tax exempt status. "We can't ask nonprofits to be more like for-profits in the ways that we like—efficient, responsive, aggressive—without expecting that they will also become more like for-profits in the ways that we don't: rapacious, hardheaded and, yes, sometimes selfish," noted Jacob Hacker.[77]

If a nonprofit family service agency bills a client's insurance company for a "usual, customary, and reasonable" fee, a fee comparable to what is charged by a private practice group that must pay taxes on such income, should this income remain tax exempt? Should tax-exempt income be limited to charitable contributions only? Do program outreach and public education activities constitute marketing and advertising? And if so, should they be limited if a nonprofit organization is to retain its tax exemption? Questions like these strike at the heart of the function of the voluntary sector. How these questions are resolved will be of great concern to nonprofit community service agencies, particularly to organizations faced with dwindling revenues.

Faith-Based Social Services

The idea of government's contracting with voluntary sector agencies is not a novel concept; through purchase-of-service agreements dating to the late 1960s, government has negotiated arrangements for delivery of a range of social services, often with sectarian agencies. This liberal mechanism for decentralization, however, has given conservatives an entrée to pose more fundamental questions about the proper role of government in social welfare. Since the 1980s conservative think tanks have, with increasing urgency, sought an alternative to federal social programs. Central to the conservative critique of conventional welfare has been William Schambra who makes a fundamental differentiation between scientific philanthropy and faith-based charity. A manifestation of Progressivism, scientific philanthropy provided the justification for elite foundations, the advocates of which believed that public problems could be analyzed scientifically and addressed effectively through social programs. By contrast, faith-based charity made no such pretense, satisfied that donations to good works from a wellspring of faith needed no further justification.[78] Compared to charity's simple, direct approach to need, Schambra characterized philanthropy as obscured by "smug, opaque, apolitical jargon—the endless, sterile, process-based chatter about collaborations, partnerings, learnings, leveragings, outcomes, and best practices."[79]

A primary proponent of sectarian nonprofit agencies is Marvin Olasky, a journalist who argues that voluntary religious agencies provided efficient and effective services to the needy before the New Deal and the deployment of the welfare state.[80] Another source of support has come from evangelical Christians, who object to the absence of moral standards that they see as characterizing traditional social service agencies managed by liberal welfare professionals. By the 2000 presidential election, centrist conservatives within the Republican Party found the voluntary sector, and in particular the religious sector, a way to appeal to independent voters. Since its resurgence with the 1980 election of Ronald Reagan, conservatism had been in opposition to liberal social policy; however, it lacked a positive stance with respect to a large segment of the electorate—the middle class, the elderly, and the ill, among others. Invoking the voluntary sector addressed this deficit, an approach that George W. Bush advanced enthusiastically during his 2000 presidential campaign as "compassionate conservatism."

As governor of Texas, Bush had had extensive experience in mobilizing the private sector to address social welfare needs. After passage of the 1996 welfare reform legislation, he had proposed contracting out all of the state's public welfare programming, a deal valued at $500 million annually; but this was vetoed by the Clinton administration. Despite this defeat, in 2000 Bush advanced "faith-based social services" as an alternative to traditional social programs.[81] Ultimately, Bush proposed a five-year, $5 billion federal program for faith-based organizations; however, Democrats objected because of the possibility of discrimination in hiring and the proposal failed. Undaunted, Bush instituted part of the plan through executive order. By 2004 over $1 billion had been awarded through Bush's faith-based initiative. (See Table 6.6.)

Enthusiasm for faith-based initiatives notwithstanding, the approach had yet to demonstrate its superiority through research. Indiana researchers evaluated 2,830 people who enrolled in 27 employment programs and found no difference between sectarian and secular organizations with respect to placement rates and beginning wages; graduates of faith-based organizations tended to work fewer hours and were less likely to receive health insurance.[82]

Regardless, proponents of faith-based social services, including many traditional sectarian agen-

Table 6.6

Federal Grants to Faith-Based Organizations

Agency	$ for Grant Programs (millions)	$ for FBOs (millions)	% for FBOs
HHS	$10,874.3	$567.9	5
HUD	2,197.7	532.1	24
Justice	791.7	51.6	7
Labor	512.4	11.3	2
Education	134.7	6.8	5

Source: Adapted from Alan Cooperman, "Grants to Religious Groups Top $1.1 Billion," *Washington Post* (March 10, 2004), p. A27.

cies with a long history of helping the needy such as the Salvation Army, insisted that government programs were too bureaucratic and impersonal, and that secular nonprofit agencies were populated by welfare professionals who failed to infuse services with adequate moral content to be effective. In office, Bush extended "compassionate conservatism" beyond the parameters of local social services to propose education reform through the No Child Left Behind Act, adding a prescription benefit to Medicare, and increasing assistance to fight AIDS in Africa.

President George W. Bush has advanced faith-based social services as an alternative to traditional social programs.

Social Entrepreneurship

Although many theologically inclined liberals endorsed the idea of faith-based social services, others pursued innovations through capital and technology. A new generation of social entrepreneurs has emerged as experiments with markets reveal untapped opportunities for program innovation, both locally and nationally. For example, the Ben & Jerry's ice cream company and Working Assets Long Distance (WALD) represent an ethic in which business praxis is inextricably suffused with social consciousness.[83] For 1996 WALD contributed $2.5 million to progressive organizations advocating in several areas: social justice, the environment, civil rights, and international justice.[84] Realizing that there was a minimal return on time invested in securing foundation grants, Peter Samuelson, founder of Starlight Starbright, an organization serving critically ill children, approached the marketing department of Colgate-Palmolive and convinced them to incorporate cause-related marketing in their products. "The results were astonishing," Samuelson reported. "Instead of receiving $25,000 from the corporation's foundation, we were suddenly receiving $250,000 from a cause-related marketing campaign."[85]

Concerned about the decline of civic institutions, particularly in urban areas, sociologists proposed "social capital" as a vehicle for revitalization. For Robert Putnam, the term *social capital* referred to "features of social organization, such as networks, norms, and trust, which facilitate coordination and cooperation for mutual benefit. Social capital enhances the benefits of investment in physical and human capital."[86] At the nexus of social capital, community-based nonprofit organizations can facilitate the development of poor neighborhoods providing they exploit new markets and technologies. An illustration of the social capital approach to community development is the work of former congressman Floyd Flake, pastor of the Allen African Methodist Episcopal Cathedral in Jamaica, New York.[87] Flake has used his position as church pastor to construct a

$34 million network of community development ventures. Seeing the future as a social entrepreneur, Flake recognizes the ideological implications of recent changes in social policy: "Those of us who have made a commitment to stay in an urban community have decided that *this* is our paradise," he observed. "We are going to rebuild that paradise—and we understand that it means some paradigm shifts, even politically, because the majority of statehouses today are in the hands of Republican governors and the majority of the assemblies are in the hands of Republicans. So we can either continue in a protest mode or we find ways to have entrée to deal with who is in power now."[88]

Table 6.7

Compensation for Victims of September 11, 2001

Income of Victim	Claims	Average Award
$4 million+	8	$6,379,288
$2 million to $4 million	17	6,253,705
$1 million to $2 million	52	5,671,816
$500,000 to $1 million	89	4,749,654
$200,000 to $499,999	310	3,394,625
$100,000 to $199,999	633	2,302,235
$25,000 to $99,999	1,591	1,520,155
$24,999 or less	163	1,102,135
0	17	788,022

Source: Adapted from Christopher Lee, "Report on Sept. 11 Fund Is Released," *Washington Post* (November 8, 2004), p. A3.

Flake served 11 years in Congress during which he authored the 1993 Community Development Financial Institutions Act which designated a revolving loan fund for economic development in low-income communities. A decade later 527 CDFIs had been established, but the number fell far short of what might have been possible. In his analysis of the fringe economy, Howard Karger has calculated that $125 billion is siphoned from poor communities by check-cashers, pawnshops, rent-to-own stores, and the like each year.[89] The National Community Capital Association reported in 2001 that a developing CDFI held capital of $7 million.[90] In other words, a fringe economy of that scale would have supported a network of over 17,500 CDFIs in 2001 alone. Unfortunately, the failure of welfare advocates to seize the promise of social entrepreneurship combined with unwillingness of the Bush administration to fully fund the CDFI program has left poor communities without financial services that could address their poverty. Exploited by the fringe economy, essential capital continues to hemorrhage from poor communities, a circumstance that is as tragic as it is unnecessary.

September 11, 2001

If the terrorist attacks of September 11 revealed the vulnerability of the nation, they also demonstrated Americans' profound sense of sympathy for the victims of the tragedy. Soon after the twin towers of the World Trade Center fell, contributions to assist victims rose to $2.3 billion. Eventually, the September 11 Victims Compensation Fund dispensed $7 billion to more than 5,000 families.[91] Yet, the upsurge in generosity was not without problems. A fundamental question arose with respect to compensation for victims: should payments be made equally or on the basis of previous earnings? In order to reduce the likelihood of litigation, a flat award was rejected; as a result, compensation varied widely as shown in Table 6.7. A dispute about the use of contributions to aid victims of September 11 led to the resignation of the director of the American Red Cross. Victims of the Oklahoma City bombing questioned why they were not able to get assistance for their losses, also attributable to terrorism.[92] Ultimately, such problems dampened Americans' support of the voluntary sector. After September 11, a poll of Americans' attitudes toward charity revealed that the number of respondents who had no confidence toward organized charities had increased from 8 percent to 16 percent, compared to a drop in those who had a lot of confidence from 25 percent to 19 percent,[93] a response that seemed to reflect the ambivalence toward the voluntary sector registered during the 1990s.

Conclusion

As commercialization, faith-based social services, social entrepreneurship, and the response to September 11, 2001 indicate, the nonprofit sector has struggled to rebound from the lethargy that characterized it during the latter decades of the twentieth century. How the voluntary sector preserves its mission of caring for the disenfranchised without succumbing to the bottom-line ethos of the corporate sector, responds to the range of diverse populations without proselytizing to unbelievers, and adapts the latest innovations in technology while putting forth a human face are challenges that remain.

Discussion Questions

1. What are the most prominent nonprofit human service agencies in your community? Are they members of the United Way? What do agencies perceive to be the advantages of United Way membership? Do they perceive disadvantages to United Way membership?
2. Has the United Way in your community failed to achieve its goals in contributions in recent years? If so, what are the causes? The proposed solutions?
3. What are the newer nonprofit agencies in your community? What populations do they serve? Are these agencies members of the United Way? If not, how do they attract the necessary resources? What is their perception of the United Way?
4. If there are unmet needs in your community, how would you create a nonprofit agency to meet them? Whom would you recruit for your board of directors? Where would you solicit resources, both cash and in-kind? Whom would you recruit for staff? What would you name your agency? Would your agency focus on providing services or on advancing social change?
5. In response to diminishing resources, many nonprofit social agencies have resorted to entrepreneurial strategies to raise money. What innovative projects have agencies deployed in your community? What entrepreneurial strategies can you think of that might be successful for nonprofit agencies in your community?
6. What are the most prominent foundations in your community? What has been the source of revenues for their activities? How would you rank them with respect to the volume of their gifts versus assets? Which foundations have been most active with respect to social welfare? Have their gifts increased or decreased in recent years?

Notes

1. Peter Berger and Richard Neuhaus, *To Empower People: The Role of Mediating Structures in Public Policy* (Washington, DC: American Enterprise Institute, 1977).
2. Kevin Eckstrom, "Helping the Poor Lift Themselves Up," *Washington Post* (February 22, 2003), p. B9.
3. David Brown, "Service Clubs Living Up to Mission," *Washington Post* (December 7, 2003), p. A1.
4. Sarah Park, "Free Medical Care Draws Thousands," *Washington Post* (July 25, 2004), p. C5.
5. David Stoesz, "A Structural Interest Theory of Social Welfare," *Social Development Issues* 10 (Winter 1985), pp. 73–85.
6. National Association of Social Workers, *Social Casework: Generic and Specific* (Silver Spring, MD: NASW, 1974).
7. *The 2001 United Way of America Annual Report* (Alexandria, VA: United Way of America, 2001).
8. Robert Alford, *Health Care Politics* (Chicago: University of Chicago Press, 1975), p. 204.
9. Roy Lubove, *The Professional Altruist* (New York: Atheneum, 1969), p. 197.
10. Walter Trattner, *From Poor Law to Welfare State* (New York: Macmillan, 1974), p. 237; and "The First Days of Social Security," *Public Welfare* 43 (Fall 1985), pp. 112–119.
11. Alford, *Health Care Politics*, p. 2.
12. Social Security Bulletin, *Annual Statistical Supplement* (Washington, DC: Social Security Administration, 1999), p. 140.
13. Ibid., p. 199.
14. Trattner, *From Poor Law to Welfare State*, p. 250.
15. Robert Barker, "Private Practice Primer for Social Work," *NASW News* (October 1983), p. 13.
16. A. Goleman, "Social Workers Vault into a Leading Role in Psychotherapy," *New York Times* (April 3, 1985), p. C-1.
17. Per conversation with NASW staff, November 16, 1992.

18. Maryann Mahaffey, "Fulfilling the Promise," *Proceedings* (Fifth Annual Association of Baccalaureate Program Directors Conference, Kansas City, 1987).
19. Donald Light, "Corporate Medicine for Profit," *Scientific American* 255 (December 1986), pp. 81–89.
20. "Generosity Index, 2004." Retrieved November 18, 2004, from www.catalogueforphilanthropy.org/ofp/olb.generosity
21. Ralph Kramer, "The Future of Voluntary Organizations in Social Welfare," in *Philanthropy, Voluntary Action, and the Public Good* (Washington, DC: Independent Sector/United Way, 1986).
22. Peter Drucker, *The New Realities* (New York: HarperCollins, 1989).
23. Peter Drucker, "It Profits Us to Strengthen Nonprofits," *Wall Street Journal* (December 19, 1991), p. 18.
24. Neil Gilbert, *Capitalism and the Welfare State* (New Haven: Yale University Press, 1983), pp. 6–7; Neil Gilbert and Harry Specht, *Dimensions of Social Welfare Policy,* 2nd ed. (Englewood Cliffs, NJ: Prentice-Hall, 1989), pp. 46–47.
25. Committee on Ways and Means, U.S. House of Representatives, Overview of Entitlement Programs, *1992 Green Book* (Washington, DC: U.S. Government Printing Office, 1992), p. 830.
26. Committee on Ways and Means. U.S. House of Representatives, Overview of Entitlement Programs, *2000 Green Book* (Washington, DC: U.S. Government Printing Office, 2000), p. 634.
27. Alan Abramson and Lester Salamon, *The Nonprofit Sector and the New Federal Budget* (Washington, DC: Urban Institute, 1986), p. xi. See also Waldemar Nielsen, *The Third Sector: Keystone of a Caring Society* (Washington, DC: Independent Sector, 1980).
28. Marvin Olasky, "Beyond the Stingy Welfare State," *Policy Review* (Fall 1990), p. 14.
29. Elizabeth Boris, "Nonprofit Organizations in a Democracy," in Elizabeth Boris and Eugene Steuerle (eds.), *Nonprofits and Government* (Washington, DC: Urban Institute, 1999), p. 10.
30. Murray Weitzman, et al., *The New Nonprofit Almanac* (New York: Jossey Bass, 2002), p. 8.
31. AAFRC, *Giving USA, 2003* (Indianapolis: University of Indiana, 2003), p. 46.
32. Virginia Hodgkinson and Murray Weitzman, *Nonprofit Almanac* (Washington, DC: Independent Sector, 1996), p. 40.
33. Robert Putnam, *Bowling Alone* (New York: Simon & Schuster, 2000), p. 122. Putnam's figures with respect to the percent of national income dedicated to charity contradict those of the American Association of Fund Raising Counsel.
34. AAFRC, *Giving USA, 2003* (Indianapolis: University of Indiana, 2003), p. 8.
35. Ibid., p. 8.
36. Ibid., p. 15.
37. "Total Giving Reaches $190.16 Billion" (New York: American Association of Fund Raising Counsels, 2000).
38. Greg Winter, "Charitable Giving Falls for First Time in Years," *New York Times* (October 27, 2003), p. A11.
39. AAFRC, *Giving USA, 2003* (Indianapolis: University of Indiana, 2003), p. 55.
40. Jacqueline Salmon, "Nonprofits Show Losses in the Public's Trust," *Washington Post* (November 9, 2002), p. A2.
41. Weitzman et al., *The New Nonprofit Almanac,* pp. 33, 73.
42. Putnam, *Bowling Alone,* p. 128.
43. Brian O'Connell, *Origins, Dimensions and Impact of America's Voluntary Spirit* (Washington, DC: Independent Sector, 1984), p. 2.
44. Steven Smith and Michael Lipsky, *Nonprofits for Hire* (Cambridge, MA: Harvard University Press, 1993), p. 184.
45. Jonathan Weisman, "Congress Votes to Extend Tax Cuts," *Washington Post* (September 24, 2004), p. A7.
46. Paul Schervish, "The Cultural Horizons of Charitable Giving in an Age of Affluence" (Cambridge, MA: Boston College Social Welfare Research Institute, September 23, 2003), p. 1.
47. Paul Schervish, "The Sense and Sensibility of Philanthropy as a Moral Citizenship of Care" (Cambridge, MA: Boston College and Indiana University Center on Philanthropy, January 2004).
48. Gardner quoted in O'Connell, *Origins, Dimensions and Impact of America's Voluntary Spirit,* p. 6.
49. John W. Gardner, *Keynote Address* (Washington, DC: Independent Sector; 1978), p. 13.
50. Irene Lacher, "Teaching America a Lesson," *Los Angeles Times* (November 11, 1990), E1; personal communication, Teach for America, October 7, 1996.
51. Teach for America, Retrieved October 3, 2004, from http://teachforamerica.org
52. "National Amounts Raised 30-Year History" (Alexandria, VA: United Way of America, n.d.).
53. David Lauter, "United Way's Chief Quits in Funds Dispute," *Los Angeles Times* (February 28, 1992), p. A1.
54. "Key Dates in the Adjudication of Former Management" (Fairfax, VA: United Way of America, 1996).
55. Karen Arenson, "Woeful '95 Leads U.S. Charities to Introspection," *New York Times* (December 10, 1995), p. 38.
56. David Johnston, "United Way, Faced with Fewer Donors, Is Giving Away Less," *New York Times* (November 9, 1997), p. 28.
57. Peter Kilborn, "Charity for Poor Lags Behind Need," *New York Times* (December 12, 1999), p. 34.
58. Judith Havemann, "Federal Charity Drive Opened to More Groups," *Washington Post* (January 2, 1988), p. A1.
59. *Designations and Donor Choice in United Way Campaigns* (Fairfax, VA: United Way of America, 1996), Table 1.

60. Tracy Thompson, "United Way Contributors Exercise Their Options," *Washington Post* (September 21, 1996), p. A-1.
61. Jean Strouse, "How to Give Away $21.8 Billion," *New York Times Magazine* (April 16, 2000).
62. Sebastian Mallaby, "Opening the Gates," *Washington Post* (April 5, 2004), p. A17.
63. Weitzman, *New Nonprofit Almanac,* p. 82.
64. AAFRC, *Giving USA,* 2003 (Indianapolis: University of Indiana, 2003), p. 13.
65. Jacqueline Salmon, "Foundations Anxious over Bill on Giving," *Washington Post* (July 8, 2003), p. A3.
66. Stephanie Strom, "Foundations Hire Ex-Lawmaker to Lobby against a Bill," *New York Times* (May 29, 2003), p. A17.
67. Teresa Odendahl, *Charity Begins at Home* (New York: Basic Books, 1990), pp. 3, 245.
68. Ibid., p. 49.
69. Ibid., p. 232.
70. Lynn Simross, "When Sharing the Wealth, Let the Donor Beware," *Los Angeles Times* (April 5, 1992), p. A6.
71. Jacqueline Salmon, "IRS to Review Pay for Executives of 2,000 Nonprofits," *Washington Post* (August 11, 2004), p. A2.
72. Jacqueline Salmon and Peter Whoriskey, "Audit Excoriates United Way Leadership," *Washington Post* (August 12, 2003), p. A1.
73. Jerry Markon, "Ex-Chief of Local United Way Sentenced," *Washington Post* (May 15, 2004), p. A1.
74. Richard Morin, "Nonprofit, Faith-Based Groups Near Top of Poll on Solving Social Woes," *Washington Post* (February 1, 2001), p. A19.
75. W. Harrison Wellford and Janne Gallagher, *Charity and the Competition Challenge* (Washington, DC: National Assembly of National Voluntary Health and Social Welfare Organizations, 1987), pp. 13–15.
76. Anne Swardson, "Hill Taking New Look at Nonprofits," *Washington Post* (June 21), 1987), p. F-9.
77. Jonathan Cohn, "Uncharitable?" *New York Times Magazine* (December 19, 2004), p. 55.
78. William Schambra, "What Philanthropists Expect from Nonprofits," comments during a panel discussion at Gallaudet University, Washington, D.C., December 2, 2004.
79. William Schambra, "The New Politics of Philanthropy," *American Outlook Today* (December 4, 2003), p. 22.
80. Marvin Olasky, *The Tragedy of American Compassion* (Washington, DC: Regenery Gateway, 1992); *Renewing American Compassion* (New York: Free Press, 1996).
81. Hanna Rosin, "Putting Faith in a Social Service Role," *Washington Post* (May 5, 2000), p. A1.
82. Alan Cooperman, "Faith-Based Charities May Not Be Better, Study Indicates," *Washington Post* (May 25, 2003), p. A7.
83. Bill Shore, *The Cathedral Within* (New York: Random House, 1999).
84. "Simple Acts, Real Progress," (San Francisco, Working Assets Long Distance, 1997).
85. Peter Samuelson, "The Robin Hood Effect," *Privilege* (November 2004), p. 1.
86. Robert Putnam, "The Prosperous Community," *The American Prospect* no. 13 (Spring 1993), p. 1.
87. Terry Neal, "Ex-Lawmaker Refuses to Be Boxed In," *Washington Post* (January 10, 1998), p. A8.
88. R. Baker, "The Ecumenist," *The American Prospect* (January 17, 2000), p. 28.
89. Howard Karger, *Shortchanged: Life and Debt in the Fringe Economy* (San Francisco: Berrett-Koehler, 2006).
90. "CDFIs Side-by-Side," (Philadelphia: National Community Capital Association, 2001), p. 48.
91. David Chen, "After Weighing Value of Lives, 9/11 Fund Completes Task," *New York Times* (July 16, 2004), p. A1.
92. Lisa Belkin, "The Grief Payout," *New York Times Magazine* (December 8, 2002).
93. Jacqueline Salmon, "Nonprofits Show Losses in the Public's Trust," *Washington Post* (November 9, 2002), p. A2.

CHAPTER 7

Privatization and Human Service Corporations

This chapter reviews the privatization of social welfare. Historically, much social welfare has been provided by the private not-for-profit sector. Since the 1980s, however, conservatives have called for downsizing government, in the process shifting service responsibility to the private sector.

In addition, the role of the business community in U.S. social welfare is described. Historically, some business leaders have made important contributions to the health and welfare of their employees by envisaging utopian work environments and pioneering the provision of benefits to employees. Business leaders were also instrumental in fashioning early governmental welfare policies. More recently, emphasis on the "social responsibility" of corporations has encouraged business leaders to assess the broader implications of corporate activities. Corporations also shape social welfare policy by influencing the political process and subsidizing policy institutes. Proprietary firms have become well established in several **human services** markets: nursing care, hospital management, managed medical care, child care, life/continuing care, and corrections. Finally, the chapter considers collective bargaining as a response to privatization. Health and human service professionals have been reluctant to join unions, primarily because they fear doing so would taint their professional status. Yet continuing privatization means that unions may be the only aggregate defense for professionals who have become employees of profit-making health and human service corporations.

As a function of public dissatisfaction with governmental social programs, increasing reliance on the private sector to finance and deliver social services has emerged as an important theme in U.S. social welfare. **Privatization,** as this idea has been termed, addresses the problem of the proper relationship between the public and private spheres of the national culture. In this case, the concept of privatization has come to involve "the idea that private is invariably more efficient than public, that government ought to stay out of as many realms as possible, and that government should contract out tasks to private firms or give people vouchers rather than provide them services directly."[1] That government should not hold a monopoly on social welfare is not a novel idea. Even liberal policy analysts have entertained ways in which the private sector could complement governmental welfare initiatives.[2] Liberal proponents of social programs are often willing to concede a viable role to the private sector—even an innovative role—but insist that government must be the primary instrument to advance social justice. Conservatives, of course, see the proper balance as one in which the private sector is the primary source of protection against social and economic calamity, and believe that government activity should be held in reserve. According to conservative doctrine, government can deploy the "safety net" of social programs, but these should provide benefits only as a last resort.

A clear articulation of the conservative vision of reinforcing the role of the private sector in social affairs appeared in the 1988 report of the President's Commission on Privatization. "In the United States . . . the growth of government has been based on the political and economic design that emerged from the Progressive movement around the turn of this century," noted the report. "The American

Spotlight 7.1

Techniques for the Privatization of Service Delivery

The President's Commission on Privatization identifies three techniques for the privatization of service delivery:

1. Selling government assets
2. Contracting with private firms to provide goods and services previously offered by the government
3. Using vouchers, whereby the government would distribute coupons authorizing private providers to receive reimbursement from the government for the goods and services they have provided

privatization movement has represented in significant part a reaction against the themes and results of Progressive thought."[3] Specifically, the report targeted government social programs and the professional administrators who manage them as the undesirable consequences of the progressive state of mind—consequences that could be corrected by privatization. The implications of this analysis are broad: Not only should benefits be removed from government and provided by the private sector, but the administration of social programs should also be removed from the public sector and placed under private auspices. Accordingly, the President's Commission on Privatization identified three "techniques for the privatization of service delivery": (1) selling government assets; (2) contracting with private firms to provide goods and services previously offered by government; and (3) using vouchers, whereby the government would distribute coupons authorizing private providers to receive reimbursement from the government for the goods and services they had provided.[4] Although all these methods had been used to restructure welfare programs at one time or another, the report introduced an unprecedented idea into the debate by characterizing social welfare as a "zero-sum game" in which an advantage to one party is always at the expense of another.

In *Reinventing Government,* David Osborne proposed a more integrated and dynamic relationship between the public and private sectors: government should establish the objectives of public policy, assigning the execution to the private sector.[5] Osborne tapped into a theme that had been integral to American social programs, reliance on the private sector to deliver the goods. Nowhere had this been more evident than in health care. When the social engineers of the War on Poverty crafted Medicare and Medicaid, they elected to reimburse private providers rather than deploy a government-owned health care system, such as the Veterans Administration. The result, as we shall see momentarily, was the emergence of a for-profit industry in health care that was uniquely American. Indeed, when the Clinton administration presented its Health Security Act, it not only conceded the existence of commercial health providers but structured the plan to amplify their position in the market.

Thus, views of privatization vary. On the one hand privatization can be viewed as load-shedding, on the other as a contractual relationship between the public and private sectors. In either event, there is no question that this relationship is being reassessed. "Governments in the United States spend roughly half a trillion dollars per year paying public workers to deliver goods and services directly," observed John Donahue. "If only one-quarter of this total turned out to be suitable for privatization, at an average savings of, say, 25 percent—and neither figure is recklessly optimistic—the public would save over $30 billion."[6] Such savings could be used to lower taxes or to extend existing programs. As state and local jurisdictions struggle to justify increasing service demand with static resources, privatization is an option that many local officials pursue.

Privatization Issues

Many health and human service professionals have trepidations about privatization. Liberal social activists have objected to privatization, for example, often citing research that identifies risks in relying on the private sector for certain activities. The irony in the critical stance toward privatization assumed by many health and human service professionals is that many of them opt for private practice as a method of service delivery, an arrangement through which government subsidizes entrepreneurs. Thus, private practice is condoned, but privatization of governmental activities is met with skepticism. This issue raises a profound concern for the social work profession: To the extent that social workers engage in private practice, there are fewer human service professionals in the public sector to work with people presenting more serious disorders. As a result, what limited influence social work has is invested in promoting its self-interest at the expense of the poor—a point underscored by the late Harry Specht and Mark Courtney in *Unfaithful Angels:*

> . . . there has been an increasing tendency of the [social work] profession to use its political power to support licensing of clinical social workers and third-party payments for social workers who are so licensed, to the relative neglect of efforts to improve the lot of social workers employed in the public social services and their clients.[7]

For many human service professionals, then, private practice represents a retreat from a service ethic that transcends self-interest: the public's welfare.

The tension between private gain and public interest surfaced in provisions of the 1996 welfare reform act which allowed states to contract with for-profit firms to not only provide social services but also determine eligibility and benefits. While privatization has evident in child support enforcement and in some sectors of child welfare, it had not been employed in public assistance previously. Not surprisingly, some corporations stood to make considerable profits from the privatization of public assistance. At the time Nina Bernstein observed, "The new [1996] welfare bill is still a matter of confusion in statehouses and city streets. But to some companies it looks like the business opportunity of a lifetime."[8]

Proponents argue that allowing private companies to run public welfare will prove to be the most cost-effective and humane way for states to implement welfare reform. For these supporters, privatization promises to deliver technological efficiency by cutting administrative costs and detecting fraud. Meanwhile, privatized operations will help recipients by offering one-stop shopping for benefits and enrollment. Supporters believe that a profit-making company has the flexibility to reward employees for positive results and to change the welfare system from one that dispenses checks to one that quickly moves people into jobs. Moreover, states that are able to reduce administrative costs will have more money available for child care, transportation, and job training programs. For state welfare administrators faced with capped block grants and substantial penalties if they fail to move recipients into jobs, a fixed-price private contract has strong appeal.

Driven by a vision of cutting administrative expenses by 20 to 40 percent (mostly by closing offices and eliminating state jobs),[9] Texas was the first state to experiment with letting a private company create and run a system to screen applicants for welfare benefits. In Texas corporations bid to manage the more than $8 billion public welfare system made up of AFDC, food stamps, Medicaid, and more than 25 other programs. The corporate players in this privatization scenario had substantial assets and included such companies as IBM, Lockheed Information Management Services (a nonmilitary division of the $30 billion Lockheed Martin), Electronic Data Systems (a $12.4 billion company formerly owned by Ross Perot), Andersen Consulting (a $4.2 billion company), and Unisys.[10] Reflecting their interest in the vast public welfare market, Lockheed hired Gerald Miller, the former director of the Michigan Family Independence Agency and president of the influential American Public Welfare Association. According to Miller, "I see this as the future of welfare reform. The private sector will ultimately run these programs," he said. Then reciting Clinton's famous phrase: "The era of big government is over."[11] In addition to Miller, Lockheed hired welfare officials from both the states and the federal government to lead its efforts to manage privatized welfare programs.

Opponents to welfare privatization voice several criticisms. First, if a corporation's profits are linked to reducing the welfare rolls, the incentive to deny aid will be significant. According to Henry Freedman of the Center for Social Welfare Policy and Law, "No company can be expected to protect the interests of the needy at the expense of its bottom line, least of all a publicly traded corporation with a fiduciary duty to maximize shareholder profits."[12] Clearly, corporations will have strong incentives to use the letter of the law to ration services to improve their profits and performance.[13] Much of this fiscal incentive will be based on the fixed-price nature of welfare contracts, which will include penalties for a failure to perform. Second, corporations are apt to reduce personnel costs. They may cut staff and replace long-term welfare workers and managers with inexperienced lower-wage workers. As a way to control salaries, corporations may try to dislodge public sector unions where they exist, and to prohibit them where they do not. One Texas union estimated that "at least half of the 13,000 state employees who now determine welfare eligibility will be cut out of the new system."[14] Third, privatization could encourage corporations to use technology to save money, such as replacing welfare offices and state workers in rural areas with automated kiosks similar to automated banking. This would have enormous implications for people who are not technologically sophisticated or who would benefit from face-to-face services. Fourth, government would find itself in a quandary if commercial providers bailed out of contracts. At worst, corporations could declare bankruptcy effectively voiding its contractual obligations, or commercial providers could reduce the availability of services as a way to leverage more resources. Finally, corporations with a major presence in a given market are in a strong position to shape social policy, defining such factors as eligibility for program benefits and allocations. Oligopolies in several markets have already emerged, such as corrections, raising the prospect of a prison-industrial complex that shapes criminal justice policy toward its own benefit. All of these corporate strategies would have a major impact on the quality of services delivered.

A new question in the debate on the balance between private and public responsibility for welfare was introduced with the recent emergence of health and human service corporations: If government is to contract out its social welfare obligations, can the business sector pick up the slack? Logically, proponents of privatization have two options: the nonprofit, voluntary sector (Chapter 6) and the for-profit, **corporate sector.** Both sectors are well-established in American social welfare. Since President Lyndon Johnson's Great Society programs, government has been contracting out services through both nonprofit and for-profit providers. The for-profit corporate sector capitalized on the contracting-out provisions of the Medicare and Medicaid programs. At the same time, through the purchase-of-service concept introduced in Title XX, nonprofit agencies became contractors providing a range of social services on behalf of public welfare departments.

Unfortunately, studies comparing the performance of these sectors have been few and their findings debatable.[15] In the absence of definitive results showing the advantages of one sector over another, the privatization debate has become heated. Advocates of *voluntarization,* or reliance on the voluntary sector to assume more of the responsibility for welfare, point to its historical contribution to the national culture, the rootedness of its agencies in the community, and the altruistic motives behind its programs. Advocates of voluntarization received a boost when the second Bush presidency advocated "faith-based" initiatives in social welfare. Proponents of *corporatization,* or dependence on the corporate sector to provide welfare, argue that corporations offer more cost-effective administration, are more responsive to consumer demand, and pay taxes. Corporatists scored a major victory in the 2003 Medicare reforms. Whether voluntarists or corporatists prevail in the privatization debate rests largely on the ability of each party to manipulate the social policy process in its favor. Whatever the outcome, this process is certain to be lengthy and complex, as one might expect with the remaking of an institutional structure that has become as essential as social welfare is in the United States. And whether voluntarization or corporatization defines the future of social welfare, privatization has already highlighted several important issues.

Commercialization

For welfare professionals the idea of subjecting human need to the economic marketplace is often problematic. For example, it is hard to condone health care advertising in view of the fact that the health care industry, notably the Health Insurance Association of America, spent millions of dollars to defeat the Clinton administration's 1993 Health Security Act—even though the United States is still without a universal program for expectant mothers and infants, to say nothing of the 40 million Americans who were then without health insurance.[16] As objectionable as market-related practices may be, the commercialization of health and human services is a reality that welfare professionals cannot simply dismiss out of a sense of moral indignation.

In one of the earliest treatments of the matter, Richard Titmuss's *The Gift Relationship* explored the differences in the ways nations manage their blood banks. Unlike the practice in the United Kingdom, blood in the United States is "treated in laws as an article of commerce"; that is, rules of the market affect the supply and quality of blood. Titmuss observed the growth of blood and plasma businesses with alarm, because these businesses bought blood from a population that was often characterized by poverty and poor health. Quite apart from the health hazard posed by a blood supply derived from such a population—a hazard highlighted by AIDS—Titmuss was concerned that the profit motive would disrupt the voluntary impulses of community life. "There is growing disquiet in the United States," he observed, that "expanding blood programs . . . are driving out the voluntary system."[17] Indeed, a majority of blood banks in the United States are commercial.[18]

Preferential Selection

The application of market principles to client service introduces strong incentives for providers to differentiate clients according to their effect on organizational performance. Such selection can be at variance with professional standards, which emphasize the client's need for service over organizational considerations. But the marketplace tends to penalize providers that are imprudent about client selection, at the same time rewarding providers that are more discriminating. The subtle or blatant practice of choosing clients according to criteria of organizational performance—as opposed to client need—is known as **preferential selection.** Under marketplace conditions, providers that do not practice preferential selection are bound to serve a disproportionate number of clients with serious problems and with less ability to pay the cost of care, thereby running deficits. By contrast, providers that select clients who have less serious problems and who can cover the cost of care often claim surpluses. For example, an analysis of psychiatric patients admitted to a public and a private hospital found that the latter selected patients of higher social status. The researchers concluded that "patients in the marginal/uncredentialed social class were comparatively more likely to be admitted to state mental hospitals than to private hospitals."[19]

Critics of privatization complain that creaming the client population through preferential selection is unethical and should be prohibited. Simply ruling out the practice is, however, easier said than done. Accusations of preferential selection are not new; private nonprofit agencies were accused of denying services to welfare recipients long before proprietary firms became established.[20] In Denver, where public hospitals have sustained heavy deficits by caring for a disproportionate burden of the medically indigent, the problem has become critical. Jane Collins, director of clinical social work for the Denver Department of Health and Hospitals, described public hospitals in the city as having become "social dumps."[21] Reports of dumping in instances when life-threatening injuries are evident have drawn the ire of many human service professionals. In some cases, private hospitals have transferred indigent patients with traumatic injuries to public facilities without providing proper medical care, thus contributing to the deaths of several patients. When the federal government prohibited such transfers, many hospitals responded by closing their emergency rooms rather than incur the cost of uncompensated care.

Preferential selection on the part of a large number of providers is likely to be adopted by others who wish to remain in a competitive position. In analyzing the practice in health care, a team of researchers from Harvard University and the American Medical Association noted that "in the same way that competition from for-profit providers leads to reduction in access, the more competitive the market for hospital services generally, the more likely are all hospitals in that market to discourage admissions of Medicaid and uninsured patients."[22] In other words, even nonprofit providers—who are exempt from taxes because they contribute to the community's welfare—are compelled to adopt the discriminatory practices of for-profit providers in a competitive market, unless the nonprofits are willing to underwrite the losses that more costly clients represent to for-profit providers. "When competitive pressures are great," researchers from Yale and Harvard universities have noted, "the behavior of for-profit and nonprofit institutions often converge."[23]

Cost-Effectiveness

Proponents of privatization frequently cite the discipline imposed on organizational performance by a competitive environment as a rationale for market reforms in social welfare. A competitive environment provides strong incentives for organizations to adopt cost-effective practices that reduce waste.

A competitive environment provides strong incentive for organizations to adopt cost-effective practices that reduce waste.

This claim has led to a handful of studies of for-profit versus nonprofit service providers. In a comprehensive review of the issue, the Institute of Medicine of the National Academy of Sciences concluded in the mid-1980s that there was "no evidence to support the common belief that investor-owned organizations are less costly or more efficient than are not-for-profit organizations."[24] Later, Robert Kuttner summarized analyses conducted by an association of nonprofit hospitals and found that "investor-owned hospitals in 1994 were 13.7 percent more expensive on a charge basis than nonprofit and public hospitals." Again, not only were for-profit hospitals more expensive, but they also provided less care to the poor, admitting only half as many Medicaid patients as nonprofit hospitals. Another analysis of proprietary hospitals by the nonprofit hospital association found that investor-owned hospitals were 30 percent more expensive than not-for-profit hospitals.[25]

Although skeptics of market strategies in welfare use such studies to criticize the supposed efficiencies of corporatization in the human services market, it appears that the practices of for-profit firms are nevertheless influencing nonprofit human service organizations. Many nonprofits have adopted features of for-profit firms—bulk buying, sophisticated information systems, staff reductions—to enhance organizational efficiency. As noted, when nonprofits compete with for-profit firms in the same market, the adoption of competitive practices is inevitable in order to ensure organizational survival. As a result, competitive practices characteristic of human service corporations may become standard organizational procedure, not because they serve the public interest better but because the rules of the marketplace require their adoption.

Nevertheless, the promise of cost containment through privatization has not been borne out, and this presents an enormous problem for the governmental sector. Under a privatized system, government is in a weak position to control the prices charged by contracting agencies unless it is prepared to deploy its own set of public institutions, thereby avoiding the private sector altogether. A good example is provided by the Medicare program. Through Medicare the government subsidizes health care for elderly people, most of which is provided by the private sector. In response to runaway Medicare costs, in 1983 Congress enacted the **Diagnostic Related Groups (DRGs)** prospective payment plan, whereby hospitals are reimbursed fixed amounts for medical procedures. Three years after the DRG system was in place, the Congressional Budget Office reported that hospitals had increased their surplus attributed to Medicare by 15.7 percent during 1985. This surplus occurred despite a reduction in the number of Medicare patients admitted to hospitals.[26]

Proponents of privatization often claim that noncompetitive markets and governmental regulation, as in the case of the DRG prospective payment system, impose additional costs that must be passed on to consumers. Research, however, does not bear this out. In a study of 6,000 hospitals sponsored by the National Center for Health Services Research and Health Care Technology Assessment, a research team found that "hospitals located in areas with 11 or more neighboring facilities within a 15 mile radius—the most competitive type of hospital market—have admission costs and patient day costs that are 26 percent and 15 percent higher, respectively, than corresponding figures for hospitals with no competitors." Significantly, the hospitals were surveyed before 1983, so governmental regulation through the DRG system could not have contributed to the higher costs.[27]

Standardization

Commercial provision of human services allows the wealthy to purchase ostentatious, customized care if they like. On the other hand, government reimbursements for care to the masses are likely to be at such low levels that they encourage standardization of care. In this way, privatization can induce human service organizations to adopt an industrial mode of production in which the accepted measure of success is not necessarily high quality of service rendered but the maximum number of people processed. Thus, corporations can generate surpluses, essential for investor-owned facilities, by increasing the intensity of production and lowering labor costs. Because the logic of the market dictates that the goal of production is to process the largest number of people at the lowest possible cost, the **standardization** of services is an important method for lowering organizational costs. Such uniformity of care has become an issue in the nursing home industry. Because Medicaid regulations stipulate standards of care, providers deriving a large portion of their revenues from Medicaid are induced to standardize care for all patients. The standardization of care has become a cause for serious concern among nursing home corporations. Richard Buchanan, professor of business administration at Bowling Green State

University, noted the social consequences of standardized care:

> The nursing home industry's identical treatment of everyone creates a one-class social system for all patients. This constitutes a denial of the affluent person's rights to purchase the quality of life that had been his or hers until stricken with illness or infirmity. This phenomenon represents creeping socialism of a major order, and creates an atmosphere ripe for either legal or market reprisal.[28]

That standardization of care within an industry dominated by for-profit firms would be equated with socialism is perhaps the best measure of the acuity of the problem.

Under these circumstances, life care—the service offered by the continuing-care retirement community—has emerged as an attractive alternative to the nursing home. Under life care plans, residents can purchase cottages or apartments in self-contained communities, at prices comparable to that of a new home, which provide a range of human services. In many respects the life care community provides more affluent residents an opportunity to purchase a higher level of long-term care. Many continuing-care facilities boast such amenities as wall-to-wall carpeting, maid service, and designer landscaping. "Already, the facility has shown its first in-house movie . . . and soon residents will be soaking up steam in the saunas, relaxing in the Jacuzzi, exercising on the mechanical bicycles, or browsing in the library," noted a visitor to one facility.[29] Found in the more posh life-care communities are cocktail lounges, billiards rooms, sports facilities, and elegantly furnished restaurants serving continental cuisine. Amenities such as these "provide a lifestyle of grace and activity for seniors with the ability to pay for it," observed an industry reporter.[30] "We sell a style of life," explained David Steel, vice president of Retirement Centers of America Inc., a subsidiary of Avon.[31]

The prospect of extensive proprietary involvement in life care troubles some analysts. Lloyd Lewis, director of a nonprofit life care community, fears that "well-funded proprietary interests" will "drain off the more financially able segment of our older population, widening the gap between the 'haves' and the 'have nots.'"[32] To a significant extent this is already occurring. Robert Ball, former Commissioner of the Social Security, noted that even life care communities operating under not-for-profit auspices are beyond the means of "the poor, the near poor, or even the low-income elderly."[33] As human service corporations divert capital to care for those who represent profit margins, economic and political support for the care of those less fortunate diminishes. "Those who cannot gain admission to [a private] institution will be forced into boarding homes . . . or bootleg boarding homes," commented Milton Jacobs, vice president of American Medical Affiliates. "These boarding homes will be filled with what are literally social rejects. We're reverting back to the way the industry was in the fifties and sixties."[34] Left unchecked, this pattern is likely to divide long-term care into two clearly demarcated systems, with the affluent enjoying the generous care of completely—some would say excessively provisioned life care communities—and the elderly poor dependent on the squalid institutions willing to accept government payment for their care.

Oligopolization

The privatization of human services invites **oligopolization:** the development of oligopolies, or the control of a market by few providers, as organizations seek to reduce competition by buying their competitors. Within the corporate sector three waves of acquisition can be identified: acquisitions affecting long-term care, hospital management, and health maintenance organizations (HMOs). As firms gain control of major shares of markets, they are in a strong position to leverage influence through trade associations to shape social policy. The consolidation of proprietary health providers has also encouraged nonprofit providers, driven by the same competitive pressures, to form franchises. Five of the 10 largest hospital systems (in terms of number of beds) are nonprofit. Of these, three are operated by religious organizations; one—the New York City Health and Hospital Corporation—is a public conglomerate; and another, Kaiser Permanente, is a private nonprofit entity. Increasingly, nonprofit health providers are joining together in order to compete with the aggressive proprietary providers, a trend that has led to oligopolies within the voluntary sector.[35] Oligopolization of human services presents a daunting specter in that a small number of wealthy and powerful organizations are in a strong position to shape social policy to conform with their interests. Within health care, this development has led Arnold Relman, editor of *The New England Journal of Medicine,* to voice alarm at the growing influence of the "new medical-industrial complex" in defining health policy in the United States.[36]

The medical industrial complex was instrumental in crafting the 2003 Medicare reforms in a manner that served its interests. Central to the passage of Medicare reform was Thomas A. Scully, the Director of the Centers for Medicare and Medicaid Services (CMS). Before taking the helm of CMS, Scully was president of the Federation of American Hospitals (FAH), a trade association of for-profit hospitals, for which he was paid $675,000 per year. At CMS, his salary was only $134,000 per year, so it is not surprising that Scully announced a swift exit after two-and-one-half years of federal service.[37] At CMS Scully battened the Medicare reform act with subsidies to healthcare corporations. Immediately after passage of the legislation, he was acquired by Alston & Bird, an Atlanta law firm specializing in health care, for an undisclosed salary, though one that probably exceeds what he made at FAH.[38] Within a year, Scully was back on Capitol Hill lobbying on behalf of the Renal Leadership Council, a kidney dialysis trade association. Joining him were other Alston & Bird acquisitions: Colin Roskey, former adviser to the Senate Finance Committee, and Marc Scheineson, former associate commissioner of the Food and Drug Administration. Alston & Bird's head of DC operations and former Clinton White House official, Marilyn Yeager stated, "It's a very nice team here. They have a lot of expertise."[39]

The 2003 Medicare reforms would have been chalked-up as another Republican maneuver to coopt a Democratic issue, had not the program's chief actuary, Richard Foster, revealed that his attempts to inform Congress of the program's true costs—$551.5 billion over ten years—had been suppressed by Scully. Foster's exposé was newsworthy since the Medicare reforms had passed by a close margin, many members of Congress voting in favor only after being assured that the health reforms were within the $400 billion parameter stated by the White House. Federal law prohibits the obstruction of communication between federal employees and Congress,[40] but that did not stop Scully from blocking access to Foster's memo explicating the costs of Medicare reform. "If Rick Foster gives that to you," a House Democratic aide who had requested the memo was told by Scully, "I'll fire him so fast his head will spin."[41] Foster, a career civil servant, stuck to his story, accusing the White House of having full knowledge of his projections, but favoring lower estimates generated by other agencies.[42] A subsequent House inquiry failed to clarify the matter, in large part because the Republican leadership was unwilling to grant subpoena power to the committee, making testimony voluntary. When the House committee asked Scully to testify about the suppression of Foster's projection, he said he was "unable to appear" because he was traveling.[43] Lacking a majority in the House, Democrats were unable to get a full hearing on the scandal.

The Challenge of Privatization

Privatization has been disquieting for health and human service professionals. For those committed to increasing government's responsibility for ensuring social and economic equality, privatization is a retreat from a century of hard-won gains in social programs. This case is argued cogently by Pulitzer Prize–winning sociologist Paul Starr:

> A large-scale shift of public services to private providers would contribute to further isolating the least advantaged, since private firms have strong incentives to skim off the best clients and most profitable services. The result would often be a residual, poorer public sector providing services of last resort. Such institutions would be even less attractive as places to work than they are today. And their worsening difficulties would no doubt be cited as confirmation of the irremediable incompetence of public managers and inferiority of public services. Public institutions already suffer from this vicious circle; most forms of privatization would intensify it.[44]

For defenders of government social programs, the problems inherent in privatization—commercialization, client creaming, inflated costs, standardization, and oligopolization—make it a poor vehicle for advancing social welfare. Most profoundly, privatization reinforces a tendency in market economies to evolve dual structures of benefits, services, and opportunities: adequate and varied services for the affluent, substandard and uniform services for the poor. As Robert Kuttner has pointed out, "in a purely for-profit enterprise or system, there is no place for uncompensated care, unprofitable admissions, research, education, or public health activities-all chronic money losers from a strictly business viewpoint."[45] For many human service advocates, the purpose of social welfare is to correct for the inherent tendency of markets to direct resources toward the affluent and away from the poor. From this left-leaning perspective, the idea of privatization of social welfare violates the essential meaning of social welfare.

Yet increased reliance on the private sector at a time when public social programs are under assault is a reality that must be faced by those concerned about social welfare. In the absence of a politically effective left and the diminishing influence of a progressive labor movement, there appears little chance of launching new government social programs, a prospect that has been preempted by tax cuts of the second Bush presidency. If the public is unwilling to authorize and pay for new governmental social programs, welfare professionals have little choice but to reconsider privatization as a basis for welfare provision. In some instances, private sector analogues to public services have demonstrated surprising success. In New York and Connecticut an innovative program called America Works has evolved through the private sector:

> Each year the company finds jobs for more than 700 of the state's hard-core unemployed, 68 percent of whom are (as a result) permanently weaned from the welfare rolls. The company gets paid only after the former welfare recipient has been working for four months and its $5,000 fee is less than half of what it costs New York State to support an average welfare family of three. All told, America Works is saving taxpayers approximately $4.5 million annually and providing many of the state's hard-core unemployed with meaningful work.[46]

Upon closer inspection, there are strong arguments in favor of privatization as a strategy for promoting social welfare. Through commercial loans and issuance of stock, for-profit organizations have faster access to capital than does the governmental sector (which requires a lengthy public expenditure authorization process) or the voluntary sector (which relies on arduous fund-raising campaigns) for purposes of program expansion. The private sector has also been the source of important innovations in programs and organizational administration that have often become models for effective administration.[47] It could be argued further that welfare-conscious administrators have missed opportunities for promoting social welfare by ignoring opportunities for professional practice associated with privatization.

Privatization will continue to challenge the moral and rational impulses of human service professionals. The President's Commission on Privatization noted in 1992 that "the impact of the privatization movement, broadly understood, is only beginning to be felt. Privatization in this broad sense may well be seen by future historians as one of the most important developments in the American political and economic life of the late 20th century."[48] How health and human service professionals choose to respond to the challenge of privatization—whether reactively or innovatively—will be critical for the future of U.S. social welfare. Privatization may come to be a rallying cry for defenders of established programs that have been discredited as being wasteful and inflexible and currying the favors of special interests; or privatization may ultimately mean discovering new ways to exploit the social carrying capacity of the private sector. As David Donnison has suggested, welfare professionals would be wiser to reconsider their aversion to the private sector and to try to find the "progressive potential in privatization."[49]

Unions and the Private Sector

Unions of health and welfare professionals are one response to privatization. Since the Depression, social welfare professionals have organized collectively in order to obtain better wages and benefits, to enhance working conditions, and improve services to clients. Two pioneers of American social welfare, Bertha Capen Reynolds and Mary van Kleek, vigorously urged social welfare workers to view unions as a vehicle for social justice. Today, members of the Bertha Capen Reynolds Society advocate collective bargaining in order to empower human service professionals. Social workers in the public sector often hold memberships in unions—most often in the American Federation of State, County, and Municipal Employees (AFSCME), with 55,000 social work members in 1993, or in the Service Employees International Union (SEIU) with 26,000 social work members. Altogether about one in four social workers belongs to a collective bargaining unit.[50] Because of the dispersion of social work activities, however, social workers have been less successful than nurses or teachers in using unions to achieve their ends.

Collective bargaining is the foundation of the union process. Collective bargaining is face-to-face negotiation between unionized employees and management for the purpose of arriving at a union contract. Such bargaining is supposed to be done in good faith, and the legal rights of workers are protected by the National Labor Relations Act. If these rights are attenuated, workers can petition the National Labor Relations Board to address grievances.

The ultimate power of unions is to exercise the right to strike when the bargaining process breaks down. Theoretically, both parties have an interest in a successful collective bargaining process, because strikes hurt both union members and their employers. Collective bargaining can also address professional issues such as caseload size, educational benefits like tuition reimbursement, conference release time and reimbursements, payment for professional dues and subscriptions, and flexible work hours. One union leader noted, "To the professional—the teacher or caseworker—things like class size and caseload size become as important as the number of hours in a shift is to the blue collar worker."[51] In one union organizing campaign, for example, caseload size, career ladders and training, pay equity, and classification downgrading were the primary issues. In a nonprofit mental health clinic, safe working conditions, benefits for part-time workers, workloads, and participation in agency decision making were the focus of organizing efforts.[52]

A significant question before human service professionals has been the extent to which union objectives are consistent with professional values. Despite the constructive influence that unions could potentially exert in response to cuts in public welfare since the Reagan presidency or wholesale privatization of state and local governmental programs, social workers have approached unions with great apprehension. Opponents to collective bargaining contend that (1) unions cost employees money; (2) strike losses are never retrieved; (3) even when they are not purposely kept uninformed by union leadership, members have little voice in union affairs; (4) bureaucratic union hierarchies control the economic destiny of members; (5) union corruption is rampant; (6) union opposition to management attempts to increase productivity arrests organizational growth; (7) union featherbedding results in unneeded employees and unnecessary payroll expenses; (8) union activities foster conflict rather than collaboration; and (9) unions fail to extrapolate the effects of wage increases on future employment, inflation, and taxes.

A fundamental concern among social welfare professionals revolves around the ultimate tactic that unions can bring to employer–employee relations: job actions, particularly strikes. For social workers who have pledged to make client welfare a priority, the prospect of denying services as a result of job actions makes union membership and professional commitment contradictory. In covering a 1984 strike by Local 1199 of the Retail Drug Employees Union that included the social work staffs of more than 50 hospitals and nursing homes, Dena Fisher wrote,

> Standards for professional practice conflict with the [NASW] Code of Ethics with regard to behavior during a labor strike when the prescribed behavior includes withholding service, failing to terminate clients properly, and picketing activity directed toward consumers. . . . The problem is that participation in a strike is a nonprofessional activity. . . . Standards of professional behavior conflict with union membership requirements.[53]

Yet proponents of union membership cite ways in which collective bargaining can complement professional objectives. In an attempt to encourage a better relationship with professional social workers, Jerry Wurf, former AFSCME president, stated that

> AFSCME's involvement [with social issues] is part of a larger commitment to improving public services and programs. But more importantly, these vital efforts prove the true mission of a labor organization to be closely linked to that of social work. AFSCME's growth in the last decade was due in large part to its role as a social missionary. This precious pursuit has undoubtedly been enhanced by the growing number of social workers in our ranks.[54]

The few studies that have examined the issue have found little incongruity between the loyalties of social workers who belong to unions. Leslie Alexander and his colleagues studied 84 union members with MSW degrees and found that "they view their work as solidly professional and, for the most part, do not see unionism and professionalism as incompatible."[55] Ernie Lightman reported similar findings when studying 121 randomly chosen professional social workers in Toronto. According to Lightman, "the vast majority saw no incompatibility; indeed, many felt unionization may facilitate service goals, offsetting workplace bureaucracy."[56] Reporting on child welfare agencies in Pennsylvania and Illinois, Gary Shaffer found that "workers did not find unionism incompatible with their educational or professional goals."[57]

Such complementarity notwithstanding, the concept of social work "exceptionalism" pervades the debate about professionalism and unions. The exceptionalism premise implies that tasks performed by social workers are more important than those performed by many other workers, especially nonprofessionals, and that normal labor relations principles are therefore not applicable. Proponents of social work exceptionalism must address two matters: First, how is it that other semi-professionals, such as teachers and nurses, have reconciled their professional priorities with union activities and become more powerful in the contexts of their work as a result? Are social service activities to be considered more essential than education or health care? Second, does the idea of social work exceptionalism contribute to the powerlessness of social workers? If social work places such value on the empowerment of clients, why should social workers themselves not also be so empowered? The idea of social work's exceptionalism was put in bold relief in 1991 when members of Canada's Public Service Alliance—many of whom are social workers—participated in one of the largest strikes in the nation's history, inspired by the government's plan to reduce wage increases.[58] If Canadian human service professionals can reconcile professional and union differences, why is this beyond U.S. social workers?

While social workers in the United States procrastinate about an alliance with unions, events such as privatization and government cuts in funding make the issue ever more urgent. Social workers and unions should be able to collaborate in problem solving, fostering a public debate on social issues and promoting class-aware groupings in an adverse social climate. Facilitating social change is a goal of several organizations, including Jobs with Justice. As Charles Heckscher points out, new approaches to unionization "are still in their infancy . . . [and] the rich variety of innovations being tried today has the potential to restore an essential pillar of labor's strength: the sense among the wider public that employee organization contributes to the general good."[59]

Corporate Welfare

The business community in the United States influences social welfare in several important ways. Benefit packages for employees, which are usually available to dependents, provide important health and welfare benefits to a large segment of the working population. Historically, this form of "welfare capitalism" has been an important complement to public social programs. "For much of the 20th century, indeed, the development of U.S. social policy has followed an identifiable second track of intervention, one to which scholars of the welfare state, orthodox or revisionist, have paid only limited attention," noted Jacob Hacker. "The legislative milestones along this track have not been large and highly prominent social programs, but public policies of diverse form—tax breaks, regulations, credit subsidies, government insurance—designed to encourage and shape private responses to public social problems."[60] The implications of this are momentous. Once private sector activities are calculated as part of the national welfare effort, the United States is similar in scale to European nations. Politically, any welfare state with competing public and private sectors can evolve separate solutions to citizens' needs, evident in liberal defense of Social Security contemporaneous with conservative preference for private alternatives, such as 401(k) plans.[61]

Corporate philanthropy has sponsored important—and, in some cases, controversial—social welfare initiatives. And policy institutes reflecting the priorities of the business community have made substantial changes in U.S. "public philosophy." More recently, the corporate sector has begun to exploit the growing human service markets in hospital management, long-term care, health maintenance, child care, public welfare, and corrections. These instances reflect the significant role that the corporate sector has played in U.S. social welfare, a role that is expanding rapidly.

Among welfare theorists, however, corporate activities have tended to be underappreciated. As discussed in Chapter 1, many progressive scholars attributed the cause of much social and economic dislocation to industrial capitalism, and there with implicated capitalism's institutional representative, the corporation. Thus, the corporation was seen not as a source of relief but rather as the perpetrator of social and economic hardship. As a result, liberal theorists concluded that the government was the only institution capable of regulating capitalism and compensating the victims of its caprices. Welfare state ideology, as it evolved, left little room for the corporation, viewing it as the source of much suffering and as generally unwilling to pay its share of the tax burden to remediate the problems it had spawned. For example, advocacy groups such as the public interest research groups (PIRGs) associated with Ralph Nader and Citizens for Tax Justice regularly criticize the corporate sector for pursuing economic and political self-interest, sacrificing the general welfare in the process. A frequent target of criticism is "corporate welfare," the direct subsidies and tax expenditures granted to businesses in the

United States, which total at least $75 billion annually.[62] In his campaigns for the presidency, Ralph Nader contended that corporate influence was unprecedented in public affairs: "Indeed the corporate government's takeover of our political government, so pronounced since 1980, has reached levels of pervasiveness without precedent in modern American history."[63] Notorious examples of the sacrifice of civic values in pursuit of profits have been well chronicled by liberal advocacy groups. These include the disruption, then abandonment, of Love Canal because of improper disposal of toxic waste; the exploitation of Mexican agricultural workers in the Southwest; the extortion of huge sums from New York City housing officials by landlords who provide single-room occupancy lodgings for the homeless; and the deceit of tobacco companies about the harmful effects of smoking. To corporate critics, CEOs flaunt their positions by commanding salaries way out of proportion to their productivity. When super-rich CEOs downsize production, lay off thousands of workers, and thereby decimate a local economy,[64] they become cultural pariahs. At the same time, few would doubt that wealth and status are enormously influential when wealthy executives leave private life and run for public office. "It's no accident that the Senate is a citadel of multi-millionaires," observed one longtime Washington journalist.[65]

Privileges, power, and wealth notwithstanding, the corporate sector has made contributions to the **commonweal,** or public good, and these are less often recognized. Consider that in 2002 corporate contributions to nonprofit activities totaled $12.19 billion, substantially more than the $3.91 billion contributed to the nation's United Ways. Virtually every large corporation has established a foundation that supports nonprofit activities. The relatively low percentage of grants in relation to total assets (as seen in Table 7.1) contributed to an unsuccessful legislative attempt to require foundations to limit their overhead expenses to five percent of operations, described in Chapter 6. Ironically, many welfare advocates who had leveled blanket indictments at the corporate sector during the 1960s found themselves furtively seeking grants from corporate foundations when government funds for new social programs dried up after the 1980s. By the end of the twentieth century, minority Americans were making their mark in corporate philanthropy. Native American tribes contributed $35 million for the new Museum of the American Indian which opened in Washington, D.C., in 2004. Jeong Kim used the sale proceeds from Yurie Systems for millions of dollars in aid to higher education. In 2003, African American publishing tycoon John Johnson contributed $4 million to Howard University's School of Communication.[66]

At this point many welfare theorists are beginning to reexamine the role of the corporate sector in American social welfare. The concept of the "mixed welfare economy" combines the corporate proprietary sector with the governmental and voluntary sectors as primary actors in social welfare.[67] And the issue of privatization has provoked a vigorous argument about the proper balance between the public and private (including corporate) welfare sectors.[68] Although Neil Gilbert's *Capitalism and the Welfare State* provided a timely review of the issues posed by "welfare capitalism,"[69] empirical investigations of for-profit human service corporations are in their infancy.[70]

History of the Corporate Sector

For most of the history of the United States, private institutions have been the basis of welfare provision. During the colonial era, the town overseer contracted out the poor to the resident who was willing to provide food and shelter at the lowest bid. Similarly, communities subsidized medical care for the poor through purchase of physicians' services. Through the eighteenth and nineteenth centuries, this practice contributed to the emergence of private institutions—hospitals and orphanages, among others—that served the needy.[71] Although many of these early welfare institutions were communal efforts and not developed as private businesses, others were precisely that. That is, many early hospitals in the United States were owned and operated by physicians, who became wealthy by providing health care to the community. By 1900 approximately 60 percent of hospitals were privately owned by physicians.[72]

With industrialization, however, the business community took a new interest in the health and welfare of employees. To be sure, certain captains of industry saw employee welfare as a concession to be made as a last resort, sometimes only after violent confrontation with organized workers. Such was not always the case, however. Early in the Industrial Revolution, before government assumed a prominent role in societal affairs, altruistically minded businessmen saw little recourse but to use

Table 7.1

Twenty Largest Foundations, 1997

Foundation	Total Assets	Grants	Ratio of Grants to Total Assets
Lily Endowment	$11,240,400,474	$249,253,042	2.2%
Ford Foundation	9,490,389,726	431,976,866	4.6
Packard Foundation	8,821,156,968	169,763,413	1.9
Rob't Wood Johnson Foundation	6,606,099,364	231,460,444	3.5
Kellogg Foundation	5,162,126,770	322,707,209	6.3
MacArthur Foundation	3,953,055,206	153,974,431	3.9
Rob't Woodruff Foundation	3,610,139,249	44,997,439	1.2
Andres Mellon Foundation	3,137,668,563	118,351,300	3.8
Rockefeller Foundation	3,035,540,414	97,364,158	3.2
Pew Memorial Trust	2,958,572,726	139,587,976	4.7
Starr Foundation	2,492,982,425	73,498,534	2.9
Kresge Foundation	2,062,753,175	13,042,851	0.6
Duke Endowment	1,942,566,287	51,483,632	2.7
Charles Stewart Mott Foundation	1,926,262,905	76,056,186	3.9
Weinberg Foundation	1,809,835,510	57,768,620	3.2
Hewlett Foundation	1,784,854,073	37,909,301	2.1
McKnight Foundation	1,677,162,841	74,719,545	4.5
Richard King Mellon Foundation	1,502,039,619	51,321,104	3.4
Carnegie Corp. of New York	1,414,100,893	36,116,572	2.6
Houston Endowment	1,299,723,058	52,203,610	4.0

Source: Internal Revenue Service, *Large Nonoperating Private Foundations Panel Study, 1985–1997* (Washington, DC: Department of the Treasury, 2001), pp. 142–151.

their business firms as an instrument for their social designs. In some cases their experiments in worker welfare were nothing less than revolutionary. During the early 1820s the utopian businessman Robert Owen transformed a bankrupt Scotch mill town, New Lanark, from a wretched backwater populated by paupers into a "marvelously profitable" experiment in social engineering. Owen abolished child labor, provided habitable housing for his workers, and implemented a system to recognize the efforts of individual employees. Soon New Lanark attracted thousands of visitors, who were as awed by the contrast between the squalor of other mill towns and the brilliance of New Lanark as they were by the substantial profits Owen realized from the venture. A humanist and an irrepressible idealist, Owen believed that the solution to the problem of poverty lay not in the stringent and punitive English Poor Laws but in "making the poor productive." Owen later transported his utopian vision to the United States, where he attempted to establish a rural planned community in New Harmony, Indiana.[73]

Although Owen's American experiment in local socialism did not survive, business leaders in the United States began to acknowledge that industrial production on a grand scale required a healthy and educated work force. Locating such workers was not easy amid the poverty and ignorance that characterized much of the population of the period. To improve the dependability of labor, several large corporations built planned communities for workers. During the early 1880s, for example, the Pullman Company, manufacturer of railroad sleeping cars, constructed "one of the most ambitiously planned communities in the United States—a company town complete with a hotel, markets, landscaped parks, factories, and residences for over 8,000 people."[74] Although some industries later built communities and facilities as a means of controlling and, in some cases, oppressing workers—as in the "company stores" operated by mining companies to keep miners forever in debt—many expressions of corporate interest in employee well-being clearly enhanced the welfare of the community.

In other instances, businesspeople experimented with alternative forms of business ownership. Current "workplace democracy" and "employee ownership" programs have a predecessor in the Association for the Promotion of Profit Sharing, established in 1892. In 1890 Nelson Olsen Nelson, a founder of this association, set aside a 250-acre tract in Illinois for workers in his company. Naming the village Leclair after a French pioneer of profit sharing, Nelson included in the town plan gardens, walkways, and a school, and he encouraged employees to build residences in the community. Consistent with his philosophy, Nelson offered employees cash dividends as well as stock in the company; and by 1893, 400 of the 500 employees held stock, thus earning 8 to 10 percent in dividends in addition to their wages. Not content with an isolated experiment in industrial socialism, Nelson advanced his ideas in a quarterly journal that promoted profit sharing. Eventually Nelson went so far as to convert his company into a wholly employee-owned cooperative, but overexpansion and irregular earnings led to his ouster in 1918.[75]

It is important to recognize that such experiments in the social function of the business firm were not solely the work of utopian crackpots, nor were they always the product of peculiar circumstances. **Welfare capitalism,** "industry's attending to the social needs of workers through an assortment of medical and funeral benefits, as well as provisions for recreational, educational, housing, and social services," was a popular idea among some business leaders before World War I.[76] Indeed, concern about the optimal purpose and value of business in the national culture was a frequent subject of discussion among the elite of U.S. commerce. Even a staunch capitalist such as John D. Rockefeller took a relatively progressive stance on the corporate role when, in 1918, he asked on behalf of the Chamber of Commerce of the United States:

> Shall we cling to the conception of industry as an institution, primarily of private interest, which enables certain individuals to accumulate wealth, too often irrespective of the well-being, the health and happiness of those engaged in its production? Or shall we adopt the modern viewpoint and *regard industry as being a form of social service* [emphasis added], quite as much as a revenue-producing process? . . . The soundest industrial policy is that which has constantly in mind the welfare of employees as well as the making of profits, and which, when human considerations demand it, *subordinates profits to welfare* [emphasis added].[77]

As fortunes, often ill-gotten, accumulated in the hands of the few, some wealthy individuals felt compelled to return a portion of their wealth to the commonwealth. In the late nineteenth century, "men who had great fortunes from the massive industrial growth of the post–Civil War period developed a humanistic concern which was manifested in lavish contributions toward social betterment."[78] Andrew Carnegie, who in 1886 had hired "an army of 300 Pinkerton detectives" to put an end to the violent Haymarket strike,[79] wrote seven years later that massive wealth was a public trust to be put toward the public interest. Carnegie eventually donated some $350 million through foundations for this purpose, most visibly for community libraries (often bearing his name) that began to dot towns across the country. For his part, John D. Rockefeller contributed about $530 million.[80]

Although largely based on the guilt associated with the great fortunes won by a handful of individuals in the midst of cruel circumstances for many, philanthropic foundations also fostered enduring contributions to social welfare. During the 1920s the Commonwealth Fund proved instrumental in the execution of a series of child guidance experiments, and these served as prototypes for today's juvenile service departments.[81] The Russell Sage Foundation funded the publication of important works on the development of social welfare, including the classic *Industrial Society and Social Welfare* as well as a series of volumes that were precursors of the *Encyclopedia of Social Work.*[82]

The Rockefeller Foundation took a leading role in providing health care to a Southern black population that was neglected by state officials.[83] The active role of the Rockefeller Foundation in the eradication of hookworm warrants particular mention. Shortly after the turn of the century, Charles Wardell Stiles was appointed zoologist of the U.S. Department of Agriculture. Hypothesizing that a disease widespread in the South was caused by a parasite, Stiles convinced his superiors to fund a research trip. He succeeded in confirming his theory, but Congress refused to finance an eradication program. So Stiles turned to the Rockefeller Foundation. In 1909 the foundation established the Rockefeller Sanitary Commission for the Eradication of Hookworm Disease, naming Stiles as an officer. By World War I, having diagnosed and treated millions of the rural poor, mostly African Americans, the commission was well on its way to eradicating the disease that had caused such extensive malaise and listlessness among the poor—in the process contributing to one of the most vicious stereotypes about blacks in U.S. culture.[84]

The business community was also involved in early insurance programs designed to assist injured workers. Although court decisions initially absolved employers of liability for injuries incurred by employees, a swell in jury-awarded settlements to disabled workers convinced corporations of the utility of establishing insurance funds to pool their risk against employee suits. Eventually companies realized that they would pay lower premiums through state-operated workers' compensation programs than they had been paying through commercial insurance. Consequently, between 1911 and 1920, all 45 of the then existing states enacted workers' compensation laws.[85] Later, when the Great Depression overtaxed voluntary social welfare agencies and when labor volatility resulting from high unemployment threatened political stability, it is not surprising that politicians, businessmen, and labor leaders drew on their workers' compensation experience in designing the New Deal. Instrumental in creating federal social programs in the Roosevelt era was Gerald Swope, an executive with the General Electric Company. Having envisaged a "corporate welfare state," including "a national system of unemployment, retirement, life insurance, and disability programs and standards," Swope helped fashion the Social Security program from his position as chairman of Roosevelt's Business Advisory Council.[86] The Social Security program clearly bore the imprint of the business community. As the plan was conceived, only workers who had contributed to a "trust fund" would be able to draw benefits; this would ensure that no public funds would be required to operate the program.[87] What became known as the "social security concept" illustrated a public pension program that was in fact modeled on programs of the private sector. As such, it "represented the acceptance of approaches to social welfare that private businessmen, not government bureaucrats had created."[88] The Social Security Act, the crown jewel of the New Deal, meant that the social and economic security of millions of Americans would be underwritten by the state.

Although benefits from programs mandated by the Social Security Act became a staple of the U.S. welfare state, the business community continued to make independent decisions regarding the welfare of workers. Major corporations, such as General Electric, General Motors, and IBM, began to offer "fringe" benefits as supplements to salaries, and these became important incentives in attracting desirable employees. By the standards of the mid-twentieth century, the benefits offered by large corporations were quite generous, including annual vacations, health care, recreation, life insurance, and housing. Business historians Edward Berkowitz and Kim McQuaid have described the conscientiousness with which some corporations cared for their employees and have suggested that it was "almost as if these firms were consciously demonstrating that the true American welfare state lay within the large and progressive American corporation."[89] Private sector activity in health, income maintenance, and education are detailed in Table 7.2.

Although private expenditures lagged behind public expenditures, the corporate share of the welfare market increased between 1980 and 1994. Continued growth of the private sector is virtually assured insofar as the service sector of the American post-industrial economy expands.

Corporate Social Responsibility

The corporation has also influenced U.S. social welfare as a result of accusations that it has been insensitive to the needs of minorities, the poor, women, and consumers. During the 1960s criticism of the corporation focused on business's neglect of minorities and on urban blight. A decade later issues relating to affirmative action, environmental pollution, and consumer rip-offs were added to the list. These

Table 7.2

Private Social Welfare Expenditures, by Category and as a Percent of GDP (in millions)

Category	1980	1985	1990	1994
Private social welfare expenditures	$254,520	471,223	727,523	924,894
Health	145,000	259,400	410,000	528,600
Personal health care	133,000	232,500	368,900	469,900
Income maintenance	53,564	118,871	164,772	204,736
Private pensions	37,605	98,570	138,114	174,452
Life insurance	5,075	7,489	9,278	11,229
Short-term disability	8,630	10,570	13,680	15,901
Long-term disability	1,282	1,937	2,926	2,895
Supplemental unemployment	972	305	774	259
Education	33,180	54,038	87,864	105,261
Welfare & other services	22,776	38,914	64,887	86,297
As a percent of GDP				
Total	27.0	28.8	31.3	34.5
Public	18.6	18.4	18.5	21.8
Private	9.4	11.7	12.8	13.5

Source: Social Security Bulletin, Annual Statistical Supplement (Washington, DC: U.S. Government Printing Office, 1995), p. 151; *Annual Statistical Supplement* (Washington, DC: U.S. Government Printing Office, 2002), p. 132.

problems contributed to a public relations crisis, as a leading business administration text noted:

> The corporation is being attacked and criticized on various fronts by a great number of political and citizens' organizations. Many young people accuse the corporation of failing to seek solutions to our varied social problems. Minority groups, and women, contend that many corporations have been guilty of discrimination in hiring and in pay scales.[90]

Melvin Anshen, a professor of public policy and business responsibility at Columbia University's Graduate School of Business, bemoaned the fact that "profit-oriented private decisions are now often seen as antisocial."[91]

In order to improve their public image, many businesses established policies on **corporate social responsibility.** Corporations that were reluctant to take seriously the social implications of their operations ran the risk of inviting the surveillance of public interest groups. As an example, the Council on Economic Priorities (CEP), founded in 1969, developed a reputation for investigating the social responsibility of U.S. corporations. CEP released *Rating America's Corporate Conscience,* which evaluated 125 large corporations based on their standing with respect to seven issues: charitable contributions; representation of women on boards of directors and among top corporate officers; representation of minorities on boards of directors and among top corporate officers; disclosure of social information; involvement in South Africa; conventional weapons-related contracting; and nuclear weapons-related contracting.[92] Social responsibility audits enable consumers to patronize (or boycott) companies according to their own social consciences and thereby create an incentive for companies to follow socially responsible practices.

Although public relations facades frequently gloss over businesses' substantive abuses, specific corporate social responsibility policies have advanced social welfare. During the late 1960s General

Electric and IBM instituted strong policies on equal opportunity for and affirmative action toward minorities and women. Under the title Public Interest Director, Leon Sullivan assumed a position on the General Motors board of directors, from which he presented principles governing ethical practices for U.S. corporations doing business in South Africa.[93] U.S. firms' adherence to the "Sullivan principles" contributed to the fall of apartheid in South Africa. More recently, financial consultants have pioneered the concept of socially responsible investing. The practice of excluding certain industries from mutual fund portfolios because their activities are contrary to those of investors gained considerable ground during the 1980s. An illustration of socially responsible investing is the Domini Social Index (DSI), an investment strategy that screens out businesses in five areas: military contracting, alcohol and tobacco, gambling, nuclear power, and South Africa. After its inception in 1988, the DSI initially performed comparably to the Standard & Poor's 500 Index, but by the early 1990s it was generating a return on investment superior to Standard & Poor's.[94] In another instance, Control Data Corporation actually sought out "major unmet social needs, designed means for serving them within the framework of a profit-oriented business enterprise, and brought the needs and the means for serving them together to create markets where none had existed before."[95] These and other initiatives demonstrate that the corporate sector has been willing to undertake significant programs to support troubled communities.[96]

Corporate practices have also been applied directly to social problems. In 1981, in a venture reminiscent of Robert Owen, developer James Rouse established the Enterprise Foundation. Although this is technically a foundation that supports charitable projects, what makes it different is that within the foundation is the Enterprise Development Company, a wholly owned taxpaying subsidiary. Profits from the Development Company are transferred to the foundation to fund projects. By the late 1980s, this fiscally self-sufficient "charity corporation" had developed innovative projects for low-income housing in dozens of cities.[97] In 1995 the Enterprise Foundation reported that since its inception, $1.7 billion had been committed for loans, grants, and equity investments in order to develop 61,000 new and renovated homes. Following the establishment of neighborhood-based employment centers in 11 cities, the Enterprise Jobs Network aided in employing 26,000 people.[98]

In the early 1980s, recognizing the tendency of community institutions in poor areas to become dependent on government or philanthropy for continuing operations, the Ford Foundation sought contributions from corporations for a program to apply business principles to social problems. By 1983 the Local Initiatives Support Corporation (LISC) had developed investment funds in 24 regions supporting 197 community development projects.[99] LISC projects provided jobs and commodities needed in disadvantaged communities, including a fish processing and freezing plant in Maine, a for-profit construction company in Chicago, and a revolving loan fund to construct low- and moderate-income housing in Philadelphia.[100] Fifteen years after its inception, LISC had helped 1,400 community-based organizations leverage $2.9 billion. LISC contributions were credited with the construction of more than 64,000 homes.[101]

The success of initiatives such as the Enterprise Foundation and LISC have led imaginative social activists to use market strategies to accelerate the upward mobility of the poor. Chicago's South Shore Bank, for example, brought $270 million in new investments to deteriorating neighborhoods and rehabilitated 350 large apartment buildings. By the end of 1990, the bank had increased its assets fivefold and contributed to two important policy initiatives of the Clinton administration: the Empowerment Zone initiative and the Community Development Financial Institution Loan Fund. By the early 1990s, South Shore Bank also was consulting with community development activists in Poland, through collaboration in the Polish-American Enterprise Fund, and in Bangladesh, in partnership with the Grameen Bank, which has pioneered peer lending among poor women and in the process become one of the largest development banks in the world. The concept of providing loans to low-income women in order to encourage self-employment also has been operationalized in the San Francisco metropolitan area through WISE, the Women's Initiative for Self-Employment. Since its inception in 1988, WISE has taught 3,500 poor women about running a business, in the process helping start or expand more than 500 businesses.[102] As South Shore Bank, the Polish-American Enterprise Fund, the Grameen Bank, and WISE indicate, the application of capital to promote social development has spawned a nascent network of international organizations.

In the light of such ventures, some business leaders have become enthusiastic about the activist responses to social problems on the part of the corporation. David Linowes, a corporate leader, foresaw a new role for business in public affairs.

> Mounting evidence proves that the private sector is uniquely well qualified to fulfill many of the social goals facing us more economically and expeditiously than government working alone. . . . I can visualize a wholesale expansion of existing incentives along with a spate of new reward strategies introduced to America's socio-economic system. Increasingly, I believe, this will help to change the attitude of businessmen regarding social involvement. I look forward to the day, in fact, when competition to engage in government-business programs will be every bit as spirited as competition for the consumer dollar is today.[103]

As chairman of the President's Commission on Privatization, during the Reagan administration, Linowes worked to define ways in which the private sector could complement the responsibilities of government.[104]

Corporate Influence on Social Welfare Policy

Corporate social responsibility notwithstanding, it would be naive to think that the corporate sector is above self-interest in its orientation toward social welfare. The conservative political economist Irving Kristol stated as much when he wrote that "corporate philanthropy is not obligatory. It is desirable if and only if it serves a corporate purpose. It is expressly and candidly a self-serving activity, and is only legitimate to the degree that it is ancillary to a larger corporate purpose. To put it bluntly: There is nothing noble or even moral about corporate philanthropy."[105] And corporate influence in social welfare is not exerted simply through myriad corporations acting independently. Special interest organizations, such as the National Association of Manufacturers and the United States Chamber of Commerce, have routinely pressed for public policies that clearly reflect the priorities of the business community. The influence that the business community brings to public policy is discussed in greater detail in Chapter 8.

Since the 1970s certain foundations have made sizeable contributions to conservative policy institutes, constructing the ideological infrastructure that would challenge liberalism in social affairs. (See Table 7.3.)

At the turn of the century, conservative foundations continued to support think tanks associated with the Right. By the end of the twentieth century, such contributions placed conservative policy institutes at the center of the social policy debate. Not only were conservative think tanks well endowed with resources, but they were dispersed throughout the United States. As a result of these investments in the marketplace of ideas, the conservative imprint on social policy has become indelible, and many of the most prominent conservative think tanks—AEI, Heritage, and Cato—have become household names. (See Table 7.4.)

Prominent policy institutes favored by the business community have been the American Enterprise Institute for Public Policy Research (AEI), the Heritage Foundation, and the CATO Institute. Established as nonpartisan institutions for the purpose of enhancing the public's understanding of social policy, these policy institutes distanced themselves from the special interest connotations of earlier business advocacy groups. At the same time, conservative think tanks served as vehicles through which the business community could take a less reactive stance regarding social policy. Conservative policy institutes, then, addressed the complaint voiced by Lawrence Fouraker and Graham Allison of Harvard's Graduate School of Business Administration: "Public policy suffers not simply from a lack of business confidence on issues of major national import, but from a lack of sophisticated and balanced contribution by both business and government in the process of policy development."[106]

Table 7.3

Top Five Conservative Foundations, 1999–2001

Foundation	Assets	Contributions
Sarah Scaife Foundation	$323,029,669	$44,800,500
Bradley Foundation	584,752,379	38,858,118
Olin Foundation	71,196,916	17,403,240
Davis Foundation	78,314,656	13,013,125
DeVos Foundation	97,048,407	12,159,101

Source: Adapted from Jeff Krehely, Meaghan House, and Emily Kernan, *Axis of Ideology* (Washington, DC: National Committee for Responsive Philanthropy, 2004), p. 14.

Table 7.4

Major Grant Recipients of Conservative Philanthropy, 1999–2001

Organization	State	Conservative Grants Received	Total Revenue, 2001
Heritage Foundation	DC	$28,569,700	$27,890,147
American Enterprise Institute	DC	7,613,741	24,095,354
Judicial Watch	DC	6,129,150	17,500,662
Manhattan Institute	NY	5,339,184	8,924,816
Cato Institute	DC	4,824,432	17,631,255
Hudson Institute	IN	4,681,592	7,818,439
Nat'l Ctr. for Policy Analysis	TX	3,818,700	4,770,562
Pacific Res. Inst. for Pub. Pol.	CA	3,272,389	4,424,316
Focus on the Family	CO	3,075,400	121,333,537

Source: Adapted from Jeff Krehely, Meaghan House, and Emily Kernan, *Axis of Ideology* (Washington, DC: National Committee for Responsive Philanthropy, 2004).

The American Enterprise Institute (AEI)

Once noted for its slavish adherence to probusiness positions on social issues, AEI, by the early 1980s, had developed an appreciation for American "intellectual politics."[107] With a budget and staff comparable to that of a prestigious college, AEI was able to recruit an impressive number of notable scholars and individuals and to maintain projects in several domestic policy areas: economics, education, energy, government regulation, finance, taxation, health, jurisprudence, and public opinion. The significance of these activities for social welfare was stated by AEI's then-president, William J. Baroody Jr.:

> The public philosophy that has guided American policy for decades is undergoing change. For more than four decades, the philosophy of Franklin Delano Roosevelt's New Deal prevailed, in essence calling upon government to do whatever individual men and women could not do for themselves.
>
> Today we see growing signs of a new public philosophy, one that still seeks to meet fundamental human needs, but to meet them through a better balance between the public and private sectors of society.
>
> The American Enterprise Institute has been at the forefront of this change. Many of today's policy initiatives are building on intellectual foundations partly laid down by the Institute.[108]

For this ambitious mission AEI empaneled a staff of influential and talented personnel. At the height of its influence, from the late 1970s through the mid-1980s, AEI maintained a stable of more than 30 scholars and fellows *in residence,* who prepared analyses on the various policy areas.[109] The institute's senior fellows included the previously mentioned Irving Kristol; Herbert Stein, an economist and chairman of the President's Council of Economic Advisors in the Nixon administration; and Ben Wattenberg, a veteran public opinion analyst. The AEI "distinguished fellow" was Gerald R. Ford, who had served as thirty-eighth president of the United States. Michael Novak, director of AEI's project on democratic capitalism, prepared analyses that focused on social welfare policy. Under the direction of Novak, the project on democratic capitalism intended to reform public philosophy by defining the corporation as a promoter of cultural enlightenment rather than as a perpetrator of inequality. "The social instrument invented by democratic capitalism to achieve social goals is the private corporation," he proselytized. "The corporation . . . is not merely an economic institution. It is also a moral and a political institution. It depends on and generates new political forms. . . . Beyond its economic effects, the corporation changes the ethos and the cultural forms of society."[110] At the same time, Novak took careful aim at the public sector, explaining, "I advise intelligent, ambitious, and morally serious young Christians and Jews to awaken to the growing danger of statism. They will better serve their souls and serve the Kingdom of God all around by restoring the liberty and power of the private sector than by working for the state."[111]

Through the late 1970s and early 1980s, AEI laid the groundwork for the conservative revolution in U.S. domestic policy. Much of the conceptual work was done by conservative scholars, but the execution depended on the building of a network between the business community and government. By the election of Ronald Reagan in 1980, that network was in place. This ensured that no social policy proposal would receive serious consideration without first passing the review and comment of AEI.

The Heritage Foundation

In 1986 AEI faltered, and organizational problems led to the resignation of Baroody. When AEI moved to the center, the Heritage Foundation assumed leadership in defining the pro-business and antigovernmental outlook favored by the Right. Established in 1973 by a $250,000 grant from the Coors family,[112] the Heritage Foundation had a 1983 budget of $10.6 million, already close to those of the liberal Brookings Institution and the conservative American Enterprise Institute.[113] Heritage espoused a militantly conservative ideology; it influenced social policy by proposing private alternatives to establishing governmental programs and by slanting its work to the religious right. By breaking new ground while building mass support for policy initiatives, Heritage complemented the less partisan analyses of AEI.

Heritage social policy initiatives emphasize privatization, which in this case means the transfer of activities from government to business. Implicit in this approach is an unqualified antagonism toward government intrusion in social affairs. Government programs are faulted for breaking down the mutual obligations between groups; for failing to attend to efficiencies and incentives in the way programs are operated and benefits awarded; for inducing dependency in the beneficiaries of programs; and for allowing the growth of the welfare industry and its special interest groups, particularly professional associations.[114]

This critique served as a basis for the aggressive stance taken by the Heritage Foundation in urban development, income security, and social welfare policies. With regard to urban development, Heritage proposed the Urban Enterprise Zone (UEZ) concept, which would enable economically disadvantaged communities to attract industry by reducing taxes, employee costs, and health and safety regulations.[115] The UEZ concept came to the attention of then Congressman Jack Kemp, who convinced the Reagan administration to make it the centerpiece of its urban policy, thus replacing the Economic Development Administration and Urban Development Action Grant programs through which government had provided technical assistance and funds for urban development.[116] When UEZ legislation stalled in Congress, Heritage changed tactics and targeted states and localities directly. By late 1984, 30 states and cities had created more than 300 UEZs.[117] As secretary of Housing and Urban Development in the first Bush administration, Kemp was well placed to reintroduce the enterprise zone concept as a way of aiding troubled communities; eventually the UEZ initiative found a home in the Clinton administration as Empowerment Zones.

In the area of income security, the Heritage Foundation—in conjunction with the conservative CATO Institute—prepared an oblique assault on the Social Security program, promoting a parallel system of individual retirement accounts (IRAs). Under the "Family Security Plan" proposed by Peter Ferrara, former senior staff member of the White House Office of Policy Development, the initial IRA provisions of the 1981 Economic Recovery and Tax Act would have been expanded to allow individuals "to deduct their annual contributions to . . . IRAs from their Social Security payroll taxes."[118] Although the idea of substituting IRA investments for Social Security contributions was blocked by liberal politicians, Heritage was clearly banking on future support from workers of the baby boom generation. "If today's young workers could use their Social Security taxes to make . . . investments through an IRA," hypothesized Ferrara, "then, assuming a 6 percent real return, most would receive three to six times the retirement benefits promised them under Social Security."[119] According to this calculus, the interaction of demographic and economic variables would lead to increasing numbers of young workers' salting away funds for themselves, spurred both by high investment returns and by the fear that Social Security would provide only minimal benefits on retirement. The result would be a surefire formula for eroding support for Social Security, a prospect that would come to fruition early in the second term of George W. Bush's presidency.

Regarding welfare policy, Heritage was instrumental in scouting Charles Murray, whose *Losing Ground* provided much of the rationale for the conservative assault on federal welfare programs. In 1982 a pamphlet Murray had written for Heritage, entitled "Safety Nets and the Truly Needy," came to the attention of the Manhattan Institute, a conservative New York think tank.[120] Traded by Heritage to Manhattan, Murray elaborated his allegation that government social programs during the War on Poverty had actually worsened the conditions of the poor. Murray's wrecking-ball thesis advocated no less than a "zero-transfer system," which consisted of "scrapping the entire federal welfare and income support structure for working-aged persons."[121] Remembering his earlier sponsor, Murray returned to Heritage on December 12, 1984, to promote his book to a standing-room-only audience at a symposium entitled "What's Wrong with Welfare?" Murray's critique of family welfare would provide the impetus for Lawrence Mead, whose recommendation that welfare recipients be mandated to work was featured in the 1988 Family Support Act, as well as Newt Gingrich's Contract with America, the outline of which foretold the end of the family welfare entitlement through the 1996 federal welfare reform.

The conservative triumph in domestic policy was not coincidental. Not long after the Reagan inauguration, Heritage Vice President Burton Pines had likened the conservative cause to a crusade. Pines noted the pivotal role of think tanks in the effort to transform public philosophy and acknowledged a debt to AEI, an organization he described as focusing "primarily on long (sometimes very long) range and fundamental transformation of the climate of opinion." Bringing the conservative Hoover Institution of Stanford into the fold, Pines characterized their work in military terms. "Together," he concluded, "Hoover, AEI and Heritage can today deploy formidable armies on the battlefield of ideas"[122]—forces that were to prove enormously influential in shifting domestic policy to the right.

The Future of Corporate Involvement in Social Welfare

Corporations will continue to influence social welfare policy, reflecting the preference of business leaders that business assumes a primary role in activities of both the voluntary and governmental sectors. It follows that human service advocates, rather than assuming a reactive role in relation to corporate involvement in social policy and programming, should engage the business community proactively. A creative illustration of this kind of engagement appears in the "Decency Principles" proposed in 1988 by Nancy Amidei, a social worker and syndicated columnist. Noting that the Sullivan principles addressed the responsibilities of firms doing business in South Africa, Amidei wondered about the responsibilities of firms doing business in the United States. Her standards for responsible business practices included:

1. *Equitable wages.* Wages should be high enough to allow workers to escape poverty; and there should be comparability across lines of race, age, sex, and handicapping conditions.
2. *Employee rights.* Employees should be provided equal opportunity, the right to organize for collective bargaining, affordable child care, safe working conditions, and health coverage.
3. *Housing.* Businesses should work for more affordable housing and help relocated or migrant workers obtain affordable housing.
4. *Environmental responsibility.* Business practices should include responsible use of resources, sound handling of dangerous substances, and conformance with environmental protection laws.

Amidei suggested that a corporation's adherence to the "Decency Principles" be a basis for government decisions on such matters as providing tax abatements to corporations to attract new industry or awarding government contracts.[123]

At the macroeconomic level, government and industry can collaborate through "industrial policy." In the 1970s and 1980s the idea that government should intervene to aid the business community was reinforced by an increasingly rapid loss of economic advantage to the economies of Japan and Germany, both of which received substantial assistance from their governments. Industrial policy was endorsed by liberal economists such as Lester Thurow, who proposed "the national equivalent of a corporate investment committee" to coordinate economic policy.[124] Thurow argued that subsequent industrialization would provide increased revenues for welfare programs but, more important, create jobs for the unemployed. In the final analysis, further improvement in the economic circumstances of the poor and the unemployed was politically feasible only under conditions of an expanding economy.

Another advocate of fusing social needs and economic requirements was Clinton administration Secretary of Labor Robert Reich. According to Reich, much of the United States' industrial malaise was attributable to underinvestment in human capital. However, human capital investments can be wasteful, leading to nonproductive dependency, when not coupled with the needs of industry. "Underlying many of the inadequacies of American social programs, in short, is the fact that they have not been directed in any explicit or coherent way toward the large task of adapting America's labor force."[125] The attachment of social needs to industrial productivity would fundamentally alter social welfare. "Government bureaucracies that now administer these programs to individuals will be supplanted, to a large extent, by companies that administer them to their employees," suggested Reich. "Companies, rather than state and local governments, will be the agents through which such assistance is provided."[126]

Significantly, industrial policy has attracted conservative adherents as well. Influential analyst Kevin Phillips proposed a more business-directed version of industrial policy. In Phillips's "business–government partnership," labor and business would agree to work cooperatively with government so that the United States could regain its dominant role in the international economy. For Phillips, however, industrial policy offers less for social welfare:

> Political liberals must accept that there is little support for bringing back federal agencies based on New Deal models to run the U.S. economy, and that much of the new business-government cooperation will back economic development and nationalist (export, trade competition) agendas rather than abstractions like social justice or social welfare.[127]

The primacy of business interests in public policy is not accepted by many social welfare advocates. While "corporatism" may seem plausible to corporate executives, government officials, and labor unions, it offers little to the unemployed or to the welfare or working poor.[128] In fact, some critics of industrial policy suggest that its very emergence signifies the inability of advanced capitalism to ensure the provision of basic goods and services to the economically disadvantaged through the welfare state.[129] Despite the downside of corporatism, there is little evidence that social policy would revert to an orientation favored by liberal Democrats. Since 1980, social policy has been reshaped according to conservative preferences. Even the Clinton interregnum succumbed to this influence, most evident in the 1996 welfare reform act. During the presidency of George W. Bush, "compassionate conservatism" provided the rationale for reforming education as well as Medicare. Shortly after his re-election, President Bush announced plans for the partial privatization of Social Security. Indeed, the increasing sophistication of the corporate sector in shaping public affairs suggests that social welfare policy of the future will show greater congruence with the priorities of the business community.

Human Service Corporations

Continued demand for human services in the post-industrial period has drawn the corporate sector directly into social welfare in the United States. Corporate exploration of the growing human services market has proceeded apace. In contrast, shackled by debt and denied revenue because of tax cuts, government social programs struggle to keep up with demand for services. Dependent on government support and on contributions of middle-income Americans who have experienced a continual erosion of their economic position, the voluntary sector is unlikely to meet future service demands. Relatively unfettered by government regulation and with easy access to capital from commercial sources, the corporate sector has made dramatic inroads into service areas previously reserved for governmental and voluntary sector organizations.

Significantly, the incentives for corporate entry into human services were initially provided through government social programs. Between 1950 and 1991, government expenditures for social welfare increased from $23.5 billion to $1.16 *trillion,* a factor of 50. As a percentage of gross domestic product, public welfare expenditures more than doubled, from 8.8 percent in 1970 to 20.5 percent in 1991. Health care allocations figured prominently in the expansion of public welfare expenditures over this period. In 1970, government spent $24.9 billion on health care; by 1991 that figure had grown to $317.0 billion.[130] The potential profits for corporations entering the rapidly expanding health and human services market were unmistakable.

Concomitantly, public policy decisions have encouraged proprietary firms to provide health and human services. This was the case when Medicaid and Medicare were enacted in 1965. By using a market approach to ensure the availability of health care for the medically indigent and the elderly, Medicaid and Medicare avoided the costs of constructing a system of public sector facilities and, in so doing, contributed to the restructuring of health care in the United States. What had been essentially a haphazard collection of mom-and-pop nursing homes and small private hospitals was transformed, in a short period, into a system of corporate franchises, complete with stocks traded on Wall Street. And almost a decade later, incentives offered through Medicaid and Medicare to encourage the corporate sector to become involved in hospital care were replicated in the health maintenance industry. The Health Maintenance Organization Act of 1973 stimulated a sluggish health maintenance industry that has since grown at an explosive rate. As Pulitzer Prize–winning journalists Donald Barlett and James Steele noted, "Wall Street reasoned that a portion of America's hospitals could be assembled into national chains, much like department stores and auto-parts distributors, and investors could make a fortune."[131]

Initially dependent on government welfare programs, the corporate sector has developed a life of its own. Exploitation of the nursing home, hospital management, and health maintenance markets has led to corporate interest in other markets. By the 1980s human service corporations had established prominence in child care, ambulatory health care, substance abuse, psychiatric care, and home health care, as well as in life care and continuing care. By the 1990s managed care firms were restructuring health and mental health services so as to fatten corporate profits; by the end of the twentieth century they had established beachheads in welfare and corrections, as well. Increasingly, proprietary firms were able to obtain funds for facilities through commercial loans or sales of stock, and to meet ongoing costs by charging fees to individuals, companies, and nongovernmental third parties. Insofar as resources for human service corporations are not financed by the state, firms are free to function relatively independent of government intervention.

How big is the corporate sector in U.S. social welfare? Early in the twenty-first century, more than 20 of the largest firms reported annual revenues that were far greater than *all* contributions to the United Ways of America.[132] These corporations employed thousands of workers, some more than the number of state and local workers for public welfare programs in any state in the union.[133] Some salient statistics on the larger human service corporations are listed in Table 7.5.

Human service corporations in the United States share several striking features. First, virtually

Table 7.5

Prominent Health and Human Service Firms, 2004

Firms	Revenues	Markets	Employees
United Health Group	$28.8 billion	HMO	33,00
HCA Inc.	21.8 billion	hosp. mgmt.	126,000
WellPoint Health	20.4 billion	health care	19,100
CIGNA Corp.	18.8 billion	HMO	32,700
Aetna Inc.	17.9 billion	health care	27,600
Anthem	16.7 billion	health care	20,130
Tenet	13.2 billion	hosp. mgmt.	109,759
Humana	12.2 billion	HMO	13,700
Health Net	11.1 billion	health care	9,053
PacifiCare Health	11.0 billion	HMO	7,700
WellChoice	5.4 billion	HMO	5,400
Coventry Health	4.6 billion	HMO	4,203
Beverly Enterprises	2.0 billion	nursing care	36,300
Magellan Health	1.5 billion	mental health	4,700
KinderCare	855.9 million	child care	24,000
Correction Corp. of Am.	1.0 billion	corrections	13,800
Psych. Solutions	293.7 million	mental health	4,810
APS Healthcare	200.0 million	mental health	1,000
Amer. Retirement	386.1 million	assist. liv.	8,700
Leisure Care	100.0 million	assist. liv.	2,000
Sunrise Senior Liv.	1.2 billion	nursing care	31,038
Interim HealthCare	600.0 million	home health	51,000
Alterra HealthCare	416.7 million	assist. liv.	11,800
MAXIMUS	558.3 million	prog. consult.	5,193
Gentiva Health	814.0 million	home health	15,100
Sierra Health	1.4 billion	HMO	3,600
Matria Health Care	326.8 million	women's health	1,452
Caremark	9.1 billion	home care, Rx	4,870
McKesson Corp.	69.5 billion	pharmaceut'l	24,600
Cardinal Health	65.0 billion	pharmaceut'l	55,000
Perot Systems	1.4 billion	systems cons.	13,500
Abt Assoc.	199.0 million	research	1,000

*Earnings for 2003.

Source: Adapted from Hoover's Inc. database. Retrieved from www.hoovers.com.

all were incorporated after World War II, the benchmark of the postindustrial era, with the great majority incorporated after 1960. Second, the for-profit sector of health and human services has matured as a major industrial sector. By the early 1980s, 34 firms reported annual revenues exceeding $10 million apiece; by the beginning of the twenty-first century, the number had risen to 241, as shown in Figure 7.1. That the number of firms in 2004 was somewhat fewer than the 286 firms identified in 2000, suggested that the sector was consolidating through mergers and acquisitions. Although most of the companies focus on health-related services, many diversify into other service areas; and in some instances, other types of corporations acquire human service firms in order to balance their operations.

Consolidation and Growth in New Human Service Markets

As mentioned earlier, human service corporations have become prominent, if not dominant, in several areas of social welfare: nursing homes, hospital management, health maintenance organizations (HMOs), child care, and home care. More recently, proprietary firms have established beachheads in other markets, notably life and continuing care and corrections.

Nursing Homes

Among corporate initiatives in social welfare, expansion into the nursing home industry is unparalleled. Between 1965 and 1978, expenditures for nursing home care increased 16.9 percent *annually*.[134] By the early 1980s, nursing homes had become a $25-billion-a-year industry, and the number of nursing home beds exceeded those in acute care facilities for the first time.[135] At that time 70 percent of nursing homes were under proprietary management. Market conditions such as these led a writer in *Forbes* magazine to observe, "This is a guaranteed opportunity for someone. How the nursing home industry can exploit it is the real question."[136] Under favorable market conditions, nursing home corporations proliferated. David Vaughan, president of a real estate firm specializing in facilities for the elderly, noted:

> The overall affluence of the over fifty-five population makes investments in special care facilities an extremely attractive venture. The need of capital in meeting the housing needs of this segment of the U.S. population has been so great that we have been able to invest in these facilities with only limited competition.[137]

Guaranteed growth of the nursing home market led to the consolidation of proprietary firms and the emergence of an oligopoly. As early as 1981, each of the following three corporations held more than 10,000 nursing home beds: Beverly Enterprises, with 38,488 beds; ARA Services, 31,325; and National Medical Enterprises (NME), 14,534.[138] Beverly Enterprises attained first ranking by its 1979 purchase of Progressive Medical Group, which was the eleventh largest chain of nursing homes. NME attained third ranking in 1979 by purchasing Hillhaven, then the third largest operation. ARA Services

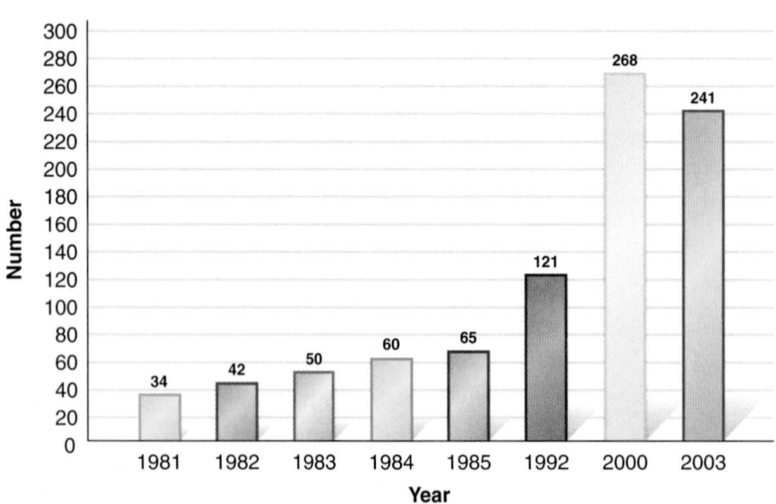

Figure 7.1

Human Service Corporations Reporting Annual Revenues above $10 Million

Sources: Standard and Poor's, 2000, and Moody's, 2004.

grew 26 percent in 1979, thereby attaining second ranking, by consolidating smaller operations in Indiana, Colorado, and California.[139] Undeterred by the filing of the first antitrust action in the nursing home industry, nursing home firms continued such acquisitions and mergers.[140] In 1984, using its Hillhaven subsidiary, NME acquired Flagg Industries, which held 12 facilities in Idaho, bringing its total holdings to 339 health care facilities with 42,000 beds. Not to be outdone, Beverly Enterprises acquired Beacon Hill America for $60 million, thereby retaining its top ranking. By the mid-1980s Beverly Enterprises controlled 781 nursing homes with a total of 88,198 beds in 44 states and the District of Columbia.[141]

Given this trend, one industry analyst believed that the industry would eventually fall into the hands of "five or six corporations."[142] A decade later, Beverly continued as the largest corporation focusing on long-term care, managing 703 nursing homes, 30 assisted living centers, 6 hospices, 11 transitional hospitals, and 4 home health centers. Yet Beverly's share of the nursing home market did not go unchallenged. On March 1, 1995, Beverly's primary competitor, NME, merged with American Medical International to form Tenet Healthcare Corporation, a $5.5 billion company.[143] Yet, Tenet would founder. In response to an FBI investigation into unnecessary heart surgeries performed at a California hospital, Tenet agreed to a $54 million penalty. Under new management, Tenet opted to sell one-third of its hospitals.[144] The nursing care industry would be shaped largely by Manor Care, the largest long-term care provider with revenues of $3.0 billion and 61,000 employees, and the somewhat smaller Beverly.

Hospital Management

The growth of the nursing home industry has been matched by corporate involvement in hospital management. Between 1976 and 1982 the number of investor-owned or investor-managed hospitals increased from 533 to 1,040, accruing gross revenues of approximately $40 billion.[145] Richard Siegrist Jr., a Wall Street analyst, concluded that the future for the industry looked bright, noting that revenues and bed ownership for the five largest companies had roughly tripled between 1976 and 1981. According to this analyst, Humana had doubled its size through an unfriendly takeover of American Medicorp (worth $450 million), gaining 39 hospitals and 7,838 beds. Meanwhile, Hospital Corporation of America (HCA) purchased Hospital Affiliates (worth $650 million), gaining 55 hospitals, 8,207 beds, and 102 hospital management contracts; General Care Corporation (worth $78 million) gained 8 hospitals with 1,294 beds; and General Health Services (worth $96 million) gained 6 hospitals with 1,115 beds. At the same time, American Medical International (AMI) acquired Hyatt Medical Enterprises (worth $69 million), with 8 hospitals, 907 beds, and 26 hospital management contracts, as well as Brookwood Health Services (worth $156 million), with 9 hospitals, 1,271 beds, and 5 hospital contracts.[146]

AMI's strategy of purchasing financially troubled community hospitals proved financially successful. Moreover, in 1984, AMI acquired Lifemark's 25 hospitals and three alcoholism treatment centers through a $1 billion stock transfer.[147] Despite such large-scale growth, AMI continued to rank second behind HCA, which owned 393 hospitals having 56,000 beds.[148] But Humana was to hold the trump card in hospital management. Boldly gambling on its offer to implant artificial hearts in 100 heart patients at no cost, Humana captured the public's attention in 1984. Even though the artificial hearts failed to perform as planned, the project reflected a management strategy that pushed Humana to the head of the pack. By 1993, Humana had forged ahead of its competitors to become the largest health and human service corporation in the world.

The mid-1990s witnessed the largest mergers among health care corporations that had occurred up to that point. As noted above, NME and AMI merged to form Tenet Healthcare Corporation, effectively approximating the market share controlled by Humana. This transaction paled, however, in comparison to the acquisition of HCA by Columbia. The Columbia/HCA merger created a $20 billion behemoth that dwarfed Tenet and Humana. By the mid-1990s the holdings of Columbia/HCA included 292 general hospitals, 28 psychiatric hospitals, and 125 outpatient and auxilliary facilities.[149] Being the largest health and human service corporation was not without its problems, however. An intensely competitive health market invited irregularities, the scale of which matched the size of the perpetrator.

> In June 2003, HCA agreed to pay $631 million in civil penalties and damages growing out of false claims to the government health care programs. That came on top of $840 million in criminal fines, civil restitution, and penalties the company paid in 2000. That same year, the company agreed to pay $250 million to settle other Medicare overbilling claims. In all, HCA has paid $1.7 billion as a result of its fraudulent practices.[150]

Despite such setbacks, HCA was well-positioned with respect to federal programs that accounted for one-third of its revenue. The son of the company's founder, Thomas Frist Jr., was none other than Bill Frist, Senate Majority Leader.

Health Maintenance Organizations

Pioneered by the nonprofit Kaiser Permanente in California, the concept of **health maintenance organizations (HMOs)** was slow to attract the interest of the corporate sector. However, from 1973 to 1981, the Health Maintenance Organization Act of 1973 authorized funds for the establishment of these membership health plans in a large number of favorable marketing areas. This funding, coupled with the growth in the nursing home and hospital management industries, reversed investor apathy. By 1983, 60 HMOs were operating on a proprietary basis.[151] By the end of the century, the HMO industry was a commercial enterprise, save Kaiser-Permanente which had to adopt for-profit strategies in order to remain competitive.

An early leader in the HMO industry was HealthAmerica, a for-profit HMO begun in 1980. Within a few years HealthAmerica enrolled almost 400,000 members in 17 locations across the nation, becoming the largest proprietary HMO (second in size only to nonprofit Kaiser Permanente). Seeking capital for further expansion, HealthAmerica offered stock publicly in July 1983 and raised $20 million for 1.5 million shares. One month later, Phillip Bredesen, chairman and president of HealthAmerica, reported that he anticipated "dramatic growth in the HMO segment of the health care business," and that "HealthAmerica [was] well-positioned with the people and systems that this growth [would] represent."[152]

HealthAmerica's growth did not go unnoticed by Fred Wasserman, founder of Maxicare, another proprietary HMO. Wasserman suspected that Bredesen had stretched his company too thin in an ambitious expansion into new market areas. In November 1986, Maxicare purchased HealthAmerica for $372 million. Coupled with the earlier acquisition of HealthCare USA for $66 million, the purchase of HealthAmerica enabled Maxicare to claim more than 2 million members nationwide and annual revenues approaching $2 billion. After the Health America takeover, Wasserman spoke optimistically about overtaking Kaiser-Permanente in pursuit of a health maintenance market[153] expected to consist

Health maintenance organizations such as Kaiser Permanente offer prepaid medical services. Members pay a monthly or yearly fee for all health care, including hospitalization. Because costs to patients are fixed in advance, preventive medicine is stressed to avoid costly hospitalization. One criticism of HMOs is that patients can use only doctors and specialists who are associated with the organization.

of 30 million members and $25 billion in revenues by 1990.[154] Wasserman's optimism was misplaced, however. The firm proved unable to manage the debt incurred by its appetite for mergers. Maxicare sought protection against creditors, filing for bankruptcy under Chapter 11 in the late 1980s. The collapse of Wasserman's HMO empire was evident in his firm's revenues. Peaking in 1987, Maxicare reported earnings of $1.8 billion; three years later, the firm earned $387 million, less than a fourth of its earlier income.

In the late 1980s managed care became the method of choice for containing health care costs, and the HMO market surged. As business and labor groups attempted to limit the fiscal drain caused by escalating costs of health care, proprietary firms stepped forward to manage care more efficiently. By the mid-1990s more than a dozen managed care companies were reporting hefty revenues. Humana, for example, controlled 17 HMOs as well as the health care provided by some 40,800 physicians, in addition to its 630 hospitals. A rapidly growing competitor, PacifiCare, had established HMOs in six states and enrolled 1.2 million members. The largest firm focusing on health management was United HealthCare Corporation, with facilities in 24 states and Puerto Rico, and enrolling 13.5 million members. FHP International was in second place, reporting annual revenues of $3.9 billion. At the beginning of the twenty-first century, the insurance giant CIGNA dominated the industry, controlling 46 HMOs in which 3 million people were subscribers.[155]

CIGNA's reign was not to last. In November 2004, WellPoint and Anthem received permission from California regulators to consummate their merger announced a year earlier. Together, the new firm will serve 28 million consumers in ten states and Puerto Rico. As a condition to the merger, the health providers agreed to pay $265 million to upgrade health care in California. Combined, WellPoint and Anthem eclipse CIGNA as the nation's largest health care insurer.[156]

Child Care

As a human services market, child care is exploited effectively by proprietary firms. In an important study of child welfare services delivery, Catherine Born showed the influence of for-profit providers relative to that of providers in the voluntary and public sectors. She noted:

> In the case of residential treatment, among all services purchased, 51 percent was obtained from for-profit firms, 26 percent from voluntary organizations, and 22 percent from other public agencies having contractual agreements with the welfare department. For contracted institutional services, 48 percent was provided by proprietary concerns, 14 percent by voluntary vendors, and 38 percent by other public agencies. The pattern was similar in the case of group home services where 58 percent was proprietarily contracted, 17 percent was obtained from the private, nonprofit sector, and 25 percent was purchased from other public agencies.[157]

The day care market, like its largest provider, KinderCare, has expanded rapidly. Begun in 1969, KinderCare has demonstrated prodigious growth, claiming approximately 825 "learning centers" representing $128 million in revenue in 1983. The net earnings for KinderCare in fiscal year 1983 represented a 68 percent increase over fiscal year 1982. The company executed a five-for-four stock split in November 1982 and a four-for-three stock split in May 1983. Also, during fiscal year 1983, the company entered the market of freestanding immediate medical care by purchasing First Medical Corporation and its 10 facilities for an undisclosed sum.[158] By the second quarter of 1984, KinderCare reported that more than 100 new learning centers and 20 new clinics were under construction.[159]

During the 1990s, KinderCare dominated the child care industry with more than 1,100 centers, but new competitors were emerging to serve a seemingly infinite need for organized child care. In 1991, Children's Discovery Centers of America claimed 93 centers and $57.2 million in revenues; Rocking Horse Child Care Center of America owned 87 preschool and elementary learning centers and reported earnings of $34.7 million; Sunrise Preschools—the new kid on the block—earned $10.4 million through its 15 preschool programs. The smaller Discovery Centers more than doubled the number of its facilities, claiming 193 centers serving 17,500 children. Sunrise Preschools actually lost market share, reporting 1995 revenues of $9.7 million from 29 facilities that cared for 2,700 children.[160]

Within a few years, KinderCare's command of the child care industry would be challenged by several upstarts which showed prodigious growth. Bright Horizons Family Solutions managed more than 500 workplace centers in 37 states, reported revenue of $423 million and 16,000 employees; La Petite Academy boasted 650 centers, $383 million in revenue, and 12,000 employees; Learning Care Group reported $206 million in revenue and 7,500 workers. The increasing participation of mothers in the labor market will increase the demand for child care. Between 1979 and 2000, the number of hours worked by wives increased 50.7 percent,[161] a figure that will likely increase as a function of stagnating family income and the work mandate affixed to welfare reform.

Home Health Care

Several companies in the **home health care** market have replicated the success of corporations in the nursing home industry. Home Health Care of America, later renamed Caremark, began in 1979. A leader in the field, the company grew particularly quickly. Caremark generated net revenues of $1 million in 1980, $35.8 million in 1983, and $133.2 million in 1986. In 1983 Caremark increased the number of its regional service centers from 10 to 31; despite the costs incurred by this expansion, net income for the year increased 129 percent. By the mid-1990s Caremark was reporting annual revenues of $2.4 billion and claimed health care facilities in Canada, France, Germany, the United Kingdom, the Netherlands, and Japan.[162]

Growth of this magnitude led Elsie Griffith, chief executive officer of the Visiting Nurse Service of New York and chair of the board of the National Association for Home Care, to observe that home health care "is expanding at a phenomenal rate."[163] Expansion continued during the early 1990s, when home health companies adjusted their services to meet earlier hospital discharges resulting from implementation of Medicare's prospective payment system. That is, as patients went home sooner, the need for a range of specialized in-home health services grew. Quickly, home health companies began to offer a variety of these services to patients. In markets where conventional home health companies failed to offer such specialized care, new firms entered the market and expanded rapidly.

The diversification of eldercare began to accelerate as if in anticipation of the retirement of the baby boomers. Apria Healthcare Group, with revenue of $1.3 billion and more than 10,000 employees included infusion and respiratory therapy in addition to medical equipment as a complement to home health. American HomePatient hired more then 3,400 caregivers to generate $336 million in 2003. To address the episodic demand for home health care, Staff Builders (now ATC Healthcare) spun off Tender Loving Care Health Care Services. New firms evolved to exploit the logical connection between home health and assisted living. Alterra Healthcare boasted 300 assisted living facilities in 20 states and generated $416 million in revenue. Enhancing its position in the market, Extendicare, a $1.7 billion company with 35,800 employees, announced plans to acquire Assisted Living Concepts, a $168 million firm with 180 assisted living centers in 14 states. Beyond assisted living, the end of the life-span has become a commercial product as well. Odyssey Healthcare, a $274 million company, provides hospice care through 70 programs in 30 states.

Increased longevity and improved health of the elderly has spawned a special market for those who can afford it: life care. Indeed, the graying of the population has led some corporations to construct special residential communities that include health care as a service. Life care, or continuing care, provides more affluent elders an opportunity to purchase a higher level of long-term care than is ordinarily found in nursing homes. And despite well-publicized bankruptcies of several retirement communities, the potentially enormous market for life care facilities has attracted the interest of several corporations. Beverly Enterprises, the largest nursing home operation, entered the life care business, and subsequently the Marriott Corporation announced plans to have 200 Lifecare Retirement Communities in operation by 2000.[164] The investment community has been enthusiastic about life care. Harold Margolin, a vice president of Merrill Lynch, stated that "the financial climate could impact on the growth of the continuing care segment of the health care industry, but only on the timing. It's going to be a very large industry."[165]

Corrections

Among the more ambitious of human service corporations is the Correction Corporation of America (CCA), founded in 1983 by Tom Beasely with the financial backing of Jack Massey, founder of the Hospital Corporation of America. CCA officials noted that many states were unable to contend with overcrowding of prison facilities and proposed contracting with state and local jurisdictions for the provision of correctional services. As CCA acknowledged in its 1986 annual report, court orders to upgrade facilities, coupled with governmental reluctance to finance such improvements, provided strong incentives for jurisdictions to consider contracting out correctional services.

> Government response to [overcrowding] has been hampered by the administrative and budgetary problems traditionally plaguing public sector facilities. Most systems have suffered a lack of long-term leadership due to their ties to the political process, and many jurisdictions have placed a low priority on corrections funding. The outcome has been a proliferation of out-dated facilities with a lack of sufficient capacity to meet constitutional standards.[166]

By 1986 CCA operated nine correctional facilities totaling 1,646 beds, and the company was negotiating with the Texas Department of Corrections "to build and manage two minimum security prisons which will provide an additional 1,000 beds."[167]

Most analysts expect that proprietary correctional facilities will continue to grow in popularity as governmental agencies recognize the cost savings of contracting out correctional services. For example, CCA's per diem charge in 1986 was $29.77, about 25 percent less than the cost in public facilities.[168] Texas, Oklahoma, and Arkansas soon put 3,000 correctional "beds" out to bid, an indication of the willingness of states to use proprietary firms on a large scale.[169] The most dramatic example of the possibilities of for-profit corrections dates from 1985, when CCA startled Tennessee state officials by offering to take over the state's entire prison system. As in 30 other states and the District of Columbia, Tennessee's system housed too many prisoners in cramped, archaic facilities and was operating under court supervision. When CCA offered the state a price of $250 million on a 99-year contract, state officials were hard pressed not to give the bid careful consideration. Ultimately, state officials balked at the idea, primarily because of a conflict of interest between CCA and leaders of state government.[170]

Undaunted, CCA moved steadily ahead, capitalizing on the dire need of local and state governments for greater prison capacity. By 1991, CCA managed 17 facilities and reported annual revenues of $67.9 million. Although these earnings were small compared with those of other human service firms, they were astonishing in light of the $7.6 million CCA had earned just six years earlier. By the mid-1990s CCA reported revenues of $207 million from holdings that had expanded to 49 correctional facilities, totaling 33,153 beds, with plans to develop or expand 16 more. Despite CCA's expansion, the largest for-profit provider of correctional services was Wackenhut, a firm with prisons and detention facilities in the United States, Great Britain, and Australia. For 1995 Wackenhut reported income of $796 million from 24 owned or managed facilities, representing 16,000 beds.[171]

Within a few years, CCA had eclipsed Wackenhut (now GEO Group) as the largest incarceration provider. Undaunted, other firms were entering the market: Correctional Services Corporation, reporting revenue of $135 million and 2,800 employees, managed 30 facilities in 14 states; Avalon Correctional Services with 430 employees and $25 million in revenue operated 12 facilities with a total capacity of 1,300 beds. Providing health care to inmates, Correctional Medical Services, claimed $150 million in revenue in 2002 and employed 6,000 workers to serve federal, state, and local prisons.

Conclusion: Implications for Health and Human Service Professionals

Most human service professionals have been skeptical about the prospect of social welfare via human service corporations. According to the critics of proprietary human service delivery, the corporate sector is the organizational manifestation of a capitalist economy that is at the root of much social injustice and human need. For these welfare advocates, professional practice within a corporate context is antithetical to the very idea of "social" welfare. In fact, studies of the organizational practices of human service corporations raise important questions about their suitability for promoting the commonweal. Human service corporations have been found to be less cost-effective than nonprofit and governmental agencies; they engage in discriminatory selection of clients, which penalizes the poor; and they attract clients away from voluntary social service agencies.

The critique of corporate incursion in social welfare is perhaps best illustrated by examining health care policy. Currently, the United States spends 15 percent of GDP on health care, yet 45 million Americans lack health insurance. Liberals who have advocated universal health care as public policy have pointed their fingers at the commercialization of health care as a primary factor for this paradox. As a result of the fragmentation of American health care, simply managing the complexity of such an incoherent arrangement imposes administrative costs of $1,059 per capita in the United States, compared to $307 in Canada.[172] David Himmelstein, a Harvard physician and universal health advocate, has estimated that the administrative savings if the United States were to adopt a single-payer system, similar to Canada's, would realize annual savings of $375 billion, sufficient to provide health insurance to every American.[173]

Despite the critique of corporate involvement in health and human services, commercial providers are likely to play an active role in defining social welfare. The economy of the United States, after all, is capitalistic, and entrepreneurs are free to establish businesses in whatever markets they consider profitable. Unless government strictly regulates—or prohibits—the for-profit provision of human services, human service corporations will influence U.S. social welfare to an even greater extent in the future. Skeptics of the commercialization of social welfare may take comfort in holding the high moral ground, but practically speaking, they are losing territory with accelerating rapidity to for-profit entrepreneurs. If the expansion of health and human service corporations during the latter decades of the twentieth century is not sufficient evidence, then consider the Medicare reforms of 2003 which subsidized the pharmaceutical industry as well as the Bush administration's efforts to partially privatize Social Security.

Despite the proliferation of human service corporations, health and human service professionals have been slow to adopt the corporate sector as a setting for practice. Considering that organizations under traditional auspices—the voluntary and governmental sectors—are increasingly limited in their capacity to provide services, it is unfortunate that health and human service professionals have been loathe to consider corporations as a suitable vehicle for delivering services and benefits. Actually, for-profit firms can be advantageous for several reasons. Proprietary firms may provide access to the capital needed for expanding social services. A primary explanation for the rapid growth of human service corporations is their ability to tap commercial sources of capital. And human service corporations can reduce the cost of commercially derived capital by depreciating assets and writing off interest payments against income during the first years of operation. This presents obvious advantages for human service administrators who are faced with diminishing revenues derived from charitable or governmental sources. Perhaps the best example of this advantage is the meteoric rise of long-term care corporations, which were almost nonexistent as recently as 1970. By convincing commercial lenders and investors that long-term care was viable, for-profit firms eventually gained control over the industry.[174]

In some instances, too, the corporate sector offers more opportunities for program innovation than are possible under other auspices. Governmental programs must be mandated by a public authority, and this requires a consensus on how to deal with particular concerns. Voluntary sector agencies are ultimately managed by boards of directors that reflect the interests of the community in organizational policy. When human service issues are controversial, welfare professionals can encounter stiff opposition to needed programs. Some of this difficulty can be obviated by a corporate structure that is not so directly wedded to the status quo. An example of how a human service corporation offers opportunities not possible through traditional human service organizations, for-profit correctional companies are able to expand the scope of correctional facilities at a time when government is reluctant to finance new construction and the voluntary sector is unable to raise the necessary capital.

The corporate sector offers greater organizational flexibility than that usually found in governmental agencies and a level of sophistication in managerial innovation not often found in the voluntary sector. To be sure, economic advantages enjoyed by the corporate sector help make this possible; but the track record in organizational experimentation by the corporate sector is undeniable. In fact, ideas that could be of value to traditional welfare organizations are frequently derived from the corporate sector, as such popular books as *In Search of Excellence* and *The Changemasters* attest.[175] That comparable books do not emerge from the voluntary or governmental sectors, reflects how noncompetitive they are with respect to entrepreneurs of the for-profit sector.

Discussion Questions

1. Privatization is a hotly debated issue in social welfare. To what extent are some of the major concerns about privatization (e.g., unfair competition between nonprofit agencies and commercial firms, preferential selection and dumping of clients, superior performance of private

providers, the emergence of an oligopoly of private providers) evident in your community? Should human service professionals practice in for-profit firms?

2. Private practice continues to be a focus of students in schools of social work. How many of your classmates are planning to become private practitioners? What are their motives? Do faculty members in your social work program who also have private practices serve as role models to students? Is there an opportunity in your studies to discuss the implications of private practice for social work?
3. How does your state regulate the practice of social work? What governmental unit is responsible for regulating social work? How is it constituted? Does your state have reciprocity arrangements with other states, honoring licenses granted in other jurisdictions? Has your state's social work licensing unit expelled professionals for unethical practices?
4. What is the position of your state chapter of the National Association of Social Workers on regulating professional practice? Are licensing and vendorship still high on the state chapter's priority list? If so, which social workers in your state remain concerned about the regulation of professional practice? Why?
5. What are the main concerns within your professional community about private practice-fees, misdiagnosis, licensing, image, competition with other professionals, vendorship? How are disagreements arbitrated, formally or informally?
6. The debate between private practice and agency-based practice continues as a heated issue within social work. What are the advantages and disadvantages of each? Is there a common base of social work practice? Can you foresee some ways to resolve the issue and bring private practitioners and agency-based practitioners together?
7. Employee ownership is a way for human service professionals to attain control over their practices. Of the prominent social service agencies in your community, which ones might be candidates for employee ownership? If such a transition were accomplished, how would you ensure accountability to consumers? To the community?
8. In order to attain job security, many human service professionals join unions. What is the largest union to which social workers belong in your community? Do issues relating to service delivery figure in the union's negotiations with management? Under what conditions would human service professionals in your community engage in a strike?
9. What are the major corporate philanthropic organizations in your community? What activities have they funded traditionally? To what extent do they incorporate social welfare projects in their funding priorities? Can you determine how priorities and funding decisions are made within these organizations?
10. If you were the director of a nonprofit welfare agency, which sources of philanthropy would you approach in your community to obtain contributions? How would you know which person or persons to approach in the organization? How would you approach them? If a major contribution were secured, how would you recognize the donor?
11. Think tanks exist in Washington, D.C., and in most state capitals. Obtain a copy of the annual report of a think tank. Who funds the think tank? Is there a relationship between the funding source and the ideological character of reports that the think tank publishes? What is the think tank's track record in social welfare issues?
12. One of the most controversial issues in contemporary social welfare has been privatization of Social Security. Where do different think tanks stand on this important issue? What are the advantages and disadvantages of allowing workers to establish private accounts as an alternative to Social Security? How would it affect you? Your classmates?
13. If you were inclined to establish a business providing a human service, what population would you focus on? How would you get capital to start the business? Would you own the business, or would you share ownership with stockholders? How would you market your service? What would you do with the profits—provide stockholders with dividends, enlarge the business, or make contributions to nonprofit agencies? What would be the name of your business?

Notes

1. Paul Starr, "The Meaning of Privatization," quoted in American Federation of State, County, and Municipal Employees, *Private Profit, Public Risk: The Contracting Out of Professional Services* (Washington, DC: AFSCME, 1986), pp. 4–5.
2. Charles Schultz, *The Public Use of Private Interest* (Washington, DC: Brookings Institution, 1977); Donald Fisk, Herbert Kiesling, and Thomas Muller, *Private Provision of Public Service* (Washington, DC: Urban Institute, 1978); Harry Hatry, *A Review of Private Approaches for the Delivery of Public Services* (Washington, DC: Urban Institute, 1983).
3. *Privatization: Toward More Effective Government* (Washington, DC: Report of the President's Commission on Privatization, March 1988), p. 230.
4. Ibid., pp. 1–2.
5. David Obsborne and Ted Gaebler, *Reinventing Government* (New York: Addison Wesley, 1992).
6. John Donahue, *The Privatization Decision* (New York: Basic Books, 1989), p. 216.
7. Harry Specht and Mark Courtney, *Unfaithful Angels* (New York: Free Press, 1994), p. 107.
8. Nina Bernstein, "Giant Companies Entering Race to Run State Welfare Programs," *New York Times* (September 15, 1996), p. 1.
9. Polly Ross Hughes, "Stakes are High as State Rushes to Privatize System," *Houston Chronicle* (October 29, 1996), pp. 1A and 10A.
10. Ibid.
11. Ibid.
12. Quoted in Bernstein, "Giant Companies Entering Race to Run State Welfare Programs," p. 1.
13. Ibid.
14. Quoted in Ibid., p. 10A.
15. See Lawrence S. Lewin, Robert A. Derzon, and Rhea Margulies, "Investor-Owned and Nonprofits Differ in Economic Performance," *Hospitals* (July 1, 1981), pp. 65–69; Robert V. Pattison and Hallie Katz, "Investor-Owned Hospitals and Not-for-Profit Hospitals," *New England Journal of Medicine* (August 11, 1983), pp. 54–65; Robin Eskoz and K. Michael Peddecord, "The Relationship of Hospital Ownership and Service Composition to Hospital Charges," *Health Care Financing Review* (Spring 1985), pp. 125–132; J. Michael Watt et al., "The Comparative Economic Performance of Investor-Owned Chain and Not-for-Profit Hospitals," *New England Journal of Medicine* (January 9, 1986), pp. 356–360; Bradford Gray and Walter McNerney, "For-Profit Enterprise in Health Care: The Institute of Medicine Study," *New England Journal of Medicine* (June 5, 1986), pp. 560–563; Regina Herzlinger and William Kradker, "Who Profits from Nonprofits?" *Harvard Business Review* (January–February 1987), pp. 554–562.
16. Douglas Frantz, "Lobbyists, Interest Groups Begin Costly Health Care Battle," *Los Angeles Times* (May 24, 1993).
17. Richard Titmuss, *The Gift Relationship* (New York: Pantheon, 1971), p. 223.
18. Theodore Marmor, Mark Schlesinger, and Richard Smithey, "A New Look at Nonprofits: Health Care Policy in a Competitive Age," *Yale Journal of Regulation* 3 (Spring 1986), p. 320.
19. Charles Muntaner et al., "Psychotic Inpatients' Social Class and Their First Admission to State or Private Psychiatric Baltimore Hospitals," *American Journal of Public Health,* 84, no. 2 (February 1994), p. 287.
20. Richard Cloward and Irwin Epstein, "Private Social Welfare's Disengagement from the Poor," in Meyer Zald (ed.), *Social Welfare Institutions* (New York: John Wiley, 1965), pp. 628–629.
21. Emily Friedman, "The 'Dumping' Dilemma," *Hospitals* (September 1, 1982), p. 54.
22. Mark Schlesinger, "The Privatization of Health Care and Physicians' Perceptions of Access to Hospital Services," *The Milbank Quarterly* 65 (1987), p. 40.
23. Marmor et al., "A New Look at Nonprofits," p. 344.
24. Gray and McNerney, "For-Profit Enterprise in Health Care," p. 1525.
25. Robert Kuttner, "Columbia/HCA and the Resurgence of the For-Profit Hospital Business," *New England Journal of Medicine* 335, no. 5 (August 1, 1996), pp. 365–366.
26. "Hospitals' Medicare Profits Up," *San Diego Union* (March 29, 1987), p. A5.
27. "Competition for Doctors and Patients Increases Hospital Costs," *NCHSR Research Activities,* no. 101 (January 1988), p. 3.
28. Richard Buchanan, "Long-Term Care's Pricing Dilemma," *Contemporary Administrator* (February 1981), p. 20.
29. Ann LoLordo, "Life-Care Centers Offer Seniors Worry-Free Living," *Baltimore Sun* (June 4, 1984), p. D4.
30. Carol Olten, "Communities Offering Seniors a Graceful Life," *San Diego Union* (March 13, 1988), p. D5.
31. Anthony Perry, "North County Housing Boom: A Lucrative Shade of Gray," *Los Angeles Times* (March 6, 1988), p. E5.
32. U.S. Senate Special Committee on Aging, *Discrimination against the Poor and Disabled in Nursing Homes,* (Washington, DC: U.S. GPO, 1984), p. 25.
33. Ibid., p. 10.

34. Quoted in William Spicer, "The Boom in Building," *Contemporary Administrator* (February 1982), p. 16.
35. Donald Light, "Corporate Medicine for Profit," *Scientific American* (December 1986), p. 42.
36. Arnold Relman, "The New Medical-Industrial Complex," *New England Journal of Medicine* 303, no. 17 (1980), p. 80.
37. Robert Pear, "Health Industry Bidding to Hire Medicare Chief," *New York Times* (December 3, 2003), p. A1.
38. Robert Pear, "Medicare Chief Joins Firm with Health Clients," *New York Times* (December 19, 2003), p. A20.
39. Judy Sarasohn, "Special Interests," *Washington Post* (June 24, 2004), p. A23.
40. Robert Pear, "Agency Sees Withholding of Medicare Data from Congress as Illegal," *New York Times* (May 4, 2004), p. A17.
41. Sheryl Stolberg and Robert Pear, "Mysterious Fax Adds to Intrigue over Drug Bill," *New York Times* (March 18, 2004), p. A1.
42. Amy Goldstein, "Foster: White House Had Role in Withholding Medicare Data," *Washington Post* (March 19, 2004), p. A2.
43. Cheryl Stolberg, "2 Decline to Testify on Drug Cost," *New York Times* (April 2, 2004), p. A15.
44. Paul Starr, "The Limits of Privatization," in Steve Hanke, *Prospects for Privatization* (New York: Proceedings of the Academy of Political Science, 1987), pp. 82–107.
45. Kuttner, "Columbia/HCA," p. 363.
46. Reason Foundation, *Privatization 1992* (Los Angeles: Reason Foundation, 1992), p. 17.
47. David Stoesz, "Human-Service Corporations: New Opportunities in Social Work Administration," *Social Work Administration* 12 (1989), pp. 35–43.
48. Reason Foundation, *Privatization 1992,* p. 251.
49. David Donnison, "The Progressive Potential of Privatisation," in Julian LeGrand and Ray Robinson (eds.), *Privatisation and the Welfare State* (London: George Allen & Unwin, 1984), pp. 211–231.
50. Milton Tambor, "Unions," *Encyclopedia of Social Work,* 19th ed. (Washington, DC: National Association of Social Workers, 1995), pp. 2418–2419.
51. J. Weitzman, *The Scope of Bargaining in Public Employment* (New York: Praeger, 1975), p. 17.
52. Milton Tambor, "The Social Service Union in the Workplace," in Howard Karger (ed.), *Social Work and Labor Unions* (New York: Greenwood, 1988).
53. Dena Fisher, "Problems for Social Work in a Strike Situation," *Social Work* 32 (May–June 1987), pp. 253–254.
54. Jerry Wurf, "Labor Movement, Social Work Fighting Similar Battles," *NASW News* 25, no. 12 (December 1980), p. 7.
55. Leslie Alexander et al., "Social Workers in Unions," *Social Work* 25 (May 1980), p. 222.
56. Ernie Lightman, "Professionalization, Bureaucratization, and Unionization in Social Work," *Social Service Review* 56, no. 1 (March 1982), p. 130.
57. Gary Shaffer, "Labor Relations and the Unionization of Professional Social Workers," *Journal of Education for Social Work* 15 (Winter 1979), p. 82.
58. "Public Service Workers' Strikes Disrupts Life in Canada," *Los Angeles Times* (September 10, 1991), p. A8.
59. Charles Heckscher, "Beyond Contract Bargaining: Partnership, Persuasion, and Power," *Social Policy* 25, no. 2 (1994), p. 29.
60. Jacob Hacker, *The Divided Welfare State* (New York: Cambridge University Press, 2002), p. 22.
61. Hacker, *The Divided Welfare State,* pp. 339, 51.
62. Stephen Chapman, "Politicians Protect Corporate Welfare," *Richmond Times-Dispatch* (October 23, 1996), p. A13.
63. Ralph Nader, ". . . And What about Corporate Welfare Reform?" *Washington Post Weekly* (October 14–20, 1996), p. 22.
64. Jinlay Lewis, "CEOs' Presence in Bush Party Draws Attention to Their Pay," *San Diego Union* (January 13, 1992), p. E3.
65. Fred Barnes, "The Zillionaires Club," *The New Republic* (January 29, 1990), p. 23.
66. Jacqueline Salmon, "Minorities Grab Fundraisers' Notice," *Washington Post* (November 7, 2004), p. F8.
67. Sheila Kamerman, "The New Mixed Economy of Welfare," *Social Work* 28 (January–February 1983), p. 76.
68. Paul Starr, "The Meaning of Privatization," and MDRC Bendick, "Privatizing the Delivery of Social Welfare Service" in *Working Paper 6* (Washington, DC: National Conference on Social Welfare, 1985); David Stoesz, "Privatization: Reforming the Welfare State," *Journal of Sociology and Social Welfare* 16 (Summer 1987), p. 139; Mimi Abramovitz, "The Privatization of the Welfare State," *Social Work* 31, no.4 (July–August 1986), pp. 257–264.
69. Neil Gilbert, *Capitalism and the Welfare State* (New Haven: Yale University Press, 1983).
70. David Stoesz, "Corporate Welfare," *Social Work* 31, no. 4 (July–August 1986), p. 86; "Corporate Health Care and Social Welfare," *Health and Social Work* (Summer 1986), p. 158; "The Gray Market," *Journal of Gerontological Social Work* 16 (1989), p. 31.
71. Abramovitz, "The Privatization of the Welfare State," p. 257.
72. Theodore Marmor, Mark Schlesinger, and Richard Smithey, "A New Look at Nonprofits: Health Care Policy in a Competitive Age," *Yale Journal of Regulation* 3, no. 2 (Spring 1986), p. 322.
73. Robert Heilbroner, *The Worldly Philosophers* (New York: Simon and Schuster, 1967), pp. 98–106.

74. Edward Berkowitz and Kim McQuaid, *Creating the Welfare State* (New York: Praeger, 1980), p. 4.
75. Ibid., pp. 5–10.
76. Gilbert, *Capitalism and the Welfare State,* p. 3.
77. Quoted in Norman Furniss and Timothy Tilton, *The Case for the Welfare State* (Bloomington: Indiana University Press, 1977), p. 156.
78. Murray Levine and Adeline Levine, *A Social History of Helping Services* (New York: Appleton-Century-Crofts, 1970), pp. 236–243.
79. Wilensky and Lebeaux, *Industrial Society and Social Welfare* (New York: Free Press, 1965), p. 88.
80. James Leiby, *A History of Social Welfare and Social Work in the United States* (New York: Columbia University Press, 1978), p. 170.
81. Levine and Levine, *A Social History of Helping Services,* pp. 236–243.
82. Wilensky and Lebeaux, *Industrial Society and Social Welfare,* p. 9; National Association of Social Workers, *Encyclopedia of Social Work,* 18th ed. (Silver Spring, MD: NASW, 1987), p. 781.
83. James Jones, *Bad Blood* (New York: Free Press, 1981), p. 34.
84. Thomas DiBacco, "Hookworm's Strange History," *Washington Post* (June 30, 1992), p. 14 (health section).
85. Berkowitz and McQuaid, *Creating the Welfare State,* pp. 33–36.
86. Ibid., p. 83.
87. Michael Boskin, "Social Security and the Economy," in Peter Duignan and Alvin Rabushka (eds.), *The United States in the 1980s* (Stanford, CA: Hoover Institution, 1980), p. 182.
88. Berkowitz and McQuaid, *Creating the Welfare State,* p. 103.
89. Ibid, p. 136.
90. Michael Misshauk, *Management: Theory and Practice* (Boston: Little, Brown, 1979), p. 6.
91. Melvin Anshen, *Managing the Socially Responsible Corporation* (New York: Macmillan, 1974), p. 5.
92. Steven Lydenberg, *Rating America's Corporate Conscience* (Reading, MA: Addison-Wesley, 1986).
93. Theodore Purcell, "Management and the 'Ethical' Investors," in S. Prakash Sethi and Carl Swanson (eds.), *Private Enterprise and Public Purpose* (New York: John Wiley, 1981), pp. 296–297.
94. Lloyd Kurtz, Steven Lydenberg, and Peter Kinder, "The Domini Social Index." In Peter Kinder, Steven Lydenberg, and Amy Domini (eds.), *The Social Investment Almanac* (New York: Henry Holt, 1992).
95. James Worthy, "Managing the 'Social Markets' Business." In Lance Liebner and Corrine Schelling (eds.), *Public–Private Partnership: New Opportunities for Meeting Social Needs* (Cambridge, MA: Ballinger, 1978), p. 226.
96. Melanie Lawrence, "Social Responsibility: How Companies Become Involved in Their Communities," *Personnel Journal* 61, no. 7 (July 1982), p. 381; James Chrisman and Archie Carroll, "SMR Forum: Corporate Responsibility—Reconciling Economic and Social Goals," *Sloan Management Review* 25, no. 2 (Winter 1984), p. 173.
97. Enterprise Foundation, *Annual Report 1983* (Columbia, MD: Author, 1983), p. 1.
98. Enterprise Foundation, *Annual Report* (Columbia, MD: Author, 1995).
99. Brian O'Connell, *Philanthropy in Action* (New York: The Foundation Center, 1987), p. 218.
100. Local Initiatives Support Corporation, *The Local Initiatives Support Corporation* (New York: LISC, 1980); "A Statement of Policy for Programs of the Local Initiatives Support Corporation" (New York: LISC, 1981).
101. Local Initiatives Support Corporation, *Making Change Happen: Annual Report* (New York: Author, 1995).
102. "Would You Like to Be Your Own Boss?" (San Francisco: Women's Initiative for Self Employment, n.d.).
103. David Linowes, *The Corporate Conscience* (New York: Hawthorn Books, 1974), p. 209.
104. *Privatization: Toward More Effective Government* (Washington, DC: U.S. Government Printing Office, 1988), pp. 2–3.
105. Irving Kristol, "Charity and Business Shouldn't Mix," *New York Times* (October 17, 1982), p. 18.
106. Lawrence Fouraker and Graham Allison, "Foreword," in John Dunlop (ed.), *Business and Public Policy* (Cambridge, MA: Harvard University Press, 1980), p. ix.
107. Peter Steinfels, "Michael Novak and His Ultrasuper Democraticapitalism," *Commonweal* (February 15, 1983), p. 11.
108. William J. Baroody Jr., "The President's Review," *AEI Annual Report 1981–82* (Washington, DC: American Enterprise Institute, 1982), p. 2.
109. Peter Stone, "Businesses Widen Role in Conservatives' 'War on Ideas,' " Washington Post (May 12, 1985), p. C5.
110. Ibid., p. 50.
111. Ibid., p. 28.
112. Richard Reeves, "How New Ideas Shape Presidential Politics," *New York Times Magazine* (July 15, 1984), p. 18.
113. Heritage Foundation, *The Heritage Foundation Annual Report* (Washington, DC: Heritage Foundation, 1983).
114. Interview with Stuart Butler at the Heritage Foundation, Washington, DC, October 4, 1984.
115. George Sternlieb, "Kemp-Garcia Act," in George Sternlieb and David Listokin (eds.), *New Tools for Economic Development* (Piscataway, NJ: Rutgers University Press, 1981), p. 42.
116. Stuart Butler, "Enterprise Zones," in George Sternlieb and David Listokin (eds.), *New Tools for Economic*

Development (Piscataway, NJ: Rutgers University Press, 1981), pp. 73–94.
117. Gilbert Lewthwaite, "Heritage Foundation Delivers Right Message," *Baltimore Sun* (December 9, 1984), p. 2.
118. Peter Ferrara, *Social Security Reform* (Washington DC: Heritage Foundation, 1984), p. 7.
119. Peter Ferrara, *Rebuilding Social Security* (Washington, DC: Heritage Foundation, 1984), p. 7.
120. Chuck Lane, "The Manhattan Project," *The New Republic* (March 25, 1985), p. 34.
121. Charles Murray, *Losing Ground* (New York: Basic Books, 1984), pp. 226, 227.
122. Burton Pines, *Back to Basics* (New York: Morrow, 1982), p. 254.
123. Nancy Amidei, "How to End Poverty: Next Steps," *Food Monitor* (Winter 1988), p. 52.
124. Lester Thurow, *The Zero-Sum Society* (New York: Basic Books, 1980), p. 95.
125. Robert Reich, *The Next American Frontier* (New York: Times Books, 1983), p. 223.
126. Ibid., pp. 247–248.
127. Kevin Phillips, *Staying on Top: The Business Case for a National Industrial Policy* (New York: Random House, 1984), pp. 5–6.
128. Yeheskel Hasenfeld, "The Changing Context of Human-Services Administration," *Social Work* 29, no. 4 (November–December 1984), p. 524.
129. James O'Connor, *The Fiscal Crisis of the State* (New York: St. Martin's Press, 1973); Ian Gough, *The Political Economy of the Welfare State* (London: Macmillan, 1979).
130. Social Security Administration, *Social Security Bulletin, Annual Statistical Supplement* (Washington, DC: U.S. Government Printing Office, 1994), p. 140.
131. Donald Barlett and James Steele, *Critical Condition* (New York: Doubleday, 2004), p. 94.
132. David Stoesz, "Human-Service Corporations and the Welfare State," *Transaction/Society* 16 (1989), pp. 80–91.
133. Bureau of the Census, *Statistical Abstract of the United States, 1986* (Washington, DC: U.S. Government Printing Office, 1986).
134. U.S. Department of Commerce, *1982 U.S. Industrial Outlook for 200 Industries with Projections for 1986* (Washington, DC: U.S. Government Printing Office, 1982), p. 406.
135. Jerry Avorn, "Nursing Home Infections—The Context," *New England Journal of Medicine* (September 24, 1981), p. 759.
136. J. Blyskal, "Gray Gold," *Forbes* (November 23, 1981), p. 84.
137. D. Vaughan, "Health Care Syndications: Investment Tools of the '80s," *Financial Planner* (December 1981), p. 49.
138. Blyskal, "Gray Gold," p. 80.
139. V. DiPaolo, "Tight Money, Higher Interest Rates Slow Nursing Home Systems Growth," *Modern Health Care* (June 1980), p. 84.
140. National Senior Citizens' Law Center, "Federal Antitrust Activity" (Los Angeles: National Senior Citizens' Law Center, 1982), p. 2.
141. "NME Makes More Health Care Acquisitions," *Homecare News* (February 17, 1984), p. 4.
142. Quoted in W. Spicer, "The Boom in Building," *Contemporary Administrator* (February 1982), pp. 13–14.
143. "Beverly Enterprises" and "Tenet Healthcare Corp," Standard & Poor's Stock Report (October 1995), p. 89.
144. Donald Barlett and James Steele, *Critical Condition* (New York: Doubleday, 2004), pp. 106–108.
145. B. Gray, "An Introduction to the New Health Care for Profit," in B. Gray (ed.), *The New Health Care for Profit* (Washington, DC: National Academy Press, 1983), p. 2.
146. R. Siegrist, Jr., "Wall Street and the For-Profit Hospital Management Companies," in B. Gray (ed.), *The New Health Care for Profit,* p. 36.
147. American Medical International, *1983 Annual Report* (Beverly Hills, CA: AMI, 1983).
148. "GAO Says Proprietary Hospital Chain Mergers Raise Medicare/Medicaid Costs," *Home-Care News* (February 17, 1984), p. 6.
149. "Columbia/HCA" *Standard & Poor's Stock Reports* (October 1996), p. 80.
150. Barlett and Steele, *Critical Condition,* pp. 70–71.
151. National Industry Council for HMO Development, *Ten Year Report* 1971–1983 (Washington, DC: Author 1983).
152. HealthAmerica, *Company Profile* (Nashville, TN: HealthAmerica, 1983).
153. M. Abramowitz, "Maxicare HMO Soars with Farsighted Founder," *Washington Post* (November 30, 1986), p. 12.
154. National Industry Council, *Ten Year Report,* p. 22.
155. "PacifiCare," "United HealthCare Corp.," and "CIGNA," *Standard & Poor's Stock Reports* (October 1996), 102.
156. Milt Freudenheim, "California Backs Merger of 2 Giant Blue Cross Plans," *New York Times* (November 10, 2004), p. C1.
157. Catherine Born, "Proprietary Firms and Child Welfare Services: Patterns and Implications," *Child Welfare 62* (March–April 1983), p. 112.
158. Kinder-Care, *Annual Report 1983* (Montgomery, AL: Kinder-Care, 1983).
159. Kinder-Care, *Second Quarter Report* (Montgomery, AL: Kinder-Care, March 16, 1984).
160. "Kinder Care," "Children's Discovery Centers," and "Sunrise Preschools," *Standard & Poor's Stock Reports* (October 1996).
161. Karen Kornbluh, "Americans Must Work Harder to Achieve the American Dream," (Washington, DC: New America Foundation, July 15, 2004), p. 2.

162. "Home Health Care of America," *Standard & Poor's Stock Reports* (March 1984, October 1995).
163. "Interview with Elsie Griffith," *American Journal of Nursing* 18 (March 1984), p. 341.
164. Paul Farhi, "Marriott Corp. Caters to America's Rapidly Aging Population," *Washington Post* (January 2, 1989), p. 5.
165. "Merrill Lynch: Bullish on Health Care," *Contemporary Administrator* (February 1982), p. 16.
166. "Digest of Earnings Reports," *Wall Street Journal* (August 13, 1987), p. 41.
167. Stephen Boland, "Prisons for Profit," unpublished manuscript, San Diego State University, School of Social Work, 1987, pp. 5–6.
168. Ibid., p. 8.
169. Eric Press, "A Person, Not a Number," *Newsweek* (June 29, 1987), p. 63.
170. D. Vise, "Private Company Asks for Control of Tennessee Prisons," *Washington Post* (September 22, 1985), p. D2.
171. "Correction Corporation of America" and "Wackenhut," *Standard & Poor's Stock Reports* (October 1996).
172. Barlett and Steele, *Critical Condition*, p. 170.
173. Steve Lohr, "The Disparate Consensus on Health Care for All," *New York Times* (December 6, 2004), p. C16.
174. D. Stoesz, "The Gray Market," p. 45.
175. Thomas J. Peters and Robert W. Waterman Jr., *In Search of Excellence* (New York: Harper & Row, 1982); and Rosabeth M. Kanter, *The Changemasters* (New York, Simon & Schuster, 1983).

CHAPTER 8

The Making of Governmental Policy

This chapter describes the process by which governmental policy is made, exploring the phases of the policy process, examining the influence of various social groups on the policy process, and accounting for the role of key organizations. The public policy process is important because many social welfare policies are established by government, and decisions by federal and state agencies have a direct bearing on the administration and funding of social welfare programs that assist millions of Americans and employ thousands of human service professionals.

In an open, democratic society, **public policy** should reflect the interests of all citizens to the greatest extent possible. For a variety of reasons, however, this ideal is not realized. Although many Americans have the right to participate in the establishment of public policy, they often fail to do so. Policy made and implemented by the governmental sector may be perceived as being too far removed from the daily activities of citizens, or too complicated to warrant the type of coordinated and persistent efforts necessary to alter it. Moreover, many Americans with a direct interest in governmental policy are not in a position to shape it, as in the case of children and the emotionally impaired, who must rely on others to speak on their behalf. Consequently, governmental policy does not necessarily reflect the interests—indeed, the welfare—of the public, even though it is intended to do so. The discrepancy between what is constitutionally prescribed in making public policy and the way decisions are actually made leads to two quite different understandings of the policy process. For welfare professionals concerned with instituting change in social welfare, a technical understanding of how policy is made is essential. It is equally important for them to recognize that the policy process is skewed to favor powerful officials and interests rather than the interests of those who lack influence. Because social workers and their clients tend to be comparatively powerless, a critical analysis of the policy process is all the more important.

Technical Aspects of the Policy Process

Public policy in the United States is made through a deliberative process that involves the two bodies of elected officials that make up a legislature. This applies both to the federal government and to the states—with the singular exception of Nebraska, which has only one deliberative body, a unicameral legislature.

Aspects of the federal policy process can be found on the policyAmerica website. Initially, a policy concern of a legislator is first developed into a legislative proposal and usually printed in the *Congressional Record*. Because every legislator has a party affiliation and a constituency, legislators' proposals tend to reflect the priorities of those stakeholders. Often, several legislators will prepare proposals that are important to similar constituencies, a phase that ensures that many aspects of an issue are considered. Increasingly, policy institutes are instrumental in developing and vetting legislative options. Through a subtle interaction of ideas, the media, and legislative leadership, one proposal—usually a synthesis of several—is presented as a policy alternative. Other legislators are asked to sign on as cosponsors, and the measure is officially introduced. After the proposed bill is assigned to the appropriate committee, public hearings are held, and the committee convenes to "mark up" the legislation so that it incorporates the concerns of committee members who have heard the public testimony. Under propitious circumstances, the committee then forwards the legislation to the full body of the chamber that must approve it. While it is being approved by the full body of one chamber, a similar bill is often introduced in the other chamber, where it begins a parallel process. Differences between the measures approved by the two chambers are ironed out in a conference committee. The proposed legislation becomes law after it is signed by the chief executive—or, if the executive vetoes the bill, passed by a two-thirds vote of each legislative chamber. This process is always tortuous and usually unsuccessful. The eventual enactment of legislation under these conditions is a true testament to legislative leadership. A third branch of government, the judiciary, assesses legal challenges to existing legislation. In the upper levels of the judiciary, members can hold their posts for life. The primary features of the policy process of the federal government are illustrated in Figure 8.1.

There are several critical junctures in a proposal's tortuous passage into legislation—or oblivion. First, most of the details in any proposal are worked out at the committee or subcommittee level. Different versions are negotiated and reconciled at the markup session, during which committee members and

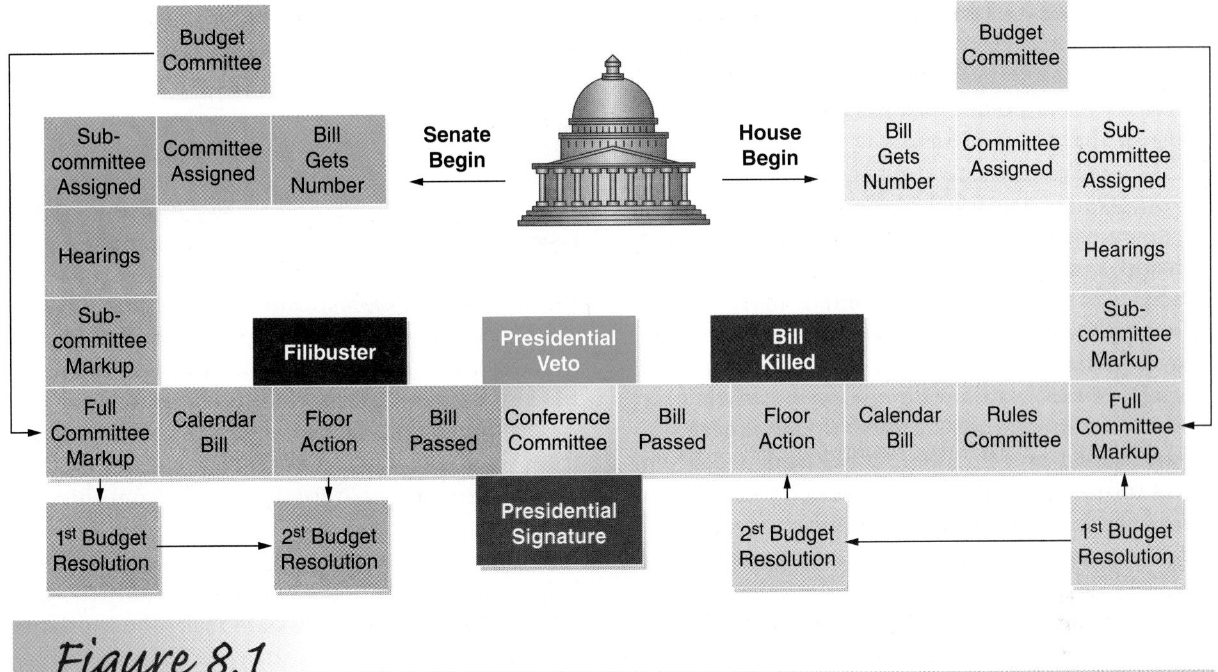

Figure 8.1

The Steps Necessary in Getting a Policy Proposal Enacted into Law

staff write their changes into the draft. This stage offers an important opportunity to inject minor, and sometimes major, changes into the substance of the bill or to alter the intent of the bill's originator(s). Second, the viability of a proposal depends to a large extent on the numbers and weight of the witnesses who testify as to its merits at subcommittee and committee hearings. Obviously, public testimony will work to the advantage of well-financed interests; such interests can afford to pay lobbyists to do this professionally, whereas advocates for the disadvantaged often rely on volunteers. Nevertheless, the public testimony stage is an important opportunity to clarify for the record the position that human service professionals may take on a given proposal. Third, budget considerations figure heavily in the likelihood of a bill's passage. Other federal spending priorities, coupled with the unwillingness of elected officials to raise taxes, increase the likelihood that legislation will be under-funded or even passed with no additional funding whatsoever. Innovative revenue "enhancers," such as earmarked taxes or user fees, can make a proposal more acceptable during periods of fiscal belt-tightening. The policy process, then, is not necessarily intended to facilitate the passage of a proposal into law. Of the tens of thousands of bills presented in Congress, only 10 percent were reported out of committee and only 5 percent became law.[1]

Beyond this general outline of the public policy process, multiple variations exist depending on historical and jurisdictional circumstances. In the federal government, all proposals related to taxation must originate in the House of Representatives, a provision the founders of the nation included in the Constitution in order to place revenue retrieval in the legislative body most representative of the people. Appointments of people for key executive posts, such as cabinet secretaries, ambassadors, and judges, must be ratified through the advice and consent of the Senate, a body less responsive to popular sentiment. States exhibit countless variations within the general outline of the tripartite balance of powers format. California, for example, has experienced chronic budget problems because the state government has been unable to raise sufficient revenue to keep up with mandated expenditures. Since the imposition of Proposition 13 in 1978, a two-thirds majority of the California legislature is required not only to raise property taxes but also to establish the state budget; this is a proportion far beyond the simple majority required in other states. Under these conditions, a small number of recalcitrant representatives can easily block the budget process. As these examples suggest, understanding the intricacies of the policy process is an essential step toward mastering public policy.

A few final points regarding the technical aspects of the policy process warrant mention. The decision-making process itself is defined by *Robert's Rules of Order,*[2] a text that lays out in detail the rules for democratic deliberation. Although *Robert's Rules* can appear obtuse, its value should not be underappreciated. Those who have mastered "the means of deliberation" are one step ahead of the rest of the crowd in seeing their ideas become public policy. Social activists who are optimistic that their proposal is working its way steadily through the legislative minefield may find their hopes exploded by an adroit procedural move on the part of an opponent who sidetracks a bill until the next legislative session. The elaborate rules of decision making, compounded by the traditions of deliberative bodies, may tend to deter citizens from participating in the democratic process. Yet there are means public policy novices can employ to become better acquainted with the ways in which elected officials go about the public's business. Citizen advocate organizations, particularly the League of Women Voters and Common Cause, can be helpful in making social policy more responsive to the public.

Congress and the legislatures of the larger states employ staff members as technical experts to aid them in decision making. Legislative staff are frequently the experts most versed in an area of legislative activity, simply because they work through policy proposals on a regular basis. Staff reports researched as part of committee deliberations can be valuable in that they often provide the most up-to-date data on particular programs or issues. A good example of this type of resource is the "Green Book" used by the U.S. House Ways and Means Committee in its consideration of social programs. Begun in the early 1980s to help committee members comprehend the vast number of social programs under their jurisdiction—Social Security, Medicare, child welfare, AFDC/TANF, SSI, and Unemployment Compensation, among others—the volume, *Background Material and Data on Programs within the Jurisdiction of the Committee on Ways and Means,* became essential reading for social program analysts. Because of its convoluted title, the volume became known by its standard-issue green paper cover, hence the Green Book. Fortunately, its popularity led to a (merciful) shortening of its title to *Overview of Entitlement Programs.*[3] In recent years the Green Book has been available online, making it more accessible.

A Critical Analysis of the Policy Process

Experience and sophistication notwithstanding, the public policy process often proves frustrating for social activists. Despite the most urgent of needs, the best of intentions, and the most strategic of proposals, the social welfare program output deriving from the legislative process often appears far short of what is required. Yet to conclude from this that public policy simply does not work would be an overstatement. A critical approach to public policy helps explain some of the limitations of the technical approach and suggests ways to make the legislative process a more effective strategy for those concerned with furthering social justice.

From a critical perspective, the policy process consists of a series of discrete decisions, each heavily conditioned by money and connections—in other words, by power. The extent to which governmental policy reflects the concerns of one group of citizens while neglecting those of others is ultimately a question of power and influence. Power is derived from several sources, and these have attracted the attention of philosophers over the centuries. Plato questioned the organization and execution of the civil authority of the state. Machiavelli focused on the limits of discretionary authority exercised by leaders of the state. The social contract philosophers of the Enlightenment—Hobbes, Locke, and Rousseau—considered the moral obligations of the state toward its citizens. Later, as the Industrial Revolution proceeded unchecked, Karl Marx attributed power inequities to control over the means of production, or capital. Subsequently, as governmental authority expanded to ameliorate the economic and social dislocation brought on by industrial capitalism, Max Weber identified bureaucratic administrators as a pivotal group. As the postindustrial era unfolded, such social critics as Marshall McLuhan and Alvin Toffler emphasized how the processing and uses of information can be a source of power and influence.

From these general speculations about social organization, other writers have turned to more specific aspects of social policy as subjects of inquiry.

Several schools of thought have emerged. According to the *elitist* orientation, individuals representing a "power structure" control social policy in order to maintain a status quo that advantages them and, in the process, excludes marginal groups. In contrast, a *pluralist* orientation assumes that social policy in a heterogeneous democratic polity is the sum total of trade-offs among different interest groups, all of which have an equal opportunity to participate. At the program level, *incrementalists* have suggested that the more important questions about social policy are the product of bit-by-bit additions to the public social infrastructure. As counterpoint, other scholars have focused on "paradigm shifts" through which major changes, such as the inception of Social Security in 1935 and the devolution of welfare to the states through the Personal Responsibility and Work Opportunity Reconciliation Act of 1996, have altered the very foundation of social policy. With regard to program evaluation, *rationalists* have used the methods of social science to determine by objective standards to what extent policy changes bring about intended outcomes. By contrast, *social activists* use the political process as the measure of program performance, assuming that the optimum in program assessment is continued recertification and refunding by public decision makers. As might be expected in the investigation of any phenomenon as complex as social policy, a comprehensive explanation is likely to incorporate elements of more than one school of thought.

Underlying these varied approaches to interpreting social policy are assumptions about its very nature. In this regard, two orientations have become prominent. The first orientation might be labeled the *liberal evolutionary perspective*. According to this orientation, social policy reflects steady progress toward a desirable condition of human welfare for all. Most liberal analysts who have promoted the welfare state as an ideal have adopted an evolutionary perspective. Believers in the evolutionary perspective expect that the national government will progressively expand social programs until, eventually, the basic needs of the entire population are guaranteed as rights of citizenship. References to welfare state philosophy appear in many chapters of this book. The liberal evolutionary perspective dominated thinking about the U.S. welfare state from the New Deal until the rise of conservative ideology in the 1980s. The demise of Catastrophic Health Insurance in 1989 and the devolution of AFDC/TANF to the states in 1996 raise fundamental questions about the validity of this perspective. The liberal evolutionary perspective has been complemented by social systems theory, which assumes that welfare consists of basic institutions and processes that are related and are changed to suit environmental conditions. Reference to "social service delivery systems" was frequent during the 1960s and 1970s, when social programs were expanding, but this approach commanded less credibility when many public programs were thrown into chaos as a result of budget cuts during the Reagan and two Bush administrations. What had once been coordinated service delivery systems suddenly became disordered and fragmented clusters of agencies struggling for survival.

A competing orientation is the *conflict perspective*, which emphasizes the differences between organized groups that compete for social resources. The conflict perspective views social policy and resultant programs as the product of intense rivalry among various classes and groups. Applied to a capitalist economy and a democratic polity, the conflict approach goes a long way toward explaining the disparate distribution of goods, services, and opportunities within U.S. society. Accordingly, conflict theory is useful in two ways: It accounts for the quite substantial disadvantages experienced by some Americans—the poor, minorities of color, people with disabilities, and women—and it shows how such groups can be empowered to achieve a measure of social justice. Obviously, a conflict perspective accounts for the behavior of for-profit providers of health and human services, which compete intensively for market share, acquire other firms, and lobby public officials to shape policy favorably. The downside of the conflict perspective is that it fails to offer a unifying vision of future social policy.

Questions of governmental decision making often focus on three central aspects: (1) the degree of change in policy represented by a decision, (2) the rationality of the decision, and (3) the extent to which the disadvantaged benefit. First, governmental policies vary in the extent to which they depart from the status quo. It can be argued that, in the final analysis, there are no new ideas, but there *are* new governmental policies that have enormous implications for certain groups. Few could dispute that the Social Security Act and the Civil Rights Act were radical departures from the status quo and substantially changed the circumstances of older people and African Americans, respectively. On the other hand, such radical departures occur only under fairly unusual circumstances, and therefore rarely.

As Charles Lindblom has observed, the great bulk of decision making is "incremental," representing only marginal improvements in social policy already in place.[4] Amitai Etzioni has proposed the term "mixed scanning" to refer to the way decision makers take a quick overview of a situation, weigh a range of alternatives—some incremental, some radical—and ultimately select the one that satisfies the most important factors impinging at the moment.[5] Thus, major shifts in public policy are the exception, rather than the rule. Most social policy changes consist of relatively minor technical adjustments in program administration and budgeting.

Second, social policy does order human affairs, and to that extent the rationality or logic underlying the policy is of great significance. Historically, two basic forms of rationality have served to justify social policy: bureaucratic rationality and market rationality.[6] **Bureaucratic rationality** refers to the ordering of social affairs by governmental agencies. Since Max Weber's work on the modern bureaucracy, this form of rationality has been central to governmental policy and hence to the maintenance of the welfare state. According to bureaucratic rationality, civil servants can objectively define social problems, develop strategies to address them, and deploy programs in an equitable and nonpartisan manner. Bureaucratic rationality takes its authority from power vested in the state, and bureaucracies have become predominant in social welfare at the federal (through the Department of Health and Human Services) and state levels. A characteristic of bureaucratic rationality is a reliance on social planning. Several social planning methods have been developed to anticipate future problems and deal with existing ones. Generally, these can be classified under two headings: technomethodological and sociopolitical.

Technomethodological planning methods emphasize databases from which projections about future program needs can be derived. Such methods place a premium on relatively sophisticated social research methods and work best with programs that can be quantified and routinized, as in the case of cash payments through the Social Security program. **Sociopolitical planning** approaches are more interactive, involving groups likely to be affected by a program. Community development activities, for example, frequently feature planners' bringing together neighborhood residents, business people, and local officials to create a plan that is relevant to the needs of a particular area.[7] Regardless of planning method, it is important to recognize the power and influence that governmental agencies have assumed in social welfare policy, much of it by exercise of bureaucratic rationality.

Market rationality refers to a reliance on the rule of "supply and demand" as a means for distributing goods and services. While on the surface this may appear to be antithetical to the meaning of rationality, a high degree of social ordering in fact occurs within capitalism. Such organization is implicit in the very idea of a market, entailing a large number of prospective consumers that businesses seek to exploit. In a modern market economy, the success of a business depends on the ability of managers to survey the market, merchandise goods and services, shape consumer preferences through advertising, and reduce competition by buying or outmaneuvering competitors. Of course, market rationality is not a panacea for providing social welfare because the marketplace is not particularly responsive to those who may not fully participate in it, such as minorities, women, children, and elderly or disabled people. Yet market rationality cannot be dismissed as a rationale for delivering social welfare benefits. Approximately half of Americans get their health and welfare needs met through employer-provided benefits that are ultimately derived from the market.[8] Since the late 1980s, commercial firms have conducted an ambitious campaign to ration health care benefits through "managed care," an idea that has become anathema to health and human service professionals. Another example of the impact of the market on social welfare benefits is the practice by governmental jurisdictions of contracting out certain human services to private sector businesses, usually with the rationale of reducing costs by taking advantage of efficiencies associated with the market.[9]

The third aspect of governmental decision making addresses disadvantaged populations. It is entirely possible, of course, for social policy to introduce radical change that is based on data but generates mixed effects with respect to the well-being of important groups. The 1996 welfare reform legislation, for example, ended the 60-year entitlement to income for poor families on the basis of evaluations of state welfare demonstrations allegedly showing that states could provide public assistance better if the federal government were not involved. Fearing the consequences of such welfare reform for poor minority children, advocacy groups such as the Children's Defense Fund lobbied ardently against the proposal, but to no avail. Of primary concern among children's advocates was the consequence of **time**

limits on the receipt of welfare for poor children. Analysts from public and private research agencies projected that 1 million to 4 million children would be terminated from public assistance if a five-year time limit on receipt of aid were imposed. The 1996 welfare reform legislation did include provisions for chronically welfare dependent families—exempting 20 percent of the AFDC/TANF caseload from time limits—but children's advocates claimed these were inadequate. The 1996 welfare reform legislation was not welfare "reform," claimed children's advocates; it was welfare termination. Several years later, the consequences of welfare reform were less clear. Those beneficiaries who had entered the labor market earned low wages, but the earned income tax credit boosted most above the poverty line. More disturbing was the subgroup that had been diverted from public assistance. Caseloads dropped more than half during the 1990s; however, most of those who left were not employed full-time, leaving their fate uncertain. Unfortunately, the scanty research on "leavers" failed to clarify the matter.[10]

The degree of change represented by any change in public policy, the extent to which it is rational with respect to bureaucratic or market criteria, and the consequences for disadvantaged populations make the social policy process a dynamic and sometimes volatile area of activity. While this process may be intimidating for the uninitiated, it is essential for achieving social justice for the simple reason that it is the only means available within the governmental arena.

The Policy Process

A critical analysis of the policy process highlights the social stratification of the society, the phases through which policy is formulated, and the organizational entities that have become instrumental in the decision-making process. This section will describe and chart these factors in order to clarify how social policy is created in the United States.

Social Stratification

A variety of **social stratification** models differentiate groups with influence from those lacking it. The most simple of these schemes consists of a dual stratification: for instance, capitalists and the proletariat, such as Marx used. A stratification familiar to Americans defines three parts: an upper class, a middle class, and a lower class. Placement of individuals in the appropriate class is usually made on the basis of income, education, and occupational status. This three-part stratification is limited in its capacity to explain very much about U.S. social welfare, however. If asked, most Americans identify themselves as middle class, even if by objective criteria they belong to another stratum. Further, the designation *lower class* is not particularly informative about the social conditions of a large portion of the population with which human service professionals are concerned.[11]

A more informative stratification consists of six social groups, which he differentiated according to wealth, internal solidarity, and control over the environment, as elaborated in Table 8.1.[12]

As this stratification model indicates, some groups—the wealthy and executives—are able to influence the environment, but other groups—the working/welfare poor and the underclass—have virtually no influence. This distinction has important implications for social welfare, because those who are of lower status tend to be the recipients of welfare benefits that are the product of a social policy process in which they do not participate. The way in which these various groups influence the social policy process will be discussed in greater detail in the following section.

With these clarifications in mind, the policy process can be divided into four stages: formulation, legislation, implementation, and evaluation. Although these terms are somewhat self-explanatory, during the decision-making process certain organizational entities exert their influence at different times, making the process an uneven one characterized by fits and starts. Organizations correspond to the stratification groups that figure prominently in their organizational activities and thereby in the policy process.

Formulation

Before the nineteenth century it would have been accurate to state that policy formulation in this country began with the legislative phase. Clearly, this was the situation envisioned by the drafters of the Constitution; but theirs was a largely agrarian society with comparatively little institutional specialization. With industrialization many complexities were injected into the society, and in time special institutions emerged to assist the legislature in evaluating social conditions and preparing policy options. Eventually, even constitutionally established bodies such as Congress lapsed into a reactive

Table 8.1

Social Stratification of the Population

Name of Group	Examples	Characteristics
The wealthy	Upper elites, the independently wealthy, large stockholders	Ownership of resources is the main source of power; control over goals is very high, but control over means is through executives
Executives	Top administrators in business, government, the military	Organizational solidarity facilitates effective policy implementation; some control over goals and a high degree of control over means
Professionals	Middle-level managers, technical experts, private practitioners, community leaders	Environment encourages limited solidarity; control over means is high, and goal setting can be influenced if collective action is undertaken
Organized workers	Semiskilled workers, civic and political clubs, social action organizations	Environment encourages solidarity, groups have some control over the means by which goals are realized
Working/welfare poor	Temporary and part-time workers earning minimum wage and who use welfare as a wage supplement	A subjugated position with with no control over the environment; frustration is shared and irrational, explosive behavior results
Underclass	Unemployables and illiterates; disabled substance abusers; itinerants, drifters migrant workers	A subjugated position with no control over the environment; a sense of failure coupled with mobility reduces social interaction and leads to retreatism

Source: Dexter C. Dunphy, *The Primary Group: A Handbook for Analysis and Field Research* (Englewood Cliffs, NJ: Prentice-Hall, 1972), pp. 42–44.

role, largely responsive to other entities that formulated policy.[13] Initially institutions of higher education provided technical intelligence to assist the legislative branch, and some still do. For example, the University of Wisconsin Institute for Research on Poverty provides analyses on important welfare policies.[14]

That legislators at the federal level, as well as those in the larger states, would rely on experts to assess social conditions and develop policy options is not surprising, given the fact that each legislator must attend to multiple committee and subcommittee assignments requiring expertise in particular matters, while at the same time contending with the general concerns of a large constituency. A typical day in the life of a legislator has been reconstructed by Charles Peters, a longtime Washington observer:

> The most striking feature of a congressman's life is its hectic jumble of votes, meetings, appointments, and visits from folks from back home who just drop by. From an 8 A.M. breakfast conference with a group of union leaders, a typical morning will take him to his office around 9, where the waiting room will be filled with people who want to see him. From 9 until 10:30 or so, he will try to give the impression that he is devoting his entire attention to a businessman from his state with a tax problem; to a delegation protesting their town's loss of air or rail service; to a constituent and his three children, who are in town for the day and want to say hello; and to a couple of staff members whose morale will collapse if they don't have five minutes alone to go over essential business with him. As he strives to project one-on-one sincerity to all these people, he is fielding phone calls at the rate of one every five minutes and checking a press release that has to get out in time to make the afternoon papers in his district.
>
> He leaves this madhouse to go to a committee meeting, accompanied by his legislative aide, who tries to brief him on the business before the committee meeting begins. The meeting started at 10, so he

> struggles to catch the thread of questioning, while a committee staff member whispers in his ear. And so the day continues.
>
> The typical day . . . usually ends around 11:30 P.M., as the congressman leaves an embassy party, at which he has been hustling as if it were a key precinct on election eve. He is too tired to talk about any but the most trivial matters, too tired usually to do anything but fall into bed and go to sleep.[15]

As a result of competing demands, legislators pay somewhat less attention to the policy process than their public image would have you believe, leaving much of the work to their staffs. Even then, public policy tends to get short shift. Because reelection is a primary concern for legislators, their staffs are frequently assigned to solve the relatively minor problems presented by constituents. In fact, placating unhappy constituents has become so prominent a concern that one legislative observer notes that constituency services—called "casework" by elected officials—have become "more important than issues" for representatives.[16]

Gradually, institutions have begun to specialize in providing the social intelligence necessary for policy formulation. These policy institutes, sometimes called think tanks, now wield substantial influence in the social policy process. Not unlike prestigious colleges, think tanks maintain multidisciplinary staffs of scholars who prepare position papers on a range of social issues. With multimillion-dollar budgets and connections with national and state capitals, think tanks are well positioned to shape social policy. Generally, financial support for these institutes comes from wealthy individuals and corporations with particular ideological inclinations that are evidenced by the types of think tanks they support. Several prominent policy institutes are located on the ideological continuum in Figure 8.2.

Within policy institutes, prominent scholars, usually identified as senior fellows, hold endowed chairs, having often served in cabinet-level positions within the executive branch. For example, when a Republican administration comes into power, large numbers of senior fellows from conservative policy institutes assume cabinet appointments; their Democratic counterparts return to liberal institutes, where senior chairs await them. For junior staffers, an appointment in a think tank can provide invaluable experience in how the governmental policy process actually works. Despite their influence in public policy, however, it is important to recognize that think tanks are private, nongovernmental institutions.

Through much of the twentieth century, a first generation of largely liberal policy institutes, such as the Brookings Institution, contributed to the formulation of governmental welfare policy. Their role was essentially reactive, in that they provided technical expertise to legislators and governmental agencies upon request. By the mid-1970s, however, a second generation of conservative policy institutes, such as the American Enterprise Institute and the Heritage Foundation, moved aggressively forward to shape a public philosophy that was more consistent with their own values. The elections of Ronald Reagan and George H. W. Bush did much to further the influence of these organizations, and the work of scholars from these policy institutes became important to the implementation and continuation of the "Reagan revolution."[17] A third generation of policy institutes emerged later to promote programs for the poor. The Children's Defense Fund and the Center on Budget and Policy Priorities endeavor to reassert the needs of the disadvantaged in social welfare policy.[18] The election of Bill Clinton to the presidency in 1992 brought to the forefront the Progressive Policy Institute, a think tank responsible for much of the

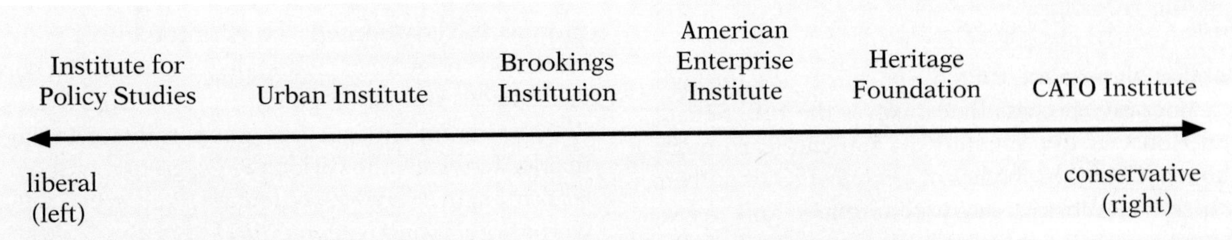

Figure 8.2

Place on the Ideological Continuum of Six Policy Institutes

policy research Clinton used during the campaign, and later influential in establishing domestic policy. When George W. Bush used conservative policy institutes to move public policy further to the right, progressive groups responded by establishing the Center for American Progress, an avowedly liberal organization. Unlike the more ideologically oriented think tanks, the New America Foundation has established itself as a policy institute with a more bipartisan agenda. Most recently, policyAmerica was established as an Internet-based think tank committed to disseminating innovations in social policy.

Legislation

The legislative phase involves two primary groups: the legislature and special interest groups that are subclassified as lobbies and **political action committees (PACs).** Much public policy work is conducted by legislators who are appointed to committees and subcommittees on the basis of their particular interests. An important and often unappreciated component of the legislative phase is the role played by the staffs of committees and subcommittees. Former legislative staffers are definitive experts in the subject area of a committee and are prized as lobbyists for special interest groups.[19] As a result of the increasing complexity of the policy process, the number of legislative staff has multiplied. In the late 1980s, 24,000 staff members served Congress, more than double the number in the late 1970s.[20] Committees are the loci of testimony on issues, and legislative hearings provide an opportunity for the official and sometimes the only input from the public on some matters. Accordingly, representatives of advocacy groups make it a point to testify before certain committees in order to ensure that their views are heard. At the federal level, the primary committees dealing with social welfare in 2000 are the following:[21]

Senate

Finance Committee. Subcommittees: Medicaid and Health Care for Low-Income Families; Medicare, Long-Term Care, and Health Insurance; Social Security and Family Policy

Agriculture. Subcommittee: Research, Nutrition, and General Legislation

Appropriations. Subcommittee: Labor, Health and Human Services, Education

Labor and Human Resources. Subcommittees: Aging; Children and Families; Disability Policy

Special Aging

House of Representatives

Ways and Means. Subcommittees: Health; Human Resources; Social Security

Economic and Educational Opportunities. Subcommittees: Early Childhood, Youth, and Families; Employer/Employee Relations; Postsecondary Education, Training, and Lifelong Learning; Workforce Protections

Appropriations. Subcommittee: Labor, Health and Human Services, and Education

The procedure by which an idea becomes legislation was described earlier, in the discussion on technical aspects of the policy process. Throughout the process, representatives of special interests

Spotlight 8.1

The Policy Process

Public policy in the United States is made through a deliberative process that involves the U.S. Senate and House of Representatives. You can learn more about each of these bodies of elected officials at their respective websites: **www.senate.gov** and **www.house.gov.** For a detailed explanation of the legislative process and how laws are made, go to **http://thomas.loc.gov/home/lawsmade.toc.html.** Political action committees (PACs) play an influential part in decisions on public policy. In the United States, PACs represent almost every group or interest imaginable. To review the various PACs, go to the Google search engine (**www.google.com**) and type in the words *political action committee.*

attempt to shape any given proposal so that it is more congruent with priorities of their members. Special interests can be classified according to the nature of their activities: Before elections, interest groups can influence the composition of legislatures by establishing PACs; in between elections, interests can exert pressure strategically through lobbying. As special interests learned to skirt federal campaign regulations, increasing amounts of "soft money" (non-regulated donations) influenced election activity.[22] As Table 8.2 indicates, during the past five years substantial funds have been expended in order to influence elections for the purpose of shaping public policy. Contributions are made to political parties and candidates who take positions that are congruent with a donor's interests. As a result larger contributors tend to prefer one political party over another by channeling contributions through political action committees (PACs), as evident in Table 8.3 on page 216. For all the money thrown into political campaigns, the consequences are remarkably static, reinforcing the status quo. In 2002, 98 percent of incumbents of the House and 86 of the Senate, were reelected.[23]

While the focus of campaign contributions is often on national campaigns, donors show considerable interest in state elections, particularly in the larger states, as evident in Table 8.4 on page 216.

In addition to contributions that are monitored by the Federal Election Commission, an increasing volume of "soft money," contributions that were not regulated flooded into campaigns during the 1990s. For example, "soft money" contributions to the major political parties more than quadrupled from $79.1 million in 1991–92 to $220.7 million in 1997–98[24] to $450 million in 2000.[25] According to Common Cause, for 1999 "soft money" contributions by business eclipsed those of labor by a factor of 10.[26] For the 2000 election year the Democratic Party received $206.6 million in "soft money," an amount eclipsed by the Republicans who received $242.5 million.[27] Other patterns in the origins of "soft money" have been discernable. While contributions on the part of individuals are evenly split between the political parties, corporations and trade associations heavily favor Republicans over Democrats almost two-to-one. The top 20 soft money contributors are depicted in Table 8.5 on page 217. Two features of soft money donations contributed to the practice becoming controversial. First, donations were often of unknown origin, raising questions about the true origins of campaign contributions. Second, soft money was clearly partisan, often aiding one particular party of campaign exclusively.

Although the "soft money" controversy commanded the headlines during the 2000 election, the real money was in lobbying. Unlike campaign contributions which are regulated, lobbyists can shift major amounts of cash depending on their particular needs. As Table 8.6 on page 218 attests, vested interests expended significant amounts to influence germane issues; in 2001, Congress deliberated the future of Medicare and considered adding a drug benefit, reviewed telecommunications deregulation, debated tort reform, and considered increasing fuel mileage requirements for passenger cars, each of which generated lobbying activity.

Given such sums, influence of lobbying on Congress is evident. Lobbying allows industries to advocate for or defend against specific bills. Thus, anticipating the Medicare reforms of 2003, the health care and pharmaceutical industries pumped almost $300 million into lobbying activities.

Table 8.2

Top 10 Donors, 1989–2004

Donor	Amount
AFSCME*	$35,222,356
National Association of Realtors	$24,598,780
National Education Association	$23,730,094
Association of Trial Lawyers of America	$23,621,116
Communications Workers of America	$22,354,566
Service Employees International Union	$22,269,375
International Brotherhood of Electrical Wkrs.	$21,861,387
Carpenters & Joiners Union	$21,168,387
Teamsters Union	$21,089,131
American Medical Association	$20,841,986

*American Federation of State, County & Municipal Employees

Source: Center for Responsive Politics. Retrieved September 2004 from www.opensecrets.org. Used by permission.

Table 8.3

Top PAC Contributors, 2003–2004

PAC Name	Total Amount	Democrat %	Republican %
Nat'l Assoc. Realtors	$2,106,733	51	49
Nat'l Beer Wholesalers Assoc.	1,993,500	23	77
Int'l Assoc. Broth'd Electrical Wkrs.	1,735,400	93	4
Nat'l Assoc. Home Builders	1,698,200	35	65
Assoc. of Trial Lawyers of America	1,668,499	92	7
Laborers Union	1,630,750	86	14
United Parcel Service	1,592,160	25	75
Nat'l Auto Dealers Assoc.	1,547,100	28	72
SBC Communications	1,531,116	32	68
Wal-Mart Stores	1,484,000	20	80
Credit Union Nat'l Assoc.	1,473,898	42	58
Carpenters & Joiners Union	1,416,500	70	30
Service Employees International Union	1,411,500	89	10
Machinists/ Aerospace Wkrs. Union	1,400,000	99	0
United Auto Wkrs.	1,338,100	99	1
American Bankers Assoc.	1,246,663	36	64
American Hospital Assoc.	1,218,526	44	56
AFSCME*	1,203,998	98	2
Airline Pilots Assoc.	1,188,000	78	22
Teamsters Union	1,184,716	88	12

*American Federation of State, County & Municipal Employees

Source: Center for Responsive Politics. Retrieved September 2004 from www.opensecrets.org. Used by permission.

Table 8.4

Contributions: Top 10 States

State	Total	To Democrats	To Republicans
Florida	$71,234,497	$33,211,130	$38,023,367
California	64,770,980	45,159,501	19,611,479
New York	44,983,877	23,833,481	21,150,396
Michigan	37,123,106	18,464,219	18,658,887
Ohio	30,021,634	11,343,926	18,677,708
Illinois	27,644,250	13,450,422	14,193,828
Pennsylvania	26,457,029	16,639,449	9,817,580
Missouri	23,753,532	14,974,999	8,778,533
Washington	22,346,694	7,097,361	15,249,334
New Jersey	19,889,321	10,066,503	9,822,818

Source: Adapted from Center for Responsive Politics. Retrieved September 2004 from www.opensecrets.org.

Table 8.5

Top 20 Soft Money Contributors, 2000

Organization	Total	To Democrats	To Republicans
Saban Capital Group	$9,280,000	$9,280,000	—
Newsweb Corp	7,390,000	7,390,000	—
Shangri-La Entertainment	6,700,000	6,700,000	—
AFSCME	6,586,500	6,586,000	—
Service Employees International Union	4,862,739	4,821,117	41,622
Freddie Mac	4,023,115	1,687,500	2,335,615
Carpenters & Joiners Union	3,868,709	3,848,709	20,000
Communications Workers of America	3,748,000	3,748,000	—
American Federation of Teachers	3,467,000	3,457,000	10,000
Pharmaceutical Rsrch & Mfrs of America	3,402,287	133,000	3,269,287
Propel	3,288,786	3,288,786	—
AT&T	3,146,971	1,389,750	1,757,221
Texans for John Cronyn	3,100,000	—	3,100,000
Philip Morris	2,901,198	604,388	2,296,816
Microsoft Corp	2,691,244	800,343	1,890,401
Ameriquest Capital	2,655,000	1,655,000	1,000,000
Williams & Bailey	2,361,400	2,361,400	—
Laborers Union	2,300,000	2,295,000	5,000
Loral Space & Communications	2,255,250	2,255,250	—
American Financial Group	2,138,108	325,000	1,813,108

Source: Center for Responsive Politics. Retrieved September 2004 from www.opensecrets.org. Used by permission.

In national politics, the key to influence is choreographing the resources of PACs, soft money, and lobbyists to attain party objectives. By way of illustration, having won control of Congress as a result of the 1994 midterm elections, Republicans moved swiftly to divert the flow of PAC money from the Democratic Party. Leading the effort was Representative Dick Armey, house majority leader, who, in April 1995, sent a letter to Fortune 500 CEOs complaining that their contributions to such "liberal" charities as the American Cancer Society were contrary to Republican intentions in social reform. In order to clarify his intentions, Armey's staff let PAC contributors know that contributions to Republican ventures were expected and that those to Democrats would also be tallied. Special interests seeking access to the new Republican leadership should be zeroing in on their contributions to Democrats. In the annals of special interest politics, Armey's brazen tactics broke new ground: "By imposing an ideological test on givers they have introduced a new level of coercion," observed journalist Ken Auletta.[28] Yet Armey's strategy violated no laws, and the money rolled in. In the first eight months of 1995 the Republican Party received $60 million in contributions, up from just $36 million in 1993.[29]

During the presidency of George W. Bush, Armey teamed up with Grover Norquist, president of Americans for Tax Reform, to launch the "K Street Project." Frustrated that lobbyists were frequently wedded to liberal social programs and the interests that sustained them, Norquist proposed routinizing Armey's vetting strategy: if the lobbying industry expected access to Capitol Hill, it needed to hire Republicans. In short order, K Street complied: virtually all new hires by lobbying firms were card-carrying

Table 8.6

Lobbying, 2002

	Expenditures (millions)
Industry	
Health care	$264.00
Communications, technology	221.48
Finance, insurance	220.93
Energy, natural resources	159.42
Transportation	147.08
Business-retail,services	140.85
Miscellaneous	134.55
Manufacturing	76.23
Agriculture	67.94
Single-issue groups	65.85
Interest Group	
U.S. Chamber Inst. for Legal Reform	$22.30
U.S. Chamber of Commerce	19.26
American Medical Association	14.84
PhRMA	14.26
Philip Morris	14.04
General Electric	13.02
National Association of Realtors	12.92
Edison Electric Institute	12.05
Business Roundtable	11.88
Northrup Grumman	11.77

Source: Adapted from "Top Lobbyists," *Washington Post* (June 24, 2003), p. A19.

Republicans. In effect, the K Street Project cemented the relationship between conservative interests and Congress.

> Now the Republican Party is using its sway over both K Street and the wider business community to build a private-sector equivalent to Roosevelt's machine. It hands out government contracts to businesses that fill its coffers: look at the way the pharmaceutical industry should gain from the new prescription-drug benefit in Medicare. It provides its most loyal foot soldiers, from congressional aides to congressmen, with a pot of gold on K Street when they retire.[30]

Having secured control of the three branches of the federal government, Republicans viewed consolidation of their power as the next goal. Strategists from the Right speculated that this could be achieved by bankrolling campaigns, coordinating lobbying, and investing in conservative think tanks. Ultimately, the objective was an era of political dominance that would rival—and reverse—the legislative triumphs of the New Deal coalition that engineered the American welfare state.[31] With the election of George W. Bush, the prospect of permanent conservative dominance in social policy became a distinct possibility. "The right has out-organized, out-fought and out-thought liberal America over the past 40 years. And the left still shows no real sign of knowing how to fight back," noted two British journalists.

> In theory, liberals have more than enough brain and brown to match conservative America. The great liberal universities and foundations have infinitely more resources than the American Enterprise Institute and its allies. But the conservatives have always been more dogged. The Ford Foundation is as liberal as Heritage is conservative, but there is no doubt which is the more ruthless in its cause.[32]

Scrambling for purchase in domestic policy, a group of philanthropists established the Phoenix Group to encourage innovative thinking among Progressives. Tycoons George Soros and Peter Lewis "had come to view progressive politics as a market in need of entrepreneurship, served poorly by a giant monopoly—the Democratic Party—that is still doing business in an old, Rust Belt kind of way."[33] For Democrats, the 2004 election had come to symbolize more than a presidential campaign, but the very relevance of the party.

The massive amounts of soft money that flooded into campaign coffers, beyond oversight of the Federal Election Commission, prompted calls for campaign reform. Pulled from the brink of legislative oblivion on more than one occasion, the McCain-Feingold campaign finance reform act was signed into law in 2002. As if to defy its provisions, President Bush promptly hosted a fund-raising dinner that generated an astonishing $33 million.[34] Although the 2002 McCain-Feingold election reform act withstood a Supreme Court challenge, many skeptics anticipated that the 2004 campaign would only generate more imaginative ways to skirt campaign finance regulations. They were not disappointed. With contributions limited to $25,000, the Bush reelection campaign began acknowledging those who had bundled contributions: Pioneers raised $100,000, Rangers $200,000 and Super Rangers $300,000. Six months before the 2004 election, the Bush reelection campaign had raised a record-breaking $296.3 million through this strategy.[35] Following suit, Democrats designated those who raised $100,000 as Patriots and Trustees for contributions of $250,000.[36]

In order to evade campaign finance reform, Democratic and to a lesser extent Republican operatives quickly employed section 527 of the Internal Revenue Service code to establish committees that could receive unrestricted funds so long as they operated independently of specific campaigns, avoided endorsing specific candidates, and honored the prohibition of airing messages 30 days prior to a primary and 60 days prior to a general election.[37] By the summer of 2002, "527 committees" were actively soliciting contributions, the largest associated with liberal constituencies: since June 2000, the AFSCME Special Account reported $16.5 million, an abortion rights group funded by Jane Fonda, Pro-Choice Vote, claimed $12.7 million, and Emily's List raised $6.2 million. 527's associated with the major parties were, for a change, behind the curve: the New Democrat Network having raised $3.6 million, the Republican ARMPAC reported $400,000.[38] Two years later, liberal 527s had already spent $50 million of an anticipated $300 million to unseat Bush, while Republicans had only just established their primary tax-exempt issue organization, Progress for America.[39] Two months before the 2004 election, labor groups were exploiting the 527-option as a way to replace contributions outlawed by McCain-Feingold significantly more than business.[40] Six months before the election, Democrats had bested Republicans in 527 fundraising by a factor of three; but Republicans still enjoyed a significant advantage in total campaign contributions, outraising Democrats $557.6 million to $393.6 million.[41]

Compared to business, labor, and lobbyists, social advocacy groups bring few assets to bear on the political process. Limited by meager resources, social advocacy groups usually rely on volunteer lobbyists. In addition to NASW, there are several advocacy groups within social welfare that have been instrumental in advancing legislation to assist vulnerable populations—among them the American Public Human Service Association, the Child Welfare League of America, the National Association for the Advancement of Colored People, the National Urban League, the National Assembly of Voluntary Health and Welfare Associations, and the National Organization for Women. Of these advocacy groups only one, AARP, ranks among the top 100 lobbyists on Capitol Hill. Despite the number of welfare advocacy organizations and their successful record in evolving more comprehensive social legislation, changes in the policy process hamper their work. Increases in the number of governmental agencies as well as in their staffs make it difficult to track policy developments and changes in administrative procedures. Worse, the escalating cost of influencing social policy, evident in the number of paid lobbyists and in the contributions lavished by PACs, is simply beyond the means of welfare advocacy organizations. As one Democratic candidate for the Senate lamented, "only the well-heeled have PACs-not the poor, the unemployed, the minorities or even most consumers."[42] Compared to more affluent interests, human service professionals have little clout. In social work, the PAC that provides assistance to candidates is Political Action for Candidate Election, or PACE, "the political arm of the National Association of Social Workers." PACE uses a variety of tactics to "expand social workers' activity in politics," including voter registration, support for political campaigns, and analysis of incumbents' voting records.[43] For the 1999–2000 election cycle, PACE budgeted total contributions of $225,000 to $240,000 to candidates running for national office,[44] an amount that, though not insignificant to candidates who received assistance, pales in comparison to the amounts wielded by more influential PACs.

This is not to say that proponents of social justice have been ineffectual. Despite their disadvantageous status, welfare advocacy groups were able to mobilize grassroots support to beat back some of the more regressive proposals of the Reagan administration. In the early 1980s, for example, scholars from the conservative Cato Institute and the Heritage Foundation proposed cutting the Social Security program. They were trounced by an effective lobbying campaign mounted by the AARP under the leadership of the late Congressman Claude Pepper (who was then in his eighties). Unfortunately, other social welfare programs did not fare as well. At the same time that Social Security was spared budget cuts, social programs for the poor were reduced by significant margins. Among the newer advocacy organizations, the Children's Defense Fund (CDF) hoped to benefit significantly from the election of Bill Clinton; First Lady Hillary Rodham Clinton had been a former chair of its board of directors, and Clinton's Health and Human Services (HHS) secretary, Donna

Shalala, had succeeded Rodham Clinton at CDF. CDF did claim a substantial victory with incorporation of the Children's Initiative in the Clinton 1993 economic package, but in 1996 children's advocates were distraught when Clinton signed the PRWORA, which they thought was injurious to poor children. CDF fared no better under the administration of George W. Bush. In search of a label on which to hang its school reform initiative, the Bush White House apprehended CDF's comprehensive Leave No Child Behind initiative, and reworked it to become No Child Left Behind.

Implementation

The fact that a policy has been enacted does not necessarily mean it will be implemented. Often governmental policies fail to provide for adequate authority, personnel, or funding to accomplish their stated purposes. This has been a chronic problem for social welfare programs. It is also possible that a governmental policy initiative will not be enforced even after it has been established. Many local jurisdictions have correctional and child welfare institutions now operating under court supervision because judges have agreed with social advocates that these institutions are not in compliance with state or federal law.

Implementation, difficult enough in the normal course of events, is that much more difficult when the public is disaffected with governmental institutions. The episodic nature of public endorsement of governmental institutions has been studied extensively by Albert O. Hirschman. In *Shifting Involvements,* Hirschman investigated the relationship between "private interest and public action." According to Hirschman, public endorsement of governmental institutions is a fundamental problem for industrialized capitalist societies, which emphasize individual competitiveness while generating social and economic dislocations that require collective action. "Western societies," Hirschman observes, "appear to be condemned to long periods of privatization during which they live through an impoverished 'atrophy of public meanings,' followed by spasmodic outbursts of 'publicness' that are hardly likely to be constructive."[45] Disenchantment with governmental solutions to social problems makes public welfare programs vulnerable to their critics, leading to reductions in staff and fiscal support, often followed by an escalation in the social problem for which the social program was initially designed. Thus, the episodic nature of public support for programs designed to alleviate social problems further impedes effective implementation.

Evaluation

The expansion of governmental welfare policies has spawned a veritable industry in program evaluation. Stung by the abuses of the executive branch during Watergate and the Vietnam War, Congress established additional oversight agencies to review federal programs.[46] As a result, multiple units within the executive and legislative branches of government have the evaluation of programs as their primary mission. At the federal level, the most important of these include the Government Accountability Office (GAO), the Office of Management and Budget (OMB), the Congressional Budget Office (CBO), and the Congressional Research Service (CRS). State governments have similar units. In addition, departments have evaluation units that monitor program activities for which they are responsible. Finally, federal and state levels of government commonly contract with nongovernmental organizations for evaluations of specific programs. As a result, many universities provide important research services to government. The University of Wisconsin's Institute for Research on Poverty is distinguished for its research in social welfare. More recently, private consulting firms, such as the Manpower Demonstration Research Corporation, Abt Associates, Maximus, and Mathematica, have entered the field, often hiring former government officials and capitalizing on their connections in order to secure lucrative research contracts. Of course, any politicization of the research process is frowned upon, because it raises questions about the impartiality of the evaluation. Is a former government official willing to assess rigorously and impartially a program run by an agency in which he or she was employed in the past or would like to be employed in the future? Questions about the closeness between governmental agencies and research firms and the validity of evaluation studies have become so common that the consulting firms located near the expressway surrounding Washington, D.C., are often referred to as "the beltway bandits."

Whether conducted in-house or contracted out to universities or commercial firms, evaluation research has become a major industry, replete with its own vocabulary. Alice O'Connor recounted in her history of poverty studies that research had become a sub-sector of the welfare state:

> The technical jargon of recent decades has taken poverty knowledge to a level of abstraction and exclusivity that it had not known before. It is a language laced with acronyms that themselves speak of particular data sets, policies and analytic techniques (PSID, NLSY, TRIM, FAP, PBJI, EITC, and, albeit without a detectable sense of irony, Five Year Plans and a model known as the KGB). It also speaks of a self-contained system of reasoning that is largely devoid of political or historical context.[47]

The influence of evaluation research in social policy was sustained by the interaction of elite university social science departments which prepared researchers and liberal policy institutes which provided the setting for the application of their analyses. Annual conferences held by professional organizations such as the Association for a Public Policy Analysis and Management, featured young researchers displaying their virtuosity in command of mathematics and logic.

Investigations by program evaluation organizations can be characterized as applied (as opposed to "pure") research, the objective being to optimize program operations. As a result of this emphasis on the function of programs, evaluation studies frequently focus on waste, cost-effectiveness, and goal attainment. Owing to the contradictory objectives of many welfare policies, the constant readjustments in programs, and the limitations in the art of evaluation research, evaluations frequently conclude that any given program has mixed results. Rarely does a program evaluation provide a clear indication for future action. Often the results of a single program evaluation are used by both critics and defenders in their efforts to dismantle or to advance the program.

The very inconclusiveness of program evaluation contributes to the partisan use to which evaluation research can be put. It is not uncommon for decision makers to engage in statistical arguments that have a great influence on social welfare policy. Of recent "stat wars," several relate directly to social welfare. One example is the question whether underemployed and discouraged workers should be included in the unemployment rate. Currently, the Department of Labor defines as unemployed only those who are out of work and actively looking for jobs; and it considers part-time workers as employed. As a result, many African Americans, Hispanic Americans, young adults, and women are not considered unemployed, even though advocates for these groups contend that they are not fully employed. Liberals argue that including underemployed and discouraged workers in the unemployment rate would produce a more accurate measure of the employment experience of disadvantaged groups. Conservatives argue that the employment rate is not a good indicator of employment opportunity anyway, citing the millions of undocumented workers who come to the United States illegally every year to take menial jobs. Further, including underemployed and discouraged workers would increase the unemployment rate by as much as 50 percent and would prove unacceptably expensive, because extensions in the number of quarters for which workers are eligible for unemployment compensation are tied to the unemployment rate. Predictably, evaluations of employment programs vary considerably. Consultants have generated considerable data about the results of state and local welfare-to-work initiatives. Their studies evince a general theme: Although welfare caseloads have dropped as much as 50 percent, heads of households who have found work (1) tend to remain stuck in sub-poverty-level wages, but (2) lose benefits such as food stamps and Medicaid—even though they remain eligible—because of efforts at caseload reduction. Such research serves ideological purposes, of course. Conservatives trumpet the reduction in welfare dependency, and liberals worry about the fate of families who continue to be poor despite full-time work.

Marginalization If the governmental decision-making process is somewhat irregular and irrational, it is also unrepresentative. As Figure 8.3 illustrates, groups in the upper levels of the social stratification populate the institutions through which policy is made. In the case of welfare policy, welfare beneficiaries must adjust to rules established by other social groups. The primary players in the social policy game are executives and professionals. The wealthy are able to opt out, leaving its social obligations in the hands of executives. Groups lower on the social stratification scale have less and less influence on governmental policy. The interests of these groups are left largely in the hands of professionals who work through advocacy organizations. Thus, the lower socioeconomic groups' lack of influence in the social policy process is virtually built into governmental decision making. The term *non-decision making* has been coined to describe this phenomenon—the system's capacity to keep the interests of some groups off the decision-making agenda.[48] Marginalization has a long history in the United States; generations of African Americans and women were legally ex-

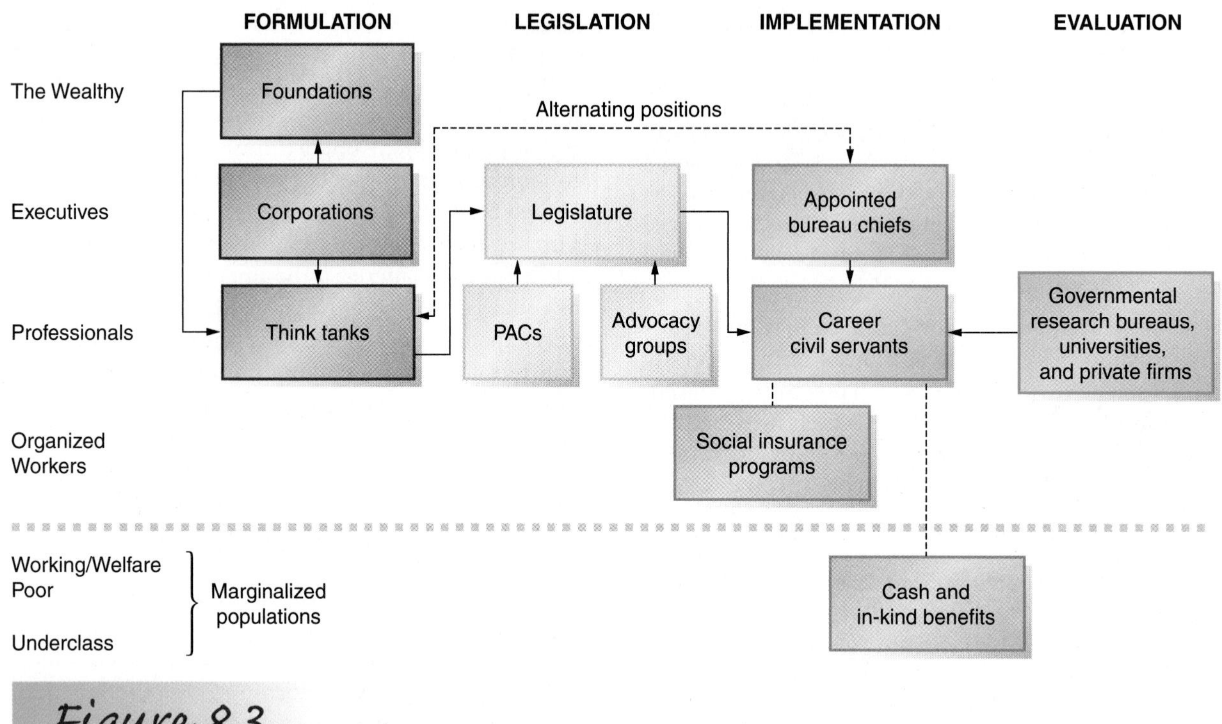

Figure 8.3

Stratification and the Public Policy Process

cluded from decision making prior to emancipation and suffrage.

Policymakers' attempts to increase the influence of disadvantaged groups in decision making have not been well received. A classic illustration of this occurred during the Great Society initiative, when poor people were to be assured of "maximum feasible participation" in the Community Action Program (CAP). This stipulation was interpreted to mean that one-third of the members of CAP boards of directors must be poor people—a seemingly reasonable idea—but the militancy of poor people in some cities at the time led to utter chaos in many CAPs. As a result of pressure from mayors and other officials, lawmakers rescinded this requirement in order to make CAPs more compliant.[49] Since then, the representation of lower socioeconomic groups in decision making has been limited, for all practical purposes, to an advisory capacity at best.

The governmental policy process also poses problems for administrators and practitioners. Policies frequently reflect assumptions about the human condition that may seem reasonable to the upper socioeconomic groups that make them but bear little resemblance to the reality of the lower socioeconomic groups that are supposed to be beneficiaries. For example, child support enforcement policy assumes that fathers of children on AFDC/TANF programs have the kind of regular, well-paying jobs that would allow them to meet the amounts of their court orders, whereas often their jobs are intermittent and low-wage. Consequently, support payments to children who are dependent on welfare have been relatively disappointing. In 1998, $14 billion in child support was collected through the Child Support Enforcement program, but most of this was for non-TANF families; only 20 percent of TANF benefits were recovered through child support enforcement.[50] An evaluation of Parents' Fair Share, a program designed to increase the child support paid by men whose dependents were on AFDC, resulted in reduced child support payments despite the multiple interventions incorporated in the program.[51] To cite another example, welfare-to-work programs assume that young women want to complete their education and gain meaningful employment—but their socialization often instructs them that school and work are irrelevant and that having a child may be the most meaningful thing they can do. For many years, AFDC/TANF has provided financial support to poor teenaged mothers, a benefit that many conservatives claim has actually induced girls to become pregnant. But an evaluation of New Chance, a teen pregnancy prevention program, resulted in outcomes that were contrary to the intent of the program: Young mothers enrolled in New Chance were more likely to become pregnant again and less likely to participate in the labor market than those in the control group.[52] In sum, the preliminary studies on child support and teen pregnancy suggest that the poor do not necessarily comply with the bourgeois assumptions that are implicit or explicit in social policy.

It is not surprising, then, that welfare programs are not well received by many of the people who depend on them. Instead of being grateful, beneficiaries are frequently resentful. In turn, upper-income taxpayers find this ingratitude offensive and are inclined to make programs more punitive. Ironically, beneficiaries of welfare programs tend to respond to punitive policies with indifference and defiance; because, for many of them, welfare programs have never been particularly helpful. The perception that welfare programs are only minimally helpful is occasionally validated when, under exceptional circumstances, someone from an upper socioeconomic group falls into the social safety net and suddenly appreciates the importance of welfare programs for daily survival.

Not all welfare programs are perceived in such a negative light. Generally, programs that benefit persons who are solidly in the working class fare better. The social insurance programs, such as Social Security, Unemployment Compensation, and Medicare, are usually regarded more highly by beneficiaries. Of course, the insurance programs require people to first pay into the program in order to claim benefits later, so they are designed to be different from the means-tested programs intended for the poor.

A particular consequence of governmental policy making falls on the shoulders of welfare professionals. "Workers on the front lines of the welfare state find themselves in a corrupted world of service," wrote Michael Lipsky in his award-winning *Street-Level Bureaucracy.* According to Lipsky, "Workers find that the best way to keep demand within manageable proportions is to deliver a consistently inaccessible or inferior product."[53] In response to the irrelevance often characteristic of governmental welfare policies, personnel in public welfare offices consequently deny benefits to people who are eligible for them, a process labeled **bureaucratic disentitlement.**[54] It should come as no surprise, then, that public welfare programs mandated by governmental policy have acquired an undesirable reputation within the professional community. The executive director of the California chapter of NASW candidly stated that "Public social services are being abandoned by M.S.W. social workers. It seems to be employment of last resort."[55] Another veteran observer was even more graphic: "To work in a public agency today is to work in a bureaucratic hell."[56] Within the context of public welfare, it is not surprising to find that burnout has become pervasive among welfare professionals. The inadequacy of public welfare policies for both beneficiaries and professionals is an unfortunate consequence of the governmental policy process as it is currently structured.

Making the public policy process more representative is a primary concern of welfare advocates. Since the Civil Rights movement, African Americans and the poor have recognized the power of the ballot, and voter registration has become an important strategy for advancing the influence of these groups. The registration of Hispanic Americans in the Southwest has been the mission of the Southwest Voter Research Institute, founded by the late Willie Velasquez. Under the visionary leadership of Velasquez, Latino voter registration grew steadily and was reflected in an increase in the number of Chicano elected officials. Fifteen years of voter registration campaigning by the institute contributed to a doubling of the number of Hispanic elected officials in the Southwest by the late 1980s.[57] The most visible example of the political empowerment of people usually excluded from the decision-making process was Jesse Jackson's 1988 campaign to be the presidential nominee of the Democratic Party. Expanding on the grassroots political base built during his 1984 bid for the nomination, Jackson's 1988 Rainbow Coalition demonstrated the support he commanded from a wide spectrum of disenfranchised Americans. Thus, mobilization of the working and welfare poor, as Velasquez and Jackson have shown, can make the policy process more representative.

As the attempts to increase the registration of minority voters suggest, reengaging Americans in the political process is a difficult undertaking. In national elections, only about half of eligible U.S. voters exercise the franchise, the lowest turnout among industrialized nations. Explanations of voter apathy are multiple. The Republican and Democratic parties have lost the allegiance of increasing numbers of voters who identify themselves as independents. Between 1987 and 2004 the number of Democratic voters declined from 52 percent to 44 percent, while Republican voters held constant at about 33 percent; yet, the unaffiliated voters increased from 17 percent to 24 percent. Although both Democratic and Republican parties boasted of modest growth during the period—4.8 percent and 8.0 percent—respectively, they were eclipsed by independent voters who grew 11.0 percent.[58] Within the voting population, more affluent voters are more than twice as likely to exercise their franchise as are those who are poor: In 1996, 65.7 percent of voters with incomes above $50,000 voted in the presidential election, versus only 28.6 percent of those with incomes less than $10,000.[59] To a troubling degree, younger voters are disengaged from the political process, a circumstance that will be exacerbated by the aging of the Baby Boomers. In 2002, voters over 65 outnumbered voters under 30 by a factor of two; in 2022, that is expected to increase to a factor of four.[60] A survey conducted by the Pew Research Center for the People and the Press revealed that substantial majorities of respondents agreed with such statements as "government is inefficient and wasteful," "politicians lose touch pretty quickly," and "government controls too much of daily life."[61] Such perceptions bode ill for the democratic process, of course. Some 30 million prospective voters are inactive, a group made up disproportionately of minorities and the poor.[62] Increasing the involvement of apathetic voters not only would make inroads against marginalization, but also would make public social programs more responsive to their circumstances.

Social Workers and Social Reform

As a result of marginalization and voter apathy, advocates of social justice are instrumental in correcting for a skewed political process. Throughout the history of U.S. social welfare, advocates of care for vulnerable populations have been shaping social policies. If we look beneath the surface of policy statements, we find a rich and often exciting account of the skirmishes fought by advocates for social justice. In some respects, social policy innovations can be looked upon as individual and collective biography written in official language. In an age of mass populations that are often manipulated by private and public megastructures, it is easy to forget how powerful some individuals have been in shaping social welfare policy in the United States. Many of these leaders are known because they achieved national prominence; yet some of the more heroic acts to advance social justice were performed by individuals whose names are not widely recognized. As just one example, not to be forgotten in this regard is Michael Schwerner, a social worker who was murdered while working in a voter registration drive in the South during the Civil Rights movement.[63]

Early social welfare leaders emerged during the **Progressive Movement,** a period when educated and socially conscious men and women sought to create structures that would advance social justice in the United States. The settlement house gained a reputation as the locus for reform activity, leading one historian to conclude that "settlement workers during the Progressive Era were probably more committed to political action than any other group of welfare workers before or since."[64] From this group Jane Addams quickly surfaced as a leader of national prominence. Through her settlement home, Hull House, she fought not only for improvements in care for slum dwellers in inner-city Chicago, but also for international peace. For Jane Addams, social work was social reform. Instead of focusing solely on restoration and rehabilitation, Addams claimed that there was a superior role for the profession: "It must decide whether it is to remain behind in the area of caring for the victimized," she argued, "or whether to press ahead into the dangerous area of conflict where the struggle must be pressed to bring to pass an order of society with few victims."[65] In that struggle Addams served nobly, receiving an honorary degree from Yale University and serving as president of the Women's International League for Peace and Freedom. In 1931, Jane Addams was awarded the Nobel Peace Prize, a suitable distinction for a social worker who once had herself appointed a garbage collector in order to improve sanitation in the slums around Hull House.

Hull House proved a remarkable institution, and among its residents were women who made lasting and important contributions to the New Deal:

> Edith Abbott, president of the National Conference of Social Welfare, dean of the University of Chicago School of Social Service Administration, and participant in the drafting of the Social Security Act of 1935

> Grace Abbott, organizer of the first White House Conference on Children, director of the U.S. Children's

Bureau, and participant in the construction of the Social Security Act

Julia Lathrop, developer of the first juvenile court and of the first child mental health clinic in the United States, and the first director of the U.S. Children's Bureau

Florence Kelley, director of the National Consumer League, cofounder of the U.S. Children's Bureau, and a member of the National Child Labor Committee

Frances Perkins, director of the New York Council of Organizations for War Services, director of the Council on Immigrant Education, and the first Secretary of Labor[66]

The activity around Hull House was never limited to those with a narrow view of reform. A regular participant in the settlement was John Dewey, in his time "America's most influential philosopher, educator, as well as one of the most outspoken champions of social reform."[67] As a result, pragmatism, America's most distinctive contribution to philosophy, was suffused with the promise of social reform.

Settlement experiences crystallized the motivations of other reformers as well. Harry Hopkins, primary architect of the New Deal and of the social programs that made up the Social Security Act, had resided in New York's Christadora House Settlement. Ida Bell Wells-Barnett led the Negro Fellowship League to establish a settlement house for African Americans in Chicago. Lillian Wald, with Florence Kelley a cofounder of the U.S. Children's Bureau, had earlier established New York's Henry Street Settlement, an institution that was to achieve distinction within the African American community. Under the guidance of Mary White Ovington, a social worker, the first meetings of the National Association for the Advancement of Colored People were held at the Henry Street Settlement.[68]

Early social welfare leaders championed causes that improved the conditions of children and immigrants, but they did not always forsake African Americans. When it became apparent that Booker T. Washington's program of "industrial education" was unable to contend effectively with ubiquitous racial discrimination, social reformers Jane Addams, Ida Bell Wells-Barnett, and John Dewey joined W.E.B. Du Bois in the Niagara Movement. The early organizations spawned by the Niagara Movement were later consolidated into the National Urban League, with George Edmund Haynes, a social worker, as one of its co-directors. In 1910 Haynes had been the first African American to graduate from the New York School of Philanthropy, so it is not surprising that an important Urban League program was the provision of fellowships for African Americans to the school.[69] Later, during the height of the Civil Rights movement, the National Urban League, under the direction of social worker Whitney Young Jr., collaborated in organizing the August 28, 1963, march on Washington, memorialized by the ringing words of Martin Luther King Jr., "I have a dream!"[70]

If the New Deal bore the imprint of social workers, the Great Society was similarly marked some 30 years later. Significantly, one leader of the War on Poverty was Wilbur Cohen, a social worker who had been the first employee of the Social Security Board created in 1935. Eventually Cohen was to be credited with some 65 innovations in social welfare policy, but his crowning achievement was the passage of the Medicare and Medicaid acts in 1965. The secretary of Health, Education, and Welfare during the Johnson administration, Cohen was arguably the nation's most decorated social worker, receiving 18 honorary degrees from U.S. universities.[71]

Social Work and Advocacy Organizations

The formulation of social welfare policy in the United States, as this chapter has shown, is a complicated and often arduous process. Much of this can be attributed to the nature of U.S. culture: to the competing interests inherent in a pluralistic society; to the multiple systems of government that make social policy at the same time; to public and private bureaucracies that serve large numbers of consumers; to economic and technological developments that lead to specialization. Under these circumstances, changing social welfare policy to improve the circumstances of disadvantaged groups can be a daunting task. Regrettably, few human service professionals consider social policy advocacy an enterprise worthy of undertaking. Most social workers prefer direct service activity, in which they have little opportunity for direct involvement in social policy. Some social workers do attain important positions in federal and state human service bureaucracies and are close to the policy process. Unfortunately, however, these managers are often administering welfare policies that have been made by legislatures and that do not necessarily represent either clients or human service professionals. Perhaps most troubling, the involvement of social workers in the formulation of social policy has been diminishing in recent years. In a provocative statement, June Hopps, dean of the Boston College School of Social Work and former editor in chief of Social Work, acknowledged that "Since the late 1960s and early 1970s, the [social work] profession has experienced a dramatic loss of influence in the arenas where policy is shaped and administered."[72] That this should occur is not only a reversal of the profession's Progressive Era legacy, but also an abnegation of a rapidly expanding service sector. Paradoxically, opportunities to enter the upper levels of the federal civil service have become available through the Presidential Management Fellows program, but social work has not found a way to systematically exploit these.

If one indicator of good social policy is the correspondence between the policy and the social reality of its intended beneficiaries, then social welfare policy should be enhanced by the input of social workers. However, social workers have left much of the decision making about social welfare to professionals from other disciplines. "There are increasing numbers of non-social workers, including psychologists and urban planners," observed Eleanor Brilliant, "taking what might have been social work jobs in service delivery and policy analysis."[73] The consequences of welfare professionals' opting to leave social policy in the hands of others are important. For direct service workers, these consequences can mean having to apply eligibility standards or procedures that, although logical in some respects, make little sense in the social context of many clients. For the public, they may mean a gradual disenchantment with social programs that do not seem to work. The causes of the retrenchment affecting social programs since the late 1970s are complex, of course; but it is worth noting that public dissatisfaction with social programs has escalated as social welfare professionals have retreated from active involvement in public policy.

The rebuilding of a role for social workers in social policy will take concerted effort. Individual leadership is a necessary, but no longer sufficient, precondition for this objective. Essential to the undertaking will be social workers' ability to understand and manipulate complex organizations and programs. In fact, this skill may be the most critical for welfare professionals to acquire if they are to advance social justice, for it addresses a question central to the postindustrial era. During the Industrial Revolution, Karl Marx suggested that the central question was "Who controls the means of production?" A mature industrial order and the expansion of civil bureaucracy led Max Weber to ask, "Who controls the means of administration?" The evolution of a postindustrial order, in which primary economic activity occurs in a service sector dependent on processed information, raises a new question: "Who controls the means of analysis?" If social workers are to shape social policy as effectively as they have in the past, they will have to learn to control the means of analysis. This means conducting research on social problems, surveying public opinion about welfare programs, analyzing existing social policy for opportunities to enhance welfare provision, and winning elected office in order to make decisions about proposed social welfare policies.

Advocacy Organizations and the New Policy Institutes

Policy analysis organizations have been instrumental in shaping social policy from as early as the New Deal period. Subsequently, policy institutes have had liberal or conservative labels ascribed to them, with the liberal organizations achieving dominance up until the late 1970s—when, as we have seen, conservative institutes began gaining popularity. The failure of government social programs to expand during the Carter presidency, followed by the profoundly negative impact of the Reagan years and the first Bush administration, led social reformers to look to traditional policy institutes such as the Brookings Institution and the Urban Institute for leadership. But the inability of these organizations to shape the debate on U.S. social welfare policy compelled increasingly impatient reformers to establish a new group of policy analysis organizations.

Children's Defense Fund Begun by Marian Wright Edelman in 1974, the Children's Defense Fund (CDF) sought to address the health, income, and educational needs of the nation's children.[74] By the mid-1980s CDF had become a major voice in children's policy and had successfully advocated programs at the federal and state levels. In 1984 CDF helped pass the Child Health Assurance Program, which expanded Medicaid eligibility to poor women and children. It also advocated for the 1998 Children's Health Insurance Program (CHIP). CDF is noted for its educational publications, particularly for eye-catching posters depicting injustices inflicted on poor, minority children. Its annual report, the State of America's Children, is an authoritative compendium of issues and programs concerning children.

The Center on Budget and Policy Priorities Established in 1981 by Robert Greenstein, former administrator of the Food and Nutrition Service in the Agriculture Department, CBPP has fought to defend social programs for low-income people against budget cuts. With a modest staff, CBPP distributes its analyses to congressional staffs, the media, and grassroots organizations. Despite its small size, CBPP provided much of the program analysis to refute arguments presented by officials of the Reagan administration in their efforts to cut means-tested social programs. Significantly, CBPP and CDF have developed a close working relationship. CBPP regularly provides data to CDF on the health and income status of children, and Greenstein is a regular contributor to CDF reports.[75]

Economic Policy Institute In 1986 Jeff Faux convinced labor-oriented liberals to establish a policy institute to represent "the perspective of working families and the poor."[76] During the subsequent decade EPI expanded rapidly and published reports depicting a widening chasm between the economic circumstances of working families and the affluent. Notable among EPI publications is its annual volume *The State of Working America,* which contains current data on income, taxes, wages, wealth, and poverty.

Institute for Women's Policy Research Created in 1987 by Heidi Hartmann, a social program researcher and director of the Women's Studies Program at Rutgers University, IWPR quickly attained a respected position in Washington, D.C. The IWPR research and advocacy agenda relating to women is extensive, including retirement, family leave, health insurance, welfare reform, and pay equity. In 1994 Hartmann received a MacArthur "genius" fellowship award for her advocacy of gender equity.

New America Foundation In 1999, Ted Halstead launched the New America Foundation in order to develop policy options congruent with the information age. With Michael Lind, Halstead wrote *The Radical Center,* a book that outlined the need for an ideological orientation that was post-liberal as well as post-conservative.[77]

policyAmerica In 2002, policyAmerica was established by David Stoesz, Howard Karger, and Jack Hansan as an Internet-based think tank designed to disseminate innovations in social policy. In addition to posting developments on it website, policyAmerica organized a well-attended conference on Bootstrap Capitalism: Financial Services in Low-Income Communities in 2004.

Center for American Progress Smarting from reversals attributed to conservative think tanks, John Podesta convinced other liberals to establish the Center for American Progress in 2003. Drawing on an annual budget of $10 million and many policy experts who had served in the Clinton administration, the Center for American Progress is well-positioned to compete with policy institutes from the Right.[78]

Political Practice

The capacity of social workers to reassert their role in social welfare policy depends on the willingness of individuals to consider public office as a setting for social work practice. Although many welfare pioneers began their careers advocating for social welfare policy and then assumed administrative positions managing social programs, others used elected office to advance social reform. The first woman elected to the House of Representatives was Jeannette Rankin, who won a seat in 1916 running as a Republican in Montana. As a social worker who had studied under Frances Perkins, Rankin voted for early social welfare legislation and against military expansion. More recently, social workers in **political practice** have included Maryann Mahaffey, a member of the Detroit City Council, and Ruth Messinger, a former member of the New York City Council.

By 2004, five social workers had attained national office:

- Edolphus "Ed" Towns received his Master of Social Work degree in 1973. Elected as a Democratic state committeeman and then as the first African American deputy borough president in Brooklyn's history, Towns was elected in 1982, with 90 percent of the vote, to serve in Congress as the representative of the eleventh Congressional District of New York. Towns's work on congressional committees overseeing government operations, public works, and narcotics directly addresses the primary concerns of his inner-city constituents.[79]

Edolphus Towns

- Barbara Mikulski received her M.S.W. degree in 1965 and then served on the Baltimore City Council and in the U.S. House of Representatives. In 1986 Mikulski became the first Democratic woman to be elected to the U.S. Senate in her own right. Through appointments to the powerful Appropriations and Labor and Human Resources Committees, Mikulski is well positioned to advocate programs in health and social services.[80]

Barbara Mikulski

- Debbie Stabenow was awarded her M.S.W. from Michigan State University, after which she was elected to the Ingham County Commission, the Michigan House, and the Michigan Senate. In 1996 Stabenow ran to represent the 8th Congressional District of Michigan on a platform opposing the extremes of the Republican Congress elected in 1994. Having won election to the House of Representatives, in 1999 Stabenow challenged an incumbent to become the second social worker to be elected to the U.S. Senate in her own right.

- Barbara Lee was elected in 1998 to fill the House seat of Ron Dellums, a social worker on whose staff she had served. Lee received her M.S.W. from the University of California, Berkeley, and established a community mental health center while completing her graduate studies. Subsequently she was elected to the California State Senate. Congresswoman Lee now serves on the House Committee on Banking and Financial Services and on the House Committee on International Relations, the Congressional Progressive Caucus, the Congressional Black Caucus, and the Congressional Women's Caucus.

Debbie Stabenow

Barbara Lee

- In 2000, Susan Davis defeated an incumbent to represent California's 49th Congressional District. Davis received her graduate degree in social services from the University of North Carolina in 1968; she subsequently moved to San Diego, where she chaired the school board. As a new member of Congress, Davis attained a coveted seat on the Armed Services Committee. Among her primary concerns are education and campaign finance reform.

Susan Davis

Conclusion

Perhaps the best indicator of social work's potential future influence on social policy appears at the local level. For example, social workers have lobbied successfully on behalf of nonprofit agencies facing threats to their tax-exempt status,[81] encouraged students to engage in election campaigns and to become more knowledgeable about politics,[82] and managed a campaign for the election of a state senator.[83] In each of these instances, social workers were gaining the kind of experience that is essential to political involvement at higher levels. By 2000 such activity was paying off: More than 200 social workers had been elected to state, county, municipal, and judicial offices. In response to increasing political activity at the state level, social work professor Robert Schneider established the collaborative organization of Influencing State Policy in order to empower human service professionals.[84]

Social workers disinclined to engage in high-visibility activities such as campaigning for public office could make their imprint on politics through legislators' "constituent services." Writing of new developments in Congress, Pulitzer Prize–winning journalist Hedrick Smith observed that members of Congress are increasingly relying on constituent services in place of pork barrel projects as domestic expenditures dry up. Using a term familiar to most social workers, politicians call constituent services "casework"; that is, "having your staff track down missing Social Security checks, inquire about sons and husbands in the armed services, help veterans get medical care, pursue applications for small-business loans."[85] The importance of political "casework" has been noted by political scientists, who attribute up to 5 percent of the vote to such activities, a significant amount in close elections. David Himes of the National Republican Congressional Committee claimed that "our surveys have shown that constituency service, especially in the House, is more important than issues."[86]

The cultivation of practice skills in the political arena at the local level offers perhaps the most promising way for social workers to regain influence in social welfare policy. Such activity can be undertaken by virtually any professional interested in the opportunity. On a volunteer basis, social workers would find few politicians who would turn down their professional assistance in the provision of constituent services. With experience, enterprising social workers might find that political practice could be remunerative, providing that they possessed skills needed by elected officials—such as conducting surveys, maintaining data banks of contributors, organizing public meetings, and keeping current on legislation important to constituents. From another perspective, however, the prospect of political practice should be taken seriously indeed. If social workers are sincere about making essential resources available to their clients—a responsibility stated in the NASW Code of Ethics—then some form of political practice is a professional obligation. "To do less," noted Maryann Mahaffey, "to avoid the political action necessary to provide these resources, is to fail to live up to the profession's code of ethical practice."[87]

Discussion Questions

1. Clicking on "For Students" on the policyAmerica website, select a social welfare policy and identify its primary components. Which elected members of Congress were cosponsors of the legislation? What committees were instrumental in its passage? Which special interests benefited from its passage?
2. Clicking on "Advocacy" on the policyAmerica website, identify your Representative and Senators. E-mail them about an issue that is important to you. Do any of your members of Congress have any important health and human service committee assignments? Do your representatives have committee assignments that could make them influential on issues important to you? Do your representatives have position statements available to constituents about specific social programs?
3. Politicians elected to your state legislature have responsibilities similar to members of Congress. Identify your state representatives. Do they have assignments on health and human service committees? Do they have position statements they could send to you on health and human service issues?
4. Select a health and human service bill of interest to you and follow it your state legislature. Which committees and interest groups supported or fought the proposed legislation? How was the bill changed to make it more acceptable to special interests? Have local interests, such as a major newspaper, endorsed or objected to the proposed legislation? Why?
5. Does your state chapter of the National Association of Social Workers make legislation a high priority for the professional community? What are the legislative goals of the state NASW chapter? How are those goals reflected in the resources allocated? How would you prioritize health and human services in your community?
6. If marginalization leaves many clients of social programs impotent in the public policy process, how could these people be made more influential? How could the local professional community assist in empowering beneficiaries of social programs? What could you do?
7. Identify social workers who serve in local elected offices. What led them to pursue elective office? What are their future political plans? Could you provide constituent services for these persons or help with their reelection?

Notes

1. U.S. Congress, *U.S. Congress Handbook 1992* (McLean, VA: Barbara Pullen, 1992), p. 184.
2. *Robert's Rules of Order* is available from several publishers.
3. The latest annual edition of *Overview of Entitlement Programs* can be obtained through the Government Printing Office in Washington, DC.
4. Charles Lindblom and David Braybrooke, *Strategy of Decision* (New York: Free Press, 1970).
5. Amitai Etzioni, *The Active Society* (New York: Free Press, 1968), pp. 282–288.
6. For a description of these forms of rationality, see Robert Alford, "Health Care Politics," *Politics and Society* 2 (Winter 1972), pp. 127–164.
7. Neil Gilbert and Harry Specht, *Dimensions of Social Welfare Policy* (Englewood Cliffs, NJ: Prentice-Hall, 1986), pp. 206–210.
8. "Nuking Employee Benefits," *Wall Street Journal* (August 29, 1988), p. 16.
9. For example, see Harry Hatry, *A Review of Private Approaches for Delivery of Public Services* (Washington, DC: Urban Institute, 1983).
10. David Stoesz, *A Poverty of Imagination* (Madison, WI: University of Wisconsin Press, 2000).
11. Even Marx, who used a two-part classification, conceded the existence of a "lumpen-proletariat," although he did little to develop the concept.
12. Dexter Dunphy, *The Primary Group* (New York: Appleton-Century-Crofts, 1972), pp. 42–44.
13. Charles Peters, *How Washington Really Works,* rev. ed. (Reading, MA: Addison-Wesley, 1983), p. 112.
14. See, for example, Sheldon Danziger and Daniel Weinberg, *Fighting Poverty* (Cambridge, MA: Harvard University Press, 1986).
15. Peters, *How Washington Really Works,* pp. 101–102, 116.
16. Hedrick Smith, *The Power Game: How Washington Works* (New York: Random House, 1988), p. 152.
17. David Stoesz, "Policy Gambit: Conservative Think Tanks Take On the Welfare State," *Journal of Sociology and Social Welfare* 16 (1989), pp. 8–16.
18. David Stoesz, "The New Welfare Policy Institutes." Unpublished manuscript, School of Social Work, San Diego State University, 1988.
19. Peters, *How Washington Really Works,* p. 114.
20. Smith, *The Power Game,* p. 24.
21. *Congress at Your Fingertips* (McLean, VA: Capitol Advantage, 1996).
22. First established in 1944, PACs are political organizations that are regulated by federal law: individual candidate contributions are limited to $5,000 per election, contributions to other PACs are restricted to $5,000 annually, and funding of national party committees cannot exceed $15,000 annually. Because of these restrictions, "soft money"—contributions outside the prohibitions of the Federal Election Campaign Act—have become more prominent in federal elections.
23. Charles Noble, *The Collapse of Liberalism* (Lanham, MD: Rowman & Littlefield, 2004), p. 36.
24. "Overall Campaign Finance Statistics," (Washington, D.C.: Common Cause, June, 11, 1999).
25. "The Power of 'Soft Money,'" *Washington Post* (February 13, 2002), p. A25.
26. Ruth Marcus and Mike Allen, "Democrats' Donations from Labor Up Sharply," *Washington Post* (July 17, 2000), p. A1.
27. "The Power of Soft Money," p. A25.
28. Ken Auletta, "Pay Per Views," *New Yorker* (June 5, 1995), p. 56.
29. Nancy Gibbs, "Where Power Goes . . ." *Time* (July 17, 1995), p. 21.
30. John Micklethwait and Adrian Wooldridge, *The Right Nation* (New York: Penguin, 2004), p. 258.
31. Adam Clymer, "Buoyed by Resurgence, G.O.P. Strives for an Era of Dominance," *The New York Times* (May 25, 2003).
32. John Micklethwait and Adrian Wooldridge, "For Conservatives, Mission Accomplished," *The New York Times* (May 18, 2004), p. A25.
33. Matt Bai, "Wiring the Vast Left Wing Conspiracy," *New York Times Magazine* (July 25, 2004), p. 34.
34. Mike Allen, "GOP Takes in $33 Million at Fundraiser," *Washington Post* (May 15, 2002), p. A1.
35. Thomas Edsall, Sarah Cohen and James Grimaldi, "Pioneers Fill War Chest, Then Capitalize," *Washington Post* (May 16, 2004), p. A1.
36. "Democrats' Secret Patriots," *Washington Post* (May 25, 2004), p. A16.
37. Juliet Eilperin, "After McCain-Feingold, A Bigger Role for PACs," *Washington Post* (June 1, 2002), p. A1.
38. Thomas Edsall, "Study Suggests Law on Campaign Finance Will Benefit Liberals," *Washington Post* (June 10, 2002), p. A19.
39. Thomas Edsall, "GOP Creating Own '527' Groups," *Washington Post* (May 25, 2004), p. A15.
40. Christopher Schmitt, "A Shift in the Balance of Power," *U.S. News & World Report* (September 20, 2004), p. 36.
41. Thomas Edsall, "Republican 'Soft Money' Groups Find Business Reluctant to Give," *Washington Post* (June 8, 2004), p. A21.
42. Smith, *The Power Game,* p. 254.
43. Interview with Toby Weismiller, NASW, Washington, DC, January 11, 1988.

44. Personal communication with Dave Dempsey, NASW, Washington, DC, July 21, 2000.
45. Albert O. Hirschman, *Shifting Involvements* (Princeton, NJ: Princeton University Press, 1982), p. 132.
46. Peters, *How Washington Really Works,* p. 111.
47. Alice O'Connor, *Poverty Knowledge* (Princeton, NJ: Princeton University Press, 2001), p. 15.
48. Peter Bachrach and Morton S. Baratz, *Power and Poverty* (New York: Oxford University Press, 1979), p. 7.
49. For a review of the CAP experience, see Daniel Patrick Moynihan, *Maximum Feasible Misunderstanding* (New York: Random House, 1973).
50. House Ways and Means Committee, *Overview of Entitlement Programs* (Washington, DC: U.S. GPO, 2000), p. 467.
51. Dan Bloom and Kay Sherwood, *Matching Opportunities to Obligations: Lessons for Child Support Reform from the Parents' Fair Share Pilot Phase* (New York: Manpower Demonstration Research Corporation, 1994).
52. Janet Quint, Denise Polit, Hans Bos, and George Cave, *New Chance: Interim Findings on a Comprehensive Program for Disadvantaged Young Mothers and Their Children* (New York: Manpower Demonstration Research Corporation, 1994).
53. Michael Lipsky, "Bureaucratic Disentitlement in Social Welfare Programs," *Social Service Review* 33, no. 4 (March 1984), pp. 81–88.
54. Quoted in Robert Kuttner, *The Economic Illusion* (Boston: Houghton Mifflin, 1984), p. 86.
55. Ellen Dunbar, "Future of Social Work," *NASW California News* 13, no. 18 (May 1987), p. 3.
56. Harris Chaiklin, "The New Homeless and Service Planning on a Professional Campus," (University of Maryland, Chancellor's Colloquium, Baltimore, December 4, 1985), p. 7.
57. "Willie's Vision for Chicano Empowerment," *Southwest Voter Research Notes* 2, no. 3 (June 1988), p. 1.
58. Rhodes Cook, "Moving On," *Washington Post* (June 27, 2004), p. B1.
59. Dale Russakoff, "Cut Out of Prosperity, Cutting Out at the Polls," *Washington Post* (October 24, 2000), p. A12.
60. Amy Goldstein and Richard Morin, "Young Voters' Disengagement Skews Politics," *Washington Post* (October 20, 2002), p. A1.
61. "Deconstructing Distrust," The Pew Research Center. Retrieved from www.people-press.org/trustrpt.htm
62. David Broder, "The 30 Million Missing Voters," *Washington Post* (July 16, 2000), p. B7.
63. Maryann Mahaffey, "Political Action in Social Work," *Encyclopedia of Social Work,* 18th ed. (Silver Spring, MD: NASW, 1987), p. 290.
64. Allen Davis, "Settlement Workers in Politics, 1890 1914," in Maryann Mahaffey and John Hanks, (eds.), *Practical Politics: Social Work and Political Responsibility* (Silver Spring, MD: National Association of Social Workers, 1982), p. 32.
65. Allen F. Davis, *American Heroine: The Life and Legend of Jane Addams* (New York: Oxford University Press, 1973), p. 292.
66. Biographical information from *Encyclopedia of Social Work,* 18th ed. (Silver Spring, MD: NASW, 1987).
67. Richard Bernstein, "John Dewey," in Paul Edwards (ed.), *Encyclopedia of Philosophy, vol. II* (New York: Macmillan and The Free Press, 1967), p. 380.
68. Mahaffey, "Political Action in Social Work," p. 286.
69. John Hope Franklin, *From Slavery to Freedom* (New York: Knopf, 1979), pp. 319–321.
70. Ibid., pp. 471–472.
71. Charles Schottland, "Wilbur Joseph Cohen: Some Recollections," *Social Work* 32, no. 5 (September/October 1987), pp. 371–372.
72. June Hopps, "Reclaiming Leadership," *Social Work* 31 (September/October 1986), p. 323.
73. Eleanor Brilliant, "Social Work Leadership: A Missing Ingredient?" *Social Work* 31 (September/October 1986), p. 328.
74. For details on CDF, see Joanna Biggar, "The Protector," *Washington Post Magazine* (May 18, 1986), p. C-4; and *The Children's Defense Fund Annual Report 1984–85* (Washington, DC: Children's Defense Fund, 1985).
75. Information on CBPP was obtained from an interview with David Kahan at CBPP on March 12, 1984.
76. *1998 Annual Report* (Washington, DC: Economic Policy Institute, 1998).
77. Ted Halstead and Michael Lind, *The Radical Center* (New York: Doubleday, 2001).
78. David Von Drehle, "Liberals Get a Think Tank of Their Own," *Washington Post* (October 23, 2003), p. A29.
79. Biographical sketch, courtesy of Congressman Ed Towns' office, n.d.
80. Biographical sketch, courtesy of Senator Mikulski's Office, n.d.
81. Elliot Pagliaccio and Burton Gummer, "Casework and Congress: A Lobbying Strategy," *Social Casework* 69 (March 1988), pp. 321–330.
82. Grafton Hull, "Joining Together: A Faculty-Student Experience in Political Campaigning," *Journal of Social Work Education* 23 (Fall 1987), pp. 116–123.
83. William Whittaker and Jan Flory-Baker, "Ragtag Social Workers Take On the Good Old Boys and Elect a State Senator," in Maryann Mahaffey and John Hanks (eds.), *Practical Politics: Social Work and Political Responsibility* (Silver Spring, MD: National Association of Social Workers, 1982).
84. For details, see the ISP website at www.statepolicy.org
85. Hedrick Smith, *The Power Game* (New York: Random House, 1988), p. 124.
86. Ibid., p. 152.
87. Mahaffey and Hanks, *Practical Politics,* p. 284. (See Chapter 10, "Political Action in Social Work.")

CHAPTER 9

Tax Policy and Income Distribution

Tax policy, the use of legislation to define how revenues are generated in order to achieve social objectives, is fundamental to the structure of social welfare in the United States. While this function may seem prosaic, in fact tax policy has been the flash-point of major historical events, as evident in the Boston "tea party" when colonists objected to taxation without representation. Recently, the massive tax cuts of the George W. Bush administration have provoked dire warnings by liberals and conservatives alike about the fiscal health of the republic. Although tax policy is an instrument of government, its influence is not limited solely to generating revenues for federal and state social programs: Through "tax expenditures," areas exempted from taxation, tax policy provides significant incentives not only for specific industries, as in "corporate welfare," but also for individual behavior, as in the mortgage interest deduction. For this reason tax policy is of increasing interest to advocates of social justice. As support for direct benefits through traditional social programs has waned, social advocates have turned to "targeted tax expenditures"—preferably, refundable tax credits—as a means to advance economic justice. As a vehicle for funding social programs, tax policy is also an important barometer for social equity; and indeed, policy analysts have long used income distribution—and more recently wealth distribution—as an indicator of how fair the economy has been for various groups.

History of U.S. Tax Policy

All governments levy taxes to meet their legislated obligations. Because taxation appropriates income from private parties—individuals and corporations—and puts it to public use, it has been controversial and, at times, volatile. Ever since the establishment of the republic, various groups have objected to government taxation, challenging the authority to appropriate private property. Such challenges usually have been sorted out through the courts; but on occasion they have led to violent armed confrontations, as in the Whiskey Rebellion that divided the nation shortly after its creation. Although tax policy has traditionally been of professional interest primarily to the "green-eyeshade" accountants at the Internal Revenue Service, the radical Right also have a keen interest in it because it recognizes that tax money is the lifeblood that allows government to function.

Ever since the creation of the welfare state with the passage of the Social Security Act of 1935, social program expenditures have grown; and all these programs have been paid for by increasing taxes. The optimal welfare state, as liberals conceived it, would provide essential benefits as a right of citizenship. These benefits would be funded by progressive taxes—taxes that derived their revenues disproportionately from the wealthy. Implicit in this vision was the political calculus that was captured by Harry Hopkins, whose synopsis has become part of welfare folklore: "Tax, tax; spend, spend; elect, elect!" For half a century, this strategy produced solid electoral support for liberal social programs: The wealthy were taxed at higher rates, the revenues were diverted to social benefits for the middle and working classes through social programs, and social program beneficiaries expressed their gratitude by voting Democratic. Ultimately, however, liberal Democratic hegemony in social policy foundered on the shoals of its own success. As working families rose into the middle class, they tended to individualize their achievements, discounting the role of social programs and, in the process, becoming more receptive to conservative proposals to reduce social programs and their tax burden. By the 1980s this scenario led to the election of Ronald Reagan, who had a visceral dislike for federal social programs. The Reagan presidency was revolutionary in several respects, one being profound changes in tax policy, increasing economic inequality. While the Clinton interregnum restored a measure of fairness in tax policy, the presidency of George W. Bush has viewed tax cuts as the centerpiece of its domestic agenda, achieving one for each year of its first term. The intent of the Bush White House has been summarized by Grover Norquist, who as president of Americans for Tax Reform has proposed that the Bush White House implement annual tax cuts: "I don't want to abolish government. I simply want to reduce it to the size where I can drag it into the bathroom and drown it in the bathtub."[1]

As a creation of the legislative process, tax policy is most visible in the passage of major bills. Over time these become the basis of the state and federal tax codes, those notoriously confounding labyrinths of accounting rules. Periodically, attempts to reform tax policy emerge, such as the 1986 federal tax reform, which simplified the tax code and eliminated—at least temporarily—provisions for special interests. Indeed, the lobbying around deletion of special tax provisions was so intense that the 1986 tax reform became known as the "showdown at Gucci gulch," after the impeccable dress of the professionals populating the lobbying firms on Washington's K Street.

As this overview suggests, tax policy is dense and at the same time dynamic. Historically, three tax policies have been central to U.S. social policy: the income tax, the withholding tax, and the earned income tax credit.

- The federal income tax was instituted after approval of the Sixteenth Amendment to the Constitution in 1914. A *progressive tax,* in that the wealthy were taxed at a higher rate, the income tax was initially levied on less than 1 percent of the population and had a top rate of only 7 percent. On average, the income tax is 8.2 percent, but it is higher for upper-income families, 11.7 percent. Because a threshold on taxable income has been set, low-income families are exempt from paying the federal income tax.[2]
- The Social Security withholding tax, the payroll tax, was established in 1935. For employed workers, the withholding tax was initially set at 2 percent of the first $3,000 in wages, paid equally between employers and workers. Since then Social Security withholding has increased and is now 15.3 percent of the first $90,000 in wages, the wage cap was established at the outset, under the presumption that Social Security was a public pension plan for workers who would not have recourse to retirement provisions available to the wealthy.[3] The withholding tax is a *regressive tax,* in that lower-income workers pay the same rate as higher-wage employees. Most taxpayers now pay more in Social Security withholding than they do in income taxes.
- The **earned income tax credit (EITC)** was enacted in 1975 after the failure of a "negative income tax" plan advanced by the Nixon administration. A *refundable tax credit,* the EITC instructs the IRS to send a check to low-wage workers, especially those with children, who have earned income below a certain level. In 2003, for example, a worker with two children could receive a maximum refund of $4,204.[4] Since the creation of the EITC, other tax credits have been introduced: A child care tax credit allows low-wage workers to deduct the costs of day care, and several states have introduced tax credits for low-income workers, some of which are refundable.

The interaction of these basic tax policies is complex, as evident in Table 9.1. While the top quintile claims almost 60 percent of income, it also bears the weight of paying most of the income, payroll, corporate, and estate taxes. On the other hand, the effective tax rate of the top quintile—almost 21 percent—is considerably less than its share of income. The negative income tax entries for the lowest quintiles can be attributed to rebates paid them through the earned income tax credit, a negative income tax for low-wage families with children.

The income tax, Social Security withholding, and the EITC have been primary elements in federal tax policy, but they should not be assumed to be the *sine qua non* of tax policy with respect to social programs. When Maryland advocates of domestic violence prevention were faced with an abrupt reduction in funding from the state in the 1980s, for example, they resorted to a clever solution: Associating domestic violence with marriage, they convinced legislators to approve an addition to the marriage license fee—a tax whose additional proceeds would be diverted to services for victims of domestic violence.

Tax provisions fund social programs that exist within an economy that is also shaped by economic policy; thus, economic policy, through tax policy, influences social programs. A classic example was the conservative enthusiasm about "supply-side economics" during the 1980s. As advocated by Arthur Laffer, optimal economic policy would consist of minimal taxation, so as not to impede capital formation and expansion. Given the relatively higher tax rates that preceded his presidency, Ronald Reagan endorsed tax reform that incorporated a one-third cut in the income tax, assuming that the cut would reinvigorate a sluggish economy.[5] But although the tax cut of 1981 jolted the economy out of recession, it also cut off tax revenues to the Treasury, which then had to sell bonds to service the federal debt. Soon the federal government plunged further into debt, the depth of which was unprecedented for peacetime. By 1983 the annual deficit was $207 billion, 6.3 percent of **gross national product,** and growing. Debt service on government bonds grew commensurately, so that by the end of the 1980s, annual interest payments on the debt were $150 billion, the second largest item in the federal budget.[6]

Annual debt service overshadowed domestic policy discussions during the early 1990s. The congressional response was to impose a cap on domes-

Table 9.1

Distribution of Federal Taxes by Quintiles, 2004

	Share of Total					
	Economic Income	Individual Income Tax	Payroll Tax	Corporate Income Tax	Estate Tax	All Federal Tax
Top quintile	59.4	85.1	48.7	77.9	99.7	69.0
Fourth quintile	19.6	14.5	26.4	9.8	—	18.9
Middle quintile	11.8	4.7	14.0	5.7	—	8.7
Second quintile	6.8	– 1.8	7.8	3.2	—	2.8
Lowest quintile	2.6	– 2.5	3.0	2.1	—	0.4
	Average Effective Tax Rate					
Top quintile		11.7	6.2	2.5	0.3	20.8
Fourth quintile		6.1	10.3	1.0	—	17.3
Middle quintile		3.2	9.0	0.9	—	13.2
Second quintile		– 2.1	8.7	0.9	—	7.5
Lowest quintile		– 7.9	8.8	1.6	—	2.5
All		8.2	7.6	1.9	0.2	17.9

Source: Adapted from "Current-Law Distribution of Federal Taxes by Economic Income Percentiles, 2004: Table T04-0093," Urban-Brookings Tax Policy Center, Microsimulation Model (Version 0304-2). Retrieved September 28, 2004 from www.taxpolicycenter.org. Used by permission.

tic spending, an effort to stem the hemorrhaging of cash leaving the Treasury during a period when inflowing revenues had been stemmed by tax cuts. Liberal Democrats insisted that entitlement spending for social programs be exempt from the spending cap, with the result that federal budget decisions subsequently penalized discretionary programs—those with fixed budgets that are subject to the appropriation process annually—disproportionately. Because discretionary programs include research and development, student loans, public transportation, and the entire defense budget, the spending cap created intense pressure between social entitlements and discretionary programs. Thus, several years after a sharp cut in federal taxes, the effects took the form of pressure to cut an array of discretionary programs.

Looming federal deficits cast a pall over the incoming Clinton administration. After campaigning on a platform that emphasized investments in human capital, President Clinton was confronted with the massive deficits left over from the Reagan and Bush administrations. Clinton's nascent liberal tendencies, evident in his support for public works and national health insurance, were redirected by Alan Greenspan, chair of the Federal Reserve. Greenspan argued that the economy in general, and financial markets in particular, would respond negatively to new social programs that carried high price tags, because such programs would either (1) worsen the federal debt or (2) require significant tax increases. Although Clinton balked at Greenspan's position, economic reality was making short work of the new president's campaign rhetoric. Cornered between forces that advocated social investments and groups demanding deficit reduction, Clinton blew up during a staff meeting, as Bob Woodward recounted in *The Agenda:*

> "Where are all the Democrats?" Clinton bellowed. "I hope you're all aware we're all Eisenhower Republicans," he said, his voice dripping with sarcasm. "We're Eisenhower Republicans here, and we are fighting the Reagan Republicans. We stand for lower deficits and free trade and the bond market. Isn't that great?"
>
> The room was silent once more.
>
> He erupted again, his voice severe and loud, "I don't have a goddamn Democratic budget until 1996.

None of the investments, none of the things I campaigned on."[7]

Capitulating to Greenspan's insistence on deficit reduction, Clinton put his social investment plans on hold, a decision that contributed to an unprecedented economic expansion that promised to make possible the eventual elimination of the federal debt by generating a surplus projected at $2 *trillion* over 10 years.

After a hotly disputed 2000 presidential election, many anticipated that George W. Bush would govern in a bipartisan manner, yet this was not the case. With Republican control of Congress, the White House was positioned to move aggressively on domestic policy; among its primary concerns was tax policy. During its first term, four tax cuts were passed reducing federal revenues $1.9 trillion over ten years. Because the federal government had to honor its obligation to social entitlements while increasing spending for national security and mounting a war on terrorism, the federal government not only spent the surplus inherited from the Clinton presidency but also slid rapidly into debt. As a result the federal debt skyrocketed. With passage of the 2004 tax cut, the federal debt was projected to increase from $4.3 trillion to $8 trillion by 2014.[8] Conservatives minimized the fiscal consequences of the federal deficit, noting that as a percentage of gross domestic product the Bush deficit was only 4.2 percent while the Reagan deficits were much higher, 6 percent.[9] Adherents to supply-side economics in the Bush White House bet that economic growth would shrink the deficit—in the words of Vice-President Cheney: "Reagan proved that deficits don't matter." Liberals were less sanguine. "Bush's policies may, in fact, best be explained by another, more radical agenda. Extensive tax cuts will require Congress to limit the growth of social programs and public investment and undermine other programs altogether," argued Jeff Madrick, "Rising deficits will inevitably force Congress to starve those 'wasteful' social programs. The prospective high deficits may even make it imperative to privatize Social Security and Medicare eventually."[10] In 2008 the first of 77 million baby boomers will begin collecting Social Security, incurring future obligations that current social insurance programs will not be able to meet. The prospects would be to either trim social insurance benefits severely or convert them to public assistance programs, neither desirable outcomes for liberals who have sought to extend social program coverage.

Tax Policy and Special Interests

Tax policy has always contained provisions that benefit specific interests. Bending the tax code in response to lobbying is a long-standing practice in the United States, though today it is most often associated with corporate influence. Actually, the exclusion of pension plans from taxation began in 1921, and these provisions have been updated to include provisions such as individual retirement accounts. Tax expenditures that benefit individuals have now grown to the point that they exceed allocations for many prominent social welfare programs. In 2003, for example, tax expenditures for pension contributions were $279.1 billion, for health insurance $561.9 billion, and for mortgage interest deductions $362.9 billion. By comparison, in 2002 allocations

Spotlight 9.1

Tax Policy

The Tax Policy Center is a joint venture of the Urban Institute and the Brookings Institution. The center is comprised of nationally recognized experts in tax, budget, and social policy who have served at the highest levels of government. The center provides analysis and facts about tax policy to policymakers, journalists, citizens and researchers. To learn more about this group, go to its website at **www.taxpolicy center.org.**

for Supplemental Security Income were $38.5 billion, Medicaid $258.2, and federal housing programs $25.7 billion. Even the largest tax credits available for low-income tax payers for 2003 are dwarfed by middle-class tax expenditures: The EITC costs $34.4 billion, child care $44.1 billion, and housing $4.1 billion.[11]

Realizing that the tax code can be manipulated to serve the interests of the affluent, many social justice advocates have targeted "corporate welfare," or the special provisions directed at specific industries, for reform. By the late 1990s corporate welfare had reached such proportions—varying from $87 billion to $150 billion annually, depending on who did the counting—that even prominent conservatives in the CATO Institute were calling for abolition of tax gifts to business. Republican John Kasich, for example, identified a dozen programs for elimination:

- Rural Utilities Services, which subsidizes loans in rural areas: $190 million
- Market Access Program, which facilitates the export of food and wine: $347 million
- Animas-La Plata Project, which diverts water to irrigate farmland: $432 million
- Pyroprocessing Program, which creates new energy from spent nuclear fuel: $100 million
- Appalachian Regional Commission, which builds roads in 13 states: $500 million
- Fossil Energy Research and Development, which encourages new technology for fossil fuels: $1.37 billion
- Timber Roads, which builds roads in remote areas: $100 million
- Clean Coal Technology, which endeavors to lower coal emissions: $500 million
- Overseas Private Investment Corporation, which provides loans to firms investing abroad: $281 million
- General Agreements to Borrow, which funds the International Monetary Fund to avert economic emergencies: $3.5 billion
- Enhanced Structural Adjustment Facility, which aids developing countries: $150 million
- Highway Demonstration Projects, which improves roads as requested by individual lawmakers: $4 billion[12]

Even this list, partial as it is, might rankle many taxpayers; but efforts at downsizing corporate welfare have proved disappointing. As long as there is pork in politics, there is the opportunity to customize tax policy to serve the concerns of individual legislators—who, after all, are often influenced by constituent requests. Thus, tax policy is crafted both to meet the Appalachian Regional Commission's need for roads and to respond to Sonoma Valley vintners' desire to export their products to France.

Tax law also has a significant influence, directly and indirectly, on the revenues of nonprofit organizations. By allowing taxpayers to deduct charitable contributions from taxable income, tax law directly encourages support of philanthropy. Lower tax rates work indirectly, at least in theory, by leaving taxpayers with more discretionary income and assets that they may then donate to nonprofit causes. Comparatively, policy analysts are more confident about the effectiveness of direct support through tax deductions than about indirect support via lower taxation. In 1981, for example, taxpayers who did not itemize their tax deductions were allowed to deduct contributions to nonprofit organizations; at the same time significant reductions in income and estate taxes were instituted. In 1986 legislation removed the deduction for charitable contributions on the part of nonitemizers; concurrently, income and corporate tax rates were reduced sharply, although many tax shelters were also eliminated. The effects on charitable giving proved ambiguous. The disallowance of charitable contributions by nonitemizers affected primarily blue-collar and middle-income families, the families that account for most of the revenues of nonprofit agencies. As a result, charitable contributions by this group of households have declined continuously since 1989. In 1990 tax policy changed the amount of the charitable deduction available to wealthier families, limiting the amount that could be deducted to no more than 3 percent of income for those earning more than $100,000 annually. Thus, incentives for charitable contributions for more affluent families were also diminished. As a result, charitable contributions by itemizers remained relatively constant through the mid-1990s.[13] Yet the charitable impulse of Americans has continued despite changes in tax policy. "Giving as a percent of income has remained remarkably constant in the face of increases in the cost of giving," concluded tax policy analysts.[14]

As noted in Chapter 6, the story on charitable giving as a function of tax reduction is less unilinear than conservatives might wish. The idea is that as taxes on individual and corporate income are lowered, private wealth increases, creating a larger pool of resources against which nonprofits can lay claim. This, of course, is a mantra that conservatives have chanted since the 1980s—indeed, to the point that some ideologues have proposed that private charity actually replace government activity in social welfare. Deep tax cuts introduced during the 1980s significantly reduced federal social welfare funding; and indeed, until the early 1990s, these were made up for by increases in charitable giving. During the 1990s, however, although both private giving and federal support of nonprofits increased significantly, these sources never compensated for the total revenue losses attributed to direct federal funding cuts. After the election of George W. Bush, conservatives proposed repeal of the estate tax, the consequence of which the Congressional Budget Office predicts would be between $13 billion and $25 billion in reduced charitable contributions since the wealthy would no longer to count gifts against their tax obligations.[15]

Table 9.2

Tax Revenue of OECD Countries as a Percent of GDP*

Rank	Country	1965	1995	1965–1995 Change
1	Denmark	29.9	51.3	21.4
2	Sweden	35.0	49.7	14.7
3	Belgium	31.2	46.5	15.3
3	Finland	30.3	46.5	16.2
5	France	34.5	44.5	10.0
6	Netherlands	32.8	44.0	11.2
7	Austria	34.7	42.4	7.7
8	Norway	29.6	41.5	11.9
9	Italy	25.5	41.3	15.8
10	Germany	31.6	39.2	7.6
11	New Zealand	24.7	38.2	13.5
12	Canada	25.9	37.2	11.3
13	United Kingdom	30.4	35.3	4.9
14	Spain	14.7	34.0	19.3
15	Switzerland	20.7	33.9	13.2
16	Ireland	25.9	33.8	7.9
16	Portugal	16.2	33.8	17.6
18	Australia	23.2	30.9	7.7
19	Japan	18.3	28.5	10.2
20	United States	24.3	27.9	3.6

*Organization for Economic Cooperation and Development

Federal Tax Policy

Despite the mammoth size of the federal budget of the United States, it is predicated on a tax base that is minimal compared to those of other industrialized nations. As Table 9.2 shows, not only was the 1995 tax burden of the United States the lowest among industrialized nations; the rate of increase during the preceding three decades was also the lowest. Another way to assess the fairness of tax policy is to compare nations with respect to their income equality by use of the Gini index. This index calibrates the extent to which a nation's income distribution varies from a perfectly equal distribution; the closer the Gini index is to zero the greater the equality, while higher values indicate greater inequality. Table 9.3 ranks the nations of the Organization for Economic Cooperation and Development (OECD), the most developed of national economies.

The relatively low tax rate of the United States largely accounts for the nation's skewed **income distribution.** A tenet of the welfare state has been the progressive taxation of income and its redistribution to the poor through social programs. By definition, a welfare state with a low tax rate is unable to generate revenues sufficient to level the differences between rich and poor; thus, the question of income distribution has become integral to the discussion of tax policy. Yet, income is only one component of economic justice; another measure of affluence is assets. Although considered in discussions of social policy less often than income, assets are important insofar as they are an indication of real wealth. Consisting of savings, real estate, stocks and bonds, and related property, assets not only can be liquidated during periods of adversity, thus offering the owner a buffer against poverty, but also appreciate in value, thus generating additional wealth. As depicted on page 239, the distribution of assets is even more skewed than income distribution, with the highest quintile owning more than 80 percent. By contrast, the wealth of the lowest quintile is negative, indicative of debt. As has been the case with income, the distri-

Table 9.3

GINI Index of OECD Member Nations

Rank	Nation	Gini Index	Rank	Nation	Gini Index
1	Denmark	24.7	11	France	32.7
2	Japan	24.9	12	Switzerland	33.1
3.5	Belgium	25.0	13	Australia	35.2
3.5	Sweden	25.0	14	Ireland	35.9
5	Finland	25.6	15.5	Italy	36.0
6	Norway	25.8	15.5	United Kingdom	36.0
7	Austria	30.5	17	New Zealand	36.2
8	Canada	31.5	18	Germany	38.2
9	Spain	32.5	19	Portugal	38.5
10	Netherlands	32.6	20	United States	40.8

Source: Adapted from United Nations Development Program, *Human Development Report, 2003* (New York: Oxford, 2003), p. 282.

bution of assets has become more skewed during recent decades, the wealthiest quintile controlling more wealth with the lowest remaining in debt. And as with income, the distribution of assets is relatively constant; moderate changes occur, but the distribution pattern remains essentially the same over time. Consider the period following the Great Society efforts of the mid-1960s: Despite a major expansion of social programs for the poor, the lowest quintile still showed negative wealth, remaining mired in debt. For these reasons, a critical examination of wealth is essential for assessing economic justice.[16] If income distribution is skewed in favor of the affluent, assets are even more so. Notably, the bottom quintile is chronically in debt, its obligations exceeding its assets. Moreover, African Americans report significantly less wealth than whites; in 1998 the median wealth of whites was $81,700, while that of blacks was $10,000.[17] The fact that assets are consistently negative for

Changes in the Distribution of Wealth (Household Assets Minus Debts), 1962–1998

	Percent Share of Wealth				Percentage-Point Change
Wealth Class	1962	1983	1992	1998	1962–98
Top 1%	33.4	33.8	37.2	38.1	4.7
Top quintile	81.0	81.3	83.8	83.4	2.4
Fourth quintile	13.4	12.6	11.5	11.9	–1.5
Middle quintile	5.4	5.2	4.4	4.5	–0.9
Second quintile	1.0	1.2	0.9	0.8	–0.2
Lowest quintile	–0.7	–0.3	–0.5	–0.6	0.1

Change in Average Wealth (Household Assets Minus Debts), 1962–1998

	Thousands of 1998 Dollars				Annualized Growth %
Wealth Class	1962	1983	1992	1998	1962–1998
Top 1%	$4,851.8	7,175.1	8,796.4	10,203.7	3.1
Top quintile	587.4	864.5	991.9	1,126.7	2.5
Fourth quintile	97.2	133.6	135.7	161.3	1.8
Middle quintile	39.4	55.5	51.9	61.0	1.6
Second quintile	6.9	12.5	10.5	11.1	1.7
Lowest quintile	–5.3	–3.2	–6.0	–8.9	–1.9

Source: Adapted from Lawrence Mishel, Jared Bernstein, and Heather Boushey, *The State of Working America: 2002–2003* (Washington, DC: Economic Policy Institute, 2003), p. 281.

the lowest quintile reflects the difficulty of poorer families to buffer themselves from economic shocks. Thus, asset poverty, the wealth needed to survive for three months at the poverty level, exceeds income-based poverty. In 1999 the official poverty level was 11.8 percent, while the asset poverty rate was 27.9 percent; however, the asset poverty rate for minorities was much higher, for blacks 57.6 percent and Hispanics 52.3 percent.[18] In 2000 the asset poverty rate was 25.5 percent, twice the conventional poverty level, 12.7 percent.[19] The consequences of the tax cuts engineered during the second Bush presidency would be expected to exacerbate the chasm between rich and poor.

State Tax Policy and the Poor

Federal taxes are important in social welfare policy because they subsidize the major social entitlements, but states also levy taxes in order to meet their legislative obligations. Historically, states have held major responsibility in social programs, areas such as mental health, child welfare, and corrections; and to a great degree the adequacy of a state's social programs depends on its tax collections. Unlike federal taxation, which is uniform across the nation, state tax policy varies significantly. By way of illustration, consider the income tax. Whereas the federal income tax is uniform nationwide, 42 states have income taxes, but 8 do not. State income taxes provide general revenues that can be used for a range of social programs, but this is not the only reason that state tax policy is important. State tax policy can establish an income floor for taxation or exempt low-income families from any tax liability altogether, thus allowing them to keep more of their income. Disparities among states are striking; in 2002, the state income threshold in Alabama was only $4,000, for example, while that of California was $39,400. Of states that levy an income tax, the more progressive jurisdictions actually provide a rebate, similar to the federal Earned Income Tax Credit. As Table 9.4 indicates, some states have been much more generous with respect to low-income families, while others have been downright punitive.

The Efficiency of Tax Policy in Reducing Poverty

In the larger context of social policy, tax policy is one of several strategies that apportion societal resources. Within social welfare, more traditional benefits have consisted of social insurance such as Social Security, cash public assistance (means-tested cash benefits) such as Temporary Assistance for Needy Families (TANF), and in-kind public assistance (means-tested noncash benefits) such as Food Stamps. These different strategies vary in terms of their efficiency in poverty reduction over time. Traditionally, social insurance—compulsory contributions to social programs like Social Security and Medicare—makes the biggest dent in poverty, more than twice that of public assistance cash and in-kind benefits combined. Note that each of these traditional means of poverty reduction have experienced declining capacities to accelerate the upward mobility of low-income families (see Table 9.5). Indeed, the efficiency of all traditional cash transfers in reducing poverty has declined from an apogee during the late 1970s.[20] Still, the focus on cash transfers addresses only a portion of what might be thought of as public investment in social infrastructure. In 2003 researchers at the Jerome Levy Economics Institute at Bard College undertook a broad investigation of public consumption as a complement to income. They reasoned that, in addition to cash transfers, investments in housing, health, and education could be computed, broken down by income strata, and calculated on a per capita basis. The result is depicted in Tables 9.6 and 9.7 on pages 242–243. Overall, upper-income groups benefit from targeted as well as general public consumption more than lower income deciles. Even though poorer strata receive more in housing, health care, and income security, these are offset by greater benefits received by upper income deciles in economic affairs and education. Beyond this generalization, there are important qualifications. For example, both targeted and general public consumption benefited the deciles in the center of the stratification, the middle class. The exception was targeted public consumption which disproportionately benefited the top decile more than other strata. This contributed to a windfall for the top decile, whose income and public

Table 9.4

State Income Tax at Poverty Line of $18,390 for Two-Parent Families of Four, 2002

Rank	State	Tax	Rank	State	Tax
1	Kentucky	$606	19	Connecticut	0
2	Alabama	478	19	Delaware	0
3	Indiana	387	19	Idaho	0
4	Virginia	379	19	Maine	0
5	Hawaii	378	19	Mississippi	0
6	Arkansas	328	19	Nebraska	0
7	West Virginia	314	19	North Dakota	0
8	Oregon	267	19	Pennsylvania	0
9	Montana	244	19	Rhode Island	0
10	Michigan	213	19	South Carolina	0
11	Louisiana	148	19	Utah	0
12	Illinois	145	33	New Mexico	(60)
13	Ohio	138	34	District of Columbia	(262)
14	Oklahoma	98	35	Maryland	(310)
15	Missouri	89	36	Kansas	(381)
16	North Carolina	83	37	Wisconsin	(423)
17	Georgia	76	38	Massachusetts	(436)
18	Iowa	63	39	New Jersey	(582)
19	Arizona	0	40	New York	(827)
19	California	0	41	Vermont	(1,064)
19	Colorado	0	42	Minnesota	(1,447)

Source: Adapted from Nicholas Johnson, Bob Zahradnik, and Joseph Llobrera, *State Income Tax Burdens on Low-Income Families in 2002* (Washington, DC: Center on Budget and Policy Priorities, 2003), p. 4.

Table 9.5

Impact of Safety Net on Poverty Reduction, 1998

Category	Individuals (thousands)	Percent Removed By
Number of poor	54,356	
Number removed due to		
social insurance	17,588	32.4
means-tested cash benefits	2,292	4.2
means-tested in-kind	3,976	7.3
federal taxes	2,112	3.9
Total removed	25,968	47.8

Source: Adapted from Lynette Rawlings, *Poverty and Income Trends, 1998* (Washington, DC: Center on Budget and Policy Priorities, 2000), p. 105.

Table 9.6

Investment in Social Infrastructure, 1989

Decile	Targeted Public Consumption: Econ. Affairs	Housing and Comm.	Health	Education	Income Security	Total Targeted Public Consumption	General Public Consumption	Mean Income	Total Public Consumption + Income	Mean Household Size	Per Capita Public Consumption + Income
Top	1,382	270	48	4,318	56	6,073	2,485	138,568	147,126	3.2	45,977
	1.0%	*0.2%*	*0.0%*	4,713	*0.0%*	*4.4%*	*1.8%*				
Ninth	1,377	265	44	*3.1%*	87	6,486	2,399	84,463	93,348	3.2	29,171
	1.6%	*0.3%*	*0.1%*	*5.6%*	*0.1%*	*7.7%*	*2.8%*				
Eighth	1,139	224	43	4,370	87	5,862	2,226	66,139	74,227	3.0	24,742
	1.7%	*0.3%*	*0.1%*	*6.6%*	*0.1%*	*8.9%*	*3.4%*				
Seventh	1,163	199	43	4,005	97	5,507	2,098	53,833	61,438	2.9	21,186
	2.2%	*0.4%*	*0.1%*	*7.4%*	*0.2%*	*10.2%*	*3.9%*				
Sixth	1,112	196	45	3,535	155	5,043	1,971	43,979	50,984	2.7	18,883
	2.5%	*0.4%*	*0.1%*	*8.0%*	*0.4%*	*11.5%*	*4.5%*				
Fifth	1,027	210	52	3,237	270	4,795	1,836	35,410	42,041	2.5	16,816
	2.9%	*0.6%*	*0.1%*	*9.1%*	*0.8%*	*13.5%*	*5.2%*				
Fourth	875	213	56	3,022	407	4,573	1,734	27,546	33,853	2.4	14,105
	3.2%	*0.8%*	*0.2%*	*11.0%*	*1.5%*	*16.6%*	*6.3%*				
Third	796	227	65	2,647	589	4,324	1,607	20,200	26,131	2.2	11,878
	3.9%	*1.1%*	*0.3%*	*13.1%*	*2.9%*	*21.4%*	*8.0%*				
Second	628	288	69	2,500	996	4,480	1,449	13,183	19,112	2.0	9,556
	4.8%	*2.2%*	*0.5%*	*19.0%*	*7.6%*	*34.0%*	*11.0%*				
Bottom	528	295	47	2,564	1,390	4,825	1,341	5,935	12,101	1.9	6,369
	8.9%	*5.0%*	*0.8%*	*43.2%*	*23.4%*	*81.3%*	*22.6%*				

Note: Figures in italics indicate mean public consumption as a percentage of mean income. All dollar amounts are in 2000 dollars.

Table 9.7

Investment in Social Infrastructure, 2000

Decile	Targeted Public Consumption: Econ. Affairs	Housing and Comm.	Health	Education	Income Security	Total Targeted Public Consumption	General Public Consumption	Mean Income	Total Public Consumption + Income	Mean Household Size	Per Capita Public Consumption + Income
Top	2,123	167	26	5,358	121	7,795	2,756	188,176	198,727	3.2	62,102
	1.1%	*0.1%*	*0.0%*	*2.8%*	*0.1%*	*4.1%*	*1.5%*				
Ninth	1,321	164	24	5,405	158	7,072	2,655	96,183	105,865	3.1	34,150
	1.4%	*0.2%*	*0.0%*	*5.6%*	*0.2%*	*7.4%*	*2.8%*				
Eighth	1,297	164	28	5,379	192	7,057	2,590	74,423	84,070	3.0	28,023
	1.7%	*0.2%*	*0.0%*	*7.2%*	*0.3%*	*9.5%*	*3.5%*				
Seventh	1,287	156	30	5,052	253	6,775	2,471	60,170	69,416	2.9	25,710
	2.1%	*0.3%*	*0.1%*	*8.4%*	*0.4%*	*11.3%*	*4.1%*				
Sixth	1,228	150	36	4,430	350	6,188	2,314	48,846	57,348	2.7	21,240
	2.5%	*0.3%*	*0.1%*	*9.1%*	*0.7%*	*12.7%*	*4.7%*				
Fifth	1,153	147	43	3,999	506	5,842	2,145	39,106	47,093	2.5	18,837
	2.9%	*0.4%*	*0.1%*	*10.2%*	*1.3%*	*14.9%*	*5.5%*				
Fourth	962	147	43	3,633	622	5,407	2,012	30,534	37,953	2.4	15,814
	3.2%	*0.5%*	*0.1%*	*11.9%*	*2.0%*	*17.7%*	*6.6%*				
Third	871	165	48	3,364	854	5,302	1,846	22,696	29,844	2.2	13,565
	3.8%	*0.7%*	*0.2%*	*14.8%*	*3.8%*	*23.4%*	*8.1%*				
Second	669	177	56	2,870	1,045	4,818	1,647	14,877	21,342	2.0	10,671
	4.5%	*1.2%*	*0.4%*	*19.3%*	*7.0%*	*32.4%*	*11.1%*				
Bottom	517	212	43	2,617	1,368	4,756	1,465	6,387	12,608	1.7	7,416
	8.1%	*3.3%*	*0.7%*	*41.0%*	*21.4%*	*74.5%*	*22.9%*				

Note: Figures in italics indicate mean public consumption as a percentage of mean income.

consumption increased 35.1 percent between 1989 and 2000, more than twice that of any other group. (See Table 9.8.) Between 1989 and 2000 per capita public consumption and income for the top decile increased 35.1 percent while that of the bottom rose only 16.4 percent. This is significant insofar as the period captures the entirety of the Clinton presidency, one widely regarded as having reduced economic inequality. The Bush tax cuts that were so favorably to the wealthy will, in all likelihood, exacerbate the economic disparity between the haves and have-nots.

Tax Expenditures as Poverty Policy

The use of federal tax policy to alleviate poverty and the increase in states' use of tax policy to augment the income of poor families are relatively new features of U.S. social policy. Indeed, the past quarter century has witnessed a significant shift in social welfare policy: gradually, direct welfare transfers are being augmented with indirect expenditures through tax credits. While the family welfare allocation was halved to $16.5 billion when AFDC was replaced by TANF, the EITC expanded to over $34 billion. This has created a major disconnect in poverty policy insofar as many of the families that are transitioning from welfare to work do not claim EITC benefits even though they would be eligible for them. In 1999, 61.6 percent of TANF/AFDC families had heard of the EITC, but only 33.3 percent had received an EITC refund.[21] If welfare departments were truly concerned about poverty, as opposed to simply distributing public assistance benefits, they would make certain that all families with earned income claimed the EITC, but few welfare workers are familiar with the program. As a result it is underutilized by the welfare poor.

Tax expenditures in the form of deductions for families' housing and health insurance costs have been enjoyed by the middle class for more than a half century, it has not been until relatively recently that tax expenditures have been targeted for low-income families. The list of tax credits available to the poor has grown to include credits for earned income, child care, the welfare-to-work transition, care for the elderly and disabled, and adoption expenses. As the number of tax credits targeted to the poor has increased, tax credits have emerged as a contender to replace, at least partially, direct income transfers to aid the poor.

Although promises of federal tax credits for low-income families were conspicuous during the 2000 presidential campaign, many advocates of social justice had already enjoyed success lobbying state legislatures. Because many state legislatures were controlled by conservatives, a tax credit strategy proved more effective than a traditional appeal for increases in welfare transfers. By 2000 almost a dozen states had complemented the federal EITC with comparable state programs, and several had introduced other tax credits. Notably, Minnesota has enacted a state EITC, a refundable child care credit, a property tax credit for renters, and a subsidized health insurance program. Paul Wilson and Robert Cline note that 27 percent of Minnesotans take advantage of at least one of these programs; the Minnesota array of tax credits thus extends important income and health assistance to families ranging from the welfare poor to the working poor.[22]

As might be expected by a transition of such magnitude, the replacement of welfare transfers with tax credits raises several policy issues:

- Tax and revenue agencies replace welfare departments as the source of benefits, a role that many departments of social services are either unprepared for or may resist outright.
- Beneficiaries of tax credits must participate in the tax system in order to claim benefits, a status that is unfamiliar for many.
- Because much tax preparation is done by commercial firms, low-income workers may fall prey to unscrupulous preparers, particularly those advancing a refund as a loan.
- Tax credit refunds are almost always paid after the fact, requiring the recipient's willingness to wait, unlike traditional welfare that arrives monthly.
- As tax expenditures, tax credits are no less consequential for the federal and state treasuries than traditional welfare transfers.

An important advantage of tax credits is that their allocations are not fixed; like open-ended entitlements, the amount awarded is determined by the volume of valid claims.

Tax credits offer new opportunities in areas historically understood as "welfare." In order to accelerate the upward mobility of the poor, for example, tax credits could be connected directly to asset

Table 9.8

Changes in Household Wealth and Public Consumption, 1989 to 2000

	General Public Consumption			Targeted Public Consumption			Mean Income			Total Public Consumption Plus Income		
Decile	1989	2000	% Change	1989	2000	% Change	1989	2000	% Change	1989	2000	% Change
Top	2,485	2,756	+10.9	6,073	7,795	+28.4	138,568	188,176	+35.8	147,126	198,727	+35.1
Ninth	2,399	2,655	+10.7	6,486	7,072	+ 9.7	84,463	96,183	+13.9	93,348	105,865	+13.4
Eighth	2,226	2,590	+16.4	5,862	7,057	+20.4	66,139	74,423	+12.5	74,227	84,070	+13.3
Seventh	2,098	2,471	+17.8	5,507	6,775	+23.0	53,833	60,170	+11.8	61,438	69,416	+13.0
Sixth	1,971	2,314	+17.4	5,043	6,188	+22.7	43,979	48,846	+11.1	50,984	57,348	+12.5
Fifth	1,836	2,145	+16.8	4,795	5,842	+21.8	35,410	39,106	+10.4	42,041	47,093	+12.0
Fourth	1,734	2,012	+16.0	4,573	5,407	+18.2	27,546	30,534	+10.8	33,853	37,953	+12.1
Third	1,607	1,846	+14.9	4,324	5,302	+22.6	20,200	22,696	+12.4	26,131	29,844	+14.2
Second	1,449	1,647	+13.7	4,480	4,818	+7.5	13,183	14,877	+12.8	19,112	21,342	+11.7
Lowest	1,341	1,465	+9.2	4,825	4,756	−1.4	5,935	6,387	+7.6	12,101	12,608	+4.2

accrual strategies such as individual development accounts. The tax preparation necessary for people to access tax credits could be one of several basic services—checking, savings, financial planning—offered by community financial services that could replace current welfare departments and serve as alternatives to marginal financial outfits that exploit the poor. Integrated with other capital formation strategies such as electronic benefit transfer, deposits by commercial banks to meet their Community Reinvestment Act obligations, and deposits by government and nonprofit agencies, tax credits could be part of a broad community development initiative that would finance projects in poor neighborhoods, thereby providing jobs to residents. In this respect, tax credits may not only begin to replace traditional welfare transfers, but in so doing may well introduce a new era of basic supports for poor families.[23]

Despite support for publicly funded social programs, there are some who believe that Americans should not pay any taxes.

Other tax credits have been proposed to augment poverty policy. Martha Ozawa and Baeg-Eui Hong have suggested using the EITC to establish a $1,000 income floor for poor children and adjusting the benefit according to family size. "The modified EITC and children's allowances combined would improve the income status of all EITC-recipient children by 23.6 percent, with black and Hispanic children benefiting more than white children," Ozawa and Hong concluded.[24] Robert Cherry and Max Sawicky have proposed a universal unified child credit that would augment the EITC and child care tax credit with an additional child credit.[25] Thus, the integration of refundable tax credits and calibrating them according to family size could reduce poverty significantly.

The Antitax Movement

Proponents of publicly funded social programs assume that tax-generated revenues are prudent investments toward the public good. Within the larger policy context, there are differing views on this assumption, however. It is worth acknowledging that some of the most egregious violations of personal decency, to say nothing of civil rights, have occurred under the auspices of public programs—such as the sterilization of "feeble-minded" people during the eugenics movement, the Tuskegee "experiment" on syphilitic African American men, and the warehousing of chronically mentally ill patients as well as of prison inmates.

For conservatives, particularly libertarians, government activities are likely to attenuate individual liberties, a likelihood encouraged by the fragmentation of modern society. The oppressive capacity of the state has long been a concern of political philosophers; in a recent statement of the issue, Jared Diamond notes that all societies try to balance the provision of essential services with measures aimed at thwarting the kleptocratic inclinations of those in power.

> These noble and selfish functions are inextricably linked, although some governments emphasize much more of one function than of the other. The difference between a kleptocrat and a wise statesman, between a robber baron and a public benefactor is merely one of degree: a matter of just how large a percentage of the tribute extracted from producers is retained by the elite, and how much the commoners like the public uses to which the redistributed tribute is put.[26]

To the extent that government enriches the powerful and mistreats citizens, a logical reform strategy is to defund the state by cutting off its tax revenues. By way of illustration, Michael Tanner of the Cato Institute calculates that $3.5 trillion has been spent on poverty programs since the Great Society period, yet with little success. "We are not going to solve our welfare problems by throwing more money at them," he concludes. "It is time to recognize that welfare cannot be reformed. It should be ended."[27]

An equally compelling critique of government taxation can be found in classic liberalism, a philosophic doctrine that emphasizes the freedom of individuals to act in their own best interests. Isaiah Berlin's distinction between "positive" and "negative liberty" was framed within the context of twentieth-century state socialism, in an era when public programs were ascendent. Advocates of public programs justified them on the basis that they protected the vulnerable from poverty, idleness, and sickness, but Berlin noted that such "positive liberty" invariably strengthened the state. Berlin preferred "negative liberty," because it emphasized the ability of free citizens to act in their own interests.[28] Although dichotomies such as Berlin's may seem to be of limited application in social work practice or, worse, to be a rationale for gutting essential social programs, it is worth noting that a primary ethical value in social work is client self-determination.

The obvious question raised by conservatives is, why tax at all? Beyond central functions of the state, conservatives contend that citizens should be allowed to retain earned income and use it as they see fit. The liberal rebuttal to this suggestion has been that unregulated capitalism inevitably skews the distribution of resources and opportunities, leaving subgroups vulnerable to insecurity with respect to income, employment, and health. The result, liberals have contended, is that specific populations suffer disproportionate and protracted poverty, thus providing the rationale for social programs. For more than a half century, they note, social insurance and public assistance programs have buffered low-income families from poverty.

Conservative ambitions in domestic policy are to reverse liberal dominance of government in the lives of citizens and allow them to do more for themselves. At best, the Right contends, government consumes tax revenues that could be otherwise used for personal purposes; at worst, social programs not only inflict acute damage on individuals but long-term harm on society as well. The inverse relationship between citizen autonomy and government social programs is at the heart of the conservative social policy strategy. By favoring autonomy, tax cuts provide individuals with discretionary income with which they can choose the services they desire. This is shrewd politics as Jonathan Rauch noted, "by repudiating the Washington-knows-best legacy of the New Deal, Republicans will empower the people, and the people will empower Republicans." And the consequences for welfare liberalism are equally profound:

> If the Democrats dig in their heels and fall back on stale rants against greed, inequality, and privatization, so much the better. The voters will know whom to thank for empowering choices that Republicans intend to give them. As for which is the "party of nostalgia," the voters will also remember who defended, until the last dog died, single-payer Medicare, one-size-fits-all Social Security, schools without accountability, bureaucratic government monopolies, static economics, and Mutually Assured Destruction.[29]

The success of the antitax movement seems evident with the relatively wide support that the Bush tax cuts have received, even if they benefit the wealthy disproportionately. In this respect voter support of tax cuts can be interpreted as a referendum on the welfare state; given the choice, rather than divert income to public programs through taxes, many voters prefer to keep their income for themselves. Having seized on the strategy, the Right has been ruthless in its application. Movement conservatives, such as Grover Norquist, have promised a new tax-cut every year of the second Bush presidency.[30] Ultimately, conservatives intend to amplify the strategy through control of state and federal legislatures, eventually securing "an era of Republican dominance."[31] In all this, the second Bush administration has not only veered farther to the Right, but shown more organizational discipline in pursuing its objectives than even the avatar of contemporary conservatism, Ronald Reagan.[32]

Upward Mobility

If people kept more of their income instead of having it taxed to support social programs, would this be prudent public policy? Obviously, there are events that afflict individuals, communities, and societies that, being unexpected, warrant a governmental safety net; but, beyond such circumstances, can people be expected to act in their own best interests economically?

Recently, economists have approached these questions through examining the concept of "social mobility." Their research has raised profound questions about the embeddedness of poverty as well as the permanence of being poor. The policy issue is simple: To the extent that poor people of working age are upwardly mobile, the case for social programs is weakened. Brad Schiller, the author of a standard text on poverty and discrimination, has examined the upward mobility of the poorest Americans and, in its absence, the intractability of the underclass. Using a national data set, Schiller examined the experience of young workers earning the minimum wage and their subsequent earnings, finding that one-third of minimum wage workers had received a raise within a year and that 60 percent were beyond the minimum wage within two years. Of those who entered the labor market in 1980, a recession year, only 15 percent continued earning the minimum wage after three years.[33] Furthermore,

> . . . the available perceptions of minimum-wage youth seem to dispel the notion that minimum-wage jobs offer low wages and nothing more. Over 85 percent of the minimum-wage entrants stated that they liked their jobs, and over 60 percent felt that they were earning skills that would be valuable in attaining better jobs. Only one out of eight minimum-wage youth perceived a total lack of on-the-job training—a condition compatible with the notion of "dead-end" jobs. Over half (56 percent) of the minimum-wage workers perceived opportunities for promotion with the same employer.[34]

Seven years after beginning a minimum wage job, the average worker had seen an increase in his or her wages of 154 percent, about 15 percent per year. Although non-minimum wage job entrants were earning more, the minimum wage entrants had closed the gap significantly. Notably, Schiller concluded that race did not appear to retard the wage increases of youth. "The longitudinal experiences of minimum-wage youth . . . refute the notion of a 'minimum-wage trap,'" concluded Schiller. "Youth who started at the minimum wage in 1980 recorded impressive wage gains over the subsequent seven years both in absolute and relative terms."[35]

The upward mobility of low-wage workers thus parallels that of the general population. Daniel McMurer and Isabel Sawhill noted that upward mobility is more pronounced than data on a stagnating income distribution would suggest. Mobility in the United States is substantial, according to the evidence. Large portions of the population move into a new income quintile, with estimates ranging from about 25 to 40 percent in a single year. As one would expect, the mobility rate is even higher over longer periods—it averages about 45 percent over a 5-year period and about 60 percent over both 9-year and 17-year periods.[36]

Mobility is also pronounced among the poor. Reporting on data from the mid-1990s, the Census Bureau found that although 30.3 percent of Americans lived below the poverty line for at least two months during a three-year span, only 5.3 percent were poor continuously for two years. On average, families were below the poverty line for four and a half months.[37] Using data from the Panel Survey on Income Dynamics, W. Michael Cox and Richard Alm conclude that upward mobility, even of the poorest Americans, is striking.

> Only 5 percent of those in the bottom fifth in 1975 were still there in 1991. Where did they end up? A majority made it to the top three-fifths of the income distribution—middle class or better. But most amazing of all, almost 3 out of 10 of the low-income earners from 1975 had risen to the uppermost 20 percent by 1991. More than three-quarters found their way into the two highest tiers of income earners for at least one year by 1991.[38]

Although the research on upward mobility suggests that low-income workers do prosper over time, its implications for tax policy are less than direct. After all, the families that make up the aggregate samples that are the basis of the research derive income from social policies, ranging from the minimum wage to family welfare, and these invariably contribute to future income gains. At the same time, the research has a profound implication: If low-income families succeed despite notoriously inadequate welfare programs, they must do so as a result of prudent decision making. If so, the optimal response is not continuing categorical welfare, but converting social programs to tax credits that allow poor families more discretionary income.

Conclusion

Tax policy, often undervalued in discussions of social welfare, serves a vital function, because it provides the revenues through which public programs operate. Increasing fluency in tax policy has significant benefits for advocates of social justice. At the national level, for example, introducing progressive features to the Social Security withholding tax, adjusting the tax rate for income and lifting the cap on taxable income-would generate significant new revenues that could make minimal Social Security benefits more adequate. This could serve a strategic purpose, as well, by providing a counterpoint to conservative contentions that Social Security should be privatized.

Leveraging tax policy to advance social justice requires sophistication in social policy, however. Historically, two streams of poverty policy have evolved in the United States. The first—public welfare—was legislated through the Social Security Act of 1935, consists of TANF, SSI, Medicaid, Food Stamps, and the like. Much of public welfare is managed by HHS and parallel agencies at the state level. The second—Bootstrap Capitalism—was enacted through the 1975 Earned Income Tax Credit, consists of an array of tax credits for individuals as well as business. Bootstrap Capitalism is operated by the Treasury Department and the Federal Reserve System. By understanding poverty policy exclusively through the public welfare paradigm, human service professionals omit from the realm of possibility a set of policy options that have enormous promise. Thus, if social welfare professionals are to enhance their role in the domestic policy debate, they will have to master the financial, procedural, and accounting nuances of tax policy. These are daunting fields, to be sure, but the potential payoff makes the effort worthwhile.

Discussion Questions

1. Click on the "For Students" link of the policyAmerica website and explore tax cuts that have passed during the Bush administration. Who have they benefited? Who has been disadvantaged? What changes in tax policy could advance economic justice?
2. Why has Harry Hopkins's political calculus, "Tax, tax, spend, spend, elect, elect!" lost its political currency in more recent times?
3. Should the federal government expand its spending on social programs despite the large and ongoing federal debt? What are the effects of increased spending, and what are the effects of stable or even decreasing spending, on social programs?
4. What are the positive and negative effects of increasing corporate taxation? How would it affect the poor in both the short-term and the long-term?
5. Should nonprofit human service corporations be required to pay taxes just as for-profit firms do? What would be the possible consequences of restructuring the tax code to mandate that nonprofits lose their nonprofit tax status?
6. Should the altruism of the population be rewarded by tax codes that permit charitable contributions to be deducted from taxes? Do the long-term effects of this tax deduction encourage or discourage real altruism?
7. Some welfare advocates concerned with income inequality argue that the function of the welfare state is to equalize incomes and assets through social welfare programs. Others believe it is unrealistic to expect that welfare state programs can do more than alleviate human suffering by providing resources to those in need. Should the goal of social welfare programs be to reduce income and asset inequality, or should that function be relegated to tax and labor policy?
8. Has the social work profession been successful in lobbying efforts and in promoting a more just society? If not, why? What strategies should social workers employ to move society toward more equitable income and asset redistribution?

Notes

1. Paul Krugman, "Duped and Betrayed," *The New York Times* (July 6, 2003), p. A31.
2. Thomas Dye, *Understanding Public Policy*, 9th ed. (Upper Saddle River, NJ: Prentice-Hall, 1998), pp. 242–243.
3. That part of the withholding tax dedicated to Medicare Health Insurance is levied on all income, though that for Social Security has a cap on taxable income. Committee on Ways and Means, *Overview of Entitlement Programs* (Washington, DC: U.S. GPO, 1998), p. 58.
4. Committee on Ways and Means, *Overview of Entitlement Programs* (Washington, DC: U.S. GPO, 2004), pp. 13–36.

5. Reynolds Farley, *The New American Reality* (New York: Russell Sage Foundation, 1996), p. 85.
6. *The Economic and Budget Outlook: Fiscal Years, 1991–1995* (Washington, DC: CBO, 1990), pp. 122, 112.
7. Bob Woodward, *The Agenda* (New York: Simon & Schuster, 1994), p. 165.
8. Jonathan Weisman, "Congress Votes to Extend Tax Cuts," *Washington Post* (September 24, 2004), p. A7.
9. David Rosenbaum and Edmund Andrews, "Bush Aide Sees Deficit in 2003 of $200 Billion," *New York Times* (January 16, 2003), p. A1.
10. Jeff Madrick, "The Iraqi Time Bomb," *New York Times Magazine* (April 6, 2003), p. 50.
11. Committee on Ways and Means, *Overview of Entitlement Programs* (Washington, DC: U.S. GPO, 20040, pp. 13-4–13-5.
12. David Rosenbaum, "Corporate Welfare's New Enemies," *New York Times* (February 2, 1997), pp. E1, E6.
13. Virginia Hodgkinson and Murray Weitzman, *Nonprofit Almanac* (Washington, DC: Independent Sector, 1996), pp. 59–63.
14. Alan Abramson, Lester Salamon, and C. Eugene Steuerle, "The Nonprofit Sector and the Federal Budget," in Elizabeth Boris and C. Eugene Steuerle (eds.), *Nonprofits and Government* (Washington, DC: Urban Institute, 1999), p. 122.
15. David Kamin, "New CBO Study Finds that Estate Tax Repeal Would Substantially Reduce Charitable Giving," (Washington, DC: Center on Budget and Policy Priorities, 2004), p. 1.
16. Thomas Shapiro and Edward Wolff (eds.), *Assets for the Poor* (New York: Russell Sage Foundation, 2001).
17. Lawrence Mishel, Jared Bernstein, and Heather Boushey, *The State of Working America, 2002/2003* (Washington, DC: Economic Policy Institute, 2003), p. 281, 284.
18. Asena Caner and Edward Wolff, "Asset Poverty in the United States," *Public Policy Brief* 76A (Annandale-on-Hudson, New York: Jerome Levy Economics Institute, 2004), p. 4.
19. Ray Boshara (ed.), *Building Assets* (Washington, DC: Corporation for Enterprise Development, 2001), p. 2008.
20. Sheldon Danziger, Robert Haveman, and Robert Plotnick, "Antipoverty Policy," in Sheldon Danziger and Deniel Weinberg (eds.), *Fighting Poverty* (Cambridge, MA: Harvard University Press, 1986), p. 65.
21. Katherin Phillips, "Who Knows about the Earned Income Tax Credit?" (Washington, DC: Urban Institute, January 2001).
22. Paul Wilson and Robert Cline, "State Welfare Reform: Integrating Tax Credits and Income Transfers." Paper presented at the 1994 National Tax Symposium, Washington, DC, May 24, 1994.
24. David Stoesz and David Saunders, "Welfare Capitalism," *Social Service Review* (September 1999).
24. Martha Ozawa and Baeg-Eui Hong, "The Effects of EITC and Children's Allowances on the Economic Well-Being of Children," *Social Work* 27, no. 3 (September 2003), p. 171.
25. Robert Cherry and Max Sawicky, "Giving Tax Credit Where Credit Is Due," (Washington, DC: Economic Policy Institute, n.d.).
26. Jared Diamond, *Guns, Germs, and Steel* (New York: Norton, 1997), p. 276.
27. Michael Tanner, "Ending Welfare as We Know It," (Washington, DC: CATO Institute,1994), p. 24.
28. Michael Ignatieff, *Isaiah Berlin* (New York: Henry Holt, 1998), pp. 202–203.
29. Jonathan Rauch, "The Accidental Radical," *The National Journal* 35, no. 30 (July 26, 2003).
30. Dana Milbank and Dan Balz, "GOP Eyes Tax Cuts as Annual Events," *Washington Post* (May 11, 2003), A1.
31. Adam Clymer, "Buoyed by Resurgence, G.O.P. Strives for an Era of Dominance," *The New York Times* (May 25, 2003), p. A1.
32. Bill Keller, "Reagan's Son," *New York Times Magazine* (January 26, 2003).
33. Bradley Schiller, "Moving Up: The Training and Wage Gains of Minimum-Wage Entrants," *Social Science Quarterly* 75, no. 3 (September 1994), p. 629.
34. Ibid., p. 627.
35. Ibid., p. 634.
36. Daniel McMurer and Isabel Sawhill, *Getting Ahead* (Washington, DC: Urban Institute, 1998), p. 33.
37. "Poverty Short-Lived for Most, Study Finds," *Richmond Times Dispatch* (August 10, 1998), p. A3.
38. W. Michael Cox and Richard Alm, *Myths of Rich and Poor* (New York: Basic Books, 1999), p. 73.

CHAPTER 10

Social Insurance Programs

This chapter explores the major forms of social insurance in the United States: Old-Age, Survivors, and Disability Insurance (OASDI), Unemployment Insurance (UI), and Workers' Compensation. In addition, this chapter explores some of the major issues and problems surrounding social insurance programs.

Definition of Social Insurance

Social insurance is the cornerstone of U.S. social welfare policy. Specifically, it is a system whereby people are compelled—through payroll or other taxes—to insure themselves against the possibility of their own indigence, such as might result from the economic vicissitudes of retirement, the loss of a job, the death of the family breadwinner, or physical disability. Based in part on the same principles used in private insurance, social insurance sets aside a sum of money that is held in trust by the government and earmarked to be used in the event of workers' retirement, death, disability, or unemployment. The major goal of social insurance is to help maintain income by replacing a portion of lost earnings. It is a pay-as-you-go system in which the workers and employers of today pay for those who have retired, are ill, or have lost their jobs. Although originally designed to replicate a private insurance fund, the Social Security program has been broadened to include a variety of programs that attempt to provide a minimal level of replacement income. Because the benefits paid to many retired workers exceed their contributions to the system, Social Security has taken on some of the characteristics of an income redistribution and/or public assistance program.

Unlike Social Security, public assistance programs are subject to **means tests** and based entirely on need. The rationale for public assistance is grounded in the concept of *safety nets,* which are designed to ensure that citizens receive basic services and that they do not fall below a given poverty level. Social insurance, on the other hand, requires beneficiaries to make contributions to the system *before* they can claim benefits. Because social insurance affects a larger number of people and benefits are generally higher, expenditures for social insurance are far greater than for public assistance (see Figure 10.1 on page 254). Social insurance is also universal; that is, people receive benefits as legal entitlements regardless of their personal wealth. Table 10.1 shows federal spending for major social insurance programs. Because the social insurance benefit structure is linked to occupationally defined productive work, most programs tend to be stigmatized little or not at all. In contrast, public assistance recipients are often highly stigmatized. Perhaps this occurs because public assistance programs are financed out of general tax revenues; they are not occupationally linked and not based on a previous work record; and recipients must be determined indigent through means tests.

Although some people complain about the costs of public assistance programs, social insurance programs are financed at more than twice the level of public welfare. For example, social insurance programs (OASDI, Workers' Compensation, Medicare, and Unemployment Insurance, among others) cost about $773 billion in 2002 compared to about $308 billion for public assistance programs (AFDC, SSI,

Table 10.1

Past, Current, and Projected Federal Spending for Major Social Insurance Programs, Selected Years (expenditures in billions)

Programs	2002	2004	2006	2008	2010
OASDI	$452	$494	$539	$598	$670
Medicare	254	287	319	366	421
Unemployment Insurance	51	46	43	45	49
Total	757	827	901	1009	1140

Source: Committee on Ways and Means, U.S. House of Representatives, *2004 Green Book* (Washington, DC: U.S. Government Office, 2004), pp. I-2, I-8.

food stamps, WIC, and others). Furthermore, social insurance programs accounted for 34.7 percent of the total federal budget in 2000, compared to 13.1 percent for public assistance programs. Finally, the average OASDI beneficiary who retired in 2003 would receive $1,150 a month compared to the national average TANF payment of $327.88 in 2002.[1] Looking at it another way, in 2001 total means-tested programs accounted for 2.5 percent of America's gross domestic product (GDP) compared to 8.3 percent of all non-means-tested programs. Broken down, Social Security accounted for 4.2 percent of the GDP; Medicare, 2.3 percent; Unemployment Compensation, 0.3 percent; and other retirement and disability, 0.9 percent.[2]

The Background of Social Insurance

The first old-age insurance program was introduced in Germany in 1889 by Chancellor Otto von Bismarck. Although that first program was originally intended as a means of curbing the growing socialist trend in Germany, by the onset of World War I nearly all European nations had old-age assistance programs of one sort or another. In 1920 the U.S. government began its own Federal Employees Retirement program. By 1931, 17 states had enacted their own old-age assistance programs, although these often had stringent eligibility requirements. For example, in some cases in which relatives were capable of supporting an elderly person, benefits were denied. These state-administered retirement programs were restrictive and often punitive; often elderly people who applied for assistance had to sign over all their assets to the state when they died.[3] Nevertheless, the concept of governmental responsibility for welfare grew during the early part of the twentieth century, and by 1935 all states except Georgia and South Carolina had programs that provided financial assistance to widows and children.[4]

Spurred on by the Great Depression of the 1930s and prompted by the growing rebellion inspired by a California physician named Francis Townsend (who advocated a flat $200 per month for each retired worker), President Franklin Roosevelt championed a government assistance program that would cover both unemployed and retired workers.[5] The result of Roosevelt's efforts was the Social Security Act of 1935, through which the federal government established the basic framework for the modern social welfare state.

The 1935 Social Security Act was relatively modest compared to its present scope. It established categorical assistance to the elderly poor, dependent children, the blind, and some disabled children. Title IV earmarked money for vocational rehabilitation, rural public health, and training for public experts. Two titles covered eligibility and financing for old-age retirement; two others established UI under joint state and federal government auspices. Title VII established a Social Security Board, whose job it was to monitor the fund. Title XI gave the legislature the right to alter any part of the act.[6]

As amended, the Social Security Act provides for: (1) OASDI; (2) UI programs under joint federal and state partnership; (3) federal assistance to aged, blind, and disabled persons under the SSI program; (4) public assistance to families with dependent children under the AFDC program (now TANF); (5) federal health insurance for the aged (Medicare); and (6) federal and state health assistance for the poor (Medicaid). Although all these programs fit under the rubric of the Social Security Act of 1935, not all are true social insurance programs (e.g., Medicaid, TANF, and SSI).

The insurance feature of Social Security emerged as the result of an intense debate: Progressives wanted Social Security funded out of general revenue taxes, whereas conservatives wanted it funded solely out of employee contributions. The compromise reached in 1935 was that old-age insurance would be financed by employer and employee contributions of 1 percent on a base wage of $3,000, with a maximum cap for worker contributions set at $30 a year. At age 65, single workers would receive $22 per month and married workers $36. No benefits were paid out until 1940 to allow the program to accumulate reserves.

The Social Security Act of 1935 has been repeatedly modified, almost always in the direction of increasing its coverage. The original Social Security Act of 1935 afforded retirement and survivor benefits to only about 40 percent of the labor force. Farm and domestic workers, mariners, bank employees, the self-employed, and state and local government employees were excluded. In 1950 farmers and self-employed persons were added, thereby bringing the coverage to more than 90 percent of the labor force. Congress made survivors and dependents of insured workers eligible for benefits in 1939, and in 1956 disability insurance was added to include totally and permanently disabled workers. In 1965 Health Insurance for the Aged (Medicare)—a prepaid health insurance plan—was incorporated into the law. In later years the act was amended to allow workers to retire as early as age 62, provided they agreed to accept only 80 percent of their benefits. In 1977 an automatic cost-of-living index was affixed to benefit payments.

With the amendments of 1939 (extending coverage to widows, elderly wives, surviving children, etc.) Social Security technically became bankrupt since it was no longer entirely self-financed. As such, the federal government assumed responsibility for any financial shortfalls and thus implicitly assumed responsibility for promoting the general welfare. By 1996, more than 43 million Americans and more than one-quarter of all U.S. households depended on a monthly Social Security check.[7] As Figure 10.1 illustrates, only 63 percent of Social Security beneficiaries were retired workers by 2002.

The Financial Organization of Social Insurance

Covered workers pay taxes into Social Security while they work, and when they retire or become disabled, they (or their family members) collect monthly benefits. Social Security taxes are used to pay for retirement, disability or Medicare benefits. General revenue taxes are used to finance Supplemental Security Income (SSI), which despite it name is actually a means-tested public assistance program rather than social insurance.

Social Security and Medicare taxes are divided among several trust funds. Two funds include: (1) the Old-Age and Survivors Insurance (OASI) trust fund (pays for retirement and survivor benefits), and (2) the federal Disability Insurance (DI) fund (pays benefits to people with disabilities and their families). There are also two Medicare trust funds: (1) The federal Hospital Insurance (HI) trust fund pays for services covered under the hospital insurance (Part A) provisions of Medicare, and (2) the federal Supplementary Medical Insurance (SMI) trust fund pays for services covered under the medical insurance (Part B) provisions of Medicare. Social Security trust fund accounts are maintained by the Department of the Treasury.

The trust funds are governed by a board of trustees made up of the secretary of the treasury, the secretary of labor, the secretary of health and human services, the commissioner of social security, and two public trustees who serve four-year terms. The board of trustees reports annually to Congress on the condition of the funds and on estimated future operations.

Before 1983 the system operated on a pay-as-you-go system, with taxes flowing into one end of the pipeline and flowing out the other end. Since 1983 Social Security has operated under a partial reserve system in which it takes in more than it pays out, thereby building up a reserve to help pay benefits to an increasing number of retired workers.

Social Security revenues are deposited daily into trust funds and benefits are paid out. Surplus income (i.e., income not needed to pay benefits) is invested in U.S. government bonds that earn the prevailing rate of interest and whose principal and interest are guaranteed by the federal government. Almost all securities held by the trust funds are "special issue" bonds available only to the funds. The DI trust fund also holds a relatively small number of public issue stocks (marketable securities

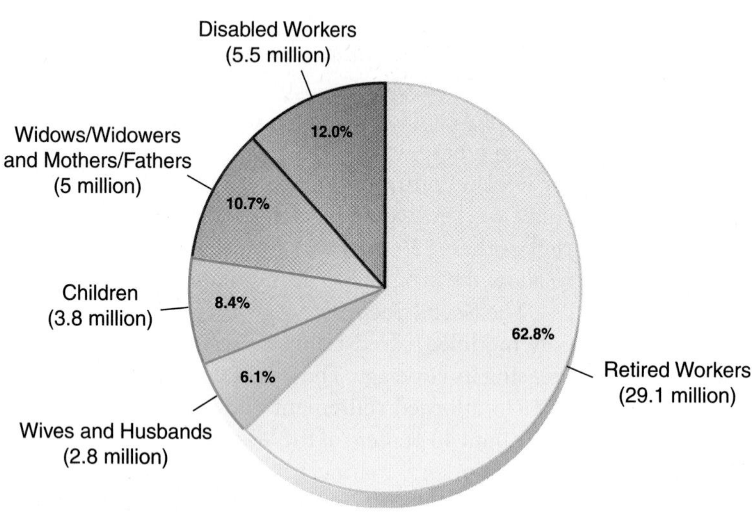

Figure 10.1

Number of Social Security Beneficiaries by Type of Benefit, December 2002

Source: Committee on Ways and Means, U.S. House of Representatives, *2004 Green Book* (Washington, DC: U.S. Government Office, 2004), pp. 1–45.

available to the general public). The OASI trust fund holds no public issue stocks. Unlike marketable securities, special issues can be redeemed at any time at face value. Consequently, investments in special issues provide the trust funds with the same flexibility as having cash. The amount of earned interest can be substantial. In 2002 the Social Security trust funds earned $80.4 billion in interest, representing an annual interest rate of 6.4 percent. In 1998 the Social Security trust funds earned $49.3 billion in interest, representing an annual interest rate of 7.2 percent.[8]

Key Social Insurance Programs

OASDI

OASDI is a combination of Old Age and Survivors Insurance (OASI) and Disability Insurance (DI). Commonly referred to as Social Security, it is the largest social program in the nation, covering approximately 9 out of 10 workers. OASDI is a federal program administered by the Social Security Administration, which in 1994 became an independent agency headed by a commissioner and a board appointed by the U.S. president for a six-year term.

Social Security is a stellar example of a program that has worked. In 2002:

- Social Security served more than 50 million people and upwards of 4 million people were awarded benefits.
- Social Security provided at least half of the income for 65 percent of the aged.
- Social Security kept 39 percent of aged persons out of poverty.
- Women accounted for 57 percent of adult Social Security beneficiaries.[9]

Moreover, the poverty rate for elderly people was 10.1 percent in 2002, lower than the poverty rate for the general population (11.7 percent). As recently as 1969, before the Social Security **cost-of-living adjustments (COLAs)** took effect, the poverty rate for the elderly was double that of the general population, 25 versus 12 percent.[10] According to the Social Security Administration, in 1996 the poverty rate for the elderly would have been 52 percent without Social Security.[11] In that sense, Social Security has a strong redistributive effect, transferring resources from those with high lifetime earnings to those with low lifetime earnings.[12]

Unlike prefunded private annuity plans, in which a worker draws off money already invested, Social Security benefits are paid by today's workers rather than by the retirees. Benefits under OASDI are entitlement based; that is, they are based on the beneficiaries' earnings, not on the amount of the revenue in the trust fund. If benefits in a given period exceed revenues, the difference is made up from the reserves in the trust funds. OASDI operates in the following manner:

- On an employee's first $87,900 in earnings, the employee and his or her employer each paid an OASDI tax equal to 6.20 percent and a Medicare hospital insurance (HI) tax equal to 1.45 percent of earnings in 2004. Employees therefore paid a total of 7.65 percent. Self-employed persons paid 15.3 percent. In general, increases in the wage base are automatic and are based on the increase in average wages in the economy each year. For example, the highest Social Security tax a worker could pay in 2002 was $5,394 (not including the HI tax), with a joint employer/employee tax of $10,788. Self-employed persons had their taxes computed on a lower base (net earnings from self-employment less 7.65 percent), and half of that tax was deductible for income tax purposes.[13]

Social Security is the key social insurance program in the United States.

- Based on their age at retirement and the amount earned during their working years, workers receive a monthly benefit payment. Retired workers aged 62 receive a reduction of 5/9 of 1 percent for each month of entitlement before age 65, with a maximum reduction of 20 percent. Benefits are modest; the average retired worker received $895 a month in 2002. The maximum benefit in 2003 for a retired worker at age 65 was $1,721 a month.[14]
- Under the OASI program, a monthly payment is made to an unmarried child or eligible dependent grandchild of a retired worker or a deceased worker who was fully insured at the time of death, if the child or grandchild is (1) under age 18; (2) a full-time elementary or secondary school student under age 19; or (3) a dependent or disabled person aged 18 or over whose disability began before age 22. A grandchild is eligible only if the child was adopted by the insured grandparent.
- A lump-sum benefit of $255 is payable to a spouse who was living with an insured worker at the time of his or her death.
- Under the Disability Insurance program (DI), monthly cash benefits are paid to disabled workers under age 65 and to their dependents. The purpose of the DI program is to replace lost income when a wage earner is no longer able to work. Monthly cash benefits are paid and computed generally on the same basis as they are in the OASI program; that is, they are calculated on the basis of past earnings. Medicare benefits are provided to disabled workers, widows or widowers, or adult children after they have been entitled to disability benefits for 24 months.
- Almost all people, whether or not they paid into Social Security, are eligible for Medicare benefits. (Medicare is treated in depth in Chapter 12.)
- Social Security beneficiaries are required to have completed at least 40 quarters of work (10 years) before they are eligible to draw benefits.[15]

Social Security, especially OASDI, has been a heated topic for much of its relatively short history. Political conservatives and laissez-faire economists are troubled because Social Security basically socializes a portion of the national income. Other critics claim that Social Security will lead to moral and economic ruin, because it discourages savings and causes retired people to become dependent on a supposedly fragile governmental system. The Social Security system, on the other hand, is popular with the elderly, who rely on it for much of their income, and with their grown children, for whom it helps to provide peace of mind.

Unemployment Insurance

The first line of defense for workers fired or laid off from their jobs is unemployment insurance (UI). Part of the Social Security Act of 1935, UI is a federal/state program whose objectives are (1) to provide temporary and partial wage replacement to involuntarily and recently unemployed workers, and (2) to help stabilize the economy during recessions. Although the U.S. Department of Labor oversees the general program, each state administers its own UI program.[16] The current guidelines of the UI program require employers to contribute to a trust fund, which is then activated if an employee loses his or her job. About 3.3 million workers were on UI in 2000, at a total cost of $4.6 billion. In 2003 the average duration of unemployed workers in the UI program was 16.4 weeks.[17]

The Unemployment Insurance System and Benefits The UI system consists of two basic parts: (1) regular state-funded benefits, generally provided for a maximum of 26 weeks; and (2) a federal/state extended benefits program. The second part provides an additional 13 weeks of benefits to unemployed workers who have used up their regular benefits and are still searching for a job. Extended benefits in the UI system are activated when the level of unemployment insurance claims in a state rises above a specified threshold. The extended benefits program is based on the assumption that when a state's unemployment rate is high, it usually takes longer to find a new job.[18] States pay 50 percent of the benefits provided by the UI extended benefits program.

To be eligible for UI benefits, a worker must be ready and willing to work, be unemployed, be registered for work with the state employment service, and have been working in covered employment during a base eligibility period. Conversely, a worker who is fired for misconduct, quits a job without a legally acceptable reason, fails to register with the state employment service, refuses a job equal to or better than the one previously held, or goes on strike is ineligible for unemployment benefits. States cannot, however, deny benefits to workers who refuse to be strikebreakers or who refuse to work for less than the prevailing wage rate.[19]

Basic decisions concerning the amount of benefits, eligibility, and length of benefit time are made by the states. Benefits are not equal to previously earned income, and in 2003 the average weekly benefit check was $262, which replaced, on average, 47 percent of a worker's previous salary.[20] State unemployment benefits vary widely, ranging in 2004 from a weekly average of $172 in Arizona to $317 in Minnesota.[21]

Problems in Unemployment Insurance Congress created the UI system in 1935, and since then the program has remained essentially the same despite changes in the economy and in the nature of unemployment. There are several problems endemic to the UI program:

1. *Part-time workers* are 59 percent less likely than full-time workers to collect UI benefits. In 23 states, people looking for part-time work are not considered to be looking for "suitable work" and are therefore ineligible for benefits. This occurs even though their employers pay UI payroll taxes for them, and they often meet minimum earnings requirements. In 2003 five states enacted laws allowing part-time workers to collect unemployment benefits while seeking part-time work.

2. *Temporary workers* are 28 percent less likely than all other workers to receive UI benefits. The number of temporary workers has been increasing, and by 2003 they totaled 2.2 million. Those who work at temporary agencies face several difficulties when applying for UI benefits. First, they may not have worked enough hours or earned enough to qualify for benefits. Second, since they were employed at temporary agencies they have difficulty proving they did not voluntarily quit the job. Lastly, to remain eligible for benefits, a worker cannot refuse "suitable work," or work of the same nature at or above the same pay rate that the worker was earning before. Some temporary workers have been denied benefits because they refused a different type of temporary assignment than they had been previously doing.

3. *Low-wage workers.* Only 18 percent of low-wage workers (those earning $8 an hour or less) receive UI benefits compared to 40 percent of high-wage workers. These workers are often ineligible because they fail to meet minimum earnings requirements. Another reason low-wage workers are often ineligible is that not all of their earnings are considered when determining eligibility. In most states, up to six months of a worker's earnings do not count toward the earnings requirements because the state ignores the last completed quarter and the current quarter of earnings. By 2003, 19 states had adopted low-wage worker eligibility reforms based on an "alternative base period," which expands eligibility for workers who need their most recent earnings to qualify for UI.[22]

4. *Limited coverage.* In 1975, 75 percent of jobless workers received benefits. By 1986, only 33 percent of jobless workers received benefits. In 2003, only 44 percent of unemployed persons received benefits.[23]

5. *Benefit decline.* In 1986 total UI benefits were 59 percent lower than in 1976 (after adjusting for inflation). Currently, about 47 percent of the average worker's lost wages are replaced by UI benefits. As such, many families cannot afford to live on these benefits. In 2004, the average weekly UI benefits are too low to lift a one-parent, one-child family above the poverty line in 22 states. In another 11 states, the benefit level is less than $1,000 above the poverty line for a two-person family. A 2004 study by the Congressional Budget Office found that almost 25 percent of UI recipients out of work for four months or more fell into poverty despite UI benefits.[24]

6. *Longer spells of unemployment.* UI was based on the assumption that layoffs are temporary and that typically employers will recall workers. Now, however, many people are losing their jobs because of long-term structural shifts in the economy. Deepening recessions, corporate downsizing (the number of workers laid off due to corporate downsizing doubled from 1984 to 1995), and increasing numbers of plant closures (1.5 million factory workers were displaced from 1991 to 1993) has strained the UI system. As a result, the average duration of unemployment has widely fluctuated over the past two decades, and periodically large numbers of people apply for extended benefits. In response, Congress passed the Unemployment Compensation Amendments of 1993, requiring new claimants to be profiled according to their demographic characteristics and work history. Those considered high risk were targeted for special job search assistance.[25]

UI is based on the belief that workers will find suitable re-employment that matches their skills and experience. However, those who receive assistance longer than the norm question this underlying assumption. While most people laid off find re-employment within 27 weeks, one study found that among the long-term unemployed, 38 percent were unemployed for 27 to 40 weeks; 28 percent, 41 to 52 weeks; and 34 percent, 53 to 100 weeks. In contrast, 41 percent of the short-term unemployed were unemployed for 1 to 5 weeks; 37 percent, 6 to 14 weeks; and 22 percent, 15 to 26 weeks. The percentage of those considered long-term unemployed rose from 6 percent in 1970 to to 22 percent by 2003.[26] By 2003, 7 states had adopted various measures to extend unemployment benefits to the long-term unemployed.[27]

7. *Women and unemployment.* Sixty-seven percent of part-time workers are women, and one-third of all women work part time. Women are also more likely to be employed by temporary agencies than are men, and their lower wages make them less likely to meet minimum UI earnings requirements. Finally, many women leave their jobs for voluntary reasons that are not considered "good cause" in many states. In many states, a woman is ineligible for UI benefits if she quits to escape a violent domestic partner, because of a schedule change that makes child care arrangements impossible, to take care of a sick child, or to follow a spouse to another location. Because of these factors, only 39 percent of unemployed women received UI benefits in 2003 compared to 41 percent of men. By 2003, 24 states had adopted family-friendly UI policies covering domestic violence as "good cause" for leaving work and collecting unemployment benefits, and 14 states adopted a "dependant allowance," permitting workers to increase their unemployment benefits based on the number of children being cared for.

8. *Meeting its financial obligations.* The UI system has difficulty in meeting its financial obligations during economic downturns without federal aid or deficit spending. Employers pay into a general fund that is supposed to have adequate financial reserves. Yet, many states borrow billions from the federal government to cover benefits in times of high unemployment. According to the Department of Labor, states have less money in their trust funds than they did in the 1940s and 1950s, thereby creating the potential for serious liability problems.[28]

9. *Tightened eligibility requirements.* In recent years, many states have tightened UI eligibility requirements. In addition, the UI program often fails to help the states with the most severe unemployment problems. For example, the calculation of unemployment rates is based on a study conducted by the Department of Labor in which 60,000 households (individuals 16 years or older are included in the survey) are interviewed each month. Part-time workers are counted as employed, and discouraged workers who dropped out of the labor force are not counted at all. Although the UI program includes mechanisms that allow states to receive more federal reimbursement when unemployment rates are unusually high, the official state rate is lowered because many of the unemployed are not counted. The consequence is that this artificially low rate of unemployment may not set off the extended benefits mechanism.[29] Furthermore, states with "pockets of poverty" receive no additional help when the overall state unemployment rate is not high enough to set off the triggers.

One conservative approach to UI reform transfers the primary responsibility for unemployment insurance to individual workers through the creation of individual unemployment accounts (IUAs). The IUA would be a portable individual trust that belonged to the employee and would work much like an individual retirement account (IRA). IUA holders would be personally responsible for investing and managing their IUA funds. The funds would be created by voluntary tax-free contributions from each worker and/or the employer. The worker would have access to the funds any time he or she was without a job.[30]

Workers' Compensation

The U.S. Bureau of Labor Statistics reported that, in 2003, 5,559 workers were killed on the job in fatal traumatic injuries—about 15 workers a day. There are roughly 6.8 million injuries and illnesses and that about 50,000 workers a year die from workplace-related illnesses.[31]

Workers' Compensation (WC) programs began in 1911 in Wisconsin and New Jersey. By 1948 every state operated some form of WC program. WC programs provide cash, medical assistance, rehabilitation services, and disability and death benefits to persons (or their dependents) who are victims of industrial accidents or occupational illnesses. In the 1990s, WC laws protected more than 97 million workers, or 87 percent of the labor force.[32] Although laws vary from state to state, the basic principle is that employers should assume the costs of occupational disabilities without regard to fault.[33] Although most workers are covered in most states, business owners and independent contractors are often excluded, as are volunteer, farm, railroad, maritime and domestic workers. Federal employees are covered under a special program.

Not only do the specific laws governing Workers' Compensation vary from state to state; there is little consistency either in benefit levels or in the administration of the programs. For example, some states require employers to carry insurance, other states provide a state-sponsored insurance fund, others allow employers to act as self-insurers, and still others do not require compulsory WC coverage. Some state programs do not cover employees of nonprofit, charitable, or religious institutions. Nevertheless, because of the potential for large claims, most employers transfer their responsibility by purchasing insurance from private companies that specialize in Workers' Compensation.

WC programs are problematic in several ways. First, benefit levels are established on the basis of state formulas and are usually calculated as a percentage of weekly earnings (generally about 66.66 percent). As such, each state sets its own annually adjusted benefit level, and these levels vary widely across states. For example, the minimum benefit level in 2003 ranged from $35 a week in Georgia to $339 in Pennsylvania. In 2003, the maximum benefit levels ranged from $323 a week in Mississippi to $1069 in Iowa.[34] Second, the cost to employers for providing WC insurance has been rising rapidly. Employers paid about $56 billion to ensure their workers in 2000, a 30 percent increase over the $43 billion it cost in 1990. Wage replacement and medical costs were the two primary factors behind the rising cost of workers' comp claims. Wage-replacement costs rose roughly 6.6 percent annually from 1996 through 2001 and medical costs jumped 11.5 percent.[35] Third, there is great variability among states in the way claims are handled. Workers are often encouraged to settle out of court for attractive lump sums, even though the amounts may not equal their lost wages. Often, benefits are uneven. For example, the price attached to the loss of a body part has been interpreted differently from state to state. Charles Prigmore and Charles Atherton note that in 1978 in Hawaii the loss of a finger was valued at $5,175, more than the courts in the state of Wyoming allowed for the loss of an eye.[36] In addition, there are often long delays between the time an injury occurs and the period in which benefits start. Finally, in some states employers are exempt from the Workers' Compensation tax if they can demonstrate that they are covered by private insurance. Unfortunately, private insurance coverage may prove inadequate after a disability benefit is determined. Even though injured workers or their survivors received $44.9 billion in benefits and medical payments in 2000, Workers' Compensation may not provide adequate protection for many disabled workers.[37]

The Social Security Dilemma

Because of its widespread public support, Social Security was long perceived by policy analysts and legislators as the third rail of politics—touch it and you die. Besides, the immediate focus of conservative Republicans and Democrats was on the more vulnerable public assistance programs, which enjoyed less public support. In the late 1990s, however, emboldened by the successful passage of the Personal

Spotlight 10.1

Major Social Insurance Programs

In the United States, there are three *major* social insurance programs:

- OASDI (also known as Social Security) covers the elderly, survivors, and those people unable to work due to a disability.
- Unemployment Insurance covers workers who have been fired or laid off from their jobs.
- Workers' Compensation provides case, medical assistance, rehabilitation services, and disability and death benefits to persons (or their dependents) who are victims of industrial accidents or occupational illnesses.

Responsibility and Work Opportunity Reconciliation Act of 1996, conservatives turned their attention to social insurance, the real welfare giant.

Criticisms leveled at the Social Security system were particularly pointed during the 1980s and 1990s. Opponents argued that Social Security was depressing private savings (and thereby providing less capital for investment) by giving people a retirement check financed by the working population rather than interest on accumulated savings. Indeed, the average Social Security recipient in 1999 would have needed a savings account of more than $190,000 (at 5 percent interest) to collect interest equal to the average benefit ($9,575) in that year.

Arguments against the Current Social Security System

As in most nations, Social Security in the United States is a pay-as-you-go system; as such, it is an intergenerational wealth transfer plan based on demographic factors. Birthrate and longevity determine the solvency of pay-as-you-go retirement systems.

The U.S. birthrate at the time of the creation of Social Security was 2.3, but it rose to 3.0 by 1950 and continued to climb throughout that decade. Today it has dropped back to 2.1. The average life expectancy in 1935 was 63; today it is about 77.5. As a result of these demographic factors, the number of workers paying Social Security payroll taxes has gone from 16 for every retiree in 1950 to just 3.3 for every Social Security beneficiary in 1997. That ratio is expected to decline to just 2 to 1 by the year 2025.

Not unexpectedly, the payroll tax has increased continuously over Social Security's history. From an original tax of just 2 percent on a maximum taxable income of $300, the payroll tax has been increased more than 30 times and in 2004 was set at 12.4 percent of a maximum income of $ $87,900. Moreover, the Social Security payroll tax would have to rise to 18 percent (if Medicare were included, nearly 28 percent) to pay all promised benefits under the current program. Obviously, this payroll tax level has a negative impact on workers' earnings. Moreover, these tax rates reflect the actuarial estimates of the Social Security system. Historically, the more pessimistic assumptions have proved to be the most accurate. Under those assumptions, the total payroll tax would rise to 44 percent—nearly triple what it is today.

Social Security is helping to exacerbate intergenerational tensions. Younger workers are skeptical about the ability of Social Security to support them when they retire. They are nervous that Social Security will buckle when the baby boomers start retiring around 2010. Some are also anxious because they are saving less than their parents. In short, some younger workers fear that they will be denied Social Security benefits despite having made enormous contributions. Ted Dimig sums up the dilemma: "So, where does this leave my generation? First of all, it leaves us with a huge resentment over the idea that our elders might saddle us with the debt for their retirement . . . while shortchanging us on our own retirement."[38]

Although OASDI is an important part of economic security for the nation's retired, serious problems threaten its future viability. The original strategy of the Social Security Act of 1935 was to create a self-perpetuating insurance fund, with benefits to the elderly being in proportion to their contributions. That scenario did not materialize. For example, in 1992 a single man retiring at age 65 would have received a maximum Social Security benefit of $13,056 per year, plus an additional $1,756 yearly in Medicare benefits. If the worker had started contributing to the Social Security fund in 1950 and contributed regularly at the maximum level until he retired in 1992, the total contribution would have been about $52,000. Yet in three and a half years this worker would have received his entire contribution back in benefits. If the worker survived to age 72, his benefits would exceed his contributions by $51,000. That amount does not include any cost-of-living increases. Put another way, a man who retired in 1980 could expect to receive Social Security benefits 3.7 times greater than his contributions would have generated if invested in low-risk government securities. For a similar woman, this ratio was even higher—4.4 times—given her longer life expectancy.[39] On the other hand, this windfall may not be true for current workers, since both the tax and the wage base upon which the tax is determined has increased dramatically since the 1970s. Whether current workers will recover their entire investment will depend on how long they live, whether they are married and whether they earned a high or low wage.

Arguments for the Current Social Security System

The Social Security program serves four main functions. (1) It supports more than 7 million survivors of deceased workers and 4 million disabled Americans. (2) Social Security is the nation's most successful antipoverty program. Largely because of Social Security, the poverty rate among the nation's elderly has fallen over the last 50 years from more than 40 percent to 10.4 percent. Today, only 40 percent of elderly Americans have access to public or private pension plans or annuities.[40] Without Social Security about half of elderly Americans would have incomes below the poverty level. For two-thirds of the elderly, Social Security is their major source of income. For a third of the elderly it is virtually their only income. (3) Social Security is important to working as well as retired Americans. Seniors who are financially solvent remain viable consumers, which is good for businesses that depend on domestic demand. In addition, given current lifestyles, few children would trade the burden of payroll taxes for the onus of supporting destitute retired parents. (4) Social Security is a special kind of "investment" unavailable in the private sector: a lifetime retirement annuity with benefits that rise with inflation. Almost all corporate pensions (many which run out after 20 years) are not indexed to compensate for the erosion of purchasing power caused by inflation. The belief that the basic protection provided by Social Security is analogous to private savings and would be unnecessary if people just saved more is spurious. And as a disability insurance policy, Social Security provides coverage equivalent to a $203,000 policy in the private sector; a similar dependent and survivor policy for a 27-year-old average-wage worker with two children would be equivalent to a $295,000 private sector policy.[41] About one in three Social Security beneficiaries is not a retiree.

Social Security has also been accused of overpaying the elderly, slighting younger workers (who could get a better return if they invested privately), and leading the nation to financial collapse. Merton and Joan Bernstein challenge these criticisms leveled at Social Security. They claim that rather than discouraging private savings, Social Security actually stimulates financial planning for retirement and thus encourages savings.[42] Others counter the overpayment argument by noting that in 2002 52 percent of families over age 65 had total annual incomes under $35,000, while only 30 percent had annual incomes exceeding $50,000. Almost 32 percent of elderly nonfamily households (persons living alone or with relatives) had annual incomes below $10,000.[43] These numbers do not suggest an elderly population that is becoming wealthy by exploiting an overly generous Social Security system.

Social Security in Trouble

Social Security began to show signs of fiscal trouble in the mid-1970s. Between 1975 and 1981 the Old-Age and Survivors Insurance fund suffered a net decrease in funds and a deficit in the reserve of between $790 million and $4.9 billion a year. This imbalance between incoming and outgoing funds threatened to deplete the reserve by 1983. Moreover, the prospects for Social Security seemed bleak in other ways. Whereas the ratio of workers to supported beneficiaries (the dependency ratio) was then three to one, estimates at the time indicated that by the end of the century (with the retirement of the baby boom generation) that ratio would be only two to one. In short, the long-term costs of the program would exceed its projected revenues. The crisis in Social Security was fueled by demographic changes (a dropping birthrate plus an increase in life expectancy), more liberal benefits paid to retiring workers, high inflation, high unemployment, and the COLAs passed by Congress in the mid-1970s.

Facing these short- and long-term problems, Congress moved quickly to pass PL 98–21, the Social Security Amendments of 1983. Among the newly legislated changes were a delay in the cost-of-living adjustments and a stabilizer placed on future COLAs. Specifically, if trust funds fall below a certain level, future benefits will be keyed to the consumer price index (CPI) or the average wage increase, whichever is lower. A second change was that Social Security benefits became taxable if taxable income plus Social Security benefits exceeded $25,000 for an individual or $32,000 for a couple. A third change increased the 2027 retirement age to 67 to collect full benefits. Although workers could retire at age 62, they would receive only 70 percent of their benefits instead of 80 percent. Finally, coverage was extended: New federal employees were covered for the first time, as well as members of Congress, the president and vice president, federal judges, and employees of nonprofit corporations.

In the mid-1990s the Social Security rules were again changed, this time easing the historic Social Security penalty for about one million beneficiaries aged 65 to 67 who are still working. Previously, annual earnings that exceeded $11,250 would result in $1.00 of benefits lost for every $2.00 earned. The new rules gradually raised the limit to $14,000, then to $30,000 by 2002. The new rules also allowed those over 70 to continue working without losing Social Security benefits.[44]

The Long-Term Prospects for Social Security

Despite these reforms, the fiscal viability of the OASDI system remains in question. Some analysts suggest that Social Security is on sound footing. They point to the fact that the income and assets reserve in the combined OASDI trust funds reached $1.53 trillion in 2003. At the end of 2003, the combined assets of the OASI and the DI Trust funds were 306 percent of estimated expenditures for 2004.[45] By 2025 that amount is projected to peak at $6 trillion.[46] Proponents maintain that the finances of the system will be in close actuarial balance for the next 75 years, with no more than a 5 percent difference between incoming and outgoing revenues.[47] Other analysts point to Congressional Budget Office (CBO) projections that by 2015, when the post–World War II baby boomers retire, OASDI benefit payments will begin to exceed taxes, and trust funds will be exhausted in 2042. At that time, Social Security will be able to pay 73 percent of benefits owed, if no changes are made[48] (see Figure 10.2). The Disability Insurance Fund (DI) will be able to pay full benefits through only 2029 (see Tables 10.2 and 10.3).[49]

The Medicare Hospital Insurance fund (HI), which pays hospital expenses, is projected to be able to pay benefits until 2025. This is longer than originally projected partly because the robust economic growth of the 1990s helped fuel the fund. Despite this, the HI program will likely require additional reforms to ensure its long-term stability. The Supplementary Medical Insurance (SMI) trust fund, which pays doctors' bills and other outpatient expenses, is expected to remain adequately funded into the indefinite future, because current law sets financing each year to meet the next year's expected costs. Despite this funding stability, SMI costs rose 38 percent from 1995 to 2000, or about 5 percent faster than the economy as a whole.

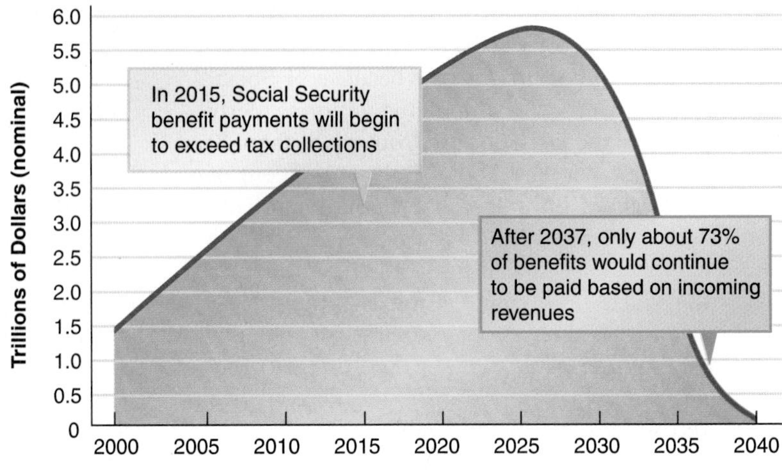

Figure 10.2

Projected Exhaustion of the Social Security Trust Fund in 2037

Source: Social Security Administration, "The Future of Social Security," Publication No. 05-10055, August 2000. Retrieved from www.ssa.gov/pubs/10055.html.

Other critics complain that the federal government is borrowing from the current Social Security surplus to fund other programs and is thereby hiding the real extent of the federal deficit. Money in the Social Security trust funds was intended to be invested and to be set aside for future years, not to

Table 10.2

Key Dates for the Trust Funds

	OASI	DI	OASDI	HI
First year outgo exceeds income excluding interest	2018	2008	2018	2004
First year outgo exceeds income including interest	2029	2017	2028	2010
Year trust funds are exhausted	2044	2029	2042	2019

Source: Social Security Administration. Retrieved September 2004 from www.ssa.gov/OACT/TRSUM/trsummary.html.

Table 10.3

Year of Trust Fund Exhaustion Using Social Security Administration Estimates

Set of Assumptions	OASI	DI	OASDI	HI
Alternative I (low cost)	Never	Never	Never	Never
Alternative II (best estimate)	2044	2028	2042	2025
Alternative III (high cost)	2033	2015	2031	2012

Source: Committee on Ways and Means, U.S. House of Representatives, *2004 Green Book* (Washington, DC: U.S. Government Office, 2004), pp. 1–60.

be used to finance other government spending. But in 1990, for example, $65 billion in Social Security surpluses went for non–Social Security spending. As a result, part of almost every federal program is paid for by the Social Security payroll tax. In that sense, the real budget deficit—and the absence of a *real* Social Security surplus to pay for future benefits—has been hidden from the public.[50]

Although some Social Security reforms have provided a short-term solution, structural problems continue to plague the system. As already discussed, one problem is the "graying of America." Since 1900 the percentage of Americans 65 years and older has more than tripled (from 4.1 percent in 1900 to 12.3 percent in 2002), and the absolute number has increased 11.5 times (from 3.1 million to 35.6 million).[51] Demographic projections suggest that by 2030 the number of persons over age 65 will increase to 70.5 million. In other words, by 2030 the percentage of elderly is expected to climb from the current rate of 12.34 percent to 19.4 percent. Furthermore, the elderly are living longer. Between 1900 and 1990 the 75- to 84-year-old group increased 16 times, and the 85-and-over group was 38 times larger.[52] These demographic trends suggest that the **dependency ratio** will significantly increase, as will the pressures on the Social Security system. For example, in 1960 the worker/beneficiary ratio was 5 to 1; by 2001 it had dropped to 3.4 to 1. By 2025 the dependency ratio is expected to be 2 to 1.[53] A question arises whether two workers in 2040 will be able to support one retired person, and whether the Social Security system—as it is presently structured—can support 20 percent of the U.S. population.

Another problem facing Social Security is the increasing tax burden. Social Security taxes on working families grew more rapidly in the 1980s than at any time since the passage of the Social Security Act in 1935. Between 1983 and 1990 the Social Security tax rate was raised six times, and from 1981 to 1992 the income level subject to the tax almost doubled. As a result, a worker's maximum payroll tax jumped from $1,502 in 1981 to more than $4,000 (including the Medicare portion of the tax) in 1996, an increase of more than 66 percent factoring in inflation. From 1937 to 1990 the maximum Social Security tax increased 100 times.[54] Social Security taxes now represent the second largest revenue producer for the federal government.

Proposed Solutions for Social Security

Several solutions have been proposed to address the impending crisis in Social Security. In 1994 President Bill Clinton appointed a Social Security Advisory Council. The mandate of the council was to focus on the future viability of the system. Three distinct proposals emerged, all of which entailed investing some Social Security funds in private financial markets.

Two of the three recommendations proposed individual investment accounts (over which the beneficiary would have some control) financed with Social Security payroll taxes. The first, proposed by former Social Security commissioner Robert Ball, called for raising Social Security taxes. In addition, Ball's plan also called for investing up to 40 percent of trust fund reserves in private capital markets.

The second solution, offered by Edward Gramlich, would trim benefits and add revenues. Gramlich called for creating a "double deck" plan: Workers would receive a basic benefit based on the number of years they worked, plus a "second deck" or add-on to their benefits equal to 15 percent of their average wages earned over their lifetime. In effect, benefits for low-income workers would remain the same, and benefits for high-income workers would be cut. Under Gramlich's proposal the retirement age would be raised to age 67 in 2027. In addition, Gramlich proposed to exclude benefits awarded to spouses of future retirees. To compensate for reduced benefits, workers would be allowed to purchase annuities from the government through defined contribution accounts established within the Social Security system and funded by a 1.6 percent increase in the payroll tax. Participants would have limited investment discretion over these accounts. Finally, Gramlich proposed that the Social Security fund be forced to invest 25 percent of its funds in stocks, which would theoretically yield a higher return over the long term than government bonds.[55] (In down times, it can also yield a lower return.)

The third option, proposed by businessman Sylvester Shieber, would replace Social Security with flat benefits independent of earnings and large mandatory personal retirement accounts. These accounts would be funded by diverting a part of the current payroll tax, and would be held and managed by individuals.[56] Significant pressure was exerted for at least a partial privatization of the Social Security system.

Projections about the future of Social Security are predicated on the belief that certain economic and demographic factors will be in play for the next 50 years, but economic and demographic shifts could easily invalidate the most earnest predictions. For example, a recession (such as the one in 2001), changing demographic trends, an oil crisis, and/or major changes in immigration patterns would all have profound consequences for the future of Social Security. However, there is nothing inviolate about the way Social Security is currently funded. An act of Congress could easily eliminate the insurance feature of Social Security and replace it with general revenue taxes. Given the widespread dependence on Social Security, it seems highly unlikely that policymakers and the public will allow the system to go bankrupt.

Another issue in Social Security involves the competition between public (compulsory) and private (voluntary) pension plans. Some critics argue that private pension plans are preferable to public plans since they are not dependent on the government and have greater potential for yielding higher returns. Private pensions originated as a means of encouraging employee loyalty and as a way of easing out aging workers. However, only about one-third of all workers and one-fourth of current employees are covered under private pension plans. Moreover, only a small fraction of these plans are indexed for inflation.

Critics of private pension plans argue that they are basically unreliable. Employees can switch jobs and thus lose their pension rights, companies can go bankrupt, corporations can raid pension funds, many are based on the vicissitudes of company stock (e.g., Enron) and workers risk losing their entire retirement if the corporate stock drops, and corrupt or incompetent pension managers can wreak havoc on pension plans. The 20 largest U.S. pension funds hold 10 percent of the equity capital of the largest U.S. companies, and in total, they own assets worth well over \$2.5 trillion.[57] Despite federal tax subsidies to private pension plans totaling more than \$64 billion in 1988, coverage under these plans has actually decreased since 1980. Supporters of Social Security argue that unlike the riskier private pension plans, OASDI benefits are portable and indexed for inflation; also, workers are immediately vested in Social Security, and benefits are not contingent on the financial condition of the employer.[58]

Although originally intended to supplement private pension funds and to operate as a pay-as-you-go insurance plan, OASDI has taken on many characteristics of a public welfare program. Specifically, most current retirees are realizing benefits far in excess of their contributions. (Those who retired in 1993 were the first group of workers to possibly receive less in benefits than they paid in taxes.)

The question remains: Should social insurance be modified to reflect social assistance and income redistribution goals? If the answer is yes, then benefits must be structured to reflect the current needs of retired workers rather than their past contributions. Furthermore, if Social Security is viewed as a public welfare program, then its regressive tax structure must be modified along more progressive lines. For example, Social Security is the single largest tax paid by a low-income worker, yet that same worker receives the lowest benefits when they retire. In short, the workers hurt most by the tax receive the fewest benefits. Using that same line of reasoning, if Social Security is designed for social assistance, then should everyone, regardless of income, be eligible? More particularly, should the very wealthy be allowed to be beneficiaries? Unfortunately, there are no simple answers to these questions.

Should We Privatize Social Security?

Proposals to fully or partially privatize Social Security with individually managed accounts have emerged from several quarters, including the Clinton administration. Supporters argue that privatization would provide the individual with control of the Social Security portion of their retirement plan, and that successful investors who never touched their

Critics of privatization argue that privatization would replace the guaranteed economic security of Social Security with risky stock market accounts.

accumulations could achieve higher rates of return and higher benefits than Social Security provides.

The question of privatizing Social Security played an important role in the 2000 and 2004 presidential campaigns. By early 2005 the largely theoretical debate about privatizing Social Security came to a head when the Bush administration released its Social Security reform plan. In one of the greatest challenges to Social Security since its inception in 1935, the Bush plan would divert some payroll taxes into private accounts that could be invested in the stock market. Specifically, the plan would let younger workers divert up to two-thirds of their Social Security taxes into private accounts, which they could invest in stocks and bonds. At the same time, the guaranteed Social Security benefit would be cut by up to 40 percent. The following is a brief summary of the Bush plan.

Overview of the Bush Plan The plan restructures Social Security to allow workers under age 55 to divert a portion of their Social Security payroll taxes into private investment accounts in exchange for lower guaranteed future benefits. Workers would invest this money in stocks and bonds in hopes of earning higher returns. There would be no change in the current system or benefit levels for those born before 1950.

Any worker born in 1950 or after would be eligible to start a voluntary personal account. A worker could choose to remain in the current system, but would not be guaranteed the same benefit levels as current retirees or those born before 1950. Participation in the plan would be phased in over three years, starting in 2009. Workers could not leave the personal account system once they entered it.

Bush's Rationale The Bush administration asserts that Social Security payroll taxes belong to the people and they should decide what to do with them. Over the long haul, individuals can expect to earn higher returns by investing in stocks, or a mix of stocks and bonds, than from what is generated now by the low-yielding Treasury bonds held by the Social Security trust fund.

Since the accounts are individually owned, they could be passed along to heirs—with certain exceptions. Supporters acknowledge that personal accounts alone will not solve the system's long-term financial problems without other structural changes.

The Mechanics of the Partial Privatization Plan Personal accounts would be administered publicly. Accounts would be modeled on the Thrift Savings Plan, a retirement system for federal workers in which there are five investment options, all mutual funds. A person could hold a mix of the funds. A sixth fund is also envisioned, whereby the ratio of stocks to bonds would change as a worker got older, becoming less risky as they approach retirement.

Workers could divert about two-thirds of their retirement taxes into personal accounts. For the first year, the total diverted into personal accounts could not exceed $1,000. This cap would rise by $100 a year. Eventually, workers at all incomes could contribute the full amount.

Workers would continue to get traditional benefits from the Social Security system because the private accounts would represent only a percentage of benefits. Future benefit levels from the traditional system would be cut.

Nothing could be withdrawn from the personal accounts before retirement, nor could money be borrowed from them. People entering retirement would have to buy an investment annuity that would assure that their income would at least reach the poverty level when the accounts and the traditional benefits are combined.

The government would borrow money to pay benefits during the phase-in to personal accounts; estimates have ranged as high as $2 trillion over 10 years.

Risks and Critique Treasury bonds are virtually risk free; stocks and corporate bonds are not. Sudden and prolonged periods of market decline, such as in 1987 and 2001, or a lack of economic growth could deplete retirement assets.

Although some conservatives want privatization and personal accounts, they favor paying for them with general revenue, which would mean borrowing the money. In that scenario, taxes collected for Social Security would be left alone to pay for traditional program benefits.

Critics argue that limited privatization would open the door to full privatization, which in the end would create a purely voluntary system that would destroy Social Security. In that scenario, worker benefits would be entirely dependent on the performance of the stock market. Critics also claim that privatization is a draconian solution to solve the problems of Social Security. The system needs changes, but not ones that are so major. Besides, the problems in the system are overblown to make the case for privatization. Lastly, they argue that for privatization to work, the economic system must be robust so that stock dividends are high. In that case, the current Social Security system would also be doing well—incomes would be rising, which would then translate into higher revenues flowing into the system.[59]

Conclusion

Social insurance programs are replete with both contradictions and difficulties. Nevertheless, social insurance programs, especially OASDI, have become a mainstay of the American social welfare state. Despite the original intent of its architects, Social Security has become a primary source of financial support for elderly Americans. Moreover, OASDI has demonstrated the ability not only to arrest the poverty rate for its constituents, but actually to reduce it. A majority of Americans have come to view Social Security as a right and to count on its benefits.

Social insurance programs represent a major source of security for both elderly Americans and present-day workers. Over the past 50 years, Americans have come to believe that regardless of the ebb and flow of economic life, Social Security and Unemployment Insurance embody a firm governmental commitment to care for workers and the elderly. Economic gains made by elderly people since the mid-1960s have validated this belief. Because Social Security is clearly linked to past contributions, beneficiaries experience little stigma. This is not true for the highly stigmatized beneficiaries of public assistance programs, and it is to this population that we will turn in Chapter 11.

Discussion Questions

1. Social insurance programs, especially Social Security, are among the most popular social programs in the nation. Part of the reason for this popularity is that unlike income maintenance programs, social insurance is not stigmatized. What are other reasons for the popularity of social insurance programs?
2. Serious questions exist about the future of Social Security. Some critics argue that Social Security is doomed, because the trust funds are

expected to be depleted by the middle of the next century. Other observers argue that Social Security is sound, because the federal government is backing it. Is Social Security on solid ground, and can we expect it to be healthy in the future? If so, why? If not, why not? What can be done to make the system more stable?

3. The Social Security system is currently plagued by several different problems. What are the three most important problems facing the system?

Notes

1. See Committee on Ways and Means, *2004 Green Book,* U.S. House of Representatives, Book, (Washington, DC: U.S. Government Office, 2004), pp. I-7, I-46, 7–37.
2. Congressional Budget Office (CBO), "The Budget and Economic Outlook: Fiscal Years 2003–2012," January 2002. Retrieved October 2004 from www.cbo.gov/showdoc.cfm?index=3277&sequence=14#tableF-10
3. Frances Fox Piven and Richard A. Cloward, *Regulating the Poor: The Functions of Public Welfare* (New York: Vintage Books, 1971).
4. David P. Beverly and Edward A. McSweeney, *Social Welfare and Social Justice* (Englewood Cliffs, NJ: Prentice-Hall, 1987).
5. Piven and Cloward, *Regulating the Poor,* p. 100.
6. W. Andrew Achenbaum, "Social Security: Yesterday, Today and Tomorrow," The Leon and Josephine Winkelman Lecture, School of Social Work, University of Michigan, March 12, 1996.
7. Ibid.
8. U.S. Census Bureau, Average and Effective Interest Rates, *Statistical Abstract of the United States: 2003* (Washington, DC: U.S. Census Bureau, 2004,) p. 361.
9. See Social Security Administration, "Fast Facts and Figures about Social Security," retrieved October 2004 from www.ssa.gov/policy/docs/chartbooks/fast_facts/2003/ff2003.pdf; and Committee on Ways and Means, *2004 Green Book,* p. A-7.
10. Department of the Census, *Current Population Reports, 1981,* Series P-60, No. 125 (Washington, DC: U.S. Government Printing Office, 1981).
11. Social Security Administration, "Fast Facts: SSI." Retrieved November 2001 from www.ssa.gov:80/statistics/fastfacts/pageii.html
12. Ibid.
13. Social Security Administration, "Fast Facts and Figures about Social Security," p. 1. Retrieved October 2004 from www.ssa.gov/policy/docs/chartbooks/fast_facts/2003/ff2003.pdf
14. Ibid.
15. Ibid.
16. U.S. House of Representatives, Committee on Ways and Means; *Overview of Entitlement Programs, 1992 Green Book* (Washington, DC: U.S. Government Printing Office, 1992), p. 485.
17. See U.S. Department of Labor, "UI Data Summary," 2000. Retrieved October 2001 from www.workforcesecurity.doleta.gov/unemploy/content/data_stats/datasum00/2ndqtr/home.htm; and U.S. Department of Labor Employment and Training Administration; Section A: Labor Force Data, retrieved October 2004 from workforcesecurity.doleta.gov/unemploy/content/chartbook/descript.asp#chta5.
18. Isaac Shapiro and Marion Nichols, *Far From Fixed: An Analysis of the Unemployment Insurance System* (Washington, DC: Center on Budget and Policy Priorities, March 1992), p. viii.
19. Diana M. DiNitto, *Social Welfare: Politics and Public Policy* (Englewood Cliffs, NJ: Prentice-Hall, 1991), p. 87.
20. Economic Policy Institute, "EPI Issue Guide, Unemployment Insurance, August 2004." Retrieved October 2004 from www.epinet.org/content.cfm/issueguides_unemployment_index.
21. U.S. Department of Labor Employment & Training Administration, "Benefits and Duration Information by State for CYQ: 2003, 2004." Retrieved October 2004 from workforcesecurity.doleta.gov/unemploy/content/data_stats/datasum03/2ndqtr/sum.asp#ben
22. See Ibid; and Economic Policy Institute, "EPI Issue Guide, Unemployment Insurance."
23. Committee on Ways and Means, *2004 Green Book,* pp. 4–7
24. Ibid.
25. Oren Levin-Waldman, "Reforming Unemployment Insurance: Toward Greater Employment," Working Paper No. 152, The Jerome Levy Economics Institute, Annandale-on-Hudson, NY, December 1995.
26. U.S. Department of Labor Employment and Training Administration, "Labor Force Data." Retrieved October 2004 from workforcesecurity.doleta.gov/unemploy/content/chartbook/descript.asp#chta10
27. Economic Policy Institute, "EPI Issue Guide, Unemployment Insurance."
28. U.S. Department of Labor, "UI Data Summary," 2000.
29. Ibid.
30. Stephen M. Colarelli and Lawrence Brunner, "Solving Problems in Unemployment Insurance," Mackinac Center for Public Policy, 1994. Retrieved October 2001 from www.mackinac.org/13

31. See Bureau of Labor Statistics, "Census of Fatal Occupational Injuries." Retrieved October 2004 from www.bls.gov/iif/oshwc/cfoi/cfch0002.pdf; and Joseph Dear, "Partner, Not Problem," *TechNews* 1, no. 1 (January/February 1995), p. 1.
32. DiNitto, *Social Welfare.*
33. Ways and Means Committee, *1992 Green Book,* pp. 1707–1709.
34. Committee on Ways and Means, *2004 Green Book,* pp. 15–140.
35. Annmarie Geddes Lipold, "The Soaring Costs of Workers' Comp," Workforce Management, 2004. Retrieved October 2004 from www.workforce.com/section/02/feature/23/39/86
36. Charles Prigmore and Charles Atherton, *Social Welfare Policy* (Lexington, MA: D.C. Heath, 1979) pp. 66–67.
37. Committee on Ways and Means, *2004 Green Book,* pp. 15–138.
38. Ted Dimig, "Social Security on the Brink," *Houston Chronicle* (August 4, 1996), pp. 1F and 4F.
39. Joseph F. Quinn and Olivia S. Mitchell, "Social Security on the Table," *The American Prospect* 26 (May–June 1996), pp. 76–81.
40. AARP, *AARP Profile of Older Persons: 2003,* 2004. Retrieved September 2004 from research.aarp.org/general/profile_2003.pdf
41. C. Eugene Steuerle, "Why Are Social Security Benefits Adjusted Every Year?" AARP Webplace, 2000. Retrieved October 2001 from www.aarp.org
42. C. Merton and Joan Broadshaug Bernstein, *Social Security: The System That Works* (New York: Basic Books, 1987).
43. AARP, *AARP Profile of Older Persons: 2003.*
44. Michael Doerflein, Angela Garner, Niki Gober, and Stacy Lochala, "Social Insurance." Unpublished paper, Graduate School of Social Work, University of Houston, Houston, TX, May 1996.
45. Social Security Administration, 2004 OASDI Trustees Report. Retrieved October 2004 from www.ssa.gov/OACT/TR/TR04/II_cyoper.html.
46. See Social Security Administration, Summary 2004, retrieved October 2004 from www.ssa.gov/OACT/TRSUM/trsummary.html; and Spenser Rich, "Plan Deepens Cuts for Future Retirees," *Washington Post* (May 22, 1995), p. A1.
47. Bernard Gavzer, "How Secure is Your Social Security?" *Parade* (Oct. 18, 1987), p. 9.
48. Social Security Administration, "The Future of Social Security," 2000. Retrieved October 2001 from www.ssa.gov/pubs/100.55.html
49. See Social Security Administration, Summary 2004; and Social Security Administration, "Social Security and Medicare Board of Trustees, A Summary of the 2000 Annual Reports, April 2000." Retrieved October 2001 from www.ssa.gov/OACT/TRSUM/trsummary.html
50. Robert J. Shapiro, "The Right Idea for 1990: Cut Social Security Taxes," *Economic Outlook,* 4 (January 29, 1990).
51. See AARP, *AARP Profile of Older Persons: 2003;* Committee on Ways and Means, *2004 Green Book,* p. A-2.
52. See AARP, *AARP Profile of Older Persons: 2003.*
53. Committee on Ways and Means, *2004 Green Book.*
54. Social Security Administration, *Social Security Bulletin, Annual Statistical Supplement, 1984–85* (Baltimore, MD: Social Security Administration, April 1986); and Shapiro, "The Right Idea for 1990."
55. Doerflein et al., "Social Insurance."
56. Quinn and Mitchell, "Social Security on the Table."
57. Peter F. Drucker, "Reckoning with the Pension Fund Revolution," *Harvard Business Review* (March 1, 1991), pp. 1–9.
58. Bernstein and Bernstein, *Social Security.*
59. Laura Meckler, "Republicans Voice Doubt about Bush Plan. And in the Senate, Not a Single Democrat Has Signed On," Associated Press (February 4, 2005); Terence Hunt, "Bush Pushes Social Security Overhaul," *Chicago Sun-Times* (February 3, 2005), p. 6; and Richard W. Stevenson, "Vast Borrowing Seen in Altering Social Security," *New York Times* (November 28, 2004), p. 2.

CHAPTER 11

Public Assistance Programs

This chapter examines key public assistance programs, including the former Aid to Families with Dependent Children (AFDC); AFDC's replacement, Temporary Assistance to Needy Families (TANF); Supplemental Security Income (SSI); and general assistance (GA). This chapter also investigates and analyzes the problems and issues inherent in public assistance programs.

The American social welfare state is a complex brew of programs, policies, and services. Perhaps few people, including many policymakers, fully appreciate the complexity of the welfare system. One reason is that unlike many European countries, which operate under a comprehensive and integrated welfare plan, the United States relies on a patchwork quilt of social welfare programs and policies. Because of the nation's historical ambivalence toward providing public relief, most welfare legislation has emerged from compromises and adroit political maneuvering rather than from a systematic plan. In short, public assistance in the United States is not a coordinated, comprehensive, integrated, and nonredundant system of social welfare services; instead, it is a disorganized mix of programs and policies.

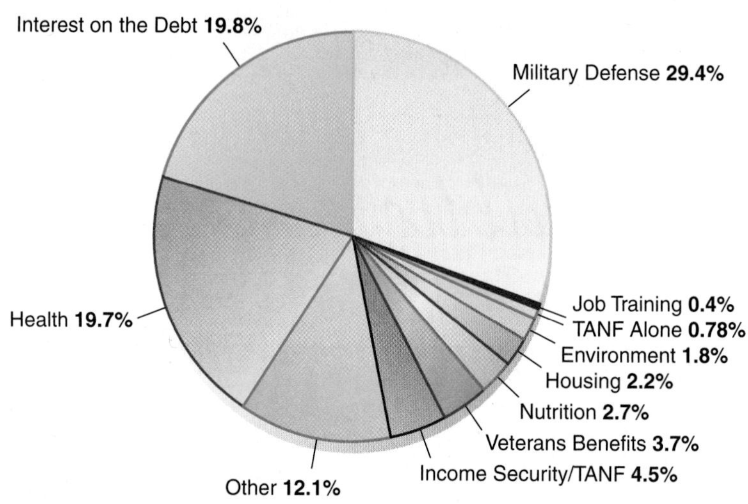

Figure 11.1

Where Federal Dollars Go, 2003

Source: National Priorities Project, "NPP Income Tax Chart," 2004. Retrieved October 2004 from www.nationalpriorities.org/taxes/IncomeTaxChart04.html?T1=10000. Used by permission.

Public assistance programs are one of the most misunderstood parts of the U.S. welfare state. Although expenditures for public assistance programs are far less than for social insurance programs, they tend to be more controversial. Unlike social insurance, public assistance programs are based entirely on need and are therefore means tested. Figure 11.1 illustrates the major federal governmental spending areas and the relative expenditures on each.

Public assistance programs that offer cash, medical, and other forms of assistance are based on

Spotlight 11.1

Key Public Assistance Programs in the United States

In the United States there are three major public assistance programs:

1. Temporary Assistance to Needy Families (TANF): a block grant based on workfare, time-limited benefits (a maximum of 5 years), and strict work participation rates
2. Supplemental Security Income (SSI): provides cash assistance to the elderly and to disabled poor people, including children
3. General Assistance (GA): state or locally run programs designed to provide basic benefits to low-income people who are ineligible for federally funded public assistance programs

the concept of safety nets: plans designed to ensure that citizens receive basic services so they do not fall below a certain poverty level. There are, however, 51 separate safety nets—one in each state and in the District of Columbia. Although federal guidelines help determine the level of aid for the poor, individual states have extensive freedom to fashion their own safety nets. States differ as to benefit levels, and the vast majority lack an adequate safety net to help the poor and the jobless.[1] Nevertheless, a major component of the safety net are programs designed to ensure that families and individuals receive the resources necessary for survival.

Assumptions and Myths about Public Assistance

Americans' attitudes toward public assistance are characterized by a mixture of compassion and hostility. This ambivalence plays out in a series of harsh and often conflicting assumptions about public assistance recipients. The struggle around public assistance programs is symbolic, reflecting the tensions in Americans' ideas about wealth, opportunity, and privilege.

On the hostility side, the argument goes like this: If privilege is earned by hard work, then people are poor because they are lazy and lack ambition. To those driven by the American spirit of competitiveness, the refusal of the poor to compete is a serious character flaw. On the other hand, only a few paychecks separate the welfare recipient from the average citizen—thus the compassion. Although democratic capitalism is based on the belief that hard work guarantees success, real life often tells a different story. The following assumptions, among others, underlie much of the discussion around public assistance: (1) Generous benefits create a disincentive to work; therefore, recipients must always receive less income benefits than the minimum wage. (2) Welfare recipients need prodding to work because they lack internal motivation. (3) Work is the best antipoverty program. (4) Public assistance programs must be highly stigmatized lest people will turn to them too readily. (5) Women receiving public assistance should work, and poor children should not have the luxury of being raised by a full-time homemaker. These assumptions about public assistance—many of which are remarkably similar to those found in the Elizabethan Poor Laws—contain numerous myths.

Because of the many myths surrounding public assistance, it is important to discriminate between fact and fiction. (In the items that follow, AFDC and TANF are used interchangeably because they served and serve the same clientele.)

Myth 1. Many families on the public assistance rolls include an able-bodied father who refuses to work.

Fact. In 2000 only 53,300 out of 2.7 million TANF families were two-parent families. This was a significant drop from the 342,000 two-parent TANF families in 1995. The vast majority of TANF families are headed by one parent—mostly mothers who are unmarried, divorced, widowed, or separated.[2] Ninety percent of TANF children live with their mothers and 10 percent with their fathers. In 2000, the total number of TANF recipients was 1,579,000 adults and 4,385,000 children. Fewer than 1 percent of all welfare recipients are able-bodied males.[3]

Myth 2. Most poor people are on public assistance, and the number is growing.

Fact. HHS data show that about half of TANF-eligible families do not receive assistance and that non-receipt among eligible families is increasing. In 2000, only about half of families poor enough to qualify for TANF received monthly cash assistance, down from nearly 8 in 10 eligible families in 1996.[4] Overall, the percentage of the poor receiving welfare has declined since the early 1970s.[5] In terms of families, the TANF rolls decreased from 1996 to 2001 by 53 percent.[6] In the mid-1990s about 85 percent of children living in poverty received cash assistance; by 2002 only 33 percent did.[7]

Myth 3. Recipient mothers have more children in order to collect greater benefits; therefore, families on public assistance are large and steadily growing in size.

Fact. The average size of TANF families in 2000 was 2.6 persons. TANF families had an average of 1.9 children, which remained unchanged from earlier years. Two in five families had only one child. One in 10 families had more than three children. The state with the largest number of TANF-dependent children was Louisiana (2.9 children), which has one of the lowest benefit levels.[8] Slightly less than half of all states have **family cap** legislation, which prohibits TANF families from receiving additional assistance for any child born after the mother has enrolled in the program.[9]

Myth 4. Once on welfare, always on welfare.

Fact. This is now a moot point, because the 1996 TANF regulations instituted a five-year lifetime benefit cap for recipients. Even before TANF, however, more than half of all AFDC recipients left the rolls within one year of going on welfare; by the end of two years, the percentage increased to 70 percent. However, within the first year after leaving welfare, 45 percent returned; almost 66 percent returned by the end of three years. Over the course of seven years, more than 75 percent of those who left welfare returned at some point.[10]

Myth 5. Welfare programs create dependency, which is transmitted intergenerationally.

Fact. Given the lifetime cap on cash assistance, the dependency issue has become less relevant. Nevertheless, even before TANF the vast majority of AFDC recipients stayed on public assistance less than four years, those who stayed eight years or more accounted for half the number of people on the rolls at any given point in time.[11]

Research on **welfare dependency** is inconclusive. Robert Moffitt found that the length of welfare spells varied with demographic characteristics, the generosity of the state's public assistance program, and local labor market conditions.[12] P. J. Leahy, T. F. Buss, and J. M. Quane found that previous work experience, age at entry to welfare, and number of children were the best predictors of long-term welfare use.[13] Mary Jo Bane and David Ellwood found that race, education, marital status, work experience, and disability influenced first-spell durations. These same variables influenced recidivism. Bane and Ellwood also point out that many of the long-term users cycled in and out of welfare, apparently trying to leave but unable to do so permanently.[14]

The phenomenon of intergenerational dependency is not yet fully understood. According to Duncan and Hoffman, only 19 percent of African American and 26 percent of white women coming from heavily dependent welfare homes were heavily dependent on welfare themselves. The 19 percent of second-generation dependent African American women was the same percentage as that of black women heavily dependent on welfare who did not grow up in heavily dependent welfare households.[15]

On the other hand, Peter Gottschalk found a positive intergenerational relationship between welfare use by mothers and daughters.[16] M. Ann Hill and June O'Neill also found persistence in welfare dependency across generations. Looking at data from the National Longitudinal Survey of Youth (NLSY), these researchers found that young white women from welfare families had a 24 percent chance of being on welfare, compared with a 2 percent chance for non-Hispanic white women coming from nonwelfare families. Comparable figures for African Americans were 42 and 15 percent; for Hispanics, 34 and 8 percent.[17] In their study of men's earnings, Mary Corcoran, Roger Gordon, Deborah Laren, and Gary Solon found that "One of our strongest results is the large negative association between a son's outcomes and welfare receipt in his family of origin."[18] While a correlation may exist between welfare receipt and family of origin, what remains unanswered is whether parental welfare receipt was the cause of the children's behavior.

Myth 6. Most welfare recipients are African Americans and Hispanic Americans.

One of the most commonly held myths about public assistance is that recipients don't want to work.

Fact. In 2001 non-Hispanic whites constituted 32.2 percent of recipients, 39 percent were black and 23.6 percent Hispanic. The remaining recipients were Asian, American Indian, or of another ethnicity.[19] Although the percentages of African Americans and Hispanics on the welfare rolls were larger than these groups' representation in the population, this is not surprising, given that people of color are generally poorer than whites.

Myth 7. Public assistance benefits provide a disincentive to work; people on welfare either don't want to work or are too lazy to work.

Fact. In 2002 the overall nationwide TANF work participation rate was roughly 33.4 percent, while the national average two-parent families work participation rate was 49.4 percent.The rate was above 50 percent in Montana (84 percent), Oregon (61 percent), Illinois (58 percent), Wyoming (83 percent), Kansas (85 percent), Massachusetts (61 percent), Iowa (51 percent), and Indiana (63 percent).[20] TANF benefits are exceedingly small. In the typical or median state, TANF benefits in 2002 for a three-person family totaled $355 per month, or 29 percent of the poverty line. Even with the inclusion of food stamps, in every state the combined benefits fell below the poverty line; and in more than half the states the combined benefits of food stamps and AFDC did not equal two-thirds of the poverty line.[21]

Myth 8. Public assistance recipients are doing better than ever.

Fact. The reverse is true. From 1972 to 1992 AFDC benefit levels failed to keep pace with inflation, falling 43 percent in the typical state. In 1992 dollars, this decline reflected a benefit loss of $279 per month, or more than $3,300 a year.[22] In 2002 the average three-person TANF family received $355 a month. The monthly benefit per recipient was $143. When adjusted for inflation this was $81 lower than the $224 received in 1978. Moreover, when adjusted for inflation the per family and individual benefit levels in 2002 were the lowest on record since 1962. Using 2002 dollars, the monthly benefit per family in 2002 ($355) was *121 percent lower* than in 1969 ($803).[23]

Myth 9. Never-married teen mothers constitute the bulk of welfare recipients.

Fact. In 2001 most adult TANF recipients were women (men represented 10 percent of adult recipients) with an average age of 31 years. Seven percent of adult recipients were teenagers and 18 percent were 40 years or older. Fourteen percent of teen recipients were also teen parents. In 2002, single never married adults accounted for 66.6 of the TANF caseload; separated adults, 13 percent; married adults, 11.5 percent; divorced adults, 8.2 percent; and widowed adults, 0.7 percent.[24] According to Duncan and Hoffman, the most important causes for beginning AFDC spells were (1) divorce or separation (45 percent), (2) an unmarried woman becoming a pregnant household head (30 percent), and (3) a drop in earnings of the female head of the household (12 percent). Conversely, the predominant reasons for terminating public assistance spells were (1) remarriage (35 percent), (2) an increase in the earnings of a female householder (21 percent), and (3) children leaving the parental home (11 percent).[25]

Myth 10. It is easy to get on public assistance and too many undeserving people are receiving benefits.

Fact. According to the Center for Local Self-Reliance, before someone can apply for TANF in Georgia they must first get a form signed by six employers stating that they applied in good faith for a minimum wage job and were turned down. Once enrolled, if they are penalized twice for failure to meet administrative/work requirements, they are barred for life from seeking aid. David Morris states that: "In the early 1990s about 75 percent of those who walked into the welfare office to apply wound up on welfare rolls. Today it is closer to 25 percent. A growing number of states (13 at last count) now drop entire families from the welfare rolls after the first instance of non-compliance by the adult recipient."[26] In addition to meeting stringent income and asset guidelines, applicants for food stamps and public assistance recipients must provide extensive documentation and meet verification requirements. In 2002, only 12 percent of food stamp beneficiaries were above the poverty line, while 36 percent had incomes at or below half the poverty line. The typical food stamp household had gross income of $633 a month and received a monthly food stamp benefit of $173. Over one-fifth of monthly funds (cash income plus food stamps) available to a typical household come from food stamps.[27]

Myth 11. Public assistance recipients migrate to states where benefits are high.

Fact. A study by economist James Walker found no compelling evidence in support of the welfare magnet theory.[28] Other studies indicate that poor people migrate for a variety of reasons, including proximity to family and friends, the desire for a better life, and the hope of finding work. Although research by the Wisconsin's Institute for Research on Poverty concluded that some poor people migrate across state lines to receive higher benefits,[29] it failed to demonstrate that high benefits per se cause migration. According to Henry Freedman of the Center for Social Policy, "Census data on migration show that poor people move in the same direction as those who are not poor, usually toward states with jobs and booming economies rather than those offering higher welfare benefits."[30] The question of whether poor people migrate for higher welfare benefits remains unanswered.

Myth 12. Welfare spending consumes a large portion of state budgets.

Fact. During the mid-1990s most states experienced large welfare-related budget surpluses. In 1999 this surplus reached $400 million in Texas alone. Specifically, federal TANF funding levels were set at 1994–95 levels, while states were experiencing a 47 percent drop in TANF caseloads. Even before the TANF surplus, states spent roughly 3.4 percent of their total budgets on AFDC in 1991. Since about 1.5 percent of state budgets came from the federal government, they only spent about 2 percent on AFDC.[31] The percent of TANF funds spent on cash assistance decreased from 73 percent in 1995 to 38 percent of total spending in 2001. However, by 2001 states overall spent more TANF funds than they received.[32]

Myth 13. AFDC benefits influence decisions relating to family composition (i.e., childbearing, marriage, divorce, and living arrangements) by encouraging women to head their own households.

Fact. Under the TANF guidelines, teenage mothers under age 18 are not entitled to benefits unless they are living at home or in a supervised facility. Although some empirical studies found a small correlation between public assistance benefits and the number of women who choose to head households or remarry, most researchers believe that the evidence does not support the view that generous benefits are responsible for high illegitimacy rates or the growth of single female-headed households. For example, although total welfare benefits have declined since 1975, the number of single female-headed households has remained relatively constant.[33]

Aid to Families with Dependent Children

AFDC was arguably the most controversial program in the U.S. welfare system. Its purpose was to maintain and strengthen family life by providing financial assistance and care to needy dependent children in their own homes or in the homes of responsible caregivers. Despite these modest goals, AFDC served as a symbol in the ideological battle between liberals and conservatives. This caused recipients to be victimized in two ways: (1) by their own poverty, and (2) by ideologically motivated assaults against their character and motives.

The requirement for receiving AFDC was that a child be deprived of the parental support of one parent because of death, desertion, separation, or divorce. (In the case of the AFDC-Unemployed Parent program, the criterion was deprivation of parental economic support because of unemployment or illness.) In 1992 AFDC served 4.8 million families (about 13.6 million individuals) at a cost of $22 billion. Of those 13.5 million recipients, about 67 percent, or 9.2 million, were children. AFDC recipients in 1992 made up about 5 percent of the U.S. population, and 13 percent of all children were receiving assistance.[34]

The Evolution of the AFDC Program

Welfare reform has been a heated topic, and most presidents since John F. Kennedy have either offered welfare reform proposals or at least given lip service to the need for reform. To understand the issues surrounding welfare reform, it is important to examine the history of the AFDC program.

Originally called Aid to Dependent Children (ADC), the AFDC program was part of the Social Security Act of 1935 and was designed to provide support for children by dispensing aid to their mothers. In 1950 the adult caregiver (usually the mother) was made eligible for ADC benefits.[35] Also in the 1950s, medical services paid for in part by the federal government were made available for ADC recipients.

Beginning in the late 1950s, some critics argued that ADC rules led to desertion by fathers, because only families without an able-bodied father were eligible. In 1961 a new component was added that allowed families to receive assistance in the event of a father's incapacity or unemployment. The new program, Aid to Families with Dependent Children-Unemployed Parent (AFDC-UP), was not made mandatory for the states, and until the welfare reform act of 1988, only 25 states and the District of Columbia had adopted it. In 1962 ADC was changed to AFDC to emphasize the family unit.

By 1962 the focus of the AFDC program had shifted to rehabilitation and new policies mandated casework and treatment services. Although historically AFDC services were delivered by one worker, beginning in 1972 federal policy dictated that the AFDC program be divided into social services and **income maintenance programs.** This policy required that one worker be assigned the AFDC paperwork while the other assumed responsibility for social services.

The number of AFDC recipients grew rapidly throughout the 1960s, then tripled from 1960 to 1970. From 1971 to 1981 that number rose another 50 percent, and in 1992 it reached an all-time high of 13.6 million recipients. In 1950 AFDC recipients constituted 1.5 percent of the population; by 1992 that number reached 5 percent.

One notorious chapter in AFDC history involved the man-in-the-house rule. This policy mandated that any woman with an able-bodied man in the house would be terminated from AFDC because, regardless of whether the man was the father, it was supposedly his responsibility to support the family. This policy was manifested in "midnight raids" in which social workers made late-night calls to determine if a man was present. Even a piece of male clothing found on the premises could justify cutting off aid. In some states the man-in-the-house rule was extended to include rules on dating. In 1968 the U.S. Supreme Court struck down the rule in Alabama, and the Court later reinforced its decision in a California case.[36]

Until the 1996 welfare reform bill, the Family Support Act (FSA) of 1988 was one of the most important pieces of welfare legislation since the New Deal.[37] The FSA (budgeted at only $3.3 billion over a five-year period) attempted to change AFDC from an income support to a mandatory work and training program. To accomplish this, the bill established the **Job Opportunities and Basic Skills (JOBS)** program, which required recipient women with children under age three (or, at state option, age one) to participate in a work or training program. By 1990 each state was to enroll at least 7 percent of its recipients (increasing to 20 percent by 1993) in a basic state education program, job training, a work experience program, or a job search program. As an incentive, recipients who were employed received 12 months of child care assistance and Medicaid benefits after they terminated AFDC.[38]

Adoption of the AFDC-UP program became mandatory for all states, although they could choose to limit enrollment for two-parent families to 6 out of 12 calendar months in a year. Moreover, one family member of an AFDC-UP household was required to participate at least 16 hours a week in a community or make-work job in return for benefits. In addition, the FSA called for mandatory child support payments to be automatically deducted from an absent parent's paycheck. Finally, the FSA allowed states to require a teenage recipient to live with a parent or in a supervised environment to be eligible for assistance.[39]

The FSA's promise soon faded. Instead of declining, AFDC caseloads actually rose by 2.1 million from 1990 to 1992. Sar Levitan and Frank Gallo wrote that "even if the program expends all the available federal funds, the total work/welfare investment will remain below the [1980] peak level of $3 billion (1992 dollars)."[40] By the end of 1991 the states had spent less than half of the available federal JOBS funds.[41] Underappreciated at the time was the FSA component that permitted states to request waivers to existing AFDC rules, which opened the door for the radical welfare reforms that emerged in 1996.[42]

In his 1992 presidential campaign, Bill Clinton promised to "end welfare as we know it" by implementing a two-year cap on AFDC benefits. In 1993 Clinton appointed a working group on welfare reform, headed by White House advisor Bruce Reed and well-known poverty researchers David Ellwood and Mary Jo Bane. Completed in 1994, the Work and Responsibility Act called for expanding the JOBS program to help recipients move from welfare to work. Based on a personal plan, each AFDC recipient would enter into an agreement with a public assistance agency in return for subsidized child care, health care benefits, and other supportive services. This plan included a two-year limit on cash assistance, after which recipients would be expected to become employed (preferably in the private sector). Those unable to find employment after two years would enter an employment program based on subsidies to public or private employers to hire recipients in "worklike" positions. In turn, employers would provide a paycheck equaling the recipient's former welfare check as compensation for a given number of weekly work hours at the minimum wage. Participants would be required to change jobs every 12 months and undergo reassessment every two years. In addition, participants would be eligible for AFDC benefits if their wages were low enough, and they would continue to receive Medicaid and subsidized child care. Although time limits and work requirements would be national, states would have had considerable flexibility for innovation.[43]

Arguably, the Work and Responsibility Act was introduced too late in the game and with too little focused effort. Specifically, the welfare reform bill was introduced in the summer of 1994, and thus competed with a faltering health care bill and a struggling crime bill. The election of the ultraconservative 104th Congress in 1994 ruled out the possibility of passing any welfare reform bill that included liberal components such as subsidized employment.[44]

The Personal Responsibility and Work Opportunity Reconciliation Act of 1996

In 1996, former President Bill Clinton signed the Personal Responsibility and Work Opportunity Reconciliation Act (PRWORA) (H.R. 3734), a complex 900-page document that confused even seasoned welfare administrators.[45] In effect, the PRWORA transformed the public welfare system by replacing AFDC, JOBS, and the **Emergency Assistance Program** with the Temporary Aid for Needy Families (TANF) program.

One of the most radical features of the PRWORA was among the least understood. Under the PRWORA there is no federal **entitlement** to assistance. In contrast, the former AFDC program operated under the principle of entitlement. This meant that states must provide assistance to anyone eligible under the law. This did not mean that states were required to provide something for nothing. In fact, states could have required recipients to participate in work, education, training, or job search programs as a condition for receiving aid. Under TANF, no family or child is *entitled* to assistance.[46] In effect, the TANF **disentitlement** rescinded the 60-year-old federal entitlement for support to poor children and families. TANF operates in the following manner:

- In order to receive a TANF grant, each state must submit a plan to the Department of Health and Human Services (HHS). In turn, HHS determines whether the plan conforms to the law. Plan requirements are generally limited, and much operational detail is omitted.
- TANF provides lump-sum federal **block grants** for states to operate their own welfare and work programs. Each state receives a block grant based on federal spending for a **fiscal year (FY)** for the state's former AFDC program, the JOBS program, and the Emergency Assistance Program. A minority of states receive annual adjustments in the form of supplemental grants; but for most states the amount of the TANF block grant is frozen, except for adjustments due to bonuses or penalties. Under limited circumstances, a state experiencing an economic downturn may qualify for additional federal funding. To be eligible, the state must maintain 100 percent of its historic spending level in the year the contingency funds are requested. A state may also apply for a loan from the Rainy Day Loan Fund, a federally based revolving loan. The maximum loan is 10 percent of a state's grant for up to three years, after which the loan must be repaid with interest.
- Maintenance of effort provisions require that to receive a full block assistance grant, the state must spend nonfederal funds at no less than 80 percent of a historic spending level based on 1994 spending. This requirement is reduced to 75 percent for a state that meets the act's **work participation rate** (percentage of TANF recipients in the workforce) requirements. A state that does not maintain the required spending level risks a dollar-for-dollar reduction in its block grant funding.
- States are prohibited from using TANF funds to assist certain categories of families and individuals. The most important prohibition involves the use of TANF funds to assist families in which an adult has received assistance for 60 months or more. (States can, however, choose to pay beneficiaries with their own monies.) States can provide exceptions for up to 20 percent of their caseloads. Although the PRWORA mandates a maximum five-year lifetime limit on cash assistance, it allows states to set a shorter time limit. Other restrictions include a prohibition on assisting minor parents unless they are attending school and living at home or in an adult-supervised living arrangement (subject to limited exceptions), and a requirement to reduce or eliminate assistance if an individual does not coop-

erate with child support-related requirements, such as identifying the father.

• The TANF block grant has four specific work requirements. First, unless a state opts out, it must require nonexempt unemployed parents or caregivers to participate in community service after receiving assistance for two months. Second, states must outline how they will require a parent or caregiver receiving benefits to engage in work not later than 24 months after they receive assistance. Third, a state must meet a work participation rate for all families that began at 25 percent in 1997 and increasing to 50 percent beyond 2002 (see Table 11.1). Fourth, states must meet different participation rates for two-parent families; for example, the rate was set at 75 percent in 1997–98 and at 90 percent in 1999. Failure to comply with the last two work requirements results in a penalty of 5 percent the first year and 2 percent thereafter (capped at 21 percent). PRWORA provides for a reduction in the minimum work participation rate standards if the state's average monthly assistance caseload decreased the previous year in comparison to its average monthly caseload in FY 1995. The all families participation rate standard is reduced by the number of percentage points the overall caseload declined. The two-parent participation rate standard is reduced, at state option, by either (1) the number of percentage points the two-parent caseload declined or (2) the number of percentage points the overall caseload declined. However, the law specifies that any caseload reductions resulting from changes in state or federal eligibility rules are excluded in calculating the credit. The act also provides states the option to retain approved welfare reform waiver provisions that are inconsistent with the TANF provisions. Such waiver provisions may affect who is required to participate, the required hours of participation, and the countable activities. Thus, the participation rate calculation may apply differently for states retaining inconsistent waiver provisions.

Table 11.1

TANF Work Participation Rates

Fiscal Year	Percentages
Work Participation for All Families	
1997	25
1998	30
1999	35
2000	40
2001	45
2002 and beyond	50
Work Participation for Two-Parent Families	
1997	75
1998	75
1999 and beyond	90

Source: American Public Welfare Association, "The Personal Responsibility and Work Opportunity Reconciliation Act of 1996 (Conference agreement for H.R. 3734)." Analysis prepared by the American Public Welfare Association, the National Governors' Association, and the National Conference of State Legislatures, August 22, 1996.

• States can spend their block grants on cash assistance, noncash assistance, services, and administrative costs in connection with assistance to needy families with children. States can also choose to spend up to 30 percent of their TANF funds to operate programs under the Child Care and Development Block Grant and the Title XX Social Services Block Grant. No more than one-third of that amount can be used for programs under Title XX, and the funds must be spent on programs for children or families whose incomes fall below 200 percent of the poverty line. Existing child care provider standards for health and safety are maintained.

• When parents participate in required work activities, the state may (but is not required to) provide child care assistance. However, a state may not reduce or terminate a family's assistance if a single parent of a child under age six refuses to comply with work requirements based on a demonstrated inability to obtain needed child care.

• In a departure from AFDC rules, TANF recipients are not automatically eligible for Medicaid. However, states are required to provide Medicaid coverage for single-parent families and qualifying two-parent families with children if they meet the income and resource eligibility guidelines that were in effect in the state's AFDC Program on July 16, 1996. (States may modify these guidelines to a limited extent.)

• When the PRWORA was enacted, most states were in the midst of welfare reform activities through the AFDC waiver process. The PRWORA provides that if a state had a waiver in place before October 1996, it can continue that waiver and is not required to comply with inconsistent provisions of the act.[47]

• The TANF program attempted to address the dramatic increase in nonmarital births (especially teen births). First, state TANF plans must demonstrate how they will establish goals and take action to prevent and reduce out-of-wedlock pregnancies. Second, states must establish actual numerical goals for reducing their "illegitimacy ratio" for fiscal years 1996–2005. Third, the act provides financial incentives to states to reduce their out-of-wedlock birth rates. On the incentive side, the act authorizes HHS to give $20 million apiece to the five states that show the greatest success in reducing their nonmarital birth rate, while lowering their abortion rate below its 1995 level.[48]

• The PRWORA allows states to impose a family cap, which denies assistance to children born into families who are already receiving public assistance.

• States must permanently deny all Title IV-A cash assistance and Food Stamp Program benefits to those convicted of felony drug possession, use, or distribution. Other members of the family can continue to receive benefits. States may opt out of this provision or limit the period of denial by passing legislation.

In addition to TANF, the PRWORA included other reforms:

• As amended in 1997, the law makes immigrants who arrived in the United States before August 22, 1996, eligible for Medicaid and SSI benefits. However, immigrants who arrived after that date are barred from all means-tested, federally funded public benefits for the first five years they are in the country. After five years states can, at their option, offer Medicaid to immigrants. Accordingly, aged, blind, and disabled immigrants are not categorically eligible for Medicaid. There are exceptions made for persons who have worked for 40 quarters in covered employment or served in the military. No state can deny coverage of emergency medical services to either illegal or legal aliens.

• Illegal immigrants are barred from the following federal public benefits: (a) grants, contracts, loans, and licenses; and (b) retirement, welfare, health, disability, public or assisted housing, postsecondary education, food assistance, and unemployment benefits.

• SSI eligibility was tightened for children. The new standard eliminated the comparable severity standard, the individual functional assessment, and references to maladaptive behavior. Specifically, the individual functional assessment (IFA) for children was eliminated. Children can qualify only if they have "a medically determinable physical or mental impairment which results in marked and severe functional limitations."

• The Food Stamp Program retained its structure as an uncapped individual entitlement. However, PRWORA included $27.7 billion in food stamp cuts, accounting for more than half of all non-Medicaid savings. The 1995 Urban Institute report on the anticipated effect of PRWORA estimated that the bill would push 1.1 million children (2.6 million people overall) into poverty and noted that the food stamp cuts were a main factor in those numbers. A substantial portion of these benefit savings would come from across-the-board reductions affecting nearly all recipient households, including families with children, the working poor, the elderly, and the disabled. In addition, Food Stamp Program benefits were limited to three months every three years for unemployed able-bodied single adults aged 18 to 50. An additional three months of eligibility was granted to adults laid off their jobs.

• Child support collection efforts were strengthened through a number of provisions. First, one condition for receiving assistance is that families must assign child support collection rights to the state.[49] Second, states must operate automated centralized collection and disbursement units. Third, noncustodial parents who are $5,000 or more in arrears are subject to passport revocation. Fourth, states must accord full faith and credit to out-of-state child support orders and liens. Federal income withholding, liens, and subpoena forms must be used for interstate cases. Fifth, states must have laws in effect that establish authority to withhold, suspend, or restrict driver's, professional, occupational, and recreational licenses of individuals who owe overdue support. Other provisions include automated state directories of new hires; expansion of income withholding requirements; access to locator information networks such as that of law enforcement; use of Social Security numbers on licenses and other government-issued documents; and expedited **establishment of paternity.**[50]

The conservative 104th Congress effectively pushed through the passage of the PRWORA. The rapidly approaching presidential election also may have played a role, especially since former President Clinton had already vetoed a similar welfare reform bill in January 1996. The rhetorical slogans of the

1992 Clinton presidential campaign, calling for "an end to welfare as we know it" and "two years and off to work," were viewed by the public as endorsements of their distaste for AFDC. Frances Fox Piven argues that Clinton's rhetoric created a maelstrom of which he eventually lost control. Moreover, by the time Clinton signed the PRWORA, he had already approved draconian state waivers that were in some cases more punitive than TANF.[51]

State Welfare Reform Waivers

Radical welfare reform was well under way even before the PRWORA became law. In fact, Clinton had granted 43 state waivers during his first term, more than all previous administrations combined. By mid-1996, 43 of the 50 states had approved or pending AFDC waivers that incorporated many of the TANF reforms. Pointing to the flood of AFDC waivers signed by the Clinton administration, the Enterprise Institute's Douglas Besharov observed, "Based on what happened in the last year, President Clinton can justifiably claim that he has ended welfare as we know it." Besharov, describing the waiver requests as "welfare reform on the cheap without an increase in spending for child care or a penny for job training," concluded that "the revolutionary result is an end to personal entitlement."[52] By 1996, state waivers that included time limits, benefit cuts, and widespread sanctions for disapproved behaviors had already resulted in a 10 percent drop in the AFDC rolls.

Many state waivers incorporate several components, including:

- Time-limited lifetime benefits (frequently a two-year cap).
- Enforcement of parental responsibility. Typical provisions include child support; family caps; required immunization of children as part of the benefit process; linkage of benefits to school attendance and grades; and requirements aimed at discouraging teenage pregnancy by obliging teen mothers on public assistance to attend school and live at home or in an approved setting.
- Simplification and efficiency in delivering benefits, such as the use of **electronic benefit transfers (EBT)** for delivering public assistance; fraud deterrent measures including the use of debit cards instead of food stamp coupons; and privatization or subcontracting out the delivery and management of public assistance programs to the private sector.
- Measures designed to move people quickly from work to welfare: incentives (often tax breaks) to encourage the private sector to hire recipients; higher limits on earnings and assets (e.g., the value of a vehicle); and job placement and training.
- Measures for promoting personal responsibility: cash-out incentives that offer beneficiaries the cash equivalent of food stamps; offers of one-time lump-sum payments (equaling total benefits for three months to a year) instead of monthly grants; help in developing asset accounts; terminating cash benefits for those who fail to comply with state welfare rules and regulations; required performance of community service; and the mentoring of recipients.
- Although not yet in effect, a plan developed in Texas calls for outsourcing the eligibility functions of the Department of Health and Human Services. In effect, this plan would close down most public welfare offices and replace them with call centers run by private providers.[53]

Has the PRWORA Worked?

Both Democrats and Republicans have pronounced the PRWORA a success. Specifically, both parties point to the dramatic decline in welfare caseloads—60 percent for individuals and 53 percent for families—since the passage of the PRWORA in 1996. The number of white families on welfare showed the steepest decline, falling by 63 percent, while the number of black families fell by 52 percent, and the number of Hispanic families by 44 percent.[54] Despite this drop, important questions remain. First, caseloads had already begun to drop—from a high of 5 million in 1994 to 4.8 million in 1995, 4.5 million in 1996, and 3.9 million in 1997. These declines occurred before the PRWORA was fully in effect. Second, other factors such as the strong labor market in the 1990s and changes in welfare policy help explain the drop in caseloads. In the late 1990s the nation was in the midst of the longest peacetime expansion in its history, with low unemployment and rising wages. Because of this, gains in employment and wages were experienced by groups with typically high rates of welfare use. Third, it is difficult to ascertain the success of the PRWORA, because it has been mainly in effect in a strong economic period. For example, beginning in mid-2001 caseloads stopped declining and rose in 28 states, most likely because of the weakening economy. In 2003 caseloads began dropping again (3 percent for individuals and 1.8 percent for families).[55] However, this drop occurred during a period of rising poverty rates and higher unemployment, which suggests that a large number of people were either discouraged from receiving public assistance, or their time limit had ran out. Perhaps more importantly, this trend broke the traditional link between increased need and increased spending.

There are three primary avenues for leaving TANF: (1) voluntary termination because of employment, marriage, and so forth; (2) reaching the end of the federal or state time limit; and (3) being terminated for failure to comply with work or administrative rules. Research on TANF has found that:

- Most recipients leaving public assistance (50 to 60 percent) take jobs that pay just over minimum wage. Because of this, many low-income families continue to receive some form of public assistance, such as food stamps. Between 2000 and 2003 the number of households receiving food stamps increased by 38 percent.
- Families that left welfare in 2000 or later were less likely to be working than families that left in the 1990s. An Urban Institute report found that the proportion of families that left welfare and were not employed rose from 50 percent in 1999 to 58 percent in 2002. Moreover, the unemployment rate of low-income single mothers increased from 9.8 percent in 2000 to 12.3 percent in 2002. Consequently, about one-third of families leaving welfare return within the first year.
- The share of families that leave welfare and are not working and without another stable source of support has increased. An Urban Institute study found that the share of leavers who were "disconnected" (i.e., not working, did not have a working spouse, and were not receiving TANF or SSI) rose from 9.8 percent in 1999 to 13.8 percent in 2002. Nearly two-thirds of disconnected leavers reported running out of money to buy food.
- Between 50 and 75 percent of welfare leavers remain poor two to three years after leaving welfare. Forty-two percent of welfare leavers remain poor five years after leaving welfare compared to a 55 percent poverty rate in the first year after leaving welfare. Most welfare leavers with incomes above the poverty level are relatively poor (about 90 percent have income below 185 percent of the poverty line) On average, household income of welfare leavers averaged about $1,000 a month.
- A study of Michigan recipients who terminated TANF in 1997 found that by 2001 only one-quarter were working in "good jobs" (i.e., jobs that paid $7 an hour or more and offered health insurance, or full-time jobs without health insurance that paid $8.50 an hour or more). This finding was similar to earlier research which found that only one in four women on welfare would be in a "good job" by their late twenties.
- A HHS-funded study of welfare reform in Wisconsin found that the net income of welfare leavers in the year after they exited welfare was lower than their income prior to leaving.
- Research suggests that time limit leavers have lower employment rates, higher poverty rates, and higher levels of material hardship than voluntary TANF leavers. A Minnesota study found that families terminated because of time limits were less likely to have jobs, and more likely to experience food insecurity, problems with housing and utilities, and unmet health care needs. Similar findings occurred in studies done in Cuyahoga County (Ohio) and Virginia.
- Families that have been sanctioned face significant hardships such as health problems, children with health problems, low basic skill levels, and substance abuse problems. A national study of mothers whose children reached age one found that those who left welfare because of sanctions were three times more likely to experience hardship, such as homelessness, eviction and hunger compared to mothers who stayed on welfare. In contrast, voluntary leavers are less disadvantaged and more employable than stayers since they are more educated; have fewer children; are less likely to have young children; and are more likely to have prior work experience.[56]

Arguably, too much emphasis is placed on caseload reduction while insufficient attention is paid to income and poverty outcomes. Between 2000 and 2003, the number and percentage of single mothers living in poverty increased while the percentage of single mothers with jobs fell. At the same time, poverty among children rose, and the number of children living below half of the poverty line increased by nearly one million. In response to this increase in poverty and need, the number of families receiving food stamps and Medicaid rose. The number of poor families receiving TANF cash assistance, however, continued to fall and it provided assistance to 845,000 fewer people in 2003 than in 2000. The Bush administration attempted to portray TANF's lower caseloads as a positive development and suggested that unemployment insurance was replacing TANF. Despite this contention, fewer than two out of every 100 poor, single-mother families were lifted out of poverty by the unemployment insurance program in 2003.[57]

Proposed Changes in TANF

Authorization for the TANF program ended in fall 2002. For it to continue, Congress must pass reauthorization legislation. In 2004, Congress approved the eighth extension of the TANF program since 2002. Although no policy changes were made the extension allowed funding to continue. Even though TANF reauthorization could simply involve extending the funding period, it is more likely that Congress will consider several key policy changes, some of which are rather technical. Based on 2004 congressional bills, some of these changes may include:

- The work participation rates states must meet is currently 50 percent. The proposed amendments would increase these rates to 55 percent in 2005; increasing by 5 percentage points each year until reaching 70 percent in 2008. Credit would be given toward the rate for employed welfare leavers.
- The hours of work required for single parents to count toward the participation rate would increase. Under the current law, a single parent with a child under age 6 is required to work 20 hours; for other single parents it is 30 hours a week and no "partial credit" is given for parents engaged in work activities for fewer than required number of hours. Under the proposed rules, single parent with child under age 6 would be required to work 24 hours and other single parents, 34 hours. Partial credit would be given for single parents who participate for at least 20 hours.
- Under the current law, vocational education training is allowed as a full-time activity that counts toward participation rates for up to 12 months. Under the proposed rules, states could count postsecondary or vocational education as a work activity for more than 12 months (capped at 10 percent of caseload).
- Under the current rules, child care funding is frozen at $2.7 billion per year (a discretionary $2.1 billion was appropriated in FY2003). Under the proposed rules, child care funding would be increased by $7 billion over five years.
- Currently, states can use TANF funds for marriage-promotion activities, but no funding is earmarked for this purpose. Under the proposed rules, up to $1.5 billion over five years would be earmarked for "marriage promotion activities. These "activities" include public advertising campaigns on the value of marriage and the skills needed to increase marital stability and health; education in high schools on the value of marriage, relationship skills, and budgeting; marriage education, marriage skills, and relationship skills programs, that may include parenting skills, financial management, conflict resolution, and job and career advancement, for non-married pregnant women and non-married expectant fathers; premarital education and marriage skills training for engaged couples and for couples or individuals interested in marriage; marriage enhancement and marriage skills training programs for married couples; divorce reduction programs that teach relationship skills; marriage mentoring programs which use married couples as role models and mentors in at-risk communities; and programs to reduce the disincentives to marriage in means-tested aid programs.[58]
- The proposed amendments include a "universal engagement" provision that would require states to assess the skills, work experience, education, and barriers to employment of adult TANF recipients and to develop self-sufficiency plans for each TANF family.[59]

Some of the challenges facing TANF reauthorization have important implications not only for cash public assistance programs, but also for the U.S. welfare state. For example, the 2004 House proposal would allow sweeping waivers that affect more than a dozen low-income programs. This superwaiver would allow social welfare programs to be substantially altered so that states and the president could effectively override congressional decisions about the level of federal resources devoted to specific programs and purposes. Moreover, if states use superwaivers to shift federal monies into an area previously funded with state resources, states could withdraw these funds and reduce overall funding for low-income programs. Such a policy would mean that federal funds targeted by Congress for low-income populations could effectively be used by states to bolster their general treasuries. Second, both the Senate and House bills devote a substantial amount of TANF ($1.5 to $1.7 billion over five years) funds to a narrow set of rigidly defined "marriage promotion" activities. Little evidence exists to support the potential effectiveness of government-funded marriage programs, particularly the narrow set of programs the bill would authorize. Even more problematic is that a substantial share of the earmarked funds would come from redirecting TANF monies that states currently can use for child care and welfare-to-work programs.[60]

Supplemental Security Income

Supplemental Security Income (SSI) is one of the more confusing social programs in the United States. In essence, SSI is designed to provide cash assistance to the elderly and to disabled poor individuals, including children. Although a public assistance program, SSI is administered by the Social Security Administration.

In 2002 the SSI program served 6.8 million people and cost the federal government almost $35 billion. Unlike OASDI, SSI is a means-tested, federally administered public assistance program funded through general revenue taxes. The basic SSI payment level is adjusted annually for inflation. A portion of elderly people receive SSI in conjunction with Social Security. Age is not an eligibility criterion for SSI, and children may receive benefits under the disabled or blind portion of the act. Among others, the following people are eligible for SSI: (1) mentally retarded individuals, (2) people who are at least 65 years old and have little or no income, (3) those considered legally blind, (4) adults (at least 18 years old) who qualify as disabled because of a physical or mental impairment expected to last for at least 12 months, (5) those who are visually impaired but do not meet the criteria for blindness, (6) drug addicts and alcoholics who enter treatment, and (7) children under 18 who have a severe impairment comparable with that of an eligible adult. In 2002 18.4 percent of the SSI rolls were made up of low-income seniors and 80.4 percent of recipients were disabled. Fifty-eight percent of SSI recipients were aged 18 to 64; 29 percent were 65 and older; and 13 percent were under age 18.[61]

To qualify for SSI, an applicant must have limited resources. In 2004, SSI applicants were allowed to own resources valued at less than $2,000 for an individual and $3,000 for a couple (excluding, e.g., a house; a car, depending on use and value; burial plots; and certain forms of insurance). SSI benefits are not generous, although they can be higher than TANF benefits. In 2002 the average monthly benefit was $407. The maximum payment for an individual in 2003 was $552 a month; for a couple, $829 a month.[62]

The SSI program began during the Nixon administration. When Richard Nixon took office in 1972, he attempted to streamline the welfare system by proposing a Family Assistance Plan (FAP). In this plan Nixon proposed a guaranteed annual income that would replace AFDC, Old Age Assistance (OAA), Aid to the Blind (AB), and Aid to the Permanently and Totally Disabled (APTD). Although Congress rejected the overall plan, the OAA, AB, and APTD programs were federalized in 1972 under a new program—Supplemental Security Income. Basically, the federal government took over the operation of those programs from the state governments. No longer would state governments set eligibility levels, establish minimum payment levels, or administer the programs.

In 1974 there were 3.25 million SSI recipients. By 2002 that number had doubled, to 6.8 million. Concomitantly, SSI expenditures increased from $5 billion in 1974 to more than $34 billion in 2002. In large part these increases resulted from the rapid growth in the numbers of disabled persons receiving SSI, a population that rose from 2.4 million in 1984 to 5.5 million in 2002.[63]

Two groups of SSI recipients that have shown dramatic growth in their numbers are children with disabilities and adults with disabilities relating to drug addiction and alcoholism. One reason for this growth was the Supreme Court's decision in the *Sullivan v. Zebley* case, which made children eligible for SSI if they had a disability that was comparable to that of an eligible adult. Children are now the fastest growing population on SSI, and by 2002 almost 1 million children were recipients. Of those children, more than 60 percent either have an emotional/mental disorder or are mentally retarded. Concomitantly, more than 50 percent of adults on SSI either have a mental/emotional disorder or are mentally retarded.[64]

The other group of SSI recipients that have drawn attention are individuals whose drug or alcohol addiction (DAA) is the primary contributing factor in their disability. Between 1980 and 1994, the number of DAA recipients on SSI rose from 23,000 to 86,000, bringing the number to more than 250,000. By 1994, this group cost the federal government $1.4 billion.[65]

As a response to SSI's rapid growth, Congress passed the Social Security Independence and Program Improvements Act in 1994, which, among other things, restricted SSI and Disability Insurance benefits to individuals disabled by drug and alcohol addiction. The new restrictions required SSI beneficiaries with a DAA diagnosis to participate in a substance abuse program. In addition, beneficiaries (except those for whom treatment was not available) would receive benefits for only 36 months. Beneficiaries removed from the SSI rolls would continue to receive Medicare or Medicaid unless they failed to comply with their treatment program for 12 successive months.[66] In addition, the law also established a Commission on Childhood Disabilities to reevaluate the SSI definition for childhood disability and to look into possible alternative definitions.[67]

Major concerns regarding SSI involve the low level of income and the stringent requirements for eligibility. SSI payments are so low that 28 states supplement them with an additional grant, with some opting to have the federal government administer the stipend. States may choose to set their own requirements for supplementary SSI payments, thereby including only certain beneficiaries or limiting disabilities.[68] Stringent eligibility requirements and complex red tape have kept many people off the SSI rolls. For example, SSI cases are reviewed every three years (a process that usually involves a medical review), and "continuing disability reviews" may be required. Some critics believe that the federal government has purposely made entrance and continued maintenance in SSI difficult to discourage participation. Moreover, only couples receiving a combination of SSI, Social Security, and food stamps are raised to or above the poverty line. In 2002, an aged individual who received SSI was raised to only 75.8 percent of the poverty threshold (see Table 11.2).

General Assistance

General assistance (GA) programs are cash and in-kind assistance programs financed and administered entirely by the state, county, or locality in which they are located. They are designed to meet the short-term or ongoing needs of low-income persons ineligible for (or awaiting approval for) federally funded assistance such as Temporary Assistance for Needy Families (TANF) or Supplemental Security Income (SSI).[69]

As of 1998, 35 states, including the District of Columbia, had state GA programs. Twenty-four of those 35 states had statewide GA programs with uniform eligibility rules. The benefit schedule is generally uniform, although some states adjust their benefits to reflect varying costs of living in different areas.

Table 11.2

Supplemental Security Income: Expenditures, Population, Benefits, and Percentages of Poverty Threshold, Selected Years, 2002 Dollars

	1974	1980	1990	1999	2002
Expenditures (in billions)	$18.6	$16.4	$23.8	$32.1	$34.6
Population (in millions)	4.0	4.1	4.8	6.6	6.8
Monthly Benefits, Aged Individuals	$78.48	$112.45	$175.29	$282.37	$322.2
Percentage of Poverty Line	74.1	72.3	73.9	75.0	75.8
Monthly Benefits, Aged Couples	$93.02	$157.56	$322.82	$642.29	$730.49
Percentage of Poverty Line	88.1	86.0	87.9	89.3	90.2

Source: Committee on Ways and Means, U.S. House of Representatives, *2004 Green Book* (Washington, DC: U.S. Government Office, 2004), pp. 3–6.

Nine of the 35 states lacked uniform state programs but required all counties to provide some form of GA. As a result, eligibility rules and benefit schedules in these states varied dramatically from county to county. Although Wisconsin and Virginia did not provide statewide GA assistance, they did provide supervision and funding for counties that chose to have the program. States lacking governmental involvement in the provision of GA were unlikely to have counties with this program.

Able-bodied adults without children (the population most often associated with GA) are the least likely to be eligible for this assistance. Although the two most populous states, California and New York, provide GA to able-bodied adults without children, few others do. Only 13 states provided GA to this population in 1998, down from 15 states in 1996. In addition, many states that provided assistance to able-bodied adults without children limited the duration of assistance and/or provided in-kind rather than cash benefits. As a rule, GA programs were more likely to provide benefits for the disabled or elderly people, children, or families with children than they were to serve the able-bodied. Thirty-four states provided GA to disabled, elderly, or otherwise unemployable individuals not eligible for (or awaiting approval for) SSI. Twenty-four states provided assistance to children or families with children ineligible for TANF, such as children living with an unrelated adult.

Most states limited GA eligibility to the severely poor. Although income eligibility varied across states, a majority of state GA programs limited assistance to only those with incomes less than half the poverty level. Most states set resource limits between $1,000 and $2,000, regardless of family size. However, states generally disregarded some earned income and certain resources (e.g., a home and a car) in determining eligibility.

Nearly all states that provided assistance to able-bodied adults in 1998 required recipients to work in order to maintain benefits. Recipients who failed to comply with the work requirements were often sanctioned, usually losing their entire benefit for a period of time.

GA benefits are low and falling. The maximum monthly benefits available to GA recipients were generally set far below the federal poverty level. Among the 27 state GA programs that provided cash benefits to individuals in 1998, the average monthly benefit maximum for an individual was only 37 percent of the federal poverty line. GA benefits were also lower than benefits in federal assistance programs. On average, GA monthly cash benefits for disabled individuals were less than 50 percent of maximum state SSI monthly cash benefits, and maximum GA benefits for families were less than 90 percent of the maximum state TANF benefits. Moreover, few states have adjusted their benefits since 1996, with the result that benefits have gradually decreased in real terms.

Most states that provide GA also provide medical assistance for GA recipients, although medical benefits are usually less comprehensive than Medicaid. In 5 of the 35 state GA programs, all recipients were eligible for medical assistance under that state's Medicaid program or Medicaid waiver program. Of the remaining 30 state programs, 26 provided medical assistance to some or all GA recipients, either through a formal state or county GA medical program or by providing benefits to cover certain medical expenses. The medical benefits varied widely in the types of services covered, but most provided more limited benefits than Medicaid.

GA caseloads are small compared to those of the major federal assistance programs. Most state GA programs provided benefits to less than 15 percent of the numbers served by TANF. In New York (which had the most extensive GA program) about 8 percent (232,000 recipients a month) of poor people received GA in 1998. This was less than one-quarter of the number of TANF recipients in New York and about one-third the number of SSI recipients.

Several states have changed their GA programs since 1996, almost always in the direction of tightening nonfinancial eligibility requirements. Connecticut eliminated eligibility for a category of employable persons without children, although it did create an additional category for persons with an impairment that interrupts employment. The District of Columbia eliminated its General Public Assistance program for persons awaiting SSI. Hawaii and Connecticut lengthened the time a person must be disabled in order to qualify for GA as temporarily disabled. Four of the 35 state GA programs established or increased time limits, raising the total number of states with time limits to 10. Three states increased or established durational residency requirements, raising the total number of states with these requirements to seven.

PRWORA-related changes to immigrant eligibility have had a significant impact on GA policies. Following the federal lead, 19 of the 35 state GA programs tightened restrictions on assistance to immigrants. New York and Washington, however, explicitly enabled immigrants no longer eligible for federal benefits to qualify for GA.

Changes to family assistance resulting from the PRWORA enabled states to shift part of the burden of providing assistance to the federal government. Nine states transferred the responsibility for providing assistance to pregnant women in their first two trimesters and/or two-parent families with little or no work history from their GA to their TANF program. Both of these categories of recipients were ineligible for federal assistance under the prior law.[70] The general trend of cutting back GA programs puts large numbers of poor people at higher risk.

Trends and Issues in Public Assistance

The basic principle underlying the PRWORA was the transference of the responsibility for managing social programs from Washington to the states. Promoted early by the Reagan administration, this ideological perspective has been labeled the "devolution revolution" or the "new federalism."[71] Energized by the omnipresent cry of "states' rights," the new federalism trades off long-term and stable federal funding for increased state control through block grants.

The use of social service block grants is not new. The last social program that was block granted and devolved to the states, the Title XX Social Services Block Grant, has been so mismanaged that it is implicated in the deaths from abuse and neglect of 2,000 children annually; almost half of such child deaths are in cases known to state children's agencies, but the agencies are unable to prevent them.[72]

The responsibility of states to care for their poor is also not new. In part, it was the failure of states to meet that responsibility that originally led to the creation of the 1935 Social Security Act, legislation that federalized most state public assistance and social insurance programs. Devolving welfare responsibility to the states is neither new nor novel. Nevertheless, the question remains: If states were unable to mount compassionate social welfare programs before 1935, why should they do so today, especially in difficult economic times?

Transforming Public Assistance Policy into Labor Policy

An argument can be made that income maintenance programs should be housed under the Secretary of Labor rather than the Secretary of Health and Human Services. Beginning almost 30 years ago, the transformation of public assistance policy into labor policy reached fruition with the passage of the PRWORA, essentially a labor policy clothed in welfare terminology.

AFDC has been an important mainstay of public assistance policy and a sore spot for conservatives since its inception. This antagonism persisted even though in 1995 combined AFDC and food stamps costs accounted for only 3 percent of the federal budget compared to 22 percent for Social Security, 18 percent for defense, and 10 percent for Medicare.[73] The real concern about public assistance was not about excessive spending; instead, it was a reaction to AFDC as a symbol of governmental responsibility to provide a cash proxy for labor market earnings. The very existence of AFDC was a thorn in the side of economic conservatives since it implied that the marketplace was somehow incapable of meeting the needs of all Americans.

Early federal attempts to transition recipients into the labor force were stillborn for several reasons. For one, between 1979 and 1994 the average wages of the lowest 30 percent of U.S. wage earners decreased by 12 percent.[74] The infusion of 3 or more million unskilled former welfare recipients into the labor force would have resulted in greater job competition and an even steeper drop in wages. Moreover, high unemployment rates in the late 1970s and early 1980s led to an oversupply of labor resulting in little incentive to drive more workers into the labor market. On the contrary, sound public policy dictated that more people be kept out of the workforce to not further aggravate unemployment. Hence, the conservative preference for labor market employment over public assistance was held in abeyance by the economic realities of the period.

In 1996, a unique confluence of events came together to complete the transformation of public assistance into labor policy. Frustrated by repeated failures of federal welfare-to-work efforts and the ignominious death of the FSA, the newly elected conservative 104th Congress was determined not to repeat past mistakes, and modified Clinton's welfare proposal in important ways. First and foremost was to disentitle public assistance. Second, the PRWORA removed the fiscal responsibility of government to provide income support to public assistance recipients beyond a five-year lifetime cap. Indeed, the Clinton welfare reform panel's proposed safety net (i.e., government as employer of the last resort) was eliminated. Under the PRWORA, the only option for those who exhaust their benefits is labor market participation or penury.

The PRWORA was passed in a period of sustained economic growth. In 1996, the unemployment rate was 4.5 percent and the economy was growing steadily at over 2.5 percent a year.[75] The low unemployment rate combined with the robust economy meant that the 138-million-member U.S. labor force could easily absorb the 4.2 million AFDC without driving down wages or increasing unemployment. The economic conditions of the middle 1990s reinforced the conservative belief that a job existed for anyone that wanted it.

Removing the federal responsibility for providing long-term cash assistance to the poor shifted the problem of poor support away from social welfare and into labor policy. The PRWORA represented the culmination of the long-standing conservative goal of deracinating public assistance: When the poor exhaust time-limited public assistance benefits they become a labor market rather than a welfare problem. With that change, U.S. public assistance policy was reduced to a short-term, transitional step in the march toward the full labor market participation of the poor.

Despite objections by welfare advocates, the conservative push toward labor policy is not without merit. First, one would be hard-pressed to argue that a well-paying job with benefits is not the best anti-poverty program. Moreover, Sweden—historically considered a progressive welfare state—has frequently used labor policy as a proxy for aggressive public assistance programs.[76] Second, the push toward workforce participation is congruent with current labor market trends for women. For instance, in 1955 only 18 percent of all U.S. mothers with children under 6 were in the labor force. By 1985 that number rose to 54 percent, and by 2002, it was 64.1 percent.[77] Given these trends, welfare advocates are hard-pressed to justify non-employment-based public assistance programs when more than three-fifths of all mothers with children under age six are in the labor force. Despite these conservative arguments, the absence of sound federal labor policy in the form of a frozen minimum wage, a lack of guaranteed health care insurance, and few workplace protections has resulted in most former recipients going from the frying pan into the fire. Specifically, many former recipients who now occupy secondary labor market jobs face an even shakier economic foundation than under tainted AFDC policies.

Despite some positive gains, the substitution of labor policy for public assistance policy has led to serious problems. For one, the absence of sound labor policy rewards low-wage employers while punishing low-income workers forced into poorly paid dead-end jobs that provide little, if any, benefits. Specifically, low-wage employers are rewarded by not being required to provide employees with a minimum number of hours, benefits or employment perks. These employers are subsidized by not having to pay the requisite salary to support a worker and their family. In effect, low-wage employers are subsidized by the earned income tax credit (EITC), child tax credit, food stamps, Medicaid, and the Child Health Insurance Program (CHIPs), which partially makes up the shortfall between low salaries and the real cost of living. For example, combined EITC and food stamp benefits alone can provide a maximum yearly supplement of $9,600 for a family of four, or almost the $10,000 minimum wage earned by a single worker.

Data from employer surveys administered in several large metropolitan areas suggests that in a severe recession job vacancy rates will decline by two-thirds or more, and by somewhat less in a milder recession.[78] Accordingly, the new hire and employment rates of former welfare recipients will decline by large amounts as well. At the same time, many unemployed low-income workers will be ineligible for TANF if they have exhausted their lifetime limits. In addition, neither TANF nor unemployment insurance benefits will be available to many non-custodial fathers whose contributions to family income are crucial. This is especially problematic since the labor market experiences of non-custodial fathers and low-income males has generally improved much less than those of single mothers in recent years.[79]

Compelling former recipients to become engaged in the workforce by way of a lifetime benefit cap will not ensure permanent labor force attachment, especially if the economy exhibits weakness. According to the U.S. Census Bureau, the poverty rate rose from 11.3 percent in 2000 to 12.1 percent in 2002, after dropping for four consecutive years. The number of poor families increased from 6.4 million in 2000 (or 8.7 percent of all families, a record low rate) to 7.6 million (10 percent) in 2002.[80] This equates to the rise in unemployment which peaked at about 6 percent in 2002. It also corresponds to a slowdown in the decline of welfare caseloads, from a reduction of 16 percent in 1998–99 to 5 percent in 2000–2001.[81]

The transition from public assistance to labor policy does not bode well for the "hard to employ," a group of recipients that have significant barriers to employment and difficultly in finding and sustaining work. Some of these barriers include substance abuse, physical disabilities, domestic violence, learning disabilities, mental health issues, language barriers, chronic health problems, and multiple barriers.[82] Many of these recipients who have been exempted from work participation under the former AFDC program are now subject to work requirements under PRWORA.

Although teenage birthrates in the United States have declined, they still remain high, exceeding those in most developed countries.

No single policy will ensure that former recipients maintain a viable attachment to the workforce. Nor can any single measure compensate for the lack of a comprehensive labor policy for low-income workers. David Stoesz sums up the dilemma: "Welfare reform that offers the welfare-poor an opportunity to become the working-poor is no *real* reform at all. The challenge that remains is to devise policies that will accelerate the upward mobility of welfare families so that they can partake in the American dream."[83] Family composition affects welfare receipt, which, in turn, is strongly influenced by teenage pregnancy.

Teenage Pregnancy

Teenage birthrates in this country have declined steadily since 1991. Although this is good news, teen birthrates in the United States remain high, exceeding those in most developed countries. For example, they are nearly twice as high as in England and Wales or Canada, and nine times as high as in the Netherlands or Japan. Nearly 11 percent of all U.S. births in 2002 were to teens (ages 15 to 19), and almost 1 million teenagers become pregnant each year, with about 446,000 giving birth.

- Eleven percent of all U.S. births are to teens. Teens account for 31 percent of all nonmarital births, down from 50 percent in 1970. Each year, almost 1 million teenage women—10 percent of all women aged 15 to 19—become pregnant. Seventy-eight percent of births to teens occur outside of marriage.
- The fathers of babies born to teenage mothers are likely to be older than the women: About one in five infants born to unmarried minors are fathered by men five or more years older than the mother.
- Between 1991 and 2000, the teenage birth rate fell by 23 percent (from 62.1 per 1,000 women to 47.7). Still, in 1998 about 5 teenage girls in 100 had a baby. Steep decreases in the pregnancy rate among sexually experienced teenagers accounted for most of the drop in the overall teenage pregnancy rate in the early to mid-1990s. Surveys indicate that 20 percent of the decline occurred because of decreased sexual activity; 80 percent was the result of more effective contraceptive practice.
- About 17 percent of teen mothers go on to have a second baby within three years after the birth of her first baby.
- Life often is difficult for a teenage mother and her child. Teens mothers are much more likely to come from poor or low-income families (83 percent) than are teens who have abortions (61 percent) or teens in general (38 percent). Teen mothers are more likely to drop out of high school than girls

who delay childbearing. Only about 64 percent of teen mothers graduate from high school or earn a GED within two years after they would have graduated, compared to 94 percent of teens who did not give birth. While 7 in 10 teen mothers complete high school, they are less likely than women who delay childbearing to go on to college. With her education cut short, a teenage mother often lacks job skills, making it hard for her to find and keep a job.

- A teenage mother may become financially dependent on her family or on welfare. Teen mothers are more likely to live in poverty than women who delay childbearing, and nearly 75 percent of all unmarried teen mothers go on welfare within five years after the birth of their first child. In part because most teen mothers come from disadvantaged backgrounds, 28 percent of them are poor while in their 20s and early 30s; in contrast, only 7 percent of women who first give birth after adolescence are poor at those ages.
- Children whose mothers were age 17 or younger when they were born tend to have more school difficulties and poorer health than children whose mothers were 20 to 21 when they were born.
- One-third of pregnant teens receive inadequate prenatal care; babies born to young mothers are more likely to be low-birth-weight, to have childhood health problems, and to be hospitalized than are those born to older mothers.
- While nearly 1 in 3 teen pregnancies are terminated by abortion, from 1986 to 2000, abortion rates among sexually experienced teens declined by 43 percent. Fewer teens are becoming pregnant, and in recent years fewer pregnant teens have chosen to have an abortion. The reasons most often given by teens for choosing an abortion are concerns about how a baby would change their lives, the feeling that they are not mature enough to have a child, and financial problems. Sixty-one percent of minors who have abortions do so with at least one parent's knowledge. Twenty-nine states currently have mandatory parental involvement laws in effect for a minor seeking an abortion.
- Both non-Hispanic white and black adolescents have experienced declines in pregnancy rates. Among black adolescents aged 15 to 19, the pregnancy rate fell 32 percent between 1990 and 2000; among white teenagers it declined 28 percent. The pregnancy rate among Hispanic teenagers increased between 1990 and 1992 but then fell 15 percent by 2000.[84]

Out-of-wedlock births have grave economic consequences. This is especially true because teenage mothers, regardless of their income, are now more likely to keep their children.[85] The high out-of-wedlock birthrate translates into important economic realities. For one, teenage mothers are twice as likely to be poor as nonteen mothers, and a teenage mother earns only half the lifetime wage of a woman who waits until she is 20 to have her first child.[86] Second, as mentioned above, a strong correlation exists between young single motherhood and high welfare dependency. In 1993, 75 percent of unmarried adolescent mothers became welfare recipients within five years of the birth of their first child.[87] Mothers with children age three and under are at the greatest risk of long-term welfare dependency. According to the Brookings Institute, teenage childbearing cost U.S. taxpayers $7 billion a year.[88] Moreover, teen mothers who grew up on public assistance were more than twice as likely to be welfare dependent themselves.[89]

Although numerous programs have been developed to reduce teenage pregnancy, evaluations of these attempts have shown mixed results. One early teen pregnancy prevention program was Project Redirection. From 1980 to 1982, 805 AFDC-eligible mothers aged 17 or younger received intensive services to optimize educational, employment, and life management skills. Evaluation of Project Redirection mothers one, two, and five years after their participation in the program was mixed. Project Redirection teens fared no better than the control group in obtaining a high school diploma or GED certificate. Although participants were more likely to be employed one year after exiting the program, their weekly earnings five years later were only $23 more than those in the control group. Five years later, the household income of the control group exceeded that of the Project Redirection group by $19. Two years after participation, 7 percent of Project Redirection teens were on welfare; five years later, 10 percent fewer of the control group were on welfare. Regarding childbearing, Project Redirection teens reported fewer pregnancies in the first and second years after the program; yet five years after the program, they exceeded the control group in their number of pregnancies as well as their number of live births. Researchers concluded that "the program impacts were largely transitory."[90]

From 1989 to 1992 researchers randomly assigned 2,322 poor young mothers, ages 16 to 22, either to New Chance—a program through which the women received health, education, and welfare assistance coordinated by a case manager—or to a control group that received no special services. At the 18-month follow-up, the experimental group fared worse than the control group in two important respects. First, New Chance mothers were less likely to be using contraception, were more likely to become pregnant, and were more likely to abort their pregnancies than the control group. Second, participants were less likely to be working after entering the program; were earning less; and, during the fourth to the sixth months, were more likely to be on public assistance.[91] To compound matters, New Chance cost $5,073 per participant, excluding child care. (If child care were included, an average of $7,646 was spent.)[92]

Not surprisingly, the anti-teen pregnancy movement is highly politicized. On one side are those that support comprehensive sex education that promotes abstinence but includes information about contraception and condoms. On the other side are those that favor abstinence-only-until-marriage programs that promote abstinence from sexual activity outside marriage as the expected standard of behavior. Proponents of abstinence-only programs believe that providing information about the benefits of condoms or contraception contradicts the message of abstinence and undermines its impact. As such, abstinence-only programs provide no information about contraception beyond failure rates. Included in the 1996 PRWORA was a provision (later set out in Title V of the Social Security Act) that appropriated $250 million over five years for state initiatives that promote sexual abstinence outside of marriage as the only acceptable standard of behavior for young people. From 1998 to 2003, almost a half a billion dollars in state and federal funds were used to support the Title V initiative. The findings of eleven states whose evaluations were available in 2003 showed few short-term benefits and no lasting, positive impact. Specifically, abstinence-only programs showed little evidence of sustained (long-term) impact on attitudes and intentions. Worse, they showed some negative impacts on the willingness of participants to use contraception, including condoms, to prevent untoward sexual health outcomes. Only in one state did any program demonstrate any short-term success in delaying the initiation of sex and none of the programs demonstrated evidence of long-term success in delaying sexual activity among adolescents.[93] The apparent failure of these prevention programs illustrates how little policymakers understand the motivation and the behaviors associated with teenage pregnancy. It also illustrates how little is known about the interpersonal, social, and cultural components that leads to teenage pregnancy.

The Underclass

The underclass was discussed in the 1980s by journalist Ken Auletta, who descriptively identified four groups that make up the underclass: (1) the "passive poor," usually those dependent on welfare; (2) hostile "street predators," often dropouts and addicts; (3) "hustlers," or opportunists, who do not commit violent crimes; and (4) the "traumatized"—alcoholics, bag ladies, and casualties of deinstitutionalization.[94] In the late 1980s William Julius Wilson revived the term, defining the underclass as

> [a] heterogeneous grouping of families and individuals who are outside of the mainstream of the American occupational system. Included . . . are individuals who lack training and skills and either experience long-term unemployment or are not members of the labor force, individuals who are engaged in street crime and other forms of aberrant behavior, and families that experience long-term spells of poverty and/or welfare dependency.[95]

Another description of the underclass is offered by Erol Ricketts and Isabel Sawhill, who define it as a subpopulation characterized by a cluster of behaviors and attitudes that are considered outside of current middle-class social norms.[96]

Relevant social science research has shown that the underclass in the United States increased from 1970 to 1980. Some researchers have estimated that in 1980 between 1 million and 2 million people could be characterized as members of the underclass. According to Ricketts and Sawhill, who are considered to have done some of the best empirical research on the subject, the "underclass" label applies to 1 percent of the U.S. population, roughly one-thirteenth of all people living under the poverty line. Using Ricketts and Sawhill's guidelines, more than 2 million people would have been classified as an underclass in 2004.[97]

Welfare Behaviorism

Behavioral Poverty The TANF program is predicated on a form of **welfare behaviorism:** an attempt to reprogram the behaviors of the poor. Current welfare reform efforts, however, are unlikely to deliver on the promises of this approach. Despite data demonstrating the marginal economic benefits of making welfare conditional, conservatives effectively leveraged a moral argument that public policy should change the behavior of the welfare poor. By the mid-1980s, conservative theorists had arrived at a new consensus on poverty; namely, that although the liberally inspired public assistance programs might once have been appropriate for the "cash poor," they were counterproductive for the "behaviorally poor."[98] As poverty programs expanded, conservatives contended, the social dysfunctions of the behaviorally poor metastasized: Beginning as teen mothers, women dominated family life, ultimately becoming generationally dependent on welfare; young men dropped out of school, failed to pursue legitimate employment, and resorted to sexual escapades and repetitive crime to demonstrate prowess; children, lacking adult role models of effective parents at home and capable workers on the job, promised to further populate the underclass.

Conservatives differed in how to respond to behavioral poverty. In *Losing Ground* Charles Murray suggested "scrapping the entire federal welfare and income support structure for working-aged persons."[99] Not long after, Lawrence Mead offered a less draconian measure in *Beyond Entitlement:* Make receipt of public aid contingent on conventional behaviors, particularly work.[100] Eventually, both prescriptions were to be incorporated in welfare policy. Following Mead's admonition, TANF required recipients to participate in work-related activities. As states secured federal waivers for "experiments," welfare mothers often had to meet a number of other requirements or risk losing aid: Through "Learnfare" children on public assistance had to demonstrate regular school attendance; through the family cap additional assistance for children born after a mother became eligible for assistance would be denied, inducing family planning; the establishment of paternity was required before a child could receive benefits, so as to enable the state to pursue child support; as a method for protecting public health, recipient children were required to have immunizations in order to attend school; to dissuade teenagers from becoming pregnant, states required teen mothers to live with their parents in order to get welfare.[101]

The ending of the 60-year federal entitlement to an income floor for poor families has had extensive political fallout. Die-hard conservatives justified the termination of welfare with George Gilder's contention that what the poor needed most was "the spur of their own poverty,"[102] and "compassionate conservatives" found a rationale in "tough love." Either way, conservative welfare reformers conceded that terminating benefits would probably worsen deprivation but argued that was necessary. Liberals were aghast.[103] Following Marian Wright Edelman's earlier demand that former President Clinton veto welfare reform crafted by the 104th Congress,[104] the *Washington Post* weighed in with an editorial declaring that Clinton's signing of the welfare reform plan would be "the low point of his presidency."[105] Liberal advocacy groups scrambled to convince the president to veto the legislation, but they failed.[106] As heat from liberal activists intensified, Clinton promised to push ameliorative action on the most controversial features of the welfare reform plan—elimination of benefits for disabled people and legal immigrants—through the incoming 105th Congress.

Personal and Parental Responsibility The welfare behaviorism inherent in TANF reflects a belief in the importance of personal and parental responsibility. This philosophy harks back to supposedly traditional "main street" values of self-reliance, independence, and individual responsibility. It is based on the idea that the U.S. offers a level playing field replete with abundant economic and social opportunities. It also includes a de facto belief in the limited role of government.

The view of parental responsibility reflected in the PRWORA focuses on several themes: (1) fathers who beget children have a responsibility to financially support them; (2) mothers requesting public aid have a responsibility to establish paternity for the purpose of collecting child support; (3) mothers who have physical custody of children have a responsibility to provide for them financially through work efforts; (4) custodial parents have a responsibility to ensure that their children receive and appropriately respond to educational opportunities; and (5) custodial parents have a responsibility to provide basic public health protection for their children, including immunizations. These tenets of parenthood are neither extreme nor especially controversial. In fact, they are in part the glue that holds society together. Controversy arises, then, not on the correctness of these values but in their operationalization. More specifically, significant controversy surrounds the question of whether attempts at engineering appropriate social behaviors are successful or whether they simply function as punishment.

Examples of social engineering as social punishment abound. Learnfare, introduced in Wisconsin in the fall of 1988, targeted teenagers who had more than two unexcused absences from school. Under Learnfare sanctions, such absences would cause the family's AFDC benefits for a dependent teen to be reduced by $77 a month; for an independent teen with a child, the penalty was $190 a month. Wisconsin officials contended that such sanctions would result in the return of 80 percent of teens on AFDC who had dropped out of school. Rhetoric notwithstanding, an independent agency's subsequent evaluation of the Milwaukee demonstration "did not show improvement in student attendance that could be attributed to the Learnfare requirement." Undeterred, state officials wrote to the evaluators and demanded that they suppress the parts of the study detailing the failure of Learnfare to enhance teen school attendance. When the researchers refused, Wisconsin officials canceled the contract, in the process impugning the professionalism of the evaluators.[107]

In Ohio, meanwhile, another demonstration program promised teens a $62-a-month carrot for good school attendance, coupled with a $62-a-month stick for truancy. Three years after the program's inception, LEAP (Learning, Earning, and Parenting) was heralded as a major victory in the battle against teen truancy. A closer examination of the LEAP evaluation is not encouraging. The glowing results were reported only for teens currently enrolled in school and excluded those who had dropped out, even though both groups were part of the study's population. Including dropouts, LEAP's outcomes plummet: The number completing high school is not 20 but 6.5 percent; the number employed is not 40 but 20 percent. Because of the benefit reduction sanction levied against truant teens, a significant number of all mothers in the study reported "diminished spending on essentials for their families, especially clothing and food."[108] In their concluding observations, evaluators conceded that changing adolescent behavior is difficult and admitted that LEAP produced some "perverse effects."[109]

Another issue underlying the new welfare reforms involves (re)marriage. According to several studies, no more than a fifth of mothers voluntarily leave public assistance as a result of earnings increases; most exits result from a change in marital status.[110] Yet public assistance programs punish marriage in two ways: (1) by how they treat a married couple with children, and (2) by how they treat families with stepparents. First, a needy two-parent family with children is less likely to be eligible for aid than a one-parent family. Although the nonincapacitated two-parent family can apply for TANF, many states' restrictions involving work expectation and time limits make the program inaccessible to many poor families. Second, a stepparent has no legal obligation to support the children of his or her spouse in most states. Nevertheless, TANF cuts or limits benefits when a woman remarries by counting much of the stepparent's income when calculating the family's countable income, thus jeopardizing the mother's eligibility status.[111] In effect, there is a strong economic disincentive for a low-income woman to marry a man with low earnings. According to the conservative Heritage Foundation's Robert Rector:

> The current welfare system has made marriage economically irrational for most low-income parents. Welfare has converted the low-income working husband from a necessary breadwinner into a net financial handicap. It has transformed marriage from a legal institution designed to protect and nurture children into an institution which financially penalizes nearly all low-income parents who enter into it. Across the nation, the current welfare system has all but destroyed family structure in the inner city. Welfare establishes strong financial disincentives, effectively blocking the formation of intact, two-parent families.[112]

Welfare to Work

TANF is predicated on the belief that recipients should be moved off public assistance and into private employment as quickly as possible, a theme that has permeated welfare reform since the 1960s. Whereas conservatives argue that paid work is the best antipoverty program, some liberals have asserted that child rearing is also a productive form of work. These liberals have contended that although it is socially acceptable for middle-class mothers to stay at home with young children, poor mothers are considered lazy and unmotivated if they try to do the same.

Workfare programs have been a constant feature of the welfare landscape since 1967, when new AFDC amendments were added to pressure recipient mothers into working. As part of those new rules, work requirements became mandatory for unemployed fathers, mothers, and certain teenagers. AFDC recipients who were deemed employable and yet refused to work could be terminated.[113] A work incentive program (WIN) was developed to provide training and employment for all welfare mothers considered employable (recipients with preschool-age children were exempt). Day care was made available to facilitate the WIN program. Partly because of a lackluster federal commitment (in 1985 the total federal contribution to WIN was only $258 million), the performance of work programs has generally been disappointing. In addition, many states were reluctant to enact mandatory job requirements, because they believed that enforcing them would prove more costly than simply maintaining families on AFDC.

Workfare again resurfaced in 1988 when it formed the backbone of the Family Support Act. By the early 1990s, however, the Manpower Demonstration Research Corporation (MDRC) had amassed considerable evidence about the performance of state welfare-to-work programs, and the results fell far short of what supporters had promised. Out of 13 welfare-to-work programs evaluated in 1991, most boosted participants' earnings little more than $700 per year. Although most programs also experienced reductions in AFDC payments, these were modest; typically, less than $400 per year. And significantly, in only two programs were AFDC payment reductions greater than the programs' cost per welfare-to-work participant.[114]

To welfare reform researchers, the welfare-to-work bandwagon was less of a star-spangled apparatus than its proponents had made it out to be. Before his assignment to the Clinton working panel on welfare reform, Harvard's David Ellwood admitted as much, writing that the typical welfare-to-work program increased earnings between $250 and $750 per year. "Most work-welfare programs look like decent investments," he concluded, "but no carefully evaluated work-welfare programs have done more than put a tiny dent in the welfare caseloads, even though they have been received with enthusiasm."[115] A similar sentiment was expressed by workfare expert Judith Gueron:

> [Although] welfare-to-work programs have paid off by increasing the employment and earnings of single mothers and reducing their receipt of public assistance . . . MDRC's research also reveals the limits of past interventions. Whether the targeted group were welfare mothers, low-income youth who dropped out of high school, teenage parents with limited prospects, or unemployed adult men, the programs had little success in boosting people out of poverty. . . . Often, welfare recipients who get jobs join the ranks of the working poor.[116]

If the reality of welfare-to-work diverges from the rhetoric of welfare reform, it is because of the assumption that TANF mothers are so welfare dependent that they have no experience with the labor market. In fact, many mothers have worked and have, as a result, come to see welfare benefits as a form of unemployment or underemployment assistance. To explain the relationship between work and welfare, labor economist Michael Piore split workers into primary and secondary labor markets. As explained in Chapter 5, workers in the primary labor market hold down salaried jobs that include health and vacation benefits, are full time, and incorporate a career track. Workers in the secondary labor market work for hourly wages—often at the minimum wage—without benefits in jobs that are part time or seasonal and are not part of a career track.

Other research has captured the erratic relationship between work and welfare for many mothers on TANF. Findings of the Institute for Women's Policy Research reveal that 43 percent of former AFDC mothers were either peripherally attached to the labor market, augmenting welfare with wages, or drifting on and off of welfare depending on the availability of work. Once AFDC mothers who were seeking work were coupled to those above, 66 percent of welfare mothers were either participating in the labor market or were trying to.[117]

But conditions of the secondary labor market make this problematic.[118] Given the reality of the secondary labor market, the trick of welfare reform is to catapult TANF mothers beyond the secondary labor market and into the primary labor market. If this could be done, earnings would increase enough to assure economic self-sufficiency. The sticking point is that substantial investments are necessary to achieve such program performance. But to do so creates two problems: First, a "moral hazard" emerges as welfare beneficiaries become recipients of benefits that are not available to the working poor not on welfare. While working people often grumble about the welfare dependent obtaining benefits not available to them, they also suspect that ample benefits induce those who should be working to apply for public assistance. Second, a "political hazard" is created for any elected official who states a willingness to support welfare recipients over the working poor. In such circumstances, the prudent politician favors the least costly and most expedient option—

push welfare recipients into the labor market and celebrate doing so with paeans to the work ethic. These moral and political hazards thus prescribe the boundaries of plausibility: perforce, welfare reform is limited to elevating the welfare poor up to the level of the working poor.

Finally, TANF work-to-welfare programs are flawed in another way. Specifically, they fail to take into account barriers to employment. A study of welfare recipients by Sandra Danziger and her colleagues found high levels of barriers to work, such as physical and mental problems, domestic violence, and lack of transportation, but relatively low levels of other barriers, such as drug or alcohol dependence or a lack of understanding of work norms. Their study also found that recipients commonly have multiple barriers, and that the number of barriers is strongly and negatively associated with employment status. Almost two-thirds of the study respondents had two or more potential barriers to work, and more than one-quarter had four or more. Finally, Danziger and her colleagues found that the barrier hypothesis is a better predictor of employment than traditional models that rely on education, work experience, and welfare history. For example, they found that the number of years of prior welfare receipt is not associated with current employment, once health and mental health factors, transportation, work skills, and perceived discrimination experiences are taken into account.[119]

Conclusion: The Evolution of Public Assistance

For a half century, AFDC did little more than dispense checks; not until relatively recently has recipient behavior been a target for systematic intervention. Because of its lack of direction, AFDC became the source for derogatory colloquialisms such as "welfare mess" and "welfare queen." Instilling some order in welfare was bound to produce some desirable outcomes. It is the extent of positive outcomes that is questionable.

Welfare analysts suspect that most of the improvement in welfare program performance is attributable to those recipients who are relatively well educated, have employment experience, and are upwardly mobile. Such welfare beneficiaries are good candidates for the secondary labor market, and some will even find secure employment in the primary labor market. Of the remaining welfare families, most may be socially mainstreamed with adequate inducements and supports. The welfare behaviorism articulated through initiatives such as welfare-to-work has been testing the malleability of this population. Some of this group will respond positively to incentives and sanctions; some will not. In all likelihood, many—perhaps 20 percent—will fail to negotiate the procedural thicket imposed by the welfare reforms of the mid-1990s. While the PRWORA allows states to exempt 20 percent of families from time limits, there is no requirement that those on the lowest social stratum be allowed to stay on aid indefinitely. And indeed, there is no assurance that states will exempt the most troubled families from time limits. It is just as plausible that savvy state welfare administrators will exempt mothers who are in lengthy educational/training programs, on the basis that they represent a better long-term investment of public resources. Even some conservatives are opposed to arbitrary time limits. At a 1996 conference on welfare reform, Lawrence Mead stated his opposition to time limits, primarily on the basis that virtually no research had been done to determine the consequences of terminating poor families from public assistance.[120]

Several features of TANF make its full implementation unlikely. A core question involves the extent to which states can be expected to comply with the federal work requirements, especially given the economic downturn that began in 2001. This problem will be exacerbated if work participation rates increase under TANF reauthorization. In 2001 the Congressional Budget Office projected that over six years PRWORA grants would fall $12 billion short of the amount necessary to enable states to provide the services and opportunities necessary to meet work requirements; yet the legislation imposes penalties—ranging from 5 to 21 percent of federal funds—for noncompliance. By 2004, most states had either exhausted their TANF funds or were approaching the need to augment federal funds with state funds. In the event of a continuing economic downswing, this will produce an enormous compression effect on the states. Squeezed between static resources and increasing demands for job placement, the initial response will be to remove families from welfare or to discourage new families from enrolling. This dilemma is already evident in the troubling trend of rising poverty rates coupled with a concomitant drop in TANF caseloads.

Whenever possible, states will attempt to transfer the most troubled families to SSI, a program that is entirely federally funded. This, however, will require certification of disability, and the federal government will resist SSI's becoming a dumping ground for the states' welfare reform failures. Indeed, PRWORA tightens the eligibility requirements for SSI in a manner that makes transfers from welfare more difficult. Without the SSI transfer option, states will be induced to reduce the number of cases not in compliance with work requirements. Given difficulties in operationalizing the federal five-year lifetime limit, states will be induced to consider ever shorter limits. Terminating families as soon as possible on the basis of noncompliance will ultimately screen out those families least likely to become employed. Eventually such families will cease seeking aid; and to the extent that large numbers of the more disorganized families disappear from state welfare rolls, states will avoid federal penalties for failing to meet employment requirements.

The future of families dumped from state welfare programs is bleak. Many have ended up in the tertiary job market, or worse, in shelters or on the streets. Like the deinstitutionalized, some former TANF families have been swallowed up in the urban landscape and have become virtually invisible, leading lives of quiet desperation. Conservative scholars, such as Marvin Olasky, have promised that private, especially religious, agencies will pick up the slack,[121] but this is doubtful. Contributions to nonprofit agencies such as the United Way have stagnated in recent years. Ineligible for state aid and unable to get necessary assistance from the nonprofit sector, former welfare families will turn to metropolitan government as the last resort. Big-city mayors are already dreading the impact that such families will have on their already over-stretched city budgets.[122]

Despite the problems, certain incremental benefits of welfare reform must be acknowledged. For example, the PRWORA allows states to establish individual development accounts (IDAs), a strategy to increase the assets of poor families and help vault them out of poverty. Unfortunately, the welfare reform plan makes no specific allocations for IDAs, leaving funding the option of state and local governments or philanthropy. PRWORA benefits are denied for life to parents convicted of felony drug offenses unless they are participating in a drug treatment program, even though family-oriented drug treatment for addicts who are also mothers is rare. Several of the provisions of PRWORA target teenagers on welfare: Teen mothers are required to live with their parents and stay in school to receive benefits; HHS is mandated to mount a teen pregnancy prevention initiative; and the Justice Department is required to identify older men who impregnate female teenagers and prosecute them for statutory rape. Several provisions address child support, including the requirement that states establish registries for child support and streamline the process for establishing paternity. States are encouraged to be more aggressive in withholding income from noncustodial parents in arrears for child support. Furthermore, more vigorous penalties are directed at noncustodial parents to encourage them to pay up, such as revocation of professional, driver's, occupational, and recreational licenses.[123]

Given the track record of demonstration programs designed to prevent teen pregnancy and increase child support, the stiff penalties directed at adolescents and deadbeat dads would seem to be more of rhetorical value to elected officials than of practical use to save the public revenues now allocated to welfare programs. Regarding a larger issue, no one seems to have taken the trouble to calculate the ultimate cost of deploying a state-administered welfare apparatus with tracking, surveillance, and sanction capacities designed to reprogram the behavior of the 2.7 million families on public assistance.

Finally, PRWORA includes funding for further research on welfare reform, most of it for the benefit of children. From 1996 to 2002, $6 million was allocated annually for the study of a random sample of abused and neglected children. The focus of this longitudinal research was child protection and out-of-home placements. An additional $15 million annually was allocated from 1997 to 2002 to track child poverty rates. If the child poverty rate increases by 5 percent or more for a given year, HHS must prepare a plan for corrective action. Significantly, there are no specific requirements for states to study the consequences of deleting families from welfare as a result of time limits, particularly as this action affects children. Moreover, while HHS has studied welfare leavers, the results of these investigations have not been translated into policy reform. On the contrary, proposed TANF reauthorization plans directly contradict research findings.

Recipients of public assistance programs do not fare as well as those covered under the social insurances. Public assistance programs involve a large dose of stigma, and the character of recipients is often maligned because of their need. Moreover, the relative success of Social Security in arresting poverty among the elderly has not been replicated in public assistance programs. In fact, the reverse is true; the poorest of the poor have endured greater levels of poverty from 1980 on. Indeed, the legacy of welfare reform engineered by the 104th Congress and signed by former President Clinton does not bode well for the future prospects of poor people in the United States.

The U.S. welfare system has undergone a dramatic transformation over the past 20 years marked by several important themes: (1) the conversion of public assistance policy into labor policy, (2) the conversion of public assistance policy into tax policy, and (3) the increased privatization of social welfare services. By converting AFDC into workfare through TANF, the PRWORA eliminated the boundary between public assistance and labor policy and became a feeder system to supply the secondary labor market with manpower. The result is fewer protected islands left for those who cannot compete in the labor market.

The conversion of public assistance policy into labor policy is shored up by tax policy through the expansion of EITC benefits, the only public assistance program that has been purposely enlarged in the past 20 years. In fact, EITC has become the largest public assistance program in the nation. By expanding EITC benefits through the tax code while at the same time eliminating AFDC, the legislature has shifted the focus from the nonworking poor to the working poor, a group more marginally acceptable to conservatives and the larger society. Public assistance payments to the poor will likely be increasingly routed through tax policy for low-income workers rather than direct cash or in-kind subsidies for the nonworking poor.

Privatized social services have encroached upon most welfare domains, including health care, public education, mental health and chemical dependency services, nursing home care, corrections, and child care. Many of these markets are already glutted by the influx of corporations seeking to increase their profits and their corporate reach. One of the last remaining frontiers is the delivery of public welfare services, an area virtually untouched by large corporations. In 1996 Texas tended its public welfare services out to public bid. Although the privatization of Texas social services was vetoed by the former Clinton administration, the concept has reappeared. Administering a multibillion-dollar public welfare apparatus is too lucrative an area for large corporations to ignore.

This is clearly a difficult time for the American welfare state. Even after huge expenditures on social welfare services, basic needs remain unmet. Given the present economic trend—in which vast numbers of service jobs are produced, many of which are part time, have few if any benefits, and pay the minimum wage—long-term welfare benefit packages will likely be required for an increasing number of citizens. How much these income benefit packages will contain, and at what cost, will be a matter for future discourse in public policy.

Discussion Questions

1. Public assistance programs are arguably the most controversial programs in the U.S. welfare state. Critics frequently lambaste them for encouraging everything from welfare dependency to teenage pregnancy. Supporters argue that public assistance programs are poorly funded and barely allow recipients to survive. Why is public assistance so controversial? What, if anything, can be done to make the TANF program less controversial?
2. Numerous myths have arisen around the TANF program. In your opinion, what myths have been the most harmful to the programs and to recipients? Why?
3. General Assistance is often the hardest hit when states decide to implement funding cuts in social welfare. What accounts for the relative unpopularity of GA? Is the GA budget the most logical place to cut when states are faced with fiscal crises? What, if anything, can be done to strengthen the image of GA?
4. Since the 1970s, most strategies for reforming public assistance have revolved around implementing mandatory work requirements. This strategy was evident in the programs of Presidents Carter and Reagan and was the centerpiece of the 1988 Family Support Act. More recently, the TANF program mandated that benefits should last for a maximum of five years, after which a recipient would be required to work. Is establishing a mandatory work requirement a viable strategy for reforming public assistance?

If so, why? If not, why not? What would be a better strategy for reforming public assistance?

5. TANF benefit levels vary widely from state to state because the federal government has refused to establish a national minimum benefit level. Moreover, there is little federal pressure on states to increase benefit levels and thereby curtail the erosion of public assistance benefits that has taken place since the 1970s. Should the federal government establish a minimum national benefit level for TANF and compel states to meet that level? If not, why not? If you agree, what should that level be?
6. Public assistance programs are increasingly being designed to change the behavior of poor recipients. Can and should the behavior of poor people be changed through social policy legislation? Will this legislation work? If not, why?
7. Although administered by the Social Security Administration, the SSI program carries a stigma similar to public assistance programs like food stamps or the TANF. Why does this stigma exist? What can be done to diminish it?

Notes

1. Isaac Shapiro and Robert Greenstein, *Holes in the Safety Nets* (Washington, DC: Center on Budget and Policy Priorities, 1988).
2. U.S. Department of Health and Human Services, Table 2, Temporary Assistance for Needy Families, Caseload Reduction Credits Total and Two-Parent Families Fiscal Year 2000, Research, Evaluation and Planning, Administration for Children and Families, Washington, DC, 2003.
3. Department of Health, Education, and Welfare, "Aid to Families with Dependent Children." (Washington, DC: Social Security Administration, Office of Research and Statistics, 1979), p. 1.
4. See Nancy Reichman, Julien Teitler, Irwin Garfinkel, and Sandra Garcia, "Variations in Maternal and Child Wellbeing Among Financially Eligible Mothers by TANF Participation Status," Center for Research on Child Wellbeing, Working Paper #03-13-FF, Madison, WI, April 2003; and U.S. Department of Health and Human Services, "Indicators of Welfare Dependence," Annual Report to Congress 2003.
5. U.S. House of Representatives, Select Committee on Hunger, "Myths and Realities: Food Stamp and AFDC Recipients" (Washington, DC: U.S. Government Printing Office, April 9, 1992), p. 59.
6. Committee on Ways and Means, U.S. House of Representatives, *2004 Green Book,* (Washington, DC: U.S. Government Office, 2004), pp. 7–3.
7. David Morris, "Ask Dr. Dave," Institute for Local Self-Reliance, 2003. Retrieved October 2004 from www.americanvoice2004.org/askdave/26askdave.html
8. Children's Defense Fund, *The State of America's Children, 1991* (Washington, DC: Children's Defense Fund, 1991), p. 156; U.S. Department of Health and Human Services, "Percent Distribution of TANF Families with No Adult Recipients by Number of Recipient Children October 1998–September 1999." Retrieved 2000 from www.acf.dhhs.gov/programs/opre/characteristics/fy99/tab03_99.htm
9. Patrick Bresette, "Testimony to the Senate Committee on Health Services: On SB 64—Relating to TANF and Medicaid Benefits for Additional Children Born to TANF Recipients," March 9, 1999. Retrieved 2000 from www.cppp.org/products/testimony/testimony/tstfamilycap.html.
10. "Welfare Reform Issue Paper," Working Group on Welfare Reform, Family Support and Independence, U.S. Department of Health and Human Services, February 26, 1994; Peter Gottschalk, "Achieving Self-Sufficiency for Welfare Recipients—The Good and Bad News," in *Select Committee on Hunger, Beyond Public Assistance: Where Do We Go From Here?* Serial No. 102-123 (Washington, DC: U.S. Government Printing Office, 1992), p. 56.
11. Mary Jo Bane and David T. Ellwood, *Welfare Realities: From Rhetoric to Reform* (Cambridge, MA: Harvard University Press, 1994).
12. Robert Moffitt, quoted in Hillary Hoynes and T. McCurdy, "Has the Decline in Benefits Shortened Welfare Spells," *AEA Papers and Proceedings* 84, no. 2 (May 1994), pp. 43–48.
13. P. J. Leahy, T. F. Buss, and J. M. Quane, "Time on Welfare: Why Do People Enter and Leave the System," *American Journal of Economics and Sociology* 54 (January 1995), pp. 33–46.
14. Bane and Ellwood, *Welfare Realities;* see also Greg J. Duncan and Saul D. Hoffman, "Welfare Dynamics and Welfare Policy," unpublished paper, Institute for Social Research, Ann Arbor, MI, 1985.
15. Ibid.
16. Peter Gottschalk, "Is Intergenerational Correlation in Welfare Participation across Generations Spurious?"

Boston College, November 1990, Conference Papers, 1990 ASPE-JCPES Conference on the Underclass (Washington, DC: U.S. Department of Health and Human Services).

17. M. Ann Hill and June O'Neill, "Underclass Behaviors in the United States: Measurement and Analysis of Determinants," City College of New York, March 1990, Conference Papers, 1990 ASPE-JCPES Conference on the Underclass (Washington, DC: U.S. Department of Health and Human Services).
18. Mary Corcoran, Roger Gordon, Deborah Laren, and Gary Solon, "Problems of the Underclass: Underclass Neighborhoods and Intergenerational Poverty and Dependency," University of Michigan, 1991, Conference Papers, 1990 ASPE-JCPES Conference on the Underclass (Washington, DC: U.S. Department of Health and Human Services).
19. See Committee on Ways and Means, *2004 Green Book;* and Department of Health and Human Services, "Percent Distribution of TANF Families by Race, October 1998–September 1999." Retrieved 2000 from www.acf.dhhs.gov/programs/opre/characteristics/fy99/tab06_99.htm.
20. U.S. Department of Health and Human Services, Table 1A, "Temporary Assistance for Needy Families TANF Work Participation Rates, Fiscal Year 2002." Retrieved October 2004 from www.acf.dhhs.gov/programs/ofa/2002/table01a.htm
21. See Michael Harrington, with the assistance of Robert Greenstein and Eleanor Holmes Norton, *Who Are the Poor?* (Washington, DC: Justice for All, 1987), p. 21; and Weingart Center, Institute for the Study of Homelessness and Poverty, "Frequently Asked Questions, 2004," retrieved October 2004 from www.weingart.org/institute/about/faq.html#Anchor4
22. Iris Lav and Steven Gold, *The States and the Poor* (Washington, DC: Center on Budget and Policy Priorities, 1993), p. 11.
23. U.S. Department of Health and Human Services, "Indicators of Welfare Dependence: Annual Report to Congress, 2004," Table TANF 6, Trends in AFDC/TANF Average Monthly Payments, 1962–2002, Appendix A, Program Data. Retrieved October 2004 from aspe.hhs.gov/hsp/indicators04/apa-tanf.htm#figtanf1
24. U.S. Department of Health and Human Services, Table 1A, "Temporary Assistance for Needy Families TANF Work Participation Rates, Fiscal Year 2002."
25. Duncan and Hoffman, "Welfare Dynamics."
26. David Morris, "Ask Dr. Dave," 2003.
27. UDSA, Food and Nutrition Service, "Summary, Characteristics of Food Stamp Households: Fiscal Year 2002, July 2003." Retrieved October 2004 from www.fns.usda.gov/oane/MENU/Published/FSP/FILES/Participation/2002AdvSum.htm
28. James R. Walker, *Migration Among Low-Income Households: Helping the Witch Doctors Reach Consensus,* Institute for Research on Poverty, Discussion Paper no. 1031-94 University of Wisconsin–Madison, April 1994.
29. Thomas Corbett, "The Wisconsin Welfare Magnet: What Is an Ordinary Member of the Tribe to Do When the Witch Doctors Disagree?" *Focus* 13, no. 3 (Fall/Winter 1991), pp. 2–4.
30. Quoted in Diane Rose, Terri Sachnik, Josie Salazar, Eunice Sealey, and Virginia Wall, "Welfare Reform II," unpublished paper, University of Houston Graduate School of Social Work, Houston, TX, 1996.
31. U.S. House of Representatives, "Myths and Realities," p. 58.
32. Jack Tweedie, "Welfare Reform: Doing Well, Trying to Do Better," *State Legislatures Magazine,* National Conference of State Legislatures, Washington, D.C., January 2003. Retrieved October 2004 from www.ncsl.org/programs/pubs/slmag/2003/103welf.htm#state
33. Robert Moffitt, "Incentive Effects of the U.S. Welfare System: A Review," *Journal of Economic Literature* 30 (March 1992), pp. 1–61; see also Barbara Vobejda, "Decline in Birth Rates for Teens May Reflect Major Social Changes," *Houston Chronicle* (October 29, 1996), p. 13A.
34. U.S. House of Representatives, *1992 Green Book,* pp. 653–687.
35. W. Joseph Heffernan, *Introduction to Social Welfare Policy* (Itasca, IL: F.E. Peacock, 1979).
36. Elizabeth D. Huttman, *Introduction to Social Policy* (New York: McGraw-Hill, 1981), p. 168.
37. William Eaton, "Major Welfare Reform Compromise Reached," *Los Angeles Times* (September 27, 1988), p. 15.
38. American Public Welfare Association, *Conference Agreement on Welfare Reform* (Washington, DC: American Public Welfare Association, September 28, 1988), pp. 1–3.
39. See David Stoesz and Howard Karger, "Welfare Reform: From Illusion to Reality," *Social Work* 35, no. 2 (March 1990), pp. 141–147; and Spencer Rich, "Panel Clears Welfare Bill," *Washington Post* (September 28, 1988), p. A6.
40. Sar Levitan and Frank Gallo, *Jobs for JOBS: Toward a Work-Based Welfare System* (Washington, DC: Center for Social Policy Studies, March 1993).
41. Ibid.
42. See David T. Ellwood, "Welfare Reform as I Knew It: When Bad Things Happen to Good Policies," *The American Prospect 26* (May–June 1996), p. 240.
43. Ellwood, "Welfare Reform as I Knew It."
44. Ibid.
45. "Legal Immigrants to Carry Burden of Welfare Reform," *El Paso Times* (August 3, 1996), p. B1.
46. Mark H. Greenberg, "No Duty, No Floor: The Real Meaning of 'Ending Entitlements,'" Washington, DC:

Center for Law and Social Policy, 1996. Retrieved 1997 from http://epn.org/clasp/clduty-2.html.

47. Mark Greenberg and Steve Savner, "The Temporary Assistance for Needy Families Block Grant," Washington, DC: Center for Law and Social Policy, August 1996. Retrieved 1997 from http://epn.org/clasp/clsummry.html
48. Paula Roberts, "Relationship between TANF and Child Support Requirements," Washington, DC: Center for Law and Social Policy, September 1996. Retrieved 1997 from http://epn.org/clasp/cltcsr.html
49. "Welfare Reform," *NASW News* (September 1996), pp. 1, 12.
50. NACo Legislative Priority Fact Sheet, New Welfare Reform Law, "The Personal Responsibility and Work Opportunity Reconciliation Act of 1996," Washington, DC: NACo, 1996.
51. Frances Fox Piven, "Was Welfare Reform Worthwhile?" *The American Prospect* 27 (July–August 1996), pp. 14–15.
52. Quoted in Ibid., p. 14.
53. Center for Public Policy Priorities, *Health and Human Services Reorganization and the Integrated Eligibility Initiative* (Austin, TX: Center for Public Policy Priorities, September 22, 2004).
54. Douglas J. Besharov, "The Past and Future of Welfare Reform," *Public Interest* (Winter 2003), pp. 18–25.
55. U.S. Department of Health and Human Services, "Secretary Thompson Announces TANF Case loads Declined in 2003," August 23, 2004. Retrieved October 2004 from www.hhs.gov/news/press/2004pres/20040823.html
56. See Shawn Fremstad, *Recent Welfare Reform Research Findings, Implications for TANF Reauthorization and State TANF Policies,* Center on Budget and Policy Priorities, Washington, D.C., January 30, 2004; Cynthia Miller, *Leavers, Stayers, and Cyclers: An Analysis of the Welfare Caseload,* Manpower Demonstration Research Corporation, New York, November 2002; Gregory Acs and Pamela Loberts with Tracy Roberts, "Final Synthesis Report of Findings from ASPE "Leavers" Grants," Urban Institute, Washington, D.C., November 2001; Rebecca Blank, "Evaluating Welfare Reform in the United States," *Journal of Economic Literature,* XL (December 2002); Maria Cancian, Robert H. Haveman, Daniel R. Meyer, and Barbara Wolfe, "Before and after TANF: The Economic Well-Being of Women Leaving Welfare," *Social Science Review* 76, no. 4 (December 2002); Maria Cancian, Robert Haveman, Daniel R. Meyer, and Barbara Wolfe, "The Employment, Earnings, and Income of Single Mothers in Wisconsin Who Left Cash Assistance: Comparisons among Three Cohorts," Institute for Research on Poverty, Madison, WI, January 2003; Pamela Loprest, "Fewer Welfare Leavers Employed in Weak Economy," Urban Institute, Washington, D.C., August 2003; Pamela Loprest, "Disconnected Welfare Leavers Face Serious Risks," Urban Institute, Washington, D.C., August 2003; Pamela Loprest, "Use of Government Benefits Increases among Families Leaving Welfare," Urban Institute, Washington, D.C., September 2003; and LaDonna Pavetti and Greg Acs, "Moving Up, Moving Out, or Going Nowhere? A Study of the Employment Patterns of Young Women and the Implications for Welfare Mothers," *Journal of Policy Analysis and Management* 20, no. 4 (Fall 2001).
57. Shawn Fremstad, Sharon Parrott, and Arloc Sherman, "Unemployment Insurance Does Not Explain Why TANF Caseloads Are Falling as Poverty and Need Are Rising," Center on Budget and Policy Priorities, Washington, D.C., October 12, 2004.
58. House of Representatives, "To Reauthorize the Temporary Assistance for Needy Families Block Grant Program through June 30, 2004, and for Other Purposes," H.R. 3897, Section 4, 108th Congress, 2nd Session, March 4, 2004. Retrieved October 2004 from www.theorator.com/bills108/hr3897.html
59. Shawn Fremstad and Sharon Parrott, "The Senate Finance Committee's TANF Reauthorization Bill," Center on Budget and Policy Priorities, Washington, D.C., May 12, 2004.
60. Ibid.
61. Committee on Ways and Means, *2004 Green Book,* pp. 3–5.
62. See Ibid.; and Social Security Administration, "Fast Facts and Figures about Social Security." Retrieved October 2004 from www.ssa.gov/policy/docs/chartbooks/fast_facts/2003/ff2003.pdf
63. See Social Security Administration, "Fast Facts and Figures about Social Security; and Committee on Ways and Means," *2004 Green Book,* pp. 3–38.
64. Ibid.
65. Ibid.
66. Jeffrey Katz, "Social Security, Conference OKs Bill Creating Independent Agency," *Social Policy* (July 23, 1994), pp. 6–9.
67. Ibid.
68. Ibid., pp. 25–30.
69. Much of the information in this section on General Assistance is taken from the excellent study done by L. Jerome Gallagher, Cori E. Uccello, Alicia B. Pierce, and Erin B. Reidy, "State General Assistance Programs 1998," Washington, DC: The Urban Institute, April 1999. The study is also available online: http://newfederalism.urban.org/html/ga_programs/ga_full.html#exesum
70. Ibid.
71. Thomas Corbett, "The New Federalism: Monitoring Consequences," *Focus* 18, no. 1 (1996), pp. 3–6.
72. See Lela Costin, Howard Karger, and David Stoesz, *The Politics of Child Abuse in America* (New York:

Oxford University Press, 1996); and Joe Sexton, "Child Welfare Chief Provides a Glimpse at Decentralization," *New York Times* (September 8, 1996), p. 5.

73. *Economic Report of the President,* (Washington, DC: U.S. Government Printing Office, 1995).
74. T. Hilton and P. Huffaker, "Welfare Reform, Low-Wage Jobs and the U.S. Economy," *The Advocate's Forum* 3 (1996), p. 1. Retrieved 2004 from www.ssa.uchicago.edu/publications/advforum/v3n1/advocates3.1.2.html
75. Public Broadcasting System, "Transcript of Economic Growth 101" (October 1996), Washington, D.C. Retrieved 2004 from www.pbs.org/newshour/bb/economy/october96/growth_10-30.html
76. Richard Friedmann, Neil Gilbert, and Moshe Sherer (eds.), *Modern Welfare States* (New York: New York University Press, 1987).
77. Infoplease.com. "Mothers Participating in the Labor Force, 1955–2002." Retrieved November 2002 from www.infoplease.com/ipa/A0104670.html
78. Harry Holzer and Michael Stoll, "Employer Demand for Welfare Recipients by Race," Discussion Paper 1213-00, Institute for Research on Poverty, Madison, WI, 2000.
79. R. Lerman, S. Riegg, and L. Aron, *Youth in 2020: Trends and Policy Implications* (Washington, DC: The Urban Institute, 2000).
80. American Public Human Services Association, *Reauthorization Roundup* 2, no. 20 (October 3, 2002).
81. Center for Law and Social Policy, "TANF Caseloads Declined in Most States in Second Quarter, but Most States Saw Increases over the Last Year: Families Hitting Time Limits May Play a Role in Declining Caseloads," Washington, D.C., October 1, 2002.
82. Office of Inspector General, "State Strategies for Working with Hard-to-Employ TANF Recipients," July 2002. Department of Health and Human Services, OEI-02-00-00630, Washington, D.C.
83. David Stoesz, *A Poverty of Imagination: Bootstrap Capitalism, Sequel to Welfare Reform* (New York: Oxford University Press, 2004), p. 106.
84. See "March of Dimes: Teen Pregnancy," retrieved October 2004 from the World Wide Web www.marchofdimes.com/professionals/681_1159.asp; and The Alan Guttmacher Institute, "U.S. Teenage Pregnancy Statistics With Comparative Statistics for Women Aged 20–24," retrieved October 2004 from www.agi-usa.org/pubs/teen_stats.html
85. "Teenaged Childbearing and Welfare Policy," *Focus* 10, no. 1 (Spring 1987), p. 16.
86. Harrington et al., *Who Are the Poor?* p. 12.
87. The Urban Institute, *Welfare Reform: Issues before the Nation* (Washington, DC: The Urban Institute, 1995).
88. See Ibid., p. 1100; and Children's Aid Society, "Adolescent Pregnancy Prevention Program, 2004." Retrieved October 2004 from www.stopteenpregnancy.com/news/news_wsj.html
89. U.S. House of Representatives, *Overview of Entitlement Programs, 1994* (Washington, DC: U.S. Government Printing Office, 1994), p. 448.
90. Denise Polit, Janet Quint, and James Riccio, "The Challenge of Serving Teenage Mothers," New York: Manpower Demonstration Research Corporation, 1988, Tables 2 & 3, p. 17.
91. Janet Quint, Denise Polit, Hans Bos, and George Cave, *New Chance* (New York: Manpower Demonstration Research Corporation, 1994), Tables 5 and 6.
92. Quint et al., *New Chance,* p. xxxi.
93. Debra Hauser, "Five Years of Abstinence-Only-Until-Marriage Education: Assessing the Impact, Advocates for Youth," October 26, 2004. Retrieved October 2004 from www.advocatesforyouth.org/publications/state evaluations/index.htm
94. Ken Auletta, *The Underclass* (New York: Vintage, 1982), p. xvi.
95. William Julius Wilson, *The Truly Disadvantaged* (Chicago: University of Chicago Press, 1987), p. 8.
96. Erol Ricketts and Isabel Sawhill, "Defining and Measuring the Underclass," *Journal of Policy Analysis and Management* 7, no. 2 (Winter 1988), pp. 316–325.
97. See Kathleen Heffernan Vickland, "Is There an Underclass: No," in Howard Jacob Karger and James Midgley (eds.), *Controversial Issues in Social Policy* (Boston: Allyn & Bacon, 1994); and Christopher Jencks, "Deadly Neighborhoods," *The New Republic* (June 13, 1988), p. 30.
98. Michael Novak, *The New Consensus on Family and Welfare* (Washington, DC: American Enterprise Institute, 1987).
99. Charles Murray, *Losing Ground* (New York: Basic Books, 1984), pp. 227–228.
100. Lawrence Mead, *Beyond Entitlement* (New York: Free Press, 1986).
101. Center on Budget and Policy Priorities, "The New Welfare Law," Washington, DC: Center on Budget and Policy Priorities, 1996.
102. George Gilder, *Wealth and Poverty* (New York: Basic Books, 1981), p. 118.
103. Daniel P. Moynihan, "When Principle Is at Issue," *Washington Post* (August 4, 1996), p. C7.
104. Marian Wright Edelman, "Say No to This Welfare Reform," *Washington Post* (November 3, 1995), p. A23.
105. "A Children's Veto," *Washington Post* (July 25, 1996), p. A28.
106. Barbara Vobejda and Dan Balz, "President Seeks Balm for Anger over Welfare Bill," *Washington Post* (August 22, 1996), p. B3.
107. Lois Quinn and Robert Magill, "Politics versus Research in Social Policy," *Social Service Review* (December 1994), pp. 83–90.

108. David Long, Judith Gueron, Robert Wood, Rebecca Fisher, and Veronica Fellerath, "LEAP," New York: Manpower Demonstration Research Corporation, 1996, p. ES6.
109. Ibid., p. ES13.
110. Robert Moffitt, "Incentive Effects of the U.S. Welfare System: A Review," *Journal of Economic Literature* (March 1992) p. 30.
111. Mark Greenberg, testimony before the Domestic Task Force, Select Committee on Hunger, U.S. House of Representatives, April 9, 1992, in *Federal Policy Perspectives on Welfare Reform: Rhetoric, Reality and Opportunities,* Serial No. 102-25 (Washington, DC: U.S. Government Printing Office, 1992), pp. 52–53.
112. Robert Rector, "Strategies for Welfare Reform," Testimony before the Domestic Task Force, Select Committee on Hunger, U.S. House of Representatives, April 9, 1992, in "Federal Policy Perspectives on Welfare Reform: Rhetoric, Reality and Opportunities," Serial No. 102-25, Washington, DC: U.S. Government Printing Office, 1992, pp. 67–68.
113. Huttman, *Introduction to Social Policy.*
114. Gueron and Pally, *From Welfare to Work.*
115. David Ellwood, *Poor Support* (New York: Basic Books, 1988), p. 153.
116. Judith M. Gueron, "Statement by the President," *Manpower Demonstration Research Corporation, 1991 Annual Report* (New York: MDRC, 1991), p. 2.
117. Roberta Spalter-Roth, Beverly Burr, Heidi Hartmann, and Lois Shaw, *Welfare that Works: The Working Lives of AFDC Recipients* (Washington, DC: Institute for Women's Policy Research, 1995), p. 18.
118. LaDonna Pavetti, *Questions and Answers on Welfare Dynamics* (Washington, DC: Urban Institute, 1995).
119. Sandra Danziger, Mary Corcoran, Sheldon Danziger, Colleen Heflin, Ariel Kalil, Judith Levine, Daniel Rosne, Kristin Seefeldt, Kristine Siefert, and Richard Tolman, "Barriers to the Employment of Welfare Recipients," Poverty Research and Training Center, University of Michigan, January 1999.
120. Personal discussion at a conference on welfare reform, the Jerome Levy Economics Institute, Bard College, Annandale-on-Hudson, N.Y., July 12, 1996.
121. Marvin Olasky, "Beyond the Stingy Welfare State," *Policy Review* (Fall 1990), p. 14.
122. Robert Pear, "Giuliani Battles Congress on Welfare Bill," *New York Times* (July 27, 1996), p. A7.
123. *Personal Responsibility and Work Opportunity Reconciliation Act of 1996* (Washington, DC: National Association of Social Workers, 1996).

CHAPTER 12

The American Health Care System

This chapter examines the U.S. health care system—specifically, the organization of medical services; key governmental health programs such as Medicare and Medicaid; the crisis in health care, including attempts to curb health care costs; the large numbers of uninsured people; the impact of the American Medical Association on health care; the growing role of managed care; and the ramifications of the AIDS epidemic in the health care system. In addition, the chapter surveys various proposals designed to ameliorate the problems in U.S. health care and considers how medical services are organized in Great Britain and Canada.

The Uninsured

Health care in the United States is marked by several contradictions. According to Census Bureau data, the number of people *with* health insurance rose to 243 million in 2003. However, the number *without* such coverage rose by 1.4 million to 45 million. The percentage of the nation's population without health care coverage was 15.6 percent in 2003, while the percentage of people covered by government health insurance programs (Medicaid and Medicare) was 27 percent. The proportion of uninsured children in 2003 was 11.4 percent of all children, or 8.4 million.[1] Although the vast majority of Americans have easy access to a wide range of health care services through employment-based or public insurance programs, more than 45 million people remain without coverage. The uninsured have the following characteristics:

- Children under 18 in poverty were more likely to be uninsured—19.2 percent in 2003 compared to 11.4 percent of all children. Children aged 12 to 17 were more likely to lack coverage than those under age 12 (12.7 percent versus 10.6 percent). Adults between the ages of 18 and 64 made up almost 20 percent of the uninsured.
- Young adults (18 to 24 years old) were the least likely of any age group to have health insurance in 2001. More than 28 percent of this group did not have coverage.
- The poor are more than twice as likely to be uninsured as those who are not poor. The percentage of uninsured poor people was 30 percent in 2002, compared to 13 percent for those with incomes above the poverty line.
- The uninsured rate for African Americans was 19.5 percent; for Asians, almost 19 percent; for whites, 11 percent; for Hispanics almost 33 per-

Spotlight 12.1

The National Center for Health Statistics

The National Center for Health Statistics (NCHS) is a key resource of information about the health of Americans. As the principal health statistics agency in the United States, the organization compiles statistical information to guide action and policies to improve the health of people living within the United States. The information provided by NCHS helps to

- Document the health status of the population and of important subgroups
- Identify disparities in health status and use of health care by race/ethnicity, socioeconomic status, region, and other population characteristics
- Describe various experiences with the health care system
- Monitor trends in health status and health care delivery
- Identify health problems
- Support biomedical and health services research
- Provide information for making changes in public policies and programs
- Evaluate the impact of health policies and programs

To learn more about NCHS, go to its website at **www.cdc.gov/nchs.**

cent; and for American Indians or Alaska Natives it was 27.5 percent.
- The proportion of the foreign-born population without health insurance (34.5 percent) was about two-and-a-half times that of the native population (13 percent) in 2003.
- The South and West have a higher uninsured rate (18 percent) than either the Northeast (12.9 percent) or the Midwest (12 percent).
- The number of people who received health insurance coverage through their employers fell by 1.3 million between 2002 and 2003, while the number of people covered by government health insurance programs (i.e., Medicare and Medicaid) rose by 3.2 million.[2]

The relatively high number of uninsured Americans is not surprising, given that family health insurance premiums cost on average $9,320 annually in 2004—a large share of income for a family trying to make ends meet.[3] The National Coalition on Health Care estimates that by 2006, the average family insurance premium will exceed $14,500.[4] In 35 states average premium costs for workers rose three times faster (36 percent) than average earnings from 2000 to 2004 (12 percent). Purchasing affordable, accessible insurance is a particular challenge for many older people, for workers in transition between jobs, and for small businesses and their employees. For example, premiums for COBRA (transitional health insurance allowed a worker when they terminate employment) averages almost $700 a month for family coverage and $250 for individual coverage, a very high price given the average $1,100 monthly unemployment check.[5]

The absence of health insurance has serious consequences. The uninsured are three times more likely then the privately insured not to receive needed medical care, 50 to 70 percent more likely to need hospitalization for avoidable acute conditions like pneumonia or uncontrolled diabetes, and four times more likely to rely on an emergency room or to have no regular source of care.[6] Approximately one million Americans seeking medical care are turned away each year because they cannot pay, and millions more forgo preventive services.[7] This exists even though every major city has at least one major medical center with an annual budget of $100 to $200 million.[8]

- Uninsured American children face a higher risk of developmental delays than those with health coverage.
- The uninsured are more likely to put off seeking care; to not receive care when needed; and to not fill a prescription or get a recommended treatment because of the expense.
- The uninsured are more likely to have problems paying their medical bills, change their way of life significantly to pay for medical bills, or to be contacted by a collection agency.
- Uninsured adults who have been hospitalized for heart attacks are over 25 percent more likely to die while in the hospital than privately insured adults. While the uninsured are just as likely to improve blood flow to their hearts in the acute stages of their heart attacks, they are less likely to undergo further costly diagnostic and therapeutic interventions.
- Uninsured adults hospitalized for a traumatic injury are more than twice as likely to die in the hospital as insured adults—even after controlling for the severity of the injury.
- The diagnosis of a serious new health condition, including cancer, diabetes, heart attack, chronic lung disease, or stroke, reduced the wealth of uninsured households by 20 percent. Insured households in which a similar diagnosis was made suffered a 2 percent decline in their overall wealth.
- Insured households paid an average of $26,957 in total medical spending after the diagnosis of a serious new health condition; uninsured households paid $42,166.
- In 2001, the cost of medical care for the uninsured totaled almost $100 billion.
- About $35 billion is spent each year to provide the uninsured with medical care, often for preventable diseases or diseases that physicians could treat more efficiently with earlier diagnosis
- Americans who lack health insurance cost the economy between $65 and $130 billion a year in lost productivity.[9]

The Organization of Medical Services

Most health care costs in the United States are paid for by private insurers, public plans, and the direct public provision of health care. Only about 25 percent of health care costs are paid for directly by consumers. The dominant form of health care coverage in the United States is private insurance, which covers about 80 percent of the population (of whom two-thirds are covered by employer-based plans). Many elderly people use private health insurance plans to supplement the coverage offered by Medicare. Medical services in the United States consist of five major components:

1. Physicians in solo practice. These are typically the traditional physicians who may employ a nurse and receptionist. This form of medical organization is becoming increasingly rare in an age of group practices and managed care.
2. Group outpatient settings, including groups of physicians sharing facilities. This setting is becoming common as physicians are forced to pool resources—capital, equipment, office staff, and so forth—in order to compete in an increasingly difficult health care marketplace. Group outpatient settings may also include health maintenance organizations (HMOs), physicians in industrial Employee Assistance Plan (EAP) settings, or doctors operating under university auspices. During the past few decades, physicians have increasingly worked in group practices or other organized settings. The federal government has strongly supported the development of HMOs.[10]
3. Hospitals—private, nonprofit, or public.
4. Public health services delivered on the state, local, regional, national, or international level. These services include health counseling; family planning; prenatal and postnatal care; school health services; disease prevention and control; immunization; referral agencies; STD (sexually transmitted diseases) services; environmental sanitation; health education; and maintenance of indexes on births, deaths, and communicable diseases. Government-sponsored health services include the Veterans Administration Hospitals (the largest network of hospitals in the United States); Community and Migrant Health Centers; services provided under the Title V Maternal and Child Health Block Grant; and the Title X Family Planning Program.
5. Sundry and corollary health services. This category includes home health services, physical rehabilitation, group homes, nursing homes, and so forth.

Major Public Health Programs: Medicare, Medicaid, and S-CHIP

Health care spending is the second fastest-growing component of the federal budget, overshadowed only by the growth in the public debt. Overall, health care spending accounts for about 19 percent of total governmental expenditures. at the state and federal levels. Almost 20 percent of the population are covered by either Medicare and Medicaid.[11]

Medicare

After Social Security, Medicare is the largest social insurance program in the United States with expenditures of $266 billion in 2002. It is also the largest public payer of health care, financing close to 20 percent of all health care spending in 2000. When Medicare began in July 1966, approximately 19 million people were enrolled; by 2003 more than 41 million people (about 35 million elderly and 6 million disabled) were enrolled in one or both of Parts A and B, and 5 million chose to participate in the Medicare+Choice (renamed Medicare Advantage) plan. In 2002, HI benefits totaled almost $150 billion.[12]

Medicare was added to the Social Security Act in 1965 and was designed to provide elderly people with prepaid hospital and optional medical insurance. The modern Medicare system is composed of four parts: compulsory Hospital Insurance (HI), known as Part A; Supplemental Medical Insurance (SMI), known as Part B; the Medicare Advantage program, known as Part C; and the Medicare Prescription Drug, Improvement, and Modernization Act of 2003, known as MMA or Part D. Although traditionally consisting of two parts (HI and SMI), Part C (established by the Balanced Budget Act of 1997) expanded beneficiaries' options for participation in private-sector health care plans. The MMA or Part D was added in 2003.

Surrounded by controversy, the MMA was signed into law in 2003. A 700 page document, this complex bill has proven to be difficult for Medicare beneficiaries to understand. Apart from prescription drug coverage, Part D also includes changes for beneficiaries such as increases in the Part B deductible, increased income standards relating to the Part B premium, and new preventive health benefits. Like SMI, participation in the MMA is voluntary.

Beginning June 2004, beneficiaries had temporary access to Medicare-endorsed drug discount cards that were estimated to save consumers 10–15 percent. For beneficiaries with incomes below 135 percent of poverty ($12,569 for a single and $16,862 for couple in 2004) the federal government provided $600 a year toward drug expenses plus the annual enrollment fee. The MMA will be fully implemented in 2006 and under the standard benefit:

- Beneficiaries will pay an estimated $35 a month ($420 a year) in premiums for basic drug coverage (these are likely to vary across plans) in addition to the Part B premium.
- Beneficiaries will pay the first $250 toward their drug costs (i.e., the deductible).
- Beneficiaries will pay 25 percent of total drug costs between $250 and $2,250. After reaching $2,250 the coverage will end and the beneficiary will pay the next $2,850 out-of-pocket. This is called the "doughnut hole." Insurance coverage will not begin again until the beneficiary has spent $3,600 of their money for prescription drugs (not including the premium). After that, beneficiaries will qualify for catastrophic coverage. For the rest of the year, they will pay a flat $2 co-payment for each generic drug and $5 for each brand-name drug, or 5 percent, whichever is greater.
- Beneficiaries will be required to find a private prescription drug plan that has contracted with the Medicare program. Managed care plans, like those currently in Medicare Advantage, may also provide the drug benefit. In areas where only one (or no) private plan exists, the government will provide a "fallback" plan that provides the standard benefit.
- Beginning in 2005, Medicare beneficiaries will receive preventive benefits, including an initial routine physical examination, cardiovascular blood screening tests, and diabetes screening tests and services.
- The deductible, the size of the "doughnut hole" and catastrophic thresholds will grow each year based on increased MMA spending. Thus, if Medicare drug costs skyrocket, the deductible and the "doughnut hole" will increase. For example, the benefit gap is projected to rise from $2,850 in 2006 to $5,066 in 2013. In addition, the annual premium is expected to grow from $420 in 2006 to $696 by 2013. Because drug costs increase faster than inflation—and are projected to continue to do so—most Medicare beneficiaries will see their drug costs rise faster than their income. In the end, it is estimated that the MMA will only pay for about 25 percent of seniors' drug costs.
- Medicare will provide additional assistance to beneficiaries who qualify based on low incomes and limited assets. There are multiple levels of low-income assistance. For example, beneficiaries with incomes below 135 percent of the poverty line and who have assets below $6,000 for an individual or $9,000 for a couple (not including the value of a home or car), will be eligible to get drugs at $1–2 per generic prescription and $3–5 per brand-name prescription. Many of these six million people (called dual eligibles) will have to pay higher co-pays for prescription drugs. This is compounded by the fact that, unlike Medicare, there are no due process clauses for lodging complaints.
- MMA plan providers are permitted to offer an alternative benefit design provided it is actuarially equivalent and does not raise the Part D deductible or out-of-pocket limit. Plan providers are also required to provide drugs in each therapeutic category but have flexibility to establish preferred drug lists. In addition, companies offering drug plans can change formularies at any time, while a beneficiary can only change cards once a year. Plans may utilize a preferred network of pharmacies to reduce beneficiary cost-sharing. They may also offer supplemental benefits for an additional premium. While Medicare has guidelines for the type of drugs plans must cover, they do not require that all plans offer the same drugs. Beneficiaries will be required to ascertain whether the plan they enroll in covers the drugs they need.

Critics charge that the MMA does not curb skyrocketing drug costs. In fact, the MMA actually prohibits Medicare from using its purchasing power to negotiate lower drug prices for beneficiaries. While private plan providers will seek discounts for enrollees, they will lack Medicare's purchasing power. This stands in contrast to the Veterans Administration which has successfully negotiated lower prices with drug companies. In effect, the "no negotiation" clause will increase program costs, which in turn will add to the federal budget deficit. In addition, consumers will not be permitted to buy cheaper drugs from Canada or other countries. Under the Medicare legislation, drugs can only be reimported from Canada, and then only if the Secretary of Health and Human

Services certifies that the reimportation is safe and it would significantly reduce costs.

Drug companies and the managed care industry stand to reap huge profits from this legislation. Not only are there no mechanisms to effectively control rising drug costs, but the new drug benefit will mean a much larger sales volume. Private insurance companies that participate in the Medicare program will also realize windfall profits as they attempt to enroll the healthiest and youngest seniors, thereby lowering their costs. The MMA also includes an opportunity for private providers to gain more ground by allowing demonstration programs that lay the groundwork for privatizing Medicare. For instance, in 2010 Medicare will begin a demonstration project in six metropolitan areas in which traditional fee-for-service Medicare will bid competitively against private plans. Since traditional Medicare serves an older, sicker and more expensive population, its costs will undoubtedly be higher.

Thomas Scully, the former Medicare director, estimated that the MMA would cost $395 billion. In contrast to this figure, federal actuaries later estimated that the MMA could cost $576 billion. At the current rate of health care expenditures, the bill could cost $1 trillion in the next century.[13] The question remained whether the Bush administration had purposely kept the real figures from the American public.[14]

Perhaps the most important part of the MMA has nothing to do with Medicare. It is a little-noticed component called health savings accounts (HSAs) that could cost the federal government $6.4 billion over the next decade. Basically, the HSAs offer a tax free shelter for those with high deductible insurance. When a person puts money into the account it is not taxed. Nor is it taxed when the money is removed to pay for medical costs. Critics argue that this will add to the federal budget deficit. Moreover, this plan removes the owners of these accounts from the shared risk that has been the core of the health insurance system. Conservatives claim health savings accounts will encourage people to more closely monitor their health care spending and bring down medical costs. Critics call the accounts a tax shelter that will benefit the wealthy and draw young, healthy workers out of health care plans, potentially doubling the cost of insurance for everyone else. For conservatives, a key selling point of health savings accounts is its potential effect on the future of health care. Specifically, polls show that two-thirds of Americans support government-run, universal health care. By giving a large segment of the population the option to withdraw from the health insurance system, health savings accounts could serve to prevent another Clinton-style health care reform proposal. Simply put, it would be hard to reform the health care system if a large number of people are self-insured.[15]

Coverage HI or Part A is provided free to persons age 65 or over who are eligible for Social Security or Railroad Retirement benefits. It is a compulsory **inpatient care** (hospital) insurance plan (it also includes some nursing and home health care) with premiums coming out of a payroll tax that is part of the Social Security deductions. While most Americans 65 or older are automatically entitled to Part A, workers and their spouses with a sufficient period of Medicare-only coverage in federal, state, or local government employment are also eligible beginning at age 65. In addition, HI coverage is provided to insured workers (and spouses and children) with end-stage renal disease (ESRD), and to some otherwise ineligible aged and disabled beneficiaries who voluntarily pay a monthly premium. In 2002, the HI program covered about 40 million people (34 million aged and 6 million disabled enrollees).[16] The following health care services are covered under Medicare's HI program:

- Inpatient hospital includes the costs of a semi-private room, meals, regular nursing services, operating and recovery rooms, intensive care, inpatient prescription drugs, laboratory tests, X-rays, inpatient rehabilitation, long-term care hospitalization, and all other medically necessary services and supplies.
- Skilled nursing facility (SNF) care is covered only if it follows within 30 days of a hospitalization of three days or more and is certified as medically necessary. Covered services are similar to those for hospitalized patients but also include rehabilitation services and medical appliances.
- Home health agency (HHA) care may be provided for a home-bound beneficiary if deemed medically necessary. Certain medical supplies and durable medical equipment may also be provided requiring a co-payment. Full-time nursing care, food, blood, and drugs are not provided as HHA services. Home health agency (HHA) care is covered by both HI and SMI and requires no co-payment or deductible.
- Hospice care is available to terminally ill persons with life expectancies of six months or

less who forego the standard Medicare benefits. Such care includes pain relief, supportive medical and social services, physical therapy, nursing services, and symptom management. If a hospice patient requires treatment for a condition not related to the terminal illness, Medicare will pay for all covered services necessary for that condition. Beneficiaries pay no deductible for the hospice program, but do pay a small coinsurance for drugs and inpatient respite care.[17]

By paying a monthly premium, U.S. citizens (and certain legal aliens) over age 65 and all disabled persons entitled to HI are eligible to enroll in the SMI program. Almost all persons entitled to HI enroll in SMI. In 2002, the SMI program covered about 38 million (33 million aged and 5 million disabled) people with benefits totaling $111 billion.[18] The SMI program covers the following:

- Physicians' and surgeons' services, including some covered services furnished by chiropractors, podiatrists, dentists, and optometrists. Also covered are services provided by non-physician Medicare-approved practitioners, such as nurse practitioners in collaboration with a physician, clinical psychologists, clinical social workers (other than in a hospital or skilled nursing facility) and physician assistants.
- Services in an emergency room or outpatient clinic, including same-day surgery, and ambulance services.
- Home health care not covered under HI.
- Laboratory tests, X-rays, and other diagnostic radiology services, as well as certain preventive care screening tests.
- Ambulatory surgical center services in a Medicare-approved facility.
- Most physical and occupational therapy and speech pathology services.
- Comprehensive outpatient rehabilitation facility services, and mental health treatment in a partial hospitalization psychiatric program.
- Radiation therapy, renal dialysis and certain (e.g., heart, lung, liver, pancreas, bone marrow, kidney, and intestinal) transplants.
- Approved durable medical equipment for home use, such as oxygen equipment, wheelchairs, prosthetic devices, and surgical dressings, splints, and casts.
- Drugs that cannot be self-administered.[19]

Funding Medicare finances are handled by two trust funds in the U.S. Treasury, one for the HI program and the other for SMI. The HI program is financed primarily through a mandatory payroll tax. Almost all employees and self-employed persons pay taxes to support benefits for aged and disabled beneficiaries. In 2004 the HI tax rate was 1.45 percent of earnings (paid by each employee with a matching amount paid by the employer) and 2.90 percent for self-employed persons. Unlike Social Security, there is no earnings cap on taxable wages.

The SMI program is financed by beneficiary payments ($66.60 a month in 2004) and contributions from general tax revenues. Beneficiary premiums are generally set at a level that covers 25 percent of the average expenditures for aged beneficiaries. As such, the contribution from general tax revenues are the largest source income for the SMI program. Beneficiary premiums and general fund payments are redetermined annually to match estimated program costs for the following year. In 2005 Medicare Part B premiums increased by $11.60 a month to $78.20, the largest single-year increase on record. Capitation payments to Medicare Advantage plans are financed from the HI and SMI trust funds.

Gaps in Medicare Coverage Fee-for-service beneficiaries pay for charges not covered by Medicare and for various cost-sharing aspects of both HI and SMI. These liabilities may be paid by beneficiaries out-of-pocket, by a third party (an employer-sponsored retiree health plan or private "Medigap" insurance) or by Medicaid (if the person is eligible). "Medigap" insurance refers to private insurance plans that pay most of the charges not covered by Medicare. For beneficiaries enrolled in Medicare Advantage plans, the beneficiary's payment share is based on the cost-sharing structure of the specific plan selected by the beneficiary. Most plans have lower deductibles and coinsurance than that required for fee-for-service beneficiaries. Beneficiaries pay the monthly Part B premium and may pay an additional plan premium.

For HI hospital care, a fee-for-service beneficiary's payment share includes a one-time deductible at the beginning of each benefit period ($876 in 2004). This deductible covers the beneficiary's part of the first 60 days of each instance of inpatient hospital care. If continued inpatient care is needed beyond the 60 days, additional coinsurance payments ($219 a day in 2004) are required through the 90th day of a benefit period. Each HI beneficiary also has a lifetime reserve of 60 additional hospital days that may be used when the covered days within a benefit period have been exhausted. Lifetime reserve days may be used only once, and coinsurance payments are required.

Medicare covers the first 20 days of skilled nursing care (SNF) in a benefit period. But a copayment is required ($109.50 a day in 2004) for days 21–100. Medicare's obligation ends after 100 days of SNF care per benefit period. Home health care has no deductible or coinsurance payment.

For SMI, the beneficiary's payment share includes one annual deductible ($100 in 2004), the monthly premiums, the coinsurance payments for SMI services (usually 20 percent of the medically allowed charges), a deductible for blood, certain charges above the Medicare-allowed charge, and payment for any services not covered by Medicare. The beneficiary is liable for 50 percent of the approved charges for outpatient mental health treatment services.

Reimbursements to Providers Medicare payments for most inpatient hospital services are made under a reimbursement mechanism known as the prospective payment system (PPS). Under PPS, a predetermined amount is paid for each inpatient hospital stay based on a diagnosis-related group (DRG) classification. In some cases the payment to the hospital is less than the actual costs, while in other cases it is more. The hospital absorbs the loss or makes a profit. Adjustments are made for unusual or costly hospital stays. Payments for skilled nursing care, home health care, inpatient rehabilitation, and long-term hospital care are made under separate PPSs. Payments for psychiatric hospital care is currently reimbursed on a reasonable cost basis, but a PPS is expected to be implemented in the near future.[20]

If a doctor or medical supplier agrees to accept the Medicare-approved rate as payment in full, they may not request any additional payments from the beneficiary. If the provider does not take assignment, the beneficiary is charged for the excess (sometimes paid by Medigap insurance). Limits exist on the excess that doctors or suppliers can charge. Medicare reimbursements to health care providers are subject to maximum payments by level of service, which are often less than some physicians will accept. In these cases, patients pay the difference between the physician's charge and the Medicare reimbursement. Because of paperwork and limited reimbursement, many physicians choose not to participate in Medicare.

Medicare payments to Medicare Advantage plans are based on a blend of local and national capitated rates. Actual payments to plans vary depending on the demographic characteristics of the enrolled population. Although Medicare provides important services, the gaps in coverage are extensive, which is why many beneficiaries opt for HMOs or supplement Medicare with private **Medigap** insurance.

Since 1980 Medicare costs have risen about 10 percent a year. Total Medicare expenditures more than doubled from 1989 to 1998, and they are rising faster than the wages on which the payroll tax is based. Medicare's annual costs were 2.7 percent of the gross domestic product (GDP) in 2004, but are expected to reach almost 14 percent by 2078. In turn, the projected date of the HI trust fund exhaustion moved from 2025 to 2019, with projected HI income falling short of outlays in 2004. Part B of the SMI trust fund and the MMA are both expected to remain adequately funded into the future because current law automatically sets financing to meet the next years expected costs (something not true for the HI program). However, this automatic provision results in rapidly growing general revenue financing, which is projected to rise from less than one percent of the GDP in 2004 to 6.2 percent in 2078. It will also result in substantial increases in beneficiary premium charges. For example, Medicare costs in 2005 will consume 20 percent of the average Social Security benefit. By 2006, that number is expected to reach 37 percent. By 2020 it will be 50 percent.[21] Medicare costs are mainly due to higher hospital expenditures and lower projected taxable payroll.[22] The Medicare program is expected to experience even greater hardships when the baby boom generation begins retiring around 2010 (see Figure 12.1).[23]

Medicaid

Before 1965, medical care for those who could not afford to pay for it was primarily a responsibility of charitable institutions and state and local governments. In 1950 the federal government authorized states to use federal/state funds under the Social Security Act of 1935 to provide medical care for the indigent. In 1957, the Kerr-Mills Act provided for a federal/state matching program to provide health care for the elderly and the poor. However, Kerr-Mills was not mandatory, and many states chose not to participate. As a compromise to ward off more far-reaching

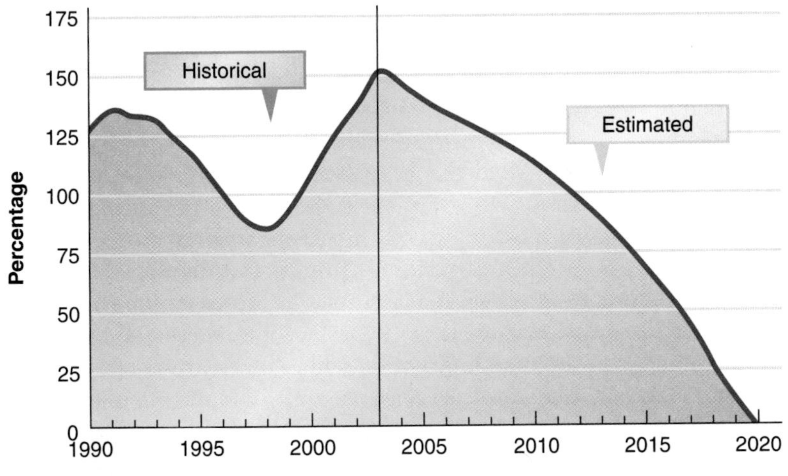

Figure 12.1

Hospital Insurance Trust Funds Assets (assets at beginning of year as percentage of annual expenditures)

Source: House Committee on Ways and Means, Statement of Rick Foster, Chief Actuary, Centers for Medicare and Medicaid Services, Testimony before the House Committee on Ways and Means, March 24, 2004.

health policies, President Lyndon Johnson signed the Medicaid and Medicare programs into law in 1965.[24] Replacing all previous governmental health programs, Medicaid became the largest public assistance program in the nation, covering about 14 percent of the population. In 2004 Medicaid served more than 42 million people at a total federal/state cost of $258 billion. Medicaid expenditures grew dramatically from 1990 to 2002 ($259 billion), and the program now accounts for about 15 percent of all health care spending.[25]

Medicaid is a means-tested public assistance program. Eligible persons receive services from physicians who accept Medicaid patients (in many places a minority of physicians) and other health care providers. These providers are then reimbursed by the federal government on a per-patient basis. Alternatively, several states are requiring Medicaid recipients to enroll in state-contracted HMOs. Medicaid is also a federal/state program. States determine eligibility within broad federal guidelines. For instance, each state establishes its own eligibility standards; determines the type, amount, duration, and scope of services; sets the rate of payment for services; and administers its own program. Medicaid policies are complex and vary among states. Thus, a person eligible for Medicaid in one state may be ineligible in another, and the services provided by one state may differ in the amount, duration, or scope of services compared to other states. State legislatures may change Medicaid eligibility, services, and/or reimbursement during the year. To be eligible for federal funds, states are required to provide Medicaid coverage for most individuals who receive federally assisted income maintenance payments, as well as for related groups not receiving cash payments. Some examples of the mandatory Medicaid eligibility groups are:

- Low-income families with children who meet certain of the eligibility requirements in the state's AFDC plan in effect on July 16, 1996
- Supplemental Security Income (SSI) recipients
- Infants born to Medicaid-eligible pregnant women. Medicaid eligibility must continue throughout the first year of life, as long as the infant remains in the mother's household and she remains eligible, or would be eligible if she were still pregnant.
- Children under age 6 and pregnant women whose family income is at or below 133 percent of the federal poverty level. The maximum mandatory income level for pregnant women and infants in certain states may be higher than 133 percent if the state has established a higher percentage for covering those groups. States are required to extend Medicaid eligibility until age 19 to all children born after September 30, 1983, in families with incomes at or below the federal poverty level. This provision phases in coverage so that by the year 2002, all poor children under age 19 will be covered.
- Recipients of adoption assistance and foster care under Title IV-E of the Social Security Act
- Certain Medicare beneficiaries and special protected groups; for example, those who lose SSI payments due to earnings from work or increased Social Security benefits
- Other "categorically needy" groups as decided by the state. These optional groups share

characteristics of the mandatory groups, but the eligibility criteria are somewhat more liberally defined. Examples of these optional groups are (1) infants up to age 1 and pregnant women not covered under the mandatory rules whose family income is below 185 percent of the federal poverty level; (2) certain targeted low-income children; (3) certain elderly, blind, or disabled adults who have incomes above those requiring mandatory coverage but below the federal poverty level; (4) children under age 21 who meet income and resources requirements for TAN; but who otherwise are not eligible for TANF; (5) institutionalized individuals with income and resources below specified limits; (6) persons who would be eligible if institutionalized but are receiving care under home and community-based services waivers; (7) recipients of state supplementary payments; and (8) TB-infected persons who would be financially eligible for Medicaid at the SSI level.[26] (Table 12.1 shows the numbers and eligibility categories of the Medicaid population.)

The medically needy (MN) option allows states to extend Medicaid eligibility to additional persons. These persons would be eligible for Medicaid under one of the mandatory or optional groups, except that their income and/or resources are above the eligibility level set by their state. Persons may qualify immediately or may "spend down" by incurring medical expenses that reduce their income to or below their state's medically needy level. By 2002, 36 states had elected to have a medically needy program. All remaining states utilize the "special income level" option to extend Medicaid to the "near poor" in medical institutional settings.

Medicaid is funded by federal/state matching funds. In every state the federal government pays at least half, and in some states far more, of state Medicaid spending. Title XIX of the Social Security Act allows considerable flexibility within the states' Medicaid plans. However, some federal requirements are mandatory if matching funds are to be received. Mandated services generally include the following:

- Inpatient hospital services
- Outpatient hospital services
- Prenatal care
- Vaccines for children
- Physician services
- Nursing facility services for persons aged 21 or older
- Family planning services and supplies
- Rural health clinic services
- Home health care for persons eligible for skilled-nursing services
- Laboratory and X-ray services
- Pediatric and family nurse practitioner services
- Nurse-midwife services
- Federally qualified health-center (FQHC) services, and ambulatory services of an FQHC that would be available in other settings

Table 12.1

Medicaid Recipients by Category, 1972–2000, Selected Years (in thousands)

Year	Total	Age 65 or Older	Blind/Disabled	Children	Adults	Other
1972	17,606	3,318	1,733	7,841	3,137	1,576
1975	22,013	3,643	2,661	9,598	4,529	1,800
1977	22,831	3,636	2,802	9,651	4,785	1,959
1980	21,605	3,440	2,911	9,333	4,877	1,499
1982	21,603	3,240	2,890	9,563	5,356	1,434
1984	21,365	3,165	2,950	9,771	5,600	1,187
1990	25,255	3,202	3,718	11,220	6,010	1,105
1993	33,432	3,863	5,016	16,285	7,505	763
1997	34,872	3,954	6,129	15,790	6,803	2,195
2000	42,763	3,731	6,889	19,723	8,750	3,761

Source: Social Security Administration, *Annual Statistical Supplement, 2003* (Washington, DC: Health Care Programs, 2004).

- Early and periodic screening, diagnostic, and treatment (EPSDT) services for children under 21 years[27]

States may also receive federal matching funds to provide certain optional services, such as:

- Diagnostic services
- Clinic services
- Intermediate care facilities for the mentally retarded (ICFs/MR)
- Prescribed drugs and prosthetic devices
- Optometrist services and eyeglasses
- Nursing facility services for children under age 21
- Transportation services
- Rehabilitation and physical therapy services
- Home and community-based care to certain persons with chronic impairments[28]

Medicaid was designed as a federal/state program to pay for health care for low-income and disabled citizens. On average Medicaid paid for about one-third of *all* births in the U.S. and, in some states, as much as 55 percent. Almost half of Medicaid recipients are children. Despite this number, the greatest single outlay of Medicaid funds goes to the elderly. For example, the elderly made up 11 percent of all Medicaid recipients in 2002, yet they accounted for about 26 percent of the Medicaid budget. Payment for long-term nursing home care alone accounted for 37 percent of the Medicaid budget. Of the almost 1.8 million nursing home beds in the U.S. in 2004, 1.33 million were certified as Medicare/Medicaid beds, and 286,000 were certified as Medicaid only.[29] Although Medicaid pays only 48 percent of the cost of nursing home care nationally, the program covers 70 percent of nursing home residents and it pays something toward the cost of nearly 80 percent of all patient days.[30] Not surprisingly, the growth of the nursing home industry parallels the creation of Medicaid. From 1965 (the year Medicaid was created) to 1970, the number of nursing home residents rose by 18 percent. From 1970 to 1975 that number rose another 17 percent; from 1975 to 1980, 14 percent; and from 1980 to 1985, about 12 percent. Because 75 percent of nursing homes are for-profit facilities, Medicaid functions as a de facto subsidy for the nursing home industry. Medicaid also functions as a subsidy for the middle class. Namely, when elderly parents of today's middle class spend down their assets they become eligible for Medicaid. Without Medicaid the children of elderly parents would be responsible for paying the average national rate of $150 a day for nursing home care. Since nursing home resident live on average 2.4 years, the total cost to a middle-class family would be more than $128,000. If their elderly parents lived in Alaska, Connecticut, District of Columbia, Hawaii, Massachusetts, New Jersey, or New York, they would pay from $189,000 to $381,000 for the nursing home care of their parents.[31]

Despite federal guidelines, four important gaps exist in Medicaid coverage: (1) the low eligibility limits set for Medicaid; (2) the refusal of many states to adopt most or all of the Medicaid options; (3) the gaps in coverage for the elderly and disabled; (4) the general ineligibility of poor single persons and childless couples for Medicaid unless they are elderly or disabled; and (5) state cutbacks in Medicaid coverage because of lower state revenues. While Medicaid covered 11.6 percent of the population in 2002, only 40.5 percent of those with incomes below the poverty line were covered.[32]

For all its shortcomings, the Medicaid program has led to important gains in the nation's health. In 1963, 54 percent of poor people did not see a physician. In that same year, only 63 percent of pregnant women received prenatal care; by 1976 that number had increased to 76 percent. Between 1964 and 1975 the use of physicians' services by poor children increased 74 percent. This increased health care utilization helped bring about a 49 percent drop in infant mortality between 1965 and 1988. For African American infants the drop in mortality was even sharper: Infant mortality dropped by only 5 percent in the 15 years before Medicaid, but by 49 percent in the 15 years after the program began. Ongoing preventive care also cut program costs for Medicaid-eligible children by 10 percent.[33] Medicaid is one of the most important governmental health programs in the United States.

The State Children's Health Insurance Program (S-CHIP)

As part of the Balanced Budget Act of 1997, Congress created the State Children's Health Insurance Program (S-CHIP), a federal-state partnership that allocated $48 billion over 10 years to expand health care coverage to uninsured children under age 19 who are not eligible for Medicaid or covered by private insurance. In 2002, $5.3 billion was spent on S-CHIPs and 5.3 million children were enrolled. The S-CHIP program gives states three options for covering uninsured children: designing a new children's health insurance program; expanding current Medicaid programs; or a combination of both strategies. By 2003, 19 states had chosen to implement a separate S-CHIP program, 17 states had a combined S-CHIP and Medicaid program, and the remainder expanded their Medicaid program. S-CHIP is a block grant program financed by federal/state matching funds. Each state with an approved plan receives enhanced federal matching payments for its S-CHIP expenditures up to a fixed state allotment. However, the largest share of S-CHIP funds come from the federal government, and in 2005 the federal share accounted for 70 percent of the program's funding.[34] S-CHIP allows states to charge premiums and copayments and covers a more limited set of benefits than Medicaid.

Before S-CHIP Medicaid eligibility was largely linked to welfare receipt. In large measure, Medicaid-eligible children had to be in an SSI or a TANF family. Perhaps the most important policy change in S-CHIP is that it delinked state-subsidized child health care from welfare receipt. Before S-CHIP only four states covered children whose family incomes were at least 200 percent of the federal poverty line. Now, S-CHIP enables states to insure children from working families with incomes too high to qualify for Medicaid but too low to afford private health insurance. By 2004, 38 states and the District of Columbia covered children in families with incomes of 200 percent of poverty or higher, making most low-income children eligible for Medicaid or S-CHIP.[35]

The Balanced Budget Act of 1997 gave states the option to enroll children in S-CHIP and Medicaid for up to 12 months, regardless of changes in income or family circumstances. Thirty-two states—more than 60 percent—have taken advantage of this new authority to ensure that children do not unnecessarily lose their coverage as a result of temporary changes in income or fluctuation in monthly paychecks.[36]

The Tobacco Settlement

Public policy is occasionally made by the court system rather than the legislature. This was the case in the 1998 tobacco industry settlement. For 40 years tobacco companies had won every lawsuit brought against them. The long march toward a national tobacco settlement began in April 1994, when representatives from seven of the leading American tobacco companies stood before Congress and swore that nicotine was not an addictive substance. The presentation was astounding even in the eyes of many people who were neutral toward cigarette companies. In 1998 the tobacco companies were forced to accept a 600-page Master Settlement Agreement (MSA) requiring them to pay $206 billion to 46 states over a 25-year period. (That amount did not include $40 billion in separate settlements reached by four other states.) From 2000 to 2004 states realized $37.5 billion in tobacco company payments. The MSA was the largest civil settlement in U.S. history. Payments are based on states' shares of the cost of smoking-related illnesses paid for through the Medicaid program. In exchange for the fine levied by the MSA, 39 states with pending individual lawsuits agreed to drop their cases. Some highlights of the MSA:

- Public health initiatives prohibit youth targeting in advertising and promotion; ban the use of cartoon characters in advertising, promotion, packaging, and labeling; restrict sponsorship by brand names; ban outdoor advertising; ban sales of merchandise with tobacco brand names; ban free samples to youth; and set minimum pack size at 20 cigarettes.
- Tobacco companies must develop corporate principles committed to compliance with the MSA, such as reducing youth smoking, designating an executive manager to identify ways to reduce youth access, and encouraging employees to identify alternative methods to reduce youth access.
- The MSA disbands tobacco trade associations, including the Council for Tobacco Research, the Tobacco Institute, and the Council for Indoor Air Research. It creates regulations and oversight for any new trade organizations.
- The settlement limits industry lobbying by prohibiting tobacco companies from opposing legislation aimed at restricting youth access and reducing consumption, specifically at the state and local levels.
- It includes the creation of a $1.45-billion public education fund to carry out a sustained nationwide advertising and education program to counter youth tobacco use and educate consumers about tobacco-related disease.[37]

States accrued significant revenues from the tobacco settlement: $6.4 billion in 2000, $6.9 billion in 2001, $8.3 billion in 2002, and $8.4 billion in 2003. Contrary to the hopes of many public health advocates, there are no restrictions on the use of MSA funds by the states. Some criticism of the tobacco settlement has centered around:

- The tobacco settlement did not require that the money be spent on antismoking or health care programs. In 2003, 31 states used their tobacco settlement funds to fill budget gaps for 2004, double the 15 states that used the funds for that purpose in 2002. Only a handful of states spent all of their tobacco money for health purposes in 2003.
- Only six states earned "A" grades from the American Lung Association in its 2004 report card for their anti-smoking programs.
- California, Connecticut, New Jersey, New York, Oregon, Rhode Island, Washington, and Wisconsin have cashed in a big chunk of their share of the settlement, selling future tobacco payments to investors for an upfront lump-sum, known as securitization.
- Fewer people are smoking and hence states receive less because their yearly allotment from the settlement fund is based on the number of cigarettes sold in the state. Nationwide, the number of smokers has dropped to 13 percent of adults, down from about 50 percent 40 years ago. State allotments also will go down as smokers turn to cigarettes from off-brand manufacturers and online retailers that do not pay into the settlement fund. Given the fiscal crunch experienced by states, many are turning to raising cigarette taxes. Studies have shown that raising cigarette taxes often causes people to stop smoking.
- The agreement has made states so dependent on tobacco settlement money that some attorney generals have gone to the aid of the tobacco industry when a jury verdict threatened industry payments to the states.
- Instead of curbing advertising, the tobacco industry actually raised its marketing budget to a record $11 billion from 1998 to 2001.[38]

(For some facts on the U.S. tobacco industry, see Figure 12.2.)

The Health Care Crisis

Health care in the United States is plagued with problems—notably, eroding coverage, rising costs, **cost shifting,** and many anxious citizens. This and the following sections explore some parameters of the health care crisis, including health care spending and cost efficiency, the effectiveness of the U.S. health care system, attempts at cost cutting, the growing role of managed care, and the impact of AIDS on the health care budget.

Cigarettes account for over 90 percent of spending on tobacco products in the United States; in 1998 Americans smoked 24 billion packs. In 1995, U.S. spending for all tobacco products totaled about $49 billion.

Five American companies—Philip Morris, R.J. Reynolds, Brown and Williamson, Lorillard, and Liggett—produce almost all of the cigarettes sold in the United States. Two companies, Philip Morris and R. J. Reynolds, account for more than 70 percent of industry sales. About 36 billion packs of cigarettes were produced by U.S. firms in 1997; about 12 billion packs were exported to other countries and about 280 million shipped to U.S. territories and to U.S. armed forces stationed overseas. The rest were consumed by domestic smokers. Smokeless tobacco products are also produced by only five domestic manufacturers: U.S. Tobacco, Conwood, Pinkerton, National, and Swisher. Over 120 million pounds of chewing tobacco and snuff were produced in the United States in 1996; in 1995, smokeless tobacco companies posted revenues of $1.7 billion. About 2.5 billion large cigars and cigarillos and 14.2 million pounds of pipe and roll-your-own tobacco were produced by U.S. companies in 1995.

The United States is the second largest tobacco producer in the world, well below China. In 1996, tobacco was grown on over 124,000 U.S. farms, with a crop value of $2.9 billion. The tobacco industry supports more than 600,000 jobs.

Figure 12.2

Tobacco at a Glance

Source: CNN, "A Brief History of Tobacco." Retrieved 2001 from www.cnn.com/US/9705/tobacco/history/index.html.

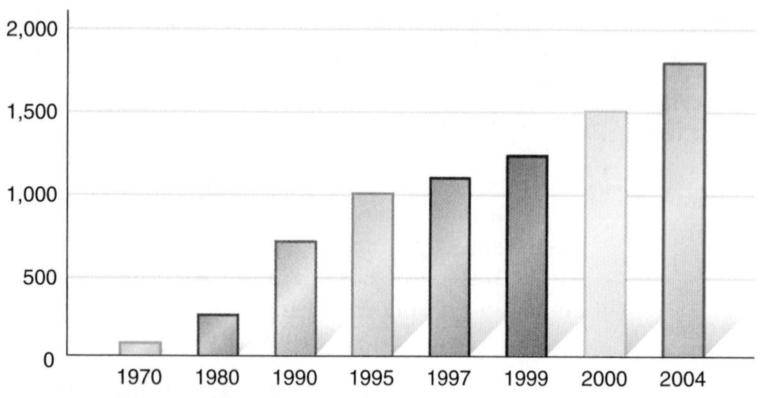

Figure 12.3

National Health Care Expenditures Selected Years, 1970–2004 (dollar amounts in billions)

Source: Compiled from Health Care Financing Administration, *Actuarial Products, N.H.E. Projections,* Table 1, retrieved 2001 from www.hcfa.gov/stats/NHE-Proj; and Centers for Medicare & Medicaid Services, *National Health Care Expenditures Projections: 2003–2013* (Baltimore, MD: Author, September 2004).

Overview of U.S. Health Care Expenditures

U.S. health care cost $1.8 trillion in 2004, up from 73 billion in 1970. This translates into 15.5 percent of the total **gross domestic product (GDP).** (Health expenditures as a percentage of the GDP measure the proportion of all resources devoted to health care.) It is projected that by 2013 health care spending will rise to $3.4 trillion and make up 18.4 percent of the GDP. In comparison, health care spending in 1970 was only 7.1 percent of the GDP. From 1970 to 2000, per capita health care costs rose from $341 to $4,611, an increase of almost 1,400 percent (see Figure 12.3). National health expenditures are expected to total $2.2 trillion and reach 16.2 percent of the GDP by 2008.[39]

Health care spending accounted for about 14 percent of the GDP in 2001. In comparison, education was only 4.8 percent of the GDP in that year.[40] Moreover, the costs of providing health care have risen faster than the rate of inflation. From 1980 to 1992, annual increases in per capita expenditures on health care were approximately 5 points above the yearly rate of inflation. Beginning in 1992, the growth in health care expenditures decelerated somewhat, registering less than 3 points above the rate of inflation[41]—then accelerated again in the late 1990s. In 2002 health care expenditures rose by 9.5 percent or more than four times the 2.15 percent rate of inflation. Although health care expenditures fell to 7.2 percent in 2004, it still remained about three times higher than the inflation rate.[42]

When health care expenditures are broken down, the largest share (31 percent) goes to hospitals.[43] (See Figure 12.4.) Increases in the cost of hospital care have been a key factor in driving up health care costs. In 2002 the growth in hospital spending was 9.5 percent. Although it fell to 6.5 percent in 2004 it continued to outpace overall inflation. In 1965 the average daily hospital room charge was $41; by 1994 it had risen to $1,127. In 1965 the average cost per hospital stay was $315. By 2003 it rose to $11,700 for an average stay of less than five days.[44]

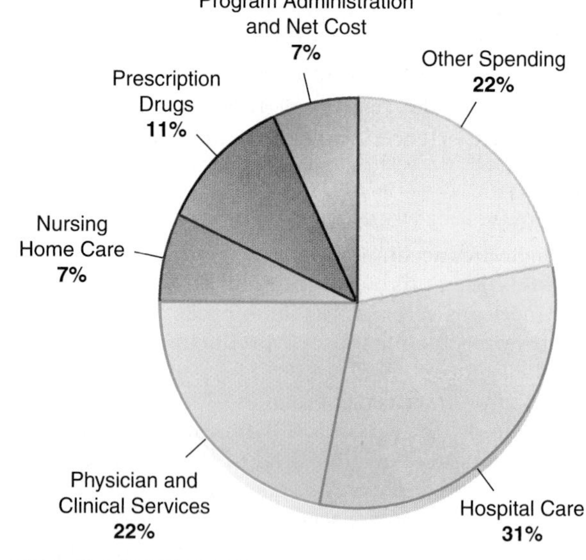

Figure 12.4

Where the Nation's Health Dollar Is Spent, 2002

Note: "Other Spending" includes dentist services, other professional services, home health care, durable medical products, over-the-counter medicines and sundries, public health, research, and construction.

Source: Centers for Medicare & Medicaid Services, *The Nation's Health Dollar: 2002* (Baltimore, MD: Author, September 2004).

Of the $840 billion spent by private sources for health care in 2002, about 60 percent ($504 billion) was spent on private health care insurance premiums. Premiums increased only 2 percent yearly from 1994 to 1998, but they jumped 8.2 percent in 1998. In 2002 premiums shot up by 11.4 percent and then dropped to about 7.1 percent in 2004.[45]

U.S. Health Care in International Perspective

Health care costs are higher in the United States than in any other industrialized nation.[46] The U.S. spends more than other countries on health care, both in absolute dollars and in the share of total economic activity. Health spending per capita in the U.S. was over $4,600 in 2000, more than twice the average of about $2,000 for the other industrial nations in the Organization for Economic Cooperation and Development (OECD). For instance, health spending in the U.S. was 13 percent of the gross domestic product, compared with Switzerland (10.7 percent), Germany (10.6 percent), Canada (9.1 percent), Japan (7.8 percent), and the United Kingdom (7.3 percent). (See Table 12.2.) Although high expenditures might be equated with excellent medical treatment, the health of the average American—as measured by life expectancy and infant mortality—is below the average of other major industrialized nations. More specifically, despite the high costs of U.S. medical care, life expectancy only ranks in the middle of the 30 OECD nations. This is due to a variety of factors, including diet, physical activity levels, births to teenager mothers, and deaths from violence.[47]

Strong evidence exists that the U.S. health care system does not perform as well as other industrialized countries. For one, the United States is the only major industrialized country that fails to provide health coverage for all, yet spending on health care totaled $4,631 per capita in 2000, 69 percent more than in Germany, 83 percent more than in Canada, and 134 percent more than the average in industrialized nations. The United States emphasizes private markets as a strategy for cost containment, yet health care costs are growing rapidly. Private spending as a share of total health care expenditures is far higher in the United States (56 percent) than in other industrialized nations (26 percent). Moreover, out-of-pocket per capita health care spending in the U.S. was $707 in 2000, more than twice ($328) that of other industrialized nations.[48]

A common perception is that other industrialized countries control costs by rationing patient care. In fact, Americans receive fewer days of hospital care than residents of other industrialized nations and have about the same amount of physician visits. Americans are, however, more likely to undergo specialized medical procedures.[49]

According to the Commonwealth Fund, the United States falls short in access to needed services. The Fund ranked the United States last among five English-speaking countries on measures of equity and first for access problems due to costs. Americans are much more likely than their counterparts in other countries to say they did not visit a physician, fill a prescription, or get a recommended test, treatment, or follow-up care because of costs. Disparities between people in above-average and below-average income groups were greatest in the United States and the uninsured were much more likely to report problems in obtaining needed care.[50]

Infant mortality rates also illustrate troubling trends. In 2002 the United States had one of the highest infant mortality rates among OECD countries (6.69 per 1,000 live births). This compared unfavorably to Greece (6.25); New Zealand (6.18); Portugal (5.84); Italy (5.76); Czech Republic (5.46); United Kingdom (5.45); Ireland (5.43); Canada (4.95); and other nations. Another health indicator is premature

Table 12.2

Total Health Care Expenditures as a Percentage of GDP

Country	1960	2002	Percentage Point Change
United States	5.2	14.0	8.8
France	4.2	9.5	5.3
OECD Median	5.5	8.0	2.5
New Zealand	4.3	8.0	3.7
Germany	4.8	10.6	5.8
Canada	3.0	9.1	6.1
Australia	4.9	8.9	4.0
United Kingdom	3.9	7.3	3.4

Source: Based on data from Uwe E. Reinhardt, Peter S. Hussey, and Gerard F. Anderson, "U.S. Health Care Spending in an International Context," *Health Affairs,* vol. 23, issue 3 (2004), pp. 10–25.

deaths, or deaths that would have been preventable had appropriate medical knowledge been applied or had risky behavior been less prevalent. The United States had the most preventable deaths per 100,000 people, and Japan had the least.[51] In short, Americans are neither healthier nor live longer than people in similar industrial nations where health care spending is lower.[52] In the end, health care spending in the United States is higher because of higher prices for services, substantially higher administrative costs, and higher rates of complex procedures.

Explaining the High Cost of U.S. Health Care

Accounting for the enormous costs of the U.S. health care system is complicated. Some policy analysts attribute at least some of these costs to the following factors.

• The Bush administration has argued that medical malpractice suits are driving up health care costs from $60 to $80 billion a year. According to the Bush Administration, this waste could be eliminated by passing legislation limiting (i.e., up to $250,000) what injured patients can collect in lawsuits. However, both the General Accounting Office and the Congressional Budget Office criticize the 1996 study the Bush administration uses as their main support. These agencies suggest that savings—if any—would be relatively small.[53]

• The treatment of people with AIDS has led to increasing fiscal strains on the health care system.[54] Although spending on HIV and AIDS victims has grown faster than some health care spending, it is still relatively small. For instance, AIDS research presently constitutes only about 5 percent of all research funded by the National Institute of Health. Overall expenditures on HIV-positive individuals increased from 1.3 to 1.4 percent of the total health care budget between 1992 and 1995.[55] Federal spending on AIDS in 1999 accounted for $10 billion.[56]

• The United States leads the world in the development and use of medical technology, but these advances have come at a high price. Between 1980 and 1991, the number of coronary bypass operations for men increased from 108,000 to 206,000; diagnostic ultrasounds for women rose from 114,000 to 652,000; and the use of CAT scans increased from 306,000 to more than 1.4 million.[57] Overall, treatment is now available for some diseases that were formerly untreatable, albeit at a high price. In addition, some technologies are introduced before being sufficiently tested to determine their cost effectiveness and superiority to existing technologies.

• The administrative costs involved in processing millions of insurance claims also adds to rising health care expenditures. Harvard Medical School researchers reported in 2004 that the United States spends $399 billion a year on health care bureaucracy, essentially the administrative costs of insurers, hospitals, doctors, nursing homes and other

The increasing costs of malpractice suits against health care providers are felt most directly by consumers, who must pay higher medical costs to offset these suits.

institutions. In California, $45 billion of the $163 billion spent on health care, or 28 percent, went to administration.[58] Despite the paperwork, the U.S. General Accounting Office estimated that in 1991 fraud cost $70 billion, or 10 percent of every health care dollar.

- Increased longevity has led to growing numbers of elderly people, many of whom have chronic diseases that are often expensive to treat. The Congressional Budget Office maintained that increases in the aged population accounted for only 5 percent of the increase in per capita health care spending between 1965 and 1990.

Hospital Costs

As noted earlier, 31.7 percent of all health care expenditures go toward hospital costs. The total costs of hospital care reached $401 billion in 1999, up from $28 billion in 1970. From 1991 to 2001 spending on hospital services grew by 61 percent. In 2002 alone hospital spending rose 9.5 percent. Although this spending is expected to drop to 6.2 percent by 2005, it will still be almost three times the rate of inflation. According to the American Hospital Association, nearly 60 percent of hospital costs go to wages and benefits of caregivers and others. Labor costs account for the largest share of spending growth for hospital services from 2001 to 2003. In addition, the costs of technology, construction, and regulatory compliance accounts for a growing share of hospital costs. Predictions from the Centers for Medicare and Medicaid Services suggest that hospitals' share of national health expenditures will decline to less than 28 percent in 2012. However, much of this decline may be attributable to cuts in federal and state health programs.[59]

Physicians' Salaries

The second largest health care expenditure is for physicians' services. From 1970 to 1999, the cost of physicians' services rose by almost 1,800 percent. From 1980 to 1990 alone, the cost of physicians' services rose by 300 percent.[60] By 2002, the average physician salary was about $261,000 (see Table 12.3).

Physician organizations argue that high salaries are necessary to repay the high debts incurred by medical students. In 2003, medical students graduated with 4.5 times more debt than in 1984. Moreover, in that same year the median debt was $100,000 and $135,000 for public school and private medical school graduates, respectively.[61] Despite this debt, the American Medical Association claims that "Even though the cost of medical school has risen faster than physician salaries, physicians still earn a decent return on their investment, roughly 6% for the $1.2 million a physician bears for the assorted costs of a public education and the wages lost while in school. Also, becoming a doctor is typically a higher paying investment when comparing average educational costs and salaries of business and law school graduates."[62]

The problem of high physician salaries is aggravated by the growth in the number of expensive medical specialists. Beginning in 1997 fewer medical students chose **primary care** tracks. In 2002, 20 percent fewer medical students were in a primary care tracks compared to 1997. For example, from 2000 to 2001 the number of medical students pursuing a family practice track dropped by 9.1 percent and internal medicine dropped by 2 percent. On the other hand, students pursuing neurological surgery increased by 36 percent, pathology by almost 27 percent, anesthesiology by almost 14 percent, and diagnostic radiology by 10 percent.[63] Today, roughly

Table 12.3

Average Salaries of Practicing Physicians, 2002

Specialty	Salary
Anesthesiology	$275,000
Cardiology	395,000
Emergency Medicine	216,000
Family Practice	204,000
General Surgery	291,000
Internal Medicine	176,000
Neurology	228,000
Obstetrics/Gynecology	261,000
Oncology	257,000
Pathology	321,000
Pediatrics	175,000
Psychiatry	244,000
Radiology	354,000

Source: Allied Physicians, "Physician Salaries and Salary Surveys, 2002." Retrieved November 2004 from www.allied-physicians.com/salary_surveys/physician-salaries.htm. Used by permission.

65 percent of medical school graduates are specialists—a reversal of the ratio that existed 30 years ago.[64]

The Pharmaceutical Industry

The high cost of prescription drugs is also driving up health care costs. Consumers pay more for medicine in the United States than in any other country. Two-thirds of doctor visits result in a drug being prescribed. Over-reliance on drugs is also a major factor contributing to medical care being the third leading cause of death in the United States. Americans filled 40 percent more prescriptions in 1998 than in 1992, and the costs of these drugs increased from $51 billion in 1992 to $101 billion in 1999. Pharmaceutical drug expenditures were $5.5 billion in 1970; by 1999 they rose to $101 billion, a 1,800 percent increase. Drug costs rose 11 percent a year between 1992 and 1997, more than twice as fast as other health care expenses. Older Americans unprotected by Medicaid spend 10 percent of their total income on prescription drugs. Many of these people are exposed to financial catastrophe as a result of highly inflated drug prices. In fact, in recent years the manufacturers of the top 20 drugs have increased their profits at five times the average rate of Fortune 500 companies.[65]

Harvard physician Marcia Angell disputes the drug industry's reputation as an "engine of innovation," arguing that the top U.S. drug makers spend 2.5 times as much on marketing and administration as they do on research. According to Angell, at least a third of the drugs marketed by the industry were discovered by universities or small biotech companies, but are sold to the public at inflated prices. Angell cites Taxol, the cancer drug discovered by the National Institutes of Health, but sold by Bristol-Myers Squibb for $20,000 a year, reportedly 20 times the manufacturing cost. Angell attacks the pharmaceutical industry—whose top ten companies make more in profits than the rest of the Fortune 500 combined—for using free market rhetoric while opposing competition.[66]

Though advertising prescription drugs has been legal for years, Food and Drug Administration (FDA) guidelines released in 1997 clarified the rules for advertising directly to consumers. Since the mid-1990s, pharmaceutical companies have tripled the amount of money spent on advertising prescription drugs directly to consumers. From 1996 to 2000, spending on these ads more than tripled, rising from $791 million to nearly $2.5 billion.[67]

In 1999 the drug industry spent $8.3 billion promoting its products—nearly half as much as the $17 billion it spent on research and development. Direct consumer advertising accounted for $1.3 billion of the total, with the rest being aimed at medical professionals. The advertising paid off. Posting huge increases in sales between 1993 and 1998 were heavily advertised drugs that included antihistamines (sales increases of $1.9 billion), antidepressants ($5 billion), cholesterol reducers ($3.4 billion), and anti-ulcer drugs ($2.7 billion).[68] Over a decade when health care costs almost doubled, prescription drug prices increased by 152 percent.[69]

Cutting Health Care Costs

There are two aspects to cutting health care costs. The first involves cutting costs for governmental health care programs; the second involves lowering overall medical costs.[70] The rising costs of Medicare led the federal government to seek alternative ways to lower hospital costs, including the Diagnostic Related Group system (DRG). In 1983 Congress enacted the DRG form of medical payment. Although earlier Medicare rules had restricted the fees hospitals could charge, the government generally reimbursed them for the entire bill. This style of reimbursement was called retrospective (after-the-fact) payment. By contrast, DRGs are a form of **prospective payment system,** or payment before the fact; the federal government specifies in advance what it will pay for the treatment of 468 classified illnesses or diagnosis-related groups.[71]

Developed by health researchers at the Yale-New Haven Hospital, the DRG system was designed to enforce economy by defining expected lengths of hospital stays. This system provides a treatment and diagnostic classification scheme, using the patient's medical diagnosis, prescribed treatment, and age as a means for categorizing and defining hospital services. In other words, the DRG system determines the length of a typical patient's hospital stay and reimburses hospitals only for that period of time. (Exceptions to the DRG classification system are made for long hospital stays, certain kinds of hospital facilities, hospitals that are the only facility in a community, and hospitals that serve large numbers of poor people.) Additional costs beyond the DRG allotment must be borne by the hospital. Conversely, if a patient requires less hospitalization than the maximum DRG allocation, the hospital gets to keep the difference. Hospitals may not charge the patient more than the DRG allotment. Hence, patients not yet ready for discharge (e.g., patients who do not have appropriate aftercare services available) may be discharged—a situation that can result in patient dumping.

Managed Care

Managed care became a household word in the 1990s. About 80 million Americans (20 percent of the population) are enrolled in HMOs, up from 33.3 million in 1990. An estimated 89 million more are enrolled in PPOs, which cost more but allow patients more flexibility. HMOs have been embraced by the nation's large employers as a way to control health costs. But although managed care cut costs for most of the 1990s, by 1998–99 costs started climbing again, increasing by about 5 percent in 1998 and by more than 7 percent in 2000.[72] From 2002 to 2004 managed care costs rose from 7 to 10 percent.

Paul Schmolling Jr., Merrill Youkeles, and William Burger define **managed care** as "an umbrella for health care insurance systems that contract with a network of hospitals, clinics, and doctors who agree to accept fees for each service or flat payments per patient. The advantage to providers is that they are given a ready source of referrals."[73] Figure 12.5 lists various types of managed care systems.

Proponents of managed care argue that the system has effectively lowered health care costs without reducing the quality of health care services. They maintain that the system encourages more efficient and less expensive medical care and that it can stress prevention over treatment. Because doctors reimbursed by managed care organizations have little incentive to overtreat patients or to recommend unnecessary medical care, the health care system is expected to be more efficient. Evidence exists that managed care lowered costs in the short term. For example:

- The per capita growth in health care expenditures was 2.7 percent in 1994, dropping from 5 percent in the 1980s and early 1990s. Per capita national expenditures on health care were $3,510 in 1994, only $100 more than in 1993 and half the increase of 1992 to 1993.

- **Health Maintenance Organization (HMO)**—a prepaid or capitated insurance plan in which individuals or their employers pay a fixed monthly fee for services rather than a separate charge for each visit or service.
- **Preferred Provider Organization (PPO)**—a type of HMO whereby an employer or insurance company contracts with a selected group of health care delivery providers for services at preestablished reimbursement rates. Consumers have the choice of who to contact to provide the service. If a doctor is not on the provider list, higher out-of-pocket expenses will result.
- **Exclusive Provider Organization (EPO)**—a type of HMO where members must get care only from the EPO doctors who may only treat members of the plan.
- **The Independent Practice Association (IPA)**—a type of HMO which has large numbers of independent doctors in private practice. Physicians are paid a fixed fee for treating IPA members but can also treat patients who are not members of the plan.
- **The Network Model**—multispecialty group of doctors who have contracts with more than one HMO. Doctors work out of their own offices.
- **Point of Service (POS)**—an option that can be offered by any type of HMO. If patients use doctors in their HMO network, and if referrals are made only by primary care physician, only nominal fees are charged. If patients use doctors outside their HMO network the cost is higher.
- **Physician–Hospital Organization (PHO)**—organized groups of doctors affiliated with a particular hospital who provide services to patients enrolled in their plan as they would in an HMO.

Figure 12.5

Types of Managed Care Plans

Source: Naomi Brill and Joanne Levine, *Working With People,* 7th Edition (Boston: Allyn & Bacon, 2001).

- Community hospital expenses grew only 2.9 percent in 1994 and 3.2 percent in 1995, a two-thirds drop from 1990 and a drop of five times from 1981. For the first time, in 1994 hospital costs per case rose more slowly than the rate of inflation. The average length of stay in a hospital dropped 4.2 percent from 1994 to 1995. For those 65 and over, the average length of a hospital stay dropped by 6.6 percent. Moreover, the occupancy rate of hospitals dropped from 74 percent in 1978 to 60 percent by 1995.
- Physicians' salaries dropped 3.6 percent from 1993 to 1994—the first recorded drop in the history of the American Medical Association.[74]

Managed care is clearly shaping U.S. medicine. According to the AMA, the percentage of doctors who had contracts with managed-care plans increased from 61 percent in 1990 to 92 percent in 1997. Among doctors with such contracts, the proportion of their income coming from those plans rose from 35 percent to 40 percent between 1996 and 1997.[75] Broadly defined, private managed plans now cover two-thirds of all privately insured Americans. Jumping on the bandwagon, the federal and many state governments have encouraged (and, in some states, required) Medicare and Medicaid beneficiaries to join managed care plans. By 1998 there were 346 Medicare HMOs with 6 million enrollees.[76] However, by 2003, that number dropped to 179 with 5 million members. By 2003, 1 million Medicare beneficiaries were dropped from their HMOs.[77] Insurers have charged that the federal government's Medicare reimbursement rate is too low to keep pace with medical inflation to ensure the financial solvency of Medicare HMOs.[78]

Critics of managed care (including HMOs) maintain that they are plagued with serious problems.[79] Indeed, managed care has not won the hearts and minds of the public. In a 1999 survey, only 46 percent of Americans said they were very confident their treatment would be based on their health care needs rather than on the cost of their care. Another national poll found that 61 percent of Americans agreed with the statement "I'm frustrated and angry about the state of the health care system in this country." In addition, only a third of people who had been ill in the previous year said they were completely happy or very happy about the care they received through their HMO.[80]

Numerous physicians say the quality of care is worse under managed care. Some have joined unions, and others have formed networks to negotiate contracts with managed care. Still others have stopped taking HMO patients. Hospitals say they are being squeezed by slow and low payments from HMOs and cuts to Medicare. Many have had to cut staff. Nurses say that hospitals often are so short staffed that patient care is being compromised. One study found that nearly 70 percent of nurses worry about inadequate staffing levels.[81]

Managed care plans generally make access to specialists difficult for consumers. Plans do this by pressuring primary physicians not to refer or by limiting specialist care to one or two visits. Some managed care plans are reluctant to cover costly procedures or experimental treatments, especially those relating to cancer. Some plans refuse to pay for medical care clients receive while out of state, even if it was required in an emergency. Other enrollees complain that managed care forces them to use only primary care physicians, hospitals, and specialists that are on an approved list, which restricts their freedom of choice. And managed care operations sometimes do not provide the same level of benefits as Medicare, especially when it comes to home health care, physical therapy, and nursing home care.[82] Critics also note that the size of managed care operations has led to greater bureaucratization and impersonality.[83]

During the late 1990s many HMOs were in financial trouble and the industry posted $1.25 billion in net losses in 1998. Some HMOs raised premiums, cut services, or sold out. Several large managed care companies across the country went bankrupt, leaving state officials and consumers scrambling to find replacement coverage. From the mid-1990s onward the health insurance market consolidated at a rapid pace. Between 1995 and 2001, there were over 350 mergers involving health insurers and managed care organizations. The result is that more than half of all commercially insured Americans are now covered by the ten largest health insurers. In many parts of the country, health insurance markets are dominated by a few companies that have significant power over the marketplace. According to an AMA study, there is at least one insurer with a market share in excess of 30 percent in 89 percent of highly concentrated metropolitan areas. In 40 percent of these markets, a single insurer has a market share in excess of 50 percent; and in 15 percent they have a market share of more than 70 percent.[84] The net result of this trend is that profit margins of health insurers have been steadily rising, despite an economic slowdown.

Health insurers experienced a 25 percent increase in profits between 2000 and 2001. Concomitantly, health care premiums increased by 11 percent—the fifth consecutive year of increases—from 2000 to 2001 and outpaced overall inflation and medical inflation.[85] One reason that managed care companies have made higher premiums stick is that there are less of them.

Managed care companies are boxed in to a degree. Specifically, HMOs can not reprise their 1990s role as gatekeepers that restrict care to boost the bottom line. Regulations on the state and federal level have dampened that idea, and after bad publicity in the 1990s, managed care companies became more lenient and paid for more care. Instead of gate-keeping, these companies simply passed along premium hikes. On the other hand, managed care companies cannot survive by simply passing along double-digit rate hikes each year. High rate increases are not feasible in an economy that is growing at 2 percent to 3 percent a year.[86]

The Underinsured

The U.S. medical system provides good care for most people in the upper and upper-middle classes, who are protected by adequate health insurance. Inadequate care, however, is the norm for some of those relying on this health care system. Although most Americans are covered by private insurance plans,[87] gaps in private health insurance may include high copayments, limits on the length of hospital stays, dollar limits on payments to hospitals and physicians, exclusion of certain laboratory tests, refusal of coverage for office visits and routine health care, noncoverage for mental health services, refusal of coverage to persons who are found to be in poor health when applying for insurance, and a lack of coverage for dental and eye care. Because privately purchased health insurance has become almost unaffordable, the availability of health insurance may be a major factor in an individual's job search or decision to continue in a job.[88] Moreover, employers may be reluctant to hire people with high-risk conditions, because of the negative effect on their insurance premiums. Finally, one of the most dramatic gaps is the frequent failure of private health insurance to cover catastrophic medical costs—those costs that could reduce a middle-class family to "medically indigent" status within only a few months.

AIDS and Health Care

The U.S. health care crisis is aggravated by the AIDS epidemic, which first surfaced during the presidency of Ronald Reagan. The Reagan administration initially saw the AIDS problem as being of little consequence. Indeed, expressing public concern for the suffering of homosexuals was a political liability—especially given that the Republican Party was actively courting the religious right, some of whose leaders saw AIDS as a divine punishment for the sin of homosexuality.[89] Unlike the Reagan and Bush administrations, the Clinton administration was not afraid to address the AIDS crisis. President Clinton pushed for full funding for the Ryan White Care Act, created the National Task Force on AIDS Drug Development, strengthened the Office of AIDS Research at the National Institutes of Health, and placed HIV/AIDS victims under the protection of the Americans with Disabilities Act.

The epidemiological data on AIDS is striking. Through 2002, 886,575 cases of AIDS in the United

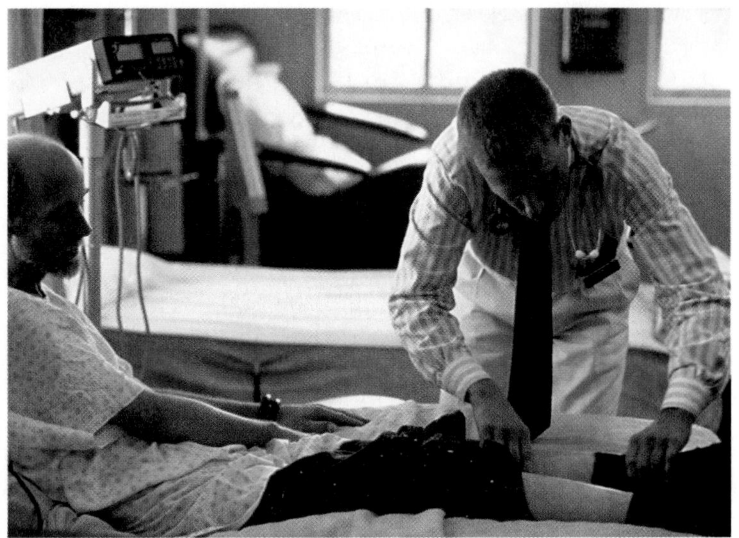

According to a Rand study, not all people with HIV are treated equally. Among adults with HIV, women receive inferior care compared to men, as do blacks and Hispanics compared to non-Hispanic whites.

States had been reported to the Centers for Disease Control (CDC); 501,669 AIDS-related deaths were reported by 2002. Five states—New York, California, Florida, Texas, and New Jersey—account for more than 45 percent of HIV/AIDS cases. Among adults and adolescents with AIDS, three exposure categories account for almost 90 percent of U.S. AIDS cases: male-to-male sexual contact (47 percent), heterosexual contact (15 percent), and injecting drug users (27 percent) (see Table 12.4).[90]

In recent years, marked declines in AIDS deaths began in 1996 and continued into 1998 in association with the widespread use of potent combination antiretroviral therapies. However, the rates of decline in AIDS incidence and deaths slowed during the latter part of 1998 and 1999. In 1999 the numbers of cases and deaths each quarter stabilized or fluctuated slightly in most populations and geographic areas. By 2002, AIDS prevalence was continuing to rise, with almost 400,000 persons living with AIDS. Although the incidence of AIDS is increasing among non-Hispanic whites, it is increasing more rapidly among blacks and Hispanics. There is an upward trend among women who were infected with HIV through sexual contact, principally with drug-using partners.[91] AIDS is the second leading cause of death in men aged 25 to 44 and one of the top five causes of death in women of the same age group.[92]

AIDS is maldistributed within racial groupings (see Table 12.4). Of the 886,575 AIDS cases reported in 2002, 323,015 occurred in non-Hispanic white males and almost 240,000 in African American men. Thus, while African American males make up only about 6 percent of the total U.S. population, they account for almost 30 percent of AIDS cases. The numbers are even more striking for women. African American women make up roughly 6 percent of the population, but they had more than 89,000 reported cases of AIDS, more than 2.5 times the number for white women (32,012).[93]

According to a recent Rand study, not all people with HIV are treated equally. Among adults with HIV in the United States, women receive inferior care compared to men, as do blacks and Hispanics compared to non-Hispanic whites. Uninsured and Medicaid-insured HIV victims receive inferior care compared to the privately insured. Patients infected through heterosexual, gay, or bisexual contacts receive superior care compared to patients infected through injection drug use. In sum, disparities in HIV care are frequently associated with insurance status, gender, race, ethnicity, exposure group, income, education, age, and even geographical region.[94]

Globally, HIV/AIDS is spreading rapidly in developing countries (see Table 12.5). In 2003, almost five million people were newly infected with HIV, the

Table 12.4

U.S. Male and Female Adult/Adolescent Cumulative AIDS Cases by Major Exposure Category and Race/Ethnicity (major population groups), 2002

	White (not Hispanic)		Black (not Hispanic)		Hispanic	
Exposure Category	Male	Female	Male	Female	Male	Female
Sex between men	237,610	NA	88,130	NA	53,547	NA
Injecting drug use	30,247	11,403	77,577	34,031	42,819	11,104
Sex between men and injecting drugs	27,264	NA	17,824	NA	8,519	NA
Hemophiliac/Coagulation dis.	3,926	1,815	590	122	441	56
Heterosexual contact	6,521	10,896	21,706	35,748	8,087	14,001
sex with inject. drug user	2,153	4,415	6,117	11,861	2,064	5,827
sex with HIV-infected person, risk unspecified	4,163	4,414	15,374	21,870	5,922	7,407
Total	323,015	32,012	239,988	89,241	126,350	29,232

Source: Centers for Disease Control, Basic Statistics, HIV/AIDS Surveillance Report, Tables A2 and A3, vol. 14 (2002). Retrieved November 2004 from www.cdc.gov/hiv/stats/hasr1402/2002SurveillanceReport.pdf.

Table 12.5

Regional HIV/AIDS Statistics, 2003

Region	Adults and Children Living with HIV/AIDS	Adults and Children Newly Infected with HIV	Adult Prevalance Rate
Sub-Saharan Africa	25–28 million	3–3.4 million	7.5–8.5%
North Africa and the Middle East	470,000–730,000	43,000–67,000	0.2–0.4%
South and South-east Asia	4.6–8.2 million	610,000–1.1 million	0.4–0.8%
East Asia and Pacific	700,000–1.3 million	150,000–270,000	0.1–0.1%
Latin America	1.3–1.9 million	120,000–180,000	0.5–0.7%
Caribbean	350,000–590,000	45,000–80,000	1.9–3.1%
Eastern Europe and Central Asia	1.2–1.8 million	180,000–280,000	0.5–0.9%
Western Europe	520,000–680,000	30,000–40,000	0.3–0.3%
North America	790,000–1.2 million	36,0009–54,000	0.5–0.7%
Australia and New Zealand	12,000–18,000	700–1,000	0.1–0.1%
Total	40 million (36–46 million)	5 million (4.2–5.8 million)	1.1% (0.9–1.3%)

Source: UNAIDS/WHO, "AIDS Epidemic Update," Global Summary of the HIV/AIDS Epidemic, December 2003. Retrieved November 2004 from www.who.int/hiv/pub/epidemiology/en/epiupdate2003_I_en.pdf. Reproduced by kind permission of UNAIDS www.unaids.org.

greatest number in any one year since the beginning of the epidemic. At the global level, the number of people living with HIV grew from 35 million in 2001 to 38 million in 2003. In the same year, almost three million died from AIDS—over 20 million have died since the first cases of AIDS were identified in 1981. According to the World Health Organization, at least 40 million people were living with HIV/AIDS worldwide in 2004.

Nowhere has the impact of HIV/AIDS been more severe than in sub-Saharan Africa.

- HIV/AIDS has reduced life expectancy by more than 20 years in Botswana, Lesotho, Swaziland, and Zimbabwe. By 2015, the disease will have reduced populations of the 38 most affected countries by 10 percent—some 91 million people.
- Young adults aged 15 to 24 account for half of all new HIV cases; the majority are women.
- Women are biologically two to four times more likely to contract HIV during unprotected sex than men, and teenagers are even more biologically vulnerable.
- AIDS has orphaned at least 14 million children. By 2010, this total will double.
- AIDS is directly or indirectly responsible for up to 60 percent of all child deaths in Africa.
- Of all the people with HIV/AIDS in the developing world who would benefit from antiretroviral drug (ARV) therapy, fewer than 5 percent have access to these lifesaving medications.[95]

Reforming U.S. Health Care

The U.S. health care system is driven by a combination of ideological and fiscal concerns. Primary among these ideological considerations is whether **health care access** should be a right or privilege. Conservatives generally believe that access to medical care is not a right but a privilege that must be earned through past or present labor force participation. Conservative democrats, in turn, believe that health care should be a right that is somehow tied to labor force participation, except in instances in which people are not linked to the workforce. Democratic socialists, grounded in a European tradition, argue that health care is a right that should be bestowed upon each individual at birth.

Another ideological engine driving debates about health care is the role of the private marketplace in the provision of medical care. Conservatives support the **commodification** of health care: They believe that the provision of medical services must be lodged squarely in the private marketplace. More specifically, health care should be provided by independent or quasi-independent medical facilities and by physicians who are either self-employed or employed by companies/organizations. Conservatives argue that medical institutions and drug companies should be free to establish the prices of health care and medical goods. They believe that in medical care, as with other commodities, increased competition lowers the price of goods and increases quality. Government regulation of the health care market is therefore seen as leading to more inefficiencies, lower quality or poorer service, and higher prices. Other conservatives, although they believe the private marketplace is the proper venue for the delivery of health care, also recognize that health care is a commodity that does not respond to market conditions in the same way as other commodities. For example, when a person is immobilized by cardiac arrest, it is unlikely that he or she will shop around for the best cardiac care prices. Likewise, most patients facing serious surgery will not choose a surgeon based on price considerations. Thus, these conservatives believe that the health care marketplace must be somewhat regulated by government to ensure quality, price, and access.

Democratic socialists argue that health care is too important to be left to the vicissitudes of the marketplace. For them, health care should be removed from the context of a market in which decisions are made purely on economic terms. They believe that the marketplace is designed not to meet the needs of people but to maximize profits. Health care must therefore be socialized; that is, it should be free or heavily subsidized at the point of access, universal in its coverage, and administered and controlled by government.

In the past 30 years, most proposals designed to reform or transform health care in the United States have been linked either directly or indirectly to the U.S. political economy. Consequently, proposals for improving health care fall into three basic categories: (1) removing health care from the marketplace through socialized medicine; (2) maintaining the private health care marketplace while providing universal coverage through national health insurance; and (3) instituting incremental reforms designed to eliminate the more egregious features in the U.S. health care system.

Socialized Medicine

The most radical proposal for reforming the U.S. health care system involved the creation of a National Health Service (NHS). Drafted in the mid-1970s by left-wing health planners and members of Congress, and proposed in the late 1970s by Congressman Ronald Dellums (a social worker), the NHS would have established health care as a right of citizenship. As with the British model, it would have provided free (no fee at the point of access and no payments from third-party vendors) and comprehensive health care coverage, including diagnostic, therapeutic, preventive, rehabilitative, environmental, and occupational health services. To improve the maldistribution of medical services, the NHS would have provided free medical education in return for required periods of service in medically underserved areas.[96] The goal of the NHS was the elimination of private profit in the health care system, and under it a national commission would have been responsible for establishing a formulary of drugs, equipment, and supplies, with regional branches purchasing these goods in their inexpensive generic forms.[97]

Another proposal for restructuring U.S. health care as a **single-payer system** was the National Health Care Act of 1992. As in the Canadian model, states would have had responsibility for ensuring the delivery of health services, for paying all providers, and for planning in accordance with federal guidelines. Although this plan would have allowed the practice of private medicine, the act would have discontinued private health insurance coverage.[98] Supporters of this bill claimed that it would immediately reduce health care spending by 18 percent, and that a single payer approach would reduce the fraud endemic to a multiple-payer system.[99]

Supporters argue that socialized health care would allow for the coordination of health services and reduce profiteering by professionals and corporations. Moreover, they contend that the experience of other countries illustrates that a system incorporating strict budgeting, nationalization, and the elimination of the profit motive arrests the growth of health care costs and, in the end, will prove less expensive than the current privatized system.

National Health Insurance

Another strategy to restructure the United States' health care system is **national health insurance** (NHI). According to Paul Starr, the United States was on the brink of establishing national health insurance several times during the twentieth century, but each time factors unique to the country's political and social institutions prevented its adoption.[100] In the 1930s, for example, NHI plans began to proliferate as part of Roosevelt's New Deal; but the idea was abandoned because of the strident opposition of the AMA—originally a supporter of NHI—and the fear that NHI's inclusion would jeopardize passage of the 1935 Social Security Act. President Harry Truman took up the NHI banner in the days following World War II, but by that time most middle-class and unionized workers were covered by private insurance plans. Moreover, the AMA again set its powerful lobbying machine into motion, this time equating national health insurance with socialized medicine and with Communism.[101]

One of the most comprehensive NHI plans was introduced in the 1970s by Senator Edward Kennedy (and successive coauthors). Supported by large segments of organized labor, the Kennedy plan included a presidentially appointed National Health Board charged with developing policy guidelines, managing the program, and planning and directing the yearly federal health budget. In addition, a national health insurance corporation would be developed to collect tax premiums from workers and disperse them to private insurance companies, which would process all claims. Under this system every American would have compulsory health insurance: Workers would be insured through their employers, the poor through a special federal insurance fund. The Kennedy plan would have eliminated the need for Medicare and Medicaid.[102]

The most recent incarnation of NHI occurred in the Health Security Act (HSA) proposed by President Clinton in 1993. Although the HSA was not a NHI plan in the strictest sense, it contained important components of national insurance. Clinton's bill was based partly on the ideas of the Jackson Hole Group, whose professionals reiterated the need for cost consciousness in health care and the need for substantial investment in outcome and evaluation research.[103]

To accomplish Clinton's health care goal, Hillary Clinton and Ira Magaziner led a 500-person task force charged with (1) extending medical insurance to the uninsured at a reasonable cost; (2) guaranteeing continued coverage when workers change jobs or get sick; (3) curbing and controlling steadily rising health care costs by developing health care networks; (4) addressing the problems of the insurance industry; (5) stopping drug companies from overinflating drug prices; (6) developing a basic core benefits package for every American; and (7) providing universal health care coverage. The result of this task force was the 1,342-page Health Security Act.

The HSA would have worked in the following manner. All citizens and legal immigrants would get a card guaranteeing them a comprehensive lifelong package of health care benefits, including inpatient and outpatient medical care, prescription drugs, dental and vision care, long-term care, mental health services, and substance abuse treatment. Coverage would be continuous regardless of employment status. All participants would buy into large purchasing pools called Health Care Alliances. Each alliance would offer separate plans for consumers: (1) a **fee-for-service** option allowing consumers to choose their doctors; (2) a plan based on joining a network of doctors and hospitals; and (3) the choice of an HMO. Consumers would then select from three levels of cost-based benefit packages, although all plans would have a yearly out-of-pocket limit of $1,500 for an individual and $3,000 for a family. Low-income self-insurers would be charged based on a sliding scale. Those on public assistance would have their fees paid by Medicaid. Employers would have paid 80 percent of the premium of the standard benefit package; workers would pay the additional 20 percent. Employers would not be charged more than 7.9 percent of their payroll costs for insuring their workers.[104]

Despite a promising start, the HSA bill faltered almost from the moment of its inception. Opposition came from several quarters. Smaller health insurers felt they were being maneuvered out of the industry and took to the airwaves. Immediately, the Health Insurance Association of America (HIAA) broadcast $2 million worth of "Harry and Louise" commercials attacking the HSA as rationing health care under socialized medicine.[105] Within days HIAA claimed that more than 40,000 callers had phoned their 800 number to register complaints about health care reform.[106] On the congressional side, small business lobbyists argued that the costs of the employer mandate would bankrupt thousands of small companies. Within weeks, dozens of lobbyists ranging from pharmaceutical companies to tobacco companies to restaurants and labor unions besieged Congress. Anticipating the 1994 elections, health industry interest groups contributed $26 million to congressional campaigns.[107] Observers put the price tag on defeating the HSA at $100 million.[108] The conservative 104th Congress of 1994 killed the possibility of comprehensive health care reform.

Critics of NHI plans charge that they would modify payment mechanisms rather than encourage major changes in the health care system. Although NHI schemes would equalize the ability of patients to pay, they would not improve the accessibility or the quality of services. Furthermore, most NHI proposals call for coinsurance (copayments) in amounts that many poor people could not afford.[109] Contrary to what some critics claim, NHI schemes are not socialized medicine: Hospitals would remain private, doctors would continue to be private practitioners, and most plans would preserve a major role for private insurance companies.

Incremental Reform

Incremental health care reform has proved more acceptable to the public and policymakers than sweeping reforms. This approach has generally focuses on remedying the more troubling aspects of the private health care system and on fine-tuning public health care programs. One example of incremental reform was the Catastrophic Health Insurance Act.

In 1988, President Ronald Reagan signed the Catastrophic Health Insurance Act, the most sweeping reform of Medicare attempted to date. This legislation was designed to provide 33 million elderly and disabled Medicare beneficiaries with protection from catastrophic hospital, doctor, and outpatient drug costs. The new Medicare benefits were to be financed by two premiums. The first was applicable to all Medicare enrollees and would have been $4 a month in 1989, rising to $10.20 in 1993. The second, income-related premium was to be paid each year in conjunction with the federal income taxes paid by the 40 percent of Medicare enrollees with the highest incomes.[110] Because of consumer pressure (i.e., the elderly refused to support the self-financing part of the reforms) and the rising deficit, the Catastrophic Health Insurance Act was repealed by Congress even before it was implemented.[111]

After the 1994 defeat of the HSA, incremental reforms were the only politically viable alternative to current health care policy. One such reform was the Kennedy-Kassebaum bill (the Health Care Coverage Availability and Affordability Act) of 1996. Although federal tax law subsidizes employer-based health insurance, it does not provide the same subsidy for insurance purchased by individuals. Hence, almost 90 percent of those who have private health insurance obtain it through their employers. To address this problem, Congress had passed the Consolidated Budget Reconciliation Act (COBRA) in 1985, which permitted individuals leaving a company of 20 or more employees to continue their health insurance benefits for up to 18 months by paying 102 percent of the premium their employer had been paying. Although this had helped some people, others remained trapped in **job lock,** fearing that if they changed jobs they would be uninsurable because of a **preexisting condition.** Passage of the Kennedy-Kassebaum bill marked the first time legislation had been enacted to protect people with preexisting medical conditions. This bill was expected to help about 25 percent of the Americans caught in job lock.[112] Although the Kennedy-Kassebaum bill was an important step, it did not address the critical issue of making health care insurance both accessible and affordable for all Americans. Nor did it address the fact that millions of Americans have no health coverage at all.

A conservative approach to incremental health care reform is based on the concept of the individual medical savings account (MSA). The MSA is a form of self-insurance whereby individuals can purchase high-deductible health insurance while setting aside pretax dollars to pay for medical expenses. Opponents of MSAs fear, however, that these plans would appeal only to the healthy and wealthy, leaving those with less money and more health problems behind in an increasingly costly insurance pool.

Congress also passed legislation in 1996 to require insurers to pay for a 48-hour hospital stay following a vaginal birth and a 96-hour stay after a cesarean section. In addition, Congress passed an amendment designed to create some level of parity between mental health and physical health benefits. The amendment requires insurers to set the same levels for annual and lifetime caps on mental health benefits as on physical health benefits. However, the bill stipulates that plans are not prohibited from requiring preadmission screening before authorization of services; nor are they prohibited from restricting mental health coverage to only those services that are medically necessary.[113]

Other incremental reforms have been enacted on state levels. In Hawaii, employers are required to insure employees who work more than 20 hours a week.[114] A Health Rights program in Minnesota extends health care coverage to all noncovered low-income residents and charges them on a sliding-scale basis.[115] On the national level, it is likely that future incremental health care reforms may involve limiting malpractice awards, extending some form of coverage to the uninsured, and instituting some limitations on the power of managed care operations to shape health care.

Comparative Analysis: Health Care in Canada and Britain

Americans often overlook what is happening in other parts of the world. This section briefly explores medical systems in Canada (a single-payer system) and Great Britain (socialized medicine).

The Canadian Health Care System

The current Canadian health care system began more than 30 years ago when a hospital insurance plan in Saskatchewan evolved into a network of plans developed by Canada's 10 provinces and 2 territories.[116] In 1966 Canada passed the Medical Care Act (Medicare), which instituted a nationwide federal/provincial health insurance system that is publicly funded, privately delivered, and free at the point of access.[117] Each province is responsible for administering its own health care plan.[118] Although each of the 10 provinces and 2 territories has it own unique plan, all plans are essentially universal and comprehensive, covering all residents for inpatient and outpatient hospital and physician services. To receive federal funds, every plan must meet basic national eligibility standards:

1. *Universal coverage.* Every provincial resident must be covered under uniform terms and conditions.
2. *Portability.* Plans must be portable, in that they must cover residents who are temporarily away from home or who have moved to another province.
3. *Comprehensiveness.* All approved hospital and physicians' services must be covered, including medical and hospital care, mental health services, and prescription drugs for those over 65 and for those with catastrophic illnesses.
4. *No cost to patient at point of access.* Services must be free at point of access and include no financial barriers to care.
5. *Nonprofit administration.* Plans must be nonprofit and publicly administered.
6. *Freedom of choice.* Each Canadian is free to choose his or her provider.[119]

Unlike the U.S. system, the Canadian system is grounded in universal entitlement rather than linked to employment. Accordingly, all of Canada's 25 million residents are eligible for provincial health insurance, regardless of their employment status, except for people covered by other federal programs such as the military.[120] Questions arose in the 1980s about direct charges made to patients beyond the level paid by the provincial health care plan. The 1984 Canada Health Act eliminated all extra billing and user charges. Today virtually every Canadian is covered by a comprehensive medical and hospital plan with no copayment.[121]

General practitioners (GPs) make up the majority of physicians in Canada and provide most of the nation's health care. Specialists can be used only if a referral is received from the GP. Although patients may choose their primary care physician, the choice is contingent upon whether the physician has openings for new patients. Patients also use the hospital in which the physician has admitting privileges. Besides providing free physician and hospital care, most provinces also cover the cost of travel and medical services if the treatment cannot be obtained in the area where the patient resides. Although covered health care is free at the point of access, some elements not covered include out-of-hospital drugs, dental care, eyeglasses, physical therapy, and chiropractic care not ordered by a medical doctor.[122]

Contrary to some misconceptions, the Canadian health care system is not a form of socialized medicine; instead, it is a social insurance model that mixes public funds with private health care delivery. Canada's single-payer model is based on the idea that provincial governments function as single-source payers of health care with a centralized locus of control. As such, Canada's provincial governments reimburse both hospitals and physicians on a prospective budgeting basis. Specifically, private physicians' fees are negotiated between the provincial governments and the medical associations. Reimbursements for physicians are on a fee-for-service basis. The salaries of physicians in Canada are generally lower than those of their U.S. counterparts. Because of budgetary problems, several provinces have limited payments to physicians who earn above a certain income by lowering the reimbursement rates. [123]

There are about 1,250 hospitals in Canada, of which 57 percent are run by religious orders or nonprofit organizations. Hospital reimbursements are made on a global prospective basis. In other words, hospitals operate on a negotiated but fixed yearly budget. As such, they must stay within the budgetary allotment granted by the province regardless of the number of patients seen in a year.[124]

Canada's Medicare system is paid for with a mixture of federal and provincial funds. Federal funds go to the provinces in the form of block grants and transfer payments. The provinces obtain funds to operate the medical system from general revenue taxes and, in the case of Alberta and British Columbia, from insurance premiums paid for by employers. Provinces that charge such premiums provide exemptions or subsidies for the aged, the unemployed, and the indigent.[125]

Critics of Canadian health care point to numerous problems facing the system. One of the most important is the question of funding. Cutbacks in government spending (from 1981 to 1992 the Canadian government cut transfer payments to the provinces by almost $8 billion), increasing demands for services, and the high cost of technology have made controlling costs the number one issue facing the Canadian health care system. The "cure" for these problems has been the replacement of federal support to the provinces with block grant transfers; a downsizing of the system, particularly the hospital sector (e.g., closing or merging hospitals, cutting staff, and shortening inpatient stays); and an increasing reliance on paraprofessional staff (e.g., replacing nurses with nursing attendants).[126]

Some critics have charged that Canada's prospective global budgeting system for hospitals has caused health care rationing. These critics argue that to cope with budgetary constraints, Canadian hospitals are closing down hospital wards during certain times of the year; filling up one-third of hospital beds with long-term elderly patients so as to keep high-volume (and expensive) traffic down; using cheaper medical materials; rushing medical procedures and thus jeopardizing accuracy; providing substandard hospital care; not investing in technology or capital improvements; and prioritizing illnesses into "urgent," "emergent," and "elective" categories, thereby causing artificial queues for treatment.[127] According to these critics, health care rationing is having a dramatic effect on Canada's medical system.[128]

Some health care analysts have suggested that the United States adopt a health care reform plan similar to the Canadian model.[129] They argue that a single-payer system allows for greater control of systemwide health care capacity—that is, supply, distribution, and costs—than does a fragmented insurance system in which no party has the overall authority for controlling the production and distribution of medical goods and services. Health care analysts also point to the uneven coverage provided to Americans under the current patchwork of private and public health insurance plans. In comparison to the universal, comprehensive, and publicly funded health care system that Canadians enjoy, most Americans are forced to purchase employer-based health insurance offering coverage that ranges from minimal to comprehensive, depending on the type of policy. Moreover, a significant number of Americans fall through the cracks in health insurance: They receive no employment-based health insurance, they cannot afford to insure themselves, and they are ineligible for Medicaid or Medicare. Critics claim that a Canadian-style universal health care policy would ensure all Americans adequate medical care without regard to their ability to pay or the generosity of their employers.

Perhaps the most formidable argument for the United States' adopting a Canadian-style health care system is provided by an examination of leading health indicators and per capita health care spending. Before the Canadian Medicare system became operational in 1971, Canada lagged behind the United States in the important indicators of infant mortality and life expectancy. Impressive gains now place Canada ahead of the United States on both health indicators. Moreover, Canada has been able to achieve those gains while spending less of its GNP on health care than the United States. Although health care costs are rising in Canada, they are doing so at a slower rate than in the United States.[130]

Factors that influence lower health care costs in Canada include lower physician and administrative costs and less concern with malpractice litigation. In 1985 the per capita physician expenditure in Canada (calculated in U.S. dollars) was $202, compared with $347 in the United States. According to the *Journal of the American Medical Association*, the higher per capita expenditure in the United States is explained entirely by higher fees, because the per capita number of physician visits is actually lower in the United States than in Canada. Fees for procedures in the United States are more than three times as high as in Canada.

In addition, fees for evaluation and management services are about 80 percent lower in Canada. Part of the difference in fee structures may be related to the lower rates of malpractice litigation in Canada. Also, because Canadian health care is based on a single-payer system, overhead costs are lower.[131] In part, this is due to the significant portion of the U.S. health care budget that is spent on advertising and billing.[132] The single-payer system also lessens the paperwork load on physicians, thereby freeing them up to see more patients. One indicator of the success of Canada's health care system is that the majority of Canadians are generally satisfied with it and show no inclination of giving it up.[133]

Britain's National Health Service

The National Health Service (NHS) is the most enduring aspect of the British Labour Party's postwar welfare state. The direct inspiration for the NHS was a 1944 white paper written for the wartime coalition government by Sir William Beveridge. The Beveridge Report maintained that a "comprehensive system of health care was essential to any scheme for improving living standards."[134]

After initial resistance from the British Medical Association, the National Health Service Act was passed in 1946 and took effect in 1948. In the words of the act, the aim was to promote "the establishment of a comprehensive health service designed to secure improvement in the physical and mental health of the people . . . and the prevention, diagnosis and treatment of illness."[135] The principle of freedom of choice was upheld in that people could either use the NHS or seek outside doctors. Doctors were guaranteed that there would be no interference in their clinical judgment, and they were free to take private patients while participating in the service. The main goal of the NHS was to provide free medical service to anyone in need. The NHS Act was based on a tripartite system: (1) hospital service with specialists; (2) general medical doctors, dentists, and eye doctors, maintained on a contractual basis; and (3) prevention and support systems, provided by local health departments.

Under the leadership of Minister of Health Anuerin Bevan, all Britain's hospitals were nationalized. Because most hospitals were owned by local governments or were heavily subsidized nonprofit institutions, nationalization was not difficult. General medical practitioners were brought into a new governmentally subsidized plan that provided universal basic medical care that was free at the point of access. This was not a major change, as physicians' services had been subsidized for industrial workers since before World War II. The NHS Act simply extended this coverage to the whole population. British physicians generally came to support the act because it guaranteed a steady income.

The NHS Act does not eliminate private medicine, and a small percentage of NHS hospital beds are reserved for private patients. As mentioned, general practitioners (GPs) and specialists are permitted to treat private patients while working in the NHS. Moreover, affluent patients are permitted to purchase private health insurance and private care. The major advantages of private care are more attractive hospital rooms and quicker service for elective surgery. About 15 percent of Britons currently have private health insurance, which businesses often provide as a fringe benefit for upper-level management.

The backbone of the NHS is the GP. Every patient in Britain is registered with a GP who provides family care. Patients may change their GPs unless they are diagnosed with a chronic illness such as AIDS. GPs are paid by the NHS on the basis of an annual **capitation** fee (per-person fee) for each registered patient. Roughly half of a GP's income comes from capitation payments, with the rest made up by allowances for services such as contraceptive advice and immunization. The role of the GP is to provide primary medical care; GPs are forbidden to restrict their practice to any special client group. Individuals can register with any GP provided he or she is willing to accept them. GPs see almost 75 percent of their registered patients at least once a year; and, because mobility is relatively low in Britain, many people retain the same GP for a considerable period of time.[136]

The GP has wide professional latitude and equips his or her own office, hires staff, and may choose to work singly, in pairs, in groups, or in a government health center. Close to 50 percent of all GPs practice in groups of three or more. Health centers, part of the original National Health Service Act, mushroomed in the late 1960s and 1970s, and by 1975 there were 600 nationally. Sweeping changes in 1967 gave GPs increased benefits, including a higher capitation rate if they had a patient load of 2,500 to 3,500. In addition, extra remuneration was provided for each person on a doctor's list who was over 65, for night calls, for transients, for maternity care, for family planning services, and for certain preventive measures. GPs also receive partial reimbursement for secretaries, receptionists, and nurses, as well as for the rental costs of their offices. Extra payments are also provided for seniority, postgraduate education, and vocational training; for working in groups of three or more; and for practicing in underdoctored areas.[137]

The second tier of the British health care system is the physician consultant (specialist). Most referrals to consultants—except for accidents or emergency care—are made through GPs. Although employed by the government and under contract to a public hospital, a physician specialist is allowed a small private practice. In effect, patients in the community are served by GPs, whereas in the hospital they are under the care of specialists. As in the U.S. health care system, physician specialists are accorded greater prestige and remuneration.[138]

The NHS is funded from general taxes, with the proceeds divided among regional health authorities that plan local health services. The regions, in turn, divide their money among districts that pay for hospitals through global prospective budgets.[139] Health services under the NHS are relatively comprehensive, with hospital and primary medical care being free. However, there are significant patient charges for adult dentistry and eyeglasses and a charge for prescriptions (in 1996, between $5 and $6). Drug prices are agreed upon between the health department and the pharmaceutical industry according to a specific pricing formula based on company profits. In addition, government subsidies for medical education mean that students' direct educational costs are low.[140]

Critics complain that NHS hospital funds are dispersed in a haphazard manner. For instance, considerable monies are spent on health care facilities in fast emptying city centers rather than in burgeoning population centers. One reform suggested to remedy this problem was the creation of "internal markets" whereby the distribution of NHS money would follow patients rather than the other way around. Another important problem was that hospitals received nothing extra for efficiently treating more patients at less cost; as a result hospitals had little incentive to improve efficiency.[141]

Another criticism of the NHS is that its funding is based not on the medical needs of consumers, but rather on how much the British treasury believes it can afford to spend on health care. The result is de facto health care rationing and long waiting lists for elective procedures—caused not by inefficiencies in the system but by limited resources. In addition, consumers complain of long waits in GP offices and of hospital buildings that are often in poor repair. There are also long waiting lists for elective surgeries such as hip replacements, routine treatment of varicose veins, and repairs of hernias. (There is believed to be little wait for urgent surgery.) Long waiting lists can be misleading to some extent, however, because they sometimes include people who have died, have moved, have already had their operations, or who have been kept waiting by consultants who want to secure more resources or private patients.[142]

Other critics charge that despite government efforts, there are serious shortages of doctors in certain parts of Britain. In addition, expenditures and resources under the NHS seem to be slanted toward hospitalization rather than toward primary, first-level care. Critics also complain about the lack of accountability of doctors and about strong unions that have supported restrictive practices and fought attempts to privatize support services.[143] Finally, other critics charge that the inequality in the British health system has resulted in higher disease and mortality rates for lower socioeconomic groups.

Under the original NHS Act, Parliament allocated money and power to local health authorities that managed the hospitals and contracted with specialists for services.[144] Passed in 1990, the National Health and Community Care Act was designed to reduce the long queues for the treatment of nonacute illnesses and procedures by introducing market efficiencies. Loosening the knot between funders and providers, this bill permitted some hospitals (called *trust hospitals*) to operate independently of the local health authority in setting fees, managing budgets, developing personnel packages, and purchasing goods. The theory was that independently managed hospitals would be more efficient than centrally planned ones. To further encourage efficiency, these trust hospitals were allowed to sell their services to any local health authority, private patients, or to private insurance companies. In addition, GPs with large practices were permitted to become fundholders of NHS grants from which they could purchase hospital or specialized services for their clients. It was expected that GPs would refer their patients to those hospitals or specialists that were the most efficient. Inefficient hospitals would get fewer referrals and thus would be forced to increase their quality of care while reducing costs.[145] Unfortunately, the hoped-for results have not been achieved.

Much of the reporting on the NHS in the U.S. press has tended to emphasize its flaws. Although some GPs express dissatisfaction with the system, however, the British people continue to use it in large numbers. For example, although 15 percent of Britons have private insurance, most use it as a supplement rather than as a substitute for the NHS.[146] Despite the criticisms, the NHS appears to be serving the majority of the British population as well as, and in some ways better than, the U.S. health care system. For instance, per capita health care expenditures are only 6 percent of Britain's GDP compared to more than 14 percent for the United States. Much of this lower cost is attributable to the success of GPs in keeping down hospital admission rates and to the relatively low administrative costs of the NHS. Notwithstanding the lower cost of the British health care system, most health indicators, such as life expectancy and infant mortality rates, are equivalent to or better than those found in the costlier U.S. health care system. Enoch Powell, a former British health minister, summed up the contradictions of the NHS: "One of the most striking features of the NHS is the continual, deafening chorus of complaints which rises day and night from every part of it, a chorus only interrupted when someone suggests that a different system altogether might be preferable . . . it presents what must be a unique spectacle of an undertaking that is run down by everyone engaged in it."[147]

It is difficult to compare the quality of the Canadian and British health care systems with that of the system in the United States. For affluent or middle-class Americans with good health insurance, the U.S. system of health care may well provide the best medical care in the world; and for complex medical procedures involving sophisticated equipment and technology, U.S. health care is unequaled. Moreover, unlike the long queues characteristic of the U.K. and Canadian systems, the waiting period for surgery, tests, and other procedures is relatively short in the United States. Finally, physicians in this country are among the best trained in the world. However, the emphasis on costly equipment and technology is not without a price. A medical approach that emphasizes specific diseases over primary care and preventive medicine usually results in good care, but for fewer people. Health care systems that emphasize personal and primary care, accessibility, and free or inexpensive services often reach more people. Given that, the health care systems of Canada and Britain appear to distribute health resources more equitably than does the U.S. health care system.

Conclusion

The examination of health care in the United States raises important questions. What is this nation's responsibility for providing health care to all its citizens? How much high-tech medicine can our society realistically afford? How should U.S. medical resources be allocated? What, if any, limitations on personal freedom are permissible in the name of promoting health and preventing disease? These and other questions require urgent answers.

The U.S. health care system is facing an acute crisis. This crisis is grounded in the failure of the marketplace to curb health care expenditures, the system's over-reliance on medical technology at the expense of providing primary health care services, the growth in health care administrative costs, and the large numbers of working people and their families who cannot afford health care coverage. Moreover, compared to industrialized countries with less-costly health care system, huge expenditures on health care in the United States are not producing greater longevity, lower rates of infant mortality, or other indicators of improved public health.

The United States is one of the few industrialized countries that does not have a comprehensive plan for national health insurance or socialized medicine. Moreover, the U.S. is one of the few industrialized nations where medical expenses can cause poverty. Terri Combs-Orme suggests that a progressive reconstruction of the U.S. health care system must be grounded in the following principles:

1. Accessible health care should be a universal right of all Americans, not a privilege to be purchased or earned.

2. The quantity, quality, and accessibility of health care should be equal for all, not dependent on income or categorical status. No health care system should result in differential quantity, quality, or accessibility of care based on income, gender, age, or any other criterion.
3. Health care should not be linked to employment. A majority of Americans purchase health care insurance through their place of employment, but the fear of job loss or other issues not under their control undermines the security of this arrangement and limits their job mobility.
4. The quality, quantity, and accessibility of health care should not vary on a state-by-state basis.
5. A progressive health care system must balance the needs and rights of children and the elderly in a fair and rational way.
6. A comprehensive health care system should include coverage for and accessibility to long-term care for the elderly.[148]

If commodification and high costs are left unchecked, health care in the United States may someday be out of reach for the majority of citizens. Although the likely outcome of the U.S. health care crisis is unknown, the situation, left solely to the caprice of the marketplace, will undoubtedly worsen.

Discussion Questions

1. In 2004, U.S. health care expenditures were $1.6 trillion a year. This cost has risen dramatically over the past 25 years in terms of the amount spent, the percentage of the GDP used for health care, and the per capita costs of health care. What are the main factors that have driven up health care costs? Can these factors be controlled? If so, how?
2. Medicaid and Medicare have experienced large increases in expenditures. What are the major factors contributing to the steep rise in Medicaid and Medicare costs? What can be done to stabilize these costs?
3. Some critics believe that the costs of Medicare and Medicaid cannot be brought under control without radically reforming the entire health care system. They argue that incremental reforms in the Medicare and Medicaid programs will have only a minuscule impact on the rise in federal and state expenditures for health care. Are these critics correct?
4. Evidence of the effectiveness of cost-controlling mechanisms such as DRGs has been mixed. Critics charge that not only has the DRG system failed to substantially reduce health care costs, but it has also led to a reduced level of patient care. Is the DRG system successful? If so, should it be a model for future health care reforms?
5. Many critics argue that there is a serious health care crisis in the United States. Describe the main characteristics of that crisis (e.g., health care costs, accessibility issues, uninsured populations, U.S. health indicators compared with those of other nations).
6. The AIDS epidemic is one of the most important public health issues facing the global community. Some critics insist that more money should be spent on basic AIDS research, outreach, and treatment. Other critics argue that AIDS is only one of many health care problems facing the United States and other countries around the world. They argue that the money spent on AIDS research should be in proportion to the numbers of people affected by the disease, which, in the United States, are relatively small compared to the numbers of those suffering from cancer and heart disease. Is AIDS a significantly more important public health problem in the U.S. than cancer, heart disease, or the effects of drugs, alcohol, and tobacco? Should the federal government spend proportionally more on AIDS research than on other diseases? If so, why?
7. Some health care analysts are calling for radical reform in the U.S. health care system. Many of these analysts insist that the nation's free market health care system should be replaced by a more cost-effective and comprehensive system. Assuming that these health care analysts are correct, which of the health care systems described in this chapter would be the best model for the United States to emulate? Why?
8. Why has the United States not developed a health care system that is universal and publicly funded, like those of its industrial counterparts? Identify the forces and interests that are shaping health care policy in the United States. What, if anything, can be done to reform or radically transform U.S. health care?

Notes

1. U.S. Census Bureau, "Income Stable, Poverty Up, Numbers of Americans with and without Health Insurance Rise," Press Release, August 26, 2004. Retrieved October 2004 from www.census.gov/Press-Release/www/releases/archives/income_wealth/002484.html
2. See Ibid. National Coalition on Health Care, "Health Insurance Coverage," Washington, D.C., 2004; and The Center on Budget and Policy Priorities, "Number of Americans Without Health Insurance Rose in 2002," Washington, D.C., October 8, 2003, retrieved October 2004 from www.cbpp.org/9-30-03health.htm
3. C. P. Pandya, "Study: Health Insurance Premiums Rising Much Faster Than Average Wages," *The New Standard* (September 28, 2004), p. 3.
4. National Coalition on Health Care; Retrieved November 2004 from www.nchc.org/facts/cost.shtml
5. National Coalition on Health Care, "Health Insurance Coverage."
6. Health Care Financing Administration, "President Clinton Announces Approximately 2.5 Million Children Have Enrolled in the State Children's Health Insurance Program, Praises the Decline in Uninsured, Urges Congress To Expand Coverage, Unveils New Funds for Outreach" (Washington, DC: Health Care Financing Administration, 2000).
7. Terri Combs-Orme, "Should the Federal Government Finance Health Care for All Americans?: Yes," in Howard Jacob Karger and James Midgley (eds.), *Controversial Issues in Social Policy* (Boston: Allyn & Bacon, 1993).
8. Irving J. Lewis and Cecil G. Sheps, *The Sick Citadel* (Boston: Oelgeschlager, Gunn, and Hain, 1983), p. 16.
9. National Coalition on Health Care, "Health Insurance Coverage."
10. Sumner A. Rosen, David Fanshel, and Mary E. Lutz (eds.), *Face of the Nation 1987* (Silver Spring, MD: NASW, 1987), p. 75.
11. U.S. Census Bureau, "Income Stable, Poverty Up, Numbers of Americans with and without Health Insurance Rise."
12. Centers for Medicare & Medicaid Services, "Medicare: A Brief Summary," September 16, 2004. Retrieved October 2004 from www.cms.hhs.gov/publications/overview-medicare-medicaid/default3.asp
13. See Families USA, "Understanding the New Medicare Prescription Drug Benefit," The Medicare Road Show, Washington, D.C., Spring 2004; Kaiser Family Foundation, "The Medicare Prescription Drug Law," March 2004, retrieved November 2004 from www.kff.org/medicare/loader.cfm?url=/commonspot/security/getfile.cfm&PageID=33325; and Egyptian Area Agency on Aging, "Medicare Prescription Drug Benefit," Cartersville, IL, May 20, 2004, retrieved November 2004 from www.egyptianaaa.org/MedicareDrugBill.htm.
14. Ceci Connolly, "OMB Says Medicare Drug Law Could Cost Still More, White House Estimates Show a $42 Billion Increase over 10 Years," *Washington Post* (September 19, 2004), p. A04.
15. Michael Scherer, "Medicare's Hidden Bonanza," *Mother Jones* (March/April 2004), p. 11.
16. Centers for Medicare & Medicaid Services, Medicare: A Brief Summary.
17. Ibid.
18. Ibid.
19. Ibid.
20. Ibid.
21. Connolly, "OMB Says Medicare Drug Law Could Cost Still More."
22. Social Security Administration, "Status of the Social Security and Medicare Programs: A Summary of the 2004 Annual Reports," Social Security and Medicare Boards of Trustees, 2004. Retrieved November 2004 from www.ssa.gov/OACT/TRSUM/trsummary.html
23. David E. Rosenbaum, "Gloomy Forecast Touches Off Feud on Medicare Fund," *New York Times* (June 6, 1996), pp. A1 and B14.
24. For a good historical analysis of the Medicare program, see Theodore R. Marmor, *The Politics of Medicare* (Chicago: Aldine, 1973).
25. Committee on Ways and Means, U.S. House of Representatives, *2004 Green Book*, (Washington, DC: U.S. Government Office, 2004), pp. 15–26.
26. Health Care Financing Administration, "Medicaid Eligibility." Retrieved 2001 from www.hcfa.gov/medicaid/meligib.htm
27. Centers for Medicare & Medicaid Services, "Medicaid: A Brief Summary," September 16, 2004. Retrieved October 2004 from www.cms.hhs.gov/publications/overview-medicare-medicaid/default4.asp
28. Ibid.
29. American Health Care Association, "Nursing Facility Beds by Certification Type," June 2004. Retrieved November 2004 from www.ahca.org/research/oscar/rpt_certified_beds_200406.pdf
30. Stephen A. Moses, "Denial Is Not a River in Egypt," *Health Insurance Underwriter* 50, no. 11 (December 2002), pp. 36–40.
31. American Association of Retired Persons, "Average Daily Cost for Nursing Home Care by State, 2001," 2004. Retrieved November 2004 from www.aarp.org/bulletin/longterm/Articles/a2003-10-30-dailycost.html.

32. Committee on Ways and Means, U.S. House of Representatives, *2004 Green Book.*
33. See Children's Defense Fund, *A Children's Defense Budget,* p. 109; and Barbara Wolfe, "A Medicaid Primer," *Focus* 17, no. 3 (Spring 1996), pp. 1–6.
34. Kaiser Family Foundation, "State Health Facts, 2004." Retrieved November 2004 from www.statehealthfacts.org/cgi-bin/healthfacts.cgi?action=compare&category=Medicaid+%26+SCHIP&subcategory=SCHIP&topic=SCHIP+Expenditures
35. Kaiser Family Foundation, "Health Coverage for Low-Income Children," Kaiser Commission on Key Facts, September 2004. Retrieved November 2004 from www.kff.org/uninsured/loader.cfm?url=/commonspot/security/getfile.cfm&PageID=46994
36. Health Care Financing Administration, "The State Children's Health Insurance Program: Preliminary Highlights of Implementation and Expansion," July 2000. Retrieved 2001 from www.hcfa.gov/init/wh0700.pdf
37. Kentucky Farm Bureau, "Summary of Master Tobacco Settlement," April 1, 1999. Retrieved 2001 from www.kyfb.org/FactTobSett040199.htm
38. See Andrew Garber, "Tobacco Settlement Gregoire Negotiated Not Popular with All," *Seattle Times* (October 04, 2004), p. A6; and Pamela M. Prah, *"Smokers Help to Balance State Budgets, Stateline,* March 3, 2004, retrieved November 2004 from www.stateline.org/stateline/?pa=story&sa=showStoryInfo&print=1&id=354303
39. See Health Care Financing Administration, "Actuarial Products, N.H.E. Projections, Table 1." Retrieved 2001 from www.hcfa.gov/stats/NHE-Proj/proj1998/tables/table1.htm
40. See Paul Starr, *The Logic of Health-Care Reform* (Knoxville, Tenn: Grand Rounds Press, 1992); and OCLC Online Computer Library Center, "Worldwide Education and Library Spending, 2003." Retrieved November 2004 from www.oclc.org/membership/escan/economic/educationlibraryspending.htm
41. U.S. House of Representatives, *Overview of Entitlement Programs: 1996 Green Book.*
42. See U.S. General Accounting Office, *U.S. Health Care Spending Trends, Contributing Factors, and Proposals for Reform* (GAO/HRD-91-102), (Washington, DC: U.S. General Accounting Office, 1991); and Centers for Medicare & Medicaid Services, "National Health Care Expenditures Projections: 2003–2013," September 17, 2004, retrieved October 2004 from www.cms.hhs.gov/statistics/nhe/projections-2003/highlights.asp
43. U.S. House of Representatives, *1996 Green Book,* p. 995.
44. See Ibid.; and U.S. Department of the Census, *Statistical Abstract of the United States, 1991* (Washington, DC: U.S. Government Printing Office, 1991), p. 107.
45. Julie Appleby, "What Happens after the Band-Aids Run Out?" *USA Today* (December 8–10, 2000), pp. 1–2.
46. See Health Care Financing Administration, "Actuarial Products, N.H.E. Projections, Table 1"; and G. J. Schieber and J. P. Poullier, "International Health Care Spending: Issues and Trends," *Health Affairs,* 10 (1991), p. 110.
47. Alliance for Health Reform, "Covering Health Issues: 2003, A Sourcebook for Journalists," January 2003. Retrieved November 2004 from www.allhealth.org/sourcebook2002/ch8_8.html
48. The Commonwealth 2003 Annual Report, "A Look in the Mirror," 2003. Retrieved November 2004 from www.cmwf.org/annreprt/2003/msg_pres02_lookinmirror.htm
49. Ibid.
50. Ibid.
51. Ibid.
52. Ibid.
53. Annenberg School of Communication, "President Uses Dubious Statistics on Costs of Malpractice Lawsuits, Two Congressional Agencies Dispute Findings That Caps on Damage Awards Produce Big Savings in Medical Costs," University of Pennsylvania, January 29, 2004. Retrieved November 2004 from www.factcheck.org/article133.html
54. See Paul Schmolling, Merrill Youkeles, and William Burger, *Human Services in Contemporary America* (Pacific Grove, CA: Brooks/Cole, 1997); and "Doctors under the Knife," p. 29. See also Leon Ginsberg, *Social Work Almanac* (Washington, DC: National Association of Social Workers, 1992), p. 123.
55. U.S. Congressional Budget Office, *Projections of National Health Care Expenditures* (Washington, DC: U.S. Congressional Budget Office, 1992).
56. Kaiser Family Foundation, "Federal HIV/AIDS Spending: A Budget Chartbook," 2000. Retrieved 2001 from www.kff.org/content/1999/2149
57. Clemens, "Rising Costs Reflect Many Instances," p. B2.
58. Victoria Colliver, "In Critical Condition: Health Care in America," *San Francisco Chronicle* (October 11, 2004), p. A8.
59. American Hospital Association, "Rising Demand, Increasing Costs of Caring Fuel Hospital Spending," Press Release, February 19, 2003. Retrieved November 2004 from www.aha.org/aha/hospitalconnect/search/pressrelease.jsp?dcrpath=AHA/Press_Release/data/PR_030219_Costs&domain=AHA
60. Health Care Financing Administration, "Actuarial Products, N.H.E. Projections, Table 2." Retrieved 2001 from www.hcfa.gov/stats/NHE-Proj
61. Myrle Croasdale, "High Medical School Debt Steers Life Choices for Young Doctors," *AMA News* (May 17, 2004), pp. 2–5.
62. Ibid., p. 6.

63. Jay Greene, "Primary Care Matches down Again; Fourth Year of Decline Worries Some," *AMA News* (April 9, 2001), p. 16.
64. J. M. Colwill, "Where Have All the Primary Care Applicants Gone?" *The New England Journal of Medicine* 326 (1992), pp. 387–392.
65. Katherine van Wormer, *Social Welfare: A World View* (Chicago: Nelson-Hall Publishers, 1997), p. 412.
66. Marcia Angell, *The Truth About the Drug Companies: How They Deceive Us and What to Do About It* (New York: Random House, 2004).
67. Meredith Rosenthal and John H. Foster "Drug Ads Take Increasing—Though Still Small—Share of Pharmaceutical Promotion Budget," *The New England Journal of Medicine* (February 14, 2002), pp. 498–505.
68. Nancy McVicar, "Drug Costs Go Up But Coverage Comes Down," *Sun-Sentinel* (February 23, 2000). Retrieved 2001 from www.sun-sentinel.com/news/daily/detail/0,1136,27000000000116737,00.html
69. "Doctors under the Knife," p. 31.
70. John H. Goddeeris and Andrew J. Hogan, "Nature and Dimensions of the Problem." In John H. Goddeeris and Andrew J. Hogan (eds.), *Improving Access to Health Care: What Can the States Do?* (Kalamazoo, MI: W. E. Upjohn Institute for Employment Research, 1992), pp. 14–15.
71. Quoted in Marie A. Caputi and William A. Heiss, "The DRG Revolution," *Health and Social Work* 3, no. 6 (June 1984), p. 5.
72. McVicar, "Drug Costs Go Up."
73. Schmolling, Youkeles, and Burger, *Human Services in Contemporary America* (Pacific Grove, CA: Brooks/Cole Publishing Co., 1997), p. 54.
74. U.S. House of Representatives, *1996 Green Book.*
75. Amy Goldstein, "Cutting Health Costs Slices into Charity," *Washington Post* (April 5, 1999), p. A1.
76. Ellyn E. Spragins, "Simon Says, Join Us," *Newsweek* (June 19, 1995), pp. 55–58.
77. Weiss Ratings Inc., "Consumers Continue to Choose Medicare HMOs Despite High Risk of Being Dropped," 2004. Retrieved November 2004 from www.weissratings.com/News/Ins_HMO/20021209hmo.htm
78. Vicki Lankarge, "Seniors Dropped from Medicare HMOs Shouldn't Rejoin Others, Weiss Warns," *insure.com* (November 14, 2000). Retrieved 2001 from www.insure.com/health/medicare/fewoptions1100.html
79. Howard Waitzkin, *The Second Sickness: Contradictions of Capitalist Health Care* (New York: Free Press, 1983), p. 220.
80. Nancy McVicar, "Medical Care Is There—If You Can Afford It," *Sun-Sentinel* (February 24, 2000). Retrieved 2001 from www.sun-sentinel.com/news/daily/detail/0,1136,27500000000104840,00.html
81. Ibid.
82. Spragins, "Simon Says, Join Us."
83. Thomas H. Ainsworth, *Live or Die* (New York: Macmillan, 1983), p. 89.
84. American Medical Association, *Competition in Health Insurance: A Comprehensive Study of U.S. Markets,* 2nd ed. (Chicago, IL: American Medical Association, January 2003).
85. Ibid.
86. Larry Dignan, "Insurers Thrive with Higher Health Costs," *Wall Street Week with Fortune* (May 6, 2003). Retrieved November 2004 from www.pbs.org/wsw/news/featurestory_20030506.html
87. John M. Herrick and Joseph Papsidero, "Uncompensated Care: What States Are Doing." In Goddeeris and Hogan (eds.), *Improving Access to Health Care: What Can the States Do?* Kalamazoo, MI: W.E. Upjohn Institute for Employment Research, 1992), pp. 139–140.
88. W. Greenberg, "Elimination of Employer-Based Health Insurance." In R. B. Helms (Ed.), *American Health Policy: Critical Issues for Reform* (Washington, DC: AEI Press, October 1992), pp. 1–4.
89. Robert Searles Walker, *AIDS: Today, Tomorrow* (New Jersey: Humanities Press International, 1992), p. 134.
90. Centers for Disease Control, "Basic Statistics," Divisions of HIV/AIDS Prevention, 2004. Retrieved November 2004 from www.cdc.gov/hiv/stats.htm
91. Ibid.
92. Walker, *AIDS,* p. 134.
93. Centers for Disease Control, "Basic Statistics, *HIV/AIDS Surveillance Report,*" Tables A2 and A3, vol. 14, 2002. Retrieved November 2004 from www.cdc.gov/hiv/stats/hasr1402/2002SurveillanceReport.pdf
94. Martin Shapiro and Samuel Bozzette, "Privileged Treatment Inequities in HIV Care Demand Remedies for U.S. Health Care," 1999. Retrieved 2001 from www.rand.org/publications/RRR/RRRfall99/privilege.html
95. World Health Organization, *The World Health Report 2003,* Geneva, 2003.
96. Ronald V. Dellums et al., *Health Services Act* (H. R. 2969) (Washington, DC: U.S. Government Printing Office, 1979). For a good summary of the act, see Waitzkin, *The Second Sickness,* pp. 222–226.
97. Dellums et al., *Health Services Act.*
98. "Summary of S. 2817, The National Health Care Act of 1992," *NASW-LA News* 16, no. 5 (September/October 1992), p. 2.
99. Daschle, Cohen, and Rice, "Health Care Reform," p. 267.
100. Paul Starr, *The Social Transformation of American Medicine* (New York: Basic Books, 1984).
101. Ibid.
102. Ibid.
103. Jeff Bingaman, Robert G. Frank, and Carrie L. Billy, "Combining a Global Health Budget with a Market-

Driven Delivery System," *American Psychologist* 48, no. 3 (March 1993), pp. 271–272.

104. Diane M. DiNitto, *Social Welfare: Politics and Public Policy* (Boston: Allyn & Bacon, 1995), pp. 270–272.
105. Robin Toner, "'Harry and Louise' Ad Campaign Biggest Gun in Health Care Battle," *San Diego Union-Tribune* (April 7, 1994), p. A7.
106. Sara Fritz, "Ads Are Designed to Counter Health Care Proposals," *Los Angeles Times* (May 15, 1993), p. A16.
107. Dana Priest, "The Slow Death of Health Reform," *Washington Post Weekly* (September 5–11, 1994), p. 11.
108. Douglas Frantz, "Lobbyists, Interest Groups Begin Costly Health Care Battle," *Los Angeles Times* (May 24, 1993).
109. Waitzkin, *The Second Sickness*, p. 218.
110. Spencer Rich, "Provisions of 'Catastrophic' Insurance Act," *Washington Post* (July 1, 1988), p. A21.
111. Ibid.
112. National Center for Policy Analysis, "Health Care Policy Brief," Dallas, TX, 1996.
113. C. Sabatino, "Kassebaum-Kennedy Health Insurance Bill Clears Congress: Medical Savings Accounts Limited to Demonstration Program," Families USA (Washington, DC: Families USA).
114. Wolfe, "Changing the U.S. Health Care System," p. 17.
115. DiNitto, *Social Welfare*, p. 270.
116. W. Barnhill, "Canadian Health Care: Would it Work Here?" *Arthritis Today* 6, no. 6 (November–December 1992), p. 8.
117. Elaine Vayda and R. B. Deber, "The Canadian Health Care System: An Overview," *Social Science and Medicine* 18, no. 3 (1984), pp. 191–197.
118. Callaway, "Canadian Health Care: The Good, the Bad, and the Ugly," *Health Insurance Underwriter* (October 1991), pp. 18–35.
119. See Tracy Falwell, Suzy Carter, Jodie Daigle, Renee Mills, Lissa Cameron, and Leticia Gonzalez-Castro, "International Health Care Systems Analysis: Canada, Britain, Germany, Sweden, France, Mexico and South Africa," unpublished paper, Graduate School of Social Work, University of Houston, Houston, TX, April 30, 1996; and T. Mizrahi, R. Fasan, and S. Dooha, "National Health Line," *Health and Social Work* 18, no. 1 (1993), pp. 7–12.
120. Jonathan S. Rakich, "The Canadian and U.S. Health Care Systems: Profiles and Policies," *Hospital and Health Services Administration* 36, no. 1 (Spring 1991), pp. 26–27.
121. Falwell et al., "International Health Care Systems Analysis."
122. Barnhill, "Canadian Health Care," p. 19.
123. Ibid.
124. Ibid.
125. Rakich, "The Canadian and U.S. Health Care Systems," p. 32.
126. See Cynthia Crosson, "Canadian Health Care Is in Critical Condition," *National Underwriter* (January 20, 1992), p. 12; and van Wormer, *Social Welfare*, p. 419.
127. See Barnhill, "Canadian Health Care"; I. Munro, "How Not to Improve Health Care," *Reader's Digest* (September 1992), p. 21; and B. Gilray, "Standing Up for American Health Care," *Health Insurance Underwriter* (February 1992), p. 10.
128. Robert E. Moffitt, "Should the Federal Government Finance Health Care for All Americans?: No." In Howard Jacob Karger and James Midgley (Eds.), *Controversial Issues in Social Policy* (Boston: Allyn & Bacon, 1993).
129. For example, David Himmelstein and Steffie Woolhandler, "A National Health Care Program for the United States: A Physicians' Proposal," *The New England Journal of Medicine* 320 (January 12, 1989), pp. 102–108; and Terri Combs-Orme, "Should the Federal Government Finance Health Care for All Americans?: Yes."
130. Combs-Orme, "Should the Federal Government Finance Health Care for All Americans?: Yes."
131. van Wormer, *Social Welfare*, p. 419.
132. See Combs-Orme, "Should the Federal Government Finance Health Care for All Americans?: Yes"; and "How Does Canada Do It?: A Comparison of Expenditures for Physicians' Services in the United States and Canada," *Journal of the American Medical Association* 265, no. 19 (May 15, 1991), p. 2474.
133. See W. Caragata, "Medicare Wars," *Maclean's* 108, no. 14 (1995), p. 4; and Leger Marketing, "Canadian Perceptions of Their Health Care System," Executive Report, Ottawa, June 2001. Retrieved November 2004 from www.legermarketing.com/documents/spclm/010709eng.pdf
134. Ruth Levitt, *The Reorganised National Health Service* (London: Croom Helm, 1979), p. 15.
135. Quoted in Ibid. p. 17.
136. Victor W. Sidel and Ruth Sidel, *A Healthy State* (New York: Pantheon Books, 1983), p. 144.
137. Ibid., pp. 144, 157–159.
138. Ibid., p. 172.
139. Ibid.
140. Sidel and Sidel, *A Healthy State*, p. 172.
141. "Nye Bevan's Legacy," *The Economist* (July 6, 1992), p. 12.
142. Ibid.
143. Ibid.
144. Levitt, *The Reorganized National Health Service*, p. 27.
145. "Nye Bevan's Legacy."
146. Ibid., p. 12.
147. Quoted in Ibid, p. 12.
148. Combs-Orme, "Should the Federal Government Finance Health Care for All Americans?: Yes."

CHAPTER 13

Mental Health and Substance Abuse Policy

This chapter reviews the provision of mental health services to people with serious mental impairments. Before the rise of the community mental health movement, states were solely responsible for the care of their mentally disturbed residents. When the movement to improve mental health services through federal assistance to the states stalled, many who suffered from serious mental illness were left without care. This lack of adequate care was made worse by a series of legal decisions that reinforced the civil rights of mental patients while requiring the states to provide adequate services. As a result of these developments, many former mental patients are now living on the streets or in squalid single-room-occupancy hotels. In 1996 mental health advocates were encouraged by passage of the Mental Health Parity Act, which mandated that employers offer employees mental health benefits that were comparable to physical health care benefits. Despite this incremental reform, problems associated with chronic mental illness as well as with alcohol and drug abuse have become more prevalent. The lack of adequate support for substance abuse prevention and treatment efforts, coupled with the economic collapse of inner-city neighborhoods, left many urban areas subject to unprecedented levels of street violence and social deterioration. And while social workers in the public sector struggled to care for their seriously impaired clients, private practitioners providing mental health services prospered—although the more recent advent of managed care has attenuated their prospects.

Throughout the history of American social welfare, states have played a prominent role in mental health services. During the nineteenth century, social problems attributable to immigration, urbanization, and industrialization overwhelmed local poorhouses that had been established during the colonial era. Dorothea Dix championed the humane treatment of people with mental illness in the United States, and by the 1840s she was instrumental in convincing many states to construct special institutions to provide asylum to the emotionally deranged. In fact, Dix's leadership was so persuasive that Congress passed legislation authorizing federal aid to the states for mental institutions. However, because President Franklin Pierce thought that the federal government should not interfere with the responsibility of the states to ensure social welfare, he vetoed the legislation in 1854.[1] It would not be until more than a century later that the federal government, through the Community Mental Health Centers Act, would assume a central role in determining mental health policy.

As a result of federal abnegation, states assumed responsibility for care of the mentally ill. During the latter decades of the twentieth century, states built large asylums for the mentally impaired to replace local poorhouses. Originally, state mental hospitals were intended to be self-sufficient communities offering good air, clean water, nutritious food, and healthful activities consistent with the dictates of "moral treatment." Considering the quality of life experienced by many Americans at that time, such refuges were sorely needed. Conditions in rural settings were no less dire than conditions in urban centers in the nineteenth century. Newspaper clippings from an immigrant community in Wisconsin, circa 1890, reveal the fate of vulnerable residents who failed to negotiate dispiriting social conditions.

> The naked body of the wife of Fritz Armbruster, a woman who had worked in Best's Butcher Shop, was found frozen by the roadside near Albion, 6 miles from Black River Falls. She and her husband had separated, he living in town, she living alone in the house. Although no one had noticed that she had been suffering from any physical or mental disorder, 2 years ago, the loss of a child is said to have affected her very deeply and may have led to her becoming partially demented. The probability is that she rose in a fit of delirium and wandered away. . . .
>
> Mr. Axel, a farmer living about 6 miles east of Kiel, Manitowoc County, cut his wife's throat a few days ago so that she might not recover and then killed himself. There were various rumors as to the cause of the tragedy such as domestic infelicity etc., but a few who had dealings with Axel of late attributed the act to an aberration of mind. . . .
>
> Milo L. Nichols, sent to the insane hospital a year or two ago after committing arson on Mrs. Nichols' farm is now at large . . . and was seen near the old place early last week. . . . He has proven himself a revengeful firebug.[2]

In response to these casualties, the state hospital served as a haven for the disturbed as well as protection for the community.

> Admitted July 19, 1893. Town of Black River Falls. Norwegian. Married. Age 29. Seven children. Youngest 8 months. Housewife. Poor. First symptoms were manifested . . . when patient became afraid of everything and particularly of mediums. She is also deranged in religion and thinks everyone is disposed to persecute her and to injure her husband. . . .

> Admitted January 20th, 1896. Town of Garfield. Age 52. Norwegian. Married. Two children, youngest 19 yrs old. Farmer. Poor. Illness began 10 months ago. Cause said to be his unfortunate pecuniary condition. Deluded on the subject of religion. Is afraid of injury being done to him. Relations say he has tried to hang himself. . . . September 29, 1896: Discharged . . . improved . . . Readmitted May 4, 1898: Delusion that he and his family are to be hanged or destroyed.[3]

An adverse social climate, coupled with the absence of welfare programs to cushion people against poverty, joblessness, inadequate housing, and illness, served to swell the population of state hospitals. Often these institutions provided care for 2,000 or more residents; and, while Dorothea Dix would have appreciated the demise of the poorhouse, she would have condemned the quality of care provided to residents. "The large state asylums for the chronic insane certainly were cold, impersonal, and often brutal bins for warehousing the mentally ill," reflected Michael Katz.[4]

In this milieu, the eugenics movement provided some of the scientifically minded reformers of the Progressive Era a straightforward and surgically precise solution to the problem of state institutions being inundated by "mental defectives." Proponents of eugenics believed that the human race could be improved by selective breeding, argued that mental patients often suffered from hereditary deficiencies, and that generational patterns of mental impairment should be eliminated by sterilization. In that adherents of eugenics were less concerned about the civil rights of individual mental patients than they were about the future of civilization, the fact that some patients might object was merely an inconvenience. In such instances, eugenicists obtained court permission to sterilize patients without their consent. Many patients, of course, lacked the mental capacity to comprehend sterilization and had no idea that the surgical procedures to which they were subjected would terminate their reproductive lives. By the 1930s 30 states had passed laws authorizing involuntary sterilization, and by 1935 20,000 patients had been sterilized, almost half of them in California. Involuntary sterilization of the feebleminded generated great controversy, eventually culminating in a Supreme Court decision, *Buck v. Bell* (1927), written by Oliver Wendell Holmes, which validated the practice.

The record case upon which Holmes based his decision had been prepared by a social worker. Tragically, the case involved a young woman in Virginia who was sterilized, only to be judged psychologically normal years later.[5] In 1906 a Charlottesville, Virginia, woman named Emma Buck had a daughter, Carrie. A widow and social outcast, Emma was brought before a Commission on Feeblemindedness in 1920 where she was committed to the Colony for Epileptics and Feebleminded. Daughter Carrie was placed in the care of a family for whom she did housework; in school, Carrie received good grades until her foster family withdrew her so that she could do housework for other families. When she was 17, Carrie became pregnant, having been raped by her boyfriend, she alleged. Such untoward behavior was unacceptable to her foster family; ominously, Carrie was brought before the same commission that had committed her mother. That same year the Superintendent of the Colony intoned on such immoral behavior: "These women are never reformed in heart and mind because they are defectives from the standpoint of intellect and moral conception and should always have the supervision by officers of the law and properly appointed custodians."[6] On January 23, 1924, Carrie was committed to the Colony; on March 28 she delivered a daughter, Vivian. Frustrated by lower court appeals to involuntary sterilization, eugenicists had been seeking a case to appeal to the Supreme Court in order to legitimize the practice, and Carrie Buck appeared an ideal candidate. Two of the Buck family women had been judged feebleminded; if Vivian were determined to be impaired as well, the mental impairment would have affected three generations. Providing questionable representation for Carrie Buck was a eugenicist and founder of the Colony. Only seven months old, Vivian was evaluated by a social worker who, when asked if the infant was normal, replied, "There is a look about it that is not quite normal, but just what it is, I can't tell."[7] But it was sufficient evidence for the justices of the Supreme Court who ruled 8 to 1 in favor of involuntary sterilization of Carrie Buck. Writing for the majority, Justice Holmes wrote famously, "Three generations of imbeciles are enough."[8] As if to rebuke the justices, Vivian did well in school, earning a place on the honor roll before dying of an infectious disease at 8.[9]

Mental Health Reform

More humane efforts to reform state institutions invariably involved the National Association for Mental Health (NAMH). Begun early in the twentieth century as an extension of the work of Clifford Beers, who had recovered after being hospitalized for mental illness, NAMH became critical of the custodial institutions operated by state governments. The issue of mental health attracted wide public attention during World War II, when approximately one in every four draftees was rejected for military service because of psychiatric or neurological problems.[10] In response to public outcry about mental health problems immediately after the war, Congress passed the Mental Health Act of 1946, which established the National Institute of Mental Health (NIMH). Accompanying the Mental Health Act was an appropriation for an exhaustive examination of the mental health needs of the nation. In 1961 NIMH released *Action for Mental Health,* a report that called for an ambitious national effort to modernize the U.S. system of psychiatric care.[11]

As David Mechanic observed, *Action for Mental Health* was a utopian vision of mental health care, the idealism of which coincided perfectly with a set of extraordinarily propitious circumstances. First, the postwar economy was booming, and, with cutbacks in military expenditures, a surplus existed that could be tapped for domestic programs. Second, a new generation of drugs—psychotropic medications—showed promise of being able to stabilize severely psychotic patients who before had been unmanageable. Third, a literature was emerging that was critical of the "total institution" concept of the state hospital and implied that non-institutional—and presumably community—care was better. Finally, because of his experience with mental retardation as a family problem, a sister who was seriously impaired after a lobotomy, President John F. Kennedy was supportive of programs that promised to improve mental health care.[12]

These political and social circumstances did not go unnoticed by Dr. Robert H. Felix, a physician who had grown up with the Menninger family in Kansas and had developed a sharp critique of the state mental hospital as an institution for the care of emotionally disturbed patients. Felix was later to become director of NIMH. A primary architect of the community mental health movement, Felix was able to draw on his extensive experience in the Mental Hygiene Division of the U.S. Public Health Service as well as on the breadth of professional and political contacts that three decades of public service afforded.[13] Felix's objective was as simple as it was radical. He intended to pick up the banner last advanced by Dorothea Dix and reassert the role of the federal government in the nation's mental health policy. Through the community mental health movement, Felix would use federal legislation to reform the archaic state mental hospitals. The laws that enabled NIMH to reform mental health care were the Community Mental Health Centers Acts of 1963 and 1965.

The Community Mental Health Centers Acts

Under the unusually advantageous circumstances of the postwar era, the first Community Mental Health Centers (CMHC) Act was passed by Congress and signed by President Kennedy on October 31, 1963. The enactment of CMHC legislation was not, however, without obstacles. To allay the American Medical Association's fears that the act represented socialized medicine, the CMHC Act of 1963 appropriated funds only for construction purposes. It was not until 1965, when the AMA was reeling from governmental proposals to institute federal health care programs for the aged and the poor, that funds were authorized for staffing CMHCs. Advocates of the CMHC Acts of 1963 and 1965 maintained that a constant target of the legislation was "to eliminate, within the next generation, the state mental hospital, as it then existed."

> The strategy of the mental health leadership and their allies was to "demonopolize" the state role in the provision of mental health services and attempt to establish a triad of federal, state, and local support for mental health services. At this time, federal bureaucrats planned to blanket the whole country with comprehensive community mental health services. Their intention was not to federalize the total program through its financing, but to obtain a degree of control through the resulting federal regulations and standards.[14]

The philosophical basis for transferring mental health care from the state hospital to the community was borrowed from public health, which had developed the concept of prevention. In adopting this formulation, proponents of community mental health presumed that services provided in the community would be superior to the warehousing of patients in state institutions. Prevention, according to the public health model, was of three types. **Primary**

prevention efforts were designed to eliminate the onslaught of mental health problems. Certain psychiatric disturbances, such as depression and anxiety disorders, seemed to be caused by stress, which could be reduced by eliminating the source of stress. **Secondary prevention** consisted of early detection and intervention to keep incipient problems from becoming more debilitating. For example, screening schoolchildren for attention deficit disorders and providing corrective treatment could enhance a child's educational career and thereby enhance development throughout adolescence. **Tertiary prevention** consisted of "limiting the disability associated with a particular disorder, after the disorder had run its course." Typically, tertiary prevention activities sought to stabilize, maintain, and—when possible—rehabilitate those with relatively severe impairments.[15] It was clear to the community mental health activists that the state hospital addressed only tertiary prevention (and then poorly), whereas community mental health offered the prospect of combining primary and secondary intervention with a more adequate effort at tertiary prevention. The structure through which prevention would be implemented was the community mental health center (CMHC).

According to the CMHC Acts, the United States was to be divided into catchment areas, each with a population of 75,000 to 200,000 persons.[16] Eventually, NIMH planned a CMHC for each catchment area, some 2,000 in all.[17] Programmatically, each CMHC was to provide all essential psychiatric services to the catchment area: inpatient hospitalization, partial hospitalization, outpatient services, 24-hour emergency services, and consultation and education for other service providers in the community. Soon after initial passage of the CMHC Act, child mental health as well as drug abuse and alcoholism services were added to the array of services provided. To make sure that patients were not lost between programs within the CMHC network, a **case management** approach was defined, whereby every case was assigned to one professional who monitored the patient's progress throughout treatment. Financially, NIMH provided funding to disadvantaged catchment areas through matching grants over an eight-year cycle. At the end of the cycle, the catchment area was supposed to assume financial responsibility for the CMHC.[18] With this framework, mental health reformers believed that the CMHC was an effective alternative to the state hospital.

Deinstitutionalization

Enthusiasm for community mental health reform ebbed when a series of circumstances that were beyond the control of the CMHC architects began to subvert the movement. Despite promising growth in the number of CMHCs during Johnson's presidency, the Nixon administration did not look favorably on CMHCs and impounded funds appropriated for mental health programs. Although funds were later released, the Nixon administration had clearly stated its disapproval of governmental mental health initiatives. Subsequent legislation to restore momentum to the flagging CMHC movement was crushed by a veto from President Ford. By the time a more sympathetic Carter administration assumed office, general economic problems were so serious that additional appropriations for mental health were not authorized.[19] Still, at the end of Carter's term, 691 CMHCs continued to receive federal assistance. With the Omnibus Budget and Reconciliation Act of 1981, however, the Reagan administration collapsed all mental health funding into a block grant available to states for any mental health services they deemed fundable. As a result, the designation of CMHCs for direct receipt of federal funds ceased in 1981.[20]

In the meantime, however, many states had planned to shift responsibility for the mentally ill to the CMHCs. In fact, the community mental health movement had proved a timely blessing for officials in states where the maintenance of archaic state hospitals was an increasing economic burden. As states discharged patients from state institutions, they realized immediate savings; essentially, "the continuing fall in the numbers of patients to be housed provided state governments with plausible reasons for abandoning expensive schemes of capital investment designed to extend and (or) renovate their existing state hospital systems."[21] In all, 14 state hospitals were closed between 1970 and 1973. The prospect of substantial cost savings through the **deinstitutionalization** of patients received wide support. As governor of California, Ronald Reagan proposed closing all state hospitals by 1980.[22] Unfortunately, the transfer of patients from state institutions to settings in the community was not well planned. Through the mid-1970s, the deinstitutionalization movement was characterized by "severe fragmentation of effort and distribution of activity broadly throughout government with little effective coordination at the state or national level."[23] For purely economic reasons, then, state officials were strongly encouraged to facilitate deinstitutionalization regardless of whether or not alternative forms of care were available for those discharged from state hospitals. Ominously, by the end of the 1990s, 93 percent of the state psychiatric beds that had existed in 1955 had been lost to deinstitutionalization.[24]

Deinstitutionalization was further confounded by a series of judicial decisions in the mid-1970s that enhanced the civil rights of mental patients while at the same time requiring states to provide them with treatment. In ***Wyatt v. Stickney,*** Alabama District Court Judge Frank Johnson ruled that the state of Alabama was obliged to provide treatment to patients in state hospitals and ordered Governor Wallace and the state to appropriate millions of dollars for that purpose—a judgment with which the state subsequently failed to comply. Shortly thereafter, in ***Donaldson v. O'Connor,*** the Supreme Court determined that "the state could not continue to confine a mentally ill person who was not dangerous to himself or others, who was not being treated, and who could survive outside the hospital." Finally, in ***Halderman v. Pennhurst,*** the Third District Court established that institutionalized patients deserved treatment in the "least restrictive alternative."

As a group, these rulings had a profound effect on institutional care for patients with mental impairments. Only persons dangerous to themselves or others could be hospitalized involuntarily. For those hospitalized, involuntarily or otherwise, states were obliged to provide adequate treatment in the manner that was least restrictive to the patient. These decisions promised to be enormously costly to state officials who were trying to curb mental health expenditures. To comply with the court decisions, states would have to pump millions of dollars into the renovation of institutions that had been slated for closure. The solution, in many instances, was to use a narrow interpretation of *Donaldson* to keep emotionally disturbed people out of state institutions. In other words, judicial decisions, coupled with the fiscal concerns of state officials, provided a convoluted logic that served to justify first emptying state hospitals of seriously disturbed patients and then requiring the manifestation of life-threatening behavior for their re-hospitalization. If people were not hospitalized in the first place, the states bore no obligation to provide the adequate, but expensive, treatment demanded by *Wyatt.* The criteria for hospitalization specified the most serious self-destructive behaviors; once admitted, however, patients were stabilized as quickly as possible and then discharged. As a result, those in greatest need of mental health services—patients who were seriously mentally ill—were often denied the intensive care they needed. The consequences for the mentally ill were substantial. In his interpretation of the legal decisions influencing mental health services, Alan Stone, a psychiatrist and a professor at Harvard Law School, observed that the true symbol of the Supreme Court *Donaldson* decision was a bag lady.[25] Thus, legal decisions favoring the mentally ill often proved illusory; in the name of enhancing the human rights of people with mental illness—but with no corresponding improvement in services—they offered those people nothing more than the right to be insane.[26]

The Revolving Door

The shortfall of the community mental health movement, states' transfers of patients from mental hospitals, judicial decisions assuring patients of their civil rights, and the deinstitutionalization movement all combined to leave tens of thousands of former mental patients adrift. Although some former mental hospital patients were able to deal with community agencies in order to obtain mental health care, many of the seriously mentally ill were left to themselves.[27] By the late 1970s some 40,000 poor, chronically ill mental patients had been "dumped" in New York City. The 7,000 on the Upper West Side of Manhattan represented "the greatest concentration of deinstitutionalized mental patients in the United States."[28] During the following decades, former patients presented such problems, that Governor Pataki authorized the designation of special units for them in nursing homes. In 2002, the *New York Times* reported that "hundreds of patients released from state psychiatric hospitals in New York in recent years are being locked away on isolated floors of nursing homes, where they are barred from going outside on their own, have almost no contact with others and have little ability to contest their confinement."[29] Of the 5,000 residents of homes, 946 had died between 1995 and 2000: "some residents died roasting in their rooms during heat waves. Others threw themselves from rooftops, making up some of at least 14 suicides in that . . . period. Still more, lacking the most basic care, succumbed to routinely

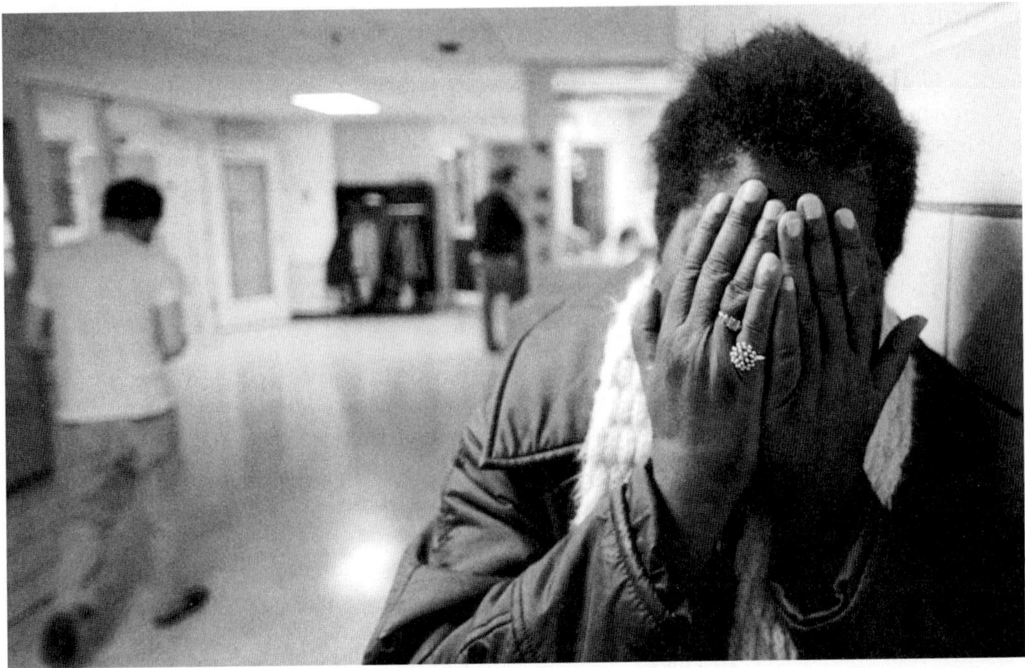

The high incidence of readmissions for psychiatric hospital patients is a chronic problem in mental health care.

treatable ailments, from bust appendices to seizures."[30] By authorizing special homes for mental patients, state officials had effectively replaced large state institutions with a dispersed network of small private ones.

New York was not alone in routinizing the neglect of those who had resided in institutions. In 1999, Katherine Boo investigated the care of retarded residents of group homes in the District of Columbia. During the 1990s, 350 incidents of theft, abuse, neglect, and molestation of residents had been reported, yet not a single fine had been levied against the companies that operated the group homes. Worse, during the late 1990s, 53 residents had died in incidents related to substandard care; of these three received only a cursory review by the District or the federal government.[31] Eventually, it was discovered that the deaths of 116 retarded group home residents had never been investigated, resulting is a series of law suits by families of the residents.[32] For her muckraking series on the subject, Boo was awarded a Pulitzer Prize.

Deinstitutionalization marginalized many patients. Reporting in *Scientific American,* two mental health researchers described their experiences with deinstitutionalized patients:

> Time and time again we see patients who were released from state hospitals after months or years of custodial care; who then survive [sic] precariously on welfare payments for a few months on the fringe of the community, perhaps attending a clinic to receive medication or intermittent counseling; who voluntarily returned to a hospital or were recommitted . . . who were maintained in the hospital on an antipsychotic medication and seemed to improve; who were released again to an isolated "community" life and who, having again become unbearably despondent, disorganized, or violent, either present themselves at the emergency room or are brought to it by a police officer. Then the cycle begins anew.[33]

The high incidence of readmissions for psychiatric patients—the "revolving door"—had become an unavoidable problem in mental health. In 1970 the ratio of readmissions per resident of a mental hospital was 1.4; in 1974 the ratio was 1.74; but by 1981 it had reached 2.83, double that of a decade earlier.[34] Through the mid-1980s the ratio of admissions per resident continued to edge up, and by 1986 it stood at 2.98.[35] By 1991, however, the ratio had fallen slightly to 2.88.[36]

Meanwhile, resources for state mental hospitals dwindled, leaving patient care uncertain. In an attempt to manage patients more cost-effectively, state mental institutions relied more heavily on psychoactive medication, sometimes with disastrous consequences. In California, for example, a federally funded group that oversees mental health care complained of unnecessary deaths of mental patients who had been left unsupervised after receiving medication:

> The 28-year-old . . . patient died December 26, 1989, while he was locked in his dorm room . . . for 3 and one-half hours, the report charges. In addition to lithium and Valium, he was given Cogentin, which can cause vomiting, and Thorazine, which can suppress the body's natural coughing reflex. He suffocated on his own vomit and a piece of Christmas candy, the report said. The [other deaths] involved a 24-year-old patient who collapsed and died after he was given five different medications, and a 21-year-old man who had a fatal heart attack after he was given an injection of the psychiatric drug Haldol, the report said.[37]

The first nationwide review of such deaths revealed that 142 psychiatric patients had died between 1988 and 1998 as a result of institutional abuses; 33 percent of the deaths were attributed to asphyxiation and 26 percent to cardiac problems. More than one-fourth were children.[38]

A coherent mental health policy had ceased to exist in the United States in the 1980s. By 1990, psychiatrist E. Fuller Torrey and his associates observed that "services for individuals with serious mental illness in the United States are a disaster by any measure used. Not since the 1820s have so many mentally ill individuals lived untreated in public shelters, on the streets, and in jails."[39] State hospitals had been divested of much of their responsibility for patients with serious psychiatric problems, but a complete system of CMHCs was not in place to care for many of those who had been deinstitutionalized. As a result of this institutional transformation, the last half of the twentieth century witnessed a radical change in mental health care. In 1955 the vast majority of mental health care was inpatient, with less intensive care representing a minority of episodes; by 1997 this had been reversed, as shown in Table 13.1.

As state hospitals converted from long-term custodial care to short-term patient stabilization, psychotropic medication came to be a routine form of treatment. But the psychopharmacological revolution, though congruent with the relatively orderly march toward deinstitutionalization in the late 1960s, actually exacerbated the psychiatric chaos of two decades later. Shown to stabilize psychotic patients until interpersonal treatment methods could be employed, the major tranquilizers—Prolixin, Thorazine, Haldol, and Stelazine, to name a few—seemed clinically indicated within the controlled environment of the hospital. In a community setting, however, psychotropic medication became problematic. Once stabilized on major tranquilizers, patients frequently found the side effects of the medication—dry mouth, nervousness, torpor, lactation in women, and impotence in men—unacceptable and stopped taking the medication.

Yet without medication such patients frequently decompensated, and without the regular supervision of psychiatric personnel, patients disappeared into inner-city ghettos or rural backwaters, adding to an already growing homeless population. Definitive data on the psychological condition of the homeless are difficult to generate, but a study of the homeless in Fresno, California, revealed that "34 percent were rated severely impaired and urgently in need of [psychiatric] treatment. An additional 33 percent were rated moderately impaired so that treatment would be of substantial benefit."[40] A Baltimore study found that 80 percent of the homeless were mentally ill, and most of these were also abusing illicit drugs and alcohol.[41] A HUD census of the homeless revealed that 62 percent had problems with alcohol abuse, 58 percent with drugs, and 57 percent with mental health.[42]

In the absence of mental health care, increasingly desperate former mental hospital patients turned to petty crime to gain income, thus clogging

Table 13.1

Type of Treatment Episodes, Selected Years

Year	Number of Inpatient Episodes	%	Number of Outpatient Episodes	%
1955	1,296,352	77.4	379,000	22.6
1965	1,565,525	59.4	1,071,000	40.6
1975	1,817,108	26.5	5,040,489	73.5
1986	2,055,571	26.1	5,830,047	73.9
1997	2,548,030	23.8	8,166,368	76.2

Source: Substance Abuse and Mental Health Services Administration, *Mental Health, United 2000* (Washington, DC: Author, 2000), Chapter 14, Table 6.

local courts. Commenting on the surge in arrests of the mentally ill, one mental health worker became exasperated: "These people are forced to commit crimes to come to the attention of the police and get help."[43] By 2000 the Justice Department reported that 283,800, or 16 percent, of inmates in local and state correctional facilities suffered from mental disorders,[44] and another 550,000 were on parole.[45] In 2003 Human Rights Watch reported that U.S. prisons contained three times more psychiatric patients than mental hospitals. This institutional mismatch had come to the point that the largest psychiatric facility in the nation was the Los Angeles County Jail which held 3,400 mentally ill inmates; second was New York's Rikers Island with 3,000.[46]

Another telling incident involved a mentally ill African American who was mistaken for a man for whom an arrest warrant had been issued. Sharing only a last name and a common birth date, Kerry Sanders was rousted from sleeping on a Los Angeles park bench, arrested as Robert Sanders, and extradited to New York, where he was incarcerated for two years before the error was noticed. In the interim, various attorneys, correctional officers, and social workers failed to recognize that the protests of Kerry Sanders were valid: He was not the man they had convicted. It was not until a records clerk realized that Kerry Sanders was not the man for whom an arrest warrant was outstanding that he was released. Later, one of Kerry Sanders's prison doctors stated condescendingly, "He got medication, free meal, food, everything. He should say 'Thank you, for two years you guys treated me very nicely.'"[47]

By 2000, reformers were attempting to change judicial policy in regard to mentally ill convicts by creating special courts to deal with nonviolent offenders who had mental disorders. Paralleling special drug courts that had emerged in several metropolitan areas during the 1990s to contend with nonviolent drug abusers, the mental health court concept was advocated by the National Alliance for the Mentally Ill (NAMI) as well as the National Mental Health Association.[48] In 2000 Congress passed America's Law Enforcement and Mental Health Project Act. Drawing on mental health courts already established in Seattle, Anchorage, Fort Lauderdale and San Bernardino, the Act instructed the Attorney General to make grants for mental health courts in other locations. The Mental Health Courts Grant Program subsequently supported the creation of 23 mental health courts in 2002 and 14 more in 2003. By the end of 2004 a consortium of mental health advocacy organizations reported that 99 mental health courts were operating.[49] Federal funding lagged behind the initiative, however; in 2003, $2.98 million was appropriated for mental health courts, but the following year the amount was zero.[50]

CMHCs under Siege

The discharge of patients from state mental hospitals imposed an enormous burden on the CMHCs. Because the seriously mentally ill were often unable to get care from hospitals, the CMHCs provided the only service these people received. A Philadelphia CMHC reported that 44 percent of its patients were chronically disturbed and that these patients consumed 70 percent of the mental health services provided.[51] CMHCs had to restructure their activities so as to focus on immediate care for seriously disturbed patients, with the result that "indirect" services, such as prevention and evaluation, were cut back. A study of 94 CMHCs showed that increasing demand for direct services to the seriously mentally disturbed began to skew mental health service delivery.[52] Thus, rather than being a mental health agency that provided a comprehensive range of services to all persons in a catchment area, the CMHC rapidly became an outpost for individuals with serious mental disturbances—a population that CMHCs were not intended to serve, at least not exclusively.

As client demand escalated, CMHCs faced significant cuts in federal funding. The Reagan administration moved to consolidate mental health funding in the form of block grants that were devolved to the states, but in the process reduced federal funding 21 percent.[53] With funding from the federal government diminishing, CMHCs became more dependent on the states, which had historically defined mental health care in the United States. CMHCs were able to compensate for federal reductions to some extent by obtaining more funding from government assistance programs. Significantly, nongovernmental sources, such as client fees and private insurance, continued to account for a relatively minor portion of CMHC operating expenses. Precisely how this reduction in federal funds affected the CMHC effort varied, of course, with individual programs. CMHCs in wealthier states, for example, were better able to weather the fiscal turmoil than were those in poorer states. Generally, however, CMHCs reduced staffing and programming through such strategies as layoffs and hiring freezes, staff reassignments, and internal reorganization.[54]

By the mid-1980s, CMHCs seemed to have made the necessary organizational adjustments to funding changes; but these were at the expense of staffing and programming needs that had been increasing. CMHCs were able to hire some new staff to make up for earlier reductions, but programming had stagnated completely. Eventually the morale of CMHC staff suffered, as mental health professionals could no longer see any relief from their inability to provide even minimal care to seriously mentally ill patients. In San Diego, for example, county officials decided to target scarce resources for only the most seriously disturbed, which drew this editorial response from a CMHC staff member:

> In the future . . . the community mental health clinics will provide little or no talking therapy to their thousands of clients. Instead, most patients will find their treatment limited to a 15-minute visit with a psychiatrist and a prescription for expensive psychotropic medications—bought, incidentally, at taxpayer expense.[55]

A decade after the devolution of mental health block grants to the states, CMHCs had adjusted by reducing professional staff; increasing caseloads; reorganizing and targeting **chronic care** services and services for people who were insured, and reducing services to children, adolescents, and the elderly who were uninsured.[56]

By 1990, mental health service delivery was diversifying. CMHCs maintained an important institutional role, yet no longer served as the focus of mental health reform as had been the case during the late 1960s and 1970s. CMHCs not only had failed to replace the state hospital system, but accounted for less than 5 percent of inpatient episodes. CMHCs were more visible in the realm of outpatient care, yet accounted for only 15.5 percent of visits, far below the 50.4 percent attributed to private practitioners.[57] Within two decades, not only had the momentum gone out of the CMHC movement, but thousands of former mental patients had been left adrift. It was perhaps inevitable that more intrusive methods would evolve to care for them.

Preventive Commitment

By the early 1990s, governmental mental health policy was in disarray. Deinstitutionalization had contributed to the homelessness problem, with at least 50 percent of the homeless being people with severe mental illness by the late 1980s.[58] When winter threatened the safety of some homeless people in New York City, a team of mental health workers were authorized to pick up those who posed a danger to themselves and to commit them to Bellevue Hospital for a three-week observation period, a policy referred to as **preventive commitment.** The first person picked up was Joyce Brown, who "was dirty, malodorous and abusive to passersby and defecated on herself."[59] To the chagrin of then Mayor Ed Koch, when Brown had been stabilized in Bellevue, attorneys from the American Civil Liberties Union challenged her involuntary commitment. The prospect that pending litigation might cancel the program led one supporter to observe that "for the severely mentally ill, liberty is not just an empty word but a cruel hoax."[60]

By late 1999, however, despite initial setbacks in preventive commitment, 41 states had authorized the practice.[61] The high number of treatment dropouts from outpatient therapy and the revolving door of hospitalization served to encourage local authorities to find some method for ensuring that seriously mentally ill persons would not deteriorate because of lack of intervention by mental health professionals. Preventive commitment provides for commitment of individuals who do not meet the statutory standard for involuntary hospitalization but who are mentally ill, are unable to voluntarily seek or comply with treatment, and need treatment in order to prevent deterioration that would predictably result in dangerousness to self or others or grave disability.[62]

A tragic incident in early 1999 strengthened the cause of preventive commitment: In New York City a 32-year-old receptionist, Kendra Webdale, was pushed under a subway train and killed by a 29-year-old mental patient, Andrew Goldstein. During the two years prior to the incident, Goldstein not only experienced persistent hallucinations, but also acted violently, once assaulting a psychiatrist. Having been discharged from inpatient care, Goldstein had fared poorly in a basement apartment without a phone; he had sought residential services in a group facility to no avail, as there were no vacancies.[63] Within a year, the New York legislature enacted Kendra's Law, authorizing $30 million for preventive commitment.[64]

An increasingly popular mental health policy, preventive commitment nevertheless presents serious problems when there are inadequate resources to ensure that it is used properly. When a facility lacks adequate staff, preventive commitment can become a form of social control—as opposed to therapy—in which treatment "consists of mandatory medication and little else."[65] One authority on preventive commitment speculated that mental health professionals would have little choice but to use "forced medication" as "the treatment of choice" for those in preventive commitment and that they would have to "actually track down noncompliant patients at their place of residence or elsewhere and administer medication as part of a mobile outreach team."[66]

For those concerned with the civil rights of the mentally impaired, such an eventuality is nothing less than ghoulish, an exercise in state tyranny in the name of social welfare.[67] Even under conditions of adequate staffing, preventive commitment remains problematic. The side effects of psychoactive medications are so pronounced for many patients that they simply refuse to take the drugs, even under duress. Among the contraindications of psychoactive medications is **tardive dyskinesia,** permanent damage to the central nervous system resulting from long-term use of medications such as Prolixin and Stelazine. Because tardive dyskinesia is irreversible and is manifested by obvious symptoms—"protrusion of tongue, puffing of cheeks, puckering of mouth, chewing movements"[68]—the disorder raises a haunting specter: In an attempt to control psychological disturbances, psychiatry has created a host of physiological aberrations. Fortunately, a new generation of psychoactive medication, such as Zyprexa, has shown less evidence of tardive dykinesia; however, they are more expensive, and this raises another problem. In 2003, Kentucky reduced the cost of its Medicaid program by excluding Zyprexa from its list of approved medication, leaving the poor mentally ill dependent on cheaper medications more likely to have adverse side effects.[69]

Mental Health Service Delivery

The Substance Abuse and Mental Health Services Administration (SAMHSA) of the Department of Health and Human Services oversees the federal Alcohol, Drug Abuse, and Mental Health block grants. These grants consolidate several separate or "categorical" programs established earlier, such as the CMHC Acts. Since 1981 all mental health expenditures have been in block grants to states. By using a block grant strategy, the federal government removed the power from federal agencies and transferred it to the individual states. Since the creation of mental health block grants, funding for mental health services has increased only incrementally, particularly in comparison with substantially greater funding for substance abuse services. During the mid-1990s the mental health block grant remained static; it began to increase slightly with the turn of the millennium, as indicated in Table 13.2.

Table 13.2

Federal Funding for Substance Abuse and Mental Health Services

Year	Amount (millions)
2002	$2,885
2003	3,056*
2004	3,174*
2005	3,203*
2006	3,251*
2007	3,305*
2008	3,360*

*Estimated

Source: U.S. Government, *Budget of the United States, 2004* (Washington, DC: U.S. GPO, 2004), p. 359.

Minimal federal funding for mental health services signaled declining leadership in mental health reform. By the 1990s several states were exploring innovative methods for delivery of mental health services.[70] One approach involved the integration of services and payment through a capitation method, a strategy developed in several localities. Under a capitation method of payment, agencies are awarded a predetermined amount per client with which they must provide a range of services. Agencies are funded the capitation amount regardless of the actual cost of serving an individual client. Capitation in mental health care would mimic health maintenance organizations (HMOs), which have a successful track record in providing preventive and primary health care. "Mental health HMOs would centralize financing and delivery system responsibility, create financial incentives to reallocate resources from inpatient to outpatient settings, and reduce system fragmentation, as perceived by patients."[71] Such an arrangement has the advantage of being easy to administer, and it builds into the reimbursement scheme certain incentives that do not exist in other arrangements. Under a capitation reimbursement method, for example, agencies are encouraged to cut down on expensive services, such as hospitalization, because a surplus can be realized when the actual cost of care is below the capitation amount. "Money can be used to develop walk-in crisis centers, step-down units that provide intermediate care after an acute hospitalization, special case management programs for coordinating services and rehabilitation or special housing services."[72] In addition, agencies are penalized for neglecting to serve clients, because every capitated client represents a resource base for the agency.

An example of how a capitation method of payment could be used in mental health service delivery was the integrated mental health (IMH) concept pioneered in New York State and Philadelphia. Capitated mental health care under IMH would have three major features. First, current **categorical grants**—Medicaid, Supplemental Security Income, Food Stamp Program, local funding—would be aggregated into a common fund from which capitation "premiums" would be paid. Second, a nonprofit planning and coordination agency would be established to oversee mental health care and in so doing negotiate contracts with providers, monitor performance, and evolve innovative programs. Third, particularly high-usage clients would be targeted for provision of less costly services in order to generate surpluses for less intensive services.[73]

The magnitude of cost savings that can be realized through IMH is illustrated by the deployment of a capitated system in two New York counties during the 1990s. In order to induce CMHCs to participate in the capitation arrangement, the counties established payment rates for levels of service for three types of patients: for "continuous patients," who had been hospitalized for some time, $39,000 per year; for "intermittent patients," who generally required intermediate care, two rates, $18,000 and $13,000; and for "outpatients," who needed the least intensive care, $5,000. State officials calculated that such payments would represent savings, because state hospital care exceeded $100,000 per patient annually. Eventually, the continuous patient rate was reduced to $28,000; the intermittent rate was combined and lowered to $15,600; and the outpatient rate was increased to $11,600. Initial assessment of the program indicated cost savings and improved patient functioning. Participating CMHCs planned to use their revenue surpluses to extend mental health services to children and the elderly.[74]

The idea of integrating services through an arrangement such as the IMH is likely to become an important source of innovation in future mental health policy. Such an eventuality has significant implications for human service professionals, who may miss an important opportunity to shape mental health programs unless they are willing to sharpen their administrative skills. The capitation of mental health services, as might be suspected, places a premium on fiscal analysis, cost accounting, and strategic planning. In a policy environment in which capitation is an increasingly prevalent method of ensuring access to service while containing program costs, mental health administrators who are not knowledgeable about fiscal management may well lose control of programs to professionals from business and public administration.

The future of mental health policy is complicated by fundamental questions. If capitation becomes a primary vehicle for reimbursing providers, should government prefer nonprofit providers, ordinarily CMHCs, or for-profit providers, usually HMOs? As the commercialization of health care demonstrates, HMOs are quick to exploit new markets, and mental health delivery is no exception. But would HMOs continue to provide services to the chronically mentally ill, or would more disturbed patients become "refugees" from the HMOs that were once eager to recruit them?[75] Under either arrangement, is it reasonable to expect mentally impaired consumers to make wise choices in selecting a mental health provider? "Many clients receiving services in managed mental health care," cautioned one observer, "may have difficulty understanding and processing" the type of information they need to make a prudent choice in service provider.[76]

Questions about the ability of the mentally disturbed to make prudent decisions about their care notwithstanding, the comparative cost advantage of community-based services remains a compelling argument in favor of capitation. For example, the Threshold Jail Program, which provides care for mentally ill inmates, calculates a per diem of $26, compared to $70 for incarceration and $400 for mental hospital hospitalization. Although the program has been extant for only a few years, it has helped all of its 45 members avoid re-arrest, an accomplishment that resulted in a grant of $495,000 from the state of Illinois.[77]

In Columbus, Ohio, another factor in the funding of mental health services emerged in 1996: the renewal of a property tax levy for mental health care.

Local taxes accounted for about half of funding for local mental health care, but the levy for mental health and substance abuse was scheduled to end in 1996. Ominously, a renewal campaign that also increased the levy failed by less than 4 percent of the vote in 1995, so mental health advocates were hard pressed to succeed in the next election cycle. Through an intensive political campaign, the levy passed in 1996 by a safe margin, 61 percent to 39 percent, guaranteeing the continuation of local revenues.[78]

Mental health policy that emphasizes innovations such as capitation presents a paradox for social workers: while they have been integrally involved in direct practice through case management, they have been less visible in program development. Thus, while case management services for people with serious mental illness "have enjoyed a rapid increase in prominence within the mental health system,"[79] social workers have been reluctant to become managers in human service corporations.[80] As conventionally structured, managed care in mental health has been subject to the same problems as managed physical health care, often attenuating services by limiting the number of therapeutic sessions. At worst a mental health corporation can collapse, as has Charter Behavioral Systems, leaving hundreds of patients adrift.[81] Regardless, unless mental health professionals increase their understanding of human service markets, they may find themselves working under the direction of business executives and using methods that are not optimal with respect to patients' well-being. Such a development is unlikely to be in the best interests of patients who are seriously emotionally disturbed.

The advent of managed care in mental health has contributed to the medicalization of psychiatry, particularly the use of psychoactive medications to control patient behavior.[82] In 2004 a controversy erupted about the use of psychoactive medication with children. While Prozac had been demonstrated to be effective in alleviating depression with adolescents,[83] the efficacy research of other medications—Paxil, Zoloft, and Effexor—had not been made public. Regardless, mental health professionals had prescribed these medications with increasing frequency, often citing research conducted by pharmaceutical companies. When British researchers reported a link between suicidal ideation and the use of unapproved medications, concerns by American parents were transmitted to the Food and Drug Administration.[84] In response to subsequent FDA queries, the pharmaceutical companies refused to release their research on clinical trials on the basis they were trade secrets.[85] As the dispute festered during the Spring of 2004, the FDA assigned an epidemiologist to evaluate 22 studies involving 4,250 children to determine the efficacy of psychotropic medication for children. When the scientist concluded that children taking antidepressants were more than twice as likely to be suicidal, the FDA refused to allow him to testify at congressional hearings on the matter.[86] In March an embarrassed FDA ordered drug companies to affix warnings of suicidal side effects on labels. Despite the publicity, the number of children on antidepressants increased 15 percent during the first three months of 2004.[87]

Parity for Mental Health Care

Although managed care defined much of the coverage for mental health care during the late 1980s and early 1990s, a reaction was building. Under aggressive managed care plans, many who had received mental health services in the past found their options rationed, attenuated, or eliminated altogether.[88] In response, a group of parents and relatives of the mentally ill organized NAMI and fought for extended mental health coverage.[89]

Advocates of extended mental health coverage were encouraged by the Clinton administration's proposed Health Security Act, a health care reform that might have placed mental health provision on a par with physical health services. The demise of the proposal left mental health advocates searching for a vehicle for obtaining parity. Health insurers opposed parity in mental health care, because it would increase the cost of premiums; the Congressional Budget Office projected that parity would raise premiums by 4 percent, or about $12 billion.[90] Given its aversion to increased health costs, to say nothing of its objections to government meddling in health care, few expected the conservative 104th Congress to move toward parity.

Yet, smarting from negative ratings associated with an overzealous conservative agenda, Congress suddenly reversed field in the closing days of the legislative session and in 1996 delighted mental health advocates by agreeing on legislation establishing parity for mental health care. Effective January 1,

1998, employers with more than 50 employees who offer any mental health coverage must include mental health benefits that are comparable to health benefits.[91] The consequences of legislatively mandating parity in mental health coverage were immediately disputed. Opponents warned of significant increases in health insurance premiums and the likelihood that employers would eliminate mental health coverage in order to dodge the parity mandate.[92] Defenders, on the other hand, minimized the implications for premium increases, noting that mental illness was, for the first time, being interpreted as a physiological disorder.

An evaluation of the Mental Health Parity Act released by the General Accounting Office in May 2000 tempered the enthusiasm of mental health advocates. Although 86 percent of employers surveyed were in compliance with the legislation, most—87 percent—had altered employee benefits so that mental health benefits were more restrictive. Significantly, only 3 percent reported that compliance had resulted in increased costs, and none had dropped mental health coverage altogether in response to mandated mental health parity.[93] Achieving parity in mental health was an important development in social policy; but, placed in context, its provisions were quite modest. Parity was predicated on employment, as such it did nothing for those who were not in the labor market; moreover, since it applied only to employers with more than 50 workers, its provisions were evaded by small employer. Thus, parity did nothing for the mentally ill who were not working, and little for those hired by small employers.

Parity for mental health care may have marked the end of the downsizing of mental health care, yet much remained to be done. The devolution of mental health care to the states beginning in the early 1980s, and the rationing of resources for mental health under managed care through the remainder of the decade, had effectively checked the expansion of mental health care, and the incarceration of mentally impaired offenders recalled the horrors against which Dorothea Dix had fought. Providing essential mental health services for poor people who evidence severe psychological disorganization remains a primary challenge to mental health advocates, although resources remained inadequate for the task at hand. In 2003, President Bush's New Freedom Commission on Mental Health released its report on the status of mental health services in the United States. For all practical purposes the report was an admission of institutional inadequacy, admitted Mike Hogan the Commission Chair, "We have an unintended conspiracy to keep people disabled."[94]

Substance Abuse

Mental health services are often associated with substance abuse. Human service professionals in direct services are familiar with clients who have chosen to anesthetize themselves from stress or misery with alcohol, tobacco, and other substances. Individuals' psychological problems are of course compounded by reliance on such substances, and these problems

Spotlight 13.1

The Substance Abuse and Mental Health Services Administration

Substance abuse is an important area of public policy not only because of the costs and appropriations for treatment programs, but also because of the enormous costs that substance abuse extracts from society. To address substance abuse issues and their toll on society, the federal government established the Substance Abuse and Mental Health Services Administration (SAMHSA) in 1992. The goal of this agency is to focus attention, programs, and funding on improving the lives of people with, or at risk for, mental and substance abuse disorders.

To learn more about SAMHSA and its programs, go to its website at **www.samhsa.gov.**

not only affect the families of substance abusers but also become more severe when addiction is manifested. Ordinarily, addiction is associated with alcohol and drugs, less often with tobacco. Substance abuse has become an important area of public policy not only because of the necessity for appropriations for treatment programs but also because of the enormous costs that substance abuse extracts from society. As these costs have escalated, substance abuse policy has attained a higher profile in domestic affairs.

The interaction of emotional difficulties, alcoholism, and substance abuse is reflected in social welfare policy and has been institutionalized in the Substance Abuse and Mental Health Services Administration. The consolidation of categorical grants into a federal block grant program under SAMHSA reflects the preference of many human service professionals for preventive programs that apply generically to all forms of substance abuse. This approach has been argued persuasively by Mathea Falco:

> An estimated 18 million Americans are alcoholics and 55 million are regular smokers, compared to 5.5 million serious drug abusers. Each year alcohol causes 200,000 deaths from disease and accidents, while more than 400,000 Americans die from smoking. By contrast, deaths from all illicit drugs range from 5,000 to 10,000. The costs of health care and lost productivity caused by tobacco-related illnesses are estimated at $60 billion a year, and those attributed to alcoholism exceed $100 billion. For all illegal drugs, the National Institute of Drug Abuse sets the annual bill to society at $40 billion.[95]

What is the logic in having separate preventive programs for tobacco, alcohol, and illegal drugs when effective prevention programs can be developed for all of them? In the light of diminishing resources for social programs, Falco's book *The Making of a Drug-Free America: Programs That Work*—a call for integrating prevention efforts—is compelling.

History of Substance Abuse

Although most societies have incorporated addictive substances into their religions or social conventions, the use of these substances is ordinarily circumscribed. For historical and demographic reasons, U.S. culture has been accepting of certain substances, ambivalent about some, and phobic about others. Tobacco, a crop the colonists were encouraged to cultivate by their European sponsors, has been a legal commodity since Europeans first settled in North America. Alcoholic beverages appear in most agrarian societies, and these are a fixture in American folklore. Still, the consequences of excessive alcohol consumption on family life led some religiously inspired Prohibitionists to call for the banning of alcohol. From 1919 to 1933, the Eighteenth Amendment to the Constitution prohibited the manufacture and sale of alcoholic beverages in the United States. Cocaine was a common ingredient in many early patent medicines and in popular beverages such as Coca-Cola. Concern about quality in production, however, led to the Pure Food and Drug Act of 1906, which required that ingredients be listed on product labels. When the public learned that there was cocaine in some products, local jurisdictions prohibited their sale. Opium, imported with the Chinese laborers who built the western rail system, was initially ignored in this country until reports surfaced that women from upright families were frequenting "opium dens." The Hague Opium Convention of 1912, of which the United States was a leader, subsequently controlled the production and sale of opium internationally. In the United States, restrictions on the manufacture and sale of cocaine, heroin, and marijuana were first established through the 1914 Harrison Narcotic Act. Marijuana was effectively made illegal through the Marijuana Tax Act of 1937.[96]

Despite this legacy, governmental control of mind-altering substances is anything but consistent. Although the federal government wages a "drug war," some states, for all practical purposes, disregard marijuana possession; some jurisdictions have legalized marijuana for medical purposes. The sale and use of cocaine and heroin have become so essential to the economy of many poor inner-city communities that the police are ineffectual in controlling trade, able at best to harass users.[97] During the 1980s cocaine was commonly used by young urban professionals (yuppies) as the drug of choice and was glamorized by Hollywood. Meanwhile, a substantial market emerged in prescription drugs, such as Valium, which were available as widely as there were corrupt physicians willing to prescribe them.

Public intolerance of drug abuse escalated because of several factors. Continued carnage on the nation's highways because of drunk drivers led to the founding of Mothers against Drunk Drivers (MADD), a voluntary group that fought aggressively for stiffer penalties for drivers under the influence of alcohol. The alcohol- and drug-related deaths of entertainers such as Janis Joplin, Jimi Hendrix, and Elvis

Presley were sobering experiences for many young people. When sports stars Len Bias and Don Rogers died from cocaine overdoses, drug abuse took center stage in the United States. In the meantime, an ominous development served to underscore drug abuse as a public health problem, not simply as an individual moral problem. AIDS, initially associated with male homosexuals in this country, was increasingly prevalent among inner-city intravenous drug users (IDUs). Needle sharing among cocaine and heroin addicts was identified as a primary means of HIV transmission. Indiscriminate injections by IDUs quickly spread AIDS within the African American and Hispanic communities in major urban centers. When IDUs practiced unsafe sex, AIDS was passed to minority heterosexuals. As women who had contracted AIDS became pregnant, they bore infants who were HIV positive. By the early 1990s concerns about substance abuse drew together diverse groups of Americans. The anguish of the white suburban mothers of MADD was shared by black inner-city mothers with AIDS.

Alcohol Abuse

Americans steadily increased their consumption of alcohol from the end of World War II until the 1980s, when drinking began to decrease. By 1987 average per capita consumption was a little more than 2.5 gallons of alcoholic beverages a year.[98] However, that amount was not evenly distributed throughout the population. One-third of the adult population abstains from alcohol consumption; one-third of people who do drink consider their consumption to be light; and the remaining third are considered moderate to heavy drinkers. The 1999 National Household Survey on Drug Abuse revealed that 45 million Americans were binge drinkers on occasion and that 12.4 million were heavy drinkers.[99]

These statistics are directly related to serious social problems. Forty-eight percent of all convicted criminals used alcohol just before committing a crime, and 64 percent of offenses against public order are alcohol related.[100] Yet substance abuse services often are not available for drinkers who are subsequently incarcerated. In 1997 substance abuse services were available at 93.8 percent of federal correctional facilities but at only 60.3 percent of state prisons, 33.5 percent of jails, and 36.6 percent of juvenile facilities.[101] Perhaps the most significant adverse consequence of alcohol consumption is highway accidents. The tragic death toll on U.S. highways not only provoked the establishment of MADD but also demands for stronger penalties for drunk drivers and public education campaigns to dissuade people from drinking while driving. This combination of motivators seemed to have a positive effect: Between 1982 and 1986 the number of inebriated drivers involved in fatal accidents dropped significantly. Even so, in 1987 approximately 23,000 people died in traffic accidents in which alcohol was implicated.[102] In 2000, Congress considered instituting a national standard of inebriation while driving.

Among the most pernicious effects of alcohol consumption is fetal alcohol syndrome (FAS), a physiological and mental deformation in infants caused by their mothers' ingestion of alcohol during pregnancy. FAS children exhibit behaviors that make them extraordinarily difficult to manage: limited attention span, slow response to stimuli, and an inability to incorporate a moral code. Because of these deficiencies, FAS children tend to have difficulty in the early socialization experiences of elementary school. Children with FAS frequently fail to understand complicated instructions; they tend to wander about, and they take the property of classmates without understanding the inappropriateness of such behavior. FAS is particularly difficult to diagnose in that its milder form, fetal alcohol effect (FAE), does not cause any physiological abnormality in facial structure. The National Institutes of Health estimated in 1990 that the incidence of FAS among children of heavy-drinking women was as high as 25 per 1,000 births and that the annual cost of coping with the disorder was almost one-third of a billion dollars.[103]

Although FAS has been recognized by pediatric researchers since 1973,[104] the syndrome was not widely known to the public until Michael Dorris's account of his adopted son's FAS condition was published in *The Broken Cord*. The husband of award-winning author Louise Erdrich, Dorris wrote poignantly about his adoption of Adam, a Native American infant. Ignorant of Adam's condition, Dorris spent years consulting with teachers, having his son tested by psychologists, and transferring Adam to special schools. It was not until he visited an Indian reservation and a special education bus discharged a group of FAS children for school that Dorris learned about FAS from a friend. Suddenly, Dorris understood that Adam was suffering from a permanent disorder brought about by his birth mother's drinking.

In *The Broken Cord,* Dorris and Erdrich wrote movingly about the consequences of FAS. Being Native Americans, their observations were as acute as they were controversial. Noting that as many as 25 percent of the children born on the Sioux Pine Ridge Reservation suffered from FAS, Dorris contended that Indian women's alcohol consumption during pregnancy represented a kind of genocide. In order to contain FAS, Dorris suggested that pregnant women who have previously given birth to FAS children and who demonstrate an inability to control their drinking be incarcerated until they give birth. Erdrich concurred, her rationale being that the health of the fetus had primacy over the mother's freedom to consume alcohol:

> Knowing what I know now, I am sure that even when I drank hard, I would rather have been incarcerated for nine months and produce a normal child than bear a human being who would, for the rest of his or her life, be imprisoned by what I had done. And for those so sure, so secure, I say the same thing I say to those who would not allow a poor woman a safe abortion and yet have not themselves gone to adoption agencies and taken in the unplaceable children, the troubled, the unwanted: If you don't agree with me, then please, go and sit beside the alcohol-affected while they try to learn how to add.[105]

The idea of restraining women during pregnancy to prevent fetal damage triggered a debate in the popular media. This controversy was fueled by two related issues. First, a rapid increase in the number of infants who tested positive for cocaine at birth raised the specter of a "bio-underclass" consisting of a generation of minority children condemned to disability by maternal substance abuse.[106] Second, arrests of women for exposing their infants to substance abuse in utero enraged feminists who had watched the cutbacks in maternal health and social services during the 1980s. "It has become trendy," columnist Ellen Goodman observed acidly, "to arrest pregnant women for endangering their fetuses."[107] By the early 1990s an unstable truce had evolved between proponents of fetal health and women's rights. Clearly, both camps favored aggressive public education and early treatment for substance abuse before, during, and after pregnancy, but lack of funding made such initiatives unlikely.

As a result, the question of how to manage substance-abusing women during pregnancy has been passed down to program managers and clinical staff. As the number of infants testing positive for substance abuse increased, opposition to social control intervention on the basis that it violated women's rights became less tenable for human service professionals. Indeed, the possibility of compulsory treatment for pregnant drug abusers became an unavoidable issue when drug abuse was associated with the transmission of AIDS.[108] Compulsory treatment, of course, runs contrary to the individual liberties guaranteed by the Constitution, because it is possible only through some commitment procedure. Proponents of compulsory treatment and preventive commitment have argued that it is the only way to protect potential victims against the uncontrolled and hazardous behavior of addicts. Critics, on the other hand, insist that effective public education and treatment would make such draconian measures unnecessary.

The issue of alcohol abuse and pregnancy was highlighted in 1996, when a 35-year-old Wisconsin woman was charged with attempted murder for going on a drinking binge shortly before giving birth. Delivered by cesarean section, the infant appeared to suffer from FAS and was placed in foster care. In prosecuting the case, the district attorney presented witnesses who testified that the mother had stated her intent to kill the fetus by drinking. By the trial date the mother had been in recovery, pleaded innocent to the murder charge, and was trying to regain custody of her child. The case broke new ground in the legal status of an unborn child and a woman's maternal responsibility during pregnancy.[109]

This dilemma has serious implications for clients of substance abuse programs as well as practitioners. Compulsory treatment is likely to deter some people from seeking treatment that they might have sought voluntarily, though perhaps at a later date. Compulsory treatment also places the practitioner in the role of social control agent, a role not conducive to building a client's trust. Compulsory treatment is likely to drive the substance abuse problem underground, further exacerbating the very problem it is intended to remedy. Without adequate investments in education and treatment, the future of substance abuse policy appears likely to be plagued by a series of such negatively reinforcing decisions.

Drug Abuse

By contrast with alcohol abuse, the prevalence of drug abuse is more difficult to ascertain because the use of controlled substances—the focus of drug abuse—is illegal. It appears that general drug abuse has begun to decline after peaking during the 1979–80 period.

In 1999 almost 15 million Americans reported use of illicit drugs, a significant decrease from the 25 million abusers estimated in 1979. Among younger Americans aged 12 to 17, drug abuse has been declining (from 11.4 percent in 1997 to 9.0 percent in 1999); that of young adults aged 18 to 25 has increased slightly (from 14.7 percent in 1997 to 18.8 percent in 1999). There is evidence that exposure to cocaine has decreased, but use of heroin has remained unchanged with an estimated 149,000 new heroin users in 1998. One-fourth of new heroin users are young and use methods other than injection.[110] Despite the reduction in the use of crack cocaine and the injection of heroin, hard drug abuse remains a serious health concern: As many as 25 percent of people who contract AIDS in this country are intravenous drug users (IDUs).[111] A haunting scenario takes shape: IDUs can no longer be thought of solely as tortured souls in the slow process of self-destruction; they have become transmitters of an epidemic that promises to be as costly as it is deadly.

The federal response to illicit drug use has been twofold, involving both interdicting the supply of illegal substances and reducing the demand through treatment and public education. Government strategies have oscillated wildly between the interdiction and prevention approaches. Before Ronald Reagan came to power, federal policy emphasized treatment and public education, assuming that these strategies would diminish demand. During the early 1970s, for example, two-thirds of federal appropriations for drug abuse were for treatment and education. A decade later, however, supply interdiction had superseded demand reduction as the prime strategy, consuming 80 percent of federal drug funds. Illegal drug use is considered in greater detail in Chapter 14.

For human service professionals an emphasis on prevention over interdiction would be a positive development in drug abuse policy. $500 million for school drug abuse prevention programs became available through the Drug Free Schools Act in the early 1990s. Applying the prevention trinity used in public health to drug abuse, it is evident that most treatment funding has been directed toward rehabilitating addicts (tertiary prevention) or treatment of abusers (secondary prevention). Limited primary prevention efforts have been field tested, but these are only now being widely adopted. Mathea Falco notes that not all have been equally effective. Life Skills Training (LST), developed in New York City, and STAR (Students Taught Awareness and Resistance), deployed in Kansas City, have been superior to DARE (Drug Abuse Resistance Education). But the real test of school prevention programs comes in poor neighborhoods where drug abuse is part of the community fabric. Programs such as the Westchester Student Assistance Program in New York, Smart Moves of the Boys and Girls Clubs, and the Seattle Social Development Project show promise; yet, upon evaluation, program graduates tend to report resistance to "soft" drugs—tobacco, alcohol, marijuana. Avoidance of "hard" drugs has not been clearly demonstrated through these programs.[112] This inability of prevention programs to produce resistance to hard drugs in high-risk neighborhoods may be due to methodological problems. High-risk youth who are susceptible to hard drug use are probably unlikely to complete a prevention program, nor are they good candidates to report hard drug usage

The federal response to illicit drug use has been twofold: cutting off the supply of illegal substances and reducing the demand through treatment and public education.

through an outcome instrument. Instead, they are likely to be casualties of the research process for the same reasons they are casualties of substance abuse. Therefore, some researchers have contended that substance abuse prevention efforts will not be successful until a much more expansive definition of primary prevention, including social, economic, and institutional factors, is adopted.[113]

In the absence of major prevention initiatives, intervention strategies focus on treatment. Generally, employees with generous health insurance have been able to gain ready admission to drug abuse treatment programs. The poor, by contrast, have found treatment available irregularly, if at all. In response to the pervasive use of alcohol and drugs, treatment facilities expanded rapidly through the early 1980s. From 1978 to 1984 the number of hospital units treating alcohol and drug abusers increased 78 percent (from 465 to 829), and the number of beds in these facilities increased 62 percent (from 16,005 to 25,981). As Table 13.3 demonstrates, more resources have been committed to treatment for alcohol abuse than for drug abuse, though the difference has been declining. Regardless, inpatient facilities provided only a fraction of treatment services to substance abusers. Perhaps half of the 5.5 million people currently using drugs would elect treatment if it were available, but that number is 1 million more than the number of available treatment slots.[114]

Although treatment lags behind demand, research continues to demonstrate the wisdom of investing in rehabilitation. Columbia University's Center on Addiction and Substance Abuse has reported that 32.3 percent of Medicaid hospitalization days were due to neonatal complications attributed to substance abuse. Cardiovascular and respiratory disorders associated with substance abuse accounted for another 31.4 percent of Medicaid hospitalization days. Significantly, when substance abuse was noted as a secondary diagnosis, the length of hospitalization doubled.[115] A comprehensive investigation of substance abuse treatment programs in California claimed savings of $7 for every $1 dollar in program costs. "Treatment is a good investment!" affirmed the California director of alcohol and drug programs. In a 1997 review of drug use treatment, SAMHSA reported that 12 months after treatment, illicit drug use dropped significantly: 48.2 percent for users of a primary drug (e.g., marijuana), 50.8 percent for crack, 54.9 percent for cocaine, and 46.6 percent for heroin.[116] As is often the case with addiction services, the subsequent question of long-term abstinence has not been thoroughly evaluated.

The extent to which substance abuse services will benefit from the 1996 legislation establishing parity of mental health services with health care remains to be seen. A major expansion of substance abuse treatment through employer insurance plans would inject substantial private resources into a service area that has been dominated by governmental programs and self-help groups. Yet because such insurance is connected to employment, it will not influence the treatment of abusers who are marginal to the labor market—those most impaired and most in need of intensive rehabilitation.

Private Practice and Mental Health Services

Mental health care has become an area in which social workers can emulate the success of psychiatrists and psychologists by establishing private practices. As a form of independent practice, private practice is influenced by the policies of the states regulating it, by professional associations, by the insurance companies that pay clinicians for their services, and managed care companies that have become established as providers of mental health services. Private social work practice in mental health has been controversial within the social work profession, as reflected in this depiction:

> In increasing numbers, social workers are flocking to psychotherapeutic pastures, hanging out their shingles to advertise themselves as psychotherapists just as quickly as licensing laws will permit. For the most part, professional associations of social workers and schools of social work are active participants in the great transformation of social work from a professional corps concerned with helping people deal with their social problems to a major platoon in the psychotherapeutic armies.[117]

Despite this kind of criticism, private practice continues to be an attractive vehicle for delivering clinical social services. In 1999, full-time social workers in private practice reported a median income of $62,500, about twenty percent higher than that of the second highest paying sector, school social work at $51,670.[118] In 2001, 23 percent of social workers

Table 13.3

1998 Treatment Episode Data

Primary Substance	1993	1994	1995	1996	1997	1998
Number Treated						
Total	1,584,033	1,635,782	1,635,963	1,601,214	1,537,143	1,564,156
Alcohol	895,523	861,108	826,037	801,538	733,300	726,800
alcohol only	542,629	506,693	477,814	458,838	413,267	411,575
alcohol + drug	351,894	354,415	348,223	342,700	320,033	315,225
Opiates	206,865	231,674	236,613	232,242	236,055	233,507
heroin	192,840	216,238	220,849	216,204	220,575	216,834
other opiates	28,050	30,872	31,528	32,076	30,960	33,346
Cocaine	277,076	293,666	272,286	256,920	230,192	233,493
smoked	201,216	217,344	202,865	190,143	169,724	170,493
non-smoked	75,860	76,322	69,421	66,777	60,405	63,002
Marijuana-hashish	111,265	139,670	170,974	192,103	198,079	208,671
Stimulants	28,907	45,167	63,217	52,893	68,048	70,618
Other drugs	21,262	21,497	20,792	18,968	17,571	19,270
Percentages						
Alcohol	56.5	52.6	50.5	50.1	47.7	46.5
alcohol	34.3	31.0	29.2	28.7	26.9	26.3
alcohol + drug	22.2	21.7	21.3	21.4	20.8	20.2
Opiates	13.1	14.2	14.5	14.5	15.4	14.9
heroin	12.2	13.2	13.5	13.5	14.3	13.9
other opiates	1.8	1.9	2.0	2.0	2.0	2.1
Cocaine	17.5	18.0	16.6	16.0	15.0	14.9
smoked	12.7	13.3	12.4	11.9	11.0	10.9
non-smoked	4.8	4.7	4.2	4.2	3.9	4.0
Marijuana-hashish	7.0	8.5	10.5	12.0	12.9	13.3
Stimulants	1.8	2.8	3.9	3.3	4.4	4.5
Other drugs	1.3	1.3	1.3	1.2	1.1	1.2

Source: 1998 Treatment Episode Data (Washington, DC: Substance Abuse and Mental Health Services Administration, 2000).

reported that their primary activity was in solo or group private practice; another 37 percent indicated they were "involved" in private practice. Of all National Association of Social Workers (NASW) members, the number working in for-profit settings increased from 19.8 percent in 1988 to 27.9 percent in 1995.[119] A more recent sub-sample of NASW members indicated that in 2000 35 percent were employed in the private, for-profit sector.[120]

For some time, many mental health services have been delivered by psychiatrists and psychologists who work predominantly out of private offices. The upsurge of social workers' interest in private practice is such that today a large portion of students entering graduate programs in social work—as many as 80 percent[121]—do so with the expressed intent of establishing a private practice. Professional schools of social work are specifically equipped to prepare graduate students for private practice. "M.S.W. programs appear to offer more to the practitioner bound for private practice than to the social worker who would prefer to work in an agency setting," concluded researchers in a study of private and agency-based social workers.[122]

The current enthusiasm for private practice can be attributed to several factors. First, private practitioners often enjoy a prestige and income that set them apart from salaried professionals.[123] In addition, private practitioners work significantly fewer hours per week compared to colleagues in public and nonprofit settings.[124] In 2002, 41 percent of social workers in private practice worked between 10 and 29 hours per week, a greater number than those working 30 hours or more, 32 percent.[125] It is not surprising that social workers, who are mostly female and usually underpaid—social work salaries are significantly less than those of nurses or teachers[126]—would see private practice as a way to increase their earnings and status. In fact, women are more likely to engage in private practice than to work in traditional social service agencies; two-thirds of private practitioners are women.[127]

Private practitioners also have a degree of autonomy that is not available to professionals who are bound by the personnel policies of traditional agencies. Srinika Jayaratne and associates found that "whereas 55 percent of the private practitioners report a high level of congruence between their expectations and their activities, only 18.3 percent of the agency practitioners do so."[128] This autonomy is important for experienced professionals who find continued supervision unnecessary or intrusive and who desire some flexibility in their work schedules to make room for other priorities. Finally, private practice allows professionals to specialize in activities at which they are best instead of having to conform to organizational requirements of the private agency or governmental bureaucracy. Again, 66.5 percent of private practitioners reported that they were able to do the things at which they excelled, whereas only 22.9 percent of agency practitioners said they could do so.[129]

The image of private practice that has emerged is one of freedom and opportunity, sans rules and regulations. This is somewhat misleading. Although private practice may involve comparatively fewer compliance requirements compared to salaried employment, it is anything but unfettered. In actuality, private practice involves many policies with which practitioners must be familiar if they are to be successful. The policies that affect private practice originate primarily from three sources: the professional community (a private entity); a government regulatory authority (a public entity); and, because of the role of managed care, corporate firms (commercial entities). This situation is complicated by the provision of service through the marketplace of a capitalist economy that traditionally discriminates against groups that do not participate fully in the labor market-minorities, women, elderly people, people with disabilities. These groups frequently lack the resources to purchase the services provided by private practitioners. For this reason, private practice is not easily reconciled with the traditional values of social work, which emphasize service to the community and to the disadvantaged. So it is paradoxical that private practice has become a popular method of social work practice, and this development remains controversial.

The private practice of social work is a relatively recent phenomenon. The National Association of Social Workers did not officially sanction this form of service delivery for its members until 1964.[130] Before that, privately practicing social workers identified themselves as psychotherapists and lay analysts. Typically, they relied on referrals from physicians and psychiatrists,[131] and after World War II they began to establish "flourishing and lucrative" practices.[132] By 1987 all 50 states regulated social workers, with the majority of states requiring a master's degree in social work (M.S.W.). However, a social work license is not automatically awarded to those holding the M.S.W. degree. Many states require candidates for licensure to have two years of post-M.S.W. experience under the supervision of a **licensed certified social worker** (LCSW) and to pass an examination. Beyond these common requirements, states vary greatly in their regulatory practices. Maryland, for example, has a three-tier system: the LCSW for M.S.W.'s who have two years of post-M.S.W. experience and who have passed an examination; the Licensed Graduate Social Worker (LGSW) for newly graduated M.S.W.'s; and the Social Work Associate (SWA) for those with baccalaureate degrees in social work.

To further complicate matters, new licensing legislation often allows candidates who have practiced professionally to become licensed without first meeting the requirements of the licensing legislation. This practice, called "grandfathering," is characteristic of new licensing legislation and, in that social work licensing is a relatively recent development in many states, there are many LCSWs in practice who would not otherwise meet the technical requirements for a license. Moreover, because some states exempt state employees from licensing requirements, many "social workers" in public welfare do not meet the licensing requirements necessary for the title of social worker. As a result, many social workers are licensed but have not met the requirements with which their colleagues must comply. Consequently, states often establish additional requirements for professionals to be eligible for vendorship. Special registries for clinical social workers may be used to identify LCSWs who are eligible for third-party payments.

Professional associations also designate practitioners who have expertise in particular areas. In social work the most common distinction is membership in the Academy of Certified Social Workers (ACSW). Requirements for the ACSW are two years of post-M.S.W. experience under the supervision of an ACSW and passage of an examination. These are similar to the requirements for the LCSW, but the two designations should not be confused. Because states have the legal authority to license professions, special distinctions established by professional associations are neither equivalent to nor a substitute for state licensure. Thus, it is common for experienced clinicians to list both LCSW and ACSW after their names as indications of professional competence. Recently the NASW (which administers the ACSW) also developed a "diplomate" designation, which identifies practitioners with skills above those required for the ACSW. Credentials such as the ACSW serve the function of distinguishing expertise among members of the professional community. But again, such credentials are determined by policies of the professional community and not by a public authority, as in the case of state licensure.[133]

Clinicians who successfully cultivate private practices stand to do quite well economically. Financial gain does not appear to be the sole motivation for social workers who enter private practice, however. In research on the motives of private social work practitioners versus social workers employed in agencies, stress reduction played an important part in the decision to go private. "Those in private practice reported fewer psychological and health strains, reported higher levels of performance, and, in general, felt better about their life circumstances," concluded researchers on private practice. "On every measure, those in private practice scored significantly better than those in agency practice."[134]

Despite the popularity of private practice, it has provoked a great deal of controversy within the professional community. There are several aspects to this controversy, not the least of which is that many practitioners who have committed themselves to helping the disadvantaged by working in voluntary and governmental sectors view the instant popularity of private practice as antithetical to everything that is "social" about social work. Donald Feldstein, head of the Federation of Jewish Philanthropies of New York, suggested that private social work practice is similar to private medical practice in that it presents "new opportunities for rip-offs by the privileged." Private practice, he maintained, was replacing social decision making with market decision making. According to Feldstein, "Social decision making is preferable to marketing human services like soap. . . . The private practice of social work is still against everything that is social about the term social work."[135] Another critic impugned the motives of social workers in private practice:

> Over 15 years ago, when I first had exposure to private practitioners, they were objects of envy, never of nonacceptance. Obviously this envy has continued. For we see more social workers developing private practices. But why all the sham? Let's be honest enough to say it's usually done for the money.[136]

Defenders of private practice emphasize the benefits of the method for practitioners and clients. Why should social workers not enjoy the same professional freedom and responsibility as other professions that use private practice extensively; for instance, law, medicine, and psychiatry? Moreover, "some clients prefer the opportunity to choose their own practitioner and a service they consider more personal and confidential."[137] Concern for the client's perceptions means that practitioners must be concerned about their image. This is evident in one privately practicing social worker's description of her office:

> It is decorated with comfortable chairs, built-in book cases, soft lighting, etc., and is arranged in such a way as to offer several different possibilities for seating. It is commensurate with most of the socio-cultural levels of my client group and provides him or her the opportunity for free expression without being overheard. . . . Dealing with only one socio-cultural client group allows me to provide physical surroundings which facilitate the client's identification with the worker.[138]

On the surface, then, private practice often provokes strong responses from welfare professionals, who perceive private practitioners as avoiding efforts by the voluntary and governmental sectors to advance social justice. On the other hand, some private practitioners believe that their work offers them an opportunity not only to enhance their status but also to provide mental health services to a middle class that the profession has neglected.

Beneath this surface issue, there are more substantive problems raised by private practice. Perhaps the most important of these is "preferential selection," the practice of selecting certain clients for service while rejecting others. In an era of specialization, professionals will refer to other providers those clients with problems that are inappropriate for their practice. An important finding of Jayaratne's research was that private practitioners do not perceive their clients in the same way that agency-based social workers do. The latter "were significantly more likely to agree with the statement that 'my personal values and those of my clients differ greatly' than those in private practice."[139] Preferential selection becomes an issue when private practitioners elect to serve less troubled clients (who are able to pay the full cost of care) while referring multi-problem clients (who are unable to pay the practitioner's fee for service directly or through insurance) to agencies of the voluntary sector. Such "creaming" of the client population places an enormous burden on public agencies, which are left to carry a disproportionate share of chronically disturbed and indigent clients. In effect, then, the public sector absorbs the losses that private practitioners would suffer if they served this population. Preferential selection has become so pronounced that researchers have facetiously identified it as a syndrome. According to Franklin Chu and Sharland Trotter, the commercialization of private practice contributes to the **YAVIS syndrome**—the tendency of clients of private practitioners to be young, attractive, verbal, intelligent, and successful. One might add W to the syndrome, because the clients also tend to be disproportionately white.[140] Consequently, clients of private practitioners are less likely to be poor, unemployed, old, and uneducated.

The Business of Private Practice

Aside from preferential selection, another set of issues relates directly to the business nature of private practice. Because private practice is a business, economic considerations figure prominently in a professional's activities. Robert Barker, an authority on private social work practice, explains how economic factors shaped a new practice he established with a colleague: "We hired a good secretary, employed interior decorators to redo our offices and waiting room. We hired an investment counselor and established retirement accounts and insurance programs. Most of all we became more serious about getting our clients to meet their financial obligations."[141]

The market nature of private practice, coupled with economic entrepreneurship, presents the possibility of questionable accounting practices, such as the creation of "uncollectible accounts," the use of "deliberate misdiagnosis," and the practice of "signing off." These practices involve income derived from third-party sources, usually health insurance. As private practitioners become dependent on insurance reimbursement, these questionable accounting practices become important for the professional community at large.

Health insurance frequently covers outpatient psychiatric care at a **usual, customary, and reasonable (UCR)** rate that is determined by the insurance companies. The UCR is what the therapist charges, not necessarily what he or she expects to collect from cash-paying clients. The practice of charging a fee higher than what is expected to be collected is termed holding an "uncollectable account," and it is frequently used with third-party fee payment arrangements. This practice is encouraged because insurance coverage rarely covers all of the practitioner's fee but leaves a certain percent to be paid by the client. For example, a social worker may have a UCR of $80 per session. The client may have insurance paying only 50 percent of the UCR, which leaves the client responsible for the remaining $40. If the client is unable to pay $40 per session but can afford $10, a clinician will bill the insurance company directly, using an assignment of benefits procedure, for $80. Meanwhile, the client pays $10 per session, as opposed to the implied obligatory contractual amount of $40. Although the therapist may collect a total of $50 per session and not the UCR of $80, it may be economical to prefer that amount over an extended period of treatment or possibly until the client can afford the full amount of the co-payment. At question here is a professional practice that is contrary to the implied contractual relationship among the client, the clinician, and the third-party payer. Yet it is in the interest of the clinician to establish this as a regular accounting procedure; the clinician depends on income from fees and may fear that the insurance company will lower the UCR if a significant number of billings (usually 50 percent) are below the customary rate.

A second questionable practice is **deliberate misdiagnosis,** an intentional error in client assessment on the part of clinicians. In a survey of clinical social workers, 70 percent of whom had engaged in private practice, Stuart Kirk and Herb Kutchins found that 87 percent of practitioners frequently or occasionally used a less stigmatizing, or "mercy," diagnosis to avoid labeling their patients. On the other hand, clinicians also frequently misdiagnose in order to collect insurance payments.

> Seventy-two percent of the respondents are aware of cases where more serious diagnoses are used to qualify for reimbursement. At least 25 percent of the respondents . . . indicated that the practices occurred frequently. Since reimbursement is rarely available for family problems, it is not surprising that 86 percent are aware of instances when diagnoses for individuals are used even though the primary problem is in the family. The majority of respondents said that this occurred frequently.[142]

Of course, such "overdiagnosis" is unethical because it places the economic benefit of the clinician before the service needs of the client. Still, overdiagnosis continues to be a prevalent practice. Kirk and Kutchins suggest that "reimbursement systems, which have become increasingly important for psychiatric treatment for the last decade, are undoubtedly a major factor in encouraging overdiagnosis."[143] The undesirable consequences of a reimbursement-driven diagnosis system are multiple. First, of course, is the possibility that clients will be done harm, particularly if confidentiality is breached and the diagnosis becomes known to others outside the therapeutic relationship. Second, if the prevalence of severe mental disorders is overreported, public officials may make errors in program planning as a result, concluding that mental disorders are worse than is actually the case. Third, and perhaps most important, overdiagnosis violates the "professionals' obligation to their profession to use their knowledge and skill in an ethical manner."[144] To be sure, individual digressions can be reported to professional and governmental bodies for investigation; but a greater problem exists for practitioners as a whole. Widespread misdiagnosis violates the social contract between the professional community and the state, and thus threatens to "corrupt the helping professions."[145] For these reasons, ethical problems associated with the relationship between diagnosis and reimbursement are of great concern to the professional community.[146]

Finally, there is the practice of signing off. Signing off has become important because some insurance covers only services provided by psychiatrists or psychologists. In other instances, insurance will reimburse at a higher rate when the services are provided by a psychiatrist or psychologist than when they are rendered by a social worker. The sign-off practice is one in which, in order to maximize reimbursement, the psychiatrist or psychologist signs the insurance claim even though the services were provided by a social worker. In some instances psychiatrists and psychologists may recruit social workers, paying them half the fees charged to insurance companies and pocketing the difference. Signing off is a type of fee splitting, and it is "unethical because it allows practitioners to refer clients not to the professional most suitable for the client's needs, but to the person who pays the highest fee."[147]

In a community in which many private practitioners compete for a limited number of paying clients, aggressive business practices, such as those above, are likely to raise questions about the ultimate concern of practitioners—whether it is the client's welfare or the clinician's income. Although the question is not ordinarily couched in such crude terms, the behavior of private practitioners may not be lost on the client population. Because clients usually seek services voluntarily, their impressions of practitioners are important; negative perceptions will eventually hurt practitioners as their clients seek services elsewhere. When unfavorable impressions emerge as a result of the practices described, practitioners will be prudent to take corrective action. Although the ethical code of the professional community can be a source for such action, much remains at the discretion of the individual practitioner.

Private practice is literally *private,* and practitioners enjoy "substantial discretion in conducting their activities."[148] Economic and other considerations may encourage private practitioners to engage in unethical or questionable practices. In such instances, other practitioners are obliged to report allegations of violations to the state licensing board or the professional association. Ultimately, it is in the interest of the professional community to address questionable practices of practitioners, and this includes the unethical business practices of private practitioners. When the media report that "routine falsification of insurance billings and other peculiarities of the mental health professions have caused acute anxiety among insurance companies . . . [who] now think they have little control over what they are paying for," more government regulation is probably not far behind.[149] In other instances the consequences are acutely embarrassing for the professional community, as when a leading proponent of third-party reimbursement for social workers in Kentucky was found guilty of insurance fraud and ordered to return $37,000 to Blue Cross–Blue Shield.[150]

The Future of the Private Sector

In response to the limitations imposed by traditional practice settings, many human service professionals have turned to private practice as a way of securing their economic and professional objectives. Private practice gives program administrators a chance to maintain their direct service skills, educators the opportunity to continue contact with clients, and clinicians with families the freedom to combine professional practice and attention to family life. More important, private practice may prove an adjunct to agency activities. "By fostering part-time practice," researchers have noted, "the profession can keep its main focus on agency services where there is a commitment to serve persons without regard to their ability to pay and where there can be a basis for social action and reform."[151]

As the growth of managed care illustrates, much of private practice is a result of larger social forces. Ellen Dunbar, former-executive director of the California chapter of NASW, observed that "The major overriding trend that engulfs all others is that social work along with other service professions is becoming more commercial . . . [and] more an integral part of the free enterprise system."[152] In fact, the commercialization of social work attracted wide attention as the profession became more immersed in private practice. "There is concern," reported *Newsweek,* "that too many social workers are turning their backs on their traditional casework among the poor to practice therapy." *Newsweek* wondered at the consequences of "an apparent middle-class therapy explosion at the expense of public welfare and grassroots service."[153] How social work will reconcile its commitment to social justice with the new opportunities presented by private practice remains a central question before the professional community.

The interest in alternative methods of service delivery represents an implicit criticism of traditional ways in which social agencies provide services. Conventional contexts of direct practice evidence several faults. First, traditional agencies place constraints on employee discretion and professional autonomy. Second, rigid agency policies make few allowances for the demands of an employee's family life and community involvements. Third, the demands of increasing caseloads compounded by diminishing resources make traditional agencies a less desirable setting in which to practice. Although nonprofit agencies have been superior to governmental programs in the quality of services provided, these traditional auspices of service delivery are beginning to merge. Consequently, social work in smaller, voluntary agencies is not very different from the "proletarianized" work in larger, public agencies.[154] To the extent that traditional agencies become less desirable as contexts in which to practice, innovative models of service delivery surface.

As researchers on private practice have noted, rather than criticizing professionals who have opted for the private sector, the social work community should make it a priority to reform the means of service provision through traditional agencies. "The goal should be to make agency practice good for the health and well-being of the practitioner, because the ultimate beneficiary would be the client."[155] Stan Taubman, who has held direct practice and administrative positions and who couples county employment with private practice, states the matter succinctly: "Private practice isn't keeping social workers out of public services. Public services are."[156]

One service delivery innovation has been employee assistance plans (EAPs). Since the 1970s, social workers have been involved in EAPs that provide a range of services to workers, a population often neglected by traditional welfare programs.[157] By the late 1980s, occupational social welfare had become a popular specialization within social work, with graduate schools offering special curricula on the subject, a national conference inaugurated for specialists in the field, and a special issue of Social Work dedicated to it.[158] Although studies of EAPs are scarce,[159] there is evidence that occupational social work is likely to expand, particularly when located within the corporation. In a modest study of 23 "private-sector, management-sponsored" EAPs, Shulamith Straussner found that in-house programs demonstrated notable advantages over those contracted out. For example, EAPs located within the corporation cost one-third as much as contracted-out services. In-house EAPs proved adaptable to management priorities, developing "short-term programs to deal with company reorganization or retrenchment, special health concerns . . . [and] other organizational needs." Significantly, union representatives approved in-house EAPs twice as frequently as they did contracted-out programs.[160] These findings suggest that EAPs that are managed by employers are perceived by management and unions as superior to services provided by an external agency. If corporate executives and labor leaders develop personnel policies consistent with these findings, welfare professionals will find the business community a hospitable setting in which to practice. In that event, occupational social work within the corporation may become as prevalent an auspice of practice as the voluntary and governmental sectors are.

Another service delivery innovation is employee ownership. Curiously, human service professionals have frequently advocated employee ownership as a method for empowering clients, yet fail to see comparable benefits for themselves. For example, Cooperative Home Care Associates (CHCA) of New York City has been co-owned by some 170 employees since its inception in 1985. CHCA offers above-average wages as well as health and vacation benefits and has, as a result, served as a vehicle out of poverty for many workers who had been on public assistance.[161]

An as yet unexplored innovation for human service professionals is the employee stock option plan (ESOP). Through ESOPs workers gain ownership of a firm by gradually acquiring stock, the acquisition of which is granted certain tax advantages. By 1990 ESOPs had been used to leverage the transfer of 11,000 companies to 12 million employees. Workers had used ESOPs to purchase wholly or in part several large corporations, such as J.C. Penney, Kroger's, Avis, and United Airlines.[162] Inexplicably, human service professionals had not used ESOPs to gain control over the organizations that employ them. In part this can be explained by the fact that the traditional auspices of practice have been the nonprofit and governmental sectors. It may seem implausible for Department of Social Service employees to seek ownership of the local welfare department or for professionals hired by the local Family Service Agency to acquire that organization. Nevertheless, recent trends in privatization make employee ownership more probable.

In the absence of employee ownership alternatives, some private practitioners have undertaken competitive strategies vis-à-vis managed care corporations. In New York, 230 therapists belonging to the American Mental Health Alliance won a contract to serve 370,000 union members; Access Behavioral Care, Inc., a therapist-owned practice in Philadelphia, has served 3 million people since its creation in 1995; and Psych Management Inc., a proprietary firm of psychiatrists, has served more than 100,000 clients through Blue Cross–Blue Shield.[163] In other instances, private clinicians have reacted defensively. The Virginia, California, New Jersey, and District of Columbia chapters of the American Psychological Association have sued HMOs for restricting the number of therapeutic sessions, limiting out-of-network referrals, and purging provider lists.[164] It remains to be seen if social workers will join psychologists in challenging the prerogatives of managed care firms.

If an issue within social work is the defection of private practitioners from their broader social responsibilities, licensing requirements could be altered to encourage involvement in community activities. Professionals are often required to demonstrate they are current with practice developments by acquiring Continuing Education Units (CEUs) for licensing. Following this logic, CEU requirements could be augmented to require professionals to demonstrate a minimal number of community service hours in order to obtain and keep a license. If mental health professionals—psychiatrists, psychologists, and social workers—were required to volunteer 100 hours annually with a nonprofit organization as a condition of licensing, a significant volume of mental health care would be available to the mentally ill.

Conclusion

Mental health and substance abuse policies have been complex in part because they have addressed behaviors that are not well understood. Compounding this have been major policy disputes that have made it more difficult to reach a consensus about optimal programming. Mental health care has been compromised by a fundamental disconnect in American social welfare policy: should responsibility for the aberrant rest with the federal government or the states? Since the 1980s, mental health care has been devolved to the states; yet, the states have been unwilling to pick up the costs for mental health services. Moreover, the aftermath of deinstitutionalization is still evident in the prevalence of homelessness and substance abuse. Substance abuse services have been compromised by a different disconnect: should the focus be on treatment or interdiction? Since the advent of the war on drugs, the emphasis has been on law enforcement, resulting in under-investment in treatment. That so many human service professionals work in mental health and substance abuse might position them well to address these problems, except many have effectively opted out for private practice.

Discussion Questions

1. Click on the "For Students" link on the policyAmerica website and identify a mental health or substance abuse policy that is of interest to you. Are the provisions of the policy adequate? What could be done to make services more effective?
2. In the early 1980s funding for community mental health centers (CMHCs) was converted to mental health block grants. To what extent did your community develop CMHCs? What has happened to them since the 1980s? What priorities have been established through the mental health block grant system? How has this changed mental health services in your community?
3. The misuse of psychoactive medication has been implicated in several undesirable consequences. Has tardive dyskinesia become a significant problem among mental health patients in your community? If so, what is being done to prevent it? Are more or fewer mental patients going through the "revolving door"?
4. The effects of substance abuse on innocent people present difficult policy dilemmas for decision makers. What policies could be put in place to prevent the birth of infants with FAS or AIDS? How could the rights of mothers be protected? What should be the role of human service professionals in such cases?
5. Prevention and treatment of substance abuse vary from locality to locality. What has your community done to dissuade young people from substance abuse? Have these initiatives been successful? According to what indicators?
6. What resources has your community committed to dealing with substance abuse? Have these resources been adequate? Which organizations support or oppose increasing treatment for substance abuse?
7. How many of the students in your social work program are planning on establishing themselves as private practitioners? To what extent are social workers in your community engaged in private practice? How has managed care attenuated their economic viability?

Notes

1. Jean Quam, "Dorothea Dix," *Encyclopedia of Social Work*, 18th ed. (Silver Spring, MD: NASW, 1987), p. 921.
2. Michael Lesy, *Wisconsin Death Trip* (New York: Pantheon, 1973), p. 33.
3. Ibid.
4. Michael Katz, *In the Shadow of the Poorhouse* (New York: Basic Books, 1986), p. 102.
5. Stephen Gould, "Carrie Buck's Daughter," *Natural History* (July 1984), pp. 85–92.
6. Quoted in Edwin Black, *War against the Weak* (New York: Four Walls Eight Windows, 2003), p. 110.
7. Black, *War against the Weak,* p. 115.
8. Ibid., p. 121.
9. Ibid., p. 122.
10. Walter Trattner, *From Poor Law to Welfare State* (New York: Free Press, 1974), p. 175.
11. Joint Commission on Mental Illness and Health, *Action for Mental Health* (New York: Basic Books, 1961).
12. David Mechanic, *Mental Health and Social Policy* (Englewood Cliffs, NJ: Prentice-Hall, 1969), pp. 59–60.
13. Henry Foley, *Community Mental Health Legislation* (Lexington, MA: D. C. Heath, 1975), pp. 13–14.
14. Ibid., pp. 39, 40.
15. Bernard Bloom, *Community Mental Health* (Monterey, CA: Brooks/Cole, 1977), pp. 74–75.
16. National Institute of Mental Health, *Community Mental Health Center Program Operating Handbook* (Washington, DC: U.S. Department of Health, Education, and Welfare, 1971), pp. 2–6.
17. Foley, Community Mental Health Legislation, p. 126.

18. The description of CMHCs is derived from the *Community Mental Health Centers Policy and Standards Manual,* 1988; see *Community Mental Health Centers Program Operating Handbook,* 1989.
19. Bloom, *Community Mental Health,* pp. 46–56.
20. U.S. Census Bureau, *Statistical Abstract of the United States,* 108th ed. (Washington, DC: U.S. Government Printing Office, 1987), p. 104.
21. Andrew Scull, *Decarceration* (Englewood Cliffs, NJ: Prentice-Hall, 1977), p. 71.
22. Ibid., p. 69.
23. Donald Stedman, "Politics, Political Structures, and Advocacy Activities." In James Paul, Donald Stedman, and G. Ronald Neufeld (eds.), *Deinstitutionalization* (Syracuse, NY: Syracuse University Press, 1977), p. 57.
24. E. Fuller Torrey and Mary T. Zdanowicz, "Deinstitutionalization Hasn't Worked," *Washington Post* (July 9, 1999), p. A29.
25. Alan Stone, *Law, Psychiatry, and Morality* (Washington, DC: American Psychiatry Press, 1984), pp. 116, 117.
26. Jean Isaac Rael, "'Right' to Madness: a Cruel Hoax," *Los Angeles Times* (December 14, 1990), p. E5.
27. Uri Aviram, "Community Care of the Seriously Mentally Ill," *Community Mental Health Journal* 26, no. 1 (February 1990), pp. 23–31.
28. Peter Koenig, "The Problem That Can't Be Tranquilized," *New York Times Magazine,* (May 21, 1978), p. 15.
29. Clifford Levy, "Mentally Ill and Locked Up in New York Nursing Homes," *New York Times* (October 6, 2002), p. A1.
30. Clifford Levy, "For Mentally Ill, Death and Misery," *New York Times* (April 28, 2002), pp. 1, 34.
31. Katherine Boo, "Forest Haven Is Gone, But the Agony Remains," *Washington Post* (March 14, 1999); "Residents Languish; Profiteers Flourish," *Washington Post* (March 15, 1999).
32. Katherine Boo, "U.S. Probes D.C. Group Homes," *Washington Post* (May 4, 1999); Marcia Greene and Lena Sun, "Deaths Put DC Group Home Firm under Scrutiny," *Washington Post* (May 18, 2000).
33. Ellen Bassuk and Samuel Gerson, "Deinstitutionalization and Mental Health Services," *Scientific American* 238, no. 2 (February 1978), p. 18.
34. Steven Segal, "Deinstitutionalization," *Encyclopedia of Social Work,* 18th ed. (Silver Spring, MD: NASW, 1987), p. 378.
35. Per September 22, 1988, conversation with Joanne Atay, research associate, author of *Division of Biometry and Applied Sciences, Additions and Resident Patients at End of Year, State and County Mental Hospitals, by Diagnosis and State* (Rockville, MD: National Institute of Mental Health, 1988).
36. Steven Segal, "Deinstitutionalization," *Encyclopedia of Social Work,* 19th ed. (Washington, DC: NASW, 1995), p. 706.
37. "State Blamed for 3 Deaths at Mental Hospitals," *Los Angeles Times* (October 2, 1991), p. A4.
38. Eric Weiss, "Mental Patients' Deaths Probed," *Washington Post* (October 11, 1998), p. A28
39. Cited in Glenn Yank, David Hargrove, and King Davis, "Toward the Financial Integration of Public Mental Health Services," *Community Mental Health Journal* 8, no. 2 (April 1992), p. 99.
40. Joseph Sacks, John Phillips, and Gordon Cappelletty, "Characteristics of the Homeless Mentally Disordered Population in Fresno County," *Community Mental Health Journal,* (Summer 1987), p. 114.
41. "Survey of Homeless Shows Mental Illness and Addiction," *New York Times* (September 10, 1989), p. 16
42. "Homeless in America: A Statistical Profile," *The New York Times* (December 12, 1999), p. WK3.
43. Hector Tobar, "Mentally Ill Turn to Crime in a Painful Call for Help," *Los Angeles Times* (August 26, 1991), p. A1
44. Edward Walsh, "16% of State, Local Inmates Found Mentally Ill," *Washington Post* (July 12, 1999), p. A6
45. Kari Lydersen, "For Jailed Mentally Ill, a Way Out," *Washington Post* (June 28, 2000), p. A3.
46. Sally Satel, "Out of the Asylum, into the Cell," *New York Times* (November 1, 2003), p. A29.
47. Benjamin Wieser, "My Name Is Not Robert," *New York Times Magazine* (August 6, 2000), p. 34.
48. "Mental Health Courts," National Mental Health Association. Retrieved October 7, 2004, from www.nmha.org
49. "Survey of Mental Health Courts," NAMI. Retrieved October 7, 2004, from http://nami.org
50. "Mental Health Courts," Bureau of Justice Assistance. Retrieved October 7, 2004, from www.ojp.usdg:gov/BJA
51. A. Anthony Arce and Michael Vergare, "Homelessness, the Chronic Mentally Ill and Community Mental Health Centers," *Community Mental Health Journal* (Winter 1987), p. 9.
52. Judith Larsen, "Community Mental Health Services in Transition," *Community Mental Health Journal* (Winter 1987), pp. 19, 20.
53. Trevor Hadley and Dennis Chulhane, "The Status of Community Mental Health Centers Ten Years into Block Grant Financing," *Community Mental Health Journal* (April 1993), p. 96.
54. Larsen, "Community Mental Health Services in Transition," p. 22.
55. Donald Woolson, "Policy Makes Short Shrift of Mentally Ill," *Los Angeles Times* (November 2, 1986), p. C4.
56. Hadley and Chulhane, "The Status of Community Mental Health Centers," p. 97.
57. Ronald Manderscheid and Mary Sonnenschein (eds.), *Mental Health, United States, 1994* (Rockville, MD, Substance Abuse and Mental Health Administration, 1994), pp. 37, 38.

58. Community for Creative Non-Violence, *Homelessness in America* (Washington, DC: CCNV, 1987).
59. Josh Barbanel, "Homeless Woman to Be Released after Being Forcibly Hospitalized," *New York Times* (January 19, 1988), p. 8.
60. Charles Krauthammer, "How to Save the Homeless Mentally Ill," *The New Republic*, (February 8, 1988), p. 23.
61. Paul Stavis, "Treatment by Cooperation," *Washington Post* (August 19, 1999), p. A21.
62. "Developments in Mental Disability Law: 1986," *Clearinghouse Review* 20 (January 20, 1987), p. 1148. Quoted in Ruta Wilk, "Involuntary Outpatient Commitment of the Mentally Ill," *Social Work* (March–April 1988), p. 133.
63. Michael Winerip, "Bedlam in the Streets," *New York Times Magazine* (May 23, 1999).
64. Stavis, "Treatment by Cooperation," p. A21.
65. "Developments in Mental Disability Law: 1986," *Clearinghouse Review* (October 1988), p. 43; and Wilk, "Involuntary Outpatient Commitment," p. 134.
66. Wilk, "Involuntary Outpatient Commitment," p. 136.
67. See, for example, Thomas Szasz, *The Myth of Mental Illness* (New York: Harper and Row, 1961); David Ingleby (ed.), *Critical Psychiatry: The Politics of Mental Health* (New York: Pantheon, 1980).
68. *Physician's Desk Reference* (Oradell, NJ: Medical Economics Company, 1986), p. 2014.
69. Gardiner Harris, "Drug Makers Resist State Efforts to Cut Medicaid Expenses," *New York Times* (December 18, 2003), p. A1.
70. Glenn Yank, David Hargrove, and King Davis, "Toward the Financial Integration of Public Mental Health Services," *Community Mental Health Journal* 28, no. 2 (April 1992), pp. 2–12.
71. Jon Christianson and Muriel Linehan, "Capitated Payments for Mental Health Care: The Rhode Island Programs," *Community Mental Health Journal* 25, no. 2 (Summer 1989), p. 122
72. A. P. Schinnar, A. B. Rothbard, and T. R. Hadley, "Opportunities and Risks in Philadelphia's Capitation Financing of Public Psychiatric Services," *Community Mental Health Journal* 25, no. 4 (Winter 1989), p. 256
73. Ibid., pp. 257–258.
74. Phyllis Marshall, "The Mental Health HMO: Capitation Funding for the Chronically Mentally Ill. Why an HMO?" *Community Mental Health Journal* 28, no. 2 (April 1992), pp. 9–14.
75. R. Thomas Riggs, "HMOs and the Seriously Mentally Ill—A View from the Trenches," *Community Mental Health Journal* 32, no. 3 (June 1966), p. 214
76. Patricia Backlar, "Managed Mental Health Care: Conflicts of Interest in the Provider/Client Relationship," *Community Mental Health Journal*, 32, no. 2 (April 1996), p. 104
77. Kari Lydersen, "For Jailed Mentally Ill, a Way Out," *Washington Post* (June 28, 2000), p. A3.
78. Janenne Allen and Richard Boettcher, "Passing a Mental Health Levy," *Journal of Community Practice* 7, no. 3 (2000).
79. Charles Rapp and Ronna Chamberlain, "Case Management Services for the Chronically Mentally Ill," *Social Work* (September–October 1985), p. 417
80. David Stoesz, "Human Service Corporations: New Opportunities for Administration in Social Work," *Administration in Social Work* (Fall 1993), pp. 8–16.
81. Barry Meier, "A Price Too High?" *New York Times* (February 16, 2000), p. C1.
82. T. M. Luhrman, *Of Two Minds: The Growing Disorder in American Psychiatry* (New York: Knopf, 2000).
83. Gardiner Harris, "Antidepressants Seen as Effective for Adolescents," *New York Times* (June 2, 2004), p. A1.
84. Shankar Vedantam, "FDA Links Antidepressants, Youth Suicide Risk," *Washington Post* (February 3, 2004), p. A1.
85. Shankar Vedantam, "Antidepressant Makers Withhold Data on Children," *Washington Post* (January 29, 2003), p. A1.
86. Gardiner Harris, "Expert Kept from Speaking at Antidepressant Hearing," *New York Times* (April 16, 2004), p. A16.
87. Milt Freudenheim, "Behavior Drugs Lead in Sales for Children," *New York Times* (May 17, 2004), p. C9.
88. Charles Hall, "What Price Peace of Mind?" *Washington Post* (April 23, 1996), p. A7.
89. Agnes Hatfield, "The National Alliance for the Mentally Ill: A Decade Later," *Community Mental Health Journal* 27, no. 2 (April 1991), pp. 89–106.
90. Robert Samuelson, "Mental Health's Gray Areas," *Washington Post Weekly* (June 10–16, 1996), p. 5
91. Helen Dewar and Judith Havemann, "Conferees Expand Insurance for New Mothers, Mentally Ill," *Washington Post* (September 20, 1996), p. A1
92. Stuart Auerbach, "The Cost of Increased Coverage," *Washington Post Weekly* (September 30–October 6, 1996), p. 19.
93. "Mental Health Parity," (Washington, DC: General Accounting Office, May 10, 2000).
94. Shankar Vedantam, "Commission Finds Disarray in Mental Health Programs," *Washington Post* (July 23, 2003), p. A24.
95. Mathea Falco, *The Making of a Drug-Free America* (New York: Times Books, 1992), p. 24.
96. Mathea Falco, *Winning the Drug War* (New York: Priority Press, 1989), pp. 19–20.
97. David Simon and Edward Burns, *The Corner: A Year in the Life of an Inner-City Neighborhood* (New York: Broadway Books, 2000).
98. *Alcohol and Health: Seventh Special Report to the U.S. Congress* (Washington, DC: U.S. Government Printing Office, 1990), p. 14.
99. "1999 National Household Survey on Drug Abuse," (Washington, DC: SAMHSA, 2000).

100. *Alcohol and Health:Sixth Special Report to the U.S. Congress* (Washington DC: Department of Health and Human Service, 1987), p. 13.
101. *1997 Survey of Correctional Facilities* (Washington, DC: SAMHSA, 1997).
102. *Alcohol and Health, Seventh Special Report to the U.S. Congress,* p. 165.
103. Ibid., pp. 140, 139.
104. Ibid., p. 139.
105. Louise Erdrich, "Foreword" to Michael Dorris, *The Broken Cord* (New York: Harper and Row, 1989), p. xviii.
106. Charles Krauthammer, "The Horror of Addicted Newborns," *San Diego Tribune* (July 31, 1992), p. B7.
107. Ellen Goodman, "Community Begs Off, But Prosecutes Mom," *Los Angeles Times* (February 9, 1992), p. B9.
108. Department of Health and Human Services, *Compulsory Treatment of Drug Abuse* (Washington, DC: U.S. Government Printing Office, 1989).
109. Edward Walsh, "In Case Against Alcoholic Mother, Underlying Issue Is Fetal Rights," *Washington Post* (October 7, 1996), p. A4.
110. "1999 National Household Survey on Drug Abuse."
111. Carl Leukefeld and Frank Tims, "An Introduction to Compulsory Treatment for Drug Abuse: Clinical Practice and Research," in *Compulsory Treatment of Drug Abuse: Research and Clinical Practice* (Rockville MD: Department of Health and Human Services, 1988), p. 2.
112. Falco, *The Making of a Drug-Free America,* Chapters 3 and 4.
113. Derek Mason, Mark Lusk, and Michael Gintzler, "Beyond Ideology in Drug Policy: The Primary Prevention Model," *Journal of Drug Issues* 22, no. 4 (Fall 1992), pp. 81–89
114. Barry Bearak, "Road to Detox: Do Not Enter," *Los Angeles Times* (September 30, 1992), p. A1.
115. Center on Addiction and Substance Abuse, *The Cost of Substance Abuse to America's Health Care System* (New York: Center on Addiction and Substance Abuse, 1993), pp. 33, 42.
116. *National Treatment Improvement Evaluation Study* (Washington, DC: SAMHSA, 1997).
117. Harry Specht and Mark Courtney, *Unfaithful Angels* (New York: Free Press, 1994), p. 8.
118. "Social Work Income 2," (Washington, DC: National Association of Social Workers, 2002).
119. Margaret Gibelman, *Who We Are: A Second Look,* 2nd ed. (Washington, DC: NASW Press, 1996), p. 69.
120. National Association of Social Workers, "Data on Practice Auspice" (Washington, DC: NASW, August 2000)
121. Philip Brown and Robert Barker, "Confronting the Threat of Private Practice," *Journal of Social Work Education* 31, no. 1 (Winter 1995), p. 106.
122. Srinika Jayaratne, Kristine Siefert, and Wayne Chess, "Private and Agency Practitioners: Some Data and Observations," *Social Service Review* 62 (June 1988), p. 331.
123. Margaret Gibelman and Philip Schervish, *What We Earn: 1993 NASW Salary Survey* (Washington, DC: NASW, 1993), pp. 25, 27.
124. Diane Vinokur-Kaplan, Srinika Jayaratne, and Wayne Chess, "Job Satisfaction and Retention of Social Workers in Public Agencies, Non-Profit Agencies and Private Practice," *Administration in Social Work* 18, no. 3 (1994), p. 103.
125. Practice Research Network, Private Practice (Washington, DC: National Association of Social Workers, 2003).
126. Gibelman, *What We Earn,* p. 32.
127. Vinokur-Kaplan et al., "Job Satisfaction," p. 103.
128. Ibid., p. 329.
129. Ibid.
130. Although Mark Courtney notes that a de facto private practice can be identified much earlier: "Psychiatric Social Workers and the Early Days of Private Practice," *Social Service Review* (June 1992), pp. 95–105.
131. M. A. Golton, "Private Practice in Social Work," *Encyclopedia of Social Work* (Silver Spring, MD: NASW, 1973), p. 949.
132. Walter Trattner, *From Poor Law to Welfare State* (New York: Free Press, 1974), p. 250.
133. For details on state licensure and professional certification, see Robert Barker, *The Business of Psychotherapy* (New York: Columbia University Press, 1982).
134. Srinika Jayaratne, Mary Lou Davis Sacks, and Wayne Chess, "Private Practice May Be Good for Your Health and Well-Being," *Social Work* 36 (May 1991), pp. 226–227.
135. Donald Feldstein, "Debate on Private Practice," *Social Work* 22, no. 3 (1977), p. 3.
136. Ibid., p. 4.
137. Patricia Kelly and Paul Alexander, "Part-Time Private Practice: Practical and Ethical Considerations," *Social Work* 30, no. 3 (May–June 1985), p. 255.
138. N. T. Edwards, "The Survival of Structure and Function in Private Practice," *Journal of the Otto Rank Association* 13 (1979), pp. 12, 15.
139. Jayaratne et al., "Private Practice," *Social Work* 36 (May 1991), pp. 228–229.
140. Franklin Chu and Sharland Trotter, *The Madness Establishment* (New York: Grossman, 1974), p. 61.
141. Robert Barker, *The Business of Psychotherapy* (New York: Columbia University Press, 1982), p. xi.
142. Stuart Kirk and Herb Kutchins, "Deliberate Misdiagnosis in Mental Health Practice," p. 230.
143. Ibid., p. 234.
144. Ibid., pp. 232, 234–235.
145. Ibid., p. 235.

146. Kimberly Strom, "Reimbursement Demands and Treatment Decisions: A Growing Dilemma for Social Workers," *Social Work* 37 (September 1992), p. 18.
147. Robert Barker, *Social Work in Private Practice* (Silver Spring, MD: NASW, 1984), p. 113.
148. Kirk and Kutchins, "Deliberate Misdiagnosis in Mental Health Practice," p. 232.
149. Kathy Sawyer, "Insuring the Bureaucracy's Mental Health," *Washington Post* (April 10, 1979), p. A8.
150. "Signing Off Fraud Charge Warns Kentucky Clinicians," *NASW News* 32, no. 6 (June 1987), p. 1.
151. Kelley and Alexander, "Part-Time Private Practice," p. 254.
152. Ellen Dunbar, "Future of Social Work," *NASW California News* 13, no. 18 (May 1987), p. 3.
153. David Gelman, "Growing Pains for the Shrinks," *Newsweek* (December 14, 1987), p. 71.
154. Michael Fabricant and Steven Burghardt, *The Welfare State Crisis and the Transformation of Social Service Work* (Armonk, NY: M.E. Sharpe, 1992).
155. Jayaratne, Davis Sacks, and Chess, "Private Practice May Be Good for Your Health," p. 229.
156. Stan Taubman, "Private Practice! Oh No!" *NASW California News* (March 1991), p. 8.
157. See Sheila Akabas, Paul Kurzman, and Norman Kolben (eds.), *Labor and Industrial Settings: Sites for Social Work Practice* (New York: Council on Social Work Education, 1979); Martha Ozawa, "Development of Social Services in Industry: Why and How?" *Social Work* 25 (November 1980), pp. 86–93; and Dale Masi, *Human Services in Industry* (Lexington, MA: D. C. Heath, 1982).
158. "Social Work in Industrial Settings," *Social Work* 33 (January–February 1988), p. 65.
159. But see J. Decker, R. Starrett, and J. Redhorse, "Evaluating the Cost-Effectiveness of Employee Assistance Programs," *Social Work* 31 (September–October 1986), p. 83.
160. Shulamith Straussner, "Comparison of In-House and Contracted-Out Employee Assistance Programs," *Social Work* 33 (January–February 1988), p. 53.
161. Francis Lappe and P. M. Dubois, *The Quickening of America: Rebuilding Our Nation, Remaking Our Lives* (San Francisco: Jossey Bass, 1994).
162. Ibid.
163. Nancy Jeffrey, "A New Balancing Act for Psychotherapy," *Wall Street Journal* (January 5, 1998).
164. Lucette Lagnado and Nancy Jeffrey, "Psychologists Sue over Managed Care," *Wall Street Journal* (December 11, 1998).

C H A P T E R 14

Criminal Justice

This chapter provides an overview of crime and corrections in the United States, beginning with the history of U.S. criminal justice. Chapter sections explore the roles of various governmental jurisdictions in criminal justice; recent data on crime and justice expenditures; important developments and issues that include juvenile justice, the underclass and crime, the War on Drugs, and the "new penology"; and the future of criminal justice in this country.

All societies respond to norm-defying behavior through sanctions, though there is considerable variation among the penalties societies apply to specific behaviors. In Western cultures irrational deviance is usually understood as a mental health matter, whereas anormative behavior on the part of a rational actor falls under the purview of law enforcement. In either case, deviance is of interest to human service professionals, because clients often engage in anormative activity. Deviance is also an issue of social justice, because poor people and minorities of color are disproportionately represented among those incarcerated in mental or correctional institutions.

History of U.S. Criminal Justice

Modern criminal justice in the United States can be traced to the faith in social science that originated in the West in the eighteenth century. Before the advent of classical criminology, justice was predicated on vengeance: Illegal acts brought the wrath of authority on the deviant. In premodern societies in which deviance was understood to be a product of evil influences, vicious and barbaric methods were justified as ways to excise Satan or to maintain archaic social structures. Thus, mutilation, torture, and capital punishment were often employed, sometimes in grotesque public displays, in order to rid society of malevolent influences.

Modern criminology dates from the Enlightenment of the eighteenth century and its notion that humankind was capable of producing the methods for its own perfectibility. The radical jurist and philosopher Jeremy Bentham (1748–1832) contended that scientific methods could be the vehicle for "the rational improvement of the condition of men." Accordingly, Bentham successfully advocated a series of reform laws in Great Britain, including several pertinent to penal institutions.[1] In the United States, Cesare Beccaria applied Bentham's utilitarian philosophy to corrections, arguing that crime could be measured in its severity, that prevention was more important than punishment, that the purpose of punishment was deterrence (not revenge), and that incarceration should segregate prisoners so as not to exacerbate lawlessness.[2] Thus, liberal, humanistic values in criminal justice can be traced to the earliest thinkers in criminology.

Nevertheless, the early American colonists had imported traditional European thinking about crime and its control. Jails were a fixture of all settlements of any size, and justice was often swift and uncompromising. In 1776, in response to the dungeons that typified colonial America, the Quakers established the Philadelphia Society for Alleviating the Miseries of Public Prisons.[3] During the following decades, institutional reformers such as Dorothea Dix sought to make jails and almshouses more humane. Unfortunately, the reformer's accomplishments were often subverted. An influx of immigrants, many of whom were unable to adjust to the American experience, became incarcerated in mental and correctional institutions. An American ethos of rugged individualism left little room for compassion, particularly when adults were concerned. In 1854, President Franklin Pierce vetoed legislation that would have involved the federal government in institutional care for people with mental illness, effectively leaving institutional control of deviants in the hands of the states.

Midway through the nineteenth century, an unlikely pioneer in U.S. corrections emerged. In 1841 a Boston shoemaker, John Augustus, agreed to supervise petty criminals, post bail, and report to the courts on his progress with the offenders' rehabilitation. The services provided by Augustus were less expensive than prison, and many of his charges seemed to benefit from rehabilitation—all the more so because Augustus used his own money. Thus, a modest shoemaker began what was to become a nationwide system of probation.[4]

Some early criminologists sought more direct applications of emerging sciences to the study of crime. The Italian psychiatrist Cesare Lombroso, for example, proposed the existence of a "criminal type," a construct of inferior intelligence, exaggerated physical features, and a taste for amoral activities, including tattooing. The idea that a criminal could be physiologically identifiable and criminal behavior genetically transmitted has preoccupied some criminologists ever since Lombroso. For example, in 1913

Charles Goring studied English convicts, and during the 1920s Earnest Hooton evaluated American criminals; both concluded that prisoners were "organically inferior" to their law-abiding compatriots.

The notion of a genetic origin of deviant behavior was popularized by the eugenics movement before World War I. Proponents of natural selection, some of them esteemed scientists and jurists, convinced state legislators to pass legislation allowing for involuntary sterilization of "mental defectives." By the mid-1950s more than 58,000 mental patients and convicts had been forcibly sterilized.[5] The practice of involuntary sterilization abated during the Civil Rights movement when it became recognized that many of the victims were women and minorities of color. That most victims of the eugenics movement were disadvantaged populations was not coincidental. Race suffused the thinking of eugenicists, as Lombroso illustrated when he wrote in 1871, "Only we white people have reached the most perfect symmetry of bodily form."[6]

The suggestion that crime was organically determined generated a firestorm of criticism during the 1960s when it was pointed out that an increasing number of criminals were minorities of color, the same populations that had been victimized by discriminative social policies. Despite this recognition, the contention that criminogenic behavior is hereditary continues to surface in the popular literature. A well-known popularization of genetically transmitted deviance was *The Bell Curve* (1994) by Richard Herrnstein and Charles Murray. The authors contended that, to a significant extent, poverty is hereditary; as a result, many social program expenditures are wasteful. Herrnstein and Murray argued that U.S. society is becoming stratified by intellectual ability, with a "cognitive elite" overseeing a degenerative underclass.[7] Another review of research on genetically transmitted crime revealed that heredity had a slightly positive influence on criminal behavior; however, the researcher suspected that future research would be more productive if it focused on the interaction between environment and genetic attributes.[8]

The Criminal Justice System

The U.S. criminal justice system is similar to education and mental health in that states and localities provide a significantly larger portion of services than the federal government. The Constitution, of course, reserves public functions to the states unless they are ceded to the federal government; in the case of criminal justice, this means that state and local government expenditures exceed those of the federal government by a factor of four.[9] During the 1980s expenditures for criminal justice more than doubled, a fact that warrants clarification. Much of the increase was attributable to corrections (as opposed to police protection and judicial and legal costs) which, on a per capita basis, increased from $30.34 in 1980 to $442.10 in 1999, increasing more than tenfold. Moreover, there was considerable variation in state expenditures. In 1999, for example, the per capita cost of criminal justice in the District of Columbia was $1,212.30; that of nearby West Virginia was $228.00.[10]

The last decades of the twentieth century witnessed a boom in prison construction, a development that drew the wrath of opponents of incarceration. Prison is an expensive way to manage deviants, costing $22,000 on average per inmate annually.[11] Since states pay most of the costs for incarceration, prisons vie with schools for funding, a competition that is decidedly skewed. "While the state government of Virginia spends upward of $70,000 per year to incarcerate each child in a juvenile prison," noted critics of imprisonment of juvenile offenders, "it contributes only about $3,400 to provide for the education of that child."[12] Such disparities have led liberals to argue for greater funding of education and youth services as a way to prevent incarceration, and some conservatives have come to appreciate the enormous expense of a criminal justice system in which prisons are dominant. Between 1995 and 2003, state correctional budgets increased by 50 percent, primarily because of prison construction and maintenance, leading several states to revise more punitive sentencing practices, such as mandatory minimums, three-strikes provisions, and abolishing parole.[13]

Both rates of crime and types of offense have varied over time. During the 1990s all categories of crime decreased significantly as shown in Table 14.1.

The reasons for the drop in crime are unclear. Demographers have noted that younger, more crime-prone people are aging and are less likely to be violent as a result; the Clinton administration cited its crime policies. In all likelihood, the proliferation of a drug economy in inner cities, the easy availability of firearms, and escalating gang violence contributed to an increasing crime rate during the 1980s.

Table 14.1

Crime and Crime Rates, by Type of Offense: 1987 to 2000

Year	Total	Murder	Rape	Robbery	Assault	Property
1987	13,509	20.1	92.1	518	855	12,025
1988	13,923	20.7	92.5	543	910	12,537
1989	15,251	21.5	94.5	578	952	12,605
1990	14,476	23.4	102.6	639	1,055	12,656
1991	14,873	24.7	106.6	688	1,093	12,961
1992	14,438	23.8	109.1	672	1,127	12,506
1993	14,145	24.5	106.0	660	1,136	12,219
1994	13,990	23.3	102.2	619	1,113	12,123
1995	13,863	21.6	97.5	581	1,099	12,064
1996	13,494	19.7	96.3	536	1,037	11,805
1997	13,195	18.2	96.2	499	1,023	11,558
1998	12,486	17.0	93.1	447	977	10,952
1999	11,634	15.5	89.4	409	912	10,208
2000	11,606	15.5	90.2	408	911	10,181

Source: U.S. Department of Commerce, *Statistical Abstract of the United States, 2002* (Washington, DC: U.S. GPO, 2002), p. 183.

But how accurate are crime figures? Traditionally, crime data have been aggregated by the FBI from the reports of state and local law enforcement agencies in the form of the Uniform Crime Report (UCR). Since 1973, however, an annual National Crime Survey (NCS) has been conducted as an alternative to the UCR. By 1990 it was evident that quite different portraits of crime were emerging from the two compilations. With regard to burglary and auto theft, shortly after its inception the NCS reported significantly higher rates than the UCR, but the path of both surveys merged by the late 1980s. With regard to larceny and assault, the NCS and UCR diverged significantly over time, failing to merge.

In the case of rape, the results were even more perplexing. In 1973 the UCR rape rate was 24 per 100,000 population; the NCS rate was more than 50 percent higher at 38. By 1990 the surveys had reversed: The UCR reported more than 105 rapes per 100,000 population, but the NCS had dropped to 24. According to the UCR, rape had increased fourfold in 17 years, but the NCS documented a reduction of 50 percent. The data indicated that law enforcement authorities were escalating their campaign against sexual assault; at the same time, households were reporting a significant decline in rape. In their attempt to sort out the differences in UCR and NCS rape rates, Gary Jensen and Maryaltani Karpos speculated that an escalating UCR documentation led law enforcement to take rape more seriously, the results eventually yielding a suppression in the rape rate reported by the NCS.[14] If this explanation endures, it is rather dramatic evidence of the possibility of the deterrence of crime when victims, in this case women, press upon law enforcement, primarily men, the import of specific types of crime.

The Jensen and Karpos interpretation of the sharp downturn in rape has policy implications as well. For example, in 1994 the Violence against Women Act (VAWA) was passed, and in the following year $26 million was allocated to the states, the first of $800 million over a five-year period.[15] During the period when the UCR documented reductions in rape, the incidence of child abuse—a different indicator of domestic violence—continued to climb. Thus, while domestic violence against women seemed to be diminishing, violence directed at children escalated. If law enforcement is effective at containing rape, then a case can be made for diverting funding to reduce domestic violence targeted at abused children.[16]

The disposition of offenders varies, of course. Those who have not been convicted of violent offenses and who have no previous criminal record are likely to be granted probation. Those who have been convicted of offenses under local or state jurisdiction may be jailed or imprisoned in facilities that have often been determined to violate minimal humane standards of care. Federal convicts, on the other hand, may be incarcerated in prisons that are qualitatively better, some of which have a decidedly pleasant ambiance. Having served time for good behavior, many prisoners earn early release and go on parole, during which they must report regularly to a supervising officer. These various statuses are depicted in Table 14.2. In less than two decades the numbers of incarcerated offenders more than tripled.

Prisons have been a signal concern in criminal justice, both because of the cost of incarceration and because of what imprisonment rates say about the preponderance of serious precipitating offenses. Among the nations of the world the incarceration rate of the United States is second only to that of Russia. Russia imprisons 687 inmates per 100,000 population; the United States 682. The rates for other nations are strikingly lower: South Africa 321, Canada 115, France 90, and Japan 39.[17] Beyond these figures, the United States passed a benchmark coinciding with the new millennium in 2000, when 2 million people were behind bars.[18] In this population, gender and race emerge prominently: roughly

Table 14.2

Adults on Probation, in Jail or Prison, or on Parole

Year	Total	Probation	Jail	Prison	Parole
1980	1,840,400	1,118,097	182,288	319,598	220,438
1981	2,006,600	1,225,934	195,085	360,029	225,539
1982	2,192,600	1,357,264	207,853	402,914	224,604
1983	2,475,100	1,582,947	221,815	423,898	246,440
1984	2,689,200	1,740,948	233,018	448,264	266,992
1985	3,011,400	1,968,712	254,986	487,953	300,203
1986	3,239,400	2,114,621	272,735	526,436	325,638
1987	3,459,600	2,247,158	294,092	562,814	355,505
1988	3,714,100	2,356,483	341,893	607,766	407,977
1989	4,055,600	2,522,125	393,303	683,367	456,803
1990	4,348,000	2,670,234	403,019	743,382	531,407
1991	4,535,600	2,728,472	424,129	792,535	590,442
1992	4,762,600	2,811,611	441,781	850,566	658,601
1993	4,944,000	2,903,061	455,500	909,381	676,100
1994	5,141,300	2,981,022	479,800	990,147	690,371
1995	5,355,100	3,077,861	499,300	1,078,541	679,421
1996	5,475,000	3,161,030	510,400	1,127,528	676,045
1997	5,725,800	3,296,513	557,974	1,176,564	694,787
1998	6,175,700	3,670,441	584,372	1,224,469	696,385
1999	6,378,000	3,779,922	596,485	1,287,172	714,457
2000	6,448,300	3,839,532	613,534	1,309,661	725,527

Source: U.S. Department of Commerce, *Statistical Abstract of the United States, 2002* (Washington, DC: U.S. GPO, 2002), p. 204.

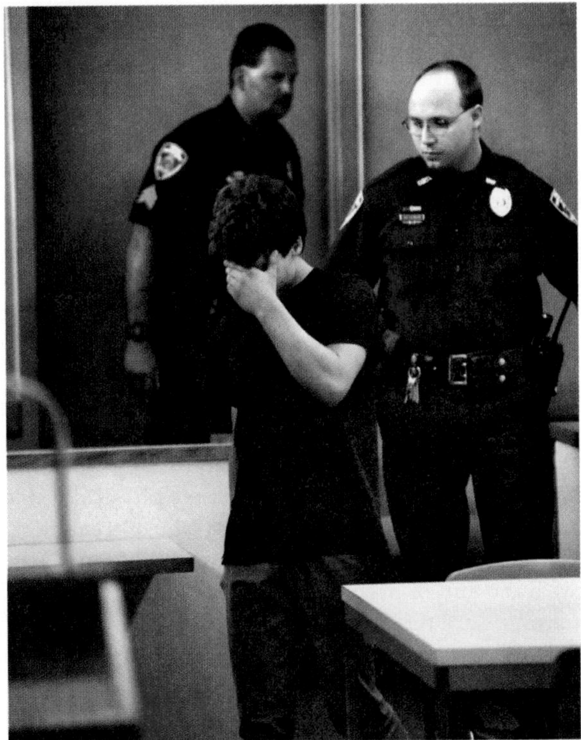

Because the majority of adult offenders were also known to the juvenile justice system, it stands to reason that diverting youngsters from juvenile crime may keep them out of the adult criminal justice system.

90 percent of inmates are men,[19] and two-thirds are minorities of color. Virtually half of all inmates are African American;[20] in 2002 about 12 percent of black men between 20 and 34 were behind bars.[21] In light of the fact that two-thirds of inmates return to prison within a few years of release,[22] recidivism poses an enormous burden on the African American community.

Juvenile Justice

Juvenile justice is a significant feature of U.S. criminal justice for several reasons. Young deviants are good candidates for becoming adult deviants, in which case they become subject to the adult criminal justice system. Because the majority of adult offenders were also known to the juvenile justice system, it stands to reason that diverting youngsters from juvenile crime may well keep them out of the adult criminal justice system. From a crime prevention standpoint, reaching young people early, when their understanding of themselves in relation to social norms is still being formed, is a more plausible strategy than attempting to intervene with adult offenders, who have a less malleable sense of themselves vis-à-vis social institutions.

The first institution for juvenile delinquency was the New York City House of Refuge established in 1825. Massachusetts followed suit with a boys' facility established in 1847 and one for girls in 1854.[23] These institutions paralleled other institutions designed to care for neglected children, such as Charles Loring Brace's New York Children's Aid Society, established in 1853. Such institutions were not known for indulging children; furnishings were spartan, the discipline harsh, and escapes common. The orphanage asylum for children became the subject of scathing parody under the pen of Charles Dickens. During the Progressive Era reformers contended that youth should be adjudicated separately from adults, and the first juvenile court was established in Chicago in 1899.[24]

Institutional care for adolescent deviants remained virtually unchanged until the 1960s, when critics of warehousing children advocated for community alternatives. In 1972 Congress passed the Juvenile Justice and Delinquency Prevention Act, a measure that intended, in part, to remove children who were "status offenders" from the more serious deviants who had actually committed felonies or violent crimes. According to Jerome Miller, a youth service advocate, the act ultimately failed. However, it gave impetus to those who were proponents of non-institutional care for delinquents.

In 1969, Miller assumed the directorship of the Massachusetts Division of Youth Services (DYS), a position that was to become symbolic of correctional reform in the United States. A social worker, Miller had been an officer in the U.S. Air Force, trained in the Menninger Clinic, and earned a doctorate at Catholic University. His initial plan, to seek incremental reforms in Massachusetts, faded as the structural flaws of state juvenile justice became more apparent. All of the personnel positions were filled through political patronage, and very few human service professionals could be found at DYS. Staff routinely resorted to cruel and inhumane treatment—such as breaking fingers of escapees, smearing feces on incorrigibles, and placing miscreants in solitary confinement—that would have been unconstitutional in an adult institution. As Miller learned during his first months on the job, rather than instituting changes, staff and administration subverted attempts to make DYS more amenable to reform. The institutional conspiracy of DYS was becoming as evident as it was implacable. At the same time, Miller was becoming aware of a compelling research finding: The longer children were institutionalized in DYS facilities, the *more* likely they were to become more serious adult offenders. As Miller saw it, not only were his reforms being disregarded, but also he was managing an institution that made youth worse. This seemed especially counterproductive when it became evident that the vast majority of adolescents in DYS institutions were not violent felons but teens who had a knack for getting into trouble.

Miller responded to the intransigence of DYS staff with the most radical of plausible solutions: If DYS was not amenable to reform and continued to damage adolescents, the most conscionable act would be simply to close it down. Thus, over a period of months, Miller and a hand-picked staff discharged the children to alternative community-based care programs. With the exception of a handful of violence-prone adolescents, all of the youth were removed from DYS by the end of Miller's tenure in the 1970s.

The consequences of such an abrupt transformation were predictable. Legislators objected to closing DYS facilities, particularly when an institution was in a legislator's district and thereby an employer of constituents. Law-and-order activists condemned Miller for turning loose on the Massachusetts public the next generation of felons. Researchers recorded a different experience. Using recidivism as an outcome measure, Lloyd Ohlin and Bob Coates of Harvard's Center for Criminal Justice found that in districts of the state in which strong community-based alternatives had been deployed, recidivism was markedly lower.[25]

Eventually the Massachusetts experiment was to become a benchmark in juvenile justice in the United States, a case study used by several prominent professional schools. In writing a postscript on the experience, Miller targeted the indiscriminate labeling of youthful deviants by human service professionals who were oblivious to the fates their judgment brought on young offenders: "Our prisons and reform schools are filled with fabricated aliens made yet more alien by those who should know better, but who insufficiently understand the subjects of their research beyond narrow methodological parameters or highly controlled settings which demean and impoverish human experience."[26]

Incarceration as the intervention of choice for youthful offenders continues to be a source of disagreement within juvenile justice. Research on conventional as well as innovative programs yields mixed outcomes. An analysis of the closing of Maryland youth detention facilities revealed that youth who were not institutionalized had higher recidivism rates—although this held only for crimes against property, not for crimes against persons or involving drugs.[27]

Early proponents of another initiative, boot camps, promised that discipline, exercise, and routine would deter adolescents from future offending. At boot camp "inmates would receive physical training, military discipline, and drug abuse treatment, all under the direction of military personnel and with the aim of preparing them for a life that would combine . . . the requirement of regular drug tests and the opportunity for gainful employment."[28] By 1993 boot camps had been established in 25 states, but just as rapidly enthusiasm faded. A study of Georgia facilities commissioned by the Justice Department concluded that boot camps failed to deter young offenders.[29] In 1994 Connecticut closed its National Guard boot camp, citing "rampant gang activity, assaults on weaker inmates, marijuana use, sexual activity, and gambling."[30] An analysis of boot camps in 8 states concluded that alumni of boot camps were neither more nor less likely to commit future offenses.[31]

Despite the lack of success of boot camps, elected officials redoubled their efforts to contain what was perceived as an explosion in the number of juveniles who were engaged in violent crime. Many resorted to treating juvenile offenders as adults. Since 1992, 45 states have altered adjudication of juveniles in order to facilitate treating them as adults. "As a result, the number of youths under 18 held in adult prisons, and in many cases mixed in with adult criminals, has doubled in the last 10 years or so, from 3,400 in 1985 to 7,400 in 1997. Of the juveniles incarcerated on any given day, one in 10 are in adult jails or prisons."[32]

Many youth advocates objected to increasing the severity of punishment for adolescents, citing evidence that some violent juvenile crime was abating. As Table 14.3 shows, juvenile arrests have changed dramatically since 1980. Murder, rape, and robbery peaked during the mid-1990s but have since dropped back to levels proximate to those of 1980. On the

Table 14.3

Juvenile Arrests for Selected Offenses

Offense	1980	1985	1990	1995	2000
Violent crime	77,220	75,077	97,103	123,131	78,450
murder	1,475	1,384	2,661	2,812	1,027
rape	3,668	5,073	4,971	4,556	3,402
robbery	33,529	31,833	34,944	47,240	24,206
assault	33,504	36,787	54,527	68,523	49,815
Weapon violations	21,203	27,035	33,123	46,506	28,514
Drug abuse	86,685	78,660	66,300	149,236	146,594
sale	13,004	14,846	24,575	34,077	26,432
possession	73,681	63,814	41,725	115,159	120,162

Source: U.S. Department of Commerce, *Statistical Abstract of the United States, 2002* (Washington, DC: U.S. GPO, 2002), p. 192.

other hand, arrests for sale and possession of illegal drugs show alarming increases; although arrests for selling drugs began to decline late in the 1990s, arrests for possession continue to climb.

Within a context of high juvenile crime and rampant drug use, Boston juvenile authorities imposed an innovation that sparked the interest of criminologists across the country. Under Operation Night Light, an aggressive initiative targeting high-risk youth, Boston juvenile authorities precipitated a reduction in youth homicides, which numbered 70 from 1992 through 1995, to zero from 1996 through 1998. As one journalist described the effort, "Juvenile law enforcement in Boston has become a community-sized octopus that embraces teenagers who are temporarily troubled and ensnares (without necessarily jailing) those who are chronically violent."[33] Subsequently, several cities have attempted to replicate the Boston model. A few year later, proponents of the Boston approach were less sanguine. By October 2004, 53 homicides had been committed in Boston, making it one of ten cities experiencing escalating rates of youth violence.[34]

The War on Drugs

By the 1980s, events had propelled the control of drug abuse to a top priority in U.S. criminal justice. The deterioration of inner cities had been accompanied by an alarming degree of social dysfunction. Illegal drugs were not only prevalent in the poorest minority neighborhoods but had also become an essential, if not the predominant, part of the local economy. As gangs vied over turf and ever more profitable drug peddling, violence exploded. Drive-by shootings became commonplace in larger cities. Gang-bangers invaded previously neutral territory—hospitals, mortuaries, cemeteries—in pursuit of enemies. Innocent people became victims of a rash of holdups, car-jackings, and seemingly random shootings. In response, President Reagan declared war on drugs. Despite unrelenting efforts to contain drug abuse, during the 1990s the Department of Justice witnessed sky rocketing increases in drug seizures. Between 1990 and 2000, the number of drug seizures increased fourfold from 745,002 to 2.98 million.[35]

Logically, two strategies dominated the War on Drugs: government interdiction of supplies, aimed at eliminating the substance, or treatment programs deployed to diminish the demand for illegal drugs. Appropriations for drug control increased substantially during the 1980s, but much of the funding was allocated for interdiction and comparatively less for treatment. For example, federal funds for law enforcement increased from $800 million in 1981 to $1.9 billion in 1986; yet funding for prevention, education, and treatment decreased from $404 million in 1981 to $338 million in 1985, a 40 percent drop when adjusted for inflation.[36] More recently, the 2001 budget of the Office of National Drug Control

Two strategies dominate the War on Drugs: government interdiction of supplies and treatment programs to diminish the demand for illegal drugs.

(ONDC) proposed $420 million for prison construction and $327.5 million for interdiction compared to $127.0 million for treatment.[37]

Despite massive infusions of funds for the Drug Enforcement Administration (DEA) and the Coast Guard, by the late 1980s most analysts agreed that supply interdiction had failed. Experts contended that emphasizing law enforcement would not solve the nation's drug problem. "It would be naive to assume that this well-meant legislative effort will be an end to our drug dilemma," concluded the late Sidney Cohen, former director of the Division of Narcotic Addiction and Drug Abuse of the National Institute of Mental Health:

> We have not yet come to understand the resolute, determined, amoral nature of the major traffickers or their enormous power. Perhaps we do not even recognize that, for tens of hundreds of thousands of field workers, collecting coca leaves or opium gum is a matter of survival. At the other end of the pipeline is the swarm of sellers who could not possibly earn a fraction of their current income from legitimate pursuits. If they are arrested, they are out after a short detention. If not, many are waiting to take their place.[38]

If efforts to reduce the propagation of coca in South and Central America proved futile, attempts to reduce street trafficking were similarly unsuccessful. A kilogram of cocaine wholesaled in Miami for $60,000 in 1981; at the height of the crack epidemic of the late 1980s, the cost had plummeted to $10,000.[39] The price of cocaine was so low that crack houses were able to offer cocaine free to new customers, charging regulars as little as $2.[40]

To compound the problem, the application of interdiction at the street level, where drugs were sold, led to arrests of users and petty distributors, swelling already overcrowded prisons. The arrest rate per 100,000 inhabitants increased from 435.3 in 1990 to 587.1 in 2000, an increase of 35 percent. In 2000,

Spotlight 14.1

The Office of National Drug Control Policy

Established in 1988, the Office of National Drug Control Policy (ONDCP) sets policies, priorities, and objectives for the nation's drug control program. The goals of the program are to reduce illicit drug use, manufacturing, trafficking, drug-related crime and violence, and drug-related health consequences.

To learn more about this federal agency, go to its website at **www.ondcp.gov.**

drug abuse violations accounted for one of eight arrests, more than another other offense. In every metropolitan area, a majority of arrestees tested positive for illegal drugs.[41] Thus, the focus on interdiction and enforcement proved perverse. To contain drug use through law enforcement, the country was imprisoning thousands of addicts at enormous cost, yet funding for prevention and treatment lagged far behind allocations for incarceration. Most ironic, drug treatment for incarcerated addicts was virtually nonexistent.

The mismatch between the needs of drug addicts and the eligibility requirements of social programs was captured by journalist Barry Bearak, who followed a group of junkies in New York City. Scavenging what funds he had left, one junkie decided to have himself admitted to a detox program. After a full day's bouncing from one welfare agency to another seeking eligibility for "special" Medicaid, which would pay for the detox services, Georgie, a middle-aged Hispanic man, found himself in a line for public assistance only a few minutes before closing time. While Georgie waited, a friend who had come with him also to get into detox was shooting up in the rest room:

> The line moved slowly. Georgie's turn finally came a few minutes before 5 p.m. It was a short discussion. He had been in the wrong spot. He needed to be at the Application Desk, back over by Table Five where he had started.
>
> He hurried across the big room. "Can I ask you a question?" he said to a clerk. "I'm sorry," she answered, her fingers busy in a file drawer. "I need to get this out of the way."
>
> Georgie spoke up with more urgency: "I want to get into detox."
>
> The woman turned to face him now. "You came too late," she said, shaking her head. "We're not giving out any more appointments."
>
> "We've been getting the runaround all day."
>
> She eyed him more carefully, looking over his sweaty face. She spoke slowly and distinctly for the junkie's benefit. "When you come back in, all they'll give you is an appointment," she said. "You won't get emergency Medicaid. Then, with an appointment, you have to come back in a week or so and see an interviewer. Then, after they have reviewed the case, the client is contacted by mail, and that takes three weeks or a month."
>
> Georgie took this in and was stunned. "So the mumbo jumbo about getting on Medicaid the same day is bull—?" he said without anger, but with resignation. "That's right. The only way to get on is with HIV [the AIDS virus]." At last, good news. His face brightened. "Well, I'm HIV," he said.
>
> The clerk took a step back from him. "You'd have to be able to prove it with a certified letter from your doctor," she said.
>
> With that, Georgie was beaten. His shoulders sagged. And the clerk knew she could shift her attention back to the end-of-the-day filing.[42]

How Georgie came to drug addiction is speculative, of course; yet many social observers cite social and economic conditions in the poorest inner-city neighborhoods that conspire to make self-administered anesthesia desirable for many adolescents. By the early 1990s, for the first time, the number of young African Americans who were neither in school nor employed exceeded 50 percent in every section of the United States.[43] During the 1980s the combination of reductions in governmental assistance to cities through social programs and the prevalence of drug trafficking had a pronounced effect on inner-city neighborhoods. Gradually, once squalid but quiet urban neighborhoods began to echo with gunfire as rival gangs fought over turf; areas in many industrial cities virtually imploded.[44] Gang killings in Los Angeles soared 69 percent during the first eight months of 1990.[45] In 1992 Los Angeles reported more than 800 drug-related homicides.[46] Gang-related murders in the nation's capital, which reached a three-year high in 1990, led a police department spokesperson to quip, "At the rate we're going the next generation is going to be extinct."[47]

Observers of urban poverty described a serious deterioration in inner-city communities of the 1980s as contrasted with those of the 1960s. When Claude Brown returned to Harlem 20 years after the publication of his *Manchild in the Promised Land,* he was shocked by the casual viciousness of gang members toward their victims.[48] "In many if not most of our major cities, we are facing something very like social regression," wrote the late Senator Daniel Patrick Moynihan. "It is defined by extraordinary levels of self-destructive behavior, interpersonal violence, and social class separation intensive in some groups, extensive in others."[49] In the socioeconomic vacuum that had developed in the poorest urban neighborhoods, the sale and consumption of drugs became central to community life. The toll this conversion has taken on young African Americans is astonishing. As of 1988, 43 percent of those convicted of drug trafficking were African American. In New York, Hispanics, and African Americans accounted for 92 percent of arrests for drug offenses in 1989. In 1990, the Sentencing Project, a criminal justice reform organization, reported that one-fourth of all

African Americans between the ages of 20 and 29 were incarcerated, on parole, or on probation. Yet the Sentencing Project data scraped only the top of what was a very large statistical iceberg.

In *Search and Destroy: African-American Males in the Criminal Justice System,* Jerome Miller identified the frequency with which young African American males were likely to run afoul of the law, reporting that

> *on an average day in 1991, more than four in ten (42%) of all the 18–35-year-old African-American males who lived in the District of Columbia were in jail, in prison, on probation/parole, or being sought on arrest warrants; on an average day in Baltimore, 56% of all its young African-American males were in prison, jail, on probation/parole, on bail, or being sought on arrest* [emphasis in original].[50]

According to Miller, incarceration was damaging enough, but simply arresting all these young men inflicted substantial harm simply because most employment applications inquire about an arrest record, and research demonstrates that employers avoid candidates with arrest records.

For Miller the War on Drugs was just another "moral panic," the sort of melodrama that an insecure middle class creates in order to retain its social standing. A moral panic is manifested by the emergence of policies and professionals that seek to re-establish social control over a phantom threat. In the case of the War on Drugs, conservative politicians and law enforcement officers convinced the public that the nation suffers from a new generation of violent minority youth that must be held in check. The evidence presented for the law-and-order agenda consisted largely of the arrest rates for violent and repeat offenders; yet Miller contended that most "violent" offenses represented the overcharging of miscreants by overzealous police, and most "repeat" offenders were re-arrested for drug-related offenses. Not coincidentally, Miller contended, blacks were the target of the War on Drugs. For 1991, he noted, "the national incarceration rate in state and federal prisons was 310 per 100,000. For white males it was 352 per 100,000. For black males age 25–29 it stood at an incredible 6,301."[51] Many of the arrests were drug related, a category that was increasing dramatically among African American youth. Per 100,000 population, drug arrests for black youth increased from 683 in 1985, to 1,200 in 1989, to 1,415 in 1991.[52] The racial disparity in juvenile drug arrests is shown in Figure 14.1.

The social consequence of the arrest and incarceration of so many black youths, Miller alleged, was the cultivation of an oppositional culture, replete with violence, in which engaging the criminal justice system was "something of a puberty rite, a transition to manhood."[53] Drawing an Orwellian conclusion, Miller predicted that jails would soon morph into "simple internment camps" for minority youth who were refugees from an alienating culture.

Other observers also documented the grim circumstances of poor minority families in urban centers. A common denominator of these portrayals was drug-related violence that seemed to metastasize throughout inner-city communities, extracting a horrifying toll on minority populations. The effect on African American family life was depicted poignantly by Alex Kotlowitz, who followed the daily activities of two youngsters, Lafayette and Pharaoh Rivers. The boys ventured out of their mother's apartment in one of Chicago's housing projects at the risk of being shot by drug dealers.[54] In New York City a popular elementary school principal, Patrick Daly, was shot to death while walking through a drug-infested neighborhood searching for a nine-year-old who had left school in

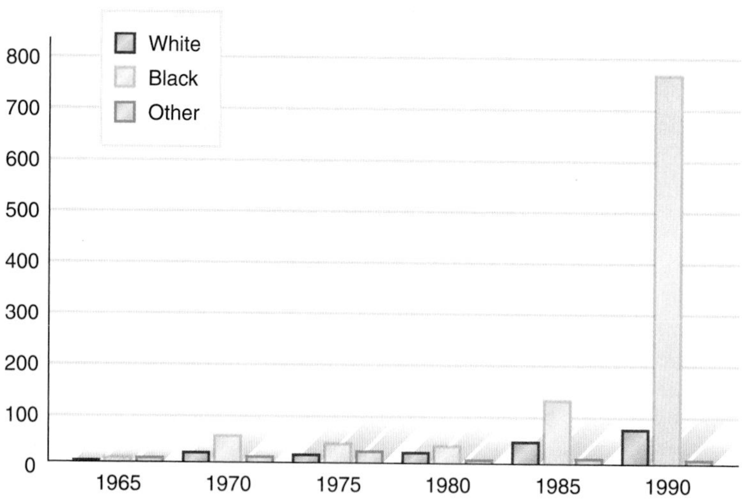

Figure 14.1

Tracking Racial Bias

Source: Adapted from Jerome Miller, *Search and Destroy* (New York: Cambridge University Press, 1996).

tears after a fight.[55] During the summer of 1992, drug-related street violence in Baltimore reached the point where the state chapter of the National Association for the Advancement of Colored People formally requested that the governor of Maryland declare a state of civil emergency and call out the National Guard to restore order in the city.

By 2000, drug abuse had stabilized, yet the war on drugs continued amid escalating controversy. Since 1985 the United States had invested several hundred billion dollars in attempting to control the drug trade, but the results were hotly disputed.[56] Most of the arrests for drug abuse occurred at the local level, and the number of offenders quickly clogged the courts.[57] High demand for drugs fueled international drug cartels, with those in nearby Mexico and Colombia provoking diplomatic tensions around extradition and interdiction.[58] More fundamental issues emerged as traditional conservatives expressed concern about involvement of the military in non-defense activities,[59] while libertarians and the Left proposed legalization of drugs as a more realistic alternative.[60]

The Underclass and "Moral Poverty"

The contention that "crime" was largely a bourgeois contrivance to maintain control over hostile minority youth, as argued by liberals like Jerome Miller, was challenged by conservative crime theorists of the 1980s. Conservatives argued that the chronic poor suffered from problems qualitatively different from those of the temporarily poor. The latter lacked basic resources, and the provision of cash benefits was a prudent response to their circumstances. The chronic poor, however, evidenced a "behavioral" poverty that differentiated them from the transient poor. The behaviorally poor engaged in habits—teen pregnancy, drug abuse, petty theft, unmarried parenthood, and welfare dependency—that not only ensured continual destitution, but also subverted the intent of well-intended social programs.[61] Behavioral poverty sustained oppositional culture, in doing so, fostered the underclass.

Accordingly, in their 1996 book *Body Count*, William Bennett, John DiIulio Jr., and John Walters argued that the upsurge in crime could be attributed to "moral poverty":

> the poverty of being without loving, capable, responsible adults who teach right from wrong; the poverty of being without parents and other authorities who habituate you to feel joy at others' joy, pain at others' pain, satisfaction when you do right, remorse when you do wrong; the poverty of growing up in the virtual absence of people who teach morality by their own everyday example and who insist that you follow suit. In the extreme, moral poverty is the poverty of growing up severely abused and neglected at the hands of deviant, delinquent, or criminal adults.[62]

To substantiate their argument, Bennett, DiIulio, and Walters cited data on the behavior of state prisoners in 1991. For that year 45 percent of prisoners were on probation or parole when they committed their latest offense. During community supervision in the previous 17 months, the 162,000 probation violators committed some 6,400 murders, 7,400 rapes, 10,400 assaults, and 17,000 robberies. During community supervision of the previous 13 months, the 156,000 parole violators committed some 6,800 murders, 5,500 rapes, 8,800 assaults, and 22,500 robberies. "Together, probation and parole violators committed 90,639 violent crimes while 'under supervision' in the community."[63]

> At the core of the crime wave is a new category of "super-predators"—radically impulsive, brutally remorseless youngsters, including ever more preteenage boys, who murder, assault rape, rob, burglarize, deal deadly drugs, join gun-toting gangs, and create serious communal disorders. They do not fear the stigma of arrest, the pains of imprisonment, or the pangs of conscience. They perceive hardly any relationship between doing right (or wrong) now and being rewarded (or punished) for it later.[64]

Bennett, DiIulio, and Walters averred that much of the increase in crime could be attributed to a proliferation of drugs that had become so extensive as to represent de facto normalization of drug abuse. The severe damage associated with heroin and cocaine justified increasing drug interdiction efforts and getting tough with street criminals who peddle drugs. Regarding treatment, Bennett, DiIulio, and Walters noted that funding increases for treatment had not been accompanied by a significant decrease in the number of addicts seeking rehabilitation. Although existing treatment capacity was serving only half the nation's addicts, the authors of *Body Count* proposed few changes other than eliminating bureaucratic waste in order to extend treatment resources. Beyond that, little could be done, given the poor track record of treatment programs in getting addicts into recovery. For many addicts, treatment was a cyclical experience, not an end to their substance abuse; the authors concluded. They cited the California Civil Addict Program, which reported that more addicts eventually died after receiving treatment (27.7 percent) than became drug free (25 percent).[65]

The conservative prescription for moral poverty was as extensive as it was sometimes implausible. Bennett, DiIulio, and Walters advocated reinforcing work as opposed to unconditional welfare, removing young children from dysfunctional homes, and encouraging adoption as an alternative to foster care. Although public policy might prove instrumental in reducing "criminogenic" influences, it was less apropos, if not irrelevant, as a vehicle for other suggestions, such as limiting children's TV time or reasserting the importance of religious values in daily life.[66] Subsequently, DiIulio moderated his position about juvenile delinquents, recognizing the environmental deficits that contributed to their misconduct. In researching programs that served delinquents, DiIulio found that religious groups were often the most effective in treating delinquents.[67] DiIulio has become an advocate of "charitable choice," the contracting out of social services through community-based religious organizations. By conceding that the compassion of religious intercession is more effective than punishment through incarceration, DiIulio has reversed his earlier position with respect to juvenile delinquency.[68]

To the extent that social and economic factors—particularly the skewing of opportunities of minority youth who become adult offenders—are associated with crime, an argument can be made for environmental influences in criminal conduct, an argument congruent with a liberal orientation to criminal justice. This is the logic that John Hagan has adopted in developing the concept of the "social embeddedness" of crime. In reviewing research on juvenile delinquency and adult offenders, Hagan noted the interaction of family and environment in the transmission of criminal behavior. Poor neighborhoods generate delinquents, often from families in which a parent has been an offender. Such intergenerational transmission of crime can be attributed to heredity; but, as noted earlier in this chapter, the relationship is too weak to be anywhere near conclusive. Consequently, Hagan takes a more direct, and more useful, route in explaining how poor communities harbor crime-prone families that produce delinquents, many of whom become adult criminals. In poor communities, Hagan contends, two developmental paths evolve for children. Kids from working families with effective adult supervision are socialized in school and through early employment into a world in which there is the likelihood of success. By contrast, children from families in which an adult is an offender are more likely to encounter the juvenile justice system; and not only does that system label them as delinquent, but the punishment of juvenile offenders-incarceration or its surrogates-also interferes with kids' completing school or building a sound foundation for future employment. Essentially, young people from families with adult offenders are doubly burdened. As Hagan writes,

> involvements of parents in crime likely provide youths with more promising connections to illegal than legal labor markets. As well, contacts with criminal friends are more likely to integrate youths into the criminal underworld than into referral networks for legal employment. And youthful delinquent acts are likely to distance actors further from the job contacts that initiate and sustain legitimate occupational careers.[69]

So oriented, it is understandable how delinquency-prone youth could find gang involvement a natural progression in socialization. Drug-related gang activities, frequently targeted by law enforcement, bring arrests and sentences that label youngsters and disrupt education and employment. Before the end of high school, a delinquent has accumulated sufficient negative attributes to subvert any interest in conventional rewards. In place of education and employment, gang activity alternates with incarceration, producing a vicious circle. Measures of the intractability of the delinquent's circumstance can be found in the "oppositional culture" that flourishes among poor minority youth. The popularization of vulgar "gangsta" rap, a pattern of claiming the loyalty of young women by impregnating them, and "dissing" enemies (including authority figures)—even at the risk of bodily harm—are all part of the capitulation that young minority males make in the face of overwhelming odds militating against traditional means of success. Oppositional culture reproduces itself in children born to young minority women whose aspirations have been sabotaged. Such children experience little that is nurturing or dependable, least of all fathers—given that their fathers, knowing the tentativeness of life on the streets, expect to be dead or incarcerated well before their offspring reach adolescence. The scenario is as tragic as it is "embedded" in the social reality of its perpetrators and victims.

The evolution of liberal policies that divert youth from delinquency and subsequently prevent adult lawlessness has been advocated eloquently by William Julius Wilson. Mainstreaming the underclass, Wilson argues, requires enhanced educational opportunity; the realization of educational standards in inner-city schools; an increase in earned income tax credits for poor working families; and, in the end, a WPA-type public employment program. Eventually, improved educational and employment opportunities will overcome current inducements to engage in lawlessness.

> As more people become employed, crime, including violent crime, and drug use will subside; families will be strengthened and welfare receipt will decline significantly; ghetto-related culture and behavior, no longer sustained and nourished by persistent joblessness, will gradually fade.[70]

Thus, Wilson reiterates a major finding from the research on opportunity and crime: Lawlessness declines as rates of employment and marriage rise.

Legalization of Drugs

During the 1980s, seemingly endless retreats in the war on drugs led some analysts to propose legalizing controlled substances.[71] Drug legalization had been a standard demand among libertarians, who argued that individuals should be free to engage in any activity so long as it does not harm others. Then, during the Reagan presidency, a small number of leaders representing law, economics, and politics complemented the libertarian position with their own arguments. Noting the massive sums pumped into law enforcement and the meager results demonstrated by interdiction and treatment, proponents of legalization argued that U.S. policy on substance abuse was at best naive and at worst counterproductive. They contended that the current policy was little more than a replication of Prohibition's futile effort to ban alcohol from American culture. A more mature and pragmatic policy would be to admit that certain substances were part of contemporary lifestyles and simply to regulate them, they contended, much as tobacco and alcohol are regulated. According to its proponents, legalization would have several benefits. Legalizing drugs would enable substantial sums to be freed from law enforcement and put toward abuse prevention and treatment programs. Legalization would decriminalize drug use, thereby cutting the prison population significantly and, by destigmatizing users, making it more likely that users would enter treatment. Additional revenues could be raised by government because illegal substances would be available legitimately and taxed accordingly. Advocates of legalization questioned the claims of the defenders of the status quo who argued that prevention, treatment, and interdiction were effective strategies that would show positive results in the long run. Legalization of drugs, claimed its adherents, could produce substantial results immediately.

Momentum toward legalizing drugs reached its peak during the mid-1980s and then flagged. Public policy scholars raised questions for which there were no ready answers. Should all drugs be legalized? Or should legalization be limited to soft drugs, such as marijuana and minor tranquilizers, while restrictions on hard drugs were maintained? Should availability be unlimited, or should age restrictions apply, as they do now with tobacco and alcohol? If there were taxes on drugs and restrictions on their purchase, would not the government still have to fund law enforcement, regulate product safety, and maintain a taxing authority in order to contain an illicit market? If the government were to attempt to counter a black market by supplying drugs directly, it would be in the contradictory position of supplying drugs while also offering treatment for users of those same drugs.[72]

Further confounding the issue of drug legalization was the firestorm of controversy over crack cocaine. Proponents of legalization visualized drugs as substances analogous to tobacco and alcohol. People dependent on marijuana, heroin, and many psychedelics could use their drugs discreetly, they contended, without disrupting society. The proliferation of crack cocaine, however, presented a completely different picture. Not only was crack implicated in violent incidents, but the craving for it was more intense than that for many other drugs. The prospect of legalizing a substance over which users seemed to have so little control and which, moreover, was connected to homicides, addicted infants, and community destruction seemed inconsistent with the vision implied by drug legalization.

By the 1990s the legalization of drugs had drifted to the margin of the substance abuse debate, although it was still advocated by a small coterie of prominent people, such as New Mexico's then-Governor Gary Johnson and financier George Soros.

Despite obvious contradictions represented by the status of tobacco and alcohol, few suggested that other substances should be legalized. In fact, pressure increased to contain the use of tobacco and alcohol. Municipalities expanded the areas they designated as smoke-free, and stricter standards and fines were established for driving under the influence of alcohol. Increasingly, authorities came to believe that soft drugs served a "gateway" function, introducing young users to more addictive substances. Rather than loosening of the regulation of such substances, continued restrictions were called for.[73] Finally, the most limited form of legalization—allowing physicians to prescribe certain substances for addicts—faltered when the country that had pioneered this strategy, Great Britain, halted the practice.[74]

If a consensus had begun to emerge about not legalizing controlled substances, there was far less unanimity about how to reclaim neighborhoods in which drugs had become central to social and economic life. Aggressive action by law enforcement officers appeared to have reached an apex, then degenerated in the face of a lawless netherworld, as when DEA agents raided the wrong house and critically wounded a San Diego man in a drug bust gone wrong. The strategy of handing down severe sentences for even first-time offenders began to lose its luster when the cost of incarceration proved to exceed by far the value of taking small-time drug traffickers off the street. The seizure of property belonging to persons who had been implicated in drug transactions became a small scandal when newspapers reported that innocent people had lost belongings to overzealous law enforcement officers.[75] The promise of paramilitary boot camps for first-time offenders who had been convicted of drug-related crimes, although it looked like an appealing solution to a public frustrated by increasing numbers of crime-prone youth, failed to demonstrate any long-term changes in behavior.[76]

In the last decade of the twentieth century, many inner-city neighborhoods were more lethal for minority Americans than they had been at any time in the nation's history. Children learned that they could make hundreds of dollars a day carrying crack between dealers, easily eclipsing the income of conventionally employed adults in the community. This made a joke of the work ethic; no one with any self-respect would consider a dead-end job paying the minimum wage. Young men who had little hope of finding a good job traded their future for quick wealth and community notoriety in the drug trade. Drug-related violence made a mockery of already fragile community institutions. Gang members were shot to death in funeral homes, schools, even hospitals. Most tragically, infants born of crack-addicted mothers writhed and screamed at birth as they experienced withdrawal, only to be diagnosed later with HIV. Unwanted, many suffered in group homes and died at an early age.

While academics debated the finer points of drug legalization, the quality of life for the urban poor grew increasingly desperate. What had once been a grim struggle to reconcile meager income with daily living requirements had become a frantic scramble for safety. At best, the drug scourge forced inner-city residents to sharply curtail their expectations. At worst, it terminated expectations altogether. Eventually, the degradation of life attributed to the proliferation of drugs entered the popular media, clashing with cherished images of America. For too many of the urban poor, the American dream had not just faded from memory; it had been replaced by an antithetical image—the American nightmare.

The "New Penology"

While academics debated the merits of the legalization of drugs, the public was growing increasingly intolerant of crime. Since the mid-1980s the nation has seen a significant increase in prison construction, the passage of new laws requiring incarceration of repeat offenders, and the reinstitution of capital punishment in some states. Approaching the end of the twentieth century, the United States boasted an incarcerated population that exceeded 2 million. In 1970 the number of inmates in state and federal correctional facilities was 96.7 per 100,000 population; by 1993 the number had more than tripled, at 352.9;[77] by 1997 it had more than quadrupled, to 445.[78] In 1994 the Violent Crime Control and Law Enforcement Act introduced the "three strikes" penalties for repeat offenders and increased the number of federal crimes to which the death penalty applies.[79] The number of prisoners under the death sentence soared. In 1980, 688 inmates were on death row; by 2000 the number had increased fivefold to 3,593.[80] Of these, 43.7 percent were nonwhite;[81] the number of people of color with death sentences thus was more than double their proportion of the general population.

The rapid expansion in correctional facilities led criminologists Malcolm Feeley and Jonathan Simon to identify the advent of a "new penology." In contrast to the old penology that focused on individual rehabilitation (via probation or parole) or deterrence (via incarceration), the new penology eschewed these for the efficient management of large populations of high-risk offenders. The mission of criminal justice, contended Feeley and Simon, was "managerial, not transformative";[82] the social function of criminal justice was "rabble management,"[83] or controlling "unruly groups."[84]

As a managerial phenomenon, the new penology required a method for classification and incarceration, and the federal sentencing guidelines incorporated in the 1984 Comprehensive Crime Control Act (implemented on November 1, 1987) served just that purpose. The U.S. Sentencing Commission established an elaborate system of 258 categories for determining the punishment for an offense according to its severity and the offender's previous convictions.[85] The guidelines generated controversy when it became evident that drug sentences varied considerably according to the type of substance and the race of the offender. For example, regular cocaine is considered less serious than crack cocaine; crack cocaine is used most widely by African Americans; thus, drug offenses by black offenders yield longer sentences. An appellate judge in Minnesota determined that the average sentence for African Americans was more than twice as long as that for whites.[86] Racial disparities in sentencing infuriate some federal judges, because the guidelines provide little latitude for the court to tailor the punishment to fit the crime.

The use of sentencing guidelines was consistent with the new penology, contended Feeley and Simon. In its new configuration, the purpose of criminal justice was not to arbitrate punishment in relation to lawlessness, but to incapacitate large numbers of high-risk offenders selectively. Accordingly, prisons became warehouses for the offenders who were judged to represent the highest risk to society. Because a high-risk designation is positively associated with race and indigence, the new penology functioned to regulate the most troublesome—and allegedly dangerous—elements of the underclass, and drug involvement served to identify those among the underclass who presented the highest risk. Thus, within the contemporary urban milieu, the new penology became an instrument of racial and class oppression.

It could be argued that in the United States prisons have historically served as institutions of last resort for incorrigible populations that have proved difficult to socialize. In that respect the large numbers of African Americans who dominate the prisons today are little different from the Irish or Italian immigrant inmates who disproportionately populated correctional facilities decades ago. If there is a qualitatively different aspect to contemporary corrections, however, it lies in the merging of systems management with the rapid expansion of the correctional corporations. The fundamental difference between the old, government-maintained penology and the new, corporate-managed penology is that the latter has a financial stake in an expanding correctional market, whereas the incentives under the old penology were such that the state attempted to limit criminal justice expenditures.

Thus, an analysis of corrections produced by Steven Donziger for the National Criminal Justice Commission targeted the emerging "prison-industrial complex." According to Donziger, the prison-industrial complex consisted of an "iron triangle" of "government bureaucrats, private industry leaders, and politicians who work together to expand the criminal justice system."[87] In the United States in 1996 there were 21 companies with annual revenues exceeding $250 million, managing some 88 prisons in which 50,000 inmates were incarcerated—a twentyfold increase in the number of inmates managed by for-profit correctional firms since 1984.[88] The passage of the "three strikes" legislation targeting repeat offenders, the war on drugs, and the consequences of the sentencing guidelines provided the prison-industrial complex with a more-than-adequate supply of inmates. Because most inmates were nonviolent offenders, incarceration in the minimum- and medium-security facilities that were favored by for-profit firms proved ideal. Contrasted to the archaic prisons typical of the old penology, the facilities managed by for-profit firms were not only more adequate with regard to basic amenities, but also more likely to provide educational and other services as methods to maintain a compliant population.

The prison-industrial complex is not without its detractors, however. Prison guard unions have emerged as staunch critics of for-profit corrections, because a primary means by which for-profit firms reduce their costs is hiring staff who are less expensive than state correctional officers who benefit from state civil service regulations and higher pay. Regardless, corrections has become big business, involving 2.2 million people in apprehending and incarcerating miscreants. "Major companies, such as Wackenhut Corrections Crop and Corrections Corporation of America employ sophisticated lobbyists to protect and expand their market share," observed Alan Elsner. "The law enforcement technology industry, which produces high-tech items such as the latest stab-proof vests, helmets, stun guns, shields, batons and chemical agents, does more than a billion dollars a year in business."[89] Although prisoners tend to benefit from correctional facilities managed by for-profit firms, especially when the alternative has been state-run facilities that are so retrograde that they have been found by the courts to violate the constitutional rights of inmates, the new penology brings with it a classic conflict between labor (prison guards) and management (CEOs).

The Future of Criminal Justice

With the expansion of correctional facilities in response to escalating crime, calls for reform of the criminal justice system have become increasingly shrill. Among the most prominent reforms are community policing, victim assistance, harsher sentences, and death sentence reviews. Competing views of criminal justice have driven these policy changes.

Community Policing Conceived in Houston, community policing reassigned law enforcement officers from patrol cars and specialty units, which had isolated them from the public, to beats on the streets of high-crime areas. As mayors[90] and the public noted the benefits of community policing,[91] the reform spread, eventually becoming a prominent feature of federal crime policy. President Clinton promised federal funding to deploy 100,000 more police officers to combat crime, and in 1995 the attorney general boasted that the Clinton administration had placed more than 25,000 police officers in the Community Oriented Policing Services (COPS) program.[92] In 2002, the Department of Justice awarded $720 million in grants through its COPS Office.

Victim Assistance Created through the 1984 Victims of Crime Act, the Justice Department's Office for Victims of Crime receives funds derived from settlements of federal civil cases and makes grants for two purposes: victim compensation and victim assistance. In 1996 the program allocated $528.9 million among 2 million beneficiaries. Because the program is not well known, outreach efforts have been undertaken to alert prospective recipients about the availability of assistance.[93] For 2003, the fund was projected to increase to $559 million.[94]

Harsher Sentences As a result of crimes committed by repeat offenders, particularly sexual offenses, jurisdictions have stiffened sentencing. Since its inception in the mid-1990s, California's "three strikes" law has resulted in a doubling of sentences for second-time offenders and mandates sentences of 25 years to life for third-time offenders, even those convicted of nonviolent crimes.[95] In response to the murders of Megan Kanka and Polly Klaas, the Violent Crime Control and Law Enforcement Act of 1994 included mandatory registration of sexual offenders with local law enforcement, information that is available to the public.[96] In 2004, harsher sentences that had been standardized through federal sentencing guidelines were found unconstitutional by the Supreme Court, throwing the policy into confusion.

Death Sentence Review During the 1990s, an increasing number of death penalty convictions were reversed, some within days, if not hours, of scheduled executions. To dramatize the prospect of executing an innocent person, the Northwestern University Law School convened a conference on the issue in November 1998, featuring more than 30 former death row inmates.[97] In a related development, the introduction of DNA evidence resulted in the release of 70 inmates, including 8 from death row, who had been wrongfully convicted.[98] In 1999 the governor of Illinois announced a moratorium on executions, because so many of the state's death row inmates had been found innocent.[99] Ultimately, an exhaustive study of capital punishment revealed that two-thirds of death sentences had been reversed on appeal, suggesting that the sentencing process was rife with irregularity.[100]

Of the 3,600 inmates on death row, approximately 10 percent are mentally retarded, a status recognized by only 13 of the 38 states permitting capital punishment; since 1976, 34 retarded inmates have been executed. As details about mentally impaired inmates became known, momentum grew to restrain capital punishment. For example, in 1995, Mario Marquez, who had an IQ of 60 and the aptitude of a seven-year-old, was executed in Texas for the murder of his niece. Hours before his execution he said, "I want to be God's gardener and take care of the animals." His attorney later said, "It was like talking to a five-year-old."[101] In 2002 the Supreme Court ruled that executing retarded inmates was unconstitutional; two years later the Court agreed to hear the appeal of an inmate who had received a death sentence for a crime committed as a juvenile, ultimately determining that the execution of inmates for crimes committed as juveniles was also unconstitutional.[102] Fundamental questions about the validity of the death penalty have contributed to the growth of mitigation investigations, in which social workers have played an important role.[103]

If conservatives defined criminal justice policy through the 1980s and 1990s, two developments marked the possibility of an ideological shift. About 95 percent of current inmates locked up during the past two decades—585,000 by 2000—will require some type of reentry service if they are to avoid notoriously high recidivism rates: Of state prisoners, for example, 62 percent are rearrested within three years, and 41 percent are reincarcerated.[104] Yet, apart from experimental pilot demonstrations such as drug courts, comparatively little attention has been directed at services for ex-cons. Among the most successful services is the Delancey Street Foundation, a nonprofessional residential program, conceived in San Francisco in 1971. Delancey Street boasts that 90 percent of its graduates become productive citizens, although its capacity is limited to only 1,000 residents.[105]

In the late 1990s charges of police misconduct, latent since the Los Angeles riot that was precipitated by the acquittal of officers charged with beating Rodney King, resurfaced. The brutality of New York police who shot and sodomized African immigrants appalled the nation, as did the wholesale corruption within the Los Angeles Police Department. Several officers from an elite Los Angeles anti-gang unit were charged with stealing drugs from an evidence locker, planting guns on suspects, even shooting unarmed gang members. Investigation of the scandal has resulted in the overturning of 100 convictions, further inquiry into the conduct of 70 police officers, and the certain prospect of millions of dollars in civil litigation.[106]

Conclusion

Despite a burgeoning population of Americans intimately acquainted with the criminal justice system, the prospect of radical reform appears dim. Other than driving down unemployment through its economic policies and encouraging community policing, the Clinton presidency was unwilling to propose any viable alternative to prison expansion. For its part, the administration of George W. Bush, intent on a "get tough" approach to crime, used the attacks of September 11, 2001 as a pretext for attenuating civil liberties through the U.S. Patriot Act. During the past two decades, the prison-industrial complex has expanded to process and capitalize on the legions of young black men sentenced and placed in its care. Despite the enormous institutional and psychological costs associated with incarceration, momentum has yet to build in the direction of community-based services. Thus, criminal justice remains one of the greatest institutional challenges facing American social policy.

Discussion Questions

1. Click on the "For Students" link on the policyAmerica website, identify legislation related to criminal justice, and trace its implications for social welfare. Has the policy been effective? What are its costs? How might it be made more adequate?
2. Crime varies considerably in terms of both the nature of offenses and the characteristics of offenders. How prevalent is crime in your community? What are the primary offenses? Who are the offenders?
3. State and local governments vary regarding the management of juvenile delinquency. Does your community have a juvenile court? Are its deliberations open to the public? What are the usual offenses that bring a youth to juvenile court?
4. Many communities are building new correctional facilities. Is your community upgrading corrections? To what extent do new facilities reflect the new penology? Are for-profit correctional firms active in your state? If not, should

they be? Should they be allowed to contract to manage probation and parole?

5. Legalization of drugs has become a heated issue. What are the implications of drug legalization for substance abuse programs? How could drug legalization be structured in your state? How would substances be taxed? How would tax revenues from legalization be allocated?
6. In many poor urban communities, drug-related street violence has escalated to unprecedented heights. How has your community balanced resource allocations for supply interdiction versus resources for demand reduction? To what extent is substance abuse treatment available to inmates in local correctional facilities? Have specific neighborhoods in your community organized to contain and reduce drug trafficking? Which agencies have supported such initiatives?
7. As the war on drugs has failed to live up to its promise, more attention has been focused on prevention, particularly among children. What models have agencies in your community adopted to prevent substance abuse among kids? How much money has been allocated for prevention programs? What is the track record of the prevention programs adopted in your community?

Notes

1. *Encyclopedia of Sociology* (Guilford, CT: Dushkin Publishing Group, 1974).
2. D. Stanley Eitzen and Doug Timmer, *Criminology* (New York: John Wiley, 1985), pp. 15–16.
3. Phyllis Day, *A New History of Social Welfare* (Englewood Cliffs, NJ: Prentice Hall, 1989), p. 181.
4. Ibid., p. 182.
5. Jerome Miller, *Search and Destroy: African-American Males in the Criminal Justice System* (New York: Cambridge University Press, 1996), p. 207.
6. Quoted in Ibid., p. 185.
7. Richard Herrnstein and Charles Murray, *The Bell Curve* (New York: Free Press, 1994).
8. Glenn Walters, "A Meta-Analysis of the Gene–Crime Relationship," *Criminology* 30, no. 4 (1992), pp. 8–16.
9. *Justice Expenditures and Employment Abstracts* (Washington, DC: U.S. Department of Justice, 1992).
10. U.S. Department of Commerce, *Statistical Abstract of the United States, 2002* (Washington, DC: U.S. GPO, 2002), p. 199.
11. "The Growing Inmate Population," *New York Times* (August 1, 2003), p. A22.
12. Andrew Block and Virginia Weisz, "Choosing Prisoners over Pupils," *Washington Post* (July 6, 2004), p. A19.
13. John Broder, "No Hard Time for Prison Budgets," *New York Times* (January 29, 2003), p. WK5.
14. Gary Jensen and Maryaltani Karpos, "Research on the Behavior of Rape Statistics," *Criminology* 31, no. 4 (1993), p. 382.
15. *Annual Report, Attorney General of the U.S.* (Washington, DC: Department of Justice, 1995), p. 4.
16. Lela Costin, Howard Karger, and David Stoesz, *The Politics of Child Abuse in America* (New York: Oxford University Press, 1996).
17. "Behind Bars," *Washington Post* (June 3, 2000), p. A9.
18. "Nation's Prison Population Climbs to over 2 Million," *Washington Post* (August 10, 2000), p. A4.
19. U.S. Census Bureau, *Statistical Abstract of the United States, 1999* (Washington, DC: U.S. Government Printing Office, 1999), p. 231.
20. David Masci, "Prison-Building Boom," *Issues in Social Policy* (Washington, DC: Congressional Quarterly, 2000), p. 138.
21. Fox Butterfield, "Prison Rates Among Blacks Reach a Peak, Report Finds," *New York Times* (April 7, 2003), p. A11.
22. "The Price of Prisons," *New York Times* (June 26, 2004), p. A26.
23. Day, *A New History of Social Welfare,* p. 180.
24. James Leiby, *A History of Social Welfare and Social Work in the United States* (New York: Columbia University Press, 1978), p. 147.
25. Jerome Miller, *Last One over the Wall* (Columbus, OH: Ohio State University, 1991), p. 222.
26. Ibid., p. 243.
27. Denise Gottfredson and William Barton, "Deinstitutionalization of Juvenile Offenders," *Criminology* 31, no. 4 (1993), pp. 98–117.
28. James Q. Wilson and John DiIulio, Jr., "Crackdown," *The New Republic* (July 10, 1989), p. 54.
29. Rhonda Cook, "Georgia's Prison Boot Camps Don't Work, Study Says," *San Diego Union Tribune* (May 8, 1994), p. A32.
30. "Connecticut Suspends Gang-Riddled Youth Boot Camp," *San Diego Union Tribune* (June 12, 1994), p. A6.
31. Doris Mackenzie et al., "Boot Camp Prisons and Recidivism in Eight States," *Criminology* 33, no. 3 (1995), p. 78.

32. Margaret Talbot, "The Maximum Security Adolescent," *New York Times Magazine* (September 10, 2000), p. 42.
33. Blaine Harden, "Boston's Approach to Juvenile Crime Encircles Youths, Reduces Slayings," *Washington Post* (October 23, 1997), p. A3.
34. Fox Butterfield, "Triple Murder in Boston Points to Unsettling Rise in Homicides," *New York Times* (October 12, 2004), p. A18.
35. U.S. Department of Commerce, *Statistical Abstract of the United States* (Washington, DC: U.S. GPO, 2002), p. 193.
36. Mathea Falco, *Winning the Drug War* (New York: Priority Press, 1989) pp. 26–27.
37. Barry McCaffrey, *The Office of National Drug Control's Fiscal Year 2001 Budget* (Washington, DC: ONDC, March 23, 2000).
38. Sidney Cohen, "The Drug-Free America Act of 1986," *Drug Abuse and Alcoholism Newsletter* (San Diego, CA: Vista Hill Foundation, 1987), pp. 1–3.
39. Falco, *Winning the Drug War,* p. 29.
40. Barry Bearak, "A Room for Heroin and HIV," *Los Angeles Times* (September 27, 1992), p. A18.
41. *Statistical Abstract of the United States,* 2002, pp. 191, 193.
42. Bearak, "Road to Detox: Do Not Enter," *Los Angeles Times* (September 30, 1992), p. A18. Used by permission.
43. John Kasarda, "Industrial Restructuring and the Consequences of Changing Job Locations," in Reynolds Farley (ed.), *Changes and Challenges: America 1990* (New York: Russell Sage Foundation, 1995), Table 5.15.
44. Christopher Jencks, "Deadly Neighborhoods," *The New Republic* (June 13, 1988), p. 18; Juan Williams, "Hard Times, Harder Hearts," *Washington Post* (October 2, 1988), p. C4.
45. Louis Sahagun, "Gang Killings Increase 69%, Violent Crime up 20% in L. A. County Areas," *Los Angeles Times* (August 21, 1990), p. B8.
46. Jesse Katz, "County's Yearly Death Toll Reaches 800," *Los Angeles Times* (January 19, 1993), p. A23.
47. Gabriel Escobar, "Slayings in Washington Hit New High, 436, for 3rd Year," *Los Angeles Times* (November 24, 1990), p. A26.
48. Claude Brown, *Manchild in the Promised Land* (New York: Macmillan, 1965); Claude Brown, "Manchild in Harlem," *New York Times* (September 16, 1984), p. 16.
49. Daniel Patrick Moynihan, *Came the Revolution* (San Diego, CA: Harcourt Brace Jovanovich, 1988), p. 291.
50. Miller, *Search and Destroy,* pp. 7–8.
51. Ibid., p. 54.
52. Ibid., p. 85.
53. Ibid., p. 99.
54. Alex Kotlowitz, *There Are No Children Here* (New York: Doubleday, 1991).
55. Barry Bearak, "Brooklyn Neighborhood Grieves for Its Mr. Chips," *Los Angeles Times* (December 19, 1992), p. A6.
56. Glenn Frankel, "The Longest War," *Washington Post Weekly* (July 7, 1997), p. 6.
57. David Simon and Edward Burns, "Too Much Is Not Enough," *Washington Post* (September 7, 1997), p. C1.
58. Pamela Frank, "Drugs across the Border: A War We're Losing," *Washington Post Weekly* (September 29, 1997), p. 27.
59. Jim McGee, "Military Seeks Balance in Delicate Mission: The Drug War," *Washington Post* (November 29, 1996).
60. George Soros, "The Drug War 'Cannot Be Won'," *Washington Post* (February 2, 1997).
61. Michael Novak, *The New Consensus on Poverty and the Family* (Washington, DC: American Enterprise Institute, 1987).
62. William Bennett, John DiIulio, Jr., and John Walters, *Body Count* (New York: Simon and Schuster, 1996), p. 56.
63. Ibid., p. 105.
64. Ibid., p. 27.
65. Ibid., pp. 175–176.
66. Ibid., Chap. 5.
67. Jim Wallace, "With Unconditional Love," *Sojourners* (October 1997).
78. James Traub, "The Criminals of Tomorrow," *The New Yorker* (November 4, 1996).
69. John Hagan, "The Social Embededness of Crime and Unemployment," *Criminology,* 31, no. 4 (1993), p. 469.
70. William Julius Wilson, *When Work Disappears* (New York: Knopf, 1996), p. 238.
71. Ethan Nadelmann, "The Case for Legalization." *Public Interest* 92 (1988), pp. 3–17.
72. James Jacobs, "Imagining Drug Legalization," *The Public Interest* 101 (Fall 1990), pp. 27–34.
73. Falco, *The Making of a Drug-Free America* (New York: Priority Press, 1989), p. 100.
74. Jacobs, "Imagining Drug Legalization," p. 30.
75. Jim Newton, "Seizure of Assets Leaves Casualties in War on Drugs," *Los Angeles Times* (October 14, 1992), p. A1; David Savage, "Drug-Case Forfeitures Will Be Reviewed," *Los Angeles Times* (January 16, 1993), p. A2.
76. David Lamb, "Last Shot to Salvage Their Lives," *Los Angeles Times* (January 17, 1993), p. A1.
77. U.S. Census Bureau, *Statistical Summary of the United States* (Washington, DC: U.S. Census Bureau, 1995), Table 349.
78. U.S. Census Bureau, *Statistical Abstract of the U.S.,* 1999, p. 231.

79. *Annual Report of the Attorney General of the U.S.*, 1995.
80. U.S. Census Bureau, *Statistical Abstract of the United States*, 2002, p. 204.
81. U.S. Census Bureau, *Statistical Abstract of the United States*, 1999, p. 233.
82. Malcolm Feeley and Jonathan Simon, "The New Penology," *Criminology* 30, no. 4 (1992), p. 452.
83. Miller, *Last One over the Wall*, p. 76.
84. Feeley and Simon, "New Penology," p. 455.
85. Mary Flaherty and Joan Biskupic, "Justice by the Numbers," *Washington Post Weekly* (October 14–20, 1996), p. 88.
86. Mary Flaherty and Joan Biskupic, "Rules Often Impose Toughest Penalties on Poor, Minorities," *Washington Post* (October 9, 1996), p. A26.
87. Steven Donziger, "The Prison-Industrial Complex," *Washington Post* (March 17, 1996), p. C3.
88. Ibid., p. C3.
89. Alan Elsner, "America's Prison Habit," *Washington Post* (January 24, 2004), p. A19.
90. Office of Community Oriented Policing Services, Department of Justice. Retrieved October 14, 2004, from www.usdoj.gov
91. Janet Vinzant and Lane Crothers, "Street-Level Leadership: The Role of Patrol Officers in Community Policing," *Criminal Justice Review*, 19, no. 2 (Autumn 1994), pp. 56–71.
92. *Annual Report of the Attorney General of the U.S.*, 1995.
93. Sharon Walsh, "Crime Does Pay . . . Its Victims," *Washington Post* (February 2, 1997), p. A1.
94. *Federal Budget of the United States, 2004*, p. 363.
95. Rene Sanchez, "A Movement Builds against 'Three Strikes' Law," *Washington Post* (February 18, 2000), p. A3.
96. Hans Selvog, "Moral Panic and Sex Offenders," (Richmond, VA: Virginia Commonwealth University School of Social Work, 2000).
97. Mary Cooper, "Death Penalty." In *Issues in Social Policy* (Washington, DC: Congressional Quarterly, 2000).
98. Brooke Masters, "DNA Testing in Old Cases Is Disputed," *Washington Post* (September 10, 2000), p. A1.
99. Bob Herbert, "Criminal Justice Breakdown," *New York Times* (February 14, 2000), p. A27.
100. Brooke Masters, "A Death Sentence, Then a Reversal," *Washington Post Weekly* (June 19, 2000), p. 34.
101. Raymond Bonner and Sara Rimer, "Executing the Mentally Retarded Even as Laws Begin to Shift," *New York Times* (August 7, 2000), p. 1.
102. Linda Greenhouse, "Justices Consider Executions of Young Killers," *New York Times* (October 14, 2004), p. A1.
103. Julie Schroeder, "Forging a New Practice Area: Social Work's Role in Death Penalty Mitigation Investigations," *Families in Society* 84, no. 3 (2003).
104. Peter Slevin, "Life after Prison," *Washington Post* (April 24, 2000), p. A1.
105. Ray Rivera, "On Delancey Street," *The Santa Fe New Mexican* (October 19, 1997).
106. William Booth, "In L. A. Police Scandal, 4 Go on Trial for Faking Cases," *Washington Post* (October 14, 2000), p. A3.

CHAPTER 15

Child Welfare Policy

This chapter examines the evolution of child welfare policy in the United States. Child protective services, foster care, adoption, and Head Start have been the focus of child welfare policy since the 1960s. The devolution of welfare to the states through the Personal Responsibility and Work Opportunity Reconciliation Act of 1996 has introduced questions about the prospects of poor children whose mothers are entering the labor market.

In U.S. social welfare, the condition of children is inextricably linked to the status of their families. Because the United States has failed to establish a family policy that ensures basic income, employment, and social service supports to parents, parents frequently have difficulty in caring for their children. As families are less able to care for their children, the demand for child welfare services escalates. The commitment that national governments make toward reducing poverty among children varies considerably. Among industrialized nations, the United States fares poorly indeed. The Luxembourg Study, which rated the number of children in poverty, found that the United States ranked last, as indicated in Table 15.1.

In the United States in recent years, the proportion of children living in poverty, the proportion of children in single-parent households, the percentage of mothers in the workforce, and the birthrate of women in minority groups have all remained high. In 2002, 12.1 million children were living in poverty in this country, a significant increase from the 10.4 million poor children in 1970.[1] Although child poverty diminishes when family incomes increase during economic expansion, improvement slowed between the 1993–1995 period, when 1.2 million children per year were lifted out of poverty, and the 1995–1998 period, when only 400,000 per year rose from the ranks of the poor.[2] More troubling, the Children's Defense Fund has reported that the number of children in families with incomes less than half of the poverty line increased sharply during the late part of the 1990s.[3]

Table 15.1

Ranking Child Poverty in 17 Developed Countries

Rank	Country	Children in Poverty*	Elderly in Poverty*	Total Poverty*
1	United States	21.9%	24.7%	17.0%
2	Italy	16.6	13.7	12.7
3	Australia	15.8	29.4	14.3
4	United Kingdom	15.4	20.9	12.5
5	Canada	14.9	5.9	11.4
6	Ireland	14.4	24.3	12.3
7	Spain	12.2	11.3	10.1
8	Austria	10.2	10.5	8.0
9	Switzerland	10.0	8.4	9.3
10	Netherlands	9.8	2.4	7.3
11	Denmark	8.7	6.6	9.2
12	France	7.9	9.8	8.0
13	Belgium	7.7	11.7	8.0
14	Germany	6.8	11.6	8.3
15	Sweden	4.2	7.7	6.5
16	Norway	3.4	11.9	6.4
17	Finland	2.8	8.5	5.4

* For purposes of comparison, poverty equals 50 percent or less of median income.

Source: Lawrence Mishel, Jared Bernstein, and Sylvia Allegretto, *The State of Working America, 2004–05* (Washington, DC: Economic Policy Institute, 2004), p. 406.

Poverty has adverse consequences for infants, contributing to insufficient prenatal care and high infant mortality. This fact explains, in part, the relatively high infant mortality rate of the United States: 6.8 deaths per 1,000 live births, compared to Japan's 3.9, Germany's 4.7, Canada's 5.0, the United Kingdom's 5.5, or the Czech Republic's 5.6.[4] Despite the chronically poor showing of child welfare in the United States relative to other industrialized nations, the most recent federal accounting that included such variables as violent crime, poverty, mortality, teen pregnancy, and overall health, indicated that U.S. children were faring somewhat better than in the past.[5] The Child Well-Being Index, which tracks the welfare of children over time through 28 variables, has shown significant improvements since the mid-1990s.[6] Between 1996 and 2001, *Kids Count,* a project of the Annie E. Casey Foundation, reported improvement on eight of ten variables used to evaluate child welfare.[7]

Although an increase in a broad range of family and child welfare services might be expected in view of the chronic negligence that has typified the nation's care for its children, the societal response has been extremely varied. As Jeanne Giovannoni notes, "at best we have a hodgepodge of funding and regulatory mechanisms, and we rely predominantly on market mechanisms dictating both the amount and variety of care available."[8] Others have been less charitable. Alvin Schorr, a veteran welfare scholar, has observed, "From the 1960s on, child welfare suffered a series of blows that left [conventional] ideology and the program in shambles."[9]

A classification of child welfare services completed by the Child Welfare League of America identified nine diverse components: services in the home, day care, homemaker services, foster care, adoption, group home care, institutional care, protective services, and services to unmarried parents.[10] Of these, protective services, foster care, and adoption are most frequently identified as being related exclusively to child welfare and, therefore, are the focus here, though emerging issues are addressed as well.

Child welfare services are often controversial, because they sanction the intervention of human service professionals in family affairs that are ordinarily assumed to be private matters and the prerogative of parents. This dilemma places extraordinary demands on child welfare professionals, who are mandated to protect the best interests of the child while not intruding on the privacy of the family.[11] Recently, this conundrum has become more pronounced: advocates for child welfare services demand more programs, but traditionalist groups attempt to cut programs that they see as designed to subvert the family. Ironically, much of this argument could be defused if the United States adopted a family policy that helped parents care for children more adequately, thus reducing the need for the more intrusive child welfare interventions. For the moment, however, the adoption of any family policy is unlikely, leaving services to children fragmented. This historical reluctance to allow government to intrude into the privacy of the family has been compounded by scandals involving under-funded, over-burdened, and mismanaged child welfare departments in New Jersey, Florida, and the District of Columbia.

History of U.S. Child Welfare Policy

Although many states established orphanages during the eighteenth century, current child welfare policy

Spotlight 15.1

The Child Welfare League of America

Established in 1920, the Child Welfare League of America (CWLA) is an association of 1,000 public and private nonprofit agencies that assist abused and neglected children and their families each year with a wide range of services. To learn more about this agency, go to its website at **www.cwla.** CWLA also offers a timeline of events in the history of child welfare at **www.cwla.org/whowhat/history.htm.**

Child welfare policy in the United States began in the 1870s. An early program led by Charles Loring Brace, founder of New York's Children's Aid Society, moved thousands of children from deleterious urban conditions in New York City to farm families in the Midwest. Under intense criticism, this program would later be replaced with programs that were less divisive to family and community.

in the United States has its origins in the 1870s.[12] The large number of child paupers led Charles Loring Brace, founder of New York's Children's Aid Society, to train thousands of children from deleterious urban conditions in New York City to farm families in the Midwest. Eventually, criticism of Brace's methods, which were divisive of family and community, contributed to more preventive approaches to children's problems. By the beginning of the twentieth century, most large cities had children's aid societies that practiced the "boarding out" of children (the payment of a fee for child rearing) to sponsors in the community.[13] The boarding out of children until adoption (except in the case of children with disabilities, who were unlikely to be adopted) was the forerunner of today's foster care and adoption programs in the United States.

Protective services for children began with one of the more unusual incidents in American social welfare. In 1874 a New York church worker, Etta Wheeler, discovered that an indentured nine-year-old child, Mary Ellen, was being tied to a bed, whipped, and stabbed with scissors. On investigating what could be done for Mary Ellen, Wheeler spoke with the director of the New York Society for the Prevention of Cruelty to Animals (NYSPCA) on behalf of the child. Although it was subsequently misreported that intervention on behalf of Mary Ellen was predicated on her status as an animal, rather than as a child, a careful review of the case indicated that Mary Ellen's case was adjudicated consistently with legal precedents involving abused children.[14] The following year, the New York Society for the Prevention of Cruelty to Children was established.[15] By 1922, 57 societies for the prevention of cruelty to children had been established to protect abused youngsters.[16]

Child welfare proved an effective rallying issue for Progressives, who advocated intervention on the part of the federal government. In 1909, James E. West, a friend of President Theodore Roosevelt and later head of the Boy Scouts of America, convinced Jane Addams and other welfare leaders to attend a two-day meeting on child welfare. This first White House Conference on Children focused attention on the plight of destitute families, agency problems with the boarding out of children, and the importance of home care. The conference proved so successful that it was subsequently repeated every 10 years—with the exception of 1981, when the conference was canceled by the Reagan administration. The White House Conference on Children served as a model for legitimating and attracting attention to social welfare needs. One significant product of the White House Conference on Children was the call to establish a federal agency to "collect and exchange ideas and information on child welfare." With an initial appropriation of $25,640, the U.S. Children's Bureau was established in 1912 under the auspices of the Department of Commerce and Labor.[17] Instrumental in the early years of the Children's Bureau were Lillian Wald, of New York's Henry Street Settlement House, and Florence Kelley, an alumna of both the Henry Street Settlement and Hull House. Julia Lathrop, a former resident of Hull House, was the bureau's first director.[18]

Because of the economic circumstances of poor families, child labor emerged as a primary concern of early child welfare advocates. The absence of public relief meant that families were compelled to work at whatever employment might be available, however wearing and demeaning. Children worked full shifts in coal mines and textile mills; women labored in sweatshops. Neither were protected from dangerous or unhygienic working conditions. Under the guidance of Florence Kelley, the National Consumer League fought for children and women using a dual strategy. First, the league lobbied for reform in the working conditions of women through regulation of sweatshops and factories, and for ending the exploitation of children by prohibiting child labor. Second, it advocated ameliorating the grinding poverty of many families by means of a family subsidy that would make such deplorable work less necessary. For Kelley, the family subsidy was a preventive measure with which she was quite familiar; in Illinois in 1911, she had successfully lobbied for passage of the Funds for Parents Act. This act was a precursor of the Aid to Dependent Children program, part of the original Social Security Act of 1935.[19]

Before the Great Depression, welfare advocates could boast of a series of unprecedented initiatives designed to improve the conditions of poor families in the United States. The Children's Bureau Act of 1912 established a national agency to collect information on children. The Child Labor Act of 1916 prohibited the interstate transportation of goods manufactured by children. The Maternity and Infancy Act of 1921 assisted states in establishing programs that dramatically reduced the nation's infant and maternal mortality rates. Yet these hard-won successes were constantly at risk of being subverted. The Supreme Court ruled the Child Labor Act unconstitutional in 1918, and the Maternity and Infancy Act was terminated in 1929, when Herbert Hoover and Congress refused further appropriations.[20] Child and family welfare initiatives remained unsuccessful until the Social Security Act of 1935 ushered in a complete set of welfare policies.

The Social Security Act addressed child welfare in two of its provisions. Title IV introduced the Aid to Dependent Children program, which provided public relief to needy children through cash grants to their families. Title V reestablished Maternal and Child Welfare Services (which had expired in 1929) and expanded the mandate of the Children's Bureau, whose goal was now to oversee a new set of child welfare services "for the protection and care of homeless, dependent, and neglected children, and children in danger of becoming delinquent."[21] Significantly, both family relief and child welfare services were to be administered by the states through public welfare departments. As a result, as of 1935 the provision of child welfare services shifted largely from the private, voluntary sector to the public, governmental sector.

Within public welfare, the responsibility for child welfare has shifted between the federal and state governments. Since 1935 the state and federal governments have shared responsibility for social services provided to families, but the role of the federal government has changed with respect to income maintenance benefits to poor families. From 1935 until 1996, federal and state government shared the funding and administration of the AFDC program. With devolution of public assistance to the states through the 1996 Personal Responsibility and Work Opportunity Reconciliation Act (PRWORA), however, the federal government limited its role to one of funding and limited oversight. PRWORA instituted a block grant program, Temporary Assistance for Needy Families (TANF), which is primarily under the control of state government. Consistent with the residual conception of welfare, primary responsibility for children rests with their parent(s) with state intervention as a backup. Ominously, in 2003 a significant number of states had reduced TANF appropriations for transition to work, assistance to the poorest families, transportation aid, and cash assistance. Thirty-two states had restricted eligibility, instituted waiting lists, and reduced payments for child care, and four states had reduced support of teen pregnancy prevention programs.[22] Thus, while PRWORA has contributed to a sharp drop in welfare rolls, reduced support for children and youth may imperil their futures.

Protective Services for Children

Through the Social Security Act, states proceeded to develop services to children independently of one another and within the relatively loose specifications of the act. In the absence of a centralized authority that would ensure standardized care throughout the United States, child welfare services varied greatly from state to state and even within states. In the two decades following the passage of the Social Security Act, child welfare services had become established within American social welfare, but with a high degree of fragmentation.

In the 1960s the status quo in child welfare was upset by increasing reports of child abuse and neglect. A pediatrician, C. Henry Kempe, identified non-accidental injuries to children as the "battered child syndrome." As more states began to address the problem, child welfare advocates built a compelling case for a national standard for child protective services. This lobbying led to the passage of the Child Abuse Prevention and Treatment Act of 1974, which established the National Center for Child Abuse and Neglect within the Department of Health and Human Services and presented a model statute for state child protective programs. All 50 states eventually enacted the model statute, which, among its provisions, specified the following:

- a standard definition of child abuse and neglect
- methods for reporting and investigating abuse and neglect
- immunity for those reporting suspected injuries inflicted on children
- prevention and public education efforts to reduce incidents of abuse and neglect

As a result of these national standards, the National Center for Child Abuse and Neglect was able—for the first time—to report trends in child abuse and the need for protective services for children. Alarmingly, the data collected by the National Center revealed a dramatic increase in reports of child abuse; these more than doubled between 1976 and 1986, when reports of child abuse numbered 2 million.[23] In 1991 Chicago's National Committee for the Prevention of Child Abuse reported that 1,383 children died as a result of abuse, 50 percent more than the number reported in 1986.[24] Most troubling was that reports of child abuse continued to climb through the mid-1980s, while at the same time expenditures for child protective services were decreasing.[25]

Increases in child abuse reports and decreases in expenditures led to a crisis in child welfare services. The magnitude of this crisis was mapped in 1987 by Douglas Besharov, an authority on child welfare policy:

> *Of the 1,000 children who die under circumstances suggestive of parental maltreatment each year, between 30 and 50 percent were previously reported to child protective agencies. Many thousands of other children suffer serious injuries after their plight becomes known to authorities. . . . Each year, about 50,000 children with observable injuries severe enough to require hospitalization are not reported* [emphasis in original].[26]

Stories of child abuse fatalities began to appear with greater frequency in the media. Shortly before Thanksgiving of 1987, the report of the beating death of a six-year-old girl under the care of a middle-class couple in Greenwich Village in New York City became a feature story in *Newsweek*.[27] Unfortunately, incidents of child abuse were too often associated with child welfare programs mandated to protect children. In Kansas City, 25 percent of the children in foster care were found to have been abused.[28] During the spring of 1988, National Public Radio broadcast a report of two Illinois state "social workers" who had been dismissed for failure to make home visits and for falsification of records associated with the deaths of two children who had been reported as victims of child abuse.[29] In Baltimore, a group of current and former foster children won a decision in the Fourth District Court of Appeals after charging that 20 administrators and caseworkers of the Baltimore City Department of Social Services had failed "to adequately monitor and protect children in foster care."[30] Such litigation placed child welfare personnel in a double bind: they were faced with increasing demands for services, yet did not have adequate staff resources to respond effectively. "If you take children out of the home, you're snatching them. If you leave them in the home [and they're abused], you didn't protect them," complained Jim Bell of the Massachusetts Department of Social Services. "We try to deal the best we can in that environment and protect the [case]workers. We don't want them hanging out there all alone."[31]

One consequence of this disintegration of children's services was a volatile debate over the definition of child abuse and neglect. One solution to the widening disparity between dwindling resources for children's services and increasing reports of abuse and neglect, of course, would be to redefine the criteria in accordance with which emergency services for children were deployed. If conservatives could promulgate a more restrictive definition of abuse and neglect, they would benefit directly, in that such a change would effectively subvert demands for greater funding for children's services and parents would retain wider latitude for their behavior in the home. Contending that confirmed reports of child abuse had consistently declined since implementation of the Child Abuse Prevention and Treatment Act, Besharov argued for a more restrictive definition.[32] Countering this claim, David Finkelhor of the University of New Hampshire's Family Research Laboratory noted that annual data from the American Humane Association indicated fairly steady rates of validated abuse and neglect, from 40 to 43 percent of all reports. Because more specific research on the nature of general abuse and sexual abuse suggested increasing incidence, Finkelhor argued for more resources for child protection.[33]

The rapid deterioration of child welfare services led children's advocates to call for more funding of social services. But proposals for increased support for child welfare services did not go unchallenged. Ambiguity in the definition of what constituted child abuse and neglect had contributed to incidents in which child welfare workers appeared to disregard parental rights in their eagerness to protect children. Perhaps the most notorious instance of such overzealousness occurred during the summer of 1984, when social workers from the Vermont Department of Social and Rehabilitation Services and the state police rounded up 112 children from "a radical Christian sect" and detained them for three days to search for indications of abuse. When the American Civil Liberties Union threatened to sue the state on behalf of the religious community, state officials reconsidered, and the children were returned to their parents.[34] Similar but less newsworthy incidents enraged parents who, feeling unjustly accused, formed VOCAL (Victims of Child Abuse Laws) in an attempt to restore traditional parental rights in the face of what they perceived to be the intrusiveness of the state.

Conservative scholars contributed to the grassroots indignation that fueled VOCAL. Sociologists Bridgitte and Peter Berger contended that social services, such as child welfare, were the vehicle through which middle-class professionals evangelized among lower-class clients. In disputes between professionals and parents over parents' versus children's rights, the Bergers' recommendation was to "trust parents over against experts."[35] With momentum building during the 1980s, the 3,000 members of VOCAL took their complaints into the public arena. In Arizona, for example, VOCAL held up a $5.4 million appropriation for child protective services.[36]

Further distracting public attention from child maltreatment, during the 1980s some family therapists suggested that therapy could "recover memories" of childhood abuse. By the end of the decade, showcase trials of child day care providers, teachers, clergy, and parents resulted in a series of convictions based on incidents that had been previously forgotten but were later retrieved during clinical treatment. Later, as appeals raised questions about the veracity of allegations, the "recovered memory" movement came under scrutiny. By the time a Wenatchee, Washington, minister and his wife were found innocent in 1996 of charges that they had run a satanic cult that abused children, judgments for virtually all of the perpetrators convicted in earlier trials had been reversed on appeal.[37]

While academics, policy wonks, and therapists debated definitional, ideological, and clinical aspects of child maltreatment, child protective services deteriorated. New York City's child welfare services became the focus of scrutiny in the cases of a series of children who died despite having been active child protection cases. In 1992 five-year-old Jeffrey Harden died from broken ribs and burns caused by scalding water. Although Jeffrey's family had been known to child welfare authorities for 18 months, intervention by four different caseworkers failed to identify the risk to the child. By the time of his death, all four workers had left the agency.[38] During Thanksgiving 1995, young Elisa Izquierdo was beaten to death by her demented mother. Despite repeated calls by neighbors and school officials, the city's child protection workers had failed to prevent her murder. Within a year, four-year-old Nadine Lockwood had starved to death. Again, child welfare workers had failed to confirm Nadine's deteriorating health even though neighbors had complained about her neglect. An investigation into the Child Welfare Administration showed the magnitude of agency failure: in a fifth of reported cases, workers failed to interview all of the children in the family; in two out of five cases, workers ignored previous reports of child abuse; almost one-fifth of cases were closed despite the risk of future abuse. Following the exposé, Mayor Rudolph Giuliani announced plans to restructure child welfare in the city.[39] Despite the appointment of a new commissioner of children's services, Nicholas Scoppetta,[40] a subsequent report found that 40 percent of abused and neglected children were returned home and mistreated again.[41]

Virtually every major metropolitan area featured at least one scandal involving a child who died while under the care of protective services. The District of Columbia's Child and Family Service Agency (CFSA) had been so mismanaged that it was in placed under a court-appointed receiver. After several years, the staff were upgraded until virtually all were MSW's, yet the agency continued to show serious performance problems,[42] chief among them high caseloads and high turnover.[43] By 2000 a deteriorating work environment had resulted in "foster care panic," in which CFSA workers removed children from parents, leading the *Washington Post* to accuse social workers of "flight from professional judgment and responsibility." "Social workers are abandoning their training as well as the children and families they've been hired to serve," the paper intoned.[44] Six months later the General Accounting Office reported that CFSA had failed to investigate 1,200 cases of suspected neglect and abuse within 30 days, among other structural problems.[45] Soon, the reporting of CFSA children placed with families outside the district was so poor that Maryland suspended accepting CFSA children for foster care. Meanwhile, another case was unnecessarily delayed, and a judge issued an order for the CFSA receiver, a social worker, to appear in court. The receiver ignored the order, which led to her arrest, handcuffing, and quick retreat to a restroom to dodge reporters.[46] More composed, the receiver announced that she would legally challenge the judge's authority to hold her accountable, a statement that was widely derided.[47] As the entire spectacle occurred in the nation's capital, congressional Republicans convened hearings to investigate misfeasance on the part of CFSA as well as the judgment of the receiver.[48] Eventually the receiver apologized to the court, paid fines that included reimbursement of parties inconvenienced by her absence at the hearing, and subsequently resigned. None of this reflected well on child welfare professionals, who appeared inept under the scrutiny of the federal lawmakers responsible for oversight of federal child welfare policy.

In 2001, the death of a 23-month-old African American infant due to child abuse, led reporters from the *Washington Post* to investigate other child deaths. Within a year, reporters had, indeed, identified the outline of a rather imposing iceberg; their research revealed that between 1993 and 2001, 229 children had died as a result of maltreatment in the District of Columbia, but the deaths had gone without proper investigation on the part of the Metropolitan Police Department and DCFS[49]—a story that would receive a Pulitzer Prize. Yet, reform of child protection in the District lagged. The State of Maryland threatened to return 1,500 District foster children because of inadequate documentation on the part of CFSA.[50] Punctuating CFSA lapses in accountability, the family of one of the children who had died of abuse—a 15-year-old whose deformed spine crushed her internal organs because corrective surgery had not been performed—initiated a $120 million suit against CFSA. In a perverse action on the behalf of the District, attorneys argued that CSFA was not liable because the agency had been placed under federal court supervision![51]

Not long thereafter, the nation witnessed another illustration of child welfare in disarray: a 5-year-old Miami girl in foster care, Rilya Wilson, had been missing for 15 months, yet Florida child welfare workers were unable to locate her.[52] Although the head of the Florida family service agency admitted that the ineptitude of child welfare workers was "appalling," she had no explanation for the whereabouts of the 374 other foster children whom the state was unable to locate.[53] Florida child welfare workers replicated the performance of those who had been encountered by reporters elsewhere: rather than admit the extent of problems in children's services, workers used confidentiality as an excuse to avoid public accountability. Two years after the exposé Rilya Wilson had yet to be found.[54]

In January 2003, the decomposing body of 7-year-old Faheem Williams was found in a Newark basement; his two brothers had been locked in a nearby room, "emaciated and with burn scars on their bodies."[55] Although Williams had been an active protective services case with the New Jersey Division of Youth and Family Services (DYFS), multiple agency errors failed to save him. Subsequently, the *New York Times* obtained case records on 17 children which documented the deaths of four children and "the sometimes brutal, prolonged abuse of 13 more."[56] As the *Times* would learn, the culture at DYFS conspired to expose children to risk. Rather than redoubling efforts to protect maltreated children, child welfare workers were so intent on closing cases that they often took short-cuts, contravening agency policy and state law. In a grim parody of street slang, workers came to refer to the rush to eliminate cases as "drive-by closings." For years, DYFS used confidentiality to avoid public scrutiny: "one of the most serious offenses committed by [DYFS] over the years has been its ability to keep the full dimensions of its failings secret—from parents of children in its care, from lawyers acting on behalf of children who have been raped or killed and from legislators seeking to reform the agency's practices." When confidentiality and stone-walling failed to discourage court inquiries into its operations, DYFS simply defied court demands to turn over records![57] Though the exposé of DYFS brought the agency's defensive practices to light, it did little to correct for its malfeasance. Within a year of the Williams tragedy, Matthew Calbi was beaten to death by his mother, despite four investigations of the family during the previous two years.[58]

In October 2003, a New Jersey couple was arrested for starving two boys they had adopted; the oldest was 19 years old, 4 feet tall, and weighed 45 pounds. Despite 38 visits by a DYFS caseworker during the previous two years, no evidence of malnourishment had been reported.[59] Although agency policies called for annual medical check-ups, none of the six children that the couple had adopted had seen a doctor during the previous six years.[60] The case file documented that one emaciated child beseeched his caseworker for food and rooted through the glove box in the caseworker's car in search of something to eat. "When he ate away from home, he begged the caseworkers not to tell his adoptive parents," reported the *New York Times*. "The family was nevertheless allowed to adopt three more children; each came with a government subsidy."[61] In fact, the previous year the couple obtained more than $30,000 in welfare benefits for the children they had adopted and one foster child.[62] Reflecting on a suit her advocacy agency brought against DYFS for its neglect of foster children, Marcia Robinson Lowry, director of a legal advocacy organization, Children's Rights, expressed her exasperation: "Either people were purposely flouting a federal court order or the depths of their incompetence was so profound that people didn't know what they were supposed to do."[63] Immediately, the governor of New Jersey announced a two-year plan to right the state's foundering child welfare agency.[64] A subsequent review of cases in which child abuse had been suspected, revealed that 110 children had disappeared from New Jersey's child protection system.[65] A year later, the four malnourished boys who had underscored New Jersey's tawdry child welfare services had doubled in weight and were recovering from years of maltreatment.[66]

In March 2004, Children's Rights filed a suit against the State of Mississippi for exposing maltreated children to further risk. The state had closed 34 child abuse prevention centers, and caseloads of child welfare workers were skyrocketing. While the Child Welfare League of America had suggested that caseloads not exceed seventeen, in several Mississippi counties caseloads had risen to 100 per worker; in Forrest County the caseload exceeded 200. Ominously, services were provided to fewer than half of families in which neglect or abuse had been confirmed. Due to a shortage of caseworkers, the state could ensure that only half of reported cases of child maltreatment were even investigated; as a result in 2004 the percent of substantiated cases was less than half what it was in 1997.[67] Mississippi would appear to be poised to replicate the debacles that have befallen Florida, New Jersey, and Washington, D.C.

Tragically, the deaths of children due to abuse and neglect were not a local problem but one that had become nationwide. By the mid-1990s the U.S. Advisory Commission on Child Abuse and Neglect concluded that some 2,000 children were dying of abuse and neglect annually,[68] far above the 1,400 deaths counted by the National Center on Child Abuse and Neglect in 2002.[69] In rating the child homicide rates for industrial nations, a British researcher concluded that the child fatality rate of the United States was double that of the second most lethal nation for children, Australia.[70] Indeed, the rate of reported as well as confirmed cases of abuse and neglect in the United States were more than double those of the United Kingdom or Canada.[71]

Regardless of increases in injury and death to children due to abuse and neglect, child welfare professionals were fancying a new approach to serving at-risk families, "family preservation." Initially demonstrated in the late 1970s through the Homebuilders program, family preservation called for the provision of intensive services for a brief period, usually six weeks, by a worker assigned four to six cases. Services provided ranged from crisis intervention to home repair to child day care—all intended to stabilize the family and prevent out-of-home placement of a child. Family preservation was greeted enthusiastically by child welfare professionals because of the multiple benefits it offered. Foremost, by keeping a family intact, this approach avoided out-of-home placement of a child who had been abused or neglected. Because of the high cost of out-of-home placement, family preservation thus offered financial benefits: the cost of mounting a family preservation program was quickly recovered through savings from the reduction in out-of-home placements. Finally, in valuing family unity over child removal, family preservation allied child welfare agencies with conservative traditionalists who placed family rights over those of children.

The relationship between family preservation and child protective services was oblique but nonetheless consequential. Child welfare professionals understood family preservation as a preventive strategy that could preclude the most dramatic disposition of child protective services, out-of-home placement. As family preservation captured the allegiance of child welfare professionals, the focus on child protection began to lapse. Even as fatalities due to child abuse mounted, children's advocates pressed for policy changes focusing on family preservation.

Consequently, when the 1993 Clinton economic package was passed, it included $930 million for family support and preservation services over five years, but only a footnote reference to child protective services.[72] After a decade family preservation had been incorporated into child welfare through the Promoting Safe and Stable Families program, budgeted at $505 million annually,[73] yet failure to intervene effectively on behalf of maltreated children contributed to CPS scandals that erupted across the United States.

Despite policies intended to ameliorate child abuse, the number of confirmed cases of maltreated children climbed steadily, more than quadrupling from 10 per 1,000 in 1976 to 47 in 1996.[74] In 2001, 2.7 million children were alleged to have been maltreated; two-thirds of those were investigated, and 903,000 were determined to have been victims of abuse or neglect. This computed to an incidence rate of 12.4 per 1,000 children. Children are much more likely to have been neglected than abused. For 2001, the rate of neglect was 7.1 per 1,000 children, while the abuse rate was 2.3. Thus, 59 percent of maltreated children had been victims of neglect, and 19 percent had been abused. Approximately 10 percent had been sexually abused, and 7 percent psychologically abused.[75] Girls (52.3 percent of victims) were more likely to be maltreated than boys (46.7 percent). Although the majority of abused children, 56.4 percent, were white, African American children were disproportionately overrepresented at 26.4 percent of victims. The vast majority of perpetrators were parents, 79.2 percent.[76]

Since 1996 the incidence of child maltreatment has decreased somewhat, although data on child abuse and neglect are notoriously inadequate. Prior to 1996, state reports on child maltreatment were voluntary; subsequently, states have been required to provide data to the "maximum extent possible." The refusal of the federal government to insist on regular reporting by the states, combined with the variation among states with respect to their data collection capacity, makes a hodge-podge of child maltreatment statistics. The result is evident in data provided by the states on alleged and founded incidents of maltreatment (see Table 15.2). The sum total of state reports would suggest slight reductions in reports of maltreatment, –1 percent, as well as confirmed cases, – 4 percent. An examination of the experiences of individual states, however, suggests a situation bordering on chaos. Several states provided suspect data or no data at all. In 1998, North Dakota reported 0 victims of maltreatment, an achievement as unprecedented as it is unlikely. For 2001 Kansas and Maryland failed to provide data on allegations of maltreatment. For those states reporting, allegations ranged from Kentucky's high of 159.5 per 1,000 children in 1998 to Pennsylvania's low of 7.9 in 1998. In 2001, founded cases ranged from Alaska's high of 82.6 per 1,000 children to Pennsylvania's low of 1.6. From these data one might conclude that in 1998 Kentuckians were 20 times more likely than Pennsylvanians to report allegations of abuse, and that in 2001 Alaskans were 50 times more likely than Pennsylvanians to victimize their children. To the contrary, it is more likely that statistics such as these reflect the failure of federal and state government to provide a minimally adequate portrait of the welfare of the nation's most at-risk population, maltreated children.

In 2003 the federal Administration on Children and Families (ACF) released an assessment of the performance of 32 states with respect to seven basic outcomes central to child welfare. The program audits included the largest states—California, New York, Pennsylvania, Michigan, Texas, and Florida—so the results summarized the experiences of a large number of vulnerable children. The subsequent report card documented that a majority of states failed to be in compliance on every outcome measure, as shown in Table 15.3. On two outcomes, not one state was in "substantial conformity."

With respect to the seven standards, *not one state was able to assure that maltreated children had a permanent and stable living arrangement; not one state was in compliance with regard to families having improved their ability to care for their children; only one state demonstrated that it adequately met a child's physical and mental health needs.* As a result of their poor performance, states risked losing million of dollars in federal funds; however, this appeared a symbolic threat since it is improbable that the federal government would step in and assume direct control of services for abused and neglected children. But there was little reason to expect dramatic improvement in state compliance with the seven standards either: "Many states said they did not have enough caseworkers to investigate reports of abuse and neglect or to monitor children in foster care. They have difficulty recruiting and retaining workers because salaries are low," reported the *New York Times*, "But some states, grappling with what they describe as their worst fiscal problems in more than 50 years, have cut spending for some child welfare services."[77]

Table 15.2

Incidents of Child Maltreatment Allegations and Victimization, by State, 1998–2001

State	Children Alleged to Be Victims per 1,000 Children		Percentage Change in Allegation Rate 1998–2001	Child Victims per 1,000 Children		Percentage Change in Victimization Rate 1998–2001
	1998	2001		1998	2001	
Alabama	33.1	26.6	–20	15.4	8.2	–47
Alaska	58.9	95.4	62	37.1	82.6	123
Arizona	48	38.4	–20	7.1	3.8	–46
Arkansas	45.2	37.6	–17	13.1	10.1	–23
California	46.4	51.7	11	17.7	13.6	–23
Colorado	37.6	27.5	–27	6.7	4.3	–36
Connecticut	51.7	56.2	9	21.4	14.4	–33
Delaware	54.1	42.8	–21	16.2	8.5	–48
DC	95.8	64.3	–33	47.7	25.5	–47
Florida	52.8	71.4	35	23.2	33.3	44
Georgia	36.7	51.7	41	12.1	16.6	37
Hawaii	12	24.2	102	7.3	13.2	81
Idaho	76	26.6	–65	22.6	9.5	–58
Illinois	34.7	44	27	11.2	8.5	–24
Indiana	67.3	33.9	–50	12.5	13.4	7
Iowa	38.9	51.6	33	10.1	17.5	73
Kansas	38.4	NA	NA	7.6	10.2	34
Kentucky	64.2	56.6	–12	23.1	16.6	–28
Louisiana	38	31.3	–18	11.6	9.2	–21
Maine	31	30.2	–3	12.3	14.4	17
Maryland	43.5	NA	NA	11.1	14.4	30
Massachusetts	36.3	40.9	13	18.9	22.1	17
Michigan	61.3	66.3	8	8.9	11.0	24
Minnesota	19.7	18.4	–7	8.4	7.6	–10
Mississippi	42.8	40	–7	8	5.9	–26
Missouri	53.4	56.4	6	8.9	6.5	–27
Montana	84.7	65.4	–23	14.7	8.4	–43
Nebraska	32.9	23.8	–28	9.5	7.4	–22
Nevada	49.7	41.9	–15	17.2	9.2	–47
New Hampshire	30.1	38.6	28	3.9	3.5	–10
New Jersey	38.2	33.8	–12	4.9	4.1	–16
New Mexico	26.6	45.6	71	8.4	13.6	62
New York	53.4	53.7	1	18.6	16.6	–11
North Carolina	65.6	61.5	–6	19.5	18.4	–6
North Dakota	43.7	43.8	0	0	8.5	NA

(continued)

Table 15.2

(continued)

State	Children Alleged to Be Victims per 1,000 Children		Percentage Change in Allegation Rate 1998–2001	Child Victims per 1,000 Children		Percentage Change in Victimization Rate 1998–2001
	1998	2001		1998	2001	
Ohio	47.7	39.5	–17	20.4	17.7	–13
Oklahoma	68.6	71.1	4	18.9	15.3	–19
Oregon	33.5	29.9	–11	12.3	10.5	–15
Pennsylvania	7.9	7.9	0	1.9	1.6	–16
Rhode Island	41.5	45.7	10	14.5	13.3	–8
South Carolina	39.9	36.2	–9	8.8	11.0	25
South Dakota	26.4	49.2	86	13.2	18.3	39
Tennessee	24.2	36.2	50	7.5	6.8	–9
Texas	30.7	32.9	7	7.1	7.4	4
Utah	38.8	39	1	11.4	14.0	23
Vermont	14	24	71	6.3	7.7	22
Washington	32.1	23.2	–28	8.8	3.9	–56
West Virginia	159.5	67.2	–58	19.3	19.8	3
Wisconsin	16.5	29.3	78	6	8.7	45
Wyoming	17.1	32.4	89	6.2	7.7	24
Total	42.5	41.9	–1	12.9	12.4	–4

Source: House Ways and Means Committee, *Overview of Entitlement Programs, 2004* (Washington, DC: U.S. GPO, 2004), p. 11-76.

Table 15.3

State Compliance on Child Protection Outcomes

Outcomes	States in Substantial Compliance	States Not in Substantial Compliance
Children are, first and foremost, protected from abuse and neglect	5	27
Children are safely maintained in their own homes whenever possible and appropriate	4	28
Children have permanency and stability in their living situations	0	32
The continuity of family relationships and connections is preserved for children	5	27
Families have enhanced capacity to provide for their children's needs	0	32
Children receive appropriate services to meet their educational needs	7	25
Children receive adequate services to meet their physical and mental health needs	1	31

Source: "Summary of the Results of the 2001 and 2002 Child and Family Services Reviews." Administration on Children and Families. Retrieved August 28, 2003, from www.acf.hhs.gov

Inadequate resources for child welfare affected the capacity of local agencies to address their mandated responsibilities. For decades the Annie E. Casey Foundation had invested tens of millions of dollars in children's services, identifying and supporting model programs across the nation. Unfortunately, the exemplary programs it subsidized remained just that, isolated from the mainstream and failing to catalyze system-wide reforms. In 2003, the Foundation identified a significant impediment to progress: the human services workforce.

> Human services is reaching a state of crisis. Frontline jobs are becoming more and more complex while the responsibility placed on workers remains severely out of line with their preparation and baseline abilities. Many are leaving the field while a new generation of college graduates shows little interest in entering the human services sector. Millions of taxpayer dollars are being poured into a compromised system that not only achieves little in the way of real results, but its interventions often do more harm than good. It is clear that frontline human services jobs are not attracting the kinds of workers we need, and that regulations, unreasonable expectations, and poor management practices mire workers and their clients in a dangerous status quo.[78]

A companion report, released by the Brookings Institution echoed the Casey Foundation's conclusions: "Unfortunately, there is a vast gulf between what these human services workers are asked to do and how they are equipped for that task," wrote Paul Light. "Workloads often exceed recommended limits, turnover rates among the most qualified workers are high, and human services employees describe their work as both frustrating and unappreciated."[79]

In 2003, Congress passed the Keeping Children and Families Safe (KCFS) Act, Public Law 108-36, as a reauthorization of CAPTA. Among its provisions, the Act doubled funding for child abuse prevention and treatment to $200 million for 2004. Funds were intended to enhance staff training and supervision as well as tracking systems. Significantly, KCFS authorized completion of the fourth National Incidence Study of Child Abuse and Neglect, updating the last such study of 1993. In order to subsume child maltreatment under the broader concept of family violence, the Act authorized $175 million to enhance public awareness about harm to families and children due to domestic violence. Finally, KCFS provided additional resources for adoption of special needs children and services to abandoned infants, particularly those with AIDS.[80] Whether the funding and compliance provisions of KCFS are sufficient to forge a more adequate network of services for maltreated children remains to be seen.

Foster Care for Children

When parents are unable to care for their children, foster care is often used to provide alternative care. As an extension of the practice of boarding out children, most foster care in the United States is at no cost to the parents, and children are placed in the homes of other families. There is an important relationship between child protective services and foster care. Foster care is primarily a service for victims of child abuse; more than half of children in foster care were placed there by child protective service workers. The second most prevalent reason for child foster care is the "condition or absence of the parent," accounting for about 20 percent of foster care placements.[81]

Spotlight 15.2

The National Foster Parent Association

The National Foster Parent Association (NFPA) is a national nonprofit organization that supports foster families through legislative advocacy, training and education, publications, networking among foster parents, state and local foster parent associations, and child welfare associations. To learn more about NFPA and read more about the history of foster care in the United States go to its website at **www.nfpainc.org.**

As in the case of protective services, foster care for children was not coordinated under the provisions of the Social Security Act. States adopted separate policies and, unfortunately, took few measures to monitor children in foster care. During the early 1960s a series of studies began to document a disturbing development: rather than being a temporary arrangement for child care, foster care had become a long-term experience for many youngsters, with 70 percent of children in foster care for more than one year.[82] Not only had states planned poorly for the reunification of children with their original families, but in many instances child welfare agencies lost track of foster care children altogether. During the summer of 1992, the District of Columbia's Department of Human Services was rocked by a foster care scandal when it was reported that the department had literally no idea of the location of one out of every four children it had placed in foster care.[83]

In response to the deterioration of children's services, several "family preservation" demonstration projects were begun. As discussed earlier, these efforts offered intensive services to families in order to prevent children from being placed in foster care or to effectively reunite children with their biological parents. The demonstrations seemed to be cost-effective. In Virginia, 14 pre-foster care placement service projects concluded that family functioning improved in 69 percent of the families receiving intensive support services. Moreover, the cost of support services was $1,214 per child, substantially less than the cost of foster care ($11,173) or residential care ($22,025) over the average length of time (4.6 years) a child was in these out-of-home settings.[84] As a result of these field experiments, "permanency planning" became a central feature of the Adoption Assistance and Child Welfare Act (ACWA) of 1980.

Permanency planning is "the systematic process of carrying out, within a brief time-limited period, a set of goal-directed activities designed to help children live in families that offer continuity of relationships with nurturing parents or caretakers and the opportunity to establish lifetime relationships."[85] ACWA was an ambitious effort, and one expert heralded it as making it "possible to implement at state and local levels a comprehensive service delivery system for children."[86] As a result of permanency planning, the number of children in foster care plummeted. In 1971, 330,400 children were in foster care; by 1982 the number had dropped to 262,000, a reduction of 20.7 percent.[87] Welfare workers swiftly removed children from foster care and reunited them with their biological families under the rationale that community support services would assist parents. Early research on family preservation services indicated cost savings; but some families needed extensive service costing as much as $2,600. As costs associated with reunification increased, public agencies struggled to pay for necessary services. An analysis of a model family reunification program found that deficits in agency resources—gaps in service, large caseloads and high worker turnover, and inadequate family preparation, among others—presented problems in more than half of all cases. The researchers were "unaware of any reported successful permanency planning program that has high caseloads as a program component."[88]

Tragically, inadequate resources sometimes created a vicious circle: When biological parents received few support services, they were less able to care for their children, thereby contributing to the need for child protective services. In the absence of intensive support services, permanency planning for many children meant a revolving door–placement in foster care, reunification with the biological parent(s), and then a return to foster care. In 1982, 43 percent of children had been in multiple placements, but by 1983 53.1 percent had been in more than one placement; 20.1 percent had been placed twice, 24.2 percent three to five times, and 8.8 percent six or more times.[89] The National Association of Social Workers newsletter reported the instance of a four-year-old New York boy who was placed in 37 different homes in two months and described another child who had been placed in 17 homes in 25 days.[90] By 2001 the number of multiple placements had dropped; 39 percent of children had been in 3 or more placements.[91]

In large measure, the permanency planning movement faltered because of lack of support services to families. Not long after passage of the Adoption Assistance and Child Welfare Act of 1980, Ronald Rooney observed prophetically that "if the promise of permanency planning is to be realized, those who allocate funds must provide money for a continuum of services that are delivered from the point of entry into foster care and include programs designed to prevent the removal of children from their homes."[92] Yet in 1981 an important source of family support services, Title XX, was cut 21 percent. For 1992 the Title XX appropriation, $2.8 billion, was $100 million less than the amount funded in 1981, despite a 58 percent increase in reports of child abuse and neglect since that time.[93] And the decline in gross appropriations for Title XX reveals only a small part of the de-funding of the program: once inflation is factored in, it can be seen that between 1977 and 1992 Title XX actually lost $3.2 billion, or 55.4 percent of its funding.[94] (By 2003, Title XX had been whittled down to $1.7 billion, further hampering child welfare service delivery.[95]) A decade after the early permanency planning demonstration projects, Theodore Stein feared that the movement was being subverted by budget cuts and a reliance on crisis services in child welfare.[96]

Limited funding for child welfare under Title XX induced states to become more dependent on other federal sources of revenue. Because it was funded completely by the federal government and did not require any state matching funds, Title XX was the optimal funding source for child welfare program administrators, but it had one important limitation: revenues were capped. Other available federal assistance included Title IV-B of the Social Security Act, which allocated a fixed amount of funds for children's services and required a 25 percent state matching contribution. Most of the programs under Title IV-E of the Social Security Act were not capped, but federal funds did require a matching state contribution ranging from 25 to 50 percent; the exception was the Chaffee Foster Care Independence Program, which was capped and required a state match of 20 percent. Moreover, the two programs that child welfare program administrators looked to under Title IV-E, foster care and adoption assistance, were reserved for poor children who would have been eligible for welfare had they stayed at home. In other words, beyond Title XX, child welfare administrators could try to address increases in service demand through other federal programs; but Title IV-B funds were capped and required a state match, and open-ended Title IV-E funds were earmarked for welfare children in addition to requiring a state match.

Under these circumstances, Byzantine patterns of service funding evolved during the 1980s as child welfare officials exploited matching formulae that optimized federal reimbursement. Imaginative program managers from affluent states first matched federal requirements for welfare children in order to capture Title IV-E funds, then funded the state match for IV-B funds, reserving Title XX funds to the extent possible for non-welfare children. Program managers from states unwilling to meet the federal matching requirements had little choice but to use scarce Title XX funds, sometimes for welfare children. Table 15.4 shows trends in three sources of federal revenues for children's services from 1986 to 1998. The rapid expansion of funds for foster care of welfare children under Title IV-E, an open-ended entitlement, contrasts with capped funding under Title IV-B and Title XX,[97] creating the risk that states may be induced to place poor, and disproportionately minority, children in foster care rather than helping them stay at home by funding in-home support services.

To compound the problems faced by foster care workers, quality foster care placements became scarce. A declining standard of living forced many women into the job market, thus restricting the pool of families with a parent at home to supervise children[98]—a requisite for desirable foster care. Between 1979 and 2000 the number of hours worked by wives increased 50.7 percent; no-longer-at-home wives were working to shore-up eroding family finances.[99] Soon the shortage of foster homes became critical. In the mid-1980s the director of the Illinois Department of Children and Family Services pleaded for 1,000 new foster parents to prevent the collapse of the state's foster care program.[100] In an investigation into the death of one foster care child, a Virginia grand jury cited "the acute shortage of suitable shelter for the 6,000 neglected, abused, and disabled children" in the state as a factor contributing to the child's death.[101] Thus, by the late 1980s, with permanency planning beset with multiple problems, foster care was an unreliable way of serving many of the most endangered children in the United States.

With passage of the Family Support and Preservation Program in 1993, extended by the Promoting Safe and Stable Families Act, policymakers gave priority to supporting troubled families in order to prevent foster care placements. Two decades after the passage of ACWA the parameters of permanency planning were fairly clear: almost half of children were returned to their immediate or extended families and slightly more than one-fifth were slated for adoption; however, more than 20 percent remained in long-term foster care or had yet to have a permanent plan established. Of plans executed, almost three-fourths remained in foster care; one in ten children remained in institutional care. (See Table 15.5 on page 405.)

Several issues have emerged to dampen enthusiasm about foster care as a solution for children from very troubled families. Although many mothers negotiate return of their children who had been placed in foster care, some overcoming the considerable hurdles associated with drug abuse,[102] others

Table 15.4

Federal Funding for Child Welfare, Foster Care, and Adoption (in millions of dollars)

Year	IV-B Child Welfare	IV-B/2 Safe & Stable Families	IV-E Foster Care	IV-E Independent Living	IV-E Adoption
1986	198	—	605	—	55
1987	223	—	793	45	74
1988	239	—	891	45	97
1989	247	—	1,153	50	111
1990	253	—	1,473	60	136
1991	274	—	1,819	70	175
1992	274	—	2,233	70	220
1993	295	—	2,547	70	272
1994	295	60	2,607	70	325
1995	292	150	3,050	70	411
1996	277	225	3,114	70	485
1997	292	240	3,692	70	590
1998	291	255	3,704	70	697
1999	292	275	4,012	70	843
2000	292	295	4,256	140	1,012
2001	292	305	4,382	140	1,197
2002	292	375	4,519	140	1,342
2003	290	404	4,690	182	1,525
2004	292	505	4,917	200	1,692
2005*	292	505	5,044	200	1,871
2006*	292	505	5,276	200	2,064

*Estimated

Source: House Ways and Means Committee, *Overview of Entitlement Programs, 2004* (Washington, DC: U.S. GPO, 2004), p. 11-5.

experience protracted difficulties. In some instances children who have been placed in foster care are returned to mothers who are poor candidates for resuming care. A celebrated case involved Cornelious Pixley, a two-year-old African American toddler who had been placed with a white policewoman after his mother was convicted of murdering his infant sister. Following a judge's order that Cornelious be returned to his mother, the foster mother challenged the decision with the assistance of child advocacy organizations. The challenge was based not only on the mother's homicide conviction, but also on her violation of probation as well as her difficulty stabilizing her household. Eventually, custody was remanded to the foster mother.[103]

Too often, foster care has emerged as the catalyst of family dramas that become the grist of journalistic accounts of a child welfare system that "is infected with mistrust, backbiting and second-guessing," hardly the ambience that builds public confidence. One reporter summarized his impression of child welfare:

> As soon as a complaint is received, a virtual industry of social workers, lawyers, judges and administrators goes to work, and no matter how pure the intentions are, the process often deteriorates into chaos. A central goal of child welfare is permanence and stability for the child, but cases routinely become so mired in complications, and legalities, and indecision, and nastiness, and the necessity of trying to understand

Table 15.5

Permanency Plans of Children (in percentages)

Disposition	1999	2000	2001
Permanency Plan			
Reunify	42	42	44
Live with relative(s)	4	4	5
Adoption	21	21	22
Long-term foster care	8	8	9
Emancipation	6	6	6
Guardianship	3	3	3
Not yet established	17	15	11
Placement Setting			
Pre-adoptive home	4	4	4
Foster home relative)	27	25	24
Foster home (non-relative)	47	47	48
Group home	7	8	8
Institution	11	10	10
Supervised independent living	1	1	1
Runaway	1	1	2
Trial home visit	3	3	3

Source: House Ways and Means Committee, *Overview of Entitlement Programs, 2004* (Washington, DC: U.S. GPO, 2004), pp. 11-105, 11-107.

> a specific moment of horror in the larger context of societal issues, that the focus can shift from the search for permanence to the mere passage of time. Months pass. Years pass. Rather than resolution, there is drift, so much that nationally, on average a third of the children entering foster care will be there in excess of two years, creating, instead of stability, an ambiguity that can be damaging.[104]

Increasing demand for foster parents and homosexual rights collided in a controversy about the suitability of gays and lesbians as parents. A Texas child welfare supervisor ordered the removal of a foster child from a lesbian foster parent, arguing that the state's anti-sodomy statutes defined homosexual households as unacceptable.[105] The *Washington Post*'s Colbert King undoubtedly spoke for many when he observed, "I couldn't care less what those [foster] parents look like as long as they are strong in themselves and are giving that kid the sense of security, belonging and love that every child on this earth needs."[106]

Adoption

From the standpoint of permanency planning, adoption has become an important child welfare service. In the early 1980s the Children's Bureau noted that 50,000 "hard-to-adopt" children were waiting for homes. Many of these children were of minority origin, had disabilities, or were older and had been in foster care for several years.[107] Because such children posed a financial burden for adoptive parents, the Adoption Assistance and Child Welfare Act of 1980 provided subsidies to adoptive parents. In 1983, 6,320 children were being subsidized each month at a cost of $12 million.[108] Between 1995 and 2002, the number of agency-involved adoptions virtually doubled from 25,693 to 50,950, respectively.[109] Providing incentives for parents to adopt hard-to-adopt children clearly supported the concept of permanency planning, as "90 percent of subsidized adoptions involve foster parents whom the subsidy has enabled to adopt children with whom they had formed a relationship . . . and most of these are minorities or have special needs."[110] Moreover, subsidized adoption proved cost-effective, costing 37 percent less than foster care.

Still, adoption is not without controversy. Because children come from a variety of racial and cultural groups, questions have been raised about trans-cultural adoption. Should agencies give consideration to maintaining the cultural identity of children placed for adoption by finding them homes in their birth culture? This question was at the heart of the Indian Child Welfare Act of 1978. Native Americans were disturbed that "25 to 35 percent of all American Indian children [were] separated from their families and placed in foster homes, adoptive homes, or institutions."[111] The fact that 85 percent of such placements were in non-Indian families and left the children "without access to their tribal homes and relationships" raised the specter of partial cultural genocide.[112] To reinforce the cultural identity of Native American children, the Indian Child Welfare Act provided for

> minimal Federal standards for the removal of Indian children from their families and the placement of such children in foster or adoptive homes which will reflect the unique values of Indian culture, and for assistance to Indian tribes in the operation of child and family service programs.[113]

Equally important, the Indian Child Welfare Act established tribes, rather than state courts, as the governing bodies responsible for Indian foster children.

A similar argument for culturally appropriate placement of children was advanced during the 1980s by the National Association of Black Social Workers (NABSW). Noting a high percentage of black children placed with white families, NABSW contended that cross-racial adoptions deprived individual children of their racial identity and would eventually result in a degree of cultural genocide for the black community. Research on cross-racial adoption, however, consistently found that African American children did not suffer adverse consequences from growing up in white families. In 1996, President Clinton signed legislation forbidding interference in child placement for reasons based on race, except by Indian tribes.[114] Although provisions to reinforce the cultural identity of children have unquestionable merit in a pluralistic society, the circumstances of many racial and cultural minorities leave the implementation of such policies in doubt.[115] Without basic health, education, and employment supports, many minority families are likely to have difficulty adopting children. For example, the number of African American children available for adoption far outstrips the number of African American families able to adopt children, despite the fact that African American families "adopt at a rate 4.5 times greater than white or Hispanic families."[116] The number of minority children not only exceeds the portion of the population represented by minorities as a whole, but the percent of adopted children as well. (See Table 15.6.)

Table 15.6

Race/Ethnicity of Children Waiting for Adoption and Adopted, 2001 (in percentages)

Race/Ethnicity	Waiting Children	Adopted Children
White	32	38
Black	42	35
Hispanic	11	16
Two or more races	2	3
Other	2	2
Unknown	4	5
Missing data	6	0

Source: House Ways and Means Committee, *Overview of Entitlement Programs, 2004* (Washington, DC: U.S. GPO, 2004), p. 11-125.

Changes in family composition further cloud the picture. The pool of adoptive families has diminished with the increase in the number of female-headed households. The combination of low wages for women and a shortage of marriageable men means that mothers are encouraged to maintain small families, not to expand them through adoption. In the mid-1980s, Esther Wattenberg of the University of Minnesota Center for Urban and Regional Affairs observed prophetically that the future of child welfare

> will be dominated by a sorting out of "the best interests of the child" in the extraordinarily complex family relationships that develop out of extending family boundaries to stepparents, several sets of grandparents, and an assortment of new siblings from remarried families that join and unjoin family compositions.[117]

Head Start

In response to concerns about the lack of educational preparation of poor children, Head Start was incorporated in the Economic Opportunity Act of 1964. The first Head Start programs were established in poor communities a year later. Intended to compensate for a range of deficits displayed by poor children, Head Start offered health and dental screening, nutrition, and socialization experiences in addition to preschool academic preparation. Of the Great Society programs, Head Start was one of a few that captured the imagination of the nation. Despite wide public support, however, participation in Head Start was somewhat uneven, as Table 15.7 shows. Significantly, it was not until 1995 that the enrollment of Head Start eclipsed that of 1966; today, fewer than half of eligible children participate in the program.[118]

During the 1980s, when government assistance to the poor was restrained, many poor families dis-

Table 15.7

Head Start: Participation and Federal Funding, Selected Years (dollars in millions)

Fiscal Year	Enrollment	Budget Authority
1965 (summer only)	561,000	$96.4
1970	477,400	325.7
1975	349,000	403.9
1980	376,300	735.0
1985	452,080	1,075.0
1990	548,470	1,552.0
1995	750,077	3,534.1
2000	857,644	5,266.2
2002	912,345	6,536.6

Source: House Ways and Means Committee, *Overview of Entitlement Programs, 2004* (Washington, DC: U.S. GPO, 2004), p. 15-124.

patched both parents to the labor market to stabilize family income, and this increased the need for Head Start. Even the Deficit Reduction Act of 1990, which held spending for most social programs in check, provided for modest increases in Head Start.[119] In large measure this funding reflected a growing appreciation that Head Start was a proven investment in human capital. Award-winning author Sylvia Ann Hewlett noted that "Head Start ($3,000 a year per child) is much less expensive than prison ($20,000 a year per inmate)."[120] The 1996 welfare reform act, which required recipients of family cash assistance to participate in the labor market, increased Head Start enrollments even further.

Since its inception, Head Start has largely become a pre-kindergarten program for the minority poor. In 2002, 52 percent of children enrolled are age four, and 36 percent are age three; 33 percent are African American, 30 percent are Hispanic, 3 percent are American Indian, and 3 percent are Asian. Thirteen percent of Head Start children have disabilities.[121] Few dispute the value of Head Start programming for at-risk children, persistent questions about the long-term benefits of the program notwithstanding. Rather than subverting Head Start, research on such questions has become central to the growing conservative critique of public education. Accordingly, in 2003 the Bush administration proposed transferring Head Start from HHS to the Department of Education, reducing health and family features in order to emphasize literacy.[122] Proponents of the transfer cited research indicating cognitive improvements among 3-year-olds enrolled in Early Head Start.[123]

Emerging Issues in Child Welfare

Changes in the economic and social circumstances of families in the United States have broadened the scope of the issues that have traditionally defined child welfare policy. Of these changes, three are likely to shape child welfare in the future: day care, maternal and child health, and teenage pregnancy.

Day Care

Day care for children has risen in importance as more and more parents with children work. In 1998 families in which both parents worked exceeded more than half of all married couples with children, up from 33 percent in 1976.[124] At the same time the number of working mothers with young children has skyrocketed; in 1947 only 12.0 percent of mothers with children under age six worked outside the home, but by 2002 64.1 percent did.[125] The need for child day care is felt both by middle-income families, in which both parents work in order to meet the income requirements of a middle-class lifestyle, and by low-income families, in which a parent is encouraged or required to participate in a welfare-to-work program. Yet the child care available is often unreliable, expensive, and of questionable quality. Thus, by 1994, almost twice as many children were cared for in a family home as in organized child care facilities.[126] Although poor families typically find family care of their children less expensive than organized child care, on average child care costs consume 28.5 percent of their income.[127] Even then, available child care often does not conform to the work schedules of parents. A study of New York City families found that half had to patch together day care from multiple providers. Low wages fail to attract the more skilled providers to the day care field, leading the Children's Defense Fund to observe ruefully that "despite their higher levels of education, child care providers are paid less than animal caretakers,

Day care for children has become more important as more and more parents with children work.

bartenders, or parking lot and amusement park attendants."[128] In 2000, the median wage for a center-based child care worker was $7.43 per hour. Low wages and poor benefits contribute to staff instability; in 1977 the turnover rate of child care staff was 31 percent.[129]

The crisis in child day care received nationwide attention in 1986 when two Miami children, unsupervised because their mother had to work and could not locate child care, climbed into a clothes dryer in which they "tumbled and burned to death."[130] This incident was cited in the introductory remarks to a proposed $375 million Child Care Services Improvement Act. An indicator of the severity of the day care crisis was that the legislation was sponsored by Orrin Hatch, a conservative senator noted for his prior opposition to social welfare legislation.[131] Regardless, by 1999 many children were caring for themselves: 3.0 percent of 5- to 8-year-olds, 14.1 percent of 9- to 11-year-olds, and 39.4 percent of 12- to 14-year-olds.[132]

The primary programs assisting parents with child care are the federal dependent care tax credit, the child care tax credit, the Child Care and Development Block Grant, and Title XX. The dependent care tax credit allows families to deduct $3,000 for one child or $6,000 for two children spent on child day care for a given year; the child care tax credit of $1,000 per child is refundable and phased out with increased income. As "tax expenditures"—de facto allocations the Internal Revenue Service creates by not taxing income spent for a specific purpose—the child care tax credit is budgeted at $44.1 billion for 2004, the largest form of federal assistance for child care.[133] Unfortunately, only a small portion of the child care tax credit is refundable, allowing poor families a cash refund for child care expenses. With passage of the 1996 welfare reform act, several child care programs were consolidated under the Child Care and Development Block Grant, funding for which was set at $3.7 billion for 2002.[134] Under Title XX states are able to purchase day care for poor families; but as of 2001, for example, only $129 million, or 7.6 percent, of the $1.7 billion in Title XX funds was expended for child care.[135]

Maternal and Child Health

Maternal and child health has emerged as an issue among child welfare advocates as younger, poor women give birth to low-birth-weight babies who have received inadequate prenatal care. Low birth weight is a concern because such infants have a higher incidence of developmental disabilities, some of which are permanent and eventually require institutional care. The relationship between low birth weight and developmental disabilities, long recognized by public health officials, resurfaced in Hunger in America, a 1985 report by the Physician Task Force on Hunger in America funded through the Harvard University School of Public Health. The task force noted that "low birth-weight is the eighth leading cause of death in the United States." Efforts to sustain premature and low-birth-weight infants are expensive and, even when successful, often cannot forestall "long-term growth and developmental problems." Infants born small and premature suffer 25 percent more major neurological problems and 117 percent more minor neurological problems than do normal infants.[136] Despite such documentation, the incidence of low birth weight among infants in the United States is relatively high, comparable to that of many poorer nations; that among African Americans parallels the rate of many African nations. Between 1996 and 2001, a period when many child welfare indicators were improving, the percent of low-birth-weight babies increased by 4 percent; for non-Hispanic blacks, 13.1 percent of babies were low birth weight, compared to 7.7 for all births.[137] Low birth weight in minority infants is of particular concern, because it relates to lack of adequate prenatal care: since 1970 the rate of late or no prenatal care among African Americans has been more than twice the rate for whites.[138] Given the relatively high number of teen pregnancies in the nonwhite population, these figures translate to a disturbing reality: substantial numbers of nonwhite infants in the United States are born with serious neurological deficits.

The primary federal program to enhance prenatal care for low-income families is WIC, the Special Supplemental Nutrition Program for Women, Infants, and Children. Under WIC, low-income pregnant and nursing women and their young children are eligible for food coupons through which they may obtain especially nutritious foods. While the WIC program would seem a logical method for addressing the low-birth-weight problem of infants born to poor women, participation in the WIC program is not at desirable levels. Nationwide, only about half of the people financially eligible to participate in WIC do so.[139] Participation and expenditures for WIC are listed in Table 15.8. Our failure to address inadequate nutrition of the most vulnerable of Americans, poor children, remains one of the most striking paradoxes of the nation's social welfare effort.

Teen Pregnancy

Problems relating to maternal and infant health are exacerbated by the sharp rise in the numbers of adolescent females having children. Out-of-wedlock births became an important family issue in the 1980s, when the incidence of unwed motherhood increased so rapidly that by 1983 half of all nonwhite births were outside of marriage.[140] In 2001, the number of births per 1,000 unmarried women was 43.8 for women of all races, 68.2 for African American

Table 15.8

WIC Participation and Spending

	Participation (thousands)				
Year	Women	Infants	Children	Total	Spending in Constant Dollars (millions)
1980	411.0	507.0	995.0	1,913.0	$1,620.5
1985	665.0	874.0	1,600.0	3,138.0	2,497.7
1990	1,035.0	1,412.5	2,069.4	4,516.9	2,955.1
1995	1,576.8	1,817.3	3,500.1	6,894.2	4,078.0
2000	1,750.0	1,894.2	3,554.0	7,198.1	4,166.0
2002	1,812.2	1,928.2	3,748.2	7,488.6	4,372.3

Source: House Ways and Means Committee, *Overview of Entitlement Programs, 2004* (Washington, DC: U.S. GPO, 2004), p. 15-115.

Table 15.9

Births to Unmarried Women by Age, 1970 and 2001

	1970		2001	
Age	Number of Non-Marital Births	% of Non-Marital Births	Number of Non-Marital Births	% of Non-Marital Births
Under 15	9,500	2.4	7,494	0.6
15–19	190,400	47.8	352,026	26.1
20–24	126,700	31.8	514,959	38.2
25–29	40,600	10.2	257,702	19.1
30–34	19,100	4.8	135,040	10.0
35–39	9,400	2.8	65,257	4.8
Over 40	3,000	0.8	16,771	1.2
Total, all ages	398,700	100.0	1,349,249	100.0

Source: House Ways and Means Committee, *Overview of Entitlement Programs, 2004* (Washington, DC: U.S. GPO, 2004), p. M–6.

women, 87.8 for Hispanic women, and 27.5 for non-Hispanic white women.[141] Even though the absolute number of births to teenagers declined between 1973 and 1991, the decline in the total number of adolescent females meant that the teen pregnancy rate was increasing substantially.[142] Most troubling was that the percentage of unmarried teenage mothers was rising so rapidly that by 1984 it was triple what it had been 25 years before.[143]

Conspicuously, the number of unwed births tripled during the last decades of the twentieth century, as seen in Table 15.9. Although the number of teen births increased substantially, those of girls under 15 declined. Moreover the modal age increased; in 1970 most unwed births were among teens age 15–19, but by 2001 most were age 20–24.

Childbearing among very young unmarried women poses a serious problem for public policy for two basic reasons. First, teenage mothers are more likely to drop out of school and thus to fail to gain skills that would make them self-sufficient. Adolescent mothers, particularly those who are African American or Hispanic, are apt to have less command of basic skills. Poor skill development represents an especially critical problem when the skills in question involve parenting. Second, teenage mothers are more likely to have to depend on welfare, the benefits of which are at levels lower than the actual cost of raising children. This combination of inadequate skill development and dependence on public welfare presents the specter of poor teenagers bearing poor children in an endless cycle of hopelessness. The consequences are particularly tragic for the children, who have little prospect of escaping the poverty trap. Reductions in the numbers of working African American and Hispanic males who are marriageable means that many of these children have little hope that their mother will marry and thus pull them out of poverty, which had been the most prevalent way for mothers to become independent of public welfare.[144] The loss of buying power of the income support provided by Aid to Families with Dependent Children (now TANF) has meant that public assistance does not provide an adequate economic base for poor children.[145]

In response to the high teen pregnancy rate, the Clinton administration moved on several fronts. The 1996 welfare reform act required that unmarried teen parents live at home or in a supervised setting in order to receive cash assistance; in addition, states were encouraged to establish Second Chance homes for pregnant teens. One billion dollars in bonuses were to be made available to states that had achieved a decline in the unwed birth while also reducing the incidence of abortions; in addition $250 million over five years was allocated for abstinence education.[146] In 1999 HHS Secretary Donna Shalala announced a national campaign to prevent teen pregnancy, focusing on the role of local nonprofit organizations in pregnancy prevention. These, initiatives, in conjunction with strengthened child support enforcement, were credited with helping sustain a steady decline in black teen pregnancy, which in 1999 fell for the eighth straight year.[147]

Conclusion: The Future of Child Welfare

After a half century of federal legislation, many child welfare advocates had become pessimistic about the care provided to youngsters in the United States. Hopes for using the family as the primary institution for child welfare had faded in the absence of economic and social supports to keep families intact. Lacking such supports, most families were reliant on the labor market to generate income to meet essential needs. Although some of the benefits of unprecedented prosperity and low unemployment began to trickle down to poor families by the end of the twentieth century, many welfare and working poor families continued to struggle. The 1996 imposition of welfare time limits cast a long shadow over poor families. In the absence of a coherent national family policy, poor families were less able to care for children; as a result, child welfare services—protective services, foster care, and adoption—have attempted to compensate for severe family deficits.

During the 1990s two strategies emerged in child welfare: the concept of child support assurance as a way to address income maintenance for poor families, and the idea of a children's authority as a way to restructure child welfare. As early as 1991 the National Commission on Children recommended the deployment of a demonstration program to test an enhanced child support enforcement and insurance scheme. Irwin Garfinkel, a social work professor at Columbia University, proposed a child support enforcement and assurance program (CSEAP) to replace family welfare. The CSEAP would reform child support in three ways: (1) The amount of child support would be calculated as a percentage of the absent parent's income; (2) support payments would be automatically withheld from paychecks; and (3) a minimum benefit to children would be provided by the federal government.[148] A federal CSEAP initiative with these components, Garfinkel reasoned, could replace most of the highly stigmatized family welfare program. The CSEAP concept is not without its critics, however. One critic opposed the idea because it placed the federal government in the same awkward position it has had with cash welfare, namely, subsidizing broken families.[149]

Meanwhile, states were experimenting with various methods for stretching their dollars to do more for children. Gradually, these efforts evolved into a potent critique of the traditional ways in which children's services had been delivered. "What's needed is a complete overhaul of children's services, bringing together public and private organizations to meet the comprehensive needs of children, adolescents, and parents," stated Stanford University's Michael Kirst.[150] Noting that many children from problem families were known to several separate health and human services agencies—none with sufficient resources to substantively help any one child—children's advocate Sid Gardner called for collaborative efforts among service providers: "In fact, we are ultimately failing our children not only because we haven't invested in them, but also because as communities we have failed to work together to hold ourselves accountable for the substantial resources we do invest—and for the outcomes of our most vulnerable residents."[151] Social worker Bonnie Bernard of the Far West Laboratory for Educational Research and Development observed that collaboration or restructuring, however defined, targets power relations. "True restructuring means the redistribution of policymaking power, not only from the central office administration to the local school," but to professionals and ultimately to consumers and their communities.[152]

In 1996 Lela Costin, Howard Karger, and David Stoesz proposed that in every jurisdiction children's services be restructured and placed under a Children's Authority, a local body that would provide a comprehensive array of services under performance-based management.[153] Since the early 1980s, the Savannah/Chatham Youth Futures Authority has demonstrated the merits of such an approach. Not only has the Youth Futures Authority integrated a variety of child and family programs, but it has been able to provide data on program outcomes. According to the Youth Futures Authority, the teen pregnancy rate for ages 10–19 decreased from 47.7 in 2001 to 42.6 in 2002, and birth rates decreased from 2.3 in 2001 to 1.2 in 2002. Unfortunately, the percent of low birth weight infants increased from 2001 to 2002. While the number of CPS investigations increased slightly during the period, the number of out of home placements fell from 450 to 360.[154] The Youth Futures Authority is not a panacea for enhancing services to vulnerable children and their families, of course, but it has shown that programming can demonstrate improvements with respect to vital indicators of child well-being. Thus, the Youth Futures Authority shows how localities can make important steps in improving child welfare services.

Discussion Questions

1. Using the "For Students" link on the policyAmerica website, identify a child welfare policy of interest to you. How has programming changed? Have budget appropriations been adequate to address the problem? What could be done to make the policy more effective?
2. Much of child welfare—protective services, foster care, and adoptions—is funded through a complex array of categorical programs. How does your welfare department optimize reimbursement through these funding sources? As a result of reimbursement systems, what are the priorities for children's services? How would you reconcile discrepancies between categorical funding priorities and community needs?
3. Maintaining the cultural identity of minority children who receive foster care and adoption services is a heated issue in child welfare. When there are too few minority families for the children needing foster care and adoption, what should the policy of the welfare department be in placing minority children? How consistent is your answer with current child welfare policy in your community?
4. Providing preschool programs for children is an increasingly important issue as more mothers enter the workforce. How adequate is day care provision in your community? Who is responsible for the oversight of day care? To what extent are the needs of low-income families considered in day care arrangements? What percentage of families eligible for Head Start actually participate in this program in your community?
5. Among health-related child welfare concerns are infant mortality and low birth weight. How do the statistics in your community compare with the state and national incidence of these two important indicators of child welfare? What are the incidences of infant mortality and low birth weight for children of teenage and minority mothers in your community? What plans does your community have for improving the health status of infants of minority and low-income families?
6. What is the plausibility of reforming child welfare by instituting a child support enforcement and assurance program or consolidating existing services under a Children's Authority? If you favor one of these, how would you convince the public that it constitutes real child welfare reform?

Notes

1. U.S. House of Representatives, Ways and Means Committee, *Overview of Entitlement Programs* (Washington, DC: U.S. GPO, 2004), p. H-5.
2. Kathryn Porter and Wendell Primus, *Changes Since 1995 in the Safety Net's Impact on Child Poverty* (Washington, DC: Center on Budget and Policy Priorities, 1999), p. v.
3. Arloc Sherman, *Extreme Child Poverty Rises Sharply in 1997* (Washington, DC: Children's Defense Fund, 1999), p. 2.
4. U.S. Department of Commerce, *Statistical Abstract of the United States, 2002* (Washington, DC: U.S. GPO, 2002), p. 829.
5. Dale Russakoff, "Report Shows Children's Well-Being Is Improving," *Washington Post* (July 14, 2000), p. A1.
6. "Child Well-Being Index," retrieved October 24, 2004 from www.soc.duke.edu/resources/child_bearing; Laura Stepp, "Baby Steps Made in Well-Being of Children, Data Show," *Washington Post* (March 25, 2004), p. A1.
7. *Kids Count* (Baltimore: Annie E. Casey Foundation, 2004), p. 33.
8. Jeanne Giovannoni, "Children," *Encyclopedia of Social Work,* 18th ed. (Silver Spring, MD: NASW, 1987), p. 247.
9. Alvin Schorr, "The Bleak Prospect for Public Child Welfare," *Social Service Review* 74, no. 1 (March 2000), p. 125.
10. Alfred Kadushin, "Child Welfare Services," *Encyclopedia of Social Work,* 18th ed. (Silver Spring, MD: NASW, 1987), p. 268.

11. Dale Rusakoff, "Assessing an Ambiguous Threat: Parents," *Washington Post* (January 19, 1998), p. A1.
12. Walter Trattner, *From Poor Law to Welfare State* (New York: Free Press, 1974), p. 100.
13. Ibid., pp. 106–107.
14. Sallie Watkins, "The Mary Ellen Myth," *Social Work* 35 (November 1990), p. 503.
15. Diana DiNitto and Thomas Dye, *Social Welfare* (Englewood Cliffs, NJ: Prentice-Hall, 1987), p. 153.
16. Kathleen Faller, "Protective Services for Children," *Encyclopedia of Social Work,* 18th Ed. (Silver Spring, MD: NASW, 1987). p. 386.
17. Trattner, *From Poor Law to Welfare State,* pp. 181, 183.
18. James Leiby, *A History of Social Welfare and Social Work in the United States* (New York: Columbia University Press, 1978), pp. 148–149.
19. June Axinn and Herman Levin, *Social Welfare* (New York: Harper and Row, 1982), p. 159.
20. Trattner, *From Poor Law to Welfare State,* p. 186.
21. Axinn and Levin, *Social Welfare,* pp. 224–228.
22. Sharon Parrott and Nina Wu, "States Are Cutting TANF and Child Care Programs" (Washington, DC: Center on Budget and Policy Priorities, 2003), pp. 1–2.
23. Barbara Kantrowitz et al., "How to Protect Abused Children," *Newsweek* (November 23, 1987), p. 68.
24. Sandra Evans, "Increase in Baby Killings Attributed to Family Stress," *Washington Post* (June 23, 1992), p. A1.
25. Faller, "Protective Services for Children," pp. 387, 389.
26. Douglas Besharov, "Contending with Overblown Expectations," *Public Welfare* (Winter 1987), pp. 7, 8.
27. Kantrowitz et al., "How to Protect Abused Children," p. 68.
28. "Foster Care: Duty v. Legal Vulnerability," *NASW News* (July 1988), p. 3.
29. "Social Workers' Neglect," *All Things Considered* (Washington, DC: National Public Radio, April 15, 1988). *NASW News* later reported that the employees cited in this broadcast were employed by the state, but were not certified social workers.
30. "High Court Review Urged on Foster Care Liability," *NASW News* (July 1988), p. 3.
31. Ibid.
32. Douglas Besharov, "Right versus Rights: The Dilemma of Child Protection," *Public Welfare* 43 (1985), pp. 19–46.
33. David Finkelhor, "Is Child Abuse Overprotected?" *Public Welfare* 48 (1990), pp. 22–29.
34. Fox Butterfield, "Sect Members Assert They Are Misunderstood," *New York Times,* (June 24, 1984), p. 16.
35. Bridgitte Berger and Peter Berger, *The War Over the Family* (Garden City, NY: Anchor, 1983), p. 213.
36. Besharov, "Contending with Overblown Expectations," p. 8.
37. William Claiborne, "Child Sex Ring or Witch Hunt: Charges Divide Town," *Washington Post* (November 14, 1995), p. A1; "A Northwest Town's Nightmare Continues," *Washington Post Weekly* (June 24–30, 1995), p. 31; Lela Costin, Howard Karger, and David Stoesz, *The Politics of Child Abuse in America* (New York: Oxford University Press, 1996).
38. Douglas Besharov with Lisa Laumann, "Child Abuse Reporting," *Society* (May/June 1996), p. 43.
39. David Stoesz and Howard Karger, "Suffer the Children," *Washington Monthly* (June 1996), p. 20.
40. Dale Russakoff, "Protector of N.Y. City's Children Knows the System Well," *Washington Post* (December 19, 1996), p. A3.
41. Rachel Swarns, "Court Experts Denounce New York's Child Agency," *New York Times* (October 22, 1997), p. A19.
42. LaShawn A. V. Williams, "A Progress Report" (Washington, DC: Center for the Study of Social Policy, March 7, 2000).
43. Sari Horwitz and Scott Higham, "Foster Care Caseloads 'Horrible'," *Washington Post* (March 27, 2000), p. A1.
44. "Foster Care Panic," *Washington Post* (March 1, 2000), p. A16.
45. Scott Higham and Sari Horwitz, "GAO Study Faults D.C. Child Care," *Washington Post* (September 20, 2000), p. A1.
46. Scott Higham and Sari Horwitz, "D.C. Child Welfare Official Arrested," *Washington Post* (August 15, 2000), p. A1.
47. Sari Horwitz and Scott Higham, "Child Welfare Chief Drops Lawsuit," *Washington Post* (August 24, 2000), p. B3.
48. Sari Horwitz and Scott Higham, "DeLay Lambastes Foster Care in D.C.," *Washington Post* (September 21, 2000), p. A1.
49. Sari Horwitz, Scott Higham, and Sarah Cohen, "'Protected' Children Died as Government Did Little," *Washington Post* (n.d.).
50. Sewell Chan, "Md. Threatens to Return D.C. Foster Children," *Washington Post* (April 18, 2002), p. B2.
51. Scott Higham, "District Says It's Not Liable in Girl's Death," *Washington Post* (March 28, 2002), p. B5.
52. Sue Pressley, "5-year-old Missing 15 Months, and No One Noticed," *Washington Post* (May 4, 2002).
53. Carol Miller, "Miami Welfare Workers Held Off Notifying Police of Missing Child," *Washington Post* (May 6, 2002).
54. Dana Canedy, "Two Years after Girl Disappeared, Little Has Changed in Florida Agency," *New York Times* (January 19, 2003), p. 18.
55. Matthew Purdy, Andrew Jacobs, and Richard Jones, "Life behind Basement Doors," *New York Times* (January 12, 2003), p. A1.

56. Richard Jones and Leslie Kaufman, "New Jersey Shows Failures of Child Welfare System," *New York Times* (Retrieved April 15, 2003,) from www.nytimes.com.
57. Richard Jones and Leslie Kaufman, "Foster Care Secrecy Magnifies Suffering in New Jersey Cases," *New York Times* (May 4, 2003), pp. 1, 32.
58. Richard Jones, "For Family of Beaten Boy, Tears, Not Finger-Pointing," *New York Times* (August 20, 2003), p. 1.
59. Lydia Polgreen and Robert Worth, "New Jersey Couple Held in Abuse," *New York Times* (October 27, 2003), p. A1.
60. Richard Jones, "Adopted Boys Were Starved, and Caseworkers Did Little, Report Finds," *New York Times* (February 13, 2004), p. A21.
61. "Watching as the Children Starved," *New York Times* (June 24, 2004), p. A26.
62. Leslie Kaufman, "Cash Incentives for Adoptions Seen as Risk to Some Children," *New York Times* (October 29, 2003), p. A1.
63. Jones, "Adopted Boys," p. A21.
64. Richard Jones, "New Jersey Plan on Child Welfare," *New York Times* (February 19, 2004), p. A1.
65. Michael Powell and Christine Haughney, "Kids in N.J.'s Care Missing," *Washington Post* (January 11, 2003), p. A8.
66. Geoff Mulvihill, "A Year Later, Four Boys Are Recovering Quickly From Neglect," *Washington Post* (October 11, 2004), p. A24.
67. Andrew Jacobs, "Lawsuit Challenges Mississippi's Short-of-Resources Child Protection System," *New York Times* (April 1, 2004), p. A14.
68. Costin, Karger, and Stoesz, *The Politics of Child Abuse in America.*
69. "The Deaths of Foster Children," *New York Times* (April 27, 2004), p. A24.
70. Costin et al., *The Politics of Child Abuse in America.*
71. Jane Waldfogel, *The Future of Child Protection: How to Break the Cycle of Abuse and Neglect* (Cambridge: Harvard University Press, 1998).
72. Costin, Karger, and Stoesz, *The Politics of Child Abuse in America.*
73. House Ways and Means Committee, *Overview of Entitlement Programs, 2004* (Washington, DC: U.S. GPO, 2004), p. 11–5.
74. Miringoff, *Social Health,* p. 75.
75. House Ways and Means Committee, *Overview, 2004,* pp. 11-75–11-77.
76. National Center on Child Abuse and Neglect, *Child Maltreatment, 1994* (Washington, DC: U.S. Department of Health and Human Services, 1996), pp. 2–10.
77. Robert Pear, "U.S. Finds Fault in All 50 States' Child Welfare Programs, and Penalties May Follow," *The New York Times* (April 26, 2004), p. A17.
78. Annie E. Casey Foundation, *The Unsolved Challenge of System Reform* (Baltimore: 2003), p. 2.
79. Paul Light, *The Health of the Human Services Workforce* (Washington, DC: Brookings Institution, 2003), p. 6.
80. *Keeping Children and Families Safe Act of 2003,* Retrieved, October 22, 2004, from www.naswdc.org.
81. Theodore Stein, "Foster Care for Children," *Encyclopedia of Social Work,* 18th ed. (Silver Spring, MD: NASW, 1987), pp. 641–642.
82. Ibid., p. 643.
83. Keith Harriston, "D.C. Foster Children Are Missing," *Washington Post* (August 6, 1992), p. C1.
84. *A Children's Defense Budget* (Washington, DC: Children's Defense Fund, 1988), p. 179.
85. Anthony Maluccio and Edith Fein, "Permanency Planning: A Redefinition," *Child Welfare* (May–June 1983), p. 197.
86. Duncan Lindsey, "Achievements for Children in Foster Care," *Social Work* (November 1982), p. 495.
87. House Ways and Means Committee, *Overview of Entitlement Programs, 2004,* pp. 11-86–11-87.
88. Peg Hess, Gail Folaron, and Ann Jefferson, "Effectiveness of Family Reunification Services," *Social Work* 37 (July 1992), pp. 306, 310.
89. Stein, "Foster Care for Children," p. 641.
90. "Foster Care Duty vs. Legal Vulnerability," *NASW News* (July 1988), p. 3.
91. House Ways and Means Committee, *Overview of Entitlement Programs, 2004,* p. 11–111.
92. Ronald Rooney, "Permanency Planning for All Children?" *Social Work* (March 1982), p. 157.
93. Children's Defense Fund, *A Children's Defense Budget,* p. 54.
94. U.S. House of Representatives, *1992 Green Book* (Washington, DC: U.S. Government Printing Office, 1992), p. 830.
95. House Ways and Means Committee, *Overview of Entitlement Programs, 2004,* p. 10-2.
96. Stein, "Foster Care for Children," p. 649.
97. Title XX amounts are not included in the table because the federal government does not collect data on how much is expended by states for child welfare.
98. Esther Wattenberg, "The Fate of Baby Boomers and Their Children," *Social Work* (January–February 1986), pp. 85–93.
99. Americans Must Work Harder to Achieve the American Dream," (Washington, DC: New America Foundation, 2004), p. 2.
100. Kantrowitz et al., "How to Protect Abused Children," p. 71.
101. Mary Jordan, "Foster Parent Scarcity Causing Crisis in Care," *Washington Post* (July 20, 1986), p. A9.
102. Dale Russakoff, "One Child's Chaotic Bounce in Mother Government's Lap," *Washington Post* (January 18, 1998); "Against the Odds, a Failed Mother Returns to Her Children," *Washington Post* (January 20, 1998), p. A1.
103. Steve Vogel, "Md. Custody Debate: Did Law Force Judge to Return Child to Killer?" *Washington Post*

(January 1, 1998), p. B1; Manuel Perez-Rias, "Pixley Denied Custody of Son," *Washington Post* (January 12, 2000), p. A1.

104. David Finkel, "'Now Say Goodbye to Diane,'" *Washington Post Magazine* (May 4, 1997), pp. 10–11.
105. Sam Verhovek, "Homosexual Foster Parent Sets Off a Debate in Texas," *New York Times* (November 30, 1997), p. 20.
106. Colbert King, "What Every Child Needs," *Washington Post* (March 11, 2000), p. A19.
107. Elizabeth Cole, "Adoption," *Encyclopedia of Social Work,* 18th ed. (Silver Spring, MD: NASW, 1987), p. 70.
108. U.S. House of Representatives, Committee on Ways and Means, *Background Material and Data on Programs within the Jurisdiction of the Committee on Ways and Means* (Washington, DC: U.S. Government Printing Office, 1985), p. 494.
109. House Ways and Means Committee, *Overview of Entitlement Programs, 2004,* p. 11-124.
110. Cole, "Adoption," p. 71.
111. Ronald Fischler, "Protecting American Indian Children," *Social Work* (September 1980), p. 341.
112. Evelyn Lance Blanchard and Russell Lawrence Barsh, "What Is Best for Tribal Children?" *Social Work* (September 1980), p. 350.
113. Fischler, "Protecting American Indian Children," p. 341.
114. Spencer Rich, "Wage Bill Includes Provisions Intended to Increase Adoptions," *Washington Post* (August 10, 1996), p. A4.
115. Patricia Hogan and Sau-Fong Siu, "Minority Children and the Child Welfare System," *Social Work* (November–December 1988), pp. 312–317.
116. Cole, "Adoption," p. 70.
117. Wattenberg, "The Fate of Baby Boomers and Their Children," p. 24.
118. *Children's Defense Fund, The State of America's Children,* 1991 (Washington, DC: Children's Defense Fund, 1991), p. 44.
119. Paul Leonard and Robert Greenstein, One *Step Forward: The Deficit Reduction Package of 1990* (Washington, DC: Center on Budget and Policy Priorities, 1990), p. 34.
120. Sylvia Ann Hewlett, *When the Bough Breaks* (New York: HarperCollins, 1992), p. 300.
121. House Ways and Means Committee, *Overview of Entitlement Programs, 2004,* p. 15-25.
122. Valerie Strauss and Amy Goldstein, "Head Start Changeover Proposed," *Washington Post* (February 1, 2003), p. A1.
123. Jay Matthews, "Early Head Start Offers an Edge," *Washington Post* (June 4, 2002), p. A9.
124. "Two-Income Families Now a Majority," *Richmond Times-Dispatch* (October 24, 2000), p. A3.
125. House Ways and Means Committee, *Overview of Entitlement Programs, 2004,* p. 9-2.
126. Ibid., pp. 9-8–9-9.
127. Ibid., p. 9-16.
128. Children's Defense Fund, *The State of America's Children,* 1988 (Washington, DC: Children's Defense Fund, 1988), p. 207.
129. House Ways and Means Committee, *Overview of Entitlement Programs, 2004,* pp. 9-18, 9-20.
130. Ibid., p. 214.
131. Ibid., p. 32; also National Association of Social Workers, *1986 Voting Record* (Silver Spring, MD: NASW, 1987).
132. House Ways and Means Committee, *Overview of Entitlement Programs, 2004,* p. 9-10.
133. Ibid., p. 13–5.
134. Ibid., p. 9–28.
135. Ibid., p. 10–9.
136. Physician Task Force on Hunger in America, *Hunger in America* (Cambridge, MA: Harvard University Press, 1985), p. 65.
137. *Kids Count, 2004* (Baltimore: Annie E. Casey Foundation, 2004), pp. 33, 34.
138. Miringoff and Miringoff, *The Social Health of the Nation,* p. 52.
139. Ibid., p. 84.
140. Michael Novak (ed.), *The New Consensus on Family and Welfare* (Washington, DC: American Enterprise Institute, 1987), p. 135.
141. House Ways and Means Committee, *Overview of Entitlement Programs, 2004,* p. M-3.
142. U.S. House of Representatives, *1998 Green Book,* p. 1245.
143. Lisbeth Schorr, *Within Our Reach* (Garden City, NY: Doubleday, 1988), p. 13.
144. William Julius Wilson, "American Social Policy and the Ghetto Underclass," Dissent (Winter 1988), pp. 80–91.
145. David Ellwood, *Poor Support: Poverty and the American Family* (New York: Basic Books, 1988), p. 58.
146. House Ways and Means Committee, *Overview of Entitlement Programs, 2004,* p. M-10.
147. "Preventing Teenage Pregnancy" (Washington, DC: U.S. Department of Health and Human Services, August 8, 2000).
148. Irwin Garfinkel, "Bringing Fathers Back In: The Child Support Assurance Strategy," *The American Prospect* (Spring 1992), p. 75.
149. Mickey Kaus, *The End of Equality* (New York: Basic Books, 1992).
150. Michael Kirst, "Improving Children's Services," *Phi Delta Kappan* (April 1991), p. 616.
151. Sid Gardner, "Failure by Fragmentation," *California Tomorrow* (Fall 1989), p. 19.
152. Bonnie Benard, "School Restructuring Can Promote Prevention," *Western Center News* (December 1991), p. 8.
153. Costin, Karger, and Stoesz, *The Politics of Child Abuse in America.*
154. "Children's Profile," (Youth Futures Authority) Retrieved October 2004 from the www.youthfutures authority.org

CHAPTER 16

Housing Policies

Most of the recent attention on housing has focused on the middle class. Yet, housing problems affect millions of Americans. Persistent problems include a lack of low-income affordable housing, dilapidated and dangerous housing, and high numbers of homeless people. Although housing discussions have frequently focused on homelessness, finding and maintaining adequate and affordable housing is also problematic for people on public assistance, for the working poor, and for a large section of the supposedly stable middle class. This chapter examines the problems of housing in the United States, with particular emphasis on low-income housing, housing affordability, homelessness, and proposals for housing reform.

Overview of Housing Legislation

Federal housing legislation began in 1937. As Figure 16.1 illustrates, this legislation developed into a tangle of laws that often evolved in conflicting directions.

In 1990 Congress passed the Cranston-Gonzales National Affordable Housing Act, which authorized housing-related block grants to state and local governments. The goals of the 1990 legislation included: (1) decentralizing housing policy by allowing states to design and administer their own housing programs; (2) using nonprofit sponsors to help develop and implement housing services; (3) linking housing assistance more closely with social services; (4) facilitating home ownership for low- and moderate-income people; (5) preserving existing federally subsidized housing units; and (6) initiating cost sharing among federal, state, and local governments and nonprofit organizations.[1] This Act also introduced the HOME investment partnerships block grant program, the Homeownership and Opportunity for People Everywhere (HOPE) program, and the national home ownership trust demonstration.

The centerpiece of the National Affordable Housing Act was the HOME program, designed to increase the supply of affordable housing for low-income families by providing federal grants to state and local governments. All states and more than 300 local jurisdictions receive HOME funds. Ninety percent of HOME-assisted units in a jurisdiction must be affordable for families with incomes below 60 percent of the area median, with the remaining units being affordable for families with incomes up to 80 percent of the median.[2]

The second component is the HOPE program, designed to facilitate home ownership by low-income families through the sale of publicly owned or held homes to current residents or other low-income households. The HOPE program has four components: (1) HOPE I finances the sales of public housing apartments to residents; (2) HOPE II finances the sales to low-income persons of other apartment buildings held by the federal government; (3) HOPE III finances the sale of single-family homes owned by federal, state, or local governments; and (4) HOPE IV represents an effort to combine social services with housing assistance for elderly and disabled households that would otherwise be unable to live independently.[3]

The linkage between housing and social services was strengthened by the Family Sufficiency program, which called for public housing authorities (PHAs) to help residents obtain coordinated social services to assist them in gaining employment. Participating families must complete these programs or risk losing their housing assistance. In return, as a participant's income increased, the money that would normally go toward a higher rent (calculated at 30 percent of income) was set aside in a special escrow account to be used for the purchase of a home. The legislation also included modest funds to create "Family Investment Centers" that provided social services in or near public housing projects.[4]

In 1998 former President Clinton signed the Quality Housing and Work Responsibility Act of 1998 (QHWRA), in some ways the housing equivalent of the 1996 PRWORA. In line with the PRWORA, the federal government devolved its responsibility as the primary agent for publicly assisted housing to 3,400 semiautonomous local PHAs. With input from public housing residents, these strengthened PHAs determine rents, admissions policies, and what (if any) social services are provided. The QHWRA also ties workforce participation into housing benefits. For example (1) PHAs can consider prospective tenants' employment history in the admissions decision; (2) TANF recipients who fail to fulfill their work requirement can lose Section 8 or public housing benefits; and (3) PHAs are encouraged to recruit "good" working-class families to act as role models for welfare-dependent families (the legislation decreases the percentage of public housing units earmarked for very low-income families from 75 to 70 percent).

The Housing Act of 1937	The United States had no national housing policy prior to the Housing Act of 1937. The objective of the act was to: "provide financial assistance to the states and political subdivisions thereof for the elimination of unsafe and unsanitary housing conditions, for the eradication of slums, for the provision of decent, safe and sanitary dwellings for families of low income, and for the reduction of unemployment and the stimulation of business activity, to create a United States Housing Authority and for other purposes."
The Housing Act of 1949 (Amended 1937 Act)	This amendment called for federal money for slum clearance and urban redevelopment and for the creation of a public authority charged with building and administering low-income housing units. Specifically, this bill required each locality to develop a plan for urban redevelopment that contained provisions for "predominantly residential dwellings." The wording of this bill was interpreted by localities to mean that only one-half of new construction was to be devoted to low-income housing.
Housing Act of 1954 (Amended the 1949 Act)	"Urban development" was changed to urban renewal, and localities were required to submit a master plan for removing urban blight and for community development. The act removed the requirement that new federally subsidized urban construction be "predominantly residential," clearing the way for massive slum clearance projects. It also allowed localities to more easily lease or sell land and to avoid the construction of public housing. Through renewal projects, localities tried to revitalize inner cities by attracting middle- and upper-income families at the expense of displaced poor families. From 1949 to 1963, urban renewal projects removed about 243,000 housing units and replaced them with 68,000 units, of which only 20,000 were for low-income families.
The Demonstration Cities and Metropolitan Development Act (Model Cities)	Passed in 1966 as part of President Lyndon Johnson's War on Poverty, the Act focused on deteriorated housing and blighted neighborhoods. The Model Cities legislation promised to "concentrate public and private resources in a comprehensive five-year attack on social, economic, and physical problems of slums and blighted neighborhoods." The Model Cities Act and virtually all neighborhood development acts were superseded by the Housing and Community Development Act of 1974.
The Housing and Community Development Act of 1974	This wide-ranging bill included provisions for urban renewal, neighborhood development, model cities, water and sewer projects, neighborhood and facility grants, public facilities and rehabilitation loans, and urban beautification and historic preservation. Although spending priorities were determined at the national level, communities were required to submit a master plan, including specific reference to their low-income housing needs.

Figure 16.1

Historical Highlights of Pre-1990 Housing Legislation

Sources: Quoted in Charles S. Prigmore and Charles R. Atherton, *Social Welfare Policy: Analysis and Formulation* (Lexington, MA: D. C. Heath, 1979), pp. 146–147; Robert Morris, *Social Policy of the American Welfare State,* 2nd edition. (New York: Longman, 1985), p. 131; Barbara Habenstreit, *The Making of America* (New York: Julian Messner, 1971), p. 46; Richard Geruson and Dennis McGrath, *Cities and Urbanization* (New York: Praeger, 1977), pp. 6–7; National Training and Information Center, *Insurance Redlining: Profits v. Policyholders* (Chicago: NTIC, 1973), p. 1.

Home Mortgage Disclosure Act (HMDA)	This Act focused on mortgage redlining. Advocates argued that a major cause of community deterioration was a "lending strike," or redlining, by financial institutions. Redlining is defined as "an outright refusal of an insurance company, bank, or other financial institution to provide its services solely on the basis of the location of a property." The term is derived from the practice of marking in red the area on a map avoided by insurance or financial institutions. As a result, families seeking to purchase a home in a redlined neighborhood may be denied a mortgage, insurance, or other necessary services. In 1976, President Gerald Ford signed the Home Mortgage Disclosure Act, which required virtually every bank or savings and loan association to annually disclose where it made its loans.
Community Reinvestment Act (CRA) of 1977	Broader than the HMDA, the CRA established the principle that each bank and savings institution has an obligation to make loans in every neighborhood of its service area. Virtually all lending institutions are covered under the CRA, and the law requires the federal government to annually evaluate the performance of each lending institution. Primary enforcement involves control by federal regulatory agencies over new charters, bank growth and mergers, relocations, and acquisitions. Only a handful of the CRA challenges result in punitive action against lenders. The power of the Act rests with the ability of community groups to win concessions from lending institutions, usually in the form of negotiated settlements.

The QHWRA also mandates that low-income tenants take personal responsibility for moving into better living conditions (e.g., a single family home).[5]

The Federal Government and Low-Income Housing Programs

For many families the cost of housing represents the single largest expenditure in the household budget.[6] It is a fixed cost that is often paid before food, clothing, and health care bills. For poor families, the precious little that remains after rent or mortgage payments is used to buy necessities for the rest of the month. The important impact of housing costs on family finances has fueled the federal government's involvement with low- and non-low-income housing programs. By 2003 the Department of Housing and Urban Development's (HUD) budget was $38 billion. Table 16.1 (pages 421–422) provides an overview of key HUD programs relating to the housing problems of low-income households.

Apart from HUD-administered programs, there is also the Low Income Housing Tax Credits (LIHTC). Created by the Tax Reform Act of 1986, the LIHTC was as a way for the federal government to encourage the development of affordable housing without having to allocate direct federal expenditures. Apartments supported by the LIHTC cannot be rented to anyone whose income exceeds 60 percent of the area median income. Each year, the LIHTC leverages about $6 billion of private investment and produces more than 125,000 affordable apartments for working families, seniors, homeless individuals, and people with special needs. Overall, the LIHTC has assisted in the production of 1.6 million apartments with affordable rents for low-income families. This has been accomplished by providing investors in eligible affordable housing developments with a dollar-for-dollar reduction in their federal tax liability. The LIHTC now accounts for most new affordable apartment production and drives up to 40 percent of all multifamily apartment development.[7]

Despite its importance, governmental assistance for housing was never provided as an entitlement to all households that qualify for aid. Unlike income maintenance programs such as SSI and the former AFDC, housing programs are not automatically provided to all eligible applicants. Congress appropriates funds yearly for various new commitments,

For many families, the cost of housing represents the single largest expenditure in the household budget.

most of which run 5 to 50 years. Because funding levels are usually low, only a portion of eligible applicants actually receive assistance. According to NLIHC's *Losing Ground,* nationally there are only 43 units both affordable and available to every 100 renter households with incomes less than 30 percent of the area median income. According to the Department of Housing and Urban Development (HUD), more than 5 million very low income renter households pay more than 50 percent of their incomes toward rent or live in severely substandard housing. Recent NLIHC research shows that waiting lists for public housing and rental assistance vouchers far surpass anticipated availability of affordable units.[8] (See Figure 16.2 on page 423.)

Relatively low levels of funding have been earmarked for housing programs. The cumulative shortfall to PHAs in operating subsidies between 1993 and 2003 was more than $1.9 billion and the cumulative shortfall in capital improvement funding was more than $20.3 billion.[9] This low funding level has also resulted in long waiting lists for

Spotlight 16.1

The Department of Housing and Urban Development

Established in 1965, the Department of Housing and Urban Development (HUD) offers various programs to increase homeownership, support community development, and increase access to affordable housing free from discrimination. To learn more HUD and its many programs, visit its website at **www.hud.gov.**

Table 16.1

Overview of HUD's Major Grant, Subsidy, and Loan Programs

The Housing Choice Voucher Program (Section 8 Rental Assistance) is HUDs largest program. The Section 8 program is based on a voucher system that allows low-income tenants (50 percent or less of the area median income) to occupy existing and privately owned housing stock. The voucher covers the difference between a fixed percentage of a tenant's income (30 percent) and the fair market rent of a housing unit. The HUD subsidy goes to the local PHA, which then pays the landlord, provided that the unit meets quality standards. Contract terms for subsidies last for from five to fifteen years. About half of Section 8 is project-based, meaning that tenants have to live in specific apartments. The other half is tenant-based, allowing tenants to take their subsidies and move. Section 8 also provides funds for new construction and for substantial and moderate rehabilitation of existing units. Only a minority of eligible applicants are served and most are on a waiting list when they apply. In 2003 about 2 million low-income families received HUD vouchers. For fiscal year 2004, the Congress provided nearly 13 billion for Section 8 renewals, an increase of 14.5 percent over fiscal year 2003.

Community Development Block Grants (CDBG) was funded at $5.3 billion in 2002. CDBGs are provided to units of local government and states for the funding of local community development programs that address housing and economic development needs, primarily for low- and moderate-income persons.

Public and Indian Housing (PIH) Grants and Loans was funded at $4.1 billion in 2002. Public Housing Operating Subsidies (totaling another $3.5 billion in 2002) are financial assistance provided for project operations to approximately 3,160 housing authorities managing approximately 1.2 million units. Public Housing was established by the U.S. Housing Act of 1937 and is restricted to households whose incomes are too low to find suitable private housing. The income of most families in public housing is less than 25 percent of the area median income and about one-half rely primarily on public assistance (TANF, SSI, and General Assistance) for their income; the other half rely on earned incomes, pensions, or Social Security. Residents pay 30 percent of their monthly adjusted income on rent. Public housing is concentrated in high poverty areas. In 1995, almost 70 percent of public housing was located in neighborhoods where the median household income was under $20,000. Contrary to popular myth, less than 10 percent of public housing units are severely degraded.

Affordable Housing Programs (HOME Investment Partnerships—see below) was funded at $1,65 billion in 2002. HOME Investment Partnership Grants provide assistance to renters, existing home owners, and first-time homebuyers, build state and local capacity to carry out affordable housing programs, and expand the capacity of nonprofit community housing organizations to develop and manage housing. The Housing Opportunities for Persons with AIDS provides affordable housing and related assistance to persons with HIV/AIDS. The Homeless Programs consists primarily of grants to public and private entitles to establish comprehensive systems for meeting the needs of homeless people.

Section 202/811 Capital Grants was funded at 1.26 billion in 2002. The program is designed to provide funds for the construction and long-term support of housing for the elderly and persons with disabilities. Advances are interest-free and do not have to be repaid providing the housing remains available for low-income persons for at least 40 years. In fiscal year 2004, $783 million was provided for elderly facilities.

Native American Housing Block Grants and Home Loan Guarantees assist Native Americans in building or purchasing homes on Trust Land; obtaining affordable housing; implementing local housing strategies to promote homeownership; and developing communities.

Fair Housing Assistance Program (FHAP) provides grants to state and local agencies that administer fair housing laws that are equivalent to the Federal Fair Housing Act.

Fair Housing Initiatives Program (FHIP) provides funds competitively to private and public entities to carry out local, regional and national programs that assist in eliminating discriminatory housing practices and educate the public and housing providers on their fair housing rights and responsibilities.

(continued)

Table 16.1

(continued)

Government National Mortgage Association (Ginnie Mae). Through its mortgage-backed securities program, Ginnie Mae facilitates the financing of residential mortgage loans by guaranteeing the timely payment of principal and interest to investors of privately issued securities backed by pools of mortgages insured or guaranteed by FHA, the Department of Veterans Affairs, and the Rural Housing Service. The Ginnie Mae guarantee gives lenders access to the capital market to originate new loans. The total amount of Ginnie Mae securities outstanding at the end of 2003 was approximately $474 billion.

Brownfields Redevelopment provides competitive economic development grants for qualified Brownfields (i.e., the cleanup and economic redevelopment of contaminated sites) projects.

Revitalization of Severely Distressed Public Housing (HOPE IV) makes awards to public housing authorities on a competitive basis to demolish obsolete or failed developments or to revitalize, where appropriate, sites upon which these developments exist.

Housing Opportunities For Persons With AIDS (HOPWA) is designed to provide states and localities with resources and incentives to devise long-term comprehensive strategies for meeting the housing needs of persons living with HIV/AIDS and their families.

The Office of Rural Housing and Economic Development (FmHA Section 502) was established to ensure that HUD has a comprehensive approach to rural housing and rural economic development issues. The office funds technical assistance and capacity-building in rural, under-served areas, and provides grants for Indian tribes, state housing finance agencies, and state economic development agencies to pursue strategies designed to meet rural housing and economic development needs. Section 502 makes low-interest loans available for home purchases in rural areas. In 2002 Section 502 supplied nearly $125 million for 1,447 loans.

Homeless Assistance Grants provides funding to break the cycle of homelessness and to move homeless persons and families into permanent housing. This is done by providing rental assistance, emergency shelter, transitional and permanent housing, and supportive services to homeless persons and families.

Empowerment Zones/Enterprise Communities (EZ/EC) is designed to create self-sustaining, long-term development in distressed urban and rural areas. The program uses a combination of federal tax incentives and flexible grant funds to reinvigorate declining communities.

Office of Lead Hazard Control is authorized to make grants to states, localities, and Native American tribes to conduct lead-based paint hazard reduction and abatement activities in private low-income housing.

Sources: U.S. Department of Housing and Urban Development, *Performance and Accountability Report Fiscal Year 2003,* 2004, retrieved November 2004 from www.hud.gov/offices/cfo/reports/2003par.pdf; Democratic Policy Committee, the Departments of Veterans Affairs and Housing and Urban Development and Independent Agencies *Appropriations Bill for Fiscal Year 2004,* retrieved November 2004 from http://democrats.senate.gov/~dpc/pubs/108–1-387.html; "Budget of the United States Government: Fiscal Year 2004," retrieved November 2004 from www.spoaccess.gov/usbudget/fy04/browse.html; "Facts about Section 8 Voucher Funding," retrieved November 2004 from www.hud.gov/offices/pih/programs/hcv/walshs8letter.pdf; "U.S. Department of Housing and Urban Development Fiscal Year 2004 Budget Summary," retrieved November 2004 from www.hud.gov/about/budget/fy04/budgetsummary.pdf; "HUD's Public Housing Program," Retrieved November 2004 from www.hud.gov/renting/phprog.cfm.

public housing and Section 8 vouchers. The Council of Large Public Housing estimated that waiting lists for public housing nationwide in 2000 included 2.35 million households, many of whom waited two or more years before getting a unit.[10]

In 2004 two similar bills (H.R. 1841 and S. 947) were introduced that would end the existing Housing Choice Voucher program (Section 8) and replace it with a block grant to the states called Housing Assistance for Needy Families (HANF). The HANF block grant would be funded at the federal level through annual appropriations. HANF funds could only be used to provide tenant-based rental assistance, home ownership assistance, cover administrative costs, or for other activities specified by HUD to further those goals. States would design their own programs based on minimal federal guidance regarding the number of families served and their income eligibility. Fami-

Section 8

- The Section 8 Housing Choice Voucher Program serves more than 4.7 million seniors, people with disabilities and low-income families with children.
- More than 324,000 seniors rely on Housing Choice Vouchers for affordable housing, representing 16 percent of all Section 8 households. Twenty-three percent of Section 8 seniors are 80 years or older. The median annual income for an elderly household in Section 8 is $8,550 and 90 percent rely on Social Security or Supplemental Security payments as their primary source of income.
- Section 8 recipients include almost 400,000 households in which one or more members has a disability, representing 22 percent of all voucher households. Almost 40,000 Section 8 households have a child with a disability.
- Sixty-one percent of all Section 8 households are families with children. More than 2.4 million children live in Section 8, representing over 50 percent of all residents. Almost 50 percent of households with children obtain their primary income from wages, with the average income being $11,390.

Public Housing

- Public housing is home to almost 3 million seniors, people with disabilities and low-income families with children. The average household size is 2.3 people.
- More than 400,000 seniors rely on public housing and supportive services. Elderly households represent 31 percent of all public housing households and 27 percent of public housing's seniors are 80 years of age or older. The median annual income for an elderly household in public housing is $8,250 and 72 percent of seniors rely on Social Security payments as their primary source of income.
- Almost 400,000 households in which one or more members has a disability live in public housing, representing 32 percent of all public housing households. Almost 18,000 public housing households have a child with a disability.
- About 1.2 million children live in public housing, representing 43 percent of all public housing residents.
- The mean income for a public housing household is $9,531, which on average is about 24 percent of the median income for their area. Close to 43 percent of non-elderly households obtain their primary source of income from wages.

Figure 16.2

Characteristics of Section 8 Recipients and Residents in Public Housing

Source: Council of Large Public Housing Authorities, *Quick Facts on Public Housing* (Washington, DC: Author, 2004).

lies who receive Section 8 assistance under the current program would continue to receive assistance subject to those requirements. Many housing advocacy groups have criticized the proposal, expressing concern that it will ultimately decrease the amount of housing assistance available to needy families nationwide. Proponents of the proposal argue that by giving states control over the administration and distribution of Section 8 assistance, many systemic inefficiencies will be eliminated. The proposal will likely reduce the number of public housing authorities nationwide, theoretically decreasing administrative costs.[11]

The United States spends less on housing assistance than any other Western industrial democracy. Not only does the U.S. government fail to adequately assist poor people with housing, but most housing subsidies benefit the nonpoor. For example, the mortgage-interest deduction cost the federal government: $372.7 billion. About 73 percent of the taxpayers who claimed this deduction on their 2002 returns earned $50,000 or more. About 47 percent of the total earned between $50,000 and $100,000. Renters and those who own their homes free and clear receive no benefits.[12]

Issues in Housing Policy

The equity in home ownership is the cornerstone of wealth for most U.S. families. According to the Joint Center for Housing Studies of Harvard University, two-thirds of Americans list their home as their single biggest asset. In 2002, home equity hit a record high of $7.6 trillion.[13]

Trends in U.S. Housing

The following represent some highlights of the often contradictory U.S. housing trends:

- The national homeownership rate reached a new annual high of 68.4 percent in 2003 and continues to climb slightly across all geographic regions, age groups, and racial/ethnic groups.[14] Home sales and the value of residential construction reached new highs in 2003.[15]
- Although persistent disparities between whites and minorities narrowed only slightly (minority home ownership was at 49.3 percent in 2002), minorities still accounted for nearly 40 percent of the net growth in owners between 1994 and 2003.[16] Rapid household growth, combined with climbing ownership rates, has boosted the minority presence in homebuying markets. On the other hand, millions of very low-income households still lack adequate, affordable housing at a time when losses of subsidized units are rising.
- Home equity remains an especially important source of wealth for low-income and minority households. In 1998, among non-elderly homeowners with incomes under $20,000, half held 69 percent or more of their net household wealth in home equity. By comparison, among homeowners with incomes of $50,000 to $60,000, half held 38 percent or less of their net wealth in home equity. For half of non-Hispanic black home owners, home equity accounted for 57 percent or more of their net wealth. For half of Hispanic homeowners, the share was even higher at 71 percent or more. Among half of non-Hispanic white homeowners, though, the contribution of home equity to wealth was 40 percent or less.
- Urban sprawl continues to increase. As employment decentralizes, families are able to live and work at greater distances from the urban core. As a result, low-density metro counties have witnessed explosive job and housing growth in recent years, whereas activity in high-density counties has been limited.
- The South and West are continuing to grow. Between 1990 and 2000, new construction added 25 percent or more to the housing stocks of 21 metropolitan areas in the South and West. No metropolitan area in the Northeast experienced housing stock growth of this magnitude. Just five states—Florida, California, Texas, Georgia, and North Carolina—accounted for 40 percent of housing permits issued in 2003.
- The exodus from central cities continues. Although most cities in the South and West registered gains, the movement away from many localities in the Northeast and Midwest pushed national net outmigration from larger cities to 1.2 million households between 1997 and 1999. In fact, between 1997 and 1999 more than a half-million households with incomes of $60,000 or more left these cities for suburban or nonmetropolitan areas. The homeownership rate in central cities increased to 52.3 percent in 2003, a slight increase of .2 percentage points from the same period in 2002.[17]
- Record numbers of very low-income households are spending more than half their incomes on housing. About 500,000 very low-income renters and nearly as many very low-income owners earning at least the equivalent of the full-time minimum wage spend this much for housing.
- While housing prices have gone up in the bicoastal regions such as New York, San Francisco, and Los Angeles, people in much of the country have little housing equity to tap for home improvements, retirement, or other needs. The prices of typical homes across most of the country's vast middle have risen just ahead of inflation and more slowly than incomes. The cost of homes in the most expensive cities is now about six times that in the least expensive, up from a ratio of three to one two decades ago.
- Five states—Florida, California, Georgia, North Carolina, and Texas—account for about 40 percent of **housing starts** nationwide in 2003.[18]
- Houses are larger today than in the past. The size of newly constructed single-family homes rose from a median of 1,385 square feet in 1970 to 2,030 square feet in 1999, a 47 percent increase. The median square footage of all homes in the United States for 2001 was 1,691 square feet.
- Overall, the number of households in the United States increased 15 percent, from 91.9 million in 1990 to 105.5 million in 2000. Family households increased 11 percent, from 64.5 million in 1990 to 71.8 million in 2000, while nonfamily households increased faster, 23 percent, from 27.4 million in 1990 to 33.7 million in 2000.
- In 1940 almost half of all housing units lacked complete plumbing facilities. The percentage of households without complete plumbing dropped from 36 percent in 1950 to 17 percent in 1960. In 1940 three-fourths of households used either coal/coke or wood to heat their homes. By 1990 fewer than 1 percent of households heated their homes

with coal/coke, and only about 4 percent with wood. More than three-fourths of households now rely on either utility-based gas or electricity to heat their homes.[19]

Problems in Home Ownership

Beginning in the 1970s, many people were forced to spend a higher percentage of their income on housing than they could reasonably afford. Some of these people became so financially overextended that they became vulnerable to mortgage default or eviction—or lacked the necessary cash to purchase other necessities.

Between 1967 and 2004 the median income for first-time home buyers rose from $28,011 to $54,500, while the median home price went from $56,466 to $168,500. In 1967 the average annual mortgage payment was $3,400; by 2004 it had risen to roughly $12,000.[20] The price increase of single-family homes is even sharper when not adjusted for inflation. In 1970 the average new single-family home cost $26,600; in 2004 it cost $263,100. For existing single-family homes the price went from $25,700 to $186,500 (see Table 16.2). The median price of housing also varies widely by city and region. For example, from 1985 to 2002 the median price for an existing single-family home in Los Angeles went from $119,000 to $382,000 (the California statewide median was $404,000); in New York City/North New Jersey, $320,000; and in Boston it rose from $134,000 to $340,000.[21]

As a result of these and other factors, home ownership rates for very low-income families with children has dropped by more than 20 percent from 1985 to 2000.[22] Some 45 percent of very low-income households are home owners. More than half of these households are headed by females or include at least one elderly member. In addition, nearly one-quarter are headed by minorities. Nearly 60 percent of very low-income home owners pay more than 30 percent of their incomes for housing; 10 percent pay more than 50 percent.[23]

Factors such as mortgage instruments also play an important role in determining housing affordability for low-income home owners. Many poor and first-time home buyers lack adequate credit, have a sketchy credit history, or lack the down payment or qualifying income necessary for a conventional mortgage. Many of the poor have turned to the fringe market, either by way of subprime or predatory loans.

Subprime mortgages include high interest rates and additional fees for borrowers classified as high credit risks. For example, a 5.5 percent APR prime rate home mortgage in early 2004 was typical for those with excellent credit. A subprime mortgage for borrowers with problematic credit might have an interest rate of 9 to 15 percent. A predatory loan (a subset of the subprime mortgage industry) could involve interest rates as high as 18 percent plus onerous loan terms. In addition to high interest, subprime mortgages also include additional fees for borrowers classified as high credit risks.

Subprime mortgage lenders were historically called "fringe" banks because they specialized in a type of lending that traditional banks rejected because of high risk levels. However, more traditional lenders were eventually enticed into the subprime market because of key developments in the banking industry. For example, the explosion in the subprime loan market occurred partly from Wall

Table 16.2

Average U.S. Housing Prices, Mortgage Rates, and Median Family Income in Non-Inflation Adjusted Dollars: Selected Years

Period	New SF Homes*	Existing SF Homes	Mortgage Rates	Median Income
1970	$26,600	$25,700	8.35%	$9,867
1975	42,600	39,000	9.21	13,719
1980	76,400	72,800	12.95	21,023
1985	100,800	86,000	11.74	27,735
1990	149,800	118,600	10.04	35,353
1995	158,700	139,000	7.85	39,558
2000	201,100	179,400	8.02	40,816
2004	263,100	186,500	5.83	43,318

*SF=Single Family

Source: Based on data from U.S. Department of Housing and Urban Development, *U.S. Housing Market Conditions* (Washington, DC: HUD, Office of Policy Development and Research, 2nd Quarter, 2004); and *The State of the Nation's Housing: 2004,* retrieved November 2004 from www.jchs.harvard.edu/publications/markets/son2004.pdf

Street's willingness to finance and securitize these loans. After years of buying only traditional mortgages from banks, bundling them into mortgage-backed securities and then selling them off to investors, investment banking firms began applying the securitization process to subprime lenders in the early 1990s. Since securitization eliminates part of a lender's risk, more financial institutions began making loans to troubled borrowers. Nationally, the number of subprime loans skyrocketed from about 100,000 refinancing and home mortgage loans in 1993 to more than one million in 2001.[24] By the late 1990s, subprime lenders became some of the highest volume originators of refinancing loans.

A 2004 report by the Association of Community Organizations for Reform Now (ACORN) found that African Americans were 2.2 times more likely than whites to be denied a conventional mortgage loan. Latino applicants were 1.6 times more likely than whites to be denied. Although minority home buyers saw a dramatically larger percentage increase than whites in the number of conventional loans they received from 1993 to 2003, a significant portion of those were high cost subprime loans. The number of conventional home purchase loans originated to Latinos grew 347 percent from 1993 to 2003, while rising 206 percent for African Americans and 64 percent for whites. However, more expensive subprime loans accounted for 23.3 percent of the conventional loans made to Latinos, 25.4 percent of the loans to African Americans, and 8.2 percent of loans to whites. Additionally, low and moderate income census tracts account for 31.3 percent of the country but received just 15.3 percent of the conventional loans in 2003. In contrast, upper-income neighborhoods make up 25.6 percent of the country and received 39.7 percent of the conventional home purchase loans.[25] These figures help substantiate the charge that subprime and predatory lenders target people of color.

The essential problem in homeownership is that in many places housing costs are rising faster than incomes. To bridge that gap, lenders and mortgage brokers have developed "creative financing." For instance, in an adjustable rate mortgage (ARM) loan the interest rate varies throughout the term of the loan, although most contain a maximum interest rate cap. The frequency of rate changes and the interest cap depends on the conditions of the loan and the buyer's credit. Subprime or predatory ARM's often involve large, explosive interest rate hikes.[26]

Another loan variation is a balloon mortgage. In this scheme, a predatory mortgage lender takes a family whose income or credit score makes them ineligible for a traditional mortgage and structures a loan that appears affordable. The mortgage is then written for a relatively short period—5 to 10 years—and the borrower pays only the interest. At the end of the loan term, the borrower faces a final balloon payment for the entire loan principal. This type of loan may also involve negative amortization, which is structuring a loan so that interest is not amortized over the term. Instead, monthly payments are insufficient to cover even the accrued interest and the outstanding loan balance increases each month. At the end of the loan term, the borrower owes more than the original amount. In either case, if the homeowner cannot afford the final balloon payment, they either lose the home through foreclosure or are forced to refinance with the same or another lender at additional costs. Some buyers are attracted to this type of high-risk loan since the low monthly payments allow them to purchase a larger house than their income or credit justifies.[27]

Yet another variation is shared appreciation mortgages (SAMs), which are fixed rate, fixed term loans for up to 30 years. These loans have more relaxed loan qualifications and smaller monthly payments than a conventional loan. In exchange for a lower interest rate, a buyer agrees to relinquish part of the future value of the home to the lender. For example, a buyer purchases a home for $100,000. After three years, they decide to move and the house has appreciated $10,000. With a 50 percent SAM loan, the homeowner would owe the lender $5,000 plus the unpaid loan balance. The reduction in the interest rate is based on how much of the property's appreciation the buyer is willing to forego—the more equity they give up the lower the interest rate.[28]

Many homeowners refinance or take out home equity loans to cash out part of the equity of their home. The cash is then used to pay off debts, remodel, pay household bills, or purchase items such as cars, vacations, and so forth. Homeowners draw out equity based on the belief that their property will continue to appreciate, although in the past housing prices have contracted, sometimes violently. If the value of a house drops, the homeowner is "upside down"—they owe more than the home's value. The prospect of quick cash is appealing to those caught up in high consumer debt. For example, Americans now have a total household debt of $7.4 trillion, almost double that of the early 1990s.[29] In 2002, homeowners initiated $97 billion in home equity loans and lines of credit, nearly five times the amount in 1993. Homeowners also converted about $180 billion of their equity into cash from 2001 to 2002.[30] Of the 3.7 million homeowners who refinanced in 1999, 60 percent had higher payments.[31] Despite the rise in home ownership (67 percent of Americans own their own homes) and rapidly rising housing prices during the 1990s, home equity has declined nationally. From 1989 to 1999, the average home equity per homeowner declined (in 1999 inflation-adjusted dollars) from $91,000 to $89,500.[32] One reason is increased home equity borrowing.

Abusive practices in the home refinancing industry involve a wide range of activities, including equity stripping, hiding loan terms, and packing loans with extra charges. One of the most prevalent is equity stripping, which operates like this. The bills of a homeowner exceed their monthly income. They have built up equity in their home and are told by a lender they are eligible for a loan, although their monthly income is insufficient to meet their current obligations. The lender is motivated to close the deal for two reasons. First, they may purposely structure unaffordable loans so that the borrower defaults and is forced continually to refinance, thereby stripping more equity from the home. Secondly, they may structure the loan so that borrower defaults and they can foreclose.

Still another variation is loan flipping, a financial scheme outlawed by the U.S. Department of Housing and Urban Development (HUD) in the 1990s but still widely practiced. Loan flipping, or multiple refinancing, works if a home has appreciated or if the homeowner did not borrow the maximum amount of equity in an earlier loan. Each time a loan is flipped more equity is stripped away as new appraisals are required; new loan origination fees, points, and closing costs are added; and the interest rate climbs upward. A higher interest rate on multiple refinancing loans is virtually assured since a homeowner's credit score goes down with each new loan. Higher interest rates are also assured since a homeowner's debt-to-asset ratio is greater because of higher loans. After several refinancing cycles, a homeowner may become ineligible for another loan, while the mortgage payments and property taxes rise to the point where the property becomes unaffordable. In the end, the homeowner loses their home and their credit. The classic example of loan flipping is Bennett Roberts, who had eleven loans from a high cost mortgage lender within four years. Roberts paid more than $29,000 in fees and charges on a $26,000 loan, including 10 points on every refinancing, plus interest.[33]

Negative equity is a new financial scheme that allows homeowners to borrow up to 125 percent of the value of their home. For example, if a house is appraised at $100,000 and the homeowner borrows the equity based upon 125 percent of the value of the home, they will have a mortgage balance of $125,000 or $25,000 more that the house is worth. If the homeowner is forced to move because of a job, health problems or other reasons, they will be unable to sell the home without adding additional money.

One of the newer variations of refinancing endorsed by HUD is a reverse mortgage for senior citizens, called a home equity conversion mortgage (HECM). This program unlocks the equity the elderly have built up in their property. Homeowners 62 or older can borrow against the value of their property. They receive payments from lenders monthly, in a lump sum, or as a line of credit. The size of the reverse mortgage is determined by the borrower's age, the interest rate and the value of the home. The older the homeowner the larger the percentage of a home's value they can borrow. For example, a 65-year-old can borrow up to 26 percent of a home's value, a 75-year-old up to 39 percent and an 85-year-old up to 56 percent. The amount owed increases over time, but no payment is due until the end of the loan term. When the loan term expires, the total loan amount plus interest is due in full. This lump sum payment is usually paid for by selling the property. No repayments are required while a borrower lives in the home and the monthly income is tax free.

For some homeowners, refinancing is a shell game whereby debt is moved from one shell to another, meanwhile growing larger as more fees are assessed, more commissions are paid, and more home equity is stripped away. Finally, the homeowner becomes asset poor and debt rich, which is appreciated only after selling a home or facing retirement. While homeownership is supposed to build assets, home equity and refinancing loans are helping to build infinite debt. Instead of creating net asset wealth, owning a home is fast becoming an albatross of debt around the necks of over-leveraged homeowners.

Problems in Finding Affordable Rental Housing

If finding affordable housing is difficult for poor and moderate-income homeowners, it has reached crisis proportions for extremely low-income (ELI) renters. There are four major reasons for the affordability gap in rental housing: (1) Real incomes of ELI renter households has dropped; (2) the number of renter households has increased; (3) the number of low-cost unsubsidized rental units is dropping (federal housing assistance has not compensated for these losses); and (4) rents have increased or remained high for much of the 1990s and early 2000s.

The standard benchmark for "affordability" is that households should pay no more than 30 percent of their after-tax income for housing. Households paying between 30 and 50 percent for housing have moderate cost burdens; households paying more than 50 percent have severe cost burdens. Almost 30 million U.S. households pay more than 30 percent of their income for housing.[34] The robust economy of the late 1990s did little to relieve the housing problems of low-income renters. Renters in the bottom quarter of the income distribution saw their real incomes decline between 1996 and 1998, while rents increased by 2.3 percent.[35] Although the rental market cooled somewhat in the early 2000s rents continued to remain high.

Although most Americans are well housed, nearly a third of all households spend 30 percent or more of their incomes on housing and 13 percent spend 50 percent or more. In addition, crowding is on the increase, some 2.5 to 3.5 million people are homeless at some point in a given year, and nearly 2 million households still live in severely inadequate units. Housing challenges are most severe among those at the bottom of the income distribution. Fully half of lowest-income households spend at least 50 percent of their incomes on housing. Severely cost-burdened households in the bottom quintile have little left over to pay for other basic necessities, spending just $161 on average each month on food and $34 on health care. By comparison, households in the bottom expense quintile that devote less than 20 percent of their budgets to housing managed to spend $80 more a month on food and $49 more on healthcare on average. Affordability pressures are likely to increase since many of the low-wage jobs created by the economy are insufficient to pay for (at 30 percent of income) even a modest one-bedroom apartment in most parts of the country. Similarly, retirement incomes are so small and stagnant that many seniors face heavy housing cost burdens on top of escalating healthcare costs.[36]

Evidence of the crisis in affordable rental housing is illustrated by the relationship of the fair market rents (FMR) to monthly minimum wage income and public assistance benefits. The FMR, a HUD designation, is defined as the dollar amount below which 40 percent of the standard quality rental housing units rent. In short, the FMR is what HUD determines it costs to rent modest, safe, and healthy housing in a specific county or MSA. The housing wage is based on the wage required by each county to rent a two-bedroom unit at the FMR. In 1999, the national two bedroom housing wage was $11.08; by 2003, it was $15.21, a 37 percent increase. This means that on average there must be almost three full-time minimum wage workers to enable a household to afford a two-bedroom unit at the FMR. The most serious housing problems are faced by the lowest income households. For ELI families—those with incomes less than 30 percent of the area median income (AMI)—the mean combined national hourly wage was $8.34 in 2003, only 45 percent of the national housing wage.[37] The loss of modest rental housing stock continues as market forces drive up the cost of housing and government fails to intervene to level the playing field.

Some states have recognized that the federal minimum wage is insufficient and have passed legislation mandating a higher wage. Still, in no state can an ELI household afford a two bedroom home at the FMR. Looking below the state level reveals greater variation. In no metropolitan statistical area (MSA) can a household earning the ELI threshold afford the FMR for a two bedroom home. In 43 MSAs, home to one-third of U.S. renters, a household earning the ELI threshold is able to afford only 50 percent or less of their MSA's FMR. At the county level, a household at the ELI threshold can afford a two bedroom home at the FMR in only 27 largely rural counties that contain less than two-tenths of one percent of the renters in the nation. In contrast, in 208 counties households at the ELI threshold can afford 50 percent or less of their area's FMR. These counties represent 8.4 million renter households, nearly a quarter of all renters in the country.[38]

As mentioned earlier, when poor households live in adequate housing, they usually pay for it by spending an excessive proportion of their income on rent. Hence, many of these households have little left over for other necessities such as heat, food, clothing, and health care. Some of these families find themselves in a "heat or eat" situation. Little research has been done on the health effects of rent burdens; but Dr. Alan Meyers, a pediatrician at Boston Medical Center, studied 200 poor children and found that only 3 percent of children whose families received rent subsidies were underweight for their age. For children whose families were on the subsidized housing wait list, in contrast, 22 percent were underweight for their age. After examining the records of 11,000 poor children, Meyers found that children were most likely to be underweight in the 90 days after the coldest month of the year; this finding bolstered his theory that families make the choice of whether to "heat or eat."[39]

Severe housing problems are related to the dwindling supply of affordable unsubsidized housing units available to very low-income households. Losses of units to either rising rents or demolition have intensified the housing problems of very low-income renters who receive no rent subsidies. Adding to the pressures on low-income households is the cost of supplying new affordable housing. Restrictive regulations and public resistance to high-density development make it difficult to replace or add lower-cost units. Between 1993 and 1995, for example, the number of unsubsidized units affordable by very low-income households dropped 8.6 percent—a decrease of nearly 900,000 units. At the same time, the number of units affordable by extremely low-income households—those with incomes less than 30 percent of the area median—fell by 16 percent.[40]

In 1999 there were 4.9 million affordable and available rental units for 7.7 ELI households. Three million low- to moderate-income working families spent more than half of their income on housing in 1997. By 2001 that number jumped to 4.8 million—a 67 percent increase. Overall, 14.4 million families have critical housing needs. It would take annual production of more than 250,000 units for more than 20 years to close the housing affordability gap. On the other hand, Congress has denied requests and provided no funding since 1995 for new rental assistance to serve families with worst case needs.[41]

Several other factors have converged to deplete low-income housing stock, including the commercial renovation of central-city downtown areas. Developments consisting of new office buildings, large apartment complexes, shopping areas and parking lots often replace low-income housing bordering on downtown areas. Traditionally affordable (and often run-down) apartment buildings, cheap single room occupancy (SRO) hotels, rooming houses, and boardinghouses are razed as new office buildings and shopping complexes are erected. Displaced longtime residents are forced to find housing in more expensive neighborhoods; to double up with family or friends; or, in some cases, to become homeless.

The loss of SROs units has exacerbated the homeless problem. In the past SROs were home to many poor people (including those suffering from substance abuse and mental illnesses) who were not living in public or low-income subsidized housing. But between 1970 and the mid-1980s, an estimated 1 million SRO units were demolished. San Francisco lost 43 percent; Los Angeles lost more than 50 percent; New York lost 87 percent; and Chicago experienced the total elimination of its SRO housing units and hotels. These demolitions left many poor persons homeless, particularly those suffering from mental illness and substance abuse.[42]

According to George Sternlieb and Jones Hughes, "a new town may be evolving in-town."[43] This new town, or "gentrified" neighborhood, is a major component of the urban renaissance taking place in many U.S. cities. Attracted by old houses amenable to restoration; good transportation facilities; and close proximity to employment and artistic, cultural, and social opportunities, young professional and white-collar workers have begun to resettle the (poor, aging, and usually heavily minority sections of central cities in the process called **gentrification.** As part of the process, upscale condos are built, houses are rehabbed, dusty lofts are modernized and sold for small fortunes, and trendy candle-lit restaurants and boutiques replace mini-marts and used furniture stores. Critics argue that a valuable piece of city real estate is being cleansed of its working class residents.

Although the renovation of central-city areas, such as New York's SoHo district, often makes a neighborhood more attractive (and potentially a tourist attraction), the effect on the indigenous—and frequently poor—population can be devastating. As homes become renovated, the price of surrounding housing increases. While low-income homeowners can command a high price for their homes, they may also find few suitable places to relocate. As neighborhoods become more affluent, property taxes rise, thus creating a burden on existing low-income homeowners. Previously affordable rental housing undergo large rent increases as neighborhoods become more desirable, thereby driving out older and poorer residents. Moreover, as the baby boomers age, the reason that many moved to the suburbs—good schools and safe neighborhoods for their children—may be eclipsed by the stress and exhaustion of long commutes and highway gridlock.

Numbers of these couples without children at home are opting to move closer to work and cultural amenities. Although gentrification has been selective, with the main demographic movement continuing to be suburban, it has had a striking impact on growing numbers of central-city neighborhoods.

The conversion of apartment buildings into condominiums represents another threat to low-income renters. As a consequence of tax breaks and income shelters, previously affordable rental housing is rapidly being turned into condominiums. Whether initiated by tenants or by developers, condominium conversion represents the serious depletion of good-quality rental stock. Because units in these conversions may cost upwards of $100,000 or more, low-income tenants can rarely afford the benefits of condominium living; and although renters are often offered a separation fee when a building undergoes conversion, this may barely cover the costs of moving, much less make up for the difference between renters' current rent and a higher alternative rent.

Overcrowded and Deficient Housing

Problems of overcrowding and structural inadequacy affect a significant number of U.S. households. HUD defines a housing unit as overcrowded if there is an average of more than one person per room. According to this definition, almost 3 million households live in overcrowded conditions, sometimes as a result of families' doubling up to avoid becoming homeless. In 1995 HUD classified 2 million housing units as seriously inadequate. "Inadequate" housing is housing with severe physical deficiencies; for example, it may lack hot water, electricity, or a toilet or may have neither a bathtub nor shower. Years of neglect have led to a serious backlog of repairs among 1.1 million assisted and 350,000 unassisted HUD-insured units. A study estimates that restoring systems in these buildings to adequate working condition would have cost $4.2 billion in 1995. In the suburbs both owners and renters make up substantial shares of households suffering from inadequate housing. That is, the number of suburban households living in these conditions equals that in central cities, but a larger share are home owners.[44]

Lead paint is one of the principal problems in units needing rehabilitation. The Centers for Disease Control and Prevention notes that lead poisoning is one of the most common and devastating environmental diseases that affect young children, causing developmental and behavior problems. Children are exposed to lead poisoning by living in older homes with peeling, chipping, and flaking paint. According to the EPA, there were nearly three to four million children with elevated blood lead levels in the United States in 1978. In the 1990s, that number had dropped to 434,000 kids. Because low-income families often occupy poorly maintained older homes, their children are four times more likely to have lead poisoning than children in high-income families.[45]

Other Factors Affecting Housing

Another problem affecting affordable housing is property taxes—the heart of local revenues. The escalating costs of providing governmental services have resulted in significant increases in property taxes, which landlords generally pass along to renters in the form of higher rents. In response, many states have tried to reduce property tax burdens for low-income households. The most common form of property tax relief occurs through **circuit breaker programs.** A typical circuit breaker program is activated when taxes exceed a specified proportion of a home owner's income, and in some states, low-income households are sent a yearly benefit check that covers all or part of the property taxes they paid. Circuit breaker programs for low-income renters operate in a similar manner. Typically, a portion of the rent paid by a low-income household is considered to represent the property tax passed on by the landlord and is thus refunded by the state or local government. Although circuit breaker programs provide relief, they are often restricted to the elderly or disabled. For example, although 31 states and the District of Columbia have circuit breaker programs, 21 states restrict eligibility to elderly and disabled households. Twenty-seven of these 31 states cover both renters and home owners; 6 states restrict eligibility to home owners.[46]

Housing costs are also aggravated by high utility rates. Nationwide, the average family paid about $2,489 in utility bills in 2004.[47] However, in many parts of the country, especially the Northeast and the Midwest, an average family may pay considerably more, because of high heating costs. For example, the Energy Information Administration forecast that heating a home with natural gas in 2005 will cost an average of $1,010; heating with oil, $1,114; and heating with propane, $1,335.[48] Low-income consumers spend anywhere from 13 to 44 percent of their total household income on utilities, whereas average-income Americans spend only 4 percent.[49] Thus, increases in home energy bills disproportionately affect the poor. In some cases the result is utility shutoffs.[50]

To mitigate the effects of the federal deregulation of oil prices and the large oil price increases of the 1970s, Congress passed the Low-Income Home Energy Assistance Program (LIHEAP) in 1981. This legislation permits states to offer three types of assistance to low-income households: (1) funds to help eligible households pay their home heating or cooling bills; (2) allotments for low-income weatherization; and (3) assistance to households during energy-related emergencies. States are required to target LIHEAP benefits to households with the lowest incomes and the highest energy costs relative to income and family size. In 2003 LIHEAP was funded at almost $2 billion (this was cut to $1.88 billion in 2004) and served roughly 4.6 million households. This was less than the $2.1 billion spent in 1985 and represents more than an 11 percent cut in LIHEAP funds.[51]

Housing discrimination is another barrier facing the poor. This discrimination takes two forms: racial discrimination and discrimination against families with children. Although illegal, racial discrimination in housing is still prevalent. In addition, many landlords and real estate agents refuse to rent to families with children. Often these families, even when they do find housing, are required to pay higher rents, provide exorbitant security deposits, or meet qualifications not required of renters without children.[52] Discrimination against families with children continues, even though Congress has banned such discrimination since 1988.[53]

Homelessness

Homelessness can be defined as simply a lack of housing. As such, it represents both a simple and a complex problem. Specifically, homeless people are not a homogeneous group. For some individuals homelessness is a lifestyle choice, the freedom to roam without being tied down to one place. For others, particularly people with mental illness and chronic alcoholism, homelessness reflects the deterioration of an overburdened public mental health system. The breakdown in the mental health system is aggravated by an influx of previously healthy people who, when reduced to economic deprivation and homelessness, develop symptoms of mental illness. For others, homelessness is rooted in cuts in federally subsidized housing programs and in the cost/income squeeze of the housing market. Finally, large numbers of people are homeless as a result of the inability of public assistance benefits to keep pace with the cost of living, especially in the area of housing and utilities. Despite the variety of causes, almost all forms of homelessness are tied to poverty. In that sense, homelessness is a manifestation of poverty.

The actual number of homeless people in the United States is difficult to ascertain for several reasons. First, definitions of homelessness vary from study to study, and different methods for counting homeless people yield different results. Second, many of the homeless are "hidden" in that they live in campgrounds, automobiles, boxcars, caves, tents, boxes, or other makeshift housing. Or they may live temporarily with family members or friends. Such

Spotlight 16.2

The National Coalition for the Homeless

The National Coalition for the Homeless (NCH) was established to end homelessness in America. To that end, this organization engages in public education, policy advocacy, and grassroots organizing. The work of NCH is focused in the following four areas: housing justice, economic justice, health care justice, and civil rights. To learn more about NCH, go to its web site at **www.nationalhomeless.org.**

Homelessness in America is both a simple and complex problem.

arrangements make it nearly impossible for agencies to count every person without stable housing. Studies of how many people are homeless on any given day or week (point-in-time studies) or of how many have experienced homelessness over a given time period (prevalence counts) are perhaps more valuable. These studies measure the magnitude of homelessness and therefore reflect the number of people who experience homelessness over a period of time, rather than an exact count. Most studies count people who are homeless in a given community by tracking people who use the services of soup kitchens and shelters.

Third, the homeless population is often undercounted in federal surveys for political reasons. Specifically, if the true extent of homelessness were acknowledged, then local, state, and federal authorities would have to target more services and funds for the homeless. For example, the U.S. Census Bureau estimated that in 2000 the homeless population numbered only 280,527, based on those counted in homeless shelters, soup kitchens, on the streets, and at other places.[54] In contrast, a study by the Urban Institute estimated that at least 2.3 million people, and as many as 3.5 million people, will experience homelessness at least once over the course of a year. The Joint Center for Housing Studies of Harvard University noted that on any given night some 850,000 Americans are homeless.[55]

Characteristics of the Homeless Population

Although homelessness has been a long-standing problem in most urban areas, it has been propelled onto center stage by media images of bag ladies, mentally ill people, chronic alcoholics, street people, and uprooted families. These images may make for interesting copy, but popular stereotypes obscure both the extent of homelessness and the true nature of the problem. The homeless are generally the poorest of the poor. They include single-parent families and, occasionally, two-parent families. They are often people who work but who earn too little to afford housing. They are women and children escaping from domestic violence. They are runaway youngsters or "throw-away kids." They are unemployed people—some who are looking for work, and some who have never worked. The homeless include retired people on small fixed incomes, many of whom have lost their cheap SRO hotel rooms to gentrification; school dropouts; drug addicts; disabled and mentally ill people lost in a maze of outpatient services; those who have worn out their welcome with family or friends; young mothers on welfare who are on long waiting lists for public housing; families who have lost their overcrowded quarters; and those who have "doubled up" and are temporarily sharing an apartment. In 2002, families comprised 41 percent of the urban homeless population, an increase of 5 percent over 2000. Nationally, children make up approximately 39 percent of the homeless population. In rural areas, families, single mothers, and children make up the largest group of people who are homeless.[56]

The list below summarizes data from the National Survey of Homeless Assistance Providers and Clients conducted by the Census Bureau in 1996 for 12 federal agencies. Released in a 1999 HUD report, this survey interviewed representatives of almost 12,000 homeless programs and more than 4,000 clients. It is the most comprehensive study conducted on the homeless population to date. The picture it paints is bleak.

- *Families.* Sixty percent of homeless women had children ages 0 to 17; 65 percent of these women lived with at least one of their minor children. Forty-one percent of homeless men had children ages 0 to 17; 7 percent of these men lived with at least one of their minor children. Most of these homeless children were young; 20 percent were ages 0 to 2, 22 percent were ages 3 to 5, 20 percent were ages 6 to 8, 33 percent were ages 9 to 17, and age was not given for 5 percent. Parents reported that 45 percent of the 3- to 5-year-olds attended preschool and that 93 percent of school-age children (ages 6 to 17) attended school regularly. Fifty-one percent of children were in households receiving AFDC, 70 percent were in households receiving food stamps, 12 percent were in households receiving SSI, and 73 percent received Medicaid.
- *Gender and marital status.* Most homeless clients (85 percent) were single (that is, they did not have any of their children with them); 48 percent never married; 9 percent were married; 15 percent were separated; 24 percent were divorced; and 7 percent were widowed. Sixty-eight percent of the homeless were male and 32 percent were female.
- *Race.* Forty-one percent of the homeless were White, 40 percent Black, 11 percent Hispanic, 8 percent Native American, and 1 percent were other races.
- *Age.* Thirteen percent of the homeless were between the ages of 17 and 24; 80 percent were from 25 to 54; and 8 percent were 55 and older.
- *Education.* Thirty-eight percent of the homeless had less than a high school education; 34 percent had completed high school; and 28 percent had some education beyond high school.
- *Food intake.* Twenty-eight percent of the homeless said they sometimes or often did not get enough to eat (compared with 12 percent of poor U.S. adults); 20 percent ate one meal a day or less. Thirty-nine percent of the homeless said that in the previous 30 days they had been hungry but unable to afford food (compared with 5 percent of poor Americans); 40 percent had gone without anything to eat for a day or longer in the previous 30 days because they could not afford food (compared to 3 percent of poor Americans).
- *Chemical dependency and mental illness.* Thirty-eight percent of the homeless reported indicators of alcohol use problems; 26 percent reported indicators of drug use problems. Thirty-nine percent reported indicators of mental health problems; 75 percent reported indicators of one or more of these problems.
- *Physical health.* Three percent of the homeless reported having HIV/AIDS; 3 percent reported tuberculosis; 26 percent reported acute infectious conditions such as a cough, cold, bronchitis, pneumonia, tuberculosis, or sexually transmitted disease other than AIDS. Eight percent reported acute noninfectious conditions such as skin ulcers, lice, or scabies; 45 percent reported having chronic health conditions such as arthritis, high blood pressure, diabetes, or cancer. Fifty-five percent had no medical insurance.
- *Crime.* Thirty-eight percent of the homeless claimed someone had stolen money or things from them; 22 percent had been physically assaulted; 7 percent had been sexually assaulted.
- *Income.* Single homeless clients reported a mean income of $348 in the previous 30 days, an amount only 51 percent of the 1996 federal poverty level of $680 a month for one person. Clients in family households reported a mean income of $475 during the previous 30 days, an amount only 46 percent of the 1996 federal poverty level of $1,023 a month for a family of three. Single homeless clients had only 12 percent of the median monthly income of all U.S. households in 1995 ($2,840), and homeless families only 17 percent.
- *Work.* Forty-four percent of the homeless had done paid work during the previous month. Twenty percent had worked in a job lasting at least three months; 25 percent worked at a temporary or

day labor job; and 2 percent earned money by peddling or selling personal belongings. Three percent reported more than one source of earned income; 21 percent received income from family members or friends; 1 percent received child support. Eight percent reported income from panhandling in the previous 30 days.

- *Public assistance.* Thirty-seven percent of the homeless received food stamps; 52 percent of households received AFDC; 11 percent received SSI; and 9 percent received General Assistance. Six percent of homeless veterans received veteran-related disability payments, and 2 percent received veteran-related pensions. Thirty percent received Medicaid, and another 7 percent received medical care from the Department of Veterans Affairs.
- *Locations.* Although there are homeless clients in every type of community, 71 percent were in central cities; 21 percent were in the suburbs and urban fringe areas; and 9 percent were in rural areas.
- *Shelter and food.* Within the week previous to the interview, 31 percent of the homeless had slept on the streets or in other places not meant for habitation; 66 percent used an emergency shelter, transitional housing program, or program offering vouchers for emergency accommodation. Thirty-six percent used soup kitchens, and 10 percent used other homeless assistance programs (e.g., drop-in centers, food pantries, outreach programs, mobile food programs).
- *Episodes of homelessness.* Forty-nine percent of clients were in their first episode of homelessness; 34 percent had been homeless three or more times. Single homeless clients and clients in families were equally likely to be in their first homeless episode, but single clients were more likely than clients in families to have been homeless three times or more. For 28 percent of homeless clients, the current episode had lasted three months or less, but for 30 percent it had lasted more than two years. Clients in families were more than twice as likely as single clients to have been homeless for three months or less; single clients were almost three times as likely as clients in families to be in homeless spells that had lasted more than two years.
- *Veterans.* Thirty-three percent of male homeless clients were veterans. Forty-seven percent of veterans had served during the Vietnam era; and 17 percent had served since the Vietnam era. Many had served in more than one time period. Thirty-three percent of the male veterans were stationed in a war zone, and 28 percent were exposed to combat.
- *Childhood.* Twenty-seven percent of homeless clients had lived in foster care or in a group home or other institutional setting for part of their childhood; 25 percent reported childhood physical or sexual abuse; 21 percent reported childhood experiences of homelessness; 33 percent reported running away from home; and 22 percent reported being forced to leave home.
- *Homeless services.* There are about 40,000 homeless assistance programs offered at about 21,000 locations in the United States. Food pantries, estimated at close to 9,000, are the most common type of program. Emergency shelters are next with an estimated 5,700 programs, followed closely by transitional housing programs (4,400), soup kitchens and other distributors of prepared meals (3,500), outreach programs (3,300), and voucher distribution programs (3,100). On an average day in February 1996, emergency shelters expected 240,000 program contacts, transitional housing programs expected 160,000, permanent housing programs expected 110,000, and voucher distribution programs expected 70,000. Expected contacts include those made by both homeless and other people who use services. Forty-nine percent of all homeless assistance programs are located in central cities, 32 percent in rural areas, and 19 percent in suburban areas. Because central-city programs serve more clients, a larger share of program contacts occur there.[57]

Trends in Homelessness

As noted earlier, homelessness and poverty are inextricably linked. Because poor families have limited resources that can cover only a portion of their basic needs, they often must make difficult choices between housing and food, clothing, or health care. Housing costs absorb the greatest percentage of a poor family's income, which can leave low-income families only a paycheck away from living on the streets if faced with a crisis. Families who have moved from welfare to work under the 1996 welfare reform law are not doing as well as projected (see Chapter 11) because of inadequate work supports and low wages. Moreover, the effects of the five-year TANF lifetime cap has not yet been fully felt, and may lead to even greater numbers of homeless people in coming years, especially in an economic downturn.

Lack of affordable health care can cause many struggling families to spiral into homelessness when a serious illness or injury causes extended absence from work, job loss, or depletion of savings to pay for health care. Mental illness and drug and alcohol addiction also play a role. The increasing number of mentally ill homeless individuals is not entirely due to the deinstitutionalization of mentally ill patients from mental hospitals; rather, homelessness results because mentally ill people experience difficulty in accessing supportive housing along with treatment services. People who are both poor and addicted also face a high risk of homelessness.[58]

Domestic violence has been linked to homelessness. Specifically, many poor women are forced to choose whether to stay in an abusive relationship or become homeless. Several studies demonstrate the contribution of domestic violence to homelessness, particularly among families with children. A 1990 Ford Foundation study found that 50 percent of homeless women and children were fleeing abuse. Another study of 777 homeless parents (the majority of whom were mothers) in ten U.S. cities, found that 22 percent had left their last place of residence because of domestic violence. In addition, 46 percent of cities surveyed by the U.S. Conference of Mayors identified domestic violence as a primary cause of homelessness.

Another disturbing trend is the rise of homeless youth. Unaccompanied youth may account for as much as 3 percent (300,000) of the urban homeless population. Many homeless youth runaway because of physical or sexual abuse, strained relationships, addiction of a family member, and parental neglect. In one study, more than half of the youth in shelters reported their parents either told them to leave or knew they were leaving but did not care. In another study, 46 percent of runaway and homeless youth had been physically abused and 17 percent had been forced into sexual activity by a household member. A history of foster care has also been correlated with becoming homeless at an earlier age and remaining so for a longer period of time. Some youth living in residential placements become homeless after discharge—they are too old for foster care and leave with no housing or income support. One national study found that more than 20 percent of youth who arrived at shelters came directly from foster care, and that more than 25 percent had been in foster care in the previous year. Many homeless adolescents find that survival on the streets requires exchanging sex for the necessities. In turn, they are at a greater risk for contracting AIDS/ HIV. Studies suggest that the HIV prevalence rate for homeless youth may be 2 to 10 times higher than for other adolescents.[59]

Attempts to Address Homelessness

On July 22, 1987, President Ronald Reagan signed the McKinney-Vento Homeless Assistance Act into law. The McKinney Act created more than 20 separate programs to be administered by nine federal agencies. (See Table 16.3.) Some highlights of the current Act include:

- *Emergency Shelter Grants Program (ESGP).* This program provides formula (block grant) funding for emergency shelter and essential services.
- *Supportive Housing Demonstration Program (SHDP).* This competitive program funds a variety of grantees to provide transitional and permanent

Table 16.3

Appropriations for Homeless Programs (in millions)

	Fiscal Year 2001	Fiscal Year 2002	Fiscal Year 2003
Homeless assistance grants (Title IV)	1,025	1,123	1,217
Emergency food and shelter (FEMA) (Title III)	140	140	152
Healthcare for the homeless (Title VI)	101	115	129
PATH	8	40	43
Treatment for the homeless	10	10	19
Education for homeless children and youth (Title VII)	35	50	54
Food stamp program (Title VIII plus non-homeless assistance)	20,074	22,849	26,250
Homeless veterans reintegration	17	18	18

Source: Based on data from National Law Center on Homelessness and Poverty, *The Mckinney-Vento Homeless Assistance Act* (Washington, DC: Author, December 8, 2003).

housing, particularly for homeless families and persons with special needs or handicaps. Initially funded as a demonstration, the program was renamed the Supportive Housing Program and made permanent in the Housing and Community Development Act of 1992. The program was also expanded to fund services only, Safe Havens, and Rural Homeless Housing.

- *Section 8 Moderate Rehabilitation for Single-Room Occupancy Dwellings.* This competitively awarded program provides funding to owners of SRO housing in the form of rental assistance payments on behalf of homeless individuals, in conjunction with the rehabilitation of the facility. The program provides permanent housing for previously homeless tenants.
- *Shelter Plus Care.* Congress added this program to HUD in 1990 and provided the first funding in 1992. Funds are competitively awarded for rental assistance. Grantees must match the value of rental assistance with an equal value of supportive services. The target population is homeless persons living on the streets or in emergency shelters with severe mental illness, chronic substance abuse problems, or AIDs.
- *Supplemental Assistance for Facilities to Assist the Homeless.* This competitive program funds projects that meet the immediate and long-term needs of the homeless, as well as projects already receiving funds under ESG and SHDP. The flexible range of assistance permits program expansion, capital improvement, and startup of new, needed supportive services. In 1992, this program was incorporated into the Supportive Housing Program.
- *Single Family Property Disposition Initiative.* Originally, this program was not a McKinney program. It was created in 1983 under the HUD Secretary's broad legislative authority to dispose of single-family properties. In 1985, it was broadened to allow HUD to sell or lease foreclosed single-family properties to nonprofit organizations, or to state or local governments to provide temporary shelter for homeless persons. In 1992, the Housing and Community Development Act recognized it as a McKinney initiative.[60]

In 1990 Congress amended the McKinney-Vento act to remove requirements that kept homeless children from attending school, including proof of immunization, former school records, and proof of residency.[61]

Apart from the McKinney Act, several broader proposals have emerged to alleviate the problem of homelessness. Chester Hartman has proposed a nine-point solution for ending homelessness: (1) Massively increase the number of new and rehabilitated units offered to lower-income households; (2) lower the required rent/income ratio in government housing from 30 to 25 percent; (3) arrest the depletion of low-income housing through neglect, abandonment, conversion, and sale; (4) preserve the SRO hotels; (5) establish a national "right to shelter"; (6) require local governments to make available properties that can be used as shelters and second-stage housing; (7) create legislation that gives tenants reasonable protection from eviction; (8) provide governmental assistance to homeowners facing foreclosure; and (9) provide suitable residential alternatives for mentally ill people.[62]

The "Federal Plan to Help End the Tragedy of Homelessness," prepared under the auspices of the Interagency Council for the Homeless, provides a set of objectives aimed at reducing homelessness: (1) Increase the participation of homeless families and individuals in mainstream programs that provide income support, social services, health care, education, employment, and housing; agencies should monitor these programs to gauge their impact on homelessness. (2) Improve the efficiency and effectiveness of homelessness-targeted programs in addressing the multiple needs of homeless persons. (3) Increase the availability of support services in combination with appropriate housing. (4) Improve access to quality, affordable, and permanent housing for homeless families and individuals. (5) Develop strategies for preventing homelessness by improving the methods for identifying families and individuals at risk of imminent homelessness; change current policies that may contribute to homelessness; and propose other initiatives to prevent people from becoming homeless.[63]

Homelessness cannot be eradicated without basic changes in federal housing, income support, social services, health care, education, and employment policies. Benefit levels for these programs must be made adequate; the erosion of welfare benefits must be stopped; residency and other requirements that exclude homeless persons must be changed; and programs (including outreach) must be made freely available to the homeless and the potentially homeless. Moreover, a real solution to the homeless problem must involve the provision of permanent housing for those who are currently or potentially homeless. Federal programs and legislation should be coordinated and expanded to provide decent, affordable housing, coupled with needed services, for all poor families. Finally, both the states and the federal government should intervene directly in the housing market by controlling rents, increasing the overall housing stock, limiting speculation, and providing income supports.

Housing Reform

The housing crisis faced by low-income people has led to numerous suggestions for housing reform. Some conservative critics argue that low-income housing assistance should be abolished, thus allowing the law of supply and demand to regulate rents and, eventually, to drive down prices. Free market economic philosophy suggests that as rents increase, demand will slacken, and eventually rents will drop. Another argument is that government intervention in housing should occur only through the supply side. In other words, the government should stimulate production of rental housing by offering financial incentives such as tax breaks to builders, entrepreneurs, and investors. If rental housing is made more profitable, more units will be built, and the increase in the housing stock will lower prices.

Some liberal critics contend that because housing is a necessity and the demand is relatively inelastic, marketplace laws should not be allowed to dominate. For example, the National Low-Income Housing Coalition has called for

- Guaranteeing housing assistance to people who need it
- Ending homelessness by linking housing with services to support recovery and self-sufficiency
- Providing a permanent and adequate supply of affordable housing
- Preserving and improving federally assisted affordable homes for people with low incomes
- providing the opportunity for resident control of housing
- preserving neighborhoods and ending displacement
- Ending economic and racial segregation through affirmative housing programs and the enforcement of fair housing laws
- Reforming federal tax laws to give priority to aiding people with the greatest housing needs
- Providing the financing needed to preserve, build, and rehabilitate housing[64]

Much of the housing innovation in recent years has come from the nonprofit sector. There are now more than 2,000 nonprofit housing groups that have built or renovated more than half a million housing units, most of them since 1990. These nonprofits operate with a combination of government subsidies and private contributions. They also get help from two important foundations—the Local Initiatives Support Corporation and the Enterprise Foundation. According to Jason De Parle, the nonprofits' "impressive track records address the fear that more subsidized housing would mean more government-financed slums."[65]

One of the largest efforts has been mounted by the Enterprise Foundation. Started by Jim and Patty Rouse in 1982, the Enterprise Foundation is a national nonprofit housing and community development organization directed by distinguished national business and community development leaders. Its goals are "First, to build a national movement to change the way life is lived in low income neighborhoods. Second, to demonstrate ourselves what can be done, and third, to communicate what works and to advocate it."[66] Specifically, the Enterprise Foundation assists community-based nonprofit organizations and state and local governments in developing affordable housing and community services by brokering low-interest loans, grants, and equity to finance affordable housing; helps with linking residents to human services; and helps train people to be effective community leaders.[67] By 2002, the Enterprise Foundation had built 144,000 affordable homes, the results of leveraging $4.4 billion in equity from 170 corporate investors. Operating with field offices in 17 cities and a network of 2,400 community organizations throughout the country, Enterprise and its subsidiaries have helped 38,000 low-income people find work and thousands to find affordable community child care.[68]

Although nonprofit housing organizations like the Enterprise Foundation are making an important impact on the country's housing problem, they have limitations. For example, many of the housing groups focus their attention on the "less needy"—those with incomes at 50 percent of the median. This occurs partly because no one group knows how to house large numbers of the poorest people, especially those on public assistance. If the poorest people are grouped together too tightly, neighborhoods may collapse. If they are spread out in the suburbs, the new neighbors complain. Perhaps more importantly, the scope and pace of building or renovating under nonprofits is inadequate to meet the need. Nonprofits are building or renovating about 50,000 units a year, and at that rate it would take a century to house the millions of families with rent burdens.[69]

Conclusion

The housing crisis is grounded in issues of availability and affordability. It is a structural problem that is based on the failure of incomes to keep pace with housing costs; an overdependence on credit to build and buy houses; a profit-making system that drives home ownership, development, and management; and the failure of states and the federal government to intervene actively in the housing market through more and higher subsidies or stricter regulation. Driven by the profit motive, speculation has forced up the price of rental and residential property faster than income growth. As a profit is made by each link in the housing chain (real estate agents and developers, lenders, builders, materials producers, investors, speculators, landlords, and home owners), renters and home buyers are forced to pay the costs. Put another way, the cost of every rental unit or home reflects the profits made by all the parties who have come directly or indirectly into contact with that property.

The provision of adequate low- and moderate-income housing is an important challenge in modern society. The poor have difficulty finding decent affordable housing; blue-collar workers and the lower-middle–class are caught in the cost/income squeeze and are having a difficult time buying and holding onto their homes. In an economic downturn, this "affordability squeeze" can result in increased mortgage foreclosures, higher rates of property tax and delinquency defaults, more evictions and homelessness, more overcrowding and doubling up of families, decreases in the consumption of other important necessities, deteriorating neighborhoods, increased business failures, higher rates of unemployment in the building trades, and the collapse of some financial institutions.

Past and current government programs have had minimal impact on the affordable housing crisis. Current housing programs are seriously underfunded, fragmentary, and without clear or focused goals. Because the federal government has often been viewed as an arbiter of last resort, some housing advocates contend that the government has the responsibility to ensure that adequate housing becomes a right rather than a privilege, and that healthy, sound, and safe neighborhoods become a reality.

An adequate housing policy for the United States must address cost burden, overcrowding, and housing quality. It must also provide opportunities for true housing choice and an end to the discriminatory practices that have led to de facto housing segregation. The nation will not have achieved the 1949 housing goal of "a decent home and suitable living environment for every American family" until all households live in adequate housing located in safe neighborhoods.

Discussion Questions

1. From 1937 until the present, the history of federal housing policy been marked by evolving priorities and programmatic shifts. Describe the dominant trends in federal housing policy from 1937 onward and show how those led to the creation of current housing policies. What, if any, ideas and programs in current housing policies have their roots in earlier federal policies? In what direction has federal housing policy evolved? What is the current emphasis in federal housing policy?
2. According to some critics, federal low-income housing policy is marked by severe inadequacies. Describe the more serious shortcomings in federal low-income housing policy and discuss alternative policies to rectify those shortcomings.
3. Home ownership is an important variable in U.S. society because it is equated with the growth of assets. For example, after paying rent for 30 years a poor family has nothing to show except 360 rental receipts. By contrast, another poor family will at least have its home as a major asset after paying off a 30-year mortgage. What are some of the obstacles standing in the way of home ownership for poor people? What

policies can be developed to help poor families overcome these barriers?

4. What are some of the most significant problems facing poor people in finding affordable rental housing of decent quality? What federal or state policies can be implemented to help poor families find such housing?
5. HUD has created a series of guidelines by which to evaluate whether a particular housing unit has "severe" physical deficiencies. Are HUD's criteria adequate? If not, what other criteria should be added to HUD's guidelines?
6. Homelessness has been described by some commentators as just another housing problem. Others argue that homelessness is primarily a manifestation of poverty. Still others contend that homelessness has psychological roots and should be seen as a social or human service problem. Where do you stand on the issue? Will the homeless problem be solved if people are simply given adequate shelter and decent jobs? Or is homelessness for many a manifestation of deeper psychosocial problems? If so, what programs, if any, should be developed for the homeless?
7. Several proposals have been offered to eradicate the problem of homelessness. Which of these programs (or combination of programs) has the best chance for eradicating homelessness?
8. Many experts argue that for low-income people, both renters and home owners, the housing situation has reached crisis proportions. Do you agree? If so, why? Moreover, what kinds of housing policies are needed to defuse this crisis and stabilize the housing market for low-income families? Should housing be considered a right and therefore be removed from the grip of the marketplace?

Notes

1. Edward B. Lazere, Paul A. Leonard, Cushing N. Dolbeare, and Barry Zigas, *A Place to Call Home: The Low-Income Housing Crisis Continues* (Washington, DC: Center on Budget and Policy Priorities and Low-Income Housing Information Service, December 1991), pp. 45–47.
2. Charles S. Prigmore and Charles R. Atherton, *Social Welfare Policy: Analysis and Formulation* (Lexington, MA: D.C. Heath, 1979), pp. 48–50.
3. National Training and Information Center, *Insurance Redlining, Profits v. Policyholders* (Chicago: NTIC, 1973), p. 1.
4. Ibid., pp. 52–53.
5. Center for Community Change, "Solutions," 1999. Retrieved December 29, 2000, from www.communitychange.org/pahcrisis2.html
6. Joint Center for Housing Studies of Harvard University, *The State of the Nation's Housing* (Cambridge, MA: Harvard University, 2003), p. 22.
7. National Low Income Housing Coalition (NLIHC), *2004 Advocates' Guide To Housing and Community Development Policy: Low Income Housing Tax Credit* (Washington, DC: NLIHC, 2004).
8. National Low-Income Housing Coalition, *NLIHC's Comments to FDIC on Proposed Changes to the Community Reinvestment Act* (Washington, DC: NLHIC September 20, 2004).
9. Council of Large Public Housing Authorities, *Quick Facts on Public Housing* (Washington, DC: Author, 2004).
10. National Coalition for the Homeless, "Why are People Homeless?" June 1999, retrieved December 29, 2000, from http:/nch.ari.net; see also Laura Waxman, *A Status Report on Hunger and Homelessness in America's Cities: 1995* (Washington, DC: U.S. Conference of Mayors, 1995); and Children's Defense Fund, *The State of America's Children*, 1991 (Washington, DC: Children's Defense Fund, 1991).
11. Florida Alliance for Assistive Services & Technology, "Congress Considers Revamping of Section 8 Program," FAAST Housing Facts, May 2003. Retrieved November 2004 from http://faast.org/bscip/pdf/May%202003.pdf
12. Jeff Schneppe, "10 Big Tax Breaks for the Rest of Us," *MSN Money*, 2004. Retrieved November 2004 from http://moneycentral.msn.com/content/Taxes/Taxshelters/P75680.asp
13. Joint Center for Housing Studies of Harvard University, *The State of the Nation's Housing* (Cambridge, MA: Harvard University, 2003), p. 22.
14. *Performance and Accountability Report Fiscal Year 2003*, The Department of Housing and Urban Development. Retrieved from www.hud.gov/offices/cfo/reports/2003par.pdf
15. Joint Center for Housing Studies of Harvard University, *The State of the Nation's Housing*, 2003. Retrieved November 2004 from www.jchs.harvard.edu/publications/markets/son2004.pdf
16. Ibid.

17. *Performance and Accountability Report, Fiscal Year 2003.*
18. Joint Center for Housing Studies of Harvard University, *The State of the Nation's Housing,* 2003.
19. Ibid.; David Leonhardt, "In Most of the U.S., a House Is a Home But Not a Bonanza," *New York Times* (August 6, 2003), p. 19; Ohio Association of Realtors, "Better, Bigger Homes Available for Today's Buyers," retrieved December 29, 2000, from www.ohiorealtors.org/news/prez_col/0403.html; George Sternlieb and James W. Hughes, "Housing in the United States: An Overview," in George Sternlieb, James W. Hughes, Robert W. Burchell, Stephen C. Casey, Robert W. Lake, and David Listokin (eds.), *America's Housing* (New Brunswick, NJ: Rutgers University, Center for Urban Policy Research, 1980), pp. 5–7; Sumner M. Rosen, David Fanshel, and Mary E. Lutz (eds.), *Face of the Nation, 1987* (Silver Spring, MD: NASW, 1987), p. 68; and Joint Center for Housing Studies of Harvard University, *The State of the Nation's Housing,* (Boston: Joint Center for Housing Studies of Harvard University, 1992), p. 12.
20. Joint Center for Housing Studies of Harvard University, *The State of the Nation's Housing,* pp. 28–31
21. See U.S. Census Bureau, *Statistical Abstract of the United States,* 1991 (Washington DC: U.S. Government Printing Office, 1991), pp. 715–717; and Sarah Max, "Top 10 Housing Markets," *CNN/Money,* February 25, 2003, retrieved November 2004 from http://money.cnn.com/2003/02/11/pf/yourhome/hotmarkets
22. Habitat for Humanity, "Poverty Housing Defeats Families." Retrieved December 2000 from www.habitat.org/Why/HW_Articles/Poverty_Housing.html
23. Joint Center for Housing Studies at Harvard University, *The State of the Nation's Housing: 2000.*
24. National Low Income Housing Coalition, *2003 Advocates' Guide to Housing and Community Development Policy,* 2003. NLIHC, 1012 Fourteenth Street NW, Suite 610, Washington, DC 20005. See also Jonathan D. Epstein, "Subprime Loan Growth Attacked Minorities in Wilmington Likely Pay Higher Fees, Group Says," *The News Journal* (November 27, 2002), p. D6.
25. Association of Community Organizers for Reform Now (ACORN), *The Great Divide: Home Purchase Mortgage Lending Nationally and in 120 Metropolitan Areas* (Washington, DC: ACORN, October 2004).
26. See Howard Karger, *Down and Out in America's Fringe Economy* (San Francisco, CA: Berrett-Koehler, 2005).
27. Ibid.
28. Ibid.
29. Robert Trigaux, "Housing Prices Could Pay Off or Pop," *St. Petersburg Times* (June 9, 2002), p. B6. See also Mike Gibb, "Consumer Credit Rockets $13b in January, Soaking Borrowers in Debt," Lending Intelligence.com, March 7, 2003. Retrieved October 30, 2003 from www.lendingintelligence.com
30. See Joint Center for Housing Studies of Harvard University, 2004; and Teresa Murray, "Experts Warn against Milking Home Equity to Extend Debt," *Minneapolis St. Paul Star Tribune* (November 4, 2000), p. B-5.
31. Murray, "Experts Warn against Milking."
32. Consumer Federation of America, "While Homeownership Rises, Home Equity Stagnates," 2000. Retrieved October 27, 2003, from www.consumerfed.org/homeowner.pdf
33. Jeff Bailey "A Man and His Loan: Why Bennie Roberts Refinanced Ten Times," *Wall Street Journal* (April 23, 1997), p. 18.
34. National Low-Income Housing Coalition, *NLIHC Background on Housing Issues* (Washington, DC: National Low-Income Housing Coalition, 2002).
35. Consumer Federation of America, "While Homeownership Rises, Home Equity Stagnates."
36. Joint Center for Housing Studies of Harvard University, 2004.
37. National Low Income Housing Coalition (NLIHC), *Out of Reach 2003,* (Washington, DC: NLIHC, 2003).
38. Ibid.
39. Tracy L. Kaufman, *Out of Reach: Can Americans Pay Rent?* (Washington, DC: NLIHC, 1996), p. 57.
40. U.S. Department of Housing and Urban Development, *Finding 2: The Stock of Rental Housing Affordable to the Lowest Income Families Is Shrinking and Congress Has Eliminated Funding for New Rental Assistance since 1995,* HUD. Retrieved November 2004 from www.huduser.org/publications/affhsg/worstcase/finding2.html
41. The National Coalition for the Homeless, "Facts About Homelessness, People Need Affordable Housing." Retrieved November 2004 from www.nationalhomeless.org/facts/housing.html
42. National Coalition for the Homeless, "Why Are People Homeless?" NCH Fact Sheet #1, June 1999. Retrieved December 2000 from http://nch.ari.net
43. George Sternlieb and James W. Hughes, "Back to the Central City: Myths and Realities." In George Sternlieb et al. (eds.), *America's Housing* (New Brunswick, NJ: Rutgers University, Center for Urban Policy Research, 1980), p. 173.
44. Habitat for Humanity, "U.S. Affordable Housing Statistics" (Washington DC: Author, 2000); Joint Center for Housing Studies at Harvard University, *The State of the Nation's Housing: 2000.*
45. See National Low-Income Housing Coalition, *NLIHC Background on Housing Issues;* and Environmental Protection Agency, "Shut the Door on Lead Poisoning," EPA November 2, 2004. Retrieved November 2004 from www.epa.gov/lead

46. Ibid., pp. 43–44.
47. U.S. Department of Labor, "Bureau of Labor Statistics Consumer Expenditures in 2002," *Report 974,* Washington, DC, February 2004.
48. U.S. Senate Committee on Energy and Natural Resources, "Senators Seek Boost for LIHEAP Funding," September 24, 2004. Retrieved November 2004 from http://energy.senate.gov/news/dem_release.cfm?id=226943
49. Carol Biedrzycki, "Residential and Low-Income Electric Customer Protection," *Texas Ratepayers' Organization to Save Energy, Inc.* Retrieved December 2000 from www.ncat.org/liheap/pubs/txreport.htm
50. Center on Budget and Policy Priorities, *Smaller Slices of the Pie* (Washington, DC: CBPP, November 1985), p. 33.
51. See Committee on Ways and Means, U.S. House of Representatives, *2004 Green Book,* (Washington, DC: U.S. Government Office, 2004), pp. 15–128, 129; and Senator Paul Wellstone, "Senate Coalition Taking Offensive in Anticipated LIHEAP Funding Fight," March 25, 1999. Retrieved December 2000 from http://wellstone.senate.gov/liheap7.htm
52. Senator Paul Wellstone.
53. Children's Defense Fund, *The State of America's Children, 1992* (Washington, DC: Children's Defense Fund, 1992), p. 38.
54. Quoted in Diana M. DiNitto, *Social Welfare: Politics and Public Policy* (Boston: Allyn & Bacon, 1995), p. 87.
55. See Joint Center for Housing Studies at Harvard University, *The State of the Nation's Housing: 2004;* and National Coalition for the Homeless (NCH), *The 2000 Census and Homelessness,* 2001. Retrieved November 2004 from www.nationalhomeless.org/census2001.html
56. The National Coalition for the Homeless, *Facts About Homelessness.*
57. U.S. Department of Housing and Urban Development, *Homelessness: Programs and the People They Serve,* retrieved November 2004 from www.huduser.org/publications/homeless/homelessness/figs_tbls.html; and National Coalition for Homeless Veterans "Background Statistics," retrieved November 2004 from www.nchv.org/background.cfm
58. See National Coalition for the Homeless, "Domestic Violence and Homelessness," April 1999, retrieved November 2004 from www.nationalhomeless.org/domestic.html; and Institute for Children and Poverty, *Homes for the Homeless—Ten Cities 1997–1998,* Homes for the Homeless and Institute for Children and Poverty, New York, 1999.
59. See National Coalition for the Homeless, "Homeless Youth," April 1999, retrieved November 2004 from www.nationalhomeless.org/youth.html; Institute for Health Policy Studies, *Street Youth at Risk for AIDS: 1995* (San Francisco: University of California, 1999); and National Association of Social Workers, *Helping Vulnerable Youths: Runaway and Homeless Adolescents in the United States* (Washington, DC: NASW, 1992).
60. U.S. Department of Housing and Urban Development, "Stuart B. McKinney Homeless Programs: Introduction," July 11, 2002. Retrieved November 2004 from www.huduser.org/publications/homeless/mckin/intro.html
61. National Low-Income Housing Coalition, *1996 Advocate's Resource Book* (Washington, DC: NLIHC, 1996).
62. Chester Hartman, "The Housing Part of the Homelessness Problem." In Boston Foundation, *Homelessness: Critical Issues for Policy and Practice* (Boston: Boston Foundation, 1987), pp. 17–19.
63. National Low-Income Housing Coalition, *1996 Advocate's Resource Book.*
64. See National Low-Income Housing Coalition, *NLIHC Background on Housing Issues;* and National Low-Income Housing Coalition, 1995 Advocate's Resource Book (Washington, DC: NLIHC, 1995).
65. Jason De Parle, *American Dream* (NY: Viking, 2004), p. 94.
66. Quoted in Len Lazarick, "Enterprise Foundation Brings Entrepreneurial Spirit to Social Causes," *The Business Monthly* (December 1999). Retrieved December 30, 2000, from www.bizmonthly.com/news1999/december/enterprise.html
67. The Enterprise Foundation. Retrieved December 30, 2000, from www.entrprisefoundation.org
68. See The Enterprise Foundation, "Annual Report: 2002," retrieved November 2004 from www.enterprisefoundation.org/about/annual/index.asp; and Len Lazarick, "Enterprise Foundation Brings Entrepreneurial Spirit To Social Causes," retrieved November 2004 from www.enterprisefoundation.org.
69. De Parle, *American Dream.*

CHAPTER 17

The Politics of Food Policy and Rural Life

The policies related to the production and distribution of food form an important part of the U.S. welfare state. For example, over the course of a year an estimated 1 in 5 Americans participates in at least 1 of the 15 food assistance programs administered by the U.S. Department of Agriculture (USDA). Expenditures for these 15 food assistance programs totaled about $46.6 billion in 2004. This chapter examines the federal response to hunger and the government's attempts to distribute foodstuffs to the poor. Topics considered include the Food Stamp Program, WIC and other food programs, U.S. farm policy, the plight of farmworkers in the United States, and the overall problems of food production and distribution. Although the issues around food may initially seem disparate, they are tied together in a complex mosaic that is basic to the well-being of the nation.

Food policy in America is marked by important contradictions. On the one hand, 33 million people live in households that are unsure where their next meals are coming from (i.e., the food insecure). On the other hand, 34 percent of all U.S. women and 28 percent of men are obese.[1] The Centers for Disease Control and Prevention (CDC) labels the obesity problem an epidemic. Almost 65 percent of Americans are either overweight or obese and the number is growing. The increase in overweight children is twice that seen in adults. In 2001, Americans spent $110 billion on fast food, more money than on higher education, personal computers, computer software, and new cars.[2] Directly and indirectly, obesity costs the U.S. $117 billion and results in 39 million lost work days a year. Three-fourths of the $1.4 trillion the United States spends on health care is to treat chronic illnesses, many of which are tied to obesity and overweight.[3] Diets of burgers and fries are bringing the nation's steady rise in life expectancy to a grinding halt. The CDC predicts that 29 million Americans will be diagnosed with diabetes in 2050 compared with about 11 million in 2003. Twenty years ago the U.S. led the world's longevity league. Today, American women rank only 19th; males only 28th, alongside men from Brunei.[4]

Hunger in the United States

One of the most striking aspects of poverty in the United States is hunger. The terms *hunger* and *malnutrition* conjure up images of emaciated Third World children with bloated bellies and protruding eyes. Americans often think of hunger as a problem that pertains mainly to developing countries. While hunger exists in the United States, it typically occurs in subtle ways. For example, poor people may eat only once a day or skip meals for several days; they may be subject to chronic malnutrition; women may bear low-birth-weight babies, and babies may be at risk from high infant mortality rates. Crossing age, race, and gender lines, hunger in the United States affects children, the elderly, the unemployed and the underemployed, homeless people, people with disabilities, and both two-parent and single-parent families. The single common thread connecting these diverse groups to the problem of hunger is poverty.

Cheap and plentiful food is an American tradition, which may partly explain why most Americans older than age 25 are overweight.[5] Americans spend a smaller percentage of their income on food than any other nation, and we feed much of the world with our surplus (the value of U.S. agricultural imports was estimated at $52 billion in 2004).[6] Consumers, retailers, restaurants, and farmers throw away one-quarter of the U.S. food stock (almost 100 billion pounds of edible food) each year. Yet in 2002, 11 percent of U.S. households were food insecure. In other words, they had one or more persons that reported experiencing reduced food intake because of a lack of financial resources. Moreover, these households were unsure where their next meal will come from. Of that number, more than 7 percent were food insecure without hunger, and 3 percent (3.3 million households) were food insecure with hunger.[7] Women and children made up 75 percent of that population.[8]

In 2002 almost 35 million Americans (21 million adults and 14 million children) lived in food insecure households.[9] This rate of food insecurity is double that of any other industrialized nation.[10] The U.S. Department of Agriculture relies on poverty statistics to determine the extent of hunger in the United States. USDA data show that only 12 percent of households with incomes below the poverty line have an adequate level of basic nutrition.[11] Moreover, food pantries, shelters, soup kitchens, and other emergency food providers serve at least 23 million people a year.[12]

Children who are denied an adequate diet are at a greater risk than other low-income children of not reaching their full potential as individuals. Undernourished youngsters have trouble concentrating and bonding with other children and are more likely to suffer illnesses that cause them to be absent from school. They consistently perform more poorly on standardized tests. Poor performance early in school is a major risk factor for dropping out of school. Studies have also shown that even mildly undernourished children may potentially suffer brain, cognitive, and psychological impairment that, if not corrected, can be irreversible. Research conducted by the Center on Hunger, Poverty and Nutritional Policy at Tufts University found compelling evidence that improved nutrition can modify and even reverse these effects. John Cook and Katie S. Martin found that millions of poor children have substandard intakes of important major nutrients. Analysis of government data revealed major differences between poor and nonpoor children's intakes of 10 out of 16 essential nutrients.

Cook and Martin also found that millions of poor children suffer from chronic undernutrition, the underconsumption of essential nutrients and food energy.[13] Intake of these nutrients is considered crucial to sound health and normal development. Inadequate food energy intake (caloric intake) can cause problems with attention, concentration, learning, and other important daily activities. For children who have not eaten breakfast, the educational value of a morning spent in the classroom may be lost. Repeated episodes of inadequate food energy intake can lead to cumulative deficits in learning, lower academic achievement, higher rates of school failure, and cognitive impairment.[14] Six- to 11-year-old children from food insufficient households have significantly lower arithmetic scores and are more likely to repeat a grade. Teenagers who were food insufficient are more likely to have seen a psychologist, have been suspended from school, and have difficulty getting along with other teenagers. Food insufficiency is also associated with increased risk of suicide in teenagers.[15]

The following data provides a snapshot of America's hungry.

- In 2002, approximately 13.1 million American children were food insecure and 10 million were malnourished. Four million children under age 12 were hungry.
- More than one-half of families with children seeking emergency food assistance are single-parent households. Single female-headed households with children had a prevalence of food insecurity of 31 percent, nearly three times the national average.
- Six percent of the nations hungry were 65 and older, 85 percent were between the ages of 18 and 65, and 9.38 percent were under 18.
- Of those hungry in the United States, 53 percent are white, 25 percent are African American, and 19 percent are Hispanic.
- Fifty percent of households affected by hunger have incomes *above* the federal poverty line. In 2000, households with incomes below the official federal poverty line had a prevalence of food insecurity that was 37 percent, three times the national average.
- About 20.5 and 21.4 percent African American and Hispanic households experienced food insecurity.
- The prevalence of food insecurity varies geographically. In 2000, central city and non-metropolitan households had a food insecurity prevalence of 14.2 and 11.5 percent respectively, compared to 7.7 percent in metropolitan households. The prevalence of household-level food insecurity was higher in the south and west (11.8 and 11.7 percent) than in the Midwest and Northeast (8.8 and 8.7 percent).
- Food insecurity is experienced when events, such as job loss, gaining a household member, or losing food stamps places stress on a household budget. Households are then faced with choices that compromise their ability to buy food. For example, clients receiving food from emergency food providers reported having to choose between food and other necessities such as utilities or heating fuel (45 percent), rent or mortgage (36 percent), or medicine or medical care (30 percent).
- In 2002 more than 39 percent of people served by emergency food centers had a high school diploma or equivalent; 37 percent had not completed high school; and only five percent had attended college or received a college degree.
- Approximately 50 percent of food insecure households participate in the Special Supplemental Nutrition Program for Women, Infants, and Children (WIC), the National School Lunch and Breakfast (NSLP) programs, or the Food Stamp program (FS). The NSLP reaches 32 percent of food insecure families, the FS program reaches 23 percent, and the WIC program reaches only 14 percent of food insecure families.[16]

The extent of hunger and food insecurity is reflected in the number of people seeking food from emergency food providers, such as food pantries and soup kitchens. America's Second Harvest, the nation's largest emergency food providers, served 23 million people in 2001. More than 9 million were children. Using the U.S. government's official food security scale, 71 percent of those individuals were food insecure and 37 percent were hungry. A 2003 study by the U.S. Conference of Mayors found that requests for emergency food assistance increased by an average of 17 percent in American cities—the second highest rate of increase since the recession of the early 1990s. The Mayors also found that 14 percent of requests for emergency food aid went unmet because local feeding organizations lacked adequate food resources. For example, requests for emergency food assistance increased by 15 percent in Los Angeles in 2003 and by 48 percent in Denver.[17]

Governmental Food Programs

The politics of food—or the way food is distributed in U.S. society—is complex. Like all resources in a free market society, food is a commodity that is bought and sold. In a pure market sense, those who cannot afford to purchase food are unable to consume it. Left to the caprice of the marketplace, many poor people would face malnutrition or even starvation. This problem is particularly acute in an urban environment, in which most people lack gardening skills and in any case have little or no access to land. Providing the poor with food is a redistributive function of the welfare state. As such, the governmental obligation to provide food to the poor is similar to its obligation to provide economic opportunity: When either or both are unavailable in adequate quantities, it is the responsibility of the welfare state to respond.

A Short History of Food Stamps and a Description of the Program

In 1933, Congress established the Federal Surplus Relief Corporation, an agency designed to distribute surplus commodity foods plus coal, mattresses, and blankets. In 1939, Congress established a food stamp program. This was terminated in 1943, when a commodity food distribution program was reestablished. A pilot food stamp program began during the presidency of John F. Kennedy, and in 1964 the current Food Stamp Act was passed.

Receiving FS increases the nutritional value of a low-income household's home food supplies by 20 to 40 percent. Food stamp households participating in the program on average spend more on food and acquire more food than low-income non-participating households. Figure 17.1 (pages 446–447) describes the current eligibility rules for the FS program.[18]

The federal government funds 100 percent of FS program benefits, with federal and state governments sharing 50 percent of administrative costs. Although administered by the USDA, state and local welfare agencies qualify applicants and provide them with Electronic Benefit Transfer (EBT) cards. (About 90 percent of FS recipients received EBT cards in 2004.) Recipients are given an allotment of stamps based on family size (see Table 17.1) and income, with eligibility requirements and benefits determined at the federal level. Food stamp eligibility is based on a means test. (See Table 17.2 on page 174.) Recipients originally had to pay a set price (depending on family size and income) for their stamps. For example, some families or individuals purchased \$75 worth of food stamps for \$35; the difference between the cost and the face value of the stamps was called a "bonus." This system proved unwieldy because many poor people could not afford to purchase stamps. Purchase requirements were dropped in 1977 and the participation rate rose 30 percent.

Table 17.1

Maximum Monthly Food Stamp Allotments—Continental United States, October 2004–September 2005

Household Size	Maximum Allotment Level (48 states and D.C.)
1	\$149
2	274
3	393
4	499
5	592
6	711
7	786
8	898
Each additional member	+112

Source: Adapted from Food and Nutrition Service, USDA, "Eligibility, 2004–2005," 2004. Retrieved November 2004 from www.fns.usda.gov/fsp/faqs.htm#7.

Assets and Income

Calculating Eligibility: Households may have no more than $2,000 in countable resources, such as a bank account ($3,000 if at least one person in the household is age 60 or older, or is disabled). Certain resources are not counted.

The *gross* monthly income of most households must be 130 percent or less of the federal poverty guidelines ($1,698 per month for a family of three in 2004–2005). Gross income includes all cash payments to the household, with a few exceptions.

The *net* monthly income must be 100 percent or less of federal poverty guidelines ($1,306 a month for a household of three in 2004–2005). Net income is figured by adding all of a household's gross income, and then taking a number of approved deductions for child care, some shelter costs and other expenses. Households with an elderly or disabled member are subject only to the net income test.

Countable assets include bank accounts, Certificates of Deposits, investments, and valuable art work, antiques, and other valuables.

Countable assets do not include:

- Homesteaded property that the claimant intends to return to if they are in a nursing home, or property occupied by a spouse, siblings, minor child, or disabled child of any age.
- Personal effects and household goods up to $2,000.
- One automobile of unlimited value if used for employment or medical purposes. The FS program currently exempts any vehicle whose equity value is less than $1,500 for persons aged 60 or older. Some states exempt all vehicles.
- Life Insurance owned by the claimant up to a $1,500 face (cash) value is exempt; however, the face value of this insurance reduces the amount of exempt burial funds described below. The claimant and spouse can both have exempted life insurance with a face value of $1,500 or less on each. Also exempt are term policies with no cash value, group policies provided by an employer or required for employment, policies on the life of an ineligible family member who is not the claimant's responsible relative, and some policies on the life of the claimant owned by someone other than the claimant.
- Funeral merchandise, such as a grave site or plot, casket, urn, vault, mausoleum, niche, headstones, markers, opening/closing the grave site, etc.
- Up to $1,500 identified in a separate account or trust as a burial fund to cover funeral services or cremation expenses (reduced by amount of Life Insurance described above) . . . or . . . $4,637 in an irrevocable prepaid burial contract with a funeral home or assigned life insurance. The interest earned on burial funds. Amounts in excess of the above limits are included as countable assets.

Deductions

- A standard deduction of $134 is allowed for most households. However, $147 is allowed for households with 5 members, and $168 for households with 6 or more members.
- Child or dependent care when needed for a job, training or school. $200 is allowed for children under 2, $175 for those 2 or older.
- Medical expenses not paid by insurance. For those 60 or older or disabled, all medical expenses over $35 are deducted.
- Child support payments will vary.
- Excess shelter costs which are more than half of the household's income after the other deductions. Allowable costs include the cost of fuel to heat and cook with, electricity, water, the basic fee for one telephone, rent or mortgage payments and taxes on the home. The amount of the shelter deduction cannot be more than $378 unless one person in the household is elderly or disabled.

Figure 17.1

Food Stamp Eligibility and Benefit Guidelines, 2004

Sources: Adapted from Food and Nutrition Service, USDA, "Eligibility, 2004–2005," 2004, retrieved November 2004 from www.fns.usda.gov/fsp/faqs.htm#7; *WorkWORLD*, Virginia Commonwealth University, VCU Employment Support Institute, Richmond, VA, 2004; and USDA, "Fact Sheet on Resources, Income and Benefits," 2004, retrieved November 2004 from www.fns.usda.gov/fsp/applicant_recipients/fs_Res_Ben_Elig.htm.

Legal Immigrants and Rules of Work

Citizenship/Alien Status

Eligible

- Pursuant to the 2002 Farm Bill, many legal immigrants became newly eligible for benefits in 2003 (as of April 2003, those residing in the US at least 5 years; as of October 2003, those under 18 regardless of date of entry).
- Born in United States or naturalized citizen.
- U.S. Veteran or on active duty in U.S. armed forces, including spouse and unmarried dependents.
- Refugee admitted under Section 207, or asylee admitted under Section 208, or Cuban-Haitian, or Amerasian, or Hmong, or Highland Laotian. Eligible for first 7 years, except Hmong and Laotian who have no limit.
- Person lawfully admitted for permanent residence unless they have less than 40 qualifying quarters.

Ineligible

- Admitted person who was paroled for at least 1 year or person granted conditional entry prior to April 1, 1980.
- Person under age 19 permanently residing under Color of Law.
- Non-citizen, age 65 or older, who legally resided in the United States on August 22, 1996, and who is ineligible for SSI due to a finding of "not disabled." Eligible if age 65 on August 22, 1996.
- Abused non-citizen or their child or parent.

Even if some members of the household are ineligible, those who are may be able to get FS. A number of states have their own programs to provide benefits to immigrants who fail to meet the regular FS eligibility requirements.

Work

With some exceptions, able-bodied adults between 16 and 60 must register for work, accept suitable employment, and take part in an employment and training program to which they are referred by the food stamp office. Failure to comply with these requirements can result in disqualification from the program. In addition, able-bodied adults between 18 and 50 who do not have any dependent children can get food stamps only for 3 months in a 36-month period if they do not work or participate in a workfare or employment and training program other than job search. This requirement can be waived in some locations.

Benefits

An individual household's food stamp allotment is equal to the maximum allotment for that household's size, less 30 percent of the household's net income. Households with no countable income receive the maximum allotment ($393 a month in 2005 for a household of three people). Allotment levels are higher for Alaska, Hawaii, Guam, and the Virgin Islands, reflecting higher food prices in those areas. The average monthly benefit was about $80 per person and almost $186 per household in 2002.

Food Stamps: Who Is in the Program and What Does It Cost?

About 23 million people participated in the FS program in 2004 at a cost of $26.4 billion. (See Table 17.3 on page 174.) This represented a significant increase from previous years (17 million people received FS benefits in 2000) and was due to continuing high rates of joblessness; states improving access to low-income populations, including legal immigrants; and better outreach. Nevertheless, nearly half of all eligible people did not receive FS benefits in 2004.[19] The FS program is targeted toward those most in need.

- In 2003 almost 54 percent of FS households included children; 67 percent were single female-headed households; and 7.7 percent were headed by married parents. The average FS family had 2.3 persons. Twenty-six percent of FS recipients were nonelderly adults; 36.1 percent were children in single-parent households; 12 percent were children in multiple adult households; and 10 percent were elderly adults. More than 27 percent of FS households contained a disabled person. Among adult participants, 60 percent were women.
- In 2003 the average household with children received $242 a month in FS benefits ($284 for a married couple household). The average monthly FS benefit was $163 per household. More than 53 percent of benefits went to households with children.
- The largest proportion of FS participants were white (41 percent); over one-third were African

Table 17.2

Gross and Net Income Eligibility Standards for the Continental United States, 2004–2005

Household Size	Gross Monthly Income (130 percent of poverty)	Net Monthly Income (100 percent of poverty)
1	1,009	776
2	1,354	1,041
3	1,698	1,306
4	2,043	1,571
5	2,387	1,836
6	2,732	2,101
7	3,076	2,366
8	3,421	2,631
Each additional member	+345	+265

*Eligibility levels are higher for Alaska and Hawaii.

Source: USDA, "Food Stamp Program: Frequently Asked Questions," October 15, 2004. Retrieved November 2004 from www.fns.usda.gov/fsp/faqs.htm#15.

Americans (35 percent), and 18 percent were Hispanic.

- In 2002 88 percent of food stamp households had gross incomes below the poverty line ($18,100 for a family of four) and approximately 36 percent had gross incomes below half of the poverty line.
- In 2002 the length of participation in the FS program was less than two years for 71 percent of recipients. Half of all new recipients stayed on the program for less than six months, and 57 percent ended participation within one year.[20]

Special Supplemental Nutrition Program for Women, Infants, and Children (WIC)

The WIC program was enacted in 1972. This program originally began as a two-year pilot program to provide nutritional counseling and supplemental foods to pregnant and breast-feeding women, infants, and young children at nutritional risk. The goal of the program is to address areas of child development that are most affected by poor health and inadequate nutrition, including impaired learning.[21] Specifically, the twin goals of WIC are (1) to enrich

Table 17.3

Food Stamp Statistics, Selected Years, 1975–2003 (participants and cost figures in millions)

Year	Total Cost of FS	Number of Participants	Percentage of Population Using FS	Average Monthly Benefits per Person
1975	$ 4,624	16.3	7.6	$21.40
1978	5,573	14.4	6.5	26.80
1981	11,812	20.6	9.0	39.50
1984	13,275	20.9	8.8	42.70
1987	13,535	19.1	7.8	45.80
1990	17,686	20.0	8.0	59.00
1991	21,012	22.6	9.0	63.90
1993	23,653	26.9	9.3	67.97
1995	20,500	26.7	8.9	71.50
2000	16,956	17.1	6.0	72.77
2003	23,880	21.2	7.5	83.93

Source: U.S. Department of Agriculture, Food and Nutrition Service, "Food Stamp Participation and Costs," October 26, 2004. Retrieved November 2004 from www.fns.usda.gov/pd/fssummar.htm.

the food intake of participants by providing them food or with coupons or food cards that they redeem at local grocery stores, and (2) to educate mothers, individually and in group classes, on how to prevent nutritional difficulties.

WIC is not an entitlement program. In other words, Congress does not set aside funds to allow every eligible individual to participate in the program. Instead, WIC is a federal grant program for which Congress authorizes a specific amount of funds each year. WIC is administered at the federal level by USDA's Food and Nutrition Service (FNS) and at the state level by 88 state WIC agencies. WIC operates through 2,200 local agencies in 9,000 clinic sites, in 50 state health departments, 33 Indian tribal organizations, American Samoa, the District of Columbia, Guam, Puerto Rico, and the Virgin Islands. There are approximately 46,000 authorized WIC retailers. Each state receives cash grants and is responsible for developing, implementing, and monitoring its WIC program.[22] Income eligibility is less restrictive than for public assistance programs; federal guidelines target families whose pretax income is at or below 185 percent of the federal poverty line. Pregnant, breastfeeding and postpartum women, infants, and children up to five years of age are eligible if they (1) are individually determined by a health professional to be at nutrition risk; (2) meet a state residency requirement; and (3) meet an income standard, or are determined automatically income eligible. A person who participates or has family members who participate in certain other benefit programs, such as the Food Stamp Program, Medicaid or Temporary Assistance for Needy Families, automatically meets the income eligibility requirement. (See Table 17.4)

Qualified beneficiaries receive supplemental foods each month in the form of actual food items or, more often, are given vouchers for the purchase of specific items in retail stores. Items that may be included in a food package include milk, cheese, eggs, infant formula, cereals, and fruits and vegetables. The USDA requires food packages that provide specific types and amounts of food appropriate for six categories of participants: (1) infants from birth to three months; (2) infants from four to 12 months; (3) women and children with special dietary needs; (4) children from one to five years of age; (5) pregnant and nursing mothers; and (6) postpartum nursing mothers. In addition to receiving food benefits, WIC participants also receive nutritional counseling.[23] In 2003, WIC served 7.6 million women and children and cost $4.53 billion.[24]

Other Food Programs

Augmenting the FS program and WIC are a range of programs targeted at various constituencies. For

Table 17.4

WIC Income Eligibility Guidelines, 2003–2004 (48 contiguous states, D.C., Guam and territories)

Household Size	Annually	Monthly	Twice-Monthly	Bi-Weekly	Weekly
1	16,613	1,385	693	639	320
2	22,422	1,869	935	863	432
3	28,231	2,353	1,177	1,086	543
4	34,040	2,837	1,419	1,310	655
5	39,849	3,321	1,661	1,533	767
6	45,658	3,805	1,903	1,757	879
7	51,467	4,289	2,145	1,980	990
8	57,276	4,773	2,387	2,203	1,102
Each additional member	+ 5,809	+ 485	+ 243	+ 224	+ 112

Source: USDA, Food and Nutrition Service, "WIC Income Eligibility Guidelines, 2003–2004," July 28, 2004. Retrieved November 2004 from www.fns.usda.gov/wic/howtoapply/incomeguidelines03-04.htm.

The National School Lunch Program is a federally assisted meal program that provides lunches to school-age children.

instance, snacks are available to children and teenagers in after-school programs through the NSLP and the CACFP, The Child Nutrition and WIC Reauthorization Act of 2004 (PL-108-265) enhances nutrition benefits for all children—with a special emphasis on older children—by authorizing reimbursement for snacks served to children through age 18 (and to individuals, regardless of age, who are determined by the state agency to be mentally or physically disabled who participate in organized after-school programs.[25]

Although some of the low-income elderly receive food stamps, they can also be served by Meals on Wheels and the Congregate Meal Dining program. Begun in 1972, the Meals on Wheels program delivers meals for adults 60 years or older unable

Spotlight 17.1

Responding to Hunger in America

The federal government's response to hunger and malnutrition in the United States consists of several major programs—the food stamp program; the commodity distribution program; the national school lunch and breakfast programs; the Special Milk Program; the Special Supplemental Nutrition Program for Woman, Infants, and Children (WIC); the Child and Adult Care Food Program; the Summer Food Service Program; Meals on Wheels; and the Congregate Dining program.

To learn more about each of these programs and the specific services they provide, go the USDA's Food, Nutrition, and Consumer Services website at **www.fns.usda.gov/fns.**

to take care of own nutritional needs. Various community agencies arrange the daily delivery of meals to elderly persons living at home, and aged persons who receive food stamps can use them to purchase the meals. In some locations, meal services are also provided for non-senior handicapped people. A donation of $2 is suggested for each meal, although there is no means test for the program. The Congregate Meal Dining program provides meals at such places as senior citizen centers. Figure 17.2 (pages 452–453) examines other food programs.

Have the Food Programs Worked?

Because WIC is a discretionary rather than an entitlement program, it can serve only as many people as its budget allows. Consequently, it is estimated that only 46 percent of those eligible receive WIC benefits.[26] Moreover, many counties have no WIC program; many others turn people away or have long waiting lists.[27] Although states may provide additional funds for WIC, only a minority of them do so.[28]

According to USDA studies, WIC saves lives and improves the health of nutritionally at-risk women, infants, and children. The results of studies conducted by FNS and other nongovernment entities demonstrate that WIC is one of the nation's most successful and cost-effective nutrition intervention programs. Some highlights of the findings are that WIC improves diet and diet-related outcomes; improves infant feeding practices; improves immunization rates and regular medical care; improves cognitive development; and improves preconceptional nutritional status. USDA research has also shown that the WIC program is playing an important role in improving birth outcomes and thus in containing health care costs. USDA reports found that Medicaid-eligible pregnant women in five states who participated in WIC during their pregnancies had longer pregnancies, fewer premature births, lower incidence of low-birth-weight infants, fewer infant deaths, and a greater likelihood of receiving prenatal care. Health care savings ranged from $1.77 to $3.13 for each dollar spent on WIC.[29]

The number of FS participants grew dramatically from 1989 (19 million) to 1994 (28 million) but has declined from that high. Food stamp caseloads decreased by 40 percent between 1994 and 2000. Studies showed that the caseload declined during this period of economic growth not only because many households' circumstances improved enough to make them ineligible for benefits, but also because a smaller percentage of the potentially eligible households were participating in the program. For example, the 33 percent decline from 1994 to 1999 was far greater than could be explained by an improving economy and welfare reform. Between 1995 and 1997, the number of people in poverty dropped by roughly 1 million people—or less than 3 percent. But the number leaving FS fell by more than 4 million people—a 15 percent drop. From 1993 to 1998 the number of children living in poverty declined by nearly 13.4 percent, whereas the number of children receiving food stamps declined by 28.6 percent. In 1994, 94 percent of eligible children were receiving food stamps; by 1998 the participation rate decreased to 75 percent for eligible children living in small families.[30] By 2003, however, participation in the FS program rose to 21.2 million cases.

In 2003, House Republicans proposed legislation that would transform the FS program into a block grant, thereby devolving responsibility to the states and letting them decide when and if they have sufficient revenues to feed people. Block grants are a means for converting an entitlement into revenue streams for states, and after a few years, states can divert money to other programs. It is not hard to imagine what will happen to America's hungry if the recession and budget deficits continue. At the same time, the USDA hopes to make it more difficult to qualify for free and reduced-price school lunches, claiming that some kids are getting cheap lunches even though their families are ineligible. Research shows that when increased documentation is required, participation rates drop for eligible children.[31]

Conservatives have also attacked the WIC program. In 2002, Douglas Besharov, director of the Project on Social and Individual Responsibility at the American Enterprise Institute, argued that the WIC program contributed to childhood obesity. He argued that real hunger is found mainly among people with behavioral or emotional problems such as drug addicts and the dysfunctional homeless. Besharov criticized liberal advocacy groups, unions, and farmers for standing in the way of "reform and modernization," code words used for dismantling a program while making it appear like an improvement.[32]

Food programs for the elderly have suffered a steep decline in federal appropriations after adjusting for inflation. In 2002 the government spent $716.5 million on home-delivered meals and on

National School Lunch Program

The NSLP program provides lunches and the opportunity to practice skills learned in classroom nutrition education. NSLP is a federally assisted meal program operating in more than 99,800 public and nonprofit private schools and residential child care institutions.

School districts and independent schools that take part in the lunch program receive cash subsidies and donated commodities from the USDA for each meal they serve. For the 2004–2005 school year, schools were reimbursed by the federal government $2.24 per free lunch served, $1.84 per reduced priced lunch, and $.21 per "paid" lunch. Free students must not be charged any amount, and reduced price students must not be charged more than 40 cents for lunch. In return, educational institutions must serve lunches that meet federal requirements. Children from families with incomes at or below 130 percent of the poverty level are eligible for free meals. Those between 130 percent and 185 percent of the poverty level are eligible for reduced-price meals. Children from families with incomes over 185 percent of poverty pay a full price, though their meals are still subsidized to some extent. Local school food authorities set their own prices for full-price meals, but most operate their meal services as nonprofit programs. During the 2002–2003 school year, 27.8 million children participated in the NSLP through more than 97,000 schools and residential child care institutions. On a typical school day, 16 million of these 27.8 million total participants were receiving free or reduced price lunches. Since the program began, more than 187 billion lunches have been served. In 2001 Congress appropriated $6.4 billion for the NSLP.

School Breakfast Program (SBP)

The SBP provides breakfasts to promote learning readiness and healthy eating behaviors. In 2002 some 8.2 million children in more than 78,000 schools and institutions use the SBP, a federal program that provides states with cash assistance for nonprofit breakfast programs in schools and residential child care institutions. Seventy-eight percent of schools that serve lunch also serve breakfast. In the 2002–2003 school year, 42 children received free or reduced-price school breakfast for every 100 who received free or reduced-price school lunch, although this ratio varied among the states from 24 per 100 to 55 per 100. The program is administered at the federal level by the USDA through its FNS. State education agencies and local school food authorities administer the program at the local level.

Breakfasts served as part of the SBP provide one-fourth or more of the daily recommended levels for key nutrients that children need. They are required to provide no more than 30 percent of calories from fat and less than 10 percent of calories from saturated fat. Research shows that children who have school breakfast eat more fruits, drink more milk, and consume less saturated fat than those who don't eat breakfast or have breakfast at home.

Children whose families meet income criteria may receive free or reduced-price breakfasts. Those from families with incomes at or below 130 percent of the federal poverty level are eligible for free meals. Children whose family income is between 130 percent and 185 percent of the poverty level are eligible for reduced-price meals. Those from families over 185 percent of poverty pay a full price, although their meals are still subsidized to some extent. Schools may not charge more than 30 cents for a reduced-price breakfast. Schools set their own prices for breakfasts served to students who pay the full meal price, though they must operate their meal services as nonprofit programs. In 2003 Congress appropriated $1.68 billion for the School Breakfast Program. In 2002 an average of 7.8 million children participated daily; of those, 6.7 million received their meals free or at a reduced price.

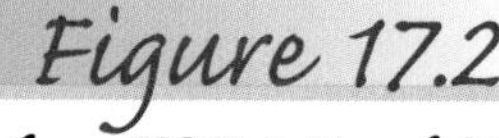

Other USDA Food Programs

Source: USDA, Food and Nutrition Service, "Fact Sheet: After-School Snacks in the National School Lunch Program." Retrieved November 2004 from www.fns.usda.gov/cnd/afterschool/factsheet.htm

Special Milk Program (SMP)	The SMP offers milk to children who lack access to other meal programs. The program provides milk to children in schools and child care institutions that do not participate in other federal child nutrition meal service programs. When local school officials offer free milk under the program, any child from a family that meets income guidelines for free meals and milk is eligible. Each child's family must apply annually for free milk eligibility. In 2001 more than 7,000 schools and residential child care institutions participated, along with 1,300 summer camps and 562 nonresidential child care institutions. Congress appropriated $15.4 million for the SMP in 2003.
Summer Food Service Program (SFSP)	The SFSP serves meals and snacks to low-income children during long school vacations. The FNS administers the SFSP at the federal level; state education agencies administer the program in most states, although in some areas the state health or social service department or an FNS regional office may be designated. Locally, SFSP is run by approved sponsors, including school districts, local government agencies, camps, or private nonprofit organizations. Sponsors provide free meals to a group of children at a central site, such as a school or a community center. States approve SFSP meal sites as open, enrolled, or camp sites. Open sites operate in low-income areas where at least half of the children come from families with incomes at or below 185 percent of the federal poverty level, making the children eligible for free and reduced-price school meals. Children 18 and younger may receive free meals and snacks through SFSP. Meals and snacks are also available to persons with disabilities who are over age 18 but who participate in school programs for mentally or physically disabled people. Congress appropriated $288.2 million for SFSP in 2003.
Child and Adult Care Food Program (CACFP)	CACFP is a key source of support for serving nutritious meals and snacks in child care centers, family child care homes, Head Start, after-school programs, shelters and adult day care centers. The program provides reimbursement for food and meal preparation costs, ongoing training in the nutritional needs of children, and onsite assistance in meeting the program's strong nutritional requirements. Children age 12 and younger are eligible to receive up to two meals and one snack each day at a day care home or center through CACFP. Children who reside in homeless shelters may receive up to three meals a day. Migrant children age 12 and younger, and persons with disabilities regardless of their age, are also eligible for CACFP. In 2002 USDA reimbursed $1.8 billion to institutions participating in CACFP; 2.9 million children and 86,000 adults were served meals.
The Emergency Food Assistance Program (TEFAP)	TEFAP was first authorized to distribute surplus commodities in 1981. The 1988 Hunger Prevention Act required USDA to purchase additional commodities for low-income households and local emergency feeding organizations. TEFAP provides USDA commodities to states who distribute the food through local emergency food providers. Available foods vary depending on market conditions. Each state determines the criteria for household eligibility, and may adjust income criteria based on need in the state. Eligibility criteria may include participation in existing food or other assistance programs for which income is considered as a basis for eligibility. An estimated 3.8 million households were served by TEFAP in FY 1997. In 1996, more than 117 million pounds of food worth more than $140 million was distributed. In 1997, total federal funding for TEFAP was $179 million.

meals provided at senior centers. Ten years earlier it spent $767 million (in 2002 dollars), which explains why older Americans remain on waiting lists for months for a home-delivered hot meal. According to Trudy Lieberman, New York City's budget for home-delivered meals illustrates the problem: "Twenty years ago Washington funded 80 percent of the program and the city funded the rest. Today the federal government provides less than 20 percent, and city and private sources provide the balance."[33]

The level of food insecurity among U.S. households changed little from 1995 to 2003. For example, in 2003 9.4 million people lived in households that experienced hunger. Moreover, the number of Americans who were food insecure rose to 34.9 million people in 2003 and has risen constantly since 1999. In addition, the demand for nationwide hunger relief services is up.[34]

Welfare reform and welfare-to-work programs are clearly not working if working people cannot afford to buy food. Hunger relief agencies report that since the early 1990s the greatest increase in hunger has been among the working poor. Among working people in emergency food recipient households, almost 56 percent work full time. According to the U.S. Conference of Mayors, 39 percent of people requesting emergency food assistance in U.S. cities are employed.[35]

A General Accounting Office (GAO) study on food stamps found that even though FS and welfare caseloads have declined, the need for food assistance has not diminished. Rather, needy individuals and families are increasingly relying on sources other than food stamps, such as food banks, soup kitchens, and emergency pantries. These findings were corroborated by other data. A Wisconsin study found that more than one-third of former welfare recipients had problems paying for food despite a high incidence of employment. Fewer than half of the former recipients reported having more money than when they were receiving public assistance, and 68 percent reported that they were "barely making it." A South Carolina Department of Social Services study reported that after leaving TANF 17 percent of former welfare recipients had no way to buy food some of the time. This is twice the number of families who reported such problems while receiving assistance. An analysis of former welfare recipients in Massachusetts found that 18 percent of families leaving the rolls were back on welfare after three months, and 21 percent were back after a year; and the same study found that food insecurity increased for many families after they went off welfare. Forty percent of the families interviewed did not have enough food or enough of the right kinds of food after being off welfare for one year. More than 20 percent of families who remained off welfare after one year used food banks or had to borrow money to buy food. In short, as poor Americans transition from welfare to work and their benefits are cut or reduced, they are finding their meager wages insufficient to meet basic needs, including child care, transportation, and housing costs. As a result, working poor families may cut their food budget or turn to local charities for aid.[36]

Food stamp participation is also hampered by excessive red tape. In reviewing the application process for food stamps in 50 states, Second Harvest found that:

- More than half of all states and the District of Columbia have FS applications that run 10 to 36 pages long.
- Food stamp applications are difficult to read and complete, and they include excessive and invasive questions—often with little or no legal connection to the FS program.
- The average length of a state food stamp application is 12 pages. Ten states have applications between 19 and 28 pages long. Most food stamp applications are longer than the applications for a federal firearms permit, a federal home mortgage loan, or a school bus driver's license.
- Only 15 states have two-part applications in which the first part, generally shorter, may be used to initiate the process and begin the accrual of benefits once certified.
- FS applications in 49 of the 50 states and the District of Columbia contain certification statements that must be signed by the applicant (under penalty of perjury) that are written at the ninth- to twelfth-grade reading level. Some state FS applications require applicants to provide accurate information (under penalty of perjury) using terms that many are unlikely to understand.
- Some applications require information regarding children's income and bank accounts; income from baby-sitting; charity and gifts from churches and synagogues; income from panhandling, bingo, and plasma donation; and garage sale receipts.[37]

Farming in the United States

The 1980s were a tumultuous time for American farmers, and in many places it rivaled the Great Depression of the 1930s.[38] Agricultural members of the American Bankers Association estimated that 3.8 percent of all farmers filed for bankruptcy in 1985 alone.[39] A 1985 USDA study of 1.7 million farms indicated that 214,000 were in serious financial difficulty, with 38,000 classified as technically insolvent.[40] Other farm indicators were equally bleak. In 1981 the total asset value of U.S. agriculture was $1 trillion; by 1985 it shrunk to $692 billion—a 30 percent drop and the steepest fall since the Great Depression. Although U.S. farms had declined in number by a modest 16,000 between 1978 and 1982, between 1982 and 1987 they declined by 151,000, or at a rate of about 30,000 annually.[41]

Despite these problems, U.S. farmers made a relative comeback in the late 1980s, due in part to the worldwide drought in 1987–1988 that depleted the grain reserves of many nations. By early 1990 farmland prices in the United States had risen, and farm exports increased to 148.5 million tons. Net cash farm income rose from $48.5 billion in 1987 to about the same level as had prevailed in the mid-1970s. More importantly, the farm debt stabilized.[42] On the other hand, the growth in farm equity was still trailing the 3 to 4 percent rate of general inflation.[43]

Of all the occupations in the United States, farming today is facing the greatest decline.

Farmers have historically demanded that agricultural commodity price supports be set at parity levels—in other words, an equal ratio between farm prices and input/output costs.[44] In 1942, Congress established the price support levels at 90 percent of parity. From 1942 to 1953, average prices paid to farmers were at 90 to 100 percent of parity, thereby raising market prices, ensuring a secure income for farmers, reducing the need for excessive debt, and encouraging stabilization in the price of grain.

By the end of World War II, powerful corporations, academics, and free traders had begun to wage war on the farm parity program. Soil conservation, supply management, and parity were characterized as socialist ideas that interfered with a free market economy. Grain companies called for lower prices to help foreign sales, arguing that expanded exports and food aid programs would compensate farmers for lower commodity prices. Industrialists argued that low food prices would translate into cheaper labor costs, and agribusiness believed that lowered commodity prices would result in more production, thereby increasing the use of their products.

The small farmer eventually lost to this powerful coalition, and farm parity was terminated in 1953. As a result, the purchasing power of net farm income decreased even as exports rose. Held constant in 1967 dollars, the purchasing power of net farm income dropped from an annual average of $25 billion in 1942–1952 (the years of farm parity) to an average of $13.3 billion in 1953–1972. In 1952 net farm income was greater than total farm debt; by 1983 net farm income was less than farm interest payments.[45]

Not all farmers were affected equally by the farming crisis of the mid-1980s. For instance, although about one-sixth of all U.S. farming households suffered net income losses in 1984[46] and many middle-sized farmers (with farms in the 80- to 500-acre range) were forced to abandon farming, very small farms endured. At the same time, very large farms were becoming more dominant in U.S. agriculture. In 1984, more than two-fifths of all U.S. farms had total annual sales of less than $10,000, accounting for only 2 percent of all farm sales. These farms experienced an overall net loss of income. By contrast, farms with sales exceeding $500,000 a year earned an average income of $219,000. Finally, in 1984 three-fifths of the total income of farming families (a proportion that is growing) came from nonfarm employment.[47]

Family farming embodies many of this nation's most cherished values—hard work, independence, strong family life, close-knit communities, and democratic institutions. For many rural families, farming is not a vocation but a way of life. Working the land, often a legacy from parents or grandparents, creates a commitment to both place and family heritage.[48] This psychological connection to farming means that many farmers see themselves as farmer–caretakers. Financial failure therefore leaves farmers not only with a sense of personal failure, but also with shame for having failed their families and their heritage. This loss can result in emotional problems ranging from stress and depression to self-destructive or aggressive behavior.[49] The Reverend Paul Tidemann, a Lutheran minister who studied the farm crisis of the 1980s, reported that "The loss of a farm . . . is not the same as a loss of a job. It signals the loss of a personal and family connection to the land. It prompts a sense of betrayal, in many cases, of generations of farmers, past, present, and future."[50]

Governmental Farm Policies

President Ronald Reagan signed the Food Security Act into law in 1985. This legislation was distinctive in three ways: (1) It was the most complicated farm bill ever passed; (2) it cost the federal government more than previous farm bills had (about $80 billion from 1986 to 1990); and (3) the price supports, at least in terms of parity, were lower than they had been in previous legislation.[51] The 1985 farm bill operated in the following way: A target price for each commodity was set by Congress and the Secretary of Agriculture; if prices fell below that level, participating farmers received a subsidy from the government. This system was connected to the Commodity Credit Corporation (CCC) loan rates. For example, in 1986 the CCC loan rate—the price to buyers—for a bushel of corn was $1.92, and the target price was $3.03. On 7 billion bushels of corn, the difference cost almost $8 billion in subsidies. Even so, the USDA estimated that the target price was 17 cents less per bushel than it actually cost farmers to raise the corn.[52] Farmers were therefore losing money on every bushel harvested and were forced to borrow to cover their losses. Grain corporations and foreign buyers were therefore allowed to purchase corn at prices below the cost of production. Federal policy was subsidizing the grain corporations at the expense of farmers, taxpayers, and the general public.

In 1990, Congress passed a five-year farm bill that made important changes in policies affecting farmers, consumers, and the environment. In particular, the 1990 farm bill reduced the number of acres for which farmers could receive deficiency payments, permitted planting flexibility, and maintained the market-oriented loan rates contained in the 1985 farm bill. The bill also contained features that improved the quality of U.S. grain, continued the protection of fragile wetlands, created new incentives to help farmers prevent the contamination of ground and surface water on 10 million acres,

Spotlight 17.2

The National Farmer's Union

The National Farmer's Union is a general farm organization that represents farmers and ranchers in the United States. The goal of this organization is to sustain and strengthen family farm and ranch agriculture. To learn more about this organization, go to its website at **www.nfu.org.**

The United Farm Workers Association

The United Farm Workers Association (UFW) represents the interests of farm workers throughout the United States. To learn more about this organization, go to its website at **www.ufw.org.**

created incentives to help farmers use fewer toxic chemicals and required farmers who used hazardous chemicals to keep records of their use, helped farmers meet environmental laws, established the first-ever national "organically grown" label, and provided a significant rural development aid package.[53] It was estimated that this bill would cost $40 billion over five years, in contrast to the $80 billion of the 1985 farm bill.

In 1996, former President Bill Clinton signed the Federal Agricultural Improvement and Reform (FAIR) Act, replacing the 1990 farm bill. This legislation enjoyed broad support from Republicans, who wanted an agricultural free market, and from urban liberals, who wanted to end farm subsidies. The 1996 farm bill was based on a similar ideological premise as the PRWORA. Namely, it was designed to wean farmers off governmental subsidies in the same way that TANF attempted to wean welfare recipients off public assistance. For free marketers, subsidy-dependent farmers were all too similar to subsidy-dependent welfare recipients.

The heart of the FAIR Act was the "Freedom to Farm" commodity program, which replaced traditional farm subsidies (i.e., those that reimburse farmers when market prices drop) with a system of fixed annual payments that decline over seven years. This legislation fundamentally changed farm policy by severing the connection between subsidies and current farm prices. The act provided for AMTA (Agricultural Market Transition Act) payments to be given annually to farmers in descending amounts from 1996 to 2002. The government delivered these payoffs to all farmers who grew wheat, feed grains, cotton, rice, and soybeans/oilseed. The total payments of $36 billion declined over a seven-year period, thus ending the open-ended entitlement of previous legislation. The success was not long lived, however. In 1998 production grew, demand fell, and prices declined. The price of a bushel of wheat at the Chicago Board of Trade dropped from $7.16 in 1996 to less than $3.00 in 1998.[54] While the 1996 farm bill was supposed to save taxpayers money, it cost more than the legislation it replaced.[55] Congress retreated from the AMTA spending caps and approved emergency relief payments. Critics believed that the goal of making farmers self-reliant and less dependent on government subsidies has not been achieved.[56]

In 2002, George W. Bush signed the Farm Security and Rural Investment Act, which governs federal farm programs until 2008. The bill altered the farm payment program and introduced counter-cyclical farm income support; expanded conservation land retirement programs; emphasized on-farm environmental practices; relaxed rules to make more borrowers eligible for federal farm credit assistance; restored food stamp eligibility to legal immigrants; added various commodities to those requiring country-of-origin labeling; and introduced provisions on animal welfare. One of the most contentious issues in the bill was mandatory country-of-origin labeling for meat and other foods, which has not been implemented. All told, the 2002 farm bill costs $248.6 billion.[57]

The Face of U.S. Farming

The following highlights important trends in U.S. agriculture.

- *Dwindling farms.* Of all the occupations in this country, farming today is facing the greatest decline. There are 2.13 million farms remaining in the United States; between 1993 and 1997, the number of mid-sized family farms dropped by 74,440. In the 1930s 25 percent of the population lived on farms; by 2004 that number dropped to 2 percent. Between 1978 and 2002, some 86,479 U.S. farms disappeared. Three hundred and thirty farm operators leave their land every week. In 1920, the United States had over 925,000 black-operated farms; by 2002, there were less than 36,000. The rate of agricultural loss by black farmers is over twice that of other American farmers. Farms operated by hobby farmers account for 35 percent of all farms.
- *Farm incomes.* More than half of all U.S. farm operators work off-farm, with 80 percent of these working full-time jobs. Nearly half of all spouses are also employed off the farm. The farm business as a source of income has played an increasingly smaller role in determining the well-being of farm households. Those farmers who remain on their land often face the prospect of working off the farm just to stay on the land. In 2004, the USDA estimated that 98 percent of total farm operator income comes from off farm sources and only 7 percent of all farm families reported 100 percent "on-farm" income. In 1999 the average farm with annual gross sales between $50,000 and $250,000 had a net income of only $23,159. More than 80 percent of a farmer's gross income is eaten up by expenses.
- *The graying of U.S. farms.* Half of all current farmers are likely to retire in the next decade. Nearly half of all farmers are between the ages of 45–65,

with the average age being 54.3. Just 6 percent of farmers are under age 35. Almost 25 percent of farmers plan to retire in the next 5 years. U.S. farmers over age 55 control more than half the farmland; since 1987 the number of entry-level farmers replacing them has fallen by 30 percent and now makes up only 10 percent of all farmers. These trends suggest an almost total absence of a new generation of beginning farmers.

- *Consolidation and control.* Nearly half of all U.S. land is farmland (more than 1 billion acres). Only 4 percent of landowners hold 47 percent of this farmland. In California, the nation's largest agricultural producer, 3 percent of California farms control 60 percent of the market. Nationwide the figures are similar—7 percent of U.S. farms received 60 percent of the net cash farm income in 1992. The top 10 percent of farm-subsidy recipients collect two-thirds of the money, and the bottom 80 percent get just one-sixth. Forty-seven percent of commodity payments go to farms with average household incomes of $135,000.
- *Women and farming.* Ownership and control in U.S. agriculture also have distinct gender biases. Of those who control U.S. farmland, only 9 percent are women. Women tend to own smaller farms; the average size of properties held by men is one-third larger than that of farms held by women.
- *Crop prices.* The small farmer's share of each food dollar has dropped steadily over the past half century. Adjusted for inflation, the price a farmer received for corn in 1999 was the lowest in 25 years. Since 1985 farm prices in inflation-adjusted dollars have dropped steadily for commodities such as corn, wheat, and soybeans.
- *Rural health and food quality.* Many rural residents are exposed to excessive odors from factory farms and often suffer from nausea, vomiting, coughing, and headaches. In more extreme cases, people living near factory farms have developed neurological diseases and women have suffered from miscarriages as a result of water and air contamination. Employees working inside factory farms have died from exposure to manure lagoons. The factory farms' extreme confinement and increased levels of production of animals intensify the opportunity for contamination of meat and poultry with bacteria, such as *E. coli* and salmonella, which can cause illness and death. Crowded livestock conditions lead to a reliance on antibiotics to maintain animal health. Over 70 percent of all antibiotics in the United States are fed to healthy farm animals. This indiscriminate use of drugs has contributed directly to the evolution of antibiotic resistant bacteria which the American Medical Association considers an impending public health crisis.
- *Farm subsidies.* Large farms receive nearly twice as much in government subsidy payments as small farms. A USDA study found that one-fourth of farm subsidies go to the largest 1 percent of producers. In 1999, the top 10 percent were paid 7.8 billion dollars, or 65 percent of all subsidies.
- *Efficiency.* Because they often farm small acreages using greater crop diversity and careful management of natural resources, family farmers are more efficient than large, industrialized food producers. Moreover, the per unit cost for agricultural production is no better in larger commercial operations than in family farms. Factory farms add many real costs, such as increased use of fossil fuels, environmental damage, health threats, and threats to the safety of the food supply.[58]

Farmworkers

The efforts of millions of farmworkers are essential to the multibillion-dollar U.S. fruit and vegetable industry. Because agricultural production depends on the influx of seasonal labor, each year anywhere from 3 to 5 million families leave their homes to follow the crops. The wages and conditions they labor under are in many cases scandalous.

The $28 billion U.S. produce industry is largely cultivated by hand, mostly through the labor of America's farmworkers. While some Americans assume that farmworker poverty results in lower food prices, Eric Schlosser notes that "Maintaining the current level of poverty among migrant farmworkers saves the average American household (just) $50 a year."[59]

Thousands of migrant farmworkers risk death and incarceration each year by crossing the U.S.–Mexico border. In the blistering Arizona heat of 2001, 14 immigrants died after smugglers abandoned them. In 2003, 17 immigrants, including a 5-year-old boy, died of dehydration in the back of an abandoned truck in Texas. Despite the danger, illegal migration rates jumped 25 percent in 2002, and almost 100 people die annually from exposure to heat, cold, and dehydration. More than two million year-round and seasonal migrant farmworkers, including 100,000 children, work in the United States. About two thirds are immigrants, of whom 80 percent are from Mexico. Just 14 percent of all farmworkers have full-time work.[60] The following represents an overview of U.S. farmworkers.

- *Demographics.* In 2002, 61 percent of farmworkers were U.S. born. The average age of farmworkers was 31, and half were under age 35. Almost 83 percent of farmworkers were men; 53.1 percent were married; and slightly less than half were parents.
- *Education and language.* In 2002, 84 percent of farmworkers spoke Spanish and they typically completed six years of education. Thirty-one percent had less than 9 years of schooling, while 52 percent had less than 12 years. Only 10 percent spoke or read English fluently.
- *Labor and conditions.* In 2002, 60 percent of all farmworkers held just one U.S. farm job a year and spent roughly half their time doing farm work. Farmworkers earned $5.94 an hour on average. About 20 percent reported being covered by unemployment insurance, but only 3 percent had employer-provided health insurance. Seventy-seven percent of farmworkers were paid by the hour and 20 percent by the piece.
- *Wages and Poverty.* Three out of four U.S. farmworkers earn less than $10,000 annually, and 61 percent of families live below the federal poverty line. The median income of farmworkers was less than $7,500 a year in 2002. In 1998 the average farm wage was just 48 percent of the average industrial wage. This is particularly striking since the largest 1.5 percent of U.S. farms employ more than half of the farm labor. Archer Daniels Midland, the world leader in the production of soy meal, corn, wheat, and cocoa, reaped $1.7 billion in profits in 2003; its CEO, Allen G. Andreas, received over $2.9 million in compensation. Dole, the world's largest producer of fresh fruit, vegetables and cut flowers generated $4.8 billion in revenues in 2003.
- *Legal status.* In 2002, 66 percent were U.S. citizens, and 8 percent were non-citizens.
- *Use of social services.* Despite their poverty, few farmworkers use social services. In 1997–98 just 20 percent of farmworkers reported using unemployment insurance. Just 13 percent of farmworker families receive Medicaid, 10 percent get food stamps, and 10 percent participate in WIC.
- *Assets.* Few farmworkers have assets. In 1997 fewer than 44 percent of farmworkers owned a vehicle. Because of this, many were forced to pay for rides to work. Home ownership also had declined. In 1994–95, one-third of all farmworkers owned or were buying a house; by 1998 that number was only 14 percent.
- *Women.* Women farmworkers had lower personal incomes than men. In 1998 the median income for women farmworkers was between $2,500 and $5,000; for men it was between $5,000 and $7,500. Only 1 in 10 women earned more than $10,000 in farm work, whereas 2 in 10 men did.[61]

Housing is a necessity for farmworkers. On average they spend more than 30 percent of their income on housing, often on sub-standard housing. In 1997, 21 percent of all farmworkers received free housing from their employers, 7 percent rented from employers, 47 percent rented privately, and 18 percent owned their own homes. One study showed that 26 percent of farmworker homes were adjacent to pesticide treated fields.[62] More than 35 percent of housing for farmworkers in eight major agricultural labor states (California, Florida, Texas, Washington, Colorado, Michigan, New York, and Ohio) lacked inside running water. Despite regulations, it is estimated that one-third of U.S. farm laborers work in fields without drinking water, hand-washing facilities, or toilets. And at the end of the workday, many farmworkers do not have a home to go to. The number of farmworkers needing housing often exceeds the available housing units. In 1980, for example, housing was available for only about one-third of the estimated 1.2 million migrant farm workers who needed it. In addition, migrant farmworkers face barriers in obtaining private housing. For example, rural communities may not have enough rental units available, or they may be unwilling to rent to migrant farmworkers because they cannot provide deposits, qualify for credit checks, or make long-term rental commitments.[63]

Education is also problematic for migrant farmworkers. Constant mobility makes it hard for the children of farmworkers to complete their education. Children who move often are two and a half times more likely to repeat a grade than children who are stationery. Changing schools is emotionally difficult for children, and youngsters are more likely to drop out of school if they change schools four or more times; educators who work with migrant children say that 55 percent of these children graduate nationwide. Migrant children also face intense economic pressure to drop out of school.[64]

Child labor is another problem. Often, the poverty encountered by migrant families requires all able family members to work. In fact, agriculture is the only industry that allows workers under age 16: The Fair Labor Standards Act sets age 12 as the legal limit for farm work, with exemptions available for children as young as 10 or 11. In 1996 an estimated 43,000 children accompanied by family members, and an additional 55,000 unaccompanied minors, were involved in farm labor. When children work in the fields, occupational injury presents an even more significant risk than for adults because of the lack of experience.[65]

The health problems experienced by farmworkers are staggering. One of the many health risks they face is the exposure to pesticides, herbicides, and fungicides. National estimates of the number of farmworkers, farmers, and their families potentially exposed to toxic chemicals range from 3.2 to 4 million people. In California, the average death rate for farmworkers is five times higher than workers in other industries.[66] Approximately 300,000 farmworkers in the United States are poisoned by pesticides annually. The Environmental Protection Agency (EPA) has estimated that 300,000 acute illnesses and injuries each year are attributable to the use of pesticides. Children work and play in the fields, and are thus exposed to the same occupational hazards as adults. Research has shown that because of lower weight and higher metabolism, children are more susceptible to the toxic effects of toxic chemicals than adults. One study found that 48 percent of children had worked in fields still wet with pesticides; 36 percent had been sprayed either directly or indirectly (by drift); and farm operators had sprayed 34 percent of the children's homes in the process of spraying nearby fields. A 2002 California study shows that 51 percent of pesticide poisoning cases were due to drift.[67] A 1988 study of 460 farmworkers in Washington State found that 89 percent did not know the name of a single chemical to which they had been exposed; 76 percent had never received any information on appropriate protection measures.[68]

As a result of the exposure to pesticides, farmworkers frequently suffer stomach ailments, headaches, rashes, burns, and other toxic chemical-related problems. Many die from environmentally caused cancer, and too often workers' babies are born with severe birth defects. Many families must sleep, bathe, and cook near the fields where they work and have no option but to use water that may be contaminated with toxic chemicals.[69] The following illustrates some of the health and safety problems faced by America's farmworkers.

- Agriculture is the most dangerous occupation in the United States; between 1979 and 1983 about 23,800 children and adolescents were injured. In 2002 an average of 103 children had died from agricultural injuries. Twenty-nine out of every 100,000 agricultural workers died of unintentional work-related injuries in 2001.[70]
- One study found that about 34 percent of migrant children were infected with intestinal parasites and/or suffered severe asthma, chronic diarrhea, vitamin A deficiency, chemical poisoning, or continuous bouts of otitis media leading to hearing loss. Other commonly reported health problems included lower height or weight, respiratory disease, skin infections, and undiagnosed congenital and developmental problems. Researchers found an 11 percent rate of chronic health conditions among migrant children, compared to the national rate of 3 percent. The majority of pre-school–age children of farmworkers are not appropriately vaccinated for their age level.
- The life expectancy of migrant farmworkers is 49 years compared to the U.S. average of 75 years.
- Water-related parasitic infections afflict migrant farmworker adults and children an average of 59 times more often than the general population.
- More than any other workers, farmworkers suffer and die from heat stress and dehydration.
- Health centers rank alcohol and drug abuse as the fourth largest health problem among adult patients of migrant health centers.
- Death rates from influenza and pneumonia are as much as 20 percent and 200 percent higher, respectively, for farmworkers than the national average.
- In a study conducted by the CDC, 44 percent of farmworkers had positive TB tests. Regional studies show that 41 percent tested positive in North Carolina, 44 percent in Florida, and 48 percent in Virginia.
- It is estimated that as few as 42 percent of female farmworkers receive prenatal care during the first trimester of pregnancy, even though many migrant pregnancies are classified as high risk with multiple indicators. The infant mortality rate among

migrants farmworkers is 125 percent higher than in the general population.[71]

In the 1960s the conditions faced by farmworkers led to the creation of the United Farm Workers union (UFW) in California, a movement led by the charismatic Cèsar Chávez. At its peak in the 1970s, the UFW had about 120,000 workers under contract, and between 1966 and 1980 it obtained two 40 percent wage increases in the grape industry, among other gains. But during the 1980s contracts began to expire and successive Republican administrations stacked the California Agricultural Labor Relations Board with pro-industry members, effectively gutting the law that had created the board. In the midst of a hostile political climate and internal differences, the UFW went into a decade-long slump. By the middle 1990s the UFW had only about 20,000 workers under contract in California, Texas, and Florida. In 2003 fewer than 10 percent of all strawberry pickers were unionized.[72]

Farm labor contractors now hire 20 percent of farmworkers nationwide and 40 percent in California. The 1980s saw the rise of independent labor contractors as key players in the farm industry. Hired by growers, these middlemen round up laborers and deliver them to the fields. Contractors pay less than growers, offer few benefits, and provide little job security. They also have a reputation for mistreating farmworkers and cheating them out of part of their wages. Contractors shield large growers from labor actions and legal claims, distancing them from the actual hiring of workers.[73] If a judgment comes down against a labor contractor, the contractor often vanishes or puts the businesses into bankruptcy, only to emerge in a new place or under a new name. The labor subcontracting system is an important obstacle to improving the welfare of farmworkers. One issue being pressed by farmworker activists is the creation of legislation that would make growers legally responsible for their workers, regardless of whether they use contractors.

Issues in American Farming

There are a number of important issues affecting U.S. farming, including the corporatization of agriculture, genetic engineering, global trade, Mad Cow Disease, local selling, organic farming, sustainable agriculture, and global warming.

The Corporatization of American Farming

U.S. family farms are rapidly being replaced by corporate farms, a trend spanning all agricultural sectors. Corporate agriculture is a system wherein the farm owner, the farm manager, and the farm worker are different people. This system represents a dramatic shift from the historic structure of traditional agriculture, in which individual farmers make the decisions and reap the profits. Industrial agriculture encourages large-scale, highly specialized farms where uniformity is emphasized over quality, and where many costs are shifted from the farm operation to society. There also attendant environmental risks in large-scale agriculture. In North Carolina, for example, a 25-million-gallon hog manure spill at a factory farm in 1995 killed thousands of fish, destroyed crops, and severely damaged a local river. A single Utah hog operation raises 2.5 million hogs a year, producing more waste than the entire city of Los Angeles.[74]

Corporatization leads to closed markets where prices are fixed not by open, competitive bidding but by negotiated contracts. Small volume producers are discriminated against in price or other terms of trade. Under these conditions, many smaller farmers who cannot participate in "vertical integration" are forced out of business because they have no place to sell their products. Moreover, in traditional food markets, 91 cents of every dollar spent on food goes to suppliers, processors, middlemen and marketers, most of whom are not based in the community. Hence, only nine cents of each dollar goes to the farmer.[75]

An integral part of corporate farming is vertical integration, whereby agricultural corporations control all aspects of production, including raising, owning, slaughtering, and marketing livestock or agricultural products. One example is ConAgra, the largest distributor of agricultural chemicals in North America and one of the largest fertilizer producers in the world. In 2004, ConAgra's gross revenues exceeded $14.5 billion and it owned more than 100 grain elevators, 2,000 railroad cars, and 1,100 barges. It is the largest of the three corporations that mill 80 percent of North America's wheat. ConAgra is also the largest turkey producer and the fourth largest broiler producer, producing its own poultry feed as well as other livestock feed. The company hires growers to raise its birds and then processes them in their own facilities. This poultry can then be purchased as fryers, under the name of Butterball, or in further processed foods such as TV dinners and pot pies under the label of Banquet, Marie Callenders, or Healthy Choice. ConAgra also owns 73 well-known brand names including Armour, Banquet, Blue Ribbon, Fleischmann's, Parkay, Hunt's, Chef Boyardee, Chung King, Wolfgang Puck, Egg Beaters, Healthy Choice, Hebrew National, Kid Cuisine, Knott's Berry Farm, La Choy, Libby's, Louis Kemp, Marie Callender, Orville Redenbacher, Peter Pan, Wesson, Reddi-Whip, and Ranch Style.[76] The extent of corporate agriculture is illustrated in Figure 17.3.

- Eight percent of farms account for 72 percent of agricultural sales. Just 2 percent of farms produce 50 percent of all agricultural products in the United States.
- By 2003, 20 large food retailers controlled nearly 50 percent of retail grocery sales. Walmart alone controls almost 20 percent of all grocery sales.
- By 2000, five grain-trading companies controlled 75 percent of the world's cereal commodity market and pricing. Four companies control 61 percent of flour milling, three companies control 82 percent of exporting, four companies control 80 percent of soybean crushing, and four companies control 60 percent of the terminal grain market. Some of the largest companies include Archer Daniels Midland (ADM), Cargill, and ConAgra.
- Four meatpacking companies—Tyson, Excel (subsidiary of Cargill), Swift, and National Beef Packing—control an estimated 81 percent of cattle slaughtering. Since 1980 their share of the beef industry has grown from 36 percent to 87 percent. By comparison, the top four beef packers slaughtered less than 30 percent of all cattle in the 1960s.
- Five companies control 78 percent of the sheep slaughter industry.
- From 1986 to 1999 the number of hog operations declined by 72 percent. Of the remaining hog operations, 2 percent control nearly half of all hog inventory. Sixty percent of pork production in the United States is owned by just four firms.
- Ninety-eight percent of all poultry is produced by large corporations, and only five companies (Tyson, ConAgra, Excel, Swift, and Smithfield) claim 50 percent of production. These companies control everything from egg-laying to marketing chicken meat. Tyson grows, kills, and processes 40 million birds a week—more than most countries produce. Farmers who are contract growers for these large companies absorb most of the risks while reaping little of the profits.
- Ten corporations supply 33 percent of the global seed market compared to hundreds of companies 20 years ago. The top ten agrochemical corporations control 84 percent of the $30 billion agrochemical market. The world's top ten seed firms control 30 percent of the $24.4 billion commercial seed market. The top two seed companies—Syngenta and Pharmacia—controlled 34 percent of the $30 billion global agrochemical market in 2000.
- The top 10 veterinary pharmaceutical companies control 60 percent of the $13.6 billion world market.
- Ninety-one percent of all genetically modified crops (GM) grown worldwide in 2001 were from Monsanto seeds. In 2002, GM crops covered an area two and a half times the size of the United Kingdom. Only 1 percent of GM research is targeted at crops used by farmers in poor countries. In 2000, six European and U.S. corporations controlled 98 percent of the market for GM crops and 70 percent of the world's pesticide market. The four corporations that control most of the GM seed market had combined sales of $21.6 billion in 2001. From 1999–2001, the United States paid out an estimated $10 billion in extra farm subsidies for corn and soy beans as a result of the low prices caused by GM crops. The loss of foreign trade due to GM crops was an estimated $1–2 billion in 2001.

Figure 17.3

Facts About Corporate Agriculture

Sources: Mafruza Khan, "What's the Beef?—Consolidation and Market Manipulation in the Beef Packing Industry," *Corporate Research E-Letter* no. 45, March 2004, retrieved December 2004 from www.corp-research.org/archives/mar04.htm; The Center for Food Safety, "Fast Facts on the Corporate Consolidation of Industrial Agriculture," 2003, retrieved November 2004 from www.ifg.org/pdf/indust_ag-fas=_facts_consol.pdf; Marlene Halverson, "The Price We Pay for Corporate Hogs, Institute for Agriculture, and Trade Policy," 2000, retrieved May 2004 from www.iatp.org/hogreport/indextoc.html; William Heffernan and Mary Hendrickson, "Concentration in Agricultural Markets," 2002, retrieved July 2004 from http://nfu.org/documents/01_02_concentration_report.pdf. Center for Food Safety text used by permission.

Genetic Engineering

Genetic engineering has sparked a global controversy since its introduction in 1995. Genetic engineering or modification is the manipulation of specific genes that are moved from one species to another to create a trait that did not previously exist. For example, crops such as corn, have been engineered to contain pesticides in every cell of the plant. As a result, these crops are not registered as food and are actually considered pesticides.[77] While the Food and Drug Administration claims GM products are safe, there has been no thorough analysis of their long-term effects. Moreover, GM products are not labeled. Critics argue that GM crops are increasingly threatening the biodiversity in the seed supply and making crops more vulnerable to disease outbreaks and pest infestations. Two multinational companies, Monsanto and DuPont, dominate the U.S. seed industry.[78]

Farmers buy GM crops based on promise of lower costs and higher yields, but they often find additional costs in veterinary bills, medications, unstable markets, and extra pesticides. Specifically, farmers that buy GM seeds enter into a contract that dictates how and when the crop can be grown. This contract also forbids the farmer to save seed, which is contrary to traditional farming practices. Many farmers have been sued for allegedly saving seeds, while neighboring farmers whose crops have been contaminated by GM pollen drift have been sued by Monsanto for unknowingly possessing GM seeds.[79]

Global Trade

The global trade in food has emerged as a serious threat facing family farmers in the United States and around the world. Agricultural free trade agreements, like the North American Free Trade Agreement (NAFTA)—which linked the economies of the United States, Mexico, and Canada—promote agricultural trade with little regard to its impact on local communities and family farmers. As a result, several countries, including the United States, have been flooded with cheap food imports (2004 was the first year since 1986 that food imports exceeded food exports). These low-cost imports has caused small farmers to lose their local markets, and family farmers worldwide have been forced off their land. In turn, this weakened local food production.[80]

Since the passage of NAFTA in 1994, family farmers in all three countries have felt the negative impacts of a free trade agreement designed to benefit agribusiness. In the United States, 100,000 family farmers were forced out of farming between 1996 and 2001. During that same period, Canada lost 11 percent of its family farms.[81] NAFTA and other liberalization policies has dramatically increased rural poverty and hunger in Mexico. Between 1992 and 2002, the number of rural Mexicans living in extreme poverty grew from 36 to 52.4 percent. In addition, 1.7 million subsistence farmers were pushed off their land and migrated to export factories, maquiladoras, or to fields and cities in the United States NAFTA critics estimate that as many as 15 million more Mexican farmers—one in six—could be displaced.[82] On the other hand, Archer Daniels Midland's profits rose from $383 million in 2001 to $451 million in 2003, while Cargill's net earnings jumped from $333 million to $1.2 billion.

Mad Cow Disease

Mad Cow Disease (Bovine Spongiform Encephalopathy, or BSE), is a neurological disease that affects cattle by attacking the brain and central nervous system. It is believed that cattle become infected with BSE by eating feed that contains remnants of other infected cattle. Humans can become infected with a BSE-like illness, called Creutzfeldt Jakob Disease (CJD) by eating meat from infected cows. There is no known cure for CJD and cooking at high temperatures or treating meat with radiation is not effective in preventing the disease. Because organic livestock producers adhere to strict feed requirements, which exclude animal by-products in the feed, it is believed by some that BSE is absent in this kind of meat.[83] Nevertheless, some consumers have become wary of purchasing beef.

Local Selling

Because many small farmers cannot compete directly with agribusiness, they are realizing the importance of selling their products locally. Since 1995 the number of farmers' markets has increased 79 percent, and in 2004, they numbered more than 3,000 nationwide. Community Supported Agriculture (CSA) programs—where local residents buy a seasonal share of produce directly from family farms—are also growing. Beginning with only one CSA in 1985, the program is now available through more than 1,000 family farms nationwide. By selling directly to consumers, farmers realize as much as 80 cents of each food dollar.[84]

Organic Farming

Started by family farmers, the organic movement is the fastest growing sector of American agriculture. Since 1992, the total number of farmland dedicated to organic crops has quadrupled. This trend has created some confusion for consumers who are unsure of what the various labels mean. (see Figure 17.4)

Sustainable Agriculture

The environmental challenges facing the United States are greater than at any time in the nation's history. Global environmental threats such as climate change; stratospheric ozone depletion; and the loss of biological diversity (through accelerating extinctions of species), forests, and fish stocks are affecting all countries regardless of their stage of economic development.

In June 1993 former President Bill Clinton appointed 25 leaders from business, government, environmental, civil rights, and American Indian organizations to the Council on Sustainable Development. Their charge was to transform the idea of sustainable development into a concrete plan of action. As a benchmark, the council adopted the definition of sustainable development proposed by the United Nations Brundtland Commission in 1987. This stated that **sustainable development** must "meet the needs of the present without com-

- *Organic:* Regulated by the USDA, the National Organic Standards assure that food products contain at least 95 percent organic ingredients and that no synthetic growth hormones, antibiotics, pesticides, biotechnology, synthetic ingredients, or irradiation were used in production or processing. Organic labels can be found on produce, dairy, meat, processed foods, condiments, and beverages.
- *Fair Trade:* Fair trade standards are enforced by the Fairtrade Labeling Organization International (FLO). Fair trade products are produced in accordance with several guidelines. For example, workers must receive decent wages, and housing, health and safety standards must be adhered to. Workers must have the right to join trade unions and child or forced labor is prohibited. Crops must also be grown, produced and processed in an environmentally friendly manner. Fair trade standards have been established for coffee, tea, cocoa, honey, bananas, orange juice, and sugar.
- *Free Farmed:* This certification program was created by the American Humane Association in 2000 to ensure that animals raised for dairy, poultry, and beef products are treated in a humane manner. These guidelines ensure that livestock have access to clean and sufficient food and water as well as a safe, healthy living environment.
- *Feel Good Buying* (not certified): Some meat and dairy products are now being marketed as hormone free. In dairy products, this means that the farmer has chosen not to inject his cows with the artificial growth hormone called rBGH. On beef products this label indicates that the animal was raised without growth hormones or steroids.
- *Raised Without Antibiotics:* This meat and dairy label indicates that the animal was raised entirely without the use of low-level and/or therapeutic doses of antibiotics.
- *GE Free, Non-GMO:* Food products that use GE Free or Non-GMO labels are regulated by individual companies, distributors or processors. Often, the companies require certification or affidavits from farmers that the materials were not genetically modified in any way.
- *All Natural:* There is no universal standard or definition for this claim.
- *Free Range:* This label claims that a meat or poultry product (including eggs) comes from an animal that was raised in the open air or was allowed to roam. However, the regulations do not specify how much of each day animals must have access to fresh air. In poultry, the USDA considers five minutes adequate exposure to be considered free range. In beef the use of the label is completely unregulated or standardized.

Figure 17.4

What the Food Labels Mean

Source: Adapted from Farm Aid, Inc., "Issues in Farming," 2004. Retrieved November 2004 from www.farmaid.org/site/PageServer?pagename=info_facts_global. Used by permission.

promising the ability of future generations to meet their own needs." The final vision statement of the council noted that: "Our vision is of a life-sustaining earth. We are committed to the achievement of a dignified, peaceful, and equitable existence. We believe a sustainable United States will have an economy that equitably provides opportunities for satisfying livelihoods and a safe, healthy, high quality of life for current and future generations. Our nation will protect its environment, its natural resource base, and the functions and viability of natural systems on which all life depends."[85]

Sustainable development theories also address the crisis of farmland mismanagement in the United States and abroad. Farming and related activities are the foundation of the U.S. food and fiber industry, which provides jobs for 17 percent of the workforce and contributes $1 trillion to the GNP. Moreover, the 1 billion acres of land in agricultural production is responsible for feeding, clothing, and housing 294 million people in the United States and millions more abroad. Yet, every minute, the United States loses 2 acres of productive farmland to urban sprawl—shopping malls, housing subdivisions, and the like. Since the first Earth Day in 1970, the United States has lost more than 40 million acres of farmland to development. Net cropland losses in the United States between 1992 and 1997 covered an area the size of Maryland.[86]

Urbanization is a leading cause of the loss of cropland. The spread of roads, buildings, and industrial parks consumes precious farmland. Cropland is also lost because of the depletion or diversion of irrigation water. In many water-scarce areas, water is supplied from nonrenewable aquifers. If farmers deplete the water stock or if it is siphoned off by large cities, agricultural land will either be abandoned or become less productive. Although irrigated land accounts for only 16 percent of all cropland worldwide, it supplies 40 percent of the world's grain.[87]

Each year the United States loses almost 3 billion tons of topsoil to wind and water erosion. As many as 1 billion tons wash into nearby waterways, carrying away natural nutrients and the fertilizers and pesticides contained in the soil.[88] This erosion damages water quality, fish and wildlife habitat, and recreational opportunities. Farmers spend an estimated $8 billion on fertilizers and $6 billion on fuel each year. Thus, the use of fertilizers, toxic chemicals, and fuel strains already tight farm budgets as well as threatening the environment. The overuse and misapplication of fertilizers and fuel threatens both the land and the farmers' profitability.[89]

The impressive success of the intensified agriculture that began in the 1960s has led to a complacent attitude toward cropland loss. Specifically, some people believed that farm yields were rising so quickly that they more than compensated for any loss of arable land. However, by 1984 the growth in crop yields had slowed. This trend was intensified in the 1990s as the amount of productive U.S. cropland per person fell to less than one-sixth the size of a soccer field.[90] Moreover, the shrinking supply of cropland and the slowing of yield increases comes on the brink of the largest projected increase in food demand in history. In 25 years farmers will be required to feed 2.2 billion more people than they do today; yet most governments continue to allow land that could be used to grow food to be developed or washed away by erosion.[91]

Sustainable development is seen by many as an alternative to environmental degradation. According to social worker Richard Estes, the concept of *sustainable development* has succeeded in uniting differing theoretical and ideological perspectives into a single conceptual framework.[92] In an ecological context, sustainable development promotes a process whereby natural resources are replenished and future generations continue to have adequate resources to meet their needs.[93] Although sustainable development is an important concept, its wide use by different groups in the development process gives some pause for concern. For example, some groups use the term sustainable development to designate a radical restructuring of society with regard to environmental development and economic growth. Others simply use the idea of sustainable development to signal a change in attitudes and emphasis. Such different approaches are sometimes labeled "dark green strategies" versus "light green strategies." Although some policy analysts claim that sustainable development can be the basis for a new developmental and ecological paradigm, others caution that the concept is not yet fully developed.[94]

Global Warming

Lastly, the greenhouse effect or global warning is having a major impact on farming and food production. The greenhouse effect—a naturally occurring phenomenon—is the way the atmosphere traps part of the sun's heat and stops it from going back into space. It makes the earth warm enough for life, and without it, the earth would be about 86 degrees F colder. Although global warming is a common term used to describe these changes, climate change is a better description since some areas may in fact cool. Global warming also describes other effects such as rising sea levels and wilder weather.[95]

Many scientists believe that increased emissions of greenhouse gases have contributed to the rise in global temperatures and sea level. These scientists maintain that we are adding dangerously to the natural greenhouse effect as the gases from industry and agriculture—chiefly carbon dioxide, methane, and nitrous oxide—trap more solar heat. Indeed, the average global surface temperature has risen by 1 degree F in the last 100 years, and scientists say the earth is warming faster than it has in the last thousand years. The Arctic Climate Impact Assessment, produced by a council of nations with arctic territory that includes the United States, Canada, Russia, and several Nordic countries, reflects the work of more than 300 scientists. Leaked in late 2004, the report found that the arctic is warming much faster than other areas of the world and that much of this change is linked to human-generated greenhouse gas emissions. The report concluded that temperature increases in some parts of the arctic increased tenfold compared with the last century's worldwide average rise of 1 degree F.[96]

The Kyoto Protocol is a global treaty on tackling climate change. It commits industrialized nations to reduce their emissions of six greenhouse gases by an average of 5.2 percent below their 1990 levels within a decade. Scientists say it would take carbon cuts of 60 percent or more to prevent dangerous climatic instability, so Kyoto is only a modest start. The United States pollutes more, absolutely and per head, than any other country. Its greenhouse emissions have risen by more than 13.1 percent from 1990 to 2002, despite the Kyoto commitment to reduce them by 6 percent.[97]

In 2001 the Bush administration rejected the Kyoto Protocol claiming that the agreement was fatally flawed because it excluded developing nations, such as China and India. Bush maintained that forcing U.S. businesses to reduce their emissions while letting companies in those countries off the hook would drive up the cost of American products and cost jobs. In effect, the Bush administration is opposed to mandatory requirements for reducing emissions, instead favoring plans to push private industry to voluntarily reduce them. Despite the U.S. rejection, the Kyoto accord will take effect in 2005 as a result of Russia's ratification.

Conclusion

The production, distribution, and consumption of food have historically been rooted in political economy. Through various forms of legislation, the U.S. government has traditionally responded to the needs of diverse groups that have an interest in food—farmers, consumers, the poor or their advocates, food distributors, grain traders, and the Third World and wealthier countries that depend on U.S. food production.

The federal government has responded to these interests by creating a patchwork quilt of policies and programs. One of the most important is the FS program, an ingenious strategy that helps keep food affordable for low-income consumers, helps stabilize farm prices, slows down agricultural surpluses by subsidizing consumption, and allows food retailers and distributors to increase their profits by ensuring a volume of subsidized consumers. The nation's food problems persist, however. These problems, which are serious for many poor people and farmers, have reached crisis proportions for others—including the very poor, farmworkers, and marginal farmers. Tragically, many farmers in the United States now profit from food stamps not because the program helps them control surplus farm goods but because it provides them with coupons. It is a sad commentary when the producers of food are unable to purchase what they grow.

Discussion Questions

1. The Food Stamp Program is currently the single most important federal program for combating hunger. Nevertheless, serious questions exist as to why about 40 percent of those eligible for food stamps are not enrolled. Why has the federal government not been more aggressive in promoting food stamps? What changes, if any, could be made in the FS program to make it

more accessible to greater numbers of eligible people?

2. WIC and the FS Program are similar in many respects. What are the specific differences between these programs? Is it necessary for WIC to be a separate program? Why?
3. Serious questions remain as to the effectiveness of U.S. food programs for the poor. What alternatives, if any, exist to the confusing matrix of food programs that make up the nutritional safety net?
4. American farming has historically been economically volatile. For example, farming was reasonably good in the 1970s, after which it spun into a depression in the early and mid-1980s. What programs and policies could be implemented to stabilize U.S. farming?
5. Some advocates claim that sustainable development should be the basis for a new developmental and ecological paradigm. Is sustainable development a theory viable enough to serve as the basis for a set of development policies? Why?
6. The problem of how to deal fairly with farmworkers in the United States is both difficult and chronic. What are some possible solutions for promoting equity and fairness for farmworkers in this country?

Notes

1. Robin McKie, "Lifespan Crisis Hits Supersize America," *Observer* (September 19, 2004), p. 2.
2. Eric Schlosser, *Fast Food Nation* (New York: Perennial, 2002), p. 3.
3. United Health Foundation, *America's Health: State Health Rankings—2004 Edition,* 2004. Retrieved November 2004 from www.unitedhealthfoundation.org/shr2004/commentary/obesity.html
4. McKie, "Lifespan Crisis Hits Supersize America."
5. CNN, "Poll: Most Americans Older than 25 Are Overweight," March 5, 2002. Retrieved November 2004 from http://archives.cnn.com/2002/HEALTH/03/05/obesity.poll
6. Scott Kilman, "U.S. Tastes Could Bring Trouble, Americans' Desire for Imported Foods May Help Worsen Trade Imbalance," *Kansas City Star* (November 10, 2004), p. A8.
7. U.S. Department of Agriculture, "Household Food Security in the United States, 2002," October 2003. Retrieved October 2004 from www.ers.usda.gov/publications/fanrr35/fanrr35.pdf
8. Ibid.
9. Christine Olson and David Holben, "Domestic Hunger and Inadequate Access to Food," *Journal of the American Dietary Association* 102 (2002), pp. 1840–1847.
10. Andrew A. Skolnick, "'More!' Cry Children as Congress Shakes Its Head," *Journal of the American Medical Association* 274, no. 10 (1995), p. 783.
11. C. Aikens, "One in Six Struggle with Chronic Hunger," *Oakland Post* (April 19, 1995), p. 6.
12. Trudy Lieberman, "Hungry in America," *The Nation* (July 31, 2003), p. 2.
13. John T. Cook and Katie S. Martin, "Differences In Nutrient Adequacy among Poor and Non-Poor Children" (Summary of Findings), Tufts University School of Nutrition—Center on Hunger, Poverty & Nutrition Policy, March 1995.
14. Ibid.
15. See Katherine Alaimo, Christine M. Olson, and Edward A. Frongillo, "Food Insufficiency and American School-Aged Children's Cognitive, Academic and Psychosocial Development," *Pediatrics* 108 (2001), pp. 44–53; and Katherine Alaimo, Christine M. Olson and Edward A. Frongillo, "Family Food Insufficiency, but Not Low Family Income, Is Associated with Dysthymia and Suicide Symptoms in Adolescents," *Journal of Nutrition* 132 (2002), pp. 719–725.
16. See Olson and Holben, "Domestic Hunger and Inadequate Access to Food"; Mark Nord, Nader Kabbani, Laura Tiehen, Margaret Andrews, Gary Bickel, and Steven Carlson, *Household Food Security in the United States, 2000* (Alexandria, VA: Food and Rural Economics Division, Economic Research Service, U.S. Department of Agriculture, 2002); Donald Rose, "Economic Determinants and Dietary Consequences of Food Insecurity in the United States," *Journal of Nutrition* 129 (1999), pp. 517S–520S; Myoung Kim, Jim Ohls, and Rhoda Cohen, *Hunger in America, 2001* (Princeton, NJ: Mathematica Policy Research, Inc., 2001); Anne Kendall, Christine M. Olson, and Edward A. Frongillo, "Relationship of Hunger and Food Insecurity to Food Availability and Consumption," *Journal of the American Dietary Association* 96 (1996), pp. 1019–1024.
17. U.S. Department of Agriculture, *Household Food Security in the United States, 2002.*
18. Ibid.
19. Food Action Research Council, "Food Stamp Program," October 22, 2004. Retrieved November 2004 from www.frac.org/html/federal_food_programs/programs/fsp.html

20. See Ibid; U.S. Department of Agriculture, *Household Food Security in the United States, 2002;* United States Department of Agriculture, "Food and Nutrition Service, Characteristics of Food Stamp Households: Fiscal Year 1999," July 2000, retrieved December 2000 from www.fns.usda.gov/oane/menu/Published/fsp/FILES/adv99char.PDF
21. Illa Tennison, "WIC Policy Analysis," unpublished paper, School of Social Work, University of Missouri–Columbia, 1987, p. 5.
22. Ibid.
23. U.S. House of Representatives, Committee on Ways and Means, *Overview of Entitlement Programs, 1992 Green Book* (Washington, DC: U.S. Government Printing Office, 1992), p. 1687.
24. U.S. Department of Agriculture, Food and Nutrition Service, "WIC Program Participation and Costs," October 22, 2004. Retrieved November 2004 from www.fns.usda.gov/pd/wisummary.htm
25. U.S. Department of Agriculture, Food and Nutrition Service, "Nutrition Assistance Programs" February 6, 2000. Retrieved January 2001 from www.fns.usda.gov/fns
26. See U.S. House of Representatives, *1992 Green Book,* p. 1688; and Kristin Cotter, "Texas WIC: Strategy for Outreach Policy," unpublished paper, Graduate School of Social Work, University of Houston, Houston, TX, Fall 1996.
27. Children's Defense Fund, *The State of America's Children, 1988* (Washington, DC: Children's Defense Fund, 1988), p. 186.
28. Isaac Shapiro and Robert Greenstein, *Holes in the Safety Nets* (Washington, DC: Center on Budget and Policy Priorities, 1988), pp. 33–34.
29. U.S. Department of Agriculture, Food and Nutrition Service, "How WIC Helps," May 15, 2000. Retrieved December 2001 from www.fns.usda.gov/wic/CONTENT/howwichelps.htm
30. U.S. Department of Agriculture, Food and Nutrition Service, "Reaching Those in Need: Food Stamp Participation Rates in the States" July 2000. Retrieved November 2001 from www.fns.usda.gov/oane/menu/Published/fsp/FILES/FSPart2000sum.HTM
31. Lieberman, "Hungry in America."
32. Douglas J. Besharov, "We're Feeding the Poor as If They're Starving," American Enterprise Institute, Washington, DC, December 2002.
33. Lieberman, "Hungry in America," p. 2.
34. U.S. Department of Agriculture. *Household Food Security in the United States, 2002.*
35. See Second Harvest, "Hunger in America, 2001," retrieved November 2004 from www.secondharvest.org/site_content.asp?s=81; and U.S. Conference of Mayors, "Hunger and Homelessness Survey," December 2003, retrieved October 2004 from www.usmayors.org/uscm/hungersurvey/2003/onlinereport/HungerAndHomelessnessReport2003.pdf
36. Second Harvest, "Who We Are," December 2000. Retrieved December 2001 from www.secondharvest.org/whoshungry/who_we_serve.html
37. Second Harvest, "State-by-State Review of Food Stamp Applications," November 2000. Retrieved November 2001 from www.secondharvest.org/policy/food_stamp_study.html
38. M. Drabenstott and M. Duncan, "Another Troubled Year for U.S. Agriculture," *Journal of the American Society of Farm Managers and Rural Appraisers* 49, no. 1 (1985), pp. 58–66.
39. Cited in Joanne Mermelstein, "Criteria of Rural Mental Health Directors in Adopting Farm Crisis Programming Innovation," unpublished Ph.D. dissertation, Public Policy Analysis and Administration, St. Louis University, 1986, p. 3.
40. Ibid.
41. "U.S. Farm Sector, in Annual Checkup, Shows Strong Pulse," *Farmline* (December–January 1991), p. 2.
42. Ibid., pp. 4–5; also see Jim Ryan and Ken Erickson, "Balance Sheet Stable in 1992," *Agricultural Outlook* 46 (January–February 1992), pp. 29–30.
43. Ryan and Erickson, "Balance Sheet Stable," p. 29.
44. United States Department of Agriculture, "History of Agricultural Price Support and Adjustment Programs, 1933–84," *Bulletin No. 485* (Washington, DC: Economic Research Service, 1984), pp. 8–9.
45. Steve Little, "Parity: Survival of the Family Farm." Unpublished paper, School of Social Work, University of Missouri–Columbia, 1986, pp. 8–9.
46. Mary Ahearn, "Financial Well-Being of Farm Operators and Their Households," United States Department of Agriculture, *Report No. 563* (Washington, DC: Economic Research Service, September 1986), p. iii.
47. Ibid.
48. Mermelstein, "Criteria of Rural Mental Health Directors," pp. 5–6.
49. Ibid., p. 7.
50. Quoted in John M. Herrick, "Farmers' Revolt! Contemporary Farmers' Protests in Historical Perspective: Implications for Social Work Practice," *Human Services in the Rural Environment* 10, no. 1 (April 1986), p. 9.
51. Ibid.
52. G. Kaye Kellogg, "The Crisis of the Family Farm in America Today," unpublished paper, School of Social Work, University of Missouri–Columbia, 1987, pp. 9–10.
53. U.S. Government, "Conference Committee Approves Five-Year Farm Bill," news release, Washington, D.C., October 16, 1990.
54. See Ford Runge and Stuart Kimberly, *Agricultural Policy Reform in the United States: An Unfinished Agenda* (Washington, DC: Center for International Food and Agricultural Policy, October 1996), pp. 1–30; and James Bovard, "Farmers Harvest Bumper Crop in

Beltway," *Wall Street Journal* (October 21, 1998), pp. 1, 2.

55. American Farmland Trust, "1996 Farm Bill Review," 1996. Retrieved December 1999 from http://farm.fic.niu.edu/aft/fbreview.html
56. R. A. Wirtz, "Farm Crisis: Here We Go Again?" *fedgazette.* Retrieved December 2001 from www.minneapolisfed.org/pbus/fedgaz/99-10/cover.html
57. Anuradha Mittal, "Giving Away the Farm: The 2002 Farm Bill," *Backgrounder* 8, no. 3 (Summer 2002), p. 1.
58. See U.S. Department of Agriculture, "2002 Census of Agriculture," Retrieved December 2004 from www.nass.usda.gov/census/census02/volume1/us/index1.htm; U.S. Department of Agriculture, "Farms and Land in Farms," February 2004, retrieved June 2004 from http://usda.mannlib.cornell.edu/reports/nassr/other/zfl-bb/fmno0204.txt; U.S. Department of Agriculture, "2002 Census of Agriculture"; U.S. Department of Agriculture, "Income, Wealth, and the Economic Well-Being of Farm Households," ERS Agricultural Economic Report No. AER812, July, 2002, retrieved May 2004 from www.ers.usda.gov/publications/AER812; U.S. Department of Agriculture, "Structural and Financial Characteristics of U.S. Farms: 2001," Family Farm Report, ERS Agriculture Information Bulletin No. 768, May 2001. Retrieved April 2004 from www.ers.usda.gov/publications/aib768; Farm Aid, "Factory Farms: The Worst of Industrial Agriculture, 2004," retrieved November 2004 from www.farmaid.org/site/PageServer?pagename=info_facts_factory; Andrew Nelson, *From a Lifestyle to a Business, Small Farming in Transition: A Case Study Analysis of Small Farming in the Upper Midwest;* Larry Keller, "Family Farming: An Endangered Career," CNN.com, October 30, 2000, retrieved October 2001 from http://fyi.cnn.com/2000/fyi/news/10/30/family.farms; Center for Rural Affairs, "Corporate Farming and Industrialization"; Farm Aid, "Family Farm Numbers," 2000, retrieved October 2001 from www.farmaid.org/org/farm/facts.asp; Farm Aid, "Factory Farming," 2000, retrieved December 2001 from www.farmaid.org/org/farm/factory.asp; Farm Aid, "Questions and Answers," 2000, retrieved December 2001 from www.farmaid.org/org/farm/q_a.asp
59. Eric Schlosser, *Reefer Madness: Sex, Drugs, and Cheap Labor in the American Black Market,* (Houghton Mifflin Company, 2003), p. 56.
60. Christine Ahn, Melissa Moore and Nick Parker, "Migrant Farmworkers: America's New Plantation Workers," *Backgrounder* 10, no. 2 (Spring 2004), pp. 2–11.
61. See Ahn, Moore and Parker, "Migrant Farmworkers: America's New Plantation Workers"; U.S. Department of Agriculture, "2002 Census of Agriculture"; U.S. Department of Labor, "Findings from the National Agricultural Workers Survey (NAWS) 1997–1998," Research Report No. 8, March 2000, retrieved November 2001 from www.dol.gov/dol/asp/public/programs/agworker/report_8.pdf; and Richard Mines, Susan Gabbard, and Anne Steirman, "A Profile of U.S. Farm Workers, Demographics, Household Composition, Income and Use of Services (April 1997), U.S. Department of Labor, Office of the Assistant Secretary for Policy, prepared for the Commission on Immigration Reform, retrieved December 2001 from www.dol.gov/dol/asp/public/programs/agworker/report/major.htm
62. Christopher Holden, "Migrant Health Series: Housing, 2001." Retrieved May 2004 from www.ncfh.org/docs/08%20-%20housing.pdf
63. See V. A. Wilk, *The Occupational Health of Migrant and Seasonal Farmworkers in the United States* (Washington, DC: Farmworkers Justice Fund, 1985); Juan Ramos and Celia Torres, "Migrant and Seasonal Farm Workers," *Encyclopedia of Social Work,* 18th ed. (Silver Spring, MD: NASW, 1987), p. 151; and National Center for Farmworker Health, *Facts about America's Farmworkers* (Washington, DC: National Center for Farmworker Health, 1996).
64. Wilk, *Occupational Health.*
65. Ibid.; and Bureau of Primary Health Care, "The Children's Health Initiative, Migrant and Seasonal Farmworker Children: The Current Situation and the Available Opportunities," Health Resources and Services Administration, October 24, 1997, retrieved December 2001 from www.bphc.hrsa.gov/mhc/MIGRANT.HTML
66. Ahn, Moore, and Parker, "Migrant Farmworkers: America's New Plantation Workers."
67. Margaret Reeves, Anne Katten, and Martha Guzman, "Fields of Poison, 2002: California Farmworkers and Pesticides," United Farmworkers, 2003. Retrieved August 2004 from www.ufw.org
68. Bureau of Primary Health Care, "The Children's Health Initiative, Migrant and Seasonal Farmworker Children: the Current Situation and the Available Opportunities."
69. Gary Huang, "Health Problems among Migrant Farmworkers' Children in the U.S." ERIC Digests, January 1, 1993. Retrieved December 1999 from www.ed.gov/databases/ERIC_Digests/ed357907.html
70. National Center for Farmworker Health, "Fact Sheets about Farmworkers, 2002." Retrieved June 2004 from www.ncfh.org/factsheets.php
71. Ibid.
72. Schlosser, *Reefer Madness: Sex, Drugs, and Cheap Labor in the American Black Market.*
73. Ahn, Moore, and Parker, "Migrant Farmworkers: America's New Plantation Workers."
74. Center for Rural Affairs, "Corporate Farming and Industrialization," 2000. Retrieved January 2001 from www.cfra.org/Issues.htm#Corporate
75. Stewart Smith, "Farming Activities and Family Farms: Getting the Concepts Right." Presented to the U.S. Congress Symposium, Agricultural Industrialization

and Family Farms, Washington, DC, October 21, 1992.

76. ConAgra, "Our Foods," 2004. Retrieved November 2004 from www.conagrafoods.com/brands/index.jsp
77. Farm Aid, "Genetic Engineering," 2004. Retrieved November 2004 from www.farmaid.org/site/PageServer?pagename='info_facts_genetic
78. Ibid.
79. Ibid.
80. Farm Aid, "Issues in Farming," 2004. Retrieved November 2004 from www.farmaid.org/site/PageServer?pagename=info_facts_global
81. Ibid.
82. Ahn, Moore, and Parker, "Migrant Farmworkers: America's New Plantation Workers."
83. Farm Aid, "Genetic Engineering," 2004.
84. Ibid.
85. The Council on Sustainable Development, "Sustainable America: A New Consensus," 1995. Retrieved December 1998 from www.whitehouse.gov/WH/EOP/pcsd/info/highlite.html
86. American Farmland Trust, "Farming on the Edge: Sprawling Development Threatens America's Best Farmland," 2003. Retrieved June 2004 from www.farmland.org/farmingontheedge/downloads.htm#foodchart
87. Ibid.
88. Richard Magleby, "Agricultural Resources and Environmental Indicators: Soil Management and Conservation," No. AH722, February 2002. Retrieved August 2004 from www.ers.usda.gov/publications/arei/ah722/arei4_2/DBGen.htm
89. American Farmland Trust, "Why Save Farmland?" 1996. Retrieved January 6, 2001, from http://farm.fic.niu.edu/aft/aftwhysave.html
90. American Farmland Trust, "What's Happening to America's Agricultural Resources?" 1996. Retrieved January 6, 2001, from http://farm.fic.niu.edu/aft/aftwhathap.html
91. Ibid.
92. Richard Estes, "Toward Sustainable Development: From Theory to Praxis," *Social Development Issues* 15, no. 3 (1993), pp. 1–22.
93. Katherine van Wormer, *Social Welfare: A World View* (Chicago: Nelson-Hall, 1997).
94. James Midgley, *Social Development: The Development Perspective in Social Welfare* (London: Sage, 1995).
95. BBC News, "Global Climate Change, A Changing World," 2001. Retrieved July 2003 from http://news.bbc.co.uk/hi/english/static/in_depth/sci_tech/2000/climate_change/impact/default.stm
96. See Stevenson Swanson, "States May Lead Action against Global Warming, Manufacturers Reduce Emissions; Local Policies Try to Bypass Bush Stance," *Chicago Tribune* (November 14, 2004), p. 8A; and Juliet Eilperin, "Cool to Global Warming, Bush Administration Challenges Evidence, Tries to Keep Council from Endorsing Plans to Curb Climate Change," *Washington Post* (November 8, 2004), p. 10.
97. Swanson, "States May Lead Action against Global Warming."

CHAPTER 18

The American Welfare State in International Perspective

Various models have evolved to depict the comparative levels of development of nations. In recent times a three-part classification has enjoyed extensive use: a First World, consisting of the industrial nations of the capitalist West; a Second World, made up of the communist nations that constructed political economies as an alternative to the market-dominated First World; and a Third World, comprising nations that were former colonies of the First World and later achieved independence, often through revolutions of liberation. This tri-part formulation became prevalent after the Second World War as the Cold War intensified. Many developing nations adopted the slogans of revolution, if not outright insurrection, in order to shed the influences of First World colonial nations. The Second World viewed the Third World as a theater of independence, an arena in which the exploitation of capitalism would be summarily ended and the colonized nations would be brought into the communist sphere of influence. On the defensive, the First World deployed foreign aid, technical assistance, cultural exchange, and, on occasion, diplomatic subterfuge to neutralize Second World incursions into the Third World. In several regions—Central America, Southeast Asia, and sub-Saharan Africa—the First and Second Worlds recruited insurgents who acted as their surrogates, engaging the opposition in armed conflict at considerable cost in arms and human life.

With the fall of the Berlin Wall in 1989, the Three World formulation lost utility. Foremost, the collapse of the Soviet Union and its Warsaw Pact satellites halved the scale of the Second World. The remaining communist nations—the People's Republic of China, Vietnam, North Korea, and Cuba—posed little immediate threat to the First World and were unlikely to serve as models for Third World nations. At the same time, some nations of the Third World had been transformed substantially from their colonial era status. Several Arab nations, despite feudal forms of governance, had prospered through oil exports, achieving levels of income that mirrored those of industrial nations. And despite the absence of natural resources, a handful of nations in Southeast Asia—Hong Kong, South Korea, Taiwan, and Singapore—experienced such consistently high levels of growth that they became known as the "Four Tigers." Tragically, many Third World nations lost ground. By the end of the millennium, several of the nations of sub-Saharan Africa and Southeast Asia were significantly less developed than they had been a generation earlier, when they achieved independence from the First World. Nations such as Cambodia, Bangladesh, Afghanistan, Somalia, and Sierra Leone had lost so much capital, their infrastructure had deteriorated to such an extent, and their polity had become so unstable that development analysts began to speculate about the emergence of a Fourth World. Further confounding the prospects of Fourth World nations, the end of the cold war led the affluent industrial nations of the First World, particularly the United States, to expend relatively less on foreign aid than they had during the Soviet threat.

Typologies of Welfare States

The welfare states of the industrialized West vary structurally. With his colleague Charles Lebeaux, Harold Wilensky sought to summarize the differences between the European and American welfare states by constructing a typology of social welfare systems. The typology contrasts **residual welfare** with **institutional welfare.** The residualist approach is concerned with providing a minimal safety net for the poorest sections of the population rather than catering for the population as a whole. Wilensky and Lebeaux believed that social policy in the United States is essentially residualist in nature. On the other hand, the institutional approach, which typifies European social welfare, seeks to provide a variety of social programs for the whole population and to combine economic and social objectives in an effort to enhance the well-being of all.[1]

These ideas were developed by the British social philosopher Richard Titmuss. Titmuss agreed that the residual approach typified social welfare in the United States and that an institutional approach was dominant in Europe. However, Titmuss noted that some countries did not fall into the residual and institutional dichotomy. For this reason he added a third category to the typology, which he called the industrial performance model. He believed that this approach characterized social policy in the former Soviet Union and communist Eastern European countries.[2]

Several subsequent attempts have been made to construct typologies of welfare states that go beyond Wilensky and Lebeaux's twofold category. One of the first was by Norman Furniss and Timothy Tilton, who provided a threefold classification that encompassed what they called the "positive state," the "social security state," and the "social welfare state." The United States exemplified the first, Britain the second, and Sweden the third.[3]

Canadian writer Ramesh Mishra, who has written extensively about international social welfare, retained the twofold approach developed by Wilensky and Lebeaux; but he stressed the efforts of some countries to forge strong alliances among government, labor, and business in order to reach a consensus on social welfare issues. This approach is known as corporatism. In corporatist societies, social welfare is integrated into the economy and other institutions of society. Countries such as Sweden, Austria, and Australia are typical of the corporatist approach. Mishra used the term *integrated welfare state* to connote the corporatist approach. On the other hand, Britain and the United States were noncorporatist in that they did not integrate social and economic policy or seek to forge a consensus around welfare issues. For this reason, Mishra called them *differentiated welfare states.* Mishra was one of the first writers to suggest that Britain was not, as Titmuss believed, like the rest of Europe but rather more like the United States in its approach to social welfare.[4]

Gosta Esping-Andersen's typology also recognized the corporatist type when classifying welfare states. However, Esping-Andersen grouped countries somewhat differently from Mishra. In addition to the corporatist category (Italy, Japan, France, and Switzerland), Esping-Andersen identified two other types, the liberal welfare state (Australia, Britain, and the United States) and the social democratic welfare state (Austria, the Netherlands, and the Scandinavian countries).[5] More recently, Norman Ginsburg constructed a fourfold typology comprising the social democratic welfare state (typified by Sweden), the social market welfare state (Germany), the corporate market welfare state (United States), and the liberal collectivist welfare state (Britain).[6] However, of the various typologies of welfare states that have been developed by social policy investigators, Esping-Andersen's is perhaps the most widely accepted.[7]

Although the typologies differ from one another, they use similar criteria when classifying countries. All place emphasis on government social programs and neglect the role of voluntary organizations and other nonstatutory activities in social welfare. The typologies also reveal the normative preferences of the authors. That is, although the typologies are intended to classify countries for analytical purposes, it is clear that they give expression to beliefs about the desirability of the role of government in social welfare. Analysts who favor extensive government involvement in social welfare have represented countries with extensive public programs more favorably in the typologies than countries that do not place as much emphasis on government involvement. For this reason, it is not surprising that most of the typologies depict the United States negatively in comparison to European welfare states.

American Exceptionalism

The apparent unwillingness of the United States to emphasize government social welfare programs has been described by Edwin Amenta and Theda Skocpol as "welfare exceptionalism."[8] These authors have also summarized explanations of the country's reluctance to create an institutional European-style welfare state. One such explanation is that the racial, ethnic, and religious diversity of the United States has prevented the emergence of a comprehensive welfare state. In European nations people are more united and have a stronger sense of civic responsibility; in contrast, the pursuit of separate interests by a great number of different groups in the United States militates against the emergence of a single national system of provision that caters to all citizens.

Another explanation is based on the country's high degree of political decentralization which impedes the emergence of strong central political institutions. Combined with a high degree of diversity, the tradition of decentralization in which the states assume much responsibility for social welfare, creates cleavages in U.S. society that effectively prevent the emergence of a strong, centralized, and comprehensive welfare state. It has also been noted that the United States does not have a long tradition of bureaucratic government that can support centralized welfare programs. Some have claimed that this is because of the absence of a feudal tradition. Developing this idea, others have pointed to the unique role of the courts in policymaking in this country, the separation of the executive and legislative branches, and the role of powerful political interest groups—all of which impede the emergence of a strong, centralized welfare state. Another factor is the role of individualism in the United States, which it is fundamentally antithetical to the collectivist assumption underlying the welfare state. It has also been argued that trade unions are weaker in the United States than in Europe and that the political left, which has played a major role in the emergence of the European welfare states, has not been strong in this country.

Although the notion of **welfare state exceptionalism** offers interesting insights into social policy in the United States, it can be criticized. For example, the idea that the United States is a welfare laggard is based largely on a comparison of social programs such as health insurance and family allowances. The absence of these programs is usually emphasized by those claiming that the United States does not have a comprehensive welfare state. Although it is true that government health care and family income maintenance programs are poorly developed in the United States, the role of indirect support for families through tax relief and tax deductions for medical expenses is often ignored, as is the significance of Medicare and state and local health care programs. Jacob Hacker evaluated the extent to which private sector health and welfare benefits effectively augmented public social programs, concluding that their inclusion put the United States on a par with European welfare states. On public benefits alone, the U.S. expended 17.1 percent of gross domestic product, less than half that of Denmark's 37.6 percent. An analysis of after-tax public and private social welfare expenditures showed a different picture, however; the U.S. expended 24.5 percent of GDP compared to Denmark's 24.4 percent.[9] Thus, the United States is different from other advanced nations with respect to social welfare provision because of its reliance on the private sector.

In addition, the United States has excelled in other social fields. During the nineteenth century it led the world in the development of public education; and it still compares favorably with many other countries in terms of access to education, particularly at the tertiary (college and university) level. The United States is also a pioneer in some aspects of environmental protection; and although environmental concerns are not always regarded as an integral part of social policy, the impact of the environment on human well-being should not be underestimated.[10] Comparative studies have also shown that when particular social programs such as retirement pensions are compared, the United States fares quite well.[11] In addition, recent historical research reveals that in the late nineteenth century, the United States was ahead of other Western countries in developing

During the nineteenth century, the United States led the world in the development of public education. Today it still compares favorably well with many other countries in terms of access to education, particularly at the college and university level.

income maintenance programs for veterans and for women with children. At the turn of the century, no other industrializing country had introduced mother's pensions, and none came as close to creating a "maternal" rather than "paternal" welfare state.[12]

Another problem is that comparisons between Europe and the United States are often characterized by strong personal biases. For example, a strong pro-British bias pervades Titmuss's writings. He has been criticized for presenting his arguments in a way that ensures the moral superiority of the institutional welfare state model.[13] It is also apparent that the European countries have widely varied welfare systems and that not all European welfare states are centralized, comprehensive, or highly activist. Studies of welfare policies in other parts of the world also have shown the U.S. welfare state in more favorable terms. For example, unlike the United States, Australia did not until recently have a universal social security system, and it relied extensively on means-tested social programs.[14] Nevertheless, it is difficult to reach the conclusion that the United States is one of the world's welfare leaders. Despite its extensive educational and Social Security provisions, the country does not compare favorably to the other industrial nations in the extent, comprehensiveness, or coverage of its welfare system. In fact, its position has deteriorated in recent years as social programs were retrenched since the Reagan administration.

Although many social policy writers in the United States have complained about their country's comparatively low level of welfare provision, however, others are not disturbed by these findings. *Welfare pluralists,* as they are known, claim that unfavorable comparisons between the United States and other countries are based on the idea that state involvement in social welfare is a good thing. They reject this assertion and do not believe that social needs should be met primarily by the government. Instead of relying only on the state for social welfare, welfare pluralists argue that people can enhance their well-being through their own efforts, through the help of neighbors or their families, by purchasing services on the market, or by obtaining help from voluntary organizations.[15] They point out that in the United States people make effective use of nongovernmental agencies, and that international comparisons should not be limited to government social programs. They also point out that although the United States may lag behind in public welfare provision, people enjoy exceptionally high standards of living and unequaled opportunities. This is why the country remains a magnet for immigrants from all over the world, people who come not to receive government handouts but to share in the American dream.

The Welfare State in Transition

As a result of the globalization of capital, welfare states—however they are classified—have made structural adjustments to remain competitive. Welfare states grew steadily during the relatively stable economic period of the 1950s to the early 1970s; but by the mid-1970s most industrial economies began to experience high inflation, high rates of unemployment, sluggish economic growth, and unacceptably high levels of taxation. During this difficult period Western governments were forced to reassess their overall economic strategies, including the resources allocated to welfare activities. Hence, beginning in the early 1970s, most Western governments either cut welfare programs or arrested their growth.[16]

All Western nations are experiencing a crisis rooted in the need to compete in a new global economy.[17] According to conservative policy analysts, national survival in the new economic order can be achieved only if government cuts costs and becomes more efficient. In addition, these analysts argue for the creation of government policies that encourage the accumulation of the capital necessary for investment, industrial modernization, and corporate growth. Conservatives maintain that this precondition for economic survival is possible only when government freezes or lowers personal and corporate tax rates. The subsequent loss of tax revenue, however, often results in heavy governmental debt, cuts in all services (including social services), a deterioration of the infrastructure, and myriad social problems. The general emphasis on efficiency and profitability also leads to industrial reorganization, which in turn leads to rapidly changing production technologies that displace workers and result in plant closures and downsizing. Thus, the effects of conservative policy changes are exacerbated as cuts in governmental services coincide with the increased demand for social services by victims of the global-based economic changes. In other words, Western industrial nations face a two-pronged assault on the welfare state: (1) the impact of the global economy on government spending, and (2) an increase in the use of social services by workers dislocated by global economic changes.

Western industrialized nations pursued liberal social policies after World War II.[18] In the United States, most presidents following Franklin D. Roosevelt tolerated—and in some cases even promoted—a liberal social welfare agenda. Although the general belief in the United States was that people should adjust to the market rather than the other way around, the social consensus also dictated that the nation should strengthen human capital in order to make people more economically competitive.[19] Thus, social welfare programs were developed to increase human capital through education, employment, health, and housing. The belief was that as human capital increased, the dependent person (or at least his or her children) would eventually be able to compete in a free market. For those who could not compete because of serious deficits (such as disabilities or old age), a system of social insurance or public assistance was developed to ensure a minimum level of subsistence. Thus, the dual focus of the welfare state was (1) to create programs to increase human capital and (2) to create programs to subsidize people unable to participate in the workforce. Even conservative presidents like Richard Nixon acquiesced to this welfare consensus.

But a more conservative welfare consensus emerged during the 1980s. This new consensus called for (1) making welfare benefits conditional on employment and other norms; (2) transforming open-ended entitlements to discretionary programs; (3) containing the growth of the governmental sector while retaining (in curtailed form) fundamental programs that affect the elderly and the working poor; (4) replacing government with other institutions, such as families and community-based organizations; and (5) contracting out services and benefits to the private sector. In effect, ideologues of the new right argued that the liberal welfare state was a failed social experiment.[20] During the 1990s, the conservative critique of the welfare state, introduced first by Margaret Thatcher in the United Kingdom and Ronald Reagan in the United States, prompted a reassessment of public welfare within liberal circles, with the result that Bill Clinton and Tony Blair (nominal liberals) essentially continued the conservative vector in social policy. Most recently, the implications of this trend have been explored by Anthony Giddens, who contends that this represents a "third way" in British social policy.[21] In the United States, Neil Gilbert has observed the emergence of an "enabling state," which conditions social welfare benefits on participation in mainstream activities, particularly work.[22]

By the end of the twentieth century, it was evident that the welfare state was on the wane. "Across all of Europe and North America, the social democratic century has come to an end," observed Alan Wolfe.

> Solidarity, social citizenship, the gift relationship, and the difference principle—as all of them representing formulations of the idea that who live in a society are obligated to insure the welfare of everyone else—are terms bandied about in academic circles, but they no longer make much of an appearance in real politics.[23]

The subsequent retrenchment of the welfare state is paradoxical. Reductions in welfare benefits have contributed to the formation of an "underclass" within the most prosperous of nations. Thus, in the major cities of the West, communities of squatters can be found, people whose poverty is not unlike that seen in the shantytowns that have been characteristic of the developing world. If the globalization of capital has resulted in the internationalization of prosperity, it has also produced an international class of paupers.

Ranking National Development

Various frameworks have been proposed to gauge the progress of nations. Among the first was the Gini coefficient, a figure denoting the extent to which the distribution of income diverges from perfect equality; a Gini ranking of developed nations appears in Chapter 9. Critics of the Gini coefficient cite the limitations of a portrait of development that is based solely on income. Other indicators, such as longevity, education, opportunity, and environment, should be included, they claim. Although this argument has obvious merit, defenders of the Gini coefficient cite its value when the disparity between the rich and poor has become such a chasm. By way of illustration, two-thirds of the world's population survives on less than $1 per day; "the assets of the world's 358 billionaires exceed the combined annual incomes of countries with 45 percent of the world's people."[24]

The Weighted Index of Social Progress

A rather more ambitious assessment of the progress of nations has been undertaken by Richard Estes, a social work professor in the United States.[25] For 1970, 1980, 1990, 1995, and 2000 Estes has ranked the social progress of nations according to their performance along 46 variables that are grouped in 10 sub-indices: education, health, women, defense, economic factors, demography, geography, political participation, cultural diversity, and welfare. Containing so many variables, Estes's scheme is much more sophisticated than the Gini coefficient. At the same time, Estes's formulation contains assumptions that are open to question. In the classic American liberal tradition, for example, Estes assumes that military expenditures are inversely related to social progress. After September 11, 2001, few Americans questioned the value of national security; yet, the balance between defense and international aid remained a matter of debate. "The United States will spend about $450 billion [in 2004] on the military but only $15 billion on official development assistance," complained Jeffrey Sachs. "The 30-to-1 ratio is mirrored by a similar imbalance in our thinking. Our military expertise is undoubted. Our ability to understand what exists before and after wars in low-income countries is nearly nonexistent."[26] As another example, the welfare sub-index consists of the foundations of the modern welfare state, another assumption of liberal ideology.[27]

Estes's analysis is as informative about international development as it is controversial. The top slots, as seen in Table 18.1, are reserved for the well-articulated welfare states of central and northern Europe. Of urgent concern are those nations at the bottom of the ranking; often their conditions have worsened. For the most part these are developing nations that have experienced internal strife, armed conflict that has further detracted from an already precarious developmental status.

In some respects, however, Estes's classification invites skepticism. Canada and the United States fall relatively far down the scale in Estes's ranking: Canada is ranked 26 and the United States is ranked 27, both below Bulgaria at 22. In 1995 the ranking of Bulgaria above the United States spurred a *New York Times* reporter to examine various development indexes. She reported that Nicholas Eberstadt of the American Enterprise Institute, a moderate-conservative policy institute in Washington, D.C., dismissed such rankings on the basis that "they pivot on arbitrary evaluations about which there is no universal consensus." In rebuttal, Estes acknowledged that "The present social situation in Bulgaria is miserable, but in terms of responding to basic human needs, Bulgaria enjoys the legacy of social provision that characterized all of the states and partners of the former Soviet Union, i.e., high literacy, high access to at least basic health care, guaranteed housing, guaranteed income support during old age and other periods of income loss, and so on."[28] The discrepancies between Estes's scale and the UN Human Development Index, discussed below, reflect different criteria in measuring development.

Because Estes has undertaken this exercise each decade, the longitudinal transformation of nations has become evident. Between 1970 and 2000 many nations have experienced substantial change in their progress. Notably, the former satellite nations of the Soviet Union have plummeted, primarily as a result of the removal of the artificial supports of command economies and their replacement with capitalism. Of the former Warsaw Pact nations, only Hungary, the former Czechoslovakia, and Poland have been able to avoid free fall since the collapse of the Soviet Union. Another group of nations have lost ground because of war. By 2000 Lebanon, Cambodia, Afghanistan, Somalia, and Ethiopia had fallen a considerable distance from their rankings decades earlier. The price of ending apartheid in South Africa also appears to have been a dramatic drop.

Several developing nations have increased their ranking positions significantly. South Korea and Singapore (and probably Taiwan and Hong Kong, had data for those countries been available in 1970) have vaulted from Third World to First World membership. Of course, Estes's 2000 ranking, fails to capture more recent events that would change nations' rankings. Overall, the consequences of the war in Iraq have worsened the circumstances of the people of that nation. While Rwanda has advanced since the 1990s genocide in central Africa, conditions in Burundi have worsened. Sierra Leone, Afghanistan, Eritrea, and Angola are among the most hopeless places on earth.

The Human Development Index

Since 1990 the United Nations has published the Human Development Index (HDI) as a register of the development of nations. The HDI is a composite of

Table 18.1

Weighted Index of Social Progress (WISP), 2000

Rank	Nation	Rank	Nation	Rank	Nation
1	Denmark	39	Lithuania	73	Peru
1	Sweden	40	Israel	78	South Africa
3	Norway	41	South Korea	78	Uzbekistan
4	Finland	41	Ukraine	78	Lebanon
5	Luxembourg	43	Croatia	81	Paraguay
5	Germany	43	Cyprus	82	Tajikistan
5	Austria	45	Argentina	82	Kuwait
8	Iceland	46	Costa Rica	84	Philippines
8	Italy	47	Russian Federation	84	Viet Nam
10	Belgium	47	Moldova	84	Malaysia
11	United Kingdom	49	Cuba	84	Suriname
11	Spain	49	Armenia	88	Egypt
13	Netherlands	49	Albania	88	Turkey
14	France	52	Singapore	90	Libya
14	Ireland	53	Macedonia	90	Iran
16	Switzerland	53	Georgia	92	Indonesia
16	New Zealand	55	Panama	93	Bahrain
18	Japan	56	Kyrgyz Republic	93	Botswana
18	Hungary	56	Mauritius	93	Honduras
20	Portugal	58	Mexico	93	Belize
20	Greece	58	Ecuador	97	Nicaragua
22	Australia	58	Azerbaijan	98	Algeria
22	Bulgaria	61	Dominican Republic	99	Jordan
24	Czech Republic	61	Jamaica	99	Cape Verde
25	Slovak Republic	61	Venezuela	99	Bolivia
26	Canada	61	Kazakhstan	102	Syria
27	Slovenia	65	Bahamas	103	Morocco
27	United States	65	Trinidad & Tobago	103	Saudi Arabia
27	Poland	67	Tunisia	105	Swaziland
30	Hong Kong	67	Mongolia	106	Lesotho
31	Estonia	69	China	106	Qatar
32	Uruguay	70	Guyana	106	Namibia
33	Belarus	71	Thailand	109	Myanmar
34	Taiwan	71	Turkmenistan	109	North Korea
34	Romania	73	Brazil	111	India
34	Latvia	73	Sri Lanka	112	Fiji
37	Yugoslavia	73	Colombia	112	Guatemala
38	Chile	73	El Salvador	114	Bangladesh

Table 18.1
(continued)

Rank	Nation	Rank	Nation	Rank	Nation
115	Oman	129	Senegal	149	Mozambique
116	Iraq	133	Cameroon	150	Burundi
116	Cambodia	134	Nigeria	150	Burkina Faso
116	Gabon	134	Papua New Guinea	152	Central African Republic
119	Ghana	134	Togo	153	Somalia
120	Zimbabwe	137	Bhutan	154	Congo, DR
121	Pakistan	137	Mali	155	Chad
121	Haiti	137	Sudan	155	Guinea
123	Congo Republic	137	Gambia	155	Niger
123	Nepal	141	Mauritania	158	Liberia
123	Comoros	141	Kenya	159	Angola
123	Zambia	141	Djibouti	159	Sierra Leone
127	Laos	141	Cote d'Ivoire	161	Ethiopia
128	Tanzania	145	Malawi	162	Eritrea
129	Madagascar	146	Yemen	163	Afghanistan
129	Benin	147	Uganda		
129	Rwanda	148	Guinea Bissau		

Source: Adapted from Richard Estes, "Weighted Index for Social Progress." Retrieved September 29, 2004 from http://caster.ssw.upenn.edu/~restes/world.html.

three variables: life expectancy, educational attainment, and income. A nation's HDI score, an average of the sum of the three variables, has a maximum possible value of 1.

In constructing the HDI, researchers arbitrarily designated the 45 nations with HDI scores above .800 as high in human development. (See Table 18.2 on pages 480–484.) Nations classified as medium, between .799 and .500, numbered 94. The 35 countries below .499 were identified as low in human development.

The HDI demonstrates that nations with somewhat lower incomes are nonetheless able to sustain longevity and mount educational programs. Despite a per capita GDP that is 63 percent that of Italy's, Greece claims comparable longevity and a comparable percentage of the population enrolled in educational programs. Similarly, Cuba's per capita GDP is one-third that of Saudi Arabia, yet Cubans enjoy greater longevity and more educational opportunity than Saudis. Still, the HDI is a less than optimal classification. An important qualification is that nations evidence significant variations internally that are not registered by the national HDI score. Ordinarily, national capitals, industrial cities, and ports elevate a nation's HDI score; rural and remote areas have a depressive affect. Although the "medium" developing nations rank higher than those ranked "low," the rural areas of the "medium" HDI-scoring nations tend to parallel those nations that rank lowest.

To address important issues related to social progress, the UN has developed other indices to assess national development. A Human Poverty Index incorporates nations' percentages of people not expected to reach age 40, their percentages of illiterate adults, the resources they have available in the form of health services and safe water, and their percentages of underweight children under age five. A Gender-Related Development Index reflects life expectancy, adult literacy, school enrollment, and income for women.

Table 18.2

Human Development Index, 2001

Rank	Nation	Life Expectancy (years)	Adult Literacy	School Enrollment	GDP Per Capita	HDI Value
1	Norway	78.7	99 %	98%	$29,620	.944
2	Iceland	79.6	99	91	29,990	.942
3	Sweden	79.9	99	100	24,180	.941
4	Australia	79.0	99	100	25,370	.939
5	Netherlands	78.2	99	99	27,190	.938
6	Belgium	78.5	99	100	25,520	.937
7	U.S.	76.9	99	94	34,320	.937
8	Canada	79.2	99	94	27,130	.937
9	Japan	81.3	99	83	25,130	.932
10	Switzerland	79.0	99	88	28,100	.932
11	Denmark	76.4	99	98	29,000	.930
12	Ireland	76.7	99	91	32,410	.930
13	U.K.	77.9	99	100	24,160	.930
14	Finland	77.8	99	100	24,430	.930
15	Luxembourg	78.1	99	73	53,780	.930
16	Austria	78.3	99	92	26,730	.929
17	France	78.7	99	91	23,990	.925
18	Germany	78.0	99	89	25,350	.921
19	Spain	79.1	97.7	92	20,150	.918
20	New Zealand	78.1	99	99	19,160	.917
21	Italy	78.6	98.5	82	24,670	.916
22	Israel	78.9	95.1	90	19,790	.905
23	Portugal	75.9	92.5	93	18,150	.896
24	Greece	78.1	97.3	81	17,440	.892
25	Cyprus	78.1	97.2	74	21,190	.891
26	Hong Kong	79.7	93.5	63	24,850	.899
27	Barbados	76.9	99.7	89	15,560	.888
28	Singapore	77.8	92.5	75	22,680	.884
29	Slovenia	75.9	99.6	83	17,130	.881
30	S. Korea	75.2	97.9	91	15,090	.879
31	Brunei	76.1	91.6	83	19,210	.872
32	Czech Rep.	75.1	99	76	14,720	.861
33	Malta	78.1	92.3	76	13,160	.856
34	Argentina	73.9	96.9	89	11,320	.849
35	Poland	73.6	99.7	88	9,450	.841
36	Seychelles	72.7	91	78	17,030	.840
37	Bahrain	73.7	87.9	81	16,060	.839
38	Hungary	71.5	99.3	82	12,340	.837

Table 18.2
(continued)

Rank	Nation	Life Expectancy (years)	Adult Literacy	School Enrollment	GDP Per Capita	HDI Value
39	Slovakia	73.3	100	73	11,960	.836
40	Uruguay	75.0	97.6	84	8,400	.834
41	Estonia	71.2	99.8	89	10,170	.833
42	Costa Rica	77.9	95.7	66	9,460	.832
43	Chile	75.8	95.9	76	9,190	.831
44	Qatar	71.8	81.7	81	19,844	.826
45	Lithuania	72.3	99.6	85	8,470	.824
46	Kuwait	76.3	82.4	54	18,700	.820
47	Croatia	74.0	98.4	68	9,170	.818
48	United Arab Emirates	74.4	76.7	67	20,530	.816
49	Bahamas	67.2	95.5	74	16,270	.812
50	Latvia	70.5	99.8	86	7,730	.811
51	St. Kitts	70.0	97.8	70	11,300	.808
52	Cuba	76.5	96.8	76	5,259	.806
53	Belarus	69.6	99.7	86	7,620	.804
54	Trinidad	71.5	98.4	67	9,100	.802
55	Mexico	73.1	91.4	74	8,430	.800
56	Antigua	73.9	86.6	69	10,170	.798
57	Bulgaria	70.9	98.5	77	6,890	.795
58	Malaysia	72.8	87.9	72	8,750	.790
59	Panama	74.4	92.1	75	5,750	.788
60	Macedonia	73.3	94.0	70	6,110	.784
61	Libya	72.4	80.8	89	7,570	.783
62	Mauritius	71.6	84.8	69	9,860	.779
63	Russia	66.6	99.6	82	7,100	.779
64	Colombia	71.8	91.9	71	7,040	.779
65	Brazil	67.8	87.3	95	7,360	.777
66	Bosnia	73.8	93.0	64	5,970	.777
67	Belize	71.7	93.4	76	5,690	.776
68	Dominica	72.9	96.4	65	5,520	.776
69	Venezuela	73.5	92.8	68	5,670	.775
70	Samoa	69.5	98.7	71	6,180	.775
71	Saint Lucia	72.2	90.2	82	5,260	.775
72	Romania	70.5	98.2	68	5,830	.773
73	Saudi Arabia	71.9	77.1	58	13,330	.769
74	Thailand	68.9	95.7	72	6,400	.768
75	Ukraine	69.2	99.6	81	4,350	.766

(continued)

Table 18.2
(continued)

Rank	Nation	Life Expectancy (years)	Adult Literacy	School Enrollment	GDP Per Capita	HDI Value
76	Kazakhstan	65.8	99.4	78	6,500	.765
77	Suriname	70.8	94.0	77	4,599	.762
78	Jamaica	75.5	87.3	74	3,720	.757
79	Oman	72.2	73.0	58	12,040	.755
80	St. Vincent	73.8	88.9	58	5,330	.755
81	Fiji	69.3	93.2	76	4,850	.754
82	Peru	69.4	90.2	83	4,570	.752
83	Lebanon	73.3	86.5	76	4,170	.752
84	Paraguay	70.5	93.5	64	5,120	.751
85	Philippines	69.5	95.1	80	3,840	.751
86	Maldives	66.8	97.0	79	4,798	.751
87	Turkmenistan	66.6	98.0	81	4,320	.748
88	Georgia	73.4	100	69	2,560	.746
89	Azerbaijan	71.8	97.0	69	3,090	.744
90	Jordan	70.6	90.3	77	3,870	.743
91	Tunisia	72.5	72.1	76	6,390	.740
92	Guyana	63.3	98.6	84	4,690	.740
93	Grenada	65.3	94.4	63	6,740	.738
94	Dominican Republic	66.7	84.0	74	7,020	.737
95	Albania	73.4	85.3	69	3,680	.735
96	Turkey	70.1	85.5	60	5,890	.734
97	Ecuador	70.5	91.8	72	3,280	.731
98	Palestinian Territories	72.1	89.2	77	2,788	.731
99	Sri Lanka	72.3	91.9	63	3,180	.730
100	Armenia	72.1	98.5	60	2,650	.729
101	Uzbekistan	69.3	99.2	76	2,460	.729
102	Kyrgyzstan	68.1	97.0	79	2,750	.727
103	Cape Verde	69.7	74.9	80	5,570	.727
104	China	70.6	85.8	64	4,020	.721
105	El Salvador	70.4	79.2	64	5,260	.719
106	Iran	69.8	77.1	64	6,000	.719
107	Algeria	69.2	67.8	71	6,090	.704
108	Moldova	68.5	99.0	61	2,150	.700
109	Viet Nam	68.6	92.7	64	2,070	.688
110	Syria	71.5	75.3	59	3,280	.685
111	South Africa	50.9	85.6	78	11,290	.684
112	Indonesia	66.2	87.3	64	2,940	.682

Table 18.2
(continued)

Rank	Nation	Life Expectancy (years)	Adult Literacy	School Enrollment	GDP Per Capita	HDI Value
113	Tajikistan	68.3	99.3	71	1,170	.677
114	Bolivia	63.3	86.0	84	2,300	.672
115	Honduras	68.8	75.6	62	2,830	.667
116	Equatorial Guinea	49.0	84.2	58	15,073	.664
117	Mongolia	63.3	98.5	64	1,740	.661
118	Gabon	56.6	71.0	83	5,990	.653
119	Guatemala	65.3	69.2	57	4,400	.652
120	Egypt	68.3	56.1	76	3,520	.648
121	Nicaragua	69.1	66.8	65	2,450	.643
122	Sao Tome	69.4	83.1	58	1,317	.639
123	Solomon Islands	68.7	76.6	50	1,910	.632
124	Namibia	47.4	82.7	74	7,120	.627
125	Botswana	44.7	78.1	80	7,820	.614
126	Morocco	68.1	49.8	51	3,600	.606
127	India	63.3	58.0	56	2,840	.590
128	Vanuatu	68.3	34.0	54	3,190	.568
129	Ghana	57.7	72.7	46	2,250	.567
130	Cambodia	57.4	68.7	55	1,860	.556
131	Myanmar	57.0	85.0	47	1,027	.549
132	Papua New Guinea	57.0	64.6	41	2,570	.548
133	Swaziland	38.2	80.3	77	4,330	.547
134	Comoros	60.2	56.0	40	1,870	.528
135	Laos	53.9	65.6	57	1,620	.525
136	Bhutan	62.5	47.0	33	1,833	.511
137	Lesotho	38.6	83.9	63	2,420	.510
138	Sudan	55.4	58.8	34	1,970	.503
139	Bangladesh	60.5	40.6	54	1,610	.502
140	Congo	48.5	81.8	57	970	.502
141	Togo	50.3	58.4	67	1,650	.501
142	Cameroon	48.0	72.4	48	1,680	.499
143	Nepal	59.1	42.9	64	1,310	.499
144	Pakistan	60.4	44.0	36	1,890	.499
145	Zimbabwe	35.4	89.3	59	2,280	.496
146	Kenya	46.4	83.3	52	980	.489
147	Uganda	44.7	68.0	71	1,490	.489
148	Yemen	59.4	47.7	52	790	.407
149	Madagascar	53.0	67.3	41	830	.468
150	Haiti	49.1	50.8	52	1,860	.467

(continued)

Table 18.2
(continued)

Rank	Nation	Life Expectancy (years)	Adult Literacy	School Enrollment	GDP Per Capita	HDI Value
151	Gambia	53.7	37.8	47	2,050	.463
152	Nigeria	51.8	65.4	45	850	.463
153	Djibouti	46.1	65.5	21	2,370	.462
154	Mauritania	51.9	40.7	43	1,990	.454
155	Eritrea	52.5	56.7	33	1,030	.446
156	Senegal	52.3	38.3	38	1,500	.430
157	Guinea	48.5	41.0	34	1,960	.425
158	Rwanda	38.2	68.0	52	1,250	.422
159	Benin	50.9	38.6	49	980	.411
160	Tanzania	44.0	76.0	31	520	.520
161	Cote d'Ivoire	41.7	49.7	39	1,490	.396
162	Malawi	38.5	61.0	72	570	.387
163	Zambia	33.4	79.0	45	780	.386
164	Angola	40.2	42.0	29	2,040	.377
165	Chad	44.6	44.2	33	1,070	.376
166	Guinea-Bissau	45.0	39.6	43	970	.373
167	Congo	40.6	62.7	27	680	.363
168	Central African Rep.	40.4	48.2	24	1,300	.363
169	Ethiopia	45.7	40.3	34	810	.359
170	Mozambique	39.2	45.2	37	1,140	.356
171	Burundi	40.4	49.2	31	690	.337
172	Mali	48.4	26.4	29	810	.337
173	Burkina Faso	45.8	24.8	22	1,120	.330
174	Niger	45.6	16.5	17	890	.292
175	Sierra Leone	34.5	36.0	51	470	.275

Source: "Table 1: Human Development Index," from *Human Development Report,* 2003. Copyright © 2003 by the United Nations Human Development Program. Used by permission of Oxford University Press, Inc.

Capability Poverty

The idea that development is a multifaceted phenomenon has eclipsed a more circumscribed notion based on simple economic parameters. Using the HDI as a basis, development researchers began to evolve a more inclusive and dynamic understanding of authentic progress and to promulgate the idea of "capability poverty." The philosophical rationale for capability poverty was stated fully by Amartya Sen, who noted two profound historical truths: There are no records of famine within democratic societies, nor are there instances of war waged between them. Rather, these most severe events can be attributed to non-democratic decision making that excludes large groups of people, who then bear the brunt of flawed policies. Sen's contention that freedom was a precondition of development, not a by-product to be enjoyed long after industrialization, earned him the Nobel Prize in economics in 1998.

Among the 10 elements of a capability approach is play—enjoying activities that are entertaining and rejuvenating.

The capability approach to development advocates "the expansion of the 'capabilities' of persons to lead the kind of lives they value-and have reason to value," Sen proposed, "Greater freedom enhances the ability of people to help themselves and also to influence the world, and these matters are central to the process of development."[29] Logically, however, deprivation of elemental requirements of survival subverts the possibility of full social participation, as do inadequate institutions that deny education, health, and recreation to subgroups. In constructing his argument for a "support-led process," Sen diverged with proponents of an economic model in which health, education, and labor benefits were viewed as being secondary. He contended that

> . . . the success of the support-led process as a route [to development] does indicate that a country need not wait until it is much richer (through what may be a long period of economic growth) before embarking on rapid expansion of basic education and health care. The quality of life can be vastly raised, despite low incomes, through an adequate program of social services. The fact that education and health care are also productive in raising economic growth adds to the argument for putting major emphasis on these social arrangements in poor economies, without having to wait for "getting rich" first."[30]

Sen's pathbreaking work was soon elaborated by his colleague, Martha Nussbaum. In *Women and Human Development* Nussbaum states the philosophical rationale for an absolute standard of social justice for the most chronically oppressed among the world's poor: women. "The core idea is that of the human being as a dignified free being who shapes his or her own life in cooperation and reciprocity with others, rather than being passively shaped or pushed around by the world in the manner of a 'flock' or 'herd' animal," contends Nussbaum. "A life that is really human is one that is shaped throughout by these human powers of practical reason and sociability."[31] Thus, optimal development is not only freedom from want but also the full enjoyment of a range of social and political opportunities. Nussbaum lists 10 elements of a capability approach to development:

1. Life: enjoying full longevity
2. Bodily health: having good health, including reproductive freedom
3. Bodily integrity: appreciating freedom of movement, security from assault, and pleasure in sexual relations

4. Senses, imagination, and thought: using the mind to explore rational and emotive bases for life as well as to advance their enhancement
5. Emotions: enjoying attachments to others that are not controlled nor censored by others
6. Practical reason: forming a conception of what is desirable and planning one's life
7. Affiliation: respecting and living with others without fear of discrimination
8. Other species: living in harmony with all features of the environment
9. Play: enjoying activities that are entertaining and rejuvenating
10. Control over one's environment: owning property and engaging politically in order to prosper[32]

So formulated, the capability approach to development provides a blueprint for achieving and maintaining progress. This approach is particularly compelling in an era of rapid international changes attributable to shifts in capital, production, and labor. "Especially in an era of rapid economic globalization, the capabilities approach is urgently needed to give moral substance and moral constraints to processes that are occurring all around us without sufficient moral reflection," Nussbaum concludes. "It may be hoped that the capabilities list will steer the process of globalization, giving it a rich set of human goals and a vivid sense of human waste and tragedy, when choices are pondered that would otherwise be made with only narrow economic considerations in view."[33]

International Aid

Historically, the most developed nations (in other words, the more advanced welfare states) have endeavored to advance development by redistributing wealth to the developing world. The traditional means of this redistribution has been intergovernmental transfers, though with increasing frequency other intermediaries are being employed. The recent performance of the industrialized nations and demonstrates several trends in international aid. Foremost, nations with the largest economies, notably Japan and the United States, lag behind other, smaller industrialized nations with respect to the percent of GNP committed to international aid. Indeed, the Scandinavian welfare states have consistently demonstrated international citizenship superior to that of the more laissez-faire economies, as is evident in Table 18.3. Compounding this pattern has been a downward trend in allocations for international aid. During the period depicted by the data, international aid from national governments dropped in 13 of the 20 nations for which longitudinal data are available. This retreat from aid has contributed to a reassessment of international assistance. As governments have donated less, reliance has increased on private **NGOs** (nongovernmental organizations) and on **quangos** (quasi-NGOs) such as the World Bank, the International Monetary Fund, and regional development banks.

Significantly, although the United States is the largest donor, not only is its percent of GNP allotted to international aid the lowest among industrialized nations, but that ratio roughly halved between 1986/87 and 2001.

Global Capital

The foundation for global markets was laid after World War II with an international agreement for currency stabilization and debt financing that was negotiated at Bretton Woods, New Hampshire. The Bretton Woods agreement established the International Monetary Fund (IMF), an international agency accountable to its member nations. With the expansion of capital to overseas markets during the 1960s, the IMF initiated a program of Special Drawing Rights (SDRs) or loans that encouraged expansionary policies in developing nations. This program, however, collided with the acute economic contraction of the 1970s due to the oil embargo, driving much of the developing world into severe debt. Subsequent IMF policies to restructure debt payments have stressed "conditionalities," or internal economic reforms, often requiring controversial reductions in domestic spending for health, education, and related social programs.

The World Bank, also accountable to its member nations, provides resources to enhance infrastructure, initially through the International Bank for Reconstruction and Development (IBRD). Following the dramatic success of the Marshall Plan that rebuilt postwar Europe, the World Bank instituted the International Development Association (IDA) in 1960 to redirect activities to developing nations. Focusing on the poorest nations, World Bank aid is

Table 18.3

Net Official Development Assistance Disbursed, as a Percent of GNP: 1986/87, 2001

Rank	Nation	Total $ (millions)	% of GNP 1986/87	% of GNP 2001	HDI Rank
1	Denmark	1,634	.88	1.03	11
2	Norway	1,346	1.13	.83	1
3	Netherlands	3,172	.99	.82	5
4	Luxembourg	141	.17	.82	15
5	Sweden	1,666	.87	.81	3
6	Belgium	867	.48	.37	6
7	Switzerland	908	.30	.34	10
8	Ireland	287	.23	.33	12
9	United Kingdom	4,579	.29	.32	13
10	France	4,198	.58	.32	17
11	Finland	389	.48	.32	14
12	Spain	1,737	.08	.30	19
13	Austria	533	.19	.29	16
14	Germany	4,990	.41	.27	18
15	Australia	873	.40	.25	4
16	New Zealand	112	.28	.25	20
17	Portugal	268	—	.25	23
18	Japan	9,847	.30	.23	9
19	Canada	1,533	.48	.22	8
20	Greece	202	—	.17	24
21	Italy	1,627	.37	.15	21
22	United States	11,429	.21	.11	7

Source: Adapted from United Nations Development Program, *Human Development Report, 2003* (New York: Oxford University Press, 2003).

often in the form of credits, long-term loans that are interest free.[34]

Both the IMF and World Bank presume that international markets will be a means for development-a strategy that, though markedly successful for industrialized nations, has been less so for developing nations. With the demise of state socialism, international markets have, nonetheless, become the primary means for economic growth of the Third World. Two entities have facilitated this growth: The General Agreement on Tariffs and Trade (GATT), established in 1947, enjoyed only modest success in reducing tariffs until 1967, but in that year impediments against international trade were cut drastically. And in 1995 the World Trade Organization (WTO) was created to accelerate the emergence of global markets, augmenting GATT. Since then membership in GATT/WTO has increased dramatically. Between 1980 and 1999 the number of GATT member nations increased from 85 to 134.[35] Globalization has accelerated with the increasing flow of private capital into developing nations. Between 1980 and 1998, governmental aid has been eclipsed by private capital.[36]

The Future

Although the unprecedented expansion of global markets has furthered economic growth internationally, the benefits have not been evenly distributed. During the last decades of the twentieth century, the per capita GDP of the most developed one-third of nations increased significantly; in contrast, that of the middle third has dropped from 12.5 to 11.4 percent and that of the lowest third fell 3.1 to 1.9 percent. "Such findings are of great concern," observed authors of the World Bank's development report, "because they show how difficult it is for poor countries to close the gap with their wealthier counterparts."[37] While the percent of people living on $1 dollar a day has decreased in Asia, it has increased significantly in Africa and Eastern Europe. (See Table 18.4.)

Critics of global capitalism perceived such disparities as more than the inevitable consequences of international markets, however. Citing a crushing debt burden that required some Third World nations to repay international lenders sums that exceeded their nation's annual economic growth, as well as the imposition of program restructuring as a condition for future loans, opponents of international capital took to the streets in a series of demonstrations. In 1999 demonstrators seriously hampered WTO meetings in Seattle; several months later attempts to disrupt meetings of the World Bank in Washington, D.C., were less successful. High on the demonstrators' lists of demands were debt relief for developing nations and a restructuring of international aid organizations in order to make assistance more just. In demanding a restructuring of global finance, many demonstrators pointed to the $1 trillion traded daily by currency speculators, on which a trivial tax of .001 percent would generate $3 billion each day that could be put to work in development projects.[38]

Given the infeasibility of deconstructing the organizations at the top of the global financial empire, development strategists have focused their energies on nongovernmental organizations. Jessica Mathews, a senior fellow at the U.S. Council on Foreign Relations, has contended that NGOs provide a bond among peoples whose relations have been abraded by the competitiveness of international markets and the retraction of aid from industrialized governments.

> At a time of accelerating change, NGOs are quicker than governments to respond to new demands and opportunities. Internationally, in both the poorest and richest countries, NGOs, when adequately funded, can outperform government in the delivery of many public services. Their growth, along with that of the other elements of civil society, can strengthen the fabric of many still-fragile democracies.[39]

Table 18.4

Percentage and Number of People Living on $1 a Day by Region

Region	Percentage		Number (millions)	
	1990	1999	1990	1999
Sub-Saharan Africa	47.4	49.0	241	315
East Asia and the Pacific	30.5	15.6	486	279
East Asia and the Pacific excluding China	24.2	10.6	110	57
South Asia	45.0	36.6	506	488
Latin America and the Caribbean	11.0	11.1	48	57
Central and Eastern Europe	6.8	20.3	31	97
Middle East and North Africa	2.1	2.2	5	6
Total	29.6	23.3	1,292	1,169
Total excluding China	28.5	25.0	917	945

Source: Adapted from United Nations Development Program, *World Development Report, 2003* (New York: Oxford University Press, 2003), p. 41.

During recent decades hundreds of NGOs have emerged to facilitate development in the Third World. As is typical of voluntary ventures, these initiatives have both positive and negative features. On the positive side, their aggregate budgets and staffs eclipse the projects of many governmental projects; on the negative side, they tend to be fragmented, any coordination being a product of volition. Three NGOs that either have become well established in development circles or show promise of breaking new ground are Habitat for Humanity, the Grameen Development Bank, and First Nations Development Institute.

• *Habitat for Humanity.* Established by Millard Fuller in 1976, Habitat for Humanity is a Christian organization that enlists volunteer labor and donated supplies to build housing for the world's homeless. On a budget of about $20 million, Habitat for Humanity had constructed tens of thousands of homes in areas from rural sub-Saharan Africa to colonias in Latin America to ghettos in the United States. Not operated as a welfare program, Habitat for Humanity requires that future home buyers provide sweat equity in constructing houses for others before they become eligible for one themselves. Home purchase is then arranged through zero-interest loans.

• *Grameen Development Bank.* In 1976, economics professor Muhammad Yunus made a small loan to a peasant woman in Bangladesh so that she could purchase materials for making bamboo stools. Pioneering a peer lending strategy whereby small groups of peasants receive a loan for which the entire group is responsible, the Grameen Bank not only enhanced the productivity of poor people but also reinforced solidarity. Soon, borrowers whom commercial banks had written off as too risky demonstrated a repayment rate above 95 percent. By 2000 the Grameen Bank boasted 1,148 branches, 2.4 million members, and cumulative disbursements exceeding $3 billion.[40] Unique to the Grameen Bank is a social compact, "the 16 decisions," to which members must subscribe in order to become members. Addressing issues ranging from sanitation to birth control, education, and nutrition, the "16 decisions" provide a moral scaffolding for the bank's social architecture. Not a welfare program, Grameen Bank loans are interest bearing; the expectation is that, once repaid, they will make the borrower's loan group eligible for larger loans in the future. As a model of micro-finance, the Grameen Bank not only inspired capital formation strategies in Africa and Latin America, but also prompted the UN to adopt it

Spotlight 18.1

Nongovernmental Organizations Making a Difference

Three NGOs that have made a difference internationally for the disadvantaged are Habitat for Humanity, Grameen Development Bank, and First Nations Development Institute.

Established in 1976, Habitat for Humanity enlists volunteer labor and donated supplies to build housing for the world's homeless. To learn more about this organization, go to its web site at **www.habitat.org**

Grameen Development Bank created a banking system based on mutual trust, accountability, participation and creativity. Grameen provides credit to the poorest of the poor in rural Bangladesh, without any collateral. To learn more about the Grameen bank, go to its website at **www.grameen-info.org**

Founded in 1980, First Nations Development Institute (FNDI) assists indigenous peoples in the control and development of their assets and, through that control, builds their capacity to direct their economic futures in ways that fit their cultures. Among its accomplishments, FNDI developed community development banks on American Indian reservations in the United States in an attempt to end the dependence of American Indians on the federal government. FNDI has also advocated the rights of Aborigines in Australia and nomads in the Kalahari Desert. To learn more about FNDI, go to its website at **www.firstnations.org.**

as a way to promote grass roots development in the poorest nations.[41]

• *First Nations Development Institute.* Established in 1979 by Rebecca Adamson, a Cherokee Indian who wanted to end forever the dependence of Native Americans on the federal government, First Nations Development Institute (FNDI) has become an advocate for indigenous peoples worldwide. In addition to organizing community development banks on reservations in the United States, FNDI has advocated the rights of Aborigines in Australia as well as nomads of the Kalahari Desert. The FNDI paradigm integrates four components—community, nature, subsistence, and culture—into a unity that is antithetical to the exploitive, individualistic model typical of the industrial West. In so doing, FNDI eschews welfare, associating it with the demise of traditional kinship patterns: "The government welfare systems, superimposed on a complex and existing system of giving, sharing and reciprocity has facilitated the breakdown of the kinship system," contends FNDI Vice President Sherry Salway Black, an Oglala Sioux.[42] In advocating for the world's indigenous populations, or first peoples, FNDI serves a population that is often neglected by traditional development projects.

NGOs cannot, of course, be expected to replace military forces or compensate for government inaction in the face of genocide. History will be a harsh judge on the West for its diffidence at Srebrenica,[43] and it will be condemning of the West's utter disinterest in the ongoing slaughter in the Congo,[44] to say nothing of its complicity in the butchery in Sierra Leone.[45] An unanswered question is whether NGOs can address the infrastructure deficits that were once the province of industrialized governments or their international intermediaries. By way of illustration, consider these situations:

- Equatorial Guinea, an African backwater best known through Robert Klitgaard's scathing caricature of corruption, *Tropical Gangsters,*[46] has been blessed by the discovery of a large oil field, yet has virtually no civic infrastructure through which to ensure that oil revenues become translated into national development.[47]
- Parasitic disease is pandemic in regions without potable water and sanitation, impeding education and productivity, as evident in Table 18.5.
- Deaths in Africa due to AIDS exceeded 2 million by 2001,[48] and the HIV infection rate for adults exceeds 20 percent in five nations in sub-Saharan Africa, constituting an epidemic that rivals the Black Death of fourteenth-century Europe; yet international efforts to contain the disease have been sporadic, resulting in the preventable infection of millions of adults and children.[49]
- Debt on development loans placed a crippling burden on several nations, prompting calls for relief. On October 1, 2004 the United States grudgingly agreed to a British plan to forgive $40 billion in loans owed to the World Bank and IMF primarily by nations in sub-Saharan Africa. The previous year African nations paid $15 billion in interest on those loans, impeding the fight against AIDS.[50]
- The widening digital divide—the disparity in access to computer technology between industrialized nations and the developing world—is furthering the gap between rich and poor nations. For example, the United States and Canada boast 1,396 Web servers, compared to 142 for Europe, 22 for Latin America, and 11 for Asia.[51]

Table 18.5

Regions without Access to Potable Water or Adequate Sanitation

Region	% of Population without Safe Drinking Water	Adequate Sanitation
Africa	36	40
Asia	19	53
Latin America and Caribbean	13	22

Source: Adapted from Worldwatch Institute, *State of the World, 2004* (Washington, DC: Author, 2004), p. 51.

As these circumstances suggest, the emerging issues in international development demand innovative solutions, and they demand them urgently.

Conclusion

Nations vary developmentally both as individual entities and as clusters. Thus, the United States is more developed than Niger, just as the countries of the industrialized West are more affluent than those of sub-Saharan Africa. At the same time, countries and regions influence one another, contributing to the dynamism of international relations. A common tendency in the West has been to regard the welfare states of North America and western Europe as ideals to which the developing nations should aspire.

Yet a series of events has challenged this assumption. First, since the 1980s the welfare states of the West have retrenched, reducing their fiscal commitments to social programs. Second, among developing nations, subgroups have emerged. The oil embargo of the 1970s highlighted a small group of nations, the oil-exporting countries, which have comparatively high per capita income despite relatively low industrialization. Another subgroup consists of Southeast Asian nations that have prospered by aggressively pursuing capitalist strategies of development. As for the nations of sub-Saharan Africa: Most of them are worse off today than when they achieved independence during the 1960s, a tragedy that has been exacerbated by the HIV/AIDS epidemic. Third, international development agencies, such as the United Nations and the International Monetary Fund, have begun to explore alternative scenarios to prosperity—scenarios, such as sustainable development,[52]—that are often contrary to the alienating individualism and narcissistic consumption characteristic of the traditional welfare state.

A world in which inequality and strife contribute to social instability poses enormous challenges for human service professionals, as regards both direct services and development theory. Social workers who have served in the Peace Corps have an immediate appreciation for the intractability of problems in the Third and Fourth Worlds, of course. But immigrants seeking better opportunities in developing nations are presenting new problems to human service workers in industrialized nations. Social workers in the United States, for example, are confronted with human trafficking, undocumented workers, and refugee families in increasing numbers.[53] As James Midgley has advised, addressing such problems requires strategies that focus on human capital, social development, and self-sufficiency, interventions that are not commonly taught in First World schools of social work.[54]

Discussion Questions

1. Which framework or index, if any, best measures international social development?
2. Is examining a nation's material conditions the best way to evaluate social development? If not, what other indicators should be used?
3. What are the main reasons that some Third World countries are less developed now than before they achieved independence?
4. Which welfare state typology provides the best explanation for the development of welfare states?
5. Compared to those of other nations, is the U.S. welfare state really "exceptional"? Why or why not?
6. How much inherent validity is reflected in national development rankings?
7. In the light of international data, how important to development is foreign aid?
8. Select a developing nation and investigate the adequacy of its social infrastructure. What is the level of provision of welfare, health, and education services? How does it compare to the benefits and services of the United States?

Notes

1. Harold Wilensky and Charles Lebeaux, *Industrial Society and Social Welfare* (New York: Russell Sage Foundation, 1965).
2. Richard M. Titmuss, *Social Policy: An Introduction* (London: Allen and Unwin, 1971).
3. Norman Furniss and Timothy Tilton, *The Case for the Welfare State* (Bloomington, IN: Indiana University Press, 1977).
4. Ramesh Mishra, *The Welfare State in Crisis* (Brighton, England: Wheatsheaf Books, 1984).

5. Gosta Esping-Andersen, *Three Worlds of Welfare Capitalism* (Cambridge, England: Polity Press, 1990).
6. Norman Ginsburg, *Divisions of Welfare: A Critical Introduction to Comparative Social Policy* (London: Sage, 1992).
7. These typologies seek to classify the social welfare systems of the industrial societies and do not refer to the developing countries of the Third World. Attempts to construct comprehensive typologies that include the developing countries are still preliminary. See James Midgley, "Models of Welfare and Social Planning in Third World Countries," in Brij Mohan (ed.), *New Horizons in Social Welfare and Policy* (Cambridge, MA: Schenkman, 1985), pp. 89–108; Stewart MacPherson and James Midgley, *Comparative Social Policy and the Third World* (New York: St. Martin's Press, 1987).
8. Edwin Amenta and Theda Skocpol, "Taking Exception: Explaining the Distinctiveness of American Public Policies during the Last Century," in Francis C. Castles (ed.), *The Comparative History of Public Policy* (New York: Oxford University Press, 1989), pp. 292–333.
9. Jacob Hacker, *The Divided Welfare State* (New York: Cambridge University Press, 2002), pp. 13–14.
10. Wilensky's comparative analysis of 64 countries rated the United State high in education and environmental protection but stated that this was at the expense of traditional social programs. See Harold L. Wilensky, *Welfare State and Equality* (Berkeley: University of California Press, 1975). See also Arnold J. Heidenheimer, Hugh Heclo, and Carolyn Teich Adams, *Comparative Public Policy* (New York: St. Martin's Press, 1975), p. 258.
11. In 1975, Wilensky (Ibid., p. 105) noted that the United States "allocates a larger fraction of its total welfare spending to pensions that any of the twenty two richest nations [in the world]." However, more recent expenditure data from the OECD show that while pension expenditures remain comparatively high, the United States is by no means a world leader. See Organization for Economic Cooperation and Development (OECD), *Social Expenditure, 1960–1990,* retrieved from www.oecd.org.
12. Theda Skocpol, *Protecting Soldiers and Mothers: The Political Origins of Social Policy in the United States* (Cambridge, MA: Harvard University Press, 1992).
13. Robert Pinker, *The Idea of Welfare* (London, Heinemann, 1979).
14. M. A. Jones, *The Australian Welfare State: Growth Crisis and Change* (Sydney, Australia: Allen and Unwin, 1980); Terry Carney and Peter Hanks, *Social Security in Australia* (Melbourne: Oxford University Press, 1994).
15. See Martin Rein and Lee Rainwater (eds.), *Public/Private Interplay in Social Protection* (Armonk, NY: M. E. Sharpe, 1986); Sheila Kamerman, "The Mixed Economy of Welfare." *Social Work* 29 (1983), pp. 5–11; David Stoesz, "A Theory of Social Welfare," *Social Work* 34 (1989), pp. 101–107; Neil Gilbert and Barbara Gilbert, *The Enabling State: Modern Welfare Capitalism in America* (New York: Oxford University Press, 1989); Richard Rose, "Common Goals but Different Roles: The State's Contribution to the Welfare Mix," in R. Rose and R. Shiratori (eds.), *The Welfare State East and West* (New York: Oxford University Press, 1986), pp. 13–39.
16. Howard Glennester and James Midgley (eds.), *The Radical Right and the Welfare State* (London: Wheatsheaf Books, 1991).
17. See Barry Bluestone and Bennett Harrison, *The Deindustrialization of America* (New York: Basic Books, 1982); Samuel Bowles, David Gordon, and Thomas E. Weisskopf, *Beyond the Wasteland* (Garden City, NY: Anchor Press, 1983); Bennett Harrison and Barry Bluestone, *The Great U-Turn* (New York: Basic Books, 1988); Robert Reich, *Tales of a New America* (New York: Times Books, 1987); and Lester C. Thurow, *The Zero-Sum Solution* (New York: Simon and Schuster, 1985).
18. See Charles Atherton, "The Welfare State: Still on Solid Ground," *Social Service Review,* 63 (Fall 1989), pp. 167–179; and Joel Blau, "Theories of the Welfare State," *Social Service Review* 63 (March 1989), pp. 226–237.
19. Atherton, "The Welfare State."
20. Martin Anderson, "Welfare Reform," in Peter Duignan and Alvin Rabushka (eds.), *The United States in the 1980s* (Stanford: Hoover Institution, 1980), pp. 145–164; George Gilder, *Wealth and Poverty* (New York: Basic Books, 1981); Lawrence Mead, *Beyond Entitlement* (New York: Free Press, 1986); and Charles Murray, *Losing Ground* (New York: Basic Books, 1984).
21. Anthony Giddens, *The Third Way* (London: Polity Press, 2000).
22. Neil Gilbert, *Transformation of the Welfare State* (New York: Oxford University Press, 2002).
23. Alan Wolfe, "Paths of Dependence," *The New Republic* (October 14, 2002), p. 41.
24. *Human Development Report* (New York: Oxford University Press, 1996), p. 2.
25. Richard Estes, *Trends in World Social Development: The Social Progress of Nations,* (Praeger, 1997).
26. Jeffrey Sachs, "Don't Know, Should Care," *The New York Times* (June 5, 2004), p. 25.
27. Ibid.
28. Barbara Crossette, "Is Life Better in Bulgaria," *New York Times* (September 7, 1997).
29. Amartya Sen, *Development as Freedom* (New York: Knopf, 1999), p. 18.
30. Ibid., pp. 48–49.
31. Martha Nussbaum, *Women and Human Development* (New York: Cambridge University Press, 2000).
32. Ibid., pp. 78–80.

33. Ibid., p. 105.
34. Todaro, 1994, pp. 476–81.
35. World Bank, *Entering the 21st Century* (Washington, DC: World Bank, 2000), pp. 6–7.
36. World Bank, *Global Development Finance* (Washington, DC: World Bank, 1999).
37. World Bank, *Entering the 21st Century,* p. 18.
38. David Stoesz, Charles Guzzetta, and Mark Lusk, *International Development* (Boston: Allyn & Bacon, 1999), pp. 260–261.
39. Jessica Mathews, "The Age of Nonstate Actors," *Foreign Affairs* 76, no. 1 (January/February 1997), p. 63.
40. Grameen Foundation," (no. 3) Grameen Connections, (Summer 2000), p. 3.
41. Felicity Barringer, "U.N. Will Back Entrepreneurs in Bid to Lift Poor Nations," *New York Times* (July 27, 2003), p. 5.
42. Cited in Stoesz et al., *International Development,* p. 191.
43. Chuck Sudetic, *Blood and Vengeance* (New York: Penguin, 1999).
44. Peter Gouveritch, *We Wish to Inform You That Tomorrow We Will Be Killed with Our Families* (New York: Farrar Straus and Giroux, 1998).
45. Ryan Lizza, "Where Angels Fear to Tread," *The New Republic* 223, no. 4 (July 24, 2000).
46. Robert Klitgaard, *Tropical Gangsters* (New York: Basic Books, 1990).
47. Norimitsu Onishi, "Oil Riches, and Risks, in Tiny African Nation," *New York Times* (July 23, 2000).
48. Worldwatch Institute, *Vital Signs, 2003* (Washington, DC: Author, 2003), p. 69.
49. Barton Gellman, "The World Shunned Signs of Coming Plague," *Washington Post* (July 5, 2000).
50. Elizabeth Becker, "Debt Relief Deal for Poor Nations Seems to Be Near," *New York Times* (October 1, 2004), p. C1.
51. Anthony Faiola and Stephen Buckley, "Poor in Latin America Embrace Net's Promise," *Washington Post* (July 9, 2000), p. A25.
52. World Bank, *Sustainable Development in a Dynamic World* (Washington, DC: Author, 2003).
53. Lynne Healy, *International Social Work* (New York: Oxford University Press, 2001).
54. James Midgley, *Professional Imperialism* (London: Heinemann, 1981); James Midgley, *Social Development* (London: Sage, 1995).

Glossary

absolute poverty A measurement and classification of poverty that is based on the minimal standard of living (including food, shelter, and clothing) necessary for survival

affirmative action Programs designed to redress past or present discrimination against minorities (including women) through criteria for employment, promotion, and educational opportunities that give these groups preferential access to such resources or opportunities

ageism Age-based discrimination against elderly persons

alleviative approach to poverty Strategies designed to ease the suffering of the poor rather than to eliminate the causes of poverty. Examples include AFDC, SSI, and the Food Stamps Program

area poverty Geographic regions that are economically depressed

block grants A method of funding social programs by which the federal government makes monies available to states for a wide range of services, including social services. Block grants usually allow states more freedom by diminishing or eliminating federal program regulations. Block grants are usually fixed in terms of the amount available

Brown v. Board of Education of Topeka, Kansas A 1954 landmark U.S. Supreme Court decision ruling that "separate but equal" facilities in education were inherently unequal

bureaucratic disentitlement The denial of benefits to eligible recipients by agents of public agencies

bureaucratic rationality The ordering of social affairs by governmental agencies

capitalism An economic system in which most of the production and distribution of goods and services occurs under private auspices

capitation The method of payment in which the provider is paid a fixed amount for each person served regardless of the actual number or nature of services delivered

case management The process by which all related matters of a case are managed by a single professional, often a social worker

case poverty Individual deficits in human capital such as illness, illiteracy, etc.

categorical grants A method of funding social services through which the federal government makes available to the states monies that must be spent for very narrowly specified service needs

charity organization society (COS) A voluntary organization active in the late nineteenth and early twentieth centuries that attempted to coordinate private charities and promote a scientific approach to philanthropy

chronic care Long-term care of individuals with long standing, persistent diseases or conditions

chronic unemployment The rate of unemployment attributable to persons who have persistent trouble finding work because of an absence of low-skilled jobs or because they have severe deficiencies in basic social and work skills

circuit breaker programs Tax rebate programs designed to relieve the low-income, elderly, or disabled homeowner or renter from the burden of property or utility taxes

clinical entrepreneurs An interest group within American social welfare that is associated with private practice and the provision of social welfare in the private marketplace

commercialization The consequence of subjecting social welfare to the marketplace, including advertising for services, marketing services, and pricing services

commodification Term describing a governmental policy that takes social needs formerly met in the public sector (e.g., health care, counseling services) and places them within the private market sector

communitarianism The political philosophy that strives to seek a middle ground between conservatism and liberalism. Communitarians are often socially liberal, although they maintain that freedom must have it bounds. They are in favor of moral education

comparable worth The idea that workers should be paid equally when they do different types of work that require the same level of skill, education, knowledge, training, responsibility, and effort

corporate sector That part of the mixed welfare economy consisting of large, for-profit human-service corporations

corporate social responsibility The concept that corporations should be held accountable for practices and decisions that adversely affect those communities in which they do business. In addition, corporate social responsibility refers to the responsibility of corporations to promote the general well-being of society

cost-of-living adjustments (COLAs) Adjustments designed to keep income maintenance and social insurance benefits in line with inflation. COLAs affect Food Stamps, Social Security, and SSI benefits

cost shifting Charging one group of patients more in order to make up for underpayment by others

culture of poverty Term used by a theoretical school that maintains that poverty is transmitted intergenerationally and that certain of its traits are found in diverse cultures and societies

curative approach to poverty An approach designed to rehabilitate the poor through attacking the causes of poverty, for example, illiteracy, poor nutrition, or lack of employment

cyclical unemployment A type of unemployment attributable to swings in economic performance, such as recessions

de facto segregation Racial segregation that is not legally mandated by the state but that characterizes school systems and residential housing patterns

deinstitutionalization Term used to describe the removal, in the late 1960s, of many mentally ill or mentally retarded patients from state institutions and their placement in community settings

deliberate misdiagnosis The intentional distortion of a diagnosis in order to avoid labeling a client or for the purpose of collecting insurance payments

democratic capitalism The type of political-economy characteristic of the United States, with a democratic polity and a capitalist economy

dependency ratio The number of workers required to pay into the Social Security system to support one retired worker living on Social Security

diagnostic related groups (DRGs) A prospective form of payment for Medicare-incurred charges. Specifically, DRGs are a classification scheme whereby hospitals are reimbursed only for the maximum number of days an illness or surgical procedure is designated to take

discouraged workers Those who have stopped seeking work out of frustration with their poor employment prospects

disentitlement The removal of an entitlement status for a group of people. Specifically, the PRWOA disentitled poor beneficiaries from receiving lifetime benefits

Donaldson v. O'Connor The court decision ruling that mental patients could not be confined unless they were dangerous to themselves or others, and also that they should not be confined unless they are being treated and cannot survive without hospitalization

dual labor market A labor market divided into two classes of workers. See Primary Labor Market and Secondary Labor Market

earned income tax credit A federal program that functions somewhat like a negative income tax. Specifically, qualified working families or single people receive a tax rebate from the federal government that exceeds the taxes they paid

electronic benefit transfers (EBT) The attempt by the federal government to use technology in the delivery of benefits. This can include automatically depositing public assistance benefits into the savings accounts of recipients, the use of debit cards in food stamp benefits, and so forth

emergency assistance program A program that operated under AFDC and was intended to provide short-term cash assistance to families in crisis

entitlements Governmental resources (cash or in-kind) to which certain groups are entitled, based on their ability to meet the established criteria. Entitlement programs have open-ended resources in that people cannot be denied benefits because of governmental resource constraints

Equal Rights Amendment (ERA) An act that if passed would give women the same rights under the law as men

establishment of paternity Policies that require unwed mothers to identify the fathers of their children in order to aid states in their efforts to collect child support

family cap Usually refers to the policy that recipient mothers will not receive any (or only partial) benefits for any children born while they are on public assistance

fee-for-service A method of reimbursement based on payment for services rendered. Payment may be made by an insurance company, the patient, or a government program such as Medicare or Medicaid

feminization of poverty A social trend marked by the increasing frequency of poverty among women. It is thought to be related to the high incidence of women relying on governmental aid, the low wages that characterize traditional female employment, occupational segregation, and family decomposition (divorce, desertion, or death)

fiscal year (FY) A term used by government and social service agencies in reference to a budgetary rather than a normal year. Fiscal years often begin on July 1 rather than January 1

frictional unemployment The rate of unemployment, usually about 3 percent, considered inevitable for a viable economy

general assistance State or locally run programs designed to provide basic benefits to low-income people who are ineligible for federally funded public assistance programs

gentrification Resettlement of existing low-income neighborhoods by middle- and upper-class home owners or investors. This development can result in forcing poor and indigenous residents out of their neighborhoods

governmental sector That part of the mixed welfare economy consisting of social programs administered by government, particularly the federal government

Great Society Formerly called the War on Poverty, the Great Society comprehended a series of social welfare programs (including community development, training and employment, and health and legal services) enacted between 1963 and 1968 during the administration of President Lyndon Baines Johnson

Greens An environmental political party. Their orientation to social policy, *greening*, often incorporates an environmental awareness with a social justice perspective

gross domestic product (GDP) A measure of the total output of goods and services produced by a country's economy

gross national product (GNP) A measure of the total domestic and foreign output claimed by residents of a country. It is made up of the Gross Domestic Product (GDP) and of incomes accruing to foreign residents

Halderman v. Pennhurst The court decision ruling that institutionalized patients were entitled to treatment in the least restrictive environment

health care access The patient's ability to obtain medical care. Access is determined by the availability of medical services, the location of health care facilities, transportation, hours of operation cost of care, and so forth

health maintenance organizations (HMOs) Membership organizations that typically provide comprehensive health care. Members usually pay a regular fee and are thus entitled to free (or minimal-cost) hospital care and physicians' services

home health care Full range of medical and other health related services such as physical therapy, nursing, counseling, and social services that are delivered in the home of a patient by a provider

homophobia The fear of (and subsequent discrimination against) homosexuals on the basis of their sexual preference

housing starts Number of new houses begun in a given period

human capital Productive investments that are embodied in humans. These include education, training, skills, experience, knowledge, and health. Increases in human capital result from expenditures on education, job training, and medical care

human service executives An interest group within American social welfare that is associated with human service corporations and advocates the provision of social welfare through large-scale for-profit programs

human services A recent concept equivalent to social welfare

ideology A set of socially sanctioned assumptions, usually unexamined, explaining how the world works and encompassing a society's general methods for addressing social problems

income distribution The pattern of how income is distributed among the various socioeconomic classes in a society

income maintenance programs Social welfare programs designed to contribute to or supplement the income of an individual or family. These programs are usually means-tested and thus based on need

Indian Child Welfare Act of 1978 Legislation that restored child-placement decisions to the individual tribes

in-kind benefits Noncash goods or services provided by the government that function as a proxy for cash, for example, Food Stamps, Section 8 housing vouchers, and Medicare

inpatient care Care given in a hospital, nursing home, or other medical institution

institutional welfare A conception of welfare holding that governmental social programs that assure citizens of their basic needs (for food, housing, education, income, employment, and health) are essential to an advanced economy. Such programs are considered a right of citizenship

job lock Individuals' inability to change jobs because they would lose crucial health benefits

Job Opportunities and Basic Skills (JOBS) This program was created in the Family Support Act of 1988. The bill required a portion of a state's welfare caseload (usually AFDC mothers) to participate in a work or training program

Keynesian economics An economic school that proposes government intervention in the economy through such activities as social welfare programs to stimulate and regulate economic growth

libertarians A small but influential group that advocates more individual responsibility and a very limited role for government in social and economic affairs

licensed certified social worker A social worker holding the Master of Social Work degree who has practiced for two years under supervision and who has passed an examination. Twenty-nine states license social workers

managed care A loose umbrella term for the organization of networks of health care providers (e.g., doctors, clinics, and hospitals) into a system that is cost-effective. Institutions or individual health care providers who are in managed care systems agree to accept set fees for each service or flat payments per patient. HMOs are one example of managed care

market rationality The ordering of human affairs by corporate institutions within the marketplace

means test Income and asset tests designed to determine whether an individual or household meets the economic criteria necessary for receiving governmental cash transfers or in-kind services

Medigap Private health insurance plans that supplement Medicare benefits by covering some costs not paid for by Medicare

mixed welfare economy An economy in which governmental, private nonprofit, and private for-profit providers of social welfare coexist within the same society

National Association of Social Workers (NASW) The major national organization of professional social workers

national health insurance Various insurance-based proposals that incorporate comprehensive health coverage for the entire nation

neoconservatism A recent American ideology, based on conservatism, that recognizes the necessity for social welfare but designs social programs so that they are compatible with the requirements of a market economy and traditional values

neoliberalism A recent American ideology, based on liberalism, that assumes that universal social programs, such as those advanced by liberals, are implausible because of current social, political, and economic limitations. Neoliberals opt for more modest changes in social welfare programs

New Deal The name given to the massive Depression-era social and economic programs initiated under the presidency of Franklin Delano Roosevelt

NGOs Nongovernmental organizations (private or voluntary) that plan, deliver, or fund social services

occupational segregation The domination of low-wage sectors of the labor market by a minority group. For example, women are thought to be occupationally segregated in "pink-collar" jobs, as secretaries, receptionists, typists, and so forth

Office of Economic Opportunity (OEO) The federal agency that was charged with the responsibility for designing and implementing the Great Society programs

oligopolization The process through which a small number of organizations effectively control a market

pay-go A system for determining federal budgetary allocations that emerged out of the 1991 Omnibus Budget Reconciliation Act. In short, funding for any new program (or enhanced funding for an existing program) must come from reallocating existing money

permanency planning A strategy for helping foster children to live in families that offer continuity of relationships and the opportunity to establish lifetime relationships

Personal Responsibility and Work Opportunity Reconciliation Act (PRWORA) Passed in 1996, the PRWORA is a comprehensive act that created the TANF program, limited benefits to both legal and illegal immigrants, changed the qualifications for SSI, and established the precedent that government no longer had the responsibility for maintaining the poor indefinitely. In effect, it disentitled the poor from income support programs

Plessy v. Ferguson The 1896 U.S. Supreme Court decision that formally established the "separate but equal" doctrine in race relations

policy framework A systematic process for examining a specific policy or a set of policies

political action committees (PACs) Organizations, usually associated with special interest groups, that divert campaign contributions to candidates running for public office in order to influence their later decisions on public policy

political economy The blending of economic analysis with practical politics. In effect, political economy views economic activity within a political context

political practice A method of social work practice by which social workers advance their priorities either by assisting those in political office or by running for office themselves

poverty line A yearly cash income threshold (based on family size) set by the federal government to determine if an individual or household can be classified as poor. Sometimes called the poverty threshold or poverty index

preexisting condition A physical condition of an insured person that existed prior to the issuance of his/her policy or his/her enrollment in a health plan

preferential selection The selection of clients for treatment according to the organizational needs of the provider as opposed to the needs of the client; usually used to describe the practice of private providers who prefer insured clients with less severe problems

preventive approach to poverty Social welfare strategies (e.g., social insurance programs) designed to prevent people from becoming poor

preventive commitment The institutionalization of persons who do not meet the requirements for involuntary hospitalization but who are likely to deteriorate without inpatient care

primary care Basic or general health care rendered by general practitioners, family practitioners, internists, obstetricians, and pediatricians

primary labor market The full-time jobs that provide workers with an adequate salary, a career track, and benefits

primary prevention Efforts designed to eliminate the causes of social problems

private practice The provision of clinical services through the marketplace by individual practitioners or small groups of practitioners

privatization The ownership or management of social services by the private sector, either nonprofit agencies or proprietary corporations. Privatization of public assistance refers to attempts by individual states to have for-profit corporations manage the delivery of their public assistance benefits

professional monopoly The right to exclusive practice granted an occupational group in exchange for its promise to hold the welfare of the entire community as its ultimate concern

progressive movement A social movement popular in the United States from the late 1800s to World War I. Progressives stressed the need for morality, ethics, and honesty in all social, political, and economic affairs. This movement advocated numerous progressive reforms. It was also successful in establishing progressive legislation, including the progressive income tax

prospective payment system (PPS) A payment method that establishes rates, prices, or budgets before services are rendered and costs are incurred

public choice school A school of political economies that suggests that because interest group demands inevitably lead to budget deficits, government should therefore limit concessions to these groups as much as possible

public policy Policies designed by government that contain a goal, a purpose, and an objective. Public policy may also incorporate a standing plan of action toward a specific goal

public transfer programs Programs such as AFDC, SSI, and Social Security that transfer money from the governmental sector to families or individuals who are either entitled to it or who have earned it

quangos Quasi-governmental organizations that have some affiliation with government but that are predominately private

racism Discrimination against or prejudicial treatment of a racially different group

relative poverty A measurement and classification of poverty that is based on and related to the standard of living enjoyed by other members of a society

residual welfare A conception of welfare holding that the family and the market are the individual's primary sources of assistance, but that governmental "safety-net" programs may provide temporary help

secondary labor market Jobs that are characterized by irregular, seasonal, or part-time employment and that pay relatively low hourly wages, provide no benefits, and offer no career track

secondary prevention Early detection and intervention to keep incipient problems from becoming more debilitating

self-reliance school A relatively new school of political-economy advocating low-technology and local solutions to social problems

settlement houses Organizations that began in the late nineteenth century as an attempt to bridge the class differences marking American society. Based on the residence of middle-class volunteers in immigrant neighborhoods, settlement houses emphasized the provision of social services as well as reform activities

sexism Discrimination against women based solely on their gender. Sexism can also be directed at men

single-payer system A centralized system of health care payment in which the government assumes the costs (but not the delivery) for health services. People choose their doctor and hospital, and the government pays the bill according to a fixed-fee schedule. Coverage is often universal and is rights-based rather than employment-based. Canada is the best-known example of a single-payer system

social insurance A system that compels individuals to insure themselves against the possibility of indigence. Similar to private insurance, social insurance programs set aside a sum of money that is held in trust by the government to be used in the event of a worker's death, retirement, disability, or unemployment. Individuals are entitled to social insurance benefits on the basis of their previous contributions to the system

socialism A school of political-economy that attributes the need for social welfare to the social problems caused by capitalism. Socialists advocate restructuring the political economy—in the American case, capitalism—as the most direct way of promoting social welfare

social justice Connotes equity and fairness in all areas of social, political, and economic life, as well as the provision of basic necessities to all without regard to their participation in the market, an objective of liberals and progressives

social services Programs designed to increase human capital by ameliorating problems in psychosocial functioning, providing necessary goods and services outside normal market mechanisms, and providing cash supplements for the lack of market income

social stratification The vertical segmentation of the population according to income, occupation, and status

social wage A term used to refer to the additional "wage" a worker receives as part of the universal benefits paid out by a welfare state (e.g., health care coverage or housing loans)

social welfare policy The regulation of the provision of benefits to people who require assistance in meeting their basic life needs, such as for employment, income, food, health care, and relationships

sociopolitical planning Methods for anticipating program needs that are interactive, involving groups likely to be affected by a program

spells of poverty Periods of time (often limited) in which individuals or families fall below the poverty line

standardization The reduction of services to a common denominator in order to lower provider costs

structural unemployment The rate of unemployment attributable to long-lasting and deep maladjustments in the labor market

supply-side economics A school of political-economy that proposes reductions in social programs so that tax dollars can be reinvested in the private sector to capitalize economic growth

sustainable development A theory that stresses the need to develop an appropriate balance between material needs and future resource availability. It calls for a form of balanced economic development

Swann v. Charlotte-Mecklenburg Board of Education A 1971 U.S. Supreme Court ruling that approved court-ordered busing to achieve racial integration in school districts with a history of discrimination

tardive dyskinesia Permanent damage to the central nervous system, evidenced by involuntary movements, caused by psychotropic medication

technomethodological planning Methods of anticipating program requirements using data bases from which projections of future program needs can be derived

Temporary Assistance for Needy Families (TANF) TANF was included as part of the Personal Responsibility and Work Opportunity Reconciliation Act (PRWOA) and is a replacement for the AFDC program. It is a block grant program based on workfare, time-limited benefits (a maximum of five years), and strict work participation rates. The TANF program was instituted in 1996

tertiary prevention Efforts to limit the effects of a disorder after it has become manifest

think tanks Popular name for policy institutes

time limits The length of time a recipient (or a recipient's family) is allowed to remain on welfare. The federal government has instituted a five-year lifetime cap on benefits; several states have set shorter caps

traditionalism A social movement that gained increased strength during the 1970s. Traditionalists seek to make social policy conform with their conservative social and religious values

traditional providers An interest group within American social welfare associated with voluntary nonprofit agencies that promotes local institutions as a preferred method of solving social problems

usual, customary, and reasonable (UCR) That fee established by a majority of practitioners in a given community for a given procedure. The UCR is defined by insurance companies to determine the proper level of payment for covered procedures

underemployed Individuals who are working at jobs in which their skills are far above those required for the position. It may also refer to those who are employed part-time when their desire is to be employed full time

unemployment The condition of individuals over 16 years of age who are looking for work

voluntary sector That part of the mixed welfare economy consisting of private, nonprofit agencies

welfare behaviorism Refers to the attempts of public officials to modify the behavioral patterns (through instituting specific social policies) of low-income people, especially beneficiaries

welfare bureaucrats Interest groups within American social welfare associated with governmental social programs that advocate the provision of social welfare through large-scale public social programs

welfare capitalism An advanced system of social welfare existing in progressive capitalist countries

welfare dependency The economic dependence of a family or individual on the provision of governmental welfare services, especially cash grants

welfare state A welfare state is one in which the national government ensures essential goods, services, and opportunities to residents as a right of citizenship

welfare state exceptionalism A term often used to characterize the U.S. welfare system and the differences between it and other welfare states, especially those of Western Europe

workfare A system begun in the late 1960s whereby AFDC or AFDC-UP recipients were required either to work or to receive work training (sometimes in the form of higher education). The concept of workfare underlies the welfare reform bills passed in 1988 and in 1996

working poor Those families or individuals who are in the work force (full- or part-time) but who are still at or below the poverty line

work participation rate This refers to the percentage of individuals on public assistance that states are required to have in the workforce under TANF guidelines

Wyatt v. Stickney The court decision requiring states to provide adequate levels of treatment to hospitalized mental patients

YAVIS syndrome The tendency of clinicians to prefer clients who are young, attractive, verbal, intelligent, and successful

Index

Photo Credits

p. 1 and p. ix (top), © Jeff Greenberg/The Image Works; p. 7, © Hulton-Deutsch Collection/CORBIS; p. 16, Lawrence Jackson/AP/Wide World Photos; p. 25 and p. ix (bottom), © Esbin-Anderson/The Image Works; p. 27, © Michael Newman/PhotoEdit; p. 38 and p. x (top), © Alan Oddie/PhotoEdit; p. 45, AP/Wide World Photos; p. 52, The Lufkin Daily News/Joel Andrews/AP/Wide World Photos; p. 58 and p. x (bottom), CORBIS/Bettmann; p. 62, GettyImages, Inc.; p. 75, © Spencer Grant/PhotoEdit; p. 90, © 2004 Marilyn Humphries/The Image Works; p. 110 and p. xi, © Tony Freeman/PhotoEdit; p. 117, © Dorothy Littell Greco/The Image Works; p. 123, © Wolfgang Spunbarg/PhotoEdit; p. 145 and p. xii (top), © Jeff Greenberg/PhotoEdit; p. 158, © Amy Etra/PhotoEdit; p. 163, Gerald Herbert/AP/Wide World Photos; p. 168 and p. xii (bottom), Mario Tama/GettyImages; p. 173, © Bill Bachman/PhotoEdit; p. 194, © PhotoEdit; p. 205 and p. xiii (top), AP/Wide World Photos; p. 228 (left, top), Dennis Cook/AP/Wide World Photos; p. 228 (left, middle), Star Democrat/Chris Polk/AP/Wide World Photos; p. 228 (left, bottom), Lawrence Jackson/AP/Wide World Photos; p. 228 (right, top) San Francisco Chronicle/Nancy Wong/AP/Wide World Photos; p. 228 (right, bottom), Lenny Ignelzi/AP/Wide World Photos; p. 232 and p. xiii (bottom), Julia Malakie/AP/Wide World Photos; p. 246, © Bob Daemmrich/PhotoEdit; p. 251 and p. xiv (top), © Mark Richards/PhotoEdit; p. 255, © Joan Slatkin/OmniPhoto; p. 265, Masahiko Yamamoto/AP/Wide World Photos; p. 269 and p. xiv (bottom), © Rob Crandalle/The Image Works; p. 272, © David Young-Wolff/PhotoEdit; p. 287, © David Young-Wolff/PhotoEdit; p. 301 and p. xv (top), Gary Kazanjian/AP/Wide World Photos; p. 316, © Jim Pickerell/The Image Works; p. 321, David Weintraub/Science Source/Photo Researchers, Inc.; p. 337 and p. xv (bottom), © Paul W. Liebhardt; p. 343, © Jim Noelker/The Image Works; p. 354, © Ken Graham/Bruce Edelman, Inc.; p. 368 and p. xvi (top), © Joe Sohm/The Image Works; p. 373, © Mitch Wojnarowicz/The Image Works; p. 376, © Syracuse Newspapers/The Image Works; p. 389 and p. xvi (middle), © David Young-Wolff/PhotoEdit; p. 392, © NMPFT/Kodak Collection/SSPL/The Image Works; p. 408, © Bob Mahoney/The Image Works; p. 416 and p. xvi (bottom), © John Nordell/The Image Works; p. 420, © Amy Etra/PhotoEdit; p. 432, Andrew Lichtenstein/The Image Works; p. 442 and p. xvii (top), © Jean-Yves Rabeuf/The Image Works; p. 450, © Michael Newman/PhotoEdit; p. 455, © Dennis MacDonald/PhotoEdit; p. 471 and p. xvii (bottom), Jose Cendon/AP/Wide World Photos; p. 474, David Butow/CORBIS SABA; p. 485, Kevin Frayer/CP/AP/Wide World Photos